International Directory of COMPANY HISTORIES

International Directory of COMPANY HISTORIES

VOLUME 97

Editor
Jay P. Pederson

ST. JAMES PRESS
A part of Gale, Cengage Learning

Detroit • New York • San Francisco • New Haven, Conn • Waterville, Maine • London

International Directory of Company Histories, Volume 97

Jay P. Pederson, Editor

Project Editor: Miranda H. Ferrara

Editorial: Virgil Burton, Donna Craft, Louise Gagné, Peggy Geeseman, Julie Gough, Linda Hall, Sonya Hill, Keith Jones, Lynn Pearce, Holly Selden, Justine Ventimiglia

Production Technology Specialist: Mike Weaver

Imaging and Multimedia: Lezlie Light

Composition and Electronic Prepress: Gary Leach, Evi Seoud

Manufacturing: Rhonda Dover

Product Manager: Jenai Mynatt

Cover Photograph: South Portico of the U.S. Treasury Department, Washington, D.C., 1941. Courtesy Library of Congress, Prints & Photographs Division, FSA/OWI Collection, reproduction number LC-USZ62-26665.

Gale
27500 Drake Rd.
Farmington Hills, MI, 48331-3535

LIBRARY OF CONGRESS CATALOG NUMBER 89-190943
ISBN-13: 978-1-55862-618-8
ISBN-10: 1-55862-618-2

This title is also available as an e-book
ISBN-13: 978-1-4144-2981-6 ISBN-10: 1-4144-2981-9
Contact your Gale, a part of Cengage Learning sales representative for ordering information.

BRITISH LIBRARY CATALOGUING IN PUBLICATION DATA
International directory of company histories, Vol. 97
Jay P. Pederson
33.87409

Printed in the United States of America
1 2 3 4 5 6 7 12 11 10 09 08

Contents

Preface vii
Notes on Contributors ix
List of Abbreviations xi

Acergy SA 1
Ackermans & van Haaren N.V. 5
Adani Enterprises Ltd. 9
AeroVironment, Inc. 13
African Rainbow Minerals Ltd. 17
Alitalia—Linee Aeree Italiane S.p.A. 21
Allegiant Travel Company 28
American Superconductor Corporation 32
Amerigon Incorporated 37
Arena Resources, Inc. 41
Arnhold and S. Bleichroeder Advisers, LLC 45
Ascendia Brands, Inc. 50
Astellas Pharma Inc. 54
Babolat VS, S.A. 59
Baldor Electric Company 63
BlueLinx Holdings Inc. 68
Bojangles Restaurants Inc. 73
Boss Holdings, Inc. 78
Bouygues S.A. 82
Burgett, Inc. 88
Cano Petroleum Inc. 92
Caribou Coffee Company, Inc. 96
Carrizo Oil & Gas, Inc. 103
Catholic Order of Foresters 107
ČEZ a. s. 112
China Nepstar Chain Drugstore Ltd. 116
Ctrip.com International Ltd. 120
Dairy Farm International Holdings Ltd. 125
DDi Corp. 129
Dreams Inc. 133
El Puerto de Liverpool, S.A.B. de C.V. 137
EMCORE Corporation 141
Energen Corporation 145
Ennis, Inc. 150
Evergreen Energy, Inc. 155
Evraz Group S.A. 160
Faegre & Benson LLP 164
Fred Alger Management, Inc. 168
Fuel Systems Solutions, Inc. 173
Galaxy Investors, Inc. 178
Greek Organization of Football Prognostics S.A. (OPAP) 182
Grupo Aeroportuario del Centro Norte, S.A.B. de C.V. 186
Hamon & Cie (International) S.A. 190
Hapag-Lloyd AG 195
Hite Brewery Company Ltd. 204

The Home Depot, Inc. 208
Houston Wire & Cable Company 214
Hummer Winblad Venture Partners 218
IDB Holding Corporation Ltd. ... 222
IG Group Holdings plc 226
INPEX Holdings Inc. 230
International Paper Company 234
Jones Knowledge Group, Inc. 244
Kolbenschmidt Pierburg AG 249
Kreisler Manufacturing Corporation 254
Madison Dearborn Partners, LLC . 258
Make-A-Wish Foundation of America 262
Malaysian Airline System Berhad .. 266
ManTech International Corporation 272
Marie Brizard et Roger International S.A.S. 276
Medifast, Inc. 281
Metalico Inc. 286
Mota-Engil, SGPS, S.A. 290
National City Corporation 294
Noah Education Holdings Ltd. ... 303
Nutrition 21 Inc. 307
Oakleaf Waste Management, LLC . 312
OOC Inc. 316
Palace Sports & Entertainment, Inc. 320
Panda Restaurant Group, Inc. 326
Redlon & Johnson, Inc. 331
Regal-Beloit Corporation 335
Rheinmetall AG 343
St. Jude Medical, Inc. 350
Salem Communications Corporation 359
Sapporo Holdings Limited 364
Selecta AG 370
skinnyCorp, LLC 374
Sonae SGPS, S.A. 378
Sterilite Corporation 382
Sub Pop Ltd. 386
SUEZ-TRACTEBEL S.A. 390
The Swiss Colony, Inc. 395
Syniverse Holdings Inc. 399
Taylor Devices, Inc. 403
Teknor Apex Company 407
Tesoro Corporation 411
Teton Energy Corporation 420
TouchTunes Music Corporation ... 424
Trend Micro Inc. 429
Tripwire, Inc. 433
USA Mobility Inc. 437
Vector Aerospace Corporation 441
Vueling Airlines S.A. 445
Webasto Roof Systems Inc. 449
Wells Fargo & Company 453
Whitbread PLC 468
Wilton Products, Inc. 477
Worldwide Pants Inc. 481
Xantrex Technology Inc. 485

Cumulative Index to Companies 489
Index to Industries 571
Geographic Index 635

Preface

The St. James Press series *The International Directory of Company Histories* (*IDCH*) is intended for reference use by students, business people, librarians, historians, economists, investors, job candidates, and others who seek to learn more about the historical development of the world's most important companies. To date, *IDCH* has covered more than 9,675 companies in 97 volumes.

INCLUSION CRITERIA

Most companies chosen for inclusion in *IDCH* have achieved a minimum of US$25 million in annual sales and are leading influences in their industries or geographical locations. Companies may be publicly held, private, or nonprofit. State-owned companies that are important in their industries and that may operate much like public or private companies also are included. Wholly owned subsidiaries and divisions are profiled if they meet the requirements for inclusion. Entries on companies that have had major changes since they were last profiled may be selected for updating.

The *IDCH* series highlights 25% private and nonprofit companies, and features updated entries on approximately 35 companies per volume.

ENTRY FORMAT

Each entry begins with the company's legal name; the address of its headquarters; its telephone, toll-free, and fax numbers; and its web site. A statement of public, private, state, or parent ownership follows. A company with a legal name in both English and the language of its headquarters country is listed by the English name, with the native-language name in parentheses.

The company's founding or earliest incorporation date, the number of employees, and the most recent available sales figures follow. Sales figures are given in local currencies with equivalents in U.S. dollars. For some private companies, sales figures are estimates and indicated by the abbreviation *est.* The entry lists the exchanges on which the company's stock is traded and its ticker symbol, as well as the company's NAICS codes.

Entries generally contain a *Company Perspectives* box which provides a short summary of the company's mission, goals, and ideals; a *Key Dates* box highlighting milestones in the company's history; lists of *Principal Subsidiaries*, *Principal Divisions*, *Principal Operating Units*, *Principal Competitors*; and articles for *Further Reading*.

American spelling is used throughout *IDCH*, and the word "billion" is used in its U.S. sense of one thousand million.

SOURCES

Entries have been compiled from publicly accessible sources both in print and on the Internet such as general and academic periodicals, books, and annual reports, as well as material supplied by the companies themselves.

CUMULATIVE INDEXES

IDCH contains three indexes: the **Cumulative Index to Companies**, which provides an alphabetical index to companies profiled in the *IDCH* series, the **Index to Industries**, which allows researchers to locate companies by their principal industry, and the **Geographic Index**, which lists companies alphabetically by the country of their headquarters. The indexes are cumulative and specific instructions for using them are found immediately preceding each index.

SUGGESTIONS WELCOME

Comments and suggestions from users of *IDCH* on any aspect of the product as well as suggestions for companies to be included or updated are cordially invited. Please write:

The Editor
International Directory of Company Histories
St. James Press
Gale, Cengage Learning
27500 Drake Rd.
Farmington Hills, Michigan 48331-3535

St. James Press does not endorse any of the companies or products mentioned in this series. Companies appearing in the *International Directory of Company Histories* were selected without reference to their wishes and have in no way endorsed their entries.

Notes on Contributors

M. L. Cohen
Novelist, business writer, and researcher living in Paris.

Jeffrey L. Covell
Seattle-based writer.

Ed Dinger
Writer and editor based in Bronx, New York.

Jodi Essey-Stapleton
Writer based in Illinois.

Paul R. Greenland
Illinois-based writer and researcher; author of two books and former senior editor of a national business magazine; contributor to *The Encyclopedia of Chicago History, The Encyclopedia of Religion,* and the *Encyclopedia of American Industries.*

Robert Halasz
Former editor in chief of *World Progress* and *Funk & Wagnalls New Encyclopedia Yearbook*; author, *The U.S. Marines* (Millbrook Press, 1993).

Frederick C. Ingram
Writer based in South Carolina.

Kathleen Peippo
Minnesota-based writer.

Nelson Rhodes
Editor, writer, and consultant in the Chicago area.

David E. Salamie
Part-owner of InfoWorks Development Group, a reference publication development and editorial services company.

Mary Tradii
Colorado-based writer.

Frank Uhle
Ann Arbor-based writer; movie projectionist, disc jockey, and staff member of *Psychotronic Video* magazine.

A. Woodward
Wisconsin-based writer.

List of Abbreviations

¥ Japanese yen
£ United Kingdom pound
$ United States dollar

A

AB Aktiebolag (Finland, Sweden)
AB Oy Aktiebolag Osakeyhtiot (Finland)
A.E. Anonimos Eteria (Greece)
AED Emirati dirham
AG Aktiengesellschaft (Austria, Germany, Switzerland, Liechtenstein)
aG auf Gegenseitigkeit (Austria, Germany)
A.m.b.a. Andelsselskab med begraenset ansvar (Denmark)
A.O. Anonim Ortaklari/Ortakligi (Turkey)
ApS Amparteselskab (Denmark)
ARS Argentine peso
A.S. Anonim Sirketi (Turkey)
A/S Aksjeselskap (Norway)
A/S Aktieselskab (Denmark, Sweden)
Ay Avoinyhtio (Finland)
ATS Austrian shilling
AUD Australian dollar
ApS Amparteselskab (Denmark)
Ay Avoinyhtio (Finland)

B

B.A. Buttengewone Aansprakeiijkheid (Netherlands)
BEF Belgian franc
BHD Bahraini dinar
Bhd. Berhad (Malaysia, Brunei)
BRL Brazilian real
B.V. Besloten Vennootschap (Belgium, Netherlands)

C

C.A. Compania Anonima (Ecuador, Venezuela)
CAD Canadian dollar
C. de R.L. Compania de Responsabilidad Limitada (Spain)
CEO Chief Executive Officer
CFO Chief Financial Officer
CHF Swiss franc
Cia. Companhia (Brazil, Portugal)
Cia. Compania (Latin America [except Brazil], Spain)
Cia. Compagnia (Italy)
Cie. Compagnie (Belgium, France, Luxembourg, Netherlands)
CIO Chief Information Officer
CLP Chilean peso
CNY Chinese yuan
Co. Company
COO Chief Operating Officer
Coop. Cooperative
COP Colombian peso
Corp. Corporation
C. por A. Compania por Acciones (Dominican Republic)
CPT Cuideachta Phoibi Theoranta (Republic of Ireland)
CRL Companhia a Responsabilidao Limitida (Portugal, Spain)
C.V. Commanditaire Vennootschap (Netherlands, Belgium)
CZK Czech koruna

D

D&B Dunn & Bradstreet
DEM German deutsche mark
Div. Division (United States)
DKK Danish krone
DZD Algerian dinar

E

EC Exempt Company (Arab countries)
Edms. Bpk. Eiendoms Beperk (South Africa)
EEK Estonian Kroon
eG eingetragene Genossenschaft (Germany)
EGMBH Eingetragene Genossenschaft mit beschraenkter Haftung (Austria, Germany)
EGP Egyptian pound
Ek For Ekonomisk Forening (Sweden)
EP Empresa Portuguesa (Portugal)
E.P.E. Etema Pemorismenis Evthynis (Greece)
ESOP Employee Stock Options and Ownership
ESP Spanish peseta
Et(s). Etablissement(s) (Belgium,

France, Luxembourg)
eV eingetragener Verein (Germany)
EUR euro

F
FIM Finnish markka
FRF French franc

G
G.I.E. Groupement d'Interet Economique (France)
gGmbH gemeinnutzige Gesellschaft mit beschraenkter Haftung (Austria, Germany, Switzerland)
G.I.E. Groupement d'Interet Economique (France)
GmbH Gesellschaft mit beschraenkter Haftung (Austria, Germany, Switzerland)
GRD Greek drachma
GWA Gewerbte Amt (Austria, Germany)

H
HB Handelsbolag (Sweden)
HF Hlutafelag (Iceland)
HKD Hong Kong dollar
HUF Hungarian forint

I
IDR Indonesian rupiah
IEP Irish pound
ILS new Israeli shekel
Inc. Incorporated (United States, Canada)
INR Indian rupee
IPO Initial Public Offering
I/S Interesentselskap (Norway)
I/S Interessentselskab (Denmark)
ISK Icelandic krona
ITL Italian lira

J
JMD Jamaican dollar
JOD Jordanian dinar

K
KB Kommanditbolag (Sweden)
KES Kenyan schilling
Kft Korlatolt Felelossegu Tarsasag (Hungary)
KG Kommanditgesellschaft (Austria, Germany, Switzerland)
KGaA Kommanditgesellschaft auf Aktien (Austria, Germany, Switzerland)
KK Kabushiki Kaisha (Japan)
KPW North Korean won
KRW South Korean won
K/S Kommanditselskab (Denmark)
K/S Kommandittselskap (Norway)
KWD Kuwaiti dinar
Ky Kommandiitiyhtio (Finland)

L
LBO Leveraged Buyout
Lda. Limitada (Spain)
L.L.C. Limited Liability Company (Arab countries, Egypt, Greece, United States)
L.L.P. Limited Liability Partnership (United States)
L.P. Limited Partnership (Canada, South Africa, United Kingdom, United States)
Ltd. Limited
Ltda. Limitada (Brazil, Portugal)
Ltee. Limitee (Canada, France)
LUF Luxembourg franc

M
mbH mit beschraenkter Haftung (Austria, Germany)
Mij. Maatschappij (Netherlands)
MUR Mauritian rupee
MXN Mexican peso
MYR Malaysian ringgit

N
N.A. National Association (United States)
NGN Nigerian naira
NLG Netherlands guilder
NOK Norwegian krone
N.V. Naamloze Vennootschap (Belgium, Netherlands)
NZD New Zealand dollar

O
OAO Otkrytoe Aktsionernoe Obshchestve (Russia)
OHG Offene Handelsgesellschaft (Austria, Germany, Switzerland)
OMR Omani rial
OOO Obschestvo s Ogranichennoi Otvetstvennostiu (Russia)
OOUR Osnova Organizacija Udruzenog Rada (Yugoslavia)
Oy Osakeyhtî (Finland)

P
P.C. Private Corp. (United States)
PEN Peruvian Nuevo Sol
PHP Philippine peso
PKR Pakistani rupee
P/L Part Lag (Norway)
PLC Public Limited Co. (United Kingdom, Ireland)
P.L.L.C. Professional Limited Liability Corporation (United States)
PLN Polish zloty
P.T. Perusahaan/Perseroan Terbatas (Indonesia)
PTE Portuguese escudo
Pte. Private (Singapore)
Pty. Proprietary (Australia, South Africa, United Kingdom)
Pvt. Private (India, Zimbabwe)
PVBA Personen Vennootschap met Beperkte Aansprakelijkheid (Belgium)

Q
QAR Qatar riyal

R
REIT Real Estate Investment Trust
RMB Chinese renminbi
Rt Reszvenytarsasag (Hungary)
RUB Russian ruble

S
S.A. Société Anonyme (Arab countries, Belgium, France, Jordan, Luxembourg, Switzerland)
S.A. Sociedad Anónima (Latin America [except Brazil], Spain, Mexico)
S.A. Sociedades Anônimas (Brazil, Portugal)
SAA Societe Anonyme Arabienne (Arab countries)
S.A.B. de C.V. Sociedad Anónima Bursátil de Capital Variable (Mexico)
S.A.C. Sociedad Anonima Comercial (Latin America [except Brazil])
S.A.C.I. Sociedad Anonima Comercial e Industrial (Latin America [except Brazil])
S.A.C.I.y.F. Sociedad Anonima

Comercial e Industrial y Financiera (Latin America [except Brazil])
S.A. de C.V. Sociedad Anonima de Capital Variable (Mexico)
SAK Societe Anonyme Kuweitienne (Arab countries)
SAL Societe Anonyme Libanaise (Arab countries)
SAO Societe Anonyme Omanienne (Arab countries)
SAQ Societe Anonyme Qatarienne (Arab countries)
SAR Saudi riyal
S.A.R.L. Sociedade Anonima de Responsabilidade Limitada (Brazil, Portugal)
S.A.R.L. Société à Responsabilité Limitée (France, Belgium, Luxembourg)
S.A.S. Societá in Accomandita Semplice (Italy)
S.A.S. Societe Anonyme Syrienne (Arab countries)
S.C. Societe en Commandite (Belgium, France, Luxembourg)
S.C.A. Societe Cooperativa Agricole (France, Italy, Luxembourg)
S.C.I. Sociedad Cooperativa Ilimitada (Spain)
S.C.L. Sociedad Cooperativa Limitada (Spain)
S.C.R.L. Societe Cooperative a Responsabilite Limitee (Belgium)
Sdn. Bhd. Sendirian Berhad (Malaysia)
SEK Swedish krona
SGD Singapore dollar
S.L. Sociedad Limitada (Latin America [except Brazil], Portugal, Spain)
S/L Salgslag (Norway)
S.N.C. Société en Nom Collectif (France)
Soc. Sociedad (Latin America [except Brazil], Spain)
Soc. Sociedade (Brazil, Portugal)
Soc. Societa (Italy)
S.p.A. Società per Azioni (Italy)
Sp. z.o.o. Spólka z ograniczona odpowiedzialnoscia (Poland)
S.R.L. Sociedad de Responsabilidad Limitada (Spain, Mexico, Latin America [except Brazil])
S.R.L. Società a Responsabilità Limitata (Italy)
S.R.O. Spolecnost s Rucenim Omezenym (Czechoslovakia
S.S.K. Sherkate Sahami Khass (Iran)
Ste. Societe (France, Belgium, Luxembourg, Switzerland)
Ste. Cve. Societe Cooperative (Belgium)
S.V. Samemwerkende Vennootschap (Belgium)
S.Z.R.L. Societe Zairoise a Responsabilite Limitee (Zaire)

T
THB Thai baht
TND Tunisian dinar
TRL Turkish lira
TWD new Taiwan dollar

U
U.A. Uitgesloten Aansporakeiijkheid (Netherlands)
u.p.a. utan personligt ansvar (Sweden)

V
VAG Verein der Arbeitgeber (Austria, Germany)
VEB Venezuelan bolivar
VERTR Vertriebs (Austria, Germany)
VND Vietnamese dong
V.O.f. Vennootschap onder firma (Netherlands)
VVAG Versicherungsverein auf Gegenseitigkeit (Austria, Germany)

W–Z
WA Wettelika Aansprakalikhaed (Netherlands)
WLL With Limited Liability (Bahrain, Kuwait, Qatar, Saudi Arabia)
YK Yugen Kaisha (Japan)
ZAO Zakrytoe Aktsionernoe Obshchestve (Russia)
ZAR South African rand
ZMK Zambian kwacha
ZWD Zimbabwean dollar

Acergy SA

200 Hammersmith Road
London, W6 7DL
United Kingdom
Telephone: (+44 (0) 20) 8210 5500
Fax: (+44 (0) 20) 8210 5501
Web site: http://www.acergy-group.com

Public Company
Incorporated: 1973 as Stolt-Nielsen Seaway
Employees: 8,000
Sales: $2.66 billion (2007)
Stock Exchanges: Oslo NASDAQ
Ticker Symbols: ACY; ACGY
NAICS: 213112 Support Activities for Oil and Gas Field Exploration; 541330 Engineering Services

■ ■ ■

Acergy SA is one of the world's leading providers of seabed-to-surface engineering, construction, and related services to the offshore oil and gas industry. The U.K.-based company, formerly part of the Stolt-Nielsen group, operates in all phases of the offshore services sector, from planning and design, to integrated turnkey construction, to abandonment services. After a restructuring effort in the early 2000s, Acergy refocused itself around four core areas of operation: SURF (subsea umbilical risers and flowlines); IMR (inspection, maintenance, and repair); Trunklines; and Conventional Field Development. The SURF segment is the company's largest, accounting for nearly 75 percent of its order backlog. Acergy operates on a global level, with operations structured into five regional divisions. The Africa & Mediterranean division, based in Suresnes, France, is the company's largest, generating more than half of its revenues in 2007. The Northern Europe & Canada division also includes the group's operations in Tunisia and Azerbaijan, and operates from offices in Aberdeen, Scotland; Stavanger, Norway; St. John's, Newfoundland, Canada; and Moscow, Russia. This division accounted for 34 percent of the group's revenues in 2007. The North America & Mexico division, based in Houston, Texas, oversees Acergy's operations in the United States, western Canada, Mexico, and Central America. This division, the company's smallest, generated just $3.2 million in revenues in 2007. The South American division is one of the group's fastest-growing, generating nearly 10 percent of revenues, with a base in Macae, Brazil. The company also maintains a presence in the Asian region, from the Asia & Middle East division's headquarters in Singapore. Acergy is listed on the Oslo stock exchange and the NASDAQ. The company is led by Chairman Mark Woolveridge and CEO Tom Ehret. The company posted revenues of $2.66 billion in 2007.

STOLT-NIELSEN EXTENSION IN 1973

Acergy's origins reach back to the late 1950s, when Norway's Jacob Stolt-Nielsen, who had been working as a shipbroker, set up a small shipping business, called Parcel Tankers Inc. Stolt-Nielsen came up with the idea to subdivide ships into several tanks, each of which could be used to ship a different material. By 1959, Stolt-Nielsen had launched his first vessel.

COMPANY PERSPECTIVES

We have a clear vision for Acergy: to be the acknowledged leader in seabed-to-surface engineering and construction. We know the actions we must take and the standards we must set to realise this vision. Acergy must be a trusted partner for clients, recognised and respected for our capabilities and resources. A provider who delivers on time, within budget and to the highest quality standards, while making safety and security an absolute priority. Our business utilises advanced, innovative technologies, delivered from one of the most versatile marine construction fleets in our industry. But above all, we depend on human imagination and endeavour to succeed. That is why Acergy is, at heart, a business driven by the passion and know-how of our people.

The idea quickly caught the attention of the international chemicals industry, and by 1963, Parcel Tankers operated a fleet of nearly 20 vessels. The company itself went global, establishing offices in Norway and Japan. By the end of the decade, the company had added both transpacific and transatlantic routes, as well as coastal routes and operations across the Great Lakes. The company also developed specifications for a new generation of tankers, featuring double hulls and other security enhancements. These features were later adapted as part of the international parcel tanker specification. In the meantime, Parcel Tankers Inc.'s success had been such that "parcel tanker" itself had become a generic industry term. In response, the group adopted the Stolt-Nielsen name in the early 1970s.

Stolt-Nielsen had also begun to explore extensions to its core chemicals shipping operations. The company set up a network of warehousing facilities in the early 1970s. At the same time, Stolt-Nielsen's Norwegian roots played a role in its extension into the offshore services sector. The discovery of significant oil and natural gas reserves off the Norwegian coast in the 1960s created a new demand for support services for the development of an offshore industry there.

At the time, the offshore market remained a fairly new industry, primarily focused on the Gulf of Mexico. Support services were largely performed manually by trained divers. Yet conditions off the Norwegian coast were vastly different from those in the relatively calm Gulf of Mexico. In response, Jacob Stolt-Nielsen led the development of new techniques, such as use of "moon pool" support ships, which featured openings in the hull of the vessel where divers could remain protected from the rough seas while entering the water. By 1972, Stolt-Nielsen had launched its first dedicated offshore services vessel, the *Seaway Falcon,* becoming one of the first to enter the Norwegian offshore market. The following year, Jacob Stolt-Nielsen established a new company, called Stolt-Nielsen Seaway (SNS).

SNS remained privately held by the Stolt-Nielsen family, and operated independently of the group's main chemicals transport business. Nonetheless, SNS was later brought under a new holding company set up by the family, Stolt-Nielsen S.A., based in Luxembourg. The new company served as the holding vehicle for the family's growing array of business interests, which included the farm fishery business, Sea Farm A/S.

EVOLVING TO MEET THE MARKET

SNS continued to evolve through the 1970s and 1980s. While remaining close to its core of diving services operations, the company expanded to include the wider North Sea offshore market. SNS also developed other support services, such as remotely operated vehicles (ROVs), in support of the ongoing exploration efforts in the North Sea. The group's operations in the region led it to add offices in Aberdeen, Scotland, in 1989. In this way, SNS established a presence in what had emerged as an important center for the global offshore industry.

Stolt-Nielsen S.A. went public in 1988, a move which served as a prelude to growth at the family's offshore services company as well. In 1991, Stolt-Nielsen acquired both SNS and Sea Farm from the Stolt-Nielsen families. Stolt-Nielsen then set out to expand its offshore operations.

In 1992, the company acquired one of its key European rivals, Comex Services, the U.K.-based offshore services arm of France's Comex Group. Comex and SNS were merged together to form Stolt Comex Seaway (SCS). The following year, Stolt-Nielsen spun off SCS as a public company, with a listing on the NASDAQ. Stolt-Nielsen retained a 54 percent stake in the newly enlarged company.

In terms of the overall offshore market, SCS remained a relatively minor player. At the same time, the company's reliance on the diving market cast a shadow over its future, as demand for these services declined toward the end of the century. Indeed, the end of the 1980s and the early 1990s witnessed a major shift in the offshore market away from the large-scale, fixed platforms of the industry's early decades, to more flex-

KEY DATES

1973: Jacob Stolt-Nielsen founds offshore services company Stolt-Nielsen Seaway.
1992: Company merges with Comex Services, forming Stolt Comex Seaway, then goes public on the NASDAQ.
1997: Company completes secondary offering on the Oslo Stock Exchange.
2000: Following the purchases of ETPM and 51 percent of NKT Flexibles, company changes name to Stolt Offshore.
2006: Parent company Stolt-Nielsen sells its remaining stake in the business and company changes name to Acergy.

ible floating and subsea installations. This trend became especially prominent as the industry moved further offshore, into deepwater fields where the construction of fixed platforms became impractical.

SCS's public offering provided the company with the fuel to respond to the industry's changes and launch a new growth drive. A centerpiece of the company's new strategy became its expansion beyond its traditional focus on diving and remote services. Instead, the company set out to redevelop itself as a full-service provider of integrated engineering and construction services focused on the offshore industry.

Backed by Stolt-Nielsen, SCS began implementing its new strategy in 1994. Among the new markets targeted by SCS was that of flexible and rigid flowline installation. The company launched the conversion of two of its existing vessels, including the *Seaway Falcon.* At the end of 1994, the company acquired another vessel, the MSS *Enterprise,* which was also converted for flowline installation.

GOING GLOBAL IN THE MID-NINETIES

SCS's expansion drive also led it to look beyond the North Sea market. In 1995, the company acquired DrillSupport International Pty Ltd. The Singapore-based company provided SCS with a springboard into the Asian Pacific region. At the same time, DrillSupport helped expand SCS's capacity in the ROV sector.

Following its expansion into the Asian Pacific, SCS turned its attention toward the Americas. In 1995, the company bought Brazil-based Monocean Oceaneering Enghehaira Submarina Ltda., part of the Oceaneering International group. Meanwhile, SCS boosted its presence in the North Sea region as well, acquiring charters for two new ROV support ships, the *Seaway Commander* and the *Seaway Surveyor,* in October 1995.

The purchase of the *Seaway Eagle* in October 1996 provided SCS with a major entry into the subsea construction sector, as well as adding flowline installation capacity. This effort was boosted by the acquisition of the *Seaway Hawk* at the beginning of 1997, then expanded with a new chartered vessel, the *Toisa Puma.* At the same time, SCS began developing its capacity as a provider of engineering, procurement, installation, and commissioning (EPIC) services, adding another major offshore market to its range of capabilities. In further support of this effort, the company launched a $14 billion investment program to expand its ROV operations to support depths ranging to 3,000 meters.

SCS began preparation for its entry into the ultra-deepwater sector, then focused primarily off the African coast. The company completed a secondary offering on the NASDAQ in March 1997; this was followed several months later with the listing of its shares on the Oslo exchange as well.

By August of that year, SCS had succeeded in winning its first contract in the West African ultra-deepwater sector. SCS then began boosting its competency in this area. In September 1997, the company agreed to exchange 12 of its ROV vessels for a 15-year charter on the *Discovery* construction vessel. SCS then completed a new acquisition of Houston-based Ceanic Corporation the following year. The Ceanic acquisition cost the company $222 million.

RESTRUCTURING FOR THE NEW CENTURY

SCS completed a number of other acquisitions at the close of the century. Purchases included diving specialist J. Ray McDermott, and ROV company Fred Olsen Energy. The two U.S. companies helped increase SCS's presence in the North American market.

By 1998, SCS's change of strategy had successfully doubled its revenues, topping $650 million for the year. The company also emerged as a major player in the ongoing consolidation of the offshore services sector. In 1999, SCS completed a new acquisition, of the ROV operations of Dolphin, another offshore services group.

By 2000, SCS's drive for scale reached a peak, when it agreed to pay more than $240 million to acquire France's ETPM. That company, part of Groupe GTM (itself part of the Suez group), added its own offshore engineering and construction operations, transforming SCS into one of the industry's leaders. Soon after, SCS added another acquisition, a 51 percent stake in NKT Flexibles. Following these acquisitions, SCS changed its name, to Stolt Offshore.

Stolt Offshore continued the group's expansion drive, buying Litwin, which specialized in the provision of turnkey engineering services, from the French Vinci group. Yet the acquisition of that financially troubled company only exacerbated Stolt Offshore's own difficulties at the start of the new century, as it began losing money. By 2002, the company's losses topped $25 million for the year. The company blamed its own rapid expansion, as well as poor management of a number of its offshore projects, on its dip into the red.

In response, Stolt Offshore brought in a new management team, led by Chairman Mark Woolveridge and CEO Tom Ehret. The company launched a major restructuring effort, regrouping its operations around four key business areas: SURF (subsea umbilical risers and flowlines); IMR (inspection, maintenance, and repair); Trunklines; and Conventional Field Development. The company also instituted a new regional operational structure based on five divisions. Each division was assigned its own geographical region, and became responsible for its own financial performance.

The restructuring effort was complemented by a move to develop a range of joint-venture operations. These included a joint venture formed with Malaysia's SapuraCrest Petroleum group, the largest oil services company in that market, in 2005. The company also became a major player in the Girassol oilfields, assuming a partnership in the Mar Profundo Girassol joint venture.

By then, the company had come into its own, after Stolt-Nielsen S.A. sold its entire stake in the company in early 2005. As part of that spinoff, Stolt Offshore was required to change its name. This led to the choice of Acergy; by the beginning of 2006, the company had rebranded its entire global operations under the new name.

Acergy maintained its focus on further expansion. In 2006, the company acquired a new heavy construction ship, in an eight-year charter for the newbuild *SkandiAcergy.* The group expected to take delivery of the vessel by the middle of 2008. Acergy also continued to win new high-profile contracts, such as the deepwater pipeline installation contract for the Kikeh Gas Pipeline Project offshore of Malaysia, in 2007, and a $700 million contract to provide services to Total in the Pazflor field off the coast of Angola, in April 2008. Acergy had proven itself a leading force in the global offshore services industry in the new century.

M. L. Cohen

PRINCIPAL SUBSIDIARIES

Acergy Havila Limited (50%); Acergy/Subsea 7 (50%); Dalia FPSO (17.5%); Global Ocean Engineers Nigeria Limited (40%); Kingfisher D.A. (50%); Mar Profundo Girassol (50%); NKT Flexibles I/S; SapuraAcergy (Malaysia; 50%); Seaway Heavy Lifting (Cyprus; 50%).

PRINCIPAL COMPETITORS

Sumitomo Corporation; China Chang Jiang Energy Corp.; Stone and Webster Engineering Ltd.; RWE AG; ThyssenKrupp Services AG; The Linde Group; Fluor Corporation; Bechtel Group Inc.

FURTHER READING

"Acergy Awarded Contracts," *Pipeline & Gas Journal,* April 2008, p. 14.

"Acergy Awarded US$700m Contract Offshore Angola," *Contracts, Tenders and Rates,* January 3, 2008.

"Acergy Expanding in Aberdeen," *Herald* (Glasgow), October 24, 2006, p. 23.

"Acergy Expands ROV Fleet with Third UHD System," *Vessel & ROV News,* September 19, 2006.

"Acergy Issues $500m CB to Pay for Buyback in US Style," *Euroweek,* September 15, 2006, p. 27.

"Acergy Wins Miskar Work," *MEED Middle East Economic Digest,* December 1, 2006, p. 23.

"Acergy Wins Trunkline Installation off Brazil," *Pipeline & Gas Journal,* May 2007, p. 12.

Kammerzell, Jaime, "Stolt Completes Salvage Project," *Offshore,* April 2004, p. 14.

"Malaysia's First Deepwater Development," *Pipeline & Gas Journal,* September 2007, p. 88.

"Name Change, New Ticker," *Oil and Gas Investor This Week,* April 10, 2006.

Paganie, David, "Acergy Charters," *Offshore,* July 2006, p. 22.

"Stolt Comex Changes Name," *Oil Daily,* May 12, 2000.

"Stolt Offshore Becomes 'Acergy,'" *Offshore Shipping Online,* February 2, 2006.

"Stolt Offshore to Begin Work off South America & Africa," *Pipeline & Gas Journal,* September 2003, p. 8.

"Stolt Spins Off Pipeline Unit with EUR 380m Marketed Sale," *Euroweek,* January 14, 2005, p. 30.

Ackermans & van Haaren N.V.

Begijnenvest 113
Antwerp, B-2000
Belgium
Telephone: (+32 03) 231 87 70
Fax: (+32 03) 225 25 33
Web site: http://www.avh.be

Public Company
Incorporated: 1876
Employees: 993
Sales: EUR 363.97 million ($550 million) (2007)
Stock Exchanges: Euronext Brussels
Ticker Symbol: ACKB
NAICS: 551112 Offices of Other Holding Companies

■ ■ ■

Ackermans & van Haaren N.V. (AvH) is an Antwerp-based holding company focused on four primary areas: Construction, Dredging and Concessions; Real Estate and Related Services; Private Banking; and Private Equity. Construction, Dredging and Concessions represents the company's historical center (AvH was founded as a dredging company in 1876) and is grouped around the company's 50 percent stake in DEME, a world-leading dredging and engineering company; its 100 percent control of construction group A.A. Van Laere, active in Belgium, Luxembourg, and part of France; and a 45 percent stake in Rent-a-Port, a port and port facilities construction and management company established in 2006. AvH's Real Estate division is focused on its ownership of real estate management and development group Extensa, active in Belgium, Luxembourg, Romania, Slovakia, and Turkey. Other real estate holdings include 30 percent of Leasinvest, which owns 49 buildings in Belgium and Luxembourg. AvH's Private Banking division focuses on the group's 75 percent control of Bank Delen, Belgium's leading private bank, and 75 percent of Bank J. Van Breda & Cie, which focuses on the small business and entrepreneur market.

Lastly, AvH is one of Belgium's most active investment groups, through its Private Equity division and its 74 percent share of Sofinim, and 50 percent share of GIB, a joint venture with Nationale Portefeuille Maatschappij. This division owns Alupa, a producer of metalized paper; Arcomet, the leading global tower crane rental company; Groupe Flo (through GIB), a leading restaurant operator in Belgium and France; IT specialist Trasys (46 percent); Spano, a wood processing group (72.9 percent); natural chemicals company Oleon (37 percent) and related company Oleon Biodiesel (60 percent); Hoet Group, a leading European truck sales and rental group (50 percent); and distribution group Distriplus (50 percent). AvH is listed on the NYSE Euronext Brussels Stock Exchange and is led by Chairman and CEO Luc Bertrand. In 2007, AvH's revenues neared EUR 364 million ($550 million).

DREDGING ORIGINS IN THE 19TH CENTURY

Ackermans & van Haaren's interest in the dredging industry began in the late 19th century, when Nicolaas van Haaren joined with Hendrik Willem Ackermans to

COMPANY PERSPECTIVES

Our mission is to create shareholder value through long term investments in a limited number of strategic participations with growth potential on an international level.

form a dredging firm in Antwerp in 1876. By then, however, the company had gained more than two decades of construction and engineering experience, with the launch of a predecessor company in 1852.

By 1900, AvH had become one of the leading players in the Flanders region, participating in the dredging of the Scheldt, starting in 1894. Because of the extensive use of canals throughout the region, dredging was an extremely important part of the construction and engineering industry there. AvH's role as a leader in the sector stemmed from the 1880s, when it became the first to introduce a new type of dredging vessel, the suction dredger. This type of vessel, as its name implies, employed a large vacuum device to perform the dredging operation.

AvH's early implementation of suction dredging techniques enabled it to expand rapidly through the end of the 19th century. By then, the company had begun developing its operations onto a global level. Over the next decades, AvH established itself as one of the world leaders in the dredging sector. Among the group's projects were the construction of the Polish ports following World War I, and operations in St. Petersburg and Helsinki. As such, the company participated in a number of monumental projects, including serving as main contractor for the expansion of the port of Antwerp starting in 1956.

Dredging remained the major focus of AvH's business until well into the 20th century. The industry was highly cyclical, however. This led the company to develop a second operational pole in the early 1960s. The strong growth of the oil exploration and drilling sector, and particularly the appearance of the first offshore oil platforms inspired AvH to extend its reach into this industry as well. In 1964, the company formed its second business, Forasol, to provide oil services.

COUNTERING CYCLES IN THE EIGHTIES

AvH's diversification served in part to expose the group to a second cyclical industry. This became especially apparent following the oil shortages of the 1970s, and the resulting global recession into the early 1980s. AvH found itself hard hit on both of its core fronts.

To reduce its exposure to the dredging sector, AvH moved to merge its own dredging business with another prominent Belgian group, Société Générale de Dragage (SGD). Founded in 1930, SGD had also developed an international reputation, participating in such major works as the dredging of Bluff Harbour, on New Zealand's South Island, in 1956. The newly expanded company became known as Dredging International.

To reduce its exposure, AvH launched a new policy of diversification in the early 1980s. As a launchpad for this effort, AvH went public in 1984, listing its shares on the Brussels stock exchange. AvH began seeking out new investment opportunities. Ultimately, the company's investment business would become the largest part of its operations; nonetheless, the company, which took an active approach to guiding the businesses in which it invested, preferred not to define itself as an investment company.

AvH's first major investment came in 1986, when the company acquired a 49 percent stake in Belgian brewer Maes Group. In 1988, AvH agreed to the merger of Maes with rival Alken-Kronenbourg, controlled by the BSN (later known as Danone) foods group. The combination of the two, forming Alken-Maes, created one of Belgium's leading brewery companies. AvH retained a 50 percent stake in the new company. By 1992, however, the company had agreed to sell its stake in Alken-Maes to BSN, realizing a gain of BEF 675 million.

AvH had been developing its future Construction, Dredging and Concessions division as well. In 1989, the company reentered the construction sector, buying a 45 percent stake in A.A. Van Laere SA. That company specialized in the civil engineering and building construction sector, focused primarily on the Flanders region. Into the early 1990s, AvH increased its stake in Van Laere, ultimately gaining 100 percent control.

Dredging nonetheless remained at the heart of the company's operations. With a new contraction in the global dredging and civil engineering sector at the beginning of the 1990s, AvH took steps to shore up its own dredging operations. For this the company joined with fellow Belgian dredging specialist Baggerwerken Decloedt, forming Dredging Environmental and Marine Engineering, or DEME, in 1991. AvH's share of the new company initially stood at 38 percent, but grew to 50 percent by the end of the decade, giving the group control of the leading Belgian dredging group. DEME in turn gained sufficient scale to compete on the global

KEY DATES

1852: Predecessor to Ackermans & van Haaren is founded in Antwerp.
1876: Nicolaas van Haaren and Hendrik Willem Ackermans form Ackermans & van Haaren (AvH) and specialize in dredging.
1964: AvH adds second pole of operations, offshore oil drilling, through Forasol.
1974: Company merges dredging operations into Dredging International.
1984: AvH goes public and launches investment operations, starting with purchase of Maes brewery in 1986.
1991: Dredging International merges with Baggerwerken Decloedt, becoming DEME (50 percent controlled by AvH).
1992: AvH enters private banking through merger with Delen.
1995: AvH acquires SNI from Belgian government, adding Sofinim private equity operations and Leasinvest real estate operations.
1998: Leasinvest acquires Extensa real estate group.
2002: AvH and CNP acquire GIB investment group.
2005: AvH spins off Extensa from Leasinvest as part of new Real Estate division.

market, especially against its main competitors in the Netherlands.

ADDING BANKING IN THE EARLY NINETIES

AvH's movement into equity investments resulted in the development of its own financial wing. This led the company to a merger with Belgian private bank Delen, founded in 1936. Delen, which went public in 1975, had originally focused on the foreign exchange market, and later teamed up with France's Paribas to form a joint venture in Luxembourg in 1987. Starting in 1990, Delen focused especially on the private banking market, emerging as the largest private banker in Belgium. This growth came especially after AvH increased its own stake in Delen to 75 percent. Through the 1990s, Delen completed a series of acquisitions, including assuming the client base from Verhaegen, Goosens, De Roeck & Co. in 1992, and buying Banque de Schaetzen, based in Liège, in 1994.

Delen next acquired Goffin, Lannoy & Cie, a publicly listed brokerage based in Brussels, in 1995, then opened a branch in Geneva, Switzerland, the following year. The company's Luxembourg operations also grew strongly, and by 1997 had been established as a separate, full-fledged bank, Banque Delen Luxembourg. In that year, AvH guided Delen into a major merger, with fellow Belgian bank J. Van Breda Group, to form a new financial holding company, Finaxis. Both Delen and J. Van Breda then operated as Finaxis subsidiaries, with Delen targeting the private banking market, and Van Breda focused on developing specialized financial products and services for the entrepreneurial market.

Through Finaxis, AvH's financial interests continued to build strongly. In 2000, the company acquired Haveaux, based in Brussels and focused on the brokerage market. AvH then moved into the insurance sector, acquiring 50 percent stakes in two companies in 2000, Asco, operating in both Belgium and the Netherlands, and BDM, which focused on providing insurance for the maritime and industrial sectors.

Through the middle of the first decade of the 2000s, AvH increased its share of Finaxis to 75 percent. Further Finaxis acquisitions followed, including that of Luxembourg's Banque BI&A in 2004, and, through Van Breda, the inland navigation operations of Ethias in 2007. In that year, also, Finaxis completed the takeover of Capital & Finance, which was merged with Bank Delen to form Capfi.

PRIVATE EQUITY FROM 1995

Despite maintaining its core dredging and construction holdings, AvH's investments increasingly turned toward the services sector in the 1990s and into the 2000s. This trend was emphasized by the group's exit from the offshore oil market, with the sale of its Forasol and other drilling holdings in 1996. AvH's willingness to divest of core holdings was also exemplified by its move into, and then exit from, the human resources market. In 1991, AvH participated in the buyout of Creyf's Interim, a publicly listed Belgian temporary employment group which at the time had been in financial difficulty. With AvH's backing, Creyf's Interim quickly regained its footing, posting profits by 1993, then launched an international expansion into the Benelux, French, German, Spanish, Austrian, and Polish markets. After gaining scale through the takeover of the Netherlands' Content Beheer in 1999, the company renamed itself as Solvus in 2002. Finally, in 2005, AvH agreed to sell its stake in Solvus to USG.

Instead, the company moved into the private equity market, paying more than $450 million to acquire the Belgian government's investment arm, SNI, and its control of Sofinim in 1995. Whereas AvH's own investments tended to be long-term, and usually sought majority control, Sofinim targeted minority positions and relatively fast exits. Over the next decade, Sofinim completed a number of important investments, buying stakes in a long list of companies. These included Aviapartner in 1995 (sold in 2005); Telenet (initial public offering, or IPO, in 2005), Atenor Group, and Mercapital SPEF in 1996; Cindu International and Hertel Holding in 1998; and Corn. Van Loocke (exit in 2007), Egemin International, and Webdiggers (sold in 2001) in 1999. Into the next decade, Sofinim's investments included AdValvas Group (sold in 2004), Cyril Finance (exited 2005) and Oleon Holding, in 2001; and NMC in 2002. Other Sofinim investments through the middle of the decade included European truck sales and rental firm Hoet Group and Oleon Biodiesel in 2006, and Spanogroup and Distriplus in 2007.

AvH's investment operations took on a new dimension in 2002, when the company launched a bid to acquire GIB, a major investment group active in France and Belgium. Faced with a rival bid from fellow Belgian group CNP, AvH eventually agreed to launch a 50-50 joint acquisition of GIB with CNP. The addition of GIB added such prominent shareholdings as the Quick Restaurant group, Belgium's leading fast-food restaurant chain, also active in France (sold in 2005) and Groupe Flo, one of the largest full-service restaurant operators in France and Belgium. Other GIB investments included Trasys, acquired in 2006.

ADDING REAL ESTATE

In the meantime, AvH had been building what was to become the fourth main pillar of its business activities, real estate. The company takeover of SNI had brought with it control of Leasinvest. Founded in 1983, Leasinvest initially focused on the leasing market, growing into one of Belgium's leading real estate investment banks. As part of AvH, Leasinvest increasingly added real estate development and management operations as well.

In 1998, Leasinvest acquired the second largest Belgian property group, Extensa, paying more than $60 million to acquire its two million square meters of building properties. The following year, Leasinvest bought the Belgian portfolios of the United Kingdom's Brixton Estate, then in the process of exiting the continental European market. This purchase, for more than $100 million, came as part of Leasinvest's buildup to its IPO, completed in 1999.

In 2005, AvH split off Extensa from Leasinvest, as part of the creation of AvH's real estate division, focused on the property management and leasing market. To boost the range of Extensa's services, AvH led the purchase of a 40 percent stake in Cobelguard, a security services firm, in 2006. Meanwhile, Leasinvest completed the takeover of Dexia Immo Lux in that year, boosting its position in the Luxembourg market. This purchase helped expand the group's portfolio beyond the Brussels market. Similarly, in 2007, the company acquired a 20 percent stake in Paris-based Financière Duval, further increasing the scope of its real estate portfolio.

By 2008, AvH had established itself as one of Belgium's most active and successful investment groups. The company boasted a wide-ranging and diversified portfolio. Yet throughout its transformation from industrial company to investment house, AvH had remained close to its historical core, guiding its main dredging holding, DEME, to a position among the global leaders in its sector into the 21st century.

M. L. Cohen

PRINCIPAL SUBSIDIARIES

Algemene Aannemingen Van Laere; Bank J. Van Breda & Cie (75%); DEME (50%); Extensa Group; Leasinvest Real Estate (29.23%); Rent-a-Port (45%); Société Nationale de Transport par Canalisation (75%).

PRINCIPAL COMPETITORS

KBC Group N.V.; Fortis S.A./NV; Argenta Bank- en Verzekeringsgroep S.A./NV; Petrofina S.A./NV; Compagnie Nationale a Portefeuille S.A.; Transcor Astra Group S.A./NV; Umicore S.A./NV; Fabricom S.A./NV; Etn Franz Colruyt S.A./NV.

FURTHER READING

"Ackermans & van Haaren Sees 'Strong' FY, 'Prudent' Due to Market Uncertainty," *Thomson Financial News,* May 26, 2008.

"Belgian Beauty Attracts Investment," *Cosmetics International,* June 8, 2007, p. 9.

"Belgian Companies Ackermans & van Haaren (Through Its 74% Subsidiary Sofinim) and Distripar Have Formed a Partnership in the Specialized Distribution Sector," *Cosmetics International,* March 23, 2007, p. 6.

Cordes, Renee, "Ackermans Bids for GIB," *Daily Deal,* September 17, 2002.

Young, Ian, "Investment Group Buys Atofina Unit," *Chemical Week,* December 6, 2000, p. 23.

Adani Enterprises Ltd.

Adani House, Near Mithakhali Cir.
Navrangpura
Ahmedabad, 380 009
India
Telephone: (+91 079) 2656 5555
Fax: (+91 079) 2656 5500
Web site: http://www.adanigroup.com

Public Company
Incorporated: 1988 as Adani Exports
Employees: 610
Sales: INR 197.44 billion
Stock Exchanges: Mumbai
Ticker Symbols: ADANIENT; ADEL
NAICS: 221112 Fossil Fuel Electric Power Generation; 221122 Electric Power Distribution; 483111 Deep Sea Freight Transportation; 311225 Fats and Oils Refining and Blending; 233110 Land Subdivision and Land Development

■ ■ ■

Adani Enterprises Ltd. is one of India's largest and fastest-growing conglomerates. Founded as a small plastics importer in 1988, Adani grew into one of the country's largest "five star export houses," trading in a wide variety of food and non-food commodities. Among the goods handled by Adani are metals, minerals, fertilizers, and other agro-industrial products and goods, textiles, steel scrap, castor oil, petrochemicals, petroleum oil and lubricants, and marine products. From its origins as a trading company, Adani has successfully diversified its holdings, starting with the construction and operation of the Mundra port complex, the largest privately managed port in India, launched in 1998. Since then, Adani has expanded its holdings to include power trading, logistics, shipping, edible oils refining, fruits and vegetables storage and handling, and real estate. Adani has further extended its operations with the decision to move into infrastructure, adding electrical power generation, natural gas distribution, coal mining, and oil exploration. In this way, Adani, like many of India's conglomerates, has followed a path of both forward and backward integration, controlling nearly the entire chain of operations within given industries. Among the principal companies in the Adani group are Adani Power, its power generation operation, which is in the process of constructing five plants with a total power generation capacity of 9,900 megawatts (MW). Adani Wilmar is the company's edible oil refining joint venture with Singapore's Wilmar, which, through its Fortune brand, has captured the leading share of the Indian edible oil market. Adani Global is India's largest scrap metal importer. The company's real estate development operations include residential and commercial projects in Mumbai and Ahmedabad, with a total surface of approximately 25 million square feet. Adani Enterprises is listed on the Mumbai Stock Exchange and is led by founder and Chairman Gautam Adani. In 2007, the company generated total revenues of INR 197.44 billion.

SCHOOL DROPOUT TO TRADING MAGNATE IN 1988

Gautam Adani was born in 1962 in Ahmedabad, in India's Gujarat region. Adani's family owned a number

COMPANY PERSPECTIVES

Our Vision: Be an entrepreneurial globally preferred business associate with responsible concern for ecology, society and stakeholders' value. Our Mission: To develop, assimilate and manage knowledge; to apply the acquired expertise across the globe, for benefit of stakeholders'; to do so profitability.

of furniture and home furnishing stores in Ahmedabad. Adani had been expected to join the family business and enrolled in the commerce department of CN Vidyalay School. In 1978, however, Adani dropped out of school to work for his cousin's diamond business in Mumbai. For the next three years, Adani worked as a diamond sorter and polisher.

In 1981, Adani's older brother acquired a small plastics company in Ahmedabad. He asked the then 19-year-old Adani to return home to run the company. Adani agreed, and quickly built up the company's production. By the middle of the decade, the plastics operation had grown into three companies, Eco Plastics, Eezy Plastics, and Elite Plastics. Total monthly production volumes by then had reached more than 20 metric tons of polyvinylchloride (PVC) based products. However, the plastic business's growth soon ran into a major obstacle. At the time, the only domestic source of PVC in India was the Indian Petrochemicals Corporation (IPC). That company's ability to supply PVC, however, fell far short of the Adani company's needs.

As a result, Adani was forced to turn to the heavily regulated import market for his PVC supply. The move proved a turning point in Adani's career, as he developed his first experience in the international import-export trading market. At the same time, Adani benefited from good timing: in 1985, the Indian government enacted new and more liberal import policies for a select number of products. PVC featured prominently on the 150-strong Open General License list, and Adani quickly moved to take advantage of the new market opportunity.

Adani had recognized that even after the company paid import duties and other fees, the imported PVC would remain far less inexpensive than the IPC-produced PVC. Adani saw an opportunity not only to supply the family's own factories, but also to sell the PVC to other manufacturers in India. Adani went in search of a larger partner, and reached an agreement with Gujarat State Export Corporation (GSEC), which agreed to supply him with a letter of credit and import PVC under its name. Even after paying a 3 percent commission to GSEC, Adani was able to achieve profit margins as high as 6 percent.

By 1988, Adani had decided to enter trading full time, and in that year founded his own company, Adani Exports, in the form of a partnership. The company was quite small at the start, with start-up capital of just INR 500,000 and revenues of just INR 22 million in its first year of operation.

Adani proved a skillful trader. The company began branching out into other products and commodities, while also adding a strong export portion as well. By 1992, Adani Exports had neared sales of INR 200 million. By then, the company was financially solid enough to pursue its own trading operations independent of GSEC.

In the meantime, the Indian government moved into a new phase of the liberalization policies launched under Rajiv Gandhi. In 1991, the government added a new series of initiatives designed to stimulate the country's exports. As part of that effort, the government dropped many of the remaining restrictions on import goods, allowing Adani to further expand the range of goods handled by his company. In 1992, the government enacted the Value-based Advance Licensing (VABAL) Scheme, which allowed companies to import goods duty-free up to a specified proportion of their exported goods. The scheme proved full of loopholes, allowing trading groups to avoid taxes and duties on most of their imports, often fraudulently. Indeed, a number of trading groups later ran into legal trouble.

Gautam Adani managed to remain on the right side of the law, while all the while leading his company on an impressive growth spree. By 1997, Adani Exports had seen its annual revenues skyrocket past INR 16 billion, and then climbed again to more than INR 24 billion by the end of the following year. By then, Adani had taken the company public, listing its shares on the Mumbai Stock Exchange in 1994. The listing proved highly successful, as the company's share price multiplied by approximately 22 times into the late 1990s.

FROM TRADING GROUP TO PORTS OPERATOR IN 1998

Adani's success had also brought a great deal of scrutiny of the company, and of Gautam Adani himself. Toward the end of the decade, Adani's company had been placed under investigation, and Adani himself had been accused of, if not formally charged with, committing a variety of crimes, ranging from fraud to importing counterfeit currency to being linked to organized crime.

KEY DATES

1981: Gautam Adani takes over as head of his brother's PVC-based plastics company.
1985: Company begins importing PVC, launching first trading operations.
1988: Adani Exports is established as a partnership.
1994: Adani Exports goes public on the Mumbai Stock Exchange.
1998: Company completes Mundra private port complex.
2001: Mundra receives Special Economic Zone designation.
2003: Company forms Power Trading division.
2006: Company changes name to Adani Enterprises as it expands into real estate, oil and gas exploration, gas distribution, and electricity generation.
2008: Adani nears completion of initial phase of 1,600 MW electrical power plant in Mundra.

Despite the intense investigation of his activities, Adani apparently had managed to remain within the law. As Adani told *Business Trader* at the time: "All this is mere speculation. Our critics plant all kinds of stories against us. None of this has ever been proved. Why doesn't anybody talk about the fact that we are India's largest foreign exchange earner?"

Indeed, by the end of the 1990s, Adani Exports' import-export operations had moved far beyond India, as the company built up a trade list of some 70 commodities from more than 60 countries. The company's growth had enabled it to earn government status as "Star Trading House" by 1993, and a "Super Star Trading House" by 1994. By 2001, Adani Exports had been awarded the status of "Golden Super Star Trading House," and finally, in 2004, was named a "Five Star Export House."

By that time, trade had become just one piece of the Adani empire. Like many of India's successful companies, Adani sought to transform itself as a diversified conglomerate. For this Adani followed a trend common among the country's largest companies, that of developing a high degree of both forward and backward integration in their operations. In this way, for example, Adani entered the shipping and logistics markets in the 1990s, becoming a major player in those sectors. The company, which had based much of its trading success on the import and export of foods, including frozen foods and marine products, entered food production itself in 1999, forming an edible oil refinery joint venture with Singapore's Wilmar Trading. The partnership, Adani Wilmar, then launched its own brand of edible oils, Fortune. That brand became the top-selling food oil brand in India.

Adani had set its sights on developing itself as a major industrial and infrastructure group. This process started in the early 1990s, when Adani received permission to build a small private jetty as part of an industrial salt operation the company proposed to build in the Mundra port zone. The salt operation itself apparently never materialized, however, the jetty was completed by 1992, when the Gujuarat state government announced its decision to privatize the region's ports. Gautam Adani, who enjoyed excellent relations with Gujarat's chief minister at the time, applied for the right to redevelop the jetty into a mega-port, designed to create a rival to India's major, and highly congested, Mumbai ports.

Adani formed a joint venture with the Gujarat Port Infrastructure Development Co., Gujarat Adani Port, and by 1998 the first phase of the Mundra port was operational. The new port offered some of the most modern deepwater facilities on the Indian continent, and also boasted an important rail link to the country's major capitals. It also filled a major gap in the group's integration efforts, which spanned import and export, shipping, port operations, and logistics. Adani next applied for, and received, Special Economic Zone (SEZ) status for the Mundra port in 2001. The new designation permitted the company to enter its next phase of development—becoming a major Indian infrastructure group.

POWER TRADING AND POWER GENERATION IN THE NEW CENTURY

The SEZ designation provided incentives for Adani's own moves into manufacturing and industrial operations. In 2001, for example, the group's Adani Wilmar joint venture established a major new edible oil refinery in the Mundra SEZ. The company then applied for the rights to import seeds, rather than crude oil, to gain full control over its edible oil operations. The new oil facility, which boasted a capacity of 600 tons per day, came in support of the group's launch of its Fortune oil brand. This naturally led Adani to push its integration model forward, and by 2001 the company owned four supermarkets in Ahmedabad. By the end of 2004, that number had grown to nearly 25 supermarkets.

Into the new century, however, Adani set its sights still higher as it sought a further extension of its integration strategy. Into the middle of the first decade of the 2000s, Adani emerged as a major infrastructure group, building a presence in the real estate development, power trading, power generation, and gas distribution sectors.

Adani at first leveraged its long trading experience, setting up its Power Trading Division in 2003. In this way, the company took advantage of the newly passed Electricity Act, which separated power trading from power generation for the first time. Adani emerged as a prominent player in the market, successfully trading more than 5,700 MW of power by 2007. The company then set its targets at achieving an average of 5,000 MW per year before the end of the decade.

From power trading, Adani, which changed its name to Adani Enterprises in 2006, leaped into power generation. These efforts had actually begun in the late 1990s, as the company gained a license to construct and operate a small naphtha-powered plant in Anjar in 1997. The following year, the group formed a joint venture with Eastern Generation of the United Kingdom to form Adani Eastern Generation Company. Yet Adani's drive into the power generation sector truly took off when the company launched a massive investment for the construction of five power plants with a combined 9,900 MW of generating capacity. The company expected these projects to be completed by 2012. The initial phase of the first plant, a 1,600 MW facility at Mundra, was expected to come online in 2008.

A TOWERING CONGLOMERATE

The move into power generation naturally led the company to integrate its fuel sources. The company moved into coal mining, buying mines in Rajasthan and Indonesia. Adani next began developing interests in the oil and gas markets. The company formed an oil exploration division, and reportedly bid $4 billion to acquire Burren Energy. Adani, through subsidiary Adani Welspun, then successfully bid for several oil and gas exploration projects in Gujarat and Assam in India, as well as in Thailand. The company also built up its own oil and gas reserves. This enabled the company to enter the gas distribution business, with contracts to supply several cities in Gujarat.

In keeping with its integration model, Adani's extension into the exploration and distribution of natural gas led the company to become involved in its destination as well. The company, although a somewhat late entrant into India's booming property development market, nonetheless arrived with a bang. Starting in 2006, the company had succeeded in building a vast land bank of 100 million square feet, including the prestigious Bandra Kurla complex. By 2008, Adani already counted among the largest real estate developers in India, with more than 25 million square feet of residential and commercial space under development in Mumbai and Ahmenabad. Gautam Adani, by then one of India's wealthiest people, had built one of the country's largest conglomerates in just two decades.

M. L. Cohen

PRINCIPAL SUBSIDIARIES

Adani Agri Fresh Ltd.; Adani Agri Logistics Ltd.; Adani Developers Pvt. Ltd.; Adani Estates Pvt. Ltd.; Adani Global FZE; Adani Global Limited; Adani Global PTE Ltd.; Adani Habitats Pvt. Ltd.; Adani Infrastructure & Developers Pvt. Ltd.; Adani Land Developers Pvt. Ltd.; Adani Power Ltd.; Adani Shipping PTE Ltd.; Adani Townships and Real Estate Company Pvt. Ltd.; Adani Virginia Inc.; Columbia Chrome (India) Pvt. Ltd.; Libra Shipping PTE Ltd.; PT Adani Global; Swayam Realtors and Traders Ltd.; Vyom Tradelink Pvt. Ltd.

FURTHER READING

"Adani Enterprises Aims 10,000MW Power Generation in 3–5 Yrs," *PTI—The Press Trust of India,* January 24, 2008.

"Gautam Adani: Another Gujarati Who Made It Big," *Economic Times,* December 8, 2007.

Mehta, Harit, "Adanis to Scale up Mundra Project," *Economic Times,* September 13, 2007.

Mishra, Ashish Kumar, "Adani Logistics to Launch Container Train Operations," *Economic Times,* July 4, 2007.

"Mundra Port IPO in Trouble," *Times of India,* May 30, 2007.

Prabhune, Tushar, and Narayan Bhatt, "Adanis Want Free Port Tag for Mundra," *Economic Times,* July 22, 2006.

Shanker, Abhishek, and Harit Mehta, "Adanis Line up Rs 2,000-cr Mundra Port Expansion," *Economic Times,* January 3, 2007.

Shukla, Nimish, "Adani Gujarat's Biggest Wealth Creator of '06," *Times of India,* January 2, 2007.

———, "Adani Topples Torrent Promoter in Rich List," *Times of India,* February 7, 2007.

———, "Adanis Plan Rs 1,500 cr IPO," *Economic Times,* March 9, 2007.

Subramaniam, G. Ganapathy, and Subhash Narayan, "Adani Group Eyes Brakel Stake in Himachal Power Projects," *Economic Times,* May 6, 2008.

Talwar, Priyanka, "Adani to Put $100m in Ports," *Economic Times,* September 1, 2006.

AeroVironment, Inc.

181 West Huntington Drive, Suite 202
Monrovia, California 91016
U.S.A.
Telephone: (626) 357-9983
Fax: (626) 359-9628
Web site: http://www.avinc.com

Public Company
Incorporated: 1971
Employees: 526
Sales: $173.72 million (2007)
Stock Exchanges: NASDAQ
Ticker Symbol: AVAV
NAICS: 335999 All Other Miscellaneous Electrical Equipment and Component Manufacturing; 336411 Aircraft Manufacturing; 336412 Aircraft Engine and Engine Parts Manufacturing; 811310 Commercial and Industrial Machinery and Equipment (Except Automotive and Electronic) Repair and Maintenance; 541710 Research and Development in the Physical, Engineering, and Life Sciences; 333611 Turbine and Turbine Generator Set Unit Manufacturing; 335911 Storage Battery Manufacturing

■ ■ ■

AeroVironment, Inc., is an innovative design, consulting, and manufacturing firm involved in aviation and alternative energy projects. Small UAVs (unmanned aerial vehicles) and fast-charge battery systems are its leading product areas, but AeroVironment has been active in a wide range of diverse research projects, including small wind turbine generators for commercial buildings. If there is a common thread through the company's various design efforts, it is efficiency.

Company founder Dr. Paul B. MacCready, who died in 2007, was an influential pioneer in the fields of human-powered and solar-powered flight. This work led to a partnership with General Motors in designing an early generation of electric vehicles. The quest for practical recharging led to the company's PosiCharge battery systems for industrial uses such as forklifts. U.S. military actions after the September 11, 2001, terrorist attacks against the United States (9/11) greatly increased interest in the company's small unmanned aircraft systems, dubbed the Raven, Dragon Eye, Swift, Wasp, and Puma, which could be launched by hand and were generally used to provide tactical reconnaissance in the field. Following a pattern set by the intellectually insatiable MacCready, the company has continued to study a wide range of energy and environmental problems.

A LEGENDARY PIONEER

AeroVironment, Inc.'s founder, Dr. Paul B. MacCready, holds a special place among aviation's greatest designers. A fascination with the nature of flight took root early in his childhood years, while growing up in Connecticut. Born in 1925, he spent much of his youth building model airplanes, a practice he never really stopped. He remained committed to aviation in adulthood, earning a Ph.D. in aeronautics from the California Institute of Technology (Caltech). In 1956 he became the nation's first world champion glider pilot.

> **COMPANY PERSPECTIVES**
>
> AV develops and produces Unmanned Aircraft Systems and Efficient Electric Energy Technologies that enable our customers to rewrite the rules—of engagement, productivity, efficiency and safety—to their advantage. AV is relentlessly committed to delivering and supporting innovations that help our customers succeed.

According to a long profile of the man in *Design News,* MacCready always intended to be a pioneer, and this led to entrepreneurship. In 1952 he formed Meteorology Research Inc. to probe storms using small aircraft. He sold this business and in 1971 launched AeroVironment, Inc., in California with Dr. Ivar Tombach and Dr. Peter Lissaman, both of Caltech. The company formed a Design Development Center in Simi Valley, California, in 1980. It was led by Ray Morgan, a veteran of Lockheed's famed Skunk Works.

ON GOSSAMER WINGS

A definitive moment in MacCready's life reads like a New Age testimonial on the power of the Universe to provide. He found himself stuck with a $100,000 debt when a relative defaulted on a loan he had cosigned. With the value of the dollar falling, this was the equivalent of a £50,000 prize U.K. industrialist Henry Kremer was offering to the first to successfully navigate a one-mile, figure-eight course with a human-powered aircraft. The debt and prize set MacCready's imagination running.

He realized that larger wings required less effort to provide lift. With a big enough wing, he could design a plane around the roughly one-third horsepower output of a competitive cyclist (in this case Bryan Allen, who was also a trained glider pilot). Working in their off hours, MacCready's team built a large, 96-foot wingspan contraption making full use of a new generation of lightweight and strong synthetic materials. This was the beginning of a profitable working relationship with DuPont, which picked up much of the tab for future projects. In 1977 the resulting *Gossamer Condor* flew into the winners' circle and into the history books, ultimately landing in the Smithsonian Institution. A few years later, MacCready's human-powered *Gossamer Albatross* flew across the English Channel, garnering another Kremer Prize.

In 1981, a derivative aircraft called *Solar Challenger* made a 165-mile flight from Paris to London using only electricity from the 16,000 photovoltaic cells lining its wings. These efforts reached their peak in 2001, when its successor, *Helios,* attained an altitude of 96,000 feet. *Helios,* which ultimately crashed off of Hawaii, was one of the biggest projects the company had undertaken, with 14 propellers mounted on a wing measuring nearly 250 feet. AeroVironment expected to eventually commercialize such high-endurance vehicles as communications satellite substitutes.

ELECTRIC VEHICLES

MacCready readily admitted there were few practical applications for human-powered aircraft, but this work led to more down-to-earth applications with electric vehicles (EVs). General Motors tapped the company to design the body for the Sunraycer solar car being developed by its Hughes Aircraft unit. In 1987 this blew the doors off the competition in a solar-powered automobile contest in Australia, averaging 41 miles per hour in the nearly 2,000-mile race.

General Motors bought a 15 percent stake in AeroVironment in 1988. In 1990 the companies partnered on the much-hyped Impact, precursor to the EV1, claimed to be the first practical electric car. Thousands were leased to drivers in California and Arizona before GM pulled the plug on the project and shredded the cars.

A SPECIALTY IN SMALL UAVS

The post-9/11 military operations in Afghanistan and Iraq produced unprecedented demand for UAVs, or what AeroVironment called UAS, or unmanned aerial systems. AeroVironment had been working with UAVs for decades before they developed into a major line of business. In the 1980s, it produced a small UAV called the Pointer that weighed just nine pounds and had a wingspan of about nine feet.

The UAVs produced by AeroVironment were much smaller than larger, headline-grabbing drones such as the Predator. AeroVironment's Raven, a smaller derivative of the Pointer with a wingspan of just four feet, could be carried into battle in a backpack and launched and recovered by soldiers in the field. Its mission was tactical reconnaissance: peering around buildings by day or night. The Army rushed the original Raven A into service in 2003 and an improved Raven B began production three years later. By mid-2007, the Army had about 350 Ravens in the field, according to *Aviation Week & Space Technology.* AeroVironment's Wasp shrank the reconnaissance drone concept further, having a wingspan of about two feet.

KEY DATES

1971: Dr. Paul B. MacCready launches AeroVironment, Inc.
1979: MacCready's human-powered *Gossamer Albatross* flies across the English Channel.
1981: *Solar Challenger* explores solar-powered flight.
1987: Sunraycer wins 2,000-mile solar-powered vehicle contest in Australia.
1990: AeroVironment helps General Motors design its Impact electric car.
2001: Solar and fuel cell-powered *Helios* attains altitude of 96,000 feet.
2005: AeroVironment makes first flight with *Global Observer,* fueled by liquid-hydrogen.
2007: AeroVironment becomes a public company, traded on the NASDAQ.

ON THE LEADING EDGE

AeroVironment continued to operate at the cutting edge of technology, and the limits of the atmosphere. It developed a liquid hydrogen-fueled vehicle called the *Global Observer* that first flew in 2005. Like the earlier, solar-powered *Helios,* it raised the prospect of aircraft that could stay aloft for months, an idea with huge implications for environmental monitoring, communications, and military surveillance applications.

Since the mid-1990s the Defense Advanced Research Projects Agency (DARPA) had AeroVironment working on miniature aircraft, or micro air vehicles (MAVs), as small as six inches. Some were propelled by a wing-flapping motion, which recalled the 18-foot flying model pterodactyl the company built in 1986 for an IMAX dinosaur documentary. The problems with sourcing reliable components at this scale level made the larger UAVs a more practical proposition. However, AeroVironment left the largest of these, such as the Global Predator, to others.

AeroVironment continued to pursue a number of varied interests. These included small power-generating "Architectural Wind" turbines for commercial buildings. In 2007 it installed 18 of the units (annual capacity 28,000 kilowatt hours) at the Kettle Foods potato chip plant in Beloit, Wisconsin.

PUBLIC IN 2007

UAV sales helped propel revenues to new heights. The company had been taking in less than $20 million even during the defense buildup of the Reagan administration. Within a few years of 9/11, revenues rose past $45 million and they more than doubled to $105 million in 2005 as net income grew sevenfold to $14.6 million. Revenues were $139 million for the fiscal year ended April 30, 2006, as net income reached $20.7 million.

Against this backdrop, AeroVironment became a public company in January 2007 upon its listing on the NASDAQ. The public offering was very well received, with the share price rising more than 50 percent (from $17 to $23) on the first day of trading. AeroVironment gleaned $113 million from the flotation. The company by then had about 450 employees, up threefold in just a few years, and it was hiring more.

The year marked another major transition. Company founder Paul MacCready passed away on August 28, 2007. He was recognized by *Time* magazine as one of the 100 greatest minds of the 20th century. He was succeeded as chairman by Tim Conver, who had been AeroVironment's president and CEO since 1991.

Frederick C. Ingram

PRINCIPAL SUBSIDIARIES

AV S.r.l.; Skytower, LLC; Skytower Inc.; AILC, Inc.; Regenerative Fuel Cell Systems, LLC.

PRINCIPAL DIVISIONS

Small UAS; PosiCharge Systems; Energy Technology Center.

PRINCIPAL COMPETITORS

L-3 Communications Holdings Inc.; Advanced Ceramics Research, Inc.; Applied Research Associates, Inc.; Elbit Systems Ltd.; Lockheed Martin Corporation; Aker Wade Power Technologies LLC; Minit-Charger, a subsidiary of Edison International; PowerDesigners, LLC.

FURTHER READING

Burke, James D., *The Gossamer Condor and Albatross: A Case Study in Aircraft Design,* Pasadena, Calif.: AeroVironment, Inc.; New York: American Institute of Aeronautics and Astronautics, 1980.

Dornheim, Michael A., "NASA Pushing Drones to Operational Use," *Aviation Week & Space Technology,* July 12, 1999, p. 42.

———, "Small Drones Mature," *Aviation Week & Space Technology,* September 15, 2003, p. 63.

———, "Special Fuel Cells Key to Months-Long Flight," *Aviation Week & Space Technology,* February 28, 2000, p. 58.

———, "Tiny Drones May Be Soldier's New Tool," *Aviation Week & Space Technology,* June 8, 1998, p. 42.

Fisher, Lawrence M., "Uniting Low Power and Efficiency," *New York Times,* Sec. 3, Financial Desk, February 25, 1990, p. 11.

"GM Buys Share of Sunraycer Ally; AeroVironment a Specialist in Environmental Management," *Automotive News,* August 22, 1988, p. 48.

HaLevey, Libbe S., "Dr. MacCready and AeroVironment: Helping Pollution Solutions Take Flight," *Southern California Business,* January 1, 1991, p. 8.

"Held Aloft by Hydrogen," *Economist,* September 17, 2005.

Helwig, David, "Work of Intrepid Birdmen Benefits Canadians," *Globe and Mail* (Canada), March 26, 1986, p. B13.

Jaroff, Leon, "Dream Makers," *Time,* December 4, 2000, pp. 102+.

LaMonica, Martin, "'Micro' Wind Turbines Are Coming to Town," *CNET News.com,* February 10, 2006.

Lindsey, Robert, "Physicist's Solar Airplane Set to Challenge the English Channel," *New York Times,* June 9, 1981, p. C1.

McCarty, Lyle H., "Lessons from an Aeronautics Master," *Design News,* August 26, 1991, pp. 138+.

Morris, Jefferson, "AeroVironment Flight-Testing Liquid Hydrogen-Powered UAV," *Aerospace Daily & Defense Report,* June 29, 2005, p. 4.

———, "'Flying Binoculars'; AeroVironment's Raven Leads Small Tactical UAVs from Novelty to Necessity in Theater," *Aviation Week & Space Technology,* June 18, 2007, p. 110.

Smith, Kevin, "AeroVironment's Wind-to-Energy System Pays Off for Its Customers," *San Gabriel Valley Tribune,* October 30, 2007.

Teague, Paul, "Model Pioneer," *Design News,* March 1, 1999, p. 92.

Tuckey, Bill, Ray Berghouse, and David G. Segal, *Sunraycer's Solar Saga,* Gordon, New South Wales, Australia: Berghouse Floyd Tuckey, 1987.

Who Killed the Electric Car?, DVD, Culver City, Calif.: Sony Pictures Home Entertainment, 2006.

African Rainbow Minerals Ltd.

P.O. Box 786136
Sandton, 2146
South Africa
Telephone: (+27 011) 779 1300
Fax: (+27 011) 779 1312
Web site: http://www.arm.co.za

Public Company
Incorporated: 1933 as Anglo-Transvaal Consolidated Investment Company Limited
Employees: 7,725
Sales: ZAR 6.15 billion ($807.8 million) (2007)
Stock Exchanges: Johannesburg
Ticker Symbol: AIN
NAICS: 212234 Copper Ore and Nickel Ore Mining; 551112 Offices of Other Holding Companies

■ ■ ■

African Rainbow Minerals Ltd. (ARM) is one of South Africa's leading mining and minerals groups, and is the country's largest black-owned mining company. ARM operates through several subsidiaries and shareholdings. ARM Platinum, which consists of a 50 percent stake in Modikwa Platinum Mine; 55 percent of Two Rivers Platinum Mine; and 50 percent of Nkomati Mine; as well as a 90 percent share of the exploration operations at Kalplat PGM. ARM Platinum, which also produces nickel, is the company's largest holding, with platinum production contributing 37 percent of the group's operating profits, and nickel production adding 20.3 percent, in 2007. ARM Ferrous generated 42.5 percent of the group's profits, through its 50 percent share of Assmang. This division produces manganese, iron ore, chrome, and manganese alloys. ARM controls 51 percent of ARM Coal, which itself holds a 51 percent stake in the Goedgevonden coal field, as well as a 20 percent stake in Xstrat Coal South Africa. ARM owns 65 percent of publicly listed TEAL Exploration & Mining Inc., which functions as ARM's vehicle for its non–South African exploration and prospecting operations. TEAL oversees projects in Zambia, Congo, and Namibia. Lastly, ARM is the largest shareholder, with a 16 percent stake, in Harmony Gold, the world's fifth largest gold producer, and the third largest in South Africa. Together these operations combined to generate more than ZAR 6 billion ($807 million) in revenues in 2007. The company has announced a goal to raise revenues past ZAR 10 billion ($1.4 billion) by 2010. ARM is listed on the Johannesburg Stock Exchange and is led by Chairman and founder Patrice Motsepe. In 2008, Motsepe became South Africa's first black billionaire.

FROM ROYAL ORIGINS TO ENTREPRENEUR

Born in Soweto, next to Johannesburg, at the height of South Africa's apartheid regime in the early 1960s, Patrice Motsepe nonetheless enjoyed a number of distinct advantages. For one, the Motsepe clan had been part of the Tswana tribe's royalty for many centuries, and Patrice Motsepe's uncle was tribal leader. For another, Motsepe's mother's great-grandfather had come from Scotland, a lineage that, after a degree of string-pulling, enabled Patrice Motsepe and his siblings to enroll in the

COMPANY PERSPECTIVES

African Rainbow Minerals Limited (ARM) is a niche, diversified South African mining company with excellent long-life, low-cost operating assets in key commodities.

prestigious St. Joseph Mission School, an Afrikaans-speaking boarding school normally restricted to so-called "coloreds" by the apartheid regime.

Perhaps the most important influence in Motsepe's later career, however, was his father, Augustine Motsepe. A vocal critic of apartheid, Augustine Motsepe had been banished to Hammanskraal, a mining region north of Pretoria, at the beginning of the 1960s. There, Motsepe set up a small grocery shop, then reinvested his profits into opening a bar and a restaurant. Motsepe later grew into one of the most successful black businessmen during the apartheid era. This success provided the Motsepe family with the resources, and political clout, to ensure their children's education.

Patrice Motsepe came to work in his father's shop during school vacations, selling alcohol to local miners. The young Motsepe quickly showed an aptitude for business, however, Motsepe's ambitions lay elsewhere. After graduating from the University of Swaziland, he applied for and received an exemption to study law at the whites-only University of Witwatersrand. After graduating in 1988, Motsepe was hired by Bowman Gilfillan, a leading corporate law firm in South Africa. By 1993, Motsepe had risen to become the firm's first black partner.

During this time, however, Motsepe had left South Africa to spend a year working for Richmond, Virginia-based McGuireWoods. While there, Motsepe began investigating the mining industry. This led him to focus on providing representation for mining companies when he returned to South Africa in 1992. In particular, Motsepe began developing an understanding of the factors behind the success or failure of a mine. Motsepe soon recognized that the smallest and leanest mining groups were also generally the most successful.

Motsepe's research whetted his own entrepreneurial spirit just in time for a sea-change in South Africa's political and economic climate. The collapse of the apartheid regime and the arrival of the African National Congress, led by Nelson Mandela, opened up new opportunities to the country's black population. Motsepe decided to leave the law firm and go into business for himself.

In 1994, Motsepe established Future Mining to provide low-level services to the South African mining industry. The company started by offering sweeping services, sending crews into gold mines to sweep up the gold dust left behind by industrial mining operations. Motsepe set up a novel pay scheme to encourage productivity. Instead of paying a standard flat wage, Motsepe established a lower base pay rate, while offering a profit-sharing scheme that could double workers' wages.

ESTABLISHING ARM IN 1997

Motsepe struggled for the better part of a year to establish his business. Unable to secure credit from the banks, Motsepe was forced to operate out of a suitcase. By the end of its first year, however, Future Mining had secured its first major contract, sweeping an Orkney-based gold mine owned by the giant Anglo-American mining company.

By the mid-1990s, Motsepe had begun laying plans to enter the mining industry outright and began looking to buy his first mine. His chance came, paradoxically, with the slump of global gold prices in 1997. Larger corporations, such as Anglo-American, then sought to exit gold mining, which had suddenly become unprofitable. The larger mining groups especially looked to shed smaller, low-yield mines such as the Orkney gold mine. Motsepe began seeking financing to buy out the Orkney operation. Yet despite the success of Future Mining, Motsepe once again found the banks reluctant to back his new venture.

Motsepe found an ally in Anglo-American's Robert Godsell, CEO of the group's gold and uranium operations. Godsell had recognized the need to support the African National Congress by fostering the emergence of a new generation of black businessmen. When Motsepe was unable to raise the purchase price for the Orkney mine, Godsell agreed to sell the mine anyway, in a deal giving Anglo-American a share of future profits.

Motsepe set up a new company, called African Rainbow Minerals, or ARMgold, bringing in André Wilkins, a mining engineer from Anglo-American, to serve as the company's CEO. Motsepe immediately set to work streamlining the Orkney mine's operations, slashing payroll by one-third and setting up headquarters nearby the mine, instead of in more distant Johannesburg. Motsepe also implemented a more intensive work schedule, boosting production from just 275 days per year to 353 days. Despite subsequent drops in the gold rate, ARMgold's low-cost operating

KEY DATES

1994: Patrice Motsepe establishes Future Services to provide sweeping and other low-level mining services.
1997: Motsepe acquires first gold mines from Anglo-American, forming ARMgold.
2001: Company enters platinum mining through joint venture with Anglo Platinum.
2003: Company merges gold interests into Harmony in exchange for 16 percent stake.
2004: Company acquires mining and exploration assets of Avmin and is renamed African Rainbow Minerals.
2005: Subsidiary TEAL Exploration goes public.
2007: African Rainbow acquires 26 percent stake in Xstrata's South Africa coal mining operations.
2008: Company launches first foreign copper mining operations in Zambia and Congo.

structure enabled the company to pay back Anglo-American's loan of more than $8 million within three years.

ARMgold acquired a number of additional gold mining shafts in the Vaal Reefs and Free State deposits from Anglo-American through the end of the decade. By then, the company had developed a growing reputation for its ability to transform marginal low-production shafts into high-production operations.

ENTERING PLATINUM IN THE NEW CENTURY

Motsepe next turned his attention to the booming platinum market. Toward this end, the company was aided by increasing pressure from the South African government on the country's industries to inaugurate black empowerment initiatives. ARM had launched negotiations with Anglo Platinum, the leading platinum producer in the world, as early as 1999. By 2001, the two companies had reached an agreement to form a new joint-venture company, a platinum mining operation at Modikwa. As part of that deal, ARM agreed to put up ZAR 100 million of the total ZAR 1.35 billion cost of the project, in exchange for a 50 percent stake. The company then formed a new business unit, ARM Platinum. Importantly, under the joint agreement, ARM had negotiated for 17 percent of the ownership of the Modikwa mine to be turned over to two local nonprofit organizations.

The Modikwa joint venture, expected to produce as much as 3.5 million ounces of platinum per year, marked an important milestone in the run-up to the Black Economic Empowerment (BEE) laws, which were finally enacted in 2005. The deal also established ARM as a major partner for companies as they rushed to comply with BEE mandates.

By the beginning of 2002, ARM had launched its next partnership. This time, the company joined with Harmony to spend $190 million to acquire another group of gold shafts, with a total production of more than one million troy ounces per year, from Anglo-American. Harmony, established in 1950 and later part of the Randgold group, had grown into one of the leading South African gold producers, and one of the top six in the global market.

The joint venture led to the creation of Free Gold, which quickly implemented ARM's low-cost operating techniques. These moves boosted not only production, but also operating margins. With its total gold output rising strongly, ARM decided to list its ARMgold subsidiary on the Johannesburg stock exchange that year.

The ARMgold listing provided ARM with a springboard into the ranks of South Africa's mining leaders. By the end of 2003, ARM had entered negotiations to acquire Anglovaal Mining, or Avmin. That company stemmed from a business established in 1933 by Slip Mennell and Bob Hersov, and had grown into one of South Africa's largest mining and industrial powerhouses, Anglo-Transvaal Consolidated Investment Company, or Anglovaal. In 1997, the Mennell and Hersov families agreed to split up the group, retaining its industrial holdings while spinning off its mining operations into Avmin.

STRATEGIZING FOR THE FUTURE

In the prelude to the Avmin acquisition, ARM merged its gold mining operations into Harmony, in exchange for a 16 percent stake in that company. Harmony consequently became the world's fifth largest gold producer. ARM then changed its name, to African Rainbow Minerals, as it integrated Avmin's operations. As part of that process, the company established a new business unit, ARM Ferrous, which took over the company's newly acquired ferrous metals operations. These included manganese and iron ore mines, as well as chrome and other production facilities. ARM Platinum was also extended to include Avmin's nickel mining business. The company also took over Avmin's exploration operations, which were focused on the Zambia, Congo, and Namibia markets. These were then placed under another subsidiary, TEAL Exploration & Mining Inc.

The deal helped to raise ARM's total revenues to nearly ZAR 5.5 billion ($700 million) by the end of 2005. In that year, encouraged by the passage of the BEE laws, Motsepe announced his plans to double ARM's size by the end of the decade. Toward that end, the company began investigating new areas of expansion. In 2005, the group, which had acquired a number of coal mining assets from Avmin, moved to extend its coal interests the following year. This was accomplished through the purchase of a 26 percent stake in the South Africa coal mining operations of Switzerland's Xstrata, in a deal worth $360 million. The deal enabled Xstrata to comply with the new BEE legislation.

ARM also targeted an entry into copper mining. This effort was led by TEAL, which went public with listings on the Toronto and Johannesburg stock exchanges in 2005. Nonetheless, ARM retained a 65 percent stake in its foreign exploration arm. By the beginning of 2007, the company announced that it was ready to launch production at its first three copper mines in Zambia and Congo, with a projected total output of as much as 70,000 tons per year by 2011.

With global prices for metals and coal skyrocketing in the second half of the first decade of the 2000s, ARM had gained a strong position for itself. By the end of 2007, revenues had soared past ZAR 6 billion ($800 million), and the company appeared on the way to achieving its growth targets by the end of the decade. In the meantime, Patrice Motsepe had established himself as a major figure in the global mining industry. By 2008, Motsepe had become South Africa's first black billionaire. ARM appeared a strong candidate to become a leader in the emerging new generation of South African mining groups.

M. L. Cohen

PRINCIPAL SUBSIDIARIES

African Rainbow Minerals Platinum (Proprietary) Limited; Anglovaal Air (Proprietary) Limited; Atscot (Pty) Limited; Avmin Limited; Bitcon's Investments (Proprietary) Jesdene Limited; Kingfisher Insurance Co. Limited; Lavino (Pty) Limited; Letaba Copper & Zinc Corp. Limited; Mannequin Insurance PCC Limited; Prieska Copper Mines Limited; Sheffield Minerals (Proprietary); South African Base Minerals Limited; Tasrose Investments (Proprietary); TEAL Exploration & Mining Inc.; Two Rivers Platinum (Proprietary) Limited; Vallum Investments (Proprietary) Limited; Venture Building Trust (Proprietary) Limited.

PRINCIPAL COMPETITORS

BHP Billiton PLC; Samancor Ltd.; Companhia Vale do Rio Doce; MB Holding Company L.L.C.; Rio Tinto Group; Freeport-McMoRan Copper and Gold Inc.; Umicore S.A./NV; Norilsk Nickel Mining and Metallurgical Co.; CODELCO Chile; Voisey's Bay Nickel Company Ltd.

FURTHER READING

"African Rainbow Minerals to Sell Part of Gold Unit," *African Mining Monitor,* May 1, 2002.

Brown, Justin, "ARM Joint Venture to Prospect in Wider Area," *Star* (South Africa), April 13, 2007, p. 3.

———, "ARM to Venture into Copper Production," *Star* (South Africa), January 30, 2007, p. 4.

"Eskom's Appetite for Coal Fuels ARM Profit," *Star* (South Africa), February 21, 2008, p. 13.

Ford, Neil, "Victory for South African Black Empowerment," *African Business,* February 2004, p. 36.

Innocenti, Nicol Degli, "AngloPlat, African Rainbow in Venture," *Financial Times,* August 22, 2001, p. 21.

Itano, Nicole, "South African Mining Giant to Emerge from 3-Way Deal," *International Herald Tribune,* November 15, 2003, p. 11.

"Metal Prices Give ARM a Boost," *Star* (South Africa), August 28, 2007, p. 3.

"S. Africa Creates Largest Black Mining Company," *American Metal Market,* April 8, 2004, p. 5.

Alitalia—Linee Aeree Italiane S.p.A.

Viale Alessandro Marchetti, 111
Rome, 00148
Italy
Telephone: (+39 06) 6562-21
Fax: (+39 06) 6562-4733
Web site: http://www.alitalia.it

Public Company (49.9% State-Owned)
Incorporated: 1946 as Alitalia—Aerolinee Italiane Internazionali
Employees: 10,240
Sales: EUR 4.86 billion ($7.09 billion) (2007)
Stock Exchanges: Italian
Ticker Symbol: AZA
NAICS: 481111 Scheduled Passenger Air Transportation

■ ■ ■

Alitalia—Linee Aeree Italiane S.p.A. is the leading airline in Italy, transporting about 24.5 million passengers in 2007. Operating principally out of a hub in Rome, Alitalia serves more than 80 destinations, including 24 within Italy and 45 throughout the rest of Europe and in North Africa and the Middle East. Intercontinental destinations number around a dozen, including Accra, Tokyo, São Paulo, Toronto, Boston, Chicago, Los Angeles, Miami, and New York. Through its membership in the SkyTeam global alliance, which also includes Air France-KLM S.A., Delta Air Lines, Inc., and Northwest Airlines Corporation, among several others, Alitalia offers service to a wider network of around 840 destinations in more than 160 countries. The company's fleet includes more than 170 aircraft, 145 of which are designed for short- and medium-haul services with the remainder capable of handling long hauls.

Beset by an aging fleet, a high cost structure, conflicts with labor unions, political interference, and intensifying competition from low-cost carriers, Alitalia spilled red ink throughout the first several years of the 21st century. A string of CEOs and restructuring plans failed to reverse the company's fortunes during this period. The Italian government, which held a 49.9 percent stake in the company and had bailed it out more than once, tried and failed several times to privatize Alitalia. Another attempt to sell the airline to Air France-KLM, collapsed in early 2008, leaving Alitalia's future in doubt given that it was reportedly losing more than EUR 2 million ($3.2 million) a day and had limited cash on hand.

POST–WORLD WAR II ROMAN ORIGINS

Alitalia was established in September 1946 as Alitalia—Aerolinee Italiane Internazionali, with financial assistance from British European Airways (BEA) consisting of an initial capital investment of ITL 900 million and an additional investment of ITL 1.5 billion by the start of 1947. BEA (a forerunner of British Airways Plc) held a 40 percent stake in Alitalia, with the Italian government owning the remaining 60 percent. The company began operations in the spring of that year with two three-engine Fiat G.12s flying routes from Turin to Rome and from Rome to Catania.

COMPANY PERSPECTIVES

We, as Alitalia employees, intend to make our Company the chosen airline for Italians and for all travelers who come to Italy as the destination for their journey; moreover we intend to develop our natural geographic vocation to serve those who choose Italy as a transit point for other destinations.

Every day we aim to win over our customers' trust, giving the experience of flying a uniquely Italian flavor, at the same time pursuing the quest for excellence in terms of safety, security and quality.

Through these actions, we intend to reconfirm Alitalia's role as an essential prime mover for Italy's social, economic and cultural growth, spreading our heritage of values and know-how all over the world.

We want to do this with a team of people who are willing to take on an ambitious challenge, people who are able to muster up courage, dedication and rigor, loyalty and determination, working with and for the country as a whole. We fully realize that total commitment is required from everyone, to enable us to achieve what we are working for: that is, creating value for our customers, our stakeholders and our colleagues.

During its first year of operation Alitalia expanded its airliner inventory through the acquisition of two G.12s, four Siai Marchetti SM.95s, and three Avro Lancastrians; by year's end it had transported a total of 10,306 passengers and 110 tons of cargo. Furthermore, in its first year of scheduled air services, the airline covered a network of over 9,000 kilometers and employed just under 300 personnel, 55 of whom were flight crew. By 1948 the airline was able to offer its first intercontinental service, introducing flights from Rome to Buenos Aires, and in fact Alitalia had been set up to concentrate principally on international routes. The Italian government partnered with the U.S. airline Trans World Airways (TWA) to create Linee Aeree Italiane (LAI) for domestic routes.

By 1950 Alitalia had substantially modernized its fleet with the addition of Douglas DC-4s and DC-3s. Expansion continued throughout the 1950s; by the tenth anniversary of the airline in 1956, its planes had traveled a total of 48,630 kilometers and had transported a total of 116,394 passengers. The number of employees had risen to 1,120 and the company's capital to ITL 4.5 billion.

MAJOR MERGER IN 1957

In 1957 Alitalia—Aerolinee Italiane Internazionali merged with LAI to become Alitalia—Linee Aeree Italiane S.p.A., the single Italian domestic and international airline. The Italian government bought out the stakes held by BEA and TWA and thus Alitalia became fully state-owned. The merger helped to centralize air transport operations in Italy, and the new entity was able to compete more effectively with other national carriers in Europe. The new company was also substantially larger, with a net capital of ITL 10 billion, an expanded network, and a staff of over 3,000. By the end of 1957 over 478,000 passengers had been carried by the fleet, which had been expanded to include Convair-Metropolitans and Viscount 785s.

The year of the Rome Olympics, 1960, was a milestone for Alitalia. Chosen as the official carrier for the games, the company introduced its first jet airliners: French-made Caravelle SE210s, which served medium-haul routes, and larger DC-8s, which were put into service on the intercontinental routes. These additions to the Alitalia inventory helped the airline achieve its goal of carrying one million passengers in one year. A year later, to facilitate the airline's expansion, company headquarters was moved from Ciampino to the recently completed Leonardo da Vinci International Airport at Fiumicino. In 1967, the same year that it introduced its new tricolored "A" on the tail fins of its aircraft, Alitalia purchased several DC-9s for its medium-haul routes in Europe and the Middle East. Two years later, with the retirement of the aging Viscount turboprop powered aircraft, Alitalia completed its transformation into an all-jet fleet consisting of 19 DC-8s, 24 DC-9s, and 19 Caravelles. Alitalia was the first European airline to go all-jet.

During this period, dramatic developments were taking place in aircraft manufacturing. In 1969 Boeing introduced the Boeing 747 "jumbo jet," an aircraft that had virtually twice the passenger capacity of the other aircraft, promising an increase in revenue for the airlines. Alitalia placed an order with Boeing and received its first 747 in May 1970. The aircraft was immediately put to work on high-density long-haul routes. In 1973 Alitalia expanded its wide-bodied fleet and took delivery of its first 275-seat DC-10/30.

A DECADE OF CRISIS: THE SEVENTIES

During the 1970s Alitalia experienced increasingly difficult financial circumstances. The price of crude oil

KEY DATES

1946: Alitalia—Aerolinee Italiane Internazionali is founded in Rome.
1947: Operations begin with routes connecting Turin to Rome and Rome to Catania.
1957: Company merges with Linee Aeree Italiane to become Alitalia—Linee Aeree Italiane S.p.A.
1960: Alitalia is the official carrier for the Rome Olympics and debuts its first jet airliners.
1969: Company becomes the first European airline with an all-jet fleet.
1997: Alitalia Express is launched as the firm's regional transportation arm.
2001: Alitalia joins the SkyTeam global airline alliance, headed by Air France and Delta Air Lines.
2004: Consistently unprofitable, Alitalia sees its net loss balloon to nearly $1 billion.
2007: Italian government places Alitalia on the auction block but fails to find a buyer.
2008: Takeover offer from Air France-KLM S.A. collapses.

quadrupled, the western economies entered a period of recession, and airlines experienced a sharp decrease in demand. For Alitalia, as well as its competitors, one solution was to furnish its fleets with more fuel-efficient aircraft. Alitalia's gas-guzzling DC-8s and Caravelles were replaced by more efficient Boeing 727s, the first of which was put into service in 1976. Inflation and political instability in Italy during the latter half of the decade left the airline facing large debts, persistent losses, and falling revenues.

By 1980, despite the partial re-equipment program of the past few years, the airline's fleet had become outdated and inefficient; the average age of its aircraft ranged from six to eight years, generally older than those of the company's European competitors. In 1982 the company was able to order McDonnell Douglas Super 80s to replace the aging Boeing 727s on medium-haul routes and also made plans to purchase more Boeing 747s to replace its fleet of DC-10s, the safety of which had been questioned following several accidents involving other airlines.

To maximize its potential for profit, Alitalia began to diversify its business interests by creating separate support companies that would provide travel services and information. These companies included Società Italiana Gestione Sistemi Multi Accesso (SIGMA), which focused on the development and management of information services in the tourist sector; Italiatour, developed to promote tourism in Italy; and Alidata, a software marketing company.

Also during this time, Alitalia went through a substantial restructuring at the hands of Luciano Sartoretti, the managing director of finance. By 1986 Sartoretti had trimmed and reshaped the company's debts. In 1987 Alitalia returned a profit of over ITL 73 billion following a period that had seen a healthy expansion across much of the European airline business. Nevertheless, the airline still faced several problems. First, although the company's performance was considered adequate, it was losing market share—both within Europe and on the transatlantic routes—to its closest rivals, Air France and Deutsche Lufthansa AG of West Germany. These two competitors had been pursuing aggressive expansion plans through major re-equipment programs and allowing for greater passenger capacity on profitable routes. Alitalia, however, had spent the past five years diversifying its interests and had failed to expand its fleet of about 123 aircraft. Alitalia was therefore less able to benefit from a number of generally profitable years in the airline business in the 1980s.

LABOR UNREST

Beginning in September 1987 Alitalia was plagued by a series of disruptive strikes by pilots, cabin staff, and ground crew, an occurrence some thought reflected both senior management's inability to deal effectively with its employees and a general weakness in its long-term planning. The following year, in an attempt to resolve some of its structural problems and intractable disputes, Alitalia recruited Carlo Verri from the executive committee of the Swedish group AB Electrolux. The appointment of Verri, a businessperson from the private sector with no previous experience in the airline business, was designed to provide Alitalia with free market know-how and top management expertise. His primary concerns were to resolve the chronic labor problems and to develop a long-term growth strategy. By May 1989 Verri had reached an agreement with the cabin crew which ran for 20 months, and in July of the same year he reached a four-year agreement with the pilots. In October he announced a plan to finance a long-term re-equipment program for both aircraft and ground equipment. Verri's plans for the rejuvenation of Alitalia, however, were brought to an abrupt end in November 1989, when he was killed in an automobile accident.

Despite Alitalia's losses from the interruption of its Mediterranean and Middle East routes during the war in the Persian Gulf in 1991, and despite its reputation for, in the words of *Forbes* writer Peter Fuhrman, "slovenly service, poisonous labor relations, and antiquated equipment," the airline experienced some financial recovery in the early 1990s. Aggressive marketing and competitive pricing in 1991 resulted in unexpectedly good results, including a 5.3 percent growth in its cargo operations against an average decrease of 2.7 percent for other European national carriers. Alitalia briefly participated in an innovative "air bridge," shipping bodies for the short-lived Cadillac Allanté from Turin to Detroit. Demand from India was expected to create the most growth for freight services.

Although sales rose 8 percent in 1991, Alitalia posted a loss like everyone else in the business during one of the industry's most catastrophic years. Alitalia relocated its headquarters to a new office complex outside Rome in 1991. At this time, the airline employed nearly 20,000; the group as a whole employed nearly 30,000.

In March 1992 Alitalia announced an ambitious five-year investment plan calling for an allocation of over ITL 4.4 trillion for expansion of the Alitalia fleet to 165 aircraft. The plan also called for the purchase of five new planes for intercontinental routes and 14 more for operations within Europe. According to Alitalia CEO Giovanni Bisignani, the expansion plan—at a time of retrenchment in the international airline business—was designed to enable the company to survive by "moving to achieve a critical mass, but staying fast and flexible."

Alitalia entered into an equity partnership with Hungarian carrier Malév in December 1992. The $77 million investment gave 30 percent of Malév shares to Alitalia and 5 percent to SIMEST S.p.A., an Italian government unit. The expectation was to develop Budapest's role as a gateway between eastern and western Europe. The two airlines together served 122 cities on five continents.

The carrier lost $203 million in 1993. Lean and effective competition from British Airways and KLM forced incoming CEO Roberto Schisano to cut about 1,500 jobs at Alitalia. The company struggled with debts of $1.8 billion. On the plus side, Alitalia inked a quite lucrative marketing deal with U.S.-based Continental Airlines in May 1994.

NEW DOMESTIC COMPETITION

In November 1995, an ambitious regional start-up began competing with Alitalia on the Milan-Rome route. Air One was one of many budget carriers launched on the wings of the economical Boeing 737, although it was the first operator of that type in Italy.

The new entrants, which also included AZZURRAair and Air Sicilia, lacked Alitalia's access to government subsidies (although AZZURRA was to become a franchisee of Alitalia). European Union (EU) commissioners, eager to promote a free market, were beginning to place a great deal of scrutiny on bailouts. Tense negotiations resulted in a 1997 recapitalization of ITL 2.75 trillion ($1.25 billion), pared from ITL 3.3 trillion. As a condition for approval, the EU required Alitalia to divest various holdings, including its stake in Malév. The airline also had to trim operations and lay off another 1,200 employees.

Domenico Cempella was named managing director and CEO after Schisano departed in 1995. He and Chairman Fausto Cereti succeeded in wringing productivity concessions for the unions in return for a 20 percent stake in the company; the Italian government's stake was thereby reduced to 53 percent. Part of the management team's recovery package included forming Alitalia TEAM, a sister company to hire "B"-scale workers. The regional subsidiary Alitalia Express was also formed in 1997. After losing $683 million in 1996, Alitalia posted its first profit (ITL 438 billion [$243 million]) in nine years in 1997.

FAILED KLM ALLIANCE, JOINING SKYTEAM

In the summer of 1999 Alitalia and KLM Royal Dutch Airlines entered into an ambitious cross-border alliance. The two companies agreed to link their networks and most of their operations and planned to act as a single airline centered on hubs in Amsterdam, Rome, and Milan. Work had already advanced on this integration when KLM terminated the alliance in April 2000. KLM had grown frustrated with an endless series of problems that had arisen at Milan's newly expanded Malpensa airport, which was slated to be one of the alliance's three hubs. In addition, the alliance plan had called for Alitalia to be fully privatized, and the Italian government had set a deadline of June 30, 2000, for the divestment of its 53 percent stake, but a deterioration of Alitalia's financial condition coupled with the travails at Malpensa made the privatization impossible. Alitalia objected to KLM's termination of their pact, and eventually an independent Dutch arbitration panel awarded the Italian airline EUR 250 million in damages while also requiring it to repay EUR 100 million for investments KLM had made at Malpensa.

In early 2001, in the wake of the collapse of this alliance, Cempella resigned and was replaced as CEO by Francesco Mengozzi, who had held the number two position at the Italian state railway company, Ferrovie dello Stato S.p.A. Under Mengozzi, Alitalia managed to enter into a new, more lasting alliance, joining the

SkyTeam global airline alliance in 2001. SkyTeam was headed by Air France and Delta Air Lines and at the time that Alitalia joined also included Aeroméxico, CSA Czech Airlines, and Korean Air Lines. The members linked their respective routing networks through codesharing arrangements, cooperated on cargo and passenger handling services, and linked their frequent-flyer programs. A number of other airlines subsequently joined SkyTeam, including Northwest Airlines and, in an ironic twist, KLM.

REPEATED TURNAROUND ATTEMPTS AT A BELEAGUERED CARRIER

By joining SkyTeam, Alitalia hoped to channel more passengers to its flights and boost its global reach. The airline continued to operate in the red, however, and it was burdened by a heavy debt load. Alitalia gained some breathing room in 2002 via a EUR 1.43 billion ($1.27 billion) capital increase. The recapitalization included a capital infusion from the Italian government of nearly EUR 900 million that boosted the state's stake to 62 percent. At the same time, Mengozzi launched a turnaround plan that featured: dropping a number of unprofitable routes, including long-haul flights to China and the U.S. West Coast; implementation of cost-cutting measures that included the elimination of 900 jobs from the payroll; and divestment of the bulk of its noncore assets, including the Sigma reservation services unit.

Late in 2003, a year in which the company suffered a widening net loss of EUR 511 million ($544 million), Mengozzi announced a further restructuring that involved slashing an additional 1,500 jobs from the workforce and outsourcing 1,200 more. The plan aimed to return the carrier to profitability by 2005. At the same time, the CEO was pushing for Alitalia's rapid privatization and also wanted the company to make the proposed merger of Air France and KLM into a three-way affair. Italy's powerful transport unions were opposed to Mengozzi's plan, however, and staged a series of strikes that eventually led the Italian government to withdraw their backing for the plan and for Mengozzi, who resigned in February 2004. Later in the year Air France and KLM merged under a holding company dubbed Air France-KLM S.A.

The unions launched another round of strikes when the new CEO, Marco Zanichelli, continued to push for the workforce reduction. In May 2004 the government ousted Zanichelli and the entire Alitalia board after the union agreed to an indefinite moratorium on strikes in exchange for reducing or deferring the proposed job cuts. Giancarlo Cimoli, who had led a turnaround of the state-run railway Ferrovie dello Stato, was named the new CEO. Verging on bankruptcy in a year in which its net loss ballooned to more than EUR 800 million ($970 million), Alitalia gained some breathing room in the form of a EUR 400 million emergency bridge loan from the government.

Cimoli managed to win union backing for a new restructuring plan that involved 3,700 job cuts, about a sixth of the overall workforce of more than 22,000, and another recapitalization. The plan, implemented in 2005, featured a reorganization that placed Alitalia's business support activities, including maintenance, airport services, and information technology operations, into the newly formed Alitalia Servizi, which was jointly owned by Alitalia and the state holding company Fintecna. This separation took about 8,600 more employees out of Alitalia's hands, shrinking the workforce to roughly 10,000. The recapitalization amounted to just over EUR 1 billion ($1.2 billion), and Alitalia at the same time secured medium- to long-term financing of EUR 370 million ($445 million). In approving this plan, the EU forced the Italian government to reduce its Alitalia stake to less than 50 percent.

FLIRTING WITH BANKRUPTCY, SEEKING A BUYER

This latest overhaul was no more successful than the previous ones, as it became apparent that a more fundamental shakeup was needed. Alitalia was deep in the red, hemorrhaging more than EUR 1 million per day. Late in 2006 the Italian government announced its intention to sell at least 30.1 percent of its stake in the company. At that level a buyer of the stake would be required under Italian law to make a formal offer for the remaining shares. Thereby on the auction block, Alitalia attracted a number of interested parties, including domestic rival Air One, Russia's Aeroflot, and the U.S. private-equity firm Texas Pacific Group. By July 2007, however, all of the bidders had dropped out, apparently put off by some of the conditions placed on a sale. The government had ruled out any takeover leading to significant job cuts or major reductions in Alitalia flights across Italy.

In the wake of this latest debacle, another new company head was named, Maurizio Prato, a former executive at the aerospace and defense firm Finmeccanica SpA. Under Prato, Alitalia attempted to stave off bankruptcy by sharply cutting flights out of Milan's Malpensa airport, essentially leaving the carrier with one main hub in Rome. With its cash reserves dwindling, a new attempt was made to engineer a sale. In March 2008 the Alitalia board accepted a EUR 747 million ($1.17 billion) buyout offer from Air France-KLM, but the latter withdrew its bid a month later when talks with Alitalia's unions over the terms of the takeover collapsed. Prato resigned, and board member Aristide Police, a lawyer and professor, was named chairman and interim CEO.

In what was likely not entirely a coincidence, the collapse of the Air France-KLM deal occurred during an Italian national election that returned Silvio Berlusconi to power, in a defeat of the outgoing prime minister, Romano Prodi. Later in April 2008, while the government was still in transition, Prodi, at the urging of Berlusconi, approved EUR 300 million ($480 million) in emergency financing for Alitalia. Berlusconi was determined to keep Alitalia both flying and out of foreign hands, and had promised to do so during his campaign. In what was potentially Alitalia's last chance for survival, the Turin-based bank Intesa Sanpaolo S.p.A. was drafted to formulate a rescue plan centering on a merger with Air One and at least 5,000 job losses from the combined workforces of Alitalia and Alitalia Servizi. Such a merger would create an airline with a domestic market share of roughly 70 percent. The unions, however, had killed off previous plans involving such steep job cuts, although in this instance the prospect of bankruptcy loomed larger than ever and might finally propel Alitalia out of government hands and toward a more stable future.

Stephen Kremer
Updated, Frederick C. Ingram; David E. Salamie

PRINCIPAL SUBSIDIARIES

Alitalia Express S.p.A.; Volare S.p.A.; Aviofin S.p.A.; Sisam S.p.A.; Alinsurance S.p.A.

PRINCIPAL COMPETITORS

Air One S.p.A.; Deutsche Lufthansa AG; British Airways Plc; Iberia, Líneas Aéreas de España, S.A.

FURTHER READING

Alitalia Forty-Five Years, Rome: Gruppo Alitalia, 1992.

"Alitalia Relies on Asian Pivot," *Asian Finance,* September 1989, pp. 26–27.

"Alitalia to Receive Emergency Financing," *Wall Street Journal,* April 23, 2008, p. B8.

"Alitalia Unveils Huge Investment for 1992," *Flight International,* March 18, 1992.

Ball, Deborah, and Daniel Michaels, "Alitalia's CEO Takes Pains to Keep Airline's Global Status," *Wall Street Journal Europe,* November 28, 2001, p. 5.

Barber, Tony, "Alitalia Unions Step Back from the Brink," *Financial Times,* September 20, 2004, p. 26.

Cook, James, "Italy's Flying Banker," *Forbes,* July 22, 1991, p. 86.

Cottrill, Ken, "KLM, Alitalia Join Forces," *Trafficworld,* December 7, 1998, pp. 37–38.

Dinmore, Guy, "Air France-KLM Withdraws Its Bid for Alitalia," *Financial Times,* April 22, 2008, p. 29.

———, "Alitalia Cuts Flights Out of Milan," *Financial Times,* February 6, 2008, p. 14.

———, "Alitalia Takeover Talks Collapse As Air France Rejects Union Proposals," *Financial Times,* April 3, 2008, p. 1.

Dinmore, Guy, and Silvia Marchetti, "Alitalia on 'Last Chance' for Survival," *Financial Times,* June 30, 2008, p. 18.

Endres, Günter, "Alitalia Cleared for Volare Acquisition," *Airline Business,* April 2006, p. 19.

———, "Alitalia Thrown Final Lifeline," *Airline Business,* September 2005, p. 24.

Feldman, Joan M., "Booting Up Competition," *Air Transport World,* October 1996, pp. 89–90.

Flint, Perry, "Alitalia's Trial by Fire," *Air Transport World,* May 1992, pp. 78–79.

———, "End of the Roman Holiday," *Air Transport World,* September 1991, pp. 22–26.

Flottau, Jens, "Alitalia Signs On, Bolstering SkyTeam's European Base," *Aviation Week and Space Technology,* August 6, 2001, p. 48.

Fuhrman, Peter, "A World Class Airline for World Cup Soccer?" *Forbes,* March 5, 1990, p. 176.

Hill, Leonard, "Malév/Alitalia: Synergies for Survival," *Air Transport World,* March 1993, pp. 90–95.

———, "Roman Remake," *Air Transport World,* December 1998, pp. 37–41, 70.

———, "Taxiing Toward Recovery," *Air Transport World,* September 1997, pp. 51–53.

"The Italian Exception," *Economist,* October 14, 2006, p. 71.

"The Italian Factor," *Flight International,* April 26, 1992.

Jennings, Mead, "Seeing the Light? Alitalia Is Still in the Throes of Recovery After the Loss of Carlo Verri and Years of Debilitating Strikes," *Airline Business,* June 1990, pp. 65+.

Johnson, Keith, and Luca Di Leo, "Alitalia Can't Stanch Red Ink," *Wall Street Journal,* April 21, 2004, p. A16.

Jones, Lois, "Renaissance or Rigor Mortis?" *Airline Business,* November 1996, pp. 24+.

Kahn, Gabriel, "Air France-KLM Withdraws Its Offer for Alitalia," *Wall Street Journal,* April 22, 2008, p. B3.

———, "Italy to Rescue Alitalia, but Exact Plan Is Vague," *Wall Street Journal Europe,* May 7, 2004, p. A1.

Kahn, Gabriel, and Charles Forelle, "Berlusconi Vows to Find New Bidder for Alitalia," *Wall Street Journal,* April 24, 2008, p. B7.

Kahn, Gabriel, and Daniel Michaels, "Ailing Alitalia Tries Again to Get Sale Aloft," *Wall Street Journal,* November 23, 2007, p. A8.

Kahn, Gabriel, and Luca Di Leo, "Alitalia's Future in Doubt As Talks Collapse," *Wall Street Journal,* April 3, 2008, pp. B1, B4.

Kahn, Gabriel, and Stacy Meichtry, "Alitalia Faces Flying Solo," *Wall Street Journal,* January 11, 2007, p. A10.

Lefer, Henry, "Alitalia Cargo Pulls Its Weight," *Air Transport World,* June 1993, pp. 195–96.

Michaels, Daniel, Susan Carey, and Deborah Ball, "KLM Ends Venture with Alitalia, Imperiling U.S. Airline Alliance," *Wall Street Journal,* May 1, 2000, p. A22.

Moloney, Liam, "Alitalia Approves Air France's Offer, but Hurdles Remain," *Wall Street Journal,* March 17, 2008, p. C6.

Pilling, Mark, "Alitalia's Long Takeover Journey," *Airline Business,* January 2008, p. 17.

Rossant, John, "Captain to Alitalia: 'We Have No Choice,'" *Business Week,* June 20, 1994, p. 166.

Salpukas, Agis, "Will Alitalia Survive Competition?" *New York Times,* June 7, 1992, p. F5.

Sparaco, Pierre, "Alitalia Pursues Strict Recovery Plan," *Aviation Week and Space Technology,* November 21, 1994, p. 91.

———, "Alitalia Targets Short-Term Recovery," *Aviation Week and Space Technology,* May 15, 1995, p. 38.

Sylvers, Eric, "Alitalia Tells Unions of Plan to Lay Off 5,000 Workers," *New York Times,* September 7, 2004, p. C1.

———, "Italy Fires Alitalia's Board and Seeks New Investors," *New York Times,* May 7, 2004, p. W1.

Trofimov, Yaroslav, and Daniel Michaels, "Alitalia Plans 'Drastic' Cost Cuts Due to Troubles at Malpensa," *Wall Street Journal Europe,* February 8, 2000, p. 1.

Visca, Lucia, and Fabrizio Spagna, *Aircrash: Anatomia di un flop,* Rome: Memori, 2004, 160 p.

Allegiant Travel Company

8360 South Durango Drive
Las Vegas, Nevada 89113
U.S.A.
Telephone: (702) 851-7300
Fax: (702) 256-7209
Web site: http://www.allegiantair.com

Public Company
Incorporated: 1997 as Allegiant Air, Inc.
Employees: 1,363
Sales: $360.57 million (2007)
Stock Exchanges: NASDAQ
Ticker Symbol: ALGT
NAICS: 481111 Scheduled Passenger Air Transportation; 481112 Scheduled Freight Air Transportation; 481211 Nonscheduled Chartered Passenger Air Transportation; 561510 Travel Agencies; 561599 All Other Travel Arrangement and Reservation Services

■ ■ ■

Allegiant Travel Company is a holding company in the business of bringing people from small U.S. towns to sunny vacation spots. Its main operating company is the Las Vegas-based airline Allegiant Air, LLC; it also sells tours through Allegiant Vacations, LLC, and has a subsidiary called AFH, Inc., for trading fuel.

Allegiant Air is markedly different from major airlines and other low-cost carriers in a number of ways. It acquires secondhand planes at a fraction of the cost of new ones. Such moves help it bring radically low fares to travelers in smaller, underserved markets. Its emphasis on leisure travel further defines its niche. The company has no nonstop competition on the vast majority of its routes and it has been quick to close routes if traffic fails to meet expectations. Ancillary revenues are a key part of the strategy. Allegiant sells everything from in-flight meals to hotel and car reservations. Its tickets are sold directly to consumers.

Now run by founders of ValuJet (renamed AirTran Holdings Inc.), the airline boasts one of the highest operating margins in the industry. It has a non-unionized workforce and several operating bases besides its Las Vegas headquarters. About three dozen MD-80 series aircraft (most of them owned) make up the fleet. The airline flies from more than 50 small cities to a number of popular vacation destinations including Las Vegas, Phoenix, Fort Lauderdale, Orlando, Tampa, Biloxi, Reno, Palm Springs, San Diego, San Francisco, and Santa Barbara.

FRESNO ORIGINS

Allegiant Air began in 1997 as a charter airline based in Fresno, California. It was originally called WestJet Express, but quickly changed its name to Allegiant Air, Inc., due to confusion with similarly named airlines. Its founder was local businessman Mitchell Allee, who hired Jim Patterson as president.

At the beginning, Allegiant had a different business model. It began by flying charters, and when it introduced scheduled service on certain regional routes, they were aimed toward the business travelers, a lucrative sector of the market that most airlines were chasing.

COMPANY PERSPECTIVES

From America's favorite small cities to world-class destinations, Allegiant Air makes leisure travel affordable and convenient. With low-low fares, nonstop, all-jet service and premier travel partners, Allegiant Air provides a complete travel experience with great value and without all the hassle.

Its emphasis on leisure travel did not come until later. Its first destination from Fresno was Las Vegas.

Allegiant began flying in 1998 with a single leased DC-9. It added a second plane the next year and had four by the end of 2000. It added service from Long Beach following the withdrawal of WinAir, a Salt Lake City charter carrier that failed after trying to navigate the difficult certification procedures for scheduled airlines that the Federal Aviation Administration (FAA) mandated following the 1996 ValuJet crash in the Everglades.

Allegiant had a much easier time with certification and won scheduled airline status in March 2000. This allowed it to list flights on the travel agents' computer reservation systems and utilize fares upon receipt rather than holding funds in escrow pending successful completion of each flight.

Allegiant soon added Reno, South Lake Tahoe, and Portland to its scheduled network (these would be short-lived excursions, however). Charters continued to be significant. Allegiant's services were also called upon for the 2002 feature film *Bounce,* which gave the airline's planes a cameo role on the silver screen.

Typical of airline start-ups, Allegiant operated in the red in the beginning, losing nearly $1 million in 1999 alone. Although it seemed to be well-financed, the carrier declared bankruptcy in December 2000, citing fuel costs that had risen more than 70 percent in one year. The young airline cut its flights with the exception of its lucrative Fresno–Las Vegas route and a few charters.

TRADING UP

Allegiant began 2001 by trading in its 1970s-vintage DC-9s for newer MD-87 aircraft, configured to seat 150 passengers. The additional range of these planes allowed the company to land a contract to fly high rollers to the Las Vegas casinos of Harrah's Entertainment. (This was expanded a few years later to Harrah's casinos in Mississippi.) These MD-80 series aircraft were not the most economical machines to operate, but they were relatively inexpensive to purchase, a mere fraction of the cost of brand-new planes.

Such aircraft burned a third more fuel and demanded more maintenance, but the lower capital burden allowed Allegiant to save money in other ways. Since new airliners were so expensive, most carriers went to great lengths to keep the planes in the air as many hours as possible. Allegiant was able to schedule its planes with greater flexibility that saved on labor and other costs.

EMERGING FROM BANKRUPTCY

Maurice J. Gallagher Jr., Allegiant's chief creditor, became majority owner in June 2001. He had owned commuter airline WestAir in the 1980s and sold it to Mesa Airlines. He was also a founder of ValuJet, Inc. (later renamed AirTran Holdings Inc.). Gallagher provided additional funds to keep the airline going during the bankruptcy. A private placement in May 2005 raised $34.5 million from other investors, including $7.5 million from the family that founded Ireland's Ryanair, Europe's influential no-frills airline.

Allegiant developed a new business model focusing on leisure, rather than business, travelers. It would operate in underserved, smaller markets. Allegiant would be quick to leave markets if competition surfaced. On the off-season, it cut frequencies and offered severely discounted fares.

Allegiant Vacations, LLC, launched in February 2002. This unit specialized in bundling airfare with stays at Las Vegas hotels. Later, the company worked out a marketing deal with Alamo Rent-A-Car.

Allegiant officially emerged from bankruptcy in March 2002. The next year, it moved its operations center to Las Vegas, Nevada, its most important destination, where the company already had some business offices. The route network, centered on Las Vegas, steadily expanded, adding connections to Colorado Springs, Wichita, and Des Moines by July 2003. A second vacation destination, Orlando, was added in 2005.

Allegiant grew increasingly profitable in the years following its bankruptcy reorganization in spite of a very difficult economic environment for airlines. Revenues were up to $132.5 million in 2005, producing income of $7.3 million. Passenger count rose 43 percent during the year, to 1.2 million. During the year, Allegiant Travel Company was formed as a holding company for Allegiant Air and Allegiant Vacations.

KEY DATES

1997: Allegiant Air begins operating charters from Fresno, California, with a single DC-9.

2000: Allegiant declares bankruptcy, citing rising fuel costs.

2001: DC-9s are traded in for larger MD-80 series aircraft.

2002: Airline is relaunched with a focus on leisure travel; Allegiant Vacations is formed.

2003: Headquarters operations are consolidated in Las Vegas, Nevada.

2005: Holding company is formed; Allegiant starts adding destinations in Florida beginning with Orlando.

2006: Initial public offering raises more than $90 million.

TAKING IT TO THE STREET

Allegiant debuted on the NASDAQ on December 13, 2006, raising $94.5 million in a successful initial public offering (IPO). Offered at $18 a share, the stock soared beyond $30 within several months. In this atmosphere Ireland's Ryan family sold their stake for $30 million, four times what they paid for it. Investors were energized by the ability of the company's new business model to weather the economic downturn. Allegiant boasted one of the highest operating margins in the industry and had posted a string of profitable quarters.

Although the company closed a few routes due to less-than-expected traffic or high fuel prices, it was expanding. After the IPO Allegiant added new destinations and service from dozens of communities. It added Tampa as its third vacation destination after Las Vegas and Orlando in November 2006. Thanks in part to its population of transplants, Florida was the company's fastest-growing market, and the company opened a new mini-hub in Fort Lauderdale a year later. It also added a base in the Phoenix suburb of Mesa, Arizona, in 2007 and another one in Bellingham, Washington, in March 2008 with flights to several California resorts.

By the end of 2006, the company had about two dozen jets, including some larger MD-83s. There were nearly 800 employees and the number of cities served had grown from one to 45 in just three years. Total revenues were $243.4 million for the year, with net income of $8.7 million. These results were exceeded in 2007, when profits more than tripled to $31.5 million as revenues expanded to $360.6 million. This was remarkable as fuel prices were hitting record levels at the same time.

BLUE SKIES IN 2008

The airline entered an innovative marketing arrangement with the Blue Man Group in March 2008. The deal put images of the cerulean-hued entertainers on aircraft fuselages and paper napkins, while the Allegiant brand got some exposure in the stage shows.

Allegiant Travel Company appeared to be thriving, with shares peaking at more than twice the offering price, as it moved into new offices in May 2008. However, the airline was grounding some of its longer flights as the price of fuel reached unprecedented levels, soaring well beyond $100 a barrel.

Frederick C. Ingram

PRINCIPAL SUBSIDIARIES

Allegiant Air, LLC; Allegiant Vacations, LLC; AFH, Inc.

PRINCIPAL COMPETITORS

Southwest Airlines Co.; AirTran Holdings Inc.; JetBlue Airways Corp.; Pace Airlines, Inc.

FURTHER READING

Bailey, Jeff, "Flying Where Big Airlines Aren't," *New York Times,* September 21, 2006, p. C1.

Cordle, Ina Paiva, "Allegiant Air Plans Mini-Hub at FLL," *Miami Herald,* August 1, 2007.

Correa, Tracy, "Low-Fare Fresno, Calif., Airline Moving Operations Base to Las Vegas," *Fresno Bee,* June 12, 2003.

Craver, Richard, "Skybus' Downfall Clears Skies for Rival: Allegiant Air Reverses Plan to Leave PTI," *Winston-Salem Journal,* April 11, 2008.

Hanigan, Ian, "Fresno, Calif.-based Airline Ends Service at Long Beach, Calif., Airport," *California,* December 9, 2000.

Huettel, Steve, "Allegiant Takes Direct Route to Profitability," *St. Petersburg Times,* November 13, 2006, p. 1D.

———, "Long-Awaited Landing," *St. Petersburg Times,* September 14, 2006, p. 1D.

Kearns, Sean, "Fresno, Calif.-based Airline Proposes Expanded Service," *Knight-Ridder/Tribune Business News; Press-Telegram* (Long Beach, Calif.), August 27, 1999.

———, "Fresno, Calif.-based Charter Airline Expands Service," *California,* January 27, 2000.

———, "Fresno, Calif.-based Charter Carrier Gets Approval for Scheduled Flights," *California,* March 15, 2000.

Knightly, Arnold M., "Allegiant Sets Course for Stock Market," *Las Vegas Business Press,* November 13, 2006, p. 16.

Nax, Sanford, "Fresno, Calif.–Area Airline Drops Four Routes," *Knight-Ridder/Tribune Business News: Fresno Bee,* December 9, 2000.

Ranson, Lori, "Allegiant Air Details Plans to Go Public," *Aviation Daily,* May 17, 2006, p. 1.

———, "Allegiant Eyes Significant Savings from Fuel Tie-Ups," *Aviation Daily,* June 14, 2007, p. 3.

Rogers, Christina, "Spreading Its Wings," *Roanoke Times,* July 8, 2007, p. 1.

"Ryan Bails Out with $30m," *Sunday Independent* (Ireland), May 27, 2007.

Smith, Darrell, "Happy Grad's Big Gift to UCD; Allegiant Air Chief Executive Donates $10 Million to Boost Business School," *Sacramento Bee,* November 1, 2007, p. D1.

Spillman, Benjamin, "Allegiant Flying Ever Higher," *Las Vegas Review-Journal,* February 1, 2007.

———, "Allegiant Has Fast Takeoff on Street," *Las Vegas Review-Journal,* December 9, 2006.

Velotta, Richard N., "Airline Expert Glories in Allegiant's Business Plan," *Business Las Vegas,* October 26, 2007, p. 11.

———, "Blue Man Group Taking Flight; Deal Between Troupe, Allegiant Air Gives Each Visibility on Other's Turf," *Business Las Vegas,* News Sec., March 21, 2008, p. 3.

———, "LV-Based Allegiant Spreading Its Wings," *Business Las Vegas,* August 10, 2007, p. 1.

American Superconductor Corporation

64 Jackson Road
Devens, Massachusetts 01434
U.S.A.
Telephone: (978) 842-3000
Fax: (978) 842-3024
Web site: http://www.amsc.com

Public Company
Incorporated: 1987
Employees: 263
Sales: $52.18 million (2007)
Stock Exchanges: NASDAQ
Ticker Symbol: AMSC
NAICS: 541710 Research and Development in the Physical Sciences and Engineering Sciences

■ ■ ■

American Superconductor Corporation develops wires and coils utilizing superconducting materials for electric power applications and designs programmable power converters that increase electrical grid capacity and reliability. The company's products enable cleaner and more efficient generation and delivery of electric power, including power derived from wind energy systems. American Superconductor is one of the world's most accomplished developers of high-temperature superconducting materials, which are substantially more efficient than conventional copper wires.

THE DEVELOPMENT OF HIGH-TEMPERATURE SUPERCONDUCTORS

In 1911, scientists first discovered that certain materials achieved superior conductive capabilities when subjected to extremely low temperatures, a phenomenon known as superconductivity. Electrical resistance disappeared and electrical capacity increased once cryogenic temperatures were reached, but the discovery did not usher in a new age of superconductivity in the commercial realm. To realize the benefits of superconductivity, materials needed to be cooled to at least −418 degrees Fahrenheit, a job that could only be performed by using liquid helium.

The high cost of liquid helium severely limited the commercial use of superconductive materials, making the groundbreaking discovery of 1911 revolutionary but largely impractical. The commercial use of superconductive materials was restricted primarily to medical applications, specifically magnetic resonance imaging (MRI) devices, but the potential for the technology transformed decidedly after the breakthrough work of two scientists, Dr. K. Alex Muller and Dr. J. George Bednorz.

In 1986, 75 years after the phenomenon had been discovered, the great hope of using superconductivity in commercial and industrial applications appeared tantalizingly close to reality. Muller and Bednorz, working in a Zürich, Switzerland-based laboratory owned by International Business Machines Corporation, discovered a new family of ceramic compounds that became superconductive at temperatures higher than

COMPANY PERSPECTIVES

HTS wire is able to transmit 150 times more energy than a copper wire of the same dimensions. This enables electric utilities to replace multiple conventional copper cables with one HTS-powered cable, leaving valuable underground real estate available for other uses—including future power upgrades. While the worldwide cable market represents a multi-billion-dollar annual opportunity for AMSC, it is just one of the many areas in which our wire is being used. Our technology also is powering a new generation of motors and generators for a variety of industries. By utilizing HTS wire, we are able to dramatically reduce the size and weight of these machines while enhancing their power and efficiency.

existing materials. Their discovery, which earned the pair the Nobel Prize for Physics in 1987, created new nomenclature for the field of superconductivity, hailing the arrival of high-temperature superconductors (HTS), which represented a decided improvement over their predecessors, low-temperature superconductors (LTS).

FORMATION OF AMERICAN SUPERCONDUCTOR

The discovery of HTS created a business opportunity Gregory J. Yurek intended to exploit. Yurek spent a dozen years as a professor of materials science and engineering at the Massachusetts Institute of Technology before founding American Superconductor in 1987, one year after the discovery of HTS materials. The materials discovered in Zürich were shown to be superconductive at −395 degrees Fahrenheit, a reading that only scientists dealing with temperatures at the cryogenic level would deem "high." Although the difference between −418 degrees Fahrenheit and −395 degrees Fahrenheit (the difference between LTS and HTS) was slight, it made a major difference in the commercial potential for superconductivity. The warmer temperature (materials with higher critical temperatures were discovered after 1986) was enough to eliminate the need of costly liquid helium. Relatively inexpensive liquid nitrogen was capable of cooling ceramic oxide compounds to levels necessary for HTS.

Through American Superconductor, Yurek intended to develop materials to distribute and to store electricity. As he set out, there was great hope for the commercial potential of HTS, which transmitted electricity with no power loss because no energy was dissipated by resistive heating. A single, thin strand of HTS wire could carry the same power load as a thick bundle of copper wire. Further, once induced in a superconducting loop, direct current could, in the company's words, "flow undiminished forever." Yurek sought to refine HTS capabilities to make wires and wire products that could be used in the power transmission and distribution market, or "power grid" market.

As is often the case with promising technology, HTS's market potential failed to deliver results as quickly as its proponents would have liked. Muller and Bednorz had made a significant discovery, but there was much work to be done to bring HTS technology into the mainstream of any of the markets—electric power, electronics, power equipment, medical, transportation—that were to be revolutionized by super-efficient conductivity. American Superconductor, which took on the role of a pioneer in the power grid market because of its early entry into the field, experienced many of the difficulties suffered by companies attempting to bring nascent technology to full commercialization. Years of heavy financial losses awaited Yurek as he contended with the developmental hurdles that blocked HTS's path to commercialization.

1990 PARTNERSHIP WITH PIRELLI CABLES AND SYSTEMS

American Superconductor was a research and development firm as it set out in 1987, a classification it was unable to shed for years. Because revenues were hard to come by and profits were nonexistent, the company's alliances with other companies interested in bringing HTS technology to market were vitally important. No strategic partnership was more important than the deal American Superconductor struck with Pirelli Cables and Systems in February 1990. Based in Milan, Italy, Pirelli ranked as the world's largest producer of power cables, giving Yurek's research and development efforts a deep-pocketed ally in developing HTS wire for use in power cables.

Although progress was slow, there were encouraging achievements in the HTS field that lifted spirits at American Superconductor's headquarters in Watertown, Massachusetts. Materials were discovered that became superconductive at temperatures above −395 degrees Fahrenheit, eventually rising to temperatures 20 times higher than the critical temperature of LTS materials. American Superconductor, meanwhile, focused on the particulars of commercializing HTS wire. In 1992, the company formed a Wire Development Group, soliciting the expertise of industry, government, and academic

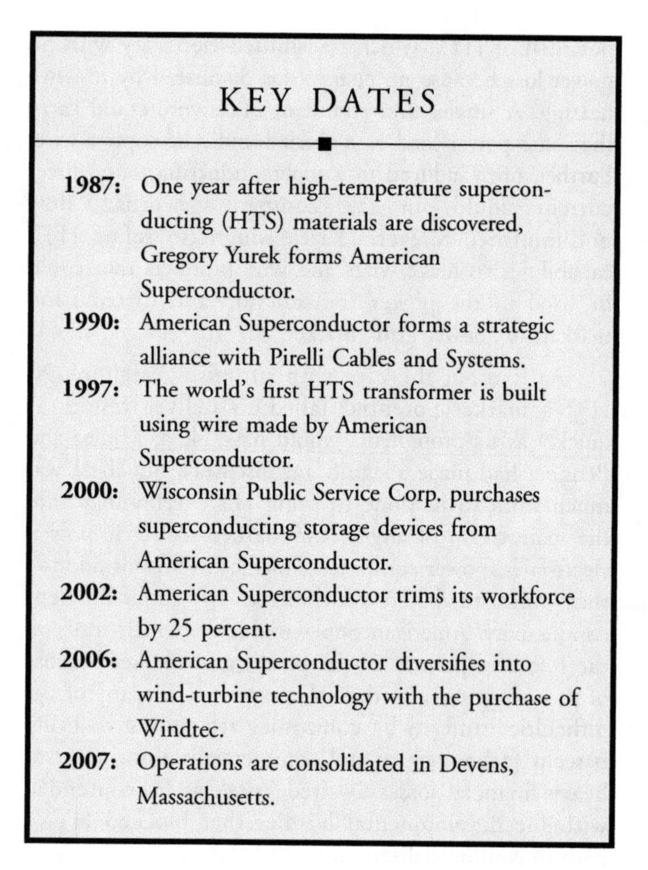

KEY DATES

1987: One year after high-temperature superconducting (HTS) materials are discovered, Gregory Yurek forms American Superconductor.

1990: American Superconductor forms a strategic alliance with Pirelli Cables and Systems.

1997: The world's first HTS transformer is built using wire made by American Superconductor.

2000: Wisconsin Public Service Corp. purchases superconducting storage devices from American Superconductor.

2002: American Superconductor trims its workforce by 25 percent.

2006: American Superconductor diversifies into wind-turbine technology with the purchase of Windtec.

2007: Operations are consolidated in Devens, Massachusetts.

representatives to develop HTS wires for electric energy applications. The focus of the group was to make fully superconducting, flexible wires that could be produced in lengths sufficiently long to be used by utilities.

An event to celebrate occurred in 1994 when American Superconductor demonstrated an HTS magnet system that surpassed a critical performance standard. The company succeeded in making an HTS magnet coil that exceeded performance criteria required of magnetic coils in commercial motors and generators. The achievement promised the development of smaller, more efficient motors and generators with 1,000 horsepower, the size typically used in industrial settings. Yurek, who served as American Superconductor's president and chief executive officer, commented on the success in an October 24, 1994, interview with *Electronic News.* "The HTS magnet coil," he said, "is a benchmark in the commercialization of HTS products. This demonstration proves that HTS materials can create larger magnetic fields than those generated with copper and iron, the traditional materials for motors and generators."

FINANCIAL HARDSHIP

American Superconductor needed further demonstrations of the superiority of HTS technology to help it record financial success. Bleak years of heavy losses continued to pock its financial record as it entered the mid-1990s. In 1994, the company generated $4.9 million in revenue, a portion of which came from its partnership with Pirelli, but the total was eclipsed substantially by its $7.7 million in losses during the year. In 1995, revenues increased to $8.5 million, but another $7 million loss greeted the company at year's end. Over the course of the next three years, American Superconductor posted more than $35 million in losses, making the need to evolve past the research and development stage a pressing objective.

American Superconductor would not make the critical leap into a fully commercial company before the end of the decade. Yurek and his team, primarily scientists and engineers with doctorate degrees, had longer to wait before their technology would be introduced into the mainstream. The company's tenth anniversary in 1997 did include an encouraging accomplishment, however. The year marked the world's first demonstration of an HTS transformer, a piece of equipment designed and built by Asea Brown Boveri that used wire developed and manufactured by American Superconductor. The demonstration, fittingly, took place in the country of HTS's birth, in Switzerland, where a 630,000-watt transformer, nearly 50 percent lighter than conventional units, was put through trials before being installed to power the headquarters of SIG, Geneva's electric utility.

OPPORTUNITIES ABOUND

As American Superconductor entered the 21st century, the prospects for the full commercialization of HTS were brightening considerably. Electric utilities were becoming increasingly interested in the capabilities of HTS, particularly as a solution for one of their most agonizing problems. Severe weather, unforeseen equipment failures, or even a traffic accident could cause momentary dips in power line voltage. Although more than 80 percent of electrical power disturbances in the United States were voltage sags that lasted less than a second, barely perceptible to residential utility customers, the dips cost commercial and industrial customers billions of dollars annually in equipment damages and lost productivity.

American Superconductor offered a solution, a Superconduction Magnetic Energy Storage (SMES) system that used superconducting magnets to deliver something akin to lightning in a bottle. The systems, housed in a semi-tractor trailer and attached to transformers at substations within a grid, stored nearly three megawatts of power, keeping electricity buzzing endlessly about inside, ready to be discharged into the grid when power fluctuations occurred. American Superconductor, which formed a marketing and sales alliance with General Electric in early 2000 to provide SMES systems to utility and industrial customers, was preparing to install its first system as the new century began. Wisconsin Public Service Corp. became the first utility to install the equipment, paying roughly $5 million to install six 2.8-megawatt storage units made by American Superconductor to make its grid more reliable. American Superconductor's vice-president hailed the event in an interview published in the July 28, 2000, edition of *Energy Daily.* "This is historic," the executive said. "This is the first time superconducting technology has been used, not as a demonstration project, but as a functioning installed component of an electric utility grid."

Yurek's company could also point to encouraging progress on other fronts. While work was being performed for Wisconsin Public Service, American Superconductor was supplying HTS wire to Reliance Electric Motor Group, a unit of Rockwell International. By the end of 2000, Reliance Electric was expected to finish building a 1,000-horsepower superconducting motor using Yurek's wire that was one-fifth the size of existing industrial motors with more torque and greater efficiency.

Arguably the most celebrated event at the time involved American Superconductor's partnership with Pirelli. The two parties renewed their commitment to each other at the beginning of 2000, signing a new agreement that provided nearly $14 million in funding to American Superconductor. The signing of the agreement shortly preceded the two partners' installation of the first HTS power cable system in a utility network. The project, slated to be completed by the end of 2000, was taking place in Detroit, which both companies hoped would serve as a model for utilities worldwide to emulate.

To add to the optimism at American Superconductor's headquarters (the company by this point had moved to Westborough, Massachusetts), there was research pointing to the increasing adoption of HTS in major markets. The government-sponsored Oak Ridge National Laboratory announced in 2000 that superconductivity was expected to save $18 billion annually once it was fully introduced into transmission lines, transformers, electric motors, and generators. Projections made by the laboratory estimated that HTS materials would penetrate 50 percent of the underground cable market by 2013, 50 percent of the transformer market by 2015, and 50 percent of the generator market by 2021. American Superconductor, girding itself for the growth of its industry, announced the site of a new manufacturing plant at roughly the same time the study was published. Located in Devens, 35 miles northwest of Boston, the 355,000-square-foot plant was to be dedicated exclusively to the production of HTS wire, equipped to manufacture more than 10,000 kilometers of wire annually. The plant was slated to commence full production by early 2002, but by the time the date arrived celebrations were soured by distressing developments.

CRISIS IN 2002

The installation of the first HTS power cable system in a utility network did not proceed as planned. The project in Detroit suffered from profound problems after unsuccessful attempts to pull three HTS cables through a serpentine, underground conduit. The twisting course damaged the vacuum seal, preventing the cables from being chilled to their operating temperature. Pirelli and American Superconductor abandoned the project in mid-2002. Privately, as reported in the May 12, 2003, issue of *Performance Materials,* officials at American Superconductor were critical of Pirelli's performance.

Shortly before stepping away from the Detroit project, Yurek dealt with another troublesome development. In March, he announced plans to eliminate 100 jobs, or one-quarter of American Superconductor's workforce. The cuts, Yurek explained in a March 27, 2002, interview with the *Boston Globe,* would change American Superconductor from "a research-oriented company to one focused on commercial products." The company, which had lost $67 million since 1998, could no longer afford to fund the relatively large research and development department that had grown during the preceding years. "I don't need Ph.D. scientists to be machine operators," Yurek informed the *Boston Globe.*

ACQUISITIONS AND DIVERSIFICATION

In the wake of the layoffs, American Superconductor completed several acquisitions, diversified, and pined for the day when its financial performance would improve. In late 2002, the company acquired Europe's sole manufacturer of powder-based, bismuth-strontium-calcium-copper oxide (BSCCO) HTS wires, Nordic Superconductor Technologies A/S, a subsidiary of Denmark's NKT Holding A/S. In 2003, the U.S. Department of Energy named American Superconductor as its primary contractor for a $30 million HTS cable project for the Long Island Power Authority, the company's first major project since the failure in Detroit. In 2006, the company entered a new field by purchasing Austria-based Windtec, a company that developed and licensed proprietary wind-turbine systems and sold wind-turbine electrical systems.

Financially, American Superconductor had not turned the corner by the time it celebrated its 20th anniversary. The company generated $52 million in revenue in 2007, but recorded a $34 million loss for the year, continuing a worrisome trend that had seen it accumulate more than $100 million in losses during the previous four years. Hoping to make his company a more financially efficient concern, Yurek announced the closure of American Superconductor's production plant in Westborough in 2007, a move made to consolidate operations in Devens, which became the new headquarters site of the company. Ahead, there was much to be done for American Superconductor to reap the rewards of its two-decade-long struggle in the HTS field. The technology continued to fuel optimism among industry observers, inspiring forecasts that HTS materials eventually would be pervasive in commercial applications, a day that could not arrive too soon for American Superconductor.

Jeffrey L. Covell

PRINCIPAL SUBSIDIARIES

American Superconductor Europe GmbH (Germany); ASC Devens LLC; ASC Securities Corp.; Superconductivity, Inc.; NST Asset Holding Corporation; Windtec Consulting, GmbH (Austria); Power Quality Systems, Inc.

PRINCIPAL COMPETITORS

SatCon Technology Corporation; Semikron Inc.; Xantrex Technology Inc.; Mitsubishi Electric Corporation.

FURTHER READING

"American Superconductor and Pirelli Energy Cables and Systems Update Strategic Alliance to Expand HTS Cable Market," *Advanced Materials & Composites News,* March 18, 2002.

"American Superconductor Buys Component Maker," *Performance Materials,* April 26, 2004, p. 5.

"American Superconductor, GE Team on SMES Effort," *Energy Daily,* April 13, 2000.

"American Superconductor Named Power Cable Lead," *Performance Materials,* May 12, 2003, p. 2.

"American Superconductor to Acquire Austria-Based Wind Turbine System Developer Windtec," *Energy Resource,* November 29, 2006.

"AMSC Completes Acquisition of Power Quality Systems," *Transmission & Distribution World,* May 1, 2007.

"ASC Forms Group to Develop Wires," *Ceramic Industry,* May 1992, p. 21.

"China Electric Locomotive Research Institute Buys Wind Energy System License from Windtec," *Energy Resource,* January 23, 2007.

Engelke, Roger, "Delivery Mechanism for Electrical Energy Being Explored," *Electronic Design,* April 19, 1999, p. 28.

"Finally, Hot Superconductors Are Heating Up," *Business Week,* November 15, 1999, p. 128.

Hawkins, Lee, Jr., "Green Bay, Wis.-based Utility Installs Devices to Prevent Voltage Dips," *Milwaukee Journal Sentinel,* August 2, 2000.

"High-Temperature Superconducting Transformer Goes On-line," *Design News,* May 5, 1997, p. 13.

Holly, Chris, "High-Tech Promise Becomes Reality: Superconductor-Based Reliability Devices Placed on Wisconsin Grid," *Energy Daily,* July 28, 2000, p. 1.

"HTS Power Cables Moving Forward," *Energy Conservation News,* January 2000.

Kerber, Ross, "Westborough, Mass.-based American Superconductor to Lay Off 100 Workers," *Boston Globe,* March 27, 2002.

"Power Cables That Squeeze More Juice into Less Space," *Business Week,* January 22, 2001, p. 4EU2.

Spoth, Tom, "American Superconductor to Devens Wire-Making Company Plans to Move Headquarters from Westboro to Site of Manufacturing Plant," *Sun,* May 30, 2007.

"Superconducting Magnet Coil Shown," *Electronic News (1991),* October 24, 1994, p. 52.

"Superconductors Put a Chill on Brownouts," *Business Week,* August 28, 2000, p. 70D.

Amerigon Incorporated

21680 Haggerty Road, Suite 101
Northville, Michigan 48167-8994
U.S.A.
Telephone: (248) 504-0500
Fax: (248) 348-9735
Web site: http://www.amerigon.com

Public Company
Incorporated: 1991
Employees: 71
Sales: $63.6 million (2007)
Stock Exchanges: NASDAQ
Ticker Symbol: ARGN
NAICS: 336211 Motor Vehicle Body Manufacturing

■ ■ ■

Listed on the NASDAQ, Amerigon Incorporated designs, develops, and markets products based on advanced thermoelectric device technologies. In essence, thermoelectric devices are composed of semiconductor elements sandwiched between a pair of substrates; when the elements are electrically connected in the proper alignment, one substrate becomes hot and the other becomes cold. A change in polarity reverses the action, making such a device ideal for heating and cooling small areas. Amerigon's primary product is the Climate Control Seat (CCS), providing heating and cooling to automobile and truck seat occupants. It is available in more than 20 vehicle lines produced by Ford, General Motors, Hyundai, Nissan, and Toyota. Through subsidiary BSST LLC, Amerigon offers a heating and cooling system that allows users to control the temperature of their personal workspace, marketed through office furniture company Herman Miller, Inc. BSST also seeks to develop other uses for thermoelectric technology, for both temperature control and power generation. Amerigon maintains an engineering and research and development facility in Irwindale, California, and a sales and technical support subsidiary in Tokyo, Japan. Manufacturing is done on a contract basis in plants in Mexico and China.

BACKGROUND OF FOUNDER, SPACE RACE TECHNOLOGY

Amerigon was founded by Dr. Lon E. Bell, who grew up in Santa Cruz, California, during the Cold War era, fascinated by rockets and the space race that developed between the Soviet Union and the United States. To further his interest he enrolled in the California Institute of Technology in 1958, graduating with a degree in mathematics in 1962. He stayed at the school to earn an M.S. in rocket propulsion in 1963, followed by a Ph.D. in mechanical engineering in 1968. While pursuing his Ph.D., Bell worked as a consultant, developing technology for some of Southern California's aerospace companies, including Jet Propulsion Labs, McDonnell Douglas Corporation, and Northrop Grumman Corporation. During this time he came across a sensing system developed by the military at Sandia National Laboratories that was used on reentry for nuclear warheads. Believing there were nonmilitary applications for the system, he formed a company called Technar Inc. in 1967. After graduating with his doctorate, Bell then determined that the technology could be used as a

COMPANY PERSPECTIVES

Amerigon designs, develops and markets products based on our advanced, proprietary, efficient thermoelectric device technologies for a wide range of global markets.

crash sensor to inflate air bags in automobiles. He developed a system that he licensed to Allied Chemical, which began manufacturing the devices that eventually became a mainstay in the automotive industry.

Bell drew on aerospace technology for other automobile devices as well. By 1986 Technar was generating $175 million in annual sales and Bell sold the business to TRW. He stayed on as president, but by the early 1990s was looking for a change of pace. It was at that point that he began working with his son David, who was studying robotics at the University of Michigan and was involved in a project to develop a solar-battery-powered electric car. Because the team had no experience in manufacturing, it enlisted the help of the elder Bell. Not only was Bell excited by the challenge, he believed that the development of an electric car was socially valuable, a way to help address the problem of pollution. The University of Michigan solar car won the GM Sunrayce USA competition in the summer of 1990 and later in the year placed third in the World Solar Challenge held in Australia.

FORMATION OF AMERIGON: 1991

In 1991 Bell sold his interest in Technar, moved back to California, and in April of that year invested $2 million to form Amerigon, Inc., in Burbank to develop components and sub-assemblies for use in an electric car. The goal was not to manufacture the vehicles but provide carmakers with the technology needed to produce electric vehicles. He hired his son Dave and several members of the Michigan solar car team, and looked to the aerospace industry for other new hires. With the end of the Cold War, the defense industry, including aerospace, was in decline, and Bell recognized that a wealth of engineering talent was available in Southern California, offering Amerigon an edge over international competitors who did not have such a resource on which to draw. Bell also knew that with California losing a large number of jobs due to cuts in defense spending, the state would likely provide financial assistance to Amerigon, which had the potential of creating a new industrial base. Democratic Congressman Howard Berman, whose district depended on the aerospace industry, became a strong supporter of the start-up and helped secure federal funding. In addition, Bell approached the president of Southern California Edison, Michael R. Peevey, whose company would be in line to benefit from the development of an electric vehicle, and he assisted in forming a nonprofit consortium called Calstart. Becoming operational in 1992, Calstart comprised about 40 sponsors and participants, including utilities, government agencies, research laboratories, and universities. Bell served as the organization's president. Within five years Calstart would be managing $80 million in 50 research projects related to electric vehicles.

Bell believed that the electric vehicle had to be developed from the wheels up. "Compared with conventional vehicles," he explained to *D&B Reports,* "electric vehicles have an incredibly different content. Batteries must change, motors, controllers must change. We'd throw out radiators, catalytic converters, tail pipes, starter motors. ... You use aluminum instead of steel to make the car lighter, extending its performance." Bell estimated that 70 percent of conventional car components would have to be redesigned and many of them radically redesigned.

COMPLETION OF INITIAL PUBLIC OFFERING: 1993

Aside from electric vehicle technology, Amerigon was founded to develop products in other areas, including radar technology, interactive voice technology, and thermoelectric technology. Amerigon set up shop, rent free, in a former Lockheed plant located near the Burbank Airport, and with Bell's seed money received about $8 million from Calstart to begin product development. He raised another $12 million in June 1993 by taking Amerigon public at $6 a share.

Amerigon developed a battery-power vehicle that according to *Forbes* resembled a dune buggy and in 1996 Bell claimed to have signed contracts from several Asian automobile manufacturers to purchase 50 aluminum electric car chassis. Enthusiasm for the electric car quickly waned, however, as it became apparent that such a vehicle would not be commercially viable for many years to come. As a result, Amerigon shifted its focus to other product areas. It developed a voice-activated automobile navigation system called Audionav that made use of electronic maps stored on compact disks and a vehicle's existing CD player. It was a low-cost alternative to systems that relied on a visual display and global positioning technology. Between 1993 and 1997, Amerigon lost about $25 million.

KEY DATES

1991: Amerigon is incorporated in California.
1993: Initial public offering of stock is completed.
1998: Company sells first Climate Control Seat (CCS) system.
2000: BSST LLC is formed to develop other thermoelectric device applications.
2002: Headquarters moves to Detroit, Michigan, area.
2004: Amerigon achieves profitability.
2007: Three-millionth CCS unit is delivered.

FIRST CLIMATE CONTROL SEAT: 1998

In 1997 Amerigon was able to complete a secondary offering of stock, raising $15.3 million. In that year the company also spun off the Audionav product into a joint venture with Yazaki Corporation to concentrate on side and rear radar-based sensing devices using the AmeriGuard Radar System and on thermoelectric technology, which was used to develop low-energy vehicle seat heaters. The result was the Climate Control Seat (CCS) system, which was manufactured at the start of 1998 for its first customer, Mark III Industries, a conversion van and truck company. Later in the year an agreement was reached with Johnson Controls, the United States' largest seating supplier, to market the CCS system. In 1999 the CCS became available with the Lincoln Navigator, the first North American vehicle to offer the seating option.

As Amerigon made the transition from development stage company to a true operating company in 1999, it experienced a number of other changes. A $9 million private equity placement resulted in TMW Enterprises gaining majority control of the company and TMW's head, Oscar Marx, took over as Amerigon's chairman. Marx was the vice-president of Ford Motor Company's automotive components group. Bell became vice-chairman and chief technology officer, replaced as CEO by Richard A. Weisbart.

Amerigon continued to lose money as it entered the new century but CCS gradually gained acceptance in the automotive industry. The first Asian car to offer the system was the Lexus 430 sedan in 2000, and in March of that year a five-year deal was reached with Ford Motor Company for the use of CCS. To further fund the development of the next generation of CCS technology, Amerigon completed a $12.5 million private placement of stock in 2000. The AmeriGuard effort, in the meantime, was shelved and Amerigon dedicated all of its resources to climate-controlled seating. Subsidiary BSST, LLC, was formed to develop other thermoelectric devices for use in the automotive as well as appliance, defense, and communication industries. Bell served as president and CEO of the unit.

Amerigon was not able to carry its momentum into 2001, however. Revenues fell from $6.9 million in 2000 to less than $6.5 million in 2001, and the company lost another $7.7 million. In October Weisbart left Amerigon, replaced as chief executive by Oscar Marx, who moved the company's headquarters to the Detroit area in 2002 to be close to its main customers, leaving the engineering and research and development unit in Irwindale, California. He also secured another $6.5 million in new equity funds and arranged for $2.5 million in bridge loans to be converted into equity. Overall, Amerigon enjoyed a strong year in 2002. In addition to Ford and Toyota, General Motors and Nissan Infiniti chose CCS as an option. As a result, sales more than doubled to $15.3 million in 2002 and Amerigon narrowed its net loss to $6.3 million.

A new chief executive took charge in March 2003, Daniel R. Coker, who had been with Amerigon since 1996, serving as vice-president of sales and marketing. Prior to that he had been vice-president and general manager of the North American operations of Arvin Meritor, a major automotive supplier. The CCS system continued to gain acceptance in the automotive industry, an option made available by five major automobile manufacturers in 14 different vehicles by the end of 2003. At the start of the year, Amerigon unveiled its new micro thermal module (MTM) product, a smaller, lighter, and less expensive seat cooling and heating system because duct assemblies were eliminated. MTM also allowed for seat backs to be heated independently of the seat cushion. It was initially offered in several Cadillac models.

ONE MILLIONTH CCS UNIT: 2004

Revenues continued to grow at a strong rate in 2003, improving to $29 million, while the net loss was reduced to $1.4 million. In 2004 Amerigon shipped its one-millionth CCS unit and achieved another significant milestone: profitability. The company netted $1 million on sales of $32.7 million, due in large measure to the addition of two new vehicle lines offering CCS as an option, the Cadillac Escalade ESV and the Nissan Fuga, and a full year of sales for five vehicles added during the course of 2003: the Cadillac DeVille, Cadillac XLR, Hyundai Equus, Mercury Monterey, and Nissan Cima. BSST was also making strides, forging an agreement with Carrier Corporation to explore the possibility of using thermoelectric devices in heating, refrigeration, and air conditioning systems for residential and commercial users as well as aerospace applications. Later in 2004 BSST began working with major automotive supplier Visteon Corporation to incorporate thermoelectric devices into other automotive heating and cooling products. At the beginning of 2005, BSST landed another major partnership with the U.S. Department of Energy to develop a system to turn hot engine exhaust into electrical power, a way to not only improve fuel economy but also reduce pollutants.

Although Amerigon enjoyed modest sales gains in 2005, to $35.7 million, it increased net income to more than $16.5 million, albeit $14 million of that amount was the result of a non-cash income tax benefit. Regardless, the $2.5 million cash the company netted was a significant improvement over the prior year. Profits continued to increase in 2006, totaling $3.5 million on sales of $50.6 million. The upward trend continued in 2007. Amerigon also shipped its two-millionth CCS unit in 2006 and three-millionth unit in 2007. While the future of the CCS system remained bright, new areas of opportunity were also opening up for Amerigon. In 2007 BSST completed the development of the first nonautomotive products, a desktop personal heating and cooling system created in partnership with office furniture giant Herman Miller. Given the spate of positive developments for Amerigon, it was not surprising that the company caught the notice of Wall Street, which bid up the price of Amerigon stock, increasing from a low of $6.24 in August 2006 to more than $22 a year later, before receding to the $11 level in 2008. Despite difficult economic conditions, especially for the automotive industry, Amerigon continued to grow sales and profits through the first quarter of 2008.

Ed Dinger

PRINCIPAL SUBSIDIARIES

BSST LLC; Amerigon Asia Pacific Inc.

PRINCIPAL COMPETITORS

Delphi Corporation; Robert Bosch GmbH; W.E.T. Automotives Systems AG.

FURTHER READING

Deady, Tim, "Inventor's New Company Is Driven by a Futuristic Idea: The Electric Automobile," *Los Angeles Business Journal,* June 10, 1991.

———, "Looking to Always Do Better," *Los Angeles Business Journal,* April 24, 1995, p. 21.

Kosdrosky, Terry, "Amerigon Gets Boost from GM," *Crain's Detroit Business,* September 26, 2005, p. 3.

———, "Amerigon's Potential Raises Its Profile," *Wall Street Journal,* April 5, 2006, p. 1.

Lubove, Seth, "A Car That Runs on Gravy," *Forbes,* July 15, 1996, p. 60.

Riggs, Carol R., "A New Auto from Aerospace," *D&B Reports,* January/February 1993, p. 30.

Arena Resources, Inc.

6555 South Lewis Avenue
Tulsa, Oklahoma 74136
U.S.A.
Telephone: (918) 747-6060
Fax: (918) 747-7620
Web site: http://www.arenaresourcesinc.com

Public Company
Incorporated: 2000
Employees: 86
Sales: $100.1 million (2007)
Stock Exchanges: New York
Ticker Symbol: ARD
NAICS: 213112 Support Activities for Oil and Gas Operations

■ ■ ■

Arena Resources, Inc., is a New York Stock Exchange–listed oil and gas acquisition, exploration, development, and production company. The Tulsa, Oklahoma-based company operates in Kansas, New Mexico, Oklahoma, and Texas, with most of its activities conducted in the Permian Basin of western Texas and southwestern New Mexico. Arena's flagship property is the Fuhrman-Mascho lease, covering some 25,000 acres in the Permian Basin. About 86 percent of its proved reserves are oil and the remainder consists of natural gas, about 55 million barrels in all in 2007.

Arena runs a lean operation, relying heavily on consultants and third-party providers to perform such functions as drilling, although Arena owns a pair of rigs. Of the company's 100 full-time employees, 40 work for its drilling subsidiary, Arena Drilling Company. Three-quarters of Arena's employees, in fact, are drillers, geologists, and engineers, most of them fulfilling multiple functions. The corporate staff numbers about 25. As needed, additional geologists, engineers, pumpers, and other employees are hired on a contract or fee basis. Frugality also extends to the base salaries of Arena's officers, whose compensation is highly dependent on bonuses and stock options and the performance of the company. Longtime CEO Lloyd "Tim" Rochford, for example, receives a base salary of just $36,000. As a result of this approach, as well as savvy acquisitions, Arena has kept debt to a minimum, allowing it to avoid hedging and to maximize profits at a time of record-high oil prices.

COMPANY FORMATION: 2000

Arena Resources was founded in 2000 by a pair of veteran oilmen, Rochford and Stanley M. McCabe. The older of the two was McCabe, who after attending the University of Maryland in the early 1960s became involved in the oil and gas industry. In 1979 he became chairman and CEO of Tulsa, Oklahoma-based Stanton Energy, Inc., a contract driller and operator of oil and gas wells. In 1989 he formed Stanton Oil & Gas, Ltd., a contract drilling company that he ran as CEO. In that same year he teamed up with Rochford to form Magnum Petroleum, Inc.

Rochford, 14 years younger, completed college business courses in California in the late 1960s and became involved in the oil and gas industry in Illinois in 1973.

COMPANY PERSPECTIVES

Management's primary goal is to enhance shareholder value through the growth of underlying proven reserves with an emphasis on positive cash flow.

He later focused his activities in the mid-continent region of the United States, organizing and funding private oil and gas drilling and completion projects. After cofounding Magnum, he became CEO, while McCabe mostly helped in the evaluation of projects and used his contacts in Oklahoma, where he lived, to bring in strategic partners. Following the acquisition of Hunter Resources, Inc., in 1995, Rochford became chairman of the resulting Irving, Texas-based Magnum Hunter Resources, Inc., and McCabe became a director. At the end of 1996 McCabe left the Magnum board and pursued independent investments and oil and gas development projects. Rochford resigned from Magnum in July 1997 and pursued a similar course as McCabe until 2000 when the two men once again joined forces.

Arena started out as a joint venture formed in March 2000, comprised of property interests contributed by the founders, including a 40 percent working interest in some Oklahoma gas properties. Arena was incorporated in Nevada in August 2000, and stock in the company was used to acquire the assets of the joint venture. A public offering of stock was also made to raise seed money, and the shares were subsequently listed on the OTC Bulletin Board. While the new business made its home in Tulsa because of the partners' extensive contacts in Oklahoma, Rochford continued to live in Rancho Mirage, California, while serving as CEO. Chairman and Secretary McCabe and Chief Financial Officer Randy Broaddrick kept watch over the Tulsa office. Altogether the partners raised $1.1 million in startup capital and in 2001 began drilling and making acquisitions. The company's business philosophy was also put in place, as Rochford explained to *Investor's Business Daily* in 2008: "I insisted from Day One we'd be in a posture of positive cash flow." Hence, the company was reluctant to take on debt and determined to get "the best bang out of every dollar."

THE FIRST WELL: 2001

In April 2001 Arena announced that it had successfully drilled its first well, located in Muskogee County, Oklahoma. A month later Arena increased its working interest in this and related properties to 70 percent. The company's first property acquisitions took place in June 2001 in both Oklahoma and Texas. In Oklahoma, Arena added the Ona Morrow Sand Unit waterflood property in Cimarron and Texas counties, receiving a 100 percent working interest and an 81.32 percent net revenue interest. A 100 percent working interest and 80 percent net revenue interest was also acquired in the Y6 lease in Fisher County, Texas, and drilling commenced in that same month. In February 2002 Sunoco agreed to purchase the oil produced on the Texas lease.

Arena completed three acquisitions in 2002. A working interest in a mineral lease in Montague County, Texas (the Dodson lease), was purchased for $200,000 in April. Next, in June a working interest in a mineral lease in Texas County, Oklahoma, was acquired for $735,000, followed a month later by another working interest in the nearby Eva South Morrow Sand Unit mineral lease at a cost of $827,500. In September 2002 Arena acquired a 24.5 percent working interest in a 600-acre lease in Cimarron County, Oklahoma, and a 100 percent working interest in an adjoining 2,600-acre lease. All told, Arena added about 5,400 acres to its position in Oklahoma and increased its daily production total by 300 barrels of oil in 2002. The company also drilled its first well in Kansas during the year.

AMERICAN STOCK EXCHANGE LISTING: 2003

Arena generated revenues of $1.7 million in 2002, earning nearly $403,000 before a preferred stock dividend of $798,000, a performance that began to attract the attention of investors. Arena received more exposure in April 2003 when its stock graduated from the OTC Bulletin Board and secured a listing on the American Stock Exchange under the ARD ticker symbol, and Arena increased investor interest as the company continued to grow at an accelerated pace in 2003. For the year the company earned $670,143 on revenues of $3.7 million, making it one of the larger Oklahoma production companies.

Arena completed another acquisition in May 2004, picking up an 82.24 percent working interest and 67.6 percent net revenue interest in a Lea County, New Mexico, 920-acre lease that was immediately put in production and helped increase Arena's revenues in 2004 to about $8.5 million while net income approached $2.5 million. The company experienced a mild setback in July 2004, however, forced to lower its estimate of reserves by 20 percent, or nearly two million barrels of oil equivalent. Arena maintained that it did indeed possess the reserves and that the lower estimate was a matter of proper paperwork filed with the Securities and Exchange Commission. Investors did not ap-

KEY DATES

2000: Company is formed.
2001: Arena drills its first well.
2003: Company is listed on American Stock Exchange.
2006: Shares begin trading on New York Stock Exchange.
2007: Revenues top $100 million.

pear to be overly concerned with the matter. In August 2004 Arena had no difficulty in completing a stock offering that raised $1.2 million for future acquisitions.

A far more important acquisition was completed in December 2004, one that would provide a turning point for Arena's fortunes. An outside consultant brought to the company's attention eight independent operations in the Permian Basin region, what would become the Fuhrman-Mascho lease, and in July 2004 Arena closed on four of the properties, comprising 10,000 acres. It was the production from Fuhrman-Mascho that provided the cash flow needed to fund a robust drilling program. Another of the operations was added in 2005 and the final properties closed in 2006, so that in the end, after some complementary acquisitions at the end of 2007 and early 2008, the Fuhrman-Mascho lease covered more than 25,000 acres.

FUHRMAN-MASCHO BEGINS PRODUCTION: 2005

The addition of the Fuhrman-Mascho lease had an even more dramatic impact in 2005, its first well beginning production in April. The company had also caught the wave of escalating commodity prices and its conservative approach to doing business began to be rewarded. Because Arena had limited its debt, it did not have to rely on hedging to lock in prices for its oil and gas to create predictable cash flow to meet interest payments. Rochford admitted that he was not opposed to hedging and might do so in the future should the company have to take on debt to acquire an attractive property, but he and Arena made the best of the current situation, selling its production at prevailing market prices. Because the price of potential acquisitions was keeping pace with commodity prices, Arena became more selective, another reason for an increasing focus on the drill bit.

In 2005 Arena posted revenues of $25.84 million and net income of almost $9.5 million. Not surprisingly, the price of Arena's stock increased, tripling in value through three-quarters of 2005 before declining somewhat later in the year. The company took advantage of its good fortune, buying a drilling rig at the end of the year for $1.5 million, again to better exploit the Fuhrman-Mascho property, production of which also allowed Arena to increase its capital expenditure budget from a slated $35 million to about $60 million.

Because of good results from Fuhrman-Mascho as well as properties in New Mexico and Kansas and the availability of drilling rigs, Arena increased its capital expenditure to $76.5 million on the fly in 2006. Funding the increase was a private placement of common stock with institutional investors that netted $30.3 million. Increased production brought escalating revenues and profits, landing Arena a coveted slot on the New York Stock Exchange in August 2006, a move that provided even greater exposure and credibility to the company. Arena was able to more than double revenues in 2006 to $59.8 million, while net income totaled a robust $23.3 million. It was a performance that would earn the company the number one slot in *Fortune Small Business* magazine's top 100 for the year, third place in *Fortune*'s 100 Fastest Growing Small Companies, 41st in *Business Week's* Hot Growth Companies, and twelfth on *Entrepreneur*'s Top 500 Companies. At the close of 2006 Arena was also able to increase its Fuhrman-Mascho lease holdings, paying about $6.1 million in cash and stock for the last of the three properties located in Andrews County, Texas, adding 4.7 million barrels of reserves.

With high commodity prices continuing to prevail in 2007 and the company's drilling sites performing well, Arena enjoyed another strong year in 2007. Not only was it able to allocate $95 million for a drilling budget, later increased to $116 million, it was able to purchase a second drilling rig for $2 million after refurbishing. Drilling time could be reduced, and increased efficiencies permitted Arena to drill about six wells per month per rig in its holdings in Andrews County, Texas. A new president and chief operating officer, Phil Terry, was named in February 2007. He had been Arena's fifth employee, joining the company in 2003 in engineering and operations. He quickly made plans for continued expansion, including the $1.5 million purchase of a 16,000-square-foot building to house the company's headquarters, large enough to accommodate the influx of new employees he began to hire to flesh out the corporate offices.

In June 2007 Arena made another stock offering to institutional investors, netting about $95 million, money earmarked for debt reduction, capital expenditures, and drilling and development projects.

Still flying high in October, Arena was able to complete a two-for-one stock split, increasing the number of shares available on the open market. Before the year was done, Arena also began to make new acquisitions. It paid $6.5 million for leases on properties in Lea County, New Mexico, and Andrew County, Texas, covering 8,900 acres. A much larger acquisition was completed in December 2007, the $49 million purchase of a 100 percent working interest and 75 percent average net revenue interest in a pair of Andrews County, Texas, properties, consisting of 5,000 acres that held an estimated eight million barrels of oil equivalent or proved reserves.

NEW CEO: 2008

Arena's revenues topped the $100 million mark in 2007 and net income totaled $34.4 million. For 2008 the company established a preliminary capital expenditure budget of $218 million, $173 million of which was allocated to the Permian Basin region of west Texas, where Arena in the previous year had drilled 133 wells. The company estimated that it had only tapped less than one-quarter of the area's potential. With high commodity prices creating stiff competition for new properties, Arena was likely in the near-term to focus most of its attention on exploring the new assets, and beefing up its in-house geology and engineering operations, while exploiting its established properties. The company would also operate with some changes at the top ranks. In May 2008 Rochford stepped down as CEO, turning over day-to-day control to Phil Terry. Rochford then replaced McCabe as chairman.

Ed Dinger

PRINCIPAL SUBSIDIARIES

Arena Drilling Company.

PRINCIPAL COMPETITORS

Murphy Oil Corporation; Cabot Oil & Gas Corporation; Pioneer Natural Resources Company.

FURTHER READING

Davis, Kirby Lee, "Tulsa-Based Arena Resources Plans to Nearly Double Cap Expenditures," *Oklahoma City (Okla.) Journal Record,* November 9, 2007.

Evatt, Robert, "Permian Properties Boost Arena Resources," *Tulsa World,* February 27, 2007, p. E4.

Kimes, Mina, "Rigged for Success," *Fortune Small Business,* May 2008, p. 39.

Murphy, Richard McGill, "Lessons from the Fastest," *Fortune Small Business,* July 2007, p. 24.

Pemberton, Tricia, "Oil-Exploration Company Arena Resources Builds Reserves, Revenues, Income," *Daily Oklahoman,* November 7, 2004.

Stern, Gary M., "A Knack for Looking Good in the Oil Patch," *Investor's Business Daily,* May 30, 2008.

Wilmoth, Adam, "The Timing Was Perfect," *Daily Oklahoman,* November 6, 2005, p. 3.

Arnhold and S. Bleichroeder Advisers, LLC

1345 Avenue of the Americas, 44th Floor
New York, New York 10105-4300
U.S.A.
Telephone: (212) 698-3000
Toll Free: (800) 800-9006
Fax: (212) 299-4360
Web site: http://www.asbai.com

Private Company
Incorporated: 1937 as S. Bleichroeder New York, Incorporated
Employees: 226
Sales: $21.4 million (2007 est.)
NAICS: 523920 Portfolio Management; 523930 Investment Advice

■ ■ ■

Based in New York City, Arnhold and S. Bleichroeder Advisers, LLC, is the final vestige of the venerable German banking houses of Gebrueder Arnhold of Dresden and S. Bleichroeder of Berlin, both of which were founded by Jewish families in the 1800s and fell victim to the anti-Semitic policies of Nazi Germany in the 1930s. While the German institutions were annexed by a non-Jewish bank, the Arnhold and Bleichroeder names continued in the New York branches the families had established as the Nazis came to power. While the parent company, Arnhold and S. Bleichroeder Holdings, Inc., sold its brokerage arm in 2002, Arnhold and S. Bleichroeder Advisers carries on the tradition, offering asset management services to institutional investors and high net-worth individual investors.

The firm, which has more than $45 billion under management, is committed to value investing, engaging in extensive research to identify undervalued companies in which to invest, and then taking a long-term approach, patiently holding on to investments until that potential is realized. Arnhold and S. Bleichroeder run the First Eagle family of mutual funds, including First Eagle Global Fund, a long-term growth fund making investments around the world in undervalued stocks and other securities as well as real estate and gold-related investments; First Eagle Overseas Fund, focusing on equities of non-U.S. corporations; First Eagle U.S. Value Fund, focusing on securities of U.S. companies; First Eagle Gold Fund, engaging in the gold and precious metals market by investing in companies involved in the trade, whether it be mining, processing, dealing, or simply investing in gold and precious metals; and First Eagle Fund of America, a U.S. equity fund that makes investments in anticipation of market changes. In addition to its midtown Manhattan headquarters, Arnhold and S. Bleichroeder maintains a satellite office in Palm Beach Gardens, Florida. The firm is owned and headed by the Arnhold family, which is also one of the firm's largest clients.

FORMATION OF ARNHOLD BRANCH: 1864

The Arnhold side of Arnhold and S. Bleichroeder's heritage was founded in Dresden, Germany, in 1864 by Max Arnhold and Ludwig Philippson. It was a prosper-

COMPANY PERSPECTIVES

We believe in buying fundamentally strong companies that are priced below our assessment of their intrinsic value. We buy the business, not the security. In other words, we tend to look at companies with the eyes of an acquirer rather than an investor, asking how the business is likely to fare over a long cycle.

ous Saxony bank whose primary customers were involved in the ceramic and brewery industries. After Philippson left in 1876, the bank took the name Gebrueder Arnhold. With no children, Max Arnhold brought his nephew Georg into the firm in 1881, who in time would bring in four sons. The oldest was Adolph, born in 1884, followed by Heinrich, Kurt, and Hans, the youngest, born in 1888. All four became partners and took on increasing levels of responsibility for the firm. Max Arnhold died in 1908 and Georg died in 1926.

Gebrueder Arnhold established the bank's branch in Berlin in 1907. According to his *New York Times* obituary, Hans Arnhold opened the office in 1911, if accurate a remarkable achievement for a 23-year-old. A 2001 article in the *Berlin Journal,* however, maintained that Hans Arnhold only took over "the increasingly important Berlin office, after receiving his training as a banker, both in Hamburg and the US." His obituary also indicated that because Gebr. Arnhold recognized the importance of the American capital market, he was dispatched to the United States to establish a branch office, primarily to develop "an old family holding, the General Ceramics Corporation in Keasbey, N.J., into a modern electronics concern."

Following Germany's defeat in World War I, Gebrueder Arnhold, due to sound management, was able to successfully navigate the ruinous inflation that gripped the country in 1919 and difficult economic conditions that persisted into the 1920s. Nevertheless, Gebrueder Arnhold was able to become active in London and Zürich as well as the United States. The same could not be said, however, for S. Bleichroeder. By the mid-1920s the Bleichroeder heirs were no longer involved in the family business, which attempted to carry on by securing new sources of capital and talent, both of which they would find in the 1930s in Gebrueder Arnhold.

ESTABLISHMENT OF S. BLEICHROEDER: 1803

S. Bleichroeder was established in Berlin in 1803 by Samuel Bleichroeder, whose father came to the city as a gravedigger. It was a modest affair, a currency exchange shop that also sold and redeemed lottery tickets. Soon Samuel Bleichroeder was claiming the title of banker, but it would be his son Gerson who truly lived up to the role. Samuel Bleichroeder, however, did make one vitally important contribution to the future banking powerhouse: He established a relationship with Vienna's Rothschild international banking dynasty. Starting in the late 1820s he became a Berlin agent for the Rothschilds and by the early 1830s his relationship became more extensive as the Berlin market began to prosper. He was typical of the Rothschilds' agents: enterprising, eager to keep the Rothschilds informed about local political and social matters, and servile to the extreme.

Samuel Bleichroeder's son, Gerson, joined the family business in 1839 and became a partner eight years later. He became the head of the bank after his father died in 1855. A younger brother, Julius, was also involved but soon left to form his own bank. Even more than his father, Gerson nurtured the relationship with the Rothschilds, but at the same time he was willing to work with other banks and develop his own base of power. He became the cofounder of a syndicate of banks, the Prussian Consortium, that raised a large sum of money to finance Prussia's military buildup, bringing him to the attention of the Prussian government, which recognized the worth of the banker, although he would never be allowed to forget that he was Jewish.

One of the rising Prussian politicians was Otto von Bismarck, who asked the Rothschilds to recommend a banker and was given the name of Gerson Bleichroeder. In 1862, with Prussia in political turmoil, Otto von Bismarck was named minister-president and foreign minister, and as he struggled to establish himself he often turned to Bleichroeder for advice. As Bismarck oversaw the unification of Germany over the next decade and emerged as chancellor, Bleichroeder became the chancellor's banker, known as the German Rothschild. He also became a nobleman, the first Prussian Jew to be accorded that honor.

Shortly after Bleichroeder's death in 1908 the banking house he founded entered decline as its ties to the German government began to loosen. Senior Director Julius Schwabach ran the business because Bleichroeder's eldest son had neither the interest nor ability to succeed his father. Schwabach's son, Paul, would later take over; after the Bleichroeder heirs were ousted in the 1920s, he attempted to run the bank by himself before seeking an

KEY DATES

1803: S. Bleichroeder banking house is founded in Berlin, Germany.
1864: Gebrueder Arnhold banking house is founded in Dresden.
1931: S. Bleichroeder and Arnhold form alliance.
1937: S. Bleichroeder New York, Incorporated is established in United States.
1938: S. Bleichroeder and Arnhold are forced to merge with non-Jewish German bank.
1939: Bleichroeder New York is renamed Arnhold and S. Bleichroeder Advisers, LLC.
1967: Company creates first offshore hedge fund.
1987: First U.S. registered mutual fund is formed.
1999: SoGen International Fund is acquired.
2002: Investment banking and brokerage business is sold.
2007: TA Associates acquires minority interest.

alliance with Gebrueder Arnhold in 1931 when Germany was enveloped in a banking crisis.

GEBR. ARNHOLD AND S. BLEICHROEDER FORGE AN ALLIANCE

The *New York Times* reported in June 1931 that Gebr. Arnhold and S. Bleichroeder "concluded an agreement for close cooperation in their domestic and foreign business activities," although "the identity and independence of each firm [was] preserved." As a result, Hans and Adolph Arnhold became partners of S. Bleichroeder, and Paul von Schwabach became a partner of Gebr. Arnhold. While this union was taking place, Adolf Hitler was rising to power in Germany, achieving his goal in 1933, at which point the process of Aryanization began to unfold, leading to the elimination of Jewish ownership of the banks in Nazi Germany. Adolph and Heinrich Arnhold were accused of fraud and bribery in a bid by the regional Nazi leadership to force them to sell the Dresden bank. Heinrich died in October 1935, according to some sources likely the result of the stress created by this persecution, and by the end of the year the Dresden bank was sold. Kurt Arnhold attempted to continue running the Berlin branch but it was only a matter of time before he too was forced to sell and flee Germany. In February 1938 what remained of Gebr. Arnhold and S. Bleichroeder in Germany was merged with the non-Jewish Hardy bank.

By the time the Arnhold and Bleichroeder names in German banking had been eradicated, both firms had moved their operations to London and New York. In April 1937 S. Bleichroeder New York, Incorporated was formed and Paul Schwabach became a partner, although he remained in Berlin. He died in November 1938, several months before the outbreak of World War II. Hans Arnhold had already left Germany for Paris and with the start of the war relocated to the United States. He was elected to the board of S. Bleichroeder New York in December 1939, and the firm was renamed Arnhold & S. Bleichroeder, Inc. It would act as correspondent for affiliated firms, including London's Anglo-Continental Exchange, Ltd., and Zürich, Switzerland-based Adler & Co. A.G.

While the Bleichroeder name was retained, there were no Bleichroeders involved, just members of the Arnhold family. In the postwar years, the New York investment bank catered mostly to a European clientele, especially West German firms after the economic recovery in the partitioned country, but it did not solicit business from the general public. Arnhold and S. Bleichroeder quietly facilitated mergers, underwrote loans and securities offerings, and became a member of all the major stock exchanges.

In 1960, Henry H. Arnhold, the son of Heinrich Arnhold and born in Dresden, was named co-chairman of Arnhold and S. Bleichroeder. His uncle, Hans Arnhold, remained honorary chairman until his death in Switzerland in 1966 at the age of 78. Henry Arnhold served in the U.S. military during World War II and joined Arnhold and S. Bleichroeder in 1947. The other co-chair was Stephen Max Kellen, the husband of Hans Arnhold's daughter, Anna Maria Arnhold. He had come to New York in 1937 to take a position with Loeb, Rhoades & Company after working a year at Lazard Brothers Ltd. in London. In the 1940s he had helped build Arnhold and S. Bleichroeder.

FIRST EAGLE FUND: 1967

It was also in the 1960s that the firm formed its first offshore hedge fund under the First Eagle name. Helping to establish it in 1967 would be the firm's most famous alumnus, George Soros, who would not only become a renowned hedge fund manager but also a financial backer for Democratic politicians and left-leaning organizations, earning the enmity of political conservatives. First Eagle was aimed at foreigners interested in investing in U.S. securities. Two years later Soros helped Arnhold and S. Bleichroeder start the Double Eagle Fund, which included securities from other countries as well. It was, in effect, an offshore mutual fund that hedged. Soros ran the Double Eagle

Fund until leaving Arnhold and S. Bleichroeder in 1973 to establish his own hedge fund.

Following the departure of Soros, Arnhold and S. Bleichroeder continued to run the First Eagle and Double Eagle funds. Also in the 1970s, due to the devaluation of the dollar, many German and European companies retained Arnhold and S. Bleichroeder to help in the acquisition of U.S. companies, as well as farmland and other real estate. In addition, the firm was a regular participant in syndicates underwriting security offerings of U.S. companies as well as foreign governments, such as the ten-year, DEM 150 million bond issue of the Province of Quebec or $300 million in debentures from Sears, Roebuck & Company.

Another generation of the Arnhold-Kellen family joined Arnhold and S. Bleichroeder in 1978 when Michael M. Kellen became a portfolio manager. He was well seasoned by this point, having graduated from Harvard University in 1966 with a degree in economics and having worked as a securities analyst at Clark, Dodge, Inc., and as a portfolio manager at private investment group William T. Golden. Another member of the new generation followed in 1983 when John P. Arnhold joined the firm. A graduate of the University of California, Santa Barbara, with a degree in English, he had worked at Chase Manhattan Bank and then became a research analyst at Lehman Brothers' Risk Arbitrage Department. Upon joining the family firm, he established the Risk Arbitrage Department. He then became co-director of institutional business in 1988 and eventually co-president and co-CEO of Arnhold and S. Bleichroeder Holdings, and chairman and CEO of Arnhold and S. Bleichroeder Advisers. In the meantime, Michael Kellen made an important contribution on his way to becoming co-president and co-CEO of Arnhold and S. Bleichroeder Holdings. In 1987 he cofounded the First Eagle Fund of America, Arnhold and S. Bleichroeder's first U.S. registered mutual fund. In effect, it was a re-creation of the First Eagle Fund that had become less appealing to investors due to tax-law changes and now emerged as a conventional U.S. fund.

It was not until the 1990s that First Eagle Fund began to appeal to the mass market, cutting the minimum account size from $25,000 to $2,500. The firm then added to its fund offerings in 1999 with the acquisition of SoGen International Fund, established by French bank Société Générale and managed since 1978 by well-regarded fund manager Jean Marie Eveillard, one of the leading proponents of value investing. Société Générale had put the fund up for sale in 1999 and reached a deal with Liberty Financial, but the buyer eventually backed out. Thus, the fund became available to Arnhold and S. Bleichroeder, which appreciated Eveillard's focus on capital preservation. SoGen did not enjoy the kind of results other funds enjoyed during the bull market of the late 1990s, but its conservative approach would pay off when the stock market collapsed in the early 2000s. SoGen was renamed First Eagle SoGen Funds.

SALE OF INVESTMENT BANKING AND BROKERAGE OPERATIONS: 2002

The early 2000s was a time of transition for Arnhold and S. Bleichroeder. The investment banking and global securities operations were sold to Natexis Banques Populaires, a unit of French bank Banque Populaire, in 2002. The combined operations took the name Natexis Bleichroeder. Arnhold and S. Bleichroeder Holdings was now left with a single focus, the asset management business of Arnhold and S. Bleichroeder Advisers. Another change occurred in February 2004 when co-chairman Stephen Max Kellen died at the age of 89. Later in the year Eveillard retired, leaving protégé Charles de Vaulx to run First Eagle SoGen.

In 2007 de Vaulx decided to leave Arnhold and S. Bleichroeder, prompting John Arnhold to reach out to Eveillard in Europe and ask him to step back into his old role. The 67-year-old agreed and returned to managing the fund that had played such a prominent role in his life. Later in the year, Arnhold and S. Bleichroeder took a major step in its development by creating a plan to provide equity incentives to retain and recruit key personnel. Part of the plan called for private equity firm TA Associates to acquire a minority interest in Arnhold and S. Bleichroeder Holdings. The Arnhold family remained majority owners of the firm, which also remained committed to the principles of value investing.

Ed Dinger

PRINCIPAL SUBSIDIARIES

First Eagle Global Fund; First Eagle Overseas Fund; First Eagle U.S. Value Fund; First Eagle Gold Fund; First Eagle Fund of America.

PRINCIPAL COMPETITORS

AXA Rosenberg Group LLC; CB Richard Ellis Investors, L.L.C.; Fred Alger Management, Inc.

FURTHER READING

"Banking Firm Is Formed," *New York Times*, April 19, 1937.

Coleman, Murray, "Back in First Eagle's Nest," *MarketWatch*, March 26, 2007.

Feldman, Gerald D., "Two German Businessmen," *Berlin Journal,* Summer 2001, p. 17.

"Hans Arnhold, 78, An Industrialist," *New York Times,* September 9, 1966.

"Jewish Banks Closed," *New York Times,* February 20, 1938.

Maidenberg, H. J., "The Firm That Bears the Name of Bismarck's Banker," *New York Times,* February 20, 1977.

Strongindodds, Lynn, "Natexis Acquires Arnhold & S. Bleichroeder in the U.S.," *Financial News,* July 3, 2002.

"Two German Banks Linked," *New York Times,* June 23, 1931.

Ascendia Brands, Inc.

100 American Metro Boulevard, Suite 108
Hamilton, New Jersey 08619-2319
U.S.A.
Telephone: (609) 219-0930
Fax: (609) 219-1238
Web site: http://www.ascendiabrands.com

Public Company
Incorporated: 1920 as Lander Company
Employees: 324
Sales: $99.6 million (2007)
Stock Exchanges: Pink Sheets
Ticker Symbol: ASCB
NAICS: 325620 Toilet Preparation Manufacturing

■ ■ ■

Ascendia Brands, Inc., is a Hamilton, New Jersey-based holding company whose subsidiaries manufacture, market, and distribute a variety of value and premium health and beauty care products. Under the Lander and Lander Essentials labels, the company offers bubble bath, bath and body products, shampoo, deodorant, ointments, oral care products, and skin care products. Other Ascendia brands include Mr. Bubble bubble bath, Baby Magic bath and skin care products, Ogilvie hair care products, Binaca breath fresheners, Dorothy Gray Moisture creams, Tussy deodorants and antiperspirants, and Tek toothbrushes. Ascendia products are available at drugstore chains, such as CVS, Rite-Aid, and Walgreen's; supermarkets chains, including Publix, Shop Rite, and Weis Markets; and mass merchants, including Wal-Mart, Kmart, and Target. Down-market Lander brands can also be found at such discounters as 99 Cent Only Stores, Dollar Tree, and Family Dollar. Manufacturing is conducted in plants located in Binghamton, New York, and Toronto, Canada. A public company, Ascendia trades on a Pink Sheet basis following a 2008 delisting from the American Stock Exchange.

COMPANY ORIGINS: 1920

Ascendia Brands traces its heritage through the Lander brands, offered by Lander Company, but its origins are far from clear. According to Ascendia, Lander was founded by Charles H. Oestreich in 1920 with two partners. A *New York Times* obituary of Oestreich indicates that he was born in New York City's Lower East Side in the late 1890s and became a self-taught accountant, landing a position with E.C. Carter & Son, a New York importer of curtain and drapery textiles, which then diversified into cosmetics and toiletries, a business that Oestreich headed and later acquired, establishing offices in Manhattan. The *Times* further maintains that Oestreich "also founded and became, in the early 1920s, president of the Lander Company, Inc." A 1991 profile of Lander published by *Drug & Cosmetic Industry* calls this account into question, however, claiming that Lander was formed by Elliott C. (E. C.) Carter and William H. Loveland. A 1986 article on the company published by the *Record* in New Jersey concurs, stating the two men "combined pieces of their names to form the company name." After Oestreich acquired the business, Loveland remained involved in cosmetic manufacturing through William H. Loveland

COMPANY PERSPECTIVES

Over the years, Lander has always remained true to its core mission; providing high quality health and beauty care products at value prices.

Company, Inc., operating out of Binghamton, New York, the two firms destined to intersect years later.

Oestreich, with his brother George Edwin Oestreich, focused Lander on value cosmetics and toiletries. Early brand names included Emily Rogers, Ruth Manner's, Dorothy Reed, Lilacs and Roses, and Elizabeth Post. The company made its mark in the industry by offering a popular ten-cent lipstick. Lander was less successful with a bath oil whose label implied it was a product of Switzerland, a misleading claim that in 1937 was brought to an end by the Federal Trade Commission. In the mid-1940s Lander began offering a fragrance and bath powder under the Spellbound label. During this period the company did well with perfumes, introducing Romantic Days in 1943 and Samezi-Soir in 1950.

EXPANDING THROUGH ACQUISITIONS: 1950

Lander enjoyed a growth spurt in 1950, adding a number of product lines through a pair of acquisitions. William H. Loveland Company was purchased in July of that year, adding Ascendia's present-day plant in Binghamton, New York. Lander also received the Old English and Speedee trade names and a wide variety of product lines, including petroleum jelly, face and hand creams, aftershave lotion, face and hand lotions, hair dressing, and wave sets. A month later Lander bought the Elizabeth Kent Company lines of cosmetics, a deal that included molds, trade names, and other materials. Other subsidiaries operated by Lander during this period included Lundborg Perfumers Inc. and MacGregor Men's Toiletries Inc.

In May 1964 George Oestreich died at the age of 61. A month later the family sold Lander to Beech-Nut Life Savers, Inc., Charles Oestreich, Lander's president, stayed on to run the business as chairman of a new Beech-Nut subsidiary. He stayed on until the business was sold in 1968 to Alvin Burack, Norman Auslander, and Herbert Paer. A year later, Oestreich suffered an aneurysm and died at the age of 72. Burack and Auslander owned a Garfield, New Jersey-based toiletries company called Scott Chemical Company, founded in 1961, which became the holding company for Lander. Burack became chairman and president for the next decade, until he was succeeded by Auslander as chairman and Paer as president. Burack and a partner then went on to acquire Helena Rubinstein Inc., eventually selling the property to French cosmetics conglomerate L'Oréal.

A pharmacist with a degree from Fordham University, Auslander had served as plant manager of Scott Chemical. Making his home in New Jersey, he moved Lander's headquarters to Englewood Cliffs in 1977. The company continued to focus on value-line products that appealed to middle-income and lower-income consumers, mostly women. The outlet for Lander's products began to change in the 1970s, however, with the demise of longtime customers, the discount and variety chains, including W.T. Grant, E.J. Korvette, and Two Guys. Wal-Mart, Kmart, and the "dollar" stores in southern states made up the difference, as did private-label sales (accounting for about 15 percent of the company's sales) to Woolworth, Shop Rite, and Kmart. Rather than spend money on advertising, Lander pushed sales by way of in-store promotions, such as crowded two-for-one table displays that invited shoppers to pick through for bargains. While Lander's products were value priced, they were not much different than heavily advertised, higher-priced branded items of other companies. "We're not selling sizzle; we sell more of the steak," Auslander told the *Record.* "We consider our lotions and creams as good as any on the market."

Lander was always willing to launch new products to cater to its core customers, although not every attempt was successful. In 1971 it brought out a line of natural products under the Mother's label but was ahead of the market by several years and the line was pulled. The company tried introducing an inexpensive nail polish every few years only to rediscover it was a highly competitive niche. Lander fared better with an Ethnic Products Division, which offered hair care products under the Black Orchid and Dixie Peach Pomade labels aimed at African Americans. Lander also did a thriving business selling health and beauty care products to institutional customers, such as the military, hospitals, and nursing homes. A silicon-based hand lotion was developed for healthcare workers and a fragrant all-purpose cleaner was developed for the nursing home market. In addition, Lander sold mouthwash and aftershave to prisons, albeit the items had to be reformulated without alcohol and the containers used no glass or metal caps that might be fashioned into weapons. The nonalcohol bases were also used to produce products that could be sold to countries in the Middle East.

KEY DATES

1920: Lander Company is founded in New York City.
1950: William H. Loveland Company is acquired.
1964: Lander is sold to Beech-Nut Life Savers, Inc.
1968: Scott Chemical Company acquires Lander.
1977: Headquarters shifts to New Jersey.
1991: Virtual Academics is formed.
2003: Virtual Academics becomes Cenuco, Inc.
2005: Cenuco and Lander merge.
2006: Cenuco changes name to Ascendia Brands, Inc.
2008: Ascendia is delisted from American Stock Exchange.

SALE OF SPELLBOUND BRAND: 1990

Lander was doing about $27 million in sales in the late 1980s and continued to mine its health and beauty care products niche in the 1990s. With sales declining for its Spellbound lines and not willing to invest in a relaunch, Lander in 1990 sold the trade name to Estée Lauder, which soon applied Spellbound to a new $200-an-ounce perfume. Lander in the meantime unveiled its Swan Lake perfume, which came in a stock design plastic swan bottle and was priced at $5.95 an ounce.

Revenues reached an estimated $66 million in 1995, one-fifth of which came from international sales. The formula of high-quality, low-cost products sold through drugstores, discounters, and mass merchants continued into the new century. In 2001 the company looked to expand into new areas, introducing Lander dog shampoos. By this time under control of CEO Joseph A. Falsetti, Lander looked to diversify far afield from the health and beauty care sector. In 2005 Lander merged with Cenuco Inc., a technology company that developed software for wireless or Internet-based streaming video aimed at cell phones and remote computers. Although Lander became part of Cenuco, as a result of the stock swap Lander owned 65 percent of the combined company and Falsetti became president and CEO, and Lander's chief financial officer, Brian Geiger, held the same post with Cenuco.

FORMATION OF CENUCO: 1991

Cenuco started out as a subsidiary of Virtual Academics, which was formed in Florida in 1991 as an online component of a distance-learning provider called Barrington University and later renamed Virtual Academic. Com Inc. Run by Robert K. Bettinger and his son, Steven M. Bettinger, Barrington and Virtual Academics were dubious enterprises, as demonstrated by investigative reporting conducted by the *South Florida Business Journal*. The *Journal* discovered that Robert Bettinger did not hold a doctorate although in the Barrington University catalog he signed as Dr. Robert K. Bettinger. Moreover, it discovered that Barrington's supposed headquarters in Mobile, Alabama, was home to the A&S Answering & Secretarial Service, and the listed university accreditation service was not based in Switzerland and Washington, D.C., but incorporated in Florida by a group that included Bettinger. Fifteen months after the *South Florida Business Journal* made these revelations, Virtual Academics changed its name to Cenuco, Inc., the name of a subsidiary formed several months earlier to create wireless solutions that would allow students to pursue education and training through PDAs (personal digital assistants) and other mobile technologies. The focus then shifted to developing a suite of fully integrated wireless solutions for the security, real estate, and insurance markets. While the plan was to remain involved in the distance-learning section, in 2004 Cenuco divested the education unit to focus on its wireless technology, which was oriented toward wireless video streaming.

The wireless business never figured much in the future of the new Cenuco following the merger with Lander. It was put up for sale, and when no satisfactory offers were fielded, the unit was shut down in the summer of 2007. Cenuco in the meantime beefed up its health and beauty care products slate. In November 2005 the company acquired several brands from Playtex Products Inc., including Mr. Bubble, Baby Magic, Binaca, Ogilvie, Tussy, and Chubs. In keeping with this focus, at the start of 2006 the company changed its name to Ascendia Brands, Inc. More brands were added in early 2007 with the acquisition of the Calgon and Healing Garden bath care brands from Coty Inc. for $125 million. In a move to take the company to the next level in light of the addition of the Coty brands, Falsetti stepped down as president and CEO in March 2007, turning over the posts to Steven Scheyer while assuming the position of executive chairman. A 25-year industry veteran, Scheyer had been president of the $1 billion Rubbermaid division of Wal-Mart.

STOCK DELISTING: 2008

The inability of the wireless unit to find traction in the marketplace and its eventual closure hurt Ascendia, which posted a loss of $48.9 million in fiscal 2007 after losing $30.2 million the previous year. As a result the company found itself in noncompliance with the American Stock Exchange in the summer of 2007 and faced the possibility of having its stock delisted. Ascendia also had to contend with impatient senior lenders. With the financial backing of Prentice Capital Management, which provided a $25 million infusion of cash, Ascendia was able to successfully recapitalize in January 2008, but because of a drop in shareholder equity the company was delisted a month later and Ascendia shares began trading on an over-the-counter basis through the Pink Sheets. In March 2008, Falsetti resigned as executive chairman and director of the company.

Ed Dinger

PRINCIPAL SUBSIDIARIES

Ascendia Brands (Canada) Ltd.; Lander Co., Inc.

PRINCIPAL COMPETITORS

Johnson & Johnson; The Procter & Gamble Company; Unilever N.V.

FURTHER READING

"Ascendia Back on Track to Restart Healing Process," *Cosmetics International,* January 11, 2008, p. 1.

"Charles Oestreich, Cosmetics Maker," *New York Times,* June 4, 1969.

Duggan, Ed, "Reality Check for Virtual Academics.com," *South Florida Business Journal,* October 13, 2000, p. 1A.

Hunter, Catherine Ellis, "Lander Co. Hits 71st Year," *Drug & Cosmetic Industry,* December 1, 1991, p. 14.

"Lander Develops Winning Formula," *Chain Drug Review,* June 23, 1997.

Lynn, Kathleen, "Low-Profile Firm Markets Cosmetics Without the Glitz," *Record* (N.J.), August 6, 1986, p. C11.

Mooney, Bill, "Ascendia Gets Listings Violation," *Trenton (N.J.) Times,* June 29, 2007, p. C08.

Astellas Pharma Inc.

2-3-11 Nihonbashi-Honcho
Chuo-ku
Tokyo, 103-8411
Japan
Telephone: (+81 813) 3244 3000
Fax: (+81 813) 3244 3272
Web site: http://www.astellas.com

Public Company
Incorporated: 2005
Employees: 13,900
Sales: ¥900 billion ($8.48 billion) (2007)
Stock Exchanges: Tokyo
Ticker Symbol: 4503
NAICS: 325411 Medicinal and Botanical Manufacturing; 325412 Pharmaceutical Preparation Manufacturing

■ ■ ■

Astellas Pharma Inc. is Japan's second largest pharmaceutical company, behind leader Takeda Pharmaceutical, with a third place position overall. (U. S.-based Pfizer is number two in Japan in terms of sales.) Astellas was formed through the 2005 merger between Fujisawa Pharmaceutical Co. and Yamanouchi Pharmaceutical Co. Astellas positions itself as an ethical (prescription) pharmaceutical developer. The company is active in a variety of health fields, including urology, cardiology, immunology, ulcer treatments, infectious diseases, Alzheimer's treatment, and cancer treatments. With patents running out on a number of Astellas' best-selling products, including immunosuppressant Prograf, Astellas has begun investing in experimental therapies. This has led to the acquisition of U.S.-based Agensys Inc., a developer of therapeutic cancer antibodies, in December 2007. In April 2008, the company announced a $760 million partnership with another U.S. company, CoMentis Inc., to develop an Alzheimer's disease therapy. The company has 13 plants and research and development facilities in Japan, China, the United States, the Netherlands, and Ireland. Astellas had combined sales of more than ¥900 billion ($8.48 billion) in 2007. The company is listed on the Tokyo Stock Exchange and is led by Masafumi Nogimori, president and CEO.

ORIGINS AND POSTWAR GROWTH

In 1894, Tomokichi Fujisawa opened the Fujisawa Shoten in Osaka as a private dealership in medicinal herbs. The business expanded rapidly during the early decades of the 20th century, its success based on the production of such widely used compounds as Camphor, a stimulant, and Santonin, a treatment for intestinal worms. Even though the company faced shortages of ingredients during World War II, it continued to prosper. It adopted the name Fujisawa Pharmaceutical Co. Ltd. in 1943.

Along with the rest of the pharmaceutical industry, Fujisawa experienced unprecedented growth in postwar Japan, mainly as a producer of antibiotics. By 1961, antibiotics accounted for 10.3 percent of Japan's total drug production. Because Japan had no effective patent

COMPANY PERSPECTIVES

Astellas will seek to enhance its enterprise value in a sustainable manner. Astellas will seek to be the company of choice among all its stakeholders, including its customers, shareholders, employees, and the global community. Astellas will strive to gain the trust of all stakeholders and thereby enhance its enterprise value.

laws, and the results of highly expensive research and development could be easily pirated, Japanese pharmaceutical companies tended to import the technology to manufacture antibiotics and other medicines from abroad.

In its early history, Fujisawa showed an impressive ability to establish good working relations with foreign firms. In 1953, Fujisawa signed a contract with the Italian company Carlo Erba to sell a broad spectrum antibiotic, Kemicetine, in Japan. Other such licensing arrangements involved Irgapyrin, an antiarthritic drug from Geigy of Switzerland, and a local anesthetic, Xylocaine, from the laboratories of Astra in Sweden. Fujisawa also began developing a number of successful drugs on its own (for example, Trichomycin, an antibiotic used in the treatment of candidiasis and trichomoniasis).

Besides the production and sale of antibiotics, Fujisawa was noted for its work with vitamin preparations. The pure synthesis of thioctic acid in company laboratories led to a highly successful product marketed as Tioctan. Neuvita, a longer-acting vitamin preparation, was added to the product line in 1961 after the firm developed a process to combine thioctic acid with vitamin B1. This new product, helpful in the treatment of liver disease, was well received by both physicians and the general public.

At the forefront of producing and marketing antibiotics and vitamins, Fujisawa reaped financial rewards. With antibiotics accounting for more than 10.3 percent and vitamins totaling more than 20 percent of the Japanese pharmaceutical industry's entire drug production in 1962, Fujisawa enjoyed an increase in profits that was 250 percent of its 1961 results.

In the late 1950s and throughout the 1960s, Fujisawa continued to expand its product line by moving into non-pharmaceutical items such as antioxidative food additives. The company's continued expansion in the 1960s, like that of many other Japanese pharmaceutical concerns, could also be attributed to the regulations of the National Health Insurance System established by the government in the early part of the decade. With the implementation of this program, the burden of public health costs fell upon the government, and people began to visit their doctors more frequently. With more patients, doctors prescribed more drugs. Because doctors operated their own drug dispensaries, the Ministry of Health and Welfare set official prices at which they would be reimbursed. These official prices were often higher than the purchase price: the profit involved obviously did not discourage doctors from generously prescribing drugs.

REAPING THE REWARDS OF RESEARCH AND DEVELOPMENT

Even as Fujisawa experienced record growth and profits, it continued, as did other Japanese pharmaceutical firms, to depend on foreign research and production technology. The result was a huge trade deficit between imported and exported drugs. The government, recognizing the potential of an active domestic pharmaceutical industry, implemented a number of measures to encourage export and to ensure that Japanese companies could withstand foreign competition. These measures included the tightening of patent laws and a restructuring of official drug pricing, which put innovative drugs at a premium.

Fujisawa's expenditure for research and development thereafter increased dramatically as it attempted to develop products that could be patented. Two new drugs to emerge from company laboratories at this time were Pyroace, an antibiotic, and Padrin, an antiseptic. By 1966, company profits were nine times what they had been a decade before, with newly developed products accounting for between 40 to 50 percent of total sales.

Fujisawa looked to foreign markets as a means of recouping its huge investments in new products. A technical cooperation agreement with Delagrange in France led to Fujisawa's licensing the manufacture and sale of the drug Primperan. In the non-pharmaceutical division, the company began to export a leavening agent for baked goods. Both of these products were well received in foreign markets.

As technology began flowing from east to west, foreign companies became particularly interested in a new class of potent antibiotics developed by the Japanese. Known as third-generation cephalosporins, these antibiotics were particularly important for their ability to combat the highly resistant strains of bacteria found in hospitals. In 1970, Fujisawa became the third

KEY DATES

1894: Fujisawa Shoten opens in Osaka.
1923: Yamanouchi Pharmaceutical Co. is founded in Osaka.
1942: Yamanouchi moves to Tokyo.
1943: Fujisawa Pharmaceutical Co. Ltd. is incorporated.
1963: Yamanouchi opens subsidiary in Taiwan.
1971: Cefazolin, a bacteria-fighting antibiotic, is launched by Fujisawa.
1977: Fujisawa establishes an American subsidiary.
1979: Yamanouchi enters U.S. market.
1990: Lyphomed Inc. is acquired and absorbed into Fujisawa's U.S. operations.
1993: Immunosuppressant Prograf hits the market in Japan.
1998: Fujisawa pleads guilty in an international price-fixing case.
2001: Protopic, a drug used to treat eczema, becomes available in the United States.
2005: Yamanouchi and Fujisawa merge to become Astellas Pharma.
2008: Astellas acquires Agensys Inc. and reaches partnership agreement with CoMentis Inc.

company in the world to develop the cephalosporin Cefamezin. This new drug, branded Cefazolin, was introduced in 1971. A joint venture between Fujisawa and SmithKline Beckman in 1977 led to the introduction of Cefazolin and other Fujisawa antibiotics on the U.S. market. This agreement also entitled Fujisawa to sell innovative SmithKline drugs in the Japanese market, including Tagamet, SmithKline's well-known antiulcer drug, and Auranofin, its popular antiarthritic medication.

Fujisawa opened a U.S. subsidiary in 1977 and established a London office in 1979. It was during this time that Mutsuya Ajisaka, Fujisawa's director of planning and coordination, outlined a new company strategy. Although much of the firm's overseas success had so far been achieved through licensing arrangements, henceforth Fujisawa would participate in more direct marketing of its products. Ajisaka also felt that antibiotics, including cephalosporins, though continuing to achieve huge sales, had saturated the market and that the company should concentrate its research in other areas. Within a few years, calcium blockers, a new class of potent drugs, emerged from Fujisawa's laboratories. These pharmaceuticals, which prevented blood vessels from constricting, were used to treat angina pectoris and hypertension.

OVERCOMING HARDSHIPS

By 1982, the per capita drug bill in Japan had reached the equivalent of nearly $100. In an effort to counter excessive profiteering and to alleviate national expenditures on medicine, the government began reducing the price of drugs. By 1987, prices had dropped 50 percent, and patients were required to pay 10 percent of examination costs. This structural change in the National Health Insurance System almost immediately affected Fujisawa's profit margins. Against this background, Fujisawa also found itself competing in a more crowded marketplace and suffering, with other pharmaceutical companies, increased costs for research and development.

Despite these difficulties, Fujisawa remained a strong and innovative competitor within the international pharmaceutical industry. The company introduced six new drugs in 1986, and it was strongly committed to developing a new class of drugs appropriate for Japan's growing geriatric population. One such drug, Gramalil, was used to treat psychotic disturbances in the elderly. Fujisawa was also developing an antitumor substance from soil bacteria, a drug that had been shown to be effective in treating leukemia and melanoma in laboratory animals.

As competition continued to heighten in the late 1980s and into the 1990s, Fujisawa made several key moves to secure its position in the industry. In 1987, it bought out SmithKline's stake in its U.S. joint venture. The company also began investing in U.S.-based Lyphomed Inc. in the 1980s. In 1990, Fujisawa acquired the drug maker in a $765 million deal. Lyphomed's operations were absorbed into the company's U.S. subsidiary, Fujisawa USA.

In 1991, the company began to focus on a promising new immunosuppressant drug used in organ transplants called Prograf. A German subsidiary was created to oversee the marketing and development of the drug, and in 1993 Prograf made its debut in Japan. It was introduced in the United States and the United Kingdom the following year and quickly became a leading drug used in liver and kidney transplants.

While the company worked to overcome the problems it faced due to deregulation in its domestic market, it dealt with bad press related to a series of scandals. In 1998, the company pleaded guilty in a price-fixing case filed by the U.S. Justice Department's antitrust division. The case claimed that Fujisawa and other leading chemical firms worked together to eliminate competition in the market for sodium gluconate, used to clean metal and glass. Fujisawa was forced to pay a $20 million fine and Akira Nakao, the executive involved, received a $200,000 criminal fine. To make matters worse, this was not the first time that Fujisawa had been involved in a public scandal. In 1983, company executives stole a rival company's data on a new drug, resulting in the arrest of several employees. Fujisawa was also forced to pay out over $100 million in damages in the early 1990s after its Lyphomed unit was found guilty of using false data to gain U.S. approval for drugs.

While these scandals tarnished the reputable image of Fujisawa, it quickly became apparent that the Japanese company had put the past behind it. In 1998, it reorganized its U.S. operations by creating Fujisawa Healthcare Inc., a unit responsible for the company's pharmaceutical business in the United States. New drugs also continued to filter out of its pipeline. Protopic, a drug used to treat atopic dermatitis, was launched in Japan in 1999, made its way to the United States in 2001, and debuted in Europe and Asia in 2002. Funguard, a drug used to treat fungal infections, was also introduced in Japan in 2002.

RESTRUCTURING FOR THE NEW CENTURY

To better position itself to compete with international drug makers in the century, Fujisawa implemented a series of restructuring efforts that included the creation of a global management system. The company continued to respond to the changing market in Japan by focusing on research and development and global expansion. A May 2003 *Business Week* article summed up industry conditions surrounding Japan's drug sector, claiming that "Japanese regulators realized that the sector needed a stiff dose of competition, and in 1998, they eased rules for new-drug approval by accepting clinical data on drugs developed outside the country. This spring, they barred physicians from collecting a commission on the drugs they prescribed—a longstanding practice that led doctors to prescribe domestic drugs, which offered higher payments. The biggest shock of all will come in 2005, when Tokyo scraps the local-manufacturing regulation." (This regulation requires companies that sell drugs in Japan to also have production facilities there.)

The looming enactment of new regulations forced Fujisawa, like the rest of the Japanese pharmaceutical industry, to react. Over the past decade, the Japanese drug companies had fallen behind their international competitors, which had carried out a series of mega-mergers creating a number of new globally operating giants. Despite their clout at home, the Japanese companies, including Fujisawa, looked like minnows in the rapidly consolidating pharmaceutical market. Fujisawa, which ranked just 14 in the Japanese market, launched a search for a partner to gain the scale it needed to survive the new realities of the global pharmaceutical industry.

MERGER ANNOUNCEMENT

At the end of 2004, Fujisawa announced that it had reached an agreement to merge its operations with those of Yamanouchi Pharmaceutical, a company of roughly the same size as itself. Founded in Osaka in 1923, Yamanouchi had moved to Tokyo in 1942. Like Fujisawa, the company turned to the international market in the postwar era, establishing its first overseas subsidiary in Taiwan in 1963. The company later entered the U.S. market, opening its first office there in 1979. The following year, Yamanouchi added operations in Europe as well, with an office in London. In 1986, the company established its first manufacturing presence in Europe, with the launch of a bulk drug production facility in Ireland.

Yamanouchi's European operations grew again in 1991, when it acquired Royal Gist Brocades, of the Netherlands. The acquisition gave the company a dedicated European marketing wing, as well as the site for its first foreign research and development center. Yamanouchi continued its expansion through the 1990s. In 1994, it launched a production arm in China, in Shenyang. The company then moved to boost its presence in the U.S. market, adding a dedicated marketing arm there, Yamanouchi Pharma America, in 2001.

By then, Yamanouchi had grown into one of Japan's top ten drug companies, with sales of more than ¥400 billion. The company had established particularly strong operations in the fields of ulcer and urinary treatments, with sales led by its urinary treatment Harnal. However, with a market share of just 2.99 percent, Yamanouchi too remained highly vulnerable to the increasingly global drugs market. To boost its position, the company sought the partnership with Fujisawa.

As part of the merger agreement, Yamanouchi acquired Fujisawa, paying ¥800 billion (approximately $6 billion) to acquire Fujisawa. The two companies viewed the operation as a merger of equals, and indeed, the start of an entirely new company. To underscore this, the newly combined company chose a new name, Astellas Pharma, adapting the name from a Japanese word that meant "shine on tomorrow."

Astellas debuted strongly, boosting its market share to 5.24 percent, giving it the second place position (behind Takeda) among Japanese drug companies, and the third place (behind Pfizer) in Japan overall. At the global level, Astellas climbed into the ranks of the top 20 drug companies. Astellas immediately began planning its expansion, announcing that it intended to borrow as much as ¥1 trillion to acquire operations outside of Japan. In 2005, the company set up a new subsidiary in Germany, which was soon followed by a subsidiary in Spain.

Into 2006, however, Astellas began readapting its international strategy. In August of that year, the company announced plans to shift production of its Prograf immune system drug to a new factory in China in 2007. Also in 2006, the company announced plans to shut down seven of its 18 factories. These included three plants in Japan, a plant in the United States, and plants in Germany, Italy, and Ireland. The plant closings were expected to be completed by 2011, eliminating 1,150 jobs from the group's payroll.

Astellas also took steps to rejuvenate its aging drug pipeline, as a number of its best-selling drugs reached the end of their patent period. Astellas began targeting investments in new generation and experimental drugs. This led the company to make two significant acquisitions in the United States. In December 2007, the company bought Agensys Inc., a California-based company that had been developing therapeutic cancer antibodies. Astellas agreed to pay $387 million to take over Agensys, plus as much as $150 million in payments as Agensys reached various milestones in its drug development.

By April 2008, the company had found its second investment, forming a partnership with another California company, CoMentis Inc., to develop Alzheimer's disease treatments. Under that agreement, Astellas paid $80 million upfront. The total deal, however, had a potential worth of $760 million, depending on CoMentis hitting milestone targets.

With these acquisitions, Astellas had begun putting into place its new long-term strategy, designed to position the company as a "Global Category Leader" in its target therapies by 2015. The combination of two of Japan's leading pharmaceutical groups had resulted in a new company prepared to meet the challenges of the pharmaceutical industry in the future.

Updated, Christina M. Stansell; M. L. Cohen

PRINCIPAL SUBSIDIARIES

Agensys, Inc. (U.S.A.); Astellas Pharma (China) Inc.; Astellas Ireland Co., Ltd.; Astellas Pharma Chemicals Co., Ltd.,; Astellas Pharma Europe B.V. (Netherlands); Astellas Pharma Manufacturing, Inc. (U.S.A.); Astellas Pharma Technologies, Inc. (U.S.A.); Astellas Tokai Co., Ltd.; Astellas Toyama Co., Ltd.

PRINCIPAL COMPETITORS

Aventis S.A.; Johnson & Johnson; Pfizer Inc.; GlaxoSmithKline; Novartis International AG; Bayer AG; Sanofi-Aventis; Roche Holding AG; Celesio AG; Idemitsu Kosan Company Ltd.; AstraZeneca AB.

FURTHER READING

"Astellas Pays $387m in Cash for Drug Company," *Private Equity Week,* December 3, 2007, p. 7.

"Astellas Pharma to Sell 3 European Plants," *Kyodo News International,* November 7, 2006.

"Astellas Sets Up Subsidiary in Spain," *Pharma Marketletter,* June 27, 2005.

"Astellas Unveils Restructuring Plan Featuring Closure of 7 Plants," *Kyodo News International,* October 4, 2006.

"A Dose of Reform for Japan's Drugmakers," *Business Week,* May 19, 2003.

"Drugmaker Astellas' Net Profit Soars 26.7% on Sale of Affiliate," *Kyodo News International,* May 15, 2007.

"Drug Maker Suffers Another Scandal Headache," *Nikkei Weekly,* March 9, 1998, p. 8.

"Fujisawa Launches Protopic in U.S.," *SCRIP World Pharmaceutical News,* February 28, 2001, p. 23.

"Fujisawa Outlines Strategic Restructuring in Interview with Marketletter," *Pharma Marketletter,* June 23, 2003.

"Fujisawa to Buy Lyphomed," *New York Times,* September 2, 1989.

"Fujisawa Unveils Restructuring Plan," *Japan Economic Newswire,* September 3, 2002.

Harbrecht, Douglas, "Japanese Company Pleads Guilty to Price-Fixing," *Business Week,* February 26, 1998.

Hirano, Ko, "Astellas Eyes Riding on Rising Health Consciousness in US," *Kyodo News International,* March 13, 2007.

"Japan's Astellas to Make Immonusuppressant Drug in China," *AsiaPulse News,* August 21, 2006.

"Japan's Next Battleground: The Medicine Chest," *Business Week,* March 12, 1990.

"Japan's 2nd Biggest Drugmaker Astellas Pharma Created," *Japan Weekly Monitor,* April 4, 2005.

Osborne, Randall, "As Much As $150M More Later Astellas Buying into Cancer," *Bioworld Today,* November 28, 2007.

"Pharma's Strength in Numbers," *Corporate Finance,* March 2004, p. 8.

Sagiike, Hideki, and Hiroshi Suzuki, "Japanese Drug Maker Seeks Loan for Acquisitions," *International Herald Tribune,* March 30, 2006, p. 17.

Young, Donna, "Astellas, CoMentis in $760M Deal for Alzheimer's Treatment," *Bioworld Today,* April 28, 2008.

Babolat VS, S.A.

93 rue André-Bollier
Lyon, F-69007
France
Telephone: (33 04) 78 69 78 69
Toll Free: (877) 316-9435
Fax: (33 04) 78 69 78 79
Web site: http://www.babolat.com

Non-Quoted Public Company
Incorporated: 1875
Employees: 200
Sales: EUR 88.0 million (2007)
NAICS: 339920 Sporting and Athletic Goods Manufacturing; 315228 Men's and Boys' Cut and Sew Other Outerwear Manufacturing; 315999 Other Apparel Accessories and Other Apparel Manufacturing; 316219 Other Footwear Manufacturing; 316211 Rubber and Plastics Footwear Manufacturing

■ ■ ■

Babolat VS, S.A., is one of the world's leading manufacturers of racket sports equipment. The company claims the invention of tennis strings in 1877, and since then it has always been represented at the highest echelons of the sport. "Tennis runs in our blood," says the company, owned by the Babolat family. The gutsy introduction of its own tennis rackets in 1994 took the firm to new levels of brand awareness and revenues. The full product line includes natural and synthetic strings; stringing machines; rackets for tennis, squash, and badminton; shoes, clothing, tennis balls, and other accessories. As one of the top three brands in tennis, Babolat makes its products available through 20,000 stores and 20,000 pro shops in more than a hundred countries.

A LONG TRADITION

Babolat VS, S.A., counts 1875 as its starting date, but its origins can be traced back even further. In 1809 an Italian named Savaresse established a workshop to make gut violin strings in Lyon, France, a city on the Rhône that was both a cultural and agricultural center.

In 1848 Savaresse's partner, Jean-François Monnier, became sole proprietor. After he brought his son-in-law Pierre Babolat into the business, the firm took the name Babolat Monnier. Babolat's parents had a butcher's shop. The company that took his name was by then making more than music from sheep intestines. It used them for sausage casings and medical sutures.

Although precursors to the equipment employed in the modern game of tennis date back hundreds of years, Babolat holds a claim as the inventor of string for tennis rackets. In 1873 the company moved to its longtime headquarters, 93 rue André-Bollier in Lyon. Several years later, after the All-England Tennis Club at Wimbledon set down the official rules of lawn tennis, an English tennis racket manufacturer named Mister Bussey approached the firm about making strings for his frames.

COMPANY PERSPECTIVES

Founded in 1875, the same year as tennis itself, BABOLAT is the first company to have specialised in racquet sports. Right from the start, the name BABOLAT has been synonymous with innovation, competition and winning. Throughout the history of tennis and throughout the world, BABOLAT has made a name for itself. From the first Davis Cup, to the Masters, Roland Garros, Wimbledon, US Open or Australian Open, the legendary VS string has been found on the most renowned podiums—sometimes even on both sides of the court! Top players like the Musketeers, Petra, Pietrangeli, Ashe, Nastase, Borg, Wilander, Becker, Sampras ... have all been winners using BABOLAT strings. And since Carlos Moya's victory at Roland Garros in 1998, BABOLAT has become the symbol of "total tennis": BABOLAT develops strings and racquets, a winning combination!

It took several years to develop a process for making an acceptable string. The company soon began equipping the famous *Mousquetaires,* the four Frenchmen Jean Borotra, Jacques Brugnon, Henri Cochet, and René Lacoste who dominated the sport. Cochet, who was from Lyon himself, actively consulted with the company. Tennis legend Suzanne Lenglen, also French, became a dedicated user as well.

In 1925 the company uncoiled its legendary VS Gut. It is impossible to overstate the importance of this string to professional tennis in the coming decades. While racket manufacturers came and went, throughout the 20th century the fabric of tennis history was woven with VS Gut. Jack Kramer, Arthur Ashe, Bjorn Borg, Pete Sampras, and many other champions insisted on it.

As worldwide demand for its gut strings grew, Babolat established several more factories, including some outside the country in Great Britain, Italy, Morocco, and Brazil. Meanwhile, Pierre Babolat was succeeded by his son Albert, who in turn was succeeded by his own son, Paul Babolat. He married Denise Witt, and the families merged their businesses into a company called Babolat-Maillot-Witt. This was split up in the early 1980s, with Babolat taking over the racket strings and medical sutures, and the other two focusing on meatpacking and musical strings. Paul Babolat's son Pierre was named chief executive in 1987. He had been working at the company since turning a teenager.

STRINGING EVOLUTION

Babolat introduced its first synthetic strings in 1954 under the Elascord name. Nylon strings became the choice of the masses because they were much less expensive. It used to require the intestines of six sheep to produce a single set of gut strings, Eric Babolat told *L'Express.* Although a refinement in the process in 1960 reduced the demand to two and a half beef guts, it still remained a costly proposition.

After having its name in front of racket technicians for 100 years, it seemed natural for Babolat to begin making its own stringing machines in 1975. In the next couple of decades, it would bring out electronic stringers and diagnostic machines for precisely calibrating individual racket characteristics such as balance and stiffness.

FOREIGN VENTURES

Revenues for Babolat were about FRF 200 million in the mid-1980s. The company then had 560 employees worldwide, almost two-thirds of them in France. Its products were sold in 30,000 locations. The company had set up a subsidiary in Germany that had grown to annual sales of FRF 12 million within its first decade. It had also established a similar-sized unit in Austria, an office in Spain, and a manufacturing operation in Brazil. In 1995 Babolat bought racket manufacturer Maxima, its Italian distributor since 1950.

Babolat expanded outside Europe by setting up marketing arrangements. It contracted Sumitomo Rubber Industries Ltd. to pitch its products in Japan beginning in 1992. Japan would be an important international market for years to come. The U.S. subsidiary's sales were up to about $4 million by 1986. However, in 1995 Babolat handed off its U.S. marketing to Penn Racquet Sports, the country's leading tennis ball manufacturer.

MAKING A RACKET

Babolat maintained utter dominance of the tiny market for natural gut, but it was also a world leader in synthetic strings. Still, the company would not become a household name (among tennis-playing families, anyway) until it started selling rackets.

Although its engineers had designed some rackets after World War II, Babolat did not really become a manufacturer until 1994, when it developed its own

KEY DATES

1809: An Italian named Savaresse establishes a workshop in Lyon to make gut violin strings.
1848: Savaresse's partner, Jean-François Monnier, becomes sole proprietor, brings son-in-law Pierre Babolat into the business.
1873: Firm moves to its longtime headquarters, 93 rue André-Bollier.
1875: At request of an English racket manufacturer, Babolat creates the first strings for the newly codified sport of lawn tennis.
1925: The evolution of gut strings produces the legendary VS Gut, the choice of champions for decades to come.
1954: Babolat introduces its first synthetic string, Elascord.
1975: Babolat begins making its own stringing machines.
1994: As the industry stumbles, Babolat introduces its own line of tennis rackets.
1998: Carlos Moya swings a Babolat racket to a French Open title and top of the world rankings.
2003: Shoes and technical clothing are introduced as Andy Roddick and Kim Clijsters, using Babolat rackets and strings, achieve number one rankings.
2005: Revenues reach EUR 60 million on strength of the fast-growing racket business.
2008: Rafael Nadal wins his fourth French Open with Babolat racket and strings.

oversized graphite racket. Following a general industry trend, production of the rackets was contracted to factories in mainland China and Taiwan.

It was, Eric Babolat later recalled in *L'Express,* an odd time to be getting into the racket business. A number of manufacturers had folded as the industry contracted after the excesses of the 1970s and 1980s. Whatever the commercial reasoning, Babolat's new rackets soon found success on the playing field. Carlos Moya wielded one to win the French Open title and a world number one ranking in 1998.

Unfortunately a year of achievement was marked by sudden loss. CEO Pierre Babolat died when his Swissair flight crashed in Canada on September 3, 1998. After a few years with an interim executive, leadership of the company went to Pierre Babolat's son Eric. Still in his late 20s, Eric Babolat represented the fifth generation of his family to head the enterprise.

DRIVING INTO THE UNITED STATES

The new line of rackets was more than just a sensible brand extension. It brought the Babolat name to new levels of recognition in the mass market. When it was just a stringing company, the brand was familiar primarily to pros and racket stringers.

The rackets, dubbed "Pure Drive," were not marketed in the United States until 2000. The particular technical attributes of the rackets helped win them wide acceptance among club players and juniors there in a short time. Built stiff with an open stringing pattern, they made it easier for everyday players to emulate the powerful topspin shots of the fast-evolving pro game.

The possibilities of the rackets were demonstrated by Andy Roddick, who claimed the record for world's fastest serve. It was particularly important to have the American Roddick on the roster to help sell the rackets in the United States, noted the *New York Times.* Babolat sought promising players such as Roddick early in their careers. They tended to remain loyal to the brand if they eventually found greater success. The company could offer discounts on its highly sought after strings as an inducement.

For the fiscal year ended August 2000, the firm reported a net profit of FRF 7.8 million on revenues of FRF 185 million. (Babolat was technically a public company, although its shares were all owned by the family.) Rackets had quickly come to represent a significant share of the business, 25 percent. By this time, natural gut accounted for only about 5 percent of the world market for strings, but it remained the choice of more than half of the leading professional tennis players.

Babolat was the number three racket brand in Europe behind Wilson and Head. At this time, the U.S. market only accounted for 10 percent of Babolat's sales. Babolat reconstituted its North American subsidiary in 2000, basing it in the sports-oriented town of Boulder, Colorado, and linking it with distributor Rocky Mountains Sports.

Babolat introduced a number of refinements to its rackets. In 1999 it debuted "Woofer" technology, named after bass speakers, which extended the active length of the strings through the racket frame. The AeroPro, launched in 2004, was designed with special attention to its aerodynamic profile to allow greater racket head speed. The company also ventured into different racket sports. It added squash rackets in 2001 after making badminton rackets for a few years.

SHOES, APPAREL, AND BALLS

In 2001 Babolat exploited an opening in the worldwide tennis ball market, which was controlled by only two or three companies (Penn, Wilson, and Dunlop/Slazenger). The company had a connection to the business via its Japanese distributor, which had also made balls under the Dunlop brand. It contracted production to Sumitomo, while focusing its marketing on France, Italy, and Spain, where it was initially aiming for a 10 percent share, reported *Les Echos.* In fiscal 2002, Babolat reported total revenues of EUR 41 million. Rackets accounted for roughly half the total, with 30 percent coming from strings and stringing machines.

The company continued to diversify. In the spring of 2003 it debuted a tennis shoe featuring a durable rubber compound from Michelin in the soles. Like the rackets, the shoes were designed in France but manufactured in China. There was also a two-year lag before they were made available in the U.S. market. Also in 2003, Babolat brought out an array of tennis clothing constructed with technical, wicking fabrics.

AIMING FOR NUMBER ONE

The year turned out to be a good one as far as publicity was concerned. In 2003 Andy Roddick won the U.S. Open with a Babolat racket and strings, while he and fellow endorser Kim Clijsters attained world number one rankings. The oldest name in tennis was aiming to become the world's largest racket manufacturer. By 2007 Babolat was number three behind Wilson Sports Co. and Head N.V. rackets accounted for 80 percent of total revenues of EUR 88 million.

With Rafael Nadal winning his fourth French Open in 2008 with a Babolat racket and synthetic strings (and rising star Dinara Safina representing the rackets in the women's final), Babolat was clearly the one to beat on the clay courts of Europe. Nadal's very first racket had been a Babolat and he had been a fan of Carlos Moya, a fellow Majorcan, while growing up. In April 2007 Nadal reaffirmed his commitment to the brand by signing a ten-year contract.

Frederick C. Ingram

PRINCIPAL SUBSIDIARIES

Babolat VS GmbH (Germany); Babolat VS Italia SpA; Babolat VS North America, Inc. (U.S.A.).

PRINCIPAL COMPETITORS

Wilson Sporting Goods Co.; Head N.V.; Prince Sports Inc.; Dunlop Slazenger Corporation; Major Sports, S.A.; Luxilon Industries NV.

FURTHER READING

Depagneux, Marie-Annick, "Babolat deviant une marque globale pour le tennis," *Les Echos,* May 30, 2003, p. 20.

———, "Babolat—du luth à la raquette de tennis," *Les Echos,* July 19, 2002, p. 15.

———, "Babolat se lance dans les balles de tennis," *Les Echos,* July 9, 2001.

———, "Le lyonnais Babolat se lance à la conquête des Etats-Unis," *Les Echos,* January 7, 2000.

Guy, Marie-Stéphane, "Babolat lance ses premières raquettes de squash," *La Tribune,* March 14, 2001.

Joly, Anne, "Babolat a diversifié son offer et ses partenariats," *La Tribune,* February 19, 2008.

"Michelin-Babolat au service de l'innovation," *La Tribune,* November 17, 2005.

Morris, Charles, "Babolat reta a las—grandes raquetas del mundo," *Expansión* (Spain), January 17, 2002.

Newman, Eric, "Babolat Seeks to Score with Roddick," *Footwear News,* August 29, 2005, p. 4.

Nocera, Joe, "Buy It and Be Great," *New York Times,* August 19, 2007.

Payot, Marianne, "Les Babolat: premiers de cordée," *L'Express.fr,* November 22, 2004.

Baldor Electric Company

5711 R. S. Boreham Jr. Street
Fort Smith, Arkansas 72908-8301
U.S.A.
Telephone: (479) 646-4711
Toll Free: (800) 828-4920
Fax: (479) 648-5792
Web site: http://www.baldor.com

Public Company
Incorporated: 1920
Employees: 8,083
Sales: $1.82 billion (2007)
Stock Exchanges: New York
Ticker Symbol: BEZ
NAICS: 335312 Motor and Generator Manufacturing; 333612 Speed Changer, Industrial High-Speed Drive, and Gear Manufacturing; 333613 Mechanical Power Transmission Equipment Manufacturing; 335314 Relay and Industrial Control Manufacturing; 333512 Machine Tool (Metal Cutting Types) Manufacturing

■ ■ ■

Baldor Electric Company is one of the leading producers of industrial electric motors, power transmission products, drives, and generators in the United States. Best known for its motors, Baldor produces a wide variety of both AC and DC electric motors ranging in size from subfractional to 15,000 horsepower. The Arkansas-based company supplies its products to more than 9,500 customers in more than 160 industries, including both original equipment manufacturers and distributors in the United States and abroad. U.S.-based customers account for about 85 percent of sales. Baldor manufactures its products at around two dozen plants in the United States, Canada, Mexico, England, and China.

COMPANY FOUNDED IN 1920

Baldor Electric was founded in 1920 in St. Louis, Missouri, by Edwin C. Ballman and Emil Doerr. Ballman was an electric engineer with a passion for inventing. He had patented a centrifugal switch that improved a motor's performance and was certain that industry could be convinced of the merits of his new device. Ballman recruited Doerr, a plant supervisor at the St. Louis Electric Company where Ballman worked, to join him in his new venture, and the two men pooled their savings to lease space in a small shop across town. The pair hired a handful of workers and persuaded a fellow St. Louis Electric employee, Oliver Baumann, to serve as office manager/bookkeeper. The new company, named Baldor after the two founders' last names, was an immediate success. The fully enclosed, low-horsepower, repulsion induction motors made by Baldor were ordered by manufacturers of such industrial equipment as floor sanders and pumps, which required high starting torque and an enclosed motor. After only one year of operation Baldor had outgrown the small leased shop, and the company purchased a factory in St. Louis that was to remain the company headquarters for the next 45 years.

Baldor's first big jump in sales came in 1924 when it agreed to manufacture motors for Williams Oil-O-

COMPANY PERSPECTIVES

Our mission is to be the best (as determined by our customers) marketers, designers and manufacturers of industrial electric motors, power transmission products, drives and generators.

Matic, a maker of oil burners in Bloomington, Illinois. Williams required so many motors that Baldor built a plant in Bloomington exclusively to accommodate orders from that company. By the late 1920s, Baldor was earning about $6 million, principally on the strength of its sales from the Bloomington plant. Baldor's prosperity came to a sudden halt in the early 1930s when the company faced the double blow of the 1929 stock market crash and subsequent Great Depression as well as the cancellation of the Williams Oil-O-Matic contract when that company decided to manufacture its own motors. On the verge of bankruptcy, company President Ballman cut wages but did not lay off any employees, a strategy that was to set a pattern for Baldor's employee/management relations for many years. Baldor recovered with the American economy but never regained the luxury of a single, large customer supplying the bulk of sales.

GROWTH THROUGH MID-CENTURY

Baldor's business grew enough during the 1930s to require multiple additions to the company's St. Louis factory, which by the end of the decade stretched over almost an entire city block. The relatively restricted line of multipurpose enclosed motors produced by the company began to be extended to include more specialized designs (such as short motors for floor sanders and vertical motors for pumps) as Baldor sought out new industries to serve.

In 1933 Baldor began to manufacture a small line of non-motor products through what became known as the company's "Apparatus Division." This virtual one-person operation was overseen by George A. Schock, who was later to become company treasurer and unofficial company historian. The division's essential role was to market the sometimes erratic offerings of company founder and President Edwin Ballman's inventive genius. "I tried to sell any product that Edwin Ballman could invent or design," Schock wrote in a company history. "Sometimes I did not do very well." Ballman's inventions included such diverse items as battery chargers, motion picture rectifiers, low-glare desk lamps, and, on one memorable occasion, an "addstick," a plastic ruler with manually operated dials for adding and subtracting. "When you saw him [Ballman] coming back from vacation you just wanted to run and hide," Schock recalled in a 1981 interview with *Forbes.* "God only knew what he'd pull out of his suitcase and ask you to build." Most of the products of the Apparatus Division were either unsalable or were such idiosyncratic pieces of what was usually a whole line of products that Schock could not lure companies away from more traditional suppliers. The division's one enduring success was its line of industrial grinders and buffers, which remained a small but consistent part of Baldor's sales into the 21st century.

When the United States entered World War II in 1941, and many U.S. companies abandoned their traditional lines to produce war products, Baldor management decided to stick with the small electric motors that the company knew best. This decision cost Baldor sales during the war years but left the company in full gear for the postwar boom. Through the late 1940s and 1950s, Baldor sales continued to grow, albeit slowly. In 1956 the company, with no more room to further expand its St. Louis factory, opened a new manufacturing plant in Fort Smith, Arkansas. In 1967 a much expanded Fort Smith facility became Baldor's headquarters, and the original St. Louis offices were closed.

Throughout this period of slow growth, Baldor continued to produce a relatively small range of motors. The company's stock-in-trade, an enclosed, durable, low-horsepower motor, sold well in the agricultural industry where it was used for crop driers and aerators but was not versatile enough to accommodate a wide range of other uses. Content with the steady profitability of his firm, Edwin Ballman refused to implement the kind of design innovations necessary to attract a wider clientele. This conservative approach served the company well during the economically buoyant 1950s, but in 1960 a price war between industry giants Gould, Westinghouse, and Emerson found Baldor stuck in the middle with little leeway to offer competitive pricing. The company, which had recorded a profit every year since 1932, lost $30,000 in 1960.

OPERATING LOSS INITIATES A NEW ERA

The 1960 loss jolted Baldor into making some profound changes in its operating philosophy. At the age of 78, Edwin Ballman stepped down as CEO of the firm to allow his son Fred to take full control of the company's management. Fred Ballman felt that Baldor's best ap-

KEY DATES

1920: Edwin C. Ballman and Emil Doerr found Baldor Electric Company in St. Louis, Missouri, to produce electric motors.
1956: Company opens a new manufacturing plant in Fort Smith, Arkansas.
1960: Net loss for the year prompts a move to transform the company into a service-oriented producer of custom-designed motors.
1967: Baldor shifts its headquarters to Fort Smith.
1976: Company goes public.
2000: Baldor enters the generator sector by purchasing Pow'R Gard Generator Corporation.
2007: Baldor acquires the Reliance line of industrial electric motors and the Dodge line of power transmission products from Rockwell Automation, Inc., for $1.83 billion.

proach for competing against the larger manufacturers was to convert the company into a service-oriented firm that could provide customers with quality, custom-designed motors where and when they needed them. Ballman quickly recruited Roland S. "Rollie" Boreham Jr., a Baldor salesman with a degree in engineering who had been complaining for some time that the company was not offering the variety of designs that his customers wanted. The two collaborated on a new business plan for Baldor that emphasized the necessity of catering directly to customer needs. Within a few years Baldor was producing one of the widest ranges of motors in the industry. Companies could go to Baldor for explosion-proof motors, lint-proof motors, motors that would work dirty, motors that could be washed, and motors that could be mounted in just about any direction. By 1965 almost two-thirds of Baldor's products were custom designed for specific applications.

The younger Ballman's reorganization of Baldor was a resounding success. Sales rose from $4 million in 1961 to $21 million by the end of the decade. New sales offices, run by independent district managers working on a commission basis, were opened across the country, and new manufacturing facilities were built in St. Louis, as well as Columbus, Mississippi; and Westville, Oklahoma. To ensure the ready availability of their products to industries that often required quick delivery to keep a factory running, Baldor also opened 23 well-stocked warehouses across the country. This system of warehouses would be maintained and expanded into the 1990s when just-in-time manufacturing made warehousing unfashionable in most industries. Baldor management felt that the advantages of their warehouse system in terms of product availability and customer service outweighed the cost and risks involved.

The energy crisis of the 1970s proved a boon for Baldor as the company's high-quality, energy-efficient motors suddenly became more cost efficient than the less expensive models put out by some large competitors. In 1976 Baldor became the first motor manufacturer to place efficiency ratings on the nameplates of all their products. During a period of recession for most motor manufacturers, the company doubled its market share in the early 1970s, with sales topping $56 million by 1975 and then more than doubling to $146 million by 1980.

ACQUISITIONS IN WAKE OF INCREASED CAPITAL

A crucial component of Ballman and Boreham's plan for growth was the insistence on research and development to bring Baldor's products and manufacturing operations to the cutting edge of technology. To finance new product development and plant modernization, company President Boreham took out Baldor's first long-term loan in 1973 and then brought the company public in 1976. With this new influx of capital, Baldor embarked on a modest program of acquisitions with the aim of vertically integrating the company's manufacturing and reducing reliance on outside suppliers. During the 1970s and early 1980s, Baldor purchased Southwestern Die Casting to supply the company's aluminum casting needs; Carolina Capacitors, a maker of motor starting capacitors; Boehm Manufacturing, a manufacturer of gears; and Nupar Manufacturing, a metal stamping company providing a wide range of Baldor's motor parts. A shift in leadership occurred during this same period, as Boreham was named CEO in 1977 and then chairman as well three years later when Ballman retired.

The early 1980s were a difficult time for the American economy in general and for the motor industry in particular. Foreign imports of industrial machinery began arriving in the United States in quantity in the 1970s as a strong dollar made offshore manufacturing relatively inexpensive. As the motors in these products wore out in the early 1980s, U.S. industry ordered foreign replacements at the expense of U.S. motor manufacturers such as Baldor. Foreign competition and a crippling slump in the agricultural industry, an important market for Baldor, took their toll. In 1982 Baldor experienced the first sales decrease since Fred Ballman's 1960 reorganization of the company and earnings were cut by a third. Fortunately for Baldor, other American motor makers were doing even worse, and in spite of the drop in sales Baldor managed to increase market share to nearly 8 percent.

RESPONSE TO MARKET DOWNTURN

Unlike many large U.S. motor manufacturers who moved production overseas, Baldor responded to foreign competition by investing more heavily in research and development and plant improvements. Management believed that Baldor's competitive advantage was the company's ability to customize its motors for specific applications. To decrease the time required to produce these specialized motors, some of which had production runs of less than 50, the company developed its own form of just-in-time manufacturing, which it called the flex-flow system. Instead of traditional progressive assembly, each motor was put together by a single worker from a tray of parts and written instructions. A wrinkle developed in this system when the company realized that some of its workers were having trouble reading the assembly instructions. Instead of terminating those who could not cope, Baldor instituted a literacy program for all of its workers and rewrote engineering documentation to a high school level. This response was typical of Baldor's attitude toward its workforce. The company, which had not laid off a single worker since the 1960 reorganization, went out of its way to give employees a sense of company loyalty and community. In addition to improving productivity, this approach helped to keep unions at bay. Baldor workers steadfastly opted to remain independent, in spite of numerous attempts at unionization. When asked by *Fortune* why the unions kept trying, Tom Netherton of the International Brotherhood of Electrical Workers quipped, "Well, you have to do something for entertainment in Fort Smith."

Baldor's determination to build the company's position as a maker of top-of-the-line specialty motors required the prompt adoption of new technologies. In the mid-1980s the company's program of acquisitions, which had begun to integrate manufacturing, began to be used as a means of extending Baldor's technological expertise. Between 1983 and 1994 Baldor acquired seven manufacturers of motors and drives whose technologies would complement those being developed at Baldor. Drives, which consist of a motor plus the controls that regulate it, were a new and important addition to Baldor's line of products in the early 1990s. Drives provide greater flexibility than fixed-speed motors by allowing the operator to regulate both the speed and torque of the motor's operation. In 1996 Baldor was predicting that drives would be the fastest-growing component of their motor business.

Baldor's investment in its plants, workforce, and new technology paid off in the late 1980s and early 1990s. Sales grew from $182 million in 1986 to $294 million in 1990, and then soared to $502.8 million by 1996. The net earnings of $35.1 million for 1996 represented an increase of 9 percent over the previous year. Even more significant, the company's share of the U.S. motor market nearly doubled to 13 percent by 1996.

In the late 1990s Baldor continued to fill out its line of products with additional strategic acquisitions. In 1997, for example, the company augmented its presence in the market for servo motors for the motion-control industry by purchasing Optimised Control Ltd. of Bristol, England. The following year Baldor purchased Santa Clarita, California-based Northern Magnetics, Inc., in what was its first acquisition completed with stock rather than cash. In this buyout, Baldor ventured outside its core business in rotary motors by gaining a specialist in linear motors. Such motors, which feature a flat coil that passes over permanent magnets, offer high speeds and high precision and are particularly suited to such applications as packaging equipment, material-handling systems, machine tools, and semiconductor manufacturing equipment.

In the fourth quarter of 1998, Baldor began feeling the effects of a slowdown in demand for motors in such industries as oil, agriculture, and semiconductor equipment. Sales and earnings fell that quarter, ending a streak of 27 straight quarters of increasing sales and earnings. The slowdown continued in 1999, leading to declines in sales and earnings for the year of 2 percent. Thus ended a string of seven consecutive years of record sales and earnings. Also in 1999, John A. McFarland was promoted from president to president and CEO; Boreham remained chairman. A Baldor veteran of nearly 30 years, McFarland over his career had helped build the firm's international business, which achieved sales of more than $80 million by 1999, and later was placed in charge of Baldor's entire sales organization.

EXPANDING INTO GENERATORS, SURVIVING ANOTHER DOWNTURN

Baldor bounced back in 2000 as revenues increased 6 percent to $621 million, topping the $600 million mark for the first time, and earnings surged by a like percent to a record $46.2 million. In November the company completed what at the time was its largest acquisition to that time, the $40 million purchase of Pow'R Gard Generator Corporation of Oshkosh, Wisconsin. Via this deal, Baldor ventured into a new, though related, business: the manufacture of generators and generator sets.

Baldor quickly began expanding the Pow'R Gard product line so that by the end of 2001 it included generators ranging from 1.3 to 150 kilowatts in four areas: military/government products, portable generators, automatic emergency generators, and industrial standby generators. Eventually, in early 2003, Baldor expanded into larger generators by purchasing Mukwonago, Wisconsin-based Energy Dynamics, Inc., for $5.8 million. Energy Dynamics specialized in industrial generators ranging in size from 30 kilowatts to 2,000 kilowatts.

In the meantime, Baldor from 2001 to 2003 was pummeled by the severe industrial downturn, during which time many companies cut their capital spending, including their purchases of motors, drives, and generators. Sales dropped by more than 10 percent in 2001 and plateaued at around $550 million for three straight years. Profits plunged more than 50 percent in 2001 and then rebounded only slightly over the next two years. Baldor reacted to this latest period of economic malaise as it had in the past: rather than instituting layoffs or closing plants, the firm maintained its previous level of investment in research and development, continued to churn out new products, and explored additional international markets, all of which left it in solid shape to bounce back once the recovery began. In addition, Baldor made up for some of the sales lost during the downturn by initiating efforts to gain new customers.

The company entered a new period of strong growth in 2004 when sales were up more than 25 percent to $648.2 million and earnings surged 41.4 percent to $35.1 million. At the end of the year, Boreham retired after more than four decades at Baldor. McFarland added the chairmanship to his CEO duties. Double-digit growth in both 2005 and 2006 pushed sales up to a record $811.3 million, while net earnings for 2006 totaled $48.1 million, another high-water mark. In addition to benefiting from the general economic recovery, Baldor was garnering rapid growth in its generator business, which pulled in $50 million in sales for the first time in 2005. During this time of escalating energy costs, customers seeking to reduce their electricity bills made Baldor's line of Super-E high-efficiency motors another major growth area. Sales of Super-E motors increased 25 percent in 2005 and 39 percent a year later.

2007 ACQUISITION OF RELIANCE AND DODGE LINES

When Rockwell Automation, Inc., placed the bulk of its power-systems business up for sale in 2006, Baldor Electric jumped at the chance for a transformative acquisition. In what was by far the largest purchase in the company's history, Baldor spent $1.83 billion in cash and stock for the Reliance line of industrial electric motors and the Dodge line of power transmission products. The deal was completed in January 2007. The addition of the Reliance brand, which traced its history back to 1904, was highly complementary to the Baldor motor line: the strength of Reliance was in motors above 50 horsepower, whereas Baldor was strongest in motors below 50 horsepower. Gaining the Dodge brand, founded in 1878, took Baldor into the new but related field of power transmission products, including mounted bearings, speed reducers, and such components as couplings and pulleys.

In addition to vastly expanding the company's product lines, this acquisition was viewed by Baldor as strategic for several other reasons. It provided the firm with a manufacturing base in China to enhance access to Asian markets, not to import goods back to the United States because Baldor planned to maintain its traditional strategy of serving its home market with U.S.-made products. Baldor also viewed the deal as strengthening its management team and providing opportunities for synergistic cost savings. The company expected to garner annual cost savings of $30 million within three years of the acquisition's completion. Although Baldor had to borrow $1.6 billion to complete the blockbuster deal, by the spring of 2008 the firm announced that it expected to reduce this debt load by $300 million by year's end.

In the meantime, the addition of Reliance and Dodge more than doubled Baldor's revenues in 2007 to $1.82 billion, while net income leaped 95 percent to $94.1 million. The revenue total was enough to push the firm onto the *Fortune* 1000 list for the first time. Looking forward, Baldor's broader array of products were expected to better insulate it against economic downturns, although rising costs of such raw materials as steel and copper were a potential trouble spot. Baldor also anticipated benefiting from the passage of the Energy Independence and Security Act of 2007, which included new efficiency benchmarks for industrial electric motors slated to take effect in 2010. The company anticipated increased sales of its Super-E high-efficiency motors, which already met the proposed standards and in 2007 accounted for 25 percent of overall sales.

Hilary Gopnik
Updated, David E. Salamie

PRINCIPAL SUBSIDIARIES

Baldor of Arkansas, Inc.; Baldor of Nevada, Inc.; BEC Business Trust; Baldor of Texas, L.P.; Baldor

International, Inc. (U.S. Virgin Islands); Southwestern Die Casting Company, Inc.; Baldor UK Holdings, Inc.; Baldor UK Ltd.; Baldor Holdings, Inc.; Baldor de Mexico, S.A.B. de C.V.; Baldor ASR AG (Switzerland); Baldor ASR GmbH fur Antriebstechnik (Germany); Baldor ASR U.K. Limited; Baldor Italia S.r.l. (Italy); Baldor Australia Pty Ltd; Baldor Electric (Asia) PTE, Ltd. (Singapore); Northern Magnetics, Inc.; Baldor Japan Corporation; Baldor Investments, LLC; Pow'R Gard Generator Corp.; Energy Dynamics, Inc.; Baldor Power Finance, Inc.; Baldor Electric India Pvt Ltd.; Baldor Panama, S.A.; Reliance Electric Company; Reliance Electric Company Europe GmbH (Germany); Reliance Electric Company Canada ULC; Dodge de Mexico S.A.B. de C.V.; Baldor Electric (Shanghai) Company LTD (China); REC Holding Inc.; Reliance Electric Technologies LLC; Baldor Electric Company de Chile Ltda; Baldor Canada Holdings, Inc.

PRINCIPAL COMPETITORS

General Electric Company; Emerson Electric Co.; Regal-Beloit Corporation; Siemens AG; WEG S.A.; A.O. Smith Corporation; TECO-Westinghouse Motor Company; Toshiba Corporation; Kohler Co.; Caterpillar Inc.; Cummins, Inc.; Honda Motor Co., Ltd.; ABB Ltd.; Danaher Corporation; Mitsubishi Heavy Industries, Ltd.; Rockwell Automation, Inc.; Altra Holdings, Inc.; Martin Sprocket & Gear, Inc.; Rexnord LLC; SEW-EURODRIVE GmbH; Aktiebolaget SKF; TB Wood's Corporation.

FURTHER READING

Bagamery, Anne, "Just a Matter of Waiting," *Forbes,* September 14, 1981, pp. 212–13.

"Baldor Jumps into Linear Motor Fray," *Design News,* June 22, 1998, p. 40.

Boreham, Roland S., Jr., *The Road Less Traveled: The History of Baldor, 1976–2000,* Fort Smith, Ark.: Baldor Electric Company, 2004, 174 p.

Brown, Alan S., "Baldor to Acquire Rockwell's Power Systems," *Mechanical Engineering,* December 2006, p. 8.

Farnham, Alan, "Baldor's Success: Made in the U.S.A.," *Fortune,* July 17, 1989, pp. 101–05.

Glorioso, Joseph A., "Baldor: Sneaking Up on the Giants," *Industry Week,* February 6, 1984, pp. 43–44.

Jaffe, Thomas, "Motormen," *Forbes,* April 29, 1991, p. 349.

Kelly, Caitlin, "Efficiency Experts," *Supply Chain Management Review,* November/December 2001, pp. S54–S55.

Mraz, Stephen J., "Teaching the Write Stuff," *Design News,* September 10, 1992, pp. 12, 14.

———, "Teaching Workers the Three Rs Is Good for the Bottom Line," *Design News,* January 24, 1991, pp. 25–27.

Muck, Tara, "Synergy Pays Off for Baldor," *Morning News of Northwest Arkansas* (Springdale), April 26, 2008.

Schock, George A., *Early History of Baldor Electric Company, 1920–1976,* Fort Smith, Ark.: Baldor Electric Company, 1992, 106 p.

Sullivan, R. Lee, "Powerhouse," *Forbes,* March 13, 1995, p. 134.

Waldon, George, "Baldor Electric Co. Rides Out Downturn," *Northwest Arkansas Business Journal,* October 15, 2001, pp. 1, 12–13.

Walter, Matthew, "Blackouts, Storms Generate Baldor Sales," *Arkansas Democrat-Gazette,* October 17, 2004, p. 76.

———, "Chairman of Baldor Set to Retire," *Arkansas Democrat-Gazette,* April 27, 2004, p. 21.

———, "While Many Manufacturers Head Overseas to Cut Costs, Baldor Electric Isn't Going Anywhere, Maintaining That Its Attention to Quality Will Pay Off," *Arkansas Democrat-Gazette,* May 23, 2004, p. 86.

Whalen, Laurie, "Baldor Gives Rosy Forecast for '08," *Arkansas Democrat-Gazette,* February 2, 2008, p. 27.

———, "Baldor's Buy at Rockwell to Double Firm," *Arkansas Democrat-Gazette,* November 8, 2006, p. 33.

———, "Powered by Vision: Baldor Electric, Now the Top U.S. Producer of Electric Industrial Motors, Is Surging Ahead Among U.S. Manufacturers," *Arkansas Democrat-Gazette,* February 4, 2007, p. 82.

BlueLinx Holdings Inc.

4300 Wildwood Parkway
Atlanta, Georgia 30339
U.S.A.
Telephone: (770) 953-7000
Toll Free: (888) 502-2583
Fax: (770) 221-8902
Web site: http://www.bluelinxco.com

Public Company
Incorporated: 2004
Employees: 2,800
Sales: $3.83 billion (2007)
Stock Exchanges: New York
Ticker Symbol: BXC
NAICS: 423310 Lumber, Plywood, Millwork, and Wood Panel Merchant Wholesalers; 423330 Roofing, Siding, and Insulation Material Merchant Wholesalers; 444190 Other Building Material Dealers

■ ■ ■

BlueLinx Holdings Inc., through its principal operating subsidiary, BlueLinx Corporation, ranks as the largest building products wholesaler in the United States. Formerly the distribution arm of Georgia-Pacific Corporation, the company owns a network of more than 80 warehouses located in every major metropolitan market in the country. BlueLinx also operates a distribution facility in British Columbia, Canada. The company's fleet of 800 trucks and 1,200 trailers delivers more than 10,000 products to building materials dealers, industrial users of building products, manufactured housing builders, and home improvement centers. BlueLinx derives 54 percent of its sales from supplying structural products such as plywood, oriented strand board, rebar, and lumber. The company generates the balance of its sales from distributing specialty products such as roofing, insulation, specialty panels, composite decking, and vinyl products.

ORIGINS

The BlueLinx name first appeared in 2004, but the business it represented enjoyed a far richer legacy. The assets that gained independence in 2004 belonged to Georgia-Pacific Corporation, the second largest forest products company in the world. Georgia-Pacific's impressive stature explained BlueLinx's towering size at its inception, a company that on its first day of business boasted $4.3 billion in revenue, operated one of the United States' largest truck fleets, and employed nearly 3,500 workers in every major metropolitan market in the country. BlueLinx, at its birth, ranked as the largest building products wholesaler in the nation, a stalwart industry position it inherited from Georgia-Pacific.

Building products distribution was at the heart of Georgia-Pacific when it was formed in 1927 as Georgia Hardwood Lumber Company. Based in Augusta, Georgia, the hardwood lumber wholesaler was founded by Owen R. Cheatham, who would lead the company until his death in 1970. Cheatham's lengthy leadership tenure witnessed profound changes and extensive growth, beginning with the diversification into building products manufacturing during Georgia Hardwood's

COMPANY PERSPECTIVES

At BlueLinx, delivering success is what our business is all about. As the leading building products distribution company in the industry, we provide the building blocks for residential and commercial construction, remodeling and repair, manufacturing, manufactured and modular housing, and homeowner projects. Look to BlueLinx for quality products, reliable distribution, knowledgeable people and innovative ideas. BlueLinx has the organization and systems to help our customers accomplish their goals, and we invite you to discover how much we can deliver.

first decade of business. Cheatham's aggressive acquisition of timberland in the 1950s led to the relocation of the company to Portland, Oregon, in 1954, the same year the distribution operations were organized formally as a division. The distribution division comprised 13 warehouses at its outset, facilities that primarily were used to distribute Georgia-Pacific's plywood products, which were manufactured at several mills in Washington and Oregon.

During the half century spanning its formation and its separation from the forest products giant, the distribution division grew alongside Georgia-Pacific's other holdings. The company's business interests became increasingly diverse following World War II, as Georgia-Pacific branched out into chemicals, consumer products such as toilet tissue, PVC products, and pulp and paper. The range of business interests led to shifting priorities for the company. A turning point occurred in 1987, when Georgia-Pacific's tissue and towel business, combined with its production of linerboard, kraft, and fine paper, generated higher profits than its wood products business. Financially, paper had become more important than wood to Georgia-Pacific, which eventually led the company to divest some of its longest-held assets, including its building products distribution business.

GEORGIA-PACIFIC LOOKS TO SELL ITS DISTRIBUTION BUSINESS

Georgia-Pacific's sweeping restructuring efforts were orchestrated by A. D. "Pete" Correll. He joined the company in 1988 as senior vice-president of pulp and printing paper, bringing with him years of experience he gained at Mead Corp., Weyerhaeuser Co., and Westvaco. In 1993, Correll became only the fifth chief executive officer in the history of Georgia-Pacific, earning a promotion that also awarded him the duties of president and chairman. Before the end of the decade, he split off the company's timber operations into a separate operating group and announced plans to divest Georgia-Pacific's commodity operations, a decision that ultimately would lead to the formation of BlueLinx as an independent company.

Correll first tried to sell Georgia-Pacific's entire building products business, both manufacturing and distribution, in 2002. He wanted to focus the company's efforts on consumer products, believing greater growth and financial stability could be enjoyed by making paper towels and toilet tissue marketed under the brand names Brawny, Quilted Northern, Angel Soft, and Dixie brand disposable tableware. The attempt to sell the building products businesses was aborted, however, scuttled because of anemic market conditions and the sale of the company's Unisource paper distribution subsidiary. In 2004, Correll made another attempt, looking to sell the distribution business to sharpen the company's strategic focus and to pay down its debt, which totaled more than $10 billion by the beginning of the year.

Based on 2003 results, the distribution business put on the auction block by Correll represented 21 percent of Georgia-Pacific's business. The division generated $4.3 billion in sales during the year, deriving the total from 63 warehouses in the United States and one location in Canada. With a fleet of more than 900 trucks and trailers, the division distributed more than 10,000 products to more than 11,000 customers, serving building materials dealers, industrial users of building products, manufactured housing builders, and home improvement centers. The inventory carried by the division included 14 product categories that composed two main lines of products: structural products and specialty products. The division's structural products, which accounted for slightly more sales than specialty products, included plywood, oriented strand board, lumber, and other products used in walls and flooring in residential construction projects. Specialty products included roofing, insulation, molding, engineered wood products, vinyl products, and metal products, which generated 43 percent of the division's sales.

CERBERUS CAPITAL MAKING A BID IN 2004

Correll found an interested buyer for his wholesale wood products business in March 2004. Cerberus Capital Management, L.P., a private, New York-based

KEY DATES

1954: Georgia-Pacific's distribution business is organized into a separate division.
2004: Georgia-Pacific sells its distribution business to Cerberus Capital Management, L.P. for $810 million; BlueLinx Holdings Inc. is formed to operate the distribution business.
2006: BlueLinx acquires Austin Hardwoods.
2007: BlueLinx reports a $27.9 million loss for the year.

hedge fund, agreed to pay $810 million for the division. Cerberus bought the division in May 2004 through a company named ABP Distribution Holdings Inc., which the investment firm subsequently merged into BlueLinx Holdings, Inc. The new name for the nation's largest wood products distribution company was derived from the blue color of its fleet of trucks and trailers and its "Linux" supply chain.

The transfer of ownership marked the beginning of a new era for the wholesale assets, but not all ties to the division's past were cut. As part of the purchase agreement, Georgia-Pacific agreed to continue selling structural panels, lumber, and other building products to BlueLinx under the terms of a five-year contract. Further, Cerberus, which focused on acquiring companies that continued to operate under existing management and staff, turned to Georgia-Pacific executives to form BlueLinx's senior management.

BLUELINX'S MANAGEMENT

George R. Judd was selected as BlueLinx's president and chief operating officer. A Georgia-Pacific veteran, Judd gave up his duties as vice-president of sales and eastern operations of the distribution division to help guide the assets under the BlueLinx banner. Before heading the division's eastern operations, Judd served as vice-president of the north and midwest regions for two years and as vice-president of the southeast division for one year. Judd was joined by BlueLinx's chief executive officer, Stephen E. Macadam, who had served as Georgia-Pacific's executive vice-president of pulp and paperboard from 2000 to 2001 and as senior vice-president of containerboard and packaging between 1998 and 2000. Immediately before joining BlueLinx, Macadam served as president and chief executive officer of Consolidated Container Company LLC.

The new era began with a sense that much would remain the same. "We worked tirelessly to make sure the transition was seamless," Judd explained in a July 2004 interview with *Prosales*. "The business is the same. All the people are there. All the management is the same. All the product offerings and services are the same. Our intent is to manage it the same way we managed GP Building Products." Macadam offered his perspective on the road ahead in an interview published in the July 2005 issue of *US Business Review*. "Our mission," he declared, "is to be the masters of the supply chain. Our role is to provide the most cost-effective way to manage all the logistics from the manufacturing facility to the job site. That's our job and opportunity."

There were, of course, differences between operating as a division of a larger company and operating as a stand-alone entity. BlueLinx did not wait long before demonstrating its independence, filing with the U.S. Securities and Exchange Commission (SEC) for a $150 million initial public offering (IPO) four months after it was formed. The company completed its IPO in December 2004, debuting on the New York Stock Exchange under the ticker symbol "BXC."

A FOCUS ON LOGISTICS

Other differences emerged soon after the company's public debut, as Macadam and Judd, unfettered by the demands of a larger organization surrounding them, concentrated solely on making BlueLinx more efficient. As Macadam had noted in his interview with *US Business Review,* BlueLinx's success hinged on the intricacies of logistics, on its ability to coordinate scores of warehouses and thousands of vehicles that made more than 1,500 deliveries each day. Distribution was a high-volume, low-profit-margin business that placed a premium on nimbleness and quick decision making, with profits and customer satisfaction vulnerable to the slightest stumble. As the stewards of a stand-alone company, Macadam and Judd were given free rein to organize BlueLinx's corporate structure to achieve optimal performance. Accordingly, they opted for a flat corporate structure that gave the company's seven vice-presidents, each of whom managed all of the business in their regions, a substantial amount of authority. "From the salesperson to the president, there are three layers," Judd said in a July 2005 interview with *US Business Review,* referring to BlueLinx's streamlined corporate structure.

The efforts to improve cost-management, decision-making processes, and communication within the organization were ongoing. At the beginning of 2006, the company created two new, senior-level positions to help it manage its business in a better way. Duane

Goodwin, a veteran of The Home Depot Inc., joined the company as senior vice-president of BlueLinx's supply chain, a position that required him to report directly to Judd. Macadam gained an aide-de-camp as well with the arrival of Steve Skinner, who was appointed senior vice-president of strategy and business development. "Our growth objectives require discipline, continuous process improvement, and comprehensive strategic planning and management," Macadam explained in a January 5, 2006, interview with *PrimeZone Media Network*. "Duane and Steve bring added strength to our management team in the crucial areas of supply chain and strategy management."

ACQUISITION IN 2006

Before the end of 2006, BlueLinx added to its stature by completing an acquisition. In August, the company purchased a privately owned hardwood lumber distributor named Austin Hardwoods. Founded in 1972 and based in Austin, Texas, the acquired company distributed hardwood boards, veneers, and plywood to cabinet makers, millwork companies, and furniture makers. Austin Hardwoods' products included ash, alder, cherry, maple, oak, and walnut. The company, with $22 million in annual sales, operated out of four facilities in Texas.

MARKET CONDITIONS STIFLING FINANCIAL GROWTH

Financially, BlueLinx did not enjoy an encouraging start to its new era as an independent company. Operating within a notoriously cyclical industry, the company felt the sting of anemic market conditions, recording declining financial totals during its first years in business. From $5.6 billion in sales in 2005, the company's business volume shrank to $3.8 billion by the end of 2007. More distressing, the company's net income recorded a sharp decline. BlueLinx posted $44.6 million in net income in 2005, $15.8 million in 2006, and ended 2007 with a numbing $27.9 million loss. Substantial declines in new home construction throughout the country were to blame, causing decreased demand for BlueLinx's structural and specialty products. Macadam and Judd, executives well versed in the damage that could be done by a depressed housing market, faced the first great challenge of their leadership tenure as they plotted a course for the future. Financial success depended on BlueLinx's ability to squeeze what it could from an inhospitable market and to be prepared for more robust conditions in the years ahead.

Jeffrey L. Covell

PRINCIPAL SUBSIDIARIES

BlueLinx Corporation; BlueLinx Services Inc.; BlueLinx Florida LP; BlueLinx Florida Holding No. 1 Inc.; BlueLinx Florida Holding No. 2 Inc.; BlueLinx Receivables Management, Inc.; BlueLinx Receivables Securitization LLC; BlueLinx Building Products Canada Ltd.; BLX Real Estate LLC; BlueLinx Landlord Agent LLC.

PRINCIPAL COMPETITORS

Weyerhaeuser Company; Boise Cascade Holdings, L.L.C.; American Builders & Contractors Supply Co., Inc.

FURTHER READING

Aronovich, Hanna, "The Chain Masters: BlueLinx Corp. Says It Is the Industry Leader, but the Company Continues to Push for Greater Levels of Success and Excellence in Building Products Distribution," *US Business Review*, July 2005, p. 128.

"BlueLinx Acquires Georgia-Pacific Distribution Business," *Wood & Wood Products*, May 2004, p. 17.

"BlueLinx Acquires Hardwood Lumber Distributor Austin Hardwoods," *PrimeZone Media Network*, August 9, 2006.

"BlueLinx Buys Georgia-Pacific Distribution Division," *Prosales*, July 2004, p. 24.

"BlueLinx Establishes Two Newly Created Positions to Support Growth Initiatives," *PrimeZone Media Network*, January 5, 2006.

"BlueLinx Gears Up for IPO," *Home Channel News NewsFax*, September 7, 2004, p. 1.

"Georgia-Pacific Selling Building Materials Distribution," *Journal of Commerce Online*, March 15, 2004.

"G-P to Sell Distribution Business," *Home Channel News NewsFax*, March 15, 2004, p. 1.

Moreira, Peter, "BlueLinx Files for $150M IPO," *Daily Deal*, September 6, 2004.

Thielemann, Alan, "Evolution to Solution: The Building Products Revolution Has Begun," *Professional Builder (1993)*, February 2004, p. 8.

Walker, Tom, "Georgia-Pacific to Sell One of Oldest Operations," *Atlanta Journal-Constitution*, March 13, 2004.

Bojangles Restaurants Inc.

9432 Southern Pine Boulevard
Charlotte, North Carolina 28273-5553
U.S.A.
Telephone: (704) 527-2675
Toll Free: (888) 300-4265
Fax: (704) 523-6803
Web site: http://www.bojangles.com

Private Company
Incorporated: 1977
Employees: 4,500
Sales: $152 million (2008 est.)
NAICS: 722110 Full-Service Restaurants

■ ■ ■

Bojangles Restaurants Inc. is a regional chain of quick-service restaurants known for its "Famous Chicken 'n Biscuits," spicy fried chicken and Southern-style biscuits made from scratch with fresh ingredients. Bojangles offers chicken in eight-, 12-, and 20-piece boxes with half as many biscuits in each box. Family meals include Southern-style side items, such as dirty rice, Cajun pinto beans, seasoned french fries, mashed potatoes, and coleslaw. Bojangles' breakfast biscuits are popular among the company's loyal customers, and Bojangles distinguishes itself from other fast-food restaurants by offering them all day. Breakfast sandwiches include a variety of filling combinations, with egg, sausage, bacon, and cheese, and biscuit sandwiches are available with country ham, steak, grilled pork chop, Cajun chicken filet, or grilled chicken filet. For dessert, customers choose from sweet potato pie or sweet biscuits in "Boberry" or cinnamon. Bojangles serves coffee made with freshly ground beans and the company's signature Sweet Tea, iced tea that is freshly steeped rather than brewed, is available by the glass or in half-gallon or one-gallon containers. Located primarily in the southeastern United States, Bojangles owns 120 restaurants and franchises more than 300 units in 12 states. International franchises are located in Mexico, Honduras, and China.

SPICING UP THE CHICKEN MARKET

In 1977, Jack Fulk and Richard Thomas noticed something missing from the food at the local chicken joints in Charlotte, North Carolina, namely spice. The two men decided to fill that gap by developing their own Southern-style chicken and a fast-food restaurant where they could sell it. Both veterans of the quick-service restaurant industry, Fulk brought experience as a Hardee's franchisee, and Thomas managed and owned Kentucky Fried Chicken and Wendy's restaurants. Fulk went to work in the kitchen, trying out different recipes for the restaurant's signature item. After much trial and error and test marketing with black pepper, jalapeno, and other flavorings, Fulk decided on red peppers as the key ingredient for the spicy chicken recipe.

The partners wanted to create a distinctive identity that would reflect the flavor of the South in a festive environment. An important part of achieving this goal involved finding a catchy name. Thomas chose the name Bojangles, after the popular song *Mr. Bojangles*

COMPANY PERSPECTIVES

The Bojangles' Recipe: No biscuit should ever be older than 20 minutes. Frozen chicken will never be as good as fresh chicken, no matter how much you bread it. Life can be bland. Our food isn't. A piece of chicken should look like a piece of chicken. Fresh ground coffee is always better. Come to think of it, fresh anything is always better. The best chicken 'n biscuits money can buy. Recipes that haven't changed in over 25 years. If it ain't broke, don't fix it. Making sweet tea is an art form. Fixin's as famous as our chicken 'n biscuits. Breakfast should never end.

performed by the Nitty Gritty Dirt Band (originally written and performed by Jerry Jeff Walker). Fulk and Thomas chose orange and yellow as the colors that would define Bojangles' atmosphere of fun and spice. Bojangles started with a simple menu that offered only chicken, buttermilk biscuits, dirty rice, and Cajun pinto beans.

The first few months of operation challenged Fulk and Thomas. Then Fulk thought of something that would lead Bojangles to success: the breakfast biscuit that would be available hot and fresh all day, every day. These sandwiches of egg, cheese, bacon, sausage, or ham were like nothing else consumers had encountered before. Using the slogan that "breakfast should never end," Bojangles attracted business in which breakfast biscuits consistently accounted for over 30 percent of overall sales.

Having solidified their success at the first Bojangles restaurant, Fulk and Thomas applied their background in franchising to expand Bojangles into a chain. The first Bojangles franchise opened in 1978, and other units quickly followed. Bojangles found franchisees already known for their management capabilities, among managers of the fast-food franchises previously operated by Fulk and Thomas. Within a few years, Bojangles owned or franchised 52 restaurants.

LEADERSHIP CHANGES, RAPID EXPANSION AND DECLINE

In 1981, Fulk and Thomas sold their small chain to Horn & Hardart, a New York company that operated a variety of businesses, including mail-order catalog company Hanover House. Horn & Hardart's Barry Florescue, who oversaw the Bojangles chain as chief executive officer, pursued a strategy of rapid growth. Franchises and company-owned stores opened along the mid-Atlantic seaboard, in Maryland, Virginia, and Pennsylvania, and west into Missouri, Tennessee, Ohio, and Texas, as well as in its home territory in the Southeast, in North and South Carolina and Georgia. Difficulty in finding prime real estate for profitable locations prompted Bojangles to purchase the Biskit chain, in northern Florida. Biskit operated 45 units, located primarily in the Jacksonville, Tampa, and Orlando markets. In 1985, the Bojangles chain operated or franchised 350 restaurants. With about 3,000 square feet of space and 80 seats each, the restaurants' sales averaged approximately $1 million. Rapid expansion of the Bojangles chain did not translate into success at each outlet, however, and a series of management changes followed.

In 1985 the company hired E. Christian Schoenleb to replace Florescue as chief executive officer. A former executive of Swenson's and Burger King, Schoenleb brought extensive experience in fast-food marketing to Bojangles. Under Schoenleb, the company sought to attract families and women with new products and a new image. Bojangles designed a new prototype building with an upscale interior that included a greenhouse look, then becoming popular in fast-food chains. Cream stucco and vibrant orange canopies extended the upmarket look to the exterior of the building. Furthermore, the prototype reduced the cost of starting a franchise. The smaller units, at about 2,700 square feet, would seat 50 to 65 customers and cost about $525,000 for land, building, and equipment.

Schoenleb began test marketing 17 new products at Bojangles' prototype in Charlotte when it opened in 1986. Of those items, six became a part of the permanent menu. For breakfast, Bojangles added the Egg Bo Biscuit, with egg, Canadian bacon, and cheese, and the company planned to offer breakfast platters by the end of the year. Other items included a chicken filet on a biscuit with Cajun marinade, country fried steak sandwich and dinner, and a mild-flavored, fried chicken. To accommodate the expanded menu, Bojangles introduced the use of automated cooking equipment to simplify cooking with fresh ingredients.

Continuing problems at the end of 1986 led Horn & Hardart to bring in one of its own fast-food executives, Carlos Garcia, to lead Bojangles. Garcia streamlined management and simplified operating systems at Bojangles. Nevertheless, rapid growth had led to poor choices in store locations; consequently, the company closed 22 stores in 1986. By the end of 1988, the company owned or franchised less than 200 units and lost $9 million.

KEY DATES

1978: The first Bojangles franchise opens for business.
1981: Bojangles is acquired by Horn & Hardart and rapid expansion begins.
1985: Growth reaches 350 units before beginning to decline.
1990: Former KFC executive Richard Campbell and private investors purchase Bojangles for $25 million.
1998: Glen Gulledge and a silent partner acquire Bojangles, with 247 units, for $85 million.
2004: International development begins with franchise deal for ten stores in China.
2008: Bojangles opens 400th restaurant in February.

Former Kentucky Fried Chicken (KFC) executive John Bifone took the helm at Bojangles in early 1989. His first step involved improving franchisee relations. Horn & Hardart alienated its franchisees when rapid expansion distracted them from existing business. Bifone initiated a three-year, 30 percent growth plan that included significant increases in advertising, an attractive solution for the franchisees. Also, Bifone visited all of the restaurants, gaining insights into how to improve operations as he stabilized franchisee relations. Under Bifone, Bojangles became profitable again, generating $1 million net income on sales of $20 million in 1989. Thus, Bifone prepared Bojangles to be put up for sale by Horn & Hardart.

CONSOLIDATION AND EXPANSION

In 1990 Horn & Hardart sold Bojangles to former KFC executive Richard Campbell and his investment partners, Los Angeles-based Sienna Holdings and Inter-west Partners. The $25 million deal gave Campbell 23 company-owned stores in Charlotte and 150 franchises in seven states. Campbell reduced overhead by 30 percent, beginning with the relocation of company headquarters from a 14,000-square-foot site in West-chase to a 6,500-square-foot office in the Pine Brook Business center. He improved corporate efficiency in operations and franchising by implementing new computer systems at the restaurant counter. A plan of slow growth allowed the company to improve operations and sales in existing markets, and to develop new store locations in contiguous markets to maximize the value of television and radio advertising. Campbell planned to purchase as many franchises as possible in order to gain revenue which, in turn, would allow Bojangles to increase its advertising budget. Also, Campbell reopened some locations in Charlotte, renovated the company-owned stores, and experimented with double drive-through windows in Charlotte.

In 1991, Campbell began his program of acquiring franchised units. In March 1991, Bojangles purchased its mid-Atlantic franchise, then in bankruptcy, with eight units in north Charlotte. The following November Bojangles purchased its second largest franchisee, Simplistic Enterprises, Inc., thus acquiring 15 restaurants in the Winston-Salem area. In 1992 the company bought back 13 restaurants in Fayetteville, Wilmington, and Jacksonville, North Carolina, from a group of investors. Bojangles obtained another 27 restaurants from its largest franchisee, Carabo, Inc., in the Greenville, Columbia, and Charleston, South Carolina, areas. With new store openings, Bojangles owned 88 of the 172 outlets in operation by the end of 1992. Store profits funded most of the expansion that followed. After Campbell's retirement in 1994, former Whataburger CEO Jim Peterson took the helm and expanded the chain to 247 units by 1998.

FOURTH SET OF OWNERS

Ownership of Bojangles changed again in 1998, as a pair of local investors purchased the company for $85 million. Investor Glen Gulledge became the company's chief executive officer and continued Campbell's strategy of company ownership of Bojangles outlets. Bojangles acquired 18 units from its third largest franchisee, Bo-Est, Inc., with stores in Asheville, North Carolina, and Greenville and Spartanburg, South Carolina. Like his predecessors, Gulledge revamped the store design with more vibrant colors. However, Gulledge sought to improve same store sales, stagnant under Campbell, by redesigning the kitchen layout for faster food preparation. The changes allowed Bojangles to update its menu without hindering employee workflow. New products included a barbeque pork sandwich and a new kids' meal, Tender Nuggets. Gulledge invested heavily in advertising that focused on the quality of the food. He increased print advertising in order to take advantage of close-up photography of Bojangles chicken and biscuit meals.

Under Jim Drury, former protégé of Wendy's founder Dave Thomas, Bojangles' strategy shifted to franchising. Drury sold company-owned stores to franchisees, and he sought new franchise opportunities in Wisconsin, Arkansas, Alabama, Georgia, and abroad. Drury found unusual locations for Bojangles franchises.

In 1999 Bojangles partnered with S-mart stores in Georgia to position restaurants in eight convenience stores.

Bojangles launched its most aggressive advertising campaign in 2003. By using unusual, wordless television commercials, the advertisements placed the focus on the food. One commercial showed an elaborate tailgate party, in which the protagonist pretends that he cooked Bojangles chicken on his grill. In another commercial, a woman consumes her breakfast biscuit, then pours the crumbs from the bag into her mouth. The advertisements concluded with the tagline "GottawannaneedagettahavaBojangles." The tagline appeared on billboards and in radio and print advertisements.

In 2004, Bojangles sought to compete with the well established Popeye's Chicken and Biscuits chain in the Atlanta market. BoJon LLC opened the first of six units in May 2004 and Contentment Foods planned to add two locations to its existing two in the southern metropolitan Atlanta area. Also, the company entered into two franchise development deals for 12 locations in Tennessee. With eight existing stores and further plans for another 20 to 30 outlets over five years, Bojangles signed its first international franchise agreement in 2004. That year the company signed a contract with Kaobita Restaurant Services Co. Ltd., to open ten stores in China over the next five years. The first outlet opened in Tianjin, the third largest city in China. Another international agreement followed in 2006, when Bojangles signed a deal with Henry Garganus to open ten stores in Central America. The first unit opened in Puebla, Mexico, and two stores opened in Honduras.

In the United States Bojangles signed franchising agreements for new outlets in Virginia. The 2005 opening of Bojangles in Elizabeth City broke all company records the first week in operation. Two more units opened over the next two years and another eight were in the planning stages. The company expanded farther afield with new store openings in Newark, New Jersey, and Scranton, Pennsylvania. Bojangles opened in the Charlotte/Douglas International Airport in a move intended to introduce the brand to the thousands of consumers who passed through the airport.

A TASTY FUTURE FOR BOJANGLES

Bojangles changed ownership again in 2007. Jerry Richardson, owner of the Carolina Panthers, purchased a 60 percent controlling interest in Bojangles Holdings Inc., with Falfurrias Capital Partners retaining the balance. Richardson planned to continue expanding Bojangles through franchising and company ownership. Bojangles planned 40 store openings for 2008. The 400th Bojangles store opened in February 2008 in Alabama, the second unit in that state. Over the next five years Bojangles planned to open 53 new outlets in Georgia, 27 in Tennessee, and 29 in northern Florida. Exploration for further expansion included the states of Texas, Oklahoma, and Louisiana.

Mary Tradii

PRINCIPAL COMPETITORS

AFC Enterprises, Inc. (Popeye's Chicken and Biscuits); Burger King Holdings, Inc.; Cajun Operating Company (Church's Chicken); McDonald's Corporation; Triarc Companies, Inc. (Arby's); YUM! Brands, Inc. (Kentucky Fried Chicken).

FURTHER READING

"Bojangles' Buys 18 Units from Franchisee," *Nation's Restaurant News,* September 14, 1998, p. 316.

"Bojangles' Chicken Eatery to Open in Milwaukee," *Milwaukee Journal Sentinel,* January 16, 2002.

"Bojangles' Eyes Tenn. Franchise Growth Plan," *Nation's Restaurant News,* May 10, 2004, p. 141.

"Bojangles' Inks Central American Expansion Deal," *Nation's Restaurant News,* April 30, 2006, p. 58.

"Bojangles' New Owners Plan up to 45 New Units in '98," *Nation's Restaurant News,* April 20, 1998, p. 4.

"Bojangles' Restaurants Inc.," *Food Institute Report,* July 9, 2007, p. 4.

"Bojangles' Signs Kaobita to 10-Unit Pact for China," *Nation's Restaurant News,* December 13, 2004, p. 60.

"Bojangles' Signs Panthers QB for Marketing Duties," *Nation's Restaurant News,* May 17, 2004, p. 14.

"Bojangles', the 'Famous' Chicken-and-Biscuit Chain, Is Poised to Start Pecking at Competitors in Hampton Roads with Plans for Eight New Restaurants This Year and 33 over Five Years," *Virginian Pilot,* April 7, 2007, p. D1.

"Bojangles' Vet Richardson Teams to Buy 60% of Chain," *Nation's Restaurant News,* September 24, 2007, p. 4.

Capshaw, Mike, "Bojangles' Bringing Biscuits to Bentonville," *Arkansas Business,* December 11, 2006, p. 12.

Carlino, Bill, "Peterson Resurfaces As CEO, President of Bojangles' Chain," *Nation's Restaurant News,* August 22, 1994, p. 1.

Cebrzynski, Gregg, "Bojangles' 'Basic' Strategy Fuels Same-Store Sales Growth," *Nation's Restaurant News,* November 29, 1999, p. 8.

Dorich, Alan, "Passion Food: Bojangles' Restaurants Inc. Says It Specializes in Doing Things 'The Old Fashioned Way,' by

Making Its Food from Scratch and Providing Top Service," *Food and Drink,* March–April 2007, p. 31.

Engel, Clint, "Bo Gets More, Targets S.C.," *Business Journal Serving Charlotte and the Metropolitan Area,* August 10, 1992, p. 1.

———, "Bojangles' Cooks Up Expansion Plan, New Prototype Store," *Business Journal Serving Charlotte and the Metropolitan Area,* January 20, 1992, p. 1.

———, "Bojangles' Feeds Growth with Franchise Buyout," *Business Journal Serving Charlotte and the Metropolitan Area,* November 4, 1991 p. 1.

———, "Making Things Happen at the 'Bo,'" *Business Journal Serving Charlotte and the Metropolitan Area,* May 13, 1991, p. 12.

Finger, Katy, "Bojangles' No Chicken When It Comes to New Competition," *Charlotte Business Journal,* June 20, 2008.

Forman, Charles, "Bojangles' Rapid Growth Pressing Segment Leaders," *Nation's Restaurant News,* January 16, 1984, p. 1.

Giannetti, Stephanie, "Southern Fried Profits," *Convenience Store News,* June 21, 1999, p. 150.

Goydon, Raymond, "Is Frank Perdue Chicken?" *Forbes,* November 5, 1984, p. 223.

Griswold, Alicia, "Bojangles' to Break New Effort," *ADWEEK Southeast,* October 13, 2003.

Hayes, Jack, "Bojangles' Risks Turf War, Targets AFC Chicken Chains' Home Market," *Nation's Restaurant News,* May 31, 2004, p. 8.

Jeffrey, Don, "Bojangles' New Image Targets Female Market," *Nation's Restaurant News,* February 3, 1986, p. 3.

———, "Bojangles' Rolls Out Nuggets; McD's Success with Chicken Puts Chain on Defensive," *Nation's Restaurant News,* January 7, 1985, p. 3.

———, "Bojangles' to Launch Six Menu Items, $8M Marketing Plan," *Nation's Restaurant News,* May 5, 1986, p. 3.

———, "Bojangles' Upgrading Its Image," *Nation's Restaurant News,* September 30, 1985, p. 3.

Labich, Kenneth, "The Allure of Hot Chicken Chain," *Fortune,* February 6, 1984, p. 129.

Littman, Margaret, "Don't Say a Word: Regional Bojangles' Quietly Hatches a New Branding Message," *Chain Leader,* December 2003, p. 22.

Lovel, Jim, "EMA's 'Campsite' Earns Kudos, Added Airtime," *ADWEEK Southeast,* August 17, 2005.

Mildenberg, David, "Chicken Vendors Hope to Grab Fast-Food Bucks in Charlotte, N.C.," *Knight-Ridder/Tribune Business News,* July 6, 1995.

Monk, Fred, "Bojangles' Chicken Franchise Cooking Up Bold Expansion in Carolinas," *Knight-Ridder/Tribune Business News,* August 11, 1994, p. 8.

Murray, Arthur O., "Mr. Bojangles': In the Fast-Food Business Since High School, Joe Drury Thinks Success Lies in Letting His Chicken and Sides Strut Their Stuff," *Business North Carolina,* October 2002, p. 54.

Price, Scott, "Bojangles' Shifts from One KFC Exec to 2nd," *Business Journal Serving Charlotte and the Metropolitan Area,* September 3, 1990, p. 5.

———, "Half Bojangles' Office Staff Lose Jobs," *Business Journal Serving Charlotte and the Metropolitan Area,* September 10, 1990, p. 1.

Telberg, Rick, and Don Jeffrey, "Garcia Plans Revamp of Basics at Bojangles'; Schoenleb Resigns Then Mulls Buyout," *Nation's Restaurant News,* November 17, 1986, p. 2.

Boss Holdings, Inc.

221 West First Street
Kewanee, Illinois 61443
U.S.A.
Telephone: (309) 852-2131
Toll Free: (800) 447-4581
Fax: (309) 852-0848
Web site: http://www.bossgloves.com

Public Company
Incorporated: 1991 as Triggerguard, Inc.
Employees: 241
Sales: $55.19 million (2007)
Stock Exchanges: Over the Counter (OTC)
Ticker Symbol: BSHI
NAICS: 424320 Men's and Boys' Clothing and Furnishings Merchant Wholesalers; 424990 Other Miscellaneous Nondurable Goods Merchant Wholesalers

■ ■ ■

Boss Holdings, Inc., operates through several subsidiaries, but generates roughly 70 percent of its sales from its main asset, Boss Manufacturing Company. Boss Manufacturing imports and distributes work gloves, boots, and rainwear in the United States and Canada. Other subsidiaries include Boss Pet Products, which imports and distributes a line of nonfood pet supplies such as pet cable restraints, shampoos, and other pet chemical products. Boss Holdings' third business segment, promotional and specialty products, consists of Galaxy Balloons, a supplier of imprinted balloons, balls, horns, and other merchandise used for advertising and promotional purposes.

ORIGINS

When the Boss Holdings' name first appeared in 1998, it was the most straightforward name the company's management could have chosen. Boss Holdings was the holding company for Boss Manufacturing Company, its primary operating subsidiary and chief asset. The choice of Boss Holdings as a corporate title was logical, but the creation of the name also served another purpose, distancing management from a troubled past. Executives in 1998 wanted to distinguish their company from its predecessor, a company rocked by financial scandal. They bore no responsibility for the problems of the past; the company itself bore almost no resemblance to the company that had suffered disgrace. By unfurling the Boss Holdings banner, everyone at the company's Kewanee, Illinois, headquarters was given a chance for a fresh start, but the adoption of a new name did not erase entirely the memories of Vista 2000, Inc.

Vista 2000 traced its roots to a Georgia corporation named Triggerguard, Inc. A consumer products company, Triggerguard was incorporated in December 1991. In August 1992, Triggerguard changed its name to Firearm Safety Products, Inc., the name of the company when, in October 1993, it merged with a newly created company, Vista 2000. The transaction, which made Firearm Safety a subsidiary of Vista 2000, put Richard P. Smyth in charge as chairman and chief executive officer of the company, setting the stage for the drama to follow.

COMPANY PERSPECTIVES

We are proud of our history as the oldest glove company in the United States. In addition to the strength and experience we've gained from our proud heritage, we are also innovative—providing functional and new vibrant products that enhance your entire glove section. At Boss, we have the flexibility to tailor our products and services for your specific needs, while maintaining the diverse resources to service our broad customer base.

RAPID EXPANSION, ADDING BOSS MANUFACTURING

Smyth had bold plans for Vista 2000. He intended to spearhead the aggressive expansion of his company. He completed the first step in his plan in October 1994 by completing Vista 2000's initial public offering (IPO) of stock. With the proceeds from the IPO, Smyth secured the fuel to drive his expansion campaign. In a five-month period, he completed four acquisitions, beginning with the purchase of PMI in May 1995. Based in Marietta, Georgia, PMI offered direct-marketing services to corporate clientele. The following month, Smyth looked to the west, purchasing Intelock, a California-based manufacturer of digital lock mechanisms that were distributed to home center and hardware retailers throughout the United States. In July 1995, Smyth completed his third acquisition, purchasing Alabaster Industries, a manufacturer based in Alabaster, Alabama, that specialized in producing injection-molded plastics products for the housewares industry.

Smyth's most important purchase, at least to the executives of Boss Holdings, followed in September 1995. He acquired ACPI for $14.2 million, a deal that gave Vista 2000 ownership of ACPI's operating subsidiary, Boss Manufacturing Company (BMC). Based in Cleveland, Ohio, ACPI manufactured and distributed consumer hardware products. The company's products included key blanks and accessories, knives, driveway markers, snow shovels, and pet products. The company also made the type of numbers, letters, and signs stocked by hardware and do-it-yourself retailers.

A COMPANY IN CRISIS

The purchase of ACPI would be Smyth's last acquisition while employed by Vista 2000. The spurt of rapid expansion quickly screeched to a halt, its progress checked by a disturbing revelation. The debacle began when Vista 2000 sought to change the end of its fiscal year from September 30 to December 30. The company hired Grant Thornton LLP to audit its financial statements for 1995, never expecting that the accounting firm would return with devastating news. In March 1996, Grant Thornton informed Vista 2000 that its prior projections of financial performance and its previously filed financial reports parted with reality. Among other discrepancies, Vista 2000's board of directors learned the company had lost $2.1 million in 1995, not the $329,000 loss it had reported.

Once Vista 2000 learned of the grievous news, it launched an investigation, seeking to determine the integrity of its financial reporting procedures. It also sought to determine the integrity of its management. Smyth was placed on a leave of absence while the company conducted its review. In mid-April, when Vista 2000 faced 17 class-action lawsuits related to the false financial reports, the company announced the resignation of Smyth and filed a lawsuit against its former chairman and chief executive officer, accusing him of a breach of fiduciary duty, among other charges. The following month, Vista 2000 was delisted by the NASDAQ.

REBUILDING PHASE

The company was in tatters, its foundation shaken by the knowledge that the fundamental indicators of its health were false. The response to the scandal was a thorough cleansing, a sweeping restructuring effort that saw Vista 2000 sell nearly everything it owned. PMI, the direct-marketing firm, was sold to a company owned by the former principals of PMI. By the fall of 1996, Intelock, which was relocated from California to Alabama after it was acquired, was closed down. In mid-1997, Alabaster Industries was sold as well, leaving Vista 2000 with only ACPI as an operating subsidiary. Management pared away at ACPI as well, divesting the keys, letters, numbers, and signs business in August 1997. After selling or closing nearly all its assets, Vista 2000 was left with BMC and the pet products division organized within BMC as its only businesses. The final move to heal the wounds from the financial nightmare occurred at the end of 1998, when Vista 2000 changed its name to Boss Holdings, ready to begin a new era of business.

In BMC, Boss Holdings possessed a venerable trade name that gave it solid footing as it began its new era of business. BMC, established in 1893, manufactured and marketed a line of gloves, boots, and rainwear, selling its products in the consumer and industrial markets. For consumers, BMC distributed its products to a variety of

KEY DATES

1991: Boss Holdings' predecessor, Triggerguard, Inc., is founded.
1992: Triggerguard changes its name to Firearm Safety Products, Inc.
1993: Firearm Safety Products merges with Vista 2000, Inc.
1994: Vista 2000 completes its initial public offering of stock.
1995: Vista 2000 acquires four companies in five months, including ACPI, owner of Boss Manufacturing Company.
1996: Vista 2000's financial reports are discovered to be erroneous, leading to the resignation of the company's chairman and chief executive officer.
1998: After restructuring in the wake of the financial scandal, Vista 2000 changes its name to Boss Holdings, Inc.
2000: Boss Holdings' primary subsidiary, Boss Manufacturing Co., closes its domestic manufacturing operations.
2002: The acquisition of assets from RocCorp, Inc., forms the basis of Boss Pet Products, Inc.
2004: Boss Holdings acquires Galaxy Balloons, Incorporated.
2005: Head-Lite, LLC, is purchased.
2007: Boss Holdings acquires Navillus Group Inc. and Dipcraft Manufacturing Company.

retailers, including mass merchandisers, and hardware, convenience, and grocery stores. BMC collected roughly 60 percent of its sales from the consumer market, relying on the industrial market for the balance of its revenue volume. For industrial sales, the company catered to commercial users of gloves and protective wear. The company distributed its products directly to companies involved in the agricultural, automotive, energy, lumber, and construction industries. Nearly all of BMC's business was conducted in the United States, although it did market a select number of items in Canada.

BOSS HOLDINGS' PET SUPPLY BUSINESS

The smaller pet products business owned by Boss Holdings and operated through BMC conducted business under the name Warren Pet. The division's products consisted of pet supplies such as toys, collars and leads, chains, and rawhide products for dogs and cats. The division, dwarfed by market titans such as Hartz Mountain Corp. and the Sergeant's Pet Products division of ConAgra Foods, Inc., made its living by competing in niche markets overlooked by the giants of the industry. Consequently, Warren Pet relied on three customers for more than 60 percent of its sales, but the new management of Boss Holdings was determined to expand the division's distributor network and redouble marketing efforts to broaden its customer base.

After the comprehensive restructuring efforts, it took some time for the dust to settle before a clear picture of Boss Holdings' financial stature could be determined. The loss of ACPI's key, letters, numbers, and signs business represented the most significant deduction on Boss Holdings' balance sheet, stripping the company of nearly half its revenue volume. The $78 million generated by the company in 1997 under the name Vista 2000 was cut to $37 million the following year under the Boss Holdings umbrella. By the end of the decade, the company relied on BMC for $30 million of its $36 million in revenue. Warren Pet contributed $3.7 million to the company's annual total, while the balance came from the sale of promotional balloons, a facet of Boss Holdings' business that would increase in size in the coming years.

BOSS HOLDINGS IN THE 21ST CENTURY: A MANUFACTURER NO MORE

Boss Holdings hit its stride as the new century began. The company diversified and expanded, adding substantially to its annual revenue volume. As the expansion campaign began, the company made a significant decision regarding its BMC subsidiary. Toward the end of the 1990s, BMC began cutting back on its manufacturing activity, replacing the supply of gloves and protective wear it made by importing finished goods. By the end of the decade, BMC relied on imported products for 70 percent of its revenues. In 2000, it shuttered its domestic manufacturing operations, closing its factory in Greenville, Alabama, that had once ranked as the largest glove production facility in the world. BMC also closed its manufacturing facility in Mexico. Asia became the sole source for BMC's products. "We can bring the product in from there for 30 cents on the dollar compared to making it here," a Boss Holdings executive explained in the August 14, 2000, issue of the *Montgomery Advertiser.* "Our competitors were already importing. We held out longer than the competition."

ACQUISITIONS: 2002–05

Boss Holdings expanded along three fronts as it progressed through its second decade of business. The company's pet supplies business was the first to benefit from an acquisition campaign. In 2002, the company used the assets acquired from Cleveland, Ohio-based RocCorp, Inc., to form Boss Pet Products, Inc. Like the Warren Pet division, Boss Pet Products was organized as part of BMC. Boss Pet Products imported and distributed pet cable restraints, shampoos, and pet chemical products, marketing the merchandise under the "Prestige" brand name. The products were sold primarily to pet supply retailers, but the subsidiary also supplied discount retailers with merchandise under several private-label brand names.

The next business to rise in stature through an acquisition was the smallest facet of Boss Holdings' operations. In 2004, the company greatly increased its involvement in the promotional and specialty products market by purchasing Galaxy Balloons, Incorporated. Based in Cleveland, Galaxy Balloons supplied a variety of items corporate customers could use for advertising and promotional purposes. The company provided imprinted balloons, mini-sport balls, exercise balls, beach balls, and other inflatable products.

One year after the Galaxy Balloons acquisition, Boss Holdings turned its attention to its mainstay business. The work gloves and protective wear segment was bolstered by the acquisition of Head-Lite, LLC, a producer of headwear outfitted with lights.

BOSS HOLDINGS IN 2007

Acquisitions helped fuel steady financial growth, compensating for the revenue lost during the restructuring efforts of the late 1990s. Revenues increased from $35 million in 2003 to $54 million in 2005 before flattening out during the next two years. In 2007, roughly a decade after Boss Holdings had reinvented itself, the company completed two acquisitions. In mid-2007, the company strengthened its small presence in Canada by purchasing Ontario-based Navillus Group Inc. The deal, conducted through Boss Canada, gave Boss Holdings an importer and distributor of safety goods and industrial workwear such as gloves, protective eyewear, and face and respiratory protection. Next, in November, Galaxy Balloons acquired Dipcraft Manufacturing Company. Based in Pittsburgh, Pennsylvania, Dipcraft had been involved in the manufacturing and printed balloon business for more than 50 years. In the years ahead, Boss Holdings was expected to complete a small number of acquisitions to fuel its growth. Pet supplies and promotional products offered the greatest room for expansion, but much of the company's future success depended on the strength of its flagship business, BMC.

Jeffrey L. Covell

PRINCIPAL SUBSIDIARIES

Boss Manufacturing Holdings, Inc.; Boss Manufacturing Company; Boss Balloon Company; Boss Canada, Inc.; Boss Pet Products, Inc.; Canadawide Safety Inc. (Canada); Galaxy Balloons, Incorporated.

PRINCIPAL COMPETITORS

The Marmon Group, LLC; Lakeland Industries, Inc.; The Hartz Mountain Corporation.

FURTHER READING

Sherman, Mike, "Greenville, Ala., Glove Manufacturing Plant Closes," *Montgomery Advertiser,* August 14, 2000.

Bouygues S.A.

32 Ave. Hoche
Paris, F-75378 cedex 08
France
Telephone: (+33 01) 44 20 10 00
Fax: (+33 01) 44 20 12 01
Web site: http://www.bouygues.com

Public Company
Incorporated: 1952
Employees: 137,500
Sales: EUR 29.6 billion ($43.49 billion) (2007)
Stock Exchanges: Euronext Paris
Ticker Symbol: EN
NAICS: 236220 Commercial and Institutional Building Construction; 237310 Highway, Street, and Bridge Construction; 515120 Television Broadcasting; 517110 Wired Telecommunications Carriers; 517212 Cellular and Other Wireless Telecommunications; 518111 Internet Service Providers

■ ■ ■

Bouygues S.A. is one of France's largest corporations, with revenues of more than EUR 29.6 billion ($43 billion) in 2007. The company operates through five distinct poles: Construction; Real Estate and Property Development; Roadbuilding; Television and Media; and Telecommunications. Road building is the group's largest division, conducted through its nearly 97 percent control of Colas SA, the world's largest road and bridge construction company. This division accounts for 39 percent of group revenues. Bouygues Construction, the group's original business, remains the world's second largest construction company, and contributes 29 percent of group turnover. Bouygues Immobilier is a leading developer of residential and commercial properties in France and elsewhere in Europe, and adds nearly 10 percent to the company's sales. Bouygues's media holdings are conducted through its 43 percent stake in TF1, the leading television broadcaster in France, which also controls Eurosport International and other broadcasting companies and channels. Lastly, Bouygues Telecom is the number three mobile telephone provider in France, with more than nine million customers, and generates nearly 17 percent of the company's revenues. In 2008, Bouygues Telecom announced its intention to enter the fixed-line telecommunications market, rolling out its own DSL-line network. Since 2007, Bouygues SA has also been acquiring a position in French high-speed rail group Alsthom, building up a 30 percent stake in that company by 2008. Bouygues is listed on the Euronext Paris, but remains under the control of the Bouygues family. Martin Bouygues, son of the company's founder and architect of its diversification, is the group's CEO and chairman.

EARLY HISTORY

Prior to 1952, Francis Bouygues worked alongside Eugène Freyssinet, a construction pioneer who revolutionized the industry through the introduction of prestressed concrete. With a sense of vision inspired by the works of Freyssinet, and an entrepreneurial spirit that would become his trademark, the young engineer used a $1,700 loan acquired from his family to set up a small

> **COMPANY PERSPECTIVES**
>
> After 37 years of listing on the Paris Bourse, Bouygues is one of the market's flagship stocks, as demonstrated by its inclusion in the CAC 40 index. Throughout this period, the Group has been committed to involving its shareholders in its initiatives, combining corporate responsibility with an entrepreneurial spirit.

firm carrying his name which operated from his apartment.

Much of Bouygues's work lacked the glamour of his future achievements. However, he immersed himself in every aspect of his business, from driving a truck to managing construction sites. His first construction jobs included the renovation of old factories and predawn repair work at the Lido cabaret.

It was not long before Bouygues had made a name for himself; positive trends in the industry afforded Bouygues many opportunities to demonstrate his business acumen. To ensure the ready identification of the company's projects, Bouygues became one of the first firms to paint its equipment uniformly in one color, "minimum orange."

As the construction industry expanded during the 1950s and 1960s, due mainly to large public works projects, the rate of employee turnover became problematic. Competition among companies to hire workers was so acute that employees of Bouygues worked an average of only six months. To halt this trend, Bouygues created an elite corps of workers in 1963 called the Compagnons du Min-orange. Identified by the company color, this cadre of membership-only employees displayed greater dedication to the company, were less likely to leave Bouygues, and asked for fewer salary increases.

Membership in the Compagnons required nomination by a site manager and approval by a committee of Compagnons. Only one in ten nominees gained admittance. Members of the corps wore uniforms with badges or stars indicating rank. Although membership assured job security, members could be demoted, if they proved unworthy of their rank. Compagnons were rewarded with long weekend holidays to such vacation spots as Sardinia, Istanbul, and Dubrovnik. Bouygues's plan worked well; employee turnover decreased noticeably.

With a force of committed workers in place, Bouygues proceeded to make impressive gains in the industry. During the 1950s and 1960s the company erected several subsidized housing projects in Paris. The company's first large-scale project was the Parc des Princes soccer stadium, awarded to Bouygues in 1969. While the contract marked Bouygues's entrance to the higher ranks of the industry, Francis Bouygues's enthusiasm failed to conceal a certain degree of inexperience.

An extremely complex design, combined with the need for custom-made precast concrete, threatened the project from the start. When the first column erected began to slide, a school near the construction site was evacuated. With his reputation at stake, Bouygues quickly assumed personal control of the project and instituted corrective measures. The project was completed, ahead of schedule; Bouygues's profit from the job was negligible. Nevertheless, the company earned great respect for its efforts, and soon new orders began to accumulate.

Unlike industry competitors, Francis Bouygues insisted on complete control of his projects. Even though he was compelled to form partnerships on several occasions, he nevertheless avoided these arrangements as much as possible. In one instance, a joint highway contract placed Bouygues at one end of a road and the company's partner at the other end. Joint work commenced only when the two roads were connected.

Another example of Francis Bouygues's management style was shown by his decision to create a company union in 1968. This came at a time when the industry was plagued with labor disagreements and strikes. As members of a separate union, Bouygues employees never joined these strikes. Bouygues later encouraged his employees to gain affiliation with the Force Ouvrière, a politically conservative nationwide union, largely opposed to the more militant Confédération Générale du Travail. Force Ouvrière organized many of Bouygues's employees, although as late as 1982, 70 percent elected to remain exclusively with the company union. Even more significant than its lack of union organization, Bouygues employees had very few grievances; all were generally well paid.

DOMESTIC AND OVERSEAS EXPANSION

Bouygues went public on the Paris stock exchange in 1970. The company's successes in and around Paris continued to grow as Bouygues completed power plants, an airport passenger terminal, a conference center, and numerous skyscrapers. In 1974 the company established Bouygues Offshore, a constructor of offshore oil rigs, barges, and other oil-related and maritime works. By the

KEY DATES

1952: Francis Bouygues founds construction company with $1,700 loan.
1970: Bouygues goes public on Paris stock exchange.
1987: Bouygues leads consortium to acquire TF1 television broadcaster.
1989: Martin Bouygues takes over as chairman and CEO from his father.
1994: Bouygues leads acquisition of mobile telephone license and launches Bouygues Telecom.
2000: Bouygues Telecom tops four million subscribers.
2006: Bouygues acquires French government's 21.7 percent stake in Alsthom.
2008: Bouygues Telecom tops nine million subscribers and rolls out fixed-line service.

mid-1970s Bouygues announced plans to expand on two fronts: in the remainder of France, and overseas. Domestic operations centered on the private home building industry. The Maison Bouygues division built homes to satisfy individual tastes at inexpensive prices. Maison Bouygues also marked the entry of Francis Bouygues's sons, Martin and Olivier, into the company's operations. Instead of receiving a direct stake in the company, the Bouygues brothers founded their own construction company, with the financial backing of Bouygues. Maison Bouygues in fact remained majority controlled by the two Bouygues brothers. By the early 1980s Bouygues had become the largest home builder in France.

The company's late entrance into overseas markets compelled Bouygues to bid lower than its competitors for an Iranian contract to build the 1974 Asian Games stadium in Teheran. Bouygues's price was 30 to 40 percent less than those of larger industry veterans such as Bechtel Group, Inc. Bouygues won the contract. This project led to further contracts to build residences in Iran and to perform repairs on the shah's palace. Using the revolutionary concrete truss design of the Asian Games stadium, Bouygues went on to complete the 1.5-mile Bubiyan Bridge in Kuwait in 1983. Business expanded to Iraq, where the company constructed a nuclear power plant (destroyed by Israeli bombing in 1984). In addition, Bouygues constructed a mosque in Jeddah, Saudi Arabia. Outside the Middle East, the company secured contracts to build power plants and universities in West Africa.

As eager as it was to enter foreign markets, Bouygues was prevented from doing so by strict financial policies which were intended to protect the company from losses in unstable countries. Francis Bouygues refused to work on credit in these high-risk markets, and always remained ready to leave them on short notice; during the Iranian revolution in 1978, Bouygues moved out without incurring any losses.

One exception to Bouygues's reluctance to work with partners came in the late 1970s, when the Saudi Arabian government opened bidding for the construction of the University of Riyadh. Bouygues's desire to maintain his independence was overridden by his ambition; when the Saudi government informed Bouygues that his company was too small to win the contract alone, he formed a partnership with Alabama-based Blount, Inc. Still, Bouygues insisted on a 55 percent controlling interest in the partnership, which gave him the final approval in all decisions. The 40-month deadline set by the Saudis for the completion of the project discouraged most bidders. By the time the $2 billion contract was to be awarded, all but two contenders had dropped out of the competition. When the contract was finally awarded to the Bouygues-Blount partnership in 1981, it was the largest fixed-price construction agreement ever. Because the two companies stood to lose money if the construction fell behind schedule, Bouygues and Blount completed the project on time and collected an additional $50 million windfall.

Bouygues entered the 1980s with impressive financial credentials and great prestige. Yet changes in both the French and world economies forced the company to change its business strategy. High interest rates, falling oil prices, and a shrinking construction market forced Bouygues to reduce its workforce. President François Mitterrand's social policies reduced the amount of government funds available for large public works projects. To compensate for the changing economic conditions, Bouygues was also forced to alter its financing methods for overseas projects; the Nigerian government paid the company four months late for a $620 million power plant.

DIVERSIFYING IN THE EIGHTIES

Bouygues initiated a program of diversification to mitigate the effects of the beleaguered construction market. An attempt to purchase Druout, a French insurance company, was thwarted when that company's former owners sued to halt the takeover. Later,

Bouygues acquired a 55 percent share of Amrep S.A., an oil services company. In an attempt to broaden its presence in the United States, Bouygues purchased a number of engineering firms and reorganized them as an Omaha-based consortium called HDR, Inc. A larger holding company, called the Centerra Corporation, was also formed to perform work in design, engineering, financing, and construction. Centerra's first large project was construction of the New World Center in Seattle.

Among other acquisitions, the more significant long-term were Saur (water treatment and supply, purchased jointly by Maison Bouygues and Bouygues SA, with Maison Bouygues as majority shareholder), ETDE (electrical power and communications networks), and Smac Acieroïd (waterproofing). However, the largest of all Bouygues's purchases of this period was in the area of construction. France's second largest construction group, Screg, accumulated a massive debt which made it vulnerable to a takeover; Bouygues thereby acquired Screg Group in 1986. With the addition of Screg, Bouygues's revenues increased to nearly $7 billion. Through three Screg Group companies (Colas, Screg, and Sacer) Bouygues became involved in the road construction industry. Bouygues also added another construction company in 1986, Dragages et Travaux Publics, which specialized in public works.

In 1987 the company failed to take over Spie-Batignolles, a large French contractor in which Bouygues claimed it had an original 10 percent interest. Not only was the attempted takeover particularly acrimonious, it resulted in an inquiry in which Bouygues was accused of failing to declare a major corporate interest. (French law required investors to declare any corporate interest in excess of 10 percent.) The Commission des Operations de Bourse, the French stock market regulatory committee, later charged Bouygues with failing to declare a 24 percent interest in Spie-Batignolles. The following year, Bouygues found itself under attack from another side, as Australian media magnate Robert Maxwell began acquiring stakes in the company. This led the Bouygues family—which despite founding the company held only a small minority of its shares—to begin a process of increasing their own shareholding position. As part of that process, Saur (controlled by Maison Bouygues, and therefore by the Bouygues brothers, and not Bouygues itself) used its subsidiary Cofipex to begin buying shares in Bouygues. Before long, Cofipex's own stake amounted to more than 10 percent by 1989. In that year, however, the Bouygues brothers transferred their stake in Maison Bouygues to a new holding company, SCDM. Through its control of Saur, and ultimately of Cofipex, SCDM took direct control of 10 percent of Bouygues.

Bouygues continued to diversify in the late 1980s. In April 1987 Bouygues and a consortium of private investors acquired a controlling interest in TF1, the leading French national television network. In 1989 the company acquired Grands Moulines de Paris, the leading flour-milling concern in France. Bouygues's construction side also completed several prestigious construction projects in the late 1990s: the Île de Ré Bridge in western France in 1988; the Grande Arche de La Défense, which was Paris's main monument to the bicentennial of the French Revolution, in 1989; and the Hassan II Mosque in Casablanca, also in 1989. In 1988 the company also moved into its impressive new headquarters, called Challenger, located in Saint-Quentin-en-Yvelines, northeast of Paris.

Perhaps the most noteworthy event of the late 1980s was the change in leadership at Bouygues. That year, Martin Bouygues, 37-year-old son of the company founder, was appointed group chairman and CEO. Francis Bouygues remained involved in the company's media activities, not only TF1 but also the 1990 launch of a start-up film production company, Ciby 2000. As chairman of Ciby 2000, Francis Bouygues helped to develop a movie company that produced such award-winning films as *The Piano* (1993), *Underground* (1995), and *Secrets and Lies* (1996). Bouygues, however, died of a heart attack at age 71 on July 24, 1993, after suffering from a long illness. He did not survive to see Ciby 2000 become profitable by 1997, at which time it had the rights to 80 films. However, Bouygues (the company) had decided to put the nascent production company up for sale.

ENTERING THE MOBILE TELECOM MARKET IN THE NINETIES

Meanwhile, under Martin Bouygues's leadership, Bouygues completed several noteworthy construction projects in the 1990s, many through partnerships: the Library of France in 1992; the Channel Tunnel, which connected England and France, and the Normandy Bridge, the longest cable-stayed structure in the world, both in 1994; the Sydney metro in 1995; the Central Railway Station in Kuala Lumpur, Malaysia, in 1997; and the Stade de France, a stadium finished in time for the 1998 World Cup (of soccer) held in France. The company also continued to expand its nonconstruction operations. In 1991 Saur entered the power supply business. In 1994 the company increased its stake in TF1 from 25 percent to 37.5 percent. Forming partnerships became increasingly common at Bouygues in the 1990s, and in 1994 the company joined with French and international partners in winning a license for the third French mobile telephone network. A mobile service was subsequently launched by Bouygues Telecom on May 29, 1996. Bouygues in May 1994 entered into a strategic alliance with French power utility EDF to develop joint operations internationally in the area of public utilities management. In 1997 Bouygues purchased another French utilities company, Cise, and merged it with Saur to create the third largest public utilities management group in France.

While this expansion continued, problems were cropping up. In 1995 Bouygues posted a net loss of $593 million resulting from writeoffs taken for losses in its property business and for start-up costs associated with Bouygues Telecom and the development of a paging service called Kobby. Several senior executives, including Martin Bouygues, were under formal investigation during 1997 for "misuse of corporate funds." In addition, the company faced pressure from one of its largest shareholders, French financier Vincent Bolloré, who purchased about 10 percent of Bouygues through the open market in late 1997 and early 1998, to divest its money-losing telecommunications businesses. However, it appeared that Bouygues had no intention to do so, and in fact announced in December 1997 that it had formed a joint venture called 9 Telecom with Telecom Italia and Veba Telecom of Germany to develop a fixed-line telephone service in France. This latest move was made in anticipation of Europe's telecommunications markets being opened to competition at the beginning of 1998. Meantime, Bouygues had improved its financial position through the late 1996 initial public offering of 40 percent of Bouygues Offshore. Bolloré's bid to gain control of Bouygues's direction failed, and in November 1998, Bolloré sold his stake to another French financial giant, François Pinault.

Bouygues returned to profitability for both 1996 and 1997. Revenues reached $15.34 billion by 1997, more than double the level of ten years earlier. Construction remained by far Bouygues's largest sector, accounting for two-thirds of overall revenue. About 15 percent came from public utilities operations, 11 percent from media, and only 4.7 percent from telecommunications.

Bolloré's attempt to acquire part of Bouygues led Martin and Olivier to unravel the somewhat complex scheme they had used over the past two decades to build up their own controlling shareholding position in Bouygues. In 1997, the brothers' SCDM holding sold its controlling stake in Saur to Saur itself. In exchange, Saur transferred its subsidiary Cofipex, as well as a cash payment, to SCDM. In this way, the Bouygues brothers publicly revealed their control over more than 46 percent of Bouygues's voting rights, effectively shielding the family's shareholding from future takeover attempts.

LEADING INTO THE NEW CENTURY

All of Bouygues's operations grew strongly into the next decade. Bouygues Telecom became one of the group's fastest-growing components. By 1998, the company had succeeded in rolling out its service on a national level, attracting more than one million subscribers by the end of that year. Just two years later, Bouygues Telecom boasted nearly five million subscribers as the mobile telecom market skyrocketed in France. Bouygues elected to sit out on bidding for the next generation of high-speed mobile telephone licenses.

This decision proved a shrewd one, as initial attempts to roll out the 3G network floundered into the middle of the decade, despite the billions of euros spent on its development. When Bouygues eventually entered the 3G market, it scooped up its own license for a fraction of the original bidding prices. Bouygues's rollout of broadband mobile telephone service enabled it to make steady gains in its subscriber base, and by 2008, Bouygues Telecom boasted more than nine million subscribers. Not content with its success in mobile telephone, the company also finally made good on its promise to add fixed-line services. In 2007, the company reached an agreement to take over the operations of a 1,000-exchange DSL fixed-line network, reaching 60 percent of the French population, from Neuf Cegetel.

Bouygues's other operations continued to build strongly into the new century as well. In 1999, the company spun off its various construction businesses into a new subsidiary, Bouygues Construction. The company completed a number of major construction projects, such as the Groene Hart Tunnel in 2001, the Budapest sports arena in 2003, an agreement to build a bridge over Masan Bay in South Korea in 2004, a project to build Thailand's three tallest residential towers starting in 2006, and the contract to build the new port of Tangiers, Morocco, in 2007. In that year, Bouygues also expanded its U.K. presence with the acquisition of Warings. Bouygues increased its stake in the Colas road building division during this time as well, gaining control of more than 96 percent of its shares.

The arrival of Nicolas Sarkozy as French president in 2007 brought new hope for the Bouygues's TF1 holding. The arrival of digital terrestrial television, which suddenly multiplied the number of available free-to-air television channels by more than four times, led to steady declines in TF1's audience share, and advertising revenues. In 2008, however, Sarkozy announced a new plan by the government to eliminate advertisements from all state-owned television stations. At the same time, the country's privately owned television stations were given the authorization to add new blocs of advertisement space in their broadcast. The move was widely seen as a gift from Sarkozy to Martin Bouygues and other TF1 shareholders for their support in his election.

In the meantime, Bouygues continued to seek new areas of operation into the later years of the first decade of the 2000s. In 2004, the company sold its Saur water business. In its place, the company received approval to acquire the French government's 21.7 percent stake in Alsthom, the electrical engineering company active in high-speed rail transport and energy generation. Bouygues completed the purchase in 2006, then began building up its positions in Alsthom. By 2008, the company had succeeded in gaining 30 percent of the company's shares. After more than 55 years, Bouygues had become one of France's largest corporations, while remaining under the control of the founding family.

M. L. Cohen

PRINCIPAL SUBSIDIARIES

Alsthom SA (30%); Bouygues Construction; Bouygues Immobilier; Bouygues Telecom (89.5%); Colas SA. (96.7%); TF1 (43%).

PRINCIPAL COMPETITORS

Vinci SA; Orange SA; SFR SA; AMEC Plc; Bechtel Group Inc.

FURTHER READING

Barbanel, Alain, and Jean Menanteau, *Bouygues: L'empire moderne,* Paris: Ramsay, 1987.

"Bouygues; Chairman and CEO, Martin Bouygues," *Business Week,* June 27, 2005, p. 52.

"Bouygues Telecom Has over 9m Customers," *Total Telecom Online,* November 29, 2007.

"Bouygues Telecom Links up with Leading French TV Channel," *Tarifica Alert,* May 9, 2006.

Campagnac, Elisabeth, and Vincent Nouzille, *Citizen Bouygues, ou, L'histoire secrete d'un grand patron,* Paris: P. Belfond, 1988, 511 p.

Cane, Alan, "Bouygues Leads New Telecoms Venture," *Financial Times,* December 10, 1997, p. 34.

Carson-Parker, John, "Francis Bouygues Reshapes Europe," *Chief Executive,* July/August 1989, pp. 34–37.

Christy, John H., "Clean Slate," *Forbes,* June 12, 2000, p. 184.

Cohen, Norma, "Lehman and Bouygues Plan East European Malls," *Financial Times,* March 13, 1998, p. 21.

Crabbe, Matthew, "A Good M&A Vintage in Prospect," *Euromoney,* January 1987, pp. 35+.

"Creative Construction—Bouygues, French Corporate Governance," *Economist,* December 2, 2006, p. 71US.

"French Company to Build Oil-Gas Complex in Ashgabat," *Times of Central Asia,* May 23, 2008.

Marray, Michael, "Build Not Buy," *Protect Finance,* March 2006, p. 78.

"Mobile Broadband from Bouygues," *Tarifica Alert,* May 27, 2008.

Owen, David, "Bouygues Quiet on Possible Revamp," *Financial Times,* April 1, 1998, p. 28.

———, "Bouygues Seeks Transatlantic Link," *Financial Times,* April 7, 1998, p. 30.

———, "Bouygues Under Pressure," *Financial Times,* April 6, 1998, p. 24.

———, "French Businessmen in Probe," *Financial Times,* February 28, 1997, p. 2.

———, "Lines to Profit Still Open As Bouygues Enters French Mobile Market," *Financial Times,* June 19, 1996, p. 31.

Ridding, John, "Bouygues-Led Consortium Wins Mobile Net License," *Financial Times,* October 5, 1994, p. 30.

"Sarkozy-ing French TV," *Video Age International,* June–July 2008, p. 6.

Schuman, Joseph, "Bouygues Bid Boldest," *Variety,* November 27, 1995, p. 76.

Taaffe, Joanne, "Bouygues Enters French Consumer Fixed-Line Market," *Total Telecom Online,* September 27, 2007.

Tully, Shawn, "France's Master Builder Is on the March," *Fortune,* May 2, 1983, pp. 210+.

Tutt, Nigel, "An Effective Performer," *Financial Times,* November 19, 1997, p. FTS6.

Burgett, Inc.

4111 North Freeway Boulevard
Sacramento, California 95834
U.S.A.
Telephone: (916) 567-9999
Toll Free: (800) 566-3472
Fax: (916) 567-1941
Web site: http://www.pianodisc.com

Private Company
Incorporated: 1988
Employees: 180
Sales: $37 million (2007 est.)
NAICS: 339992 Musical Instrument Manufacturing

■ ■ ■

Based in Sacramento, California, Burgett, Inc., doing business as PianoDisc, is a leading manufacturer of player piano systems that allow listeners to enjoy "live" music from virtually all genres. The company's products, which are available through some 600 dealers in 40 countries worldwide, provide entertainment in a wide variety of settings, from restaurants and hotels to music schools and individual homes.

PREHISTORY

PianoDisc's roots can be traced to a chicken ranch in Southern California, where Gary Burgett and his younger brother, Kirk, each developed individual talents that would later serve them in the business world. Encouraged by his mother, Gary flourished as a piano player, while Kirk honed his mechanical aptitude by working on farm equipment under his father's tutelage.

Following the death of their father, Gary studied both music and accounting at Bob Jones University, worked as a church music director, and in 1978 opened what quickly became a thriving teaching studio in Sacramento.

Although Kirk did not know how to play the piano like his brother, he became interested in rebuilding the instrument after meeting Paul Magee, a well-known piano rebuilder. After gaining an appreciation of the piano's mechanical features, Kirk left his job in a machine shop, and the Burgett brothers opened a small, 750-square-foot store named Burgett Pianos in 1979.

A critical development occurred in 1983, when Burgett Pianos became a Marantz Pianocorder franchise and began selling player piano devices. Showing off the technology at a variety of venues, from home shows and model homes to shopping centers and local fairs, the Pianocorder soon generated 40 percent of sales. Consumers who otherwise would have never even considered buying a piano were captivated by the entertainment value offered by a player piano, and by the late 1980s Burgett Pianos saw its annual piano sales grow from 50 units to 400.

In the midst of this success, the Burgetts were encouraged when Yamaha acquired Marantz's Pianocorder Division in October 1987. Although it seemed that a good situation was about to get even better, things took a turn for the worse in November, when Yamaha pulled the Pianocorder off the market and introduced the Disklavier, a computer-driven player

COMPANY PERSPECTIVES

At PianoDisc, we are committed to leading our industry by serving our customers, our dealers, our employees, and our vendors all over the world. Our servanthood is manifested through superior products, excellent service and honest communication. There is no better example of the servant leader than the Lord Jesus Christ. Our business is dedicated to Him, and we have dedicated ourselves to modeling His examples—with His help and to the best of our ability.

piano. Because they were not Yamaha dealers, selling the Disklavier was not an option for Burgett Pianos. With less than a two-month supply of Pianocorders on hand, the Burgett brothers suddenly faced the real possibility of losing almost half of their sales.

Realizing that many other non-Yamaha dealers throughout the country shared in their plight, Kirk Burgett convinced Gary that they should design and produce their very own player piano system. Because they were located in California, the brothers had easy access to software and mechanical engineers, as well as those with electronic manufacturing knowledge.

FORMATIVE YEARS: 1988–89

Gary and Kirk Burgett embarked upon what proved to be a difficult journey, establishing PianoDisc in 1988. They reached an important milestone that year, debuting at an industry trade show a semifunctional player piano unit named the PDS-1000. Some 80 dealers placed orders for 100 units, to be delivered that October, in advance of the holiday retail season.

"The delivery commitments we made almost killed us," Gary Burgett said in the November 1993 issue of *Music Trades.* "We were naive to think that we could finish engineering the PDS-1000, build a software library, and have a factory setup in three months."

In addition to the incredibly complex task of designing a computer system that could control thousands of mechanical parts inside a piano, as well as the challenging tasks associated with getting a new business up and running, the Burgetts had to contend with patent issues. Taking great care to avoid infringing upon Yamaha's player piano patents, they developed their own patented Pulse Mapping technology to power PianoDisc player systems.

Legal and patent issues caused delays, and the October 1988 delivery target came and went. The Burgetts weathered a difficult time as they worked to prepare their new product for the marketplace and ultimately produced the first system in March 1989.

EARLY INNOVATIONS: 1990–97

During the 1990s, PianoDisc made a name for itself in the music industry by introducing a steady stream of new products. In a pioneering move, the company became the first to include a built-in soundcard in a player piano unit when it rolled out the PDS-32 in 1990.

In many ways, 1993 was a pivotal year for PianoDisc. The company unveiled a piano performances library called the Artist Series, which allowed customers to enjoy "live" performances by famous artists from virtually every genre in their businesses and homes. That same year, the company achieved another breakthrough with the PDS-128, which at the time was the industry's smallest player system. The following year, the PianoDisc experience was improved again via the introduction of PianoVideo, a system that synchronized a videotaped performance with the "live" PianoDisc performance.

By this time PianoDisc had become the nation's leading player piano systems manufacturer, with revenues of about $13 million, a workforce of some 75 employees, and a new 50,000-square-foot factory in Sacramento.

Breakthroughs continued during the mid-1990s. In 1995 the company's Pedal Adapter System made it possible for disabled individuals to operate piano pedals. That same year, PianoDisc introduced an acoustic/electric hybrid piano unit named QuietTime, which enabled users to play a piano normally or like a keyboard by using headphones to hear the sound. In 1996 the company introduced the PDS-128, which allowed both CD and diskette playback from a single device.

Midway through the decade, several important developments occurred on the corporate front. The subsidiary Music Systems Research, formed in 1995, was created to market the company's Impact Series line of powered speakers, which could be used with the PianoDisc system, as well as computers and other products. The following year, PianoDisc made a successful $905,000 bid to acquire the assets of bankrupt piano manufacturer Mason & Hamlin Piano Co. The company's roots dated all the way back to 1854, when it was established in Boston by Henry Mason and Emmons Hamlin.

During the late 1990s, PianoDisc continued to make breakthroughs with new products and technolo-

KEY DATES

1988: Gary and Kirk Burgett establish PianoDisc.
1989: The first PianoDisc system is produced.
1993: A new, 50,000-square-foot factory opens in Sacramento, California.
1996: PianoDisc makes a successful bid to acquire the assets of bankrupt piano manufacturer Mason & Hamlin Piano Co.
2005: The Mason & Hamlin brand turns 150.
2008: PianoDisc celebrates 20 years of operations.

gies, such as the 1997 introduction of SilentDrive, which improved the performance of the PianoDisc player systems through greater pedal and key control, with the added benefit of reducing the piano's mechanical noise.

A SECOND DECADE: 1998–2008

PianoDisc celebrated ten years of operations in 1998. That year, the company exhibited a new technology called PianoLink, which allowed audio, video, and musical instrument digital interface (MIDI) signals to be transmitted at the same time. This technology enabled customers to watch a pianist at a remote location, such as a concert hall, via television and hear the "live" performance on their piano in real time. MIDI is a communications protocol that facilitates communication between computers and musical instruments.

The economic prosperity of the late 1990s, coupled with low interest rates and continued focus on innovative products, including a PianoCD system containing some 4,000 different songs, had a positive impact on sales. From the first quarter of 1997 to the first quarter of 1998, the company's revenues skyrocketed 37.6 percent. Sales continued to soar in 1999, with first quarter figures rising 38 percent over 1998 levels. As demand for PianoDisc products exceeded production, the company instituted a swing shift in order to double its output. By this time, PianoDisc also had acquired the piano brands Knabe, which had roots stretching back to 1837, and George Steck, which originated in 1857.

The early 2000s were accompanied by an economic slowdown that impacted virtually every industry. However, despite flatter piano industry sales, PianoDisc continued to do well. The company moved ahead by targeting affluent customers who could afford its cutting-edge products.

By 2003 PianoDisc revenues exceeded $20 million, and the company sold its products through a network of approximately 600 distributors in 45 countries worldwide. Early that year, PianoDisc introduced the Opus7. The new player system, the company's seventh, was housed completely inside the piano. In addition, customers were able to download system upgrades and new music to the Opus7 directly from the Internet. This was accomplished with a combination remote control/handheld computer called the Conductor Tablet that offered additional functionality, such as the ability to control a customer's household appliances.

The emotional power of PianoDisc products was demonstrated during Television Night at the Hollywood Bowl II in 2004, which included a special tribute to actor, comedian, musician, and writer Steve Allen (1921–2000), the original host of the *Tonight Show.* The tribute involved a Mason & Hamlin piano that played a song Allen himself had recorded years earlier.

By the middle of the first decade of the 2000s PianoDisc had successfully restored Mason & Hamlin to its former glory. Of approximately 300 piano manufacturers that were in business in 1911, Mason & Hamlin was one of only four still operational in 2005, when the brand celebrated its 150th birthday. Its pianos, some of which cost more than $50,000, were considered to be investment grade. In recognition of its heritage, the Mason & Hamlin Historical Preservation Society was established in 2005.

In addition, international expansion occurred at PianoDisc in 2005, when the company opened offices in Beijing and Shenzhen, China. These locations were formed to help the company tap into China's growing market for luxury products. They also served as a base for expanding support, services, and training there.

By 2006 PianoDisc sales were roughly $25 million. Unfortunately, in September of that year, a fire destroyed some of the company's operations in Sacramento. Resulting in about $8 million worth of damage, the fire consumed 100 new grand pianos and 16 Model 50 professional upright pianos, the company's entire fourth-quarter supply.

Fortunately, though, the fire's impact on operations was minimized because hardware for PianoDisc systems, which then cost between $5,000 and $20,000, was manufactured in Shanghai, China, and the company's administration, purchasing, software development, and accounting operations were spared from the blaze.

As PianoDisc headed toward 2010, the company employed a workforce of approximately 115 people in Sacramento. By this time, its products were sold via its dealer network and also through piano manufacturer Steinway, among others. The company rounded out

2006 by unveiling Original Artist PianoSync, a new product for the Opus7 system that synchronized music CDs from popular artists such as Frank Sinatra, Ray Charles, Billy Joel, and The Eagles with separate piano accompaniments for the PianoDisc player that could be downloaded from the PianoDisc web site.

In 2007 the Burgetts continued to leave their mark on the piano industry. At Mason & Hamlin, the brothers introduced the third new grand piano, the Model B baby grand, since 2004. The new product came on the heels of a successful 2006, when the Mason & Hamlin business saw its net sales increase 22 percent.

Late in 2007, PianoDisc introduced PianoVideo HD, an offering that made it possible for people to view high definition piano concert videos in tandem with corresponding "live" performances on their player-equipped pianos.

PianoDisc celebrated 20 years of operations in 2008. Some two decades after deciding to make their own player piano system, the Burgett brothers had raised the bar in their industry through a steady stream of innovative products. As the 21st century's second decade approached, their company appeared to be well positioned for continued success and innovation.

Paul R. Greenland

PRINCIPAL SUBSIDIARIES

Music Systems Research; PianoDisc - Europe (Germany); PianoDisc - China; PianoDisc - Seoul (South Korea).

PRINCIPAL COMPETITORS

Baldwin Piano Inc.; Steinway Musical Instruments Inc.; Yamaha Corporation.

FURTHER READING

"An All-New Concert Grand Debuts at NAMM to Celebrate Mason & Hamlin's 150th Anniversary: With a Passion for Pianos, the Burgett Brothers Have Carefully Nurtured Mason & Hamlin Back to Health and Burnished One of the Most Illustrious Traditions in the Piano Industry," *Music Trades*, February 2005.

"PianoDisc Bids for Mason & Hamlin," *Music Trades*, April 1996.

"PianoDisc Marks 15th Year: How Founders Gary & Kirk Burgett Turned a Retail Piano Shop into a Technology Pioneer," *Music Trades*, June 2003.

"The PianoDisc Story: How Two Brothers Transformed a Dream into a Lucrative Hi-Tech Player Piano," *Music Trades*, November 1993.

Cano Petroleum Inc.

Burnett Plaza
801 Cherry Street
Unit 25, Suite 3200
Fort Worth, Texas 76102-6882
U.S.A.
Telephone: (817) 698-0900
Fax: (817) 698-0796
Web site: http://www.canopetro.com

Public Company
Incorporated: 2004
Employees: 114
Sales: $28.35 million (2007)
Stock Exchanges: American
Ticker Symbol: CFW
NAICS: 211111 Crude Petroleum and Natural Gas Extraction

■ ■ ■

Based in Fort Worth, Texas, Cano Petroleum Inc. is an energy producer that uses secondary enhanced oil recovery (EOR) methods to obtain oil from "mature" U.S. oilfields. In other words, the company extracts additional oil from fields that have already been worked by major oil companies employing traditional methods. Cano Petroleum uses special technology to obtain oil not recoverable using standard methods. One recovery technique the company uses is called waterflooding, in which water is injected into the earth under high pressure to flush oil from porous rocks.

Cano Petroleum operates in a highly specialized niche that is largely ignored by bigger oil companies. The company minimizes risk by focusing on domestic operations, as opposed to doing business in international zones where risks, political or otherwise, are much greater.

ORIGINS: 2004

Cano Petroleum, which takes its name from the 16th-century Spanish explorer Juan Sebastian del Cano (1476–1526), was established in 2004 by oil and gas entrepreneur Jeff Johnson. Prior to forming Cano Petroleum, Johnson worked in the corporate finance field. Early in his career, he was successful in securing funds for partnerships related to Chesapeake Energy's south Texas projects.

Johnson honed his experience in the gas and oil industry by acquiring undervalued properties, increasing their value, and then selling them. After forming an independent oil and gas exploration venture in 1993, he was involved in the acquisition of a company named Scope Operating Inc. four years later, the oil production assets of which he eventually sold.

After securing $8.75 million in start-up capital, Cano Petroleum began trading on the NASD's OTC Bulletin Board under the symbol CAOP in June 2004. The company was initially named Huron Ventures Inc., and adopted the name Cano Petroleum Inc. as a condition of its acquisition of Davenport Field Unit Inc., which gave the company a 2,178-acre site in Lincoln County, Oklahoma's Davenport field, a formation that then contained an estimated 48 million barrels of oil.

COMPANY PERSPECTIVES

Cano Petroleum's business model is well-focused, as is its mission: to build shareholder value.

After generating $8 million from its initial public offering, and with Johnson at the helm as CEO, the company made its first acquisition under the Cano Petroleum banner on June 30, 2004, snapping up Edmond, Oklahoma-based Ladder Energy Co. for $2.2 million. The deal gave Cano Petroleum 51 producing oil and gas wells in the 4,500-acre Rich Valley field.

More developments continued during the latter part of the year. In September Cano Petroleum acquired $2.5 million in assets from the Bartlesville Sandstone operation in Nowata County, Oklahoma's Nowata field. In October Cano Petroleum drilled its first new oil well at the Davenport field, and commenced drilling of a second well. That same month, the company applied for a listing on the American Stock Exchange.

INITIAL GROWTH: 2005–06

Progress continued in 2005. Early in the year, Cano Petroleum acquired central Texas-based Square One Energy. The $8 million cash and stock deal included approximately 10,300 acres of fields in Texas' Comanche, Eastland, and Erath counties, with 34 wells, a gas processing plant, and a variety of other assets. Following the acquisition, Square One's assets became Cano Petroleum's Desdemona Unit.

Continued growth was aided by the company's initial wave of institutional funding in March 2005. Totaling $5.1 million, the financing was provided by Wellington Management.

Cano Petroleum's request for a listing on the American Stock Exchange was fulfilled midway through 2005. The company's common stock was listed on May 5 under the ticker symbol CFW, making it visible to a wider range of potential investors. Cano Petroleum executives celebrated by ringing the opening bell on July 12.

The fall of 2005 was marked by a flurry of important developments at Cano Petroleum. The company's continued expansion prospects were aided by more institutional investments in September, totaling about $19.5 million. That same month, Cano Petroleum spent $55.24 million to acquire an unnamed oilfield.

The Union Bank of California awarded Cano Petroleum with $100 million in credit in October, leading up to a major deal for Pampa, Texas-based WO Energy the following month. The acquisition caused the company's total proved reserves to reach 40.02 million barrels, up from 5.52 million barrels before the deal. The term "proved reserves" essentially refers to oil that can be recovered from the earth with existing technology, and under existing economic conditions, with a high degree of certainty. Daily production tripled from the equivalent of 400 barrels per day to 1,200, pushing the company's operating revenues to about $800,000 per month.

The WO Energy deal gave Cano Petroleum a sizable number of new assets in Texas' Carson, Gray, and Hutchinson counties. In addition to ten workover rigs and a wide range of equipment and vehicles were 480 producing wells, 380 idle wells, and 40 water disposal wells located in the 20,000-acre Panhandle field. From an original estimated equivalent of 600 million barrels of oil, Cano Petroleum estimated that some 90 million barrels had already been recovered over the years via primary methods. The company's engineers estimated that the equivalent of 34.5 million barrels of proved reserves remained in the field, a figure that Cano Petroleum said could be even higher via the use of better recovery methods.

In addition to the WO Energy deal, in November 2005 Cano Petroleum revealed that it would ramp up production by pouring $13.6 million into five of its existing fields in Oklahoma and Texas. The capital investments were slated to occur over the course of a 12-month period.

Cano Petroleum was in a good position in early 2006. As oil prices continued to soar, the future looked very promising. The company's workforce had grown to include 85 workers, up from only six 18 months earlier. Since the acquisition of WO Energy, Cano Petroleum's stock price had catapulted 82 percent, to $8.68 per share.

The company moved forward with approximately $65 million in credit at its disposal, $6 million in cash, and limited competition in its niche (acquiring fields that produced daily equivalents of about 1,200 barrels of oil per day). While lucrative for a smaller firm like Cano Petroleum, such fields were well off the radar screen of major oil firms, which were forced to seek large oil discoveries to maintain their production levels.

Despite its stable footing, Cano Petroleum was forced to contend with a difficult situation in April, when the company and three of its subsidiaries were sued by owners of the Four Sixes Ranch in the Texas Panhandle for allegedly causing wildfires that erupted at

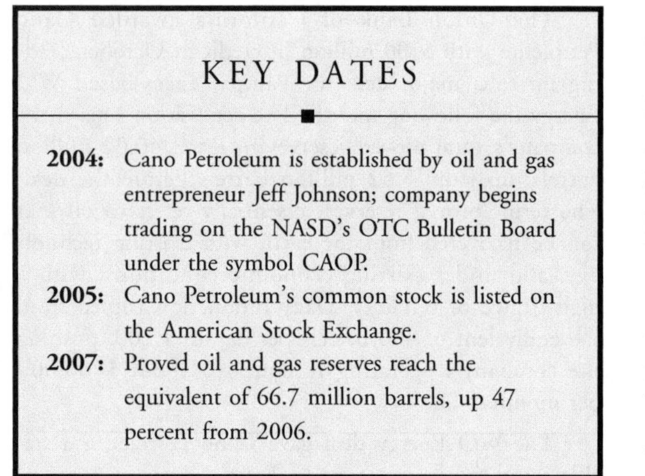

KEY DATES

2004: Cano Petroleum is established by oil and gas entrepreneur Jeff Johnson; company begins trading on the NASD's OTC Bulletin Board under the symbol CAOP.

2005: Cano Petroleum's common stock is listed on the American Stock Exchange.

2007: Proved oil and gas reserves reach the equivalent of 66.7 million barrels, up 47 percent from 2006.

the ranch in March, destroying more than 475,000 acres of land. Specifically, the suit laid blame on electrical lines supplying power to the company's gas and oil operations.

Filed a mere 11 days after the fires, the lawsuit stunned Cano Petroleum Chairman and CEO Jeff Johnson. Commenting on the situation in an April 18, 2006, *Business Wire* release, he said: "We don't understand it. It looks like they want to fight fires with lawsuits. Our focus has been on protecting the land and the people during this extraordinary drought. Over the past four months, hundreds of grass fires in the Texas Panhandle have been blamed on careless cigarette disposal, fireworks, trash burning, and, even, arson. The claims in this lawsuit are an unbelievable stretch."

While the wildfire-related litigation was a sore spot for Cano Petroleum in the Texas Panhandle, the company continued to make meaningful progress in that region. In May the company closed a $24 million deal for oil and gas properties located across 9,700 acres in the Texas Panhandle field. In addition to increasing net daily production by about 400 barrels, the deal also pushed Cano Petroleum's total proved reserves up by the equivalent of seven million barrels.

PREPARING FOR THE FUTURE

Institutional investors continued to pump money into Cano Petroleum in 2006. In September the company sold more than 6.6 million shares of stock for net proceeds of $76 million, about $69 million of which was earmarked for debt reduction. Cano Petroleum moved into its 2007 fiscal year with no debt and announced a $41 million capital budget. While operating revenues soared 235 percent for the 2006 fiscal year, to $18.41 million, the company recorded a net loss of $1.84 million.

Cano Petroleum capped off the year with news that it had discovered new gas in the Barnett Shale on its Desdemona field. The discovery was an added perk for Cano Petroleum, because the company did not acquire the field for the gas. Making the find even sweeter were existing pipelines on the land, which made transporting the gas easier.

By the second quarter of the 2007 fiscal year, Cano Petroleum's capital plan was on-target. Of $40.9 million in planned expenditures, about $10.5 million had been invested in the company's fields. While no expenditures had been made on the Rich Valley and Pantwist fields, $6.4 million had been invested in the Desdemona field, where ten Barnett Shale wells had been drilled to capitalize on the new discovery there. Following Desdemona were investments in Davenport ($1.5 million), Panhandle ($1.1 million), Corsicana ($1.0 million), and Nowata ($0.5 million).

In April Cano Petroleum announced it had acquired properties situated on 20,000 acres in New Mexico's Roosevelt and Chavez counties for $7 million in cash and 404,204 shares of stock. The deal gave the company roughly 12 million barrels of additional proved oil reserves, about 11 million of which were still undeveloped.

Midway through 2007, Cano Petroleum's legal entanglement related to the Texas Panhandle wildfires was finally resolved when the 100th District Court in Carson County, Texas, dismissed the case on June 21. Cano Petroleum was not found responsible for negligence and the plaintiffs' attempt to terminate oil and gas leases with the company were unsuccessful.

During the later years of the first decade of the 2000s, Cano Petroleum operated in a climate where global oil production was near its peak. In the September 2007 issue of *US Business Review,* Jeff Johnson shared his views on the future in an article by Alan Dorich, commenting: "As a society and a human race, we had better figure out for the next generation where fuel is going to come from. Unfortunately, here in America, we're addicted to it [oil]. We're going to have problems if we don't figure out another source for fuels. … We need to squeeze out every barrel we can, from every place on Earth. Every barrel we produce here in America is one less barrel we need to worry about in the Middle East."

At the end of its 2007 fiscal year, Cano Petroleum reported that its proved oil and gas reserves had reached the equivalent of 66.7 million barrels. This was a 47 percent increase from the previous year, when reserves were the equivalent of 45.4 million barrels. Following capital spending of more than $51 million in 2007, the company earmarked $60 million for its 2008 capital budget, the majority of which was slated for its Desdemona Barnett ($21.9 million), Panhandle ($20.3 million), and Cato field ($10.0 million) operations.

Late in the 2007 calendar year, Cano Petroleum announced that a research alliance the company had formed with the University of Texas at Austin's Center for Petroleum and Geosystems Engineering was producing results. In October the company revealed that researchers from the university had provided the company with findings regarding potentially new EOR efforts at its Desdemona, Davenport, Panhandle, and Nowata fields.

In November, Cano Petroleum generated $25 million from the private placement of its common stock. At the same time, the company increased its capital budget by $21 million, with $11 million earmarked for its Cato field in New Mexico, and $10 million for its Panhandle field. These developments preceded an agreement for an additional $25 million in financing in early 2008.

Moving forward, Cano Petroleum seemed to be on strong footing as the company's prior investments began to show results. Importantly, Cano Petroleum had resources to continue expanding and improving its operations.

Paul R. Greenland

PRINCIPAL SUBSIDIARIES

Cano Petro of New Mexico Inc.; Ladder Companies Inc.; Pantwist LLC; Square One Energy Inc.; W.O. Energy of Nevada Inc.

PRINCIPAL COMPETITORS

Credo Petroleum Corp.; Newfield Exploration Co.; Noble Energy Inc.

FURTHER READING

"American Stock Exchange Lists Common Stock of Cano Petroleum Inc.," *PR Newswire,* May 9, 2005.

"Cano Petroleum Begins Trading on OTC Bulletin Board Under Symbol CAOP," *Business Wire,* June 4, 2004.

"Cano Petroleum CEO Responds to Lawsuit from Texas Panhandle Landowner on March Fires; Panhandle Production at 95% of Normal Operation," *Business Wire,* April 18, 2006.

"Cano Petroleum Closes $55 Million Acquisition of WO Energy & $115 Million Financing Facility: Boosts Production 200%, Proved Reserves Grow 700%," *Business Wire,* November 30, 2005.

Dorich, Alan, "Cano Creates Value: Cano Petroleum Has Focused Its Efforts on Recovering Oil in the United States and Reducing the Nation's Reliance on Foreign Sources," *US Business Review,* September 2007.

"Enhanced Recovery; Cano Petroleum Sees Huge Potential for Domestic Enhanced Oil Recovery," *American Oil & Gas Reporter,* February 2006.

Caribou Coffee Company, Inc.

3900 Lakebreeze Avenue North
Brooklyn Center, Minnesota 55429
U.S.A.
Telephone: (763) 592-2200
Toll Free: (888) 227-4268
Fax: (763) 592-2300
Web site: http://www.cariboucoffee.com

Public Company
Incorporated: 1992
Employees: 6,616
Sales: $256.8 million (2007)
Stock Exchanges: NASDAQ
Ticker Symbol: CBOU
NAICS: 722213 Snack and Nonalcoholic Beverage Bars

■ ■ ■

Caribou Coffee Company, Inc., ranks second among company-owned and operated gourmet coffeehouse chains in the United States, in terms of number of coffeehouses operated. However, it remains a fraction of the size of the market's dominant player, Seattle-based Starbucks Corporation. The smaller chain of coffeehouses maintains a lead in its home base of Minnesota but has yet to find comparable success outside the state. Caribou Coffee has partnered with well-known national brands in coffee-related products in order to gain broader name recognition and has reevaluated its coffeehouse expansion strategy.

FIRST YEARS: 1992–93

The Caribou story begins, as legend has it, with an Alaskan wilderness vacation. Kimberly and John Puckett were inspired during the trip to do something larger with their lives and consequently formulated an idea for a business of their own.

The Pucketts, both graduates of Dartmouth College's school of business, gained experience in finance and marketing prior to striking out on their own. Kim worked for General Mills, Dunkin' Donuts, and the Chase Manhattan Bank, and John served as a consultant with Bain & Company and as an investment banker for Merrill Lynch Capital Markets where he specialized in mergers, acquisitions, and leveraged buyouts.

The Pucketts, onetime regulars at the Coffee Connection, a small Boston chain, spent about a year researching the coffeehouse concept and looking for ways to improve on it. "What really interested us in coffee was, at the time, it was just booming in Boston, same thing that's happening in Minneapolis [now]," John Puckett said in a January 1994 *Twin Cities Business Monthly* article by Allison Campbell.

The pair moved to Minneapolis in the summer of 1992, following a six-month analysis of potential markets. In addition to possessing positive demographics, the region was a known commodity: the home turf of Kim Puckett. Family, social, and school connections paved their way into the investment community and allowed the Pucketts to open their first coffeehouse that December.

In general, the gourmet coffee business was on an upswing. While overall U.S. coffee consumption had

COMPANY PERSPECTIVES

Here at Caribou Coffee, we believe this to be true: that if passion, hard work and excellence go into an endeavor, the outcome will be a quality experience, and therefore rewarding.

In 1990, during an adventure through the Alaskan wilderness, our founders journeyed to the top of Sable Mountain. After a strenuous climb, they reached the summit and were rewarded with a sensational view: the boundless mountains, a clear blue sky, and a herd of caribou thundering through the valley. That was truly the "aha" moment.

The breathtaking panoramic view became the entrepreneurial vision for Caribou Coffee—a company that believes excellence is a product of hard work, and that life is too short for anything else. This vision serves as a guide as we strive to create a special experience for you here at Caribou coffee.

fallen during the 1960s, 1970s, and 1980s, the decline took the biggest bite out of the mass-produced ground variety of coffee sold in supermarkets. High gross profit margins on individual cups of specialty coffees, plus good return on investment, and relatively low start-up costs, drew scores of entrepreneurs such as the Pucketts to the business.

In the Twin Cities, the Pucketts' first shop, located in the affluent suburb of Edina, joined other coffee vendors on the scene. They ranged from eclectic neighborhood hangouts with such names as Muddy Waters to locally owned microroaster/coffee shops such as Dunn Bros. Coffee Co. and franchise operations including Chicago-based Gloria Jean's Coffee Beans. On a larger scale, Folgers, Kraft General Foods, and Nestlé, entered the market with their own gourmet grinds, and the Seattle-based Starbucks coffeehouse chain went public in a push to become a national chain. The specialty coffee industry's annual sales were about $780 million in 1993.

BREWING UP A STORM: 1994–95

The Pucketts opened their second shop in the robust Uptown area of Minneapolis. Site selection was utmost on their minds. A key ingredient for the success of the coffee shops was location, and the couple was determined to lock in good sites before Starbucks arrived on the scene.

Four Caribou Coffee shops marketed espresso drinks, baked goods, coffee beans, and branded merchandise as a new round of financing was put in motion in September 1993. Two earlier rounds netted $600,000, but in their third the company received commitments for $3 million, more than double the target figure of $1.2 million. Opening costs for a Caribou Coffee shop ranged from $175,000 to $200,000. In a short time, the company established itself as a top player in the Twin Cities market.

Unlike other locally based competitors Dunn Bros. and Kafte Inc., Caribou Coffee purchased rather than roasted its own beans, choosing instead to concentrate on service and quality control. The mystery shopper was one technique used to ensure good customer service: loyal customers trained to critique their Caribou experience regularly visited the shops. Kim, who was in charge of personnel, received the historically low score when she filled in for an ailing employee, according to the Campbell article.

While the Pucketts strived for product and customer service consistency from store to store, they also wanted each location to reflect the personality of the neighborhood. "All ours do now," said John Puckett in *Twin Cities Business Monthly.* "That's how we'll compete with what I'm sure will be ultra-deep pockets that come into this business, as the big chain companies see the growth." Neighborhood locations, preferably in older buildings, staffed by people with an affinity to the community, helped create a unique feel at each location, according to Campbell.

As Kim managed the personnel aspects of the stores, John tended to coffee quality, real estate acquisition, and finances. A fourth self-managed private placement brought in $7.3 million in the spring of 1994. Some of the new capital was earmarked for expansion into a new market: Atlanta.

Bringing ten stores into operation in a relatively short period gave the couple ample learning opportunities. For example, they discovered downtown Minneapolis shops pulled in morning customers but slacked off over the rest of the day, thus proving to be poorer performers than the neighborhood shops. To facilitate growth the company made some internal adjustments, including the establishment of a central roasting facility and the hiring of a chief financial officer.

As expected, Starbucks came on the scene and opened shops in downtown Minneapolis in March 1994, providing competition for Caribou but also up-

KEY DATES

1992: Kimberly and John Puckett open their first coffeehouse in Minneapolis.
1994: Self-managed private placements continue to fund growth.
1995: First institutional money flows into Caribou.
1996: Regional chain gains notice with new Alaskan lodge concept.
1997: Investors push for overhaul of operations.
1999: McDonald's executive takes charge.
2000: Caribou comes under new majority ownership.
2003: Drive for growth prompts another change in leadership.
2005: Coffeehouse chain goes public.

ping interest in specialty coffee. Kafte closed its Minneapolis locations a few months later, claiming competition among the larger players had inflated real estate prices for choice sites. Owner Joe Anderson, who established his first shop in 1985, also said in a November 1995 *Minneapolis/St. Paul CityBusiness* article that Caribou Coffee had cornered the market on investment dollars as well.

The Pucketts continued to seek opportunities that would strengthen their position in the market. In September 1994, Caribou Coffee entered into a joint agreement with Byerly's Inc. for shops in or adjacent to four of the upscale supermarkets; competitor Starbucks had similar arrangements with independent supermarkets in Seattle and Chicago. In addition to serving beverages to Byerly's shoppers, Caribou shelved branded coffee beans and merchandise. Caribou had other synergistic relationships with retailers, including bagel shops and bookstores.

Twenty-one Caribou Coffee shops pulled in a total of $6.45 million in sales in 1994, according to an April 1996 *Corporate Report Minnesota* article by Lee Schafer. The investment community, eager to send up the next Starbucks, continued to pump money into Caribou Coffee. The enterprise also drew interest, Schafer surmised in an earlier article, because of the caliber of investors on board, such as John Puckett's uncle Dr. Thomas F. Frist, founder of Hospital Corporation of America, and asset manager James R. Jundt, who was well-known on Wall Street. A round of funding in 1995 brought in about $18 million including the first institutional dollars. Oak Investment Partners of Newport, Connecticut, contributed $3.5 million.

ADJUSTING THE BREW: 1996–97

A new look helped earn Caribou Coffee a spot on the 1996 "Hot Concepts!" list compiled by *Nation's Restaurant News*. An Alaskan lodge format replaced the slick urban look Caribou Coffee had cultivated. The change differentiated Caribou from Starbucks and brought the concept more in line with the experience that originally inspired Kim and John Puckett's enterprise. The Alaskan lodge concept, showcased in Caribou's larger shops, featured rough wood and stone decor, comfortable seating, cozy fireplaces, and live music for evening patrons. A running caribou continued to dominate the company's logo, and the Pucketts' Alaskan photo hung in each store along with a request for outdoor vacation shots of customers wearing Caribou Coffee T-shirts.

On average, beverages pulled in 60 percent of revenue, food 20 percent, coffee beans 15 percent, and merchandise 5 percent. Total sales reached $15.46 million in 1995, but the developing company continued to lose money.

By May 1996, the Pucketts' grand adventure had spun off 58 units, including four Detroit-area Coffee Exchange stores acquired and converted to the Caribou Coffee format, but repeated rounds of financing had diluted their ownership to less than 20 percent. Board member James Jundt, who personally invested $1.65 million, held more than 10 percent of the company. Representatives of three venture capital firms, including Oak Investment Partners, also sat on the board.

The influx of funds from the investment firms put pressure on the Pucketts to reach the 100-store mark and take the company public, as had Starbucks at that watershed. However, internal changes such as executive management turnover (the head of store operations and the chief financial officer departed) and the revamping of the concept slowed the growth rate. Predictions that the last round of funding would bring Caribou to the 100-store mark by the end of 1996 failed to pan out, and some investors expressed concerns regarding the Pucketts' ability to manage a larger company, reported Schafer.

Twenty-five store openings pushed the count to 89 by the beginning of 1997. In May, Jay Willoughby, a 24-year veteran of chain restaurant management, joined Caribou as president and partner. Willoughby previously headed the 1,000-plus Boston Market chain and PepsiCo restaurant ventures. Willoughby took command of all operations. Kim Puckett, as chair of the board, concentrated on corporate culture and communications, and John Puckett, as CEO, focused on raising funds.

Caribou's 89 units, located in the Twin Cities, Atlanta, Detroit, Chicago, North Carolina, and Ohio, placed the company in the number two spot among all U.S. company-owned coffeehouses. Market leader Starbucks owned and operated 1,140 stores and San Francisco-based Pasqua Inc.'s held third place with 55. Two franchise operations, Gloria Jean's and Coffee Beanery, held the number two and three spots, respectively, behind Starbucks, when considering all U.S. coffeehouses.

Estimated to be the nation's fifth largest coffee shop chain, Caribou Coffee ranked among the top 20 percent in the country among any business when it came to raising private funds. "Caribou might not have achieved that ranking if things had gone more smoothly," wrote Terry Fiedler for the *Star Tribune* in June 1997. "Because the company didn't have its cups in a row, it enlisted existing private investors for another round of financing—$12 million—this year instead of selling shares to the public." Caribou did finally top the 100-store mark in 1997, and total sales were about $40 million.

A deal with Delta Airlines in early 1998 promised the company some welcome exposure. Most of the Atlanta-based carrier's domestic flights would offer Caribou brand coffee. The coffee company had a strong presence in the region: Caribou operated 18 Atlanta stores, second in number to the Twin Cities. Starbucks coffee had been aboard United Airlines flights since 1996, part of a growing trend in the airline industry to offer brand-name products.

The sheer number of tasting opportunities afforded by the airline deal outweighed anticipated sales gains: only about $4 million but for an estimated 60 million cups of coffee. Caribou Coffee sold just ten million cups in its stores on an annual basis but based on gross profit margins of up to 80 percent the stores earned the lion's share of revenues. Direct-mail sales also got a boost when Caribou gained access to Delta's preferred customer list.

Another opportunity to build recognition as a national brand came by way of an agreement with Target stores. Caribou began test marketing bags of coffee beans in 20 Target stores across the country in July 1998 and then in all Target stores during the holiday season.

PUSHING TOWARD THE PEAK: 1999

Caribou ads hit the airwaves for the first time in February 1999, beginning in the Atlanta area. Nationally recognized Twin Cities-based ad agency Carmichael Lynch handled the radio campaign which was slated for other major Caribou markets in the spring. Caribou used its "Life is short: Stay awake for it," slogan from print, outdoor, and direct-mail ads in conjunction with slice of life scenarios.

The $3 billion gourmet coffee market steamed along but remained highly fragmented as the century wound down. Meanwhile, Caribou continued to position itself for the move from a regional to a national chain. Willoughby worked to create internal stability capable of supporting the leap. He brought the business to profitability for the first time by strengthening existing markets and working to retain and satisfy employees. Growth scheduled for 1999 was to be funded internally, but Willoughby had his eye toward that long-promised public offering as a vehicle to move Caribou to the next level.

A new CEO came aboard in July 1999 to lead the charge. Don Dempsey, head of McDonald's China, was enticed by a 5 percent ownership stake to come back stateside. The Pucketts held 15 percent of the company with an additional 15 percent controlled by Puckett family members and close friends.

"Dempsey first spurned Caribou's offer last year, criticizing the company's losses, overexpansion and lack of discipline. But since then, Caribou has cleaned up its operations under a former PepsiCo executive, Jay Willoughby, who was hired two years ago and help put the company in the black," Jill J. Barshay recounted in a July 1999 *Star Tribune* article. Willoughby retained his posts of president and chief operations officer. The coffeehouse chain brought in more than $75 million in revenues for the year.

FOUNDERS STEP ASIDE: 2000

The Pucketts exited board and management roles in late 2000. Unable to raise additional funds from existing investors, Caribou Coffee turned to Atlanta-based Crescent Capital. The U.S. investment arm of a Bahrain-based investment bank, Crescent purchased a majority stake in the midwestern company for an estimated $75 million. The $200 million-asset firm kept Dempsey in place as CEO. The Pucketts, money manager Jim Jundt, and some other original individual investors retained some ownership of the company, according to the *Star Tribune*.

Crescent Capital increased its holdings in Caribou Coffee in 2001, and also faced some unanticipated challenges. In the days, weeks, and months following the September 11 terrorist attacks on the United States, people of Middle Eastern descent and those with ties to Islamic countries came under close scrutiny.

Inflammatory statements by an adviser to First Islamic Investment Bank of Bahrain and subsequent rumors regarding Caribou Coffee touched off a boycott of the chain within some Jewish communities. Conversely, comments by Starbucks Coffee's CEO prompted a boycott of that chain by some Arabs, Jon Tevlin reported for the *Star Tribune.* Michael J. Coles inherited the problem when he accepted the CEO post in June 2003.

Coles, cofounder of the successful chain Great American Cookie Co., had less than stellar results when he tried to add gourmet coffee. "What I knew about coffee then was enough to go into the eye of a sewing needle," Coles said in the *Atlanta Journal-Constitution* in June 2003. "I know so much more now." Coles, who first came on as interim CEO following Dempsey's departure in early 2003, faced some industry-related challenges as well. Coffee consumption was falling, while the number of retailers with premium coffee offerings was rising.

Dempsey had differed with the owners about the rate of growth. He maintained that adding 50 stores a year, versus a more aggressive 100 stores, was best for the company. Coles planned to open up to 75 sites, in 2004, and as many as 100, in 2005.

Caribou Coffee dominated its home market and had a significant presence in locales it entered ahead of Starbucks. However, since going public in the early 1990s, Starbucks had adeptly snapped up choice high traffic locations elsewhere. Caribou Coffee countered by bringing in new real estate experts to help compete for locations, John Reinan reported in a January 2004 *Star Tribune* article.

In other moves to drive growth, Caribou Coffee established a commercial division to capitalize on coffee-related opportunities with businesses such as restaurants and grocery stores. Caribou Coffee also had coffee shops within corporate settings including Best Buy, General Mills, and West Publishing. Franchising was also in the works, both domestically and internationally.

The Arab world's rich and ancient tradition of the coffeehouse made it a tempting location for gourmet coffee retailers to expand. Starbucks began selling specialty coffee in Kuwait City in 1999. The enterprise drew investors with the promised high margins, but net profits varied greatly depending on operating costs and the price of coffee beans, according to the *Financial Times.* Caribou planned to enter the region through franchised operations, despite increased regional instability and a significant decline in global public sentiment toward the United States since the invasion of Iraq.

"I am not worried about anti-American sentiment at all. Survey upon survey has proven that the Middle East is against U.S. policy but not against U.S. brands or culture," Bachir Mihoubi, vice-president of global franchising, told the *Financial Times.* "For the Arabs, it is all about the experience, the cleanliness, the service, the American brand." Crescent Capital, established by affluent Middle Easterners in 1997, held 87 percent of the company.

AN IPO: 2005 AND BEYOND

The 330-plus coffeehouse chain set the terms of its initial public offering (IPO) in September 2005. The existing shareholders were expected to retain about 72 percent of the company after the sale. Net proceeds would be used to retire debt, fund expansion, and support general corporate needs. Initially, Caribou Coffee's market capitalization would be about $270 million. Starbucks' capitalization, by comparison, was more than $18 billion, according to Susan Feyder of the *Star Tribune.*

Shares, which opened at $15.51, dropped to $11.35 by the end of day two. The fall continued into October. Growth and a positive coffeehouse climate drove the timing of the Caribou Coffee IPO. Yet investors were put off by the coffeehouse chain's history of poor returns and limited national name recognition.

Also at issue were possible limitations placed on some aspects of the business by the Islamic principles followed by Arcapita Bank (formerly First Islamic Investment Bank). "For example, the principles don't allow the company to engage in derivative transactions, which some have speculated could hurt Caribou's ability to hedge coffee prices," Terry Fiedler explained in the *Star Tribune.* "Coles, however, said that the company buys coffee contracts 12 months out, so price fluctuations are not a big factor for the business."

Arcapita also had significant holdings in Duluth, Minnesota, aircraft maker Cirrus Industries; Church's Chicken stores; and specialty retailer Loehmann's. In another side note, the bank's home of Bahrain served as base to the U.S. Navy's Fifth Fleet.

Caribou Coffee shares dropped 21.6 percent with news of losses for 2005. Analysts had predicted a slight profit. At year-end, the company's stock price received a positive jolt, in conjunction with the announcement of a deal with Coca-Cola North America. The pair planned to enter the ready-to-drink iced-coffee market dominated by a Starbucks and PepsiCo partnership.

Caribou Coffee had previously engaged in other alliances to increase brand awareness, including one with Kemps for ice cream and another with Generals Mills for snack bars. A deal with Keurig Incorporated would put Caribou Coffee in single-cup servings.

Coles added free wireless Internet, emphasized customer service, maintained an inviting store atmosphere, offered high-quality coffee, and doubled the number of Caribou Coffee locations. Nevertheless, Starbucks continued to be the king of convenience: a big draw for busy consumers. In November 2007, Coles stepped aside as CEO and chairman but continued to serve on the board. President and COO Rosalyn Mallet, a food and hospitality veteran who joined Caribou Coffee in March, took on the added position of interim CEO.

The company's operating margin was negative 4 percent versus a plus 10 percent for Starbucks, according to the *Star Tribune*. Robert W. Baird & Co. analyst David Tarantino said of Coles: "There was a lot of top-line related expansion that came under his leadership, but the market is still waiting to see the profitability from that."

The company posted a net loss for 2007. Weakened consumer spending did nothing to help Caribou Coffee's comparable store sales. By March 2008, its stock was trading below book value.

Franchise fees, royalties, and sales to commercial customers and franchisees produced significant gains but were only a small part of overall revenue, according to the *Star Tribune*. Underperforming stores were being axed and the company focused on maintaining its strongest regions, primarily Minnesota and areas of Illinois and Michigan.

Kathleen Peippo

PRINCIPAL COMPETITORS

Dunkin' Donuts, Inc.; Dunn Bros Coffee Franchising, Inc.; Starbucks Corporation; McDonald's Corporation; Kraft Foods Inc.; Nestlé Inc.; The Procter & Gamble Company.

FURTHER READING

Barshay, Jill J., "Caribou Coffee Hires CEO from McDonald's," *Star Tribune* (Minneapolis), July 21, 1999, p. 1D.

Campbell, Allison, "Good As the Last Cup," *Twin Cities Business Monthly,* January 1994, pp. 32–36.

Carideo, Tony, "All Eyes on Piper Capital Fixed-Income Fund Losses," *Star Tribune* (Minneapolis), April 23, 1994, p. 3D.

———, "Rothmeier, 46, Suing Noel Rahn on Charge of Age Discrimination," *Star Tribune* (Minneapolis), September 28, 1993, p. 1D.

Cummins, H. J., "WHO'S the BOSS?" *Star Tribune* (Minneapolis), December 16, 2006, p. 1D.

Davoudi, Salamander, "Coffeehouses Defy Anti-US Sentiment: Case Study Caribou," *Financial Times* (London), June 16, 2004, p. 34.

De Young, Dirk, "Caribou Coffee Gets Nice Perk—Test Roll-out in Target Stores," *Minneapolis/St. Paul CityBusiness,* November 20, 1998, pp. 1, 44.

Feyder, Susan, "Caribou Coffee Sets Terms for Its IPO," *Star Tribune* (Minneapolis), September 7, 2005, p. 2D.

Fiedler, Terry, "Caribou Off to Bitter Start," *Star Tribune* (Minneapolis), October 14, 2005, p. 1D.

———, "Minneapolis-Based Caribou Coffee to Fly with Delta," *Star Tribune* (Minneapolis), January 8, 1998.

———, "Riding Herd on Caribou," *Star Tribune* (Minneapolis), June 22, 1997.

Finke, Gail Deibler, "An American Coffeehouse," *Visual Merchandising and Store Design,* November 1996.

Harper, Roseanne, "Caribou Coffee Bars Set to Bubble Up at Most Lunds Units," *Supermarket News,* January 19, 1998, pp. 27, 31.

Huber, Tim, "Caribou Sips $12M in Venture Financing," *Minneapolis/St. Paul CityBusiness,* May 9, 1997, pp. 1, 36.

"Industry Veteran Jay Willoughby Is Joining Caribou," *Star Tribune* (Minneapolis), May 3, 1997, p. 1D.

Kempner, Matt, "Caribou Strives to Become 'No. 1 in Experience,'" *Atlanta Journal-Constitution,* June 3, 2007, p. C1.

Khermouch, Gerry, "Caribou Goes Mellow in New Pitch," *Brandweek,* February 15, 1999, p. 9.

Kleiman, Carol, "Management Diversity in Caribou Brew," *Chicago Tribune,* October 5, 2004, p. 2.

Lee, Thomas, "Caribou Stock Is Roasted After Company Predicts Loss, *Star Tribune* (Minneapolis), January 12, 2006, p. 1D.

Maler, Kevin, "Caribou Drinks in $18M," *Minneapolis/St. Paul CityBusiness,* November 10, 1995, p. 10.

———, "Kafte Is Casualty in Local Coffee War," *Minneapolis/St. Paul CityBusiness,* June 17, 1994, p. 9.

Marcotty, Josephine, "Brewing Success," *Star Tribune* (Minneapolis), July 9, 1993, p. 1D.

McCartney, Jim, "The Buzz on Caribou Coffee," *St. Paul Pioneer Press,* March 14, 1999.

McKinney, Matt, "Caribou Stock: Half Full or Half Empty?" *Star Tribune* (Minneapolis), March 9, 2008, p. 2D.

———, "Caribou's CEO Isn't Saying Why He Resigned," *Star Tribune* (Minneapolis), November 14, 2007, p. 1D.

———, "CEO Leaves a Sagging Caribou," *Star Tribune* (Minneapolis), November 13, 2007, p. 1D.

"NRN Names Eight to '96 Hot Concepts! Roster," *Nation's Restaurant News,* April 15, 1996, pp. 1, 82.

Peterson, Susan E., "Caffeine Combo," *Star Tribune* (Minneapolis), December 1, 2006, p. 1D.

Reinan, John, "Ready to Lock Horns,"*Star Tribune* (Minneapolis), January 26, 2004, p. 1D.

St. Anthony, Neal, "Building a Coffee Empire, Take Two," *Star Tribune* (Minneapolis), January 26, 2004, p. 1D.

———, "Caribou Must Pay Supplier $900,000; Bakery Contract Was Breached, Jury Says," *Star Tribune* (Minneapolis), March 23, 2000, p. 1D.

———, "Venture Firm Buys Caribou," *Star Tribune* (Minneapolis), December 9, 2000, p. 1D.

Schafer, Lee, "Caribou Runs with New York Banker," *Corporate Report Minnesota,* April 1995, p. 83.

———, "Coffee Clutch," *Corporate Report Minnesota,* August 1996, pp. 36–43.

Schmeltzer, John, "Caribou Grinds Away at Rumor," *Knight-Ridder/Tribune News Service,* July 8, 2004.

Shah, Allie, and Chris Havens, "I-35W Bridge Collapse: The Aftermath," *Star Tribune* (Minneapolis), August 3, 2007, p. 6A.

Stafford, Leon, "Cookie Jar to Coffee Cup: Java 'Nut' Hopes to Lead Caribou on Path of Market Leader Starbucks," *Atlanta Journal-Constitution,* June 18, 2003, p. D1.

Tevlin, John, "Caribou Severs Ties with Islamic Advisor," *Star Tribune* (Minneapolis), July 4, 2002, p. 1B.

Walkup, Carolyn, "Caribou Coffee: Taking the Coffeehouse 'On the Road,'" *Nation's Restaurant News,* May 20, 1996, pp. 56, 58.

———, "Drive-Thru Java Craze Hits the Ground Running, Heads East," *Nation's Restaurant News,* May 12, 1997, p. 6.

Walsh, Paul, "CFO Leaves As Caribou Reports Tepid Sales," *Star Tribune* (Minneapolis), January 12, 2008, p. 1D.

Waters, Jennifer, "Caribou Mugs It Up with Byerly's," *Minneapolis/St. Paul CityBusiness,* September 23, 1994, p. 2.

Woodward, Curt, "Coffee Wars Brew New Drink Choices," *Journal-Gazette* (Fort Wayne, Ind.), January 21, 2007, p. 3H.

Carrizo Oil & Gas, Inc.

1000 Louisiana Street, Suite 1500
Houston, Texas 77002-5018
U.S.A.
Telephone: (713) 328-1000
Fax: (713) 328-1035
Web site: http://www.carrizo.com

Public Company
Incorporated: 1993
Employees: 75
Sales: $125.8 million (2007)
Stock Exchanges: NASDAQ
Ticker Symbol: CRZO
NAICS: 211111 Crude Petroleum and Natural Gas Extraction

■ ■ ■

Carrizo Oil & Gas, Inc., is a Houston, Texas-based independent oil and natural gas exploration, development, and exploitation company. The bulk of the company's operations are conducted in the Barnett Shale region of north Texas and the Miocene, Wilcox, Frio, and Vicksburg onshore trends located in Texas and Louisiana. In addition, Carrizo has interests in the Rocky Mountains and the North Sea of the United Kingdom. What has been the key to the company's success is its extensive 3-D seismic data, covering more than 10,000 square miles, and expertise in analyzing the data to find pockets of untapped oil and natural gas previously neglected in the licenses the company holds.

INCORPORATION BY FORMER SHELL OIL EXECUTIVES

Carrizo Oil & Gas, Inc., was incorporated in Texas in late 1993 by former Shell Oil Company executives and investors to take advantage of 3-D seismic data to exploit proven but mature natural gas and oil properties in the Miocene, Wilcox, Frio, and Vicksburg trends. Heading the group was S. P. "Chip" Johnson IV, who served as chief executive. A graduate of the University of Colorado with a degree in mechanical engineering, Johnson became a registered petroleum engineer and spent 15 years at Shell, holding a number of positions, including manager of planning and finance, and manager of development engineering. Joining him as CFO at Carrizo was Frank A. Wotjek, another industry veteran. Paul B. Loyd Jr. was also a founder and served as president for the first two months. At the time he was also CEO and chairman of Reading & Bates Corporation and the former CEO of Chiles-Alexander International, Inc. Another founding investor was Steven A. Webster, who had previously founded Falcon Drilling Company and also served as CEO of R&B Falcon Corporation.

Initially, Carrizo concentrated on acquiring producing properties but soon changed course, looking to scout for drilling opportunities using 3-D seismic data. The use of 3-D seismic technology at the time had been solely the province of the large exploration companies, those that could not only afford to pay for the information but had the specialists who could interpret the data to find unexploited reserves of oil and natural gas. Because of its seasoned leadership, Carrizo possessed the knowledge and when the costs of 3-D data began to fall

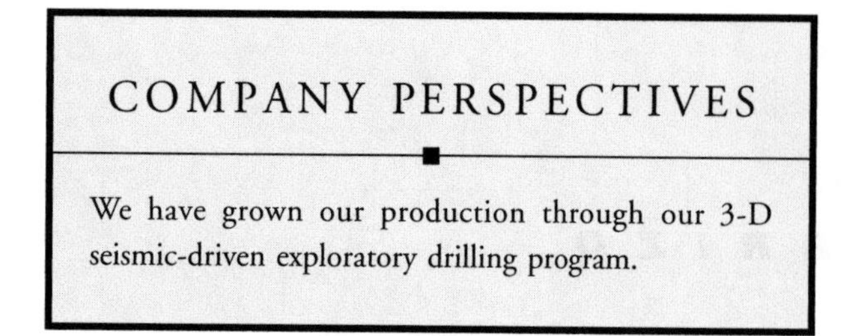

COMPANY PERSPECTIVES

We have grown our production through our 3-D seismic-driven exploratory drilling program.

the company was quick in 1995 to acquire a sizable library of information covering the Texas-Louisiana onshore trends it had targeted, providing a head start in some regions that many in the industry had assumed had been tapped out.

DRILLING BEGINS: 1996

After determining some prospects using the 3-D data, Carrizo began drilling them in 1996. To help in the effort, George F. Canjar was hired to head exploration activities and was later named president of exploration development. A Colorado School of Mines graduate, Canjar was a colleague of Johnson at Shell Oil, where he spent 15 years. All told, 20 wells were dug in 1996, leading to a significant increase in revenues, which more than doubled, from $2.43 million in 1995 to nearly $5.2 million in 1996. Moreover, Carrizo turned profitable, netting $1.1 million after losing $467,000 the previous year. The company's aggressive drilling program carried into 1997 when after five months Carrizo drilled as many wells as it had in all of 1996.

The company took advantage of its momentum, as well as a good marketplace, by conducting an initial public offering (IPO) of stock in the summer of 1997 that netted $28.1 million. Most of the money was used to pay down its revolving credit line and repay loans to directors and officers, but $8.4 million was also set aside for capital expenditures. Revenues increased to $8.71 million in 1997, leading to operating income of $2.43 million and a modest net profit after deferred income tax was applied. Carrizo also strengthened its executive team in 1997 with the addition of Kendall A. Trahan, who became vice-president of land to head the company's land activities. A certified professional landman, Trahan was another seasoned industry veteran, with stints at Arco Oil & Gas Company and Vastar Resources, Inc.

TOUGH MARKET: 1998

The year 1998 proved to be a tough patch for both Carrizo and the oil and gas industry due to lower commodity prices that had an adverse effect on the capital markets. As a result, the company was unable to take advantage of some prospects and revenues fell to $7.86 million and the company posted a net loss of $19.33 million. On the positive side, Carrizo received 14 3-D surveys covering 695 square miles in south Texas and Louisiana in 1998 that led to the identification of nearly 300 possible drilling candidates.

Because oil and gas prices began to pick up in mid-1999, Carrizo was able to overcome a lack of capital to drill exploratory wells by tapping into the resources of major shareholders and outside partners. Revenues increased to $10.2 million and the company returned to profitability, netting $1.7 million. More importantly, these successful new wells allowed Carrizo to secure new capital from investors, led by Chase Capital Partners, which brought an infusion of an estimated $30 million. Carrizo was able to retire some preferred shares held by Enron Corp., restructure its bank debt, and develop plans for a more aggressive drilling program in the new century.

Carrizo enjoyed a banner year in 2000. The company drilled 39 wells, 24 of which were successful. Revenues soared to $26.8 million and net income to nearly $12 million. Another 60 new potential drill sites were also determined, bringing the number of prospects to 250, and 438 square miles of 3-D seismic data was acquired during the year to provide the company's geoscientists with more material from which to develop further drilling candidates. Also in September 2000 Carrizo received a majority stake in Houston-based Michael Petroleum Corp. as a finder's fee. A year later the asset was cashed in for about $5.5 million.

Falling gas prices in 2001 trimmed Carrizo's momentum in 2001, but the company still enjoyed a very successful year. It posted an 80 percent success rate on the 25 wells it drilled, which included some important new discoveries. Revenues were essentially flat for the year, totaling $26.2 million, and net income dipped to $9.5 million. The pipeline of potential drill sites still numbered 250, boding well for the future, and Carrizo achieved some diversity in its portfolio by acquiring 50 percent of the working interests in 107,000 mineral acres, coalbed methane, held by Rocky Mountain Gas Inc. for a $7.5 million promissory note.

BARNETT SHALE: 2003

Carrizo's performance reached a plateau in 2002, with revenues increasing to $26.8 million while net income fell to $4.8 million. Although low gas prices hurt the balance sheet, the company took heart in a 34 percent increase in production levels and a sizable replacement of its reserves. Carrizo also purchased 2,174 square miles of 3-D seismic data to bolster its position for future

KEY DATES

1993: Carrizo is founded.
1995: Company begins acquiring 3-D seismic data.
1997: Initial public offering of stock is completed.
2003: Carrizo becomes involved in Barnett Shale play.
2004: Secondary stock offering nets $23.5 million.

growth. The "program was working well," Johnson told *Oil & Gas Journal* in a 2005 profile, but touting a deep database of seismic information was not easy for a public company to sell to investors "because things aren't very predictive, and sometimes you have ups and downs in production." Johnson added, "What we needed was a resource play, a gas play that was very predictable that could be a nice steady growth, which we then could put the onshore Gulf Coast higher-potential discoveries on top of." What Carrizo found was the Barnett Shale field in North Texas, which offered a great deal of promise because of new technologies. Improved fracturing methods freed up pools of oil and natural gas, and horizontal drilling techniques provided access to bring the commodities to the surface. In 2003 Carrizo acquired 7,500 net acres in the region, including 23 producing wells and 150 possible drilling sites.

Also during the year, Carrizo acquired development licenses in the U.K. sector of the North Sea, including 200,000 acres in productive areas. The plan for these assets was to partner with larger companies which would finance drilling activity. Although they were speculative plays, Carrizo stood to garner an attractive return with little investment. In another development in 2003 Carrizo contributed its coalbed methane properties in the Rocky Mountains to a joint venture called Pinnacle Resources, which had $30 million in backing from a private equity investor. In 2003 Pinnacle drilled 124 wells, while Carrizo drilled 39, achieving an 87 percent success rate. With natural gas prices riding higher, Carrizo was able to grow revenues to $38.5 million in 2003 and post earnings of $7.2 million.

Carrizo completed a secondary stock offering in early 2004, netting $23.5 million for the company, which paid down debt and earmarked the rest of the proceeds for the drilling budget and an effort to retain larger interests in some of its drilling prospects. The company's ability to take advantage of its 3-D data was again borne out in 2004 when 32 of the 38 wells drilled in the onshore Gulf Coast area were successful, a 92 percent success rate. In the Barnett Shale location, all 33 wells were successful. With high oil and natural gas prices, Carrizo was able to post record revenues of $51.4 million in 2004, resulting in net income of $10.5 million.

Drilling costs and acquisition costs increased in 2005. Although Carrizo bid on several properties it failed to win any of them, but fortunately the company, unlike many of its rivals, was well stocked with drilling prospects after a decade of assembling seismic data and securing licenses ahead of the crowd. Drilling costs were up 10 percent, but that did little to hamper Carrizo in 2005, when it recorded oil and natural gas revenues of $78.1 million and net income of $10.6 million.

CONTINUING WITH RECORD RESULTS: 2006

The Barnett Shale field played an increasingly important role for Carrizo. After drilling 37 gross and 22 net wells in 2005, the company drilled 46 gross and 34 net wells in 2006. Moreover, about 70 percent of all reserves came from Barnett. The Gulf Coast area also produced record results for Carrizo in 2006, when 16 out of 19 wells drilled during the year were successful. Record production was matched in 2006 with record revenues, approaching $83 million, and record earnings of $18.2 million.

Carrizo began receiving production from nine new wells in the Barnett Shale field in May 2007. The company also received favorable news from its North Sea interests, with two major discoveries announced in the Huntington Prospect in June 2007. Overall, it was another year of record production for Carrizo. With the high price of oil and natural gas, the company was able to increase revenues to $125.8 million, resulting in net income of $15.5 million.

High times for Carrizo continued in the first quarter of 2008. Production was almost double that of the same period in 2007 and revenues were 137 percent higher. The company looked to take advantage of its position to again tap the equity markets. In February 2008, 2.3 million shares at $54.50 per share were put on the block, and in May, $325 million worth of Convertible Senior Notes were offered to investors.

Ed Dinger

PRINCIPAL SUBSIDIARIES

CCBM, Inc.; Pinnacle Gas Resources, Inc.

PRINCIPAL COMPETITORS

Abraxas Petroleum Corporation; Brigham Exploration Company; Newfield Exploration Company.

FURTHER READING

"Carrizo Oil and Gas Inc.," *Oil & Gas Investor,* November 1997, p. 80.

"Carrizo Oil and Gas Inc.," *Oil & Gas Investor,* September 2000, p. 4.

"Carrizo Oil and Gas Inc.," *Oil & Gas Investor,* August 2005, p. 28.

Fletcher, Sam, "Carrizo Blends Predictability and Potential," *Oil & Gas Journal,* October 24, 2005, p. 34.

Oberweis, Jim, "The Hardy Boys (Companies That Survived Slump)," *Forbes,* April 7, 2008, p. 114.

Perin, Monica, "Carrizo Oil & Gas Lays IPO Plans to Finance Increases in Exploration," *Houston Business Journal,* June 23, 1998.

White, John, "The Shale Shaker," *Oil & Gas Investor,* January 2006, p. 3.

Catholic Order of Foresters

355 Shuman Boulevard
P.O. Box 3012
Naperville, Illinois 60566-7012
U.S.A.
Telephone: (630) 983-4900
Toll Free: (800) 552-0145
Fax: (630) 983-4057
Web site: http://www.catholicforester.com

Nonprofit Company
Incorporated: 1883 as Illinois Catholic Order of Foresters
Employees: 380
Total Assets: $618.79 million (2007)
NAICS: 524210 Insurance Agencies and Brokerages

■ ■ ■

Catholic Order of Foresters (COF) is a nonprofit fraternal insurance organization offering term, whole life, and annuity insurance plans. Each COF member is eligible for the societies' fraternal benefits, which include scholarships and educational awards, newborn and orphan benefits, and tuition assistance for Catholic school students and public school students attending Catholic religious education programs. The organization operates through "courts," or branch locations, that sponsor social, educational, religious, and benevolent activities, such as raising money for school, parish, community, and humanitarian needs. COF operates 400 courts in 31 states and the District of Columbia, serving more than 140,000 members.

THE EARLY YEARS: 1883–1920

During the latter part of the 19th century, the United States was still recovering from the Civil War and the financial panics of the 1870s. Railroads had connected the Eastern states with the Western states, which were rapidly being populated by people taking advantage of liberal homestead laws. Impoverished immigrants from Europe were streaming into this country; many were settling in large cities such as Chicago, where common problems and hardships bound them in mutual dependence. Rich with dreams but poor in financial resources, these immigrants were devastated when death struck. The time was ripe for the establishment of fraternal benefit societies that operated for the mutual benefit of their members by providing insurance coverage and a structure to involve members in charitable, educational, patriotic, and, very often, religious activities within their own communities.

In 1883, when Chicago was celebrating its half-century mark, Irish immigrant Thomas Taylor set about realizing his dream of founding a Catholic benevolent society. Accompanied by two Jesuit priests of Chicago's Holy Family Parish, Taylor presented his plan for "Fraternalism in Action" to 42 men gathered in the parish hall. Each man paid dues of $1 to become a charter member of the society being proposed. According to Julius A. Coller's *A Century of Fraternalism,* seven of these pioneer members applied to the state of Illinois for a charter to establish an association for "the promotion of fraternity, unity, and true Christian charity; the establishment of a fund for the relief of the sick and the distressed members" and of a widow-and-orphans'

COMPANY PERSPECTIVES

As a fraternal benefit society, the Catholic Order of Foresters is committed to planting the seeds of community and caring by offering valuable benefits that provide a solid base of lifetime financial stability to our members. The word fraternal refers to brotherhood and friendship—and that's what Catholic Order of Foresters is all about. We're people helping people, bonding together for mutual support, loving and serving God by giving of our physical, financial and spiritual resources to make a difference.

benefit fund for the surviving dependents of a deceased parent.

Upon receipt of certification in 1883, Illinois Catholic Order of Foresters was launched on the insurance world. Seventy-four members established Holy Family Court Number One; in a relatively short time other courts (branches) sprang up in Chicago and throughout Illinois. When a court was organized in Milwaukee in 1887, the Order dropped the word *Illinois* from its name. COF opened in many other states and grouped them into State Courts bearing the name of each state. In 1888 COF received a charter to open a court in Canada.

COF had expanded rapidly. By the end of the century the Order had 79,895 members. Initially, dues consisted of a per-capita assessment collected upon the death of a Forester. This system of replenishing the treasury, however, soon became cumbersome for the expanding business of the Order. In 1896 a graded-assessment system was adopted: each Forester was assessed a fixed monthly payment (determined by his age at the time of entry) that would remain the same throughout his lifetime. To maintain the Order's financial stability, a reserve fund was established in 1899. Between May 13, 1883, and January 1, 1901, COF disbursed $3.5 million to beneficiaries of deceased Foresters. Although no provision had been made for payment of insurance if death occurred because of war or any related incident, during the last three months of 1918 COF paid out $1.1 million in death claims, an amount that included $354,250 of war claims.

PEAK, DECLINE, AND REGROUPING: 1921–33

Catholic Order of Foresters continued its phenomenal growth: membership peaked at 163,248 in 1921. As early as 1905 there had been heated discussions about the need to readjust assessment rates but no action had been taken. In 1922, however, at the insistence of the Illinois Insurance Department, delegates to a special COF session voted to upgrade insurance rates to keep the society financially sound. They adopted the 4 percent American Experience Mortality Table for all Foresters (as of their attained age) but allowed exceptions for members enrolled under the National Fraternal Congress Rates; for other members over 61 years of age, a maximum rate of $4.80 per thousand was established. Bitter reaction to this change of rates had an adverse effect on membership. Although the majority of Foresters remained committed to the organization, many others surrendered their insurance policies; some members remained in the society but took no part in its activities; and still others stayed on but were harshly critical of almost everyone and everything. By year-end 1923, COF membership was down to 127,461.

Dedicated officers and members journeyed from court to court and meeting to meeting to explain the change of rates and to emphasize the advantages of remaining Foresters. At first COF had been open only to men but in 1928 it offered boys a $600 "juvenile policy" carrying a fixed annual fee of $3 from birth to age 16. The Order weathered the time of discontent and, although membership losses continued for several years, paid all claims in full and continued its fraternal activities, including large donations, such as $50,000 for the Shrine of the Immaculate Conception in Washington, D.C., and $25,000 toward the building of the Seminary of St. Mary of the Lake, an institution for training Catholic priests.

THE ORDER TURNS 50

At its golden anniversary in 1933, Catholic Order of Foresters had 135,000 members in courts located in 28 states and in all the provinces of Canada. The Order had set up a Juvenile Division for Boy Rangers, the name given to boys insured from birth to age 16. To men between the ages of 16 and 60, the Order offered eight forms of insurance policies ranging from term- and whole-life insurance to endowments. After three years, all policies acquired a reserve value. COF also provided total disability benefits, premium loan privileges, old-age cash surrender benefits, and paid-up insurance benefits. The maximum insurance any Forester could carry was raised to $10,000. From 1923 to 1933, annual dividends remained at approximately 8⅓ percent of premiums. Dating from the founding of the Order in 1883, a total of $52.2 million was paid to widows, orphans, and other beneficiaries. The initial treasury of $42 grew to invested reserves of over $28

KEY DATES

1883: Illinois Catholic Order of Foresters, comprising 42 members, is established.
1887: Illinois Catholic Order of Foresters shortens its name to Catholic Order of Foresters (COF).
1928: COF opens membership to males under the age of 16.
1952: Membership is opened to females.
1967: COF begins awarding scholarships to Forester children.
1971: COF ends its involvement in Canada.
1984: New headquarters are established in Naperville, Illinois.
2004: COF merges with National Fraternal Society of the Deaf.
2005: For the fifth consecutive year, COF's membership increases.
2006: COF merges with Catholic Knights of Ohio.
2008: COF celebrates its 125th anniversary.

million, an amount more than 25 percent above the society's total insurance liability.

THE WAR YEARS

For everyone, the years after the Great Depression were a time of long, uphill struggle against unemployment. Financial insecurity and social unrest ran rampant. Historian Coller wrote that "this was an era when Fraternalism was sorely tried and not found wanting" and quoted Past High Chief Ranger Richard T. Tobin as saying that during these adverse circumstances "the practice of Fraternalism brought brilliance where there was darkness." When the Foresters met for the 1940 Convention, harmony again reigned in the Order and drives to increase membership were underway.

Then came the 1941 attack on Pearl Harbor and the Foresters added another dimension to their activities: promotion of investment in War Savings Bonds and Stamps. By November 1945 a total of $10.55 million in Victory Bonds had been purchased by the COF High Court, its employees, and other COF members. The U.S. Treasury Department sent a special representative to present an official commendation to COF employees and a Silver Award, the Treasury's highest award for volunteer patriotic service, to Thomas H. Cannon and Thomas R. Heaney for their outstanding leadership in the bond program.

At the end of all hostilities a total of 13 million American men and women had served in the war; 11,185 of these people were Foresters. As stated above, during World War I the Order had not included a war clause in its Constitution. Nonetheless, COF had paid war-related claims amounting to $362,000 by implementing a patriotic assessment of $1 per member. During World War II the Order was in such excellent financial position that it paid war claims from the Reserve Fund. Also, COF donated $25,000 to the Chicago archdiocesan seminary, St. Mary of the Lake in Mundelein.

FIRST FEMALE MEMBERS: 1952

An amendment to the COF Constitution in 1952 gave the Foresters a new look: membership was opened to women and girls. Two new all-women courts were formed but, for the most part, women and girls joined existing courts and held important offices not only in these subordinate courts but also in the State Courts. Another innovation occurred in 1965 when Catholic Central Union, a Czech ethnic fraternal society organized in 1877, merged its entire membership into Catholic Order of Foresters, thereby adding 3,383 adults and 850 youths as members. The adopted members received all the Forester benefits, including cash dividends on insurance certificates.

Another significant event was the 1967 establishment of the COF Scholarship Program. From then on, the Order awarded annual scholarships of $2,000 ($500 for each of four years at college) to Forester children. The total amount of the scholarships was increased to $4,000 in 1980 and then to $5,000 in 1996. A committee of educators, basing their evaluation on grades and extracurricular activities, selected the winners of the scholarships.

AN EXIT FROM CANADA

Review of the COF operation in Canada brought about another change. When the 1922 rate adjustment became effective, Canadian membership, which had peaked at 22,156, immediately began to decline. Attrition continued steadily; by 1973 total Canadian membership had fallen to 3,118. Operating in Canada had always been expensive because Canadian law required that a Canadian COF agent maintain complete membership files in that country. Since the COF Home Office in the United States had to keep all records for the entire

Order, Canadian requirements necessitated duplication of all Canadian files.

Furthermore, in 1964 Canada made a radical revision of its tax laws, removing all tax exemptions from fraternal organizations. In 1971 COF, with no net gain from its Canadian business, had to pay taxes amounting to $20,532. Separation from the Canadian operation became financially necessary. To take care of its remaining Canadian members, COF made reinsurance arrangements for them with the Artisan Life Insurance Cooperative, a Montreal-based Catholic fraternal society similar to Catholic Order of Foresters. This transfer ended COF's function as an international society.

During the first years of its existence COF moved its home office several times, going from a single room in 1883 to office suites in various Chicago office buildings until it relocated in its own four-story building in 1952. By 1975 the ever increasing cost of transportation became a serious problem for COF employees of the Home Office; furthermore, the COF building was soon to be dwarfed by skyscrapers. In 1981 the Order accepted an offer for its property (now worth 4½ times book value), stipulated right of occupancy for a flexible period not to exceed four years, and began to look for a new location.

As COF's first 100 years came to a close, the Order was competing with banks, savings and loan organizations, money-market funds, retail and mail-order companies, to name but a few rivals for dollars. Nevertheless, the Order's financial results for 1982 broke all records. Assets totaled $178.2 million; dividends paid to members reached an all-time high of $7.3 million meaning Foresters received 55 cents for every dollar they had put into the Order; and there was a net surplus of $32.1 million. Insurance in force, one of the criteria by which the size of a life insurance company is measured, totaled $627.65 million.

NURTURING FRATERNALISM INTO THE 21ST CENTURY

COF bought land and built its new headquarters in Naperville, Illinois, a site about 30 miles west of Chicago. The 1984 relocation came after 100 years of COF's founding, explosive expansion, and decline and resurgence of membership. Throughout those years the Order never reneged on its commitment to the financial security of its members, or the support of their spiritual growth and involvement in civic, social, educational, and humanitarian needs.

Over the years, COF gradually increased its operating efficiency by taking advantage of developing technologies; for instance, COF implemented a computerized membership database, direct billing, and the mailing of premium notices. However, social changes—for example, the weakening of family units as a result of divorce and of having both parents in the work force—left less time for supporting the kind of local-court activities defined by an earlier generation.

The Order responded by strengthening its Youth Courts through the offer of financial incentives, such as college scholarships, educational awards, and federal student bank loans to young adults who became members with the purchase of a low-cost whole-life insurance policy. COF also set up new programs, such as recognition dinners and awards to members involved in civic, social, athletic, and humanitarian activities. Membership in the Adult Courts was stimulated by updating and expanding existing programs and by reaching out with new financial products, such as loans to churches and other Catholic organizations; a Matching Funds Program for Catholic and community causes; a Newborn Infant Benefit; an Orphan Benefit Program; and an Accelerated Death Benefit Rider for eligible COF policies. This rider allowed members diagnosed with a terminal illness to receive advance payments of up to 75 percent of their insurance proceeds.

COF ensured continuing financial stability by adhering to a strategic business plan based on conservative investments and business practices. To absorb fluctuations in market values of investments, insurance companies, unlike other businesses, were required to keep a reserve for asset valuation and another reserve for interest maintenance. At year-end 1997, the COF total reserved for this requirement was $6.05 million, a sum that, when added to surplus funds, amounted to an adjusted surplus of $51.08 million and indicated a new level of financial strength for the Order. Total COF assets amounted to $381.57 million and insurance in force stood at $1.97 billion.

MEMBERSHIP AND MERGERS

As COF entered the 21st century and neared its 125th anniversary, increasing its membership remained high on the organization's list of priorities. A perennial struggle, increasing enrollment ensured the longevity of the organization, providing the fuel that powered its advancement. Toward that end, COF recorded encouraging success, increasing its membership during the first five years of the decade. The organization attracted new members by introducing new financial products. In 2005, for instance, COF introduced "Forester Guardian Level Term" and "Forester Guardian Plus Return of Premium," which were credited for attracting new policy holders and for driving an 18 percent increase in sales during the year.

COF also attracted new members by joining forces with other fraternal organizations. In 2004, COF merged with the National Fraternal Society of the Deaf. In late 2006, national convention delegates approved the merger between COF and Catholic Knights of Ohio.

One source of distress during the period involved the potential loss of COF's tax-exempt status. In January 2005, a Congressional Joint Committee on Taxation recommended abolishing fraternal benefit societies' federal tax-exempt status. COF, fearing a crippling blow to its way of operating, joined a national campaign led by the National Fraternal Congress of America, the chief advocate for the country's 76 fraternal societies, to lobby against changing the law. The effort succeeded, but COF's High Chief Ranger, David E. Huber, was not about to celebrate. "I must caution, however," Huber wrote in COF's 2005 annual report, "although we won the battle, the war goes on ... at some point, we will again need to justify our tax exempt status."

COF TURNS 125

For the first time in five years, COF's membership declined in 2006. Enrollment dropped by nearly 2,000 during the year, but the organization responded by recording a banner 2007. Membership increased by nearly 4,000 during the year, lifting net insurance sales back above the $200 million mark. On that cheerful note, COF celebrated its 125th anniversary in 2008, able to look back on a legacy of benevolence and financial resiliency. Since the last time the organization had celebrated a major anniversary (its centennial in 1983), it had returned $248 million in dividends to members, an average of nearly $10 million for the previous 25 years. The figures reflected astute management, ensuring that COF would continue to aid members and their communities for decades to come.

Gloria A. Lemieux
Updated, Jeffrey L. Covell

PRINCIPAL COMPETITORS

Woodmen of the World Life Insurance Society; Modern Woodmen of America; Nationwide Mutual Insurance Company.

FURTHER READING

Cannon, Thomas H., "Confidence Reborn," *Catholic Forester,* April 1933, p. 3.

Ciesla, Robert, "Sharing Our Successes: Building on Our Foundation," *Catholic Forester,* March/April, 1997, pp. 6–9.

"COF Cash Dividend Equal to 8 1/3% of Annual Premium," *Catholic Forester,* June 1933, cover page and p. 9.

Coller, Julius A., II, *A Century of Fraternalism,* Chicago: c. 1984, pp. 4–6, 44.

"Did You Know That COF Has a War Memorial in Washington, D.C.?" *Catholic Forester,* January/February 1983, pp. 22–25.

Gorski, John A., "1982 Annual Report," *Catholic Forester,* March/April 1983, pp. 4–5.

Heaney, Thomas R., "A Half Century of Catholic Forestry," *Catholic Forester,* May 1933, p. 2.

Huber, David E., "Yesterday - Today - Tomorrow," *Catholic Forester,* Spring 2007, pp. 16–17.

Wimmer, Don H., "Modernizing Fraternal Accounting," *Catholic Forester,* July 1933, p. 9.

ČEZ a. s.

Duhova 2/1444
Prague, 140 53 4
Czech Republic
Telephone: (+420 211) 041 111
Fax: (+420 211) 042 001
Web site: http://www.cez.cz

Public Company
Incorporated: 1992
Employees: 31,161
Sales: CZK 174.56 billion ($9.39 billion) (2007)
Stock Exchanges: Warsaw
NAICS: 221122 Electric Power Distribution

■ ■ ■

ČEZ, a. s. is the Czech Republic's leading electrical power producer and distributor, accounting for more than 60 percent of the national market. ČEZ (the full name stands for Czech Energy Works) has also positioned itself as the largest electrical power group in the Central and Eastern European markets, with operations in Bulgaria, Poland, and Romania, as well as a partnership agreement with Hungarian counterpart MOL. ČEZ operates more than 55 power plants. The group's network includes 32 hydroelectric power stations, 15 coal-based plants, and two nuclear facilities. The company has begun investing in renewable energy sources, operating a wind farm and one solar power plant. Altogether, ČEZ boasts plant capacity of more than 15,000 megawatts (MW). In 2007, the company distributed more than 80 terrawatts. This strong production capacity has also enabled ČEZ to position itself as the second largest electricity exporter in Europe, behind France's EdF. Created from the state-run electricity monopoly under the former Czechoslovakia, ČEZ remains held at more than 60 percent by the Czech government. The company is considered the largest corporation in the Central European region, with a market capitalization of more than CZK 738 billion ($36 billion). The company is listed on the Warsaw Stock Exchange and is led by Chairman and CEO Martin Roman. In 2007, ČEZ posted total revenues of CZK 174.56 billion ($9.39 billion).

FORMATION WITH THE CZECHOSLOVAKIA BREAKUP IN 1992

Even prior to the breakup of Czechoslovakia, the country operated two distinct electrical power entities, the Czech Energy Works (ČEZ), and Slovak Power Enterprises. ČEZ was further divided into eight distinct regional companies, each overseeing power generation and distribution in their individual markets. The Czech region benefited from strong resources, with plentiful coal deposits and a river system spanning most of the region. As a result, the country developed a vast network of both coal-fired and hydroelectric power plants.

Among the earliest of the country's hydroelectric plants was one at Cenkova Pila, a small facility capable of generating 0.1 MW. Larger plants were constructed in the years leading up to World War II, including a 13.9 MW facility built in Vrané in 1936. Following the war, as the country fell under the domination of the

COMPANY PERSPECTIVES

As a powerful, dependable, and stable partner, we are ready to help you realize your power supply plans and concepts.

Soviet Union, the country experienced a surge in both electrical generating capacity, and demand for electricity. Among the first large-scale plants was a 48 MW facility built in Štěchovice in 1948. In the mid-1950s, ČEZ completed construction of a hydroelectric works at Slapy, capable of generating 144 MW. By the late 1970s, the country boasted a 450 MW facility at Dalešice.

While hydroelectric power represented a renewable energy source, the country's primary fuel source remained coal, and specifically brown coal from the Upper Silesia region. The postwar era witnessed the construction of the bulk of ČEZ's coal-fired plants, including a complex built at Dvůr Králové nad Labem in 1955. The use of coal permitted the construction of larger plants. The group's construction efforts took off into the 1970s, starting with the development of the Mělník II facility, which grew into a total capacity of more than 220 MW. A series of plants built in Počerady during that decade added a further 1,000 MW to the company's electrical power generation capacity. By 2000, ČEZ's coal-based electricity production would top 7,000 MW, and account for 70 percent of its total power generation capacity. In comparison, the company's total hydroelectric power capacity barely cleared 800 MW by then.

ČEZ began a move toward nuclear power generation in the 1970s. Work on the group's first nuclear facility began in 1974 at Dukovany. That project was soon put on hold, however, following the decision to abandon the original project design. Construction on the new design started in 1978, and the first phase was finally completed in 1985. The company commissioned the fourth and final reactor at the Dukovany plant in 1987. Total power output at the Dukovany site reached 1,700 MW.

By then, ČEZ had been at work on a second nuclear facility, in Temelín. Design and engineering began on that plant in 1979, and was largely completed in 1985. In 1987, the company launched construction of the site's first operating units. Yet the disaster in Chernobyl, and the collapse of the Soviet regime at the end of the 1980s, cast a pall on the Temelín project. In the end, the project was scaled back, then put on hold. Over the next decade, however, the facility was modernized. By 2000, ČEZ had commissioned the site's two reactors, with a total output of 2,000 MW.

PRIVATIZATION IN 1992

The collapse of the Soviet Union in the meantime had led to the breakup of Czechoslovakia itself. The government of the new Czech Republic restructured its electricity monopoly under the National Property Fund. In the process, a new company was created, ČEZ a. s., as the largest of the country's power generators and distributors.

ČEZ was faced with the daunting task of updating the dilapidated and highly inefficient power grid left over from the Communist era. With over 7,000 kilometers of power lines under its control, the company inherited a nonstandardized system, with different parts of the network operating at different voltage rates. At the same time, the political upheavals during the 1980s meant that little money had been spent in maintaining and upgrading the country's electrical power network. Consequently, nearly all of the group's plants and equipment were antiquated and in need of repair or replacement.

The Czech government responded to the need to improve the country's infrastructure by launching a wide-ranging privatization program. Under this effort, most of the formerly state-owned industries, including ČEZ, were converted into private corporations. This allowed ČEZ to bring in foreign shareholders and the investment capital required to carry out the modernization of its network. The Czech government nonetheless retained more than 60 percent of ČEZ, guaranteeing control over its former monopoly.

ČEZ invested heavily over the next decade, carrying out a network-wide improvement program, spending more than EUR 3.5 billion ($3 billion) on refurbishing its coal-fired plants during the late 1990s. As part of this program, ČEZ also instituted new environmental protection measures, earmarking more than EUR 1.5 billion toward this effort between 1992 and 1998. The group continued its environmental protection into the next decade, ultimately spending more than EUR 7 billion. It could thus claim to have reduced its sulfur dioxide emissions by 92 percent, its carbon dioxide by 77 percent, ash particles by 95 percent, and nitrogen oxide by 50 percent.

In another environment-related effort, ČEZ began investing in renewable energies during the 1990s as well. In 1993, the company completed construction on the Czech Republic's first wind power plant. The model

KEY DATES

1992: ČEZ a. s. is created following breakup of Czechoslovakia.
2003: ČEZ merges with five regional electrical power companies, forming ČEZ Group.
2004: First foreign expansion occurs with acquisition of three electricity distributors in western Bulgaria.
2005: Company acquires Romania's Electrica Oltenia.
2006: Company enters Poland, then lists shares on Warsaw Stock Exchange.
2007: ČEZ forms joint venture with Austria's MOL to build gas-fired power plants.
2008: ČEZ announces plans to build up to five new gas-fired plants in the Czech Republic.

plant, which produced just 315 KW, provided the company with an in-field research and development laboratory for its later wind farming efforts. The company later built a full-scale wind power facility at Nový Hrádek, which was commissioned in 2002. That plant produced just 1.6 MW, however, in contrast with its latest generation of coal-fired plants, which boasted capacity of as much as 660 MW.

ČEZ also launched a limited entry into solar power generation in the late 1990s. Starting in 1997, the company built its first solar power facility, located at the Dukovany nuclear power site. Commissioned in 2002, the solar power plant produced just 0.01 MW of power; however, the plant's true purpose was to operate as a research and educational facility.

BECOMING A CENTRAL EUROPEAN LEADER IN THE NEW CENTURY

The Czech government began restructuring its electricity industry in the early 2000s in anticipation of the country's entry into the European Union (EU). As part of that effort, ČEZ merged with several of the country's smaller regional power companies, forming the ČEZ Group, with ČEZ a. s. as its centerpiece, in 2003. In so doing, ČEZ boosted its share of the Czech electrical power market to 73 percent. The Czech government also announced plans to continue ČEZ's privatization. However, that effort was aborted after bids fell short of the government's targets. In the meantime, in accordance with EU rules, the Czech government carried out the "unbundling" of its electric utilities. ČEZ restructured, placing its distribution and generation operations into a separate, independently operating subsidiary.

The failure of its privatization effort led ČEZ to turn the tables, as the company asserted its intention to redevelop into a leading player in the Central European market. Exports became a key part of that strategy, and by the early 2000s the company had begun to export more than 30 percent of its total power generating capacity.

ČEZ prepared to take the next step in 2003, when it earmarked more than EUR 600 million to fund a foreign acquisition drive. The company's first target was its Slovak counterpart, and former sister company, Slovenske Elektrarne (SE). In the end, however, the company's bid proved too cautious, and SE instead was sold to Italy's ENEL.

NEW LEADERSHIP UNDER MARTIN ROMAN

By then, ČEZ had taken on a new chief executive, Martin Roman, after Jaroslav Mil was dismissed by the Czech government, ostensibly for being too independently minded. Then just 34 years old, Roman had been educated in the West and represented a new generation of businessperson in the Czech Republic. Roman's career credentials included the dramatic turnaround of the Skoda automotive group.

Roman led the company on a renewed foreign expansion drive. By July 2004, the company had won its bid for three electricity distribution companies in western Bulgaria, paying nearly EUR 282 million. ČEZ next turned to Romania, where it won the auction to buy that country's Electrica Oltenia in 2005. The addition of that company's customer base helped raise ČEZ's total to 6.8 million, placing it as the eighth largest in Europe.

The continued privatization of the region's electricity sector brought ČEZ a number of new acquisition prospects at mid-decade. By the end of 2006, the company had completed the acquisition of two coal-fired power plants in Poland, Elektrownia Skawina S.A. and Elektrocieplownia Chorzow Sp. z.o.o. (Elcho), adding another 830 MW to the group's total capacity. The company then acquired a black-coal plant in Varna, adding nearly 1,300 MW, raising the group's total capacity past 15,000 MW.

ČEZ made a new move toward full privatization in October 2006, when the company listed its stock on the Warsaw Stock Exchange. The Czech government nonetheless maintained control of the company, with a 60 percent stake. The choice of listing its shares in Poland, meanwhile, underscored the group's intention to position itself as a dominant player in the Central and Eastern European electricity markets.

In 2007, ČEZ entered Bosnia, forming a joint venture with that country's Elektroprivreda to build a new 700 MW power plant and upgrade an existing 300 MW plant, both in Gacko. Later that same year, the company teamed up with Hungary's MOL, forming a joint venture to build gas plants at that company's Bratislava and Szazhalombatta refineries. Under the agreement, ČEZ acquired a 10 percent stake, in part to protect MOL against the takeover ambitions of Austria's OMV.

In May 2008, ČEZ announced its intention to convert more of its domestic generating capacity to low-carbon gas-firing plants, with plans to build as many as five plants in the foreseeable future. Nonetheless, the company remained committed to exploring the expansion of its renewable energy resources, including nuclear power facilities. At the same time, ČEZ expected to continue to consolidate its Central European leadership, announcing its interest in pursuing acquisitions in Albania, Macedonia, Turkey, and elsewhere.

M. L. Cohen

PRINCIPAL SUBSIDIARIES

ČEZ Bulgaria EAD; ČEZ Chorzow B.V.; ČEZ Ciepło Polska sp. z o.o. (Poland); ČEZ Deutschland GmbH; ČEZ Distribuce, a. s.; ČEZ Distribuční služby, s.r.o.; ČEZ ELECTRO BULGARIA AD (67%); ČEZ Energetické služby, s.r.o.; ČEZ FINANCE B.V.; ČEZ Hungary Ltd.; ČEZ Laboratories Bulgaria EOOD; ČEZ MH B.V.; ČEZ Poland Distribution B.V.; ČEZ Polska Sp. z o.o.; ČEZ Romania S.R.L.; ČEZ Silesia B.V.; ČEZ Slovensko, s.r.o.; ČEZ Správa majetku, s.r.o.; ČEZ Trade Bulgaria EAD; ČEZ Trade Polska Sp. z o.o.; ČEZ Trade Romania S.R.L.

PRINCIPAL COMPETITORS

Unipetrol A.S.; E.ON Energie A.S.; Severomoravska energetika A.S.; Prazska energetika A.S.; Severoceska energetika A.S.; E.ON Distribuce A.S.; Dalkia Ceska republika A.S.; Vychodoceska energetika A.S.; Sokolovska uhelna, pravni nastupce, A.S.; Coal Energy A.S.; Prazska teplarenska A.S.; E.ON Ceska republika A.S.

FURTHER READING

Anderson, Robert, "ČEZ Powers Ahead with Central European Expansion," *Financial Times,* February 23, 2006, p. 24.

———, "New Turnaround Man at ČEZ," *Financial Times,* February 25, 2004, p. 20.

Andress, Mark, "ČEZ Has Plans to Be Regional Powerhouse," *Financial Times,* January 6, 2004, p. 26.

"ČEZ and SE Invest EUR 3.5bn in Plants," *Utility Week,* May 25, 2007.

"ČEZ A.S. Seeking to Expand Its Activities in Poland," *Utility Week,* March 9, 2007.

"ČEZ Coals Up," *Utility Week,* May 12, 2006.

"ČEZ Earmarks EUR 1.5bn for Bosnia," *Utility Week,* February 3, 2006, p. 10.

"ČEZ Increases Central Europe Stake," *Utility Week,* September 7, 2007.

"ČEZ Is Likely to Bid for Turkish Mining Company," *Utility Week,* May 23, 2008.

"ČEZ Poised to Double Up in Renewable Capacity," *Utility Week,* April 28, 2006.

"ČEZ Reveals a Plan to Lead in Central Europe," *Utility Week,* March 18, 2005, p. 12.

"ČEZ Takes on Carbon Capture Agenda," *Utility Week,* July 20, 2007.

"ČEZ Unveils Overseas Acquisition War Chest," *Utility Week,* September 26, 2003, p. 12.

D'Amico, Mary Lisbeth, "A State Utility Turns up the Juice," *Business Week,* April 4, 2005, p. 28.

Hawkins, Nigel, "ČEZ (a Profile of the Company)," *Utility Week,* June 13, 2003, p. 29.

China Nepstar Chain Drugstore Ltd.

Xinnengyuan Building, Tower B, 6th Floor
Nanhai Road, Nanshan District
Shenzhen, Guangdong 518054
China
Telephone: (86 755) 2643 3366
Fax: (86 755) 2640 1549
Web site: http://www.nepstar.cn

Public Company
Incorporated: 1995 as Shenzhen Nepstar Medical Co. Ltd.
Employees: 9,096
Sales: $268.0 million (2007)
Stock Exchanges: New York
Ticker Symbol: NPD
NAICS: 446110 Pharmacies and Drug Stores

■ ■ ■

Listed on the New York Stock Exchange, China Nepstar Chain Drugstore Ltd. is the People's Republic of China's largest retail drugstore chain. At the start of 2008 the company owned and operated more than 2,000 stores located in 62 cities. The largest contingency consists of more than 300 stores located in Shenzhen, where the company maintains its headquarters. Merchandise includes about 1,200 prescription drugs, accounting for nearly one-quarter of sales; another, 1,200 over-the-counter drugs, providing about 35 percent of sales; more than 600 nutritional supplements, contributing some 18 percent of sales, and herbal products, less than 3 percent of sales. Another 20 percent of revenues come from other products, including beauty, hair care, skin care, and family care products, as well as packaged snacks, soft drinks, stationery products, cleaning supplies, and seasonal and promotional items. Wall Street giant Goldman Sachs is a major investor. Although a public company, China Nepstar is majority owned by its founder and chairman, Simin Zhang, one of China's richest entrepreneurs.

BIRTH OF NEPSTAR FOUNDER: 1962

Simin Zhang was born in the city of Changchun in China's Jilin Province in 1962. He attended Harbin Institute of Technology, graduating in 1983 with a degree in precision instruments. He found a job at the PRC Space Administration and in 1986 went to work for CITIC Group (China International Trust and Investment Company). CITIC was established in China in 1979 to attract foreign capital as well as introduce advanced technologies and modern business practices to the country. In the late 1980s Zhang was dispatched by CITIC to fast-growing Shenzhen, China, to receive further training, but in 1989 he left the company to form Shenzhen Haiwang Pharmaceutical Corporation. According to *Fortune International,* Zhang started out with a single product "evolved from a hangover cure, based on a traditional medicine made of oyster extract."

A budding entrepreneur, Zhang was not content with just one product, and one company. He built up a slate of over-the-counter products, traditional Chinese medicines, and active pharmaceutical ingredients, and created Neptunus Group as a holding company for his

COMPANY PERSPECTIVES

High quality product offerings, professional service and convenience are among our promises to our customers and the foundation of our drive to be the leader in China's pharmaceutical retailing business.

ventures. It was not surprising that eventually Zhang would want to develop a retail outlet for Neptunus products by establishing a drugstore chain. Moreover, the industry was highly fragmented and regional in China, offering a great deal of promise for a Western-style drugstore chain that could establish a national footprint and perhaps act as a consolidation vehicle. The opportunity was further enhanced by the sheer size of the population, one-fifth of the world's people, and an aging population that would be increasing expenditures on pharmaceutical products.

OPENING OF FIRST STORE: 1996

The first step in building a retail drugstore chain was taken in June 1995 with the creation of Shenzhen Nepstar Medical Co. Ltd. Several months later, in January 1996, the company became the first Chinese member of the National Association of Chain Drug Stores. The first Nepstar store then opened in June of that year in Shenzhen under the name Shenzhen Guiyuan Store. For the next 18 months the chain opened additional stores in Guangdong Province where Shenzhen was located. It was not until late 1998 that the first unit outside the province was opened in Kumming, the capital of Yunnan Province, the first step in breaking out of the regional confines of the Chinese drugstore business. The stores typically ranged in size from 80 to 120 square meters and offered a uniform look and layout. They were brightly lit, opened seven days a week from 8:30 A.M. to 10:30 P.M. They were also the first drugstores in China to offer over-the-counter drugs on open shelves. Other than prescription drugs, all other merchandise was, as in Western stores, easily accessible to customers.

China Nepstar spread along coastal cities and adjoining provinces, opening units as quickly as possible with little regard for profitability at this stage. Starting in the new century, the company began forming subsidiaries to operate the stores on a regional basis. The first of these was Ningbo Nepstar. The following year brought the creation of Dalian Nepstar, Hangzhou Nepstar, Sichuan Nepstar, Shenzhen Nepstar, and Guangzhou Nepstar. In 2002 Shanghai Nepstar was added. Also in 2002 China Nepstar bought out the ten-year franchise in China held by The Medicine Shoppe International, Inc., part of Ohio-based Cardinal Health, Inc., and the largest franchiser of independent community pharmacies in the United States. Medicine Shoppe entered mainland China, focusing on professional drugstores and Western medicines, while Nepstar opted for more of a convenience style for its units to limit direct competition. Another regional operating company, Jiansu Nepstar, was established in 2003.

RESTRUCTURING AND INCORPORATION IN CAYMAN ISLANDS: 2004

China Nepstar underwent a restructuring in 2004 when Zhang formed China Neptunus Drugstore Holding Ltd. in the British Virgin Islands, which in turn incorporated China Nepstar in the Cayman Islands. Later in the year, in October, China Nepstar entered into a $40 million investment agreement with New York-based The Goldman Sachs Group, Inc., that included the purchase of $15 million in redeemable convertible preferred shares in the company and another $10 million a year later.

Investing in China Nepstar was in keeping with Goldman Sach's view of the growing importance of the Chinese economy. In 2003 the firm's economists issued a position paper arguing that the economies of Brazil, Russia, India, and China—the "BRIC" countries, as they were known—had the potential over the next four decades of becoming larger than the world's six most developed countries, provided their governments made decisions supportive of growth and, in the case of China, avoided instability caused by social unrest over the lack of political reform. The idea of the BRIC economies struck a chord with investors, who began to direct their attention to these emerging-market countries.

By the start of 2005 China Nepstar owned and operated 668 stores through its network of regional companies. Three more regional companies were added during the year, albeit one, Shandong Nepstar, was under common control. The others were Quindao Nepstar and Tianjin Nepstar. All told, China Nepstar opened 423 stores in 2005, acquired 47 others (Shandong Nepstar), and closed or relocated another 23, ending the year with 1,115 units. As part of its agreement with Goldman Sachs, China Nepstar remained committed to rapid expansion (while targeting good locations in large cities), as part of a commitment to grow the chain to at least 2,000 units within five years. It also began to pay more attention to improving margins. A new line of private-label products was launched, including over-the-

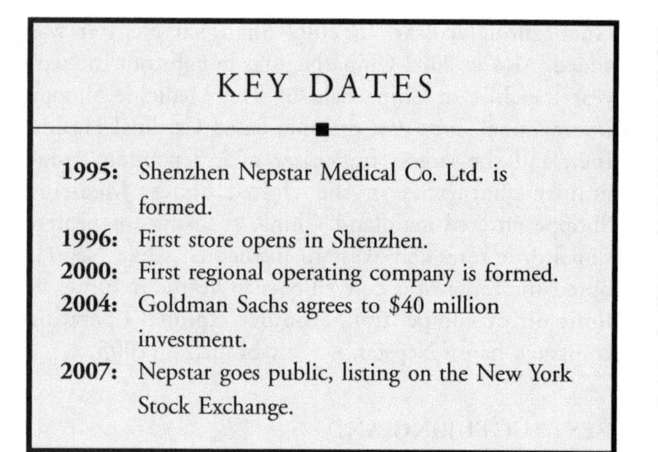

KEY DATES

1995: Shenzhen Nepstar Medical Co. Ltd. is formed.
1996: First store opens in Shenzhen.
2000: First regional operating company is formed.
2004: Goldman Sachs agrees to $40 million investment.
2007: Nepstar goes public, listing on the New York Stock Exchange.

counter drugs and nutritional supplements, and helped improve the balance sheet. While private labels would soon account for about one-fifth of sales, they contributed almost one-third of gross profit. Revenues increased from RMB 843 million in 2004 to RMB 1.3 billion in 2005, while gross profit during this period grew from RMB 223 million to more than RMB 381 million.

NEW CEO: 2005

The strategy of improving operations while maintaining growth continued in 2006. In March, China Nepstar reached an agreement with three Sichuan Province drug makers to produce drugs for the chain, again a move to pad margins. The company also began to emphasize professional training for frontline employees to improve customer service and customer loyalty. To lead China Nepstar into this next stage, a new chief executive officer, Jiannong Qian, had been hired in August 2005. He was a man well versed in Western retailing. After graduating with a degree in economics from Shandong University in 1983 and staying to teach economics for four years, he continued his education in Germany, earning a master's degree in economics from the University of Essen in 1992 and spending another two years in the doctoral program in economics at the University of Duisburg-Essen. In 1994 he became senior manager at Weixing Company Group, and in 1997 moved to Metro AG, one of the largest retailers in the world, operating supermarkets, hypermarkets, and other stores. Qian was manager of the food purchasing department until 2002. He also worked for another German company, Heimwerkermaerkte AG, a home improvement retailer, and just prior to joining China Nepstar, served as vice-general manager of Wumart Stores, Inc., a Chinese chain of supermarkets, hypermarkets, and convenience stores.

In 2006 China Nepstar opened 370 new stores, acquired nine others, and closed or relocated 48, bringing the total number of units at year's end to 1,446. Revenues during the year improved to RMB 1.73 billion and the company posted its first net profit, RMB 13.6 million. Management was talking about opening 10,000 stores in five years and, in order to achieve that ambitious goal, began reorganizing its management structure at the start of 2007. The expansion pace picked up significantly during the year. By June, when China Nepstar celebrated its 12th anniversary, the number of units reached 1,600, but by the end of the year that number would swell to 2,002. None were acquired and 594 were opened from scratch.

COMPLETION OF ADS OFFER: 2007

Before 2007 came to a close, China Nepstar and Goldman Sachs, along with co-underwriter Merrill Lynch & Co., took advantage of the company's momentum to conduct an initial public offering (IPO) of American Depositary Shares (ADS). Each ADS was worth two ordinary shares. When the offering was completed in November 2007, China Nepstar netted $334 million, a better performance than the $250 million the company had expected.

Given the circumstances, investor enthusiasm was understandable. China's population was aging at the same time that per capita income was increasing, leading to a forecast of 18 percent per capita drug spending in the country over the next five years, but China Nepstar was expected to experience even greater results because the government was making an effort to create a divide between prescribers of drugs and providers of drugs. Hence, the traditional system of hospital distribution would give way to pharmacy distribution. To make matters even more favorable, China Nepstar was the only retailer in the country that had been able to negotiate direct purchasing agreements with drug manufacturers and was involved in private-label products. It also paid taxes, unlike hospitals, making the government an interested party in its growth.

China Nepstar shares were listed on the New York Stock Exchange and wasted little time in rising in value by as much as 24 percent on the first day of trading. When the final numbers were tallied in 2007, China Nepstar posted revenues of nearly RMB 2 billion, or about $268 million. Earnings also improved to RMB 148.2 million, or $20.3 million.

According to the prospectus for China Nepstar, $52 million of the IPO proceeds were earmarked for new stores, $27 million to construct a pair of distribution centers, and another $11 million to upgrade the chain's inventory control and information management systems. At the start of 2008, the company announced an ambitious plan to add more than 1,000 new stores during the year, bringing the total to more than 3,000. To help achieve that goal, China Nepstar began aggressively pursuing acquisition opportunities, targeting cities where it already had a presence. In March 2008, the company acquired 18 drugstores in Dongguan City from Dongguan Hui Ren Tang Pharmaceutical Co. Ltd., expanding the number of units in the city to more than 120. Later in the month 68 drugstores were acquired in Ningbo in Zhejiang Province from Ningbo New Century Medical Ltd. After bolstering its existing footprint, China Nepstar was expected to expand into new territories in 2009, including provincial capitals as well as Beijing, the capital of the country and China's second largest city.

Ed Dinger

PRINCIPAL SUBSIDIARIES

Nepstar Commerce; Nepstar Electronics; Nepstar Jinfu Logistics; Nepstar Wisconsin Trading.

PRINCIPAL COMPETITORS

A.S. Watson & Company, Limited; Dairy Farm International Holdings Limited; WuMart Stores, Inc.

FURTHER READING

Beltran, Luisa, "China Nepstar Worth $4B in IPO," *TheDeal.com,* November 12, 2007.

"China Nepstar Buys 68 Stores for 30 million Yuan," *Xinhua Economic News,* March 3, 2008.

"China Nepstar to Open over 1,000 Drug Retail Stores This Year," *China Business News,* January 7, 2008.

"Chinese Pharma Companies Eye Overseas Stock Market," *China Business News,* October 22, 2007.

Dorfman, Brad, "China Nepstar Plans Expansion As Shares Jump," *Reuter News,* November 9, 2007.

Hjelt, Paola, "40 Under 40," *Fortune International,* September 16, 2002.

"Nepstar Expanding Business Through Policy of Acquisitions," *China Business News,* March 3, 2008.

"Nepstar to Set Up 10,000 Stores in 5 Years," *Alestron,* January 19, 2007.

"Sichuan Drug Makers and Nepstar Sign Outsourcing Agreement," *China Business News,* March 29, 2006.

Ctrip.com International Ltd.

90 Fu Quan Road
Shanghai, 200235
China
Telephone: (86 21) 3406 4880
Fax: (86 21) 5426 1600
Web site: http://www.ctrip.com

Public Company
Incorporated: 2006
Employees: 5,500
Sales: $164.38 million (2007)
Stock Exchanges: NASDAQ
Ticker Symbol: CTRP
NAICS: 561510 Travel Agencies

■ ■ ■

Ctrip.com International Ltd. is the largest online travel service in China, with more than 19 million registered users, primarily independent business and leisure travelers. Ctrip customers have access to accommodations at more than 28,000 hotels in 134 countries, and they book more than nine million hotel room nights annually. Ctrip offers airline ticketing for all Chinese airlines and many international airlines with flights originating in China; Ctrip sells more than ten million airline tickets each year. The company offers packages for independent and group travel. Ctrip offers travel services through branch offices in Beijing, Guanzhou, Shenzen, and Hong Kong, and sales offices in 30 cities in China, including partnership and franchise offices. Car rental and limousine services are available in 18 cities. The company's English-language web site offers international customers access to hotels and airline reservations worldwide, as well as in China.

MEETING CHINA'S CHANGING TRAVEL NEEDS

James Jianzhang Liang and Min Fan founded Ctrip in 1999, combining their complementary talents in computer technology and the Chinese travel industry, respectively. Liang's experience included management of the Enterprise Resource Platform division at Oracle China. Fan brought more than 15 years of travel industry experience, and his positions included chief executive officer of Shanghai Travel Service Company and a variety of managerial positions at Shanghai New Asia Hotel Management Company. Their formation of Ctrip consolidated a wide range of travel services into one web site, where customers could easily book hotel and airline reservations.

When business operations at Ctrip began in October, the company offered hotel reservations and airline ticketing. The majority of Ctrip's hotel inventory derived from block reservations obtained for its exclusive use for sale to the public, but the company also accessed hotel rooms on a space-available basis. With funding from foreign investors, such as the Carlyle Group, which purchased $8 million in Series B Preferred Stock in November 2000, Ctrip expanded rapidly. The company added more suppliers, continually broadening its hotel and airline offerings.

One limitation at this time involved the lack of automatic pay systems in China, such as credit cards or

COMPANY PERSPECTIVES

The company's business philosophy focuses upon: *C*ustomer: Customer needs guide Ctrip. *T*eamwork: Ctrip creates a seamless collaborative system between customers and partners. *R*espect: Ctrip treats customers with the utmost respect. *I*ntegrity: Ctrip puts integrity first in its cooperation with its partners. *P*artner: Ctrip pursues win-win cooperation with all its partners.

debit cards. This required customers to purchase tickets in person. Through franchises and partnerships, Ctrip established a network of local offices in 20 cities, so customers could go to Ctrip, its partners, or franchises to pay for and pick up airline tickets. Later, Ctrip introduced door-to-door delivery in 35 cities in China. After booking and paying for their airline tickets, customers in the major cities could request ticket delivery to their homes. Door-to-door delivery overcame the hesitation many customers felt toward electronic tickets; they preferred a regular ticket.

In 2002, Ctrip purchased an air ticketing agency, becoming a full-service travel agency. The company developed packaged trips for independent travelers, providing air transportation, hotel reservations, and airport-to-hotel transportation. The company offered some group travel packages with guided tours, considered the traditional form of travel in China. Primarily, Ctrip focused on providing travel services to independent business and leisure travelers, and services covered both domestic (Chinese) and select international travel destinations.

By the end of 2002, Ctrip reported sales of RMB 100 million ($12.1 million). Hotel commissions accounted for 85 percent of revenues, and most of these derived from three-star, four-star, and five-star hotels. Liang and Fan attributed their success to the technological infrastructure, which eased reservation fulfillment and air ticketing.

PUBLIC FUNDING SUPPORTS EXPANSION

As Ctrip continued to grow, the company attracted more foreign investment to support expansion. In September 2003, the offer of Series C Preferred Stock raised $10 million. Then, on December 9, 2003, Ctrip debuted on the NASDAQ. The initial public offering (IPO) of stock started at $18 per share and nearly doubled to $37.35 before settling at $33.94 at the end of the day. Ctrip planned to apply the proceeds towards working capital, sales and marketing, and acquisitions. Also, Ctrip's private equity partner, the Carlyle Group, raised $75.6 million from the sale of their American Depositary Shares. In June 2004, Ctrip additionally raised funds through a private placement of 6.6 million shares for $54.8 million, to Rakuten, of Japan.

Ctrip continued to grow as discretionary income rose and the Chinese government eased restrictions on travel within and outside of China. Moreover, Ctrip's early entry in serving the growing number of independent travelers in China gave the company a competitive edge. In 2004, hotel commissions increased 80 percent and accounted for 78 percent of total revenue. Revenues from airline tickets increased 210 percent and accounted for 18 percent of sales. Sales from package tours rose 119 percent and accounted for 3 percent of total sales. Overall, revenues at Ctrip reached RMB 333.8 million ($40.3 million), nearly double 2003 revenues. Net income of RMB 133.1 million ($16.1 million) contrasted with 2003's RMB 53.8 million ($6.5 million).

DIVERSIFYING AS TRAVEL SERVICE SUPPLIER

With an established reputation in the Chinese travel market, Ctrip began to diversify its travel offerings. In February 2004, Ctrip formed a partnership with Shanghai Cuiming International to provide a wider range of group tours. Also, Ctrip obtained exclusive rights in mainland China to provide reservations to Disneyland Hong Kong when it opened in the fall of 2005. Ctrip prepared a variety of special-rate packaged trips for independent travelers for sale to customers in the mainland. The Chinese government eased restrictions on independent travel from China to special administrative regions, such as Hong Kong and Macao, which were officially opened on July 1, 2004.

In preparation for future growth, Ctrip began construction on a reservations center in Shanghai, a $20 million project. Existing infrastructure, including bilingual web sites and a 24-hour customer service center, handled 100,000 callers daily. When completed in 2007, the new center would provide 2,000 seats for customer service representatives. The largest call center in Asia, the center would include capacity to add another 3,000 seats.

To expand its share of the Asian market, Ctrip acquired an interest in ezTravel.com.tw in Taiwan. An online service similar to Ctrip, ezTravel.com supplied

KEY DATES

1999: Company is formed.
2000: Foreign investment helps support business development.
2002: Ctrip becomes a full-service travel agency.
2004: Ctrip increases group tour offering for upscale market.
2006: Ctrip launches new hotel reservation system, adding 25,000 hotels worldwide.
2007: Ctrip launches English-language web site.

the Taiwanese market with individual and group travel packages, and hotel reservation and airline ticketing services. Each company would provide local travel services to the customers in the other company's home country.

Ctrip upgraded its technological search capabilities for hotel information and improved its international hotel offerings in 2006. Google applied its bendi.google.com search engine to Ctrip's web site, to enable customers to search hotel-related information rapidly; the system covered 3,000 hotels. In September Ctrip launched a new hotel reservation system as it added 25,000 hotels from outside of China. Through direct contact with hotels or in cooperation with international hotel suppliers, Ctrip offered its customers a centralized place to search for hotel accommodations. With more Chinese traveling abroad, Ctrip offered convenience through its centralized search capabilities.

As the e-commerce travel market in China developed, new technology facilitated its expansion. Ctrip began to accept a new method of payment through China UnionPay's EasyPay system. To use EasyPay, a customer booked an airline ticket, which was then delivered to the customer's home. The customer swiped a bankcard on their home telephone to pay for the ticket. This fixed-line payment system would become available as customers acquired the proper telephone technology. UnionPay considered this method safer than the Internet.

CULTIVATING TRAVEL SERVICES WITH NEW BUSINESS OPERATIONS

Ctrip's development as a travel service matured as the company added new business operations targeted to independent and leisure travel. In December 2006, Ctrip formed Shanghai Ctrip Charming International Travel Service Company. The new agency intended to increase Ctrip's 10 percent share of the high-end tourism market to 50 percent. Hotels offered with these packages were rated with at least three stars. Ctrip also introduced two new transportation services, car rentals and limousine service, in April. The company also began offering business trip management services to large corporations at this time.

Ctrip bolstered its competitiveness with traditional travel agencies in China, which focused on group tourism. In June 2007 Ctrip opened a group tour service in Shanghai and Beijing, for travel to Japan, Australia, and Europe. The service was oriented to high-end travel products, at 10 to 15 percent above average rates from bricks-and-mortar travel agencies. The company introduced three group tours to Europe, available for departure from Chengdu, Shanghai, or Beijing. Ctrip planned to offer the tours from as many as 20 cities.

Ctrip itself faced increasing competition from other online services, such as eLong, as well as hotels which began to focus more on direct and online sales. Through direct sales to customers, hotels sought to sidestep high commission rates charged by Ctrip. Ctrip, however, offered increasingly improved online services. The company introduced a hotel search service using Baidu.com, the largest Internet search engine in the Chinese language. At map.baidu.com, customers linked web sites of 5,000 hotels, obtaining information on hotel accommodations, hotel atmosphere and amenities, as well as videos of many of the hotels.

Despite new competition in the Chinese travel market, Ctrip held 56.3 percent of the market for Chinese online travel services. In contrast, the second largest online travel company, eLong, carried 13.7 percent of the market. Hotel reservations and airline ticketing accounted for 92 percent of sales. The company benefited from a rapid increase in travel outside of China, up 19 percent in 2007. Package tours to Thailand and other Asian countries were popular among Chinese travelers. The Thailand trip included elephant rides and sightseeing to Buddhist temples, as well as air travel and hotel accommodations.

INTERNATIONAL TRAVEL, SPECIAL EVENTS PROVIDING A FOCUS FOR EXPANSION

With the 2008 Summer Olympic Games set to take place in Beijing, Ctrip took steps to leverage its local knowledge to attract business from international travelers. Hence, Ctrip launched an English-language web site in 2007; however, it represented a direct translation from Ctrip's Chinese-language site. The company's strategy involved increasing brand awareness among expatriates in China, then marketing its services in Hong Kong and Macao, before seeking customers in the United States and elsewhere. Also, Ctrip waited for approval for Chinese companies to market travel packages in the United States. In anticipation of higher demand, Ctrip expanded its car leasing business to six major cities, with locations in Shanghai, Hangzhou, Nanjing, Wuxi, Suzhou, and Kunshan.

In May 2008, the company relaunched the web site applying a Western style to the look and language of the site. Content fit the needs of Ctrip's international customer base. Customers benefited from Ctrip's wide array of hotel accommodations as well as locally derived information on places of interest in China.

The Olympic Games promised high returns for hotels in 2008. Premium prices on Beijing hotels indicated high commissions in 2008, as hotel rates increased 400 to 1,000 percent. Ctrip expected further opportunities for business growth during the World Expo Shanghai 2010.

Ctrip's plans for future international expansion involved formation of beneficial local partnerships in order to expand its travel service supply base. The company rejected the idea of expansion through acquisition, despite increased competition from its nearest competing Chinese online travel agency, eLong, which had been acquired by Expedia.com. Also, Ctrip planned to open another call center in Nantong, near Shanghai, adding 7,000 customer service representatives, to the 3,500 employees at its new Shanghai facility.

Mary Tradii

PRINCIPAL SUBSIDIARIES

C-Travel International, Ltd.; Nantong Tongchen Information Technology Co. Ltd.; Shanghai Ctrip Charming International Travel Agency Co. Ltd.; Shanghai Huacheng Southwest Travel Agency Co. Ltd.; Shenzhen Ctrip Travel Agency Co. Ltd.; Nantong Tongchen Information Technology Co. Ltd.

PRINCIPAL COMPETITORS

eLong, Inc.; Hotels.com; Hotwire; Mangocity.com.

FURTHER READING

"Beijing Hotel Room Prices Rise 400–1000 Percent for Olympics," *Xinhua News Agency,* March 7, 2008.

"China UnionPay Partners with Ctrip.com for Fixed-Line Network Payment Service," *China Business News,* September 8, 2006.

"Ctrip Becomes Exclusive Mainland Online Travel Services Provider for Disneyland Hong Kong," *Chain Business News,* July 12, 2005.

"Ctrip Builds Booking Center with USD20mm," *Alestron,* December 19, 2005.

"Ctrip Expands Car Rental Services," *Xinhua Economic News,* March 25, 2008.

"Ctrip Faces Challenges from Direct Sale by Airlines and Hotels," *Xinhua Economic News,* August 27, 2007.

"Ctrip Going Public at NASDAQ," *Alestron,* December 15, 2003.

"Ctrip Initiates Asia's Largest Call Center," *Xinhua Economic News,* June 18, 2007.

"Ctrip into High-End Overseas Tourism Market," *Alestron,* December 11, 2006.

"Ctrip Invests in Taiwan-Base Counterpart," *SinoCast, LLC China IT Watch,* March 15, 2006.

"Ctrip Launches Door-to-Door Delivery in 35 Chinese Cities," *China Business News,* October 27, 2003.

"Ctrip Marches into Traditional Tourism with Cash," *SinoCast, LLC China IT Watch,* August 9, 2007.

"Ctrip Offers Intercity Car Leasing Service in East China," *Alestron,* March 26, 2008.

"Ctrip Taps Outbound Travel Market in SW China," *Xinhua Economic News,* July 5, 2007.

"Ctrip to Relaunch English Website, Target International Market," *China Business News,* March 19, 2008.

"Ctrip.com Announces Entry into Car Rental Business," *China Business News,* April 4, 2007.

"Ctrip.com Goes Abroad," *SinoCast, LLC China IT Watch,* September 27, 2006.

"Ctrip.com International Ltd., an Online Travel Company in China, Established Franchises and Partnerships in 20 Major Cities in China," *Hotel & Motel Management,* July 17, 2000, p. 44.

"Ctrip.com International Rolls Out Business Travel Service," *Alestron,* March 26, 2007.

"Ctrip.com Launches Outbound Group Tour Service in Beijing," *Xinhua Economic News,* June 7, 2007.

"Ctrip.com Named Fan Min New CEO," *Alestron,* January 25, 2006.

"Ctrip.com Starts Hotel Search Services," *Alestron,* October 22, 2007.

"Ctrip.com Teams Up with Google to Upgrade On-line Search for Chinese Hotels," *Xinhua News Agency,* May 9, 2006.

"Ctrip.com to Fight Against Traditional Travel Services," *Alestron,* June 8, 2007.

"Ctrip.com Unveils Q4 and Full-Year Earnings of 2007," *SinoCast, LLC China IT Watch,* February 29, 2008.

"ELong to Sell Super-Low Air Tickets, Challenging Ctrip," *Alestron,* March 5, 2008.

Liu, John, "Ctrip Says Tour Sales May Triple As More Chinese Travel Abroad," *Bloomberg.com,* March 11, 2008, http://www.bloomberg.com/app/news?pid=20670001&refer+asia&sid=apDgvQu5QpJ8.

"Nanhu Travel Agency Challenges Ctrip.com's Monopoly," *Alestron,* May 28, 2007.

"Room at the Inn; Chinese Hotels," *Economist,* January 26, 2008, p. 64US.

Whiteman, Lou, "Bubble-Era Debut for Ctrip.com," *Daily Deal,* December 10, 2003.

Dairy Farm International Holdings Ltd.

7/F Devon House, Taikoo Place
979 King's Road-Quarry Bay
Hong Kong,
Hong Kong
Telephone: (+852) 2299 1888
Fax: (+852) 2299 4888
Web site: http://www.dairyfarmgroup.com

Public Company
Incorporated: 1986
Employees: 69,000
Sales: $6.8 billion (2007)
Stock Exchanges: London Singapore Bermuda
Ticker Symbol: DFI
NAICS: 445110 Supermarkets and Other Grocery (Except Convenience) Stores; 442110 Furniture Stores; 442299 All Other Home Furnishings Stores; 446110 Pharmacies and Drug Stores; 452910 Warehouse Clubs and Superstores; 722110 Full-Service Restaurants

■ ■ ■

Dairy Farm International Holdings Ltd. is one of the largest operators of supermarkets, hypermarkets, and other retail formats in the Asian region. Based in Hong Kong but registered in Bermuda, Dairy Farm's operations span most of the principal Asian markets, including mainland China, Taiwan, Singapore, Vietnam, Malaysia, Indonesia, India, Macau, and Brunei. The company's network includes more than 2,200 retail outlets, which combined to generate total revenues of $6.8 billion in 2007. Dairy Farm's retail formats include supermarket brands Wellcome (Hong Kong, Taiwan, Vietnam); ThreeSixty (Hong Kong); Jasons Marketplace (Singapore, Taiwan, Hong Kong); Giant (Malaysia, Indonesia); Shop N Save (Singapore); Hero (Indonesia); and Foodworld (India). The company's hypermarket offering is focused on the Giant brand, present in Indonesia, Singapore, and Malaysia, while the company operates the Mannings health and beauty store format in Hong Kong, Macau, and China. Dairy Farm also holds the license for operating the 7-Eleven convenience store format throughout much of Asia, including in Hong Kong, southern China, and Singapore. The company also holds the IKEA franchise rights for Hong Kong and Taiwan. Lastly, Dairy Farm owns a 50 percent share of restaurant chain Maxim's, in Hong Kong. Listed on the London stock exchange, with secondary listings in Singapore and Bermuda, Dairy Farm International is itself part of the Jardine Matheson trade group. The company is led by CEO Michael Kok.

BRINGING FRESH MILK TO HONG KONG IN 1886

Although Dairy Farm International grew into one of the Asian region's, and the world's, largest retail groups, the company literally started out as Hong Kong's first dairy farm. In 1886, renowned Scottish physician Patrick Manson led a group of five Hong Kong businessmen in a venture importing a herd of 80 dairy cattle to the British colony. Born in 1844, Manson had traveled to Taiwan to serve as a medical officer for the Chinese Imperial Maritime Customs. Manson developed an

COMPANY PERSPECTIVES

Our goal is to satisfy the appetites of Asian shoppers for wholesome food and quality consumer and durable goods at competitive prices.

expertise in tropical diseases, becoming one of the field's foremost experts.

The creation of Dairy Farm came as part of Manson's effort to improve colonial life in the late 19th century. Milk and dairy products remained scarce in Hong Kong, and imported dairy products were prone to contamination. The farm, located in Pok fu-lam, began breeding its own herds under supervision from British-trained staff. In this way, Manson hoped to ensure a plentiful supply of less expensive milk and dairy products for the colony.

By the early 1890s, the company had succeeded in adapting its herd to the difficult tropical climate. Before long, the company was able to meet the steadily rising demand with increases in its own dairy production. By 1892, Dairy Farm's sales had grown sufficiently to build a cold storage facility in Hong Kong itself. The new icehouse, located in the city's Central District, also enabled the company to begin developing its own import operations, such as butter from Australia starting in 1899. Just five years later, Dairy Farm added the import of frozen meat. The addition of these new products led the company into retail sales, with the opening of its first store at its icehouse.

Retail increasingly became a company focus in the early decades of the 20th century. In 1913, the company launched the first of a series of extensions of the Central District facility, adding a butcher shop and a smoked meat processing room. The site became the company's headquarters as well, and was also expanded to provide accommodations for the company's general manager. Other products and services added by the group during this time were the production of fresh pies, and a storage service for winter clothing.

RETAILING FOCUS IN THE POSTWAR ERA

During World War I, Dairy Farm founded its own ice production plant, with which it began supplying the island's fishing fleet. By 1918, the company had also opened a second retail shop, in Kowloon. Further store openings continued through the 1920s, and by the end of the decade the company boasted six stores in operation. The company had also created a number of subsidiaries, adding operations both on the Chinese mainland and in Macau.

Following the end of the war, however, and after the Communist revolution in mainland China, Dairy Farm's retail store operations had slipped back to just three stores. Nonetheless, the period marked a new era of economic boom as Hong Kong began to establish itself as a major financial center in the Asian region. Into the 1950s, Dairy Farm began to focus its growth on its retailing wing, expanding its range of goods and food products. Dairy Farm's transition to retailing took off especially in the 1960s, following the acquisition of the Wellcome grocery group. The acquisition was particularly significant in that it enabled the company, until then largely focused on the island's English-speaking population, to become a major retailer for the Chinese population as well. By the mid-1970s, Dairy Farm's holdings included 19 supermarkets across Hong Kong and Kowloon.

Dairy Farm, which had gone public some years before, had by then become part of a larger group, when the Jardine Matheson trading group acquired the company in 1972. Dairy Farm was then placed on Jardine's Hongkong Land subsidiary, while continuing to operate autonomously. With backing from its powerful parent, Dairy Farm began a new era of international expansion.

The company first turned toward Australia, acquiring that country's Franklins supermarket group, a chain of 75 discount stores. In 1980, Dairy Farm returned to the Chinese mainland, becoming the first company to enter a joint venture there as part of the Communist government's new reform policies. Dairy Farm accelerated its international expansion through the middle of the 1980s, adding operations in Taiwan, Singapore, and elsewhere in the Asian Pacific.

Dairy Farm's total retail network soon topped 300 stores by 1986. In that year, the company was spun off from Hongkong Land, and instead was listed as an independent company on the Hong Kong stock exchange. As part of its demerger, Dairy Farm took over a 50 percent stake in the Maxim's restaurant chain in Hong Kong. Despite its public offering, Dairy Farm remained part of the Jardine Matheson group, which retained a 78 percent stake into the next century.

INTERNATIONAL RETAIL GIANT IN THE NINETIES

The presence of Jardine Matheson in Dairy Farm's holding played a role in a new company expansion in 1989,

KEY DATES

1886: Patrick Manson leads founding of small dairy farm in Pok-fu-lam, Hong Kong.
1892: Dairy Farm opens cold storage facility in Hong Kong's Central District.
1904: Company opens first retail shop in Central District facility.
1918: Company opens second retail shop in Kowloon.
1964: As part of focus on retailing, Wellcome supermarket group is acquired.
1972: Jardine Matheson acquires Dairy Farm through Hongkong Land subsidiary.
1979: First international expansion occurs with purchase of Australia's Franklin supermarket group.
1986: Dairy Farm lists stock on Hong Kong stock exchange.
1989: Company acquires 7-Eleven franchise from Jardine Matheson, then expands in Spain, England, and New Zealand.
1996: Dairy Farm introduces 7-Eleven franchise to Guangdong Province in China.
2001: Company refocuses operations around Asian markets.
2006: Company opens first store in Vietnam.

when the trading company transferred its franchise for the operation of 7-Eleven convenience stores to Dairy Farm. The acquisition gave Dairy Farm control of nearly 230 7-Elevens throughout Hong Kong.

By then, the company had also entered the United Kingdom, buying a 25 percent stake in the Kwik-Save supermarket network in 1987. The company next targeted Spain, adding control of Simago, a chain of nearly 110 stores in that country. In that same year, Dairy Farm took a major step toward a leadership position in the Australasian region, picking up Woolworths in New Zealand. The acquisition made Dairy Farm one of the top two retailers in that country.

Closer to home, Dairy Farm reached a joint-venture agreement with Nestlé to produce and distribute that company's brand ice cream and other dairy products for China and Hong Kong. Dairy Farm then began expanding its 7-Eleven franchise into other markets, starting in Shenzhen, China, in 1992. The company later expanded the chain throughout southern China, and into Singapore and other Asian markets. Singapore became an especially important market for the country, as the company built up a significant presence there. In 1993, for example, the company bought Cold Storage, which operated a network of 142 stores. The acquisition also formed the springboard for Dairy Farm's entry into Malaysia the following year.

The mid-1990s saw a dramatic expansion of Dairy Farm's international holdings. In China, the company formed a joint venture to develop its supermarket network there. The company also created a joint venture with France's Casino SA to build a network of hypermarkets in Taiwan. That country played an important role in Dairy Farm's international growth plans, as the company sought to expand its operations to more than 200 supermarkets across the island by the end of the decade.

At the same time, the company moved into Indonesia, with an agreement to manage the 11-store chain of Mitra supermarkets for PT Hero, which operated 71 Hero supermarkets. That deal led Dairy Farm to acquire a 32 percent stake in Hero itself in 1998. Similarly, the group formed a technical assistance partnership with the RPG group to develop a chain of supermarkets in India. While most of the group's expansion during this period took place in developing markets, Dairy Farm also tried its luck in Japan, forming a joint venture with that country's Seiyu to open four Wellsave discount stores there.

FOCUS ON ASIA IN THE NEW CENTURY

Dairy Farm expanded into the Malaysian supermarket sector in 1999, buying 90 percent of Giant TMC Bhd, an operator of hypermarkets and supermarkets built by that country's prominent Teng family. By 2000, the company had brought the Giant hypermarket format brand to Singapore as well. The company then planned to open as many as ten hypermarkets in Malaysia and Singapore through the decade.

Back in Hong Kong, Dairy Farm celebrated the opening of its 400th 7-Eleven store, claiming the market lead in the convenience store segment. The company further consolidated its leadership position through the acquisition of rival Daily Stop in 2004. At the same time, the company laid out plans for a wider rollout of the 7-Eleven franchise in Guangdong, forming a joint venture with Guangdong Sinogiant. The deal called for the opening of as many as 350 7-Eleven stores in that province.

With its Asian operations expanding strongly, Dairy Farm decided to refocus its operations around that fast-growing region into the new century. As such, the company began selling its non-Asian holdings, including its operations in Australia, New Zealand, Spain, and the United Kingdom.

Dairy Farm increased its position in Singapore in 2003, acquiring that country's third largest supermarket group, Shop N Save Pte. Ltd. That deal added 35 supermarkets to Dairy Farm's Singapore operations. The strong growth of its retail operation encouraged the company to narrow its focus, leading to the sale in 2004 of the ice manufacturing company founded nearly 90 years earlier.

Dairy Farm had also continued to seek new horizons for its retail empire. In 2002, the company reached an agreement to take over the franchise to operate IKEA stores in Hong Kong and Taiwan from Jardine Matheson. In Indonesia, the company gained majority control of PT Hero, then entered new supermarket joint ventures in India, which brought 43 Foodworld and 32 Health and Glow stores within its sphere of operations. By 2006, the company had targeted entry into Vietnam, opening its first store in Ho Chi Minh City. The following year, the company added Brunei to its list of markets. Dairy Farm also caught the spirit of the times, founding ThreeSixty, a natural and organic foods retailer. After more than 120 years, Dairy Farm International had grown from a small Hong Kong-based dairy farm to one of the Asian region's leading retail groups.

M. L. Cohen

PRINCIPAL SUBSIDIARIES

CJ Olive Young Limited (Korea); Dairy Farm Management Limited (Bermuda); DFI Home Furnishings Taiwan Limited; Foodworld Supermarkets Private Limited (India); GCH Retail (Malaysia) Sdn Bhd; Giant South Asia (Vietnam) Limited; Giant TMC (B) Sdn Bhd; Guangdong Sai Yi Convenience Stores Limited (China); Hayselton Enterprises Limited; Mannings Guangdong Retail Company Limited (China); Maxim's Caterers Limited; PT Hero Supermarket Tbk (Indonesia); Shop N Save Pte Limited (Singapore); The Dairy Farm Company, Limited; Wellcome Company Limited; Wellcome Taiwan Company Limited.

PRINCIPAL COMPETITORS

China Resources Enterprise Ltd.; Lianhua Supermarket Holdings Company Ltd.; Guangdong Nan Yue Logistics Company Ltd.; Chaoda Modern Agriculture (Holdings) Ltd.; Chia Tai Enterprises International Ltd.; Convenience Retail Asia Ltd.

FURTHER READING

"Asia Growth," *Grocer,* March 5, 2005, p. 11.

Bow, Josephine J., "Dairy Farm Expanding in Asia," *Supermarket News,* October 9, 1995, p. 16.

"Dairy Farm Acquires Shop N Save Supermarkets in Singapore," *AsiaPulse News,* November 17, 2003.

"Dairy Farm Plans More Giant Hypermarkets," *Straits Times,* December 14, 2001, p. 17.

"Dairy Farm Sells Hong Kong Distribution Unit to Citic Pacific," *AsiaPulse News,* February 6, 2001.

"Dairy Farm to Buy Ikea Businesses in Hong Kong, Taiwan," *AsiaPulse News,* October 31, 2002.

"Dairy Farm to Open New Hypermarket," *Straits Times,* February 27, 2002.

Hong, Nguyen, "The Price Is Right," *Vietnam Investment Review,* May 29, 2006, p. 12.

"Indonesia's Hero Supermarket to Open 60 New Retail Outlets," *AsiaPulse News,* May 12, 2006.

Pearce, Jean, "Defying Rules Brings Success to Supermarket Chain," *Japan 21st,* July 1996, p. 60.

Turcsik, Richard, and Jenny Summerour, "Dairy Farm to Develop 300 New C-stores in China," *Progressive Grocer,* October 2001, p. 12.

———, "Dairy Farm to Expand Hypermarkets in Asia," *Progressive Grocer,* September 2000, p. 18.

DDi Corp.

1120 Simon Circle
Anaheim, California 92806-1813
U.S.A.
Telephone: (714) 688-7200
Toll Free: (800) 491-9766
Fax: (714) 688-7400
Web site: http://www.ddiglobal.com

Public Company
Incorporated: 1978 as Details Inc.
Employees: 1,300
Sales: $181.1 million (2007)
Stock Exchanges: NASDAQ
Ticker Symbol: DDIC
NAICS: 334412 Bare Circuit Board Manufacturing

■ ■ ■

DDi Corp. is a fast-turnaround multilayered printed circuit board (PCB), engineering, and manufacturing service provider, involved in the wireless telecommunications and networking, military and aerospace, semiconductor development and testing, industrial equipment, and computing industries. DDi works with clients in the design stage to avoid unnecessary costs and delays and also offers testing services to provide greater control and cost certainty. The company's manufacturing facilities are geared either to produce PCBs for immediate delivery needs or higher volumes for extended periods of times, and DDi provides transition services to transfer PCB production to long-term, high-volume offshore contract manufacturers. In addition to its Anaheim, California, headquarters, DDi maintains PCB fabrication operations in Milpitas, California; Sterling, Virginia; and Toronto, Canada. Ohio-based subsidiary Sovereign Circuits serves the military, aerospace, and high-durability commercial markets. DDi is a public company listed on the NASDAQ.

COMPANY FOUNDED: 1978

DDi traces its origins to 1978 when James I. Swenson founded a company called Details Inc. in Anaheim. Swenson grew up in Superior, Wisconsin, the son of a baker. In 1955 he enrolled at Wisconsin State College–Superior in pre–chemical engineering and in his senior year transferred to the University of Minnesota–Duluth, graduating in 1959 with a degree in chemistry. After fulfilling his military obligation, Swenson went to work as a researcher in the Minneapolis–St. Paul area for such firms as Honeywell and Univac. He was not particularly comfortable with corporate life and politics, however. He found himself repeatedly thwarted in his efforts to be promoted to full scientist at Honeywell. In 1968 he and his wife relocated to California, where he continued to work for major corporations. Finally in 1978 he decided to start his own business, focusing on the commercialization of high-technology printed circuits that had long been relegated to the research lab.

With $15,000 drawn from a second mortgage on his house, Swenson hired four employees and established a small printed circuit shop in Anaheim. Because they were creating the inner layer details for PCBs, he named the company Details Inc. The shop produced engineering PCB prototypes used in computers and other

COMPANY PERSPECTIVES

Count on DDi to engineer and manufacture your complex, technologically advanced, multi-layer printed circuit boards to meet your prototype, quick turn, and volume production needs.

electronic devices, serving such major customers as Apple, Compaq, IBM, and Motorola.

SALE OF BUSINESS: 1997

Swenson considered selling Details in the early 1990s but instead installed a new president, Bruce D. McMaster, whose team expanded the company's quick-turn capabilities. By 1997 Details was generating $80 million in annual sales. Swenson sold the business to McMaster and other managers, and they subsequently refinanced Details for $62.4 million. The money was provided by Bain Capital Funds of Boston, which took a 26.4 percent stake in the business; Chase Manhattan Entities of New York (8.5 percent); and Celerity Partners LLC of Los Angeles (5.2 percent).

Celerity also owned Dynamic Circuits Inc., a Milpitas, California-based quick-turnaround PCB manufacturer acquired in 1996. Celerity had targeted this specialized industry because it was a $1 billion market growing at an annual rate of 20 percent and dominated by hundreds of small companies, making it ripe for consolidation. Dynamic Circuits was acquired to serve as a platform in an industry consolidation effort. The company was established in San Jose, California, in 1991 by Charles D. Dimick, a former senior vice-president of sales and marketing at Sigma Circuits. In addition to its Silicon Valley plant, the company added facilities in Georgia, Massachusetts, and Texas. Dynamic Circuits designed and produced PCBs, and it did prototype manufacturing of back panels, card cages, and wire harnesses.

After Celerity and the other equity firms acquired interests in Details, the company became a consolidator itself, paying $38.9 million for Colorado Springs Circuits Inc. in December 1997. Seven months later, in July 1998, Details and Dynamic Circuits merged, creating Dynamic Details Incorporated. Dimick became chairman of the board while McMaster served as chief executive of the combined businesses. In 1999 the Colorado Springs facility began moving its operations to the Dynamic Circuits plant in Texas. The transfer was completed in March 2000.

INITIAL PUBLIC OFFERING: 2000

Also in March 2000, Dynamic Details reached an agreement to acquire a U.K. time-critical PCB service provider, MCM Electronics Limited, for about $86 million, a move that included four U.K. facilities and which management hoped would double business in Europe. In order to pay for the deal and pare down debt, Dynamic Details prepared to make an initial public offering (IPO) of stock. In April 2000 the company was reincorporated in Delaware as DDi Corp. On the day that the company set the price of its IPO, 14.7 million shares at $16 to raise $235 million, the NASDAQ fell 300 points and continued to erode as DDi launched its road show to promote the offering. Because the MCM acquisition depended on the IPO, DDi had no choice but to proceed. It settled for selling 12 million shares at $14 a share, raising $168 million.

After the disappointment of the IPO, the price of DDi stock soared as investors rewarded the company for being involved in one of technology's hottest sectors. DDi and the equity firms that had invested in it took advantage of the situation by making a secondary offering of stock in October 2000, raising $128.5 million. With this cash at its disposal, DDi went on a yearlong acquisition spree. In August 2000 the company paid $20 million to acquire the assets of bankrupt Virginia-based Automata International Inc. A month later, at the cost of $14.9 million, DDi added Garland, Texas-based Golden Manufacturing Inc., maker of engineered metal enclosures and assembly service provider to communications and electronic original equipment manufacturers (OEMs) such as Alcatel, Ericcson, and Motorola. For the year, DDi posted sales of nearly $500 million.

DDi completed five more acquisitions in 2001. DDi Europe bought Thomas Walter Limited in March for $30 million. The Marlow, U.K., quick-turn PCB provider served the European electronics industry. A month later DDi acquired Nelco Technology, an Arizona-based manufacturer of semifinished wiring boards. Also in April 2001, DDi formed a joint venture with a Japanese software designer of PCBs and interconnect packages and systems, Zuken Inc., the two companies agreeing to work together to serve Japanese OEMs. The Kabushiki Kaisha DDi venture then opened a sales office in Tokyo.

DDi next turned its attention to Canada and in May 2001 acquired Olympic Circuits Canada Inc., a quick-turn prototype PCB manufacturer based in Toronto, for $12.8 million. The deal provided DDi with a 50,000-square-foot manufacturing facility and, more important, access to markets in the northeastern United States and Canada that it had previously lacked. Finally, in June 2001 Southern California-based Altatron

KEY DATES

1978: James Swenson founds Details Inc.
1991: Dynamic Circuits Inc. is formed.
1997: Swenson sells Details.
1998: Details and Dynamic Circuits merge to form Dynamic Details Inc.
2000: Business is reincorporated as DDi Corp. and taken public.
2003: Company declares Chapter 11 bankruptcy protection.
2005: European operations are sold.
2006: Sovereign Circuits Inc. is acquired.

Technology, provider of assembly services to electronics OEMs, was acquired for $4.8 million. Later in the year DDi also opened a fast-track assembly plant in San Jose to serve OEMs in northern California, especially start-ups. The company also engaged in some restructuring in 2001 as business conditions began to deteriorate and the price of DDi stock began to tumble. Facilities in Garland, Texas, and Marlborough, Massachusetts, were closed in October of that year. Sales fell to $361.6 million in 2001.

CHAPTER 11 BANKRUPTCY: 2003

In early 2002 Dimick retired to complete a management transition plan that had been put in place at the time of the Details and Dynamic Circuits merger. McMaster became DDi chairman and CEO. He did not face an enviable task, however. As high technology companies endured a deep slump and tightened their belts, reducing demand for DDi's services, commodity-oriented PCB manufacturers in Asia invaded DDi's quick-turn niche, increasing supply and causing further harm to pricing. DDi initiated another restructuring effort, resulting in the closure of plants in Moorpark, California, and Dallas, Texas, in June 2002, but revenues continued to fall, dipping below $250 million in 2002. In the first half of 2003 DDi lost $40 million on sales of $117.8 million, much of that due to the servicing of the company's $285 million debt load.

The company's stock, which was worth around $46 a share in September 2000, lost 99.9 percent of its value. By August 2003, a day after DDi filed for Chapter 11 bankruptcy protection, it was worth a nickel a share. Once a $1.7 billion company, DDi now had a market capitalization of less than $3 million. The bankruptcy was prearranged and called for the company's lenders to receive almost all of the equity, 94 percent. DDi's management received 5 percent, leaving just 1 percent for DDi's pre-bankruptcy shareholders. As a result DDi's debt was also reduced to $91 million when it emerged from bankruptcy in December 2003. Sales for the year totaled $159.6 million.

McMaster remained chief executive as DDi rebounded somewhat in 2004, and the price of the company's stock peaked at $19.50 per share in the first quarter of the year. Due to improved market demand and higher selling prices, revenues increased $29.4 million to $189 million in 2004, but business tailed off as the year wore on, and in the end DDi posted a $45.9 million loss and the price of shares fell below $2.50.

A soft PCB market carried into 2005, resulting in a dip in sales to $184.6 million for the year and the loss of a further $64 million. Well before the results were in, the European operation was closed to eliminate about $38 million in debt, and the price of DDi stock traded below $1 per share and was in danger of being delisted by the NASDAQ. In November 2005, McMaster resigned to "pursue other opportunities." He was replaced as president and CEO by Chief Financial Officer Mikel Williams.

ACQUISITION OF SOVEREIGN CIRCUITS: 2006

Business picked up in 2006 when DDi generated $198.1 million in sales, the increase mostly due to the engineering and manufacture of multilayer PCBs, and the company narrowed its loss to $7.2 million. The company also avoided having its stock delisted by engineering a one-for-seven reverse stock split, a maneuver that reduced the number of shares to increase the stock price above the $1 per share level. Then, too, DDi elected to exit the lower-margin assembly business, selling it to Veritek Manufacturing Services for $12 million in cash in September 2006. Devoted entirely to its core time-critical PCB business, DDi bolstered its position in October 2006 by acquiring North Jackson, Ohio-based Sovereign Circuits Inc. in a $14.8 million cash and stock transaction plus the assumption of about $2.5 million in debt. The 20-year-old Youngstown-area company brought with it a 75,000-square-foot facility and provided DDI with inroads into the key aerospace, military, and high-reliability commercial markets. Moreover, Sovereign added expertise in flex and rigid-flex technologies.

The divestiture of the assembly business resulted in a drop in revenues to $181.1 million in 2007, but for the first time in several years DDi turned a profit, albeit a modest $688,000. It took some time for the price of

DDi stock to reflect this improvement in business, and management took advantage of the situation to launch a stock repurchase plan. The year 2008 started well, and in the first quarter alone the company more than matched the profits from all of 2007, recording a net income of $718,000 on sales of $47.4 million, a 9 percent improvement over 2007's first quarter. Williams expressed optimism that DDi had finally turned the corner after several years of painful restructuring, telling the *Orange County Business Journal,* "There's plenty of room for us to grow our business, even in a tough market, if we do our job right."

Ed Dinger

PRINCIPAL SUBSIDIARIES

Sovereign Circuits Inc.

PRINCIPAL COMPETITORS

Merix Corporation; SigmaTron International Inc.; TTM Technologies Inc.

FURTHER READING

Brennan, Peter, "Growth by Design," *Orange County Business Journal,* September 25, 2000, p. 1.

Chuang, Tamara, "CEO of Anaheim, Calif.-based DDi Resigns," *Orange County Business Journal,* November 1, 2005.

"DDi Corp., Lord of the Boards," *Manufacturer US,* August 2006.

Finkle, Jim, "Anaheim, Calif., Electronics Maker Issues Request to Reorganize," *Orange County Register,* August 21, 2003.

Hollingsworth, Jana, "UMD Alumnus Gives Millions for Building, Scholarships," *Duluth News Tribune,* September 21, 2007.

Serant, Claire, "DDI Flies IPO in Face of Market Storm," *Electronic Buyers' News,* April 17, 2000, p. 5.

———, "DDI to Stick with Tried-and-True," *Electronic Buyers' News,* June 5, 2000, p. 72.

Tolkoff, Sarah, "Circuit Board Maker DDi Eyes Comeback—Again," *Orange County Business Journal,* February 25–March 2, 2008.

Woodard, Chris, "Tech Company Comes to Rescue in a Hurry," *Investor's Business Daily,* August 23, 2000, p. A12.

Dreams Inc.

2 South University Drive, Suite 325
Plantation, Florida 33324
U.S.A.
Telephone: (954) 377-0002
Fax: (954) 475-8785
Web site: http://www.fieldofdreams.com

Public Company
Incorporated: 1996
Employees: 255
Sales: $59.7 million (2007)
Stock Exchanges: American
Ticker Symbol: DRJ
NAICS: 453998 All Other Miscellaneous Store Retailers (Except Tobacco Stores)

■ ■ ■

Dreams Inc. is a leading player in the $4 billion market for sports memorabilia. Through licenses with the National Football League, Major League Baseball, the National Hockey League, the National Basketball Association, and NASCAR, the company's Dream Products arm, which operates under the banners of Schwartz Sports and Mounted Memories, handles the merchandise side of the business. Goods are sold via a chain of 15 company-owned, mall-based Field of Dreams stores and another ten franchised locations, which the company markets via its Dreams Franchise Corp. business.

In order to maximize the potential of its retail stores, which are based in high-traffic shopping malls, Dreams Inc. uses a computerized point-of-sale system to help store owners track sales and make adjustments to their inventories based on trends and other factors. Field of Dreams stores are marked by upscale décor and attention-grabbing window displays and offer a wide range of merchandise that appeals to both casual gift buyers and serious collectors.

BUILDING THE BUSINESS: 1990–99

The company took its present form in April 1996, when StratAmerica Corp., which owned Shari's Franchise Corp. (Shari's Restaurants), changed its name to Dreams Inc. StratAmerica formerly owned the National Basketball Association's Utah Jazz franchise.

StratAmerica entered the sports memorabilia market when it acquired an 80 percent stake in Palm Desert, California-based Sports Archive Inc. in August 1990. In exchange for 200,000 shares of restricted common stock, StratAmerica gained a baseball card and memorabilia store in Palm Desert named Field of Dreams, which had secured a license from the Merchandising Corporation of America Inc. (MCA) and Universal City Studios Inc. to use the name of the well-known film starring Kevin Costner.

Sports Archive Inc. was established by Richard J. Heckmann and Gregory T. MacDonald. Heckmann was senior vice-president of investments and branch manager for Prudential-Bache Securities and chairman of American Toxxic Control Inc. In addition, he owned the nation's largest ski goggle manufacturer, Smith Sports Optics Inc., as well as several large agricultural

COMPANY PERSPECTIVES

Memorabilia has a unique appeal, because a single item can sum up a lifetime of heroic accomplishments. And, this memorabilia "magic" is fueling our growth from coast to coast.

enterprises in California, and had served as associate administrator of the Small Business Administration.

MOVIE AN INSPIRATION FOR THE BUSINESS

MacDonald's colorful background included a 12-year stint as the personal manager for rock star Rick Nelson, as well as time managing the legendary Elvis Presley in association with Col. Tom Parker. In addition to promoting concerts for many leading names in the music business, MacDonald headed an independent television production and phonograph packaging business focused on direct-to-consumer broadcast advertising. He coproduced a documentary titled *A Tribute to Ricky Nelson,* which was nominated for best music documentary by the American Film Institute and *Billboard Magazine* in 1989.

Sports Archive Inc. had been planning to expand. StratAmerica saw the Field of Dreams store as a prototype that it could use to grow the business through its financial resources and experience in the field of business and sports. In a July 13, 1990, *Business Wire* release, StratAmerica President Sam D. Battistone envisioned a chain of memorabilia stores with design elements related to positive aspects of the *Field of Dreams* movie. Each location would offer a selection of merchandise that appealed to both beginning and investment-level collectors.

PLANS FOR GROWTH

Following the deal, Sports Archive Inc. became a subsidiary of StratAmerica. Several key developments occurred in the latter part of 1990 as the company made plans to grow. In August Beverly Hills, California-based Quantum Marketing International Inc. was chosen to produce a 30-minute infomercial about baseball card collecting that offered a starter kit to would-be collectors. By this time the company also had its eye on about ten sites for new stores in Southern California shopping malls.

In September StratAmerica differentiated itself from competitors by introducing an authenticity guarantee for certain cards and collectibles. In addition, the company guaranteed that its packs and boxes of sports cards had not been opened prior to the sale to remove the most valuable cards. Together, these efforts meant greater peace of mind for customers.

THE FIELD OF DREAMS FRANCHISE

In October, Olympia Fields, Illinois-based Francorp Inc., the nation's largest franchise development consulting firm, was chosen to develop a franchise plan for Field of Dreams. Two months later StratAmerica selected Portland, Oregon-based SiBer Properties Inc. to find and secure locations for new Field of Dreams stores.

StratAmerica's first expansion effort bore fruit in December 1990, when the company opened an 800-square-foot retail location in the Fashion Mall in Indio, California. A third store was slated to open around the same time in the Glendale, California, Galleria.

Developments continued to unfold in 1991. In April, the company announced that requirements for selling Field of Dreams franchises had been completed in 30 states and that preparations were underway to meet similar requirements in 18 other states. A new warehouse facility with $2.5 million worth of memorabilia also was established around this time.

After acquiring full ownership of Sports Archive Inc. in May, StratAmerica announced the sale in July of its first two franchises, located near Omaha, Nebraska. By this time, franchise approval had been secured in 36 states, including the company's home state of California.

In April 1992 StratAmerica announced that it had sold a total of 18 Field of Dreams franchises. In addition to nine existing locations, new sites were planned for markets such as Chicago and Las Vegas, where a site had been secured in the Forum Shops Mall connected to the Caesars Palace and Mirage Hotels. At the same time, StratAmerica changed the name of its Sports Archive Inc. subsidiary to Dreams Franchise Corp., which was a more accurate description of its business model.

Another significant development in 1992 was an exclusive agreement with basketball legend Bill Russell, which involved his signing 5,000 autographs over a two-year period. Russell's autograph was highly prized because he had not signed one for 28 years. At the same time, however, during its 1992 fiscal year, StratAmerica lost $4.95 million on sales of $16.99 million.

By mid-1993 StratAmerica had sold 37 Field of Dreams franchises and 18 stores were in operation, including new locations near Minneapolis at the Galleria

KEY DATES

1990: StratAmerica Corp. acquires an 80 percent stake in Sports Archive Inc., which operates a baseball card and memorabilia store named Field of Dreams; StratAmerica opens second Field of Dreams store in Indio, California.
1991: Sports Archive Inc. is acquired.
1992: Subsidiary Sports Archive Inc. is renamed Dreams Franchise Corp.
1996: StratAmerica changes its name to Dreams Inc.
1998: Mounted Memories Inc. is acquired.
2002: Dreams Inc. focuses on company-owned stores via new subsidiary named Dreams Retail Corp.

of Edina and the Ridgedale Center. The company had established a presence at the Mall of America near Minneapolis and in the Woodfield Mall near Chicago.

MID-NINETIES DOWNTURN

During its 1993 fiscal year, StratAmerica continued its downturn, losing $2.86 million on sales of $16.62 million. The company remained unprofitable during the mid-1990s. In 1994 it lost $3.4 million on sales of $15.96 million. The following year, losses totaled $2.1 million on sales of $14.49 million.

On March 28, 1996, a pivotal development unfolded when StratAmerica's shareholders approved the sale of the company's Shari's Franchise Corp. subsidiary to Portland, Oregon-based Shari's Management Corp. The sale signified StratAmerica's intent to focus on sports and celebrity memorabilia, as it said goodbye to the restaurant operations that generated about $11.42 million of its annual revenues. This focus was formalized when StratAmerica changed its name to Dreams Inc. The company recorded a net loss of $721,000 for the year, on revenues of $13.83 million.

A potential snag occurred in August 1997, when Universal Studios Licensing Inc. suspended Dreams' license to use the Field of Dreams name over accounting-related matters. For a short time, the development prevented the company from opening any new franchises using the movie title. However, in October an agreement was reached with Universal that enabled the company to continue using the Field of Dreams name.

By early 1998, Dreams had 27 franchised locations throughout the United States. At this time the company also signed a memorandum of understanding to facilitate the purchase of Sunrise, Florida-based Mounted Memories Inc., which manufactured and distributed acrylic cases and merchandise for the protection and display of collectibles, as well as licensed and autographed sports memorabilia. In addition to bringing in a 17,000-square-foot facility, the deal with Mounted Memories gave Dreams an existing lineup of sports personalities who had agreed to do private signings.

The acquisition of Mounted Memories, which had annual sales of about $7 million, involved 15 million shares of Dreams stock and $2.3 million in cash. It was completed in November 1998, by which time Dreams had 47 stores, including 34 franchised sites in the United States and 13 affiliated stores in Australia. The company ended its 1998 fiscal year in the black, with a net income of $432,000 on sales of $1.9 million.

SPORTS COLLECTIBLES LEADER: 2000–08

The new millennium brought new partnerships to Dreams. In April 2000 the company announced a strategic partnership with Major League Baseball (MLB) intended to generate more in-store appearances by current and former ball players, as well as new product offerings.

In June, Dreams inked a deal with Green Diamond Sports Inc. and became the master distributor of authentic memorabilia from baseball legend Ted Williams. Around the same time, Dreams teamed with the National Hockey League Players Association to produce and market *For the Love of Hockey,* a 200-page commemorative hardcover book signed by 92 of the game's most legendary players. About 300 of the books were available only at Field of Dreams stores.

Early in the calendar year, pro football legend Dan Marino became part of Dreams when he was named director of business development and was added to the company's board of directors. In November, Dreams announced that it had teamed with MLB to offer bases from opening day 2000, the first MLB games played during the 21st century, at 11 of its stores. Bases were offered from the Chicago Cubs, Chicago White Sox, Florida Marlins, Minnesota Twins, San Diego Padres, Tampa Bay Devil Rays, Los Angeles Dodgers, Seattle Mariners, Texas Rangers, Detroit Tigers, and Cincinnati Reds. Around the same time, Dreams made an exclusive one-year deal with football legend Johnny "The Golden Arm" Unitas to market authentic memorabilia and collectibles from his 18-year career.

Dreams capped off its 2000 fiscal year on a high note. Revenues skyrocketed 90 percent to $13.4 million, and net income rose 55 percent to $936,000. By this time the company had completed the integration of Mounted Memories and Field of Dreams. In addition, Dreams began pursuing e-commerce opportunities, such as wholesale arrangements with CBS SportsLine and ESPN.com.

On the leadership front, Ross Tannenbaum served as Dreams' president and CEO in 2000, and Sam Battistone remained chairman. In December, an important executive development occurred when Field of Dreams Executive Vice-President John F. Walrod was named as the subsidiary's president. Walrod had been with the company since 1992.

Relationships with well-known sports celebrities continued in 2001, as the company secured exclusive product agreements with basketball superstar Shaquille O'Neal, who also joined Dreams' advisory board.

The following year, an important strategic shift occurred when Dreams began to acquire some of its franchised stores and make them company-owned enterprises. This goal was accomplished via a new wholly owned subsidiary named Dreams Retail Corp., which agreed in March to acquire locations in Denver, Colorado's Park Meadows Mall and Somerset Mall just north of Detroit. A third company-owned location was secured in November, when Dreams agreed to acquire a store in San Diego, California's Horton Plaza.

Promotional deals with well-known sports celebrities continued during the middle of the first decade of the 2000s, including an arrangement with Bill Cowher, coach of the 2005 Super Bowl Champion Pittsburgh Steelers. In early 2006, the company revealed a major three-year expansion plan that identified about 120 potential locations for new stores.

By this time Dreams had ten company-owned locations, as well as 19 franchised sites. In March, the company named Jorge Salvat as president of its growing franchise business. The company was doing well on all fronts and capped off its 2006 fiscal year with record revenues of $42.7 million, up 29 percent over the previous year's total of $33 million.

In early 2007 Dreams acquired all three Field of Dreams stores in the lucrative Las Vegas market. By mid-2008 the company had 16 company-owned Field of Dreams stores to its name, as well as ten franchised locations, one FansEdge store, and an e-commerce operation that included the web sites ProSportsMemorabilia.com and FansEdge.com. As 2009 approached, Dreams seemed to have the formula down for selling authentic sports collectibles of every stripe.

Paul R. Greenland

PRINCIPAL SUBSIDIARIES

Dreams Franchise Corp.; Dreams Retail Corp.; Field of Dreams; Mounted Memories Inc.

PRINCIPAL COMPETITORS

Donruss Playoff L.P.; The Sports Authority Inc.; The Upper Deck Company LLC.

FURTHER READING

"StratAmerica Acquires Sports Archives; 'Field of Dreams' Name Rights Included," *Business Wire,* August 9, 1990.

"StratAmerica Announces 'Field of Dreams' Authenticity Guarantee for Sports Collectors Cards," *Business Wire,* September 5, 1990.

"StratAmerica Announces First Franchise Sale for Its 'Field of Dreams' Sport Card and Sports Personality Gift Store; California Approves Franchise Sales," *Business Wire,* July 10, 1991.

"StratAmerica Corp. Acquires 100 Percent of Sports Archives Inc.," *Business Wire,* May 22, 1991.

"StratAmerica Corp. Changes Name to Dreams Inc.; Shari's Restaurants Sold," *Business Wire,* April 8, 1996.

Liverpool®
ES PARTE DE MI VIDA

El Puerto de Liverpool, S.A.B. de C.V.

Avenida Mariano Escobedo 425
Mexico City, 11570
Mexico
Telephone: (52 55) 5328-6862
Toll Free: (800) 713-55-55 (within Mexico)
Fax: (52 55) 5254-8339
Web site: http://www.liverpool.com.mx

Public Company
Incorporated: 1944
Employees: 30,000
Sales: MXN 43.12 billion ($3.97 billion) (2007)
Stock Exchanges: Bolsa Mexicana de Valores OTC
Ticker Symbols: LIVEPOL; LIVPP
NAICS: 452111 Department Stores (Except Discount Department Stores); 522210 Credit Card Issuing; 531120 Lessors of Nonresidential Buildings (Except Miniwarehouses); 531312 Nonresidential Property Managers; 551112 Offices of Other Holding Companies

■ ■ ■

El Puerto de Liverpool, S.A.B. de C.V., is Mexico's leading department store chain. A holding company, it is engaged through its subsidiaries not only in the management and operation of department stores but also of shopping centers in which its stores are located; the management and leasing of real estate; and the offer of financing to its customers by means of its own credit cards. El Puerto de Liverpool's retail sales of family and home products include women's fashion and furs, men's sports apparel and shoes, handcrafts, furniture, lamps, home appliances, kitchenware, glassware, children's toys, cosmetics, accessories, and restaurant gourmet foods.

MEXICO CITY INSTITUTION: 1847–1980

El Puerto de Liverpool (Liverpool) got its start in 1847, when Jean-Baptiste Ebrárd opened a clothing store near the Plaza Mayor, or Zócalo, the huge public square in central Mexico City bordered by the National Palace and the largest and oldest cathedral in the Americas. It first occupied a space of only 65 square meters. The goods consisted of a grab bag of silks, linens, and other fabrics, plus laces, sashes, straps, and other such accessories. These products, which met a demand from the city's more affluent residents, were imported mainly from France. Eventually this store, and others of the same type, were divided into specific departments.

Ebrárd's store came to be called El Puerto de Liverpool because the goods principally first passed through this port, the main one for commercial traffic to the Americas. Its chief competition came from German merchants who then controlled the clothing trade in Mexico City. El Puerto de Liverpool began carrying goods wholesale in 1862. Ten years later, it was housed in a two-story building, which by 1900 had departments for hats, suits, dresses, coats, fabrics, white goods, and accessories, among others. Two more stories were added to the building in 1920. In 1934 it moved into a new building, also in the heart of Mexico City, that consisted of six floors and a commercial basement and that housed the first escalators in the city. El Puerto de

COMPANY PERSPECTIVES

We are the leader, at the national level, of constantly growing department stores, founded in 1847.

We offer families a selection of products for clothing and the home that exceeds their expectations of quality, fashion, value, and retention, within an agreeable environment.

Collaborators, shareholders and suppliers, we form a human community in which we realize ourselves personally and professionally, generating high economic value, with a sense of our responsibility to our surroundings.

Liverpool was incorporated in 1944 and abandoned wholesaling the following year. It was listed the Bolsa Mexicana de Valores, Mexico City's stock exchange, in 1965.

During the postwar years Sears Roebuck de México became the country's first department store chain. El Puerto de Liverpool did not open a branch until 1962, when its second store appeared on Avenida de los Insurgentes, Mexico City's busiest commercial street. The third store was Liverpool Polanco, which opened in 1970 in one of the city's wealthiest neighborhoods.

Mexico City's well-to-do residents were moving away from the central neighborhoods to the outskirts and needed space to park their cars when they went shopping. In 1969 the first shopping center appeared, partly backed by Sears. Two years later, the second, Plaza Satélite, opened its doors, with investment from a bank and three department stores, including Sears and El Puerto de Liverpool. In 1980 Liverpool opened its own commercial center, Perisur, with the collaboration of three other department stores, including Sears. Perisur, called the largest commercial center in Latin America, had parking for 6,000 automobiles.

GOING NATIONAL: 1980–2000

El Puerto de Liverpool was ready to breach the confines of the capital city. The first provincial branch opened in 1982 in Villahermosa, the state capital of Tabasco, where the chain also opened its own shopping center, Galería Tabasco 2000. It was followed the next year by a store in Monterrey, where Liverpool's Centro Comercial Galerías Monterrey was opening, and in 1985 by a store in Tampico. In 1988 the company purchased a rival department store chain, Fábricas de Francia. Based in Guadalajara, this chain dated back to the 1860s and consisted of eight stores. Like the Liverpool units, they were aimed at an upper- and upper-middle-class clientele.

El Puerto de Liverpool, in 1992, inaugurated Galerías Coapa and Galerías Insurgentes, Mexico City commercial centers that included two more of the chain's stores. The following year it opened a store in Centro Comercial Santa Fe, located in an affluent area on the outskirts of Mexico City. The company was coproprietor of this shopping center. El Puerto de Liverpool was by that time Mexico's largest shopping center owner, leasing space for more than 400 stores.

Kmart Corporation entered the Mexican marketplace in 1993 with the opening of a Super Kmart Center as a joint venture with El Puerto de Liverpool. Over the next four years the joint venture, Kmart de México, S.A. de C.V., opened four hypermarkets (three in Mexico City and one in Cuernavaca), with a fifth in Puebla almost completed. This was not an auspicious period for business, however, since a financial crisis in late 1994 led to a devaluation of the Mexican peso and a subsequent national recession.

Liverpool projected a drop in sales of 22 to 25 percent during 1995, despite cutting prices for its articles for the home by 20 percent and offering credit customers six interest-free months for purchases in this department. It also entered negotiations with the foreign banks to which it owed $100 million. In early 1997, Kmart de México was sold to Controladora Comercial Mexicana, S.A. de C.V. (Comerci), one of the nation's largest self-service retail chains, for $148.5 million.

As the national economy recovered, El Puerto de Liverpool resumed its expansion, opening its fourth store outside Mexico City in León in 1996. The following year it purchased eight stores in the southeastern part of the country from Grupo Comercial Chedraui, S.A. de C.V., which was operating them under the Las Galas name. Liverpool paid about $41.5 million for the acquisition and turned the Las Galas units into Fábricas de Francia stores. Ending its centennial year, Liverpool had 28 stores and five commercial centers.

El Puerto de Liverpool had 31 stores in the spring of 1999, when it purchased 11 Salinas y Rocha department stores for about $27 million from Grupo Elektra, S.A. de C.V., which owned four of the properties and rented the other seven. The stores reopened under the Fábricas de Francia name. The acquisition reinforced the Liverpool chain's presence in such important markets as León and Monterrey and helped it to enter new markets such as Acapulco.

KEY DATES

1847: Small fabrics and notions store, the predecessor to El Puerto de Liverpool, opens in Mexico City.

1872: El Puerto de Liverpool occupies a two-story building.

1934: Liverpool moves into a bigger building that includes the first escalators in Mexico City.

1962: Liverpool opens a second store on Mexico City's busy Avenida de los Insurgentes.

1965: El Puerto de Liverpool is listed on the Bolsa Mexicana de Valores for the first time.

1970: The third El Puerto de Liverpool opens in the city's affluent Polanco neighborhood.

1971: Liverpool has its own store in one of the city's earliest shopping malls, Plaza Satélite.

1980: Liverpool develops a giant Mexico City commercial center, Perisur.

1982: First Liverpool store opens outside Mexico City, in Villahermosa, Tabasco.

1988: Company purchases rival department store chain Fábricas de Francia.

1993: Liverpool opens the first of several hypermarkets in collaboration with Kmart Corporation.

1997: The hypermarkets are sold; Liverpool buys the Las Galas department store chain.

1999: Liverpool purchases 11 Salinas y Rocha department stores.

2007: Liverpool is the sixth largest retail enterprise in Latin America.

LIVERPOOL IN THE 21ST CENTURY

El Puerto de Liverpool continued to grow in the first decade of the 21st century, reaching a total of 68 stores and 13 shopping malls in 2007. It was the sixth largest retail enterprise in Latin America and had more than doubled its net profit over a five-year period. Liverpool held an estimated market share of 63 percent in its field, considering only its main department store competitors (and about half overall).

About 59 percent of its retail sales were being made with its own branded credit cards. Some 2.4 million had been issued, and the company had a credit portfolio of more than $1.4 billion, of which about $300 million had been securitized. Some 43 of the stores were under the Liverpool name, with the remainder under the Fábricas de Francia name. Liverpool owned and operated ten commercial centers and had a minority participation in three more. It was the anchor tenant in each. The centers were attracting approximately four million visitors a year.

El Puerto de Liverpool initiated a mail-order service in 2006 that targeted Mexicans living in the United States. It also had a program to aid its suppliers, some of whom were artisans who needed access to credit on affordable terms. Some items were always said to be welcome, such as good quality moccasins and classic cut shirts. Of the company's 4,500 suppliers, almost 3,600 were small- to medium-sized enterprises that together accounted for 20 percent of company sales.

Liverpool listed 12 different departments on its web site in 2008. These included toys, sporting goods, home furnishings, children, and luggage. The items in the men's department included toiletries, fragrances, watches, wallets, and ties, while those in the women's department included cosmetics, perfumes, purses, watches, and earrings. (The web offerings did not include men's and women's clothing.) The gift department concentrated on wines, liquors, and food baskets. The health department carried many medical devices as well as supplies. The technology department featured cameras, television sets, video games, and cell phones. Many similar items were in the outlet department, which also carried computers and DVD/VCR recorders.

The closely held enterprise was still chiefly in the hands of persons of French origin. The Michel, David, Guichard, and Bremond families controlled more than three-quarters of the shares. The two biggest financial institutions, Grupo Financiero BBVA Bancomer, S.A. de C.V., and Grupo Financiero Banamex, S.A. de C.V., held almost 18 percent, while the remainder were owned by individuals. The chief executive was for many years Max Michel Suberville, who retired in 2004. His son, Max David Michel, was chairman of the board.

The secret of El Puerto de Liverpool's continued success was said to be its emphasis on novelty and variety of goods and attention to service, with the goal of the highest profit per square meter of selling space. A Liverpool executive said that the company sought to augment its selling space by double digits each year, implying the opening of ten new stores annually. Although already in almost all large Mexican cities, Liverpool saw a potential to expand in 50 more cities. New stores, although in smaller locations, would offer the same quality of products as in existing stores, the same attention to service, and the same credit terms. The only variable would be the smaller size of the store.

To counter fashion retailers such as Zara, Mango, Bershka, C&A, and Massimo Dutti, El Puerto de Liverpool had introduced, in partnership with the Spanish retailer El Corte Inglés, a chain called Sfera Joven. Liverpool considered this chain indispensable to compete for the youth market, which was drawn to fashion brands and not much disposed to shopping in department stores. A retail consultant told Norma Lezcano of the business magazine *Expansión* that there was little risk for Liverpool in launching Sfera Joven because "The manufacturer is responsible for the stock, the staff, the space, the margins ... it's like a concession."

Financial analysts described as one of El Puerto de Liverpool's best features its knowledge of the middle class, which demanded credit extended quickly and efficiently. The company was one of Mexico's five leading issuers of credits and was considering opening its own bank. Credit was being extended on the basis of fixed payments over 48 months. Liverpool's monthly rate of 3.15 percent was lower than any of its competitors except Sears. The credit division was accounting for 5 to 6 percent of the company's annual revenues. (The shopping centers accounted for 3 percent.)

Liverpool's chief competitor was Carlos Slim Domit, the wealthiest individual in Latin America. Slim's Grupo Carso, S.A. de C.V., roster of retail stores included Sears, Dorian's, and a Saks Fifth Avenue that opened in 2007 in the Santa Fe shopping mall. Wal-Mart de México, S.A. de C.V., was rumored to be repositioning its Suburbia retail chain to compete with Liverpool. Other big retailers were oriented toward a lower socioeconomic level.

Robert Halasz

PRINCIPAL SUBSIDIARIES

Bodegas Liverpool, S.A. de C.V.; Operadora Liverpool, S.A. de C.V.; Servicios Liverpool, S.A. de C.V.

PRINCIPAL DIVISIONS

Credit; Real Estate; Retail.

PRINCIPAL COMPETITORS

El Palacio de Hierro, S.A. de C.V.; Sears Roebuck de México, S.A. de C.V.

FURTHER READING

Castillo Méndez, Laura Elena, *Historia del comercio en la ciudad de México,* Mexico City: Colección Popular, 1973, pp. 46–51.

"Compra Liverpool tiendas Chedraui," *Reforma,* April 22, 1997, p. 31.

"Kmart Enters Mexico with First Supercenter," *Discount Store News,* January 4, 1993, pp. 1, 87.

Lezcano, Norma, "La Reina de la moda," *Expansión,* June 25–July 9, 2007, pp. 132, 134, 136.

Montes de Oca, José Antonio, "150 años de ofrecer moda," *Reforma,* December 6, 1997, p. 2.

Ugarte, Jesús, "Toma Comerci Kmart y deja Auchan," *Reforma,* February 21, 1997, p. 21.

———, "Transforman tiendas SyR," *Reforma,* August 3, 1999, p. 4.

Vargas, Elena, "Almacenes de prestigio tienen en la mira a las Pymes," *Entrepreneur* (Mexico City), October 2004, pp. 94+.

Zuñiga, Maria Elena, "Pelea Liverpool por mercado," *Reforma,* September 18, 1995, p. 37.

EMCORE Corporation

10420 Research Road, S.E.
Albuquerque, New Mexico 87123
U.S.A.
Telephone: (505) 332-5000
Toll Free: (888) 726-3472
Fax: (505) 332-5038
Web site: http://www.emcore.com

Public Company
Incorporated: 1986
Employees: 750
Sales: $169.6 million (2007)
Stock Exchanges: NASDAQ
Ticker Symbol: EMKR
NAICS: 334413 Semiconductor and Related Device Manufacturing

A onetime New Jersey-based company, EMCORE Corporation (Emcore) is an Albuquerque, New Mexico, company involved in two business segments: fiber optics and photovoltaics. The company designs, manufactures, and markets its semiconductor-based products for broadband, fiber-optic, satellite, and solar power customers. Emcore's fiber-optics products facilitate the transmission of information in the form of light signals. Customers include cable television, fiber-to-the-premises networks, and high-speed data communications and telecommunications networks. Emcore's photovoltaics operating segment offers gallium arsenide solar cells, covered interconnect cells, fully integrated solar panels, and receivers. They are used in satellites as well as in terrestrial applications. A public company listed on the NASDAQ, Emcore maintains domestic operations in Albuquerque; Ewing, New Jersey; Warminster, Pennsylvania; and Newark, Alhambra, San Diego, and Sunnyvale, California. The company also maintains two plants in China.

FORMATION IN 1984 BY AT&T SCIENTISTS

Emcore was established in Somerset, New Jersey, in 1984 by a group of scientists from nearby AT&T Bell Laboratories to produce machinery used to make gallium arsenide and other compound semiconductors and provide manufacturing services. Heading the group was Norman E. Schumaker, the manager of the New Materials and Technology Group at Bell Labs, where he was employed for 16 years. He served as Emcore's president, chief executive officer, and chairman. Another cofounder was Richard A. Stall, who served as vice-president–technology for the start-up. At Bell Labs, Stall was responsible for the development of molecular beam epitaxy (MBE) technologies, and was also an expert in metalorganic chemical vapor deposition (MOCVD) technologies. For seed money, Emcore raised about $10 million from a pair of venture capital firms and another 60 investors, including more than a dozen executives from the Price Waterhouse accounting firm. One of the firm's partners had learned Emcore was looking for investors from Schumaker at a Little League baseball game while watching their sons play. It was a chance encounter that would have serious repercussions a dozen years later.

COMPANY PERSPECTIVES

Emcore business—connected by the power of light.

Emcore was incorporated in New Jersey in 1986 and conserved its cash while pursuing preliminary research. A year later the company generated about $3 million in sales. That amount would double to $6.3 million in 1988. Sales increased to more than $10 million by 1992, and then receded to $8.2 million a year later. Most of the sales during these years were research and development systems and small pilot production systems, but the emphasis began to change in 1994 when growing demand for compound semiconductor devices resulted in Emcore selling larger production platforms. Revenues increased to $9 million in 1994 and doubled to more than $18.1 million in 1995. Emcore also turned a $1.5 million profit in 1995. A year later, though, it posted a $3.2 million loss despite growing revenues to $27.8 million.

JESUP & LAMONT GAINS CONTROL OF EMCORE: 1995

In 1995 a controlling stake in Emcore was acquired by the investment banking and brokerage firm of Jesup & Lamont. The president of the merchant banking division, Reuben F. Richards Jr., became president and COO in October 1995. Emcore's customers, which included Hewlett-Packard, Lucent Technologies, Texas Instruments, Westinghouse, and IBM, had an increasing need to get their new high-performance products to market. Thus in 1996 Emcore supplemented its product offering, adding design and production of wafers and package-ready devices. In order to expand the business further, Emcore prepared to make an initial public offering of stock. To shepherd the company through this next stage in its development, Richards replaced Schumaker as CEO in December 1996.

With an underwriting group led by Donaldson, Lufkin & Jenrette Securities Corporation and Needham & Company, Inc., Emcore's initial public offering (IPO) of stock was completed in March 2007, netting about $22.8 million. The money was not only used to pay off some debt, but was also earmarked to expand the company's manufacturing capabilities and fund acquisitions of complementary businesses. After recording an increase in sales to $47.8 million when fiscal 1997 came to a close on September 30, 1997, Emcore acquired Albuquerque-based MicroOptical Devices, Inc. (MODE), for $32.8 million in stock. MODE was one of the pioneers in vertical cavity surface emitting lasers (VCSELs), using the technology to develop microlasers and subsystems. The addition of MODE was intended to help Emcore establish a dominant position in the promising optoelectronic laser market.

START OF PHOTOVOLTAICS DIVISION: 1998

Emcore soon began making plans to expand the Albuquerque operation, turning to the local government for $55 million in industrial revenue bonds, providing lower tax rates as well as reduced interest rates, in order to build a new solar-cell plant in a proposed scientific and technology park located close to Sandia National Laboratories, from which MODE had been a spinoff two years earlier. The new facility opened in October 1998. In the meantime, the MODE plant was also expanded by 20,000 square feet. In another development, Emcore started a photovoltaics division in Albuquerque in 1998. With this launch, the MODE acquisition, and plant expansion, Emcore transformed itself from a capital equipment company into a vertically integrated producer of a full line of compound semiconductor products, including solar cells, VCSELs, high brightness and blue LEDs, and TurboDisc systems.

In 1998 revenues fell to $43.8 million, due in part to a strike suffered by one of the company's major customers, General Motors Corporation, and a change in the company's product mix. It was also during this fiscal year, in December 1997, that the matter of Price Waterhouse executives owning stock in the company became an issue.

Coopers & Lybrand had audited Emcore's books since it was incorporated in 1986, but Emcore's CFO, Thomas Werthan, became concerned about merger plans between Price Waterhouse and Coopers & Lybrand. To make sure there would be no conflicts of interest, he contacted the Coopers & Lybrand partner who oversaw Emcore's audits, Brendan Dougher, and agreed that executives holding Emcore stock would have to comply with independence rules. A few weeks later the accounting firm insisted that Emcore either change auditors or cover the partners' costs of selling their stock, but in the end agreed that the executives would have to foot the bill themselves.

In February 1999, however, Emcore was on the verge of filing for a $97.5 million secondary stock offering, looking to take advantage of a rise in price following the IPO, when it learned that in fact the PricewaterhouseCoopers' partners had not sold their Emcore

KEY DATES

1984: Emcore is founded in Somerset, New Jersey.
1986: Company is incorporated.
1995: Jesup & Lamont acquires majority control.
1997: Company goes public.
2002: Tecstar assets are acquired.
2004: MOCVD business is divested.
2007: Corporate headquarters is moved to Albuquerque.
2008: Planning begins to split EMCORE into two separate companies.

stock. Consequently, Emcore was forced by the Securities and Exchange Commission to re-audit its 1998 books, delaying the offering to June, when the asking price fell $5 per share, costing Emcore a considerable amount of money. Not only did Emcore dismiss PricewaterhouseCoopers as its auditor, it filed a civil racketeering suit against the accounting firm and ten of its top executives before the matter was settled.

PLUMMETING REVENUES: 2002

Revenues improved to $58.3 million in 1999, the start of a major growth spurt that increased revenues to $104.5 million in 2000 and $184.6 million in 2001. To keep pace with demand, Emcore added more space to its Albuquerque operations. The company's losses continued to accumulate, however, totaling $60 million during this three-year-period. Matters grew far worse in 2002. With the economy in recession, and the telecommunications industry especially hit hard, Emcore had to contend with a dramatic fall in capital equipment spending by its customers. Revenues plummeted to $87.8 million, and $10.3 million of that amount was contributed by a midyear acquisition, the Applied Solar Division of Tecstar, Inc., and Tecstar Power Systems, Inc., an old-guard solar panel manufacturer, serving the satellite market since 1958. To deal with the sudden drop in business, Emcore launched a restructuring program that cut expenses as much as possible. Not only were there layoffs and a realignment of the engineering, manufacturing, and sales/marketing units, the company changed its research focus. Going forward Emcore would fund only projects that could be expected to generate returns in just one year.

Although difficult business conditions persisted in 2003, Emcore was able to rebuild sales to $113.1 million. It also completed three acquisitions to position the company for success in the high-growth markets in which it participated. In December 2002 Sunnyvale, California-based Alvesta Corporation was acquired to bolster the fiber-optic product lines, especially receivers. A month later the West Coast optoelectronics business of Agere Systems was purchased for $26.2 million in cash. Finally, in October 2003 the Ethernet transceiver business of Milex Inc. was added to the Fiber Optics division. Fiscal 2003 also brought the sale of the TurboDisc Metal Organic Chemical Vapor Deposition business, the MOCVD business deemed not to offer the same high-growth future as Emcore's other product lines.

Emcore was repositioning itself as a provider of compound semiconductor solutions for the broadband, fiber-optic, satellite, and wireless communications markets. To help in completing this transformation, in 2004 Emcore acquired Corona Optical Systems, a four-year-old Lombard, Illinois-based company that made laser modules for launching light into fiber-optic equipment. Due to the divestiture of the MOCVD business, revenues fell to $93 million but continuing operations enjoyed strong growth with sales increasing by more than $30 million.

More acquisitions followed during 2005 and 2006. In May 2005 Emcore supplemented its fiber-optics unit by acquiring the analog cable TV and radio frequency over fiber specialty businesses of JDS Uniphase Corp. for $1.5 million. Phasebridge, Inc., a Pasadena, California-based maker of multi-chip optical modules and subsystems for the defense and optical networking markets, was purchased in November 2005. A month later Christiansburg, Virginia-based Force, Inc., was added in a stock swap, bringing the maker of advanced fiber-optic-based signal transport equipment into the fold. At the start of 2006, Emcore also acquired K2 Optronics, Inc., for $4.1 million in stock. The Sunnyvale, California, company specialized in analog and digital transmission lasers for the cable television, sensing, and test and measurement industries. Emcore also sold the assets of its Electronic Materials Division in 2006 as well as an interest in a solid state lighting joint venture with General Electric. The funds received were then used to start a new division, Emcore Solar Power, to take advantage of its solar power technology for terrestrial applications. As a result of these acquisitions and divestitures, sales grew to $115.4 million in 2005 and $143.5 million in 2006. Moreover, Emcore turned a profit in 2006, netting almost $55 million, due primarily to $100 million in cash it received from General Electric for its share of the joint venture.

NEW HEADQUARTERS IN ALBUQUERQUE: 2007

In 2006 Emcore announced that it would move its corporate headquarters to Albuquerque in 2007. Solar panel operations were also consolidated at the Albuquerque plant and in 2007 further changes were made. The fiber-optics engineering facilities and design centers in Virginia, Illinois, and Northern California were closed and relocated to Alhambra, California, and Albuquerque. Emcore also completed another acquisition, paying $4 million in April 2007 for San Diego-based Opticomm Corporation, which produced advanced optical communications systems.

Revenues increased to $169.9 million in 2007. Both the fiber-optics and photovoltaics operating segments enjoyed strong growth, but it was the solar business that many analysts believed held the most promise, even though some investors were losing confidence and bidding down the price of Emcore stock. In the first four months of 2008, the company lost about half of its market value. To unlock the value of both business segments, Emcore, as authorized by the board of directors, began developing a plan to split the fiber-optics and photovoltaics business into two separate companies.

Ed Dinger

PRINCIPAL SUBSIDIARIES

Corona Optical Systems, Inc.; Velox Semiconductor Corporation; K2 Optronics, Inc.; EMCORE IRB Company, Inc.; Opticomm Corporation; EMCORE Solar Power, Inc.

PRINCIPAL COMPETITORS

Lattice Semiconductor Corp.; Opnext, Inc.; Semitoll Inc.

FURTHER READING

Alpert, Bill, "Laser Shootout," *Barron's,* January 1, 2001, p. 19.

Amedeo, Michael, "Emcore Moves to Albuquerque," *Albuquerque Tribune,* October 31, 2006, p. C3.

Baca, Aaron, "Solar-Cell Plant Seeks Big Bond Issue," *Albuquerque Journal,* April 7, 1998, p. A1.

Duffy, Maureen, "Ma Bell's Kids Contribute to Jersey's High-Tech Rep," *Crain's New York Business,* February 23, 1987, p. 15.

MacDonald, Elizabeth, "Called to Account," *Wall Street Journal,* February 18, 2000, p. A1.

Philbin, Brett, "Emcore Believers Bank on Bright Future in Solar," *Wall Street Journal,* May 7, 2008.

Stets, Dan, "Chips Off the Old Block; N.J. Firms Trying New Materials," *Philadelphia Inquirer,* November 13, 1988.

Energen Corporation

605 Richard Arrington Jr. Boulevard North
Birmingham, Alabama 35203
U.S.A.
Telephone: (205) 326-2700
Toll Free: (800) 654-3206
Fax: (205) 326-2704
Web site: http://www.energen.com

Public Company
Incorporated: 1978
Employees: 1,542
Sales: $1.43 billion (2007)
Stock Exchanges: New York
Ticker Symbol: EGN
NAICS: 221210 Natural Gas Distribution

■ ■ ■

Energen Corporation is a diversified holding company involved in the exploration, development, production, and distribution of natural gas, oil, and natural gas liquids. At the heart of Energen is its subsidiary, Energen Resources Corporation, a nonregulated oil and gas company that generates the vast majority of the holding company's sales and profits. Nearly all of Energen Resources' reserves are located in the San Juan Basin in New Mexico, the Black Warrior Basin in Alabama, the Permian Basin in Texas, and in northern Louisiana and eastern Texas. Energen's operating utility is the Alabama Gas Corporation (Alagasco), the largest distributor of natural gas in Alabama. Alagasco serves 450,000 residential, business, and industrial customers in a 22,000-square-mile service territory.

ALAGASCO IN THE SEVENTIES

During the 1970s, Alagasco was a mature natural gas utility with limited growth prospects. A poor regulatory environment existed in Alabama, with its public service commission committed to the traditional utility rate case process. Shareholder values were negatively affected by this limited growth potential, so in 1979, a year after incorporating, Energen was organized as a holding company for Alagasco's increased earnings and enhanced shareholder value.

Energen dedicated itself to oil and gas exploration and production as a nonregulated energy business seeking diversified growth. Energen added other energy-related businesses over time; however, these were mostly short-term enterprises that were sold or discontinued. "We learned that growing diversified earnings was not easy," Energen executives revealed in an annual report.

Thereafter, Energen concentrated on oil and gas exploration and production for diversified growth. "Over the years," company management explained in an annual report, "a variety of opportunities and challenges have influenced Energen's operations, but our basic strategic focus has not changed. ... [W]e continue to work to provide shareholders with earnings growth superior to that offered by a 'pure' utility by combining the strength of our utility with profitable diversification."

COMPANY PERSPECTIVES

Energen Corporation dramatically expanded its oil and gas focus over the past dozen years and is, today, among the Top 20 independent exploration and production companies on the basis of U.S. reserves.

CHANGES IN THE EIGHTIES

Pivotal changes occurred in the 1980s, accentuating the need for Energen to remain keenly competitive. First, gas prices collapsed early in the decade, leaving utilities to sort out messy legal and contractual problems with gas producers. State government regulators became more sympathetic to utilities at this time and were more willing to pass some costs of legal settlements to utility customers.

The regulatory mood in Alabama began to shift. Energen found itself in a progressive regulatory environment. In particular, Rate Stabilization and Equalization (RSE) activity enacted by the Alabama Public Service Commission (APSC) affected Energen positively. In 1983, the APSC abandoned the traditional utility rate case process in favor of a rate-setting mechanism, RSE, to give state utilities opportunities to earn a return on average equities within a specified range. The commission approved quarterly adjustments in order for utilities to earn a return on equity by the end of a given year. Rates increased annually depending on projected costs. A quarterly review of rates ensured that earnings fell within the allowable range.

Deregulation of well-head prices and interstate pipelines also proved beneficial to Energen. In the turbulent times of deregulation, Energen cooperated well with state agencies, which further enhanced the company's position in the new regulatory environment.

Operational changes initiated during the 1980s formed the foundation of Energen's future business strategies. Energen began unbundling its services to large commercial and industrial customers at this time. The company first introduced flexible rate strategies to attract large customers in the deregulated market. Later the flexible rate strategies helped Energen address the possibility of released pipeline capacity from other utilities. In addition, Energen started the P Rate, which decreased pipeline costs for large transportation customers and lowered gas supply costs for residential customers.

Energen worked to keep gas utility rates low, since competition increased between gas utilities and the low-cost electricity providers in residential and small commercial markets. For example, Energen diversified its gas portfolio and took other measures to decrease gas costs.

After a long decline through the decade, the oil and gas industry reached its lowest point in 1986. U.S. consumption of gas dropped below any previous level. Although consumption of gas in the United States rose 4.8 percent in 1987, demand projections for future years showed no more than a 3 percent increase annually, beginning in 1988. (Utility stocks were sensitive to inflation, so rates were expected to increase in 1988 as well.) In 1988, most state utility commissions agreed on a 13 percent rate of return on shareholder's equity, so shares yielded about 7 percent.

During the mid- and late 1980s, Energen focused on growth and diversification to intensify shareholder value. In 1988 specifically, Energen grew through acquisitions. The company bought and improved local city gas systems throughout Alabama. Energen's oil exploration activities also secured the company's footing. Energen found gas in northern Alabama that was easily accessible and had the potential to increase earnings when gas prices recovered. In light of these developments, industry analysts expected Energen's earnings to increase about 16 percent in 1988.

In addition, federal tax credits were available for nonconventional fuel production until 1992, so Energen's gas exploration and production subsidiary became increasingly important during the 1980s. Taurus Exploration took advantage of the tax credits and became a leading developer of coalbed methane in Alabama's Black Warrior Basin by the end of the decade.

GROWTH DURING THE NINETIES

Early in the 1990s, Energen stopped developing one coalbed methane project. When the tax credits ceased in 1992, the project was no longer a viable vehicle for long-term growth. The company nevertheless continued operating coalbed methane wells in Alabama, but counted on conventional oil and gas for its long-term growth prospects.

In May 1994, Energen offered a stock repurchase plan. The company intended to buy back shares to fund its employee savings plan and to meet other corporate obligations. At the time, Energen had 10.9 million outstanding shares.

In July 1994, Conoco, Inc., and Energen agreed to a five-year strategic alliance for coalbed methane programs. Under the agreement, Taurus Exploration provided consulting services for Conoco's acquisition,

KEY DATES

1978: Energen Corporation is incorporated in preparation for its organization as a holding company the following year.
1988: Energen acquires several gas systems in Alabama.
1994: Energen and Conoco, Inc., form a five-year alliance for coalbed methane programs.
1995: Energen commits $500 million to purchase oil and gas properties.
1997: Michael Warren Jr. is promoted to the post of chief executive officer of Energen.
2000: After spending more than $500 million on property acquisitions during the previous five years, Energen's oil and gas reserves reach 1.1 trillion cubic feet equivalent.
2005: Another five-year spending spree, totaling roughly $700 million, increases oil and gas reserves to 1.72 trillion cubic feet equivalent.
2007: Revenues reach a record high of $1.43 billion.

exploration, and development activities. Conoco's U.S. coalgas production came from the central Appalachian Basin, the San Juan Basin in New Mexico, and the Pocahontas gas project in Virginia. Conoco concentrated its overseas coalbed methane activities in France, Germany, and the United Kingdom. Taurus held about 1,000 coalbed methane wells in the Black Warrior Basin of Alabama and in Europe. (Until 1992, the company relied on the Section 29 tax credit to develop these coalbed methane holdings economically.)

In 1995, Energen introduced a strategic plan for developing Taurus as an oil and gas exploration and production subsidiary. In fact, Energen initiated an overall diversified corporate growth plan beginning that year. The company planned to invest $500 million to the year 2000 to acquire additional properties, for offshore exploration and for other developments. An early part of the plan included a three-and-a-half year agreement with Sonat Exploration regarding ongoing reserve acquisitions. Energen's annual investment in the agreement was projected between $25 million and $50 million from 1996 through 1998. Energen bought oil and gas properties using $100 million of short-term credit throughout 1995 and 1996.

Energen offered $250 million of debt and common stock at varying terms in 1996 to finance its acquisition of properties, reduce debts, or meet other corporate needs. For instance, in September, the company sold $125 million in medium-term notes. Energen invested $26 million on conventional oil and gas reserves in 1996, but also allocated funds for an unexpected opportunity to develop nonconventional fuel through Taurus Exploration. In July, Energen purchased 105 billion cubic feet of coalbed methane reserves in the Black Warrior Basin from Houston-based Burlington Resources, Inc., at a cost of $61 million. Energen received a 100 percent working interest in 100 wells on 19,000 gross acres with proven reserves in west central Alabama. Net annual production from the property exceeded 4.5 billion cubic feet, and production on 43 percent of the wells qualified to receive the nonconventional fuels tax credit through the year 2000.

In 1996 alone, Taurus spent $108 million on producing properties with development potential and another $18 million on offshore exploration and development of 12 wells in the Gulf of Mexico. From 1996 through 2000, Energen expected to invest $400 million buying properties to develop through its subsidiary. Energen committed another $100 million to offshore exploration and development in the Gulf of Mexico by Taurus.

Results in 1996 were remarkable. Taurus added 172 billion cubic feet of gas equivalent in 1996, increasing its total year-end reserves 164 percent. The subsidiary's oil and gas production rose 60 percent, and net income grew 28.5 percent.

Alagasco likewise earned 13.2 percent return on average equity in 1996, marking a record net income for the sixth consecutive year. Moreover, the Alabama Public Service Commission continued 1996's Rate Stabilization and Equalization through the year 2000, giving Alagasco the opportunity to earn between 13.15 percent and 13.65 percent return on earnings in the future. This ensured good service for Alagasco's customers and also guaranteed shareholders a healthy return on investments. "Everything seems to be going fine on the utility side," Michael C. Heim of A.G. Edwards and Sons told *Petroleum Finance Week*. "Alagasco got an extension of its rate stabilization structure, which allows it to make adjustments annually to offset expenses and earn close to its authorized rate of return."

Overall, Energen's earnings rose from $19.3 million in 1995 to $21.5 million in 1996. "Fiscal 1996 was an excellent year for Energen from a financial perspective," said Energen Chairman and CEO Rex J. Lysinger in *Petroleum Finance Week*. "But it was an even better year in terms of the tremendous success we achieved in implementing the first year of our aggressive, five-year diversified growth strategy." Energen expected 1997 to be another exceptional year.

In July, Taurus acquired coalbed methane properties in the Black Warrior Basin owned by Amoco Corporation. Energen paid $72 million for the properties (260 producing wells on 100,000 gross acres in Jefferson County, Alabama) with the potential to produce more than seven billion cubic feet annually. (Taurus had operated 170 Amoco wells since 1988.) Production from the wells qualified for nonconventional fuel tax credits, which would increase annually with inflation, until the year 2000. Taurus expected about $6 million in tax credits related to its coalbed methane production and anticipated a 70 percent increase in oil and gas production. According to Morgan Keegan and Company's David H. Tannehill, a gas utility analyst based in Memphis, in *Petroleum Finance Week,* "Taurus' management is good and the unit is run well. It's more conservative than other oil and gas producers because it has focused on acquiring properties to develop instead of to explore. So Taurus' emphasis on producing properties with development potential makes its strategy reasonably low risk."

LOOKING TO THE NEW CENTURY

Industry analysts warned that the future of Energen could be quite different as it faced new challenges. For example, gas utilities throughout the nation considered implementing residential unbundling in the late 1990s. Residential unbundling called for offering separate services at separate prices to residential customers or offering them a choice of energy providers in order to gain market-driven pricing and improved efficiencies. "We do not need to unbundle our residential rates to be motivated to keep costs down and operate efficiently—long-standing competition has provided that impetus," explained Lysinger and William Michael Warren Jr., president and chief operating officer, in Energen's 1996 annual report. "Neither do we see residential unbundling in Alabama generating significant earnings for Alagasco, as we already have extremely good market penetration."

Another challenge was the possible threat of consolidation within the industry. Energen, however, only saw itself bigger and stronger in the future. As corporate executives explained in the 1996 annual report: "By the end of the century, we expect Taurus and Alagasco to be contributing about equally to consolidated earnings, and we are targeting consolidated ROE [return on equity] to exceed the utility's return. Finally, we envision Energen as a much larger company, having a market capitalization of more than $500 million. As we move into the twenty-first century, Energen will continue to rely on its strategic planning process to guide the company's operations and to evaluate future opportunities for enhancing shareholder value."

A NEW ENERGY GIANT TAKES SHAPE

The one fault in management's vision of the future was underestimating its abilities. The senior officers projecting a market capitalization of $500 million stood atop a company with a $4.5 billion market capitalization 12 years later, as Energen thoroughly transformed itself through aggressive expansion. The company, once just a local utility serving Alabama, became one of the 20 largest independent energy concerns in the United States, achieving its impressive growth by leaning on its most important subsidiary, Energen Resources.

During the second half of the 1990s, Energen more than made good on its promise of spending $500 million on acquiring energy properties. Preferring gas assets to oil assets, the company spent the years entrenching its position in the San Juan Basin, the Black Warrior Basin, and the Permian Basin. It supplied Energen Resources with the capital to pursue an extraordinarily aggressive expansion campaign. Between 1996 and 2000, Energen Resources spent $510 million on property acquisitions, $185 million in related development, and $80 million in exploration and associated development. By the end of 2000, Energen Resources' oil and gas reserves totaled 1.1 trillion cubic feet equivalent.

Energen had no intention of slowing its pace of expansion in the new century. Warren, who had been promoted from chief executive officer of Energen Resources and Alagasco to chief executive officer of Energen in 1997 and chairman of the holding company in 1998, led the charge forward. He directed his senior officers to scour the North American energy market for new properties with significant amounts of proved undeveloped (PUD) reserves. The search uncovered a wealth of suitable acquisition candidates, primarily gas properties that became part of Energen Resources' portfolio. Between 2000 and 2005, Energen Resources' spent roughly $700 million on new property acquisitions, which lifted revenues in 2005 above the $1 billion mark for the first time in the holding company's history. After spending $1.2 billion on property acquisitions during the previous decade, Energen Resources possessed oil and gas reserves with 1.72 trillion cubic feet equivalent.

Aggressive expansion continued after 2005, fueled by the $1 billion Energen Resources intended to spend on property acquisitions by 2010. The growth enabled Energen to post record high financial totals in 2007, when the holding company generated $1.43 billion in revenues and collected $309 million in net income. The completion of Energen Resources' third five-year plan by the end of the decade promised to make the company one of the largest competitors in the country, lifting it toward heights few observers could have anticipated a decade-and-a-half earlier.

Charity Anne Dorgan
Updated, Jeffrey L. Covell

PRINCIPAL SUBSIDIARIES

Alabama Gas Corporation; Energen Resources Corporation; Energen Resources TEAM, Inc.

PRINCIPAL COMPETITORS

EnergySouth, Inc.; Pioneer Natural Resources Company; Southern Company.

FURTHER READING

"Conoco, Energen Make Global Coalgas Pact," *Coal & Synfuels Technology,* August 1, 1994, p. 6.

"Conoco, Energen Set Alliance," *Oil Daily,* July 6, 1994, p. 5.

"Conoco, Inc.," *Oil and Gas Journal,* July 11, 1994, p. 30.

"Energen Files Shelf Registration to Sell up to $250 Million of Debt and Common Stock," *Petroleum Finance Week,* September 9, 1996.

"Energen Registers to Sell $125 Million of Medium-Term Notes," *Petroleum Finance Week,* September 23, 1996.

"Energen to Buy Amoco Properties," *Oil Daily,* July 10, 1997, p. 8.

"Energen to Buy Back Stocks," *Oil Daily,* May 27, 1994, p. 7.

"Energen's Taurus Exploration Unit Acquires Burlington Resources' Black Warrior Assets," *Petroleum Finance Week,* July 22, 1996.

Mendes, Joshua, "Gas Stocks with Glowing Dividends," *Fortune,* June 20, 1988, p. 111.

"Taurus Supplies Much of Energen Corporation's Fiscal 1996 Upward Earnings Kick," *Petroleum Finance Week,* November 11, 1996.

Ennis, Inc.

2441 Presidential Parkway
Midlothian, Texas 76065
U.S.A.
Telephone: (972) 775-9801
Toll Free: (800) 752-5386
Fax: (972) 775-9820
Web site: http://www.ennis.com

Public Company
Incorporated: 1909 as Ennis Business Forms, Inc.
Employees: 6,256
Sales: $610.61 million (2008)
Stock Exchanges: New York
Ticker Symbol: EBF
NAICS: 323116 Manifold Business Form Printing

■ ■ ■

Ennis, Inc., is a leading wholesale manufacturer of printed business products and apparel. The company sells a comprehensive line of stock and custom business forms, checks, commercial printing, office supplies, presentation products, and multimedia packaging. Ennis's printed business products operations generate nearly 60 percent of its annual sales. Apparel sales account for the balance. The company's apparel business, operated under the name "Alstyle Apparel," makes a line of knit basic activewear, generating 95 percent of its revenues from T-shirt sales. Ennis operates through 44 facilities in the United States and Mexico.

ORIGINS

Ennis Business Forms was founded in Texas in 1909, eventually serving customers both in the United States and Mexico. Ennis printed and nationally distributed a line of business forms and products such as hand- or machine-written records and documents. The majority of the company's products were custom or semicustom jobs based on customer specifications regarding size, color, number of parts, and quantities.

In fact, Ennis historically offered the most diversified line of business forms in the industry. The company utilized various weights, widths, colors, sizes, and qualities of paper when producing printed products. Unlike other business forms companies, Ennis sold its products solely through local printers, stationery shops, and other independent dealers.

SEASONAL SALES AND OVEREXTENSIONS IN THE SEVENTIES

Ennis experienced seasonal fluctuations in sales throughout its history. In particular, the raw cotton industry affected sales annually, with most forms selling prior to harvesting season. However, the economy in general was by far the predominant factor in the company's quarterly sales fluctuations. By the 1970s, Ennis had expanded and financially extended itself beyond safe limits. Change was on the horizon.

Kenneth A. McCrady joined Ennis in 1970, serving as vice-president of finance. In May 1971, he became an executive vice-president and treasurer of the company.

COMPANY PERSPECTIVES

From a small, rural company serving the cotton industry to a complete printed products manufacturer, Ennis has always strived to increase the success of our distributors. Dedicated to serving the wholesale printing industry for over 96 years, we bring together a unique mix of experience, distinction and innovation to simplify the way you do business and maximize your profits. Ennis is your expert for forms, promotional and financial printing solutions and now apparel!

Then that same year McCrady was named president and chief executive officer, positions he retained until April 1985 when he was elected chairman.

Charged with revitalizing the company, McCrady redirected Ennis from large, low-margin accounts in metropolitan areas during the 1970s to small businesses in the 1980s. Earlier, Ennis had conducted about 50 percent of its business in metropolitan areas. Now the company concentrated on specialized forms for small businesses in rural locations or small cities. Less price competition in these areas made price increases possible for the company.

From 1980 through 1989 earnings per share rose 20 percent annually. Dividends also increased at a 30 percent compound rate, and McCrady ably decreased outstanding stock shares by four million.

McCrady achieved a debt-free, cash-abundant company by 1989. That year, only about 25 percent of Ennis's business came from metropolitan areas. The company operated with a net margin of about 15 percent, twice the industry average. According to Katarzyna Wandycz of *Forbes,* since McCrady "was named chief executive in 1971 with a mandate to straighten out the overextended company. ... [H]e has run it with ultraconservatism. ... But there is nothing conservative about Ennis' results." Stock shares purchased in 1980 were valued somewhere around ten times that amount by 1989.

RESPONDING TO THE CHANGING INDUSTRY IN 1989

At the end of the 1980s, the business forms industry began stagnating. In the past, the industry grew faster than the overall economy, but 1989's projections showed future growth in line with the economy's.

In addition, competition increased for Ennis. Historically, one of the company's major strengths was its network of dealers. When other business forms firms were selling through mail order, Ennis developed healthy relationships with local printers and stationery shops. At the end of the 1980s, though, other industry players began working through dealer networks in efforts to expand their channels of distribution.

McCrady needed another survival plan for Ennis. "Since the industry is slowing," he told *Forbes* in 1989, "the only way to increase sales is to take somebody else's market share by cutting prices. But if you do that, margins are going to suffer. And we are not interested in sales just for the sake of increasing sales." Instead Ennis responded to sluggishness in the business forms industry by launching new products; for example, pressure-sensitive labels and advertising specialties such as pens and key chains.

A GROWTH PLAN FOR THE NINETIES

McCrady also decided to shrink the company in the next decade. In May 1996, Ennis enacted a new growth plan, which included generating more orders through lower selling prices and improved service time. This resulted, however, in higher costs as more employees were needed to carry out the plan.

Nevertheless, Ennis established a growth target of 10 percent annually in 1996, an aggressive target given the mature industry and shrinking market. (Half of Ennis's fiscal 1997 revenues, for example, came from products whose usage was declining, but in a market still worth about $7 billion at retail prices.) Ennis worked to gain market share and to expand into non-form products and services.

Initially, the company emphasized sales growth. Then Ennis redirected its attention to profits. In 1996, for example, Ennis spent $13.6 million on equipment, especially for process-color commercial printing, label/form combinations, variable data printing, and bar codes. The company also completed production improvements for business forms, labels, and presentation products. Ennis invested both in computer systems for customer service and in production equipment. (An additional $6.9 million was allocated for production improvements later in the decade as well.)

TWO ACQUISITIONS IN 1996

Until 1996, Ennis maintained one subsidiary, Connolly Tool and Machine Company, which complemented its business forms operation. Connolly Tool and Machine

KEY DATES

1909: Ennis is founded.
1971: Kenneth A. McCrady, Ennis's new chief executive officer, shifts the company's focus from large corporate accounts to small businesses.
1989: To invigorate sales, the company introduces new product lines.
1997: Ennis forms a commercial printing products business unit, marking its entry into software development.
2000: Ennis acquires Northstar Computer Forms Inc.
2004: The purchase of Alstyle Apparel and Activewear Manufacturing Co. marks Ennis's entry into the apparel business.
2008: Revenues surpass $600 million, having more than doubled during the previous four years.

designed and manufactured tools, dies, and machinery per customer specifications at a production facility in Dallas, Texas. Throughout its history, Connolly Tool and Machine mostly served clients in the southwestern United States. It became known as one of the leading independent machinery designers and manufacturers in the region.

The subsidiary distributed its tools, dies, and special machinery on a contract basis to individual customers. It utilized various types and grades of metals as raw materials for production, as well as purchased electrical and mechanical components at market prices from major suppliers. Then in April 1996 Ennis purchased a presentation folder manufacturer located in Los Angeles, California. Ennis expected to gain better growth for its product line in the West Coast market through this acquisition. The company also purchased a commercial printing operation located in Seattle, Washington, in April 1996. Ennis viewed this acquisition as an opportunity to enter into short-run, high-quality process color printing, since the acquisition provided production and marketing expertise in a high-potential area.

COMMERCIAL PRINTING VENTURES IN 1997

In 1997, Ennis earned the highest sales in the history of the company, with net sales rising 8.2 percent. Net earnings, however, declined due to lower selling prices and higher costs, which frustrated company leaders. McCrady, by that time chairman of the board and chief executive officer, and Nelson Ward, president and chief operating officer, wrote in one of the company's 1997 interim reports that "We continue to achieve sales growth; however, we are disappointed with the rate of growth. … We continue to believe that we can reasonably expect 3 percent to 4 percent unit sales growth on our traditional business forms products. We are also continuing to search for acquisitions which meet our strategic requirements."

Ennis's leaders planned to bring consistent growth in sales and earnings in the near future through the development of its commercial printing business. Committed to enlarging its commercial printing business, Ennis appointed Keith Walters as vice-president of commercial printing operations. (Walters formerly was a vice-president of manufacturing at Atlas/Soundalier, one of American Trading and Production Company's divisions.) The company also engaged in software development as part of the same strategy.

Ennis developed the InstaLink software system, which provided a communication network through which customers could conduct business with Ennis. The system operated through the Internet. A customer could send orders or make inquiries about an order, while Ennis plants provided proofs, quotes, and order status reports through InstaLink. The company also developed its Printers' Mall software in 1997. An internally developed software system, Printers' Mall was used by dealers and their customers to design and order process-color commercial printing.

Ennis targeted these efforts to small and medium-sized businesses. The Printers' Mall system greatly reduced the cost of four-color printing for smaller businesses, and Ennis's InstaColor production process allowed users to create custom postcards, brochures, and catalogs using personal computers, and pre-designed templates. Ennis achieved smaller order quantities and affordable prices through commercial printing, providing its dealers with a viable option for serving small businesses. As Ward noted in a press release: "Direct-selling commercial printers often require minimum quantities that far exceed the needs of smaller businesses. With our new software and production process, however, we have the capability of providing these businesses, which are served by our dealers in all fifty states, easy design capability, low-quantity orders, and the selling power of color."

PLANTS AND FACILITIES IN 1997

In 1997 Ennis operated 16 manufacturing facilities in 12 states and Mexico City, including a manufacturing facility and general offices in Ennis, Texas. The company owned most of these facilities, except for the Portland, Los Angeles, Seattle, and Mexico City plants, which were leased. (Another plant in Boulder City, Nevada, closed in November 1995. The company leased this property to a third party.)

A PLAN FOR THE 21ST CENTURY

As Ennis approached the end of the 20th century in 1997, the company began to change in order to lessen its dependence on the business forms market. (In 1997, business products still accounted for 96 percent of the company's net sales.) Although fully committed to marketing its existing products and services, Ennis executives also vowed to seek acquisitions and to improve the company's efficiency to achieve targeted sales growth.

The search to find new avenues of financial growth would lead to arguably the boldest move in Ennis's lengthy history, but the company did not make its leap of faith until its centennial neared. Until that signal moment arrived, Ennis played the role of a consolidator in the business forms industry, completing a series of small acquisitions that eliminated competitors and increased its market share. The company that entered 1996 with only one subsidiary controlled 30 subsidiaries a decade later, as acquisitions broadened Ennis's product offerings, paved its entry into new markets, and added thousands of new employees.

One of the largest acquisitions during the period was the $42 million purchase of Northstar Computer Forms Inc. in 2000. Itself a consolidator in the business forms industry, Northstar employed 320 workers at two plants in Minnesota, where it primarily made bank forms. The acquisition gave Ennis a total of 17 production facilities in 12 states. By the time it acquired Calibrated Forms Co., Inc., in 2002, Ennis operated 29 production facilities in 12 states. The company's annual sales had climbed to $229 million by the time it completed the Calibrated Forms deal, a volume that would nearly triple in the next five years.

ALSTYLE ACQUISITION IN 2004

In November 2004, Ennis made the move that would change its corporate profile dramatically. The company, which was ranked as one of the largest business forms concerns in the country, jumped into the apparel business. Ennis acquired Alstyle Apparel and Activewear Manufacturing Co., an Anaheim, California-based manufacturer of T-shirts, tank tops, and fleece garments. Alstyle knitted cotton and polyester fibers into tubular material and dyed the materials at a manufacturing facility in Anaheim before shipping the materials to its facilities in Mexico, where the materials were cut and sewn into finished apparel items. The company generated nearly all its revenue from the sale of T-shirts in the United States.

The addition of Alstyle changed the face of Ennis. The company restructured itself, organizing its business into two segments: print and apparel. By the time it submitted its annual filings for 2004 to the Securities and Exchange Commission, it had changed its name from Ennis Business Forms, Inc., to Ennis, Inc. The company's payroll grew exponentially as well, increasing to more than 6,000 employees, roughly half of whom worked in Mexico.

In the wake of the Alstyle acquisition, Ennis pressed ahead with its acquisition campaign in the business forms industry. Numerous, small acquisitions were completed that steadily added to the company's stature. In January 2006, it paid $1.2 million for Tennessee Business Forms, Inc. Two months later, it paid $4.6 million for Specialized Printed Forms, Inc. In September 2007, Ennis paid $2.7 million for Trade Envelope, Inc. The following month it paid $12.5 million for B&D Litho, Inc.

EMBARKING ON A NEW CENTURY

The acquisitions, coupled with the foray into the apparel business, fueled the greatest financial growth in Ennis's history. The company had ended the 1990s with $150.9 million in revenues. Nearly a decade later, on the eve of its centennial, Ennis generated $610.6 million in revenues. In the years ahead, the company was expected to continue acquiring business forms competitors while building its apparel business. After a century of business, Ennis showed no signs of slowing down. The company was demonstrating a drive for growth that was bringing it close to the $1 billion sales mark, a target it likely would hit during its second century of business.

Charity Anne Dorgan
Updated, Jeffrey L. Covell

PRINCIPAL SUBSIDIARIES

Ennis Business Forms of Kansas, Inc.; Calibrated Forms Co., Inc.; Connolly Tool and Machine Company; Admore, Inc.; PFC Products, Inc.; Ennis Acquisitions, Inc.; Texas EBF, LP; Ennis Sales, LP; Ennis Management, LP; Adams McClure, LP; American Forms I, LP; Northstar

Computer Forms, Inc.; General Financial Supply, Inc.; Crabar/GBF, Inc.; Royal Business Forms, Inc.; Alstyle Apparel, LLC; A and G, Inc.; Alstyle Ensenada LLC; Alstyle Hermosillo LLC; Diaco USA LLC; Cactex S.A.B. de C.V. (Mexico); Cactex de Mexico S.A.B. de C.V.; Alstyle International de Mexico S.A.B. de C.V.; Alvest, S.A.B. de C.V. (Mexico); Diaco International S.A.B. de C.V. (Mexico); Tennessee Business Forms, Inc.; TBF Realty, LLC; Specialized Printed Forms, Inc.; Block Graphics, Inc.; Trade Envelope, Inc.; B&D Litho, Inc.; Skyline Business Forms.

PRINCIPAL DIVISIONS

Print Segment; Apparel Segment.

PRINCIPAL COMPETITORS

Deluxepinpoint; Delta Apparel, Inc.; Cenveo, Inc.

FURTHER READING

"Competitor Acquired," *Graphic Arts Monthly,* November 2002, p. 24.

"Ennis Expands Product Offerings," *Graphic Arts Monthly,* December 1999, p. 32.

"Ennis in $18 Million Deal," *Office Products International,* August 2004, p. 24.

"Ennis Inc. Buys Assets of 2 Business Forms Makers," *Dallas Morning News,* October 8, 2007.

"Ennis Is Purchasing Kansas Rival," *Daily Deal,* August 27, 2002.

"Ennis Pays $3 Million for Royal Business Forms," *Graphic Arts Monthly,* December 2004, p. 17.

Levy, Melissa, "Texas Company to Acquire Northstar Computer Forms in $42 Million Transaction," *Star Tribune,* February 22, 2000, p. 10B.

Quinn, Steve, "DeSoto, Texas-based Paper Products Firm Defies Critics with Success," *Dallas Morning News,* May 24, 2002.

"USA: Ennis Consolidates East Coast Operations," *just-style.com,* March 22, 2005.

Wandycz, Katarzyna, "Limited Options," *Forbes,* November 27, 1989, p. 166.

Evergreen Energy, Inc.

1225 17th Street, Suite 1300
Denver, Colorado 80202
U.S.A.
Telephone: (303) 293-2992
Fax: (303) 293-8430
Web site: http://www.evenergy.com

Public Company
Incorporated: 1984 as Kfx, Inc.
Employees: 200
Sales: $48.7 million (2007)
Stock Exchanges: New York (Arca)
Ticker Symbol: EEE
NAICS: 212111 Bituminous Coal and Lignite Surface Mining

■ ■ ■

Evergreen Energy, Inc., is a leading developer of a coal refining technology that produces cleaner and more affordable fuel out of coals with a high water content. The company owns patents for processes that produce what it calls "K-Fuel," a refined coal. Evergreen owns a pilot coal processing plant in Gillette, Wyoming, and also runs coal laboratories and coal certification centers in Gillette and in Rapid City, South Dakota. Through its Ohio-based subsidiary, Buckeye Industrial Mining Co., Evergreen does business in coal marketing and logistics. Another subsidiary, C-Lock Technology, operates in the field of automated measurement of greenhouse gas emissions and carbon emissions. Evergreen also investigates coal and energy development abroad, principally in the Asia-Pacific region, through its Evergreen Energy International subsidiary.

EARLY YEARS

Evergreen Energy was founded by Theodore Venners and partners in 1984 as Kfx, Inc. Venners had long been involved in mining and real estate in the West. He began his working life as an aide to the governor of South Dakota, and later cofounded a Wyoming strip mine company, Fort Union Mine Partnership. He sold his mines in 1980 to the French company Compagnie Française des Petroles. National Public Radio reported in a profile on Venners in 2003 that the entrepreneur had made "tens of millions of dollars" on the sale. Although he could easily have retired with this fortune, Venners instead sought another investment opportunity.

Venners was very knowledgeable about Western coal, which varies greatly from the coal mined in the eastern United States. The coal mined in Wyoming's vast Powder River Basin is low in sulfur, which makes it less of a pollutant than Eastern coal. However, it is also high in moisture. Powder River Basin coal has a moisture content of about 30 percent by weight. This kind of coal also has a low heating value. It is difficult to transport as well, because it is unstable, with a tendency to self-ignite (catch fire). Thus, although the western United States has plentiful deposits of this so-called low rank (low grade) or subbituminous coal, it has historically not been in high demand. Powder River Basin coal sells for a fraction of the price of higher-grade Eastern (or bituminous) coal.

COMPANY PERSPECTIVES

Evergreen Energy refines coal into a cleaner, more efficient and affordable fuel. Using a patented process involving heat and pressure, Evergreen makes coal cleaner before it's burned, which helps coal-fired facilities operate cleaner and more efficiently. Evergreen's K-Fuel refined coal process is available on a near-term basis for addressing both our nation's growing energy demands and important environmental concerns. For utilities and industry—we're a near-term solution to coal-fired efficiency and environmental concerns. For consumers, we help meet their energy needs, keep utility rates low and make their communities cleaner. For the country, we improve the energy and environmental qualities of our largest domestic energy source.

COAL BENEFICIATION

When Venners sold his mines, he became interested in the possibility of making something out of low-rank coal. Coal is used for 50 to 60 percent of the energy needs of the United States, and demand for coal is growing as parts of the Third World industrialize rapidly. Coal-burning plants release greenhouse gases which contribute to global warming, and can also release toxins including sulfur and mercury into the air. Accordingly, Venners speculated in the mid-1980s that there would be growing need for inexpensive coal, especially if it was cleaner-burning than high-grade coal. He began to investigate what is known in the industry as coal beneficiation or the process of making something better out of raw coal.

Work on coal beneficiation began in earnest in the 1970s, when the rising cost of imported oil spurred research into domestic energy sources. Venners was soon drawn to the research of Edward Koppelman, a prolific inventor who worked out of the Stanford Research Institute (SRI) in Palo Alto, California. Koppelman had worked on many projects since the 1920s. He was well known for developing deicing and defogging equipment for the Air Force during World War II. He had also developed aircraft insulation and antenna systems, patented a process that dried wood using radio waves, and found ways to recover valuable minerals from rice hulls. His interests also extended to mining. In the 1970s, he worked on coal beneficiation.

At SRI, Koppelman patented several processes that produced high-energy, clean-burning fuel from organic materials, waste materials, and from low-rank coal. In 1984, Venners and partners bought interests in Koppelman's low-rank coal patents. They founded Kfx, Inc., and began building a pilot coal plant to test out the beneficiation process. The goal was to reduce the water in the low-rank coal using heat and pressure. The resulting material bore the patented name K-Fuel, the K standing for Koppelman. In 1986, the pilot plant was moved to its current site in Gillette, Wyoming.

INITIAL RESULTS

Kfx spent approximately $50 million over the next decade to develop the K-Fuel process. The company learned a lot along the way. Kfx was at first most interested in reducing the water content of Powder River Basin coal. However, the company soon learned that its refining process had a side benefit of also significantly reducing pollutants. Venners explained in an interview with *Waste News* (October 27, 2003), "When we use the temperatures and pressure to remove moisture from the coal, it squeezes out and vaporizes the pollutants. Mercury removal is kind of like what the Post-It note is to 3M: not what we intended to do, but a nice benefit." The environmental aspect of the K-fuel process became an important element in the firm's marketing.

By the late 1990s, the company was able to boast that it could improve the heating ability of its low-rank coal by a marked amount. The Wyoming coal typically produced 8,400 British thermal units (Btu) per pound in its raw state. After being processed into K-Fuel, the coal produced about 11,400 Btu per pound. This was almost as high as Eastern coal, which averaged about 12,000 Btu when mined. Because K-Fuel already had much of its pollutants removed in processing, plants burning K-Fuel did not need to spend money on scrubbers and other equipment that removed pollutants emitted during burning. The economics of the process looked feasible.

INVESTORS AND CUSTOMERS

Kfx attracted several large investors. Thermo Ecotek Corporation, a division of the Waltham, Massachusetts power company Thermo Electron, put $60 million into Kfx while its K-Fuel process was being developed. The leading coal company Kennecott Energy and Coal also provided technical assistance to the Gillette pilot plant. However, Kfx was slow to attract major customers for K-Fuel. A fire at the Gillette plant in 1996 may have unsettled potential investors, as spontaneous combustion was a dreaded problem with refined coal.

KEY DATES

1984: Company is founded.
1986: Pilot K-Fuel processing plant moves to Gillette, Wyoming.
1996: Fire occurs at Gillette pilot processing plant.
2004: Company announces Alaska coal deal with Kanturk Partners.
2005: Founder Theodore Venners steps down as CEO.
2006: Name changes from Kfx to Evergreen Energy.
2008: Evergreen shuts down pilot processing plant.

Despite several setbacks and grueling years perfecting the pilot plant, Venners was a tireless advocate for Kfx and K-Fuel. After the terrorist attacks against the United States on September 11, 2001, the Bush administration turned its attention more closely to domestic energy supplies. Venners was quick to promote Kfx as an alternative to imported oil. Venners referred to the American West as "the Saudi Arabia of coal," (*Rocky Mountain News,* November 16, 2001), and claimed that "the reserves in Wyoming would be enough for 200 years of U.S. power supply." Following this with a glowing account of K-Fuel's environmental benefits, Kfx seemed to have an increasingly desirable product. However, while Venners told the *Rocky Mountain News* in 2001 that Kfx was in the final stages of negotiation with several utilities for large-scale production of K-Fuel, he declined to name these partners. Several years later, these customers still had not materialized. The company listed revenue of $4 million for 2000, and had a total of 50 employees.

WORKING WITH ALASKAN COAL

After working on the beneficiation process for 20 years, finally in 2004 Kfx announced it had a tentative agreement to license its technology to a firm that would process low-rank coal from Alaska. Alaska had abundant coal in its Beluga coal fields, but this, like Wyoming coal, had a high water content. The government of Taiwan had just announced an agreement with Alaska state officials to purchase Beluga coal. Kfx's license agreement with a Washington firm, Kanturk Partners LLC, would have given Alaska a way to make its coal more attractive to the Taiwanese.

However, there were two major problems with the Taiwan-Kanturk-Kfx deal. One was that Alaska's attorney general, Gregg Renkes, had a conflict of interest. Although he represented the state of Alaska to Taiwan, he had performed consulting for Kfx since 1990, and he held a lot of Kfx stock. He stood to gain considerably from even the hope of Kfx pulling off the deal, as its stock price soared on the news.

The other problem was that Kanturk was not so much a third party as it had appeared. An industry player licensing Kfx technology would have granted the company some legitimacy. This was not the case, though. One of the Kanturk principals turned out to be John Venners, brother of Kfx chief executive Theodore Venners, and a founding partner of Kfx himself. Kfx revealed the close ties between Kfx and Kanturk only after it had announced the deal. It also became public at this time that John Venners had paid a $10,000 fine in 2000 to settle allegations by the Securities and Exchange Commission that he had fraudulently manipulated Kfx's stock price.

Venners had not admitted wrongdoing in the 2000 case. Nevertheless, the Alaska deal very quickly looked sour. Kfx had enjoyed a rising stock price over the previous year, up 73 percent in 2003. Longtime stockholders were in a position to make a lot of money off Kfx, as they had bought low and could sell high. Yet the company itself was not making money off refining coal. In a combined statement for 2001 through 2003, Kfx claimed to have revenue of $78,000, and losses of $63.4 million.

MOVING ON

In September 2005, Theodore Venners stepped down as Kfx's CEO. He remained chairman of the board, and was still the company's single largest stockholder. Venners was replaced by Mark Sexton, who had been head of Evergreen Resources, a Denver-based natural gas company. This was seen as good news by Kfx investors, as Venners was tarred by the dealings with his brother, Kanturk Partners, and Gregg Renkes in Alaska. Kfx's stock price continued to rise sharply. By late 2005, its price had gone up 150 percent over the past year. The company's fortunes were bolstered by an investment of $3 million from one of the world's leading coal companies, Arch Coal. Shortly after the Arch deal was announced in the fall of 2005, Kfx entered an agreement with another Western energy company, Black Hills, to do a test burn of K-Fuel.

Kfx had a troubled past and decades of losses. Still, investors seemed to think its technology was promising. The factors that had made coal beneficiation seem a good bet in the 1980s were even stronger at the midpoint of the first decade of the 2000s. Energy demand was rising worldwide, environmental concerns were even more compelling, and Kfx had a fix on a clean, and inexpensive, refining process. A profile of Kfx in *Barron's* (August 22, 2005) characterized the K-Fuel refining process as "transformative" of the coal industry, if it was successful. Kfx seemed a high-risk gamble, but one that promised large returns if it could do what it hoped to do with low-rank coal.

MEDIA IMAGE

Venners and Sexton continued to talk up Kfx. Its stock price was still buoyant into 2006, and the company's market capitalization approached $1 billion. A reporter for the regional business magazine *Colorado Biz* (January 2006) claimed that "Kfx's decades-long investment is about to pay off." The deal with Arch Coal seemed to show that the Kfx process was about to reach a new level of feasibility. At an alternative energy conference in the spring of 2006, Mark Sexton claimed that the company could transform Wyoming coal into Eastern-grade coal at only a fraction of the price, and that the company was in the final stages of testing at its Gillette plant.

Much of Kfx's share price seemed to rest on the company's hopes, rather than on what it was actually producing. Perception was important to investors. This was shown when Kfx's share price dropped sharply in September 2006 after a test burn of K-Fuel at an Ohio utility. Although the burn seemed to have gone well, Kfx did not immediately reveal that there had been some problems in shipping the K-Fuel. Sexton characterized the problems with excessive dust and heat as minor. However, wary investors dumped the stock, and the price slid 18 percent in one day.

A few weeks after the Ohio test burn, Kfx announced that it was changing its name to Evergreen Energy. At the same time, it moved its stock from the American Stock Exchange to the electronic NYSE Arca exchange. The new name had connotations of clean, green energy. It also tied into the past of Mark Sexton, who had led Evergreen Resources before moving to Kfx. Theodore Venners also stepped down as board chairman, although he remained a board director and the company's chief technology officer. These changes seemed to signal a break with the controversy that had dogged the Kfx name in the past.

SENSE OF URGENCY

Several developments ensued after the name change. In January 2007, Evergreen announced that it had formed an arrangement with a subsidiary of TXU Corporation, TXU Generation Development Co., to explore refining K-Fuel at TXU power plants. TXU, a Texas firm, was particularly interested in the environmental benefits of Evergreen's technology. A few months later, the major Japanese conglomerate Sumitomo entered into a deal with Evergreen to buy a 4 percent share in a new subsidiary, Evergreen Energy Asia-Pacific, which would investigate business opportunities in Asia. These partnerships seemed to show an increasing possibility that the K-Fuel process would gain commercial viability.

Although these deals looked promising, the company was evidently still not moving swiftly enough into commercial operations. Evergreen's board of directors let chief executive Mark Sexton go in April 2007. Sexton had been in place less than two years. He was succeeded by COO Kevin Collins, who was named interim CEO. The reason given for Sexton's ouster was that the company needed to accelerate its search for new customers.

Evergreen soon had a deal penciled with an Indonesian mining firm, brokered through Sumitomo and the company's Asia-Pacific subsidiary. In addition, the Bechtel Power Corporation lent technical expertise to Evergreen, in order to solve some lingering problems at the Gillette pilot plant.

In March 2008, Evergreen announced that it was closing down the Gillette plant. It took a write-down of $109 million. The company's 2007–08 shareholders' letter had made developing new commercial opportunities a top priority. The letter also stated, "we do have a sense of urgency" about reaching construction agreements with customers, either domestically or abroad. Market factors continued to make K-Fuel a promising investment: coal prices were rising worldwide, and environmental controls were increasingly necessary and expensive. K-Fuel offered a less expensive, clean energy solution. By the spring of 2008, though, the company's stock price had dropped 90 percent from its high two years earlier. With its pilot plant shuttered, Evergreen seemed to face even more barriers to reaching commercial viability.

Evergreen had gained important technological insight from its partnership with Bechtel. CEO Collins told shareholders that the company could apply this technology elsewhere. He also left the door open for restarting the Gillette plant, should the opportunity arise.

Angela Woodward

PRINCIPAL SUBSIDIARIES

Buckeye Industrial Mining Co.; C-Lock Technology, Inc.; Evergreen Energy International, LLC.

PRINCIPAL COMPETITORS

Arch Coal, Inc.; PacifiCorp.; Rhino Resource Partners, L.P.

FURTHER READING

Bradner, Tim, "Alaskan Coal Developer Watches New Processing Plant Progress in Wyoming," *Alaska Journal of Commerce,* January 2, 2005.

Buchsbaum, Lee, "Energy Innovators," *Colorado Biz,* January 2006, pp. 42–47.

Chakrabarty, Gargi, "Evergreen Energy CEO Leaves Company," *Rocky Mountain News,* April 25, 2007.

Dobbyn, Paula, and Bill White, "Experts Question Renkes' Large Holding of Kfx Stock," *Anchorage Daily News,* October 31, 2004, p. A1.

Draper, Heather, "The Mr. Clean of America's Coal," *Rocky Mountain News,* November 16, 2001, p. 7B.

"Evergreen Energy Advances Proposed Coal Refinery Project with Sumitomo and Major Indonesian Mining Group," *Business Wire,* January 31, 2008.

"Evergreen, TXU Explore Use of K-Direct Coal Refining Process," *Energy Resource,* January 31, 2007.

Hayhurst, Tracy, "Firm's System Boosts Coal Energy," *Waste News,* October 27, 2003, p. 2.

Jakab, Spencer, "Arch's Kfx Move: Unconvincing," *Barron's,* October 17, 2005, p. 18.

———, "Fueling a Controversy," *Barron's,* August 22, 2005, p. 24.

Merriam, Norman W., *Upgrading Low Rank Coal Using the Koppelman Series C Process,* Laramie, Wyo.: Western Research Institute, 1997.

Milstead, David, "Evergreen Energy Idles Wyoming Coal Refinery," *Rocky Mountain News,* March 21, 2008, p. 4Business.

Norris, Michele, "Analysis: Several Entrepreneurs Have Brought to the Marketplace Systems That Can Eliminate Mercury from Coal," *All Things Considered* (National Public Radio), December 12, 2003.

Raabe, Steve, "Coal-Processing Company Kfx Inc. Changes Name to Evergreen Energy Inc.," *Denver Post,* September 27, 2006.

———, "Kfx on Defense After Slide," *Denver Post,* September 15, 2006, p. C3.

Salpukas, Agis, "Energy for a Power Source," *New York Times,* January 2, 1998.

Seelig, Fred, "Coal Cleaning Cheaper Than Clean Coal," *Chemical Market Reporter,* May 22, 2006, p. 6.

Weil, Jonathan, "Moving the Market," *Wall Street Journal,* September 29, 2004, p. C3.

Evraz Group S.A.

Ulitsa Dolgorukovskaya 15, Bldg. 4
Moscow, 127006
Russia
Telephone: (+7-495) 232-1370
Fax: (+7-495) 232-1359
Web site: http://www.evraz.com

Public Company
Incorporated: 1992 as EAM Group
Employees: 110,000
Sales: $12.8 billion (2007)
Stock Exchanges: London Moscow
Ticker Symbol: EVR
NAICS: 331111 Iron and Steel Mills; 331221 Cold-Rolled Steel Shape Manufacturing

■ ■ ■

Evraz Group S.A. is one of the world's largest vertically integrated steel groups. The Moscow-based company's production volumes include more than 16 million metric tons of crude steel each year, nearly 13 million metric tons of pig iron, and more than 15 million metric tons shipped in 2007. The company is also one of the world's leading producers of high-strength vanadium steel and steel products. Evraz operates steelmaking companies in Russia, including the Nizhny Tagil (NTMK), Zapsib (ZSMK), and Novokuznetsk (NKMK) steel mills. Evraz's international steel holdings include Evraz Oregon Steel Mills, Claymont Steel in Delaware, and Strategic Minerals Corporation (Stratcor) based in Danbury, Connecticut; Highveld Steel and Vanadium Corporation in South Africa; Palini & Bertoli in Italy; Evraz Vitkovice in the Czech Republic; Delong Holdings in China; and the North American operations of IPSCO Tubulars. Evraz Group's strong vertical integration strategy allows it to control both its iron ore supply and its fuel supply. The company's mining operations include the Kachkarnasky mining concern (KGOK), one of Russia's largest, which also controls the sole source of vanadium ore in the country; the Vysokogorsky iron mines (VGOK); and the Evrazruda group of mines. Taken together, the group's mining output tops 18 million metric tons per year. At the same time, Evraz controls several coal mines, including Mine 12, Raspadskaya, and Yuzkhkuzbassugol, ensuring its supply of coking coal.

Evraz was founded by Alexander Abramov, who worked as a physicist before becoming one of Russia's most powerful steel traders. The company is led by Alexander Frolov, chairman and CEO, and includes among its major shareholders Roman Abramovich, one of Russia's top tycoons. Evraz is listed on the London and Moscow stock exchanges. In 2007, the group posted total revenues of $12.8 billion.

FOUNDING A STEEL TRADING GROUP IN 1992

Alexander Abramov was a physicist trained at the elite Moscow Institute of Physics and Technology (the Russian equivalent of the Massachusetts Institute of Technology), where he earned his Ph.D. in 1985. Abramov initially worked for the Soviet government and by 1990 had risen to become deputy chief of the Institute

COMPANY PERSPECTIVES

EVRAZ' Vision is to be: a world-class steel and mining company, one of the top five most profitable steelmakers globally; a leader in the construction and railway steel product markets in Russia and CIS; a global player with strong position in flat product markets of Europe and the United States; the lowest cost producer of crude steel in Russia and CIS through superior efficiency and vertical integration; a leading global producer of vanadium products.

of High Temperatures. That body, which worked primarily for the country's aerospace and defense industries, gave Abramov a strong network of connections. In particular, his work brought Abramov into contact with the Russian steel industry, which included major clients of the institute.

At just 31 years of age, therefore, Abramov appeared on track to become one of Russia's leading scientists. However, the collapse of the Soviet Union and the economic upheavals in Russia at the beginning of the 1990s forced Abramov to look elsewhere to earn a living. In an August 2003 *Financial Times* article he was quoted as saying, "By 1990, it became clear that there [would] be no money for science in Russia. It was a simple choice—either I had to leave the country as many of my colleagues did, or to go into business."

Abramov chose the latter route. Initially, Abramov was interested in finding commercial applications for the technologies under development at the institute. Yet Abramov quickly recognized that the lead time for such development was much too long. Any hope for building a revenue stream would require four to eight years of development.

This reality forced Abramov to seek new horizons. The early 1990s witnessed the first wave of Russian entrepreneurs and a growing number of trading groups. Abramov recognized the opportunity to build his own trading company, based on his contacts in the steel industry. In 1992 Abramov and a group of scientists from the Institute of High Temperatures founded the predecessor to the Evraz Group, the metal trading company Evroazmetall. "We had good contacts with the directors of those plants," Abramov told the *Financial Times*, "They knew me personally and this helped me to get my first trading contracts."

The extreme shortage of cash positioned trading groups such as Evroazmetall as central players in Russia's economy during the early to mid-1990s. The former Soviet-era factories were desperate for funds as the country shifted toward a free-market economy. The trading group provided a means for factories to generate the needed cash for raw material purchases and payroll requirements more quickly than having to develop their own distribution side. Evroazmetall thus established a steady supply of steel and steel products for its trading operations.

BECOMING A STEEL PRODUCER IN 1998

The tide began turning against the trading companies, however, as the Russian economy floundered in the second half of the decade. The country's often antiquated and poorly run factories found it hard to compete within the increasingly international and competitive markets. As a result, traders such as Evroazmetall found that their customers owed them huge sums of money. At the same time, an increasing number of producers began buying their own trading operations, cutting out independent traders such as Evroazmetall.

Abramov, who was on his way to becoming one of Russia's leading steel industry figures, had no intention of allowing his company to be acquired. Instead, he decided to transform the company from a steel trader into a steel producer. He worked out a series of agreements by which he converted customer companies' debts into equity in their operations. In this way, the company quickly built a portfolio of stakes in leading steel producers, mining companies, and steel products manufacturers. The company established a new holding group, EAM Group, to bring together these production assets.

The companies themselves, many of which had declared bankruptcy, were eager to accept EAM's offer. By 1997, EAM had completed its first truly significant takeover, the Nizhny Tagil steel plant (NTMK), located in the Sverdlovsk region. Founded in 1940, NTMK originally specialized in the production of armor plate and served as a major producer for the Soviet army. Later, the steel group produced steel rails for the railroad industry. NTMK had been privatized in 1992, but it already faced bankruptcy by 1995. As part of EAM, the NTMK operations were rationalized, and by the end of the decade NTMK had become profitable.

Unlike most of Russia's new oligarchs who built up vast and highly diversified conglomerates, Abramov chose to focus the EAM operations on a core of rail and construction steel production. This interest brought Abramov to western Siberia and specifically to the Kemerovo region, the site of Russia's largest rail steel

KEY DATES

1992: Physicist Alexander Abramov founds steel trading group Evroazmetall.
1998: Evroazmetall becomes EAM and transitions into steel production with acquisition of NTMK.
1999: EAM restructures steel holdings under Evraz.
2005: Evraz registers in Luxembourg and lists shares on London Stock Exchange then acquires steel mills in the Czech Republic and Italy.
2006: Evraz acquires 73 percent of Stratcor in the United States.
2007: Evraz acquires Oregon Steel Mills in the United States.
2008: Evraz acquires IPSCO steel group in the United States and Canada and 51 percent of Delong Holdings in China.

producers. The region also contained the country's largest coal mines.

With contacts in the steel industry Abramov was able to establish a relationship with the region's governor, Aman Tuleev, who in turn assisted the EAM takeover of two of the region's largest steel groups. Both the Novokuznetsk Iron and Steel Plant (NKMK) and the Zapsib Iron and Steel Plant (ZSMK) had gone bankrupt by the late 1990s. NKMK, founded in the 1930s, had grown into one of the world's top five manufacturers of rail steel products. ZSMK launched production in 1964, ranking as the largest steel mill in Siberia at the time. It was privatized in 1992 but went bankrupt four years later. In 1999, EAM took over the management of both NKMK and ZSMK and exchanged debt for equity in both companies.

By the turn of the millennium, EAM had succeeded in paying off both companies' debts, while gaining controlling stakes in both. The company founded by Abramov just ten years before had grown into one of Russia's leading steel groups, accounting for some 22 percent of the country's total steel output. The company then was restructured, becoming Evraz, and serving as a holding for NTMK, ZSMK, NKMK, as well as the group's growing list of other operations.

GOING INTERNATIONAL IN THE NEW CENTURY

These other operations included mining. In the Kemerovo region Evraz was in a prime position to accomplish Abramov's second goal for the company: developing vertical integrated operations. Through the end of the 1990s and into the early 2000s, Evraz acquired stakes in a number of mining and ore processing companies, including in Vysokogorsky and Kachkanarsky. In 2002, the company founded Evrazruda, which took over the operations of a number of mining and ore processing companies in the Kemerovo, Khakassia, and Krasnoyarsk Kai regions.

Evraz moved closer to achieving self-sufficiency in its raw material supply as it completed a series of acquisitions through 2004 and 2005. These included Mine 12, situated near both the ZSMK and NKMK steel works. First excavated in 1917, Mine 12 reached outputs of more than 800,000 metric tons of coal per year, including more than 700,000 metric tons of coking coal. Evraz then acquired 50 percent of the Yuzhkuzbassugol mining group. With 12 coal mines, Yuzhkuzbassugol had a total annual output of 16 million metric tons, making it Russia's largest coal mining company. Evraz acquired full control of Yuzhkuzbassugol in 2007. By then, the company had also completed its acquisition of Raspadskaya, the second largest coal company in the Russian Federation.

Evraz had also been building up its ore mining resources especially in Kachkanar, the sole known vanadium ore source in Russia. By 2006, Evraz had gained control of the main mining company in the region, KGOK, which produced a total output of nearly nine million metric tons per year.

In the meantime, Evraz's steel expansion had hit something of a wall in Russia. The company's dominant position, especially in the rail steel sector, meant that its future growth in the domestic market had become limited. At the same time, the company's exports were heavily dependent on Asian markets, as that region accounted for 90 percent of the group's exports. However. the rising power of the Chinese steel industry, both domestically and on the export market made it necessary for Evraz to develop new export possibilities. Europe was an obvious target for the company, but the high import tariffs in place in the region made entry difficult. In order to overcome these obstacles, Evraz launched the next phase of its development: international expansion.

In 2005, Evraz reincorporated in Luxembourg as Evraz Group S.A. and launched an initial public offering (IPO) on the London Stock Exchange. Soon after the listing, founder Abramov announced his plans to retire. Alexander Frolov took over as group CEO and chairman. Evraz began looking for acquisition targets, starting in Europe, to overcome the region's import duties. The company's search took it first to the Czech

Republic, where it bought newly privatized Vitkovice Steel from the Czech government. Next, Evraz turned to Italy, acquiring Palini & Bertoli, based in San Giorgio di Nogaro.

ENTERING NORTH AMERICA IN 2006

Evraz's vanadium production led to its next growth moves. Despite its control of the Russian vanadium market, Evraz lacked the capabilities for processing the ore. For this task, the company began scouting for potential acquisition targets. In the United States, Evraz acquired a 73 percent stake in Strategic Minerals Corporation (Stratcor), a leading producer of vanadium, as well as vanadium and tungsten steel products. Evraz then moved into South Africa, acquiring nearly 25 percent of Highveld Steel and Vanadium. By 2007, Evraz had gained a 54.1 percent stake in Highveld.

At the same time, the company had also entered the general U.S. steel market, with the acquisition of Oregon Steel Mills, originally founded in 1926 as Gilmore Steel Corporation. Evraz's appetite for the U.S. steel market remained strong. In March 2008, the company acquired 93 percent of Clamont Steel holdings, based in Delaware, for $565 million. By May of that year, the company had agreed to pay $4.03 billion to buy 12 U.S. and Canadian steel mills, part of the IPSCO Tubulars group, from parent SSAB. Also during this period, Evraz entered the Chinese market, paying more than $1.5 billion for a 51 percent stake in that country's Delong Holdings. From a small steel trader, Evraz had grown into one of the world's steel giants at the beginning of the new century.

M. L. Cohen

PRINCIPAL SUBSIDIARIES

Evraz Oregon Steel Mills (U.S.A.); Evraz Vitkovice Steel; Highveld Steel and Vanadium (South Africa); Nizhny Tagil Iron and Steel Plant; Palini & Bertoli; Strategic Minerals Corporation; West Siberian Iron and Steel Plant.

PRINCIPAL COMPETITORS

GTR Inc.; Libyan Iron and Steel Co.; Qingdao Iron and Steel General Corp.; Guangdong Shaoguan Iron and Steel Group Company Ltd.; Machine Sazi Arak; ArcelorMittal (MT); Cargill Inc.; Reinforcing Steel Contractors; BHP Billiton Ltd.; Groupe PX–PX Holding S.A.; Ahwaz Rolling and Pipe Mills Co.; Nippon Steel Corp.; Trident Steel (Proprietary) Ltd.; Tata Sons Ltd.

FURTHER READING

Bush, Jason, "A Man of Steel Who Keeps a Low Profile," *Businessweek,* June 6, 2005.

———, "Russian Steel Is on the Acquisition Trail," *Business Week Online,* December 4, 2006.

Carney, Seth B., "Testing the Road to Oligarchy," *Czech Business Weekly,* August 8, 2005.

Chuvala, Bob, "Danbury Firm Strikes It Rich," *Fairfield County Business Journal,* April 17, 2006, p. 1.

"Evraz Group Buys Claymont Steel," *Metal Producing & Processing,* January–February 2008, p. 6.

"Evraz Group to Buy 51% Stake in Steelmaker Delong Holdings," *Economist Intelligence Unit,* February 27, 2008.

"Evraz Jumps on Russian IPO Wave with $6.6bn Flotation," *Euroweek,* May 13, 2005, p. 27.

"Evraz Purchase of Claymont Steel Finalized," *American Metal Market,* January 29, 2008, p. 6.

"Evraz to Buy SSAB's North American Pipe, Plate and Tube Business," *Economist Intelligence Unit,* March 20, 2008.

Haflich, Frank, "Evraz Buy of Oregon Steel Fills Void at Both Producers," *American Metal Market,* November 21, 2006, p, 1.

Hartley, Rob, "Evraz Hunting Feedstock to Fuel Higher Output," *American Metal Market,* October 9, 2007, p. 8.

"IPSCO Tubulars Sold to Russian Steel Makers," *Supply House Times,* May 2008, p. 16.

Mackenzie, Michael, "$50bn in Deals Grabs Attention," *Financial Times,* November 21, 2006, p. 38.

"Oregon Steel Purchase Completed," *American Metal Market,* January 25, 2007, p. 6.

Robertson, Scott, "Evraz Posts Big '07 Gains on High Prices, Key Buys," *American Metal Market,* April 3, 2008, p. 8.

"The Science of Forging a Steel Empire," *Financial Times,* August 27, 2003.

Faegre & Benson LLP

2200 Wells Fargo Center
90 South Seventh Street
Minneapolis, Minnesota 55402
U.S.A.
Telephone: (612) 766-7000
Toll Free: (800) 328-4393
Fax: (612) 766-1600
Web site: http://www.faegre.com

Private Company
Incorporated: 1886 as Cobb & Wheelwright
Employees: 1,200
NAICS: 541110 Offices of Lawyers

■ ■ ■

Faegre & Benson LLP is the second largest law firm in Minnesota, employing approximately 525 attorneys who serve clients in the United States, Europe, and Asia. Faegre & Benson's legal services cover roughly 70 areas of specialization, including environmental law, patent prosecution, banking, and finance, but its principal services are related to transactions and litigation. The firm serves clients in more than 60 countries through U.S. offices in Minnesota, Colorado, and Iowa, and international offices in England, Germany, and China. Faegre & Benson is a member of the United States Law Firm Group and the World Law Group, both of which refer commercial attorneys to clients worldwide.

ORIGINS AND EXPANSION

Faegre & Benson's ties to Minneapolis began in 1886, when the firm was established as Cobb & Wheelwright. More than a century later, the firm's historians would be hard pressed to find a trait that connected Cobb & Wheelwright and Faegre & Benson. Although the firm remained in practice from the late 19th century into the 21st century, an achievement not to be dismissed, the only continuity in the firm's history was its headquarters location in Minneapolis. In name, in the areas of its legal practice, and, most assuredly, in size, Cobb & Wheelwright and Faegre & Benson shared little in common. Perhaps because of the sweeping differences separating the firm's origins from its modern guise, Faegre & Benson pays little attention to its early years in its advertising, noting its founding date and nothing more.

By the end of the 1960s, the firm had developed into a recognizable legal force in Minneapolis, a point in the firm's development that marked the beginning of robust growth to follow. By the end of the decade, Faegre & Benson employed 45 lawyers who required a similarly sized support staff to perform their work. All the firm's employees worked on a single floor in the Northwest National Bank Building in downtown Minneapolis. Faegre & Benson's biggest rival, Dorsey & Whitney LLP, shared ties with a bank as well, the First National Bank of Minneapolis.

Both firms grew at a fantastic rate during the next quarter-century. Surging nationwide demand for legal services between the mid-1960s and mid-1980s provided the fuel for expansion. "If you were successful and people knew your name," the chairman of Faegre & Benson's management committee recalled in the November 1994 issue of *Corporate Report-Minnesota,*

COMPANY PERSPECTIVES

Approximately half of our lawyers focus on litigation. We've achieved some of the nation's most significant victories and highest recoveries ever in intellectual property litigation. We represented the plaintiffs in the *Exxon Valdez* litigation, which resulted in what was for many years the largest punitive damage award in the history of American law. We've handled pioneering litigation defending free speech rights. We have served as national counsel in complex class actions for companies like Novartis and 3M. Our litigators have handled cases in nearly every state and at every level of the state and federal court systems, including the United States Supreme Court.

"you could expect your volume to grow 10 percent per year."

However, the demand for legal services began trailing off by the late 1980s. Faegre & Benson responded to its flagging business volume by hiring its first marketing director, aping the corporate reaction to diminishing sales, but more important, the firm had steadily branched out into new practice areas before the late 1980s. "When I came here," a Faegre & Benson attorney told *Corporate Report-Minnesota,* describing his arrival in 1972, "there were no labor, environmental, construction, or health care practices, and certainly no international practice." Faegre & Benson recruited attorneys trained to serve the differing needs of its clientele, perpetuating its growth and staying abreast of Dorsey & Whitney.

Faegre & Benson's diversification into various practice areas also drew its impetus from the needs of its clients. Most significantly, Faegre & Benson's clients established their own in-house counsel over the years. "They're much more sophisticated now than they were 25 years ago," a Faegre & Benson partner was quoted as saying in the November 1994 issue of *Corporate Report-Minnesota,* referring to the firm's clients. "And they are far less willing to pay you to get smart. They expect you to know their business. And know it in detail." Company-funded legal staffs stripped Faegre & Benson of the type of general legal work that had provided a steady stream of income, which forced the firm to expand its range of specialty legal services, becoming adept in a variety of legal areas.

HEADQUARTERS UP IN FLAMES: 1982

Faegre & Benson's maturation was also aided by an event entirely out of its control. On Thanksgiving Day in 1982, a fire destroyed the Northwestern National Bank Building, leaving the firm without a home. Ultimately, the fire was a blessing, forcing the firm's management to reassess every facet of operation, everything from the technology it used to the areas in which it practiced. Having to start over (the firm settled into the Norwest Center, built on the same site as its former headquarters) accelerated the pace of change at the firm, leaving an indelible mark on its culture and its way of doing business. "Law firms don't change radically, they change incrementally," the chairman of the firm's management committee explained in the November 1994 issue of *Corporate Report-Minnesota,* before adding, "but the fire changed us radically."

The various forces driving the firm's expansion between the late 1960s and early 1990s led to impressive growth. By 1994, Faegre & Benson was six times larger than it had been at the end of the 1960s, employing 275 attorneys and 375 support personnel, enough to make it the second largest law firm in Minnesota, trailing only Dorsey & Whitney. Roughly 75 percent of the firm's payroll worked on eight floors in the Norwest Center, while the remainder worked in branch offices that had opened primarily during the 1980s. Faegre & Benson had offices in Des Moines, Iowa; Denver, Colorado; and Washington, D.C. It had also expanded overseas, establishing a presence in London; Frankfurt; and for a brief period, in Almaty, Kazakhstan. Clients by the 1990s included its landlord, Norwest Corporation, and numerous well-known corporations such as Dayton Hudson Corporation, Cowles Media Company, Piper Jaffray Companies, and International Multifoods Corporation.

MANAGEMENT STRUCTURE

Faegre & Benson's partners, attorneys, and support personnel took their orders from the firm's all-powerful management committee. The management committee consisted of eight members elected to four-year terms, with two positions scheduled for election each year. Aside from taking responsibility for guiding the firm's direction, the committee also controlled Faegre & Benson's system of distributing earnings to its partners, a system regarded as unique within the legal community. The distribution of profits was determined by a subjective point system that took into consideration seniority and performance over an extended period, yielding compensation rates that awarded the highest-rated attorney roughly six times more than what the lowest-

KEY DATES

1886: Faegre & Benson is founded as Cobb & Wheelwright.
1982: The firm's headquarters is destroyed by fire.
1990: Faegre & Benson attorneys begin the discovery phase of the lawsuit against Exxon.
1994: A federal jury awards $5 billion in punitive damages and $287 million in compensatory damages against Exxon.
2001: Faegre & Benson establishes an office in China.
2008: The U.S. Supreme Court cuts the punitive damages in the *Exxon Valdez* case to just over $500 million.

rated attorney collected. To foster harmony within the firm, only the members of the management committee knew how much was awarded to each partner.

FAEGRE & BENSON AND *EXXON VALDEZ*

Faegre & Benson's secretive point system was one area of concern when the firm became involved in a landmark case whose magnitude threatened to disrupt its accustomed manner of existence. Faegre & Benson was one of two corporate law firms that sued Exxon Corporation for the 1989 *Exxon Valdez* oil spill that sent nearly 11 million gallons of crude oil into Prince William Sound in Alaska. In 1994, a federal court jury in Anchorage, Alaska, determined the monetary toll to be exacted from the oil company, awarding $5 billion in punitive damages and $287 million in compensatory damages, the largest lawsuit in the history of commercial litigation.

Faegre & Benson's involvement in the *Exxon Valdez* case originated from the efforts of Brian O'Neill, who became the lead trial attorney in the lawsuit. After the oil tanker ran aground, O'Neill flew to Alaska, where he made contact with a small, three-partner law firm in Soldotna named Robinson, Beiswenger & Ehrhardt. The Robinson firm, representing Alaskan fishermen, needed help in bringing action against British Petroleum, an oil company whose tanker had spilled oil into Glacier Bay, near Prince William Sound, in 1987. O'Neill offered the help of Faegre & Benson, won settlements of $51 million for clients, and endeared himself and his firm to the fishermen who were clamoring for action against Exxon. The case also formed the basis for Faegre & Benson's relationship with the Robinson firm, which would serve as Faegre & Benson's local counsel in the *Exxon Valdez* lawsuit. The two firms reached an agreement—a deal, fittingly, negotiated on an Alaskan dock—that called for Robinson to collect 30 percent of clients' fees and Faegre & Benson to collect 70 percent of clients' fees.

When the punitive and compensatory damages were determined in 1994, the prospect of the massive sum Faegre & Benson stood to gain sparked some skepticism about the profits' effect on the firm. The financial gain from the lawsuit, estimated to be in the $150 million range, would be accepted gladly, to be sure, but its deposit into Faegre & Benson's coffers threatened to change the firm radically. The firm's partners were expected to gain $1 million payments from the lawsuit, a sum large enough to foment anxiety about the firm's secretive system for distributing profits. "It may well be that people simply aren't going to be satisfied with not knowing how the other folks are doing," the president of a Minneapolis law firm observed in the December 1997 issue of *Corporate Report-Minnesota,* referring to the distribution of profits at Faegre & Benson. Further, the prospect of the firm's partners receiving such large lump sums sparked concern that a substantial percentage of the firm's greatest talent would opt for retirement or a prolonged sabbatical.

A member of the Exxon trial team, in the same issue of *Corporate Report-Minnesota,* conceded the riches to be gained presented causes for concern. "The Exxon award will create a challenge to the culture and the fabric of the firm, but we've faced a lot of challenges before. … This is something that we'll live with, and we'll continue to operate as a group of colleagues who enjoy practicing law together."

The ultimate lesson learned from the *Exxon Valdez* case is contained in the adage, "Don't count your chickens before they hatch." It was a view expressed by Faegre & Benson's chairman of the management committee in 1997, quoted in the December issue of *Corporate Report-Minnesota,* who said the firm had made one decision about the Exxon award: "We've decided not to spend it, because we don't have it." The settlement of the case dragged on throughout the 1990s and into the following decade, held in limbo by endless appeals, rulings by various courts, including the U.S. Supreme Court, and recalculations of the punitive and compensatory damages awarded.

EXPANSION INTO THE NEW CENTURY

Faegre & Benson, as its most spectacular piece of litigation wended its way through the judicial system, enjoyed strong growth while O'Neill and his team tended to the *Exxon Valdez* case. At the beginning of the 2000s, the firm was in expansion mode, pressing ahead despite the standstill status of what promised to be its largest profit gain ever. The firm tripled the size of its Frankfurt office in early 2001 by merging with the German firm Brendel Ekkenga Daniel. Weeks later, Faegre & Benson received approval from China's Ministry of Justice to open an office in Shanghai, getting the go-ahead shortly after Dorsey & Whitney received permission. The firm also expanded its headquarters during the year, taking another three floors in the Wells Fargo Center, the name of the former Norwest Center. The most significant move on the expansion front occurred in late 2001, when Faegre & Benson's Denver office merged with Bynum & Johnson in Boulder, Colorado, one of the largest law firm mergers in the history of Colorado. The merger added 37 attorneys to Faegre & Benson's Colorado operations, making it one of the five largest law firms in the state.

Faegre & Benson celebrated its 120th anniversary in 2006. Throughout its more than century-long existence, the firm had remained in Minneapolis, establishing itself as a fixture in the midwest legal community and making great strides toward becoming a prominent player in the global legal arena. Although the firm developed its reputation and earned its financial standing from work entirely separate from its involvement in the *Exxon Valdez* lawsuit, the largest lawsuit in the history of commercial litigation had a way of overshadowing everything not related to the lawsuit. The preeminence of the lawsuit persisted because of its size and because of its longevity. By 2008, 18 years after the discovery phase of litigation began, Brian O'Neill was still behind his Faegre & Benson desk tending to the details of the lawsuit.

According to his estimation, O'Neill had logged more than 24,000 hours on the *Exxon Valdez* lawsuit by 2008, watching the punitive assessment against Exxon drop, rise, and fall again to $2.5 billion. In June 2008, the U.S. Supreme Court gave its final say on the matter, slashing the charges against Exxon to just over $500 million. The venerable midwest firm, after the nearly two-decade ordeal, could focus entirely on the many areas of legal practice in which it excelled.

Jeffrey L. Covell

PRINCIPAL COMPETITORS

Oppenheimer Wolff & Donnelly LLP; Lindquist & Vennum PLLP; Dorsey & Whitney LLP.

FURTHER READING

Austin, Marsha, "Montano Calls It Quits After a Lifetime of Law," *Denver Business Journal,* January 1, 1999, p. 10A.

Branaugh, Matt, "Boulder, Colo., Law Firm to Merge with International Firm's Denver Office," *Daily Camera,* November 16, 2001.

"Faegre & Benson LLP; Established 1886," *China Law & Practice,* August 15, 2003, p. 46.

Fletcher, Amy, "Local Law Firm Merges," *Denver Business Journal,* November 16, 2001, p. 10A.

Fudge, Tom, "Waiting for Payday: Will Greed Rock the Boat at Faegre & Benson?" *Corporate Report-Minnesota,* December 1997, p. 50.

Hoogesteger, John, "Faegre Triples Frankfurt Office to Meet Demand," *CityBusiness,* March 2, 2001, p. 2.

Jones, Barbara L., "Statistics Show Minnesota's Biggest Law Firms Are Getting Bigger," *Minnesota Lawyer,* July 23, 2007.

Lore, Michelle, "Clients Claim Against MN Law Firm Dismissed," *Minnesota Lawyer,* May 20, 2002.

———, "A Slippery Verdict for Minnesota Lawyer," *Minnesota Lawyer,* November 19, 2007.

"MN Law Firm to Open Office in China," *Minnesota Lawyer,* March 26, 2001.

Nelson, Rick, "Once Burned-Out, Faegre Keeps Growing," *Corporate Report-Minnesota,* November 1994, p. 34.

Pribek, Jane, "Two Midwest Law Firms, Two Successful Diversity Models," *Minnesota Lawyer,* May 31, 2004.

Smith, Scott D., "Faegre Expanding Headquarters, Staff," *CityBusiness,* April 27, 2001, p. 4.

Fred Alger Management, Inc.

111 5th Avenue
New York, New York 10003
U.S.A.
Telephone: (212) 806-8800
Toll Free: (800) 992-3863
Fax: (212) 806-2942
Web site: http://www.alger.com

Private Company
Incorporated: 1964 as Fred Alger & Co.
Employees: 170
Sales: $27.2 million (2007 est.)
NAICS: 523920 Portfolio Management; 551112 Offices of Other Holding Companies

■ ■ ■

Fred Alger Management, Inc., is a New York City-based investment advisory firm that caters to both individuals and institutional investors, including corporate pensions, foundations, and government entities. Focusing on growth stocks and priding itself on original research, the firm manages ten mutual funds, six institutional funds, six offshore funds, seven Alger American Funds, the China-U.S. Growth Fund, and the Castle Convertible Fund (dealing in convertible debt and convertible preferred securities). All told, Fred Alger has about $14 billion in assets under management. One of the tenants of the ill-fated towers of the World Trade Center, the firm has successfully recovered from the terrorist attacks of September 11, 2001, in which 35 key employees were killed, including David Alger, executive vice-president and chief financial officer and brother of the firm's founder.

LOSS OF FAMILY FORTUNE A MOTIVATING FORCE

Fred Alger Management was founded by Frederick Moulton Alger III in 1964. The member of a prominent Michigan family that was involved in both business and politics, Alger was born in Detroit in 1934 and raised in the affluent Grosse Pointe suburb. After a prep school education he enrolled at Yale University, graduating with a degree in American studies. In the summer of his junior year, at the behest of his father, he worked at a regional stock brokerage, First of Michigan Corp., and began to learn the basics of investing as well as the value of research. Lacking any prior career ambitions, Alger enrolled in the business school at the University of Michigan, earning an M.B.A. in 1958 while confirming a talent for finance. By that time, Alger knew that the family fortune had been dissipated and that a life of idle wealth was not an option, and so he began a business career, determined to rebuild, and hold onto, the family fortune.

After making his mark with First of Michigan while still in graduate school, Alger went to work for Wells Fargo Bank in San Francisco in November 1958 for further seasoning before taking on Wall Street. Seven months later, however, he was called to active duty in the Marine Corps and upon his return found himself without a job at the bank. He then went to work for a San Francisco mutual-fund management company, North American Securities Co., as a securities analyst. It

COMPANY PERSPECTIVES

At Alger, our primary focus is in assisting our clients and financial professionals in making the best possible investment decisions.

was here that Alger refined his understanding of the stock market and approach to investment.

FORMATION OF FRED ALGER & CO.: 1964

Alger moved to another mutual fund company, Winfield & Co., in 1962 and was soon handed the responsibility of managing one of the firm's three mutual funds, Quality Distribution Shares (QDS). He then convinced his superiors to dispatch him to Wall Street to establish a research operation and a toehold in the East. Hence in the spring of 1963 Fred Alger made his debut on Wall Street, ready for a star turn. In short order Alger left Winfield to directly run QDS for its parent Security Management Company, Inc., and also took charge of the Security Equity Fund. As a result he formed Fred Alger & Co. in October 1964 and with $3,000 in the bank set up shop as a one-man operation at 56 Pine Street.

A strong performance for Security Management quickly established Alger as a rising Wall Street money manager, garnering him some industry attention and in late 1965 led to the management of two mutual funds (one of which took the name the Alger Fund) controlled by Bernie Cornfeld, the "king of mutual fund operators" who made his mark pitching mutual funds to military personnel and others abroad. Two months later Alger took on a partner, William Scheerer, a respected Wall Street veteran who, ten years older, provided a good balance to the sometimes brash Alger. Moreover, while Alger was drawn to growth companies, Scheerer focused on undervalued companies. Later in 1966 Alger signed up his first high-net-worth individual, Chat Hickox, a friend and business associate who had inherited $1 million and had not been satisfied with the performance of Smith Barney in growing his assets. A second employee was taken on at the start of 1967 and during the spring the growing operation moved to larger accommodations at 120 Broadway.

Media attention, such as a 1968 cover story in *Institutional Investor,* turned Alger into a well-known figure, the epitome of the "go-go money manager" of the period, often admired and sometimes criticized. Alger took on another Cornfeld fund, Canadian Venture Fund, at the close of 1968, and a year later became investment adviser to Security Ultra Fund. The stock market soon hit a rough patch late in 1969 and into 1970 and just as quickly as his star ascended, Alger found himself struggling to maintain his reputation. He was fired by Cornfeld in March 1970, and only months later Cornfeld suffered the same fate as his empire of mutual funds folded.

DAVID ALGER JOINS FIRM: 1971

In July 1970 Alger registered with the Securities and Exchange Commission (SEC) as an investment adviser and the company took its first seat on the New York Stock Exchange. By the end of the year, the ten-person firm managed $160 million in assets and had a net worth of $550,000. It was at this point, at the start of 1971, that Fred Alger's brother, David Dewey Alger, joined the firm. Nine years younger than his brother, David Alger received a degree in history from Harvard University and, like Fred, worked summers at First of Michigan. He planned to become a criminal lawyer but soon became interested in an investment career after his brother provided him with a hot stock tip that his girlfriend took advantage of and provided him with a share of the profits. Again like his brother, David Alger earned an M.B.A. from the University of Michigan. He then went to work at New York's Irving Trust Co., which was just forming a research department. After a year of learning the ropes in Wall Street he went to work for a boutique investment firm, and then joined his brother in a junior research position to help support the firm's growing business that resulted from being a registered investment adviser.

Asking quickly to be put in charge of a planned hedge fund, he was put in his place by his older brother, who told him, "You don't just show up and automatically become good at the stock market. This is a trade you learn after many years of beating your head on the floor." While occasionally harsh on David, sometimes upbraiding him in front of the research department, Fred Alger also took his brother under his wing and provided him with a thorough understanding of the trade.

The early 1970s were a difficult time for Fred Alger Management. After losing the Cornfeld funds, the firm was fired by Security Management Co. in 1972. The business was rebuilt over the next few years. A European investment banking venture, Lansdowne Ltd., was launched, and in 1974 the Percy Friedlander brokerage was acquired from City Investing as well as a pair of closed-end funds: Spectra Fund and CI Fund (which was renamed Castle Convertible Fund). The brokerage

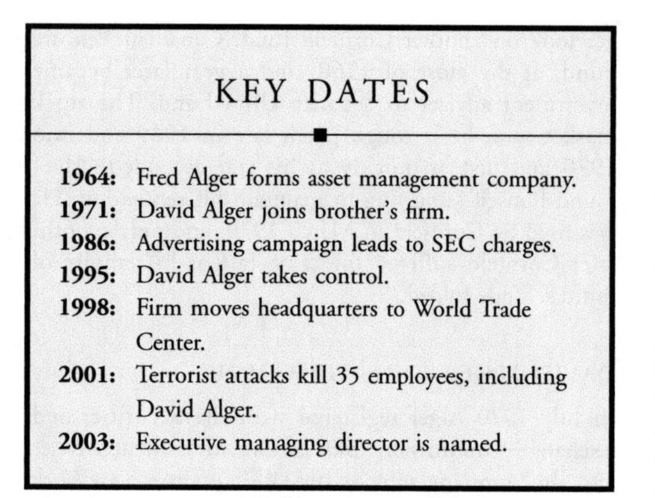

KEY DATES

1964: Fred Alger forms asset management company.
1971: David Alger joins brother's firm.
1986: Advertising campaign leads to SEC charges.
1995: David Alger takes control.
1998: Firm moves headquarters to World Trade Center.
2001: Terrorist attacks kill 35 employees, including David Alger.
2003: Executive managing director is named.

would leave two years later, however. Fred Alger also began seeking institutional accounts: in 1976 the company signed its first major client, Celanese, and also courted pension accounts. Late in the 1970s Fred Alger enjoyed a strong rebound that carried into the next decade and reestablished his reputation as a premier stockpicker.

Scheerer retired from the firm in 1982 and a third of his shares were divided among David Alger and two other key employees. In time David Alger's stake would grow to 20 percent. Also in the early 1980s the firm beefed up its infrastructure to position it for continued growth. A search firm for analysts was established and the Alger brothers, according to *Baron's,* "shamelessly mined their alma maters, Yale and Harvard, for musicians, poetry majors, actors and jocks with high grade-point averages"—anyone, in short, who was smart and accustomed to putting in long hours and working hard. A brokerage clearing operation was opened in New Jersey with settlement capabilities in 1980. David Alger was also made the head of the research unit during this period.

AD CAMPAIGN BACKFIRES: 1986

In 1986 Fred Alger looked to stimulate further growth with a television and print advertising campaign that used as its theme, "A Genius for Managing Money." It was not an approach that was well received by Wall Street competitors or the SEC, however. The firm, and Fred Alger in particular, was taken to task for misleading claims about the performance of funds since the 1960s. An article in *Barron's* written by Benjamin J. Stein was especially scathing. What was more important was the reaction of the SEC, which in October 1987 charged the firm with deceptive advertising. A settlement was reached in March 1990 in which Fred Alger neither admitted nor denied the allegation.

Fred Alger's hot streak continued into the mid-1980s. Crocker Investment Management Corp. was acquired from Wells Fargo & Co. in 1986, and in that same year six mutual funds were unveiled. The good times came to an abrupt end in October 1987 with what became known as "Black Monday" when the stock market crashed. The U.K.-based firm of Dawnay Day attempted to acquire the firm in early 1988, but the bid did not come to fruition. Two years of subpar performances, due in large measure to the decline of growth stocks, led to the withdrawal of $1.1 billion, or 44 percent, of the money the firm had under management, according to the *Wall Street Journal.* One bright spot during this period was the performance of David Alger's Small Cap Fund, which in 1989 posted a gain of more than 65 percent, the country's best performing mutual fund.

The firm's net worth was $62.6 million in 1990, representing a 15 percent drop over the $73.7 million recorded two years earlier. With the United States in recession, the early 1990s were tough times for everyone and Fred Alger was no exception. In 1993 the World Trade Center was bombed by terrorists, prompting the firm to take measures to prepare for future disasters. A back office was established in Morristown, New Jersey, and each day research data and account information was backed up and transferred to it. A substitute stock trading operation was put in place and regular drills were conducted to make sure all was ready.

Around this time Fred Alger also began making plans to preserve his wealth. Because of high federal estate taxes, as much as 55 percent, Alger elected in 1995 to renounce his U.S. citizenship and in April of that year, to avoid publicity, moved to Geneva, Switzerland, while taking citizenship in St. Kitts-Nevis at the cost of a fee of $50,000 and the ownership of $150,000 in local property. Alger continued to visit the United States, maintaining a home on Long Island, but his stays by law were limited in time. Although retired, Alger did not completely withdraw from the firm he founded, using his European base to help promote Alger Fund portfolios.

David Alger replaced his brother as the head of Fred Alger Management and quickly made his mark, helped in large part by an improving economy. He also increased the firm's stature by becoming a frequent guest on the increasingly important television financial programs, and in time he overcame the tag of being the younger brother of Fred Alger and gained a reputation in his own right. He took over a firm with $3 billion in assets under management and enjoyed steady growth in the mid- to late 1990s, benefiting greatly from the performance of technology stocks. By the end of 1998 the firm had $10 billion of assets under management, a number that would swell to $16 billion early in the new century before a collapse in the tech sector led to a severe drop in the stock markets, especially the NASDAQ.

TERRORIST ATTACKS LEAD TO LOSS OF 35 EMPLOYEES: 2001

In late 1998 Fred Alger Management relocated its headquarters to new offices high in one of the twin towers of the World Trade Center in lower Manhattan, which was ironic given that the firm's backup plans were formulated in response to the 1993 bombing of the complex. Irony would give way to tragedy, however, on September 11, 2001, when terrorists flew a pair of airliners into the towers. The firm was devastated: 35 out of the 55 headquarters' employees were killed, including David Alger. Fred Alger was in the country at the time, packing up to leave his Long Island home for Switzerland after a vacation. The catastrophe plans that he had spearheaded after 1993 were put into effect. The employees working in the firm's Jersey City offices that handled administrative, marketing, and fund pricing were ordered to move to the Morristown facility even before the towers collapsed.

Not only did the firm have the Morristown and Jersey operations to fall back on, it retained some key employees who happened to be away from the World Trade Center office on September 11. Fred Alger was also available to step in to fill the leadership void and the firm was soon able to bring back several former employees to help in the recovery. Moreover, these people brought with them new experiences to help the firm improve its business model. "In returning from the brink," according to *Pensions & Investments,* "Alger's senior management took a long, hard look at the business. They analyzed every aspect of the fee structure of institutional accounts and mutual funds, looked critically at trading, and took apart all investment processes." Consequently, Alger emerged stronger in some ways. A decision to establish a management committee in charge of day-to-day activities after Fred Alger stepped away in 2002 did not work, however. The situation was rectified a year later when for the first time in the firm's history an executive managing director was named.

Staying in business was a significant accomplishment for Alger, but there was little the firm could do to overcome a poor economy and a downturn in the stock market. Assets under management receded to $9 billion five years after the events of September 2001, the firm's situation exacerbated by changes in the insurance industry and a number of mergers and acquisitions among clients that forced them to choose between asset managers. All too often, Alger lost out. The firm's focus on growth stocks also did not do well during a time when value investing returned to favor, but the pendulum would swing once again and by 2006 Alger's fortunes began to improve. On the other hand, the firm again had to contend with the SEC and charges of mutual-fund "market timing" and late trading. After three and a half years, the matter was settled in January 2007 when Alger agreed to pay a $10 million penalty and return $30 million, the money earmarked for affected investors. Improving fund performance led to an increase in assets under management to $16 billion by 2008.

Ed Dinger

PRINCIPAL OPERATING UNITS

The Alger Funds; The Alger Institutional Funds; China U.S. Growth Fund; Alger American Fund; Offshore Funds; Castle Convertible Fund.

PRINCIPAL COMPETITORS

AXA Rosenberg Group LLC; Old Mutual (US) Holding, Inc.; Wells Capital Management.

FURTHER READING

Anders, George, and Beatrice E. Garcia, "Making Claims: Fred Alger Regains Wall Street Spotlight, but His Ads Rile Some," *Wall Street Journal,* October 1, 1986, p. 1.

Atlas, Riva D., "A Firm Adds Staff and Woos Veterans Back into the Fold," *New York Times,* September 10, 2002, p. C6.

Atlas, Riva D., and Geraldine Fabrikant, "After Havoc, Reviving a Legacy," *New York Times,* September 29, 2001, p. C1.

Brown, Ken, "Rebuilding Wall Street: At Fred Alger, Close Ties Lure Back Alumni," *Wall Street Journal,* November 15, 2001, p. C1.

———, "Rebuilding Wall Street: Six Months After: For Alger, the Return of Founder, Alumni Helps Stabilize Ship," *Wall Street Journal,* March 8, 2002, p. C11.

Bruner, Jon, "In the Sunshine," *Forbes,* October 29, 2007, p. 78.

"From the Ashes; Fred Alger Management," *Economist,* September 7, 2002, p. 85.

Gertner, Jon, and Ilana Polyak, "The Reincarnation of Fred Alger," *Money,* February 2002, p. 84.

Hoover, Ken, "Alger MidCap Growth on the Mend," *Investor's Business Daily,* July 14, 2002, p. A08.

Martin, Douglas, "David Alger Is Dead at 57," *New York Times,* September 25, 2001, p. A27.

McReynolds, Rebecca, "The Hard Road of Recovery: How One Firm, Fred Alger Management, Has Survived the Devastation of 9/11," *Buyside,* September 2002, p. 34.

Mirchandani, Dilip K., *One Way Up Wall Street: The Fred Alger Story,* New York: Fred Alger Management, 1999, 496 p.

Norton, Leslie P., "The Legacy," *Barron's,* October 8, 2001, p. F5.

Peek, Liz, "Five Years Later, Fred Alger Has Made a Comeback," *New York Sun,* September 11, 2006.

Smith, Anne Kates, and David Landis, "Deaths in the Family," *Kiplinger's Personal Finance,* November 2001, p. 34.

Stein, Benjamin J., "A Hard Look at Fred Alger's Performance," *Barron's,* November 3, 1986, p. 14.

Williamson, Christine, "Introspective Alger Returns from Brink with Renewed Energy," *Pensions & Investments,* June 10, 2002, p. 28.

Fuel Systems Solutions, Inc.

3030 South Susan Street
Santa Ana, California 92704-6435
U.S.A.
Telephone: (714) 656-1300
Fax: (714) 656-1401
Web site: http://www.fuelsystemssolutions.com

Public Company
Incorporated: 2006
Employees: 1,002
Sales: $265.33 million (2007)
Stock Exchanges: NASDAQ Global Market
Ticker Symbol: FSYS
NAICS: 336399 All Other Motor Vehicle Parts Manufacturing

■ ■ ■

Fuel Systems Solutions, Inc., operates the largest alternative fuel technology research facility worldwide and is the holding company for two of the leading gaseous fuel system technology companies in the world, IMPCO Technologies, Inc., and BRC S.r.l. IMPCO Technologies, of Santa Ana, California, designs, tests, manufactures, and markets alternative fuel systems for heavy duty and industrial equipment applications, such as forklifts, and other material handling equipment, small portable engines, and large stationary generators. BRC, of Cherasco, Italy, designs, manufactures, and markets alternative fuel systems for automobiles, buses, and fleet delivery vehicles. The company offers fuel systems integration for gaseous fuel storage, fuel delivery, and electronic control for original equipment manufacturing and aftermarket conversion. The company's products are distributed through more than 140 dealers in 53 countries. Sales and marketing offices as well as assembly facilities are located in the Netherlands, Italy, Australia, Japan, Argentina, and the United States.

COMPANY EDGE IN EXPANSION OF ALTERNATIVE FUELS

The history of Fuel Systems Solutions, Inc., begins with the formation of Impco Carburetion in 1958. A manufacturer of original equipment for the automotive industry, Impco produced aftermarket kits for converting cars and trucks to alternative fuel usage. Over the years, Impco established a worldwide reputation for producing quality applications for low-emission, alternative fuel engines, including those used in forklifts and other industrial equipment, as well as cars and trucks. In 1989, AirSensors, Inc., an electronic fuel injection manufacturer, purchased Impco, then a subsidiary of A.J. Industries that generated annual sales of $18.5 million.

AirSensors and Impco, the latter renamed IMPCO Technologies, Inc., combined their knowledge to create state-of-the art electronic fuel systems for low emission, alternative fuel technology. After passage of the National Energy Policy Act of 1992, AirSensors and IMPCO found many new opportunities for product development. Adapting to new regulations for low-emission engines and air quality improvement, automotive manufacturers invested in alternatives to the

COMPANY PERSPECTIVES

Fuel Systems Solutions, through its subsidiary companies, offers the industry's most extensive solutions within the alternative fuels markets, including: automotive and mass transportation vehicles, heavy duty, industrial equipment, power generation and stationary engines.

gasoline-powered, internal combustion engine. The quality of IMPCO products attracted new business. For instance, in July 1993, General Motors contracted with IMPCO to engineer an electronic fuel system for natural gas vehicles. The two-year agreement included testing, production, and installation.

Other high-profile contracts followed. IMPCO retrofitted fleet vehicles for the Texas Department of Transportation for use with liquid petroleum gas (LPG). The U.S. Department of Energy (DOE) National Renewable Energy Laboratory hired IMPCO to develop an LPG ultra-low emission rehicle. IMPCO applied its gaseous fuel technology to transform a Chrysler LH sedan, with a 3.3 liter V-6 engine. With the Southern California Gas Co., IMPCO created a natural gas vehicle upfit and conversion center. The three-year contract involved operation of the 60,000-square-foot Ecotrans center. Plans included a 24-hour-a-day testing facility to certify emissions on engine families, such as compressed natural gas engines.

As a leader in alternative fuel systems, IMPCO expanded its distribution in the United States and worldwide. An agreement with Cummins Power Systems spread IMPCO's alternative fuel systems market to the East Coast, from Boston to Washington, D.C., and west into eastern Ohio. Mikuni Corp. signed an agreement to distribute IMPCO fuel conversion products in Japan. Mikuni customers included Mitsubishi, Honda, Nissan, Suzuki, and Yamaha Motor companies. During the fiscal year ended April 30, 1995, IMPCO shipped 262,327 gaseous fuel management systems, the largest number to date in a one-year period. That year sales reached $45.23 million.

To accommodate anticipated growth, AirSensors acquired three fuel systems companies. A 51 percent interest in Technisch Bureau Media B.V. of the Netherlands expanded distribution of IMPCO products to Germany, France, and the United Kingdom. The acquisition of Garretson Equipment Company, Inc., of Mt. Pleasant, Iowa, gave AirSensors additional manufacturing capacity. In 1997, AirSensors acquired certain assets of Automotive Pty. Ltd. (Ateco), a longtime distributor of IMPCO products in Australia. To further build business on the strength of the IMPCO brand, AirSensors consolidated all of its business operations under the IMPCO Technologies name in 1997.

ADVANCES IN ALTERNATIVE FUELS–RELATED MARKETS

With a solid base of income from its fuel systems, IMPCO took a long view toward expected changes in energy use and air quality improvements by increasing its investment in research. In September 1997, IMPCO established the Heavy Duty Engine Division, intended to focus on alternative fuel systems for trucks and buses, as well as large stationary gas engines used by industry. In November, IMPCO's Technology and Automotive OEM Division opened the Advanced Technology Center in Irvine, California. The 80,000-square-foot facility housed the largest staff of alternative fuel engineers and technicians in one place. The center provided state-of-the-art laboratories and equipment for emissions control and alternative fuel assembly and testing. Technology development involved clean-burning fuel systems for trucks, taxis, delivery trucks, passenger vehicles, forklifts, stationary engines, and other indoor vehicles and portable engines. The center represented IMPCO's intent to develop alternative fuel storage systems, metering, and delivery, particularly for hydrogen fuel cell technology.

In the company's core fuel systems business, IMPCO expanded globally through acquisition, joint venture, and new distributors. In 1998 and 1999, IMPCO obtained several orders from its new Venezuelan distributor, NATURGAS. To strengthen its European distribution, IMPCO formed a joint venture with BERU Aktiengesellschaft, of Germany. IMPCO-BERU Technologies B.V. combined the two companies' complementary product capabilities, such as BERU's ignition technology with IMPCO's alternative fuels technology. In April 1999, IMPCO acquired the alternative fuels division of Mikuni Corp., its Tokyo distributor. Later, in October, IMPCO opened an office in Mexico City for Latin American business. The Mexico City operation provided distributors assistance with technical development, sales and marketing, training, and administration.

Meanwhile, research was leading to several innovations. In November 1999, IMPCO announced that its engineers had made a significant advance in the hydrogen storage technology for automotive usage. The storage cylinder addressed problems of permeability and diffusion of hydrogen fuel, as well as hydrogen's chemi-

KEY DATES

1989: AirSensors, Inc., acquires Impco Carburetion, renamed IMPCO Technologies.
1992: IMPCO Technologies obtains new business after National Energy Policy Act prompts investment in alternative fuel systems.
1997: IMPCO Advanced Technology Center opens in Irvine, California.
1999: IMPCO announces several new alternative fuel technologies.
2005: IMPCO completes merger with BRC S.r.l. and forms Fuel Systems Solutions holding company.
2007: Sales outside the United States reach 77 percent of revenues.

cal damage to metal, by employing a composite material resistant to becoming brittle. The technological breakthrough brought hydrogen fuel one step closer to practical usage as an automotive fuel.

IMPCO developed a new gaseous fuel injector, the IPR Injector Regulator, designed for high pressure injection in fuel cell or internal combustion engines. IMPCO employed electromagnetic technology and fuel metering innovation to produce the multi-point system. The injector could be used with natural gas, propane, and alcohol fuels and, with some modifications, hydrogen fuel.

In April 2000, IMPCO introduced two new products directed toward reducing carbon monoxide in the industrial workplace. Co-Trac monitored carbon monoxide levels in the industrial facility and Co-Trend software analyzed the data to ensure that environmental air quality in the workplace met Occupational Safety and Health Administration requirements. Co-Trac was designed as a compact piece of equipment, to be used on a mobile device, such as a forklift, or from a stationary position. The FGA-4000/4005 gas exhaust analyzer provided repair technicians with updated equipment to diagnose IMPCO's alternative fuel systems.

In July 2001, a yearlong collaboration with Ford Motor Company resulted in development of an alternative fuel system for the F-150 full-size truck, and the Ford Crown Victoria passenger car. Ford began testing both vehicles, which used fuel-injected liquid propane gas instead of gasoline. Several contracts between General Motors and IMPCO initiated collaboration to advance GM's alternative propulsion system with an alternative fuel storage system.

In September 2004, after ten years of research and development, IMPCO introduced an alternative fuel product for the diesel bus and truck market. The Eclipse Heavy Duty Engine Management System utilized clean-burning natural gas and propane in diesel engines. Three years of testing revealed a reduction of nitrous oxide, hydrocarbons, and carbon monoxides by 85 percent compared to diesel engines. Moreover, carcinogenic particulate matter was almost entirely eradicated. Fuel economy was comparable to diesel.

VACILLATING INTEREST BY WALL STREET

Throughout this period of expansion and product development IMPCO attracted the attention of Wall Street investors who became interested in new developments in hydrogen fuel and other fuel alternatives. IMPCO's stock value rose 200 percent in late 1999 and early 2000, from $13 to $44 per share. While questions of feasibility and practical usage arose, the stock price fluctuated wildly. Nevertheless, IMPCO attracted funding from private placements of common stock. In July 2000, IMPCO raised $53 million in private equity, most of it allocated to technological research. In January 2002, IMPCO sold two million shares at $11.25 per share, for a total investment of $22.5 million from institutional investors. In December 2003 another private placement of common stock raised $9.6 million in funding from large institutional investors.

Investor support continued despite IMPCO's debt load and year-over-year losses. In 2000, IMPCO revenues increased to $113 million, nearly double 1995 revenues.

A variety of business losses plus significant research investment led to losses of $6.9 million and $14.2 million in 2003 and 2004, respectively. Also, sales had declined but rebounded to $118.29 million in 2004. As energy independence became a priority in the United States and worldwide, however, IMPCO held an excellent position for future success, with its worldwide distribution capabilities and its technological lead.

ACQUISITION POSITIONS IMPCO FOR EUROPEAN EXPANSION

When the European Union committed to energy independence through alternative fuels, IMPCO acted to capitalize on the opportunities overseas. In October 2002, IMPCO began a merger process with BRC S.r.l., one of the leading manufacturers of automotive alternative gaseous fuel products and systems worldwide. In

July 2003, IMPCO purchased a 50 percent interest in the Cherasco, Italy-based company. BRC customers included major automotive manufacturers, such as Peugeot-Citroën, Jaguar, DaimlerChrysler, FiatTofas, Mitsubishi, Daewoo, and Ford. The following January, BRC began manufacturing IMPCO products for sale in the European market. In February, BRC and IMPCO introduced the first product developed collaboratively, an electronic fuel control valve designed for transportation and industrial uses. IMPCO and BRC planned to market the product in Europe, Latin America, and the United States.

IMPCO continued the process of acquiring BRC in October 2004 in a stock transaction valued at $27.6 million. In early 2005 BRC cofounder and President Mariano Costamanga became CEO of IMPCO, and IMPCO CEO Robert M. Stemmler retained his position as chairman of the board. A February public offering of 4.6 million shares garnered $24.86 million, of which $10.02 million was allocated to the cash portion of the acquisition of BRC. The combination of two leading alternative fuel companies created the largest such company worldwide, with $120 million in revenue. The combined facilities included 17 manufacturing and assembly sites and 27 office locations in more than 50 countries.

In August 2006 IMPCO reorganized under the name Fuel Systems Solutions, Inc., as a holding company for IMPCO and BRC. Stock distribution involved an exchange of two shares of IMPCO common for one share of Fuel Systems Solutions common.

REBOUNDING SALES IN EUROPE AND ASIA

As countries worldwide sought to reduce pollution, to become energy efficient and independent, and to find alternatives to higher gasoline and diesel prices, business development at Fuel Systems Solutions became more global. For instance, European Union guidelines for conversion from liquid fuel vehicles to gaseous fuel vehicles targeted 20 percent of vehicles by 2020. Moreover, governments in Europe subsidized conversion. Similarly, the Australian government encouraged conversion to LPG by eliminating excise tax on LPG until 2011. Hence, Fuel Systems Solutions experienced a steady rise in the proportion of revenues derived from outside the United States to 77 percent in 2007, even as revenues increased significantly, from $118.29 million in 2004 to 265.33 million in 2007.

Product development at Fuel Systems Solutions naturally fit the changing fuel habits overseas, particularly in Australia, where the company held a 30 percent share of the vehicle conversion market. After BRC introduced its state-of-the-art "Sequent" electronic gaseous fuel injection system in June 2005, several original equipment manufacturers selling vehicles in Australia purchased the Sequent for 2005–06 production. Also, in late 2006, BRC introduced the Sequent Direct Injection system. The conversion equipment allowed gasoline-powered direct injection vehicles to operate on LPG, an industry first.

In September 2006, Fuel Systems Solutions introduced its compressed natural gas (CNG) refueling station. The company opened a 15,000-square-foot manufacturing facility in Cherasco, Italy, for production of the refueling equipment. Developed at the company's BRC facility, the three-cylinder, W-shaped compressor was priced to sell for $80,000 to $400,000, depending on the specific model and size. With CNG's popularity amid rising petroleum prices, Fuel Systems Solutions expected significant sales in the years ahead.

In May 2007, BRC expanded its vehicle conversion kit manufacturing capacity when Fuel Systems Solutions acquired Zavoli S.r.l. A manufacturer and distributor of alternative fuel conversion kits in Cesena, Italy, Zavoli produced kits that converted internal combustion engines for usage with LPG or CNG.

IMPCO's growth in the industrial manufacturing segment increased in both the United States and Asia. In Asia, IMPCO gained two significant new customers in forklift manufacturing. The company began distributing emission certified LPG engines to Anhuo HELI Forklift Truck Group in Hefei, China. In April 2008, Hyundai Heavy Industries of Korea signed a contract to purchase components and systems to convert 2.0 liter engines in forklifts to operate on LPG.

In the United States, new regulations from the Environmental Protection Agency and the California Air Resource Board prompted IMPCO to open a new state-of-the-art manufacturing facility in Santa Ana. The facility enabled the company to handle an expected 20 percent increase in demand for conversion kits for industrial equipment. At the end of November, the company reported $6 million in sales for the newest, low-emission equipment for original manufacturers of forklifts, sweepers, and other mobile industrial equipment. New technology at this time included power generation fuel systems designed to meet emissions regulations scheduled to take effect in July 2008. In addition, a fuel system in General Motors' new 3.0 liter engine, also used in industrial equipment, met low-emissions standards effective in January 2010.

Mary Tradii

PRINCIPAL SUBSIDIARIES

BRC S.r.l.; IMPCO Technologies, Inc.

PRINCIPAL COMPETITORS

Aisan Industry Company; Landi Group; Lovato Company; Nikki Company; OMVL, S.r.l.; A.M.T. Tartarni, S.r.l.; TeleflexGFI.

FURTHER READING

"AirSensors to Acquire Firm," *Wall Street Journal,* March 2, 1989, p. 1.

Darmiento, Laurence, "Fuel-System Maker Enjoys Stock Rise Despite Losses," *Los Angeles Business Journal,* February 19, 2001, p. 45.

"Fuel Systems Solutions Adds Korean Industrial Forklift Customer, Introduces New Low Emissions 3.0 Liter GM Engine, More Stringent Power Generation System," *PrimeZone Media Network,* April 3, 2008.

"Fuel Systems Solutions' Chief Executive to Oversee Industrial Subsidiary on Interim Basis; Company Appoints Vice President of Business Development," *PrimeZone Media Network,* February 20, 2007.

"Fuel Systems Solutions Introduces CNG Refueling Station Product; Production Ramping Up; Initial Orders Shipped to Customers," *PrimeZone Media Network,* September 26, 2006.

"Fuel Systems Solutions Signs Agreement to Acquire Italian Gaseous Fuels Aftermarket Business; Transaction Would Expand Company's Leadership Position for System Conversion in Italy and International Markets," *PrimeZone Media Network,* May 14, 2007.

"IMPCO Announces Completion of Quantum Spin-Off," *Advanced Materials & Composites News,* August 5, 2002.

"IMPCO Technologies Forms Two Joint Ventures with India's Minda Industries," *AsiaPulse News,* June 22, 2001.

"IMPCO Technologies Gets Awards from General Motors and Others," *Advanced Materials & Composite News,* August 6, 2001.

"IMPCO Technologies, Inc.—Sees Increased Sales in Power Generation Market," *Market News Publishing,* June 8, 2001.

"IMPCO Technologies' Stockholders Approve Reorganization and Establishment of Holding Company—Fuel Systems Solutions; Highlights Recent Australian Initiatives to Convert Vehicles to Gaseous Fuel Systems," *PrimeZone Media Network,* August 24, 2006.

Moore, Brenda L., "Fuel-Cell Mania Is Powering IMPCO, but Feasibility Questions Remain," *Wall Street Journal,* February 23, 2000, p. CA2.

Potkewitz, Hilary, "Investors Wait for Dust to Settle As Impco Hits Several Setbacks," *Los Angeles Business Journal,* May 9, 2005, p. 33.

Roberts, Allen P., Jr., "Oil Prices, Advances in Europe Fueling Turnaround at IMPCO," *Los Angeles Business Journal,* May 15, 2006, p. 12.

Galaxy Investors, Inc.

3801 Lockport Street, Suite 2
Bismarck, North Dakota 58503
U.S.A.
Telephone: (701) 223-2412
Fax: (701) 223-2744
Web site: http://www.spacealiens.com

Private Company
Incorporated: 1996
Employees: 210
Sales: $17 million (2007 est.)
NAICS: 722211 Limited-Service Restaurants; 722410 Drinking Places (Alcoholic Beverages)

■ ■ ■

Galaxy Investors, Inc., through its Space Aliens Grill & Bar restaurant concept, is the first successful franchise operation to come out of Bismarck, North Dakota. In addition to the original Bismarck location, the company owns and operates a second location in Fargo. Another North Dakota unit, as well as three in Minnesota, are franchised. The founders, all with extensive experience in the industry, plan to take the concept beyond North Dakota and Minnesota in coming years.

TAKING FLIGHT: 1994–97

Mort Bank channeled his creative energy into fast-food restaurants in Bismarck, Minot, and Mandan, North Dakota, for more than two decades. McRock 'n' Roll, McSports Dome, and Western-theme McDonald's were hits in the region, attracting the attention of corporate headquarters. The *Bismarck Tribune* recounted the story: "'We were doing very well at that point,' said Gene Holwegner, one of three franchise owners of seven McDonald's restaurants in the area. 'They offered to buy them back.'" The franchised stores were repurchased by McDonald's Corporation in 1994.

Following the sale of the McDonald's locations, Bank turned to developing a concept he had been considering for quite some time but not yet implemented: an outer space theme. Bank joined forces with Holwegner and another McDonald's veteran, Dave Glaser. Both Holwegner and Glaser had accumulated extensive operations and administration experience. The trio worked the next two and a half years to bring the idea to reality. Bank, a travel and cooking aficionado, concocted recipes for the restaurant the team envisioned.

Galaxy Investors, Inc., opened its first restaurant in January 1997. Decked out in an out-of-this-world décor and serving up Southern barbecued ribs, the Space Aliens Grill & Bar became a fixture in Bismarck. "Aliens never go out of style. People are interested in aliens and whether there's other life out there," Glaser told the *St. Cloud Times.*

THE PRIME DIRECTIVE: 1999–2002

The aliens landed in Fargo next. The second corporate location opened in December 1999. Perched on the gateway to the wild, wild West, the grill and bar

COMPANY PERSPECTIVES

There is intelligent life down here and they know where to eat, and that's because Space Aliens Grill & Bar channels in children and adults alike with its alien-induced aura and out-of-this-world food.

Each of our restaurants has been created to beam up the imagination of the earthlings that walk into our world. The décor features a 30-foot-high domed ceiling that displays a view of outer space. Plus we have a force field of alien sculptures in the dining room, bar and arcade, showcasing a variety of extraterrestrial settings and distinct personalities.

And the food ... earthly explorers can enjoy a menu ranging from Martian Munchies to Alien Burgers. It's enough food to fuel them up for their next endeavor.

featured a motorcycle-riding alien, a rodeo-cowboy alien, and a scene of three earthling doctors named Mort, Gene, and Dave tending to survivors of a crash landing.

Seeking to go where no Bismarck restaurant had gone before, the three owners turned to a business model with which they were all well acquainted. Galaxy Investors sold its first franchise unit in 2002, to Eric and Doni Rogneby and Chris Lind. The Rognebys each were 20-year veterans of McDonald's Corporation. Eric, a consultant to McDonald's restaurants in Minnesota and North Dakota, would head the operation. "These are quality people with extensive restaurant backgrounds, successes and a great work ethic," Bank said of the Rognebys in the *Bismarck Tribune.*

Galaxy Investors initially limited franchise opportunities to Minnesota. Waite Park was tapped as the home for the first Space Aliens Grill & Bar located outside of North Dakota. The community of Waite Park was located near St. Cloud and in the rapidly growing area of central Minnesota. The Rognebys lived in Maple Grove, a northwest tier suburb of the nearby Twin Cities metropolitan area, connected to the St. Cloud area by Interstate 94 (I-94).

Patterned after the company-owned restaurants, the site would feature outer space décor, barbecued meats, including Bank's award-winning ribs, rotisserie chicken, and fire-roasted pizza.

BLENDING IN: 2003

The Waite Park restaurant opened in May 2003, tapping into an aspect of the area's culture. The Waite Park Space Aliens Grill & Bar greeted patrons with a sports lover (anglers, snowmobilers, golfers, college athletes) meets alien motif. The 9,200-square-foot operation encompassed seating for 300, a bar, a retail area, a game room, and brought about 100 jobs to the local economy. According to Eric Rogneby, the restaurant was sure to be a draw for out-of-towners. "When aliens come to Earth, this is where they eat," he said in the *St. Cloud Times.*

To entice the more earthly customers, the restaurant sought the help of Rebekah Glasmann and James Lundberg, owners of St. Cloud-based Traumen Glasberg design company. The husband and wife team looked to Hollywood for inspiration in creating a unique look for the space.

"The artists who worked with Rogneby have created a friendly yet mysterious space for diners," Liz Kohman explained in the *St. Cloud Times.* "Think *Men in Black* meets the Muppets," said Glasmann.

Like some other themed restaurants, settings changed from room to room in the Space Aliens Grill & Bar. A Mars Band played above the bar, while a three-dimensional face looked out from the surface of the red planet. The adult patrons could entertain themselves with an interactive game network offering trivia and golf. An outer space theme dominated the domed dining area, complete with sunken seats and an echo chamber. In addition, "The Galaxy of Games" offered everyone a chance to play some 75 arcade games and earn prizes.

Another feature encouraged customers to completely immerse themselves in the otherworldliness of the place. "We have no windows," Rogneby said in the *St. Cloud Times.* "We want the attention to be kept in the building."

While the décor was out of this world, the food was down to earth and included such offerings as chicken noodle soup, stuffed baked potatoes, burgers, salads, and quesadillas. Specializing in barbecue, the restaurant smoked meat on the premises and sold barbecue sauce and spice mixtures. Appetizers, such as seasoned and smoked pork strips dubbed Martian Munchies, appeared on the menu as did alien-inspired desserts and drinks. Kids and lunchtime customers had their own menu.

"People come here because they're curious and the food is great," Rogneby told the *St. Cloud Times.* Beyond food and décor, the restaurant offered birthday party packages and a gift shop with alien-related items for sale.

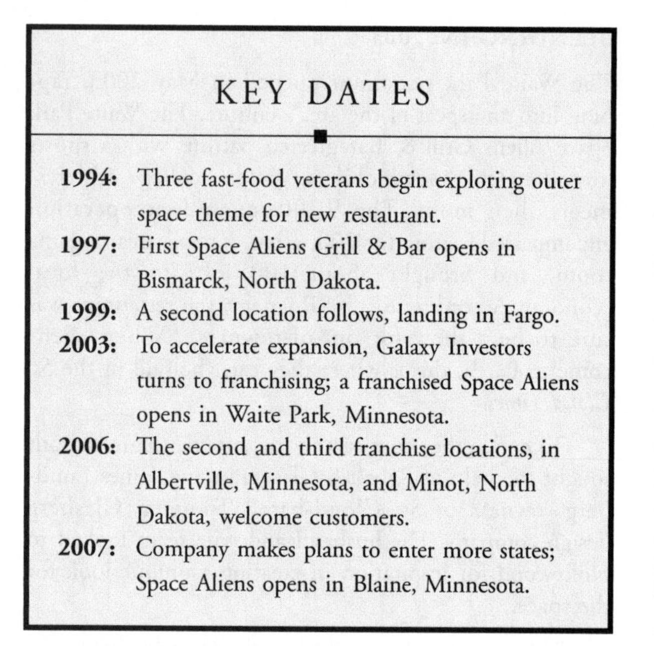

KEY DATES

1994: Three fast-food veterans begin exploring outer space theme for new restaurant.

1997: First Space Aliens Grill & Bar opens in Bismarck, North Dakota.

1999: A second location follows, landing in Fargo.

2003: To accelerate expansion, Galaxy Investors turns to franchising; a franchised Space Aliens opens in Waite Park, Minnesota.

2006: The second and third franchise locations, in Albertville, Minnesota, and Minot, North Dakota, welcome customers.

2007: Company makes plans to enter more states; Space Aliens opens in Blaine, Minnesota.

HOMETOWN SUCCESS: 2004–06

Keeping pace with the area's development, Galaxy Investors expanded the Bismarck location in 2004. The original building was 6,400 square feet, but additional footings had been poured in anticipation of future space needs. The 1,600-square-foot addition allowed Galaxy Investors to double the size of the game room, add 80 more seats for dining, and reconfigure the bar. The redesign, resembling the newer Fargo and Waite Park sites, included "Area 51" seating. A general building facelift of new carpeting, ceramic tile, and paint was also on the docket.

New franchise operations opened in Albertville, Minnesota, and Minot, North Dakota, in 2006. Galaxy Investors' efforts had produced the first successful franchise to come out of the small city on the I-94 corridor. The accomplishment gave the founders reason to be proud. When asked by the *Bismarck Tribune* to name a comparable theme-restaurant, Space Aliens Grill & Bar cofounder Holwegner said, "Wouldn't compare it to anything."

The company was banking on future growth in markets similar to Bismarck. A city of fewer than 60,000, its demographics included a mix of older people, families, and young adults. A menu with broad appeal and age-specific attractions had kept customers coming in the door.

CAREFULLY PLANNED FUTURE: 2007–08

The owners counted on their extensive experience in the world of restaurant franchising to help successfully lift off future locations. They envisioned at least 20 more restaurants in Minnesota, Wisconsin, Iowa, South Dakota, and Colorado within the next decade, according to a February 2007 *Bismarck Tribune* article. A Blaine, Minnesota, location opened in mid-2007. "We're doing well," Holwegner said in the hometown paper. "We decided we would take a good, slow approach initially."

Once well-qualified franchisees came on board, the company made available its accumulated know-how. In the construction realm, Galaxy Investors provided franchisees with information including site selection guidance and prototype building plans. Under operations and training, they assisted with the menu, kitchen layout, equipment selection, and systems development. Furthermore, Galaxy Investors struck contracts with manufacturers and distributors that helped keep costs down for the new owners. Franchisees also received marketing and advertising assistance for electronic and print media.

Galaxy Investors lent a hand elsewhere in 2008. The Bismarck Space Aliens Grill & Bar helped sponsor a humanitarian aid fund-raiser, an effort prompted by a Bismarck soldier who wanted to aid poor families in Iraq. While on leave, she and some friends organized "Operation Flip Flop" and lined up support in an effort to bring footwear, stuffed animals, and food to inhabitants of the Iraqi countryside.

Chief Warrant Officer Theresia Hersch wrote in the *Bismarck Tribune:* "As we traveled down the road, the area was flat like North Dakota, had a few palm trees, sand, some fields of green and a stillness that one can't forget. We approached the first village and you could see the kids running toward us, waving their hands. For us who were in the vehicles for the first time, smiles came to our faces when we could finally see the little people—the kids." The family-friendly restaurant, while paying attention to its future back home, had taken some time to improve the here and now for some needy families far beyond its realm of operations.

Kathleen Peippo

PRINCIPAL COMPETITORS

McDonald's Corporation; Doctor's Associates Inc. (Subway); QIP Holder LLC.

FURTHER READING

Hanson, Mark, "Space Aliens Making Room for More Earthling Customers," *Bismarck Tribune,* May 30, 2004, p. 1.

———, "Space Aliens Sells First Franchise for Theme Restaurant," *Bismarck Tribune,* November 10, 2002.

Helena, Sue, "Space Aliens Comes to Area," *St. Cloud Times,* November 3, 2002, p. 1E.

Hersch, Theresia, "In January, a Six-Person Team Was Put Together … [Derived Headline]," *Bismarck Tribune,* April 21, 2008, p. A6.

Kohman, Liz, "Welcome Home, Aliens," *St. Cloud Times,* May 7, 2003, p. 1C.

Reid, Crystal R., "They'd Had All the Other Themes for a McDonald's … [Derived Headline]," *Bismarck Tribune,* February 4, 2007, p. B1.

Greek Organization of Football Prognostics S.A. (OPAP)

62 Kifissou Ave.
Athens,
Greece
Telephone: (+30 210) 579 8000
Fax: (+30 210) 579 8982
Web site: http://www.opap.gr

Public Company
Incorporated: 1958
Employees: 813
Sales: EUR 5.06 billion ($6.39 billion) (2007)
Stock Exchanges: Athens
Ticker Symbol: OPAP
NAICS: 713990 All Other Amusement and Recreation Industries

■ ■ ■

Greek Organization of Football Prognostics S.A. (OPAP) is the only company authorized to operate lotteries and sports betting games in Greece. The company operates a variety of games, ranging from Propo, the group's original sports-betting game focused on soccer, to its biggest selling, Pame Stihima, a fixed-odds betting game covering the international sports market. Other offerings include more traditional lottery type games, such as Lotto, Joker, Kino, Super3, and Extra5. Tickets to the company's games are sold through a national network of nearly 5,000 agents; the company also sells tickets through online and portable telephone platforms.

Formerly the state-owned and nonprofit numerical gaming monopoly, OPAP was privatized in 1999. As part of its privatization, the company purchased a 20-year exclusive franchise to the country's gaming market. This gives the company control of more than 42 percent of the total legal gaming market, with horse racing and casino operations making up the rest. When horse racing is excluded, OPAP controls 68 percent of the lottery and betting market in Greece. The government's position as OPAP's majority shareholder enables the Greek government to block access to the domestic market by foreign competitors. OPAP itself has been preparing an international expansion, building its gaming technology and platforms, with an eye toward entry into Bulgaria, Turkey, and other markets. The company has long been active in Greek Cyprus, however, having established operations there in 1969. Sotirios Kostakos is group chairman, and Basile Neiadas is OPAP's chief executive officer. Listed on the Athens Stock Exchange, OPAP posted revenues of nearly EUR 5.1 billion ($6.4 billion) in 2007.

SPORTS-BETTING BEGINNINGS IN 1958

The Greek government responded to two national passions, football (as soccer is known in Europe) and betting, by establishing its own gambling franchise in 1958. For this, the government's General Secretariat of Athletics Resources created a new body, Organization of Football Prognostics (OPAP), incorporated in 1958. OPAP was granted the monopoly for the right to operate legal sports betting and lottery games in Greece. In addition to developing a legal structure for gambling in Greece, OPAP was also formed as a nonprofit organization, with the proceeds of its operations targeted toward

KEY DATES

1958: Organization of Football Prognostics (OPAP) is founded by Greek government to launch betting and lottery games.
1969: OPAP introduces Propo, its original game, to Cyprus.
1990: Company launches its first numerical lottery game, Lotto.
1999: OPAP is privatized as a limited liability company.
2000: Fixed-odds betting game Pame Stihima is created as a joint venture, in partnership with Intralot.
2001: OPAP is listed on the Athens Stock Exchange.
2003: OPAP begins operating on for-profit basis in Cyprus.
2007: OPAP acquires full control of Pame Stihima.

funding and supporting sports in Greece.

By 1959, OPAP launched its first, and only game, called Propo. This game operated as a football pool, in which bettors placed bets on which teams would win a series of football matches. At first focused on the Greek football circuit, Propo immediately attracted a large, primarily masculine, clientele. By the end of its first year, OPAP held 33 Propo games. Over the next decades, OPAP gradually increased the scope of the Propo pools, extending the game to cover football matches throughout much of Europe, and including major events, such as the European Championships and the World Cup.

At the beginning of the 1990s, OPAP held nearly 135 Propo games per year. By then, the company had built a national network of more than 5,000 agents. OPAP also extended its reach into Cyprus in 1969; the company continued to served the Greek Cypriot population on a non-profit basis following the island's division in the 1970s.

The Greek government began preparations to loosen control over the country's gambling sector in the 1990s. The prospect of new competition for the Greek gambler's budget forced OPAP to begin developing a new range of products. At the same time, OPAP seized an opportunity to extend its sales beyond the male market (men accounted for the overwhelming majority of Propo ticket sales). In 1990, OPAP introduced its first new game in more than 30 years, the numerical lottery game, the twice-weekly Lotto. This game took the form of a traditional lottery, requiring players to match six numbers from a total of 49.

The new game was an instant success, and within its first year netted more than GRD 100 million (the equivalent of roughly $275,000). Yet within a few years, Lotto sales began to decline. Despite a small pickup in sales in 1996, sales of Lotto tickets continued their downward trend through the 1990s.

NEW GAMES IN THE NINETIES

In order to provide a new boost to Lotto sales, OPAP launched Proto, in 1992. While it was possible to play Proto as an independent game, its primary purpose was to function as an add-on game for Lotto, Propo, and later tickets. Every Lotto and Propo ticket featured a second set of seven numbers, which players could then choose to activate in return for a small charge. The launch of Proto played a role in the resurgence of Lotto popularity into the mid-decade.

By then, the government's liberalization of both the casino and horse-betting sectors had placed OPAP under new competitive pressure. The company also suffered from the surge in illegal gambling activities, especially the increase in the numbers of illegally installed slot machines. Estimates of the number of illegal slot machines in operation by 2000 ranged from 150,000 to 300,000.

While the government launched a crackdown on illegal gambling, OPAP continued to seek the winning combination to draw the country's gamblers to its own products. The company added an extension of Propo in 1996, called Propo Goal. This game required bettors to forecast the eight teams (from a pool of 30) scoring the highest number of goals in a given week. Propo Goal appealed to only a small segment of the population, and into the 2000s remained the company's least-played game.

A more successful launch for the company came in 1997, with the arrival of Joker. Also a numerical lottery game, Joker required players to choose five numbers correctly from a field of 45, as well as a sixth number from a field of 20. Joker tickets also featured the Proto extension. The new game quickly became the company's most popular, before falling to a third-place position in the years ahead.

GOING PUBLIC IN 2001

Until the end of the 1990s, OPAP retained its status as a state-owned corporation, operating on a nonprofit basis. This meant that the company returned all proceeds to the government, minus the costs of its own operations. In this way, OPAP played a significant role in the development of Greece's sports sector.

In 1999, however, the Greek government moved to privatize OPAP, to pave the way for the company's future growth. In that year, OPAP was converted to a limited liability company, and began operating on a for-profit basis. Under the terms of the privatization, the Greek government agreed to sell OPAP the exclusive concession to the country's numerical lottery and sports betting market for a period of 20 years. In return, OPAP agreed to pay nearly EUR 323 million ($300 million).

The privatization also paved the way for OPAP to launch its first fixed-odds betting product. For this, the company partnered with rival Greek company Intralot SA, which had been formed to develop gambling software and technology for international markets. Among Intralot's successes into the 2000s was an entry into the U.S. market, where it gained contracts with four states to provide lottery software platforms and services. More than 83 percent of Intralot's revenues came from overseas.

OPAP and Intralot formed a joint venture to launch Pame Stihima, Greece's first legal fixed-odd betting game, in 2000. Pame Stihima allowed players to place bets, against fixed odds, on a variety of sporting events, including football, basketball, Formula 1 racing, tennis, and others, both in Greece and abroad. The pent-up demand for this product, and the large installed base from a history of illegal betting, brought instant success for the game.

By 2004, Pame Stihima generated more than EUR 1.6 billion per year in ticket sales, accounting for more than half of the company's total revenues. In contrast, the popular Joker lottery game generated just EUR 250 million in sales that year. The success of Pame Stihima also played a major role in the success of OPAP's public offering, completed in 2001.

The Greek government launched a new crackdown on illegal betting in the early 2000s, in part in preparation for OPAP's secondary offering, completed in 2003. At that time, the Greek government reduced its stake in OPAP to just 51 percent. Under European Union convention, however, this was enough to allow the Greek government to guarantee OPAP's monopoly on the market, by banning entry to foreign players.

INTERNATIONAL ASPIRATIONS FOR THE NEW CENTURY

OPAP continued to expand its range of games into the 2000s. In November 2002, the company introduced two new games, Super 3 and Extra 5. Both were lottery games. Super 3 required players to guess up to three numbers drawn in each game, which were held three times daily. In Extra 5, players picked five numbers from three fields of 35 numbers each.

OPAP began rolling out the more complex Kino game in 2003. Another fixed-odds numerical lottery game, Kino featured daily draws of 20 numbers from a pool of 80 every five minutes over a five-hour period. Players were able to choose from among 12 different levels, depending on how many numbers they wished to select.

Kino was first launched in Rethymno, on the island of Crete, in November 2003. By the end of the year, the game had been introduced across the whole of the island, and then into the regions of Larisis and Magnesia. The full national rollout of Kino was completed by the end of 2004, at which time the game play was extended to seven hours per day. Kino became another major hit for OPAP, generating nearly EUR 900 million in its first full year of play.

In the meantime, OPAP had embarked on its own internationalization strategy. In 2003, the company renegotiated its presence in Cyprus, converting its operations there to for-profit status. The company then acquired stakes in the Cypriot companies OPAP Glory Ltd. and Glory Technology Ltd., which had been responsible for collections and payouts in Cyprus as well as development of software platforms supporting these games. Following the acquisitions, OPAP received permission from the Cyprus government to establish fixed-odds gambling operations there.

OPAP next founded two new companies in Cyprus, OPAP International and OPAP Services. The first of these was to serve as OPAP's springboard into the larger international market. The second was formed to provide a range of services to sports teams and other athletic organizations, ranging from ticket issuing and sales to branding consultation and services.

OPAP began investigating potential new markets in the middle of the first decade of the 2000s. However, the company soon recognized that its technology was not yet strong enough to support a launch into developed markets. At the same time, more accessible markets such as Bulgaria, and elsewhere in the Balkans and Central and Eastern Europe, lacked the necessary infrastructure and economic advancement to support a wide-scale rollout of OPAP's operations.

OPAP was subsequently forced to maintain its focus on the domestic market. The company began developing two more games for growth at home, Bingo and Super 4, included in its package of lottery concessions. OPAP also moved to take full control of Pame Stihima, which had begun showing signs of weakening, in 2007. In this way, OPAP brought Pame Stihima's technology in-house, which could then be deployed for its operations in Cyprus, and future expansion elsewhere.

OPAP also began to address the softening of its Pame Stihima sales. In late 2007, the company reached an agreement with Intralot to provide nearly 29,500 new terminals, for use both in the company's agent network, as well as in self-standing kiosks. Under the terms of the agreement, Intralot would update the Pame Stihima game, providing new gameplay features. Intralot also agreed to share its technology with OPAP, including jointly developing a new generation of OPAP's Lotto game.

OPAP remained the dominant player in Greece's gambling market, commanding 42 percent of the total market, and 68 percent of the market with the exclusion of horse racing. The company had also begun to position itself as player in a new and more competitive international betting market. With sales of nearly EUR 5.1 billion in 2007, OPAP's future growth appeared a reasonable bet.

M. L. Cohen

PRINCIPAL SUBSIDIARIES

OPAP (Cyprus) Ltd.; OPAP Glory Ltd. (90%); OPAP International Ltd.; OPAP Services S.A.

PRINCIPAL COMPETITORS

Intralot S.A.; Betting Company S.A.; Parnitha Casino S.A.; Rodos Casino S.A.

FURTHER READING

"Greece Finishes Fourth OPAP Privatisation in EUR 1.1bn Deal," *Euroweek,* July 22, 2005, p. 26.

"Greece Sells Betting Shop," *International Financial Law Review,* August 2002, p. 8.

"Greek Lottery Operator OPAP Bets on Good Performance to Draw Investors," *Institutional Investor International Edition,* October 2004, p. SS3.

"Greeks Are Projected to Spend 8.5 Billion [euro] This Year Gambling in Casinos," *International Gaming & Wagering Business,* February 2007, p. 10.

Hope, Kerin, "Opap Bets on Growth with Moves Towards a Secondary Listing," *Financial Times,* July 11, 2003, p. 27.

———, "Opap Offering Reaches Goal," *Financial Times,* July 16, 2002, p. 28.

———, "Opap Sale Raises Euros 735m for Greece," *Financial Times,* July 14, 2003, p. 24.

———, "Price Range Set for Greek State Lottery," *Financial Times,* July 8, 2003, p. 27.

"Interview with Dr. Anestis Fillipidis, Chairman of OPAP," *Euromoney,* July 2004, p. S8.

"Intralot Wins OPAP Contract Worth 96.5m [euro]," *IGWB: International Gaming & Wagering Business,* October 2007, p. 8.

"OPAP Soars to Success with New Eu763m Greek Offering," *Euroweek,* July 18, 2003, p. 23.

Grupo Aeroportuario del Centro Norte, S.A.B. de C.V.

Aeropuerto Internacional de Monterrey
Zona de Carga
Carretera Miguel Alemán, Km. 24 s/n
Apodaca, Nuevo León 66600
Mexico
Telephone: (52 81) 8625-4300
Web site: http://www.gacn.com.mx; http://www.ir.oma.aero

Public Company
Incorporated: 1998
Employees: 944
Sales: MXN 1.9 billion ($173.75 million) (2007)
Stock Exchanges: Bolsa Mexicana de Valores NASDAQ
Ticker Symbols: OMA; OMAB
NAICS: 488112 Airport Operations, Except Air Traffic Control; 531190 Lessors of Other Real Properties; 551112 Offices of Other Holding Companies

■ ■ ■

Grupo Aeroportuario del Centro Norte, S.A.B. de C.V. (GACN), is a holding company that, through its subsidiaries, is engaged in the operation, maintenance, and development of 13 airports in northern Mexico. Better known by the acronym OMA (for Operadora Mexicana de Aeropuertos, S.A. de C.V., the former name of the operating company), it operates these airports under a 50-year concession from the Mexican government. OMA charges fees to airlines, passengers, and others for the use of airport facilities. The company also derives rental and other income from commercial activities conducted at its airport terminals, such as the leasing of space to restaurants and retailers.

OMA's chief source of revenue is the airport at Monterrey, which is Mexico's third largest city and an important destination for business travelers. The Ciudad Juárez and Reynosa airports are located very close to the Rio Grande, which forms the border with Texas. The airport at Mazatlán serves Mexico's chief Pacific Ocean port city, and the one at Tampico, an important Atlantic Ocean port. Those at Acapulco and Zihuatenejo draw many vacationers arriving and departing from Pacific beach resorts. OMA's airports at Chihuahua, Culiacán, Durango, San Luis Potosí, and Zacatecas all serve state capitals. The one at Torreón is a transportation hub for many communities of north central Mexico.

THE ROAD TO PRIVATIZATION: 1995–2000

Aeropuertos y Servicios Auxiliares (ASA) was the name of the federal agency established in 1965 to administer 33 Mexican airports. By 1977 this number had grown to 47, and by 1995, to 68. The bulk of ASA's revenues came from landing fees, rent from airport shops, and airport-located government facilities such as postal, telephone, and telex offices. Although only seven Mexican airports were profitable, they accounted for 65 percent of the nation's air traffic, and ASA was making a profit of about $200 million a year. Nevertheless, Mexico's Congress approved a constitutional amendment in December 1995 authorizing privatization of the airports.

COMPANY PERSPECTIVES

Mission: To provide world class airport facilities and services in terms of quality and safety that meet the needs of our clients and promote sustainable development.

The secretariat of communications and transport then divided 35 of Mexico's most valuable airports into four regions. Excluding Mexico City, each regional division contained both profitable and unprofitable airports so that the holding companies for each group would receive an overall annual return on their investment that ASA officials calculated at about 15 percent. Three of these regions took in Mexico's main southeast, northern, and Pacific airports. The central region consisted only of Mexico City's airport, which was not privatized.

The next stage of the privatization process authorized strategic partnerships between foreign and Mexican investors as official operating service providers. The investing partners were restricted to a 15 percent share of the holding company, with the remaining shares to be publicly sold later. Foreign investment was limited to 49 percent of the holding company, which in the case of the 13 airports of the northern region to be privatized was GACN, incorporated in 1998 as a wholly owned entity of the federal government.

OMA AS OPERATING CONSORTIUM: 2000–06

OMA was incorporated in 1998 to bid for the concession to operate the 13 airports to be privatized in the northern region. It was awarded the concession in 2000 in return for a payment of MXN 864.06 million ($76 million). For this sum it gained 15 percent of GACN's capital and control of the operation and administration of the 13 privatized airports for at least 15 years. Empresas ICA Sociedad Contraladora, S.A. de C.V., the largest engineering, construction, and procurement company in Mexico, held 49 percent of OMA's shares. Vinci, a French parking lot operator, also had 49 percent of the shares, and Aéroports de Paris, S.A., operator of the Charles de Gaulle and Orly airports in France, had the remaining 2 percent. In 2001 ICA sold 11.75 percent of its shares in OMA to Aéroports de Paris, which, exercising the option it held, paid the company $11.4 million for the shares.

OMA was charged with the task of providing the technical, operative, administrative, and financial capacity to improve the security, access, and efficiency of the airports under the concession, as well as to provide suitable, modern, and efficient infrastructure. The company even sought to make a visit to its facilities a cultural experience. By mid-2002 most of OMA's airports had devoted space usually given over to businesses for displays such as the exposition of northern Mexican painting presented in Monterrey's terminal building.

OMA's early years as an airport concessionaire were dogged by the effects of a recessionary climate in the U.S. economy and the decline in air travel that followed the September 11, 2001, terrorist attacks on the United States. Like the other two concessionaires, OMA signed, in late 2002, an agreement with the Mexican government's secretariat of communications and transport and the national chamber of air transport to reduce the rates it charged airlines and passengers. The company also agreed to apply other strategies to encourage the use of its airports by airlines and passengers. Rubén López Barrera, an ICA executive who became OMA's chief executive officer, maintained that the company's rates were 11 to 30 percent lower than those of U.S. airports.

Conditions remained so unfavorable that the government, in early 2003, postponed its intention of selling its 85 percent holding in GACN during the year. With passenger volume lagging, OMA displayed special interest in developing other aspects of its business. In 2004 the company announced that it was investing MXN 110 million ($9.77 million) in infrastructure for air cargo facilities, with half the funds destined for Monterrey. This airport was Mexico's third most important for moving air freight, with double-digit growth in each of the previous five years. With an area of 60,000 square meters for freight operations, it was the leading air cargo terminal in northern Mexico and served both as a final destination and as a logistical hub for freight.

Commercial receipts not directly related to air transport were also gaining increasing attention, especially since, unlike plane parking, cargo handling, and refueling, rates were not regulated by the government. Most of this income was coming from the rental of commercial spaces in the terminals, although in some cases the concessionaires were exacting a percentage of sales. On average, airline passengers were spending two-and-a-half hours in the terminal and were generally accompanied by other persons. Grupo Aeroportuario del Sureste, S.A. de C.V. (Asur), was seemingly the most adept at exploiting this business opportunity, earning 25 percent of its revenue from the rental of commercial space in 2004, compared to only 7 percent before it started managing the nine airports

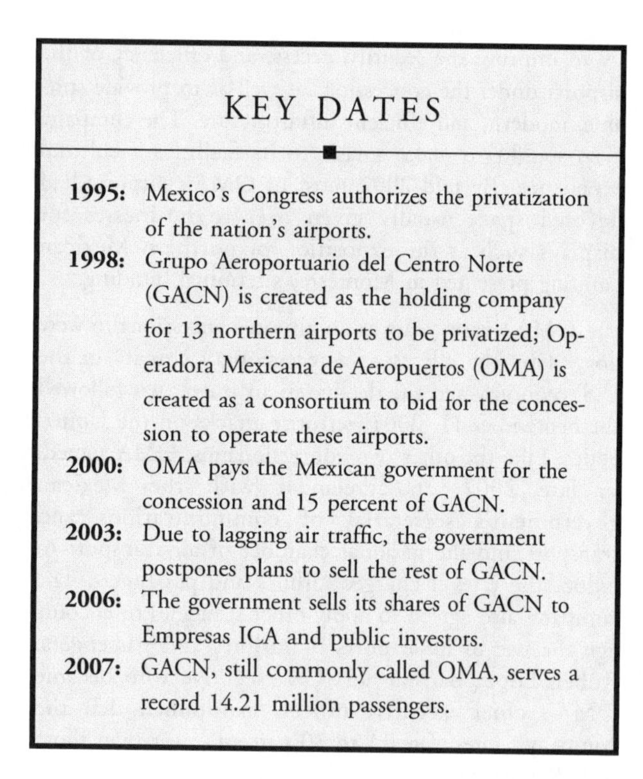

KEY DATES

1995: Mexico's Congress authorizes the privatization of the nation's airports.
1998: Grupo Aeroportuario del Centro Norte (GACN) is created as the holding company for 13 northern airports to be privatized; Operadora Mexicana de Aeropuertos (OMA) is created as a consortium to bid for the concession to operate these airports.
2000: OMA pays the Mexican government for the concession and 15 percent of GACN.
2003: Due to lagging air traffic, the government postpones plans to sell the rest of GACN.
2006: The government sells its shares of GACN to Empresas ICA and public investors.
2007: GACN, still commonly called OMA, serves a record 14.21 million passengers.

within its concession. For OMA, the figures were 20 percent and 7 percent, respectively. Unlike the other two concessionaires, OMA charged rent in dollars and put a ceiling on prices charged by retailers.

In 2005 ICA acquired an additional 37.25 percent of the stock of OMA, which now was officially named Servicios de Tecnología Aeroportuaria, S.A. de C.V., by purchasing the shares held by Vinci. ICA paid $38 million for Vinci's holding, which gave it 74.5 percent of the shares. (Aéroports de Paris held the remaining 25.5 percent.) ICA had invested heavily in infrastructure projects and was the only Mexican construction contractor to be actively engaged in airports. In 2006, for example, it won a MXN 1.9 billion ($181 million) contract to complete the construction of a new second terminal at Mexico City's Benito Júarez International Airport. Bernardo Quintana Isaac, chief executive officer of Empresas ICA, S.A.B. de C.V., became OMA's chairman of the board in 2004.

PUBLICLY TRADED ENTERPRISE: 2006–08

ICA neared majority control of the holding company in early 2006, when one of its subsidiaries, exercising an option, purchased 36 percent of GACN from the Mexican government for $203.3 million. At the same time, another ICA subsidiary acquired Vinci's 37.25 percent holding in the operating company (SETA) for $37.7 million. In November 2006 the government sold its remaining 48 percent of GACN on stock exchanges in Mexico City and New York for a total of about $432.2 million. The share price increased by 16 percent within a few hours and had almost doubled by the end of May 2007. ICA, through its wholly owned subsidiary Autoinvest, S.A. de C.V., was OMA's controlling shareholder, with 56 percent of the company's capital stock, counting both the SETA shares and the shares and American Depositary Receipts sold in Mexico City and New York, respectively.

OMA did very well in 2006 by focusing on flights within Mexico. Although its revenues and the number of passengers it served were not as large as the two other concessionaires, the company's profit margin was higher. Monterrey, through which almost half of OMA's passengers set foot, was increasingly a haven for low cost airlines. Volaris began flying from and to the airport in March; Alma, in September; Viva Aerobús in November, and Aladia in December. Interjet and Avolar had begun service from there at the end of 2005. In all, these second-tier airlines accounted for almost 10 percent of passenger traffic at Monterrey.

By that time, Monterrey was serving as the point of departure for 17 airlines flying directly to Mexico's other main cities and to most of the leading U.S. destinations—including New York, Los Angeles, Chicago, Atlanta, Dallas, Houston, Las Vegas, Miami, and Phoenix—as well as Madrid, where service to and from Monterrey had begun in 2005. However, a major expansion of the airport was needed to avoid an increase in flight delays. At the end of 2006 a new temporary terminal, mainly used by low cost carrier VivaAerobús, began operations. The demand was so great that work on an expansion of this terminal began in late 2007. Construction also began in 2007 on Terminal B of the airport, with operations expected to commence in 2009. Terminal B would have the capacity to serve two million passengers annually.

According to forecasts by financial analysts, flights within Mexico were expected to increase at a greater rate than international flights until 2010. Also, some foreign travelers headed for the Pacific beaches served by OMA's Acapulco, Mazatlán, and Zihuatanejo airports after Hurricane Wilma struck the Atlantic coast "Mexican Riviera" in the spring of 2006. The company also saw a market in U.S. cruise ship customers docking in Acapulco who might choose to return by air, boarding a U.S. Airways flight to Los Angeles. OMA saw opportunity at Culiacán, where the airport serving Sinaloa's state capital was experiencing an increase of 40 percent in its operations with the entry of Mexicana, Interjet, and VivaAerobús. An additional platform for commercial airplanes was to be constructed there and at Ciudad Juárez, which was also receiving funds for a rehabilitation of the runway and an expansion of the terminal.

OMA was taking measures to reduce the potential problem resulting from the growth of residential housing adjacent to its airports. In its financial report for the first quarter of 2008, the company announced that it had invested about $60 million, of which the purchase of lots accounted for more than half. OMA intended in this way to secure room for further airport expansion. Specifically, the document pointed to the problem of crowding caused by new housing surrounding the airports of Tampico and Torreón.

OMA served 14.21 million arriving and departing passengers in 2007, with Monterrey accounting for about 45 percent of the total. Five of its nine airports (Chihuahua, Ciudad Júarez, Monterrey, Reynosa, and San Luis Potosí) also housed terminals for handling and storing freight. Of OMA's revenues in 2007, nonaeronautical sources such as automobile parking, restaurants, retailers, and advertising accounted for about 18 percent. The principal fees for aeronautical services, charged to the airlines using OMA's facilities, were passenger charges; landing charges; aircraft parking, boarding, and unloading charges; aircraft long-term parking charges; passenger walkway charges; and airport security charges. Passenger charges accounted for 75 percent of revenue from aeronautical services and 61 percent of total revenue.

By 2007 OMA had increased the total area available for commercial activity in its airports by about 50 percent since 2000 and had more than doubled the commercial area in the Monterrey airport. The company was renegotiating its agreements with tenants of commercial space in its terminals. It had adopted a new type of contract providing for royalty payments based on a percentage of revenues, subject to a minimum fixed amount based partly on square footage, as opposed to the customary airport leases based solely on square footage.

OMA was also making an effort to lease space to more established, internationally recognized businesses. Retail tenants were offering such upscale brands as Hermès, Mont Blanc, Swatch, Christian Dior, Lancôme, L'Oréal, Swarovski, and Lacoste. The company also had developed its own "OMA Plaza" brand for its commercial space. It had encouraged car rental companies to establish onsite automobile pick-up and drop-off facilities at the airports. OMA had also consolidated most of the telephone and Internet service with a single provider and was offering Internet access at all 13 airports, either wireless or at service kiosks.

Robert Halasz

PRINCIPAL SUBSIDIARIES

Servicios Aeroportuarios del Centro Norte, S.A. de C.V.

FURTHER READING

Bibian, Cinthya, "Pretende ICA controlar OMA," *Reforma,* July 29, 2005, p. 3.

Calderón, Lino Jávier, "Air Pressure," *Business Mexico,* September 1995, pp. 12, 14–15.

Cepeda, Francsco, and Miriam Pineda, "Toman control de aeropuertos," *Reforma,* September 14, 2000, p. 7.

Cruz, Lilian, "Encuentran 'mina de oro,'" *Reforma,* June 20, 2005, p. 12.

———, "Va ICA por participación de Gobierno en Grupo Aeroportuario Centro-Norte," *Reforma,* January 23, 2006, p. 2.

Morales, Roberto, and Marina Delaunay, "Aire caliente," *Expansión,* June 25–July 9, 2007, pp. 162, 164, 166.

Nirdlinger, Dan, "In Flight," *Business Mexico,* April 1998, pp. 54–55.

Hamon & Cie (International) S.A.

Axisparc, Rue Emile Francqui 2
Mont Saint Guibert, B-1435
Belgium
Telephone: (+32-010) 39-04-00
Fax: (+32-010) 39-04-01
Web site: http://www.hamon.com

Public Company
Incorporated: 1904
Employees: 912
Sales: EUR 432.64 million ($488.7 million) (2007)
Stock Exchanges: Euronext Brussels
Ticker Symbol: HAMO
NAICS: 333415 Air Conditioning and Warm Air Heating Equipment and Commercial and Industrial Refrigeration Equipment Manufacturing

■ ■ ■

Hamon & Cie (International) S.A. is a pioneering manufacturer of industrial cooling systems and other specialized equipment and systems for the engineering, procurement, and contracting (EPC) sector. Founded at the beginning of the 20th century, Hamon remains one of the largest producers of cooling systems in Europe, specializing in large-scale installations necessary for releasing the heat produced in most industrial processes. Hamon is one of Europe's leading developers of cooling systems, primarily focused on the wet-cooling segment. In this area, the company commands a 21 percent market share. While cooling systems operations generates 37 percent of the group's revenues, Hamon has built a diversified operation around three other niche markets. The fast-growing Air Pollution Control division accounts for approximately 40 percent of Hamon's total revenues, but more than 80 percent of the company's EBIT (earnings before interest and taxes). This division focuses on particulate management using electrostatic precipitators as well as fabric filters, and it is also active in the flue gas treatment sector. The United States represents Hamon's primary air pollution control market, accounting for 29 percent of group sales and 63 percent of EBIT, compared to its European operations, at 11 percent of total revenues and 18 percent EBIT. The North American markets are also the primary theater for the third Hamon division, chimneys. Through subsidiary Custodis, Hamon designs, builds, repairs, and maintains both concrete and steel-based chimneys, stacks, and silos. This division controls a 32 percent share of the U.S. and Canadian markets and represents 16 percent of Hamon's total revenues.

The fourth and smallest Hamon division is its France-based heat exchanger operation, which produces heat exchanger systems based on state-of-the-art air cooler and other technologies. This division added 7 percent to company sales. Hamon is listed on the Euronext Stock Exchange, but more than 50 percent of the company's stock is held by the founding Hamon family, through their holding company Sopal. Jacques Lambilliotte, grandson of the founders, remains Hamon's chairman, while his son, Francis Lambilliotte, serves as managing director. In 2007, Hamon posted revenues of nearly EUR 433 million ($489 million).

COMPANY PERSPECTIVES

Hamon positions itself as one of the main worldwide players in the niche markets for which it provides specific process equipment and the associated after-sales services. Hamon aims to create value for its shareholders and to offer them a return above the current one of its business sector, whilst offering to its customers innovative systems and leading edge technology at competitive prices. This is achieved by completely fulfilling the requirements of its leading customers by the strict control of its costs and quality.

Hamon aims to ensure the satisfaction and the development of its personnel, and more generally, the satisfaction of all partners. It does so whilst respecting the sustainable development of the environment in which it operates.

COOLING THE INDUSTRIAL REVOLUTION

Hamon & Cie was founded by brothers Achille and Fernand Hamon, originally from France's Brittany region. Their family's involvement in France's industrial sector dated from the 19th century, when members of the family participated in the construction of the Eiffel Tower. Achille and Fernand, who became engineers, formed their first company together about 1900, building and assembling wood-based structures.

Early in the 20th century, however, the brothers recognized that increasing industrial production techniques, especially in steel production and mining and power generation facilities, had created a demand for new types of support equipment and structures. In particular, the dissipation of high temperatures generated during industrial production and power generation presented an important engineering problem. In response, engineers sought to develop efficient cooling solutions.

Achille Hamon became the first of the two brothers to focus on this new sector; in 1904 he founded a new company in Paris dedicated to designing, engineering, and constructing water cooling towers. Two years later, Fernand Hamon joined his brother in this effort. Instead of becoming part of the Paris company, though, Fernand Hamon founded a company in Belgium. The two businesses remained highly connected, however, and later merged. Both companies profited from the early 1900s surge in industrial activity in France and Belgium.

Hamon's towers were initially constructed of wood. With the outbreak of World War I, the brothers joined together at the Paris business and converted their production to manufacture support structures needed for building military trenches. By the war's end in 1918, the company had also launched the manufacture of prefabricated, temporary housing.

The Hamons returned to their main cooling tower business after the war and soon distinguished themselves as innovators in the field. The company adapted new construction materials and were able to build the ever larger cooling towers required by steel, mining, and power generation industries. In the late 1920s, the group was joined by Maurice Hamon, son of Fernand, who emerged as an important figure in the Hamon group. In 1927, however, Maurice decided to set up in business for himself, creating Sobelco in Brussels. The new company also produced cooling towers, but it focused especially on electrical power generating, producing condensers and other components and systems as well. In this way, Sobelco prospered from the boom in the electricity sector in the 1920s and 1930s.

POSTWAR INTERNATIONALIZATION

Achille and Fernand Hamon died in the 1950s, leaving both the Belgian and French Hamon companies under the leadership of Maurice Hamon, who also remained as head of Sobelco. The merger of these operations took place at the end of the 1960s. By then, Hamon had asserted itself as a leading name in the global cooling tower sector, in part through its commitment to innovative technologies. Among them, the company had become the first to develop so-called natural draft water cooling techniques.

Timing once again played a crucial role in the group's success. In the 1950s and 1960s the French government was determined to develop greater self-sufficiency in its energy supply. Given that the country had few natural resources, the company launched one of the world's most ambitious nuclear power generation programs. Hamon worked closely with the state-owned Electricité de France (EDF), a partnership that enabled the company to take the lead in cooling tower innovation.

Backed by its strong technologies, Hamon began developing a wider international presence. During the 1950s, for example, the company entered Spain, forming a partnership with that country's Esindus to introduce Hamon's technologies there.

KEY DATES

1904: Achille Hamon establishes a business in France for building cooling towers; brother Fernand founds Belgian sister business two years later.
1927: Maurice Hamon founds Sobelco in Belgium, then becomes head of both Hamon businesses.
1958: Hamon sells U.S. license to its technologies to Research-Cottrell.
1968: Hamon and Sobelco merge to become Hamon Sobelco.
1985: Hamon repurchases North American license from Research-Cottrell, then launches diversification strategy.
1997: Hamon lists stock on Brussels Stock Exchange and begins new acquisition drive.
2003: Heavy debts and falling profits force company to restructure operations.
2007: Hamon returns to profitability, with growth driven by Air Pollution Control sector.

Hamon also became attracted to the U.S. market and set up a sales operation in the United States in the 1950s. The company was soon overtaken by its success, however. As orders began to build, the company sought a means to launch manufacturing of its cooling towers in the United States. Yet the company's relatively small size meant that banks were unwilling to provide backing for the expansion.

Hamon pursued a domestic partner and settled on Research-Cottrell Corporation. That company had been founded as Research Corporation in 1912 by Frederick Cottrell, a chemistry professor and inventor at the University of California at Berkeley. Cottrell had patented a number of devices, notably an electrostatic precipitator, invented in 1907. In 1952, the Research Corporation, which had largely confined itself to commercializing its inventions, decided to enter manufacturing directly and founded Research-Cottrell.

In 1958 Hamon and Research-Cottrell reached an agreement that gave the latter company the manufacturing and commercialization rights for Hamon's cooling tower technologies for the North American market. The partnership got off to a rocky start, however; after five years, Research-Cottrell had still not generated any orders for Hamon's cooling towers. Becoming impatient, Hamon nearly terminated the agreement. Maurice Hamon decided to hold firm, though, and by 1963, Research-Cottrell had at last completed its first cooling tower order. Over the next decades, Research-Cottrell succeeded in building its operation into one of the leading U.S. cooling tower companies. Indeed, by the early 1980s, the company had built more than 60 percent of all cooling towers in the United States.

The Hamon Sobelco merger was completed in 1968, and the company's base became Belgium. Hamon's foreign expansion effort next turned to Germany, where the partnership with EDF enabled it to secure its first major order in the early 1970s. In 1974, Hamon created a dedicated German subsidiary, Hamon Kühltürme und Apparatebau, based in Bochum. Hamon also recognized the opportunities in South Africa, which, in addition to its important mining industry, was then witnessing a new industrialization drive. By the mid-1970s, Hamon succeeded in winning an order worth $60 million, one of the company's largest to that date. Over the next decade, the company entered Australia and the United Kingdom, and, into the 1980s, a joint venture got underway in Japan as well. By 1987, the company had also added operations in South Korea, again through a joint venture with a local partner.

DIVERSIFYING IN THE EIGHTIES

Maurice Hamon died in 1973, leaving his widow, Louisette Hamon, as head of the company. Louisette Hamon remained in charge of the company until 1985. In that year, Francis Lambilliotte, great-grandson of Fernand Hamon, who joined the company in 1980, took over as its managing director. His father, Jacques Lambilliotte, then became the company's chairman.

The new management team set out to transform the company. In 1985, Hamon repurchased the license to its technology from Research-Cottrell and instead set in place its own manufacturing and marketing subsidiary for the North American market. The company thus initiated a strategy for controlling the global rights to its cooling tower technology.

Concerned about having focused too much on a single sector, Hamon launched a diversification strategy in 1985. For this move, the company identified complementary systems and technologies. Hamon acquired France's Spiro-Gills, which specialized in the production of heat exchangers. The company then added Belgium's d'Hondt, which supplied heat exchangers and air coolers for petrochemical installations.

Next, Hamon targeted heat recovery technologies, buying France's Air Industrie Thermique. Hamon then bought several other companies involved in this sector, becoming a major player in the French thermal exchange systems sector.

Into the 1990s, Hamon decided to extend its offering with dry cooling tower technologies. Hamon formed a joint venture in 1992 with dry cooling specialist ABB-Lummus of Sweden. At the same time, Hamon expanded its water cooling component. This move was accomplished especially through a deal worked out with Alstom Group, in which Hamon sold the French group its Sobelco subsidiary and in turn purchased Alstom's water cooling tower unit, Scam. The purchase transformed Hamon into the global leader in its sector.

STUMBLING AND RECOVERING

Hamon leveraged its reputation and leadership status with an entry into the fast-developing Asian market. Through the mid-1990s, the company put into place a series of partnerships in Thailand, Malaysia, Indonesia, China, and elsewhere in Asia. This expansion led the company to target still further growth, which led Hamon to the stock market. In 1997, Hamon listed its shares on the Brussels Stock Exchange.

The public listing permitted the group to shift its expansion into overdrive. Between 1997 and 2001, Hamon made a number of major acquisitions. These included heat exchanger group FBM Hudson Italiana and in 1997 a 30 percent stake in India's GEI, which specialized in air-cooled heat exchangers. The following year, the group returned to India, adding Thermopack Engineers, as well as setting up a new subsidiary in Brazil. Other acquisitions included Brandt & Kritzler in Germany and Mariana Battista in Italy in 2000 and Entech and ZBD Constructor, both in the United States, in 2001.

Along the way, Hamon's U.S. operations came full circle, when it acquired Research-Cottrell in 1998. The former partner had fallen on hard times during the 1990s, but over the past decades had established itself as a leading player in the air pollution control (APC) sector. Research-Cottrell also brought to Hamon its control of Custodis, the leading manufacturer of industrial chimneys in North America.

Hamon's rapid growth came at a heavy cost. By 2002, the group was saddled with debt and faced an economic slowdown. This decline was especially sharp in the United States, where the Enron scandal all but halted construction of new power plants and their cooling towers.

In order to survive, Hamon was forced to undergo a radical restructuring starting in 2003. As part of that effort, the company sold a number of its prized companies, including its entire dry cooling tower component and its North American water cooling tower operations. Hamon regrouped its four core operations: water cooling towers in Europe, chimneys in North America, heat transfer systems in France, and the APC market in the United States and Europe.

The APC operation was to prove the company's most dynamic into the first decade of the 2000s. By 2008, the group's APC operations represented more than 40 percent of its revenues and more than 80 percent of its pretax profits. In the meantime, the company had carried out a series of capital increases, helping to pay down most of its debt load. By 2007, the company was once again posting profits and had regained its revenue growth. After more than 100 years, Hamon remained a leading name in the global engineering industry.

M. L. Cohen

PRINCIPAL SUBSIDIARIES

Brown Fintube (France) S.A. (99.1%); Compagnie Financière Hamon S.A. (France; 99.1%); Hacom Energiesparsysteme GmbH (Germany); Hamon–B. Grimm Ltd. (Thailand; 49.2%); Hamon (Nederland) B.V.; Hamon (South Africa) Pty Ltd. (70%); Hamon Australia Pty Ltd.; Hamon Cooling Towers Inc. (U.S.A.); Hamon Corporation Inc. (U.S.A.); Hamon Custodis Cottrell (Canada) Inc.; Hamon Custodis Inc. (U.S.A.); Hamon D'Hondt S.A. (France; 99.1%); Hamon Do Brazil Ltda.; Hamon Dry Cooling Ltd. (U.K.); Hamon Environmental S.A.R.L. (France; 99.95%); Hamon India PVT Ltd.; Hamon Korea Co Ltd. (South Korea; 89.73%); Hamon Korea Youngnam Ltd. (South Korea; 45.76%); Hamon Malaysia SDN. BHD; Hamon Polska Sp.Zo.O (Poland); Hamon Research-Cottrell Inc. (U.S.A.); Hamon Research-Cottrell SA (99.95%); Hamon Thermal & Environmental Technology (Jiaxing) Co. Ltd. (China; 70%); Hamon Thermal Europe (France) S.A. (99.1%); Hamon Thermal Europe SA; Hamon Thermal Germany GmbH; Hamon U.K. Ltd.; Heat Transfer Ré Services S.A. (Luxembourg); Thermal Transfer Corporation (U.S.A.).

PRINCIPAL COMPETITORS

United Technologies Corporation; Fujitsu Ltd.; DENSO Corporation; ABB Ltd.; Mitsubishi Heavy Industries Ltd.; The Linde Group; ThyssenKrupp Technologies AG; Linde AG; Danaher Corporation; Carrier Corporation; Metso Corporation; Dalkia S.A.S.; Daikin Industries Ltd.; Trane Inc.

FURTHER READING

"Belgium-Based Hamon Company Est. Branch in Taiyuan," *IRP Strategic Business Information Database,* October 13, 2003.

De Groote, Peter, "Hamon Presteert in Lijn met Verwachtingen," *De Tijd,* March 4, 2008.

Georis, Vincent, "Hamon Monte dans la Spin-off Xylowatt," *L'Echo,* April 9, 2008.

———, "Hamon s'Engage dans les Energies Renouvelables," *L'Echo,* April 9, 2008.

"Shiriam EPC Enters JV with Belgian Co Hamon," *Economic Times,* February 20, 2007.

"Single Row Condensers Build on Success," *Modern Power Systems,* July 1998, p. 43.

"SPX Completes Acquisition of Hamon CIE Global Dry and NAFTA Wet Cooling Businesses," *PR Newswire,* December 19, 2003.

Hapag-Lloyd AG

Ballindamm 25
Hamburg, D-20095
Germany
Telephone: (+49 40) 3001-0
Fax: (+49 40) 33 00 53
Web site: http://www.hapag-lloyd.com

Wholly Owned Subsidiary of TUI AG
Founded: 1847
Incorporated: 1970
Employees: 8,400
Sales: EUR 6.2 billion ($9.06 billion) (2007)
NAICS: 483111 Deep Sea Freight Transportation

■ ■ ■

Hapag-Lloyd AG is the fifth largest container line shipping company in the world. The company operates more than 140 container ships with a total capacity of 514,000 standard containers. Operating globally in the Far East, Transpacific, Atlantic, Latin America, and Australasia, Hapag-Lloyd maintains about 340 sales offices in more than 100 countries on five continents. The firm was formed in 1970 from the merger of Hamburg-Amerikanische Packetfahrt-Actien-Gesellschaft (Hapag), based in Hamburg, and Norddeutscher Lloyd (NDL), based in Bremen, with the two predecessors tracing their origins back to 1847 and 1857, respectively. In 1997 Hapag-Lloyd was acquired by the German industrial conglomerate Preussag AG, which later shed its industrial side and emerged as a tourism and shipping group known as TUI AG. In 2005, as a wholly owned subsidiary of TUI, Hapag-Lloyd was bolstered through the acquisition of the Anglo-Canadian container carrier CP Ships Limited. By mid-2008, however, Hapag-Lloyd was verging on being absorbed itself by one of its competitors after TUI placed its shipping arm up for sale.

EARLY HISTORIES OF HAPAG AND NDL

Hapag and Norddeutscher Lloyd were established in the mid-19th century to accommodate the escalation in European migration to North America. Hapag was founded in Hamburg on May 27, 1847, by a group of German merchants and shipowners led by Ferdinand Laeisz, August Bolten, Dr. Adolph Halle, and Ernst Merck; prominent businessman Adolph Godeffroy was named the first chairman. Ten years later, on February 20, 1857, Norddeutscher Lloyd (North German Lloyd) was founded in Bremen by Eduard Crüsemann and Hermann Henrich (H. H.) Meier. NDL a year later inaugurated a transatlantic passenger service between Bremerhaven and New York with its first steamship, *Bremen.*

Initially Hapag used sailing ships to provide passage from Hamburg to New York. A trip to New York generally took 40 days, and the return trip 28 days. The time onboard was reduced to two weeks for a roundtrip when, in 1856, Hapag's first steamship, *Borussia,* completed its inaugural run. In contrast to the shoddy, cramped, and life-threatening conditions of the typical transatlantic passenger ships of the time, many of which treated passengers as little better than freight, Hapag

COMPANY PERSPECTIVES

We began by transporting emigrants to the "New World," then served as a bridge for the emerging global trading sector and today offer worldwide container transport services and luxury cruises. Hapag-Lloyd is one of the leading and most innovative companies in shipping. In our over 150-year history, we have continually responded to technical and market challenges and gone on to develop solutions for our customers. We regard the ongoing globalisation of the economy as an opportunity to be seized, just as much as the continuing advance of information technology. We owe our success to our customer orientation, quality awareness and highly motivated staff. Our services are based on the successful international cooperation of many people, so we are basically cosmopolitan in our approach.

from the start offered higher quality service, such as better accommodations, including separate berths for every passenger, better food, and improved relations between crew and passengers. Hapag owed much of its early success to this emphasis on quality and distinction. Eventually, the North Atlantic route on which Hapag was founded was commonly called the Hamburg-American Line.

In 1872 several Hamburg merchants founded the Deutsche Transatlantische Dampfschiffahrts-Gesellschaft, or the Adler Line, to serve the transatlantic trade. The Adler ships were bigger, faster, and generally of a higher quality than those of Hapag. Unprofitable times ensued, characterized by increased competition, price wars, and the mid-1870s economic depression in the United States, during which passenger rates fell drastically. Hapag bought the Adler Line in 1875 to prevent it from falling into the hands of stronger competitors, particularly NDL. The purchase necessitated a major restructuring of the Hapag fleet; the number of passenger ships was reduced and smaller cargo vessels were introduced on routes to the West Indies and the Caribbean.

In 1886 the passenger manager of the Carr-Union Line, Albert Ballin, also became Hapag's passenger manager. Ballin's dual appointment reflected the wish of both companies to avoid further rate wars, which Ballin achieved by operating the Hapag and Carr-Union Line ships as a pool. In 1890 Hapag bought Carr-Union Line's ships and integrated them into the existing fleet, effectively ending the separate existence of the Carr-Union Line. By 1892 Hapag had carried 526,000 passengers across the Atlantic, approximately 200,000 fewer than NDL.

In the meantime, Ballin, who had been named managing director in 1888 and was destined to exert a major influence in the company's development, essentially "invented" the modern-style cruise. At his behest, despite the opposition of some members of the company board, who thought absurd the idea of taking a long sea voyage for pleasure alone, Hapag's then flagship, the steamship *Augusta Victoria,* set sail in late January 1891 on a two-month pleasure cruise from Cuxhaven to the Mediterranean. The 174 passengers aboard were treated to a luxurious voyage, among the highlights of which were the ample food and the daylong shore excursions at 13 ports of call, from Portugal to the Middle East. The trip was a resounding success, prompting Hapag to continue offering cruises. NDL soon followed with its own cruise offerings.

In 1892 Ballin played the central role in the formation of the North Atlantic Steamship Lines Association. Original members were Hapag, NDL, Holland America, and Red Star. This organization pooled resources to avoid duplication of effort and competition, which would push down rates.

Similarly, NDL experienced growth during this time. Finding cargo and mail links between Germany and the East to be inadequate, German traders were forced to rely on British and French mail services, which were run to suit their own national requirements. In 1885 a law providing for imperial German mail steamer subsidies to East Asia and Australia was enacted, and NDL was awarded the contract. In return for an annual subsidy of 4.4 million marks, NDL agreed to run a monthly service from Bremerhaven to China with feeder services to Hong Kong and Japan as well as a monthly service to Australia with feeder service to several South Sea islands. The early years of the trade were difficult. NDL's ships proved unsuitable for the tropics and had too much passenger accommodation relative to cargo space. The need to purchase new ships placed a strain on NDL's finances. In 1892, however, following an agreement with the government, the service was streamlined and became profitable in 1893. NDL's mail contract was subsequently renewed until 1914.

Hapag had been too weak to compete for the original mail contract following the rate battle with the Carr-Union Line. Concerned that Hapag was too dependent on trade with the Americas, Ballin instituted a monthly freight service between Hamburg and eastern destinations, including Singapore, China, Hong Kong,

KEY DATES

1847: A group of German merchants and shipowners form Hamburg-Amerikanische Packetfahrt-Actien-Gesellschaft (Hapag), initially providing passage between Hamburg and New York on sailing ships.
1856: Hapag's first steamship, *Borussia,* completes its inaugural run.
1857: Norddeutscher Lloyd (NDL) is founded in Bremen by Eduard Crüsemann and Hermann Henrich Meier and soon offers a transatlantic passenger service between Bremerhaven and New York.
1891: Hapag's *Augusta Victoria* embarks on the first modern-style cruise, steaming from Cuxhaven to the Mediterranean Sea.
1914: World War I erupts, eventually resulting in Hapag and NDL losing most of their fleets.
1930: An international shipping crisis prompts the formation of the Hapag-Lloyd Union.
1935: The Nazi government, having taken majority control of Hapag and NDL, orders the dissolution of the union.
1945: Potsdam Agreement requires all German ships be turned over to the Allies and forbids German shipping companies from engaging in overseas trade activities for five years.
1968: A joint venture of Hapag and NDL launches fully containerized transport services in the North Atlantic trade.
1970: Hapag and NDL merge to form Hapag-Lloyd AG; the transatlantic passenger business, the foundation for both predecessors, is discontinued.
1997: German industrial conglomerate Preussag AG acquires Hapag-Lloyd for about DM 2.8 billion ($1.54 billion).
1999: Preussag restructures the core of its portfolio into a shipping and logistics arm, Hapag-Lloyd, and a tourism arm, TUI Group GmbH; Hapag-Lloyd retains its cruise business, but the remainder of its tourism operations are transferred to TUI.
2002: Reflecting its largest operation, Preussag is renamed TUI AG.
2005: Hapag-Lloyd sells the last of its logistics businesses, leaving it focused solely on shipping and cruises; TUI acquires the Anglo-Canadian shipping firm CP Ships Limited and then merges it into Hapag-Lloyd, which now ranks number five in the world among container shippers.
2008: TUI announces its intention to divest the Hapag-Lloyd container shipping operations while keeping the Hapag-Lloyd cruise business.

and Japan. In 1898 Hapag also bought the Kingsin Line which had been operating a Far Eastern service out of Hamburg for some years, and thus acquired 13 ships and became a major player in the Far East market. In order to avoid a rate war during this time, NDL offered Hapag a share in the imperial mail contract. The service was pooled with alternate fortnightly departures from Bremen and Hamburg.

EARLY 20TH-CENTURY DEVELOPMENTS

The era of close cooperation between the two companies lasted until 1903. In the early 20th century, Hapag was the world's largest shipping company, owning 190 deep-sea vessels, operating on 74 routes, and calling at over 350 different ports worldwide. NDL had 135 deep-sea vessels and coastal ships, bringing the NDL fleet total to 494 ships. Hapag and NDL together employed 51,000 staff members, including 30,000 seafarers. In addition to their superiority in cargo shipping, Hapag and NDL were by 1914 the undisputed world cruise leaders. Both companies took great pride in operating cruise ships of a most luxurious standard and offering the most imaginative itineraries. At the outbreak of World War I, however, their liner services were largely curtailed. NDL's and Hapag's first postwar cruises did not take place until 1925 and 1926, respectively.

During the war, vessels from both fleets contributed to Germany's war effort by acting as blockade runners, auxiliary cruisers, troop carriers, and supply ships. Many of these ships were lost during the conflict. After the war, however, the fleets of NDL and Hapag were considerably diminished; most ships remaining in the German merchant fleet and all new vessels manufactured before armistice day had to be transferred to the Allies. The companies were left with a handful of small ships suitable only for coastal services.

Hapag and NDL, along with all other German shipping companies, had to rebuild from scratch after 1918. They began by taking over the agencies for the British companies Alfred Holt & Co. and Ellerman & Bucknall Steamship Co. Ltd. Hapag acquired the Hamburg line of Japanese company Nippon Yusen Kaisha (NYK) while NDL obtained NYK's Bremen line. In 1920 Hapag managed to reestablish its North Atlantic service through a joint agreement with United American Lines. A year later, Hapag's first postwar passenger liner, *Bayern,* joined the fleet. By 1925 the Hapag fleet had reached 45 ships, and purchases and construction continued.

The largest postwar addition to Hapag's fleet took place in 1926, when it acquired Deutsch-Australische Dampfschiffs-Gesellschaft (DADG), at one time Germany's third largest shipping company with 51 vessels. During this time NDL was also steadily regaining some lost ground. NDL purchased some of its former vessels from the Allies, and, in January 1922, it resumed transporting mail and freight to the Far East. Later that year, NDL recommenced passenger services to the Far East with its first vessel assembled after World War I, the *Weser.* Newer ships were deployed to the Far East by NDL as German trade in the region experienced a sustained upturn.

CRISIS, UNION, AND NAZI TAKEOVER

A worldwide economic slump from 1930 to 1932, however, created an international shipping crisis. Hapag, in particular, remained under financial pressure from the merger with the heavily indebted DADG. In addition to falling rates and volumes, and other financial pressures, both Hapag and NDL suffered severe liquidity problems, forcing them to apply for loans, restructure their capital, and mortgage some of their tonnage. In response to their financial plight and the depressed state of the market, Hapag and NDL formed the Hapag-Lloyd Union in 1930. The union went much further than typical pooling arrangements. Both partners retained their individual company identities, but all services and activities were operated jointly and all profits and losses shared. Furthermore, representatives of each company sat on the other's board, and a program to sell unused tonnage for scrap was set in motion. Services were further streamlined as other rationalization measures were adopted.

The union, however, proved transitory. In 1935 the Nazi government, which had taken a 51 percent stake in both companies, ordered an end to the agreement and all other shipping partnerships and cartels. The total breakup of Hapag and NDL into a number of smaller operators was prevented only by the determined intervention of respective chairpersons Emil Helfferich and Karl Lindemann. Despite restrictions, Hapag and NDL were still able to operate several joint overseas services, a practice necessitated by the intense international competition of the 1930s. Toward the end of the decade, NDL placed orders for three combined passenger cargo vessels; the *Scharnhorst, Gneisenau,* and *Potsdam* were among the most advanced of the time and were among the most famous vessels ever owned by either of these companies. At the onset of World War II, Hapag and NDL were once again ranked with the world's greatest shipping companies. The Hapag fleet consisted of 108 deep-sea vessels, while NDL owned and deployed 73 deep-sea vessels servicing a wide range of international routes.

Throughout World War II, the German merchant fleet and the country's navy worked together closely. Merchant ships were dedicated to supplying the German war effort and to breaking blockades in the Far East. Some ships were converted to armed merchant cruisers or were used as naval auxiliaries. In 1941, however, the state sold its majority stakes in both Hapag and NDL, and in the end, the Potsdam Agreement of 1945 required all German ships and related installations that had survived the war to be handed over to the Allies, forbidding German shipping companies to engage in overseas trade activities for five years.

POSTWAR RECONSTRUCTION

In the interim NDL began a towage service between Hamburg and Bremen, which it later extended to other German ports, and both Hapag and NDL became involved in parcel carrying services and catering. Hapag started its first postwar overseas service in 1950 with chartered ships to the West Indies. Within a year Hapag was again active in the North Atlantic cargo trade and had restarted service from Cuba to Mexico. Three years passed, however, before either Hapag or NDL were in a position to resume their trade with the Far East, one of their most important prewar routes. The almost complete loss of assets by the end of the war made external aid crucial for German shipping companies trying to reconstruct their fleets. An act of Parliament was passed on September 27, 1950, that empowered the federal government to offer favorable long-term loans for ship construction. By 1951 tax relief became available for shipbuilding loans, and both companies began steadily rebuilding their fleets. The Hapag fleet grew from seven ships in 1951 to the postwar peak of 67 vessels in 1960.

When Hapag and NDL resumed liner services to the Far East, they employed large combined passenger-cargo vessels with accommodations for around 90 passengers. On the North Atlantic route, however, only NDL resumed passenger service to New York as Hapag concentrated on the cargo business. Hapag also reentered the tourism business when it placed the 250-passenger luxury cruise liner *Ariadne* into service in February 1958.

The postwar reconstruction of Hapag and NDL services had, in most cases, progressed on a joint basis, and the "containerization revolution" provided impetus for additional cooperation. The shift from conventional cargo shipping to container shipping offered many benefits including cost savings, reduced transit and warehousing times, safer transhipment, reduced losses from damage and theft, and lower labor costs. This transition, however, initially involved a large investment of capital in new container ships (which were typically significantly larger than conventional freighters), the containers themselves, and the infrastructure needed to load and unload the new ships. Hapag and NDL therefore combined their two North Atlantic lines as Hapag-Lloyd Container Linien. In 1968 this joint venture, using two new container ships, became the first European entity to launch fully containerized transport services in the North Atlantic trade.

1970 MERGER FORMS HAPAG-LLOYD

The two companies in September 1970 formalized their cooperation with a complete merger, forming Hapag-Lloyd AG and ending more than a century of rivalry and sometime partnership. Hapag-Lloyd immediately ranked as one of the largest liner companies in the world, with combined revenues of more than DEM 1 billion, around 11,300 employees, and a fleet of 112 oceangoing vessels. In addition to the core shipping and cruise lines, the combined operations also included a number of other businesses, including port companies in Hamburg and Bremen, a container leasing company, a travel agency, and a 12.9 percent stake in Touristik Union International GmbH (TUI), the largest tour operator in Germany. One other business was discontinued in 1970, shortly after the merger was consummated. NDL's transatlantic passenger liner business had since the mid-1960s faced increasing competition from both scheduled and charter airline flights and eventually began operating in the red. Thus, soon after the formation of Hapag-Lloyd, the business upon which both predecessor companies had been founded was shut down.

In 1971 Hapag-Lloyd became involved with four other partners (NYK and Mitsui O.S.K. Lines, both of Japan, and Overseas Containers Ltd. and Ben Line of the United Kingdom) in the multinational TRIO consortium. The TRIO service, which operated between Europe and the Far East, involved 18 gigantic containerships (four contributed by Hapag-Lloyd), replacing 60 conventional vessels, and represented the largest investment ever in the history of liner shipping. Hapag-Lloyd was also able to rejoin the China trade by entering into a long-term cooperation agreement with a longtime player in that trade, the Rickmers Line. Hapag-Lloyd also acquired a 70 percent stake in Rickmers and took full control of the company in 1988.

In 1973, meanwhile, Hapag-Lloyd launched a charter airline called Hapag-Lloyd Flug, a move inspired by the holiday package boom. The business expanded rapidly. By the end of 1991 Hapag-Lloyd owned 20 aircraft with a combined seating capacity of 3,573. By that time, the majority of Hapag-Lloyd's aircraft fleet had come into service after 1988.

The first years of Hapag-Lloyd's merger were difficult. Worldwide, shipping was in a slump resulting from overtonnage; German shipping, in particular, was hit by the strength of the deutsche mark. After a flurry of construction in the 1970s as containerization took root, Hapag-Lloyd took delivery of only two new ships between 1978 and 1989. Deliveries resumed in the late 1980s as Hapag-Lloyd put some of the world's largest and most advanced containerships into service.

In the meantime, the company entered a new sector via the 1980 acquisition of a majority stake in the freight forwarding and logistics firm Pracht Spedition + Logistik GmbH, which ran sea, air, and land forwarding services in Europe, North America, Asia, and Australia and warehousing and furniture transport operations in Germany. Hapag-Lloyd purchased full control of Pracht in 1986. Around this same time, however, Hapag-Lloyd was narrowing its focus to two main areas: container transport and tourism, the latter including the airline, cruise ship, and travel agency operations. Among the businesses jettisoned at this time were the port facilities and container leasing. In the dismantling of the latter business, Hapag-Lloyd increased the stock of containers it owned to around 80,000.

The fortunes of the shipping industry improved in the second half of the 1980s, but Hapag-Lloyd's turnover remained flat and profits disappointing. The

1990 results of the liner shipping division were the worst since the introduction of containerization. The results for 1991, however, exceeded expectations: In the liner sector, profits in eastern trades more than compensated for the disappointing results on the North American routes, contributing to the net income figure of DM 65 million ($49 million). Despite the Gulf crisis, tourism developed favorably in 1991 and accounted for nearly one-third of the group turnover of DM 3.7 billion ($2.2 billion).

FORMATION OF THE GRAND ALLIANCE

In early 1991 the TRIO consortium was disbanded. In Hapag-Lloyd's case, it was replaced in 1993 by a new alliance that was eventually dubbed the Grand Alliance. The other initial partners were NYK and Singapore-based Neptune Orient Lines Limited. Hapag-Lloyd contributed six container ships to the venture, which launched a two-way service linking Europe, the U.S. East and West coasts, and Asia via the Panama Canal. The alliance thus enabled Hapag-Lloyd to return to the transpacific trade eight years after abandoning it following heavy losses. The Grand Alliance added a route between Europe and the Far East in 1996, the same year that a fourth member joined, P&O Containers, later P&O Nedlloyd.

In the summer of 1993 an important management transition occurred when the longtime head of Hapag-Lloyd, Hans Jakob Kruse, was succeeded as chairman of the executive board by Bernd Wrede. Unlike the previous leader, who had deep ties to the shipping industry, Wrede had a background in finance and was therefore more likely to initiate the changes that were needed at a time when profits at the shipping business were lagging, particularly the North Atlantic route, which was operating in the red. Among Wrede's first steps were to decentralize the shipping operations, overhaul the shipping side's approach to sales and marketing, and launch a number of cost-cutting initiatives, including a 20 percent slashing of the payroll. By 1996 the company was making some progress on the profit front and its shipping revenues were on the rise despite a difficult market environment in which freight rates were falling and Hapag-Lloyd faced ever larger competitors thanks to significant mergers in the industry.

The difficulties in the shipping business meant that even though it generated a little more than half of the overall company revenues for 1996 of DM 4.5 billion ($2.8 billion), it was responsible for only around a fifth of the operating profits. Hapag-Lloyd's tourism side had steadily grown in importance to account for an increasing amount of revenues and the bulk of the profits. Hapag-Lloyd had expanded its investment in the tourism industry late in 1993 when it increased its interest in TUI to 30 percent, giving it a stake equal to that of the tour operator's largest shareholder, Westdeutsche Landesbank Girozentrale. The Hapag-Lloyd cruise business, already the leader in the German market, was further bulked up in early 1997 via the acquisition of Hamburg-based Hanseatic Tours, which was the general agent in the German-speaking market for a number of U.S. cruise ships and also owned Hanseatic Cruises, operator of the cruise ship *Hanseatic.* With the chartering of the newly built, 420-passenger *Columbus* in mid-1997, Hapag-Lloyd's cruise business, generator of DM 300 million in revenues in 1996, boasted four top-class cruise ships designed for a variety of requirements and destinations.

1997 TAKEOVER BY PREUSSAG

Shortly after celebrating its 150th anniversary, Hapag-Lloyd in October 1997 gave up its independence by agreeing to be taken over by Preussag AG, a German industrial conglomerate with interests in steel, coal, shipbuilding, and logistics. The deal was valued at about DM 2.8 billion ($1.54 billion). To gain regulatory approval for the takeover, Westdeutsche Landesbank, a major shareholder in both Preussag and TUI, sold its TUI shares to Preussag, which transferred them to Hapag-Lloyd, giving the latter majority control of TUI.

In 1999 Preussag gained full control of TUI, but that same year Preussag restructured its tourism, shipping, and logistics assets. A new tourism holding company, later named TUI Group GmbH, was formed as a direct subsidiary of Preussag and comprised not only TUI itself but also Hapag-Lloyd's tourism operations, including its travel agencies and Hapag-Lloyd Flug airline. (The travel agencies were soon operating under the TUI brand, but the airline continued as Hapag-Lloyd Flug for several more years before being renamed Hapagfly in 2005 and then evolving into TUIfly in 2007.)

Hapag-Lloyd AG remained centered on its core container shipping business but also retained the Hapag-Lloyd Cruises and the Pracht freight-forwarding businesses and assumed control of two Preussag logistics companies, VTG-Lehnkering and Algeco. Hapag-Lloyd also initially held onto the conventional shipping line Rickmers but then sold this business in 2000 to concentrate solely on container-based shipping. In the meantime, in 1998 the Grand Alliance was reformulated to include Hapag-Lloyd, NYK, P&O Nedlloyd, Malaysia-based MISC Berhad, and Hong Kong-based Orient Overseas Container Line Limited.

The acquisition of Hapag-Lloyd was the first step in

Preussag's transition into a services group. Preussag gradually divested itself of its once-core industrial holdings while at the same time making a series of acquisitions in the tourism sector that substantially bulked up the TUI side. By 2002 TUI was responsible for more than 60 percent of Preussag's revenues (with Hapag-Lloyd contributing around 19 percent), and so Preussag elected to change its name to TUI AG that year to signal the company's new era and to reflect its leading business.

In the meantime, in 2000 Preussag announced plans to float up to 49 percent of the shares of Hapag-Lloyd on the stock market but canceled the initial public offering (IPO) for tax reasons. The following year, Hapag-Lloyd placed into service *Hamburg Express,* the first of four massive new ships it had ordered to increase its overall shipping capacity and keep pace with the global growth in container shipping; each of the vessels were capable of carrying 7,500 standard containers. Wrede had continued to head the company after the Preussag takeover, but at the end of 2001 he stepped down from the post of executive chairman and was succeeded by Michael Behrendt. The new leader was a former head of VTG-Lehnkering and had served as a member of Hapag-Lloyd's executive board since 1999.

Despite an ongoing worldwide economic slowdown, Hapag-Lloyd in 2003 enjoyed the best year in its 157-year history, generating a record operating profit of EUR 343 million ($432 million) on revenues of EUR 3.9 billion ($4.9 billion). Early in 2004 TUI announced plans to narrow Hapag-Lloyd's focus to container shipping and cruises in preparation for another anticipated partial flotation of the company's stock. TUI wanted to use the proceeds from the IPO to reduce its debt and also wanted to increase its concentration on tourism. Most of Hapag-Lloyd's logistics operations, including Pracht, Algeco, and the bulk of VTG-Lehnkering, were divested in 2004 and the remainder was jettisoned a year later. In September 2004, however, TUI postponed the Hapag-Lloyd IPO citing an adverse stock market environment.

2005 ACQUISITION OF CP SHIPS

Plans for an IPO were still on the table in the early months of 2005, but TUI then reversed course from its intended de-emphasis of its shipping side by acquiring the Anglo-Canadian shipping firm CP Ships Limited late in 2005 for EUR 1.7 billion ($2 billion) in cash and the assumption of about EUR 260 million ($305 million) in debt. Spun off from railway firm Canadian Pacific Limited in 2001, CP Ships had been based in the U.K. town of Gatwick, but its stock had traded on the Toronto and New York exchanges. Its history dated to 1886, when Canadian Pacific Railway began chartering oceangoing vessels to transport tea and silk from Asia to the west coast of Canada. By 2005 the company was the 16th largest container carrier in the world, with a capacity of around 187,000 standard containers.

TUI subsequently merged CP Ships into Hapag-Lloyd. The latter instantly leaped up the chart of the world's shipping leaders, vaulting from the 13th position to number five on the basis of its enlarged capacity of more than 410,000 standard containers. CP Ships' 78 vessels, most of which were of the smaller variety, boosted Hapag-Lloyd's fleet total to 133. Hapag-Lloyd had a number of additional ships on order, including three 8,000-container-capacity behemoths. The addition of CP Ships' lines solidified Hapag-Lloyd's position as the largest player in the transatlantic trade while also providing it with new north-south routes linking both Europe and North America with South America and Australasia.

The deal came at a crucial time of industry consolidation headlined by world leader A.P. Møller - Mærsk A/S's takeover of P&O Nedlloyd, which led the latter to leave the Grand Alliance. The four remaining members of this consortium, one of the largest such alliances in container shipping in the world, carried on with Hapag-Lloyd enjoying greater leverage thanks to P&O Nedlloyd's departure. In 2007 the members signed an agreement extending their cooperation for ten more years. At the time the alliance was operating about 140 vessels with a capacity of between 2,700 and 9,000 standard containers, offering customers 20 services, mainly on major east-west routes.

However necessary the takeover was from a competitive standpoint, Hapag-Lloyd's integration of CP Ships did not go entirely smoothly mainly because of the need to combine CP Ships' numerous and overlapping information technology systems and to trim the firm's bloated workforce. High integration costs, coupled with rising operating costs and declining freight rates, sent Hapag-Lloyd into a net loss of more than EUR 100 million ($132 million) for 2006. The addition of CP Ships helped send revenues up more than 63 percent to EUR 6.25 billion ($8.25 billion).

Continuing to invest in upgrading its fleet, Hapag-Lloyd by early 2008 had increased its overall capacity to more than 514,000 standard containers with the launching of the 8,750-container-capacity *Bremen Express.* The company had orders in place for 15 more similarly sized vessels for delivery through 2011. Some TUI investors, however, had grown increasingly disenchanted with the parent company's shipping side, having concluded that the company had overpaid for CP Ships given the integration problems Hapag-Lloyd had encountered and that TUI would be more valuable if Hapag-Lloyd were divested. TUI's board was eventually won over by such arguments and confirmed in March 2008 that it did indeed intend to sell Hapag-Lloyd. Only the container shipping operations were to be included in the sale as the Hapag-Lloyd cruise business was to be retained by TUI. Singapore-based Neptune Orient Lines quickly emerged as the frontrunner in the subsequent bidding, with TUI hoping for a sale price as high as EUR 5 billion ($7.8 billion). A consortium of investors backed by the Hamburg state government was also attempting to pull together an offer to keep Hapag-Lloyd from falling into foreign hands. The ultimate outcome of the auction was thrown into further doubt in July 2008 when TUI's largest shareholder, Norwegian shipping magnate John Fredriksen, announced his opposition to the sale in part because weak market conditions were indicating the sale price for Hapag-Lloyd was likely to be much lower than originally anticipated.

Debra Johnson
Updated, David E. Salamie

PRINCIPAL SUBSIDIARIES

Hapag-Lloyd (Italy) s.r.l.; Hapag-Lloyd (America) Inc. (U.S.A.); Asia: Hapag-Lloyd (Asia) Pte. Ltd. (Singapore).

PRINCIPAL COMPETITORS

A.P. Møller - Mærsk A/S; Mediterranean Shipping Company, S.A.; CMA CGM S.A.; Evergreen Marine Corp. (Taiwan) Ltd.; China Ocean Shipping (Group) Company; China Shipping Container Lines Co., Ltd.; Neptune Orient Lines Limited; Hamburg Süd.

FURTHER READING

Atkins, Ralph, "TUI Bids EUR 1.7bn for CP Ships to Bolster Container Business," *Financial Times,* August 22, 2005, p. 17.

Barnard, Bruce, and Peter T. Leach, "Who Will Buy Hapag-Lloyd?" *Florida Shipper,* April 28, 2008.

Berkenkopf, Katrin, "TUI Cancels Hapag-Lloyd IPO As Behrendt Jumps on Board," *Lloyd's List,* September 8, 2004, p. 1.

Berkenkopf, Katrin, and Patrick Hagen, "Hapag-Lloyd Lines Up for Sale As TUI Seeks a Quick Separation," *Lloyd's List,* March 19, 2008, p. 3.

Bonney, Joseph, "NYK, NOL, Hapag-Lloyd Form Three-Continent Alliance," *American Shipper,* November 1992, pp. 20+.

———, "Prudent Policies Pay Off for Ship Line Hapag-Lloyd," *Journal of Commerce and Commercial,* December 23, 1987, pp. 1A+.

Bowley, Graham, "Preussag Takes Controlling Stake in Hapag-Lloyd," *Financial Times,* September 3, 1997, p. 38.

Canna, Elizabeth, "Balancing the Scales at Hapag-Lloyd," *American Shipper,* February 1995, pp. 67–68.

———, "Hapag-Lloyd Makeover," *American Shipper,* December 1993, pp. 40B–40D.

Cockrill, Philip, *The Woermann Steamship Line of Hamburg, 1890–1965,* Newbury, U.K.: Philip Cockrill, 1980, 34 p.

Damas, Philip, "Hapag-Lloyd: Single but Choosy," *American Shipper,* June 1997, pp. 54, 56–57.

Drechsel, Edwin, *Norddeutscher Lloyd, Bremen, 1857–1970: History, Fleet, Ship Mails,* 2 vols., Vancouver, B.C.: Cordillera Publishing, 1994–1995.

Erdogan, Bülent, "Hapag-Lloyd Expects Loss of EUR 100m After CP Ships Buy," *Lloyd's List,* November 10, 2006, p. 2.

Fisher, Andrew, "Hapag-Lloyd Finds Calmer Waters: Rehabilitation of a West German Shipping Group," *Financial Times,* November 3, 1987, p. 32.

———, "Pacific Minnow Finds the Going Too Rough: Hapag-Lloyd of West Germany Pulls Out of One Area of the Container Shipping Market," *Financial Times,* October 16, 1985, p. 6.

Fleming, Stewart, "Banks to Aid Hapag-Lloyd," *Financial Times,* March 4, 1983, p. 16.

———, "Hapag-Lloyd Cuts Operations to Ride Out Storm," *Financial Times,* December 3, 1982, p. 21.

Graham, Rachel, "TUI Cancels IPO for Shipping Unit," *Wall Street Journal Europe,* September 8, 2004, p. M3.

Hamburg-Amerikanische Packetfahrt-Actien-Gesellschaft, *Sixty Years of Ocean Navigation and the Half Century Anniversary of the Establishment of the First Line of Steamships Flying a German Flag,* New York: Hamburg-America Line, 1906, 63 p.

Hapag-Lloyd, *100 Jahre Kreuzfahrten, 1890–1990,* Bremen: Hapag-Lloyd-Kreuzfahrten, 1990.

"Hapag-Lloyd's Integration of CP Ships Not All Plain Sailing," *Lloyd's List,* August 29, 2007, p. 14.

Koenig, Robert, "Friendly Deal Puts Hapag-Lloyd Under Preussag AG Ownership," *Journal of Commerce and Commercial,* September 3, 1997, pp. 1A+.

Leach, Peter T., "Hapag-Lloyd Steps Up: $2.3 Billion Acquisition of CP Ships Would Produce Fifth-Largest Container Carrier," *Journal of Commerce,* August 29, 2005, pp. 10–12.

Paris, Costas, and John Jannarone, "Neptune, TUI Weigh Options for a Shipping Merger," *Wall Street Journal,* February 7, 2008, p. C5.

Paris, Costas, and P. R. Venkat, "Neptune Orient Is Set to Bid for Hapag-Lloyd," *Wall Street Journal,* May 22, 2008, p. B2.

Rhoads, Christopher, "Preussag Aims to Acquire Travel Firm Hapag-Lloyd," *Wall Street Journal Europe,* September 3, 1997, p. 3.

Seiler, Otto J., *Bridge Across the Atlantic: The Story of Hapag-Lloyd's North American Liner Services,* Herford, Germany: Verlag E.S. Mittler & Sohn, 1991, 81 p.

———, *Hapag-Lloyd: A Century of the Australia Service, 1886–1986,* Hamburg: Hapag-Lloyd, 1986, 109 p.

———, *Hapag-Lloyd: A Century of the Far East Service, 1886–1986,* Singapore: Hapag-Lloyd, 1986, 144 p.

Thiel, Reinhold, *Die Geschichte des Norddeutschen Lloyd, 1857–1970,* 5 vols., Bremen: H.M. Hauschild, 2001–2006.

Toll, Erich E., "Hapag-Lloyd's Goal? Diversify," *Journal of Commerce and Commercial,* January 26, 1988, p. 3B.

Vail, Bruce, "Hapag-Lloyd Looks for Future Growth on Far East Route," *Journal of Commerce and Commercial,* April 27, 1990, pp. 1A+.

Wiborg, Susanne, *Albert Ballin,* Hamburg: Ellert & Richter, 2000, 144 p.

Wiborg, Susanne, and Klaus Wiborg, *1847–1997: The World Is Our Oyster; 150 Years of Hapag-Lloyd,* Hamburg: Hapag-Lloyd, 1997, 435 p.

Wiesmann, Gerrit, and Robert Wright, "TUI Puts Hapag-Lloyd Shipping Unit on the Auction Block," *Financial Times,* June 19, 2008, p. 20.

Wright, Robert, "Port City Braced for Fight with NOL to Keep Vital German Asset," *Financial Times,* May 21, 2008, p. 20.

———, "TUI Sets Course for CP Ships Purchase," *Financial Times,* September 5, 2005, p. 25.

Hite Brewery Company Ltd.

Hite Bldg.
132-12 Cheongdam 1-dong
Gangnam-gu
Seoul, 135 957
South Korea
Telephone: (+82-2) 32190114
Fax: (+82-2) 34422683
Web site: http://www.hite.com

Public Company
Incorporated: 1933
Employees: 1,565
Sales: KRW 962.9 billion ($969.7 million) (2007)
Stock Exchanges: Korea
Ticker Symbol: 000140
NAICS: 312120 Breweries; 312111 Soft Drink Manufacturing; 312140 Distilleries

■ ■ ■

Hite Brewery Company Ltd. is South Korea's leading beer and alcoholic beverages company. Through its Hite lager brand, Hite dominates the beer segment, with a market share of more than 60 percent. In addition to the European-styled Hite, the company brews and markets several other beer brands, including Max Prime, the only 100 percent malt beer in Korea, launched in 2007; S, marketed toward female beer drinkers; and Stout. Nonetheless, the Hite brand accounts for 92 percent of the company's beer sales. Hite is also the leading player in South Korea's *soju* market, the country's traditional beverage, through its control of Jinro Ltd. Hite's *soju* production has led the company into the international market, especially into China, where the company established a subsidiary in Beijing in December 2007. Hite operates breweries in Kangwon, Masan, and Jeonjoo.

The company also bottles and markets its own mineral water brand, Puriss. In addition, Hite distributes the Kingdom, Lancelot, and Cutty Sark whiskey brands and wine brands, including Kangaroo Ridge and Rutherford Hill. Hite is listed on the Korea Stock Exchange and has applied for permission to relist Jinro as well. In July 2008 the company restructured its operations, creating a separate holding company, Hite Holding, for three of its subsidiaries, Hite Distillers, Hite Alcohol, and Hite Industrial. The company is led by CEO Park Moon-Deuk. In 2007, Hite posted total revenues of KRW 963 billion ($970 million).

BEER BREWER DURING THE JAPANESE OCCUPATION

Hite Brewery originated as a result of the Japanese domination of Korea in the early part of the 20th century. Into the 1930s, there were no domestic Korean beers. Instead, the country's most popular alcoholic beverage was *soju,* a traditional Korean beverage distilled from sweet potatoes. The tightening of Japan's military control over Korea and its institution of anti-Korean measures designed to eliminate Korean culture favored the creation of a domestic brewing industry. This situation led Japan's Sapporo to launch a brewery in Korea in 1933. By December of that year, Sapporo had completed construction of its Korean brewery in Yeongdeungpo, Gyunggi.

COMPANY PERSPECTIVES

Management Policy: To maintain highest quality; to satisfy the needs of customers; to become a creative and reliable company.

Following Japan's defeat in 1945, the U.S. military took control of the brewery and placed Min Dukgi in charge of its operations. At that time, the company changed its name to Chosun Beer Brewery Co. Ltd., after the name of a former Korean dynasty. Chosun then rebranded its beer under the Crown label.

Crown did not remain Korea's sole domestic beer for long. In 1948, Oriental Brewery (OB) appeared and launched its own brand, OB. Korean beer drinkers flocked to the new brand, and by 1952 OB had captured the lead in the growing Korean beer market. Before long, OB came to dominate the market, grabbing as much as a 70 percent share, a position it would maintain into the early 1990s. During this time, Korean consumption habits changed as well, and by the end of the 20th century, beer had become the alcoholic beverage of choice, representing 49 percent of the market, compared to just 32 percent for *soju*. Chosun attempted to capture a share of the latter market, building a *soju* distillery and launching the Namsung brand in 1957. In 1965, the company changed its *soju* brand to Bobae.

Chosun's own fortunes fell in proportion to OB's growth. The Korean military government, which frowned on alcoholic beverage production, moved to separate itself from the company, which became a privately held firm in 1952. Yet the original owners were unable to counter the swift rise of its new competitor. Instead, the Park family increasingly gained control of the company. Under its new ownership, Chosun upgraded production facilities and equipment. By 1962 Chosun had developed sufficient production technologies to launch its brand on the export market. Chosun also invested in new packaging types, including a new bottle design specifically for the United Nations peacekeeping troops in South Korea. In 1965 the company became the first in South Korea to package its beer in flip-top cans. An important milestone for the company came in 1968, when its Crown label won a gold medal at the ICSP international competition. This success paved the way for the group's entry into the export-beer market.

EXPANSION IN THE EIGHTIES

When Park Kyeong-Bok was named company president in 1969, he launched Chosun's gradual return to market dominance. Park quickly led the group on an expansion drive, doubling the capacity of its main Yeongdeungpo brewery. The company also began building up its Bobae *soju* operation, carrying out an expansion of its facilities over several phases through the 1970s and into the 1980s. In 1973, the company became the first in Korea to build its own malting plant, near its Yeongdeungpo brewery. The company's malting plant was at the time the largest in Asia. Fueling this expansion, the company went public in 1973. However, the Park family remained the company's major shareholder.

In 1978 Chosun took over the Masan brewery, which at the time produced its own beer brand, Handok. Chosun invested in doubling the capacity of its new brewery; in the 21st century, the Masan brewery became responsible for supplying beer for the group's export sales. In 1980 the company also added a second malting plant, in Jinju.

Chosun's expansion continued through the 1980s. The company entered a number of technical partnerships, most notably with Sapporo, which provided engineering assistance in the expansion of the group's brewing capacity. In 1986 Chosun teamed up with Carlsberg, acquiring the Danish company's brewing technology. These partnerships enabled the company to launch several new beer types during the 1980s, including Crown Light and Saeng in 1982; Carlsberg under license from 1986; Super Dry in 1989; and the popular Dry Mild in 1991. The latter label sold more than ten million cases by the end of its first year. Nonetheless, Chosun remained a minor player in the Korea market, as its market share dropped to just 15 percent at the beginning of the 1990s.

NEW LABEL IN 1993

A new generation of the Park family took over the Chosun leadership during the 1980s. It was the arrival of Park Moon-Deuk as company president in 1991 that signaled the start of a new era for the company. In 1993 Chosun recognized a new market opportunity: It adopted the sterile filtration brewing method, as opposed to the older pasteurization technique. The company developed an entirely new lager beer, based on pure mineral water, called Hite. The name was reportedly formed from the words "Humanity, Innovation, Trust, and Excellence."

The Hite advertising campaign emphasized its use of high-quality water and appealed to the growing environmental awareness in South Korea at the time.

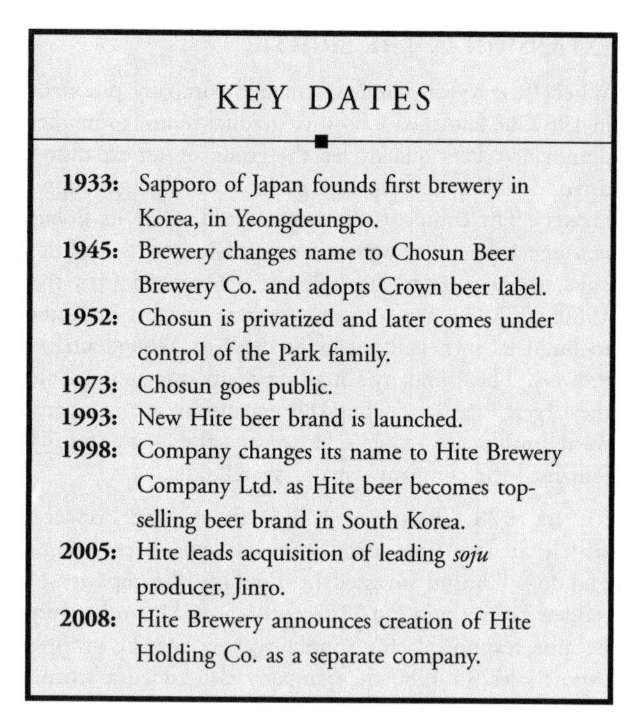

KEY DATES

1933: Sapporo of Japan founds first brewery in Korea, in Yeongdeungpo.
1945: Brewery changes name to Chosun Beer Brewery Co. and adopts Crown beer label.
1952: Chosun is privatized and later comes under control of the Park family.
1973: Chosun goes public.
1993: New Hite beer brand is launched.
1998: Company changes its name to Hite Brewery Company Ltd. as Hite beer becomes top-selling beer brand in South Korea.
2005: Hite leads acquisition of leading *soju* producer, Jinro.
2008: Hite Brewery announces creation of Hite Holding Co. as a separate company.

The Hite launch was accompanied by a stroke of luck. In the early 1990s, chief rival OB found itself at the center of a national controversy, when its parent company accidentally released phenol into Nakdong River. The toxic substance quickly entered the country's water supply, sparking a scandal. The Hite brand's advertising campaign, which emphasized its use of natural spring water, capitalized on OB's problems.

The launch of Hite and the massive investment in its promotion helped to depress Chosun's earnings and share price through much of the 1990s. By 1997, however, the tide had begun to turn. In that year, Hite succeeded for the first time in claiming the number one position in market share. By 1998, the brand had confirmed its leadership, and the company adopted a new label emphasizing its number one position. In that year as well the company changed its name to Hite Brewing Co.

By then, the company had expanded into other areas. The company began importing and distributing whiskey, in partnership with the United Kingdom's United Distillers, introducing its Dimple brand to the South Korean market in 1985. Hite's whiskey subsidiary, called Hiscot Co., later developed its own import labels for the Korean market, including Launcelot, introduced in 2002, and Kingdom, in 2007. Hite also branched out into bottled water, buying the mineral water company Noksuwon in 1996. In 1997, the company rebranded its bottled water under the Puriss brand.

DUAL MARKET LEADERSHIP

Hite continued to develop new beer labels into the early 2000s. The company launched a black beer, called Stout, in 2000. The following year, in celebration of Japan and Korea's joint hosting of the World Cup, the company launched the K&J brand. Hite also developed a brew specifically for the Japanese market, a dry malt beer with lower malt content to appeal to Japanese consumer tastes. In Korea, meanwhile, the company prepared a 100 percent pure barley beer, Prime, and launched it in 2002.

Through the middle of the decade, Hite continued to develop its beer brands. In recognition of the growing consumption of beer among Korean females, the company launched a number of targeted labels. These included the Exfeel line of beers, including a low-carbohydrate version and S, a light beer specifically marketed to younger and female consumers. At the same time, the company sought to position itself in the premium beer category, launching its Max Prime label in 2006. Nonetheless, the Hite label remained the company's flagship brand, accounting for 92 percent of its total beer sales. By 2008, Hite had boosted its share of the Korean beer market past 60 percent.

By then, too, Hite Brewery had grown into the country's leading producer of *soju.* This achievement took place in 2005, when the company won the right to acquire that segment's leader, Jinro Ltd., which had collapsed into bankruptcy two years earlier. Founded in 1924, Jinro had long dominated the *soju* market, before teaming up with Coors in the United States in an attempt to break into the South Korean beer market as well. The upheavals caused by the Asian economic crisis in the late 1990s had taken their toll on Jinro, however, and by 2003, the company had been forced into liquidation, removing its listing from the Korea Stock Exchange.

In order to acquire Jinro, Hite raised KRW 3.4 trillion ($3.4 billion) in conjunction with a group of investors, including Korean Teachers Credit Unit, Korean Federation of Community Credit Cooperatives, Korea Development Bank, and the Military Aid Association. Hite's own stake in Jinro topped 40 percent. By 2008, the company had increased its holding to more than 48 percent. Hite then applied for permission to relist Jinro. Under the relisting, expected to be completed in 2008, Hite anticipated increasing its own stake in the *soju* maker to more than 50 percent. In preparation for the public listing, Hite announced its plans to restructure parts of its operations in July 2008. As part of this effort, the company separated a number of its existing subsidiaries into a new holding company, Hite Holding Co.

Having gained undisputed dominance in the two primary alcoholic beverage categories in South Korea, Hite began looking for new horizons. To expand beyond South Korea, Hite looked toward its popular Jinro brand, which had established itself as a major brand in the Japanese market. Hite next turned to China, which, like Japan, boasted a strong ethnic Korean population. In December 2007, the company established a new subsidiary in Beijing, to boost its distribution of *soju* in that market. From there, the company announced its interest in further international expansion with plans to add operations in Russia and the United States, along with other Asian markets. As Korea's oldest brewer, Hite hoped to extend its dominant position into new markets in the 21st century.

M. L. Cohen

PRINCIPAL SUBSIDIARIES

Hiscot Co.; Hite Alcohol Co.; Hite Development Inc.; Hite Distillers Co.; Hite Industrial Co.; Hite Soju Co.

PRINCIPAL COMPETITORS

Doosan Corp.; MH Ethanol Company Ltd.

FURTHER READING

"Can Hite Drink the Toast?" *Business Korea,* July 2005, p. 53.

"Carlsberg Sells $235m Stake in Hite As Froth Comes Off Asia," *Euroweek,* June 16, 2006, p. S7.

"Hite Brewery Poised to Buy Jinro for $3.4 Billion," *Bloomberg,* June 4, 2005.

"Hite Brewery's Honourary Chairman Dead at 85," *AsiaPulse News,* July 25, 2007.

"Hite Opens Spirits Unit in China," *just-drinks.com,* December 13, 2007.

"Korea's Hite Brewery to Acquire Liquor Distiller Jinro," *AsiaPulse News,* July 21, 2005.

"Max Prime (Acid Test)," *Grocer,* March 15, 2008, p. 67.

"S. Korea's Hite Opens in China to Expand Overseas Liquor Sales," *AsiaPulse News,* December 11, 2007.

"Shareholders Okay South Korea's Hite Brewery Holding Firm Plan," *AsiaPulse News,* May 29, 2008.

"Song, Juna A., "Hite Brewery Consortium to Buy Jinro," *Financial Times,* June 4, 2005, p. 8.

"'3-Way Competition in Beer Market to Cost Consumers,'" *Korea Times,* May 6, 1999.

The Home Depot, Inc.

2455 Paces Ferry Road, NW
Atlanta, Georgia 30339-4024
U.S.A.
Telephone: (770) 433-8211
Toll Free: (800) 430-3376
Fax: (770) 384-2356
Web site: http://www.homedepot.com

Public Company
Incorporated: 1978
Employees: 331,000
Sales: $77.35 billion (2007)
Stock Exchanges: New York
Ticker Symbol: HD
NAICS: 444110 Home Centers

■ ■ ■

The Home Depot, Inc., the largest home improvement retailer in the world, operates more than 2,200 warehouse stores in the United States, Canada, Mexico, and China, the vast majority of which operate under the Home Depot name. In the United States, where the firm ranks as the second largest retailer behind only Wal-Mart Stores, Inc., there are about 1,950 Home Depot stores spread across all 50 states, while the foreign operations include roughly 165 units in Canada, more than 60 in Mexico, and about a dozen in China. Home Depot warehouses, which on average consist of about 105,000 square feet of enclosed space plus another 23,000 square feet of outside garden area, stock between 35,000 and 45,000 products in a typical year, including building materials, hardware and tools, wall and floor coverings, paint, plumbing and electrical supplies, home appliances, and landscaping and gardening items. In addition to serving do-it-yourselfers and commercial customers, Home Depot stores also cater to so-called do-it-for-me customers by offering a variety of installation services.

ROOTS IN HANDY DAN

The company was incorporated in June 1978 as a result of a corporate management shake-up by new ownership of the Handy Dan home center chain. As a result of the managerial shuffle, Bernard Marcus and Arthur Blank found themselves out of work. With backing from a New York venture capital firm, Marcus and Blank formed The Home Depot, Inc., and opened the company's first two outlets in the Atlanta, Georgia, area, in June 1979. The concept that had helped secure financing for the project was that when the price of merchandise was marked down, sales increased while the cost of making those sales decreased. The major problem that had plagued most cut-rate retail operations, however, was poor service at the operations level, which hired unskilled, low-paid employees to keep costs down.

Marcus and Blank realized that recognizing customers' needs was one of the most important elements in a company's growth. They were aware that at the time do-it-yourselfers made up more than 60 percent of the building supply industry's sales volume, but the majority of them did not have the technical knowledge or

COMPANY PERSPECTIVES

The Home Depot is in the home improvement business and our goal is to provide the highest level of service, the broadest selection of products and the most competitive prices. We are a values-driven company and our eight core values include the following: excellent customer service; taking care of our people; giving back; doing the "right" thing; creating shareholder value; respect for all people; entrepreneurial spirit; building strong relationships.

expertise to accomplish most home repair or improvement projects.

The Home Depot management team set about to solve this problem in two ways. First, they made sure that all Home Depot stores were large enough to stock at least 25,000 different items. Their competitor locations normally had room for only 10,000. The second solution was to train the sales staff in each store to help remove much of the mystery attached to home improvement projects from the minds of consumers. Marcus and Blank believed that, with the education provided by knowledgeable sales staffers, Home Depot customers would gain the confidence to take on more projects at home, coming back to Home Depot outlets to purchase what was needed and get additional advice from sales staff.

Home Depot built its sales staff from both dedicated do-it-yourselfers and professional tradespeople, hiring most employees in full-time capacities. Only 10 percent of Home Depot's sales personnel were part-time. Whenever possible, each store had a licensed plumber and electrician on staff, and customers were urged to call the Home Depot store in their area if they had any problem or questions while they were doing their home repair or improvement projects. The company also scheduled in-store instructional workshops for its customers and in some cases brought in local contractors as teachers.

This approach paid off. By 1984 the company was operating 19 stores and reported sales of $256 million, a 118 percent increase over 1983. In 1986 Home Depot's sales reached the $1 billion mark, and the company was operating 60 retail outlets by year's end. In the meantime, the company was taken public in September 1981 on the NASDAQ, and then the stock was shifted to the New York Stock Exchange in 1984.

TROUBLES DURING THE MID-EIGHTIES

The company's growth was not without its problems, however. In 1984 Home Depot paid $38.4 million for the nine-store Bowater warehouse chain, with outlets in Texas, Louisiana, and Alabama. The acquisition created immediate difficulties. Bowater's reputation with consumers was shoddy, and the merchandise in its stores did not match what Home Depot carried in its other outlets. In addition, Bowater's employees did not meet Home Depot's standards; Home Depot eventually was forced to dismiss almost all of them.

During these years Home Depot's sales continued to climb, but for the first time in the company's history the cost of sales also increased. In 1985 the company's earnings fell 42 percent, and with the ever increasing costs of opening new outlets (at that time it was more than $8 million per store) the company's long-term debt rose from $4 million to $200 million in just two years. By the end of 1985, the company's stock price had plummeted. It was clear that changes were needed if Home Depot was to continue to grow and prosper.

The company slowed down its expansion. In 1986 Home Depot opened only ten new stores, all in existing, established markets. A stock offering of 2.99 million shares at $17 per share helped reduce and restructure the company debt. Marcus also installed a computerized inventory control system and upgraded the company's management training programs. In keeping with Marcus's commitment to slower, more conservative growth, the company continued opening new stores to completely capture existing markets instead of striking out into new regions of the country.

1989: A BREAKTHROUGH YEAR

By 1989 Home Depot had surpassed Lowe's Companies, Inc., in sales, becoming the largest home-repair chain in the United States. By year's end almost all outlets were using the company's new satellite data communications network. The fast and accurate exchange of information linking stores permitted continued growth by enhancing the company's responsiveness to market changes. The satellite also served as a foundation for the Home Depot television network, a system that produced and transmitted live programming by top management to each outlet. The company's net earnings increased 46 percent in 1990, and Home Depot effected a three-for-two stock split that same year. Sales increased 38 percent over 1989. With the trend for continued growth in the do-it-yourself (DIY) market shown by a 33 percent increase in the number of customer transactions logged by the

KEY DATES

1978: Bernard Marcus and Arthur Blank found The Home Depot, Inc.
1979: The partners open the first two Home Depot outlets in Atlanta, Georgia.
1981: Company goes public.
1986: Sales reach $1 billion.
1994: Home Depot enters the Canadian market via the purchase of a 75 percent stake in Aikenhead's Home Improvement Warehouse.
2000: 1,000th store opens; former General Electric Company executive Robert L. Nardelli is brought onboard as CEO.
2006: HD Supply, the company's wholesale supply business, is bolstered via the $3.5 billion acquisition of Hughes Supply, Inc.
2007: Nardelli resigns under pressure, and Frank Blake is named his successor; HD Supply is sold for $8.3 billion; annual sales decline for the first time in the company's history.

company in 1990, with an increase of 4 percent for the average customer sale, Home Depot seemed to be an emerging giant in the U.S. retail marketplace.

The company began the 1990s with the goal of doing more than $10 billion in sales from 350 locations by 1995. Part of this plan included a 75-store expansion into the northeastern United States, one of Home Depot's strongest markets despite the region's economic setbacks. Company officials believed the area's dense population and large number of older homes would generate impressive results. Expansion plans also included the state of Washington.

Despite the continued health of the home remodeling market, the company's stock flattened out in 1993, as the firm began to saturate its market. Along with superstores such as Bed Bath & Beyond, Home Depot suffered from consumer reaction to the proliferation of large warehouse megastores. In reaction, the company began to search for ways to redefine its marketplace, and to develop enhancements to its three-tiered "price, assortment, and service" strategies.

PERIOD OF SUSTAINED STRONG GROWTH

Throughout the 1990s Home Depot tested several programs designed to determine where business could grow next. In 1991 it sampled customer interest in an installation program for items such as carpets, doors, and windows. The program met with success and was adopted throughout Home Depot stores. A bridal registry was tested, as well as a drive-in lumberyard and a delivery service. Home Depot also established an environmental marketing department to help educate consumers about what product choices are more environmentally friendly. Over 70 hardware products, from lightbulbs to paint, were identified for customers via in-store flyers and posters. Customer satisfaction again came under consideration in a program called S.P.I. (store productivity improvement) in which cleaning, restocking, and other routine tasks were scheduled after store hours. In 1995 Home Depot opened its first 24-hour store and published a book on home repair, the 480-page *Home Improvement 1-2-3,* compiled with *Better Homes and Gardens* magazine publisher Meredith Corporation.

In addition to entering new U.S. markets, Home Depot began to examine other options. In 1994 the company spent approximately $161.5 million on a 75 percent share of Aikenhead's Home Improvement Warehouse, a Canadian chain of seven hardware stores, which were subsequently converted to the Home Depot name. While Home Depot examined the possibility of expansion both north and south of the border, by the following year plans to open outlets in Mexico had been put on hold, and the number of planned Canadian openings had been reduced to 25 through 1996. Instead, the company added to the number of its EXPO Design Centers, bringing the total to five. Begun in 1991 and located throughout the United States, these stores concentrated on the upscale interior design market and further expanded the company's sales base. In addition, efforts to court the commercial market also began to reap profits; overall, Home Depot net earnings achieved a five-year compound growth rate of 35 percent over the first half of the 1990s.

In addition to its dual concerns of maintaining both the bottom line and customer satisfaction, Home Depot continued to take a leadership role in many of the communities its stores had entered. Under the leadership of Blank, who contended that corporate America had a responsibility to give back to the society within which it flourished, Home Depot's Team Depot had become involved in humanitarian causes ranging from local welfare organizations to Habitat for Humanity and the Boys and Girls Clubs of Canada and the United States. In addition to encouraging the continuous volunteer efforts of its employees, the company also employed 1996 Olympic hopeful athletes, paying them competitive wages as part-time employees during their training for the Atlanta-based games, of which Home Depot was a corporate sponsor.

Although some forecasters continued to shed doubt upon the company's ability to maintain its phenomenal level of growth, company management remained confident. By 1996 Home Depot's profits were approaching $1 billion, while revenues amounted to $19.54 billion, a 26.3 percent increase over the previous year, as the store count passed the 500-unit mark. The company had also pushed its way into the rankings of the ten largest retailers in the United States.

In 1997 the top management at Home Depot changed for the first time in the firm's 19-year history. Blank, who had been serving as president and COO, succeeded Marcus as the company CEO, with Marcus remaining chairman. That same year, the company entered into one of the largest employment-discrimination settlements in U.S. history, although it admitted no wrongdoing in the matter. The agreement settled a class-action sex-discrimination suit filed in 1994 charging Home Depot with discriminating against female employees in the area of advancement and promotion opportunities. The terms included payments to plaintiffs and plaintiff attorneys totaling $87.5 million, and the company also earmarked an additional $17 million for internal costs, including the implementation of new employment procedures at Home Depot stores across the country.

By 1998 the company was operating more than three dozen Home Depot stores in Canada, and that year it bought out its minority partner in the Canadian unit, the Molson Companies Limited, for $261 million. In the booming economic times of the late 1990s, when Americans bought new homes and remodeled existing ones at record rates, Home Depot benefited by well over $38 billion in revenues by 1999, when net earnings surged more than 43 percent to $2.32 billion. Also contributing to these results, in addition to the opening of 160 new Home Depot stores and seven more EXPO Design Centers, were efforts to beef up the stores' product and services offerings. For instance, Home Depot successfully tested the addition of home appliances to its warehouse stores, taking a page out of the playbook of archrival Lowe's, which had long sold washing machines, refrigerators, and other major appliances. Home Depot rolled appliances out into its full network of stores during 2000. The company's status as a retailing powerhouse was confirmed in 1999, meantime, when its stock became a component of the Dow Jones Industrial Average.

THE NARDELLI ERA

In 2000, when the firm opened its 1,000th store, Home Depot's earnings growth slowed considerably as net income increased just 11.3 percent to $2.58 billion. Home remodeling slowed that year, and the company was also hurt by an industry-wide collapse in the price of lumber, which comprised nearly 20 percent of Home Depot's sales. In December 2000 Blank stepped aside to enable the company to nab a new CEO from outside the ranks, Robert L. Nardelli, the former head of General Electric Company's GE Power Systems division and one of the runners-up in the struggle to determine a successor to legendary GE leader John F. "Jack" Welch Jr. Marcus and Blank served as cochairmen after Nardelli's arrival, but both founders left the company board during 2001, and Nardelli assumed the chairmanship as well. Also in 2001, Home Depot expanded its e-commerce web site to cover the 48 contiguous states, and it expanded into Mexico via the purchase of the four-unit TotalHOME home improvement chain, subsequently rebadged under the Home Depot name.

Over the next several years, Home Depot rode the booming housing market steadily higher, reaching $5.84 billion in net income and $81.51 billion in revenues by 2005 and firmly entrenching itself as the number two retailer in the United States, behind only Wal-Mart Stores, Inc. At the same time, however, some of Nardelli's attempts to rein in the entrepreneurial culture that had been entrenched at Home Depot since its founding and to improve operational efficiencies backfired. A move by Nardelli early in his tenure to quicken the pace at which inventory flowed through stores led a number of store managers to simply reduce inventory, resulting in stocking shortages, lost sales, and angry customers. Customer service eroded when more part-timers were hired as part of a cost-cutting effort and when a new salary cap prompted a number of veteran workers to leave. Lowe's gained ground on its much larger rival during this period by emphasizing customer service and stores touted as cleaner, better organized, and better lit. Nardelli did launch a store refurbishment program, but critics charged that the effort was belated.

In another of Nardelli's key initiatives, Home Depot pushed aggressively via acquisition into the wholesale supply business in part as a hedge against a future falloff in the housing market and as a way to maintain the company's historic rate of growth. In 2004 Home Depot acquired the Costa Mesa, California, firm White Cap Construction Supply, Inc., a major supplier of specialty hardware, tools, and materials to construction contractors. The following year, in a $1.4 billion deal, National Waterworks Holdings, Inc., of Waco, Texas, was purchased. This firm was a leading supplier of pipes, fittings, and other parts used in municipal water-transmission systems. In the biggest deal of this spending spree, and the firm's largest ever, Home Depot acquired Hughes Supply, Inc., for $3.5 billion in March 2006. Based in Orlando, Florida, Hughes was one of the nation's biggest distributors of construction, repair, and maintenance-related products, serving local governments, contractors, and other customers in 40 states. Hughes was integrated into Home Depot's HD Supply unit. As this unit was built up, Nardelli slowed down the rate of new store openings in the United States, and he also pursued a new avenue of potential future growth: China. Late in 2006 Home Depot gained a toehold in that potentially lucrative market by buying the Home Way, a home improvement retailer operating 12 stores in northeastern China. These outlets were rebranded with the Home Depot name the following year.

REFOCUS ON RETAILING UNDER NEW LEADERSHIP

Early in January 2007 Nardelli resigned under pressure from the company board. The precipitating event in his departure was a dispute over his hefty pay package, which was the subject of escalating disenchantment among investors, but Nardelli had also endured a barrage of criticism for his autocratic management style and the depressed level of Home Depot's stock. Investors expressed additional outrage at the size of his exit package: $210 million. Francis S. "Frank" Blake was named the company's fourth CEO, and chairman as well, having previously served as vice-chairman and executive vice-president.

Blake came onboard just after the U.S. housing market had entered into a deep decline, an economic environment that had pushed Home Depot's comparable-store sales into the negative during 2006. Determined to refocus the company on its core retail business, the new leader moved quickly to reverse one of his predecessor's biggest initiatives, the move into the wholesale supply sector. Blake viewed HD Supply as a distraction from the retailing core, and although the business had contributed 15 percent of the company's revenues in 2006, it was responsible for only about 9 percent of the operating profits. In August 2007, Home Depot sold HD Supply to a consortium of private-equity firms for $8.3 billion. Proceeds from the sale helped fund $10.8 billion in share repurchases during 2007 as part of a massive plan to repurchase $22.5 billion in shares and, it was hoped, boost the stock price.

At the same time, Blake attempted to reinvigorate the Home Depot stores with a number of initiatives. To tackle the key challenge of improving customer service, a number of steps were taken, including the chainwide hiring of more than 2,500 licensed plumbers and electricians not only to provide better service to customers but also to serve as expert trainers for other employees on the floor. Home Depot also embarked on a major overhaul of its supply chain that included the investment of $260 million to build eight new distribution centers to better control inventory at the stores. Product lines were also overhauled to try to drive customers into the stores, and the company boosted its spending on store maintenance.

For 2007, a year in which comparable-store sales fell 6.7 percent, Home Depot saw its total sales decline for the first time in its history, a drop of 2.1 percent to $77.35 billion. Net earnings plunged 20.1 percent to $4.21 billion. In the spring of 2008, as the U.S. home improvement retail market remained in the doldrums, Home Depot announced plans to close 15 underperforming stores and canceled plans to open 50 new U.S. stores that had been in the pipeline. While moving quickly in an attempt to spark a turnaround, Home Depot had clearly been forced into a mode of entrenchment, not unlike that of many debt-strapped Americans no longer able to afford the costly home improvement projects that had fueled much of Home Depot's historic growth.

William R. Grossman
Updated, Pamela L. Shelton; David E. Salamie

PRINCIPAL SUBSIDIARIES

Home Depot International, Inc.; Home Depot U.S.A., Inc.; HD Development of Maryland, Inc.

PRINCIPAL COMPETITORS

Lowe's Companies, Inc.; Menard, Inc.; True Value Company; Wal-Mart Stores, Inc.; Ace Hardware Corporation; Sears, Roebuck and Co.; Costco Wholesale Corporation.

FURTHER READING

Barmash, Isadore, "The 'How' in Home Improvement: No. 1 Home Depot Now Aims to Provide Old-Fashioned Service with a Style," *New York Times,* June 14, 1992, p. F5.

Bauerlein, Valerie, "Home Depot to Buy Hughes Supply for $3.19 Billion," *Wall Street Journal,* January 11, 2006, p. A3.

Brooks, Rick, "Hammer and Tongs: Home Depot Turns Copycat in Its Efforts to Stoke New Growth," *Wall Street Journal,* November 21, 2000, p. A1.

Bueno, Jacqueline, "Home Depot's Agreement to Settle Suit Could Cut 3rd-Quarter Earnings by 21%," *Wall Street Journal,* September 22, 1997, p. B18.

Carrns, Ann, "Home Depot to Buy Commercial Seller of Water Pipes," *Wall Street Journal,* July 20, 2005, p. B2.

Darrow, William P., Raymond D. Smith, and Ross A. Fabricant, "Home Depot and the Home Center Industry," *Mid-Atlantic Journal of Business,* December 1994, pp. 227+.

Doherty, Jacqueline, "Chipping Paint?" *Barron's,* June 25, 2001, pp. 21–22.

Facenda, Vanessa L., "Cowboy Culture/GE Mentality," *Retail Merchandiser,* August 2002, pp. 23–24, 26, 28.

Fong, Mei, "Home Depot Joins Push into China," *Wall Street Journal,* December 14, 2006, p. B2.

Greenwald, John, "Shelter from the Recession," *Time,* June 10, 1991.

Grow, Brian, "Out at Home Depot: Behind the Flameout of Controversial CEO Bob Nardelli," *Business Week,* January 15, 2007, pp. 56–58, 60–62.

———, "Renovating Home Depot," *Business Week,* March 6, 2006, pp. 50–56, 58.

———, "Thinking Outside the Big Box: Home Depot Ratchets Up Growth—by Moving Past the Lumberyard Look," *Business Week,* October 25, 2004, pp. 70, 72.

Hagerty, James R., "Tough As Nails: Home Depot Raises the Ante, Targeting Mom-and-Pop Rivals," *Wall Street Journal,* January 25, 1999, p. A1.

Hawkins, Chuck, "Will Home Depot Be 'The Wal-Mart of the '90s?'" *Business Week,* March 19, 1990, pp. 124+.

"The Home Depot," *Management Horizons,* July 1990.

Hudson, Kris, and Ashby Jones, "New Leader Is Renowned for Vision," *Wall Street Journal,* January 4, 2007, p. A12.

Jaffe, Greg, "Home Depot Names Arthur M. Blank As Chief Executive, Succeeding Marcus," *Wall Street Journal,* May 29, 1997, p. B6.

Kimbrough, Ann Wead, "Home Depot's Do-It-Yourself Retail Success," *Atlanta Business Chronicle,* March 21, 1988, pp. 1B+.

Lamm, Marcy, "The Nuts and Bolts of Hardware Success: How Home Depot Captured Imagination," *Atlanta Business Chronicle,* November 6, 1998, p. 3A.

Lublin, Joann S., Ann Zimmerman, and Chad Terhune, "Behind Nardelli's Abrupt Exit: Amid a Pay Dispute, Home Depot's Chief Faced Board Tensions," *Wall Street Journal,* January 4, 2007, p. A1.

Lublin, Joann S., Matt Murray, and Rick Brooks, "Home Depot Nabs GE's Nardelli As CEO," *Wall Street Journal,* December 6, 2000, p. A3.

Marcus, Bernie, and Arthur Blank, with Bob Andelman, *Built from Scratch: How a Couple of Regular Guys Grew the Home Depot from Nothing to $30 Billion,* New York: Times Business, 1999, 332 p.

McCarthy, Michael J., "Home Depot's Do-It-Yourself Powerhouse," *Wall Street Journal,* July 17, 1990, p. B1.

Morse, Dan, "Home Depot to Buy White Cap in Bid to Sell More to Builders," *Wall Street Journal,* May 7, 2004, p. B2.

———, "Under Renovation: A Hardware Chain Struggles to Adjust to a New Blueprint," *Wall Street Journal,* January 17, 2003, p. A1.

Murray, Alan, "Executive's Fatal Flaw: Failing to Understand New Demands on CEOs," *Wall Street Journal,* January 4, 2007, p. A1.

Pascual, Aixa M., "Can Home Depot Get Its House in Order?" *Business Week,* November 27, 2000, pp. 70, 72.

———, Nardelli: Taking on a Fixer-Upper," *Business Week,* December 18, 2000, pp. 216, 218.

Roush, Chris, "Home Depot OKs Sex Bias Settlement," *Atlanta Journal-Constitution,* September 20, 1997.

———, *Inside Home Depot: How One Company Revolutionized an Industry Through the Relentless Pursuit of Growth,* New York: McGraw-Hill, 1999, 266 p.

Saporito, Bill, "The Fix Is in at Home Depot," *Fortune,* February 29, 1988, pp. 73+.

Sellers, Patricia, "Can Home Depot Fix Its Sagging Stock?" *Fortune,* March 4, 1996, pp. 139+.

Shutt, Craig A., "Home Depot Aims to Stay on Top," *Building Supply Home Centers,* June 1988, pp. 58+.

Sutton, Rodney K., "Growth at Home Depot Shows No Limit," *Building Supply Home Centers,* February 1995, pp. 22+.

Terhune, Chad, "Home Depot Buys a Mexican Chain of Home Centers," *Wall Street Journal,* May 3, 2001, p. B9.

———, "Home Depot's Home Improvement: Retail Giant Aims to Spur Sales with Less-Cluttered Stores, Increased Customer Service," *Wall Street Journal,* March 8, 2001, p. B1.

———, "Home Depot Slows Store Openings, Looks to Build Industrial Business," *Wall Street Journal,* January 20, 2006, p. A3.

Terhune, Chad, and Dan Morse, "Refinishing Home Depot: Former GE Exec Bob Nardelli Trims Retailer's Expansion As Pace, Economy Take Toll," *Wall Street Journal,* June 25, 2002, p. B1.

Thompson, Roger, "There's No Place Like Home Depot," *Nation's Business,* February 1992, pp. 30+.

Zemke, Ron, *The Service Edge,* New York: NAL Books, 1986.

Zimmerman, Ann, "Home Depot Chief Renovates," *Wall Street Journal,* June 5, 2008, pp. B1, B2.

———, "Home Depot Tries to Make Nice to Customers," *Wall Street Journal,* February 20, 2007, p. D1.

Zimmerman, Ann, and Dennis K. Berman, "Home Depot Boosts Buyback, Sets Unit Sale," *Wall Street Journal,* June 20, 2007, p. A3.

Zimmerman, Ann, and Joann S. Lublin, "Home Depot Bows to Whitworth Again: Chain May Sell or Spin Off Wholesale-Supply Unit in a Reversal of Strategy," *Wall Street Journal,* February 13, 2007, p. A3.

Zimmerman, Ann, and Mary Ellen Lloyd, "Home Depot Net Falls 66% As Store Growth Brakes," *Wall Street Journal,* May 21, 2008, p. B3.

———, "Nardelli's Flawed Strategy Hits Home Depot Profit," *Wall Street Journal,* February 21, 2007, p. A2.

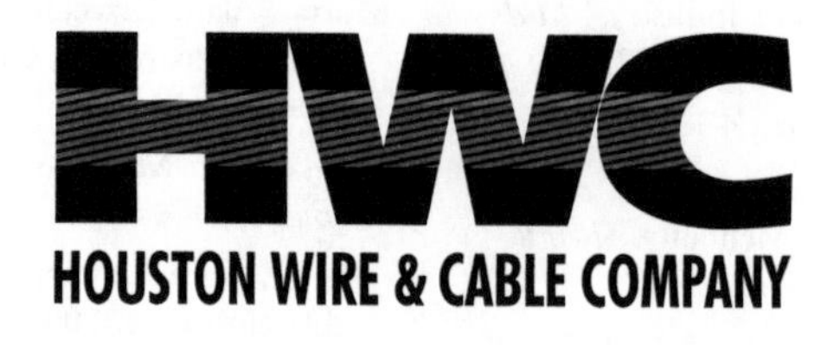

Houston Wire & Cable Company

10201 North Loop East
Houston, Texas 77029
U.S.A.
Telephone: (713) 609-2100
Toll Free: (800) 468-9473
Fax: (713) 609-2101
Web site: http://www.houwire.com

Public Company
Incorporated: 1975
Employees: 304
Sales: $359.1 million (2007)
Stock Exchanges: NASDAQ
Ticker Symbol: HWCC
NAICS: 423610 Electrical Apparatus and Equipment, Wiring Supplies, and Related Equipment Merchant Wholesalers

■ ■ ■

Listed on the NASDAQ, Houston Wire & Cable Company (HWC) is a master distributor of specialized electrical and electronic wire and cable, serving the power generation, industrial, infrastructure, and environmental compliance markets through local electrical distributors. Products include control, instrumentation, low- and medium-voltage power, industrial-armored control and power, voice, data communications, fire, alarm, and security cable. The company's $60 million inventory of more than 23,000 products is supplied by the industry's top manufacturers, including Belden, General, Cable USA, AmerCable, Dekoron, Olflex, and Alpha. The company also offers some private branded products, the most prominent of which is LifeGuard, a low-smoke, zero-halogen cable, but it also offers the HOUWIRE and DataGuard lines.

In addition to its Houston, Texas, headquarters, HWC maintains ten distribution centers, strategically located in Philadelphia, Charlotte, Chicago, Atlanta, Tampa, Baton Rouge, Denver, Los Angeles, San Francisco, and Seattle. As a result, 95 percent of customers receive shipments within 24 hours. In addition, HWC offers value-added services, such as engineering support, custom cutting of wire and cable, and job-site delivery. Custom programs include a cable management program to provide customers with materials for major projects on a just-in-time basis; an Internet-based cable selection system that allows customers greater control over their cable needs and the ability to release shipments as needed; and an asset management program in which HWC will audit customers' wire and cable inventories and create a pool of necessary items at its own distribution center for later resale at discounted prices.

COMPANY FOUNDED: 1975

Houston Wire & Cable Company was founded in Houston, Texas, in 1975 by one of the more flamboyant figures in the wire distribution business, Terrence Michael Hunt, who was known to fly a skull and crossbones flag above his company headquarters, and his partner Hugh Robertson. Born in Oklahoma City, Oklahoma, in 1947, Hunt graduated from Southern Methodist University in 1972. He then went to work

COMPANY PERSPECTIVES

The HWC team is committed to providing great customer service and top quality products—shipped correctly and on time.

for Anixter Brothers Inc., a major wire and cable distributor, and soon headed a regional office. In 1975 he struck out on his own to form HWC with Robertson and made a mark in the industry by establishing a policy of only selling to electrical distributors. In the first year as a master distributor, HWC generated $1 million in sales. Business grew at a steady pace, spurred by the opening of new distribution centers. The company also expanded into Canada, but the Texcan Cable Ltd. unit was sold in 1986. Sales reached $81.4 million and net income totaled $2.5 million in fiscal 1986, making HWC the second largest U.S. cable distributor, trailing only Anixter Brothers.

Hunt and Robertson sold Houston Wire & Cable to a group of investors led by New York-based Bradford Associates, who formed HWC Distribution to make the transaction. Hunt and Robertson stayed on to run the company and a year later shepherded it through an initial public offering (IPO) of stock, to raise capital for expansion and provide a payout for its backers. The IPO was completed in June 1987, netting the company $6.8 million.

ALLIED ACQUISITION OF HWC: 1989

Demand for specialized wire and cable remained high, leading to the addition of new warehouses for HWC as well as renovations of existing facilities. Space was leased in Chicago, Dallas, Houston, Philadelphia, Seattle, Baton Rouge, and San Francisco. Revenues topped the $100 million mark in fiscal 1988. That number reached $140 million a year later. Then the company's performance caught the attention of Little Rock, Arkansas-based Alltel Corporation, which in 1989 bought HWC stock for $142.8 million.

Alltel was a fast-growing company with a group of young, ambitious executives. It had been formed in 1983 through the merger of Little Rock-based Allied Telephone Company and Hudson, Ohio-based Mid-Continent Telephone Corporation. Allied had started out during World War II as an Arkansas-based telephone service company performing work for many local mom-and-pop independent phone companies, whose operations were hampered by the lack of qualified telephone repairmen due to military service. After the war the founders took over the management of a small phone company, establishing the foundation for an independent regional carrier. Mid-Continent was established in 1960 when five small independent telephone companies in Ohio consolidated. When Allied and Mid-Continent merged, Mid-Continent was four times the size of Allied, but the deal was made because in large part Mid-Continent faced a succession problem, and Allied was stocked with executive talent. Hence, the chief executive of Allied, Joe T. Ford, was soon running Alltel. By the time HWC was acquired, Alltel had become the fifth largest non-Bell telephone company and 12th largest nationwide.

RECESSION HURTS BUSINESS

Also involved in the 1983 merger were the supply businesses of the two companies, Southern Supply for Allied and Buckeye Supply for Mid-Continent. Their combined operations created Allied Supply, which served Alltel subsidiaries as well as other independent telephone companies. Stiff competition in the field in the mid-1980s hurt sales, though, prompting Alltel to grow the supply business through acquisitions. In late 1987 the supply business of Contel Corporation was purchased. The acquisition of HWC in 1989 then greatly expanded Allied Supply's distribution network, adding 13 sales and warehouse facilities. While HWC had been growing annual revenues at a rate of 30 percent in the five years before the acquisition, sales growth fell to the 15 to 20 percent range in the first few years under Alltel, but the slump was primarily the result of a poor economy. The company's specialty business, in fact, was a thriving niche that boded well for the future of HWC.

The sale of HWC to Alltel also put an end to Hunt and Robertson's connection to the company they founded. Hunt signed a noncompete clause and retired to his ranch in Montana, but still in his early 40s grew bored there, and in 1991 he launched Futronix Corporation in Houston to distribute surplus electric supplies. After his noncompete agreement expired in 1994, he returned to the wire and cable business and built up the operation, which he sold to another Houston firm, Kent Electronics, in 1996. He continued to run Futronix as a division president.

MANAGEMENT-LED BUYOUT: 1997

HWC did well under Alltel's ownership, but major changes in the telecommunications industry made the

KEY DATES

1975: Houston Wire & Cable Company is founded.
1987: Company is taken public.
1989: Alltel Corporation acquires the business.
1997: Company is taken private.
2000: Futronix is acquired.
2006: Company goes public once again.

supply business expendable in the mid-1990s. Alltel had grown into an awkward size for the times, too large to be acquired except by the giants of the industry but too small to succeed in a consolidating telecommunications arena. Alltel was better positioned to sell individual units rather than the entire company, and so HWC was put on the block in 1996. In July 1997 a former HWC executive, John Myers, and a team of executives acquired HWC for an undisclosed amount with financial backing from Code, Hennessy, and Simmons LLC, a Chicago-based investment firm that had pursued the distribution niche since 1993 when it became involved in the swimming pool supplies business. Meyers had been with HWC for 14 years and spent three years as vice-president and general manager under Alltel's ownership, leaving in 1992 to run the wire and cable division of Houston's Graybar Electric Company. He was recruited by Code, Hennessy, and Simmons to become involved in the buyout because of his familiarity with HWC and extensive industry experience, more than 40 years in the wire market.

HWC Distribution returned to its original name of Houston Wire & Cable, a move to take advantage of the company's strong name recognition. Myers did not, however, intend to alter the company's master distributorship approach to business. During his previous four years purchasing wire and cable for Graybar, Myers had learned a great deal about what distributors needed from a master distributor. "I found out that the biggest thing was a logistical problem," he told *Electrical Wholesaling* in September 1998. "Distributors have to stock material, take it off the floor, package it, ship it and put that reel back into stock. They are looking for someone to help reduce transaction costs." What HWC developed, in essence, was a virtual warehouse network that customers could make their own without the cost and bother. HWC warehouses would stock the wire and cable and the local distributor could tap into it as orders were placed. HWC's task was to convince distributors to give up one of their core responsibilities, keeping inventory, but by demonstrating that they would actually save money by relying on HWC, the company gradually created converts. "I am trying to get them to outsource," Myers explained. "I am not selling wire and cable. I am selling value-added services."

In 1998 Myers turned over the helm to Charles A. Sorrentino, who became president and CEO. Sorrentino was the former president of Pameco Corporation, a national heating, ventilation, air conditioning, and refrigeration distributor. He carried on the strategy outlined by Myers, who left to become an industry consultant. HWC established a national account sales force in 1999, as well as a national service center. A year later the company acquired a distant cousin, and chief direct competitor, the Futronix division of Kent Electronics. HWC also introduced its first private brand, HOUWIRE.

NEW SALES AND MARKETING STRATEGY: 2003

In the early 2000s poor economic conditions hurt the electrical distribution market. HWC improved operating efficiencies while strengthening its infrastructure, implementing a state-of-the-art coding system in 2001, and introducing a new product catalog in 2002, but the most important step taken came in 2003 when a new sales and marketing strategy was put in place. The sales force was expanded, and HWC began to work with its distributor customers to stimulate demand from end-users, especially in the utility, industrial, and infrastructure markets. Moreover, HWC sought to promote new private branded products, which offered higher margins to the company. To accompany the HOUWIRE product, HWC introduced the LifeGuard brand in 2003 and DataGuard in 2005.

Due to the poor economy, revenues sagged to less than $150 million in 2003, when the company netted just $216,000. With its new strategy in place, however, HWC began a strong comeback in 2004, increasing revenues to $172.7 million and net income to $4.8 million. A new online cable selection system helped bring in more business, and in 2005 sales grew to $214 million and profits more than doubled to $12.5 million. The upward trend continued in 2006 when HWC posted a record $323.5 million and net income of $30.7 million.

The company took advantage of its performance in an IPO of stock completed in June 2006, which netted $49.9 million. A subsequent offering conducted in March 2007 provided Code, Hennessy, & Simmons with a payout on its investment. Although HWC failed to meet its objectives in 2007, due to challenging business conditions, it still managed to produce record sales of $359.1 million and net income of $30.2 million. In the first quarter of 2008 the company continued to grow, posting a 9.4 percent increase in revenues over the same period from the prior year, almost entirely the result of organic growth, resulting in record profits. HWC also took advantage of its strong results to continue a program of buying back its stock, the price of which, management believed, did not accurately reflect the company's underlying strength.

Ed Dinger

PRINCIPAL SUBSIDIARIES

HWC Wire & Cable Company; Advantage Wire & Cable; Cable Management Services Inc.

PRINCIPAL COMPETITORS

W.W. Grainger, Inc.; Anixter International Inc.; Graybar Electric Co., Inc.

FURTHER READING

Antosh, Nelson, "Local Cable Firm on a Roll," *Houston Chronicle,* November 27, 1988, p. 1.

Badillo, Francisco, "Alltel to Buy Wire Firm for $130 Million," *Akron Beacon Journal,* February 4, 1989, p. A8.

Chandler, Douglas, "Wire World," *Electrical Wholesaling,* September 1998.

Darwin, Jennifer, "Rewired to Houston," *Houston Business Journal,* July 7, 1997.

"Entrepreneur Enterprise Awards Runners-Up," *Houston Business Journal,* February 27, 1989, p. 13.

Funk, Dale, "Houston Wire & Cable Files IPO for $112.7 Million in Stock," *Electrical Wholesaling,* May 1, 2006.

Klempin, Raymond, "HWC Plans $16 Million Public Offering," *Houston Business Journal,* June 22, 1987, p. 1.

Lucy, Jim, "Wire? What Wire?" *Electrical Wholesaling,* September 1998, p. 33.

Hummer Winblad Venture Partners

1 Lombard Street, Suite 300
San Francisco, California 94111
U.S.A.
Telephone: (415) 979-9600
Fax: (415) 979-9601
Web site: http://www.humwin.com

Private Company
Incorporated: 1989
Employees: 50
Operating Revenues: $63 million (2007 est.)
NAICS: 523999 Miscellaneous Financial Investment Activities

■ ■ ■

Hummer Winblad Venture Partners (HWVP) is a venture capital firm focused exclusively on investing in software ventures. The firm helps start-up companies involved in desktop software, embedded systems, client-server, Internet, and distributed network computing. Led by founders John Hummer and Ann Winblad, the firm's portfolio of investments includes Widgetbox, Voltage Security, Cittio, and Kwiry among roughly 35 companies that it has funded. HWVP is the first venture capital company to invest solely in software companies. Aside from its cofounders, the firm's principal partners are Mark Gorenberg, Doug Hickey, Mitchell Kertzman, Prashant Shah, Todd Forrest, and Lars Leckie.

THE FOUNDERS OF HWVP

HWVP owes its successes and failures to the decisions made by its senior executives, a corollary applicable to all companies but one of exceptional significance in the operation of a venture capital firm. Decisions determine where a venture capital firm invests its money, to which company, market, product, or technology a firm hitches its fortunes to, entailing a risk-reward scenario akin to a high-stakes poker game. Accordingly, any assessment of a venture capital firm invariably becomes an assessment of its principal partners' ability to gamble in the marketplace, an ongoing evaluation in which HWVP's founders and partners have alternately earned top honors and failing grades during the first 20 years of the firm's existence.

When institutional investors, industry onlookers, and hopeful entrepreneurs assayed Ann Winblad, they found an executive worthy of their esteem. A Minnesota native, Winblad was born in Red Wing, but grew up in Farmington, a small town in the suburban Minneapolis–St. Paul area that was home to fewer than 3,000 people during Winblad's youth. "The universe was very, very small," Winblad recalled in an interview published in the September 27, 1999, edition of *Business Journal.* "The perimeter of your life in Minnesota is the next farm. There was not a lot of diversity in Farmington—in careers, in conversation."

Winblad excelled in school, enabling her to break free from the confines of Farmington, but she did not stray far at first. Valedictorian of a graduating class of 110 students and head cheerleader, Winblad (whose father was coach of the high school football and

COMPANY PERSPECTIVES

Hummer Winblad Venture Partners was founded in 1989 as the first venture capital fund to invest exclusively in software companies. Through our history, we've had the opportunity to invest in the pioneers and leaders of several generations of software applications, architectures, delivery methods and business models.

basketball team) enrolled at The College of St. Catherine, a private Catholic college for women located in St. Paul. In 1973, she earned degrees in math and business administration before becoming one of the first women to earn a master's degree at the University of St. Thomas, a then all-male Catholic college located in St. Paul. Winblad achieved the feat by officially registering at St. Catherine, but attending classes at St. Thomas, earning degrees in international economics and education.

While she was pursuing her education, Winblad received numerous offers from recruiters. Among the solicitations were promises of prestigious positions by 3M Corp. and the Federal Bureau of Investigation, both beginning to implement affirmative action hiring programs, but Winblad chose to make her future at the Federal Reserve Bank of Minneapolis. The "Minneapolis Fed" was one of the dozen regional reserve banks composing the Federal Reserve System, the United States' central bank. She was hired as a systems analyst, but almost immediately she regretted her decision. "I thought I was joining a football team," she said in her interview with *Business Journal,* "but it was a bowling team." Bored, Winblad resigned after 13 months, ready to begin a career as an entrepreneur.

Winblad wanted to start a business that would allow her to explore her love for writing software, a passion she had developed while in college. To help her start the enterprise, Winblad turned to her colleagues at the Minneapolis Fed, convincing three associates, including her former boss, to take a one-year sabbatical to launch Open Systems Inc. Winblad used what little savings she had, borrowed $500 from her brother, and formed Open Systems in 1976. The company essentially took the contents of accounting textbooks, converted the information into software code, and made the program available for the microcomputers of the era. Winblad, who served as vice-president of marketing for Open Systems, figured as the dominant personality within the company, leading it through years of success. Open Systems lost $85 during its first year, but was profitable every subsequent year until it was sold to UCCEL Corp. in 1983. UCCEL paid $15 million for Open Systems, not the last time Winblad would record a substantial return on investment.

WINBLAD-HUMMER MEETING LEADS TO PARTNERSHIP

Winblad moved to California after selling Open Systems. She started consulting independently in what would become her new home state, developing marketing strategies for a number of well-known clients such as Microsoft, International Business Machines, and Apple Computer. While establishing a new career for herself, she met venture capitalist John Hummer. At Hummer's repeated urging, Winblad agreed to form a partnership and join Hummer in a business venture, a firm that was christened Hummer Winblad Venture Partners.

Winblad's decision to form a business with Hummer must have excited her father, for reasons entirely separate from a business perspective. Hummer, born in Washington, D.C., attended high school in Arlington, Virginia, where he distinguished himself academically and athletically. He was recruited by Princeton University, where in 1969 the six-foot, nine-inch Hummer led the school's basketball team to a berth in the National Collegiate Athletic Association's basketball tournament during his junior year. After earning a degree in English the following year, Hummer was selected by the National Basketball Association's Buffalo Braves in the first round of the college draft, as the 15th pick overall. Hummer spent six years as a professional basketball player, ending his career in 1976 after a three-year stint with the Seattle Supersonics. After he retired, Hummer continued his education, earning a master's degree in business administration from Stanford Business School in 1980. He entered the venture capital business in 1982, which eventually led to his introduction to Ann Winblad, the daughter of a high school basketball coach.

HWVP SETS ITS STRATEGY

Hummer and Winblad formed their firm in 1989 with a specific mission. They intended to focus solely on software companies for their investments, becoming the first venture capital firm to target the software sector exclusively. A year after starting the firm, they recruited Mark Gorenberg, who would become HWVP's third senior partner. Once an influential engineer at Sun Microsystems, Gorenberg studied at the Massachusetts Institute of Technology and earned postgraduate degrees

KEY DATES

1976: Winblad and colleagues form Open Systems.
1983: Open Systems is sold to UCCEL Corp.
1989: John Hummer and Ann Winblad form Hummer Winblad Venture Partners (HWVP).
2000: HWVP invests in Napster Inc., touching off a torturous period for the firm.
2003: After straying into the retail consumer sector, HWVP's partners decide to invest solely in software ventures.
2005: HWVP accelerates its pace of investing.
2007: Investments during the year include Move Networks, Kwiry, and Aria.

from the University of Minnesota and Stanford University.

Together, the three partners recorded encouraging success during their first years in business. The firm's first investment, a November 1989 funding of a desktop software start-up, T/Maker, was followed by roughly two to three major investments annually, a pace the firm would keep throughout most of the 1990s. Companies that were part of HWVP's portfolio during the first half of the 1990s included Netopia, Wind River, Powersoft, and Viewpoint, all involved with some aspect of the software business. Roughly half of the companies in the firm's portfolio at any given time were ventures that Hummer and Winblad backed financially before the start-ups had collected their first dollar. The partners gambled and they usually won. Companies that joined the firm's portfolio during the latter half of the 1990s, including software-related ventures such as Liquid Audio, Net Perceptions, and AdForce, strengthened the firm's reputation. Hummer, Winblad, and Gorenberg could look back on the 1990s with pride, having made investors such as 3M Corp., Hughes Aircraft, Princeton University, and the Mellon Foundation handsome profits on their original investments.

FROM SUCCESS TO FAILURE

Unfortunately for the partners at HWVP, their glowing success quickly lost its luster. There were several investments that tarnished the firm's reputation, but one in particular stood out from the rest, a blemish that confounded critics. In April 2000, HWVP invested $13.5 million for a 21 percent stake in Napster Inc., the controversial file-sharing software provider that had the music industry seething over piracy and copyright infringement issues. A major legal battle loomed, as the record labels and artists marshaled their forces to stamp out peer-to-peer networks that, according to their argument, facilitated the illegal distribution of copyrighted content. Napster was the company directly in their sights, promising a legal war aimed at its destruction.

Industry observers wondered why HWVP would invest in a company on the verge of being attacked by the deep-pocketed music industry. Their befuddlement was exacerbated when a HWVP partner, Hank Barry, was installed as interim chief executive officer of Napster and Hummer was named as a director of the company as part of the investment deal. The move, critics argued, exposed HWVP to being liable in the court proceedings set to occur. Dan Beldy, an HWVP partner, tried to calm fears that the firm had made a disastrous move in an October 23, 2000, interview with *Private Equity Week:* "No investor wants to take on market risk, let alone legal risk," he said. "But we are very confident in this company and, for us, we wouldn't have made the investment if we thought there was even a chance of something happening from the liability perspective. Of course," he added, "you can't prevent someone from suing you, but we don't see it happening."

Beldy's lack of foresight was soon confirmed. Universal Music Group and EMI Recorded Music, as part of their showdown with Napster, filed a lawsuit against HWVP, Barry, and Hummer for contributing to copyright infringement by giving Napster financial support. The lawsuit dragged on until 2006, when the record labels won sanctions against HWVP, settling with the firm out of court for an undisclosed sum.

The Napster investment was not the only thorn in HWVP's side. At the beginning of the new millennium, the firm began to stray from its original mission of investing exclusively in software companies, dabbling disastrously in consumer retail businesses. HWVP took its first step outside the software sector with a $20 million investment in gourmet grocer Dean & Deluca, but its real troubles stemmed from investments in companies such as Pets.com, HomeGrocer, Gazoontite, and Mombo. To compound matters, its investments in software companies were not panning out either: By 2000, all four HWVP-backed software ventures that had gone public during the previous two years were trading below their initial public offering prices. The firm was caught in the middle of the dot-com implosion, and it was sent, like several of the companies in its portfolio, cascading downward. "We invested in the poster children for failure," Hummer conceded in a March 14, 2005, interview with *Private Equity Week.*

RESETTING A STRATEGIC COURSE

Hummer, Winblad, and the other HWVP partners gathered at the firm's headquarters in San Francisco in 2003 and conducted a thorough analysis of their investment strategy, scrutinizing every financial commitment they had made since 1989. They left the meeting vowing to return to their exclusive focus on software companies. "We'll never do anything but software again," Hummer informed *Private Equity Week*.

HWVP, steeled by the hard lessons it had learned, began investing in earnest in 2005. After making just five first-round investments during 2004, the firm set a goal of completing one deal per month as it entered 2005. Armed with a more than $400 million fund, HWVP invested in Cittio, a network monitoring and operations software start-up; Akimbi Systems, a developer of virtual infrastructure management software; and Palamida, a developer of software that functioned as an antivirus scanner. The firm was back to its old self, enjoying the level of success it had recorded throughout most of the 1990s.

As HWVP neared its 20th anniversary, it had put the tumult in the late 1990s and early 2000s behind it. During the first half of 2007, the firm invested $22.4 million in 13 companies, including Move Networks, an Internet-services company providing online video broadcasting and streaming capabilities; Kwiry, a mobile phone note-taking venture; and Aria, a developer of billing and customer-management software. In the years ahead, the ever changing composition of its portfolio promised to include market winners and market losers—more of the former than the latter, its partners hoped—but one defining trait of its investment strategy was guaranteed not to change. HWVP, the first venture capital firm to invest solely in software ventures, intended to stay close to its roots.

Jeffrey L. Covell

PRINCIPAL COMPETITORS

Kleiner Perkins Caufield & Byers; Internet Capital Group, Inc.; Draper Fisher Jurvetson.

FURTHER READING

"Ann Winblad: VC with a View," *CioInsight*, April 6, 2006.

Carlsen, Clifford, "Hummer Winblad Adds $20M Zip to Gourmet Venture," *San Francisco Business Times*, February 4, 2000, p. 5.

———, "Winblad Returns with Voltage Deal," *Daily Deal*, July 8, 2003.

Chmielewski, Dawn C., "Left for Dead, Napster Gets New Life," *San Jose Mercury News*, May 18, 2002.

"Fallen Back to Earth," *Business Week*, July 9, 2001, p. 104.

Fox, Pimm, "Ann Winblad," *Computerworld*, September 30, 2002, p. 66.

Fugazy, Danielle, "Should Hummer Pay for Its Poor Judgment on Napster?" *Private Equity Week*, April 28, 2003, p. 1.

Gardner, Jim, "Hoopster VC Finds the NCAA Plays Some Fierce Defense," *San Francisco Business Times*, January 28, 2000, p. 4.

Haislip, Alexander, "Hummer Winblad Refocuses, Reloads: Firm Raises $185m for Fund VI Eight Months After Settling Napster Suit," *Private Equity Week*, August 27, 2007, p. 1.

"Hum, Baby!" *PC Week*, August 9, 1993, p. A7.

Knorr, Eric, "Veteran Venture Capitalist Is Sold on SaaS," *InfoWorld*, March 20, 2006, p. 4.

Kraeuter, Chris, "Gazoontite Ingests $26.5M," *San Francisco Business Times*, December 24, 1999, p. 14.

Levine, Daniel S., "Hummer Sued for Defying Zero Gravity," *San Francisco Business Times*, June 1, 2001, p. 1.

———, "Hummer Winblad Investments Go South," *San Francisco Business Times*, October 6, 2000, p. 1.

———, "Power Play: VC Hummer Seizes Board," *San Francisco Business Times*, June 22, 2001, p. 1.

Loizos, Constance, "Hummer: 'We Are Far from Blowing Up,'" *Private Equity Week*, March 14, 2005, p. 1.

Nash, Jim, "Ann Winblad: Small-Town Native," *Business Journal*, September 27, 1993, p. 12.

"Price Steps Down from Hummer Winblad to Join Widgetbox," *Private Equity Week*, March 24, 2008, p. 3.

Primack, Dan, "Hummer Winblad Defends Napster Move," *IPO Reporter*, October 23, 2000.

———, "Hummer Winblad Still on Hook for Napster," *Private Equity Week*, July 19, 2004, p. 1.

———, "Why Hummer Winblad Shared with Napster," *Private Equity Week*, October 23, 2000, p. 1.

Winblad, Ann, "My Biggest Mistake," *Inc.*, December 1999, p. 151.

IDB Holding Corporation Ltd.

3 Azrieli Center, The Triangle Tower, 44th Floor
Tel Aviv, 67023
Israel
Telephone: (+972 03) 607 5666
Fax: (+972 03) 607 5667
Web site: http://www.idb.co.il

Public Company
Incorporated: 1969
Employees: 45
Total Assets: ILS 105.4 billion ($31.23 billion) (2008)
Stock Exchanges: Tel Aviv
Ticker Symbol: IDBH
NAICS: 523999 Miscellaneous Financial Investment Activities; 551112 Offices of Other Holding Companies

■ ■ ■

IDB Holding Corporation Ltd. is Israel's largest financial and investment institution. The holding company oversees five primary, publicly listed investment vehicles: IDB Development Corp. (IDBD); Discount Investment Corp. (DIC); Clal Industries and Investments (CII); Clal Insurance Pensions & Finance Group; and Koor Industries. In addition, IDB Holding directly or indirectly controls majority stakes in a number of leading Israeli corporations, including Clal Tourism (100 percent); Property and Building Corporation (68 percent); Golf & Co. Group (74 percent); Cellcom Israel (53 percent); Gav Yam Bayside (67 percent); Netvision (75 percent); Clal Insurance (56 percent); Clal Finance (77 percent); Ellron (49 percent); and Nesher Israel Cement Enterprises (75 percent). Through these operations, IDB holds stakes in hundreds of Israeli corporations, in virtually every sector, and has long played a major role in Israel's financial, technological, and industrial development.

Founded as an offshoot of the Israel Discount Bank, IDB Holding is itself listed on the Tel Aviv Stock Exchange. Majority control of the group is held by an investment consortium, including the Ganden Group, the Dankner family investment vehicle. Nochi Dankner is IDB Holding's chairman. At the beginning of 2008, IDB Holding reported total assets of more than ILS 105 billion ($31 billion). IDBD reported roughly the equivalent in total assets.

INVESTING IN ISRAEL IN 1935

IDB Holding Corporation was founded in 1969 as an investment offshoot of Israel Discount Bank. That company had been founded in 1935 by Leon Y. Recanati. Born in Thessalonika, Greece, in 1890, Recanati became one of the leaders of the Greek Jewish community in the early 20th century, helping to found the Greek B'nai B'rith in 1911, later acting as Greek representative to the World Jewish Congress in 1933, and also as president of the Greek Jewish community. Recanati's family owned a merchant's business, serving as local trade representative for foreign companies in Greece; Recanati himself became head of that business after his older brother's death. Among the Recanati family's other businesses was the Fumero tobacco factory.

COMPANY PERSPECTIVES

Vision. The IDB Group will continue to be Israel's leading investment company—holding the largest and most diversified portfolio in the Israeli economy. We will continue to actively pursue significant expansion opportunities in the global marketplace. The IDB Group remains committed to ongoing involvement in the community in the fields of health, education, culture, environment and welfare.

One of the founders of Greece's Zionist movement, Recanati recognized the dangerous rise of Nazism, and in 1934 decided to move to what was then Palestine, leading a group of Saloniki Jews. Many of them were workers in the region's ports, and became instrumental in building the port at Haifa.

At the time of Recanati's arrival in Palestine, there were almost 70 Jewish-owned banks in operation. However, Recanati quickly realized that none of these were owned by Sephardic Jews (i.e., Jews of Spanish and Middle Eastern origin), and therefore did not address the particular needs of that growing community. In 1935, therefore, Recanati decided to create his own bank, called Palestine Discount Bank.

Recanati drew on his own trade experience, and oriented the new bank toward a focus on foreign trade. Nonetheless, the bank also became highly involved in supporting the growth of the Greek community in Israel, in particular by underwriting the "man of means" requirement demanded by the British mandate for new immigrants. In the years leading up to and during World War II, Recanati was instrumental in rescuing hundreds of Greek Jews, as well as Greek naval officers.

DEATH OF FOUNDER, CONTINUING GROWTH

Recanati himself did not live to see Israel's independence, dying suddenly in 1945. The then modest-sized bank was taken over by his four sons, and eventually came under the leadership of Daniel Recanati. At the time, the bank operated from its headquarters in Tel Aviv, and a branch in Jerusalem, opened in 1943. In 1948, as the bank became Israel Discount Bank (IDB), it opened a second branch office in Tel Aviv.

IDB opened its first Haifa branch one year later. The company also tapped into the U.S. market for the first time, opening a representative office in New York City. IDB later added operations in Latin America, with an office in Montevideo, Uruguay, opened in 1958. In the meantime, IDB became a major force behind Israel's rapid economic and industrial growth through the 1950s, investing heavily in the country's development.

The bank also invested in its own growth, acquiring control of a number of other banking institutions, including Palestine Mercantile Bank, and the Israeli branch network of Ottoman Bank. Under Daniel Recanati, IDB grew strongly, and by the time of its public offering in 1963 had already become one of Israel's largest banks.

FOUNDING AN INVESTMENT GROUP IN 1961

IDB's new financial clout enabled it to become a central figure in Israel's continuing industrial, technological, and economic development. The bank became a major source of loans and investments to the business community. In 1961, the bank decided to establish its first dedicated investment company, Discount Investment Corp. (DIC). That company became a new force in Israel, backing a large number of companies in a wide variety of industries. DIC's investments included those in retailing, through a controlling stake in the Super Sol supermarket group; real estate, through its control of Property and Building Corp., one of the largest in Israel; and agrochemicals, through Makhteshim Agan, one of the world's largest agrochemical manufacturers.

DIC represented only part of IDB's sprawling investment portfolio. In 1962, the bank teamed up with a group of Latin American investors to form the Clal group, later to be represented by Clal Industries and Investments (CII), Clal Insurance, and Clal Finance. Clal Industries invested in a variety of sectors, including basic industries such as cement production (Nesher), paper manufacturing (American Israeli Paper), and transportation and infrastructure (Taaavura), before adding high-technology (Netvision, FundTech) and retail (Golf & Co.) investments as well. Clal Insurance grew into one of Israel's leading insurance companies, claiming nearly one-third of the total market. Clal Finance grew into a leading provider of mortgage lending, credit, pension funds, and other financial services.

By the end of the 1960s, IDB's range of investment holding companies had grown to the extent that they required their own holding company. In order to simplify its operations, IDB restructured its operations, creating IDB Holding Corporation as the holding company for its investment businesses. IDB Holding's importance to the Israeli economy was underscored with

KEY DATES

1935: Leon Recanati founds Palestine (later Israel) Discount Bank.
1961: Company, now known as IDB, creates first investment holding company, Discount Investment Corp.
1969: IDB forms holding company for investment operations, IDB Holdings.
1981: Non-finance holding company IDB Development Corp. is established.
2003: Recanati sells its 52 percent stake to Ganden Group consortium led by Nochi Dankner.
2008: Company raises $1.5 billion to acquire stakes in two European banks.

the government's own stake of more than 40 percent in the company. IDB Holding later oversaw the public listing of all of its five investment holdings, while nonetheless maintaining majority control in each.

IDB Holding continued to grow strongly through the 1970s, developing both its industrial and financial investments. At the end of the 1980s, IDB Holding restructured. This led to the creation of a new holding vehicle, IDB Development Corporation (IDBD), which then took over all of IDB Holdings' non-financial investments in 1981. Soon after, IDB and a number of other Israeli banks became ensnared in a share trading scandal, that later resulted in the convictions of two members of the Recanati family. The restructuring also led to the family's steady exit from control of IDB, in favor of increased ownership of IDB Holdings. By 1991, the founding family had gained a 52 percent stake in IDB Holdings.

TRANSFERRING OWNERSHIP IN THE NEW CENTURY

IDB Holding was led by Daniel Recanati's son Raphael as CEO through most of the 1990s. In 1998, Raphael Recanati retired from the company, and transferred leadership to his son Oudi, named DIC's chairman, and nephew Leon, who took over as Clal's chairman. Overseeing IDB Holding's sprawling investment empire proved too much for Oudi Recanati, and in 2002, he resigned his position to focus on other activities. Soon after, his cousin Leon follow suit, announcing his decision to put the family's stake up for sale.

IDB Holding found a buyer in Ganden Group, another Israeli holding conglomerate established in 1996 by Nochi Dankner and Avi Fischer. Ganden Group led a buyer consortium including Avraham Livnat and Yitzhak Manor, both prominent Israeli industrialists. Negotiations dragged out for another year, in part because the proposed sale fell under the oversight of various Israeli agencies. The merger was completed in May 2003 for $548 million.

As CEO, Nochi Dankner set into place his own vision of IDB Holding's future direction. Dankner attempted to gain control of Israel's largest bank, Bank Hapoalim, in 2006. That deal, however, quickly fell through. Dankner also indicated the group's interest in selling its struggling Clal Insurance holdings, which had fallen into the red by 2008. At the same time, Dankner launched a new effort to expand IDB Holding into international markets. The company announced its interest in entering the Las Vegas real estate development market in 2008. IDB Holdings also planned to gain a position in the European investment market. To that end, the company raised more than ILS 1.75 billion in debt on the Tel Aviv Stock Exchange in 2007. Then in May 2008, the company raised a $1.5 billion credit facility from Goldman Sachs to acquire stakes in Credit Suisse and Barclay Bank. Already Israel's largest holding company, IDB Holding sought to assert itself on a world level in the new century.

M. L. Cohen

PRINCIPAL SUBSIDIARIES

Clal Industries and Investments; Clal Insurance Pensions & Finance Group; Discount Investment Corp.; IDB Development Corporation Ltd; Koor Industries.

PRINCIPAL COMPETITORS

FIBI Holding Company Ltd.; Delek Group Ltd.; Israel Corporation Ltd.; ICL-Israel Chemicals Ltd.; Fishman Holdings; Elco Holdings Ltd.; Granite Hacarmel Investments Ltd.; Strauss Ltd.; Housing and Construction Holding Company Ltd.; Africa Israel Investments Ltd.

FURTHER READING

Baider, Sharon, "Discount Investment Makes Super-Sol Offer," *Globes,* May 25, 2008.

———, "Koor Gets $1.5b Backing for European Investment," *Globes,* May 18, 2008.

"Discount Investments Sells IDB Holdings," *Israel Business Today,* May 15, 1998.

"Ganden to Acquire 52% Stake in IDB," *Jerusalem Post,* October 11, 2002.

"Goldman-Sachs Weighs IDB Share Buy," *Israel Business Today,* November 30, 1997, p. 15.

"IDB Acquires 23 Percent Holding in Sipchem," *Chemical Market Reporter,* September 1, 2003, p. 3.

"IDB Increases YLR Holding," *Israel Business Today,* January 31, 1997, p. 23.

Kedian, Amir, "IDB Profit Soars," *Globes,* November 29, 2006.

Meltzer, Roy, and Erez Peer, "Nochi Dankner Mulls Sale of Clal Insurance," *Globes,* March 7, 2007.

"Recanati, Leon," *Encyclopaedia Judaica,* edited by Michael Berenbaum and Fred Skolnik, vol. 17, 2nd ed., Detroit: Macmillan Reference USA, 2007.

"A Round of Applause for Mr. Leon Recanati," *Israel Business Today,* December 31, 1998, p. 4.

Shmoul, Avi, "Leon Recanati (1948–)," *Lifestyles Magazine,* January 2005.

"Toolmaker Buys into Israeli Giant," *International Herald Tribune,* May 27, 1996, p. 16.

Wollberg, Erez, "Clal Insurance Moves into Red," *Globes,* May 25, 2008.

Yoshai, Michal, "IDB Development Continues to Raise Capital," *Globes,* June 24, 2007.

———, "Nochi Dankner Mulls Las Vegas Expansion," *Globes,* March 23, 2008.

IG Group Holdings plc

Friars House
157–168 Blackfriars Road
London, SE1 8EZ
United Kingdom
Telephone: (+44 020) 7896 0011
Fax: (+44 020) 7896 0010
Web site: http://www.iggroup.com

Public Company
Incorporated: 1974
Employees: 404
Sales: EUR 184.0 million (2008)
Stock Exchanges: London
Ticker Symbol: IGG
NAICS: 713990 All Other Amusement and Recreation Industries

■ ■ ■

IG Group Holdings plc is one of the United Kingdom's pioneering and largest spread-betting groups, offering a variety of "speculative investment" services and products. In this sense, IG Group's operations are closer to traditional stockbroking and related investment vehicles than to traditional fixed-odds gambling. IG operates across two broad categories: financial, which includes financial spread-betting, foreign exchange (forex) trading, Contracts for Difference (CFD) and financial binaries; and sports spread-betting. These activities are conducted through several brand names, including IG Index, the group's original name, which handles most of its financial spread-betting, forex trading, and related services; IG Sports, created in 2008 as a dedicated division for the group's sports spread-betting services; IG Markets, which oversees CFDs for share prices, forex, commodities, and related sectors; Binarybet.com, through which the company has pioneered a hybrid betting service combining traditional fixed-odds betting and spread-betting for both the financial and sports markets; and Extrabet.com, an online betting service that provides fixed-odds betting facilities for sports events up to the final moments of play.

IG Group supports its operations through the development of its own online trading platform, PureDeal, launched in 2007. More than 90 percent of client bets are placed online. Nonetheless, IG Group continues to provide other support services, including telephone, PDA, and mobile services. Long focused exclusively on the United Kingdom, IG Group has been exporting the spread-betting concept in the 2000s, establishing subsidiaries and offices in Australia, Singapore, Germany, France, and Spain. In 2008, the company also entered the United States, where spread-betting is illegal, with the acquisition of Chicago-based HedgeStreet. The United Kingdom remains the group's largest market, generating 79 percent of its revenues. Of these, the financial market represents by far the largest part of the group's operation, accounting for 90 percent of IG's total sales. Founded in 1974, IG Group is listed on the London Stock Exchange. The company is led by J. R. Davie, chairman, and Tim Howkins, CEO.

COMPANY PERSPECTIVES

IG Group Holdings plc offers speculative investment products to a retail and professional client base, through a number of well-known brands. The group's principal businesses give clients the ability to trade on financial markets. Our longest established business is financial spread betting, where we are the world's leading provider (based on turnover), servicing a retail client base, primarily in the UK. Our rapidly growing Contracts For Difference (CFDs) and foreign exchange business services retail clients and market professionals around the world from offices located in the UK, Australia, Singapore, Germany, France, Spain and now the USA.

BETTING ON BETTING IN THE SEVENTIES

IG Group was the brainchild of Stuart Wheeler, who became one of the pioneers of spread-betting in the United Kingdom. Wheeler had been raised by adoptive parents (his mother was the daughter of a baronet) and educated at Eton and then Oxford. From there, Wheeler practiced as a barrister for three years before entering the financial services sector in the 1960s. After working six years as a merchant banker for Hill, Samuel & Co., Wheeler then joined First National Finance Corporation. At the beginning of the 1970s, however, Wheeler had been fired from that job.

Forced to find new work, the 40-year-old Wheeler recognized an opportunity to combine his two interests of finance and gambling. Indeed, into the early 1970s, Wheeler had developed something of a reputation for his gambling skills. In 1965, Wheeler was asked to leave Caesar's Palace in Las Vegas because he had been winning too much against such opponents as Omar Sharif, Ian Fleming, and financier James Goldsmith.

London's emergence as one of the world's major financial services capitals coincided with its relatively liberal betting laws. Where gambling remained strictly legislated, if not illegal, in many of the world's markets, in the United Kingdom gambling came to be seen not only as a form of amusement, but also, in the case of spread-betting, as a financial service. U.K. gamblers also became accustomed to placing a wider variety of bets, from sports events to the length of the government's annual budget speech.

The first to match betting with financial markets was Coral Index, established by bookmaking group Coral as an extension of its traditional betting operations. Coral recognized the potential of enabling gamblers to place bets on the performance of share prices on various stock market indices, such as the Dow Jones and FT 30 indices. Spread-betting involved establishing a spread at which, for example, the index was expected to rise or fall during a given period of time. Bettors could then place their bets for or against the spread. Their gains, or losses, were then determined by whether the index exceeded or fell short of the spread limit. Winnings were more or less unlimited, as were losses.

Wheeler too spotted the potential of the new type of wager, and attempted to persuade a number of other bookmaking firms, including sector leaders Ladbroke and William Hill, to back him in setting up spread-betting operations for them. Unable to raise interest, Wheeler decided to go into business for himself. In 1974, Wheeler established a small business in the attic of his home, taking bets on the price of gold.

The effort quickly turned to disaster, as the price of gold dropped sharply that year. That disaster ultimately inspired Wheeler's success. A major attraction of spread betting was its treatment by British tax law. Unlike fixed-odds gambling, where winnings were subjected to capital gains taxes, spread-betting winnings remained tax free. (On the other hand, losses could not be recovered against the gambler's taxes.) Despite his own losses, Wheeler's clients had happily pocketed their winnings tax-free, and sought to win more.

Gathering a group of investors, who each invested £100 for a stake in the company, Wheeler launched IG Index in 1975. The company slowly built a client base through the decade. For the most part, clients came from the ranks of London's City financial professionals and the well-to-do. Entry into the spread-betting market presented a number of obstacles. Among these was the need to possess an understanding of financial markets. Prospective clients were also required to submit to credit checks, and to meet minimum income requirements. Lastly, unlike traditional fixed-odds betting, in which a loss involved only one's initial wager, in spread-betting, losses could far exceed the original wager.

GROWTH INTO THE EIGHTIES

Risks existed for the spread-betting company as well. A mistake in establishing the spread could quickly prove costly for the company. Spread-betting groups, like traditional gambling outlets, also faced the potential of bad debts, with little recourse under the law. IG Index itself hit a rough patch soon after its founding, to the

KEY DATES

1974: Stuart Wheeler begins offering spread-betting services on international gold prices, then forms IG Index.
1986: IG Index acquires rival spread-betting service from Ladbrokes.
1998: Company launches online trading service.
2000: IG Group goes public on London Stock Exchange.
2003: Company is delisted from London Stock Exchange following management buyout.
2005: IG is relisted on London Stock Exchange.
2008: IG acquires HedgeFirst in Chicago.

extent that a friend wrote Wheeler a check for £1,000 to keep the company afloat. Instead, Wheeler paid a visit to London's Portland Club, where he succeeded in raising the needed capital by playing bridge.

Into the 1980s, IG Index began diversifying its own spread-betting operations. In 1982, the company began taking bets on the performance of the FT 30 and Dow Jones indices. The company emerged as a leader in the sector, which by then counted three major companies: Ladbroke, which had acquired Coral Index; City Index; and IG Index. Through the middle of the decade, IG Index followed the market, widening its range of bets to include a variety of financial indices, including commodities, options, and currencies. The company also joined in the growing sports spread-betting market, in which clients placed their bets not so much on which team might win, but by how much they might win. Companies also took bets on political events, such as the timing for the next general election.

IG Index moved into the lead in the sector in 1986, when it reached an agreement to acquire Ladbroke. The purchase of Ladbroke, which took bets on the FT 30, FTSE 100, gold prices, the spread between both the dollar and the mark and the dollar and the British pound, doubled IG Index in size.

The year 1986 represented something of a turning point for the spread-betting market. In that year, the British government passed the Financial Services Act. The new legislation, among other aspects, provided a more solid foundation for the spread-betting market, as spread-betting became classified as an investment business. Among other rules put into place by the legislation, all spread bets were legally enforceable as debts.

DEVELOPING NEW PRODUCTS AND SERVICES

Despite its rise as Britain's leading spread-betting operation, IG Index remained a relatively small company through much of the 1990s. By 1998, the company's total revenues only neared £6 million. However, IG Index had spent much of the previous decade preparing for a new era of growth.

IG Index began developing new products and services during the 1990s, including establishing a dedicated sports spread-betting division in 1993. In 1995, the company became the first in the sector to take bets on individual share prices, rather than on an entire stock market index. The following year, IG Index also added foreign exchange trading, allowing private clients and smaller institutional investors to trade in a market previously accessible only to large-scale banks.

After adding forex trading, IG Index continued to branch out from its spread-betting core. The company created a new product, Contracts for Differences (CFD), in order to add margin trading for its clients in 1999. CFDs were not considered betting, and therefore were subject to taxes, and were more attractive to offshore investors not subject to British capital gains tax laws. Also in 1999, IG Index created a new subsidiary, Index Direct. This operation extended the company's spread-betting services to a wider client base by offering lower entry bets. These efforts helped the company achieve growth rates of more than 100 percent in its 1999 and 2000 fiscal years.

Perhaps the most significant factor in IG Index's growth in this period was its move online. In 1998, IG Index became the first of the United Kingdom's spread-betting groups to launch an online betting platform. The automated system allowed bettors to trade in real-time and around-the-clock, and in general without requiring any personal contact. Leading much of this innovation was Nat Le Roux, who joined the company in 1992 as its financial dealing director, before being named deputy chief executive in 1999. Le Roux had spent more than ten years working in the futures and stockbroking markets before joining IG Index.

IG Index's move online coincided with the great dot-com boom at the end of the 20th century. The company's client base began to swell with new clients, and by the beginning of the 2000s topped 15,000. IG Index itself moved to capitalize on its success, and in 2000 the company went public, becoming IG Group and listing its shares on the London Stock Exchange. The listing made fortunes for the company's original investors, who each saw their original £100 investment grow to be worth £12.5 million. Wheeler himself continued to control more than one-third of the company after the listing.

INTERNATIONAL HORIZONS FOR THE NEW CENTURY

IG Index initially appeared immune to the crash of the technology sector at the beginning of the 2000s. By 2002, however, the crisis in the investment community finally caught up with the company, which was forced to post profit warnings. With its share price slipping, the company was rocked by Wheeler's sudden announcement March 2002 that he had decided to step down as the company's chief executive. Wheeler also announced his intention to sell nearly 25 percent of the company. After he was unable to find a buyer for the stake, Wheeler agreed to support a management buyout of the company led by Le Roux, who had taken over as group CEO. In 2003, therefore, IG Index removed its stock listing from the London exchange.

Under Le Roux's leadership, IG Group regained its momentum. By 2004, the company's revenues neared £50 million. Just two years later, IG Group's sales had jumped again to £89 million, before topping £120 million in 2007. Fueling this growth was the company's decision to develop its operations on an international level. For this, the company targeted Australia, then the English-speaking Asian markets, including Singapore and Hong Kong. IG Group also began extending its business into the largely untapped European market, establishing offices and desks in Germany, the Netherlands, France, Spain, Italy, and elsewhere. By 2008, the company had made its first move into the U.S. market, acquiring Chicago-based hedge fund specialist HedgeFirst.

Le Roux led the company back to the London Stock Exchange in 2005. The following year, Le Roux left the group, which appointed Tim Howkins in his place. Under Howkins, IG Group continued to bet on a strong future. The company launched a new hybrid product, binary betting, combining aspects of fixed-odds and spread betting. IG also established a new dedicated sports betting brand in 2007, IG Sports. In that year, also, IG Group unveiled its new online trading platform, PureDeal. The extended its technology in 2008 to the mobile telephone market, rolling out spread-betting software created for the new Apple iPhone. In this way, IG Group expected to hold onto its title as the global spread-betting leader.

M. L. Cohen

PRINCIPAL SUBSIDIARIES

extrabet Limited; IG Asia Pte Limited (Singapore); IG Australia Pty Limited; IG Finance; IG Financial Markets Inc. (U.S.A.); IG Group Holdings plc; IG Group Limited; IG Index plc; IG Markets (Deutschland) AG; IG Markets Limited; IG Nominees Limited; ITS Market Solutions Limited; Market Data Limited; Market Risk Management Inc (U.S.A.).

PRINCIPAL COMPETITORS

CMC Markets Plc; IFX Plc; City Index Plc; Camelot Group Plc; Ladbrokes Plc; Coral Eurobet plc; Sportingbet.com (UK) Plc; Stanley Leisure PLC; Victor Chandler International Ltd.

FURTHER READING

Blackwell, David Harold, "Wheeler Hands in His Cards," *Financial Times,* March 14, 2002, p. 21.

Cope, Nigel, "Where Bookie Meets Broker," *Management Today,* May 1995, p. 76.

Crosland, Jonas, "IG Group Spends Its Way to Growth," *Investors Chronicle,* February 19, 2008.

———, "Solid Growth at IG Group," *Investors Chronicle,* January 14, 2008.

Dey, Iain, "IG Bets on Volatility and China," *Daily Telegraph,* January 15, 2008.

Hasell, Nick, "IG Worth a Punt As It Places Bet on Regulatory Changes," *Times,* November 20, 2007, p. 61.

———, "IG's Global Gamble on Spread Betting Pays Off," *Times,* July 24, 2007, p. 43.

"IG Group Going Private," *Acquisitions Monthly,* August 2003, p. 50.

"IG Group Seeks Agency for £12m Global Media Account," *Marketing Week,* May 29, 2008, p. 10.

Parkinson, Gary, "Spread Betting Boss Throws in His Hand," *Daily Telegraph,* March 14, 2002, p. 63.

"Re-listing IG Sets Spread at £400m," *Leisure Report,* May 2005, p. 1.

Simpkins, Edward, "Wheeler's New Dealer," *Sunday Telegraph,* March 17, 2002, p. 10.

Smith, Philip, "Betting Game," *Accountancy Age,* July 20, 2006.

Spikes, Sarah, "Star-Gazing Howkins Has Clear Vision for IG," *Financial Times,* October 7, 2006, p. 20.

Waller, Martin, "IG Founder Prefers to Be King of His Own Castle," *Times,* January 21, 2003, p. 21.

Warwick-Ching, Lucy, "IG Group Bolstered by Growth in Online Betting," *Financial Times,* January 24, 2006, p. 21.

INPEX Holdings Inc.

4-1-18 Ebisu
Shibuya-ku
Tokyo, 150-0013
Japan
Telephone: (+81 03) 5448 1201
Fax: (+81 03) 5448 1259
Web site: http://www.inpex.co.jp

Public Company
Incorporated: 1966 as North Sumatra Offshore Petroleum Exploration Co. Ltd.
Employees: 400
Sales: ¥969.71 billion ($7.55 billion) (2007)
Stock Exchanges: Tokyo
Ticker Symbol: 1605
NAICS: 211111 Crude Petroleum and Natural Gas Extraction

■ ■ ■

INPEX Holdings Inc. (Inpex) is Japan's leading oil and gas importer, responsible for ensuring a large part of the country's energy supply. As such, Inpex is active on a global basis in both the exploration and operation of oil and gas fields. The company controls or participates in more than 75 projects in 25 countries, including in the Asian Pacific, South America, the Caspian Sea region, and the Middle East. Indonesia has long been the company's major market, especially for natural gas. The company is a leading supplier to the Bontang LNG (liquefied natural gas) factory, one of the largest in the world, and in turn imports as much as 25 percent of the LNG imported into Japan from Indonesia. Inpex also sells LNG to other markets, including Australia, Singapore, and Malaysia. The group operates LNG and petroleum exploration and production units in Indonesia's Masela block and Australia's WA-385-P block.

Inpex has also been involved in a number of major discoveries, including in the Kazakhstan and Azerbaijan regions of the Caspian Sea, the Azadegan Oil field in Iran, and offshore fields in Abu Dhabi. Altogether, Inpex controls probable reserves of 1.61 billion barrels of crude oil, LPG, and condensates, and nearly 2.1 trillion cubic feet (equivalent to 1.96 billion barrels) of natural gas. The company's total production in 2007 reached 418 million barrels. Of this, 44 percent was generated from the Asia/Oceania region, while the Middle East and North Africa contributed 36 percent. Formerly a state-controlled company, Inpex went public in 2004, listing on the Tokyo Stock Exchange. A year later, the group merged with domestic rival Teikoku Oil Co. under a newly formed holding company, Inpex Holdings. The Japanese government retains a golden share in Inpex, in order to prevent a takeover by a foreign entity. Kunihiko Matsuo is the company's chairman, and Naoki Kuroda serves as its president. Inpex Holdings posted total revenues of nearly ¥970 billion ($7.55 billion) in 2007.

ENSURING JAPAN'S ENERGY SUPPLY IN 1966

Japan's rapid industrialization during the 1950s and 1960s forced the country to secure sufficient energy

COMPANY PERSPECTIVES

The mission of INPEX is to secure a stable and efficient supply of oil and natural gas for Japan, a nation poor in energy resources. INPEX was established in 1966 as a pioneering Japanese company to promote the development of oil resources in an international context. Over the course of our history, we have overcome many difficulties, and since 1970, we have discovered a number of large oil and gas fields in Indonesia.

reserves to sustain its growth. Yet the lack of natural resources in Japan—the country was able to provide just 4 percent of its total energy needs, placing it among the lowest in the developed world—meant that the country was highly dependent on imported fuels. In order to minimize its dependence on foreign oil companies, the Japanese government began developing its own oil and gas exploration, operations, and importing businesses.

Among these was the North Sumatra Offshore Exploration Co. Ltd. Created in 1966, that company formed a partnership with Japan's main exploration company, Japex, to develop the Bunju and Mahakam blocks off the coast of Indonesia. The partnership transferred the exploration and production rights to the company, which renamed itself as Offshore Petroleum Exploration Co. in 1967. The company adopted its future name, Indonesia Petroleum Ltd., or Inpex, only in 1975.

By then, Inpex had developed a new series of partnerships, including with Unocal to explore the Attaka field, in the Mahakam block, in 1970. That partnership quickly struck success, with the discovery of the Attaka natural gas field. By 1972, Inpex had joined the ranks of producer operators, launching production at the Attaka field. Inpex formed a second exploration partnership, with CFP, in 1970; that company transferred its share of the partnership to fellow French group Total in 1971.

Through the 1970s, Inpex succeeded in discovering several new fields in the Mahakam offshore block, including the Bekapai field, in 1972, and the Handil field in 1974. Most of Inpex's production was destined for the newly built Bontang LNG Plant in Indonesia, which became one of the largest of its type in the world. Production at the Bontang plant started in 1977. Inpex quickly became one of the largest suppliers to the Bontang plant, which in turn became a major source for imported natural gas for the Japanese market. Inpex started shipping from Bontang in 1988.

Inpex continued to add new operations through the end of the 1970s and into the 1980s. In 1977, the company teamed up with Gulf (later ChevronTexaco) to take over the rights to the South Natuna Sea block B. The two companies then formed a joint venture partnership, Inpex Natuna Ltd. In 1986, the company added a stake in two more Indonesian offshore projects, Northwest Java and Southeast Sumatra, both acquired from Reading & Bates. Inpex then established two new subsidiaries for these shareholdings, Inpex Jawa and Inpex Sumatra.

Into the early 1990s, Inpex completed several production sharing agreements with Pertamina. These included the Northwest Java block, the South Natuna Sea block B, the Attaka field, the Southeast Sumatra block, and the Mahakam block. By 1992, the company launched production at the Belida field, in the Natuna block.

EXPANDING BEYOND INDONESIA IN THE NINETIES

Despite its success in Indonesia, Inpex increasingly recognized that it needed to build a more geographically diverse portfolio of oil and gas fields in the light of the new economic and political realities of the late 20th, and early 21st, centuries. Into the 1990s, the company began to seek new regions for its development. Among its first targets was Australia, where the company formed a partnership with BHPP, through subsidiary Inpex Alpha. That partnership began developing the WA-210-P area in 1989. By 1994, these efforts paid off, with the launch of production at Griffin fields.

Inpex also sought an entry into the Persian Gulf region. In 1996, the company reached an agreement with Amerada Hess to buy the concession for the Abu Al Bukhoosh block off Abu Dhabi in the United Arab Emirates. Two years later, Inpex returned to Australia, winning a bid for the exploration and production rights in the WA-285-P offshore block in Western Australia. By 2000, the company had succeeded in locating its first natural gas and condensate deposits there.

Inpex's search for geographic diversity continued as well. In 1998, the company joined the rush to the huge gas and oil deposits in the Caspian sea. In that year, the company reached an agreement with the Kazakhstan government to develop the Offshore North Caspian block. This led to the discovery of crude oil deposits in the Kashagan fields in 2000. By 2002, the company had discovered a second crude oil field, Kalamkas. In that year, too, Inpex extended its Caspian Sea interests with

KEY DATES

1966: Company is founded as North Sumatra Offshore Petroleum Exploration Co. Ltd.
1975: Company changes name to Indonesia Petroleum Ltd. (Inpex).
1989: Inpex enters Australian offshore exploration market as part of geographical diversification drive.
2004: Company acquires JODCO and goes public on Tokyo Stock Exchange.
2006: Company merges with Teikoku Co., forming INPEX Holdings.

the creation of a partnership with Lukoil in Azerbaijan.

In the meantime, Inpex had also ventured into the South American market. In 1999, the company teamed up with Texaco and Nissho Iwai to buy the exploration and production rights to Frade block and BC-4 block in Brazil. Inpex also continued to find success in its core Indonesian region. The company discovered a new natural gas and condensate field in the Timor Sea Masela block at the end of 2000. In 2001, the company added a stake in the Berau block, also in Indonesia.

MOVING UPSTREAM

Having successfully developed a geographically diverse range of exploration and production interests, Inpex began extending its operations upstream. Already a major supplier of natural gas to Japan, Inpex began positioning itself as a supplier to other markets as well. In 2001, for example, the company began piping its first shipments of natural gas to Singapore. The following year, the company began adding Malaysia as well. This extension of its markets also encouraged the company to gain more control over its transporting infrastructure. The company moved to add its own pipeline operations, buying the BTC (Baku-Tblisi-Ceyhan) pipeline in 2002.

The move upstream was accompanied by continued increases in production. The company launched production at the Bayu-Undan Condensate field, part of its Timor Sea operations, in 2004. The company also began producing crude oil and condensates in the Belanak oil and gas field, part of Inpex Natuna's operations. In 2005, Inpex's active operations grew through the launch of natural gas production at the APN field, in northwest Java. The company also added production at its operations in the Central Azeri field of the Caspian Sea.

Despite its success, and despite its importance to Japan's energy supply, Inpex remained a small player in the global market. However, the international energy market was already beginning to witness the effects of the emergence of two new major players in the world's economy, China and India. The rapid economic development in both countries, which together represented one-third of the total world population, had also transformed them into major new competitors for the increasingly limited fossil fuel resources.

If Inpex had managed to hold its own in the energy market in the last decades of the 20th century, its lack of scale made it vulnerable to the new realities of the global oil and natural gas markets. In recognition of this, the Japanese government began taking steps to restructure and consolidate parts of its energy import infrastructure. This led to the takeover by Inpex of Japan Oil Development Co., Ltd. (JODCO), in 2004. That company, founded in 1973, had focused its own operations on the Persian Gulf region, particularly in the Abu Dhabi offshore market. The addition of JODCO's operations at five fields in the ADMA block helped to solidify Inpex's geographic diversification.

Following the JODCO merger, the Japanese government moved to boost Inpex's industry profile. Inpex was privatized, listed on the Tokyo Stock Exchange in November 2004. Despite the public offering, the Japanese government retained a so-called golden share in the company, which enabled the government to block any takeover attempt of Inpex by a foreign company.

JOINING FORCES FOR THE NEW ENERGY ERA

Soon after its merger with JODCO, Inpex moved to join forces with another of Japan's oil and gas groups, Teikoku Co. That company, founded in the 1940s, had also developed exploration and production operations. The combination of Inpex's operations and those of Teikoku proved highly complementary, as the two companies shared similar operations but in different locations. As a result, through Teikoku Inpex gained entry into the African markets, with operations offshore of Congo, as well as in Algeria and Egypt. Following the merger agreement, completed in 2005, Inpex and Teikoku merged their operations under a newly created holding company, Inpex Holdings, in 2006.

In that year, Inpex added another major new oil project—the massive Azadegan field in Iran. Inpex won a 75 percent stake in the project, in partnership with the National Iran Oil Company. However, Iran's position on the United States' list of terrorist states placed Inpex in a delicate position. The reluctance of the Japanese government to go against the United States forced Inpex to postpone its development of the Azadegan field. Inpex sought unsuccessfully to bring in a partner to develop the site. By the end of 2006, however, the impatient Iranian government stripped Inpex of its $2 billion contract to lead the development of the Azadegan field. Inpex was nonetheless allowed to retain a 15 percent stake in the future project.

Inpex was buoyed again the following year, when it discovered new natural gas reserves at the Abadi field, in the Masela block. The new discovery helped boost the total probable reserves under Inpex's control to 1.61 billion barrels of crude oil, LPG, and condensates, and nearly 2.1 trillion cubic feet (equivalent to 1.96 billion barrels) of natural gas. As a major supplier of Japan's energy resources, Inpex remained a central player in the country's economy.

M. L. Cohen

PRINCIPAL SUBSIDIARIES

Azadegan Petroleum Development, Ltd. (Iran; 15%); INPEX Alpha, Ltd. (Australia); INPEX Browse, Ltd. (Australia); INPEX Jakarta Office (Indonesia); INPEX Libya, Ltd.; JODCO Abu Dhabi Branch; Teikoku Oil Co., Ltd.

PRINCIPAL COMPETITORS

Exxon Mobil Corporation; Royal Dutch Shell PLC; BP PLC; Chevron Corporation; ConocoPhillips; Saudi Arabian Oil Co.; Total S.A.; Sumitomo Corporation; Nippon Oil Corporation; Apache Corporation; Japan Petroleum Exploration Co., Ltd.; AOC Holdings, Inc.; Uehara Sei Shoji Co., Ltd.

FURTHER READING

Clark, Martin, "On the Prowl," *Petroleum Economist,* February 2006, p. 31.

"The Dash to Kazakhstan," *Financial Times,* January 23, 2007, p. 25.

"Inpex Corp. Continues IPO Success in ¥ 160bn Share Sale," *Euroweek,* November 12, 2004, p. 21.

"Inpex Mulls Azadegan Phase 1 Bids," *MEED Middle East Economic Digest,* April 15, 2005, p. 11.

"Inpex Signs Agreement to Investigate Darwin LNG," *ABIX News Summary,* April 22, 2008.

Jack, Andrew, and Bayan Rahman, "Inpex Set to Buy Stake in Lukoil Project," *Financial Times,* November 19, 2002, p. 30.

"Japan's Inpex Finds More Indonesian Gas," *Natural Gas Week,* August 20, 2007, p. 13.

"Japan's Inpex Has Lost a $2bn Contract to Develop the Giant Onshore Azadegan Oilfield," *Petroleum Economist,* November 2006, p. 44.

Jopson, Barney, "Inpex Debut Success Calms Tokyo Fears," *Financial Times,* November 18, 2004, p. 33.

Juji, Nobuko, and Mariko Sanchanta, "Inpex IPO Faces Months of Delay," *Financial Times,* June 29, 2004, p. 31.

Pilling, David, "Inpex and Japan Inc.'s Energy Security," *Financial Times,* November 14, 2005, p. 26.

International Paper Company

6400 Poplar Avenue
Memphis, Tennessee 38197
U.S.A.
Telephone: (901) 419-9000
Toll Free: (800) 223-1268
Fax: (901) 214-9682
Web site: http://www.ipaper.com

Public Company
Incorporated: 1898
Employees: 51,500
Sales: $21.89 billion (2007)
Stock Exchanges: New York Swiss Amsterdam
Ticker Symbol: IP
NAICS: 113110 Timber Tract Operations; 321113 Sawmills; 322110 Pulp Mills; 322121 Paper (Except Newsprint) Mills; 322130 Paperboard Mills; 322211 Corrugated and Solid Fiber Box Manufacturing; 322212 Folding Paperboard Box Manufacturing; 322213 Setup Paperboard Box Manufacturing; 322214 Fiber Can, Tube, Drum, and Similar Products Manufacturing; 322215 Nonfolding Sanitary Food Container Manufacturing; 322224 Uncoated Paper and Multiwall Bag Manufacturing; 322226 Surface-Coated Paperboard Manufacturing; 423840 Industrial Supplies Merchant Wholesalers; 424110 Printing and Writing Paper Merchant Wholesalers; 424130 Industrial and Personal Service Paper Merchant Wholesalers

■ ■ ■

International Paper Company (IP) is one of the world's largest forest products companies, battling for the top spot with Finland's Stora Enso Oyj. IP focuses principally on two main sectors within the forest products industry: uncoated papers, from which about 30 percent of overall revenues are derived, and industrial and consumer packaging products, responsible for nearly 38 percent of sales. Another one-third of revenues stem from the firm's distribution business, which operates mainly in the United States under the xpedx name. This unit distributes printing paper, packaging, graphic arts, maintenance, and industrial products to a variety of industrial wholesalers and end users. After selling the vast majority of its land holdings in 2006, IP owns or manages about 300,000 acres of forestlands in the United States and roughly 250,000 acres in Brazil. The company also maintains harvesting rights on more than 500,000 acres of government-owned forestlands in Russia. International Paper began as a major player in its core industry and expanded through mergers, acquisitions, and product development. By the early 21st century, IP had operations in North America, Latin America, South America, Europe, and Asia that included about two dozen pulp, paper, and packaging mills and around 130 converting and packaging plants. Around 22 percent of its revenues originated outside the United States.

EARLY HISTORY

Established on January 31, 1898, in Albany, New York, International Paper Company resulted from a merger of 17 pulp and paper mills located throughout five northeastern states. The new company had 1.7 million

COMPANY PERSPECTIVES

Our Mission: Why We Exist, What We Do, and How We Do It. International Paper is dedicated to making people's lives better. Our employees use renewable resources to make products people depend on every day. Our customers succeed because our innovative products and services make their businesses better. Our communities welcome us as neighbors, employers and environmental stewards. Our shareowners benefit from our superior financial performances. By keeping our promises, we deliver results.

acres of timberlands, with the properties ranging as far north as Canada, and streams running through the properties were used to run the mills with hydroelectric power. By 1900, the mills provided 60 percent of U.S. newsprint. In 1901, in order to enhance its research and development efforts, the company opened the Central Test Bureau in Glens Falls, New York. This was the U.S. pulp and paper industry's first laboratory.

The company's power interests played a dominant role in its early years. As household electricity demand grew in the 1920s, the firm established large hydroelectric plants and power companies. At one time, it produced enough electricity to light all of New England and most of Quebec and Ontario. In 1928 International Paper & Power Company was organized in Massachusetts to acquire International Paper. IP continued to operate as a subsidiary of International Paper & Power. In 1935 the United States passed the Public Utility Holdings Act, making it illegal for an organization to run both an industrial firm and a power company. The law signified the end of International Paper's involvement in the energy and power business. Instead, the company began to focus on key areas such as paper and packaging.

The company expanded into the southern United States in the 1920s and 1930s, primarily because trees could be grown more quickly and in greater volume than they could in the North. It also maximized its use of the trees through the kraft process, which involved use of a very strong pulp to manufacture packaging materials.

In June 1941 a new company was incorporated to acquire the assets of International Paper & Power Company. The new parent company was named International Paper Company to reflect the change from a paper and power company to a manufacturer devoted solely to paper. During World War II, International Paper did what it could to support the war effort. Its contributions included the development of nitrate pulp for use in explosives and the development of a waterproof board called V-board, or victory board, which was used to make boxes to send food and other supplies to the troops. The new technology, along with the wartime inventions of other manufacturers, led to increased competition after the war. As a result, IP began to invest more capital in research and development. Shortly after the war, it established a research laboratory in Mobile, Alabama, which was later renamed the Erling Riis Research Laboratory to honor a former company vice-president.

An emphasis on packaging products also characterized the firm's progress in the 1940s. In December 1940 it acquired the Agar Manufacturing Corporation, which included three subsidiaries and four container plants in Illinois, Kansas, Massachusetts, and New Jersey. In June 1941 the Southern Kraft Corporation was merged into IP and became the Southern Kraft Division. Previously a subsidiary, Southern Kraft owned eight kraft board and paper mills in the southern United States. IP also bought the assets of a shipping-container maker, the Scharff-Koken Manufacturing Company.

In 1947 IP merged with Single Service Containers, Inc., a manufacturer of milk containers, and in 1953 it founded the International Paper Company Foundation, a nonprofit organization developed to support charitable, educational, and scientific efforts. IP acquired the capital stock of a specialty coated paper manufacturer, A.M. Collins Manufacturing Company, of Philadelphia, in 1955. In 1957 the latter merged with IP. In 1958 IP bought Lord Baltimore Press, Inc., a Maryland manufacturer of cartons and labels.

In an attempt to diversify beyond paper production and conversion, IP acquired Long-Bell Lumber Company in a $117 million deal completed in 1957. At the time Long-Bell was the world's largest lumber company, producing plywood, hardwood lumber, and building products. Among its assets were sawmills, manufacturing plants, wholesale and retail distribution networks, and 450,000 acres of timberland. The Federal Trade Commission (FTC) launched an investigation into the takeover of Long-Bell, concerned about its potential antitrust implications given that IP was three times larger than its closest rival. The deal was approved only after IP promised not to acquire any other major competitor for the next ten years.

IP's Canadian subsidiary, Canadian International Paper Company, also made its share of acquisitions in the 1950s. These included Brown Corporation in 1954; Hygrade Containers Ltd. in 1955; and Anglo American

KEY DATES

1898: International Paper Company (IP) is formed from the merger of 17 pulp and paper mills in the northeastern United States.
1928: With IP's power business growing, International Paper & Power Company is formed as a holding company for IP and its power operations.
1935: Passage of the Public Utility Holdings Act makes it illegal for an organization to operate both industrial and power businesses, leading to the divestment of IP's power interests.
1941: A new International Paper Company is incorporated to acquire the assets of International Paper & Power and to signal the new focus on paper.
1957: IP acquires Long-Bell Lumber Company.
1981: Canadian International Paper subsidiary is sold to help fund a major plant modernization program in the United States.
1986: Hammermill Paper Company is acquired.
1988: Masonite Corporation is acquired.
1989: IP acquires Aussedat Rey of France and Germany's Zanders Feinpapiere AG.
1993: North American distribution operations are consolidated as ResourceNet International.
1995: IP gains majority control of New Zealand-based Carter Holt Harvey.
1996: Montvale, New Jersey-based Federal Paper Board Company is acquired for $3.5 billion.
1998: ResourceNet International changes its name to xpedx.
1999: Union Camp Corporation is acquired for $7.9 billion.
2000: IP acquires Shorewood Packaging Corporation for $920 million and Champion International Corporation for $10.2 billion; IP announces plans to divest $5 billion in assets by year-end 2001.
2001: Divestments include Masonite and Zanders Feinpapiere.
2005: IP sells its majority stake in Carter Holt Harvey; major business transformation is launched refocusing the company on uncoated paper and industrial and consumer packaging.
2006: Headquarters are relocated to Memphis, Tennessee; divestments include 5.6 million acres of U.S. forestlands and coated paper businesses in the United States and Brazil.
2007: Among further divestments, the company exits from the wood products sector.
2008: IP agrees to buy Weyerhaeuser Company's containerboard, packaging, and recycling operations for $6 billion.

Paper Company, Mid-West Paper Ltd., Vancouver Pacific Paper Company, and Victoria Paper Company in 1959. International Paper ended the 1950s with its first year of sales in excess of $1 billion.

DIVERSIFYING BEYOND THE CORE, WITH MIXED RESULTS

During the following decade, new technology improved both product design and manufacturing processes. In 1962, for example, IP began using computers to control paper machines at its mill in Georgetown, South Carolina. A year later, it introduced polyethylene-coated milk cartons. In addition to new products, the 1960s presented IP with challenges, including development of new production and management techniques. Since 1943 IP had been headed by the Hinman family; John Hinman was chief executive from 1943 to 1961, and his son, Edward B. Hinman, held the post from 1966 to 1969. Various associates appointed by the elder Hinman ran the company from 1961 to 1966.

During the 1960s IP continued to grow internally and took giant leaps toward diversification, many of them in haste, and learned that bigger is not always better. IP had emphasized production efficiency as a means of increasing output for most of the century. IP's production muscle came at the expense of marketing expertise, which lagged. The production emphasis led to overexpansion of paper plants, which in turn resulted in low profit margins. To increase profitability, IP diversified, with little success, into areas as far ranging as residential construction, prefabricated housing, nonwoven fabrics, consumer facial tissue, and disposable diapers. Its move into lumber and plywood was only somewhat more successful. White paper, paperboard, and pulp still accounted for more than half of the company's sales during the early 1970s; converted paper products comprised one-third; lumber, plywood, and other building products totaled 9 percent; and the remaining sales came from real estate, packaging systems, and nonwoven fabrics.

By 1971 IP's long-term debt, which had been almost nonexistent in 1965, reached $564 million. When Edward Hinman took over in 1966, the company's greatest asset was its large share of real estate, including eight million acres that it owned and 15.5 million that it leased. In 1968 Hinman sought the help of Frederick Kappel, formerly chairman of AT&T. The two ran the company together, but after earnings declined by 30 percent in 1970, Kappel and a team of outside directors replaced Hinman the following year with Paul A. Gorman, another AT&T executive. Gorman faced the challenge of returning the company to profitability.

Gorman started the long-term task by setting up a $78 million reserve to cover writeoffs of inefficient facilities; closing a specialty mill in York Haven, Pennsylvania; and closing various plants in Ecuador, Italy, Puerto Rico, and West Germany. In 1972 he also sold most of Donald L. Bren Co., a southern California house builder acquired in 1970, and Spacemakers Inc., a prefabricated-housing subsidiary. The company also sold its interest in C.R. Bard, Inc., a medical equipment manufacturer.

From 1966 to 1972, IP had spent $1 billion to increase its papermaking and paper-converting capacity by 25 percent. During the early 1970s the paper industry headed toward cyclical recession. IP laid off 7 percent of its employees. Gorman felt that the firm needed more financial control and saw to it that decisions made by the company's manufacturing groups were reviewed from a financial, marketing, and manufacturing perspective. In addition, all projects had to show a minimum after-tax profit of 10 percent. Ailing plants were improved, sold, or shut down. Gorman also reorganized international operations on a product line basis. His efforts were successful. Earnings of $69 million in 1971 were the lowest in ten years, despite record earnings just two years earlier, but they jumped 30 percent the first six months of 1972.

In 1973 J. Stanford Smith joined IP as vice-chairman. Previously a senior vice-president with General Electric Company, Smith replaced Gorman as chairman and CEO in 1974. Smith felt that one way to increase profitability was to develop natural resources on the company's land. He devised a plan to purchase General Crude Oil Company, which IP did in 1974 for $489 million. The business was unsuccessful, however, in locating major oil or gas deposits on IP's land. Five years later, in order to raise capital for acquisitions and internal growth, the company sold General Crude Oil's oil and natural gas operations to Gulf Oil Corporation for $650 million. In addition, IP sold a Panama City, Florida, pulp and linerboard mill to Southwest Forest Industries for $220 million. In the meantime, in 1976 IP completed a major corporate reorganization that saw the Southern Kraft Division and the Northern Division replaced with five product-centered business units focusing on white papers, consumer packaging, industrial packaging, specialty packaging, and wood products.

MAJOR PLANT MODERNIZATION PROGRAM

Between 1975 and 1980, IP's operating profits were mediocre. Again it turned to new management for help, and in 1980 Edwin A. Gee stepped in as chairman. A chemical engineer, Gee recognized that many of the company's 16 pulp and paper mills, all built in the 1920s and 1930s, were wasting labor and energy. Immediately, he instituted a $6 billion program to modernize the plants. Gee's goal was to turn the world's largest paper company into one of the lowest-cost producers of white paper and packaging materials, thus making it one of the most profitable papermakers as well.

To raise money for Gee's plan IP sold its remaining interest in General Crude Oil Company for $763 million and used the profits to buy Bodcaw Company of Dallas in 1979. Bodcaw added a highly efficient linerboard mill in Pineville, Louisiana, and 420,000 acres of prime timberland. In 1981 IP sold Canadian International Paper for $900 million. In addition, Gee increased the research-and-development budget and reduced IP's labor force by 20 percent. By 1982 he had raised $2 billion, aided by sales of land, timber, and other subsidiaries.

After determining that only two of the six major packaging mills were operating efficiently, Gee sold one mill, shut down three others, and invested $600 million in the Mansfield, Louisiana, mill. In April 1981 IP unveiled a new southern pine plywood and lumber manufacturing plant in Springhill, Louisiana. The $60 million facility, the brainchild of Gee, featured the latest computerized process controls and supplied the containerboard mill in Mansfield plus paper and pulp mills at Camden, Arkansas, and in Bastrop, Louisiana.

In the same year, John A. Georges became president and COO. His solution to IP's production problems was not to build new plants but to remodel existing facilities. The company also spent $500 million on remodeling a Georgetown, South Carolina, mill, changing its product focus in the process. Instead of brown linerboard, a cyclical product, part of the plant was set up to make white papers. The white paper business was to offer a faster-growing and more stable market.

In addition, Georges began a $350 million project to convert another mill in Mobile, Alabama. The 60-year-old facility, which housed the company's last remaining newsprint machine, was also remodeled to produce white papers in 1985, thus marking the end of the company's longstanding newsprint business. In 1987, newsprint prices began a steady decline.

A recession in the early 1980s meant further delays, but the investments began to bear fruit in the mid-1980s. As a result of new automation, IP's production costs decreased 11 percent between 1981 and 1987 and its mills were able to use 25 percent less energy. Georges was named CEO in 1984 and chairman a year later, succeeding Gee in both cases.

DIVERSIFYING GEOGRAPHICALLY AND IN PRODUCT MIX

Georges's promotions had been preceded in 1984 by a decline in linerboard and pulp prices and a 14-year low in earnings. The white-paper market seemed to be one of the few that was profitable, so Georges hired a team of scientists and technicians to promote business in that area. Their work led to a major acquisition in 1986: Hammermill Paper Company. The $1.1 billion purchase increased IP's white-paper capacity by 750,000 tons and provided the technology to produce premium paper lines. Georges also reduced the number of salaried employees from 12,000 in 1981 to 9,200 in 1988, and streamlined management. Under his leadership, the firm also acquired Anitec Image Technology Corporation, maker of photographic film, papers, and darkroom chemicals; Avery Corporation, a Chicago-based envelope manufacturer; and Kendall Company's nonwoven fabrics division. IP also purchased Masonite Corporation, maker of composite wood products, in 1988. As a result, profits improved in 1988 and set a record in 1989.

In addition to the company's recovery, however, it also weathered several crises. These included a 1984 fire that destroyed its Nacogdoches, Texas, plywood-manufacturing plant, causing $32.5 million in damages. The facility reopened in 1986 after being equipped to produce oriented strand board, an alternative to plywood. In 1987, to protest inadequate wages and benefits, 2,200 workers went on strike at paper mills in Alabama, Maine, Mississippi, and Wisconsin.

Under Georges's leadership, the watchword at IP in the late 1980s and early 1990s was diversity, both in geography and product mix. His aim was to lessen the firm's vulnerability to the cyclical nature of its core paper, packaging, and forestry operations. Many of the international acquisitions that Georges pursued were aimed at expanding IP further into the area of specialty products, which generally produced higher margins. These products included photographic paper and films, specialty industrial papers, molded-wood products, laminated products, and nonwoven fabrics such as disposable diapers. Although similar in some ways to the firm's diversification of the 1960s, this round of expansion proved more successful.

Heading into its overseas spending spree, International Paper already owned box-manufacturing facilities in Italy, the Netherlands, Spain, Sweden, and the United Kingdom. In 1989 it acquired three major European manufacturers: Aussedat Rey, the second largest paper company in France; the Ilford photographic-products division of Ciba-Geigy; and Germany's Zanders Feinpapiere AG, a high-quality coated-paper company. In 1990 IP bought the French operations of Georgia-Pacific Corporation.

The following year, in addition to bolstering its domestic base with the purchase of three U.S. paper distribution companies—Dillard Paper, Leslie Paper, and Wayne Paper—and its European holdings with the acquisition of Scaldia Paper BV of the Netherlands and the packaging equipment business of Dominion Industries Ltd., IP gained a presence in the Pacific Rim through a $258 million purchase of a 16 percent interest in the leading New Zealand forest products company, Carter Holt Harvey Ltd. (CHH). IP increased its stake in CHH in 1992 to 24 percent by investing an additional $298 million. Not only dominant in its home market, CHH was a major exporter of forest products to Australia and Asia. Also in 1992, IP paid $209 million for an 11 percent stake in Israel's Scitex Corporation Ltd., a world leader in color electronic-imaging equipment. The stake was increased to 12 percent the following year. The company also purchased Kwidzyn from the government of Poland for $150 million and the promise to invest $75 million more in the firm, the country's largest white-paper manufacturer and operator of one of the most modern paper mills in Eastern Europe.

SURVIVING SEVERE CYCLICAL PAPER-INDUSTRY DOWNTURN

IP's diversification program appeared to pay off in the early 1990s when the paper industry encountered one of its worst cyclical downturns in 50 years. While competitors Boise Cascade Corp. and Champion International Corp. posted huge losses, IP continued to report profits, albeit smaller than those of the period from 1988 to 1990. Sales in 1992 hit a record $13.6 billion, although earnings were reduced substantially by a $263 million restructuring charge for the closure and consolidation of 20 underperforming mills and sales offices worldwide. In 1993 IP folded its North American distribution business into ResourceNet International, with more than 250 locations.

IP continued to expand aggressively in the mid-1990s. In 1994 ResourceNet International picked up two paper-distributing companies in Mexico, while in the area of liquid packaging, a new plant was built in Brazil and a joint venture was formed in China to build and operate a plant near Shanghai. IP made its biggest purchases to date in 1995, however. The firm spent $1.15 billion to attain majority control of Carter Holt Harvey and $64 million to acquire DSM, a producer of ink and adhesive resin based in the Netherlands. IP attempted to acquire Holvis AG, a Swiss fiber and paper company, for $422 million but was rebuffed by the Holvis board. Late in 1995 IP announced a $3.5 billion purchase of Federal Paper Board Company, based in Montvale, New Jersey, and the 15th largest paper company in the United States. Federal Paper specialized in bleached paperboard used for cigarette cartons, laundry detergent, and other consumer products, and, added to IP's packaging operations, gave IP about one-third of the bleached board market. Through the transaction, IP gained mills in Augusta, Georgia; Riegelwood, North Carolina; and Versailles, Connecticut.

Fittingly, the Federal Paper acquisition was consummated nearly simultaneously with the announcement of Georges's retirement as chairman and CEO, both of which occurred in early 1996. Georges's diversification program had increased non-U.S. sales to 30 percent of total revenues by 1994. While IP's core paper, pulp, and paperboard businesses accounted for 78 percent of sales in 1988, they accounted for only 52 percent of sales by 1994. During the same period, IP's specialty products' share of sales increased from just 3.7 percent to 17.3 percent. Overall, during Georges's leadership tenure, annual revenues at the company quadrupled to nearly $20 billion.

RESTRUCTURING AT BEGINNING OF DILLON'S TENURE

John T. Dillon, previously president and COO, succeeded Georges as chairman and CEO of International Paper. In addition to working to consolidate the Federal Paper acquisition, Dillon's initial months of leadership focused on divesting some operations, in part to offset the approximately $800 million in long-term debt incurred with the purchase of Federal Paper. In the most significant divestment of 1996, International Paper sold about 300,000 acres of timberlands in Oregon and Washington, booking a $592 million pretax gain in the process. Also in 1996, IP took a $515 million restructuring and asset impairment charge as part of an ongoing cost-cutting program. A large proportion of the charge went toward the writing off of assets in the company's struggling imaging products business, maker of printing plates, films, chemicals, and paper for the photography and commercial printing market. With market conditions suddenly deteriorating after a record-setting year for the paper industry in 1995, IP saw its net earnings drop to $303 million in 1996 from the $1.15 billion of the previous year.

Conditions failed to improve in 1997, and Dillon responded midyear with a major restructuring plan that aimed to divest more than $1 billion in underperforming assets or businesses. By mid-1998 IP had sold its imaging products business; Veratec, its nonwovens business; two of its four box plants in California; and small paper mills in France and Colombia. The company's workforce was reduced by about 10 percent. Restructuring and other charges led to a net loss of $151 million for 1997. Among the other charges that year was $150 million set aside as a legal reserve as part of the settlement of a class-action lawsuit brought against Masonite Corporation. The suit alleged that pressed-wood exterior siding made by Masonite was failing prematurely, allowing moisture to be retained and causing damage to the underlying structure. In September 1996 a jury found that the siding was defective, leading to the settlement in January 1998. Two other similar suits—one also involving siding, the other a roofing material—against Masonite were settled in similar fashion in January 1999.

Concurrent with the restructuring efforts were targeted acquisitions. IP's North American distribution business, which changed its name from ResourceNet International to xpedx in January 1998, expanded in July of that year with the purchase of Mead Corporation's Zellerbach distribution unit for about $261 million in cash. This acquisition increased xpedx's 1998 revenues to $5.2 billion, a 22 percent increase over the previous year. The combination was expected to result in annual savings of $100 million in operating costs, and IP shut down 25 facilities and eliminated about 1,000 jobs following the deal's closure. Also added in 1998 was Weston Paper and Manufacturing Company, acquired through a stock deal valued at $232 million. Based in Terre Haute, Indiana, Weston operated 11 corrugated-container plants in the South and Midwest. In December 1998 International Paper expanded in Eastern Europe with the purchase of Svetogorsk AO, a Russia-based pulp and paper firm.

TAKEOVERS OF UNION CAMP (1999) AND CHAMPION (2000)

Dillon moved beyond these smaller deals in April 1999 with a blockbuster stock-swap acquisition of Union Camp Corporation for about $7.9 billion, including the assumption of about $1.6 billion in Union Camp debt. Although much larger than the previous several acquisitions, this deal was also targeted in the sense that Union Camp's operations meshed so well with those of International Paper. Two of Union Camp's strengths, uncoated paper and containerboard, were strengths of IP as well. Union Camp's Alling and Cory distribution business was merged into xpedx. The merger also added 1.6 million acres of timberlands to IP's holdings, with most of the new lands adjacent to the previously held ones. Union Camp also held a 68 percent stake in Bush Boake Allen, Inc., a leading producer of flavors and fragrances, and this concern was seen as complementary to IP's Arizona Chemical unit, a product of an early diversification effort dating back to the early 1930s. In the wake of the Union Camp acquisition, IP eliminated more than 3,600 jobs from its workforce and closed a number of unprofitable plants in an effort to eliminate excess capacity.

IP's acquisition spree continued in 2000, with the company picking up Shorewood Packaging Corporation in March for about $640 million in cash plus assumed debt of $280 million and Champion International Corporation in June for about $5 billion in cash and $2.4 billion in IP stock and the assumption of $2.8 billion in debt. Both acquisitions involved third parties. In the case of Shorewood, the company had been fending off a hostile takeover by Chesapeake Corporation before agreeing to be acquired by IP. The addition of Shorewood greatly expanded IP's position in the high end of the consumer packaging sector, making it a leading provider of high-quality printing and paperboard packaging for home entertainment, cosmetics, health and beauty, pharmaceutical, sporting goods, tobacco, and other consumer products.

Champion had agreed to be acquired by UPM-Kymmene Corporation of Finland in February 2000 in a stock-swap deal originally valued at $6.6 billion. UPM's stock had fallen significantly in price, reducing the value of the deal, by April 2000, which is when IP stepped in with its first offer, a combined cash and stock transaction valued at $6.2 billion. UPM responded with an all-cash offer of $70 per share, or $6.8 billion. In May International Paper emerged the winner of a tense takeover battle with a revised offer of $75 in cash and stock, or $7.4 billion.

Champion was a company with 1999 revenues of $5.27 billion and papermaking capacity of 4.79 million tons a year. It ranked as the second largest producer of magazine paper and the sixth largest maker of office paper in North America. Champion (and Shorewood) had distribution operations that were absorbed by xpedx postmerger. The five million acres of U.S. timberlands controlled by Champion greatly increased IP's land holdings. Champion also had key assets outside the United States. Its Weldwood of Canada Limited subsidiary was a manufacturer of pulp, lumber, plywood, and engineered wood products with operations centered in British Columbia and Alberta. Brazil-based Champion Papel e Celulose Ltda. was one of South America's leading makers of office paper and a major producer of magazine paper with a total of 600,000 tons of annual capacity. IP also gained the significant timber holdings in Canada and Brazil controlled by these two companies, and even more importantly it had a major presence on three continents: North America, Europe, and South America. International Paper also gained a new headquarters through the Champion deal as the company moved its head offices from Purchase, New York, to the former headquarters of Champion in Stamford, Connecticut, later in 2000.

MAJOR DIVESTITURE PROGRAM

During 2000 IP also launched a major divestiture program. It was originally aimed at eliminating $3 billion in assets but this figure was increased to $5 billion following the acquisition of Champion. The divestitures were originally slated to be completed by the end of 2001. The program had a number of goals: cutting down the debt incurred from the string of acquisitions; paring the company's operations to three core areas: paper, packaging, and forest products; and reducing capacity in an attempt to break free of the ups and downs of the paper industry cycle. In November 2000 IP sold its interest in Bush Boake Allen for $640 million. During 2001, IP completed a series of divestitures, selling its petroleum and minerals business, 265,000 acres of forestlands in Washington and 800,000 acres in east Texas, Masonite Corporation, Zanders Feinpapiere, a hydroelectric facility in the state of New York, a water company in Texas, and its flexible packaging business. The company also closed down a number of mills and announced plans to lay off about 3,000 workers in the United States, or about 10 percent of the workforce there.

For 2001 IP reported revenues of $26.36 billion, a decline from the previous year's total of $28.18 billion. Thanks to restructuring and other charges of $1.12 billion and losses on the sales of businesses totaling $629 million, the company posted a net loss of $1.27 billion for the year. Despite this volley of red ink, under the continued leadership of Dillon, International Paper had made great strides in its ambitious restructuring program, and it remained the world's largest forest products company while appearing to have transformed itself into a much nimbler, more competitive, and potentially more profitable giant.

In 2002 the company continued its divestiture program, selling its oriented strand board facilities to Nexfor Inc. for $250 million and its decorative products unit to an affiliate of Kohlberg & Co. for approximately $113 million. IP had also hoped to sell its industrial papers business and Arizona Chemical but took these units off the market after failing to corral sufficient offers for them. Late in 2002 the company shut down its Hudson River mill in Corinth, New York, eliminating nearly 300 jobs and 100,000 tons of paper production capacity. Prior to the closure, the Hudson River facility had been the only one of International Paper's original 17 mills to still be owned and operated by the company.

In the midst of the biggest downturn in the forest products industry in half a century, IP in 2002 saw its sales fall 5 percent while posting another net loss of $880 million primarily because of a number of special charges, including an after-tax total of $278 million set aside as a further legal reserve relating to the Masonite class-action settlements and a $1.2 billion charge for goodwill impairment. IP managed a return to modest profitability in 2003 despite the continuation of the historic industry downturn: a net gain of $302 million on sales of $25.18 billion. During the year, the company announced a further workforce reduction of about 5 percent, or 3,000 jobs, as part of a plan to cut costs and boost sales and thereby increase profits by $1.5 billion over a three-year period. In October 2003 Dillon retired as chairman and CEO, having reached the company's mandated retirement age of 65 for its top executive. IP veteran John V. Faraci, who had joined the firm in 1974, was named Dillon's successor, promoted from president.

In 2004 International Paper, under its new leader, launched modernizations of three of its U.S. paper mills located in South Carolina, Maine, and Michigan. The firm also bolstered its packaging business by acquiring Box USA Holdings, Inc., a leading corrugated box maker based in Northbrook, Illinois, in a deal valued at around $400 million. IP also elected to trim its wood products operations by divesting Weldwood of Canada, the former Champion subsidiary. In a deal completed at the end of 2004, Weldwood was sold to West Fraser Timber Co. Ltd. for $1.17 billion. IP recorded an after-tax loss of $711 million on this sale. In another year-end divestment, IP sold 1.1 million acres of forestlands in Maine and New Hampshire to GMO Renewable Resources, LLC, a private forest investment management company, for roughly $250 million.

IP pared its operations further in 2005, selling its fine papers business and its industrial papers business in May and June, respectively. Much more dramatic changes were soon in store, starting with IP's June announcement of its intention to sell its majority stake in Carter Holt Harvey. This move was designed to enable the company to shift its focus in that region of the world to the faster growing Asian market. During the third quarter of 2005 IP sold this stake to Rank Group Investments Limited, a unit of Rank Group plc, for $1.14 billion.

2005 LAUNCH OF BUSINESS TRANSFORMATION

In July 2005 International Paper launched a major transformation of its business. The firm announced a plan to sell a number of additional units to narrow its focus to uncoated paper (the type used in office printers and for printing books) and industrial and consumer packaging, while also retaining its distribution business. In a further aspect of the transformation, IP began a realignment of its U.S. mills within these core areas to reduce higher-cost capacity, slash the operations' overall cost structure, and increase productivity. Four mills were subsequently closed, laying off thousands from the company workforce. The overall plan was originally expected to raise as much as $10 billion in after-tax proceeds and yield annual cost savings of about $400 million. Much of the proceeds was earmarked for debt reduction, but IP also used a portion for stock repurchases, investments in the remaining operations, and targeted acquisitions. In a further streamlining effort, International Paper in mid-2006 moved its corporate headquarters from Stamford to Memphis, Tennessee, where its operational headquarters had been based since 1987.

More than $11 billion was garnered in 2006 and 2007 from the subsequent string of divestments. IP sold the bulk of its U.S. forestlands, approximately 5.6 million acres, in a series of deals that yielded proceeds of $6.6 billion and were said to comprise the nation's largest land sale since the Louisiana Purchase. The firm's U.S. coated paper business was sold to an affiliate of the investment firm Apollo Management L.P. for approximately $1.4 billion, while its Brazilian coated paper unit went to Stora Enso in a $420 million deal. During 2007 IP completed four more significant divestments: 13 sawmills in the southern United States, to West Fraser Timber, for $325 million; its beverage packaging operations, to Carter Holt Harvey, for $500 million;

Arizona Chemical, to Rhone Capital, for $485 million; and five U.S. wood products mills, to Georgia-Pacific Corporation, for $237 million. The Georgia-Pacific deal essentially marked International Paper's exit from the wood products sector.

The 2007 sales wrapped up the divestiture portion of IP's transformation, and by the end of that year the company had managed to slash its long-term debt load to $6.35 billion, down from $13.5 billion. Faraci had guided International Paper into becoming a smaller but more profitable corporation, with the results for 2007 showing net income of $1.17 billion on sales of $21.89 billion. By this time Faraci had begun making additional investments in his company's core businesses, concentrating initially on bolstering the international operations, particularly in emerging markets.

During 2006 IP invested $140 million into a joint venture with China's Shandong Sun Paper Ltd. to produce coated paperboard for packaging applications, such as milk cartons and cigarette boxes. In a complicated swap of assets with the Brazilian firm Votorantim Celulose e Papel S.A., IP traded its pulp mill in the state of Mato Grosso do Sul for a pulp and uncoated paper mill in the state of São Paulo. IP also ventured further into Russia, where since 1999 it had operated a mill near St. Petersburg producing copier paper. In October 2007 the company spent $620 million for a 50 percent stake in Ilim Pulp, Russia's largest forest products concern and the operator of four pulp and paper mills in that nation's European and Siberian regions. The partners in the resulting joint venture agreed to invest $1.5 billion into these mills over the following five years to upgrade equipment, improve productivity, and boost capacity by 40 to 50 percent. The Ilim deal expanded IP's presence not only in Russia but also in China because Ilim was selling more pulp and paper in China than in its home market.

International Paper's improved balance sheet and cash flow also enabled it to pursue a significant deal to expand its North American packaging business. In March 2008 the company entered into an agreement to buy Weyerhaeuser Company's containerboard, packaging, and recycling operations for $6 billion. Included in the transaction were nine containerboard mills, 76 box plants in the United States and Mexico, ten specialty packaging plants, four kraft bag and sack facilities, and 19 recycling plants. The acquisition, which was approved by the U.S. Department of Justice in May 2008 and expected to close in that year's third quarter, promised to double the size of the industrial packaging unit of IP. That unit had generated sales of $5.25 billion in 2007, or about one-quarter of the firm's overall total. Because it was set up as a purchase of assets, International Paper expected to realize a tax benefit of around $1.4 billion from the deal, reducing the purchase price to $4.6 billion.

While some analysts praised the deal as a bolstering of a key core unit, others raised concerns about the added debt IP needed to take on to complete the purchase. In the meantime, IP's profits for the first quarter of 2008 were down sharply because of rising raw material and energy costs. Also clouding the company's future at this time were the shaky state of the economy and the potential for additional low-cost competition from such emerging markets as Brazil and China.

Kim M. Magon
Updated, David E. Salamie

PRINCIPAL SUBSIDIARIES

IP Pacific Timberlands, Inc.; Shorewood Packaging Corporation; The Branigar Organization, Inc.; International Paper do Brasil Ltda. (Brazil); International Paper Investments (France) S.A.S.; International Paper Investments (Luxembourg) Sarl; IP Singapore Holding Pte. Ltd.; OAO Svetogorsk (Russia); International Paper Group (UK) Limited.

PRINCIPAL OPERATING UNITS

Printing Papers; Industrial Packaging; Consumer Packaging; Distribution (xpedx); Forest Products.

PRINCIPAL COMPETITORS

Stora Enso Oyj; Georgia-Pacific Corporation; Weyerhaeuser Company; UPM-Kymmene Corporation; Smurfit Kappa Group; Svenska Cellulosa Aktiebolaget SCA; Jefferson Smurfit Corporation; Smurfit-Stone Container Corporation; MeadWestvaco Corporation; Nippon Paper Group, Inc.; Oji Paper Co., Ltd.

FURTHER READING

Bush, Jason, "Now It's Really International Paper," *Business Week,* December 17, 2007, pp. 63+.

Byrnes, Nanette, and Michael Arndt, "John Dillon's High-Risk Paper Chase," *Business Week,* January 22, 2001, pp. 58, 60.

Carlton, Jim, "International Paper Thinks Inside Box, Buys Package Rival," *Wall Street Journal,* March 17, 2008, pp. B1, B2.

Deutsch, Claudia H., "International Paper Offers $6.2 Billion for Champion," *New York Times,* April 26, 2000, p. C2.

Flaum, David, "IP Buys Weyerhaeuser Division," *Memphis (Tenn.) Commercial Appeal,* March 18, 2008, p. C1.

Generations of Pride: A Centennial History of International Paper, Purchase, N.Y.: International Paper Co., 1998, 209 p.

Heinrich, Thomas, "Product Diversification in the U.S. Pulp and Paper Industry: The Case of International Paper, 1898–1941," *Business History Review,* Autumn 2001, pp. 467–505.

Hessel, Evan, "Paper Cuts: John Faraci Has Whacked Billions from International Paper's U.S. Operations; Can He Succeed Abroad?" *Forbes,* June 18, 2007, pp. 118, 123–24.

International Paper Company After Fifty Years, 1898–1948, New York: International Paper Company, 1948, 110 p.

"IP Aims to Chop Debt, Boost Investments," *Pulp and Paper,* August 2006, pp. 6–8.

"IP Buys Zellerbach Merchant from Mead," *Pulp and Paper,* August 1998, pp. 15, 17.

"IP Deal with VCP Will Grow Company's Uncoated Papers Presence in Brazil," *Pulp and Paper,* November 2006, p. 6.

"IP Inks Second Major Global Move with Ilim Pulp Venture in Russia," *Pulp and Paper,* December 2006, p. 6.

"IP Planning to Take a $500-Million Charge," *Pulp and Paper,* April 1996, p. 23.

"IP's Transformation Plan Nearly Complete," *Pulp and Paper,* February 2007, pp. 9–10.

"IP to Further 'Transform' Itself by Selling, Spinning Off, or Closing Capacity," *Pulp and Paper,* September 2005, p. 6.

Killian, Linda, "A Walk in the Woods," *Forbes,* September 30, 1991, pp. 78–79.

Kimelman, John, "Slash and Build: While Restructuring at Home, International Paper Is Investing Overseas," *Financial World,* April 13, 1993, p. 28.

Loeffelholz, Suzanne, "Putting It on Paper," *Financial World,* July 25, 1989, p. 26.

Maki, Amos, "Two More Sales Continue IP 'Transformation,'" *Memphis (Tenn.) Commercial Appeal,* December 20, 2006, p. C1.

Mies, Will, "IP Pushing into Global Markets," *Pulp and Paper,* December 2006, pp. 23–26.

Osborne, Richard, "An Unpretentious Giant: John Georges Has Quietly Built International Paper into a Diversified $15 Billion Corporation," *Industry Week,* June 19, 1995, pp. 73–76.

Palmer, Jay, "No Lumbering Giant: International Paper Races to New Peaks in Earnings," *Barron's,* January 2, 1989, p. 13.

Perez, Evan, "International Paper to Jettison Assets in Restructuring Effort," *Wall Street Journal,* July 20, 2005, p. B2.

"Pulp Friction," *Economist,* November 11, 1995, p. 66.

Scinta, Christopher, "International Paper Sets Sales of Timberland for $6.1 Billion," *Wall Street Journal,* April 5, 2006, p. B2.

Shaw, Monica, "Big and Better," *Pulp and Paper,* April 2004, pp. 24–29.

Starkman, Dean, "International Paper Has Its Work Cut Out for It," *Wall Street Journal,* May 15, 2000, p. A4.

———, "Shorewood Agrees to International Paper Acquisition," *Wall Street Journal,* February 17, 2000, p. C15.

"Stora Buys IP's Coated Business in Brazil," *Pulp and Paper,* October 2006, pp. 11–12.

Sullivan, Allanna, "International Paper Shutting Plants to Cut Supply," *Wall Street Journal,* October 19, 2000, p. A4.

Tan, Kopin, "Putting It Down on Paper," *Barron's,* August 7, 2006, pp. 15–16.

"'Transformation' Sales Could Hit $9.1 Billion As IP Sells Coated Unit," *Pulp and Paper,* July 2006, p. 6.

Welsh, Jonathan, "International Paper Settles Suit on Masonite Siding," *Wall Street Journal,* July 15, 1997, p. B3.

———, "International Paper Unveils Revamping and Posts Better-Than-Expected Results," *Wall Street Journal,* July 9, 1997, p. A4.

———, "IP Agrees to Acquire Union Camp Corp.," *Wall Street Journal,* November 25, 1998, p. A3.

Willoughby, Jack, "Paper Tiger: A Dow Dowager No More, International Paper Works Itself into Fighting Trim," *Barron's,* July 9, 2001, pp. 21–22.

Young, Jim, "International Paper Co.: Worldwide Expansions Gear for Economic Recovery," *Pulp and Paper,* May 1994, pp. 32, 35.

Jones Knowledge Group, Inc.

9697 East Mineral Avenue
Centennial, Colorado 80112
U.S.A.
Telephone: (303) 792-3111
Toll Free: (800) 350-6914
Fax: (303) 784-8579
Web site: http://www.jonesknowledge.com

Wholly Owned Subsidiary of Jones International, Ltd.
Founded: 1987 as Mind Extension University
Employees: 330
Sales: $26.3 million (2007)
NAICS: 611310 Colleges, Universities, and Professional Schools; 611710 Education Support Services

■ ■ ■

Jones Knowledge Group, Inc., is a global leader in online education and related education enhancing products. Jones Knowledge organizations include Jones International University, an accredited, online university offering bachelor's, master's, and doctoral degrees. Undergraduate majors include bachelor of arts degrees in business communication and business administration and a bachelor of science in information technology. Master's degrees are offered in business administration, business communications, and education. Doctorates are offered in business administration and education. In order to accommodate a worldwide student base, courses are offered in English and Spanish.

Related products include Jones e-global library, which provides research materials in a virtual environment. College Connection provides students with a school directory. In the area of professional development, Jones International Academy and Jones/NCTI offers custom or standard courses that address the training needs of specific industries, such as telecommunications, healthcare, consumer electronics, and customer service call centers. Courses apply to certification or degree credit at Jones International University. Jones Knowledge Integration Group provides consulting for implementation of online educational systems. The Knowledge Store offers products created by the Jones family of companies, such as prepared online curriculum.

DISTANCE LEARNING ON CABLE TELEVISION

The forerunner to the online education system formed by Glenn R. Jones, Mind Extension University, originated at Jones Intercable, Inc., one of the largest cable television management companies worldwide. Started in 1967, the company expanded when Jones pioneered the use of public limited partnerships to raise equity capital. Applied to the acquisition of cable television systems during the 1970s and 1980s, the partnerships enabled Jones to develop Jones Intercable into a billion-dollar company.

During the late 1980s, after becoming one of the wealthiest people in the United States, Jones began to pursue philanthropic interests. The inspiration for education courses broadcast over cable television occurred during a trip to the Vietnam War Memorial in Washington, D.C. In a contemplative moment, Jones

COMPANY PERSPECTIVES

Since 1987, Jones Knowledge, Inc., has been a leading innovator in the development and delivery of end-to-end learning solutions. Glenn R. Jones, our founder and CEO, has devoted much of his life to his passionately held belief that education should be available to everyone, everywhere.

felt a desire to facilitate communication and human understanding for a more peaceful world through education. Also, he had a longstanding interest in promoting equal educational opportunity for all. Hence, Jones established the Mind Extension University (MEU) in 1987, offering college credit courses through televised classroom instruction. Jones Intercable subsidized the institution.

To legitimize the coursework offered at MEU, Jones partnered with Colorado State University in Fort Collins, where correspondence and audio-taped courses were available for college credit. Jones hired faculty at the university to design the television cable courses, and faculty member Don Sutton became the managing director of MEU. Sutton established another 18 college and university partners to assist in developing a curriculum. Such broad participation enabled MEU to offer courses in English, mathematics, science, foreign languages, arts, humanities, linguistics, health, political science, anthropology, history, business, and social services, as well as teacher recertification. The curriculum included undergraduate and graduate level classes. In addition to watching the courses over participating cable networks, credit-earning students conferred with professors by telephone.

Within three years, MEU had 5,000 students enrolled and taking courses. An M.B.A. course, established with the same criteria as on-campus coursework, quickly filled its maximum participation of 120 enrolled students. In 1991, the University of Maryland offered a bachelor of arts completion curriculum and a master's in education. MEU attracted subscribers interested in watching the courses, even without the college credit. A Graduate Equivalency Degree (GED) preparation course and non-credit self-improvement courses, such as Let's Learn Japanese, were offered for free. Before the transition of Internet education, MEU taught 30,000 students through 30 colleges and universities.

TRANSITION TO THE ONLINE UNIVERSITY

As personal computers became more widespread, Jones Knowledge began to transfer the distance-learning curriculum to software for computer-based education. Moreover, Jones saw the emergent Internet technology as a natural evolution of distance learning in the information age, and software courseware provided the foundation for offering college classes over the Internet. E-education software provided the tools to manage online courses for faculty and administration. Tests, grade books, and chat rooms eased faculty teaching. The software included administrative tools for admissions, registration, and financial aid offices as well as a course catalog. College Connection software provided students with an online directory of the schools' facilities, online registration and enrollment, class add and drop forms, and computer assistance.

E-education software supported the technical basis for the establishment of Jones International University (JIU) in 1993. JIU was the first virtual institution of higher education to exist solely online. Initially, JIU offered courses toward certification, but not to a degree. In 1995, JIU began to offer courses toward a master of arts degree in business communication. Then, in 1999, JIU became the first online educational institution to earn accreditation, granted by the North Central Association of Colleges and Schools (NCA), a member of the Higher Learning Commission responsible for authorizing degree granting schools. Accreditation allowed JIU to confer undergraduate and master's degrees. In March 2000 the NCA approved the M.B.A. degree at JIU, and classes began in April.

Other educational curricula gained NCA approval during the early 2000s. In 2001, JIU obtained NCA approval to offer a master of education in e-Learning and in 2002 the bachelor of business administration (BBA) program. The BBA program, the first complete online degree in business, offered specializations in marketing, finance, entrepreneurship, global business, human resources, and e-commerce. In 2003, JIU began to offer specialized education curriculum within its degree programs, such as the M.B.A. in finance. Three specialized bachelor of arts in business communication and master of arts in business communication degrees were offered.

While development continued toward the company becoming an online credit-granting, educational institution, Knowledge TV continued to offer for-credit courses via cable. When Comcast bought Jones Intercable in 1999, Jones International retained Knowledge TV.

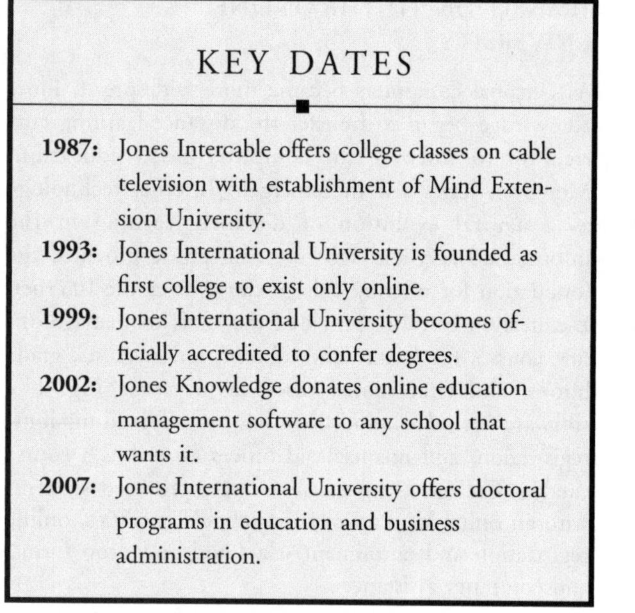

KEY DATES

1987: Jones Intercable offers college classes on cable television with establishment of Mind Extension University.

1993: Jones International University is founded as first college to exist only online.

1999: Jones International University becomes officially accredited to confer degrees.

2002: Jones Knowledge donates online education management software to any school that wants it.

2007: Jones International University offers doctoral programs in education and business administration.

OFFERING E-EDUCATION SOFTWARE TO EDUCATIONAL INSTITUTIONS

Jones Knowledge branded its course management software e-education and sold licenses to schools, colleges, and universities. By 1999, 18 colleges and universities used Jones Knowledge software, including nine institutions in the state of Colorado. Software-based courses included online chat sessions with professors and other students, as well as individual attention from professors through e-mail.

E-education attracted program administrators because of the flexible adaptation for individual professors. Jones offered the e-education program for colleges' direct management of course content. E-education offered more than 700 courses derived from the 18 colleges and universities that began the MEU classes. Customer service and technical support for both the institutions and the students ensured the software would be successfully applied to distance learning.

In November 2002, Jones Knowledge decided to donate its e-education, course management software to educational institutions worldwide. The source code, referred to as Jones Standard, became available on CD-ROM. The donation allowed schools to host their own courses, saving as much as $50,000 annually on software license fees. More than 200 educational institutions requested the software. Jones continued to offer its advanced version, which contained third-party technology that could not be offered for free. In general, Jones Knowledge abandoned the software business altogether in order to concentrate on other aspects of online education. In February 2004, Jones offered free technical support as well.

NEW TOOLS ENHANCE ONLINE LEARNING EXPERIENCE

In August 2000, Jones International announced that it had allocated $60 million toward the advancement of online education at Jones Knowledge. The funds supported the curriculum development at JIU as well as the development of technologies to enhance online education.

In December, Jones Knowledge introduced its e-global library, a virtual research library intended for online students. A staff of 30 librarians sorted through information from the Internet to find resources considered appropriate to academic and professional quality research. They organized content to make it useful for teachers and students at JIU and other online education settings. The E-global library included research guides on 65 topics covering all academic disciplines, as well as tutorials on how to conduct research, how to use the Internet, and how to use libraries. Student information included financial aid, career development, and other education-related concerns. In addition to providing educational support at JIU, the e-product was sold to corporations and other educational institutions through an annual subscription. The delivery platform allowed licensees to custom organize content to the specific needs of their online learning environment or business usage.

Jones e-global library developed a line of "Life and Leisure" research guides, designed to be used by librarians and the general public. Topics covered included gardening, volunteerism, genealogy, travel, food and cooking, health, death and dying, pregnancy and childbirth, consumer law, small business law, bankruptcy law, and personal finance. Similar guides being developed included arts and crafts, collecting, childcare and child safety, homeschooling and homework assistance, marriage and divorce, event planning, pets, and retirement planning.

Jones Knowledge tools, such as the e-education software, e-global library, JIU, and Jones Knowledge Store were applied to professional development in the knowledge-based business. In June 2001, RNL Design and Scott Rice of OfficeScapes applied these tools to create a prototype of the office of the future. Known as the work(place) 2010 Learning Center, the prototype showed how online learning could be integrated into the office environment for continuing education and professional training. Such a center would provide online degree and certification programs through JIU and a virtual library for research through the e-global library.

Product development involved expansion of Jones Knowledge's curriculum for teacher education. Through an agreement with Apex Learning, Jones Knowledge gained access to 25 courses for professional development for K–12 teachers. To be delivered through the Jones e-education program, the online courses included classroom management, student assessment, and advanced placement.

Jones Knowledge introduced the "Quick Start" program in June 2002. Designed for students, teachers, administrators, and curriculum developers of K–12 education, Quick Start provided an easy-to-use tool for implementing online educational courses at low cost. Quick Start offered more than 60 accredited courses in language arts, mathematics, science, foreign languages, social studies, computer science, and other education-related courses. Courses for educators included classroom management, teaching methods, leadership, and professional certification. These were provided by the Florida Virtual School, Apex Learning, Sagemont Virtual School, and JIU.

In June 2002, subsidiary Jones International Academy introduced the Jones Technical Training Series, a safety training course designed for telecommunications technicians, equipment installers, and subcontractors. Jones Knowledge found that the cable training program from MEU was still relevant to the current market. The company remastered the work for digital transmittal over the Internet or on CD-ROM.

JIU EVOLVES AS AN ACCREDITED UNIVERSITY

JIU continued to develop as an accredited university by providing new educational opportunities. In July 2003, JIU introduced three new master of education program majors, in elementary curriculum, assessment, and instruction, in secondary curriculum, assessment, and instruction, and in educational leadership and administration. In 2005, the Colorado State Board of Education authorized JIU's Teacher Licensure and Principal and Administrator Licensure degrees as valid to meet the state's requirements for content for K–12 education. Also, in the state of Colorado, JIU signed an agreement to accept coursework from the Colorado Community College system for matriculation to JIU degree programs.

For the first time, federal student aid became available to JIU students in the United States in 2004. The U.S. Secretary of Education waived the "50 percent rule," which required at least half of a student's education take place at a physical campus location in order for students to obtain federal aid. Widespread use of the Internet changed attitudes toward distance education. JIU was one of 29 institutions to become eligible for low-interest student loans through the Stafford Loan or Direct PLUS Loan programs. JIU students received tuition assistance through the Federal Pell Grant program, which did not have to be repaid.

The American Academy of Financial Management recognized JIU's M.B.A. in finance as qualifying graduates for its Master Financial Profession (MFP) Designation and board certification. The Project Management Institute (PMI), which certifies professional project managers, accepted JIU as a Registered Educational Provider (REP). PMI provided project management certification to graduates of qualified M.B.A. programs.

Jones Knowledge sought to bring students the full experience of a university education. Toward that end, the company launched the "Cyberdome" where students gathered in a virtual arena for graduation ceremonies. The first commencement ceremony for the class of 2005–06 took place in the spring of 2006. The cyberdome also provided a virtual space for special events, such as entertainment or education productions. Also completing the university experience was the opportunity to earn a Ph.D. In May 2007, JIU began to offer its first doctoral programs, in education for K–12 education leadership and in business administration.

In cooperation with Mid-continent Research for Education and Learning (McREL), Jones Knowledge provided the popular Classroom Instruction That Works (CITW) through its delivery platform at JIU. The four-week course included interactive activities, self-reflective journaling, and discussion boards for interaction among teachers. Teachers who took the course received three graduate level credits for a master of education degree at JIU. Developed by McREL, CITW was one of the best-selling teacher development courses worldwide, and online access would further expand participation in CITW. Indeed, in October 2007, more than 90 teachers in the Arctic Circle accessed CITW via JIU. Located at North Slope, the northernmost community in the United States, with a population of 4,200, the teachers taught a student body that was over 90 percent Inupiaq Eskimo.

EXPANDED GLOBAL FOCUS

Always oriented to providing education on a global basis, Jones Knowledge sought opportunities for cross-cultural collaboration. In September 2005, JIU announced that it would be offering a joint M.B.A. degree with the Universidad Centroamericana (UCA) in Managua, Nicaragua. UCA provided the foundation courses, and JIU provided the curriculum to complete an M.B.A. with an emphasis in e-commerce. Students in

Nicaragua would otherwise have to leave the country to gain a specialized education. JIU and UCA planned to offer a joint master's degree in Spanish taught by bilingual faculty at JIU. UCA students benefited from the collaboration with access to the e-global library.

In October 2007, Jones Knowledge introduced a new course, Understanding Islam: An Introduction, in October 2007. To design the class, the company hired Islamic scholar Akbar Ahmed, former High Commissioner of Pakistan to Great Britain and Khaldun Chair of Islamic Studies at American University in Washington, D.C. The online course included modules on history, religious beliefs, women, and terrorism, as well as communication skills for interacting with Islamic people. Hence, the class furthered Glenn Jones's original vision for distance education, to facilitate communication and human understanding.

Mary Tradii

PRINCIPAL SUBSIDIARIES

College Connection; Jones e-education; Jones e-global library; Jones International Academy; Jones International University; Jones Knowledge Integration Group; Jones/NCTI; Knowledge Store.

PRINCIPAL COMPETITORS

Blackboard, Inc.; eCollege.com; PRC, LLC; WebCT, Inc.

FURTHER READING

Cantwell, Rebecca, "Learning Unlimited Cable Visionary Glenn Jones Helps Expand Educational Horizons with Virtual University," *Rocky Mountain News,* April 12, 1999, p. 1B.

Felix, Kathie, "Free Online Course Delivery Platform," *Multimedia Schools,* November–December 2002, p. 13.

Forgrieve, Janet, "A Degree of Freedom," *Rocky Mountain News,* January 14, 2002, p. 1B.

"Glenn Jones," *Denver Business Journal,* December 7, 1990, p. 20.

"Jones Debuts Safety Education Course," *CED,* June 2002, p. 91.

"Jones Intercable Inc.," *Denver Business Journal,* March 12, 1990, p. 28.

"Jones International Becomes First Accredited Virtual University," *EDP Weekly's IT Monitor,* March 15, 1999, p. 3.

"Jones Knowledge, McREL Bring Online Learning to Teachers in the Arctic," *US Newswire,* October 1, 2007.

"Jones Pushes Ahead on Cable Training," *CED,* August 2003, p. 12.

"Jones Releases 'Life and Leisure' Guides," *Computers in Libraries,* April 2002, p. 52.

"Migrate Online," *District Administration,* September 2002, p. 78.

Neff, Todd, "Jones Knowledge Leaves Learning Software Market, First Giving Away Its 'Jones Standard' to Schools, Colleges," *Rocky Mountain News,* December 16, 2002, p. 3B.

"Service Learning Online," *District Administration,* July 2002, p. 48.

Sullivan, Tom, "Dreams Turn to Reality: Glenn Jones Turns All of America into a Classroom Through Cable," *Cable Television Business,* December 1, 1990, p. 26.

Thompson, Rachel W., "Mind Extension University Clears 9M Sub Mark," *Multichannel News,* September 17, 1990, p. 4.

"'Understanding Islam' Course Creates Awareness and Improved Relations," *US Newswire,* October 11, 2007.

Kolbenschmidt Pierburg AG

Karl-Schmidt-Strasse
Neckarsulm, D-74172
Germany
Telephone: (+49 7132) 33 3140
Fax: (+49 7132) 33 3150
Web site: http://www.kspg-ag.com

Wholly Owned Subsidiary of Rheinmetall AG
Incorporated: 1998
Employees: 11,900
Sales: EUR 2.25 billion ($3.5 billion) (2007)
NAICS: 336311 Carburetor, Piston, Piston Ring, and Valve Manufacturing; 331521 Aluminum Die-Castings; 333618 Other Engine Equipment Manufacturing; 336399 All Other Motor Vehicle Parts Manufacturing; 423120 Motor Vehicle Supplies and New Parts Merchant Wholesalers

■ ■ ■

Kolbenschmidt Pierburg AG is one of the world's largest suppliers of automotive components, producing pistons, aluminum-based engine blocks, pumps, air supply systems, actuators, solenoids and emissions control components, and bearings, as well as aftermarket components. The Neckarsulm, Germany-based company is organized into six independently operating divisions. Through KS Kolbenschmidt, the company is one of the world's leading piston manufacturers, with plants in Germany, France, the United States, the Czech Republic, Brazil, and Japan, as well as joint ventures in China and Japan. Pierburg focuses on air management and emissions control systems and components, with factories in Germany, the United States, Spain, India, and the Czech Republic. The Pierburg Pump Technology division is a global leader in automotive pumps, including oil, vacuum, and coolant pumps, with factories in Germany, the United Kingdom, France, Mexico, Italy, and Brazil. KS Aluminium-Technologie is one of Europe's leading producers of aluminum-based engine blocks. This division operates primarily in Germany and through a joint venture in China. KS Gleitlager oversees Kolbenschmidt Pierburg's production of plain bearings, as well as Permaglide bearings, continuous castings and large bearings, with facilities in Germany, the United States, and Brazil. The last division is Motor Service, which produces aftermarket engine repair components from sites in Germany, France, Brazil, China, and Turkey. Kolbenschmidt Pierburg is itself a 100 percent subsidiary of Rheinmetall AG, and serves as the company's Automotive products division, alongside its Defense division. In 2007, Kolbenschmidt Pierburg generated total revenues of nearly EUR 2.25 billion ($3.5 billion), representing 56 percent of Rheinmetall's total turnover.

BUILDING A GERMAN PISTON MAKER IN 1910

Kolbenschmidt Pierburg was created through the merger of two of Germany's oldest and largest automotive components manufacturers in 1998. Both companies originated in the early years of the 20th century, and played crucial roles in the development of the German automotive industry. While Kolbenschmidt had come under the control of the now-defunct Metallge-

COMPANY PERSPECTIVES

We are a global automotive supplier with exceptional powertrain expertise. We provide innovative solutions. We are committed to performance, quality and the environment. Our independent business units strive for leadership positions in their worldwide markets. We welcome change and achieve success through our highly skilled, dedicated and empowered associates. We work as a team—with open communication and mutual respect. We willingly accept our social responsibilities as good corporate citizens. Customer satisfaction and trust is the foundation of our sustained success.

schellschaft conglomerate, Pierburg was taken over by another major German conglomerate, Rheinmetall. The two component suppliers' merger was carried out following the collapse of Metallgesellschaft and Rheinmetall's takeover of Kolbenschmidt.

That company had been founded by Karl Schmidt, son of Christian Schmidt, who had founded German industrial giant NSU Motorenwerke in the late 19th century. The younger Schmidt started his own career at NSU, where he completed his apprenticeship at its site in Neckarsulm, before working at the Austin automotive company in Birmingham, England. Returning to Germany, Schmidt eventually became NSU's chief engineer. In 1910, however, he left the company to found his own business, Deutschen Ölfeuerungswerke, based in Heilbronn. In the meantime, Schmidt had patented a new smelting technique, using lightweight scrap metals. Schmidt initially produced furnaces. By 1917, the company had adapted the smelting technology for the production of piston blanks. The company moved to a new and larger works in Neckarsulm, and then grew into a major supplier of pistons to German automotive industry.

Deutschen Ölfeuerungswerke, later known as Kolbenschmidt (Kolben is the German for piston), became part of Metallgesellschaft AG, after the Frankfurt-based metals giant acquired majority control of the company in 1927. By 1934, Kolbenschmidt had discontinued its furnace production, and focused its operations entirely on piston manufacturing. The group's location in Neckarsulm, close to the Audi automotive works, enabled it to emerge as a leading piston producer in Germany, and Europe, before World War II.

During the war, Metallgesellschaft had been taken over by the Nazis and converted its production to support the German war effort. Allied bombing raids more or less destroyed Kolbenschmidt's operations in 1945. Following the war, Metallgesellschaft underwent a process of "de-nazification," then focused its efforts on rebuilding its heavily damaged empire. Kolbenschmidt too rebuilt its operations into the 1950s. The company once again emerged as a major piston supplier for Germany's automotive industry. The company also expanded its production to include a wide range of pistons, for industrial vehicles and machinery, aerospace engines, and even lawnmowers. In this way, Kolbenschmidt grew into one of the largest and most diversified piston companies in Germany and Europe.

INTERNATIONAL GROWTH IN THE POSTWAR ERA

By the late 1960s Kolbenschmidt had also begun to target a more global automotive market. In 1968, the company set up its first operations in South America, in São Paulo, Brazil. The group's subsidiary there, KS Pistoles Ltda., initially began producing ring-belt pistons. That company later expanded, and moved to larger production facilities in Nova Odessa. The new plant became Kolbenschmidt's largest, producing a full range of pistons not only for the Brazilian market, but for all of South America. The Brazilian subsidiary also became a major supplier of pistons for the export market beyond South America, especially to the North American, Australian, and European markets.

Kolbenschmidt targeted the North American market as well, and set up its first subsidiary there in 1978, in Marinette, Wisconsin. That operation grew steadily through the 1980s. The shift in the U.S. automotive industry, which saw the country's automakers turn increasingly toward third-party manufacturers for its components and systems, provided new room for the U.S. unit's growth, and in 1990 the company teamed up with a Japanese partner, Unisia Jecs Corp., to form the piston production joint venture Karl Schmidt Unisia (KUS). That company then built a new factory in Marinette, which then became one of the world's largest and most diversified piston plants. By then, Kolbenschmidt had also extended its operations into France, where in 1989 it bought Société Mosellane Mécanique (subsequently renamed Société Mosellane de Pistons) in Thionville, near the German border, from Renault.

Kolbenschmidt's fortunes soured, however, amid the crash of the European automotive sector and the economic recession of the early 1990s. Encouraged by its highly diversified parent Metallgesellschaft, Kolben-

KEY DATES

1909: Steel trading company Stahlhandelsunternehmen Gebr. Pierburg oHG is founded in Berlin.
1910: Karl Schmidt founds Deutschen Ölfeuerungswerke in Heilbronn.
1917: Company launches production of pistons, becomes Kolbenschmidt and is acquired by Metallgesellschaft.
1928: Pierburg launches production of carburetors.
1968: Kolbenschmidt opens production facility in Brazil.
1978: Kolbenschmidt enters United States.
1986: Pierburg is acquired by Rheinmetall.
1998: Kolbenschmidt is acquired by Rheinmetall and merges with Pierburg.
2003: Company acquires pistons business from Microtechno (Mazda) of Japan.
2008: Kolbenschmidt opens new 60,000-square-foot engineering and design center in Michigan.

schmidt attempted its own diversification, quickly buying a number of new operations, including airbag systems, steering wheels, plain bearings, aluminum castings, and pumps. However, the diversification drive came at a heavy cost and, saddled with debt, Kolbenschmidt slipped into losses into the middle of the decade.

While Kolbenschmidt's business was nonetheless considered ultimately sound, parent Metallgesellschaft was not. Following an unfortunate move into hedge funds, resulting in a loss of $1 billion in a single year, and itself saddled with debt, Metallgesellschaft launched a major restructuring in the mid-1990s. As part of that effort, Metallgesellschaft began selling a number of its holdings, including its 47 percent stake in Kolbenschmidt. After a protracted bidding process, including a blocked bid by the U.K.'s T&N, which controlled the number one piston maker in Germany, Kolbenschmidt was taken over by Rheinmetall. The new parent, with a 74 percent stake in Kolbenschmidt, then merged the company with its own automotive component subsidiary, Pierburg.

PIERBURG CARBURETOR LEADER IN 1909

The merger with Pierburg created one of Germany's and the world's leading diversified automotive components manufacturers. Pierburg's own origins reached back to 1909 when Bernhard Pierburg, with brothers Heinrich-Hermann and Wilhelm, founded the steel trading firm Stahlhandelsunternehmen Gebr. Pierburg oHG. Based in Wilmersdorf, near Berlin, the company became a major supplier of steel to the country's fledgling automotive and aeronautics industries.

The Pierburg company reincorporated as a limited liability company in 1923, in part to survive the period of hyperinflation. A major turning point for the company came in 1926, when it took over the bankrupt Arthur Haendler & Cie. That company had earlier acquired the license to produce Solex carburetors, a revolutionary French design introduced in the previous decade. Bernhard Pierburg sent his son Alfred to France to study carburetor design. Returning to Berlin, the younger Pierburg oversaw construction of the company's first factory and launched production in 1928. When Pierburg's trading business foundered during the Great Depression, the company decided to split off its healthy carburetor operation into a separate company, called Deutsche Vergaser Gesellschaft mbH (DVG), created in 1931. Pierburg itself never recovered, and by 1938 had been liquidated.

In the meantime, DVG became the leader of the German carburetor market, and even before the outbreak of World War II supplied carburetors to nearly all of the country's automakers. From 1935, DVG also began manufacturing fuel pumps as well. The company then became a major contributor to the German military buildup and to the Nazi war effort, producing both carburetors and fuel pumps for the military. Alfred Pierburg himself received the title of Wehrwirtschaftsführer, becoming responsible for overseeing arms production in France. In this capacity, Pierburg was at least able to protect the Solex company.

Most of DVG was destroyed in the Allied bombing raids. Alfred Pierburg was banned from rejoining the company by the Allied authorities. Yet Alfred Pierburg's protection of Solex led the French company to transfer the license to Pierburg's own name. This permitted him to launch a new company, Deutsche Vergaser Gesellschaft mbH & Co. KG, in Neuss, near Düsseldorf. Over the next decade, Pierburg regained control of the group's former Berlin works, adding production of Pallas and Zenith carburetors, as well as the company's own Paita design, introduced in 1956. Once again, Pierburg grew into Germany's leading manufacturer of carburetors, and one of its largest fuel pump suppliers by the early 1960s.

Pierburg emerged as a leading innovator in carburetor technology after the 1959 launch of the PICT carburetor, the first to feature an automatic starter. In

1972, the company introduced another successful design, the 4A1 double register downdraft carburetor, used in BMW, Audi, and Rolls-Royce models. The company later teamed up with rival Bosch to introduce the Ecotronic carburetor, the first to be controlled by microprocessor.

Along the way, Pierburg had steadily diversified its production, and by the late 1970s produced fuel and vacuum pumps, solenoid valves, throttles, as well as engine castings, among other products. This diversification played a part in Pierburg's survival as its mechanical carburetors, which continued to account for 60 percent of its revenues, increasingly became obsolete following the introduction of the Bosch-dominated electronic fuel-injection system. Following Alfred Pierburg's death in 1975, however, Bosch had succeeded in gaining a 20 percent stake in Pierburg, including a seat on its board of directors, presenting an obstacle for the company's development of its own electronic fuel-injection technology.

Leading the company by that time was Alfred's son Jürgen Pierburg, who led a major restructuring of the group's operations which, in 1978, became unified under the Pierburg AG name. Pierburg attempted to join forces with Siemens for its entry into electronic fuel technology. That move was blocked by Bosch, however. By 1986, Pierburg instead agreed to be acquired by German industrial giant Rheinmetall AG. Following that acquisition, Pierburg abandoned its now outmoded carburetor business altogether in 1990.

GERMAN AUTO COMPONENTS LEADER IN THE NEW CENTURY

The merger between Pierburg and Kolbenschmidt not only created one of Germany's leading automotive components groups, but one with a global reach. Despite the difficult economic period, both companies had continued to expand during the 1990s. Pierburg added the DC Motor factory, in Hartha, in the former East Germany in 1990. By 1995, the company had added operations in the United States, establishing production facilities in South Carolina. Kolbenschmidt, meantime, had entered the Czech Republic, buying one of that country's leading piston manufacturers.

Kolbenschmidt Pierburg's U.S. operations took a major step forward in 1999, when it bought Zollner Pistons. That company had long been one of the country's leading pistons makers. The Zollner company was then merged into the KUS joint venture, which took on the name Karl Schmidt Unisia Inc. Kolbenschmidt later increased its share of its U.S. pistons business to 100 percent.

In the meantime, the company continued to seek new markets. The company entered China in 1997, establishing Kolbenschmidt Shanghai Pistons Co. in a joint venture with Shanghai Piston Works. The company added a second joint venture there, in 2001, with Shanghai Automotive Industry Corporation. The move into China came in part due to pressure from U.S. automakers seeking to source a greater percentage of their vehicle components from China's low-cost production centers.

Kolbenschmidt Pierburg next targeted the Japanese market, buying the pistons production unit of that country's Microtechno Corp., part of the Mazda automobile group. Next, the company boosted its Czech presence in 2004. Two years later, Kolbenschmidt Pierburg entered Mexico, acquiring Pistones Moresa in Celay.

In 2007, Rheinmetall moved to take full control of Kolbenschmidt Pierburg, buying out the group's minority shareholders and delisting the company from the Frankfurt stock exchange. Following the takeover, Kolbenschmidt Pierburg was then restructured as the parent company to Rheinmetall's Automotive Division. The new division was also Rheinmetall's largest component, generating nearly EUR 2.25 billion in revenues, worth 56 percent of the group's total turnover.

Kolbenschmidt Pierburg continued to seek new growth outlets, using its aluminum technologies to develop new lighter weight and more fuel efficient component designs in order to woo automakers. The company also targeted new markets, particularly fast-growing India, where it established a new subsidiary in 2006. The company continued to build its presence in the U.S. market, still the world's largest, as well, setting up a new 60,000-square-foot engineering and design center in Michigan. Combining nearly a century at the heart of the world's automotive industry, Kolbenschmidt Pierburg looked forward to the road ahead.

M. L. Cohen

PRINCIPAL SUBSIDIARIES

Karl Schmidt Unisia Inc. (U.S.A.); Kolbenschmidt K.K. (Japan); Kolbenschmidt Pierburg AG; KS Aluminium-Technologie AG; KS Gleitlager GmbH; KS Kolbenschmidt Czech Republic a.s.; KS Kolbenschmidt France S.A.S.; KS Kolbenschmidt GmbH; KS Pistões Ltda. (Brazil); MS Motor Service International GmbH; Pierburg GmbH; Pierburg Inc. (U.S.A.); Pierburg S.A. (Spain); Pierburg S.à.r.l., (France); Pierburg S.p.A. (Italy).

PRINCIPAL COMPETITORS

Faurecia S.A.; Mahle GmbH; TRW Automotive GmbH; Bosch Corporation; Keihin Corp.; Sauer-Danfoss Inc.; SFS Holding AG; Siemens VDO Automotive S.A.S.; Walbro Corporation.

FURTHER READING

Bongard, Arjen, and Edmund Chew, "Aluminum Drives Kolbenschmidt's Growth," *Automotive News Europe,* May 15, 2006, p. 18.

Brezonick, Mike, "Many Paths to Growth for Piston Maker," *Diesel Progress North American Edition,* June 1999, p. 114.

Chew, Edmund, "Carmakers Push Suppliers into China," *Automotive News Europe,* June 30, 2003, p. 1.

Floerecke, Klaus-Dieter, "Japanese Acquisition to Drive Kolbenschmidt's Asian Ambitions," *Automotive News Europe,* March 24, 2003, p. 4.

"German Supplier Finally Gets NA Tech Center," *Ward's Auto World,* May 1, 2008.

Munford, Christopher, "MG Hastens Effort to Sell Kolbenschmidt Unit," *American Metal Worker,* February 1, 1994, p. 9.

Ostle, Dorothee, "German Parts Maker Has Lofty Acquisition Goals," *Automotive News,* January 8, 2001, p. 18.

"Pierburg Accelerates Internationalization Efforts," *AsiaPulse News,* October 31, 2006.

"Pierburg Merges with Kolbenschmidt," *Ward's Auto World,* March 1998, p. 127.

"Raw Materials Drag Down Kolbenschmidt Pierburg," *just-auto.com,* November 7, 2006.

Schweinsberg, Christie, "KP Upbeat After Massive Restructuring," *Ward's Auto World,* May 1, 2005.

Snavely, Brent, "German Suppliers Adapt to Expand in US," *Automotive News,* April 24, 2006, p. 22B.

Kreisler Manufacturing Corporation

180 Van Riper Avenue
Elmwood Park, New Jersey 07407
U.S.A.
Telephone: (201) 791-0700
Fax: (201) 791-8015
Web site: http://www.kreisler-ind.com

Public Company
Incorporated: 1914 as The Stern-Kreisler Jewelry Company
Employees: 200
Sales: $23.85 million (2007)
Stock Exchanges: NASDAQ
Ticker Symbol: KRSL
NAICS: 336412 Aircraft Engine and Engine Parts Manufacturing; 336419 Other Guided Missile and Space Vehicle Parts and Auxiliary Equipment Manufacturing

■ ■ ■

Kreisler Manufacturing Corporation is a manufacturer of precision metal parts for the aerospace, marine, and energy industries. The company has capabilities for a number of manufacturing processes including bending, welding, brazing, heat treating, forming, and machining. It also provides engineering and testing services. About 90 percent of the company's production goes toward components for aircraft engines.

Originally a jewelry manufacturer, in World War II the company began making tubing and manifolds for aircraft engines as well as parts for cathode-ray tubes. It later added a leather watchband operation in Florida but the 1979 closure of its jewelry operations left the company with a single operating subsidiary, Kreisler Industrial Corporation. In 2005 the company added a Polish subsidiary, Kreisler Polska, Sp. z o.o., as a source of machined parts.

ORIGINS IN JEWELRY

Kreisler Manufacturing Corporation's history begins in 1914, when Marcus Stern and Jacques Kreisler launched The Stern-Kreisler Jewelry Company in New York City. In 1933, after the jewelry business floundered in the Great Depression, Jacques Kreisler launched a watchband business with Stern's son Tobias. Most of the production was slated for use in Bulova watches, but the company also supplied jewelry retailers.

In 1940 Kreisler moved to New Jersey due to the high cost of doing business in the Big Apple. Employment peaked at 1,000 workers during World War II as the company made tubing for aircraft engines and other strategically important components. The postwar years produced an immediate demand for the finer things in life, such as jewelry and cufflinks, among a generation of men deprived by years of military austerity.

The company ran into stiff competition from Speidel in the watchband business. In the early 1950s the company switched production from jewelry to cigarette lighters under the name Colibri by Kreisler. It also moved a leather watchband operation from Brooklyn to St. Petersburg, Florida, and established its Crest Leather Manufacturing unit. It added pens to its product line a few years later. Another subsidiary, Kre-

COMPANY PERSPECTIVES

Kreisler supports its customers in all phases of product development from conception to design, manufacturing and inspection. The company does this by offering the manufacturing experience, engineering know-how and certified quality systems that provide each Kreisler customer with a reliable and cost efficient product. Beginning with the aircraft engine industry a half century ago, Kreisler earned a first rate reputation for engineering and manufacturing the best tubular fabrications while using the most advanced technologies available. Today the company is active in other industries using advanced materials and processing methods that meet the needs and cost parameters of many power generation programs.

isler Industrial Corporation, was formed in New Jersey in July 1956.

PUBLIC IN 1968

Revenues were $18 million by the late 1960s. In 1968 Kreisler had an initial public offering that raised $6 million. A Delaware corporation named Kreisler Manufacturing Corporation was formed in December of that year as a successor to entities set up earlier in New Jersey (1940) and New York (1930).

Edward L. Stern, who had worked at the company since 1948, became company president in 1972 upon the death of his father, Tobias. Although a public company, Kreisler was thinly traded and remained very much family-controlled. As the *St. Petersburg Times* noted, Stern wore many hats, including chairman, chief executive officer, chief financial officer, secretary, and director. A short time later, Stern relocated the company's headquarters to St. Petersburg, Florida.

In 1979 the jewelry and wristband operations were shuttered in face of inexpensive competition from abroad. This left the company with a single subsidiary, Kreisler Industrial, dedicated to aerospace components. Edward Stern still wanted to live in St. Petersburg, and the headquarters remained there with just a few administrative personnel.

The Reagan years produced ample demand for its aerospace components. In the early 1990s the company was posting annual revenues of about $5.7 million and pulling in income of $1 million. Kreisler began the 1990s with annual revenues of $8 million, but it would be a decade of transformation. Pain is often a harbinger of the need for change, and that was evident in Kreisler's case, as it consistently posted annual losses throughout the first half of the 1990s.

The end of the Cold War and a mid-1990s glut in aircraft production hit the company hard and revealed inefficiencies in its production methods. In addition, most of its business was with Pratt & Whitney (owned by United Technologies Corp.); when Pratt & Whitney decided to take production of tubular products in-house in 1993, Kreisler was devastated. Annual sales fell to just $4 million in 1994.

A SUCCESSFUL TURNAROUND

In order to survive, the company adopted modern approaches to operations management such as Toyota-style lean manufacturing and Dr. Eliyahu M. Goldratt's Theory of Constraints. It lowered inventory levels, invested in new equipment, rationalized plant layout, and fired almost everyone.

All the remaining managers were trained in Theory of Constraints methodology by the AGI-Goldratt Institute. They found that the output of the whole plant was being limited by the time it took their machinists to locate and assemble their tools and materials. Pregrouping these reduced setup time and made the whole process flow more smoothly.

In all, Kreisler managed to cut production times by two-thirds. It also cut administrative costs by 30 percent. One of the biggest improvements was using newfound in-house capacity as a hedge against unreliable suppliers, who had been the chief cause of late deliveries. On-time deliveries rose from 65 percent to an industry-leading 97 percent, according to AGI-Goldratt.

The retooled company succeeded in winning back Pratt & Whitney. It also supplied most of the other major jet engine manufacturers, including Rolls-Royce PLC, General Electric Co., and AlliedSignal Inc. However, it continued to look for ways to diversify, such as supplying components for electric generators and even producing lighting for the movie industry.

The turnaround effort won praise from observers such as *Forbes* as the company's share price peaked at $56 in 1997. Sales for the year rose more than a third to $10.8 million while profits grew to a healthy $1.8 million. Revenues reached $13 million in 1998. Kreisler had about 100 employees in New Jersey and another two or three at the tiny headquarters in St. Petersburg, Florida.

The results attracted a $25.5 million buyout offer from the John Wood Group, an aerospace contractor

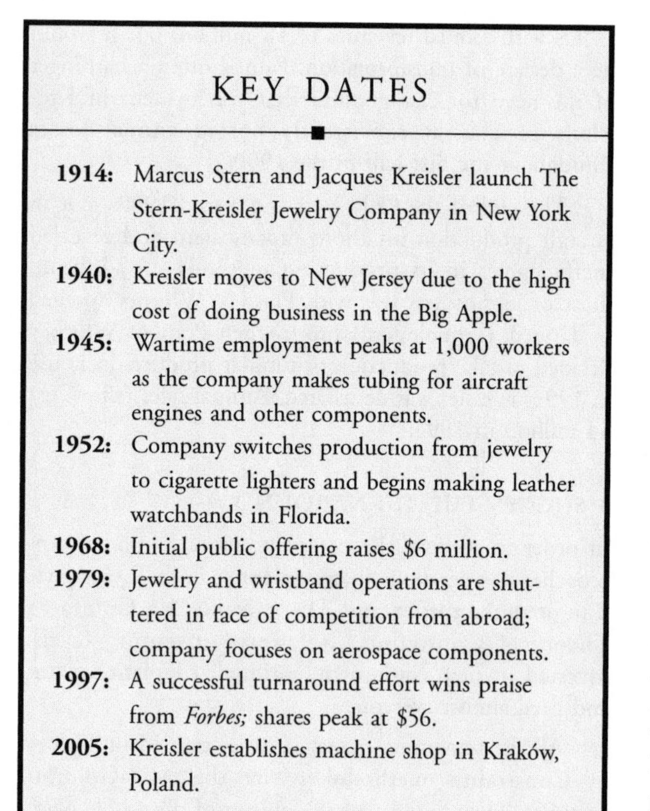

KEY DATES

1914: Marcus Stern and Jacques Kreisler launch The Stern-Kreisler Jewelry Company in New York City.

1940: Kreisler moves to New Jersey due to the high cost of doing business in the Big Apple.

1945: Wartime employment peaks at 1,000 workers as the company makes tubing for aircraft engines and other components.

1952: Company switches production from jewelry to cigarette lighters and begins making leather watchbands in Florida.

1968: Initial public offering raises $6 million.

1979: Jewelry and wristband operations are shuttered in face of competition from abroad; company focuses on aerospace components.

1997: A successful turnaround effort wins praise from *Forbes;* shares peak at $56.

2005: Kreisler establishes machine shop in Kraków, Poland.

based in Scotland. However, Wood balked upon discovering environmental contamination (from the solvent tetrachloroethylene or PCE) at Kreisler's Elmwood Park, New Jersey, manufacturing site. Although Kreisler maintained its insurance would cover at least some of the estimated $1.5 million cleanup cost, the parties failed to agree on a price after that. Kreisler officials later bemoaned the Garden State's environmental standards as an impediment to running a manufacturing business, along with high corporate taxes.

CHANGING TIMES

Difficulties in the global airline industry after the September 11, 2001, terrorist attacks on the United Sates were felt acutely at Kreisler. Sales plummeted nearly a third in 2003, to $12.5 million. The next year revenues slipped only 2 percent as military-oriented engine programs began to make up the difference.

Edward L. Stern died in June 2004 after leading the company through three decades. After his death his sons Edward A. (Ned) and Michael became chief executive officer and chief financial officer, respectively, while sharing the title of president. Wallace N. Kelly, an aviation industry consultant with an engineering background, was named chairman. In October of that year, the company closed the Florida office and settled all administrative functions at its plant in Elmwood Park, New Jersey.

A recovery was just around the corner. Revenues were $14.4 million in fiscal 2005, producing income of $169,590. By 2006 the company had sales of $19.7 million and more than 120 employees. Officials forecast a favorable decade to come for the aviation industry. Kreisler was consistently making *Aviation Week & Space Technology*'s list of best-performing smaller aerospace companies, while in 2008 *Fortune Small Business* pronounced Kreisler one of the 100 fastest-growing small public companies in the United States. Revenues rose 21 percent in 2007 to nearly $25 million, while net income climbed 69 percent to about $2 million.

Kreisler for a long time had enjoyed a diverse workforce. Bergen County's *Record* reported the company's New Jersey operation included 20 nationalities among just 120 employees (most of them union members). The company had in the 1950s been known for hiring disabled workers for the intricate tasks involved in assembling mesh wristbands. The business was starting to become more global in nature. In 2005 Kreisler established a machine shop in Kraków, Poland, primarily as a supplier for the U.S. plant.

Frederick C. Ingram

PRINCIPAL SUBSIDIARIES

Kreisler Industrial Corporation; Kreisler Polska, Sp. z o.o. (Poland).

PRINCIPAL COMPETITORS

Argo-Tech Corporation; Magellan Aerospace Corporation; Pacific Aerospace & Electronics, Inc.; Triumph Group, Inc.

FURTHER READING

AGI-Goldratt Institute, "Kreisler Manufacturing—Success with TOC," New Haven, Conn., c. 1998, http://www.goldratt.com/kreisler.htm.

Boyte, Ken, "Changing Course: Kreisler Manufacturing Has Survived by Adapting," *Tampa Bay Business Journal,* February 19, 1999, p. 4.

Carew, Dorothy, "Men Decide to Dress Up After Drab GI Garb," *Waterloo (Iowa) Daily Courier,* March 18, 1946, p. 7.

Demarrais, Kevin G., "Fortune Smiling on Kreisler; Aerospace Firm Bounces Back Again," *Record* (Bergen County, N.J.), June 18, 2006, p. B7.

"Dull Duds Disappear; Drab Dans Don Dress Duds, Develop into Dapper Dandies," *Chester Times,* July 30, 1947, p. 17.

Goldratt, Eliyahu M., and Jeff Cox, *The Goal: A Process of Continuing Improvement,* Great Barrington, Mass.: North River Press, 2004.

Green, William, "Fasten Your Seat Belts," *Forbes,* December 15, 1997, pp. 47+.

Harrington, Jeff, "Chemical Problems May Hurt Sale Talks," *St. Petersburg Times,* October 1, 1999, p. 6E.

Huntley, Helen, "Death Could Spell End of Kreisler in Bay Area," *St. Petersburg Times,* June 18, 2004, p. 1D.

"Kreisler Manufactures Successful Turnaround," *Tampa Tribune,* May 17, 1998, p. 33.

"Kreisler Shareholders in the Driver's Seat," *Tampa Tribune,* May 17, 1998, p. 13.

"Military Holds Up Kreisler's Revenue," *Tampa Bay Business Journal,* September 28, 2004.

"Stern Family Members Fill Key Roles at Kreisler Manufacturing," *Weekly of Business Aviation,* July 5, 2004, p. 6.

Torbenson, Eric, "Kreisler Manufacturing Corp.: Soaring with New Strategy," *St. Petersburg Times,* June 7, 1998, p. 4H.

Trigaux, Robert, "Kreisler Takes $25.5-Million Buyout Offer," *St. Petersburg Times,* July 2, 1999, p. 1E.

"Work Performance of Handicapped Elates Plant Head," *El Paso Herald-Post,* December 3, 1954.

Madison Dearborn Partners, LLC

3 First National Plaza, Suite 3800
Chicago, Illinois 60602
U.S.A.
Telephone: (312) 895-1000
Fax: (312) 895-1001
Web site: http://www.mdcp.com

Private Company
Incorporated: 1992
Employees: 4,158
Sales: $566.0 million (2007 est.)
NAICS: 523999 Miscellaneous Financial Investment Activities

■ ■ ■

Madison Dearborn Partners, LLC, is a private equity investment firm focused on management buyouts of other companies. Madison Dearborn concentrates on six broadly defined industries: basic industries, which includes natural resources, energy, and building products; consumer, a collection of retail, restaurant, and consumer products companies; financial services; communications; real estate; and healthcare. The firm raises money from institutional investors to build a portfolio of investments. Between 1992 and 2006, the firm raised nearly $14 billion, which it invested in companies such as Ruth's Chris Steak House, PayPal, and Nextel Communications. Among the company's largest transactions have been those for Boise Cascade ($3.7 billion), Jefferson Smurfit Group ($3.5 billion), Cinemark USA Inc. ($1.5 billion), and Yankee Candle ($1.4 billion).

FROM THE HALLS OF FIRST CHICAGO

Madison Dearborn, a specialist in management-led buyouts, came into existence in a manner similar to the type of deals it completed. The private equity firm sprang from the offices of First Chicago Corporation, a bank that later became known as Bank One Corporation. In 1980, the bank formed its own equity investment arm, a sideline business named First Chicago Venture Capital (FCVC) that served as an incubator for the future Madison Dearborn. There, in the offices of FCVC, the foundation for Madison Dearborn was set, establishing the predecessor to the private equity firm that would excite industry observers, their attention drawn to the firm because of its penchant for completing massive transactions. FCVC also served as the proving ground for the future principals of Madison Dearborn. The migration of two or three executives from FCVC to Madison Dearborn would have been worthy of note, but the connection between the two firms was far thicker than a thread. Madison Dearborn, essentially, was FCVC operating under a different corporate banner.

FCVC operated between 1980 and 1992, a 12-year existence that ended when 14 FCVC executives left First Chicago Corporation and formed their own firm. They settled into new offices at the intersection of Madison

COMPANY PERSPECTIVES

All investments made by MDP have as a central element the partnering of MDP with a strong management team. We seek experienced managers who have a solid understanding of their businesses and track records of building shareholder value. As evidence of our commitment to management, each MDP principal makes a significant personal investment in every transaction MDP undertakes. MDP has demonstrated over its more than two decades of investing experience that the combination of a talented and motivated management team with the capital and resources of MDP is a powerful formula for success.

and Dearborn in downtown Chicago, a location that served as the inspiration, however, straightforward, for the name of the new firm. Of the 14 executives who left FCVC to become principals of Madison Dearborn, ten would be present to cut the cake during the firm's 15th anniversary celebrations. James N. Perry Jr., David F. Mosher, Benjamin D. Chereskin, Nicholas W. Alexos, Samuel M. Mencoff, and Paul J. Finnegan composed the group that guided Madison Dearborn during its prolific first 15 years. These men were led by their former president, the executive *Chicago Crain's Business* trumpeted as "the dean of Chicago's private-equity community" in its December 15, 2003, edition.

John A. Canning Jr. headed the group that made the small alteration in their morning commute to the offices of Madison Dearborn. A graduate of Denison University and Duke University, where he earned his law degree, Canning spent nearly a quarter-century working for First Chicago, eventually rising to the posts of executive vice-president of First National Bank of Chicago and president of FCVC. At Madison Dearborn, he spearheaded efforts to raise the first of five funds that would be invested during the firm's first 15 years of operation, a $550 million fund organized as Madison Dearborn Capital Partners, L.P., which the firm would use to execute its strategy. Madison Dearborn searched for management buyouts, looking to gain control of private or publicly held, middle-market companies or divisions of larger corporations. The firm focused on industries such as communications, healthcare, financial services, as well as segments composing what it defined as basic industries: natural resources; chemicals; energy; automotive; paper, packaging, and forest products; food; automotive; building products; and metals and mining.

SECOND FUND: 1996

Madison Dearborn launched its second fund, a $925 million war chest christened Madison Dearborn Capital Partners II, L.P., in 1996. Within two years of the fund's creation, 85 percent of the money had been funneled into a variety of companies both large and small. At that point in the fund's employment, five years after Madison Dearborn had gained independence from First Chicago, the first meaningful assessment of the investment firm's performance could be gauged. Canning's group had recorded annualized returns of nearly 40 percent, assembling a $1.5 billion portfolio that ranged from catalog retailing companies to Carrols Restaurant Group, Inc., the Syracuse, New York-based company that ranked as Burger King Corporation's largest franchisee in the world with 335 locations.

Madison Dearborn's impressive start encouraged Canning to amplify his efforts substantially. In 1998, he began gearing for the firm's third fund, Madison Dearborn Capital Partners III, L.P., a $2.2 billion undertaking that rivaled in size the largest U.S. buyout funds and entirely surpassed any previous attempts by a Chicago-based fund, whose efforts had not eclipsed the $1 billion mark. Canning's confidence was fueled by the performance of his firm and the decided increase in investor enthusiasm for private holdings. Madison Dearborn, only a few years out on its own, was perceived as savvy and aggressive, creating ideal conditions for the firm to leap forward with its investment activities.

SURVIVING TURBULENT TIMES

The timing of the second fund's launch, which occurred at the beginning of 1999, put Madison Dearborn on a collision course with the spectacularly bad collapse of the technology sector as the new millennium began. Madison Dearborn directed its investments toward communications concerns during the debacle and paid the price for imprudent investments. A $15 million investment in Focal Communications Corp., for instance, which skyrocketed to a value of $1.4 billion on paper, became essentially worthless a short time later. As James Perry, a Madison Dearborn managing director, told *Telephony* in a June 4, 2001, interview, "Valuations got way out of whack a year and a half ago when everyone thought that within six months you could go public even if you hadn't proven anything in terms of a busi-

KEY DATES

1980: First Chicago Corporation forms an equity investment subsidiary, First Chicago Venture Capital, the predecessor to Madison Dearborn.
1992: A group of First Chicago Venture Capital principals led by John A. Canning Jr. forms Madison Dearborn.
1996: After raising $925 million, Madison Dearborn launches its second fund.
1999: The firm's third fund totals $2.2 billion.
2000: Madison Dearborn closes its fourth fund after raising $4 billion.
2002: The firm invests $3.5 billion in Jefferson Smurfit Group.
2004: For $3.7 billion, Madison Dearborn gains control of paper, packaging, and timberland assets from Boise Cascade Corp.
2006: The firm's fifth fund totals $6.5 billion.
2008: Madison Dearborn posts its largest gain ever, $1.2 billion from the sale of Intelsat Ltd.

ness model." He added, "We were all seduced into thinking you had something with value way above what you paid for it."

ACQUISITION OF JEFFERSON SMURFIT GROUP IN 2002

Despite making some regrettable errors with its third fund, Madison Dearborn overall delivered enviable results with its investments. Arguably its smartest move during the period was a $200 million investment in 1999 for a 42 percent stake in Packaging Corp. of America, an Illinois-based producer of paper products. Over the life of the investment, the firm made approximately $950 million from the deal, enjoying tremendous success in an industry that became a focal point of its investments. After raising $4 billion in 2000 to launch its fourth fund, Madison Dearborn Capital Partners IV, L.P., the firm completed the largest deal in its history, entrenching its position in the paper and packaging business. In 2002, Madison Dearborn invested $3.5 billion in a leveraged buyout of Ireland-based Jefferson Smurfit Group, the world's largest manufacturer of containerboard, corrugated containers, and other paper-based packaging products. The firm's involvement in the industry began with the 1993 acquisitions of two pulp mills from Procter & Gamble Co. By the time it purchased Jefferson Smurfit Group, Madison Dearborn ranked as the industry's second biggest acquirer, trailing only International Paper Co.

A decade after it gained independence from First Chicago, Madison Dearborn ranked as the sixth largest buyout firm in the country. The firm had its hands in paper and packaging and in telecommunications, having invested in more than 40 such companies, Nextel Communications, Omnipoint Corporation, and PowerFone Holding representing just a few of the communications companies in Madison Dearborn's portfolio. Aside from the firm's heavy involvement in paper and telecommunications, its portfolio contained a diverse collection of other companies, ranging from Hines Horticulture, the largest commercial nursery operation in the country, to Ruth's Chris Steakhouse, a chain of fine-dining restaurants, to Family Christian Stores, the largest Christian-related products retailer in the country.

The $3.5 billion investment in Jefferson Smurfit Group set the tone for Madison Dearborn's investment activity in the years to follow. The firm completed a series of massive transactions that attracted the attention of the global investment community. The scale of the firm's investments appeared to surprise even Canning, who remarked, "I never thought we'd get this big, or stay together as long as we have," in a December 15, 2003, interview with *Crain's Chicago Business.* Madison Dearborn's aggressive campaign continued in March 2004, when the firm signed an agreement to acquire a majority stake in Cinemark, Inc. The Plano, Texas-based company operated a chain of movie theaters, operating 3,142 screens in the United States and South America. Madison Dearborn invested $1.5 billion in the company, greatly strengthening the consumer segment of its portfolio.

BOISE CASCADE IN 2004

The investment in Cinemark was merely a prelude to the firm's major investment of 2004. In July, the firm completed the largest investment in its history, acquiring the paper, forest products, and timberland assets belonging to Idaho-based Boise Cascade. The transaction was part of Boise Cascade's efforts to separate its distribution businesses, which became part of Boise Office Solutions, from its manufacturing operations, which became part of Boise Cascade Holdings, LLC, a new company formed by Madison Dearborn. The firm paid $3.7 billion to acquire the assets, adding substantially to its formidable presence in the paper, packaging, and wood products industry.

Having returned to a familiar investment area with the Boise Cascade deal, Madison Dearborn next moved into uncharted territory. In October 2005, the firm agreed to acquire three power plants for $975 million. The plants supplied nearly one-fourth of the power-generating capacity in New York City.

FIFTH FUND IN 2006

By 2006, Madison Dearborn had raised capital for its fifth fund, Madison Dearborn Capital Partners V, L.P., attracting eager support from institutional investors such as endowments, pension plans, and financial services companies. The pattern of huge increases in the size of the firm's funds continued, giving Madison Dearborn principals $6.5 billion to invest. The firm's financial wizards did not wait long before completing their first major deal. In October 2006, Madison Dearborn reached an agreement to acquire The Yankee Candle Company, Inc., for $1.4 billion. Based in South Deerfield, Massachusetts, Yankee Candle made and sold scented candles and related items through a network of more than 17,000 outlets, including a chain of 400 company-owned stores.

Celebrations were justified when Madison Dearborn ended its 15th year of business in 2007. The firm stood among the elite in the global investment community, having posted an enviable performance record. The majority of the 22 principals who directed the firm's investments had worked alongside one another for decades, each possessing expertise in at least one of the six areas of Madison Dearborn's investment activity. They celebrated a memorable start to their next 15 years working together when the firm collected a massive profit at the start of 2008. The firm, in January 2005, had made an initial investment in Intelsat Ltd. The Pembroke, Bermuda-based company ranked as the world's largest commercial satellite operator, providing fixed satellite services to media broadcasters, telecommunications companies, corporations, and Internet service providers through its network of in-orbit satellites. At the beginning of 2008, Intelsat was sold to a group of private equity companies for $5 billion, a transaction that gave Madison Dearborn approximately $1.2 billion. "It's the largest gain ever," Canning noted in a February 5, 2008, interview with the *Chicago Tribune.*

More deals were guaranteed to take place as Madison Dearborn prepared for the future. The Canning-led group demonstrated a disciplined approach to investing combined with a willingness to enter into mammoth transactions. The years ahead were expected to see the firm at the forefront of investment activity in the United States and abroad, its prominence virtually assured because of the enormous financial resources at its disposal. In 2008, Madison Dearborn was in the midst of raising money for its sixth and largest fund, a $10 billion supply of capital that Canning and his team were waiting eagerly to put to use.

Jeffrey L. Covell

PRINCIPAL SUBSIDIARIES

Madison Dearborn Capital Partners, L.P.; Madison Dearborn Partners II, L.P.; Madison Dearborn Partners III, L.P.; Madison Dearborn Partners IV, L.P.; Madison Dearborn Partners V, L.P.

PRINCIPAL COMPETITORS

Apollo Advisors, L.P.; Bain Capital, LLC; Thomas H. Lee Partners L.P.

FURTHER READING

Bates, Patricia, "Madison Dearborn Owns Stake in Family Christian," *Billboard,* April 3, 1999, p. 67.

Berg, Natasha, "Madison Agrees Terms with Jefferson Smurfit," *Acquisitions Monthly,* July 2002, p. 51.

"Biggest Euro LBO Ever," *Investment Dealers' Digest,* June 24, 2002.

DiOrio, Carl, "Deal's on the Mark: Madison Inks $1.5 Billion Deal for Exhib Chain," *Daily Variety,* March 15, 2004, p. 9.

"Jim Perry; Madison Dearborn Partners," *Telephony,* June 4, 2001, p. 182.

Johnson, Jim, "Bid for Jefferson Smurfit Causes Ripple Effect in U.S.," *Waste News,* June 24, 2002, p. 6.

Lewis, Diane E., "Illinois Company to Pay $1.4 Billion for Yankee Candle Co.," *Boston Globe,* October 26, 2006.

"Madison Dearborn Buys JSG," *Official Board Markets,* June 22, 2002, p. 1.

Miller, James P., "Madison Dearborn Comes Out on Topps," *Chicago Tribune,* September 20, 2007.

Ryan, Kate, "Madison Dearborn Makes Power Play," *Crain's Chicago Business,* October 17, 2005, p. 3.

Strahler, Steven R., "After the Gold Rush," *Crain's Chicago Business,* December 15, 2003, p. 13.

———, "Firm's $2-Bil. Buyout Fund Sets Record: Investor Interest Fattens Madison Dearborn Kitty," *Crain's Chicago Business,* November 23, 1998, p. 1.

———, "Seeing Gold on the Silver Screen," *Crain's Chicago Business,* May 3, 2004, p. 4.

———, "Street Talk: Management Changes Afoot Down at Madison Dearborn," *Crain's Chicago Business,* November 17, 2003, p. 42.

Tita, Bob, "Big Payoffs for Madison in Boise IPO," *Crain's Chicago Business,* May 9, 2005, p. 4.

———, "Madison Dearborn's Paper Gain," *Crain's Chicago Business,* August 9, 2004, p. 4.

"US Investor Group Is Smurfit Bidder," *Print Week,* May 10, 2002, p. 8.

Yerak, Becky, "Madison Dearborn Partners Posts Its Biggest Investment Gain Ever," *Chicago Tribune,* February 5, 2008.

Make-A-Wish Foundation of America

3550 North Central Avenue, Suite 300
Phoenix, Arizona 85012
U.S.A.
Telephone: (602) 279-9474
Toll Free: (800) 722-9474
Fax: (602) 279-0855
Web site: http://www.wish.org

Private Company
Incorporated: 1983
Employees: 35
Operating Revenues: $182.9 million (2006)
NAICS: 813219 Other Grantmaking and Giving Services

■ ■ ■

Make-A-Wish Foundation of America is a charitable organization that grants wishes to children suffering from life-threatening medical conditions. Make-A-Wish serves as the national body overseeing 67 local and regional chapters throughout the United States and in Guam and Puerto Rico. Its sister organization, Make-A-Wish Foundation International, promotes the growth of affiliated Make-A-Wish organizations worldwide. Make-A-Wish grants wishes to ailing children older than two-and-a-half and younger than 18 at the time of the child's referral, which must include a certification of medical eligibility from the child's physician. The organization raises money through donations from individuals, corporate sponsorships, planned gifts, and grants. It does not raise funds by soliciting door-to-door or by telephone. It does not receive federal, state, or local funding. Make-A-Wish spends 76 percent of the money it raises on granting wishes. The organization grants a wish an average of every 40 minutes.

THE INSPIRATION: CHRISTOPHER JAMES GREICIUS

Fittingly for an organization that relied largely on grass-roots support, Make-A-Wish did not begin as a formally organized national body. Instead, its roots sprang from the ad hoc efforts of family and friends focused on the plight of one child, a single cause that served as the inspiration for the formation of a national foundation. Make-A-Wish owed its existence to the compassion of a small group of Phoenix, Arizona, residents and how they put a smile on a dying boy's face.

In 1980, seven-year-old Christopher James Greicius was being treated for leukemia. The prognosis was bleak, offering scant hope of the boy fulfilling his dream to one day become a police officer. His mother, Linda Bergendahl-Pauling, and friends of the family could only hope to ease Chris's suffering by making sure his last days were as enjoyable as possible. A friend of the family, U.S. Customs Officer Tommy Austin, knew one way to lift Chris's spirits: give him a ride in a police helicopter. Austin promised Chris he could arrange for a flight over downtown Phoenix, an offer that led to the creation of Make-A-Wish.

What originally started as a ride in a helicopter quickly developed into a much grander plan for Chris, as friends and those who heard of the child's dream to become a police officer banded together and created a

COMPANY PERSPECTIVES

Since 1980, the Make-A-Wish Foundation has given hope, strength and joy to children with life-threatening medical conditions. From our humble beginnings with one boy's wish to be a police officer, we've evolved into an organization that grants a child's wish in the U.S. every 40 minutes.

series of memorable experiences for the boy. Austin used his contacts at the Arizona Department of Public Safety (DPS) to help bring his plans to fruition, asking a DPS officer he knew for the use of a department helicopter. Word of Chris's illness quickly spread within DPS, giving birth to a group of DPS personnel committed to the cause of making Chris's wish come true.

On April 29, 1980, the plan was put into action. Chris's day started with a tour of Phoenix in a helicopter, which ended its flight at DPS headquarters. There, three police cruisers and a motorcycle officer, Frank Shankwitz, greeted Chris and escorted him to a meeting with DPS command staff. At the meeting, Chris was sworn in as the first honorary DPS patrolman in state history.

On May 1, Chris received a custom-tailored DPS uniform, which he wore while he took a proficiency test on his battery-powered motorcycle. After passing the test, Chris earned his motorcycle "wings," which he was given the following day when his illness forced him back into the hospital. His room was arranged with the mementos of his experience: his uniform was hung in the window, his motorcycle helmet and trooper hat were placed on top of his dresser so he could see them. Chris died the following day.

A TRIBUTE TURNS INTO A FOUNDATION

The homage to Chris Greicius continued after his death. The DPS dispatched two officers, Shankwitz, and Scott Stahl, to Kewanee, Illinois, to take part in Chris's funeral procession. On the flight back to Arizona, Shankwitz and Stahl reflected on their experience and became convinced the suffering of other stricken children and their loved ones could be eased by making wishes come true. Shankwitz and Stahl approached Chris's mother, Linda Bergendahl-Pauling, about their idea and the trio presented the plan to all those who had made Chris's dream as close to reality as possible. The response led to the formation of the Chris Greicius Make-A-Wish Memorial, the precursor to the Make-A-Wish Foundation of America.

Initially, the Chris Greicius Make-A-Wish Memorial confined its work to the Phoenix area. Its first donation came from a grocery store manager, who contributed $15 to the cause of granting wishes to severely ill children. In November 1980, five months after Chris's death, the organization received its tax-exempt status as a nonprofit entity from the Internal Revenue Service, a designation that made contributions tax-deductible. Various media outlets in Arizona began covering the formation of the foundation and the story of Chris's wish, which brought in a steady stream of donations. By March 1981, the Chris Greicius Make-A-Wish Memorial had raised more than $2,000, enough to grant its first wish dedicated to the memory of Chris Greicius.

FIRST OFFICIAL WISH IN 1981

Like Chris, Frank "Bopsy" Salazar was a seven-year-old diagnosed with leukemia. Instead of dreaming to become a police officer, Frank wanted to be a firefighter. The foundation sent its first "wish-granting" team into action, enlisting the support of the Phoenix Fire Department (PFD), which presented Frank with a full uniform, including equipment and a helmet. Frank became a member of Engine 9's ladder truck, sounded the vehicle's horn, operated its 75-pound hose, and at the end of the day earned his firefighter's badge, becoming the city's first honorary firefighter.

Media coverage of the event aroused the empathy of others, adding unplanned events to Frank's wish. Pilots of a hot-air balloon donated their craft, taking Frank on a flight over Phoenix. Most significantly, The Walt Disney Company learned of the special events planned for Frank and offered a private tour of Disneyland, meals, and gifts to the child, marking the beginning of a relationship between Disney and Make-A-Wish that would endure into the 21st century. After his trip to Disneyland, Frank returned to the hospital, fell asleep, and was awakened by a knock on his window. Using the ladder on their truck parked below, five PFD firefighters entered Frank's room, capping a perfect day for the child. Hours later, Frank Salazar died.

INCORPORATION IN 1983

By 1982, one year after granting its first official wish, the foundation had granted eight wishes to children in the Phoenix area. The organization's efforts attracted the attention of *NBC Magazine,* a national new program, which featured Make-A-Wish, giving it invaluable

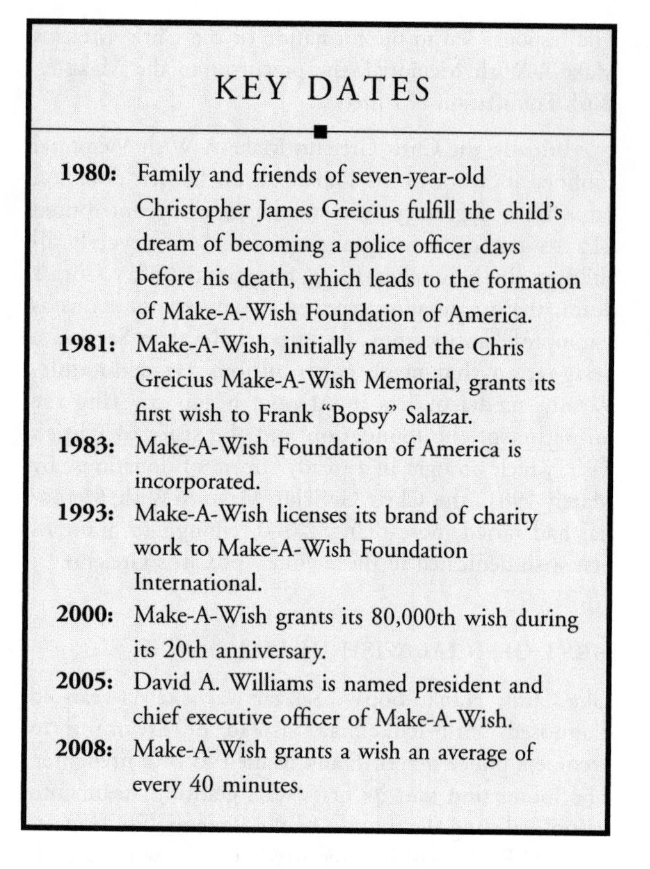

KEY DATES

1980: Family and friends of seven-year-old Christopher James Greicius fulfill the child's dream of becoming a police officer days before his death, which leads to the formation of Make-A-Wish Foundation of America.

1981: Make-A-Wish, initially named the Chris Greicius Make-A-Wish Memorial, grants its first wish to Frank "Bopsy" Salazar.

1983: Make-A-Wish Foundation of America is incorporated.

1993: Make-A-Wish licenses its brand of charity work to Make-A-Wish Foundation International.

2000: Make-A-Wish grants its 80,000th wish during its 20th anniversary.

2005: David A. Williams is named president and chief executive officer of Make-A-Wish.

2008: Make-A-Wish grants a wish an average of every 40 minutes.

exposure that soon led to its expansion outside Phoenix. Local chapters were formed, staffed primarily by volunteers who raised money and formed wish teams to grant wishes within their state or region. By May 1983, when the Make-A-Wish Foundation of America was incorporated, there were six official chapters in operation. The year also marked the exportation of the concept when Nigel Brown and Robb Lucy formed Make-A-Wish Foundation of Canada, a chapter that granted its first wish the year of its formation. Meanwhile, in the United States, the number of chapters increased to 22 by 1984, the foundation embarking on steadily paced expansion that would eventually create nearly 70 chapters serving every community in the United States, Guam, and Puerto Rico.

FOUNDATION'S ROLE

As the number of Make-A-Wish chapters increased, the foundation, based in Phoenix, governed the charitable network. The foundation was responsible for providing operational, financial, training, marketing, and developmental guidance to its chapters. The chapters raised money, dispatched wish teams, and followed the foundation's guidelines for awarding wishes. The first step in the wish-granting process was the referral of a candidate, which could come from only three sources: a medical professional treating the child, the child's parents or legal guardians, or the potential wish child. Next, the eligibility of the child was determined. A candidate had to be older than two-and-a-half and younger than 18 at the time of referral and diagnosed with a life-threatening medical condition; wish children, contrary to popular belief, did not have to be terminally ill. A candidate also could not have received a wish from another wish-granting organization. The third step in the process involved approving the wish. Once a Make-A-Wish chapter approved a child's wish, it worked closely with the foundation in Phoenix to develop a plan of execution. Make-A-Wish assumed responsibility for all expenses associated with the wish, regardless of the financial capabilities of the wish child's family.

As the years passed, Make-A-Wish volunteers discovered nearly all wishes fell within four categories. Children typically wanted to take on another guise, such as become a superhero or a police officer; travel to a favorite destination, such as Disneyland, the most common wish granted by Make-A-Wish; meet a celebrity; or receive a gift item. The number of wishes granted by the foundation's chapters soared into the tens of thousands over the years, but one wish stood out from the rest, exemplifying the Make-A-Wish mission. A 12-year-old named Hope, after asking how many other children in her home state of North Carolina were waiting for wishes to be fulfilled, used her wish to help her local chapter raise enough money to pay for 155 pending wishes.

THE 21ST CENTURY

Make-A-Wish granted its 80,000th wish during its 20th anniversary in 2000. Less than a decade later, the foundation had granted more than 165,000 wishes, more than doubling the volume of its charitable work. Leadership of the foundation, its nearly 70 chapters, and nearly 25,000 volunteers, was in the hands of David A. Williams, who held the titles of president and chief executive officer. Williams, a veteran of the nonprofit arena, joined Make-A-Wish in January 2005 at the start of the foundation's 25th anniversary. Before taking the helm, he spent more than a decade as the executive director of the Houston Food Bank, and ten years as an executive at Habitat for Humanity International, rising to the posts of vice-president and chief operating officer.

Under Williams's stewardship, Make-A-Wish enjoyed spectacular financial health. During the first three years of his tenure, the foundation's national office revenue more than doubled from $25 million to $52 million, distributions to chapters nearly tripled from $8.8 million to $24 million, and the foundation's total revenue swelled from $144 million to $183 million. The foundation granted 12,691 wishes in 2006, the most in its history, setting a record that was broken the following year when it granted 13,007 wishes. By 2008, the foundation was granting one wish an average of every 40 minutes, at an average cost of $7,017 per wish.

Supported by thousands of volunteers, donations from individuals, and an impressive list of corporate sponsors, Make-A-Wish conducted charitable work from a position of strength. The organization was financially sound, well managed, and its concept, copied by numerous other charitable entities, enjoyed widespread appeal, both in the United States and abroad. Make-A-Wish, in 1993, licensed the wish-granting model to Make-A-Wish Foundation International, which promoted the formation of Make-A-Wish chapters worldwide. By 2008, Make-A-Wish chapters were in operation in more than 30 countries, each delivering memorable experiences to youngsters in great need. For both ailing children and their grieving family and friends, Make-A-Wish provided a way to inject happiness and inspiration into the darkest hours, offering solace to all those involved in the organization's approach to giving. The human need to find joy in the midst of despair was answered by Make-A-Wish, ensuring that the charitable work inspired by Chris Greicius would continue for decades to come.

Jeffrey L. Covell

PRINCIPAL COMPETITORS

A Wish Come True, Inc.; A Wish With Wings, Inc.; Children's Dream Fund; Dare To Dream Foundation; Wishes Can Happen, Inc.

FURTHER READING

Aragon, Lawrence, "Make-A-Wish Wishes Grant-A-Wish Would Go Away," *Business Journal,* March 19, 1990, p. 4.

"Make-A-Wish Foundation of America Appoints Mary Kay Phelps Vice President, Marketing and Development," *PrimeZone Media Network,* September 25, 2001.

"Make-A-Wish Foundation Selected As Among 'America's Greatest Brands,'" *PrimeZone Media Network,* December 27, 2004.

Morain, Erin, "Make-A-Wish Brings Joy in Times of Hardship," *Business Record,* November 14, 2005, p. 6.

Pope, Tom, "Coordinating Your Message: Getting Chapters on the Same Marketing Page As National," *Non-Profit Times,* February 15, 2008, p. 10.

Malaysian Airline System Berhad

3rd Floor, Administration 1 Building, MAS Complex A
Sultan Abdul Aziz Shah Airport
Subang, 47200
Malaysia
Telephone: (+603) 7840 4550
Fax: (+603) 7846 3932
Web site: http://www.malaysiaairlines.com

Public Company
Incorporated: 1937 as Malayan Airways Limited
Employees: 19,423
Sales: MYR 15.3 billion (2007)
Stock Exchanges: Kuala Lumpur
Ticker Symbol: 3786
NAICS: 481111 Scheduled Passenger Air Transportation; 481112 Scheduled Freight Air Transportation; 453220 Gift, Novelty, and Souvenir Stores; 481211 Nonscheduled Chartered Passenger Air Transportation; 485111 Mixed Mode Transit Systems; 488119 Other Airport Operations; 488510 Freight Transportation Arrangement; 493110 General Warehousing and Storage Facilities; 541990 All Other Professional, Scientific, and Technical Services; 551112 Offices of Other Holding Companies; 561520 Tour Operators; 721110 Hotels (Except Casino Hotels) and Motels; 722110 Full-Service Restaurants; 812332 Industrial Launderers

Malaysian Airline System Berhad (MAS) is the holding company for Malaysia Airlines, Malaysia's national airline. Through several subsidiaries and associate companies, the company manufactures aircraft parts, offers trucking and cargo transportation services, caters food, and provides laundry and dry-cleaning services for airlines and other industrial institutions. A newly formed holding company, Penerbangan Malaysia Berhad, took over MAS's debt and assets after the Malaysian government bought out private shareholder Tajudin Ramli in 2000. A few years later, its new managing director and CEO, Idris Jala, instituted a Business Turnaround Plan to address longstanding internal problems. MAS flies more than 14 million passengers a year.

ORIGINS

The history of Malaysia Airlines dates back to 1937, when the Straits Steamship Co. of Singapore joined forces with two British companies, Ocean Steamship Co. and Imperial Airways, and won approval from Singapore's government to operate an airline in the region. Malayan Airways Limited was registered on October 21, 1937.

Receiving clearance and placing planes in the air, however, proved to be two different things for Malayan Airways Ltd. Operations did not begin until 1947, well after the Japanese occupation had come to an end, when a twin-engined Airspeed Consul lifted off from Subang International Airport in Kuala Lumpur, linking that city with Singapore, Ipoh, and Penang in the north of the country. In 1947 the fledgling airline added a 21-seater

COMPANY PERSPECTIVES

A journey of unexpected pleasures and delightful rewards.

DC-3 to its fleet of three Airspeed Consuls. By the end of the year the airline was flying to Jakarta (then called Batavia), Palembang, Bangkok, Medan, and Saigon (later called Ho Chi Minh City). Jointly controlled by the intercontinental carriers BOAC and Qantas, Malayan Airways was for a time run by Keith Hamilton, who would later become head of Qantas.

INDEPENDENCE

Following Malaysia's political establishment in September 1963 (the new country comprised the former states of Malaya and Singapore, and the onetime colonies of North Borneo, Sabah, and Sarawak), Malayan Airways became Malaysian Airways and was reorganized to focus on connecting the new country's disparate regions. Expansion brought more aircraft into the fleet after Borneo Airways was purchased and folded into Malaysian Airways in 1965. This brought four Dakota jets and two Scottish Aviation Twin Pioneer aircraft to the carrier's stable of aircraft.

More organizational changes for the airline occurred in 1966, a year after Singapore seceded from Malaysia to become a sovereign state. That year, the governments of Singapore and Malaysia jointly bought a controlling stake in the airline and renamed it Malaysia-Singapore Airlines Ltd. (MSA). Powerful Boeing jets then entered the fleet and enabled flights to reach a number of far-flung Asian destinations. However, differences between Kuala Lumpur and Singapore over the future direction of MSA prompted a split in 1972. Lee Kuan Yew, prime minister of Singapore, desired a truly national carrier for his country, the aim being to fly a small fleet of Boeing 707s displaying the yellow and blue colors of Singapore Airlines.

Malaysia likewise chose to go its own way. In October 1972, Malaysian Airline System (MAS) was established. (The acronym MAS means gold in the Malay language.) Each of its aircraft would henceforth sport a winged tiger logo, a stylized form of the traditional Kelantan "wau" or Malaysian kite.

The split was crucial to the future fortunes of MAS. From 1972, the airline continued to see itself as a regional carrier, connecting a myriad of remote destinations in Peninsular Malaysia, including Sabah and Sarawak. Singapore Airlines, on the other hand, was committed from its inception to becoming an international success. By 1975, Singapore Airlines was flying to Seoul, Hong Kong, and Taipei. A year later, that airline was carrying passengers to Paris, Dubai, and New Zealand.

REGIONAL EMPHASIS

Unlike Singapore, Malaysia looked to focus on exploiting its vast reserves of natural resources: petroleum and petroleum products, natural gas, timber products, and rubber. The country's government would choose much later than Singapore had to attempt competing with Western companies in manufacturing and high-tech markets.

Thus, maintaining a successful regional airline was judged the best strategy for Malaysia during the 1970s. The company slowly built up its regional services to Jakarta and Medan in Indonesia. Later the destinations of Bangkok, Hong Kong, Manila, and Singapore were added.

Expanding as a regional airline was not without incident for MAS. In 1978, the company's low-wage policy met with a setback. Kuala Lumpur had set out rules limiting union activity at the national air carrier as a means of keeping wages and costs down, and a bitter and disruptive labor dispute occurred in 1978. Events surrounding a strike at the national airline prompted the government to intervene and cite MAS workers as being engaged in illegal activity. Several union officials were subsequently arrested.

ECONOMIC BOOM

An economic boom in Malaysia during the 1980s helped spur growth at Malaysia Airlines. By the end of the decade, MAS was flying to 47 overseas destinations. These included eight European cities: London, Zürich, Paris, Frankfurt, Istanbul, Vienna, Amsterdam, and Brussels. MAS also flew at this time to six Australian cities (Brisbane, Adelaide, Darwin, Perth, Melbourne, and Sydney) as well as to Auckland, New Zealand. Besides flights to such Asian hubs as Hong Kong, Tokyo, and Peking, MAS also connected with Los Angeles and Honolulu. By 1992, MAS had added scheduled flights to Madrid and Rome, and plans were in motion to reach at least one destination in Eastern Europe. Moreover, a new service to South Africa and Brazil was scheduled for 1993. The airline would also look to reach one city on the eastern seaboard of the United States.

MAS also chose during the early 1990s to expand by teaming up with other airlines to make additional

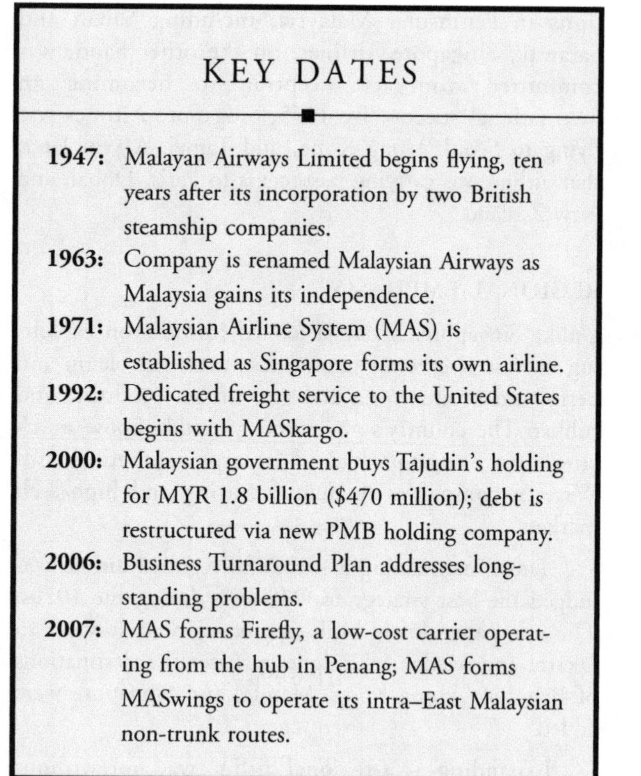

KEY DATES

1947: Malayan Airways Limited begins flying, ten years after its incorporation by two British steamship companies.
1963: Company is renamed Malaysian Airways as Malaysia gains its independence.
1971: Malaysian Airline System (MAS) is established as Singapore forms its own airline.
1992: Dedicated freight service to the United States begins with MASkargo.
2000: Malaysian government buys Tajudin's holding for MYR 1.8 billion ($470 million); debt is restructured via new PMB holding company.
2006: Business Turnaround Plan addresses long-standing problems.
2007: MAS forms Firefly, a low-cost carrier operating from the hub in Penang; MAS forms MASwings to operate its intra–East Malaysian non-trunk routes.

destinations available for its customers. For example, Iran Air connected Kuala Lumpur with Tehran, and Royal Jordanian connected MAS flights with Amman. In addition, joint services to Chile and Argentina were discussed in late 1991.

The impetus for this expansion came from Malaysia's burgeoning economy. Between 1986 and 1991, the country's export-oriented economy posted an average real growth of 9 percent. Changes to Malaysia's foreign investment rules during the mid-1980s were designed to help speed a shift from an economy previously dependent on natural resources to a finely tuned industrialized economy. At the same time, a number of large Asian and Western corporations such as Sanyo, NEC, Toshiba, and Philips established branch plants in Malaysia. The extra traffic of company officials flying back and forth from their headquarters to Malaysia, and the transportation of their high-tech goods, boosted ticket sales for the airline. The number of business passengers MAS accommodated was underscored by gross foreign investments in Malaysia that rose 30 percent in 1991 to MYR 10.7 billion ($5 billion).

TOURIST TRADE

As the country's export trade thundered ahead in the late 1980s, so did the domestic passenger traffic in and out of Malaysia, and naturally tourism also provided a springboard to expansion for MAS. By the late 1980s Malaysia began to go after the prized Western tourist, a market already well exploited by neighboring Thailand and the Philippines. Nearly 5.5 million travelers visited Malaysia in 1991. Although the country, and its airline, were hit by the effects of the Gulf War and global recessionary conditions, tourism contributed MYR 5 billion, or $2.4 billion, to the country's trade balance in 1991. The bulk of these tourists came from neighboring Brunei, Indonesia, the Philippines, Singapore, and Thailand. Kuala Lumpur's plans to build a number of luxury golf courses in the country were expected to help secure growing numbers of Japanese tourists.

Getting into the package tour business also helped MAS encourage increased passenger traffic. Malaysia Airlines Golden Holiday packages and Malaysia Stopover packages were established in 1984. These encouraged European and Australian travelers in transit between the two continents to take a break in Malaysia before carrying on to their final destination. To further stimulate tourism, a joint campaign was run by the Malaysian government and MAS to declare 1990 Visit Malaysia Year. During the year, some 7.4 million tourists flew into and out of the country, as compared with the 4.8 million tourists who visited Malaysia in the previous year.

Another source of new traffic for the airline was the growing number of foreign students attending educational institutions in Malaysia. In September 1989 the International School of Kuala Lumpur registered 700 students; a year later, the school had doubled its enrollment. By the same token, young Malaysians were studying in Europe and North America. In Canada, where many Malaysian students attended universities, it was thought, in early 1992, that this new traffic source might warrant regular service between the two countries.

Canada's own national airline, Air Canada, which was suffering from economic recession and increasing global competition, was slow to grant Malaysian Airlines landing rights. The Canadian government felt that allowing MAS to land in Vancouver would encroach on territory commanded by Canadian Airlines International Ltd., while Toronto International Airport was considered the preserve of Air Canada. Malaysia's case at the time was not helped by Ottawa having a year earlier announced the cancellation of Singapore Airline's landing rights in Toronto. Even so, Kuala Lumpur officials reasoned that Canada was out-of-step in trying to protect its national airline carriers. The global airline industry as a whole was going the opposite way, toward increased deregulation and competitiveness. Malaysia was prepared to wait for Canada to accept its growing economic might and grant reciprocal landing rights.

Intercontinental traffic for the airline was encouraged by the purchase of Boeing 747 wide-body jets. By 1991, the airline had four of them, and three more were added a year later with an average of two more due for delivery each year until 1995. In 1992, a tightening labor supply in Malaysia, in part the result of its increasingly prosperous economy, was cited by international corporations as the prime obstacle standing in the way of future expansion plans. Manpower shortages were especially acute at the middle management and technical levels. All of these circumstances would impact MAS's passenger and cargo traffic figures as the country's economy moved from the farm to the factory and beyond.

Amid this backdrop, the Malaysian government in 1992 forecast that passenger traffic on the country's combined airways, international and regional, would grow 10 percent annually in the five years before 1997. International freight volume in the same period was expected to rise 13 percent annually.

Officials in Kuala Lumpur announced in 1992 that they had plans to build a new international airport in Sepang, adding that all other airports in the country were expected to cope with the increased passenger demand of the 1990s without the need for expansion. Government forecasts in 1992 pointed to 9.5 million passengers to be carried by MAS that year, a figure expected to jump to approximately 15 million by 1995.

Cargo was also identified as an expanding source of revenue for the airline in the 1990s. In recognition of this potential, MAS in 1992 introduced MASkargo in order to begin providing a full cargo service to the United States and Europe. A DC-10-30 jet was fitted to carry up to 60 tons of cargo per flight. Further plans were announced to purchase an additional Boeing 747-400 freighter to carry 45 tons of extra cargo per flight. In 1992 MASkargo also opened a fully automated cargo handling center in Penang. The new facility complemented the expanded MAS Cargo Center at Subang Airport, which provided semiautomated and computerized facilities including elevating transfer vehicles and electronic scissor lifts fitted with computerized scales. Expansion at the cargo center brought MASkargo's total warehouse storage space to 150,000 square meters.

The ambitious expansion plans taxed the carrier's profits, which were nearly halved, from MYR 206 million to MYR 120 million, between 1991 and 1992. Turnover increased 23 percent in 1992, however, reaching MYR 3.6 billion. Correspondingly, employment at MAS rose from 17,869 workers in 1992 to 19,509 in 1993. Demand for flight crews was so great that the carrier contracted for 35 percent of these positions with overseas personnel, mostly Australian. Fifteen hundred of the employees worked in the airline's unique flight kitchen, which served 22 airlines. All 17,000 meals a day were *halal,* that is, observing Muslim dietary restrictions such as those that prohibited pork.

During this time, MAS hired *Star Wars* producer George Lucas's special-effects unit to create a stunning sci-fi television commercial. The spot, which aired around the world, was commissioned to present MAS as a modern, world-class airline and featured a huge kite-shaped space station. The cost was estimated between $2 million and $4 million.

In 1993, MAS bought a 24.9 percent interest in U.S. charter operator World Airways. The company also leased five of its MD-11 aircraft. Operations personnel, in high demand at MAS, were also made available.

PRIVATE OWNERSHIP 1994–2000

In 1994 Malaysian entrepreneur Tajudin Ramli bought a 32 percent controlling interest for MYR 2 billion ($745 million) worth of stock. The government retained an 11 percent interest. Tajudin, who had earlier put together a mini-aviation empire in preparation for competing with MAS, was saddled with an overly large fleet and diminishing profits. Although sales rose to MYR 4.1 billion ($1.6 billion) in the fiscal year ending March 3, 1994, profits fell from MYR 145.4 million ($56.4 million) to MYR 7.7 million ($2.9 million). The carrier was still receiving large shipments of new aircraft, including Boeing 747s, and sales of its used aircraft were slow. (Some of MAS's new A330 aircraft were delivered late, resulting in penalty payments from Airbus.)

Tajudin immediately set out to trim the fat. He introduced a more businesslike attitude and required better reporting from the company's managers. Aircraft utilization was increased. The carrier signed code-share agreements on transpacific routes and promoted its Kuala–Lumpur–Los Angeles route to attract more business passengers.

Virgin Atlantic Airways teamed with MAS in 1995 to operate joint London–Kuala Lumpur flights. The service proved convenient for Virgin's Australia-bound passengers. Planes stayed just as full after the number of flights was increased from eight to 14 a week, although the two carriers faced very formidable competition from the British Airways/Qantas alliance, which operated the only single-plane service between London and Australia.

MAS recorded its highest ever pretax profit in 1997 of MYR 349.4 million ($120 million). The company continued to buy new planes and relocated to Kuala Lumpur International Airport (KLIA) in Sepang, a move expected to further enhance its reputation.

Depreciating Malaysian currency brought MAS's debt up to MYR 12 billion by 1998. Debt servicing helped MAS lose MYR 260 million ($62 million) in 1998. In response, the carrier deferred new aircraft purchases, sold old planes, and slashed underperforming routes.

RESTRUCTURING

With most of its financing denominated in U.S. dollars, the carrier was quite vulnerable to the Asian financial crisis. To cope in 1999 it deferred delivery of a dozen of the 25 new planes it had on order while selling three B747-Combi aircraft, while three new B747-400s were delivered in 2002. Passenger count nevertheless steadily grew through the late 1990s, reaching 38 million in 2001, reflecting improvements MAS was making to the quality of its product. Revenues increased as well, to MYR 9.1 billion. However, the airline was racking up losses throughout this time. The fiscal year ended March 31, 2001, was particularly bleak, with the net loss of MYR 1.32 billion.

A restructuring plan put forth by Tajudin, whose hands were tied by the government when it came to cutting jobs, was at first rejected on the grounds it would rescue Tajudin at the expense of minority shareholders. Foreign airlines with an eye toward global expansion (such as Thai Airways and British Airways) seemed interested in investing in MAS, but were leery of inheriting the unprofitable domestic operations. As debt mounted to $2.5 billion, the government ultimately stepped in, buying out Tajudin's 29.09 percent holding for MYR 1.8 billion ($470 million, or double the market value) in December 2000. The need to protect KLIA's development into a regional hub was the explanation.

Mohamed Nor Yusof became MAS's next chief executive. A former banker, he arranged a financial restructuring program called "Widespread Asset Unbundling." A new holding company called Penerbangan Malaysia Berhad (PMB) was created that took over MAS's debts and assets in exchange for a 69 percent equity holding.

MAS cut a number of money-losing secondary destinations from the international network, while entering codeshare arrangements with KLM, Garuda Indonesia, and Vietnam Airlines. It also won government approval to raise fares for the first time in more than a decade. It raised international fares in 2000 and increased fares in peninsular Malaysia by 52 percent in 2001. MAS remained saddled with unprofitable domestic routes in the economically depressed eastern part of Malaysia, however.

BUSINESS TURNAROUND PLAN

MAS managed to post gains in 2003 and 2004, in spite of SARS and the war in Iraq. However, it was on a course for bankruptcy when it lost MYR 1.3 billion in the first nine months of 2005, its new CEO Idris Jala told *Air Transport World.* Idris, a veteran of Shell Oil, took over in December 2005.

The management addressed four critical issues the airline faced; low yield, lack of cost control, inefficient network, and low productivity (overstaffing) under a new Business Turnaround Plan which helped MAS become one of the country's best-performing stocks. Over the last two years, passenger yields improved 32 percent and cost reduced by some MYR 1.3 billion. The network was streamlined, with unprofitable routes suspended; more capacity was added within Asia, however, and the entire network was rearranged as a hub-and-spoke system leading to Kuala Lumpur. Domestic routes were rationalized in August 2006 as a result of the government-initiated reorganization in which MAS was allowed to operate 25 domestic routes. Late 2007, the government asked MAS to take back the rural air services, and MAS then created a subsidiary called MASwings Sdn. Bhd. to assume control of this subsidized business.

Earlier in April 2007, MAS created its own low-cost carrier to explore new growth opportunities. Based in Penang, Firefly offered very low-priced service to a half-dozen destinations in Malaysia and Thailand.

The workforce, long considered bloated, was allowed to shrink 15 percent through a mutual separation scheme and attrition. Even as the company was economizing, it invested in improved information technology systems to better manage its yields and enhance its customer service experience. It also bolstered its third-party maintenance capabilities.

By the end of 2007, the airline posted its highest profit in the 60-year history of the company, MYR 851 million. This achievement capped a complete turnaround of its business.

Malaysia Airlines announced its second Business Transformation Plan in January 2008. The aim was to transform the Malaysian national airline into a Five Star Value Carrier, one that delivered the highest quality of products and services at affordable prices, without compromising safety or quality, and achieved an annual profit of MYR 1.5 billion by the year 2012.

Etan Vlessing
Updated, Frederick C. Ingram

PRINCIPAL SUBSIDIARIES

Malaysia Airlines Cargo Sdn. Bhd.; MAS Aerotechnologies Sdn. Bhd.; Syarikat Pengangkutan Senai Sdn. Bhd.; MAS Golden Boutiques Sdn. Bhd.; MAS Golden Holidays Sdn. Bhd.; MASkargo Logistics Sdn. Bhd.; MAS Academy Sdn. Bhd.; MAS Aerotechnologies Sdn. Bhd.; FlyFirefly Sdn. Bhd. (formerly known as Kelas Services Sdn. Bhd.); Malaysia Airlines Capital (L) Limited; Macnet CCN (M) Sdn. Bhd.; Malaysian Aerospace Engineering Sdn. Bhd.; MASwings Sdn. Bhd.; Abacus Distribution Systems (Malaysia) Sdn. Bhd. (80%); Aerokleen Services Sdn. Bhd. (51%); MAS Catering (Sarawak) Sdn. Bhd. (60%); Aerofine Meat Sdn. Bhd. (49%); GE Engine Services Malaysia Sdn. Bhd. (30%); Hamilton Sundstrand Customer Support Centre (M) Sdn. Bhd. (49%); Honeywell Aerospace Service (M) Sdn. Bhd. (30%); LSG Sky Chefs-Brahim's Sdn. Bhd. (30%); Pan Asia Pacific Aviation Services Limited (25.53%); Taj Madras Flight Kitchen Limited (20%).

PRINCIPAL COMPETITORS

Singapore Airlines Limited; Cathay Pacific Airways Limited; Thai Airways International Public Company Limited.

FURTHER READING

Abdullah Mat Zaid, "Malaysia Airlines' Corporate Vision and Service Quality Strategy," *Managing Service Quality,* Vol. 4, No. 6, 1994, pp. 11–15.

———, "Measuring and Monitoring Service Quality at Malaysia Airlines," *Managing Service Quality,* Vol. 5, No. 2, 1995, pp. 25–27.

Daneels, Jenny, "Operator Gears Up to Be High Flier," *Asian Business,* October 1997.

Donville, Christopher, "Malaysian Airlines Spreads Its Wings Internationally," *Globe and Mail,* July 7, 1992.

Feldman, Joan, "Malay Makeover," *Air Transport World,* June 1995, pp. 37–42.

Forward, David C., "Critical MAS," *Airways,* January 1999, pp. 45–51.

"Fresh Start," *Airline Business,* February 1, 2005, p. 31.

Hill, Leonard, "Asia's Newest 'Dragon,'" *Air Transport World,* September 1993, pp. 66–74.

Hoon, Lim Siong, "Make or Break for Tajudin and MAS," *Asiamoney,* July/August 1994, pp. 35–37.

Jayasankaran, S., "Unhappy Landings," *Far Eastern Economic Review,* July 23, 1998, pp. 52–53.

Malaysia—A Special Study by Corporate Location, London: Century House Information Ltd., 1991.

"MAS Takes Tough Cost-Cutting Measures to Face Gloomy Outlook," *AsiaPulse News,* June 2, 2008.

Mecham, Michael, "MAS Profits Slide, but Worst May Be Over," *Aviation Week and Space Technology,* June 6, 1994, pp. 33–36.

———, "777 Wins Key Round of Asian Face-Off," *Aviation Week and Space Technology,* January 15, 1996, p. 34.

"Nation Can Afford to Pick and Choose Among Investors," *Globe and Mail,* July 7, 1992.

"Operator Gears Up to Be High Flier," *Asian Business,* October 1997, pp. 10–12.

Putzger, Ian, "Malaysian Limbo," *AirCargoWorld,* February 2001, pp. 19+.

Shifrin, Carole, "Virgin Atlantic, Malaysia Team to Gain Global Strength," *Aviation Week and Space Technology,* January 23, 1995, pp. 43–44.

Thomas, Geoffrey, "Juggling Act," *ATW,* November 2008, pp. 32–34, 37.

———, "Return to Sender," *ATW,* July 2001, pp. 26–30.

———, "Transforming Malaysia Airlines," *ATW,* May 2007, pp. 44–46.

Tsuruoka, Doug, "Flying High," *Far Eastern Economic Review,* January 13, 1994, pp. 77–78.

———, "Go Fly a Kite," *Far Eastern Economic Review,* September 30, 1993, p. 70.

Vandyk, Anthony, "Going Technical," *Air Transport World,* May 1991, pp. 80–81.

Vatikiotis, Michael, "Financial Headwinds: Malaysian Carrier's Expansion Hits Profits," *Far Eastern Economic Review,* June 1992, pp. 65–68.

ManTech
International Corporation

ManTech International Corporation

12015 Lee Jackson Highway
Fairfax, Virginia 22033
U.S.A.
Telephone: (703) 218-6000
Fax: (703) 218-8296
Web site: http://www.mantech.com

Public Company
Incorporated: 1968
Employees: 7,400
Sales: $1.8 billion (2008 est.)
Stock Exchanges: NASDAQ
Ticker Symbol: MANT
NAICS: 518210 Data Processing, Hosting, and Related Services; 541511 Custom Computer Programming Services; 541512 Computer Systems Design Services; 541519 Other Computer Related Services; 561110 Office Administrative Services; 561499 All Other Business Support Services

■ ■ ■

ManTech International Corporation is a leading contractor for the defense and intelligence communities. It is active in a variety of technical areas including secure communications and database management. Nearly two-thirds of the company's employees hold top-secret clearances with the U.S. government, which typically accounts for about 98 percent of revenues. Based near Washington, D.C., ManTech operates from nearly 300 locations around the world. The company is not to be confused with the Manufacturing Technology initiatives of the U.S. Air Force, also referred to as ManTech.

SHADOWY ORIGINS

ManTech International Corporation was formed in 1968 as a tiny engineering services contractor for the U.S. Navy (there were initially just two employees). In keeping with the spirit of its work, which involved such projects as making submarines stealthier, the company maintained a very low profile.

When an article on ManTech surfaced in the *Washington Post* in 1988, the writer commented how Chairman and cofounder George Pedersen avoided having his picture taken. ManTech was a long way from the scrutiny of being a public company.

The firm was nevertheless growing quickly. It had a number of offices in the Washington, D.C., area and the West Coast by the end of its first decade. With a headquarters in Rockville, Maryland, it changed its name from ManTech of New Jersey Corp. to ManTech International in 1979. Pedersen became chairman of the company around this time, and added the titles of president and chief executive officer in 1995. (Company cofounder Franc Wertheimer had held the office of president earlier.)

THE REAGAN ERA

As the company's prospectus later noted, the federal government began a long period of increasing information technology (IT) spending every year around 1980.

COMPANY PERSPECTIVES

Whether we are providing risk management solutions, cyber or physical security for the U.S. Department of State and its embassies around the world—or delivering advanced information technology solutions for the U.S. Army, Navy, Air Force or the Intelligence Community, ManTech is committed to helping our customers accomplish their critical national security missions. We support the advanced telecommunications systems that are used in Operation Iraqi Freedom and in other parts of the world. ManTech has developed a secure, collaborative communications system for the Department of Homeland Security that will significantly strengthen the exchange of real-time threat information used to combat terrorism. The Department of Justice's U.S. Marshall Service relies on ManTech to help them deploy a common, office automation system. We also provide extensive, advanced information technology support to the National Security agency and other Intelligence Community customers.

ManTech accelerated its growth via acquisitions. In 1979 it bought the Annapolis, Maryland-based engineering services division of CADCOM, Inc. This unit, formed around 1970, was involved in a variety of engineering and statistical studies. It had about 30 employees. ManTech added the Seed Software unit of Control Data Corp. in 1984. Seed produced software for managing very large databases such as those used by the Navy to track its spare parts. ManTech had annual revenues of about $100 million by 1986.

The 1993 acquisition of some assets and rights of Alexandria, Virginia-based Accel Inc. gave ManTech a production line for building customized PCs. Accel had been formed by Ali Jani and Bijal Mehta and quickly became successful manufacturing IBM clones, reaching revenues of $33 million in 1992. Pittsburgh's Revive Technologies, a specialist in database management, was acquired in 1999.

ManTech's total revenues exceeded $200 million a year in the mid-1990s and the company was consistently profitable. The Reagan years had been good to it, and the company also prospered through the post–Cold War defense cutbacks due to the military's emphasis on using technology to maximize its resources. The growth of the Internet was making ManTech's computer security business increasingly relevant.

By 2000 ManTech's revenues were $379 million, producing income of $1.7 million. The company then had about 3,500 employees, nearly half of them with some kind of government security clearance.

PUBLIC IN 2002

ManTech had posted a rare annual loss in 2001 as it sold some foreign subsidiaries and commercial units early in the year. Investors did not seem too troubled by this, and the company's subsequent initial public offering (IPO) was successful. It valued the company at more than $250 million.

Originally registered in New Jersey, ManTech International was reincorporated as a Delaware corporation in 2002. The February IPO raised $115.2 million from investors who were eager to get a piece of the windfall from the War on Terror. George Pedersen still owned a majority of shares after the offering.

Much of the cash reaped in the IPO was slated for acquisitions. ManTech soon added Aegis Research Corporation, another defense and intelligence support contractor, in an all-cash deal worth $69.1 million. Aegis employed 500 people and had annual revenues of $60 million. ManTech also acquired CTX Corporation by the end of 2002. The deal was worth about $35 million. CTX had 188 employees and annual revenues of $24 million, mostly derived from government intelligence agencies. Founded in 1993, it specialized in IT.

Another Washington area contractor was acquired in February 2003: Integrated Data Systems Corporation (IDS), part of Affiliated Computer Services, Inc. ManTech paid about $60 million for the unit, which was oriented toward defense and intelligence agencies. IDS, launched in 1990 by its CEO, Robert Coleman, had grown to 230 employees and annual revenues of $40 million. It focused on secure communication software and systems engineering.

Some acquisitions were less successful than others. ManTech purchased MSM Security Services Inc. for $5 million in March 2003, believing that technology would take much of the grunt work out of its business of performing background checks. This did not happen within a suitable time frame, and the unprofitable business was sold to ManTech CEO George Pedersen for $3 million in 2007.

With total revenues approaching $1 billion, ManTech underwent another round of restructuring in 2005. By this time it had about 6,000 employees. ManTech Environmental Technology Inc. was sold to Alion Sci-

KEY DATES

1968: ManTech is formed by George Pedersen in New Jersey as an engineering contractor for the U.S. Navy.
1976: Company headquarters moves to Washington, D.C., area.
1979: ManTech buys CADCOM's engineering division.
1984: ManTech buys Seed Software Corp. from Control Data Corp.
2002: ManTech becomes a public company.
2005: Company sells some holdings in a minor restructuring.
2006: Annual revenues exceed $1 billion; company has 5,600 employees.
2007: SRS Technologies becomes ManTech's largest acquisition to date; McDonald Bradley Inc. is also acquired.

enc'e and Technology Corp. in February 2005. In December it sold its 40 percent share of a U.K. intelligence services joint venture it had formed nine years earlier with Vosper Thornycroft. In November 2006 the company spun off its NetWitness Security Product Group, a maker of network forensics tools. ManTech continued to acquire companies, such as Gray Hawk Systems, another Washington area IT contractor it bought for $100 million in June 2005.

A $1 BILLION COMPANY

The divestments did not prevent ManTech from becoming a $1 billion company in 2006. In fact it continued to expand at a rapid pace, and its purchases grew increasingly larger. At a price of about $195 million, SRS Technologies, Inc., became ManTech's biggest acquisition to date in May 2007. SRS specialized in systems engineering for the military, intelligence, and space communities. Another defense IT firm, McDonald Bradley Inc. (MBI) of Herndon, Virginia, was acquired in December 2007 for $76.5 million. MBI had been formed in 1985 and had annual revenues of about $50 million.

At the time of its 40th anniversary in 2008, ManTech had much to celebrate. It had grown from two employees to 7,400, and posted record revenues of about $1.5 billion for the previous year. Its prospects for the immediate future were bright, and the company was forecasting revenues of $1.8 billion for 2008.

Some analysts believed that even if political changes resulted in a major cutback in ground troops in Iraq, the company's intelligence-oriented products and services would remain in demand for years.

Frederick C. Ingram

PRINCIPAL SUBSIDIARIES

ManTech Command Control Systems Corporation; ManTech Information Systems &Technology Corporation; ManTech Security & Mission Assurance Corporation; ManTech Solutions & Technologies Corporation; ManTech Systems Engineering Corporation; ManTech Environmental Corporation; ManTech Support Technology, Inc.; NSI Technology Services Corporation; ManTech Advanced Systems International, Inc.; ManTech Telecommunications and Information Systems Corporation; ManTech Europe Systems Corporation; ManTech Australia Pty. Ltd.; ManTech Australia International, Inc.; ManTech U.K. Systems Corporation; ManTech Advanced Development Group, Inc.; ManTech Security Technologies Corporation; ManTech Gray Hawk Systems, Inc.; ManTech GRS Solutions, Inc.; ManTech SRS Technologies, Inc.; ManTech Global Services Corporation; ManTech MBI, Inc.

PRINCIPAL DIVISIONS

Intelligence Analysis and Mission Operations; Information Technology Solutions; Systems Engineering and Integration Solutions; Global Logistics and Supply Chain Management.

PRINCIPAL OPERATING UNITS

ManTech Defense Systems Group (DSG); ManTech Information Systems & Technology (MIST); ManTech Security & Mission Assurance (MSMA); ManTech SRS (MSRS).

PRINCIPAL COMPETITORS

Computer Sciences Corporation; Northrop Grumman Corporation; Booz Allen Hamilton Inc.; Stanley, Inc.; CACI International, Inc.; SRA International, Inc.; General Dynamics Corporation; Lockheed Martin Corporation; Science Applications International Corporation.

FURTHER READING

Day, Kathleen, "Accel's Founders Leave Va. Computer Firm; Alexandria Plant, Rights to Name Turned Over to Fairfax's Mantech," *Washington Post,* April 6, 1994, p. D3.

Grocer, Stephen, "ManTech Investigates Selling Security Unit," *Mergers & Acquisitions Report,* March 14, 2005.

Higgins, Marguerite, "Fairfax, Va.-based Technology Contractor Needs Time to Recover," *Washington Times,* June 22, 2004.

Johnston, Nicholas, "ManTech International Shares Post First-Day Gain of 13%," *Washington Post,* February 8, 2002, p. E5.

"ManTech Completes Spin Out of NetWitness Security Product Group," *InDefense,* November 8, 2006.

"ManTech Focuses HQ Hunt in Chantilly's Westfields," *Washington Business Journal,* April 12, 2004.

"ManTech's $92M Filing a Sign of the Times," *IPO Reporter,* December 3, 2001.

McCarthy, Ellen, "Contractors to Join Forces As ManTech Buys Aegis," *Washington Post,* July 2, 2002, p. E6.

Merle, Renae, "ManTech to Purchase Software Firm CTX," *Washington Post,* December 7, 2002, p. E3.

Moore, Heidi, "ManTech IPO Rises 14% on First Day," *Daily Deal,* February 7, 2002.

Ramstack, Tom, "ManTech Revenue Nears $1 Billion," *Washington Times,* June 28, 2005, p. C9.

Rowland, Kara, "ManTech Focuses on More Growth," *Washington Times,* November 28, 2006.

———, "ManTech Poised to Thrive in Defense; Election Unlikely to Have Effect," *Washington Times,* April 8, 2008, p. C9.

Sinha, Vandana, "Navy Intranet Subcontractor Prepares to Move to Norfolk, Va.," *Virginian-Pilot,* June 6, 2001.

Willoughby, Jack, "Security Offering: ManTech Looks to Cash In on Concerns," *Barron's,* February 4, 2002, p. 34.

Marie Brizard et Roger International S.A.S.

BP 557, 130–142 rue Fondaudege
Bordeaux, F-33002 Cedex
France
Telephone: (+33 05) 56 01 85 85
Fax: (+33 05) 56 01 85 99
Web site: http://www.mariebrizard.com

Wholly Owned Subsidiary of Belvedere S.A.
Incorporated: 1755
Employees: 600
Sales: EUR 328 million ($450 million) (2006 est.)
NAICS: 424820 Wine and Distilled Alcoholic Beverage Merchant Wholesalers; 312130 Wineries; 312140 Distilleries

■ ■ ■

Founded in 1755, Marie Brizard et Roger International S.A.S. remains one of France's oldest and most well-known drinks groups, especially for its range of fruit- and spice-flavored liqueurs. The company's flagship product is its anisette, an anise-flavored liqueur, produced according to the same recipe since the company's founding. Other liqueurs include Manzanita, Hot Mint, Litchao, Chocolat Royal, and Charleston Follies, among many others. Marie Brizard's spirits include Old Lady's gin, Berger Pastis (an aniseed-flavored liqueur), Gautier cognac, William Peel, the number one-selling whiskey brand in France, San José tequila, Pitters Port, and others. The Bordeaux-based company also markets a variety of wines, and operates one of France's largest wine bottling plants, Les Chais Beaucairois. Other Marie Brizard operations include three production sites in France, and two in Spain. International sales has long formed an important part of Marie Brizard's business, and continues to account for approximately one-fourth of its total sales, estimated at EUR 328 million ($450 million) in 2006. The company's products reach more than 120 countries, and each year Marie Brizard sells more than 200 million bottles. Marie Brizard is a subsidiary of Belvedere S.A., which acquired the company in 2006.

A TASTE FOR THE 18TH CENTURY

Marie Brizard represented a rarity in 18th-century French economic life. Where women were, for the most part, shut out of commerce, Marie Brizard not only led her own company, but founded the company herself. Unmarried at the age of 41, Marie Brizard (according to company legend) gave part of her time nursing the ill in Bordeaux's hospitals. One of her patients had come to France from one of the country's colonial islands. Grateful for her care, the patient gave Marie Brizard the recipe for an elixir popular in his home country, a beverage purported to possess all manner of properties conducive to good health. Marie Brizard's determination to perfect and produce this beverage, as the legend continued, came more from altruism than from commercialism.

In reality, anise-flavored drinks had already made their appearance earlier in the century. Marie Brizard's father, Pierre, owned a small distillery and produced anisette prior to his death in 1743. The distillery would

COMPANY PERSPECTIVES

The brand, created by Marie Brizard in Bordeaux, a region renowned throughout the world for its tradition of quality wines, is one of the world's most venerable producers of liqueurs and drinks based on plants, fruits and spices. Originally, the firm made its name with the aniseed liqueur that was later to become the Marie Brizard anisette, but its real growth period came when it branched out into a wide range of cocktail-based liqueurs, spirits, syrups, and more recently wines.

eventually be transferred to Marie Brizard's name in 1755, coincidentally when Pierre's creditors won a judgment demanding that Pierre's debts be paid. In that year, Marie Brizard joined with Jean-Baptiste Roger, married to one of her nieces, who brought in a supply of capital, while Marie Brizard supplied the family-owned distillery equipment. The company's operations officially started in 1755, purchasing green anise from Spain and installing itself in a distillery in Bordeaux to produce its anisette. The beverage proved a quick success in the court of King Louis XV, and became a popular liqueur among France's privileged class.

The company soon added the "international" element to its name. At the time, Bordeaux was one of the most important ports in Europe, particularly through its position in the spice trade. As Marie Brizard's anisette recipe was dependent on imported spices, the company began trading bottles of its anisette for spices, bringing the Marie Brizard label to such French territories as Haiti and Louisiana by the early 1760s. By the end of the century, the company was firmly established and prosperous.

Jean-Baptiste Roger died in 1795, and his share of the company was transferred to his widow. Marie Brizard would die in 1801, at the age of 87. By then, however, Marie, with no children of her own, had transferred the company to Roger's widow and sons. While prosperous, the company entered the 19th century a relatively modest concern in a field crowded with anise-flavored drinks. By the end of the century, Marie Brizard had seen most of its competitors disappear. Marie Brizard itself had earned a reputation for its quality, top-shelf liqueur. Another factor in the company's success was its longstanding refusal to allow nepotism to play a part in its management. Family members wishing to enter the business were required to gain a strong degree of experience. At the same time, the company showed no reluctance in hiring talent from outside the family. The company had also begun diversifying beyond anisette, launching its own cognac in the 1860s, bitters in the 1870s, a creme de cocoa in 1880, a creme de menthe in 1890, while also producing cherry and apricot brandies and other fruit-flavored liqueurs. The diversification performed well for the company, which saw sales rise from 21 million ancient francs in the 1870s to 71 million ancient francs at the end of the century.

EXPANDING IN THE 20TH CENTURY

While exports had continued to grow during the 19th century, it was in the early decades of the 20th century that foreign sales began to take on a true importance for the company. Marie Brizard first looked toward Spain, a premier producer of anise and one of the largest markets for anise-flavored drinks. In 1904, Marie Brizard opened its first foreign sales branch and warehouse, in the Spanish Pyrenees region. In 1924, the company installed its first Spanish distillery. Over the next 60 years, the company would expand its Spanish production capacity to three plants, and capture more than 30 percent of Spain's anise-beverage market. As Marie Brizard continued to build its sales of anisette to the foreign market, the company also recognized the need to diversify its offerings.

By 1900, the company had launched a new creme de cocoa label, Topaze, which proved a strong success. Following World War I, Marie Brizard began developing its product line, clinging to alcoholic beverages, starting with rum, with the Charleston label, and soon followed by gin, under the Old Lady's label, the latter expanding in sales to become the top-selling gin in France. The company also launched an intensive expansion program, modernizing and building new production facilities. Growth slowed during the Depression years and sales continued to remain slow through the years following World War II. Nonetheless, by the late 1950s, the company's sales were topping 100 million ancient francs. During the 1950s, the company also began making a strategy shift, adding the distribution of other brands to its own brand names. One of the first of these came in 1956, when Marie Brizard sought to add a new spirits category, Scotch whiskey. For this, the company teamed up with another family-run enterprise, the William Grant Company of Scotland, becoming the exclusive French distributor for that company's Grant's whiskey, which would become the largest-selling whiskey in France, and the eighth largest worldwide, and later Glenfiddich and Clan MacGregor labels.

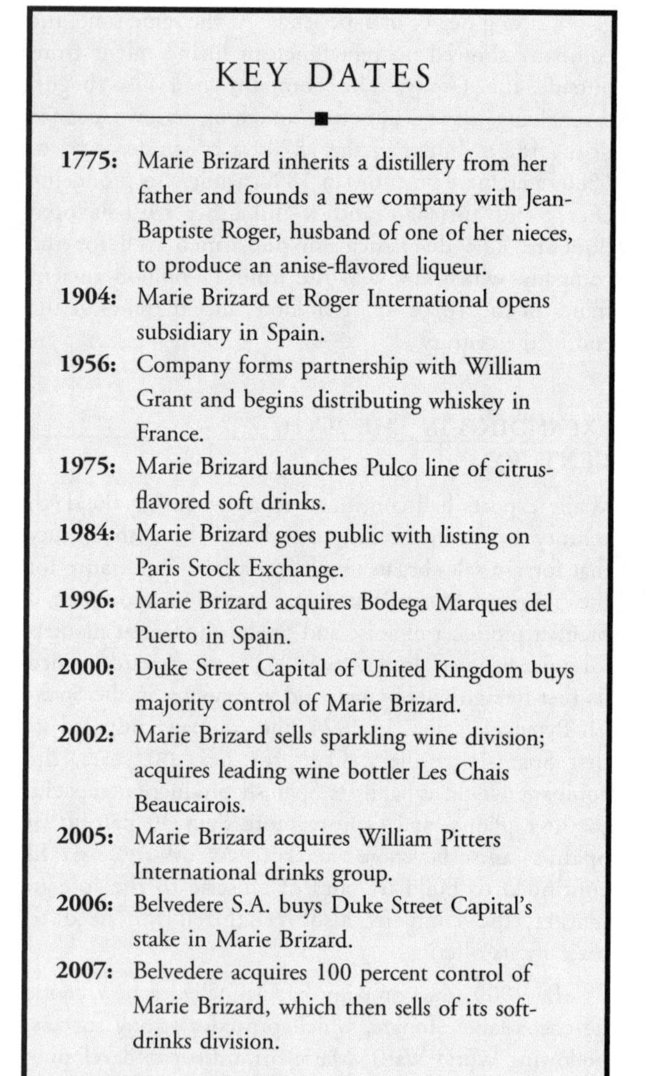

KEY DATES

1775: Marie Brizard inherits a distillery from her father and founds a new company with Jean-Baptiste Roger, husband of one of her nieces, to produce an anise-flavored liqueur.
1904: Marie Brizard et Roger International opens subsidiary in Spain.
1956: Company forms partnership with William Grant and begins distributing whiskey in France.
1975: Marie Brizard launches Pulco line of citrus-flavored soft drinks.
1984: Marie Brizard goes public with listing on Paris Stock Exchange.
1996: Marie Brizard acquires Bodega Marques del Puerto in Spain.
2000: Duke Street Capital of United Kingdom buys majority control of Marie Brizard.
2002: Marie Brizard sells sparkling wine division; acquires leading wine bottler Les Chais Beaucairois.
2005: Marie Brizard acquires William Pitters International drinks group.
2006: Belvedere S.A. buys Duke Street Capital's stake in Marie Brizard.
2007: Belvedere acquires 100 percent control of Marie Brizard, which then sells of its soft-drinks division.

In the early 1970s, however, Marie Brizard was quick to recognize the clouds looming over the alcoholic beverages industry. A number of factors were beginning to place pressure on liquor sales: the rising health concerns, particularly the recognition of alcoholism as a disease, coupled with increasing dietary and weight consciousness, which saw digestif consumption, the primary market for anisette, decline in favor of continued aperitif consumption. The 1970s also saw the first in a long series of increasing tax burdens on alcohol sales. In 1973, Marie Brizard took the first step beyond the alcoholic beverage category, forming an association with the fruit juice specialist Ralli, of Aubagne, to create a line of citrus-flavored fruit juice drinks. In 1975, the company launched the first in its line of Pulco concentrated fruit juice drinks, Pulco Citron, which was followed by Pulco Orange. The Pulco launch was a success: in four years, sales of the fruit juices quadrupled, reaching FRF 58 million, and Marie Brizard captured some 90 percent of the category it had invented. The Pulco brand also found success beyond the French border in Belgium, Germany, and Spain. In 1980, Marie Brizard acquired Ralli, marking the company's first acquisition.

GOING PUBLIC IN 1984

The company remained a fairly modest operation, with sales of FRF 360 million and 350 employees in the early 1980s. However, Marie Brizard, by then led by Paul and Gérard Glotin, the eighth generation of the Roger line, was preparing to expand the company. The first step toward this end came in 1981, when the family-owned company opened its capital to outside investors, selling 6 percent of the company. This step was followed by a public offering in 1984, when the company was listed on the Paris secondary market. This move, however, would introduce waves in the longstanding relationship between Marie Brizard and William Grant. At the offering, the Grant family company, wary of this breach in the tradition of family ownership, bought up the majority of the shares introduced to the public. Yet even with nearly 9 percent of Marie Brizard's shares, the Grant family found itself excluded from Marie Brizard's board of directors and its decisions regarding the company's future.

Meanwhile, Marie Brizard was preparing to round out its beverages offerings. In 1987, the company moved into the champagne category, acquiring the Champagne Philipponnat label and production operations. Two years later, Marie Brizard added the company Grand Champagnes de Reims and its Abel Lepitre label. While the move into champagne proved less than successful—and would eventually drag the company into the red in the 1990s—Marie Brizard found fortune through a number of other expansion moves. In 1988, the company acquired SLJFB Vedrenne, the leading producer of cassis de Bourgogne liqueurs.

Other acquisitions followed in the early 1990s. In 1991, the company expanded its nonalcoholic beverages sales with the purchases of the Abel Bresson line of syrups, popularly mixed with carbonated and non-carbonated water, and the Cidou brand of fruit juices. At the same time, Marie Brizard was also putting in place a distribution network that would enable it to survive as an independent despite massive consolidation in the distribution industry. Faced with competing against global goliaths such as Seagram and Guinness, Marie Brizard began developing what it dubbed its "spiderweb strategy," establishing through joint ventures and alliances a European distribution network among other independent and family-owned beverage producers, including Codorniu of Spain, Peter Eckes of Germany, and O'Darby of Ireland. Meanwhile, Marie Brizard also set up a Netherlands-based holding company, Marie Brizard European Development, to oversee the company's future acquisition activities.

Between 1991 and 1995, the company stepped up its expansion, both in France and overseas. The company acquired Mohawk, a vodka producer and distribution network in the United States, renamed as Marie Brizard Wines and Spirits USA, and purchased a distributor, Pat Foods, for its products in Australia. The company also acquired Caves Altovisto, adding that company's wines, sparkling wines, and other liqueurs and spirits, as well as a distribution arm in Portugal. In Belgium, the company added the Cinoco distribution network. By 1993, the company's sales reached FRF 1.8 billion, more than four times its revenues just ten years earlier.

LOSING A PARTNER IN 1994

The tensions building between Marie Brizard and William Grant, however, came to a head at the beginning of 1994. As of January 1994, the Grant family announced that it was ending its 35-year relationship with Marie Brizard, having secretly reached an agreement with another French distributor. The loss of the Grant distributorship caused a crisis at Marie Brizard, which saw its revenues plunge to FRF 1.4 billion for the 1994 year.

Nonetheless, by the end of 1995, Marie Brizard was able to overcome the Grant loss, rebuilding revenues to more than FRF 1.9 billion. In 1994, Marie Brizard found a new Scotch whiskey distribution partner in Whyte and Mackay, and also added several other labels, including Janneau amargnac, Ferrieira port, and La Mauny rum. Also aiding the company's sales was its January 1995 purchase of Marseille-based Berger, a producer of anise drinks, syrups, and sparkling wines founded in 1923.

Absorbing Berger, which posted FRF 815 million in sales in 1994, would give Marie Brizard a slight case of indigestion, coupled with continued losses in its champagnes segment, the restructuring effort following the Berger merger would dip Marie Brizard into the red, with net losses of FRF 24 million and FRF 37 million for 1995 and 1996, respectively. In February 1995, however, Marie Brizard was buoyed somewhat when it was awarded damages of FRF 130 million in its breach-of-contract lawsuit against Grant.

NEW OWNER IN THE NEW CENTURY

Strengthened by the Berger merger, Marie Brizard looked for new growth opportunities. The company extended its operations in Spain in 1996, acquiring Bodega Marquès del Puerto, a producer of Rioja wines. In 2002, the group's wine business expanded again, through the purchase of Les Chais Beaucairois (LCB), one of the leading wine bottlers in France, from retail distribution giant Groupe Casino. LCB added sales of EUR 150 million to Marie Brizard's total, as well as giving the company a major new distribution outlet, more than 80 percent of LCB's revenues came from stock Casino's store shelves.

The growth of Marie Brizard's wine business encouraged the company to launch a reorganization of its product line in 2003. The company decided to focus on just three categories: wines, spirits, and fruit-based soft drinks. This led to the sale of its sparkling wine operations, starting with Les Caves de la Bouvraie, sold to Boisset in October 2003. Next, the company disposed of its two remaining sparkling wine companies, Sorevi and SNCB Grandin, added at the time of the Berger acquisition, to Kriter-Patriarche at the beginning of 2004. Also at the time, Marie Brizard exited the U.S. market, selling its Florida-based subsidiary.

Marie Brizard boosted its spirits portfolio the following year, acquiring William Pitters International. That purchase brought a number of important brands to the company, including its William Peel whiskey, the number one selling whiskey brand in France. In this way, Marie Brizard at last filled the gap left after the rupture of its contract with Grant's. Other Pitters brands included San José tequila, Odin vodka, and a line of William Pitterson cocktails, among others. The addition of Pitters added another EUR 100 million to the Brizard group sales.

The new century also meant new ownership for the company. This process started in 2000, when U.K. investment group Duke Street Capital bought 67.83 percent of Marie Brizard. By 2006, Duke Street was prepared to exit this investment, and in April of that year found a buyer in French-Polish vodka champion Belvedere S.A. The purchase, for EUR 141 million, enabled Belvedere to emerge as one of the fastest-growing diversified drinks groups in Europe.

Belvedere moved to acquire complete control of Marie Brizard in 2007, when it launched a buyout of the company's minority shareholders and removed its listing from the Paris stock exchange. Belvedere transferred Marie Brizard's duty-free operations to its own duty-free subsidiary that year as well. Also in 2007,

Marie Brizard exited the soft-drinks segment, selling its Pulco and Sirop Sport operations.

Next, the company began attacking the problem of the steady decline in anise-flavored drinks. The association with Belvedere, which had originated as a vodka marketing company before developing its own drinks production operations, provided Marie Brizard with the resources to aid it in redeveloping its anise brands. This led to the relaunch of the Berger pastis brand, featuring a new high-end and modernized design, in May 2008. With new owners and a 233-year history, Marie Brizard remained a major name in the French and international drinks industry.

M. L. Cohen

PRINCIPAL SUBSIDIARIES

Berger S.A.; Champagne Philipponnat S.A.; Sorevi S.A.; S.N. Caves de la Bouvraie S.A.R.L.; Danflou Vedrenne S.A.; Cognac Gautier S.A. Gemaco; Cidou S.A.; Marie Brizard Espana S.A. (Spain); Bodega Marques del Puerto (Spain); Caves Altoviso Vinicola do Passadouro LDA (Portugal); Caves Quinta da Corga LDA (Portugal); S.A. Cinoco N.V. (Belgium); Marie Brizard European Development N.V. (Netherlands); Marie Brizard Wines & Spirits USA; Pat Foods Pty Ltd. (Australia); M.B.R.I. Japan.

PRINCIPAL COMPETITORS

SHV Holdings N.V; Wray and Nephew Group Ltd.; Pernod Ricard S.A.; Palmer and Harvey McLane Ltd.; REWE-Zentral AG; Scottish and Newcastle PLC; Musgrave Group PLC; Maxxium Worldwide B.V.; Greene King PLC; Davide Campari-Milano S.p.A.; A F Blakemore and Son Ltd.

FURTHER READING

"Belvedere Bids to Buy Out Marie Brizard Shareholders," *just-drinks.com,* April 20, 2006.

"Belvedere Closes Marie Brizard Soft Drink Sales," *just-drinks.com,* September 25, 2007.

"Belvedere Takes Over Marie Brizard Duty Free Distribution," *just-drinks.com,* January 25, 2007.

"Blavod Signs Marie Brizard Distribution Deal," *just-drinks.com,* March 16, 2004.

"Brands Respond to Stagnant Pastis Market," *Les Echos,* July 12, 2002.

"Brizard Purchase Helps Belvedere Sales Soar," *just-drinks.com,* February 15, 2007.

Durieux, Isabelle, "Guerre de familles," *L'Expansion,* October 24, 1994, pp. 78–80.

Kevany, Sophie, "Future of Marie Brizard Unit in Doubt," *just-drinks.com,* March 22, 2007.

"Marie Brizard Sells Sparkling Wine Arm," *just-drinks.com,* December 19, 2003.

"Marie Brizard Set for Duty-Free Relaunch," *Duty Free News International,* September 15, 2007, p. 18.

"Marie-Brizard: une recette de longevité," *L'Expansion,* October 1982, pp. 227–29.

Orozco, Stacie, "Firm Has 240 Years of Spirited Expertise," *South Florida Business Journal,* April 14, 2000, p. 18A.

Todd, Stuart, "Marie Brizard in Pitters Acquisition Talks," *just-drinks.com,* December 7, 2004.

Medifast, Inc.

11445 Cronhill Drive
Owings Mills, Maryland 21117-2270
U.S.A.
Telephone: (410) 581-8042
Toll Free: (866) 463-3432
Fax: (410) 581-8070
Web site: http://www.medifast.com

Public Company
Incorporated: 1980 as HealthRite, Inc.
Employees: 245
Sales: $83.8 million (2007)
Stock Exchanges: New York
Ticker Symbol: MED
NAICS: 311423 Dried and Dehydrated Food Manufacturing

■ ■ ■

Medifast, Inc., designs and manufactures a variety of weight-loss products, which the company distributes through physicians, its own weight control centers, retail stores, and direct-to-consumer through the Internet and advertising-generated marketing. The core of the weight-loss program is a protein shake that provides low-calorie, balanced nutrition for complete meal replacement and serves as part of a daily meal plan. Medifast produces more than 70 varieties of protein shakes, available in chocolate, vanilla, or strawberry flavors. Many address specific health needs, such as Medifast Plus for Diabetics, Medifast Plus for Appetite Suppression, and Medifast Plus for Coronary Health. Weight-loss products, such as snack bars, soups, powdered scrambled eggs, and soy crisp snack chips, support a healthy diet and nutrition during weight loss and for weight management. Medical supervision for weight loss is available through the company's Take Shape for Life program, a network of physicians and health coaches, or at Medifast Weight Loss Clinics or Hi-Energy Weight Loss clinics. The company operates more than 20 Medifast Weight Control Centers in Texas and Florida, and nine Hi-Energy Weight Loss clinics in Arizona, Georgia, and South Carolina. Medifast franchisees operate more than 100 weight-loss clinics.

CONSUMER POPULARITY, THEN UNCERTAINTY

The Medifast Take Shape Weight Loss program was created by Dr. William Vitale who formed HealthRite, Inc., in 1980, just as nutritional protein shakes as a meal replacement became popular with dieters. Vitale designed the program for rapid weight loss, his products to be combined with a restrictive 800-calorie diet. Vitale intended the program to be operated under physician supervision and distributed Medifast through medical doctors who sold the product at a price markup. HealthRite expanded its product line with complementary foods that assisted the weight-loss process, such as low-calorie snack bars.

HealthRite experienced sudden, unexpected growth in 1988, when television show host Oprah Winfrey lost 67 pounds on the Optifast weight-loss program. Winfrey's success prompted a rapid increase in consumer demand for meal replacement products. During this

COMPANY PERSPECTIVES

Your health is your most prized possession and Medifast is here to help you make the right choices to take control of your health. We teach people that the challenging environment you face everyday is so often not your fault and that your health really does matter to us. Medifast conveniently allows you to lose weight quickly, safely and more effectively than traditional weight loss plans and we are committed to teaching you how to maintain a healthy body long term. At Medifast, we are on a mission to enrich lives by providing innovative choices for lasting health.

time HealthRite developed a sales network of 15,000 physicians who sold Medifast, and sales soared to $50 million.

The company's fortunes reversed just as quickly, however, when the meal replacement craze lost credibility after Winfrey and other dieters regained lost weight upon returning to normal eating habits. The company struggled as many doctors stopped selling Medifast, leading to a steep decline in sales. HealthRite survived bankruptcy proceedings in the early 1990s, but by 1998 sales had declined to $15 million.

Seeing potential for the nutritional weight management system, shareholder Bradley T. McDonald gained control of the company in 1998, as it again verged on bankruptcy. McDonald became the CEO and began to restructure. McDonald, who first invested in the company in 1997, found venture capital as he held creditors at bay. Bank refinancing and additional investment from McDonald solidified the company's solvency. Liquidation of the herbal products subsidiary provided cash for product development, and McDonald added several new shake and snack bar flavors. Development of complementary products involved specialty diet foods, such as oatmeal and soups, which provided HealthRite with premium priced products.

Medifast regained its reputation as a trustworthy meal replacement product after Johns Hopkins Weight Management Center gave Medifast products a positive review. The visibility increased sales among doctors who sold nutritional products; medical supervision of the products renewed the company's credibility with consumers.

HealthRite expanded its market base during the late 1990s, as medical insurance programs stopped paying for weight-loss programs. The steep decline in sales prompted HealthRite to seek other sales outlets. Internet sales and a multilevel marketing program expanded the market range, and the company entered the retail sector for the first time in late 1998. This step required the company to meet Food and Drug Administration (FDA) standards for caloric content. For retail distribution, the caloric content of the protein shake increased to meet the needs of a 1,200-calorie diet for women and 1,500-calorie diet for men. The FDA required inclusion of daily meal planning and nutritional recommendations with the product, in order to safely support these caloric restrictions.

REVIVING THROUGH DIVERSIFIED PRODUCTS AND PROGRAMS

In 2001, McDonald solidified the restructuring process by changing the company name to Medifast, in line with the product brand name. By this time, the company had added another 40 products after a market study showed that consumers wanted a broad range of weight management foods. Medifast developed products for specialized needs. The *Fit!* product line, designed for adolescents ten to 16 years of age, included a chocolate-flavored shake in a box for easy carrying, as well as energy bars in chocolate and peanut butter flavors. Medifast Plus for Diabetics included a soy-based nutritional drink, snack bars, soups, oatmeal, chili, and beverages. Low in fat, sugar, carbohydrates, and calories, the products featured a low glycemic index, meaning that the food minimized the rise in blood sugar level.

To offset the loss of business from physicians, in 2002 Medifast launched its Take Shape for Life program, intended to specifically address problems of obesity. Customers obtained supervision from certified health advisers and medical professionals for a program of shakes and meals at new Medifast Weight Loss Clinics and through a network of health coaches. Clinic professionals monitored meal planning and weight-loss progress and provided motivational support, as well as fitness and disease prevention programs. Medifast selected Orlando, Dallas, and Houston as its entry markets. Take Shape for Life included a network of trained health coaches, who could support customers during their weight-loss process regardless of location.

Medifast expanded it product line and sales and distribution capacities through a series of acquisitions. In June 2003 the company purchased Women's Choice Systems, which sold the Women's Wellbeing brand. Marketed in 18,000 food and drugstores, the product line included items for women's special needs, such as addressing symptoms of menopause. The acquisition of

KEY DATES

1988: Oprah Winfrey introduces the public to meal replacement weight-loss programs when she loses 67 pounds on Optifast program.
1998: Company faces bankruptcy after decade of sales declines due to public concerns about meal replacement programs.
2001: Medifast takes product name as company name.
2004: National advertising campaign begins major growth cycle.
2007: Sales increase 85 percent, to $74.1 million.

Hi-Energy Weight Control Centers, which added 50 weight-loss clinics nationwide, cost Medifast $1.5 million plus liabilities, capital expenditures, and fees. Medifast revamped the Hi-Energy weight-loss program, incorporating 20 years of physicians' experience into the procedures and monitoring of customer targets for weight loss. To support expansion, Medifast acquired distributor Duns and Associates, as well as a 119,000-square-foot distribution facility in Ridgley, Maryland.

SUCCESSFUL NATIONAL MARKETING CAMPAIGN

With new products, sales outlets, and support mechanisms in place, Medifast began a period of increasing investment in advertising. In 2003 sportscaster Dick Vitale, former coach of the Detroit Pistons, signed a three-year agreement to be a spokesman for Medifast. Also, Medifast tripled its marketing budget from $1 million in 2002 to $3 million in 2003. Touting the company's medical reputation, Vitale appeared in advertisements in *Newsweek, Parade,* and *National Enquirer* as well as on CBS radio. After testing television commercials in the fall of 2003, Medifast launched a full-scale advertising campaign on Direct TV and several top national cable networks in January 2004. The 60-second commercials ran ten times per day on each channel. Strong consumer response required the company to add a third-party call center, but the large number of medical questions required additional training for call center employees. Medifast reduced its advertising replay until late February, when training of a dedicated call center staff was completed. Advertising boosted the company's clinical businesses as well as direct-to-consumer sales.

Medifast expanded its national advertising efforts with the development of a 30-minute infomercial to market the company's Medifast Plus for Diabetics. The long-form commercial highlighted information from a two-year clinical trial at the prestigious Johns Hopkins University Bloomberg School of Public Health to ascertain the weight loss and weight maintenance effectiveness of the products for type 2 diabetics. The study showed Medifast Plus for Diabetics aided weight loss, participating patients losing twice as much weight as the control group, which followed only nutritional guidelines from the American Diabetics Association. Moreover, 24 percent of the participants using the Medifast program either reduced the diabetic tendency or eliminated the problem altogether.

In May, Medifast expanded its advertising campaign to network television. These ads were designed to stimulate sales at physicians' offices, for the Take Shape for Life Network of certified health advisers, and at the Hi-Energy clinics, which had expanded in number from 40 to 80 clinics since the summer of 2003. Medifast planned to expand the Hi-Energy and Medislim clinic network to 125 outlets by the end of 2004. Advertisements included a 60-second spot on NBC's popular *Today Show,* with approximately 4.3 million viewers. Print advertising included national Sunday news magazines.

Before Medifast introduced its Maintain by Medifast product line of low carbohydrate shakes, bars, and soups in January 2005, it test marketed the line in July 2004 on National Multi-Channel Television Retailer, a cable network. Medifast sold $1,800 of products per minute. Satisfied with the results, Medifast followed with a national print, radio, and television campaign.

Advertising supported Medifast's expansion of the Hi-Energy brand to regional drugstore chain Kerr Drug. The Weight Control Centers were located in drugstores, as a "store-within-a-store." In April 2005, Medifast opened three such outlets in Raleigh and one in Greensboro, North Carolina. Outlets ranged from 500 to 1,000 square feet in size. Five Hi-Energy clinics opened in DrugMax in Hartford, Connecticut, the following July.

Medifast expanded its product line with a special brand for All-Pro National Football League linebacker Ray Lewis. The Ray Lewis Take Shape America Nutrition line, introduced in October 2005, provided products designed to support sports performance and weight management. These included the Pro Drink for Men, Pro Drink for Women, with a mix of soy and whey protein, and Balanced Nutrition Energy Bars.

Medifast's marketing efforts resulted in a sales increase of 47 percent in 2005, to $40.1 million, compared to $27.3 million in 2004. Even more phenomenal improvement resulted in 2006, with revenues increasing another 85 percent, to $74.1 million.

Medifast prepared for continued growth by expanding its manufacturing capacity. New equipment included a mixer capable of producing a 5,400-pound batch of nutritional shake powder, twice the capacity of its two largest blenders. To accommodate the new production capacity, the company added two production lines and two packaging lines, as well.

EXPANDING ON SUCCESS

With Michael S. McDevitt as the new chief executive officer, Medifast continued to employ the methods that regenerated the company's viability during 2007. The company introduced new products, such as powdered scrambled eggs and soy crisp snack chips. Marketing strategy involved a new infomercial format, shifting from 30 minutes of testimonials to a talk-show style discussion of how Medifast products can alleviate the dangers of obesity.

With an advertising budget of $28 million, Medifast employed two high-profile spokeswomen, Genie Francis and Kristy Swanson. Francis, known for more than 20 years for her role as Laura on the daytime soap opera *General Hospital,* became a weight-loss model when she shed more than 30 pounds on the Medifast plan. Francis shared her experience with customers through an online blog and real-time chats. Swanson, known for her role as Buffy Summers in *Buffy the Vampire Slayer,* provided a younger role model and shared her experience through a personal journal on the company web site. After successfully completing their weight-loss programs, both Francis and Swanson were featured in various publications: *People Magazine, Soap Opera Digest,* and *Life and Style Weekly* chronicled their weight-loss process. They were covered on national television by programs such as *The View, E! News,* and *Inside Edition.*

Medifast sought new outlets for its products and services. The corporate wellness program was designed to provide companies with an obesity program for their employees. A variety of support included medical supervision and a health coach, along with online access to nutritionists, information, and support groups. There was also access to a Medifast Weight Loss Clinic, available for participants wanting more personal attention. CareFirst Blue Cross/Blue Shield of Maryland was among Medifast's first customers.

During 2008 Medifast obtained approval to franchise weight-loss clinics in California, Illinois, Maryland, Minnesota, New York, Rhode Island, and Virginia, bringing the total to 47 states. Medifast's first franchise sold was located in the Baltimore area, and it included up to four Medifast Weight Loss Clinics in the metropolitan area. A new franchiser planned to open four clinics in Southern California and three clinics in central California within two years; rights included four clinics in the San Diego area. Corporate-owned weight-loss clinics opened in Orlando, Houston, and Dallas, bringing the total to 21 Medifast Weight Loss Clinics. The company planned to open another 20 stores over the next two years in select markets.

Mary Tradii

PRINCIPAL SUBSIDIARIES

Jason Pharmaceuticals, Inc.; Jason Properties, LLC; Seven Crondall, LLC; Take Shape for Life, Inc.

PRINCIPAL OPERATING UNITS

Medifast Direct; Take Shape for Life; Medical Physicians and Clinics; Medifast and Hi-Energy Weight Control Centers.

PRINCIPAL COMPETITORS

eDiets; Herbalife Ltd.; Jenny Craig, Inc.; LAWeight Loss; NutriSystem, Inc.; Slim-Fast Foods Company; Weight Watchers International, Inc.

FURTHER READING

Connolly, Allison, "Mainstream Medifast: Owings Mills Firm Is Using Outlets, Franchises, National Ads to Market Its Weight-Loss Products," *Baltimore Sun,* May 4, 2007.

———, "Medifast Promotes McDevitt to Chief Executive," *Baltimore Sun,* January 6, 2007.

"DrugMax Gains Weight Loss Program," *Drug Store News,* July 11, 2005, p. 3.

Hammock, Jay, "Stock of Owings Mills, MD-based Diet Supplement Maker Leaps Ahead," *Baltimore Sun,* July 23, 2003.

"HealthRite, Inc.," *Baltimore Business Journal,* February 9, 2001, p. 7.

Levy, Sandra, "Medifast's Weight Control Centers to Debut in Kerr Drug," *Drug Topics,* April 4, 2005, p. 49.

"Low-Carbohydrate, Diabetic Friendly Products Launched on Television Retailer," *Biotech Week,* August 11, 2004, p. 407.

"Maryland-Based Owings Mills Signs Actress Genie Francis As Its New Spokesperson," *Baltimore Sun,* May 31, 2007.

"Medifast Acquires Hi-Energy Weight Loss Control Centers," *Health & Medicine Week,* December 1, 2003, p. 610.

"Medifast Bradley McDonald," *MMR,* April 25, 2005, p. 64.

"Medifast Finishes Warehouse Purchase," *Daily Deal,* September 16, 2003.

"Medifast Forms Strategic Alliance with Xl Health, Inc.," *Drug Week,* April 9, 2004, p. 144.

"Medifast Restyles Weight Loss Line for Mass Channel Sales Effort," *Drug Store News,* July 20, 1998, p. CP45.

"Medifast's Soy-Based Meal for Diabetics," *Nutraceuticals International,* May 2002.

"Medifast Taps New Spokeswoman," *Marketing to Women: Addressing Women and Women's Sensibilities,* August 2007, p. 3.

Much, Marilyn, "Medifast, Inc. Owings Mills, Maryland: It Enjoys a Steady Diet of Top-Line Growth," *Investor's Business Daily,* August 8, 2003, p. A05.

"New Products," *Nutraceuticals World,* July/August 2003, p. 81.

Swibel, Matthew, "Glutton for Growth," *Forbes,* November 10, 2003, p. 177.

"Take Shape America," *Nutraceuticals World,* October 2005, p. 86.

Metalico Inc.

186 North Avenue East
Cranford, New Jersey 07016-2143
U.S.A.
Telephone: (908) 497-9610
Fax: (908) 497-1097
Web site: http://www.metalico.com

Public Company
Incorporated: 1997
Employees: 391
Sales: $334.2 million (2007)
Stock Exchanges: American
Ticker Symbol: MEA
NAICS: 3331419 Primary Smelting and Refining of Nonferrous Metal (Except Copper and Aluminum)

■ ■ ■

Metalico Inc., is a Cranford, New Jersey-based company that recycles ferrous and non-ferrous scrap metal and fabricates lead metal products. Recycling centers are maintained in New York, Ohio, and Pennsylvania and serve the United States' and Canadian markets. Sources of scrap metal include demolition contractors, manufacturers, small scrap dealers, peddlers, and even local residents looking to sell old siding, window frames, and doors. The materials are then processed into reusable forms and sold to foundries, electric arc furnace mills, secondary smelters, aluminum recyclers, and metal brokers. Metalico also manufactures deoxidizing aluminum for the steel industry. Metalico's Tranzact, Inc. operation recycles high-temperature refractory metals, including chromium, molybdenum, rhenium, tantalum, and tungsten. Some of the lead metal scrap Metalico collects from such sources as automobile and truck batteries is used by Metalico's five product fabrication operations located in four states. As the largest lead fabricator in the United States, these units supply the plumbing, marine, radiation shielding, and roofing trades. In addition, Carson City, Nevada-based West Coast Magnum Shot and Granite City, Illinois-based Lawrence Brand Shot produces lean magnum shot used in shotgun shells.

FOUNDER, A CUBAN EXILE

Metalico was founded by Carlos E. Aguero, a native of Cuba who fled the island with his family following the Communist revolution in 1959 and the rise to power of Fidel Castro. He came to the United States, where he received his education, graduating with a degree in accounting and international business from Upsala College, a private college in East Orange, New Jersey, which later closed. He then went to work as an accountant for Coopers & Lybrand in 1973, staying until 1981, and rising to the rank of audit supervisor. He returned for a brief stint in 1983 before joining the accounting firm of Gralnick, Strauss, D'Angerio, where he was named a partner and specialized in the waste management field. Although he remained with the firm, Aguero also served as comptroller for the Pennsauken Solid Waste Management Authority in New Jersey in 1985, a post he held until 1990. In 1988 he left Gralnick Strauss to start his own waste management business called Continental Waste Industries, Inc.

COMPANY PERSPECTIVES

The Company pursues its growth strategy through acquisitions and investments in strategic products, markets and geographic areas. Metalico is committed to proving that the American manufacturing sector can compete in a global economy through dedicated employees and management, capital and technology investments, and careful control of inventory and energy costs.

Based in Clark, New Jersey, Continental Waste was a hauler of nonhazardous waste, an industry that had been consolidating since the 1965 Solid Waste Disposal Act, which imposed higher hygiene standards, thereby increasing the cost of doing business and squeezing out smaller operators. While there had been a great deal of consolidation in the hazardous waste collection field, there remained opportunities in the nonhazardous waste field, and Aguero formed Continental Waste to serve as a consolidation vehicle. Over the next decade he engineered the acquisition or merger of more than 30 companies, pursuing a "hub and spoke" strategy, and in 1993 took the company public. By 1996 the company was doing about $80 million in business, operating landfills, transfer stations, collection services, and recycling centers in ten states as well as Costa Rica and Mexico. It ranked 47th on the Waste Age 100 issued in 1995. The company's success attracted the attention of an even larger player in the industry, Florida-based Republic Services Inc., controlled by well-known businessman H. Wayne Huizenga. In 1996 Aguero agreed to sell Continental Waste to Republic for $350 million.

FORMATION OF METALICO: 1997

Aguero signed a non-compete agreement with Republic, but because he was just 43 years old, he was not ready to retire. A year after selling Continental Waste, in August 1997, he formed a new company, Metalico Inc., to become a consolidator in a field related to waste management: metals reclamation and recycling. Contributing some of the startup funds, Aguero became chairman, CEO, and president. He raised further funds by selling $18 million of convertible preferred stock to a group of venture capital firms that included RFE Investment Partners, Seacoast Capital, and Kitty Hawk Capital Inc. Shares were also purchased through funds managed by First Analysis Corp. The money, as well as stock, was soon put to use. In December 1997 Metalico acquired from Taracorp Inc. two lead fabrication plants in Granite City, Illinois, and Atlanta, Georgia, producers of lead sheet, roof flashing, solder alloys, shot and lead, and tin alloys. College Grove, Tennessee-based General Smelting & Refining Inc., a secondary lead smelter and refiner, was also acquired. Combined, these businesses generated more than $45 million in annual sales.

In February 1998 Metalico completed four more acquisitions. Rochester, New York-based Lyell Metal Co. Inc. was a 20-year-old metal processor of both ferrous and non-ferrous scrap. In addition, Aguero beefed up the manufacturing component, acquiring a pair of Healdsburg, California, sister companies: Santa Rosa Lead Products Inc. and W.W. Nelson Inc., makers of lead-based products, including roof flashings and lead-lined doors. Metalico also acquired West Coast Shot Inc., a Carson City, Nevada, manufacturer of lead shot. The acquisition spree continued in April 1998 with the purchase of Bloomfield, Connecticut-based Stanley Sack & Co., a scrap metal recycler. Two upstate New York scrap companies were also added in July of that year: Buffalo-based Lake Erie Recycling Corp., which processed copper, aluminum, and other non-ferrous metals; and Tonawanda-based Louis Levin & Co. Inc., a collector of industrial ferrous scrap in the Buffalo area.

SLOWING EXPANSION: 1999

Metalico cut back on expansion in 1999, due in part to a softening in the market related to the Asian financial crisis. Demand for recycled metal fell and prices followed suit. The selling price for high-temperature alloy scrap, for example, dropped from $4 a pound in 1998 to just 75 cents by the start of 1999. As a result, the workforce at Stanley Sack was trimmed and some work moved to Metalico yards in Buffalo and Rochester. At the time, Metalico was negotiating a union contract with workers at Stanley Sack, the first ever for the Connecticut business, and the changes resulted in complaints issued by the National Labor Relations Board, alleging that Metalico had fired workers in retaliation for organizing. Metalico insisted that the changes were due purely to economic factors beyond its control. Metalico did complete one significant acquisition during 1999, however. In August 1999 it purchased Gulf Coast Recycling Inc. in East Tampa, Florida, adding about $25 million in annual sales.

Metalico's revenues totaled $67 million in 1999, accompanied by a net loss of $5 million. Demand for recycled metal increased in 2000, but prices were kept down by the availability of large quantities of recycled

KEY DATES

1997: Company is founded.
2000: Gulf Coast Recycling is acquired.
2004: Stock is listed on Pink Sheets.
2005: Metalico shares begin trading on the American Stock Exchange.
2008: American CatCon is acquired.

ferrous metals from countries that had once been part of the Soviet Union. In addition, increasing domestic demand for finished steel products in the United States was offset by low-cost imports, mostly from Asia, resulting in prices that continued to fall for Metalico. On the strength of the Gulf Coast Recycling acquisition, Metalico was able to grow revenues to $81.3 million in 2000, but the company lost $4.7 million.

Low prices continued in 2001, leading to a drop in Metalico's sales to $71.4 million. The company was, however able to record earnings of $10.2 million. With the economy in recession, sales continued to trend downward in 2002, dipping to $59.3 million, while net income fell to $2.8 million. Because of these poor conditions, Metalico during this period idled its secondary lead smelting subsidiary in College Grove, Tennessee. The company was able to seize an opportunity in 2002 to form a joint venture with Birmingham, Alabama-based Mayfield Manufacturing, creating a lead products fabricator under the Mayco Industries, L.L.C., name.

AMERICAN STOCK EXCHANGE LISTING: 2006

Sales continued to decrease in 2003 to $51.4 million, and net income dipped below $2 million. In 2004 Metalico bought out its partner in Mayco Industries, a move that helped improve revenues to $104.8 million and net income to $6.7 million in 2004, but higher average selling prices were also a factor, as was the $4 million contributed by a pair of acquisitions completed during the year. A Lackawanna, New York, scrap handling company was purchased for $1.6 million, and a Rochester, New York, scrap yard, Samuel Frank Metal Co., was added for another $4.9 million. Metalico also took steps in 2004 toward full public trading of its common stock when it secured a listing on the Pink Sheets reporting system. A year later Metalico received approval from the American Stock Exchange to list its shares on the high-profile exchange.

Sales continued to climb in 2005, topping $155 million, while net income totaled $5.6 million. Returning to expansion mode in 2006, Metalico acquired Roth Brothers Smelting in DeWitt, New York, near Syracuse. This 22-acre site became the home to Metalico Syracuse Inc., and the Lackawanna deox aluminum smelter was relocated there. It would serve auto wreckers and other accounts, and the automobile hulks and light iron it received would be transferred to a new shredding operation in the area. Metalico engineered another acquisition in July 2006, agreeing to purchase Ohio-based Niles Iron & Metal Co. Inc. and its two scrap yards for a reported $44 million, but by the end of August the deal was scrapped after Metalico had second thoughts about the potential profitability of the assets. The owners of Niles Iron responded by filing suit against Metalico, alleging breach of contract.

Higher sales volumes combined with higher prices resulted in a 33.8 percent increase in revenues in 2006 to $207.7 million. The company all but doubled net income as well to $10.3 million. With conditions more conducive to acquisitions, Metalico resumed its aggressive growth push. In May 2007, Quarryville, Pennsylvania-based Tranzact, a $30-million-a-year recycler of molybdenum, tantalum, and tungsten scrap, was added for $10 million. A month later the assets of Rochester, New York-based Compass Environmental Haulers Inc., a construction and demolition debris transfer station, was bought. Metalico then spent $36 million to acquire Annaco, Inc., an Akron, Ohio-based scrap metal recycler that was a major motor block processor, and $40 million for Totalcat Group, Inc., a Newark, New Jersey-based recycler and manufacturer of catalytic devices. Together Annaco and Totalcat brought in revenues of more than $90 million. Moreover, they fit with a strategy of expanding Metalico's reach along the Great Lakes corridor while also providing some diversity to the company's product lines. In 2007 Metalico's revenues surged to more than $334.2 million and net income improved to $14.8 million.

FORMATION OF METALICO CATCON: 2008

An emphasis on external growth carried into 2008. At the start of the year Metalico paid $35 million for American CatCon Holding, LLC, and American CatCon, LLC, both owned by Allen W. Hickman Jr. and his family. With its main operation located near Austin, Texas, and a buying center in Dallas and another facility in Gulfport, Mississippi, American CatCon recycled catalytic converters and also recovered platinum group metals. With more than $122 million in sales, American CatCon was Metalico's most significant acquisition to date. The assets became the foundation for a new subsidiary, Metalico CatCon Inc., with Allen Hickman serving as general manager.

To fund further deals, Metalico raised about $28.7 million in a private placement of stock in April 2008. A month later the company raised another $100 million through the private placement of 7 percent senior convertible notes. Out of the net proceeds, Metalico used $69 million, along with $7 million in stock, to complete the purchase of Snyder Group Inc., a Brownsville, Pennsylvania-based operator of two western Pennsylvania scrap yards, four feeder yards, and a shredder operation. The new units, Metalico Neville Inc., added $120 million to Metalico's annual revenues.

Ed Dinger

PRINCIPAL SUBSIDIARIES

Metalico Buffalo; Metalico Rochester; Metalico Aluminum Recovery; Metalico Neville Inc.; Metalico Transport; Mayco Industries, Inc.; American CatCon, Inc.; Metalico Syracuse; Metalico Annaco; Tranzact, Inc.; Santa Lead Products; West Coast Shot; Lawrence Brand Shot.

PRINCIPAL COMPETITORS

Commercial Metals Company; OmniSource Corporation; Philip Services Corporation.

FURTHER READING

Corder, David R., "N.J. Firm Acquires Gulf Coast Recycling," *Tampa Bay Business Journal,* August 23, 1999.

Geiselman, Bruce, "New Consolidator Buys Scrap Firm," *Waste News,* March 2, 1998, p. 7.

Nicholson, Gilbert, "Mayfield Merger Creates Mayco," *Birmingham Business Journal,* May 27, 2002.

Schaffer, Paul, "Metalico Caps Acquisition of Snyder Scrapyards in Pa.," *American Metal Market,* May 7, 2008, p. 14.

———, "Metalico Forms New Unit to Run Hickman Assets," *American Metal Market,* January 8, 2008, p. 6.

———, "Metalico Reticent over $76m Yard Acquisition," *American Metal Market,* April 25, 2008, p. 1.

———, "Metalico Sells Stock to Build War Chest," *American Metal Market,* March 31, 2008, p. 11.

———, "Metalico Thinks Pink in Likely First Step Toward Public Trade," *American Metal Market,* July 6, 2004, p. 7.

Worden, Edward, "Metalico Buys Two Companies," *American Metal Market,* July 16, 1998, p. 7.

———, "Metalico Still on Growth Track," *American Metal Market,* February 23, 1998, p. 7.

Mota-Engil, SGPS, S.A.

Rua do Rego Lameiro 38
Oporto, P-4300-454
Portugal
Telephone: (351 22) 519-0300
Fax: (351 22) 519-0303
Web site: http://www.mota-engil.pt

Public Company
Incorporated: 1987 as Mota & Companhia
Employees: 15,938
Sales: EUR 1.4 billion (2007)
Stock Exchanges: Euronext Lisbon OTC
Ticker Symbols: EGL; MTELF
NAICS: 236116 New Multi-Family Housing Construction (Except Operative Builders); 236210 Industrial Building Construction; 237110 Water and Sewer Line and Related Structures Construction; 237310 Highway, Street, and Bridge Construction; 237990 Other Heavy and Civil Engineering Construction; 488490 Other Support Activities for Road Transportation; 541330 Engineering Services; 551112 Offices of Other Holding Companies; 562111 Solid Waste Collection

■ ■ ■

Mota-Engil, SGPS, S.A., is a Portuguese holding company whose engineering and construction division makes it Portugal's leading construction company. It also has holdings in transport concessions, environment and services, industry and energy, tourism, and shared services. In all, the holding company has interests in 90 companies. It is active on three continents and, besides Portugal, is especially strong in Spain, Central and Eastern Europe, and Angola. The companies under the control of Mota-Engil collectively form what is called the Mota-Engil Group.

FORTY YEARS OF MOTA AND ENGIL: 1946–86

Mota & Companhia was founded in 1946 by Manuel António da Mota, who immediately established a branch of the company in Portugal's colony of Angola, where his firm was engaged in timber exploitation and public works construction until Angola achieved independence in 1975. Portugal's five African colonies were home to millions of Portuguese, many employed in the building trades, who had not been able to find work in their own poverty-stricken country.

Mota & Companhia won its first major contract in 1952, when it was charged with the construction of the international airport at Angola's capital, Luanda. The importance of Portuguese contractors in Portuguese-speaking Africa continued after independence. "Portuguese emigrants," wrote a *Financial Times* correspondent in 1982, "will—out of economic necessity—go on serving as a kind of roving international workforce of builders, because they are willing, plentiful, inexpensive and hard-working." Portuguese firms had the great advantage of speaking a common language with their hosts and considerable experience in completing projects in these countries. For many years after independence Mota and Paviterra UEM, a company engaged in earthmoving that Mota established in as-

COMPANY PERSPECTIVES

The Mission is directed all times towards achieving total customer and shareholder satisfaction, the basic principles being to provide utmost quality under the very best safety conditions, with full regard for the environment and with no discouragement of the human spirit that we wish to retain in our relations with our employees.

Against a background of profound alterations, we are fully prepared to look into any changes in an endeavor to transform them into sustained growth opportunities for the Group.

sociation with the government of Angola in 1980, were the only corporate structures engaged in public works in that country.

However, after the independence of the colonies, Mota also became active in other African countries. In 1975 the firm began constructing the Dreihuk Dam in Botswana, the Matooster-Bierkrall Highway and, subsequently, the Lonhlupheko-Lomahasha Highway in neighboring Swaziland. Mota also became active in Portugal. In 1976 it was awarded the contract to construct a small dam in southern Portugal. Soon after, it won its first major public works contract there, involving changes in the course of the lower Mondego River. The company's performance resulted in commissions of every kind, and very quickly Mota was Portugal's third largest company in its field.

Engil, a civil engineering firm, was founded in 1952 by Fernando José Saraiva and António Lopes de Almeida. Two new shareholders, Simões Cúclo and António Valades Fernandes, joined the company in 1954, and Valades Fernandes took control of its destiny in this period. In 1961 Engil won its first major contract outside the Lisbon area, to build an industrial and commercial school. It also constructed the bridge over the Tua River in Mirandela. Under an agreement with a foreign firm, the company in 1969 won exclusive rights for Portugal of a sliding formwork patent. This allowed Engil to erect a large number of silos and chimneys.

THE ROAD TO MERGER: 1987–2000

Mota & Companhia was incorporated in 1987 and entered the Lisbon stock exchange. Beginning in 1990 it branched out from civil construction. Its activities included property development and the manufacture of highway signing and marking, precast structural elements, ceramic products, and asphalt compounds. In 1994 Mota won the contract, in conjunction with other companies, for the Vasco da Gama bridge project. This bridge, the longest in Europe, spanning the Tagus River estuary at Lisbon, was completed in 1998. This commission led to the creation of Lusoponte, a concessionaire for the highways that crossed the Tagus downstream from Vila Franca de Xira.

Engil was incorporated as a holding company in 1987 and in the next few years acquired Sociedade de Empreltadas, Gerco, Sociedade de Engenharia Eletrotécnica, and Ferroviase Construções. During this period Engil built the Alto do Lindoso Dam. Engil entered the African market in 1989. In that year the British engineering and construction group AMEC plc acquired a half-share of the Engil construction group, which had entered the Lisbon stock exchange. Portugal, financed with an infusion of funds from the European Union, was entering a prosperous period for construction.

In 1994 AMEC sold its stake in Engil for PTE 2.7 billion ($17.2 million). Engil also spent about PTE 3 billion ($19.1 million) to take complete control of three associated companies. The holding company, in which Portugal's Geril group had a controlling interest, began projects in Germany and Peru in 1996. In 1999 two companies belonging to the Mota family, Algosi SPGS and Vallis SPGS, made a bid to acquire Engil. The hostile takeover, although bitterly contested by Geril, resulted in the formation of the Mota-Engil group, Portugal's largest construction company, the following year.

BRANCHING OUT: 2002–08

Newly merged Mota-Engil began to diversify into the fields of transportation, environment, and services in 2002. The following year it became a holding company with four distinct and autonomous business areas: engineering and construction; environment and services; real estate and tourism; and transport concessions. By 2004 Mota-Engil was active in Eastern Europe, and, after the integration of two group companies, it created Mota-Engil Polska, S.A., the fourth largest building company in Poland.

In 2005 the holding company's Martifer SPGS metallic-structures company established a strategic partnership with REpower Systems, AG, the third largest European company in the production and assembly of air generators for wind power. Founded in 1990, Martifer had grown from 18 to 1,500 employees and

KEY DATES

1946: Mota & Companhia is founded and becomes active in Portugal's African colony of Angola.
1952: Mota wins its first major contract, to build the airport at Angola's capital, Luanda; Engil is founded as a civil engineering firm.
1987: Mota is incorporated and joins the Lisbon stock exchange.
1989: Engil is incorporated and joins the Lisbon stock exchange.
2000: The merger of Engil into Mota results in the creation of Portugal's largest construction firm.
2003: Mota-Engil becomes a holding company with four distinct, autonomous lines of business.
2004: Active in Eastern Europe, the company's holdings include Mota-Engil Polska.
2006: Acquisition of the Tertir Group makes Mota-Engil the leading port operator in Portugal.

had invested in energy equipment, the production of biofuels and electricity, and retail warehousing. Its goal was to further develop activities in the field of renewable energy, and it was also forming partnerships in the construction of wind power towers and the development of biodiesel fuels, in the form of oilseeds added to diesel fuel.

In 2007 Martifer was one of three companies that agreed to foster REpower's growth, establishing REpower Portugal, a joint venture. Another joint venture in which Martifer took a one-third stake was Ventinvest, which obtained a license to operate wind farms having a production capacity of 400 megawatts. Martifer had also contributed to the construction of the Oporto airport and the Lisbon stadium where the Euro 2004 soccer championship was held.

Mota-Engil, in 2006, acquired the Tertir Group, which enhanced its position in the sectors of environmental protection and water treatment. Tertir was a leader in loading and unloading cargo at port terminals, with controlling positions in Lisbon facilities and those of Maputo, Mozambique. This acquisition made Mota-Engil the largest port operator in Portugal. Also in 2006, Mota-Engil started work on a bridge spanning the Zambezi River in Mozambique. This was the biggest public-works project in the history of the country.

Malawi was another African country in which Mota-Engil had, since 1989, been active, and in 2006 it completed a road between Kamphata and Nkhoma. The following year, it received an eight-year contract for works to be undertaken at a uranium mine in Malawi. Mota-Engil also was responsible for the renovation and expansion of the Midima Highway linking Balantyre, Malawi's largest city, to Mozambique and its Indian Ocean ports. Funded by the European Union, the road was renamed the Robert Mugabe Highway and dedicated in 2008 by none other than the Zimbabwean president himself. In Portugal, the Lusolisboa consortium won a 30-year toll-road concession in the Lisbon metropolitan area. Mota-Engil held 36 percent of this consortium.

The company's U.S. associate, MK Contractors LLC (MKC), was engaged in the construction of residential real estate. By 2003 the firm had constructed two apartment condominium buildings in Coral Gables, Florida, and had practically completed Bentley Beach, a five-star hotel in South Miami Beach. Work was underway on Brickell Bay, a 36-story residential building in downtown Miami. In 2005 MKC won contracts to build two more residential condominiums, one in Miami, the other in Coral Gables.

Martifer was spun off in an initial public offering on the Lisbon stock exchange in 2007, but Mota-Engil continued to hold 37.5 percent of the shares and to influence the management of the company. In 2008 a consortium in which Mota-Engil held a half interest won a 30-year toll-road concession to build a highway between Perote and Xalapa in Mexico. The company also had a half stake in a $400 million residential construction project in Angola.

Engineering and construction represented 75 percent of Mota-Engil's sales in 2007. Environment and services accounted for 18 percent, and transport concessions for the remaining 7 percent.

The toll-road concessions were more important than revenue figures indicated, however, because they were highly profitable and therefore made Mota-Engil's stock a favorite among international investors. In addition to company sales of EUR 1.4 billion, other income came to EUR 132.81 million.

By area, countries outside Spain and Portugal were significant for Mota-Engil's operations. Central and Eastern Europe accounted for 20 percent of the company's sales in 2006, while Africa and the Americas accounted for nearly 18 percent. The Eastern European countries, besides Poland, where Mota-Engil had a presence were the Czech Republic, Hungary, Romania, and Slovakia.

Mota-Engil announced in 2008 that it aimed to reach EUR 3.65 billion in annual revenue in 2013, of which countries outside Spain and Portugal would account for more than half. The company expected growth to come from the construction of a new international airport in Lisbon and the development of a high-speed train in Portugal. It expected to bid with partner ES Concessões for work on these infrastructure projects. Mota also said it would analyze prospects in the Indian and Ukrainian markets and would seek to develop new partnerships with Martifer in Portugal and abroad. Approximately 75 percent of Mota's stock was held by family-owned corporations. The chairman of the board was António Manuel Queiros Vasconcelos da Mota.

Robert Halasz

PRINCIPAL SUBSIDIARIES

Mota-Engil, Ambiente Serviços, SA; Mota-Engil, Engenharia e Construção, S.A.; Mota-Engil Serviços Partilhados, S.A.; MEESWAY, Concessões de Transportes, SA.

PRINCIPAL DIVISIONS

Engineering and Construction; Environment and Services; Industry and Energy; Transport Concessions.

PRINCIPAL COMPETITORS

Somague SPGS; Teixeira Duarte SPGS.

FURTHER READING

Bugge, Axel, "Portugal's Mota Aims to Boost Revenues, Diversify," *Reuters,* May 30, 2008.

"Construction Looks to Ex-Colonies," *Financial Times,* September 29, 1982, p. 19.

"Mugabe Defends Malawi Road Naming," *BBC News,* May 4, 2006.

Ward, Sandra, "Europe-Bound," *Barron's,* May 1, 2006, p. 38.

Wise, Peter, "Portugal: The Ones to Watch," *Banker,* May 2008, pp. 92, 94.

Wise, Peter, and Andrew Taylor, "Amec Sells Engil Shareholding," *Financial Times,* October 13, 1994, p. 27.

National City Corporation

1900 East 9th Street
Cleveland, Ohio 44114-3484
U.S.A.
Telephone: (216) 222-2000
Fax: (216) 575-9957
Web site: http://www.nationalcity.com

Public Company
Incorporated: 1845 as City Bank of Cleveland
Employees: 32,064
Total Assets: $155.04 billion (2008)
Stock Exchanges: New York
Ticker Symbol: NCC
NAICS: 551111 Offices of Bank Holding Companies; 522110 Commercial Banking; 522292 Real Estate Credit; 523110 Investment Banking and Securities Dealing; 523120 Securities Brokerage; 523920 Portfolio Management; 523930 Investment Advice; 524210 Insurance Agencies and Brokerages; 525910 Open-End Investment Funds; 525920 Trusts, Estates, and Agency Accounts; 532420 Office Machinery and Equipment Rental and Leasing

■ ■ ■

With more than $155 billion in assets and over 1,400 branch offices in Ohio, Florida, Illinois, Indiana, Kentucky, Michigan, Missouri, Pennsylvania, and Wisconsin, National City Corporation is the largest bank holding company headquartered in Ohio and ranks among the top dozen banks in the United States in terms of assets. As is typical of U.S. regional banks, National City concentrates primarily on its own region, offering retail banking, commercial banking, mortgage banking, and asset management services within its nine-state geographical footprint. In addition, the company operates nationwide in selected sectors, most notably mortgage banking, an area supported by more than 400 National City offices across the country, as well as certain financial services within commercial banking. The 160-plus-year-old institution grew rapidly in the late-20th-century era of bank consolidation, and then launched an aggressive move into mortgage banking at the very end of the century. Subsequently, National City was hit hard by the 2007 meltdown in the mortgage market and had to be bailed out the following year via a $7 billion infusion of capital.

1845 ORIGIN AS CITY BANK OF CLEVELAND

The company was founded in 1845, shortly after the Ohio Bank Act of that year brought a measure of stability to the state's banking system. Cleveland had endured three years without a bank of any kind and the City Bank of Cleveland, as National City Bank was initially known, was the first to be chartered under the new law. Ruben Sheldon and Theodoric C. Severance, both of the Fireman's Insurance Company, led the new institution. Formerly president of Fireman's Insurance, Sheldon assumed those same duties at City Bank. Severance, formerly secretary at the insurance company, started his career in banking as a teller.

City Bank opened for business in July, providing its clients with secured paper money, a safe place to deposit

COMPANY PERSPECTIVES

We care about doing what's right. At National City, we are committed to employing a talented workforce, partnering with diverse business owners, and investing in the communities we serve.

savings, and a source of funds for commercial loans. Its function as a lender supported the oil, iron, steel, shipping, and railroad industries that would be vital to Cleveland's development as an important midwestern city. During its first five years in operation, City Bank's capital stock tripled from $50,000 to $150,000. Lemuel B. Wick served as president in the 1850s, during which time the bank's growth propelled two moves to successively larger headquarters.

1865 RECHARTERED AS NATIONAL CITY BANK OF CLEVELAND

Rampant inflation during the Civil War crystallized formerly divided opinions on a unified currency structure, prompting the 1863 ratification of the National Banking Act. The new law created a national currency secured by U.S. bonds, as well as a new system of federally regulated banks. These "national" banks were required to purchase bonds worth up to one-third of their capital stock and to deposit those bonds with the U.S. Treasury as security for a new system for national currency. City Bank waited until its original state charter expired in 1865 before complying with the new law and becoming National City Bank of Cleveland that year.

W. P. Southworth succeeded Lemuel Wick as president upon the latter's death in 1873. In 1889 longtime employee John F. Whitelaw became president. A 1995 company history credited Whitelaw with establishing the conservative character that continued to distinguish National City Bank throughout most of its history.

National City Bank grew and profited throughout the late 19th century but remained one of the smaller commercial banks. Assets rose steadily, passing the $1 million mark in 1881, $1.5 million in 1890, and $2 million in 1901. This consistent rate of growth would have been admirable during a normal period, but was especially extraordinary given the severe panic (or national recession) of the mid-1890s, when almost 500 banks failed nationwide.

Whitelaw died in 1912 after serving the bank for more than half a century. His abrupt departure opened the door to a takeover by James M. Hoyt, who purchased a total of 1,000 shares (including Whitelaw's 842) to gain control of National City. The new stockholder moved the business, increased its capital stock to $500,000, expanded the board of directors from five to 25, and got Charles A. Paine elected president by the end of the year. National City opened an imposing new headquarters in 1913, replete with tile floors, marble, and luxurious fixtures. Rapid asset growth during this period seemed to reflect the bank's new image, doubling from $2.5 million in 1912 to $5.7 million in 1914. By that time, National City Bank ranked fourth among Cleveland's banks in terms of combined capital and surplus, and sixth in deposits and total assets. Nevertheless, a centennial history characterized the institution at this juncture as "plodding along nicely, but down among the minors," having not participated in the wave of mergers and acquisitions that characterized this period in banking history.

In an effort to decentralize and stabilize the nation's monetary system (which was then concentrated in New York City) the U.S. government ratified the Federal Reserve Act in 1913, creating a system of 12 regional banks. This new organization bolstered the public's confidence in national banks by requiring all, including National City, to deposit 3 percent of their capital and surplus with the regional Reserve bank for safekeeping. Although many bankers initially opposed the creation of the Federal Reserve, the agency helped prevent panics and runs on banks, gave the federal government more control over the country's money supply, made commercial credit more available, and inhibited venturesome banking practices.

National City grew quickly during World War I, and shared its good fortune by purchasing $100 million in U.S. bonds in support of the country's war effort. Assets increased from $4.5 million in 1913 to $15.5 million in 1919. Bank President Paine was elected to the newly created title of CEO and chairman in 1918, and Hoyt V. Shulters, formerly of East Ohio Gas Co., advanced to the presidency.

SURVIVING THE GREAT DEPRESSION

Assets nearly doubled to $30.6 million by 1925 and totaled about $40 million by the end of this prosperous decade, when National City ranked second among Cleveland's national banks and fifth overall. The institution's conservative management sheltered it from the financial crisis of October 1929 and the devastating

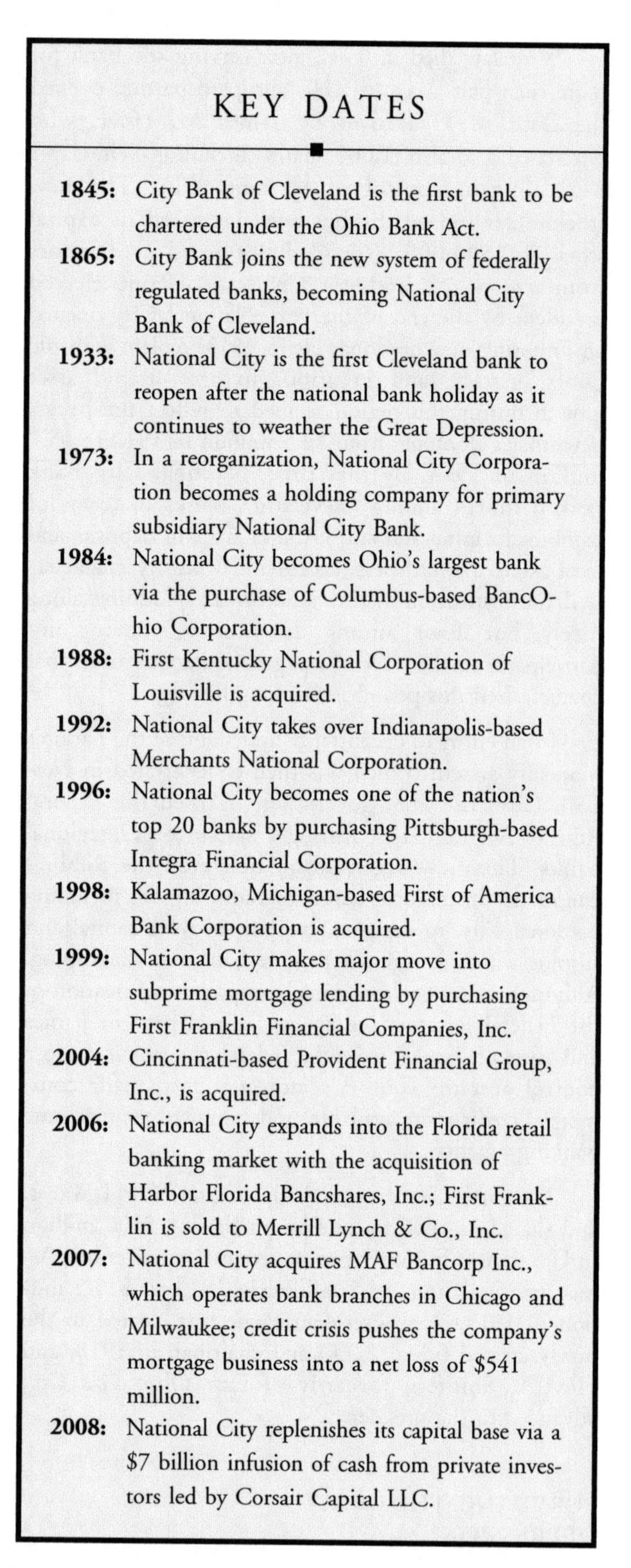

KEY DATES

1845: City Bank of Cleveland is the first bank to be chartered under the Ohio Bank Act.
1865: City Bank joins the new system of federally regulated banks, becoming National City Bank of Cleveland.
1933: National City is the first Cleveland bank to reopen after the national bank holiday as it continues to weather the Great Depression.
1973: In a reorganization, National City Corporation becomes a holding company for primary subsidiary National City Bank.
1984: National City becomes Ohio's largest bank via the purchase of Columbus-based BancOhio Corporation.
1988: First Kentucky National Corporation of Louisville is acquired.
1992: National City takes over Indianapolis-based Merchants National Corporation.
1996: National City becomes one of the nation's top 20 banks by purchasing Pittsburgh-based Integra Financial Corporation.
1998: Kalamazoo, Michigan-based First of America Bank Corporation is acquired.
1999: National City makes major move into subprime mortgage lending by purchasing First Franklin Financial Companies, Inc.
2004: Cincinnati-based Provident Financial Group, Inc., is acquired.
2006: National City expands into the Florida retail banking market with the acquisition of Harbor Florida Bancshares, Inc.; First Franklin is sold to Merrill Lynch & Co., Inc.
2007: National City acquires MAF Bancorp Inc., which operates bank branches in Chicago and Milwaukee; credit crisis pushes the company's mortgage business into a net loss of $541 million.
2008: National City replenishes its capital base via a $7 billion infusion of cash from private investors led by Corsair Capital LLC.

depression that followed. While over 30 percent of the country's banks failed from 1929 to 1933, National City fared considerably better: its assets declined only 25 percent, to $29 million. In fact, National City was Cleveland's only major bank to maintain full access to accounts and was first to reopen after the March 1933 bank holiday.

The company also endured an unexpected management shakeup during this period. In 1932 President Hoyt Shulters died and was replaced on an interim basis by Charles B. Reynolds. Sidney B. Congdon, who had served as a national bank examiner for the Cleveland, Pittsburgh, and Cincinnati region throughout the fiscal crisis, was elected president of National City in 1933. His long list of credentials, including chief examiner of the Reconstruction Finance Corporation, further bolstered National City's reputation for stability. The bank quickly resumed its rapid growth pattern, with assets ballooning from $35 million in 1932 to $475.5 million by 1944.

Like many other national commercial banks, National City began to move decisively into full-service retail banking in the post–World War II era, adding a trust department, personalized checks and check sorting, home service representatives, and 24-hour depository services at each branch. The company also began investing in automation, purchasing its first computer in 1959. By the 1960s, National City had 24 branch offices and had crossed the $1 billion asset mark.

1973 REORGANIZATION AS NATIONAL CITY CORPORATION

The bank took its first step toward becoming a major regional player in 1973, when it created National City Corporation as a holding company and made National City Bank its primary subsidiary. This new corporate structure enabled the company to bypass some of the most stringent banking regulations and begin what it called a "cautious, well-planned strategy of acquiring affiliate banks." The charge was led by Julian McCall, who had begun his banking career at First National Bank of New York (later Citibank) in 1948 and joined National City as a first vice-president in 1971. He advanced to president and was elected to the board of directors within five months, and became chief executive in 1978 and chairman a year later. McCall guided National City Corp. through an intense series of in-state acquisitions. From 1974 to 1984, National City acquired 11 relatively small ($300 million to $750 million asset) banks, thereby increasing its asset level to about $6.5 billion. Unlike many of its competitors, National City maintained its affiliates' historical names and autonomous marketing programs, forming a federation of banks with unified back-office operations.

Throughout this period of expansion, however, the Cleveland bank remained unable to break into Ohio's vital Columbus and Cincinnati markets. Then, in 1984,

National City burst onto the state capital scene through the $315 million purchase of Columbus's BancOhio Corporation. This union of Ohio's second and third largest banks created a $12.5 billion asset powerhouse that was 30 percent bigger than its next largest Ohio rival, Banc One Corporation. BancOhio also gave National City a leading 35 percent share of Columbus's deposits. The combination of National City's strength in commercial banking with BancOhio's retail forte more than doubled the resulting entity's number of branches and expanded its geographic reach to 53 of Ohio's 88 counties, or over 80 percent of the state's population. While McCall acknowledged that these increases were important, he characterized the union as an anticipation of the industrywide shift to interstate banking that occurred throughout the late 1980s. By 1990, federal strictures against interstate banking became practically irrelevant. The merger with BancOhio not only shielded National City from acquisition by an out-of-state bank, it also set the Cleveland institution up as a regional leader.

Aside from these positives, however, a December 1984 *Forbes* article pointed out a few drawbacks to the union, including BancOhio's marginal profitability in the early 1980s (.32 percent, compared to a peer group average of 0.8 percent), and the fact that National City's long-term debt doubled to $200 million with the acquisition. The new parent addressed these problems quickly, closing 70 branches and furloughing 700 full-time employees in an effort to cut costs by reconciling overlapping operations. By 1985, BancOhio contributed $30 million of National City's $108 million in earnings, and helped it become Ohio's second bank to be listed on the New York Stock Exchange in 1986. During this period, cautious midwestern banks such as National City began to attract analysts' attention because many did not buy into the risky lending and investment strategies that ruined so many financial institutions in the 1980s.

In the meantime, National City had shored up its internal operations through joint ventures in electronic banking, including charter membership in Money Station, Ohio's largest system of automatic teller machines, as well as point-of-sale debit cards. The company forged strong ties with its locales by creating National City Community Development Corporation, a for-profit development corporation that infused low and moderate income neighborhoods in the bank's key metropolitan markets with almost $50 million from 1982 through 1995. This and other community-conscious efforts earned the bank an outstanding rating from the Office of the Comptroller of the Currency for complying with the Community Reinvestment Act.

J. Robert Killpack, National City Corp. president since 1980, succeeded Julian McCall upon his 1986 retirement. Killpack served in that capacity only until the fall of 1987, when he retired and was succeeded by Edward B. Brandon. Called "the most popular executive at National City Corp." in an August 1986 article in the *Cleveland Plain Dealer,* Brandon had earned his undergraduate degree in economics at Northwestern University and an M.B.A. from the Wharton School of Banking and Finance. He moved up through National City Bank's ranks, becoming president of National City Corp.'s largest affiliate in 1984 and CEO one year later. He advanced to the parent company's presidency in 1986, and had a brief wait in the wings until Killpack's retirement. According to an October 1987 article in the *Cleveland Plain Dealer,* Brandon's "one overriding priority" was "an interstate bank merger to get back into the running for status as a super-regional bank."

ACQUISITIONS IN KENTUCKY (1988) AND INDIANA (1992)

In pursuit of that goal, Brandon engineered several major acquisitions, both within and across Ohio's borders, in the late 1980s and early 1990s. One of the most significant of these came in 1988, when National City beat out four other bidders to win the hand of $6 billion (asset) First Kentucky National Corporation of Louisville. Like the BancOhio acquisition, the addition of First Kentucky boosted National City's size (making it the country's 11th largest bank, according to market capitalization) and helped it remain independent of the even larger national banks then moving into the Midwest.

Nevertheless, the acquisition drew criticism from some industry analysts and stockholders because it diluted National City's stock by 11 percent during a "banking bust" that *Fortune* magazine characterized as the industry's most difficult period since the Great Depression. More than a thousand U.S. banks failed from 1985 to 1992. Nonperforming loans and correspondingly high loan loss provisions during this period battered National City's net. Earnings flattened, then started to erode in 1989, as nonperforming assets rose to peak at $468 million in 1991.

Brandon incurred more criticism that year when, after eight months of behind-the-scenes negotiations, National City pursued a hostile, highly publicized takeover of Ameritrust Corporation, another Cleveland bank. National City was soon joined by Society Corporation, Banc One, and NBD Bancorp, Inc., in competition for Ameritrust. Society won the rivalry in September, and the rebuffed National City reached a deal to acquire Indianapolis-based Merchants National

Corporation in October. In the two months that followed, Wall Street registered its disapproval, driving the bank's stock down 20 percent. The $640 million acquisition of Merchants National, an institution with assets of $5.4 billion, was completed in May 1992.

While Brandon continued to defend his acquisition strategy, he acknowledged some of the criticism, telling Brian Hellauer of *American Banker* that "We had acquired an awful lot of banks in a ten-year period, and in the process had gone from one of the most efficient banks in the industry to where we were at best mediocre." National City hired top consulting firm McKinsey & Company, Inc., to help guide a two-year reorganization dubbed the "Vision" plan. Economizations, especially at BancOhio, where costs ran up to 20 percent higher than National City's other subsidiaries, helped cut from $65 million to $120 million in annual operating costs. Between 1992 and 1994, all of the holding company's major affiliates took on the National City name, presenting a unified marketing front. National City also continued to decrease its dependence on interest income (already battered by loan losses) and focus more strongly on fee income. Interest income declined 24 percent from 1990 to 1993, while noninterest income increased by 48 percent. During this same period, National City's net grew over 72 percent, from $249 million to $430 million. By early 1993, the company's stock price reflected these improvements, having recovered 71 percent from its late 1991 low. Brandon had repudiated his detractors by mid-1995, having boosted National City's stock 178 percent from 1985 to 1995 and increased assets from $14 billion to $35 billion.

David A. Daberko succeeded Brandon as president of National City Corp. in 1993 and CEO in 1995. The Phi Beta Kappa graduate of Denison University with an M.B.A. from Case Western Reserve University had made his entire professional career at National City, advancing through the investment and corporate banking ranks of National City Bank. Upon his ascension to the presidency in 1993, Daberko asserted that "There will always be strong regional banks, and we will be one of them."

Although Daberko had previously maintained that market share gains would fuel National City's growth in the mid-1990s, the $2.1 billion acquisition of Pittsburgh's Integra Financial Corporation announced in August 1995 and completed the following May pushed the Cleveland bank over the $50 billion asset mark and into the list of the nation's top 20 banks. Faced with a new chorus of criticism, Daberko quickly announced a 29 percent cut in Integra's staff and rationalization of its 260 western Pennsylvania branches.

As federal regulators began dismantling the Glass-Steagall Act of 1933, which had separated commercial and investment banking, National City was one of the first U.S. banks to venture into the once-barred areas. With its 1995 purchase of Indianapolis-based Raffensperger, Hughes & Co., Inc., National City became the first commercial bank to acquire a retail brokerage with investment banking capabilities since the Great Depression. The acquisition of Raffensperger, which was renamed NatCity Investments, Inc., provided National City with the ability to issue stocks and bonds to help corporate clients buy other companies. The deal also greatly enhanced the breadth of mutual funds that National City brokers could offer to their customers.

MORTGAGE PUSH, FURTHER RETAIL BANKING ACQUISITIONS

The purchase of Raffensperger was part of a larger effort to become a full-fledged financial services institution with greater fee income. Another fee-based business earmarked for expansion in the late 1990s was mortgage banking, and in this area National City sought to become a national player. In early 1997 the company purchased 61 mortgage offices from Bank United of Texas, a deal that gave National City a total of nearly 100 mortgage offices in 33 states. Between 1996 and 1998 net income from fee-based businesses nearly doubled to $210.8 million thanks in large measure to the boost in the mortgage business.

As the banking industry continued to consolidate, National City pursued additional acquisitions in its core retail banking sector in order to keep from being swallowed by its increasingly larger peer institutions. In March 1998 the company completed its largest purchase to that time, the $7.7 billion acquisition of First of America Bank Corporation, based in Kalamazoo, Michigan. With this addition, National City gained its first presence in retail banking in Michigan and Illinois while also augmenting its position in Indiana. First of America ran about 540 bank branches and had assets of $21 billion. Also in March 1998, National City further bolstered its position in northern Indiana by spending nearly $800 million for Fort Wayne National Corporation, a $3-billion-asset bank based in Fort Wayne, Indiana, with more then 60 branches. Upon completion of these deals, National City ranked as the nation's 13th largest bank with assets approaching $80 billion. It ranked number two among banks operating in Indiana, number three in Michigan, and number five in Illinois.

National City ended the 20th century with a further push into the mortgage market. In November 1999 the company's mortgage unit gained additional scale in the western United States via the $42.3 million acquisition of Dallas-based AccuBanc Mortgage Corporation, operator of 100 retail and 15 wholesale offices in 27 states with particularly strong positions in Texas, California, Washington, and Maryland. By the end of 1999 National City was offering mortgages through its own bank branches and through 260 retail and wholesale mortgage offices in 38 states, and it ranked as the seventh largest mortgage originator in the United States. The company also made a big move into the subprime mortgage market, subprime being that sector of the lending market serving higher-risk individuals with lower credit ratings. The August 1999, $266.1 million purchase of First Franklin Financial Companies, Inc., based in San Jose, California, vaulted National City into the top ten among subprime mortgage lenders.

RIDING THE MORTGAGE BOOM TO NEW HEIGHTS

National City's retail banking business entered the 21st century with a reputation for mediocrity, and the company set about changing that. Over the next several years, National City spent more than $500 million to enhance customer service, improve the product offerings, upgrade technology (both that used by customers and that used by employees), substantially increase the marketing and promotion of the bank's products and services, and make enhancements in employee-oriented areas such as increases in compensation and better training. National City credited this program with boosting its market share in its core markets.

In the meantime, in the booming housing market of the first years of the 21st century, fueled by historically low interest rates, the mortgage industry thrived from the spate of home buying and refinancing. National City rode this wave to new heights, by 2003 netting around $1 billion in profits from its mortgage operations alone, about half of its record net income that year of $2.12 billion. Its mortgage volume for 2003 reached $130 billion, up from just $12.5 billion in 1998. A significant portion of this increase stemmed from an aggressive expansion at First Franklin, which wrote around $30 billion in subprime loans in 2003, compared to only about $4 billion in 1999.

As it contended with slow growth in its core retail banking business in the economically distressed Midwest, and in anticipation of an expected cooling of the red-hot mortgage market, National City began another spate of acquisitions. In April 2004 the company extended its retail banking footprint into Missouri for the first time by purchasing Allegiant Bancorp, Inc., for $493 million. Allegiant operated about three dozen branches in metropolitan St. Louis and had assets totaling about $2.5 billion. In July 2004 National City filled a longstanding hole in its network of bank branches, the Cincinnati/northern Kentucky market, via the $2.2 billion acquisition of Provident Financial Group, Inc. The $17-billion-asset Provident operated 65 branches, mainly in Greater Cincinnati. National City filled another void in northeastern Ohio later in 2004 by purchasing Wayne Bancorp, Inc., a bank with $825 million in assets and 23 branches, for $182 million.

At the end of 2004, National City's assets had reached $139.28 billion, making it the tenth largest bank in the United States; its 2004 deals also propelled it into the number one spot in the Ohio market. National City's net income that year soared to a record $2.78 billion in part thanks to an after-tax gain of $477 million recorded from the $1.2 billion sale of the majority-owned National Processing, Inc., a merchant and debit-card processing company, to Bank of America Corporation. The proceeds from this divestment helped offset a sharp decline in net income from the firm's mortgage business as rising interest rates slowed down refinancing activity. This trend continued in 2005 when National City's prime mortgage business saw its earnings fall further to $284 million, while the earnings for subprime specialist First Franklin slid 28 percent, to $397 million. National City paused its acquisition drive that year, although it did open 29 new retail branches, mainly in the bank's newer markets of Cincinnati, Chicago, and St. Louis.

In 2006 National City continued to grow organically in these same markets and also gained another eight branches in St. Louis by purchasing Forbes First Financial Corporation. Midyear, National City completed the move that most other multistate banks had taken in the late 1990s of consolidating its various state-chartered banks into a single national bank subsidiary, National City Bank. The company in December of that year made its first foray in retail banking outside the Midwest, acquiring Fort Pierce-based Harbor Florida Bancshares, Inc., which operated 42 branches along the central east coast of Florida and had assets of $3.2 billion. National City followed up this $1.1 billion purchase with the January 2007 acquisition of Fidelity Bankshares, Inc., for a further $1 billion. Fidelity, based in West Palm Beach, operated 52 branches along Florida's southeast coast and had $4.2 billion in assets. Florida was an attractive market for National City because unlike its core midwestern markets it offered the potential for faster-than-average growth and because the state was a retirement haven for midwestern snowbirds and thus banking relationships established in the Midwest might be continued in Florida.

In 2006 National City continued an effort begun a year earlier to gradually narrow the company's focus to "direct" businesses where it had a direct, personal relationship with the customer. This included such areas as retail, corporate, and small-business banking as well as wealth management and the prime mortgage business. The largest of National City's "indirect" businesses, in which transactions flowed through a broker or other intermediary, was First Franklin, which the bank sold to Merrill Lynch & Co., Inc., in December 2006 for $1.3 billion. National City also sold to Merrill Lynch a portion of the loans that First Franklin had originated, but about $7.5 billion of these subprime loans remained on National City's balance sheet at the end of 2006.

In May 2007 National City entered into an agreement on another major acquisition, a $1.9 billion purchase of MAF Bancorp Inc., based in Clarendon Hills, Illinois. Taking over MAF and its 82 branches and $11.1 billion in assets boosted National City into the number four position in the Chicago banking market and also provided it with its first branches in Wisconsin, specifically the Milwaukee market. This acquisition was completed in September 2007.

VICTIM OF SUBPRIME CREDIT CRUNCH

Peter E. Raskind succeeded Daberko as CEO of National City in July 2007 and assumed the chairmanship as well at year-end. During Daberko's dozen years at the helm, the company grew about fourfold, from $36 billion in assets to $140 billion, while expanding from 645 branches in three states to around 1,400 branches in nine. Raskind had a 17-year stint at U.S. Bancorp before joining National City in 2000, eventually serving as vice-chairman starting in 2004 and as president beginning in December 2006.

The new leader almost immediately had to contend with the rapidly deteriorating housing market, the implosion in the subprime mortgage market, and the wider credit crunch that ensued. Having sold First Franklin, National City pulled back further from its riskier lending strategies, announcing in August 2007 that it would stop offering second mortgages through brokers. It later did the same for first mortgages. While the company moved quickly to tighten its lending standards, the rapid emergence of the credit crunch left National City, and numerous other industry players, holding billions of dollars in shaky loans that in previous years it would have been able to sell to Wall Street investors. The collapse of the secondary market for mortgages thus left National City quite vulnerable, as did the bank's exposure to two markets with higher-than-average foreclosure rates: the Midwest and Florida. National City further weakened its own financial position with an ill-timed stock buyback plan totaling around $3 billion that was launched soon after the divestment of First Franklin. The company paid as much as $38 a share for its own stock, which by the end of 2007 had plunged to around $16.50.

As its financial position deteriorated, National City announced a string of layoffs in the later months of 2007 into the beginning of 2008 that eventually totaled 3,200, or 10 percent of the workforce. The poor environment for originating mortgages coupled with a huge increase to $579 million in its provisions for bad loans sent the mortgage banking business of National City into a net loss of $541 million for 2007. Although National City still managed to report overall net profits of $314 million for the year, this represented an 86 percent plunge from the previous year.

By early 2008 the credit crunch had depleted National City's capital and left its balance sheet littered with as much as $25 billion in bad loans. In mid-March investors sent the company's stock plunging by 43 percent in one day, down to $7.52, the lowest level since 1991 and an 80 percent drop from a year earlier. Regulators began prodding National City officials to either replenish its capital base or sell itself to a rival. Crosstown rival KeyCorp, Cincinnati-based Fifth Third Bancorp, and Toronto-based Bank of Nova Scotia all pored over National City's books but eventually walked away.

Finally, in a deal announced in April and completed in early May, National City retained its independence by securing a $7 billion infusion of cash from private investors, who paid about $5 per share for what amounted to about 70 percent of the company's equity. Joining the lead investor, private-equity firm Corsair Capital LLC, a spinoff from JPMorgan Chase specializing in ailing financial institutions, were a number of smaller investors, mainly institutional investors. This infusion provided National City with capital to cover future loan losses while also buying it some time to possibly offload some of its troubled loans. The company was expecting that its mortgage business would lose between $2 billion and $2.4 billion in 2008, an amazing reversal from the heyday of just a few years earlier. Going forward, National City planned to rely on mortgages for only 5 to 10 percent of its profits, compared to the 50 percent level of 2003 and 2004. Raskind intended to concentrate on the firm's core, nine-state retail banking operation. He also had to contend, however, with a spate of lawsuits filed by shareholders charging that National City officers and directors had failed to fully disclose the problems the company faced and therefore cost them millions of dollars as the stock plunged.

April Dougal Gasbarre
Updated, David E. Salamie

PRINCIPAL SUBSIDIARIES

National City Bank; National City Mortgage Co.; Allegiant Asset Management Company; NatCity Investments, Inc.

PRINCIPAL COMPETITORS

KeyCorp; Fifth Third Bancorp; U.S. Bancorp; Citizens Financial Group, Inc.; The PNC Financial Services Group, Inc.; JPMorgan Chase & Co.; Wells Fargo & Company; Bank of America Corporation; Huntington Bancshares Incorporated; TD Commerce Bank; Wachovia Corporation.

FURTHER READING

Andrews, Greg, "Merchants Deal 'a Blockbuster,'" *Indianapolis Business Journal,* November 4, 1991, p. 1.

Bennett, Robert A., "Brandon Dreams Expansion," *United States Banker,* March 1992, p. 27.

Benton, Elbert J., *A Century of Progress: Being a History of the National City Bank of Cleveland from 1845 to 1945,* Cleveland: National City Bank of Cleveland, 1945.

Byrne, Harlan S., "National City Corp.," *Barron's,* September 17, 1990, pp. 56–57.

Carrns, Ann, and David Enrich, "How Safe Bank Tried Subprime and Got Singed," *Wall Street Journal,* January 3, 2008, pp. C1, C3.

Chase, Brett, "National City CEO Has Takeovers Down Pat," *American Banker,* January 17, 1996, p. 4.

Enrich, David, and Jed Horowitz, "Merrill Lynch to Pay $1.3 Billion for National City Mortgage Unit," *Wall Street Journal,* September 6, 2006, p. C3.

Foster, Pamela E., "National City Sharpens Ax," *Business First Columbus,* August 12, 1991, pp. 1, 9.

Fuller, John, "BancOhio, National City Wed," *Cleveland Plain Dealer,* September 29, 1984, p. 3B.

———, "Banks Map Big Future with Merger," *Cleveland Plain Dealer,* October 2, 1984, p. 1E.

———, "A Tale of Two Bankers," *Cleveland Plain Dealer,* September 30, 1984, p. 1E.

Hallinan, Joseph T., "National City Reaches Accord to Buy Provident," *Wall Street Journal,* February 18, 2004, p. B2.

Hellauer, Brian, "National City's Vision: A Strong, Independent Regional Bank," *American Banker,* November 8, 1993, p. 1A.

Hill, Miriam, "Mergers Help Bank Industry," *Cleveland Plain Dealer,* May 22, 1991, p. 1G.

———, "National City Becomes 17th Largest Bank with Purchase," *Cleveland Plain Dealer,* August 28, 1995, p. 1A.

———, "National City CEO Passes the Baton," *Cleveland Plain Dealer,* July 25, 1995, p. 1C.

———, "National City Chief Pushes Bid," *Cleveland Plain Dealer,* May 16, 1991, p. 1A.

———, "National City to Buy Ohio Bancorp," *Cleveland Plain Dealer,* April 3, 1993, p. 1C.

———, "National City to Slash Costs, Jobs," *Cleveland Plain Dealer,* August 14, 1991, p. 1H.

Klinkerman, Steve, "It's Back to Basics for National City Chief," *American Banker,* November 29, 1993, p. 4.

———, "National City's Brandon Is Winning Bet in Indiana," *American Banker,* March 23, 1993, pp. 1, 13.

Mahoney, Mike, "Brandon Is Contender," *Cleveland Plain Dealer,* August 5, 1986, p. 1D.

———, "Deregulation Will Test New Leaders of Banks Here," *Cleveland Plain Dealer,* October 13, 1987, p. 1E.

Maturi, Richard J., "Buckeye Banker: National City Corp. Thrives in Ohio," *Barron's,* November 24, 1986, p. 54.

Mazzucca, Tim, "Nat City Doubles Down in Fla.," *American Banker,* July 28, 2006, p. 1.

Miller, Jay, "Lawsuits Still Nat City Thorn," *Crain's Cleveland Business,* April 28, 2008, p. 1.

Murray, Matt, "National City Is No Longer Just a Big Midwestern Bank," *Wall Street Journal,* February 5, 1998, p. B4.

———, "National City to Acquire First of America in a Stock Swap Valued at $6.78 Billion," *Wall Street Journal,* December 2, 1997, p. A3.

———, "A Newcomer to Pittsburgh Finds It Has a Lot to Prove," *Wall Street Journal,* June 3, 1996, p. B5.

Murray, Teresa Dixon, "How National City's Mortgage Division Lost Half a Billion Dollars," *Cleveland Plain Dealer,* February 12, 2008, p. A1.

———, "National City Buys Provident Financial," *Cleveland Plain Dealer,* February 18, 2004, p. A1.

———, "National City Reports Big Loss As Market Takes Ride," *Cleveland Plain Dealer,* January 23, 2008, p. A1.

———, "National City to Buy Chicago Competitor," *Cleveland Plain Dealer,* May 2, 2007, p. C1.

———, "National City to Cut Another 1,200 Jobs," *Cleveland Plain Dealer,* October 25, 2007, p. A1.

———, "National City Will Purchase Fla. Bank," *Cleveland Plain Dealer,* July 12, 2006, p. C1.

———, "Raskind Adds Title of CEO at National City," *Cleveland Plain Dealer,* July 24, 2007, p. C1.

———, "Retiring National City CEO Reflects," *Cleveland Plain Dealer,* December 29, 2007, p. C1.

Murray, Teresa Dixon, and Peter Krouse, "Hard Work Isn't Over for Bank: National City Must Keep Cutting, Work on Public Standing, Experts Say," *Cleveland Plain Dealer,* April 27, 2008, p. A1.

———, "National City Will Retain Control After $7 Billion Infusion," *Cleveland Plain Dealer,* April 21, 2008, p. A1.

"National City Bank 150th Anniversary," *Cleveland Plain Dealer,* May 17, 1995, p. S1.

National City: 150 Years, 1845–1995, Cleveland: National City Corporation, 1995, 52 p.

Rieker, Matthias, "Infusion at Nat City Settles One Question, Raises Another," *American Banker,* April 22, 2008, p. 1.

Serwer, Andrew E., "Banking Boom in the Heartland," *Fortune,* July 18, 1988, p. 21.

Shingler, Dan, "Same Bank, Two Views," *Crain's Cleveland Business,* p. 11.

Sidel, Robin, David Enrich, and Peter Lattman, "NatCity Close to $6 Billion Cash Infusion," *Wall Street Journal,* April 21, 2008, pp. C1, C2.

Silvestri, Scott, "National City Banks on Corporate, Non-prime," *American Banker,* May 22, 2000, p. 1.

Sundaramoorthy, Geeta, "Will Retail Be the Answer for Nat City?" *American Banker,* April 5, 2004, p. 1.

Tippett, Karen, "National City: No-Thrills Banking," *FW,* August 21, 1990, p. 19.

Turner, Shawn A., "National City Continues Shift from Mortgage Profit," *Crain's Cleveland Business,* April 3, 2006, p. 4.

Weberman, Ben, and John Heins, "The Doughnut or the Hole," *Forbes,* December 17, 1984, pp. 94+.

Noah Education Holdings Ltd.

Building B, 10th Floor
Futian Tianjian Hi-Tech Venture Park
Shenzhen, Guangdong Province
China
Telephone: (+86 755) 8343 2800
Fax: (+86 755) 8204 9504
Web site: http://www.noahedu.com.cn

Public Company
Incorporated: 2004
Employees: 907
Sales: $72.8 million (2007)
Stock Exchanges: New York
Ticker Symbol: NED
NAICS: 511210 Software Publishers

■ ■ ■

For most of the late 20th and early 21st centuries, the People's Republic of China experienced social, political, and economic reforms to maintain a competitive position in the world market. Labor unrest, encroaching Westernization, and an increased interest in establishing a market-oriented economy caused the country to bolster international relations. As a result, China joined the World Trade Organization in 2001, finally acknowledging its status as a worldwide economic power. During this time, digital technology represented one of the fastest growing industries throughout the world. Three engineers recognized the value of this burgeoning field while responding to the emerging need for supplemental education in China. Noah Education Holdings Ltd., a leader in the Chinese educational electronics market, is the result of their efforts. In 2007, the company posted sales of $72 million.

FOUNDING FATHERS, 1999 TO 2004

Dong Xu, Benguo Tang, and Xiaotong Wang were in their early 30s when they recognized the need for English-language translation products in China. Xu and Tang each held degrees in engineering physics from Tsinghua University in Beijing, and Wang was trained at Tianjin University, in precision instruments. For nearly ten years, Xu, Tang, and Wang had worked as engineers and executive managers in technologically advanced companies: Xu was branch manager of Chengdu Enwei Group, a leading Chinese provider of healthcare products, and VP of sales at Tibet Medicine Company; Tang specialized in technical engineering at Dongguan Yimeida Electronic Factory and managed the Guangdong office of Gansu Duyi Medical Company; while Wang supervised electronic products and software as senior engineer and manager at Yimeida Electronic Company and served as vice-general manager of Hubei Xiangfan Tianhui Medical Instrument Company.

In 2004 the three men combined their engineering expertise and business experience to form Shenzhen Noah Industrial Company, Ltd., to design, produce, and distribute educational translation devices. Their first invention, the NH 2000 electronic dictionary, was a handheld device programmed with pronunciation technology to translate Chinese words into English.

Noah's product launch came at an opportune time as China had undergone several significant social and

COMPANY PERSPECTIVES

Noah is a leading provider of interactive education content in China. The Company develops and markets interactive, multimedia learning materials. The majority of Noah's offerings are designed to complement prescribed textbooks used in China's primary and secondary school curriculum, covering subjects such as English, Chinese, mathematics, physics, chemistry, biology, geography, political science and history. Noah delivers content primarily through handheld digital learning devices, or DLDs, into which content is embedded or subsequently downloaded at over 8,500 points of sale, approximately 2,000 download centers, or through the Company website, www.noahedu.com.

economic changes. Chinese families enjoyed a nearly 7 percent increase in disposable income from 2002 to 2006 and because education had always been held in such high esteem, families were willing to invest more in their children's education. Since Chinese students were required to complete nine years of formal education, a compulsory stipulation in place since 1986, increasing numbers of children began attending schools. As students became more educated, many sought higher learning at colleges overseas and found universities required English proficiency for admission.

This growing emphasis on education spurred Xu, Tang, and Wang to focus their products and services on the educational electronics market. In April 2004, with the help of a $16 million investment from Baring Asia II Holdings Limited and Alpha Century Assets Limited from the British Virgin Islands, Noah Education Holdings Ltd. was established. The umbrella company, incorporated in the Cayman Islands, acquired the assets of the original Noah Industrial Company Ltd., and established three wholly owned subsidiaries to conduct business in China: Innovative Noah Electronic Company Ltd.; New Noah Technology Company Ltd.; and Noah Education Technology Company Ltd. Xu, Tang, and Wang became, respectively, CEO and chairman, COO and director, and CTO and director.

EDUCATION FOR ALL, 2005

Targeting school-aged children in urban areas of China, Noah designed and developed an affordable, interactive, portable way for students to practice the skills they learned in the classroom. In 2005 the company unveiled a proprietary software platform, NP-I TECH, to be run on a Digital Learning Device (DLD). Equipped with a multimedia format that combined text, graphics, flash animation, sound, and video, the DLDs delivered content such as English, Chinese, math, physics, chemistry, biology, geography, political science, and history. Different versions of each subject area corresponded directly to the specific textbook and curriculum adopted by individual cities and provinces within China. The first Noah DLD was sold in March 2005.

Consumers could either receive DLDs with the selected content already embedded or have the DLD programmed at a download center. Points of sale and download centers were primarily located in urban areas throughout China. The DLDs soon became available in department stores, Noah-branded stores, bookstores, electronic chain stores, and mall-based kiosks. The growing line of DLD products was actively promoted through television and newspaper advertisements, campus billboards, and popular Internet portals.

Noah's management carefully researched and identified appropriate markets for their products. According to the National Bureau of Statistics in China, nearly 300 million children between the ages of five and 19 lived in China in 2005. Almost 75 percent of the child population was enrolled in primary and secondary schools, and within ten years the Chinese government had plans to require 100 percent compliance of its nine-year compulsory education. Noah placed high emphasis on the English language training market, as it was valued at $1.9 billion in 2005 and the company expected the lucrative niche to nearly double within five years.

By the end of 2005 Noah's products were widely accepted and the business was financially stable. The company reported annual revenue of $25.2 million and had sold nearly 11,000 DLDs and over one million electronic dictionaries. Its success earned Noah a place among the "Technology Fast 500 Asia Pacific," an award given to the fastest-growing technology companies by Deloitte Touche Tohmatsu. With a solid start, Noah was poised for a profitable future.

PRIVATE TO PUBLIC, 2006 AND BEYOND

Responding to the lifestyles of its young audience, Noah kicked off 2006 with several improvements to the DLD. One of the first enhancements was to upgrade previous models' black-and-white screen with a color screen. While the black-and-white screens were still available, with high resolution and contrast, the company believed

KEY DATES

2004: Engineers Dong Xu, Xiaotong Wang, and Benguo Tang found Noah Education.
2005: Noah releases proprietary software NP-I TECH multimedia technology.
2006: The company introduces the first color DLD (digital learning device).
2007: Noah announces its initial stock offering on the New York Stock Exchange.
2008: Noah remains in the black despite its share price falling below $5.

most users would appreciate and prefer a color screen. Other trends included adding more characters and design elements reflecting popular culture, and a partnership with Taiwan-based mobile phone manufacturer OKWAP to create a mobile phone compatible with Noah's learning content software. Less expensive than personal computers, the DLDs gave active students a user-friendly interface to learn on the go.

Noah also offered improved ease in accessing content. The company launched a web site, www.noahedu.com, in June 2006. While consumers could still retrieve content from download centers, the web site provided a more convenient avenue for purchasing and downloading learning materials. The web site also featured online communities, chat rooms, bulletin boards, and online tutoring sessions. Tutors from Noah's newly established Teacher's Alliance were also available to answer students' questions posted on the web site. The Alliance was made up of 250 teachers throughout China who had contractual arrangements with Noah to offer tutoring support as well as assist in the development of the courseware.

As 2006 drew to a close, Noah's growth and success had skyrocketed. Annual revenue reached $49.1 million, nearly twice that of 2005, and the company had sold over 300,000 DLDs, a 96 percent increase from 2005. The increase of DLD sales was offset by a decrease in electronic dictionary sales by 12 percent from 2005. The decrease, however, could be explained because many of the DLDs offered dictionary content.

By mid-2007 Noah offered 28,000 courseware titles, half of them covering English language learning; had 30 provincial distributors and 300 local distributors; and operated more than 8,500 points of sale and about 2,000 download centers across China. The firm's growing line of eDictionaries numbered 12 different DLD models, which had sold over two million units. In addition, Noah had licensed and compiled over 150 dictionaries total, including 16 related to the English language, almost a dozen corresponding to other languages, and nearly 125 dictionaries covering professional terms ranging from engineering to medical and legal terminology.

The company had established two after-school tutoring centers where teachers worked with primary and secondary students and had plans to open more tutoring centers in other areas of China. In addition to providing English-language training to primary and secondary students, courseware was developed to reach college students and young professionals in China. Likewise, Noah planned to create language study courseware for the increasing numbers of international students seeking to learn Chinese. With education on the minds of the Chinese public, plans were underway to test the interest of the international investment community.

In October Noah took the plunge and went public on the New York Stock Exchange. Trading under the ticker symbol NED, share prices began at $14 each and rose as high as $19.85 on opening day, earning the company $137.9 million. By the following day, stock prices soared to $23.70, prompting analyst Trace Urdan to comment to the *Wall Street Journal* (October 20, 2007), "As hot as Chinese consumer stocks are, the stocks of Chinese companies in the education segment are hotter still." While the prediction seemed sound, the stock market proved brutal and the new stock began to tumble. Following the bear market afflicting most stocks in 2007, Noah stock plummeted to a low of $7 by the end of the month.

Despite its dismal stock performance, Noah still operated in the black. The company's 2007 year-end revenue had risen to $72.8 million, about a 30 percent increase from the year before. Sales were also solid with over 550,000 DLDs sold, a nearly 40 percent increase from 2006. Again, electronic dictionary sales decreased about 16 percent from 900,000 in 2006 to 770,000 in 2007. In 2008 Noah sales were steady, but its stock price continued to fluctuate wildly in the volatile market, reaching an all-time low of $4.76 on March 18.

By May Noah had announced its products were being used in 600 schools throughout China, reaching over 1.4 million students according to Jennifer Schonberger of the online *Small Cap Investor* site (May 16, 2008). By the following month, Noah's share prices had leveled off to $5.56 with management confident the stock would soon rally, reflecting strong sales and an even stronger balance sheet (projected revenues for fiscal 2008 were estimated at $93 million). Thus, despite a less than stellar worldwide economic outlook, Noah Education remained in a unique position to close the language gap in China and elsewhere and to meet the growing needs of a global economy in the 21st century.

Jodi Essey-Stapleton

PRINCIPAL SUBSIDIARIES

Innovative Noah Electronic (Shenzhen) Company Ltd.; New Noah Technology (Shenzhen) Company Ltd.; Noah Education Technology (Shenzhen) Company Ltd.

PRINCIPAL COMPETITORS

Global View Co. Ltd.; Guangdong Bubugao Electronic Industry Limited; Guangdong Dongtian Culture Enterprise Co., Ltd.; Houghton Mifflin Harcourt Publishing Company; HUMAN Education & Technology Co., Ltd.; Kaplan, Inc.; New Oriental Education & Technology Group Inc.; Princeton Review, Inc.; Shanghai Ozing Digital Technology Limited.

FURTHER READING

Cowan, Lynn. "The Buzz: Noah Education's IPO Soars," *Wall Street Journal,* October 20, 2007, p. B4.

Haruni, Ron, "Noah Education Holdings: A Promising Chinese IPO," *SeekingAlpha,* October 17, 2007.

"Noah Education IPO Raises $137.9 M, Above Range," *Reuters,* October 18, 2007.

Schonberger, Jennifer, "Noah Education Holdings Higher After Posting Q3 Earnings," *SmallCapInvestor.com,* May 16, 2008.

Nutrition 21 Inc.

4 Manhattanville Road
Purchase, New York 10577-2197
U.S.A.
Telephone: (914) 701-4500
Fax: (914) 696-0860
Web site: http://www.nutrition21.com

Public Company
Incorporated: 1983 as Applied Microbiology, Inc.
Employees: 30
Sales: $42.2 million (2007)
Stock Exchanges: NASDAQ
Ticker Symbol: NXXI
NAICS: 325414 Biological Products (Except Diagnostic) Manufacturing

■ ■ ■

Nutrition 21 Inc. is a nutritional biosciences company that develops, markets, and distributes products that target conditions related to diabetes as well as arthritis, cardiovascular health, immune function, metabolic syndrome, and obesity. After focusing on the sale of patented ingredients, primarily chromium-based, to vitamin and supplement manufacturers, the company has shifted its strategy to devote more resources to the development of higher-margin therapeutic brands. They include Chromax chromium picolinate, promoting healthy blood sugar and cardiovascular health; Core4Life, a chromium-based nutritional product targeting improved memory and "brain health"; Diachrome Diabetes Essentials Blood Sugar Health, controlling blood sugar and cholesterol levels in people with type 2 diabetes; Diabetes Essentials Heart Health, a combination of magnesium and taurine to lessen the danger of heart, muscle, and kidney function problems resulting from diabetes complications; Diabetes Essentials Nutrition to Go, a multivitamin for diabetes' patients, offering 14 essential vitamins and minerals; Iceland Health Joint Relief; and Iceland Health Maximum Strength Omega-3, supporting joint health, heart health, a more robust immune system, and better memory; and Selenomax, a highly absorbable selenium yeast intended to promote a healthy immune system.

Nutrition 21 products are sold through major mass merchants, including Wal-Mart and Walgreens. In addition, the company is developing other patented mineral compounds. Nutrition 21 is a public company listed on the NASDAQ based in Purchase, New York.

BROOKLYN BIOTECH ORIGINS: 1983

Following a 1997 acquisition, the Nutrition 21 name was assumed by AMBI Inc., which was originally incorporated in New York in June 1983 as Applied Microbiology, Inc., by David Guttman. In his mid-30s at the time, Guttman, a businessman who once imported pantyhose from Brazil, had become fascinated with biotechnology companies in the mold of Genentech and Biogen that offered such great promise and captured the attention of venture capitalists. He sensed an opportunity when he learned of the work being done at

COMPANY PERSPECTIVES

Good science is the Nutrition 21 hallmark that distinguishes the Company as an innovator and a leader in the nutritional supplement industry.

the Public Health Research Institute (PHRI) in New York City. More importantly, research allocations from the city had dried up and the institute was eager for new sources of funding.

PHRI had been founded in 1942, but its roots reached back to 1892 when a cholera epidemic in Germany forced New York City to establish an emergency diagnostic laboratory to determine if ocean-liner passengers from Germany were infected with the disease. The operation was retained following the crisis, becoming the Bureau of Laboratories, which would include a research department. Out of this endeavor grew PHRI and a long-term contract with New York City, initially $100,000 a year to conduct research related to public health problems in the city, making it the only medical organization in the country that received major municipal support. Over the years, the institute produced and distributed smallpox vaccine, developed ways to increase antibody response to infection, contributed to the development of a vaccine for dengue fever, and in the 1970s cancer-causing oncogenes were identified. By this time city funding had reach $700,000 a year, but when New York was faced with a financial crisis in 1977 and no help was forthcoming from Washington, sharp budget cuts had to be made and city payments to the institute were suspended.

Guttman struck a deal with PHRI, receiving a 20-year license to commercialize its research in exchange for stock in Applied Microbiology and royalties from product sales. Guttman established offices in Brooklyn but for the first two years struggled to find a focus for the company, which was involved in diverse research projects. That would change in 1985 when Peter Blackburn joined the company. Born in the United Kingdom, Blackburn received a Ph.D. in biochemistry from the University of Sheffield in England and came to the United States to become an assistant professor of biochemistry at the Rockefeller University in 1979. Five years later he left to become a senior investigator with Enzo Biochem, Inc. At Applied Microbiology, Blackburn was named senior scientist and co-director of research. He narrowed the company's focus to PHRI's work with bacteriocins, toxins that inhibited the growth of bacteria. A year after going to work for Applied Microbiology, Blackburn was appointed associate member in applied genetics at PHRI.

APPLIED MICROBIOLOGY, GOING PUBLIC: 1986

The company narrowed its focus further by seeking out niches in which larger competitors were not interested, as well as product applications that required the minimum amount of regulatory approval. To raise money, Applied Microbiology was taken public by Brooklyn's Datek Securities Corporation in 1986, raising $3.3 million from the sale of units (two shares and a warrant) at $6 a piece and the company's shares began trading on an over-the-counter basis. The initial public offering was hardly in the same league as Genentech, which had gone public in 1980 at $35 a share and quickly soared to $89. "It was hard to get Wall Street interested," Guttman told the *New York Times*. "We were small. We weren't pursuing something like AIDS or cancer. And we didn't bring any venture capitalists to the table."

What Applied Microbiology was able to accomplish, however, was to attract the attention of larger pharmaceuticals and other companies who agreed to partner with the small company on particular projects related to bacteriocins. The company worked with Pfizer Inc. to develop an antibacterial mouthwash, and Calgon Vestal Laboratories, a Merck & Company unit, to produce hospital lotions to fight antibiotic-resistant bacteria. Australian food processor Burns, Philp & Company, owner of Fleischmann's yeast, also acquired a 14 percent stake in the company and made its fermentation plants available to nurture bacteria that produced the proteins that killed other bacteria. The company's most significant product, developed with Swiss pharmaceutical and chemical company Ciba-Geigy, was a treatment for bovine mastitis. It was a teat dip that did not have to contend with extensive regulatory approval and could be put on the market quickly to generate income to fund other research projects.

CONSERVING CASH: 1991

In 1990 sales reached $915,000 and Applied Microbiology lost $1.2 million. Guttman spoke of growing revenues to $1 billion within the decade, but in the meantime he gave up his $150,000 salary at the start of 1991 to conserve cash, the company's president left and

KEY DATES

1973: Nutrition 21 is formed in San Diego, California, as partnership.
1983: Applied Microbiology, Inc., is founded in Brooklyn, New York.
1986: Applied Microbiology goes public.
1997: Applied Microbiology is renamed AMBI Inc., acquires Nutrition 21.
2001: AMBI changes name to Nutrition 21 Inc.
2006: Iceland Health, Inc., is acquired.

was not replaced, two senior executives accepted steep pay cuts, and half the ten-person research staff was laid off. Bringing products to market also proved elusive. The company could not reach an agreement with Pfizer on how to conduct product trials for an antibacterial mouthwash. Procter & Gamble then tested the formula but soon terminated the agreement. After numerous delays, Applied Microbiology was able to launch its teat dip product in August 1991 through Babson Brothers Company. To generate further cash flow, Applied Microbiology used $40 million in stock to acquire U.K.-based Aplin & Barrett, Ltd., a profitable biotech company that generated $5 million in annual cash flow, a move Guttman hoped would keep the company afloat until other products were brought to market.

Applied Microbiology posted sales of $10.2 million in 1994 and turned its first profit, netting nearly $1.8 million, but it was far from clear that the company had finally turned the corner. Guttman was replaced as chief executive in 1994 and a year later, after the company generated sales of $11.7 million and net income dipped to $283,000, he resigned from the board of directors. The new management team forged a fresh strategy in 1996. It called for the company to develop antibacterial drug candidates only to the "proof of principal" stage and then allow partners to complete development and commercialize the products. Because the preservatives business inherited from Aplin & Barrett was not related to the healthcare field, it was divested, sold for $13.5 million to Burns, Philp & Company for $13.5 million and the return of 2.42 million shares of stock. The most significant change was the decision to focus on the development and marketing of proprietary nutrition products, such as the Cardia Salt Alternative product the company had developed. The salt substitute targeted patients with high blood pressure who had difficulty lowering their sodium intake.

GROWTH IN NUTRITIONAL SUPPLEMENTS THROUGH PURCHASE OF NUTRITION 21: 1997

In keeping with its modified mission, in early 1997 Applied Microbiology changed its name to AMBI Inc. Later in the year it strengthened its ties to the nutritional supplements business by acquiring Nutrition 21 for $10 million in cash and 500,000 shares of stock. Based in San Diego, California, Nutrition 21 had been founded in 1973. It provided raw materials to vitamin manufacturers and was a major supplier of chromium picolinate, a dietary supplement that had been receiving a great deal of attention, touted as a "medical miracle" by some, a claim that drew the attention of the Federal Trade Commission (FTC). For its part, Nutrition 21 made weight-loss and other health claims that it could not substantiate to the FTC's satisfaction and in November 1996 agreed to settle the resulting charges. At the time Nutrition 21 was slated to be acquired by Vyrex Corporation of La Jolla, California, but a year later found a home with AMBI instead.

What AMBI found attractive about chromium picolinate was its ability to control glucose in diabetic and prediabetic patients. Another supplement picked up from the Nutrition 21 acquisition was selenium, an antioxidant that was found in seafood, organ meats, and cereals but as a dietary supplement had been shown to help protect cells in the circulatory system and was believed to be an aid in warding off cancer. These supplements were added to AMBI's proprietary products, which included nisin, an antibacterial peptide that offered promise as an oral treatment for infectious disease of the colon, capable of killing harmful bacteria while sparing harmless bacteria.

With a shift in direction came a change in the type of partners AMBI sought. In September 1998 American Home Products Corporation invested in AMBI and its Whitehall-Robins Healthcare Division acquired a license to market Cardia Salt to retail customers. The following month Cultor Food Sciences, Inc., a major food ingredients company, agreed to market the product to food manufacturers. In the meantime, AMBI began developing other new nutrition products, including a beverage to maintain glucose control and another beverage to maintain good cardiovascular health. Revenues in 1998 totaled $20.8 million, resulting in net income of $1.1 million.

At the start of 1999 AMBI acquired Optimum Lifestyle Inc., maker of dietary supplement bars marketed under the Lite Bites label. The products were then reformulated with chromium picolinate. Another important development in 1999 was an alliance forged with QVC, Inc., the popular television retailer. AMBI began selling Lite Bites through QVC as well as a new product, Sweet Support dietary supplement bars, which were formulated to meet the needs of people cautious about their blood sugar levels. Sales continued to rise for AMBI in 1999, reaching $28.3 million, while earnings increased to $5.9 million. A year later sales totaled $32.8 million and net income improved to $6.5 million.

Pleased with its nutritional supplements business, AMBI decided to sever ties with its pharmaceutical origins, selling the rights to its Wipe Out Dairy Wipes teat dip product to ImmuCell Corporation and its nisin and lysostaphin antibacterial technologies for both animal and human uses to Rockville, Maryland-based Biosynexus. AMBI was free of the burden of further development costs yet remained in line for future milestone payments and royalties. Because of the change in focus, AMBI also switched chief executives. In September 2000 Gail Montgomery, a veteran of the commercial weight loss industry, took over as president and CEO. She streamlined the organization, laying off workers, which resulted in restructuring charges that adversely impacted earnings in 2001. In addition, the company's patent on Chromax Chromium expired, leading to price reductions. As a result revenues fell to $23.3 million that year and net income slipped to $1.1 million.

Fiscal 2001 also brought another name change as AMBI decided to adopt the name of its lead subsidiary, becoming Nutrition 21 Inc. in March 2001. It was a move partially made to help boost the stock price, which had been lagging because investors were confused about the company's business. Moreover, in October 2001, a new chairman was elected, 71-year-old John H. Gutfreund, the former bond trader who had been chairman and CEO of Wall Street giant Salomon Inc. In 1991 he became embroiled in a scandal involving illegal bidding on Treasury bonds and resigned from Salomon, replaced by financier Warren E. Buffett.

Having cut the cord to its biotech past, Nutrition 21 introduced new supplements, including Diachrome for diabetics and Metabolic Makeover, but with a declining economy revenues began to fall off, hovering around $10.5 million through 2005. The company also suffered net losses of $10.5 million in 2003, $5.9 million in 2004, and $7 million in 2005. Further, the company had to contend with a lawsuit filed by a former employee who charged that Montgomery had unfairly fired him. Weeks after an appeals court in 2005 upheld an arbitrator's decision that awarded the plaintiff $709,000 related to stock options, plus interest, Montgomery resigned. According to the company the timing was a coincidence, Montgomery's departure merely a reflection of Nutrition 21 reaching a new stage in its development and requiring a chief executive with a different skill set.

Succeeding Montgomery was Paul Intlekofer, who had been with Nutrition 21 since 2002. He quickly moved to once again shift the company's focus, from ingredients provider to becoming a consumer healthcare company that developed and marketed finished products for the prevention and management of diabetes. Chromium was the keystone to the strategy, a substance that Intlekofer insisted was as important to insulin health as calcium was to bone health. With this message he was able to secure shelf space in the vitamin and mineral supplement aisle at CVS, Rite Aid, Duane Reade, Albertsons, and elsewhere.

ACQUISITION OF ICELAND HEALTH: 2006

In fiscal 2007 (August 2006), Nutrition 21 expanded its product offerings with the acquisition of Iceland Health, Inc., a New York company that manufactured fish oil and omega-3 fatty acids to pharmaceutical standards, mostly sold through infomercials and the Internet. The deal provided Nutrition 21 with entry into the promising omega-3 heart health market. As a result of the deal, revenues soared to $42.14 million in fiscal 2007, although the net loss widened to $19.15 million, mostly due to the restructuring changes related to transforming Nutrition 21 into a marketing-driven company.

Nutrition 21 became involved in another product category in November 2007 with the introduction of Core4Life, a product aimed at improved memory and brain health. Later in fiscal 2008, Nutrition 21 introduced Iceland Health Cholesterol Health, Iceland Health Joint Relief Plus Sleep Support, and Iceland Health Skin Rejuvenation. Through the first half of fiscal 2008 the new strategy appeared to be paying off as sales were showing an 83 percent improvement over the same period the previous year.

Ed Dinger

PRINCIPAL SUBSIDIARIES

Nutrition 21 LP.

PRINCIPAL COMPETITORS

NBTY, Inc.; Perrigo Company; Schiff Nutrition International, Inc.

FURTHER READING

Barnaby, Feder, "An Urban Start-Up's Rural Twist," *New York Times,* June 6, 1991, p. D1.

Drury, Allan, "Nutrition 21's Montgomery Quits," *News Journal* (Westchester County, N.Y.), November 5, 2005, p. 1D.

Gupta, Udayan, "Watching and Waiting: Biotechnology Holds Great Promise, but Investors Are Still Waiting for the Payoff," *Wall Street Journal,* November 13, 1989.

Kass, Rochelle, "AMBI Selects New Top Chief," *News Journal* (Westchester County, N.Y.), October 3, 2000, p. 1D.

Mele, Christopher, "Nutrition 21 Turns to Science," *News Journal* (Westchester County, N.Y.), January 21, 2002, p. 1D.

"Nutrition 21 Tackles Age-Related Health Issues," *Chain Drug Review,* June 25, 2007, p. 85.

Sabra, Chartrand, "A Company Has Found Protein Compounds That Could Join Antibiotics in Fighting Infections," *New York Times,* October 21, 1996, p. D2.

Weiss, Tara, "Nutrition 21 Focusing on Insulin Health," *News Journal* (Westchester County, N.Y.), June 11, 2006, p. 1D.

Oakleaf Waste Management, LLC

One Oakleaf Center
800 Connecticut Boulevard
East Hartford, Connecticut 06108
U.S.A.
Telephone: (860) 290-1250
Toll Free: (888) 625-5323
Fax: (860) 290-1251
Web site: http://www.oakleafwaste.com

Private Company
Incorporated: 1995
Employees: 450
Sales: $600 million (2007 est.)
NAICS: 562998 All Other Miscellaneous Waste Management

■ ■ ■

Oakleaf Waste Management LLC manages national waste service contracts for retail, restaurant, hospitality, manufacturing, and property management customers. The company serves national companies with multiple business locations. Oakleaf performs a site audit to determine the proper solution to handling a client's waste needs and uses a network of independent, certified waste haulers to remove debris and recyclable materials. The company serves more than 90,000 locations in North America through contracts with 4,800 haulers. Through The Home Depot Inc., Oakleaf provides dumpster rental services to contractors and do-it-yourself customers involved in home renovation projects. The company also offers The Tire Shark, a hydraulically driven compactor that punctures and compresses a tire to one-third its size in 12 seconds.

ORIGINS

From James R. Barnes's perspective, waste management operated according to a flawed business model before Oakleaf emerged on the scene. Judging by the size and financial performance of his company, Barnes was right. Nearly 5,000 certified haulers; an impressive, ever expanding list of national and multinational corporate clients; and exponential revenue growth offered tangible proof that the Oakleaf way of managing waste represented an evolutional, if not a revolutionary, improvement over traditional waste-management practices.

The success of Oakleaf turned Barnes into a hometown hero. Born in East Hartford, Connecticut, Barnes attended college in Poughkeepsie, New York, earning a degree in business in 1984 from Marist College. After college, Barnes rose to the post of director of marketing at Coldwell Banker Real Estate and spent time working for a regional hauler of waste, the experience that led him to form Oakleaf. As the headquarters for his company, Barnes chose East Hartford, a decision that proved to be a boon to East Hartford's economy and gave the city the darling of the business press who would be featured in *Fortune, Business Week, FAST Company, Chain Store Age,* and *Inc.,* among numerous other publications.

Barnes's experience in the solid waste industry alerted him to the gross inefficiencies inherent in the traditional way waste was removed. Companies, such as

COMPANY PERSPECTIVES

Waste is a terrible thing to waste. That's why Oakleaf will help you turn your trash into cash. We're not a broker. We're not a hauler. We don't own any trucks or have any landfills to feed. Instead, we earn our keep by helping you reduce, divert and monetize your waste flow, and by helping you meet your environmental goals. We'll provide you with a complete turn-key solution, from evaluation and design to implementation and management. With Oakleaf, you'll produce less trash, pay less to haul it—and you'll put up with fewer hassles along the way. In other words, you'll finally be doing waste outsourcing right.

retailers, restaurant operators, distributors, and other generators of garbage, typically contracted with waste haulers to dispense with steady streams of garbage, old corrugated containers, and other materials. Companies either contacted the haulers themselves or used the services of a broker, who found a hauler to perform the work and earned a commission from introducing the two parties. For a company operating out of a single location, the arrangement worked well, but for a company with multiple locations the arrangement led to burdensome problems. For instance, a retailer such as The Gap Inc., which operated at 3,000 locations, conceivably would have to pay 3,000 invoices to local haulers.

BARNES'S NEW APPROACH

Barnes envisioned a better way to conduct business for both companies and haulers. He cast Oakleaf as an orchestrator of waste management, a company that would handle all aspects of waste disposal for its clients, including contracting with haulers. This approach distinguished Oakleaf from its competitors: The company did not operate as a broker in the traditional sense because it signed ongoing contracts with companies and with haulers. Further, Barnes was spared the expense of maintaining trucks, landfills, and the workforce incurred by haulers operating nationally. "We decided to become more of a general contractor," he said in a January 8, 2007, interview with the *Hartford Business Journal.* Oakleaf would make its living in dealing with waste without ever deploying a truck, baler, or compactor.

Barnes believed he had developed a business model that would make money for all parties involved: Oakleaf, its corporate customers, and waste haulers. Once they hired Oakleaf, companies no longer had the burden of dealing with the waste produced by their businesses. "We can manage this aspect of their business nationwide without them expending their resource of time," Barnes explained in an August 2007 interview with *Recycling Today.* Barnes also intended to save companies money by assessing their waste, identifying recyclable materials, and channeling the materials to sources paying optimal prices. For haulers, Oakleaf's ties to national companies meant increased and steady business as well as significant improvements in their route densities. "They do get you accounts that as small haulers are hard to get into," one hauler said, referring to Oakleaf in a January 8, 2007, interview with the *Hartford Business Journal.* "I can't go out and get all the Cumberland Farms [accounts], but I can tell Oakleaf, 'I'm in Willimantic, and I'll take all the ones in my area.'"

The outsourcing business model appealed to all parties, but when Barnes formed Oakleaf in 1995 the benefits were not apparent immediately to either companies or haulers. He had to sell the novel approach to an industry inured to the conventional way of doing business. Companies had to be convinced outsourcing waste management made financial sense; haulers had to be convinced to sign contracts with a new company preaching a new way to do business. Barnes promised prospective clients they would pay Oakleaf less than what they were paying for their existing waste removal service, a guarantee that forced him to go out and search for ways to save his clients money. Targeting retail clients with multiple locations, Barnes signed his first customer in 1995, a chain of convenience stores operated by Xtramart. Once he had secured Xtramart as a customer, he focused on getting a number of clients in the same geographic area to concentrate truck pick-ups and realize greater efficiency. Trash containers and compactors, ordered by Oakleaf, were installed and collections were scheduled.

RAPID GROWTH

The chore of convincing companies and haulers of the merits of Oakleaf's strategy became easier with each passing year. Haulers, in particular, increasingly became receptive to Oakleaf's presence. Between 1996 and 2001, the company attracted new business in droves, recording annualized growth of a staggering 6,330 percent that gave Barnes the critical mass to realize the efficiencies of scale that underpinned his business model. Recycling in the workplace became more prevalent during the period, further endearing Oakleaf

KEY DATES

1995: James Barnes founds Oakleaf.
2001: Oakleaf's customer base exceeds 120 companies representing more than 60,000 locations.
2003: A private equity firm, Charterhouse Group, invests in Oakleaf.
2004: Oakleaf acquires an equipment rental firm, Greenleaf Corp.
2006: Oakleaf begins courting property management companies after purchasing Valet Waste.
2007: Charterhouse Group sells its stake in Oakleaf to New Mountain Capital.

to the customers it courted. Although the company's corporate title included the word "waste," Oakleaf stressed recycling, helping its clients to save money and project a positive corporate image. "We want to divert as much of that material as possible," Barnes noted in his August 2007 interview with *Recycling Today.* "We don't own a landfill, so we're not motivated to fill up that landfill."

By 2001, Oakleaf served more than 120 customers, managing waste at more than 60,000 locations through its internal programs and contracts with certified haulers. Revenues were projected to be $135 million by the end of the year, giving Barnes the confidence and the resources to expand Oakleaf's services. The company would develop its own innovative waste and recycling services; for other capabilities, it expanded via acquisition, enabling it to cater to a wider audience. In May 2001, in what touched off an acquisition spree that would continue for the next several years, Oakleaf purchased National Mall Monitor. Based in Hartford, Connecticut, National Mall provided trash management services to shopping malls, generating $20 million in annual revenue. Another $60 million in revenue was secured the following year when Oakleaf purchased Refuse Environmental Systems Inc. in December. Based in Agawam, Massachusetts, Refuse Environmental operated as a waste broker serving 6,000 locations. The acquisition made Oakleaf three times the size of its closest competitor in managing waste.

ACQUISITIONS EXPANDING OAKLEAF'S SERVICES

Barnes's success attracted the interest of a New York-based private equity firm, Charterhouse Group, Inc., in 2003. The investment firm, impressed by Oakleaf's growth and the potential of its business model, invested $30 million in the company, giving Barnes the resources to continue expanding into new markets. In mid-2004, he acquired Greenleaf Compaction, Inc. Based in Phoenix, Arizona, Greenleaf rented stationary compactors, containers, and balers to commercial businesses and haulers, serving 1,750 customers in 45 states. In early 2006, Barnes completed a complementary acquisition, purchasing Valet Waste, which supplied small trash bins to condominiums and removed the bins once they were filled with trash. Valet Waste served more than 40,000 residential units in Alabama, Florida, and Georgia, giving Barnes entry into a market well suited for the assets gained in the Greenleaf acquisition. "Valet Waste fits perfectly with our full-service waste outsourcing business model," he said in a February 13, 2006, interview with *Waste News.* "Combined with our compactor fleet rental business, Oakleaf can now provide a turnkey solution to the residential property management market."

In August 2006, Barnes turned his attention back to Oakleaf's shopping mall business. The purchase of National Mall Monitor in 2001 had paved the company's entry into the market, and Barnes sought to strengthen Oakleaf's presence in the field by acquiring International Environmental Management. Based in Roswell, Georgia, International Environmental specialized in serving shopping malls, counting more than 300 malls as customers.

Oakleaf's expanding service offerings, given new dimensions by acquiring other firms, also broadened in scope through internal means. In late 2006, Oakleaf signed an agreement with The Home Depot, Inc., to provide dumpster rental service to customers of the chain, which ranked as the world's largest home improvement retailer. Oakleaf also partnered with Wal-Mart Stores, Inc., the world's largest retailer of any type, to promote "The Tire Shark," a hydraulically driven compactor that punctured and compressed discarded tires. For retailers such as Pier 1 Imports, Inc., Oakleaf developed the "Pack-A-Drum," a manual-powered compactor designed to turn pallet wrap and other plastics into a dense bale of recyclable plastic.

AMBITIOUS GOAL FOR THE FUTURE

By 2007, 12 years after he started his company, Barnes was projecting $1 billion in sales by the end of the decade. He was more than halfway toward his goal, as Oakleaf continued to record torrid financial growth, generating $600 million in sales. The company, whose network of certified haulers had expanded to 4,800 operators, served more than 90,000 locations, having attracted a customer base of corporate luminaries that included General Electric Company, Sears, Roebuck and Co., PepsiCo, Inc., and Triarc Companies, Inc., among roughly 500 other customers.

Speculation about Oakleaf's potential debut on Wall Street was a subject of interest as the company plotted its future course. Barnes, in an interview with *Business Week* published on August 3, 2006, referred to a possible initial public offering, saying, "it certainly has been an interest of ours and I'm certain that it's something that we will consider in the future." The proceeds from a stock offering would bring in cash to fuel the company's expansion, but in the interim it enjoyed the financial backing of private placements. In 2007, Charterhouse Group sold its interest in Oakleaf, ending its four-year affiliation with the company after recording a sevenfold increase on its investment. Charterhouse Group sold its interest to two private equity funds, New Mountain Partners II, L.P. and New Mountain Partners III, L.P., for $655 million. The two funds were sponsored by New Mountain Capital, LLC, a New York-based private equity firm with more than $6 billion in aggregate commitments.

Looking ahead, Oakleaf faced a promising future. As the company's client roster grew longer and its instances of saving money increased, the corporate world remained enticed by the prospects of outsourcing its waste management practices and policies. The road ahead did have some potential obstacles, however, those addressed by Oakleaf's director of marketing, Marc Okrant, in an interview published in the Summer 2006 issue of *Energy Business.* "We're an entrepreneurial firm that has evolved into a professionally managed company," Okrant said. "We realize that as we grow the challenge is to ensure that the customer experience is maintained and is consistent. Our systems development team works on ensuring that we have proper tools in place. This is an exciting time for us, showing leading companies not only how to improve their waste disposal but also how to actually make money at it."

Jeffrey L. Covell

PRINCIPAL SUBSIDIARIES

Oakleaf Global Holdings, Inc.

PRINCIPAL COMPETITORS

Allied Waste Industries, Inc.; Republic Services, Inc.; Waste Management, Inc.

FURTHER READING

Brown, Matthew L., "Rubbish to Riches," *Hartford Business Journal,* January 8, 2007.

"East-Hartford, Conn.-based Oakleaf Management Buys Waste-Hauler Equipment Firm," *Hartford Courant,* July 28, 2004.

Gershon, Eric, "New Money, New Jobs: Waste Company May Hire Up to 100," *Business Week,* August 2, 2006.

Johnson, Jim, "Got an Ally? These Firms Now Do," *Waste News,* May 9, 2005, p. 1.

———, "Oakleaf Acquires Mass. Broker," *Waste News,* December 9, 2002, p. 1.

"Oakleaf Waste Management, East Hartford, Conn., Is Merging with Refuse Environmental Systems, Agawam, Mass.," *Chain Store Age,* February 2003, p. 63.

Taylor, Brian, "At the Source: Oakleaf Waste Management Brings an Outsourcing Model to Retailers and Other Large Waste and Scrap Generators," *Recycling Today,* August 2007, p. 46.

Toushek, Gary, "Well Disposed," *Energy Business,* Summer 2006, p. 89.

"Trash Broker Planning to Go Public?" *Solid Waste Report,* June 13, 2003.

Truini, Joe, "Oakleaf, Greenleaf Merge," *Waste News,* August 2, 2004, p. 4.

"Waste Industry Briefs," *Waste News,* February 13, 2006, p. 6.

"Waste Management," *Chain Store Age,* May 2001, p. 213.

OOC Inc.

1052 Folsom Street
San Francisco, California 94103
U.S.A.
Telephone: (415) 703-8122
Toll Free: (866) 695-5595
Fax: (415) 503-1633
Web site: http://www.extremepizza.com

Private Company
Incorporated: 1994
Employees: 150
Sales: $8 million (2007 est.)
NAICS: 722110 Full-Service Restaurants; 533110 Owners and Lessors of Other Non-Financial Assets

■ ■ ■

OOC Inc., operator of the Extreme Pizza chain, presides over 32 company-owned and franchised restaurants that offer dine-in, take-out, and take-and-bake service. The restaurants are located in California, which is home to 22 Extreme Pizza units; Colorado; Oregon; Texas; Virginia; and Washington. There is one Extreme Pizza restaurant operating in Kilkenny, Ireland, which is expected to serve as the European headquarters of the concept. The restaurants offer nearly 20 different styles of pizzas as well as a broad selection of toppings that customers can combine to create their own pizzas. The menu also features calzones, salads, and submarine sandwiches. Beer and wine are sold at selected locations.

ORIGINS

Todd Parent's first entrepreneurial business model failed, but after altering his strategy the former finance executive scored great success, creating one of the fastest-growing franchise concepts in the United States. The inspiration for his business occurred in 1987, when Parent, a University of Vermont student, was studying abroad at the Collège de Sorbonne in Paris, France. There, the 21-year-old was struck by a ubiquitous sight on Parisian streets, the French version of gourmet, take-out dining: crepe stands. "Pizza wasn't my first choice," Parent recalled in a July 1, 2003, interview with *Inc.* magazine. "In college, when I was studying in Paris, I ate crepes every day. I thought I could bring the crepe stand concept to the United States, but crepes were only a fad for about a month. They never caught on."

Pizza was not Parent's first choice, nor was a career as a restaurateur his first choice after earning a degree in economics from the University of Vermont. He headed south after college and found employment on Wall Street, where he worked for a brief period at U.S. Trust Corporation. Parent's short career in finance and money management ended once his desire to become an entrepreneur and restaurateur overtook him, but he did not go it alone after leaving Wall Street. He realized he needed to gain experience in the restaurant business before launching his own company.

First in New Jersey, next in Colorado, Parent learned the nuances of operating a restaurant by taking any job he could in the business. He spent stints working as a bartender, dishwasher, sous chef, prep cook, line cook, waiter, and as manager for several different

COMPANY PERSPECTIVES

If you want to get a sense of our business philosophy, all you have to do is pick up a slice. There's no better testament to "Dedication to Quality, Commitment to Innovation" than the pizza itself. Our dedication to quality comes from a strict policy to use only the freshest ingredients, the tastiest combinations of toppings, and a mouth-watering store-baked crust. As for the innovation side of things, well that's easy. Think about it ... what does an office full of freethinking, pizza connoisseur daredevils get you? It gets you mandarin oranges, Canadian bacon, pineapples, mozzarella, and cheddar (Paia Pie). It gets you black beans, ground beef, olives, onions, cilantro, and cheddar (California Cactus). And for the politically savvy pizza-eaters, it gets you homemade hummus in place of tomato sauce, tomatoes, olives, feta, fresh basil, pepperoncinis, and mozzarella (Peace in the Middle East). This is the sort of pizza invented by people who sail from kites, who snowboarded before there were snowboards, and who learned to always color outside the lines.

restaurants. His efforts to learn every aspect of the business eventually took him to San Francisco, where he joined Noah's Bagels, operator of a chain of deli restaurants. Parent worked his way up through the ranks, earning the admiration of the company owners. While at Noah's, Parent drafted a business plan for his Extreme Pizza concept, which combined gourmet, take-out pizza with an "extreme" sports motif (Parent enjoyed snowboarding, windsurfing, surfing, and kite sailing). He showed the business plan to his employers, who encouraged him to press ahead as an entrepreneur. "The owners of Noah's were good mentors and sources of support," Parent said in an interview published in the January/February 2005 issue of *Food and Drink*. "They said, 'If you don't try it now, you might not ever have this opportunity again.'"

FAILURE AT FIRST

In 1994, after six years of working for others, Parent launched his business, making an entrepreneurial debut riddled with mistakes. His first misjudgment, which he referred to as his "biggest mistake" in a June 2, 2006, interview with the *San Francisco Business Times*, was asking a friend to be his business partner. For undisclosed reasons, the partnership never worked, prompting Parent to buy out his partner's 50 percent stake in 1997, which he deemed his "smartest move" in the *San Francisco Business Times* article. Despite the fact that Parent had later misgivings, the assistance of a financial partner at least enabled the Extreme Pizza concept to get up and running. Parent used his personal savings and bank loans to provide his half of the start-up capital and opened a 1,100-square-foot pizza shop on Fillmore Street. Incorporating an extreme sports theme, the small shop offered take-and-bake service, supplying premade pizzas customers purchased to cook at home. With that style of service, Parent made his second error, a decision he also characterized as his biggest mistake in another interview with the *San Francisco Business Times.*

The decision to focus on take-and-bake gourmet pizzas may have worked in another type of market, but it failed miserably in the heart of metropolitan San Francisco. "Our biggest mistake was thinking take-and-bake would succeed on its own," Parent conceded in an October 27, 2000, interview with the *San Francisco Business Times*. "Papa Murphy's has built a 300-location chain on the concept, but those are all in suburbia," he explained. San Franciscans shunned the new pizza shop on Fillmore Street.

A CHANGE IN STRATEGY

With his Fillmore restaurant floundering, it was time for Parent either to shut down operations or to revamp his business model. He chose the latter and approached the pizza business from another angle. Take-and-bake, although it remained as an option for Extreme Pizza customers for years to come, was replaced by traditional take-out and dine-in service as the primary focus of the shop. Parent also invested heavily in new baking equipment; initially, the Fillmore shop had only the capability to heat and to serve one slice at a time. To invigorate demand, Parent made arguably his most astute move, promoting Extreme Pizza to corporations in San Francisco, offering his gourmet pizzas as lunch fare for office workers. Corporate accounts managers, or company employees themselves, turned in droves to Extreme Pizza for lunch or for a snack. The dot-com industry, which established a major presence in San Francisco, was expanding rapidly, creating a wealth of new business that few pizza operators other than Parent courted aggressively.

All the adjustments made by Parent would have failed to produce results if the product he was selling did not find a receptive audience. In creating Extreme Pizza's menu, he favored eccentric combinations of toppings, creating memorable pizzas that differed substantially from the products offered by his

KEY DATES

1994: Todd Parent opens the first Extreme Pizza in San Francisco.
1999: After a 400 percent increase in sales during the previous two years, revenues reach $1.6 million.
2003: The number of Extreme Pizza restaurants reaches 15.
2008: An Extreme Pizza opens in Kilkenny, Ireland.

competitors. Traditional toppings such as pepperoni, black olives, and onions, sat alongside peculiar items such as mandarin oranges, roasted walnuts, and new potatoes. Instead of traditional tomato sauce, customers could choose pesto, hummus, or black beans and salsa. The names of the pizzas lent a distinctive quality to Parent's business as well, featuring recipes created by Extreme Pizza employees and their customers, whose suggestions occasionally were incorporated into the company's menu. Names such as "Drag It Thru the Garden" (mushrooms, green peppers, onions, marinated artichoke hearts, broccoli, tomatoes, basil, and mozzarella); "Poultry Geist" (marinated chicken, broccoli, onion, Swiss, fontina, Gorgonzola, mozzarella, and sage); and "Yard Sale" (every available topping), left a lasting impression in the minds and on the palates of customers.

RAPID GROWTH

Parent's efforts to find a viable business model succeeded. Between 1997 and 1999, Parent's company, which operated under the name OOC Inc., recorded a 400 percent increase in revenues, generating $1.6 million by the end of the decade. The period also saw Extreme Pizza garner a coveted prize when it was voted as the "Best Pizza in San Francisco" in 1998, providing a marketing boon that Parent used to court corporate clientele. In 2000, when sales were expected to double during the year, Extreme Pizza enjoyed a wealth of business from the "south of Market [Street] dot-com hordes," as the *San Francisco Business Times* noted in its July 6, 2001, edition. The company had secured accounts with 127 technology companies by 2000, giving Parent the business volume and the confidence to expand his restaurant concept. By late 2000, he planned to open two to three restaurants in the San Francisco Bay area during the next 12 months.

BEGINNING OF FRANCHISING

Parent's burgeoning business hit an unexpected snag when the dot-com industry it supported collapsed suddenly at the start of the 21st century. The number of the company's corporate accounts plunged from 127 to 72 during the first half of 2001, as many of the companies Extreme Pizza served shut down, leaving their pizza bills unpaid. Despite losing scores of customers and finding itself awash in unpaid invoices, Extreme Pizza pressed ahead, as Parent began franchising his pizza concept to aspiring entrepreneurs. The decision to franchise Extreme Pizza gave Parent a new way to spur expansion, particularly because he stipulated that franchisees agree to open multiple locations.

By the fall of 2001, those considering opening their own Extreme Pizza restaurants could find encouragement in the vitality of the developing chain. There were five locations in California in operation, each recording between $18,000 and $25,000 per week in sales. The menu had expanded to include a selection of salads, calzones, and 14-inch-long submarine sandwiches. Each of the company's restaurants could accommodate up to 50 seated customers, a type of service (dine-in) that accounted for 25 percent of Extreme Pizza's business. Take-and-bake, the initial service offered by Parent, continued to demonstrate its unpopularity, representing less than 1 percent of sales, which made take-out service the company's most important revenue generator, accounting for 65 percent of sales.

There was no greater testament to the public's affection for Extreme Pizza than an award the business received as Parent began to franchise his concept. Extreme Pizza was voted the best pizza in Calgary, Alberta, a remarkable achievement considering the company did not operate a restaurant in Calgary, or in Canada, or anywhere close to Calgary. The nearest restaurant, which opened in Colorado Springs, Colorado, in early 2002, was the company's second franchised unit, its seventh restaurant in total, and its first outside its home state of California. Parent's brainchild, after initially struggling to get noticed, was enjoying a level of recognition accorded to hot dining trends, and he made sure to capitalize on the popularity of his concept. A commissary was established, functioning as the hub of operations for both company-owned and franchised units, used to store, prepare, and distribute all the produce and goods needed for the retail locations. Parent, meanwhile, began exploring franchising interests in San Diego, California; Portland, Oregon; El Paso, Texas; Tampa, Florida; and Las Vegas, Nevada, intent on spreading Extreme Pizza's presence throughout the country.

As Parent pursued expansion, he favored franchising restaurants over opening company-owned stores. Extreme Pizza was a 15-unit chain by 2003. By the end of the following year, there were 21 restaurants in operation, 17 of which were franchised locations. Parent planned to open two company stores and ten to 12 franchised units in 2005. His plan was to open at least ten restaurants annually, which would bring him to his goal of 50 Extreme Pizza units by 2007.

Parent fell short of reaching his target, but his expansion efforts reached far geographically, giving Extreme Pizza a sprawling, ungainly posture as it neared its 15th anniversary. Between 2005 and 2008, restaurants opened in Colorado, home to four units. Next to California, where 22 units were in operation, Colorado contained the greatest concentration of restaurants, making the two units in Texas and single locations in Oregon, Washington, and Virginia look like lonely sentinels waiting for reinforcements. Parent, as it became clear in early 2008, did not worry about fleshing out Extreme Pizza's geographic presence. In April, he sold the European rights to the Extreme Pizza concept to a California native named Carla Freely. Freely opened an Extreme Pizza outpost in Kilkenny, Ireland, which she intended to use as the chain's European headquarters for selling franchises and hosting training courses. The bold move promised more to come from the dining concept born on Fillmore Street. The years ahead would determine if Parent's business model had the capability to become an international phenomenon.

Jeffrey L. Covell

PRINCIPAL COMPETITORS

Z Pizza Corporation; Wahoo's Inc.; Tin Star Restaurants.

FURTHER READING

Boyles, Tom, "An Extreme Pizza Concept," *Pizza Marketing Quarterly,* Fall 2001.

Dunn, Michael, "Fun, to the Extreme," *Tampa Tribune,* September 29, 2005, p. 1.

Gardner, Jim, "Deadbeat Dot-Coms Make Pizza Chain's Dough Fall," *San Francisco Business Times,* July 6, 2001, p. 4.

Ginsberg, Steve, "Extreme Pizza Cooking Up Pie-in-the-Sky Success," *San Francisco Business Times,* October 27, 2000, p. 7.

Gurwell, Lance, "Extreme Pizza Enters the Colorado Springs Market," *Colorado Springs Business Journal,* April 26, 2002.

Jergler, Don, "Long Beach, Calif., Eatery Offers Extreme Pizza Experience," *Press-Telegram,* May 2, 2004.

———, "San Francisco-based Chain to Open Extreme Pizza Parlor in Long Beach, Calif.," *Press-Telegram,* May 3, 2004.

Keys, Laura, "US Pizza Giant Enters Local Market," *Kilkenny People,* April 4, 2008.

Knudson, Brooke, "To the Extreme: Extreme Pizza Defines Its Niche in the Gourmet Pizza Market," *Food and Drink,* July–August 2007, p. 90.

Philipps, Dave, "Dude, There's a Pizza Place Just for You," *Colorado Springs Gazette,* January 21, 2005, p. G2.

Platt, Kayla, "Entrepreneur Profile: Todd Parent," *San Francisco Business Times,* June 2, 2006.

Robinson, Kathryn, "Daring Combinations Make Sense to the Taste Buds," *Seattle Times,* August 12, 2005, p. I16.

Rodriguez, Robert, "Taking Pizza to an Extreme," *Fresno Bee,* December 29, 2001, p. C1.

Srinivasan, Kirsten, "To the Extreme: Extreme Pizza Reinvents the Pizza Industry with Extreme Sports," *Food and Drink,* January–February 2005, p. 162.

"Things I Can't Live Without," *Inc.,* July 1, 2003.

Palace Sports & Entertainment, Inc.

4 Championship Drive
Auburn Hills, Michigan 48326
U.S.A.
Telephone: (248) 377-0100
Fax: (248) 377-3260
Web site: http://www.palacenet.com

Private Company
Incorporated: 1978 as Arena Associates, Inc.
Employees: 350
Sales: $170 million (2007 est.)
NAICS: 711310 Promoters of Performing Arts, Sports, and Similar Events with Facilities; 711211 Sports Teams and Clubs

■ ■ ■

Palace Sports & Entertainment, Inc., is a Detroit-area holding company that owns and/or operates sports teams and entertainment facilities. The company runs the business operations of the National Basketball Association's Detroit Pistons and owns and manages its home arena, the 21,000-seat Palace of Auburn Hills, which also plays host to the firm's Women's NBA team the Detroit Shock as well as numerous concerts and other events. Other Palace Sports & Entertainment properties include the 15,000-seat DTE Energy Music Theatre, consistently named the top-grossing outdoor music venue in the United States; The Asheville (North Carolina) Tourists minor-league baseball team; several Palace Locker Room retail shops; and a growing marketing division. The company also manages the Meadow Brook Music Festival, which presents live music at a 7,500-seat outdoor venue owned by Oakland University. Billionaire Guardian Industries owner William Davidson holds controlling interest in the firm.

BEGINNINGS

Palace Sports & Entertainment (PS&E) can trace its origins to the $6 million purchase of the National Basketball Association's (NBA) Detroit Pistons by William Davidson in 1974. The team was founded in Fort Wayne, Indiana, in 1939 as a semi-pro outfit by Fred Zollner, and later became a member of the NBA before moving in 1957 to Detroit. The Pistons' owner had met Davidson in Florida, where they were summer neighbors.

Athletic from his youth, William Davidson had served in the Navy in World War II and earned a business degree from the University of Michigan and a law degree from Wayne State University. After briefly practicing law, he successfully helped turn around troubled drug and surgical supply firms. In 1957 he was named president of the floundering Guardian Glass, an auto windshield maker which an uncle had founded in 1932. Davidson guided it through bankruptcy and then helped transform the business into a major publicly traded international glass and photographic products supplier under the name Guardian Industries.

After Davidson's purchase of the Pistons was completed he began seeking ways to improve the money-losing team's fortunes, both at the ticket booth and on the court. The team was then playing games at Cobo Arena in downtown Detroit, but attendance had

COMPANY PERSPECTIVES

"In the 20 years we've run The Palace, and in the 17 summers we have operated DTE Energy Music Theatre, we have worked hard to provide the concert programming to satisfy our area's love of live music. Through all of the challenges our area has faced, we are grateful to the concert-goers and sponsors who have continued to support the shows at our venues. Without their enthusiastic patronage, we would be unable to host the quantity and quality of concerts which has earned us our honors."—Tom Wilson, president and CEO

declined as the middle class abandoned the troubled city for its northern suburbs. In the fall of 1977 Davidson announced he would move the team a half-hour north to the Pontiac Silverdome, an 80,000-seat stadium that had been built to house the Detroit Lions. The following year he also formed a company called Arena Associates, Inc., with developers David Hermelin and Robert Sosnick. Over the next decade the team's won-loss record improved but the makeshift space (which utilized only a portion of the giant covered stadium and had inadequate heat and poor lighting) proved a sore spot with both fans and management.

PALACE OF AUBURN HILLS OPENS: 1988

After the Silverdome's roof suffered severe storm damage in March 1985 the Pistons took up temporary quarters in Detroit's Joe Louis Arena, but the city had deteriorated to the point that many suburban fans felt unsafe there, and Davidson decided the time was right to give the team a home of its own. Arena Associates soon began making plans to build a new facility for the Pistons that could also be used for concerts and other events. It would be located just east of Pontiac in Auburn Hills, also the home of Guardian Industries. The plan to create a privately financed arena was unusual, as most such facilities were built in part with civic funds.

The $70 million-plus venue was designed by Rossetti and Associates of Detroit with significant input from Davidson and Pistons CEO Tom Wilson, none of whom had worked on such a facility before. To its more than 21,000 seats would be added 180 corporate entertainment suites on three levels, a radical departure in both quantity and placement. Davidson and Wilson were gambling on renting the latter as a means to boost revenues at a time when other arenas offered only a limited number of suites and placed them high in the rafters.

Although rentals were slow at first, they picked up after Chrysler CEO Lee Iacocca took one, and more were grafted on during the construction process. The groundbreaking design would prove a key component in the company's financial success, and it was subsequently copied around the league as other teams replaced their aging arenas.

The name of the new venue would be the Palace of Auburn Hills, which was chosen in a contest whose winner received two lifetime tickets to all future events. In keeping with its name, the firm sought to offer patrons a high level of service and amenities, and the brick-and-concrete-faced building included a restaurant, cocktail lounge, and television production studio, with comfortable padded seats and large ceiling-mounted video screens that offered instant replays and other content.

The Palace opened on August 13, 1988, with a concert by Sting, and during its first year in operation it hosted more than 160 events, half of them sellouts, which were attended by 2.5 million patrons. In addition to 50 sold-out Pistons games, the facility played host to concerts by Michael Jackson, Elton John, and Eric Clapton, as well as a tennis match between Jimmy Connors and Andre Agassi.

For its first year the arena grossed approximately $40 million, and it was honored by trade journals *Performance* and *Pollstar* as Best New Venue for 1988, the first of many such industry awards it would receive.

PURCHASE OF PINE KNOB MUSIC THEATRE: 1990

In the spring of 1990 Arena Associates announced plans for a new $30 million outdoor amphitheater adjacent to the Palace called Palace Gardens, but in November the idea was dropped when the firm paid approximately $20 million to buy Pine Knob Music Theatre in nearby Clarkston, Michigan, a 16,646-seat outdoor arena that hosted a summer concert series. Opened in 1972, it had been owned since 1984 by the Nederlander Organization.

Over the years the venue had developed a reputation for long lines, unfriendly staff, and poorly organized parking, and its new owners vowed to implement the Palace model of gracious service, rechristening the facility New Pine Knob to drive this point home. A $6 million improvement program was soon begun that

KEY DATES

1974: William Davidson buys Detroit Pistons of the National Basketball Association.

1978: Davidson, David Hermelin, and Robert Sosnick found Arena Associates, Inc.

1988: Palace of Auburn Hills opens as Pistons' new home.

1990: Firm buys Pine Knob Music Theatre in Clarkston, Michigan.

1994: Company takes over management of Meadowbrook Music Festival in Rochester, Michigan; firm adds Detroit Neon soccer and Detroit Vipers hockey teams; combined sports, venue operations take name Palace Sports & Entertainment.

1997: Detroit Neon (subsequently known as the Safari) folds.

1998: Women's NBA team the Detroit Shock is founded, begins playing at Palace.

1999: Palace Sports buys Tampa Bay Lightning of National Hockey League.

2001: Pine Knob becomes DTE Energy Music Theatre in $10 million deal; Detroit Vipers team ceases operations.

2004: Pistons, Lightning, Shock each win league championships.

2005: Firm buys North Carolina minor-league baseball team the Asheville Tourists.

2008: Tampa Bay Lightning is sold for $200 million; William Davidson is named to Basketball Hall of Fame.

would double the number of restrooms, triple the amount of food concessions, boost parking and ticket booths, and add giant video screens, new exterior landscaping, and improved sound. Some 2,000 of the 10,000 lower-priced lawn seats were removed to decrease crowding, while the number of audio speakers directed toward the area was doubled. The firm also shifted its bookings to include a wider range of pop-rock acts that attracted a larger audience.

In 1991, its first season under Arena Associates management, Pine Knob hosted 75 shows that drew 600,000 attendees, and was declared the top-grossing outdoor amphitheater in the United States by industry observers, a position it would retain on an annual basis. Additional improvements would be made to the venue almost every year, and before the 1992 season the firm boosted capacity to 15,253 and began installing padded seats near the stage, also increasing the number of handicapped spots. Meanwhile, at the Palace, an ice floor and ice rink capabilities were installed, which would allow it to host hockey games and figure skating events.

BIRTH OF DETROIT NEON, VIPERS: 1994

In early 1994 the company joined with Chrysler Corporation to launch a new Continental Indoor Soccer League team, the Detroit Neon, which was named after a Dodge car. The firm also acquired an International Hockey League (IHL) team, the Salt Lake Golden Eagles, and renamed it the Detroit Vipers, after the Dodge Viper automobile. Both would play their home games at the Palace.

In March the firm agreed to take over management of Meadowbrook Music Festival, a summer concert series at a 7,500-seat outdoor venue at Oakland University, located in nearby Rochester, Michigan. It featured a diverse mix of more than two dozen rock, jazz, classical, and children's concerts, which complemented the offerings of Pine Knob and the Palace.

During the year the organization officially took the name Palace Sports & Entertainment (PS&E). Along with managing its own venues and sports teams, its duties also included running the business operations of the Pistons. Pistons and Arena Associates CEO Tom Wilson would also head PS&E.

In April 1995 a new sponsor-supported $15 million, 100,000-square-foot addition was announced for the Palace, which would include an atrium lobby, arcade, theater, and Pistons memorabilia display area. The firm also invested $3.5 million to add video screens to Pine Knob's lawn area and enlarge some of its restrooms. Revenues for the year reached an estimated $100 million.

In November 1996 PS&E announced plans to build a 30,000-seat auto racetrack at the Michigan State Fairgrounds in Detroit, which would cost upward of $40 million. Community opposition was fierce, however, and in late January the proposal was dropped.

In 1997 the Detroit Neon became the Detroit Safari, after its naming rights were sold to General Motors, maker of the GMC Safari minivan. The team folded at the end of the season, however, when the Continental soccer league went belly up.

In 1998 PS&E grew again with the creation of the Detroit Shock of the Women's National Basketball

Association. The Palace-based expansion team posted a 17–13 record its first season and within six years would win the league championship.

Starting in the early 1990s PS&E had opened a small handful of sports merchandise retail stores called Palace Locker Room, and by 1998 there were three in suburban shopping malls and two at the Palace, which generated about $4.5 million in revenues per year.

ACQUISITION OF TAMPA BAY LIGHTNING: 1999

In March 1999 the firm bought the Tampa Bay Lightning, a National Hockey League (NHL) team based in Tampa, Florida, also taking leasehold rights to the 21,500-seat Ice Palace arena, which was owned by the county. The total cost was approximately $100 million. The Lightning were the poorest-performing team in the NHL and had posted a $20 million loss the year before, but PS&E officials expressed optimism about quickly turning its fortunes around. The firm also announced plans to boost the number of suites at the Ice Palace, add more live events, and seek a buyer for the naming rights. At the same time the company took a minority ownership stake in an Arena Football League team based there, the Tampa Storm, in exchange for performing its sales and marketing duties.

In November PS&E was awarded a contract to oversee advertising at Detroit's Metro Airport, where the number of displays would be boosted from 100 to 300. A month later the firm partnered with Detroit Lions owner William Clay Ford Jr. to buy a new Arena Football League franchise that would become known as the Detroit Fury, whose games would be played at the Palace. Revenues for the year were undercut by a three-month NBA player lockout, which had shortened the Pistons' 1998–99 season.

During the year the firm worked with a consultant to sell the naming rights to the Palace for as much as $100 million, but the effort was dropped at the beginning of 2000.

In March, partner Robert Sosnick died at the age of 66, and in November David Hermelin passed away at the age of 63. William Davidson would continue to hold controlling interest in the firm, with CEO Tom Wilson also owning a stake.

For 2000 PS&E was ranked the fourth largest concert promotion firm in the United States, with revenues from this category surpassing sports. The Pistons, who had sold every available ticket in their early years at the Palace, were averaging about 14,000 fans per game as their success declined.

In January 2001 Pine Knob, the number one U.S. outdoor amphitheater for ten years running, took the name DTE Energy Theater in a ten-year, $10 million deal with a local power company. During 2000 nearly one million concertgoers had attended shows there, with gross revenues topping $24 million.

DETROIT VIPERS FOLD: JUNE 2001

In June the Detroit Vipers closed up shop as the IHL ceased operations. The team had won several division titles, but after becoming a farm team for the Lightning had lost key players and finished its final season in last place.

In the fall the National Labor Relations Board charged that the Ice Palace in Tampa had unfairly treated workers who wanted to join the IATSE stagehands union. The facility became known as the St. Pete Times Forum, after a $30 million, 12-year deal was cut with the *St. Petersburg Times* newspaper.

In June 2003 PS&E took to the Florida courts in a bid to reduce its property tax bill for the Forum, citing losses of as much as $40 million in the most recent year, and $100 million since it had purchased the Lightning. The firm claimed the facility was worth only about $20 million, while it was assessed by the county at more than five times that amount. Also during the year, Michigan mortgage lender Rock Financial (known nationally as Quicken Loans) signed on as presenting sponsor of the Pistons, which gave it a presence at games that fell just short of naming rights. Its logo would appear on Pistons tickets, signs, programs, and ads. The innovative deal, which was reportedly worth more than $1 million per year, was soon copied by other professional sports teams.

In 2004 PS&E celebrated championship wins of its three main teams, the Pistons, the Lightning, and the Shock. At the same time DTE Energy Music Theatre continued its streak of being the top-attended or top-grossing amphitheater in the United States, while the Palace ranked second in the arena category and the St. Pete Times Forum made the top ten. In the fall the Detroit Fury football team ceased operations, having never risen above a .500 winning percentage.

Late in the year another $5 million round of improvements to the Palace was announced. Although only 16 years old, the facility was one of the older arenas in the NBA, and the firm constantly worked to keep it current.

On November 19 the venue, and the Pistons, received an unwelcome dose of negative publicity from a fan-initiated fight with players at a Pistons–Indiana Pacers game. The melee eventually resulted in the prosecution of several fans, two of whom were banned from Palace events for life, and the suspension of nine players. The firm had always sought a "fan-friendly" ambience that played down the presence of security personnel at games, but it sought to assure the public, and boosted security presence to playoff game levels. The NBA later called for increased player security and new limits on alcohol sales at games league-wide.

Another setback for the organization was the cancellation of the 2004–05 NHL season after owners locked out players following a breakdown in negotiations over salaries. The Lightning, which had broken even for the first time during its championship run the year before, recorded a substantial amount of red ink.

In March 2005 PS&E reached an agreement with Hillside Productions to book and market events at the 7,000-seat Jerome Duncan Ford amphitheater in Sterling Heights, Michigan, which had formerly been known as Freedom Hill. The deal was the first step in a plan to buy a 90 percent stake in the facility.

ASHEVILLE TOURISTS JOINS THE FOLD: SUMMER 2005

In August the firm bought minor-league baseball team the Asheville Tourists of Asheville, North Carolina, for approximately $6.5 million, later adding $800,000 worth of enhancements to its stadium. During the year another $25 million upgrade to the Palace was announced that would add a new atrium and food court as well as 13 new corporate suites under the stands, which would be rented for up to $500,000 per year. The back-to-back championships of the Pistons had helped spur the move.

In March 2006 Belle Tire was signed as presenting sponsor of concerts at DTE Energy and Meadowbrook theaters for five years. A month later PS&E dropped its contract with Hillside Productions to manage Freedom Hill amphitheater, after its partner fell out of compliance with the agreement by suing Macomb County over parking revenues. With attendance falling as the Michigan economy worsened, in July the firm ran a two-day sale that slashed ticket prices up to 75 percent at Meadowbrook and DTE Energy.

During 2006 a new unit, Palace Ventures LLC, was formed to pursue marketing opportunities as part of a corporate strategy to move deeper into this area. In May 2007 the firm bought Troy, Michigan, graphics/digital imaging company Meteor LLC for an amount put at less than $2 million. Other acquisitions, including a mobile marketing company and clothing and merchandise manufacturers, were rumored to be in the offing. PS&E worked with nearly 500 corporate sponsors, and was seeking to broaden their marketing opportunities through the new ventures.

In 2007 another $6 million in upgrades began at DTE Energy, including a new pavilion roof, food concessions, and landscaping. In the fall a new company division was formed that would provide sports marketing services to college and university teams.

2008: SALE OF LIGHTNING; DAVIDSON INDUCTED INTO BASKETBALL HALL OF FAME

After a mid-2007 deal to sell the Lightning fell apart, in early 2008 a new agreement was reached with *Saw* film producer Oren Koules and former NHL player Len Barrie. Their OK Hockey group would pay $200 million and absorb existing debt in exchange for the Lightning and leasehold rights to the St. Pete Times Forum. After several lenders backed out, Koules received funding assistance from PS&E and Galatioto Sports Partners. In June the sale was approved by the NHL board of governors.

Meanwhile, in April PS&E founder William Davidson, now 85, was named to the Basketball Hall of Fame. His visionary leadership of the Pistons and construction of the trendsetting Palace had helped change the face of professional basketball.

Two decades after the opening of its first sports arena, Palace Sports & Entertainment, Inc., had become one of the most successful managers of teams and entertainment venues in the United States. With a portfolio of stellar properties and a reputation for developing innovative marketing strategies, the firm was positioned solidly for continued success.

Frank Uhle

PRINCIPAL DIVISIONS

Detroit Pistons; Detroit Shock; The Palace of Auburn Hills; DTE Energy Music Theatre; Meadowbrook Music Festival; Palace Sports & Entertainment Service Co.; Palace Sports & Entertainment Restaurant Management Group; Palace Ventures LLC; Palace Promotions; Palace Publications; Palace Creative Group; Palace Locker Room; Asheville Tourists.

PRINCIPAL COMPETITORS

Ilitch Holdings, Inc.; Detroit Lions, Inc.; Live Nation, Inc.; General Sports and Entertainment LLC; Hillside Productions; Detroit Opera House.

FURTHER READING

"Asheville Tourists Sold to Owner of Pistons, Lightning," *Associated Press Newswires,* August 12, 2005.

Atkins, Harry, "Ford, Palace Buy Arena Football League Team," *Associated Press Newswires,* December 1, 1999.

Barkholz, David, "Big Three Mulled Track Investments," *Crain's Detroit Business,* February 3, 1997, p. 26.

———, "Distractions Keep Palace from Scoring on 'Hail Mary,'" *Crain's Detroit Business,* January 24, 2000, p. 100.

———, "Palace Net Gain: Entertainment, Not the Pistons," *Crain's Detroit Business,* January 22, 2001, p. 8.

Boers, Terry, "Pistons' Palace No Fly by Night," *Chicago Sun-Times,* August 24, 1988, p. 134.

Dietderich, Andrew, "Palace Goes Ultra-Luxury with Suites, Club," *Crain's Detroit Business,* October 24, 2005, p. 27.

Dietderich, Andrew, and Jenette Smith, "Palace Guard? Arena Says In-Your-Face Security Isn't in the Game Plan," *Crain's Detroit Business,* November 29, 2004, p. 3.

Emmons, Natasha, "PS&E Takes Over Marketing to Keep Arena League's Storm in Tampa Bay," *Amusement Business,* September 13, 1999, p. 16.

Erlendsson, Erik, "NHL OKs Bolts Sale to OK Hockey," *Tampa Tribune,* June 19, 2008.

———, "Vipers Fold As IHL Collapses," *Tampa Tribune,* June 5, 2001, p. 6.

Fricker, Daniel G., "Detroit Airport Awards Advertising Contract to Sports Firm," *Knight-Ridder/Tribune Business News,* November 16, 1999.

Graham, Adam, "Music Venues Slash Concert Prices," *Detroit News,* July 8, 2006, p. 3.

Halcom, Chad, "Talks on Hold for Palace to Operate Freedom Hill," *Crain's Detroit Business,* August 13, 2007, p. 20.

Hinsberg, Claire M., "Business Arena," *Corporate Detroit Magazine,* November 1, 1995, p. 8.

Langlois, Keith, "Shock and Pistons Owner's Hall of Fame Candidacy Began with a Stroll on a Florida Beach" (Four-Part Series), http://www.wnba.com/shock/news/davidson_partone.html, July 4, 2008.

Morath, Eric, "Palace Adds New Wrinkles for Fans," *Detroit News,* November 1, 2006, p. 1C.

Muret, Don, "Another Record Year for Pine Knob," *Amusement Business,* November 1, 1993, p. 6.

———, "Arena Associates Adds Michigan's Meadow Brook to Venue Roster," *Amusement Business,* March 14, 1994, p. 10.

———, "Palace, Chrysler Corp. Teamwork Results in New CISL Franchise," *Amusement Business,* January 24, 1994, p. 17.

———, "Palace's $15 Million Atrium Nears Completion," *Amusement Business,* June 3, 1996, p. 14.

———, "Playing the Name Game," *Amusement Business,* February 5, 2001, p. 1.

———, "PS&E Purchases Ice Palace, Lightning," *Amusement Business,* March 15, 1999.

"Naming Rights," *Florida Trend,* November 1, 2002, p. 32.

"Palace Sports Goes to Court," *St. Petersburg (Fla.) Times,* June 2, 2003, p. 1E.

Pullen, Doug, "Pine Knob Readies New Season As Renovations Continue," *Grand Rapids Press,* April 4, 1991, p. D5.

Shea, Bill, "Palace Adds Marketing Arm," *Crain's Detroit Business,* October 1, 2007, p. 3.

Smith, Jennette, "Postseason Prospects: Pistons Likely Will See Profits, While Lightning Probably Won't," *Crain's Detroit Business,* March 29, 2004, p. 3.

Zepp, Louise, "Pistons & Family Show Biz Highlight Debut Year for Palace of Auburn Hills," *Amusement Business,* August 19, 1989, p. 13.

Panda Restaurant Group, Inc.

1683 Walnut Grove Avenue
Rosemead, California 91770
U.S.A.
Telephone: (626) 799-9898
Toll Free: (800) 877-8988
Fax: (626) 403-8688
Web site: http://www.pandarg.com

Private Company
Incorporated: 1973 as Panda Management Company, Inc.
Employees: 13,000
Sales: $1.2 billion (2007 est.)
NAICS: 722110 Full-Service Restaurants; 722211 Limited-Service Restaurants

■ ■ ■

Panda Restaurant Group, Inc. (PRG), owns and operates the largest Chinese quick-service restaurant chain in the United States, with more than 1,000 Panda Express restaurants in 35 states, the District of Columbia, and Puerto Rico. A franchise operates several outlets in Japan. Panda Express Restaurants are located in five basic operating environments: mall food courts; supermarkets and retail chain stores; shopping centers and key intersections; university and college campuses; and airports, casinos, and sports arenas. PRG also owns and operates seven Panda Inns, full-service restaurants that serve gourmet Mandarin and Szechuan meals in a fine dining atmosphere; all Panda Inns are located in Southern California. The company's 27 quick-service, Hibachi-San Grill restaurants feature Japanese cuisine and are found at shopping mall food courts in Maryland, California, Nevada, Minnesota, Oregon, Arizona, and Georgia. In association with EATertainment International, the company owns Orleans Express, a quick-service Cajun food restaurant.

BEGINNINGS AS PANDA'S FULL-SERVICE RESTAURANTS

Before opening his first Panda Inn restaurant, Andrew J. C. Cherng, who emigrated from China to the United States via Hong Kong, Taipei, and Japan, studied mathematics at Baker University in Baldwin City, Kansas. After graduation in 1970, Cherng and his new wife, Peggy, moved to Los Angeles, where Cherng began managing his cousin's Hunan restaurant. In 1973, after raising $60,000 in capital from family and friends, Cherng and his father, master Chinese chef Ming-Tsai Cherng, opened the first Panda Inn restaurant in Pasadena, a suburb of Los Angeles, one of the United States' great ethnic melting pots. The Panda Inn was among the first such eateries in Southern California to modify authentic Mandarin and Szechuan dishes to complement the area's Asian cuisine.

Initially, the Cherngs were determined to expand in the full-service Chinese restaurant market, a tough business in California, due to its large Asian American population. Although the new company was able to open six additional full-service restaurants, Cherng soon saw that fast-food, drive-through restaurants were a national craze in the United States. He also realized that Southern California offered an excellent market for

COMPANY PERSPECTIVES

Mission: Deliver exceptional Asian dining experiences by building an organization where people are inspired to better their lives.

experimenting with an Asian food version of that kind of operation. Accordingly, he set out to expand into the quick-service restaurant field.

1983–92: STEADY EXPANSION WITH PANDA EXPRESS CHAIN

The opportunity to develop a fast-food business originated with a mall developer who asked Cherng to modify his menu for a shopping mall food court. In 1983, Cherng launched Panda Express, opening the first unit at the then new Galleria mall in Glendale, California. It proved to be a very successful beginning for what would become Panda Management Company's (PMC) chief chain. Panda Express was one of the few quick-service restaurants to evolve from a full-service concept. The dishes featured at the various Panda Inn restaurants originated in three regions of China: Canton, Beijing, and Szechuan. Although less inclusive, the dishes at the Panda Expresses were the same as those served at the original Panda Inns and were prepared on the site of each unit. The company introduced a new food to that market, and it found a good market niche, a wide-open field, in fact. Panda Express joined authentic Mandarin cuisine to a sector historically dominated by hamburgers and fried chicken. Because few concessions were made to expediency, the food quality remained high and quickly won the new chain a loyal customer base. Panda Express attracted customers in the 18 to 34 age bracket, the upwardly mobile segment of the working population most likely to adapt to a nouveau, fast-food cuisine.

PMC opened 13 units over the next five years. These were usually located in shopping malls, but eventually Panda Express spread into a variety of locales, where potential customers were on the move. Starting in 1988, the company placed outlets in grocery stores when the Cherngs introduced a Panda Express to a Vons supermarket.

Its success led the company to expand its new chain outside of Southern California, spreading to Nevada, Arizona, Colorado, and Utah and eventually to the East Coast, where it would meet stiffer competition from a rival chain, Toronto-based Manchu Wok, which was well established east of the Mississippi River. By the end of 1992, the Panda Express chain numbered just over 50 units.

1993–2000: MARKET FACTORS ENCOURAGE CHAIN EXPANSION

Market indicators for Asian fast food were very strong, encouraging rapid expansion for Panda Express. Notably, the National Restaurant Association issued a report indicating that between 1987 and 1990 there was a 31.5 percent gain in the Asian segment of the fast-food business. Overall, Asian restaurant sales in the United States rose from $7.5 billion in 1990 to $8.3 billion by August 1995.

Panda Management responded to the market surge with very quick growth. By April 1994, it operated 125 units in 21 states, Washington, DC, and Japan. Sixty of these were financed by money generated internally. Panda Express ran neck and neck with Manchu Wok, which, with far more units, just kept even in sales. Manchu Wok soon fell far behind Panda Express in the number of new openings, although it still dominated the express Chinese food market in the eastern part of the United States.

One factor contributing to the rapid increase in the number of Panda Express units was the chain's versatility. Its five different footprints, ranging from 400 to 2,000 square feet, allowed it to find unit sites in a wide variety of places and to adjust size to sales, which in 1994 ranged from $350,000 to more than $1.5 million per unit.

In 1994, in part to help make its expansion and diversification plans go smoothly, Panda revamped its upper management team. In January of that year, it recruited and hired Joseph Micatrotto as president and chief operating officer. Although Andrew Cherng remained chairman and CEO, he gave Micatrotto considerable latitude in mapping out new directions for the company. Micatrotto, who grew up in a "little Italy neighborhood" of Cleveland, came to Panda from a 14-year career at Chi-Chi's, a Louisville, Kentucky-based chain of Mexican restaurants. The company also hired Russell Bendel as senior vice-president of operations. He joined Panda after resigning his post as COO at El Torito, another chain of Mexican restaurants based in Irvine, California. Although neither Micatrotto nor Bendel had knowledge of Oriental cuisine, they had the managerial, organizational, and leadership skills that PMC needed.

At the time Micatrotto took the reins as president, PMC had an enviable history of minority employment. About 45 percent of the workers were Hispanic and 40

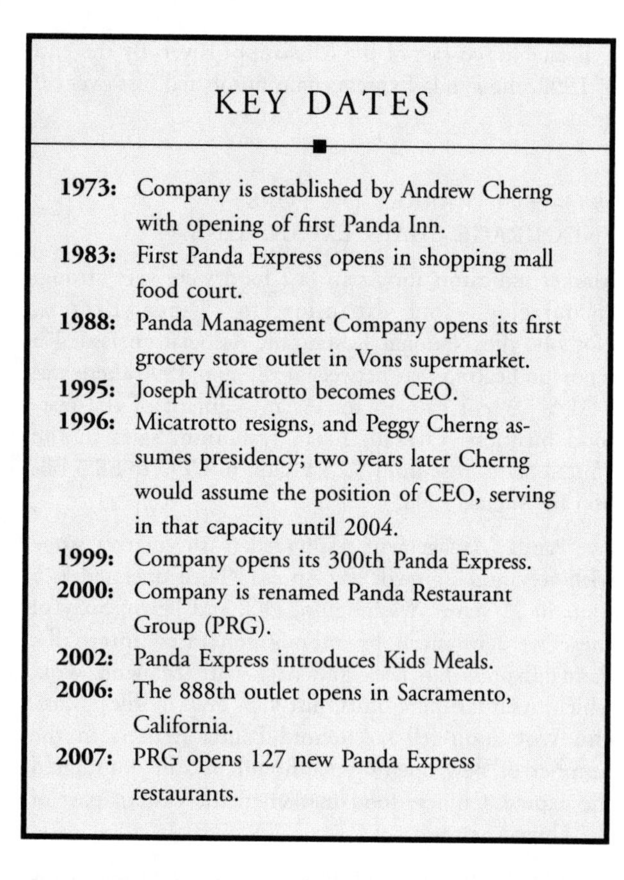

KEY DATES

1973: Company is established by Andrew Cherng with opening of first Panda Inn.
1983: First Panda Express opens in shopping mall food court.
1988: Panda Management Company opens its first grocery store outlet in Vons supermarket.
1995: Joseph Micatrotto becomes CEO.
1996: Micatrotto resigns, and Peggy Cherng assumes presidency; two years later Cherng would assume the position of CEO, serving in that capacity until 2004.
1999: Company opens its 300th Panda Express.
2000: Company is renamed Panda Restaurant Group (PRG).
2002: Panda Express introduces Kids Meals.
2006: The 888th outlet opens in Sacramento, California.
2007: PRG opens 127 new Panda Express restaurants.

percent Asian. As part of his program, Micatrotto scheduled "cultural diversity" lunches, sensitivity training experiences through which workers developed their awareness of their diverse cultures.

Although Micatrotto resigned the presidency of PMC in 1996, relinquishing it to Peggy Cherng, one of the things that he had recommended was an increase in the number of street-level, freestanding stores offering dine-in, drive-through, and carry-out services. By the end of 1998 these accounted for only about 80 Panda Express units, most of which were located in malls and other, less traditional places. By adding more standalone units, the company sought to offer stiffer competition to such fast-food giants as McDonald's and Taco Bell as well as traditional Chinese restaurants.

During the 1990s, PMC also took steps to increase the percentage of take-out orders. In 1995, its 173 Panda Express units were averaging only a 30 percent volume in take-out sales, considered rather low for limited-service Chinese food restaurants. In addition to a "Flavors of China" campaign, stressing Panda's authentic regional foods, it promoted a home meal replacement family dinner featuring two entrees, rice or chow mein, and appetizers for $12.99. Also, to improve its efficiency, the company modified its distribution channel. The company reduced the number of dealers it used from 70 to just a single, central company to distribute its raw products.

By the mid-1990s, PMC had begun committing more of its revenue to its marketing budget, which until then had been very small. It also started conducting market research through focus group sessions, using questionnaires to evaluate the quality of its foods. By 1999 the company produced its first block of television ads. These were initially limited to the Las Vegas area, where, in a relatively new market for the company, the company operated 19 Panda Express units. At that time, Peggy Cherng (who had been elected CEO in 1998 and would serve in that capacity until 2004) said that the campaign was a test of the medium's ability to bolster sales and "the commercials' ability to deliver the brand message."

Maintaining authenticity in Chinese cooking challenged PMC, especially since some concessions had to be made to American tastes and preference for quick service. Simply put, the fast-food format required a kind of juggling act between quality and speed. Among other things, reflecting health-conscious trends in the United States, Panda Express restaurants used no MSG in any of its foods. In order to preserve the authenticity of its dishes, the restaurants also kept recipe modifications to a minimum, using only minor adjustments to suit the American palate. Most importantly, even as the chain entered its period of explosive growth in the 1990s, its restaurants continued to prepare foods from scratch, maintaining what Micatrotto called "a quick service environment with a full-service kitchen."

In 1998, celebrating its 25th anniversary, PMC redesigned and reopened its flagship Pasadena Panda Inn, the first of its restaurants. The renovation was in a way symbolic, reflecting the company's desire to preserve tradition even as it ventured into new culinary and geographic areas. Although the restaurant was one of the first to serve foods from diverse Chinese provinces, its kitchen also produced several original dishes, including Tea Smoked Duck, Creamy Mustard Shrimp, Lotus Leaf, and Sizzling Crispy Garlic Chicken.

Throughout its history, PMC worked diligently to play a significant, good neighbor role in its host communities. Under the rubric "Panda Cares," it undertook many initiatives to improve the quality of life for children in those communities. In addition to contributions of money, the company urged its employees to volunteer their time and labor. An example of PMC's commitment occurred in February 1999 in Las Vegas, when it opened its 300th restaurant with a gala celebration. PMC donated 20 percent of its opening day profit to the Candlelighters for Childhood Cancer of Southern Nevada.

BUILDING MARKET BASE, ACCELERATING THE PACE OF GROWTH

Beginning in 2000, the newly renamed Panda Restaurant Group (PRG) sought to accelerate the pace of expansion. To finance this growth, Cherng considered various options, including a public offering of stock and franchise development. However, Cherng preferred direct ownership to maintain control over consistency and quality. To facilitate access to real estate locations, PRG invested in FoodBrand, a food court operator and a subsidiary of Mills Corporation, a shopping center developer. PRG planned to open Panda Express and Hibachi-San restaurants in newly developed food courts.

At this time, Panda Express sought to build on the company's family-oriented customer base with new promotions and marketing. In 2002, the company began offering kids meals at shopping mall outlets. Special fortune cookies focused on children with sayings such as, "Your mom is probably right," and "Sweet dreams come to those who sleep." Rather than include a plastic toy, a Panda Express kids meal was accompanied by crayons and a newsletter filled with educational games and activities centered on endangered animals, the natural world, and Asian culture. Television advertisements designed to attract families followed the new product introduction. The "Be Fulfilled" campaign emphasized joy and happiness. In one television commercial, a mother was happy to bring home the family meal at the end of the workday. The tagline read, "Joy. Now available in convenient little takeout containers."

PRG's expansion strategy involved development of restaurants in freestanding locations or endcap locations, at the outer edge of strip shopping malls. Such locations made it possible to incorporate drive-through sales windows for take-out orders. With more space, ranging from 2,000 to 2,500 square feet, the stores offered seating for 40 to 60 diners. Areas for expansion included Texas, Illinois, Missouri, Ohio, Minnesota, North Carolina, Georgia, Florida, Maryland, Hawaii, and the District of Columbia. Density in certain markets increased significantly. For example, with 35 stores in the Chicago area, PRG planned to open another 20 stores over the next two years. PRG also continued to pursue specialized locations, such as Dodger Stadium in Los Angeles and Edwards Air Force Base in Lancaster, California, where Panda Express outlets opened in 2005.

New restaurant openings accelerated as PRG expanded the Panda Express restaurant base by about 100 stores annually. From operating 400 locations in 34 states in 2001, and generating $300 million in revenue, the number increased to 700 locations by March 2005. The company marked the opening of the 888th store in Sacramento, California, in October 2006 (the number 8 is considered a lucky number in China). In 2007, the company opened 172 Panda Express restaurants. By mid-2008, the company operated more than 1,000 outlets and revenues more than tripled, to over $1 billion.

Part of the success of the Panda Express concept stemmed from the difficulty competitors experienced in operating an Asian fast-food outlet. That the chain succeeded where others failed was partly due to PRG's focus on employee happiness. The company paid a dollar more per hour than other fast-food restaurants, and it provided healthcare benefits to employees working 30 or more hours. Also, Andrew Cherng concerned himself with the personal well-being of employees, encouraging participation in meditation, hobbies, charity work, and other life-enhancing activities. The company promoted from within its employee base and provided management training. Cherng encouraged employees at all levels to read self-improvement books. In addition to PRG experiencing a very low rate of employee turnover, the other likely benefit was that the company would remain solidly committed to its promise of delivering exceptional dining within its chosen niche.

John W. Fiero
Updated, Mary Tradii

PRINCIPAL OPERATING UNITS

Hibachi-San Grill; Panda Express; Panda Inn.

PRINCIPAL COMPETITORS

Benihana Inc.; McDonald's Corporation; Manchu Wok; P.F. Chang's China Bistro, Inc.; Subway; Taco Bell Corporation; Wendy's International, Inc.

FURTHER READING

Bernstein, Charles, "Manchu Leads the Working Race," *Restaurants & Institutions,* August 1, 1994, p. 30.

Cebrzynski, Gregg, "Panda Express Breaks TV Ad Campaign As Test to Raise Brand Awareness," *Nation's Restaurant News,* August 9, 1999, p. 11.

"Chinese Restaurant Chain Looks for Further Expansion," *Food Institute Report,* October 22, 2001, p. 5.

Farkas, David, "Fast and Friendly," *Chain Leader,* March 2000, p. 72.

"Fast Food Chain Opens 500th Store Here," *San Diego Business Journal,* October 21, 2002, p. 14.

Glover, Kara, "Success on Oriental (Food) Express," *Los Angeles Business Journal,* September 25, 1995, p. 21.

Hessel, Evan, "Kung Pao Chicken for the Soul," *Forbes Global,* April 21, 2008, p. 106.

Jennings, Lisa, "Having Words with Peggy Tsiang Cherng: Chief Executive and Co-Chair, Panda Restaurant Group," *Nation's Restaurant News,* August 1, 2005.

Krantz, Matt, "Panda Express Spreads Chinese Food Across USA," *USA Today,* September 11, 2006, p. 4B.

Marchetti, Michele, and Lucas Alisson, "Creating *Panda*-monium," *Sales & Marketing Management,* January 1996, p. 14.

Martin, Richard, "Panda Express: Bullish About the Bear," *Nation's Restaurant News,* May 16, 1994, p. 86.

———, "Top Chi-Chi's, El Torito Execs Tackle Panda Push," *Nation's Restaurant News,* August 7, 1995, p. 18.

Mullman, Jeremy, "Panda Express Plans to Add 23 Area Eateries: Asian Fast-Food Chain Looks to Double Outlets over Next Three Years," *Crain's Chicago Business,* October 3, 2005, p. 24.

Norris, Maya, "Leading Role: Panda Express Offers Leadership Training to Help Keep Its Managers Around," *Chain Leader,* June 2005, p. 40.

"Panda Express Emphasizes Joy and Harmony in New TV Spots," *Nation's Restaurant News,* May 6, 2002, p. 18.

"Panda Group Buys 40% of Mills' FoodBrand Arm," *Nation's Restaurant News,* November 5, 2001, p. 45.

"Rosemead, Calif.—Rapidly Expanding Panda Express, Based Here, Is Scheduled to Open Its First Military Base Location Today at Edwards Air Force Base in Lancaster, Calif.," *Nation's Restaurant News,* July 5, 2006.

Ruggless, Ron, "Panda Express Takes to Street with Push for Freestanding Units," *Nation's Restaurant News,* August 9, 2004, p. 4.

Spector, Amy, "Panda Express Gears Up for Fast Lane, Tests Drive-Thru in 2nd Unit," *Nation's Restaurant News,* November 15, 1999, p. 4.

Walkup, Carolyn, "Panda Express Promo Targets Takeout Business," *Nation's Restaurant News,* February 28, 1994, p. 7.

Redlon & Johnson, Inc.

172–174 St. John Street
Portland, Maine 04102
U.S.A.
Telephone: (207) 773-4755
Toll Free: (800) 905-5250
Fax: (207) 871-8675
Web site: http://www.redlon-johnson.com

Private Company
Incorporated: 1887 as Foote Bros.
Employees: 260
Sales: $104.4 million (2005)
NAICS: 421700 Hardware, and Plumbing and Heating Equipment and Supplies Wholesalers

■ ■ ■

Redlon & Johnson, Inc., is a Portland, Maine-based regional wholesale distributor of plumbing, heating, air conditioning, water systems (pumps, tanks, water treatment, drilling supplies, and well accessories), PVF (pipes, valves, and fittings), and industrial products. The company serves professional contractors, eschewing retail sales to avoid competing against its customers. Redlon & Johnson maintains operations throughout Maine and New Hampshire as well as Pennsylvania, and Maryland, including five showrooms, located in Lewiston and Portland, Maine; and Laconia, Manchester, and Portsmith, New Hampshire. They are not open to the general public, requiring a referral from a local contractor and an appointment. The showrooms essentially drive sales for contractors, showing off major brand products while acting as a design center to help homeowners and building owners design their own kitchens and bathrooms. A retail quote on selected products is then drawn up and submitted to the contractor, again making sure the company is not competing for retail business. Redlon & Johnson sales offices and distribution centers are also located in Augusta, Bangor, Bath, Presque Isle, and Rockland, Maine; Manchester, New Hampshire; Altoona and Grove City, Pennsylvania; and Cumberland, Maryland. Branches make deliveries within a 30- to 80-mile radius, depending on the location. Redlon & Johnson is a privately held company, formerly known as The Gage Co.

19TH-CENTURY ROOTS

Redlon & Johnson was created in 1984 through the merger of Redlon's Supply and Johnson Supply, the former some 40 years older than the latter. Redlon's Supply traces its history to Bath, Maine, when in 1887 William M. Sparks joined a company called Foote Bros. This plumbing company was also involved in lead working and steam fitting. Sparks then bought out one of the Foote brothers, and the company was renamed Foote and Sparks. The Redlon family, which hailed from China, Maine, became involved with the company in 1893. Their members included Osgood Morrill Redlon, J. A. Redlon, and A. H. Redlon. Osgood then married Sparks's daughter. Osgood Redlon emerged as a mechanical genius who would receive numerous patents over the years for the devices he invented, including boiler stands, pipe hangers, closet bends, adjustable roof collars (a weatherproof flange that created a seal around the plumbing vent stack where it emerged through the

COMPANY PERSPECTIVES

Redlon & Johnson's Mission is to provide VALUE to Our Customers. Value in the form of Quality Products; extensive and dependable product and application Knowledge; and Dependable Delivery. We also provide value added services such as, Quick Pick-Up Counters, Showroom Centers, Engineering and Fabrication Services, as well as Marketing Information and Promotion. We also make the commitment to Inventory, both in breadth and availability, in every market we serve.

roof), and adjustable legs for sinks, trays, and other articles. His most recognizable invention was the Redlon Roof-Collar.

OSGOOD REDLON BECOMES SOLE OWNER: 1914

In 1906 when Sparks retired, Osgood Redlon and J. A. Redlon became co-owners of the business, known as Redlon's Supply. Osgood Redlon then became the sole owner in 1914. In addition to being a manufacturer of plumbing products, including his own inventions, Redlon served as a wholesale distributor of plumbing supplies. By 1936 distribution was the focus of the company, rather than manufacturing. Operations spread throughout Maine, and eventually Redlon's Supply served the entire state. Osgood Redlon headed the company until his death in 1955. His son Abbott Redlon now took charge, and then in 1961 grandson Richard O. Redlon assumed control. Under the direction of the third generation, Redlon's Supply enjoyed strong growth in the 1960s and 1970s, adding branches in Augusta, Portland, and Rockland, and emerging as Maine's largest plumbing and heating distributor.

In Portland, Redlon's Supply met with stiff competition from another well-established heating and plumbing wholesaler: Johnson Supply. It had been founded in 1939 in Portland by George Finberg. In 1969, a Boston-area building supplies company, Westco Corp., acquired Johnson Supply. A decade later Westco was in turn acquired for $14.3 million by Amstelland Corcernbeheer BV, a Netherlands-based construction firm and building materials company. With the financial backing of its Dutch parent, Westco was able to acquire Portsmouth, New Hampshire-based Moulton Supply, followed by the purchase of Redlon's Supply in 1984. Redlon's Supply, Johnson Supply, and Moulton Supply were then merged to form Redlon & Johnson Supply. The combined company established its headquarters in Johnson Supply's seven-story warehouse in Portland.

Richard Redlon stayed on with Westco after the Redlon & Johnson merger, serving as vice-president of the plumbing and heating division before going into semiretirement and continuing to provide advice to the Portland office. Moreover, his wife would run the Portland showroom and his son, Stephen, became the manager of the Portsmouth, New Hampshire, branch. Another Redlon's Supply employee, Lee C. Moulton, would also become president of Redlon & Johnson. A 1974 graduate of Bowdoin College, and a Vermont native, Moulton spent two years with another Portland distributor before joining Redlon's Supply.

Although Amstelland Corcernbeheer provided funds for Redlon & Johnson to expand, it gave Moulton a free hand in running the business. In 1986 the company acquired other New England plumbing, heating, and industrial operations that were brought into the fold, so that by the end of the decade Redlon & Johnson, in addition to its home office in Portland, maintained wholesale branches in Augusta, Bangor, Bath, and Rockland, Maine; Manchester, New Hampshire; and Lawrence, Massachusetts. In addition, it operated a pair of industrial supply companies under the Westco International name, located in Portland and Bangor.

FIRST SHOWROOM OPENED: 1987

Having outgrown its main Portland operation, Redlon & Johnson opened a new 52,000-square-foot warehouse in 1987. Because of the breadth of styles and models of plumbing and heating equipment on the market, the company continued to lease two floors of the old building as well. The new Portland facility also included a 5,000-square-foot bath and kitchen showroom on the second floor, Redlon & Johnson's first and the largest in the state. It was not open to the public, and required a referral from a contractor.

The addition of the showroom made sense on a number of levels. First, it provided the company's customers, primarily small contractors, with a service that proved mutually beneficial to both parties. Moulton told *Business Digest of Southern Maine* in a 1990 company profile that the small contractors "either have to sell fixtures out of a catalog or have their clients visit a competitor's showroom, if they don't have one of their own. Our showroom helps contractors upgrade their sales by letting customers see and experience a full range of products, and helps educate their customers so they leave here understanding what they are buying and feeling good about it." Moreover, people wanted to see

KEY DATES

1887: Foote Bros. is founded in Bath, Maine.
1893: Osgood N. Redlon joins company.
1914: Redlon assumes sole ownership of what becomes Redlon's Supply.
1939: Johnson Supply is established in Portland, Maine.
1955: Osgood Redlon dies.
1984: Westco Corp. acquires Redlon's Supply, merges it with Johnson Supply to form Redlon & Johnson.
1987: First showroom opens.
1990: Gage Co. of Pittsburgh, Pennsylvania, acquires Redlon & Johnson.
1998: Gage moves headquarters to Portland.
2007: New showroom opens in Manchester, New Hampshire.

what they were buying and in the 1980s the amount of money they were spending on bathroom and kitchen projects was growing ever higher.

Homeowners were especially willing to foot the bill for bathroom renovations because, as Moulton explained, "People have found that the bath is the only area of the home where they can fully realize their investment at the time of sale." As a result, homeowners were opting for increasingly expensive and elaborate equipment, such as saunas, whirlpools, tanning salons, and luxurious baths and showers. Not only did the showroom feature multiple bathroom ensembles, kitchen products, and other product groups, it included a comfortable conference room where orders could be finalized, and a play area for children, including a television and VCR to keep them occupied while their parents conferred with Redlon & Johnson's design consultants. Retail quotes were drawn up later and supplied to the local contractor that had arranged the visit to the showroom.

With the new showroom in operation, Redlon & Johnson increased sales to some $35 million in 1987. At the end of the decade that number grew to about $50 million. Of that amount about 38 percent came from plumbing supplies and fixtures, an equal amount from in-home heating supplies, 9 percent from residential well equipment, and approximately 15 percent from industrial supply products. The company employed 210 people at the end of the 1980s, most of them natives of the communities where the branches were located. "We staff them with local people who know the contractors and maintain the element of friendliness that goes with a family business. ... We are also willing to sacrifice short-term gains in favor of long-term relationships," Moulton explained.

THE GAGE CO. ACQUIRES REDLON & JOHNSON: 1990

With the arrival of the European Economic Community slated for 1992, Amstelland Corcernbeheer focused more attention on its domestic affairs at the start of the 1990s and merged with another Dutch firm to become NBM/Amstelland. It was not surprising, therefore, that in June 1990 the Redlon & Johnson operations, including Westco Industrial Supply Distribution, was sold to Pittsburgh, Pennsylvania-based The Gage Co. The old-guard company, established in 1892, was originally involved in the production of brass gauges (or "gages," hence the name of the business) for railroad locomotives, steam engines, and other applications. Over the years it ventured into manufacturing, assembling "Duquesne" automobiles in the early 1900s and later producing Gainaday washers. Eventually the focus shifted to the distribution of plumbing, piping, and industrial products.

Gage used Redlon & Johnson as a base for a New England division. At the same time it acquired Redlon & Johnson, it also supplemented the operation with the purchase of several other New England suppliers that would form the foundation of the present-day operation. They included Pennsylvania branches from Gage, as well as Hartford, Connecticut-based Park West Plumbing Supply and Worcester, Massachusetts-based Grace Plumbing Supply Company. In early 1993 Redlon & Johnson expanded beyond New England and Pennsylvania into the mid-Atlantic region with the acquisition of Hagerstown, Maryland-based Western Maryland Supply Corp., a well-established company that had been in business since 1923.

It was also in 1993 that Redlon & Johnson's current chief executive, Thomas E. Mullen, a 15-year Gage employee, began his tenure with the company when Gage appointed him corporate vice-president and general manager of the New England division. Not only did Mullen deepen his ties to Redlon & Johnson during the 1990s, so too did Gage. In January 1997 Mullen was named president of Redlon & Johnson, and in the autumn of that year he opened a corporate purchasing headquarters in Portland for Gage.

GAGE BRANCHES TAKE REDLON & JOHNSON NAME: 2000

In 1997 Gage, with operations in the mid-Atlantic region, Michigan, Indiana, and Ohio, as well as New England, operated 38 branches and generated $213 million, a 7 percent increase over the year before. The following year was a time of considerable change for the company. Seven branches were sold or closed, reducing employment from 600 to 550, and revenues fell to $175 million. During the year Gage also moved its headquarters from Pittsburgh to Portland. Further downsizing took place in 1999, when 19 branches were sold or closed; 11 of them (nine in Michigan and two in Indiana) were sold to Ferguson Enterprises Midwest. Gage's revenues fell to $140 million and the number of employees was cut to 360. It was also in 1999 that Mullen was elected president and chief operating officer of Gage, but it was a distinction with little difference. In 2000 all of the remaining branches assumed the Redlon & Johnson name and in effect the Gage Company was doing business as Redlon & Johnson.

Despite a downturn in the economy the construction market in the Northeast remained strong, allowing Redlon & Johnson to enjoy something of a rebound in 2000, when sales increased to $150 million. In 2001, however, the full effect of a poor economy began to be felt. Redlon & Johnson closed six of its branches and employment was slashed to 245. Revenues were cut by a third to $95 million. To stimulate business the company adopted a new logo with the tagline "Partnering with Professionals," and also launched a new web site. The company then upgraded its computer system at the start of 2002.

Revenues again topped the $100 million mark in 2003, and grew to $108.4 million in 2004. With business picking up, another branch was added in 2005 when sales totaled $104.4 million, according to information the company provided trade publication *Industrial Distribution*. Because Redlon & Johnson elected not to provide financial data beyond 2005, it was difficult to determine how the company fared beyond that point. What was certain was that in late 2007 Redlon & Johnson opened a new showroom in Manchester, New Hampshire. Because of the popularity of home makeover shows, especially those on cable television's HGTV, homeowners were becoming increasingly aware of the resale value of home improvements and gaining an education on the types of projects to pursue and products to acquire. Because of that trend, it was likely that Redlon & Johnson and its contractor customers would place a growing emphasis on the showrooms to stimulate business for both parties.

Ed Dinger

PRINCIPAL COMPETITORS

Ferguson Enterprises, Inc.; F.W. Webb Company; HD Supply, Inc.

FURTHER READING

Charest, Bob, "Cutting-Edge Showroom Has Bold Bathroom Designs," *New Hampshire Union Leader,* April 30, 2008, p. C3.

"Gage Buys Company," *Bangor Daily News,* February 23, 1993.

Hyde, Christopher, "Redlon & Johnson Supply Is a Permanent Fixture," *Business Digest of Southern Maine,* March 1, 1990, p. 24.

Paiste, Denis, "Two Firms to Relocate to Manchester Airpark," *New Hampshire Union Leader,* June 14, 2006, p. B4.

Regal-Beloit Corporation

200 State Street
Beloit, Wisconsin 53511-6254
U.S.A.
Telephone: (608) 364-8800
Fax: (608) 364-8818
Web site: http://www.regalbeloit.com

Public Company
Incorporated: 1955 as Beloit Tool Corporation
Employees: 17,900
Sales: $1.8 billion (2007)
Stock Exchanges: New York
Ticker Symbol: RBC
NAICS: 335312 Motor and Generator Manufacturing; 333612 Speed Changer, Industrial High-Speed Drive, and Gear Manufacturing; 333613 Mechanical Power Transmission Equipment Manufacturing; 333995 Fluid Power Cylinder and Actuator Manufacturing; 335314 Relay and Industrial Control Manufacturing; 336350 Motor Vehicle Transmission and Power Train Parts Manufacturing

■ ■ ■

Regal-Beloit Corporation is one of the world's largest manufacturers of electric motors, motion-control products, and power generation equipment. Among the company's main product lines are motors for heating, ventilating, and air conditioning (HVAC) applications, a full range of AC and DC industrial motors, electric generators and controllers, gears and gearboxes, marine transmissions, and high-performance automotive transmissions. The facilities of Regal-Beloit include around three dozen main manufacturing plants located in the United States, Canada, Mexico, Germany, Italy, the United Kingdom, India, Thailand, and China. Founded in 1955 as a producer of high-speed cutting tools (an area since divested), Regal-Beloit later ventured into power transmission equipment and then, via a string of acquisitions starting in 1997, into its largest segment in the early 21st century, electric motors.

ORIGINS IN CUTTING TOOLS IN MID-FIFTIES

Regal-Beloit Corporation was founded in 1955 by entrepreneur Kenyon Y. Taylor as the Beloit Tool Corporation in the southeastern Wisconsin community of Beloit. Working from his home with three friends, three desks, and three telephones, Taylor manufactured specially designed metric and decimal-dimensioned cutting tools from a "plant" in his garage. Emphasizing superior customer service from the start, Taylor offered 24-hour delivery of his special taps to his mostly local customers. Within six months of the company's inception, orders were multiplying, and Taylor hired more workers to expand his production capacity. Quickly running short of space, he moved Beloit Tool to an old abandoned roller-skating rink east of downtown Beloit. By the end of its first full year in business, Beloit Tool had posted losses of $40,000, the first and only time it registered an unprofitable year. From its earliest days, Beloit Tool marketed its products under the Regal brand (named, some said, after a type of flower).

In 1957 Taylor acquired Crest Tool Industries, a cutting tool company that specialized in providing tools

COMPANY PERSPECTIVES

Our Vision: We will clearly distinguish our products and services as the best value to our customers, as measured by our customers. We will maintain a sustainable, competitive advantage through the excellence of our people and our processes—creating value for all our stakeholders.

Our Mission: We will live our values, demonstrating integrity in all our actions. We will function with a high level of personal energy, energizing those around us. We will have the courage to make difficult decisions and execute to accomplish our vision.

to U.S. government purchasing agencies, and two years later Beloit Tool had passed the $100 million sales level. The same year, it demonstrated its early commitment to employee-sensitive management by establishing a profit-sharing plan, a byproduct of Taylor's reaction to the treatment of workers as "commodities and clock numbers" that he had experienced firsthand during the Great Depression.

With sales soaring, in 1961 Taylor moved his corporate headquarters to a new location in an old farmhouse in nearby South Beloit, Illinois, and in 1967 acquired the historic Durst Foundry and Machine Works of nearby Shopiere, Wisconsin. That company's founder, Walter Durst, had established Durst in 1932 and built a significant niche manufacturing equipment for the farming industry, mostly in the form of pump drives, large specially designed transmissions, forklift axles, and a variety of standard and custom gearboxes. Taylor kept Durst on as a consultant and renamed the new operation Durst Power Transmission Division.

GOING PUBLIC, CHANGING NAME TO REGAL-BELOIT

In 1969 Beloit Tool completed its first public offering of stock, selling 120,000 shares over-the-counter at $12.48 per share. In 1972 Taylor officially changed Beloit Tool's name to Regal-Beloit Corporation, an alteration that was primarily intended to dispel the erroneous notion that the company specialized in machine tools. The firm's stock began trading on the NASDAQ in 1973; three years later, the company moved to the American Stock Exchange.

Throughout the 1970s, Taylor continued his strategy of expanding his firm's market share and product lines by acquiring promising companies mainly in the cutting tools area. In this segment, Regal-Beloit had absorbed such small players as Empire Gage Company (Detroit, Michigan), Walter T. Cole Tool Company (Scottsdale, Arizona), Quality Tool Works (Waukegan, Illinois), QT Tool Company (Bedford, Indiana), and Standworth Tool (Lebanon, Indiana) before adding several more in the 1970s, including M.E.C. Corporation, Caladak Gage Company, the Connecticut-based Douglas Tool, Inc., and Los Angeles-based Premium Cutting Tools, Inc. In the early 1970s Regal-Beloit also made a short-lived foray into the consumer hardware market via the purchases of Standard Fasteners, Inc., Standard Packaging Service, and American Fastener Corporation, which were placed into a new Fastener Division. After the sales for these businesses proved disappointing, this division was divested in deals completed in 1975 and 1978.

The U.S. power transmission market, meantime, had traditionally been fragmented among dozens of smaller manufacturers, and the pickings for an acquisition-minded, cash-heavy firm such as Regal-Beloit seemed ripe. In mid-1978 Regal-Beloit purchased Orbmark Company, the developer of a high-torque, low-speed hydraulic motor. A year later Taylor brought James L. Packard, a seasoned corporate manager from PepsiCo, Inc.'s Frito-Lay division, onboard Regal-Beloit's management team. Initially heading Durst, Packard was quickly promoted to company president and chief operating officer during 1980. In expectation of the huge sales potential of foreign markets, Taylor in 1979 also unveiled Regal-Beloit International Sales Corporation, which he headquartered in the firm's Beloit offices.

PUSH INTO POWER TRANSMISSION PRODUCTS

Regal-Beloit was hit hard by the deep recession of the early 1980s, and its cutting tools business faced a less prosperous future because of its place within a mature industry whose products were improving in quality and thus lasting longer, resulting ultimately in a reduction in sales. In a crucial shift in the company's history, Packard pushed for a concerted acquisition-driven expansion of Regal-Beloit's more promising power transmission business, building on the Durst and Orbmark foundation, in order to reduce the firm's reliance on cutting tools. This drive commenced in 1981 with the acquisition of Grove Gear Corporation of Union Grove, Wisconsin, a manufacturer of standard and special worm gear speed-reducing gearboxes, adaptors, and accessories, founded

KEY DATES

1955: In Beloit, Wisconsin, Kenyon Y. Taylor founds Beloit Tool Corporation, specializing in high-speed cutting tools.
1967: Beloit first enters the power transmission product business via purchase of Durst Foundry and Machine Works.
1969: First public offering of stock is completed.
1972: Company's name is changed to Regal-Beloit Corporation.
1981: Grove Gear Corporation is acquired.
1991: Regal-Beloit ventures overseas for the first time, acquiring the U.K. firm Opperman Mastergear, Ltd.
1997: Company makes entrance into electric motor manufacturing via purchase of Marathon Electric Manufacturing Corporation.
2000: Leeson Electric Corporation is acquired.
2004: Regal-Beloit doubles in size by acquiring two General Electric Company units.
2006: Company sells the remainder of its founding business, cutting tools.
2007: Fasco Motors and Jakel Incorporated, producers of motors and blower systems for air-moving applications, are acquired.

in 1947. It continued the following year when Regal-Beloit purchased Rockwell International's Off-Highway Division, which specialized in heavy-duty gearing for agricultural and construction equipment, hydraulic pump drives, and power transmissions.

Also in the early 1980s, Regal-Beloit began a program of plowing $7 million to $8 million annually into new equipment to ensure that its manufacturing processes were as efficient and modern as possible. At the same time, it was also earning a reputation as the only firm in the industry that purchased *used* equipment from machinery dealers and auctioneers, at a 30 percent savings, to keep operating costs down. Buying only bug-free products from reliable dealers, Regal-Beloit by 1996 was saving $3 million annually on equipment purchases. It also began adopting the low-inventory technique later known as "just-in-time delivery" several years before it became de rigueur among American corporations.

In 1984 Taylor stepped down as CEO while remaining chairman of the board and turned Regal-Beloit's reins over to Packard, who continued the company's grand acquisition strategy as sales broke the $57 million mark, a company record. Throughout the 1980s, 12 firms were purchased and absorbed, substantially expanding the firm's market share, manufacturing capability, and profitability. As Packard later commented, "by quickly instituting effective cost controls, more efficient manufacturing methods and our strong customer service philosophy, these new divisions became strong contributors to the company's overall performance." Moreover, by holding out for a reasonable selling price, paying only cash (rather than stock), and considering only firms that could generate earnings in the first year following acquisition, Regal-Beloit recouped its acquisitions costs quickly and kept its debt low. Finally, by preserving the identity of the acquired company's product line and assiduously applying "lean" manufacturing techniques (such as "just-in-time"), its new acquisitions could grow rapidly once in the corporate fold.

Although the purchases of power transmission businesses were ultimately more strategic, Regal-Beloit's acquisitions of this period also included a number of firms within the founding area of cutting tools. In 1984, for example, the company bought Glenbard Manufacturers, Inc., a venerable manufacturer of reaming tools based in Chicago. Packard returned to the acquisition waters again one year later with the purchase of National Twist Drill of Columbia, South Carolina, a producer of large-volume drills, taps, end mills, gages, and reamers. Meanwhile, on the power transmission side, Regal-Beloit in 1985 also added Noster Industries, Inc., of Garden City, Michigan, a producer of specially designed heavy-duty automotive transmissions for military vehicles.

By 1985, its 30th anniversary year, Regal-Beloit was employing 1,250 people working out of 18 manufacturing and customer service facilities nationwide. Packard led its large facilities through a major improvement program, incorporated new products and related manufacturing equipment into the company's plants, and began a systematic workforce flexibility program in which nearly a third of Regal-Beloit's employees were training for new positions at any given time. After three decades at Regal-Beloit's helm, Taylor finally relinquished the chairmanship to Packard in 1986. As sales reached $78 million, Packard installed the first U.S. computer-controlled manufacturing process for grinding threaded tools in 1986, and the Power Transmission Group won several major contracts, including a $5.5 million agreement with the federal government to design and test transmissions for refueling vehicles.

Beginning in the early 1980s, the power transmission equipment industry had become mature—growth was slow, sales were declining, and the profusion of industry firms led to excess manufacturing capacity. The industry, which had long been dominated by old line and "captive" manufacturers (companies manufacturing equipment exclusively for their parent firm), began to undergo a radical transformation in which foreign and domestic competition intensified and new specialized product niches began to emerge. In this new competitive environment, some smaller companies failed because they were unable to afford new equipment, and some larger firms began to outsource their work to cut costs. Regal-Beloit exploited both opportunities: The failing smaller firms made attractive acquisition targets, and Regal-Beloit's experience with diverse product lines enabled it to claim the outsourced work of the larger firms. Packard led it into a wider and wider series of product markets in which, although it often was not the largest firm, its flexibility, customer service performance, and streamlined manufacturing processes could find a very profitable niche. The power transmission equipment industry was inexorably contracting, but Regal-Beloit seemed to face only opportunity.

As the company adjusted to its 1985 acquisition of National Twist and Noster's product lines, in 1986 it began a string of five plant expansions in five years and a year later acquired four more firms: Paterson Gearmotor, Inc., a manufacturer of fractional-horsepower gear motors; Illinois Gear of Chicago, a manufacturer of a variety of gears for heavy industrial use; Ohio Gear of South Carolina, a manufacturer of standard and special worm gear and concentric shaft speed reducers; and Richmond Gear of South Carolina, a producer of high-performance ring and pinion gear sets and transmissions. The additions broadened Regal-Beloit's product line, pumped up its financials, and enabled it to minimize its dependence on any single one of its markets.

Surveying his firm's new profile, Packard commented to the *Beloit Daily News,* "all things considered, we think we're going to be an exciting company." As if to drive home the point, he had added three more companies by decade's end: New York Twist Drill (1988), Foote-Jones Gear (1989), and Electra-Gear (1989). Founded in 1949, New York Twist Drill (Ronkonkoma, New York) manufactured drills, taps, end mills, reamers, and gages for high-volume applications and filled out Regal-Beloit's Cutting Tool Group. Electra-Gear, of Anaheim, California, and Foote-Jones Gear, of Chicago, Illinois, expanded the Power Transmission Group product lines. By 1991, Regal-Beloit's growth-through-acquisition strategy had amounted to 20 individual acquisitions, and in August 1989 it was named to *Financial World* magazine's "Growth 500," finishing 261st on the strength of its 23 percent five-year annual earnings-per-share growth rate. By the end of the 1980s, Regal-Beloit was able to report record profits of $11.5 million on record sales of $167.4 million; the Power Transmission Group, which had begun the decade generating only 35 percent of overall sales, was responsible for 65 percent of revenues.

NEW HEADQUARTERS AND FURTHER ACQUISITIONS

In May 1990 Regal-Beloit broke ground on a new $2.4 million world headquarters building in downtown Beloit, signaling its aim to return to its original Wisconsin roots after nearly three decades on the other side of the Illinois border. When it opened in March 1991, the 24,000-square-foot building housed Regal-Beloit's corporate offices, data processing center, and advertising, accounting, and personnel departments in a light-flooded design intended to avoid a "factory" feel. The much-ballyhooed move, however, was clouded by uncertainty. Regal-Beloit's capital expenditures for 1990 were expected to hit $8 million to $10 million, a ten-year high, and amid rumors of a potential takeover bid, management could only confirm that 30 percent of company stock was in "friendly" hands. Moreover, a contract to build replacement transmissions for the U.S. Army had been poorly bid, and Regal-Beloit was forced to swallow the loss. Finally, because of its broad product diversification, the recession of the early 1990s dragged at Regal-Beloit's profits, which dropped to $5.5 million in 1991, while revenues were off as well, totaling just $152.2 million that same year.

Nevertheless, the company's fundamental financial conditions remained positive. It had achieved an average annual return on investment of 17.2 percent (despite little use of debt) between 1955 and the move to the new building, had raised cash dividends 26 times in those 31 years, and had declared 123 consecutive quarterly payments without a dividend reduction. Although Packard was forced to admit that because of the recession Regal-Beloit's sales volumes were "significantly reduced," it had done better than many of its smaller competitors, which presented themselves as attractive acquisition targets. Moreover, with healthy operations in Illinois, New Jersey, Texas, California, South Carolina, North Carolina, and New York, its long pursued acquisition strategy seemed as viable as ever. "We are still looking at companies to purchase," Packard told an interviewer in 1991. "Our ability to grow will come through acquisitions. Right now we have a strong cash position, virtually no debt, and we are pretty well poised to be aggressively seeking out acquisitions at this point."

Consequently, in July 1991 Packard completed Regal-Beloit's first overseas acquisition with the purchase of Opperman Mastergear, Ltd., of Newbury, England. The acquisition added 220 employees (most in England, the rest at Opperman's German operation) to the company's ranks. Two more acquisitions—hydraulic pump drive manufacturers Hub City, Inc., of Aberdeen, South Dakota, in April 1992 and Terrell Gear Drives, Inc., of Charlotte, North Carolina, in November—boosted Regal-Beloit's sales to $199.8 million by year-end. In 1993 price increases in the used metal-cutting machine tools industry were offset by increased sales figures for the Power Transmission Group, all of whose units posted improved numbers. With exports accounting for roughly 3 percent of company sales and rising, Packard began casting about for another likely acquisition target in Europe, where the power transmission market was scattered among several small firms. By the end of 1993 Regal-Beloit's total sales had edged up to nearly $220 million.

Packard strengthened Regal-Beloit's profit margins throughout the 1990s by continuing to install computer-aided manufacturing systems, dropping non-performing products and unveiling new ones, and restructuring facilities. He also began implementing "cell" manufacturing techniques in which a wider variety of products could be manufactured by abandoning the traditional practice of committing entire plants to the production of a single product in favor of divvying up each facility into flexible manufacturing cells to produce multiple products as needed. As Regal-Beloit's sales jumped to $242.6 million in 1994, Packard found another market-share-broadening target in the marine and industrial transmission operations of Borg-Warner Automotive, Inc., which unit Regal-Beloit acquired in January 1995. Christened the Velvet Drive Transmission Division, the operation contributed mightily to Regal-Beloit's 21.9 percent increase in sales for 1995, which was further boosted by the progress of Regal-Beloit's new Italian operation, Costruzioni Meccaniche Legnanesi S.r.L., acquired in late 1994.

Aborted merger talks with Brad Foote Gear Works of Illinois, material and labor shortages, power outages and extreme heat, and slowing sales of Regal-Beloit's agricultural power transmission products all seemed to doom management's optimistic sales forecasts for 1995. Nevertheless, by the close of the year strong demand from virtually all industrial customers and the increasing progress of Regal-Beloit's foreign subsidiaries (which were closing in on 10 percent of all power transmission sales) had produced new records for sales, net income, and earnings per share.

If anthropologist Margaret Mead was correct in describing the city of Beloit as a "microcosm" of American society, Regal-Beloit had served as a kind of microcosmic barometer of the U.S. industrial economy throughout its history. Its markets were so diverse and its products so essential and varied that its quarter-by-quarter performance could reliably be used as an index of the condition of U.S. industry. By the 1990s, it had become a Wall Street darling (since 1992 its stock had been significantly outstripping the Dow Jones factory equipment index), and in 1996 *Forbes* magazine named it among the "200 Best Small Companies in America." Moreover, more than one industry analyst shared the opinion that Regal-Beloit was an "extremely well-run company ... a low-cost, efficient manufacturer" managed by "capable" executives with an eye toward the "long haul."

ENTRANCE INTO ELECTRIC MOTORS IN 1997

As successful as Regal-Beloit had been throughout its history, it was at a key juncture in the late 1990s because its two core businesses, cutting tools and power transmission products, both had limited prospects for future growth. In 1997, the company shifted gears again making a dramatic plunge into a new, though highly complementary and faster-growing, sector: electric motors. The selection of electric motors as Regal-Beloit's new growth engine made perfect sense given that 70 percent of the gearboxes the firm had been churning out were ultimately connected to an electric motor.

Regal-Beloit's March 1997 purchase of Marathon Electric Manufacturing Corporation for $279 million in cash, at the time by far the largest acquisition in company history, marked the firm's inaugural move into electric motors. Founded in 1914, the Wausau, Wisconsin-based Marathon produced electric motors, generators, and related products. In the domestic market for industrial electric motors, it had ranked fourth, producing AC electric motors ranging in size from 1/12 horsepower to more than 500 horsepower for such applications as heating, ventilating, and air conditioning (HVAC) products, pumps, commercial laundry equipment, and floor-care products. Marathon had also developed into a major supplier of generators, ranging in size from 5 kilowatts to 2.3 megawatts, to the Department of Defense, generator-set assemblers, and original equipment manufacturers. Marathon maintained ten manufacturing and warehousing facilities, including eight in the United States and one each in Singapore and the United Kingdom.

Regal-Beloit nearly doubled itself via this deal, adding Marathon's $245 million in 1996 revenues to its own sales of $281.5 million. Marathon Electric became the center of a newly formed Electrical Group, while the company's cutting tools and power transmission units were combined as the Mechanical Group. By 1998, Marathon's first full year under Regal-Beloit, revenues for the two groups were nearly equal: $280.2 million for the Mechanical Group and $263.4 million for the Electrical Group. Net income that year set a record of nearly $42 million.

Over the next decade, Regal-Beloit completed a string of acquisitions that ultimately made it one of the largest producers of electric motors in the North American market. In May 1999 the company spent $32.1 million for the Lincoln Motors business of Cleveland-based Lincoln Electric Holdings, Inc., gaining a line of AC motors ranging from 1 horsepower to 1,000 horsepower. The addition of Lincoln Motors, which had been generating annual sales of $50 million, pushed the revenues of Regal-Beloit's Electrical Group beyond those of the Mechanical Group. The former received another large boost in September 2000 in the form of the purchase of Leeson Electric Corporation for $260 million. Founded in 1972 and based in Grafton, Wisconsin, Leeson had garnered revenues of $175 million in fiscal 2000 from the sale of a variety of smaller electric motors (up to 350 horsepower). The acquisition of Leeson, operator of eight plants throughout the United States and Canada, propelled Regal-Beloit into the number two position among manufacturers of industrial electric motors in the United States, trailing only Baldor Electric Company.

Regal-Beloit's operations suffered during the first years of the 21st century as the manufacturing sector fell into a deep recession. Revenues grew in 2001 to $663.6 million thanks to the Leeson acquisition, but in the poor economic climate profits plunged 42 percent, to $19.6 million. Profits improved slightly the following year, but sales fell 8.8 percent. The company took a charge of $725,000 in the fourth quarter of 2002 to cover the costs of plant consolidations and the closing of four facilities, including a Leeson plant in Saukville, Wisconsin. At this same time, Regal-Beloit was seeking opportunities for expansion in global markets with faster growth potential than North America and was looking to widen its international manufacturing network. Toward these goals, the company at the beginning of 2003 entered into a joint venture with the Chinese firm Shanghai Jinling Co., Ltd., to manufacture subfractional and fractional electric motors in China. Additional joint ventures and acquisitions in China followed over the next several years.

DOUBLING IN SIZE WITH 2004 GE DEALS

As the economic climate began to improve for Regal-Beloit in 2004, the company turned aggressively acquisitive once again, completing two separate deals with General Electric Company (GE). In August 2004 Regal-Beloit paid $72 million in cash for GE's Commercial AC motor division, producer of motors, pumps, and processors for commercial heating and air conditioning units. In addition to its headquarters in Fort Wayne, Indiana, the GE division operated a major manufacturing plant in Juárez, Mexico, and a technical resource center in Hyderabad, India. This unit had annual sales of $144 million. In the second deal, valued at approximately $400 million in cash and stock, Regal-Beloit gained GE's HVAC motors and capacitors businesses, which produced a full line of motors and capacitors mainly for residential HVAC systems. Also based in Fort Wayne, these operations included four plants, located in Springfield, Missouri; Faridabad, India; and Reynosa and Juárez, Mexico. Sales for the operations were around $442 million.

Regal-Beloit was essentially able to double itself with the GE deals as revenues jumped from $619.1 million in 2003 to $1.43 billion in 2005. Out of the 2005 revenue total, 86 percent of the sales stemmed from the Electrical Group. In addition to greatly bolstering the company's position in the HVAC motor market, these acquisitions significantly enlarged Regal-Beloit's profile as a multinational company. They also turned out to be the final ones of Packard's deal-filled tenure as CEO. In April 2005 Packard handed the corporate reins to Henry W. Knueppel after having shepherded Regal-Beloit through more than two dozen acquisitions and shifted the firm's focus twice, toward power transmission products beginning in the early 1980s and toward electric motors starting in 1997. Since joining the company in 1979, Knueppel had worked his way up to president and COO by April 2002. Packard remained chairman until his retirement at the end of 2006, when Knueppel assumed that position as well. In the meantime, Regal-Beloit transferred its stock from the American Stock Exchange to the New York Stock Exchange in January 2005.

In 2006, when revenues reached $1.62 billion and net income surpassed the $100 million mark for the first time, Regal-Beloit made a number of additional strategic moves overseas. Among these were the startup of a generator manufacturing plant in Monterrey, Mexico, additional capital investments in India, and the acquisition of the Sinya group, a Changzhou, China-based manufacturer of fractional and subfractional HVAC motors. Back home, Regal-Beloit rolled out the largest product launch in its history, the introduction of the X13, a line of high-efficiency HVAC motors that was quickly adopted by the seven leading makers of HVAC equipment. The year also marked the end of an era as Regal-Beloit sold what remained of its cutting tools business. By the time of the divestment, the firm's founding business was generating annual sales of only about $17 million.

During 2007, the company continued to churn out new energy-efficient motors in response to increased demand stemming from rising energy costs. Regal-Beloit also completed four more acquisitions, including the French firm Alstom's motors and fans business in India, and Morrill Motors, a producer of fractional-horsepower motors for commercial refrigeration and freezer equipment. Morrill, based in Erwin, Tennessee, had additional manufacturing capacity in Jiaxing, China. In two separate transactions completed in August 2007, Regal-Beloit acquired two businesses specializing in motors and blower systems for various air-moving applications such as alternative fuels systems, water heaters, and HVAC systems: Fasco Motors and Jakel Incorporated. Fasco, purchased from Tecumseh Products Company for $220 million, maintained manufacturing and distribution facilities in Missouri, Mexico, Thailand, and Australia, while Regal-Beloit gained a plant in Piedras Negras, Mexico, through the Jakel deal. These two businesses, which together generated annual sales of more than $350 million, were amalgamated under the Fasco name in January 2008.

The turmoil in the U.S. housing market wreaked havoc with the residential HVAC sector in 2007, but Regal-Beloit overcame this challenge to post record results thanks to its balanced portfolio of businesses. Buoyed by strong results in commercial and industrial motors, power generation products, and overseas markets, sales were up 11.3 percent, to $1.8 billion, and net income grew 7.7 percent, to $118.3 million. The difficulties in the residential HVAC motor sector continued in 2008 as Regal-Beloit also contended with the rising costs of raw materials such as steel and copper. In the meantime, Regal-Beloit remained on the acquisition trail, picking up another Chinese electrical motor maker, Hwada, in the spring of 2008.

Paul S. Bodine
Updated, David E. Salamie

PRINCIPAL SUBSIDIARIES

Hub City, Inc.; Costruzioni Meccaniche Legnanesi (Italy); Mastergear GmbH (Germany); Opperman Mastergear Ltd. (U.K.); Marathon Electric Manufacturing Corporation; Regal-Beloit Holdings Ltd. (Canada); Thomson Finance Ltd. (Canada); Regal-Beloit Asia Pte. Ltd. (Singapore); Changzhou Modern Technologies Co. Ltd. (CMT) (China; 95%); Changzhou Regal-Beloit Sinya Motor Co. Ltd. (China); Regal-Beloit Mexico Holding S. de R.L. de C.V. (99.9%); Thomson Technology Shanghai Ltd. (China); Regal-Beloit Electric Motors, Inc.; Morrill Motors, Inc.; Regal Beloit Holding BV (Netherlands); Regal Beloit Finance BV (Netherlands); RBC Australia Holding Company Pty. Limited; Marathon Electric Motors (India) Ltd. (99%); RBC Horizon, Inc.

PRINCIPAL COMPETITORS

Baldor Electric Company; Emerson Electric Co.; A.O. Smith Corporation; General Electric Company; Cummins, Inc.; Siemens AG; Toshiba Corporation; WEG S.A.; ABB Ltd.; Altra Holdings, Inc.; Peerless-Winsmith, Inc.; SEW-EURODRIVE GmbH; Getriebebau Nord GmbH & Co. KG; Sumitomo Corporation; ZF Friedrichshafen AG.

FURTHER READING

"The CEOs of Wisconsin: James Packard," *Business Journal of Milwaukee,* March 27, 1993, p. 33

Content, Thomas, "Regal-Beloit Partners with Chinese Manufacturer," *Milwaukee Journal Sentinel,* November 11, 2002, p. 4D.

Doherty, Chuck, "Regal-Beloit Plans Purchase," *Milwaukee Sentinel,* February 25, 1992, p. 1D.

Goc, Michael J., *Take an Idea and Make It Go: Regal-Beloit Corporation, 1955–2005,* Friendship, Wis.: New Past Press, 2005, 95 p.

Gordon, Mitchell, "Cutting Edge," *Barron's,* May 26, 1986, pp. 45–46.

———, "The Cutting Edge: Regal-Beloit Is Carving Out a Lush Market," *Barron's,* December 21, 1981, pp. 32+.

Hajewski, Doris, "Firm's Frugality Pays Off," *Milwaukee Journal Sentinel,* October 8, 1995.

Jones, John A., "Regal-Beloit Keeps Profits Up As Heavy Industry Rolls On," *Investor's Business Daily,* January 2, 1996, p. A33.

Krantz, Matt, "How One Firm Saves a Third by Buying Used," *Investor's Business Daily,* October 15, 1996, p. A4.

Lank, Avrum D., "Regal-Beloit Set to Pay $379 Million to Acquire Motor Businesses from GE," *Milwaukee Journal Sentinel,* November 16, 2004, p. 1D.

Nelson, Brett, "The Sweet Smell of Oil," *Forbes,* December 29, 1997, pp. 63+.

"Newest 'Kid' on a Super Block," *Beloit Daily News,* April 24, 1991, special issue on Regal-Beloit Corporation.

Osenga, Mike, "Pump Drives Key to Expanding Off-Road Program," *Diesel Progress,* September 1993, pp. 52–55.

Ostrander, Kathleen, "The Big Move: Regal-Beloit's New Headquarters Reflects Its Philosophy," *Milwaukee Sentinel,* March 28, 1991, sec. 4, p. 1.

———, "Regal Dips, but Seeks Acquisition," *Milwaukee Sentinel,* April 25, 1991, sec. 4, p. 3.

Romell, Rick, "Fit for *Forbes:* Bottom Line Helps Regal-Beloit Make List," *Milwaukee Journal Sentinel,* October 25, 1996, p. 9D.

———, "Regal Beloit Finds Fire Sale: Tecumseh Sells Subsidiary for About Half Purchase Price," *Milwaukee Journal Sentinel,* July 4, 2007, p. D1.

———, "Regal-Beloit to Buy Marathon Electric," *Milwaukee Journal Sentinel,* February 27, 1997, p. 1D.

Rondy, John, "Regal-Beloit Corporation," *Business Journal of Milwaukee,* July 31, 1993, p. 17.

Sandler, Larry, "Regal-Beloit Eyes Growth in Europe," *Milwaukee Sentinel,* March 18, 1993, 3D.

Savage, Mark, "Motor Maker Steps Up: Leeson Purchase Boosts Regal-Beloit," *Milwaukee Journal Sentinel,* August 9, 2000, p. 15D.

———, "Regal-Beloit Plans Acquisitions," *Milwaukee Sentinel,* December 16, 1994, p. 2D.

———, "Regal-Beloit Plans to Buy Motor Unit," *Milwaukee Journal Sentinel,* April 7, 1999, p. 1D.

Schmid, John, "Regal Beloit Makes Acquisition," *Milwaukee Journal Sentinel,* September 5, 2007, p. D3.

Rheinmetall AG

Rheinmetall Allee 1
Düsseldorf, D-40476
Germany
Telephone: (+49 0211) 4 73 01
Fax: (+49 0211) 473 47 46
Web site: http://www.rheinmetall.com

Public Company
Incorporated: 1889 as Rheinische Metallwaaren- und Maschinenfabrik AG
Employees: 19,185
Sales: EUR 4.01 billion ($5.88 billion) (2007)
Stock Exchanges: Frankfurt
Ticker Symbol: RHM3
NAICS: 332995 Other Ordnance and Accessories Manufacturing; 336399 All Other Motor Vehicle Parts Manufacturing; 336992 Military Armored Vehicle, Tank, and Tank Component Manufacturing; 551112 Offices of Other Holding Companies

■ ■ ■

Rheinmetall AG is a holding company focused on two core industries: Automotive and Defense. The group's Automotive division is conducted through Kolbenschmidt Pierburg AG, one of the world's leading suppliers of pistons, pumps, air supply systems, actuators, solenoids and emissions control components, and bearings, as well as aftermarket components. Kolbenschmidt Pierburg in turn operates through six main divisions, KS Kolbenschmidt, Pierburg, KS Aluminium-Technologie, KS Gleitlager, Pierburg Pump Technology, and Motor Service. Rheinmetall's automotive holdings include production facilities in Germany, the Czech Republic, Italy, Spain, the United Kingdom, France, Mexico, the United States, Brazil, India, and China. Kolbenschmidt Pierburg generated 56 percent of Rheinmetall's total turnover.

Rheinmetall's Defense division is a leading European arms manufacturer, with a focus on land forces equipment, including land defense systems, weapons and munitions, propellants, air defense, and simulation and training products. The Land Systems division is based on Rheinmetall Landsysteme GmbH, and produces armored vehicles, combat support vehicles, such as mine-clearing systems, bridge-laying tanks, and recovery vehicles. The Weapons and Munitions includes the company's production of the 120mm cannon for the Leopard 2 tank, the PzH-2000 self-propelled howitzer, countermeasure systems, as well as advanced laser and microwave weapons technologies. Rheinmetall's Propellants division includes artillery and mortar charge systems, propellants, charges, as well as cartridge cases, and civil applications of its technologies, such as for medical, automobile and aviation, and other uses. Rheinmetall's Air Defense division is largely conducted through its Swiss subsidiary, Oerlikon Contraves, which produces short-range cannon, missile-supported antiaircraft systems, guided missile launchers, and ammunitions. The company's C4ISTAR division develops command & control and reconnaissance systems, as well as surveillance and sensor equipment, such as thermal imaging systems and drones, among others. The last division, Simulation and Training, produces these systems for Germany and its allies.

COMPANY PERSPECTIVES

Internationalization—People and Markets. It is the people and the products that shape the profile, reputation and distinctiveness of a company. Being present in a market, living and working there, understanding and fulfilling the needs of our customers—this is our philosophy. The way we think and act in the various countries is a factor that lends the Rheinmetall Group its international competence.

We observe national and international markets and competitive scenarios and explore growth opportunities surfacing in the relevant economic regions of Europe, America, and Asia. With the aid of regional and segmental analyses we assess and evaluate technology, market and industry trends and their implications for our worldwide operations.

With application-driven R&D focused on our core capabilities and by reaching out internationally we aspire to uncover new growth areas, access promising neighboring market segments in line with our strategy and by converging and focusing our resources, substantially extend market shares in the various product groups.

We have sown the seeds for expansion into new markets and for our operations to branch out regionally. Rheinmetall is braced for new challenges—across borders and beyond frontiers.

Once a sprawling conglomerate with diversified interests including paper and packaging, office products, and electronics, Rheinmetall underwent its major restructuring at the beginning of the 2000s. That process, led by CEO Klaus Eberhardt, was completed by 2005. Since then, Rheinmetall's turnover has nearly recovered to its levels of the early 2000s, topping EUR 4 billion ($5 billion) in 2007. Rheinmetall is listed on the Frankfurt Stock Exchange.

BEGINNINGS IN 1878

The company's founder, Heinrich Ehrhardt, was an industrial engineer from Zella in central Germany's Thüringen region. After starting out as a sales representative and completing his higher education on the side, Ehrhardt worked for a number of years as an engineer for a cast steelworks in Witten, where he improved the production of train axles. In 1878 the 38-year-old Ehrhardt founded his own small machine tool factory in Zella. He quickly attained an excellent reputation as a designer and industrialist, and the granting of licenses for his patents brought him into contact with directors of foreign enterprises.

Ehrhardt had become mutual friends with the manager of a munitions factory, Josef Massenez. When Massenez's company, Hörder Bergwerks- und Hüttenvereins, won a contract from the War Ministry that it could not fulfill, Massenez offered it to Ehrhardt in exchange for a commission. Although Ehrhardt lacked the technical expertise and production capacity, as well as sufficient capital, he was willing to take the risk. Accepting the job, Ehrhardt brought together a group of venture capitalist associates and on April 13, 1889, founded Rheinische Metallwaaren- und Maschinenfabrik AG (Rhine Metalware and Machine Factory Joint-Stock Company), which was registered on May 7 as a business in Düsseldorf on the Rhine.

At first Ehrhardt was completely occupied with the government contract, untiringly developing an appropriate manufacturing method. In December 1889 production started in rented space in Düsseldorf. Only three months later the young enterprise had 1,400 employees and supplied the war ministry with 800,000 projectiles a day.

Ehrhardt's ingenuity had paid off. On June 28, 1891, he received a patent for a "technique for simultaneous perforation and modelling of iron and steel ingots in heated condition." Having begun the search for resourceful engineers two years before while still in Zella, Ehrhardt took his employees' talents further with the development of seamless tubing for gun barrels. His company next developed a drawing technique, which received a patent in April 1892. Ehrhardt's pressing and drawing methods for the production of metal tubing and hollow parts garnered strong sales not only in the military, but also in the shipping and railroad industries and in gas and water utilities.

MOVING TO DÜSSELDORF

With the completion of his first government contract, Ehrhardt began construction of Rheinische Metallwaaren- und Maschinenfabrik's own factory in Düsseldorf-Derendorf, to which production gradually shifted. A metal tubing manufacturing facility and an iron foundry enabled production of nonmilitary products as well. The expansion of the production programs had led to increasing needs for steel, so in 1892 Ehrhardt and his son-in-law Paul Heye acquired a

KEY DATES

1878: Heinrich Ehrhardt founds a machine tool factory in Zella, Germany.

1889: Company begins producing munitions as Rheinische Metallwaaren- und Maschinenfabrik AG.

1951: Company reincorporates as Rheinmetall-Borsig AG following World War II.

1986: Rheinmetall acquires Pierburg automotive components group.

1997: Rheinmetall acquires majority share of Kolbenschmidt, which then merges with Pierburg.

2001: Rheinmetall launches major restructuring, streamlining operations to focus on Automotive and Defense sectors.

2007: Rheinmetall acquires 100 percent control of Kolbenschmidt Pierburg.

small forge in Rath that they named Rather Metallwerk Ehrhardt & Heye. In 1896 the forge was merged into Rheinische Metallwaaren- und Maschinenfabrik as the Rath division. Thus, Ehrhardt controlled a secure, integrated output of quality steel and semifinished products that rendered him independent from suppliers.

In 1896 Ehrhardt developed a 7.5cm field cannon into the first barrel recoil cannon suitable for field service, a significant technical development at that time. It brought Ehrhardt high accolades from Norwegian kings, Austrian emperors, and finally German Kaiser Wilhelm II. With this development, Ehrhardt's company was guaranteed great business success.

For the field testing of weapons and ammunition, in 1899 Rheinische Metallwaaren- und Maschinenfabrik took a lease on a large track of land near the village of Unterlüß in Lower Saxony. A small manufacturing facility was also established there for the production of ammunition and cartridge cases. In subsequent years the testing grounds were enlarged and ultimately reached an area of 15 kilometers (km) long and 5 km wide.

Rheinische Metallwaaren- und Maschinenfabrik expanded its production program and strengthened its market share with its acquisition in 1901 of Munitions- und Waffenfabrik AG in Sömmerda in Thüringen. At its factory, Dreysesche Gewehrfabrik, Munitions- und Waffenfabrik produced hand weapons, cartridges, and shell fuses. In the following years until the outbreak of World War I, Rheinische Metallwaaren- und Maschinenfabrik's manufacturing operation, partly through further acquisitions, developed considerably.

At the beginning of 1914 the Rheinische Metallwaaren- und Maschinenfabrik factories had nearly 8,000 workers. One year later, following the outbreak of World War I, there were 11,000 employees, and by 1918 the workforce had grown to approximately 48,000, including about 9,000 women. Then, with the Armistice in November 1918, military production came to a sudden standstill. The Düsseldorf enterprise, which had virtually quadrupled its staff during the war years, had to dismiss 22,000 employees.

With the signing of the 1919 Treaty of Versailles, prohibiting Germany from manufacturing large caliber weapons, Rheinische Metallwaaren- und Maschinenfabrik was deprived for a time of a substantial part of its business. Although small and midsized weapons could still be produced (beginning in 1921 it built mid-caliber guns for the navy), the company took a major turn toward augmenting its nonmilitary production capacity. Steel production at Rath was considerably strengthened to support civilian production. Meanwhile, the company was able to stay financially liquid by issuing public bonds, and in 1924 the majority of its stock was acquired by the state.

RHEINMETALL BRANDING IN THE TWENTIES

In the first half of the 1920s agricultural machinery, such as heavy steam-powered plows, railroad cars, and locomotive engines, were built in the company's Düsseldorf factories, while precision mechanical apparatus, including typewriters, calculating machines, and principal motor vehicle parts, were assembled at the Sömmerda plant in Thüringen. By 1921 the motor vehicle division had developed into a large and significant business within its industry in Germany. At the beginning of the 1920s the name Rheinmetall began to be used as a trademark.

Ehrhardt continued into old age to direct his creativity toward weapons technology development. In 1922 at the age of 81 he finally retired from Rheinmetall's board of directors and returned to his native Thüringen. He died on November 20, 1928, at age 88.

Meanwhile, Germany's economic crisis had intensified. As a result of the lack of orders, the civilian production division in Düsseldorf began showing losses, and, with the exception of the profitable steam-plow, production lines gradually ground to a halt. However, Rheinmetall did not suffer as greatly as some other enterprises did. In April 1933 it acquired another major company facing liquidation, August Borsig GmbH, one of Germany's leading manufacturers of locomotive engines. Two years later the merger led to a new name, Rheinmetall-Borsig AG, and in 1938 the headquarters of the firm moved from Düsseldorf to Berlin.

From the middle of the 1930s, Rheinmetall-Borsig, as with many other industrial enterprises at the time, developed and produced weapons and munitions in response to orders from the Reich War Ministry. Production included machine guns, tank guns, mortars and field artillery, antiaircraft guns, and railroad guns.

With the outbreak of World War II in September 1939, Rheinmetall-Borsig restructured itself into a Regular Works and an Affiliated Works. Regular Works comprised the facilities in Düsseldorf, Sömmerda, Unterlüß, and the Borsig plant in Berlin-Tegel, with separate divisions in Derendorf, Rath, Grafenberg, Halver, Gruiten, and Oberkassel. Affiliated Works consisted of eight facilities that since 1936 had been used as production plants for weapons and munitions. By the first year of the war, all ordnance factories came under the control of institutions of the German armed forces. In March 1940 the newly created Ministry of Armaments and Munitions began to coordinate the arms efforts.

As the war dragged on, the Nazi state demanded ever greater efforts from the industry to increase its weapons production. Demands of the commanders of the navy and air force for technical innovations compelled Rheinmetall-Borsig's research and development department to work under intense pressure. By July 1944 the company had introduced nearly 20 different weapons systems into the armed forces. Its chief engineer since 1938, Carl Wanninger, was a talented and creative designer who provided a strong stimulus to the development of military technology. An example of the high level of Rheinmetall's research and development was its varied rocket projects, although there was only one rocket production line. At the beginning of the war, the factories of Rheinmetall-Borsig had about 47,000 workers, a number that climbed to 85,000 by October 1944.

Toward the end of the war, air raids left their mark on the Rheinmetall plants and impaired production considerably. Thus, numerous production activities of the Düsseldorf facilities were relocated to the central and eastern regions of Germany. Later, factories in Berlin and Sömmerda also prepared themselves to move. In November 1944 British air raids caused heavy damage to the factories in Derendorf and Rath. In March 1945 the last smelting at the foundry in Derendorf took place, as Düsseldorf lay under severe artillery bombardment. Two months later the German Reich capitulated.

Under the occupation of Allied forces, Rheinmetall-Borsig had to give up its armaments production completely. A total production prohibition temporarily ceased all activities, and the company ended the war with a loss of 620 million reichsmarks. Many of Rheinmetall-Borsig's factories were completely dismantled by the Allies; it would not be until the 1950s that it was possible to begin normal business activities.

POST–WORLD WAR II REORGANIZATION

In order to resume civilian production, Rheinmetall-Borsig was reorganized and reincorporated in 1951. Borsig AG in Berlin and Rheinmetall AG in Düsseldorf were established as separate subsidiary operating companies of the same group management company, Rheinmetall-Borsig AG, a newly incorporated entity. In the following economically difficult years up until 1956, the Rheinmetall group undertook significant rebuilding. A small enterprise of civilian machine manufacture was started at the company's two main locations, Düsseldorf and Berlin. Production in Düsseldorf centered on loading and transport equipment, while steam boilers and refrigerators were manufactured in Berlin.

On June 23, 1956, the majority share of Rheinmetall-Borsig AG, which had been controlled by the federal government since 1951, was purchased by Röchlingsche Eisen- und Stahlwerke GmbH and would eventually go to the latter's holding company. In August of that same year, the subsidiary Borsig AG was sold after two eventful decades with Rheinmetall. With Borsig gone, the company was renamed Rheinmetall Berlin AG at the next general shareholders' meeting in November. The Düsseldorf subsidiary Rheinmetall AG became Rheinmetall GmbH in 1957. Soon, with the establishment of the Bundeswehr (federal armed forces), Rheinmetall again took up military production while also continuing its civilian industrial machine manufacturing activities.

With the acquisition of Benz & Hilgers, a leading manufacturer of bottling and packaging machinery for the food industry, Rheinmetall diversified into packaging technology. Leading the business strategy of increasing nonmilitary industrial production were Chairman of the Board Ernst Röchling, board member Otto Kranzbühler, and veteran board member Otto Paul Caesar, who became chairman in 1968. In subsequent years more small machine manufacturing enterprises were founded or purchased, although they did not justify any change in the corporate structure.

Meanwhile, the military production sector expanded through Rheinmetall Berlin's traditional means of acquisition. In 1970 the company took over a majority share of Nico-Pyrotechnik, which was later transferred to Rheinmetall GmbH. In 1975 Rheinmetall GmbH acquired the munitions manufacturer NWM de Kruithoorn in Hertogenbosch of the Netherlands. Moving beyond guns and ammunition, in 1979 Rheinmetall delivered its first battle tank, Leopard 2, to the Bundeswehr. It was equipped with Rheinmetall's 120mm smooth-bore gun, a noteworthy technological innovation in NATO (North Atlantic Treaty Organization) tanks.

By 1979 there were approximately 5,700 employees in the Rheinmetall group, bringing in sales of DM 735.5 million ($401.3 million), 70 percent of which was in military production and 30 percent in industrial equipment manufacturing.

DIVERSIFYING IN THE SEVENTIES

Rheinmetall Berlin tested the limits of its diversification with the 1979 acquisition of Württembergische Metallwarenfabrik (WMF), a manufacturer of such consumer durables as cutlery, silverware, glass, and hotel furnishings. The federal antitrust commission, however, withheld its approval of the acquisition, and in 1985 WMF was sold. The later acquisition in 1981 of majority shares in Ganzhorn & Stirn GmbH and Jagenberg AG propelled the Rheinmetall group more decisively in the direction of packaging technology. Ganzhorn & Stirn, subsequently renamed Gasti-Verpackungsmaschinen GmbH, ranked among the leading suppliers of bottle filling and capping machinery for the food industry. Jagenberg was a leading manufacturer of paper treating and converting machinery.

The acquisition of a controlling share in Jagenberg, a move initiated by Hans U. Brauner, chief executive of Rheinmetall Berlin since 1980, also necessitated restructuring the machine manufacturing business of Rheinmetall Berlin. A new independent profit center called Machinery was created at the same administrative level of the military equipment subsidiary Rheinmetall GmbH. The management of this new profit center was to be undertaken by the Jagenberg subsidiary.

The next major acquisition of Rheinmetall Berlin was the 1986 purchase of an 80 percent share of Pierburg GmbH in Neuss, a manufacturer of carburetion systems and motor components. Pierburg's activities were consolidated into the Rheinmetall group's third major business center, Automotive Components. Brauner, having become chairman of Rheinmetall Berlin in 1985, continued to spearhead the company's diversification as a means of balancing financial risk.

In the late 1980s more emphasis was put on research and development. In May 1986 construction began on a new research and development center in Unterlüß, TZN Forschungs- und Entwicklungszentrum Unterlüß. The facility, which developed applied electronic technologies, was supported by Rheinmetall GmbH, the state of Lower Saxony, and a regional manufacturers' association. Meanwhile, the new subsidiary Pierburg GmbH was developing into an electronics-oriented enterprise in the field of carburetion technology. In 1988 Pierburg introduced the multipoint injection system Ecojet M and a lambda-controlled carburetor, Pierburg Ecotronic. In addition, Jagenberg introduced Jagmatic, a system for controlling squareness in the process of manufacturing paper. Other technological developments of Rheinmetall Berlin at this time included the introduction of compact lasers and automated control systems using five-axis robots in their production processes. By 1992 Rheinmetall Berlin was spending approximately 5 percent of its income on research and development.

With the 1988 acquisition of the Kampf group of companies, a leading manufacturer of foil machines, Jagenberg entered a new phase in machine construction. Machines for paper processing and rolling, foil-laying, plastic laminating, and packaging became the primary equipment types constructed. The movement toward packaging machinery was reinforced with the 1989 acquisition of Automation und Fördertechnik ELM GmbH, a packaging equipment firm. Acquisitions and careful management contributed to Rheinmetall Berlin's postwar record sales of DM 3.25 billion ($1.85 billion) in 1988. Pretax profit was DM 171.8 million ($97.82 million), and at the close of that year the group employed 15,465 people.

In the early 1990s the Machinery and Automotive Components sectors suffered as a result of the German and global recession. In 1992 Jagenberg's sales fell 12.6 percent, resulting in a net loss of DM 7.5 million ($4.8 million), and Pierburg's sales fell 12.8 percent, causing a net loss of DM 6.6 million ($4.2 million). Both subsidiaries reduced their workforces by 7 percent and 11.6 percent, respectively. Consolidated group sales fell 9.8 percent to DM 3.1 billion ($2.01 billion) with a net income of DM 20.2 million ($12.93 million).

With the end of the Cold War and resulting cutbacks in military spending, not only the group as a whole, but even the Defense Technology subsidiary Rheinmetall GmbH began to look for ways to expand into related nonmilitary technology. In April 1992 Rheinmetall Berlin established Rheinmetall Machine Vision GmbH, an industrial image processing business with about 140 employees. Rheinmetall GmbH also entered the fields of nonmilitary explosives with the acquisition of Pyrotechnische Fabrik Oskar Lünig GmbH; propellent chemicals with the acquisition of WNC-Nitrochemie GmbH; and security systems, including video surveillance and metal detectors, with the purchase of Heimann Systems GmbH. Other product developments were in the fields of computerized control and signal systems. In July 1992 Rheinmetall won a contract for disposal of former East German army ammunition. Also in 1992, Rheinmetall GmbH discontinued its historic Düsseldorf facilities and moved its headquarters to Ratingen.

GERMAN CONGLOMERATE IN THE NINETIES

In March 1993 Rheinmetall Berlin acquired a 63 percent share in the electronics company Preh-Werke GmbH, which expanded Pierburg's production into the field of electronic components. Preh manufactured digital input systems and control and indicator systems, used in automobile heating, ventilation, and air conditioning systems. Preh's sales prior to its acquisition were about DM 220 million ($141 million), and it employed 2,000 people.

In February 1993 Rheinmetall Berlin moved into an entirely new field of business with its acquisition of a 75 percent share of Mauser Waldeck AG, Germany's largest manufacturer of office furniture with sales of DM 400 million ($256 million). This subsidiary, Office Systems, was established as Rheinmetall Berlin's fourth independent business sector and accounted for approximately 12 percent of the group's business. At that time Automotive Components of Pierburg GmbH contributed 28 percent, Machinery of Jagenberg AG 27 percent, Defense Technology of Rheinmetall GmbH 26 percent, and nonmilitary diversifications of Rheinmetall GmbH 7 percent of the group's business.

Rheinmetall invested strongly in building up its automotive division through the 1990s. Pierburg, which had exited the by then outmoded carburetor sector, targeted new areas of the automotive market, focusing on pumps and valves, particularly with an eye toward reducing emissions and improving fuel efficiency. Pierburg successfully entered the United States, setting up a factory in South Carolina in 1995.

Two years later, Rheinmetall's automotive division grew into one of its largest, when the company acquired majority control of Kolbenschmidt. Founded in 1910, Kolbenschmidt had long been Germany's leading piston manufacturer, before developing a position among the global leaders in this sector. Kolbenschmidt had fallen on hard times in the early 1990s; when its parent, the Metallgesellschaft (MG) conglomerate, collapsed in the mid-1990s, Kolbenschmidt, a public company, was put up for sale. Rheinmetall then acquired MG's 74 percent stake and merged its automotive operations as Kolbenschmidt Pierburg (KP).

FOCUSING ON THE DEFENSE AND AUTOMOTIVE INDUSTRIES IN THE NEW CENTURY

KP quickly asserted itself on a global level. The company solidified its position in the United States, buying one of that market's leading piston manufacturers, Zollner, in 1999. KP also added operations in China and Japan a year later, then expanded into the Czech Republic in 2004.

Rheinmetall continued to build its other operations as well. In 1999, the company acquired Zürich, Switzerland-based Oerlikon Contraves AG, which focused on developing guided missile systems for the air defense market. The company also expanded its electronics wing, buying Richard Hirschmann & Co. in 1997. The company then created a dedicated division for all of its electronics holdings, called Rheinmetall Electronics.

Into the new century, however, Rheinmetall's status as a highly diversified conglomerate had come under fire from the investment community. The company's share price slumped, to the extent that the company found itself worth much less than the total value of its assets. In addition, the company had a heavy debt load, which represented more than its total equity. The appearance of U.S. investor Guy Pratte-Wyser in Rheinmetall's shareholding, coupled with the desire by the company's majority shareholder, the Rochling family, to sell its stake in the company, led Rheinmetall to take action.

In 2001, the company appointed a new CEO, Klaus Eberhardt, who orchestrated a dramatic restructuring of the company's operations. Over the next several years, Eberhardt led the progressive sell-off of three of its five divisions, starting with its paper and packaging division. The company then divested its office products division. By 2005, Rheinmetall had sold its electronics division as well, completing the restructuring. With the Rochling family's exit, the company was also able to convert its share structure from a two-tier to a single-tier system in which all shares possessed full voting rights. The streamlined Rheinmetall saw its share price grow strongly, and by the end of 2005 the company's stock had been admitted to the Frankfurt exchange's MDAX index. Then, in 2007, Rheinmetall further simplified its structure, buying up the minority shareholders in KP, which was then delisted from the stock exchange.

Rheinmetall continued to look for new growth opportunities for its two divisions into the second half of the decade. The company's defense division grew with the purchase of a 51 percent stake in Chempro GmbH, as well as a minority position in ADS Gesellschaft fur aktive Schutzsystems GmH, helping to solidify the company position as a leading European supplier of land forces systems. The company also bought Zaugg Electronik, based in Switzerland, a major producer of military-grade safety fuses. At KP, meanwhile, Rheinmetall expanded with new operations in Mexico in 2006, an entry into India, and the construction of an expanded production facility in Brazil in 2007. Rheinmetall could look back on 130 years of history as a focused automotive and defense group in the 21st century.

Heather Behn Hedden
Updated, M. L. Cohen

PRINCIPAL SUBSIDIARIES

CHEMPRO Gesellschaft für kunststoffgebundene Produkte mbH; Karl Schmidt Unisia Inc. (U.S.A.); Kolbenschmidt K.K. (Japan); Kolbenschmidt Pierburg AG; KS Aluminium-Technologie AG; KS Gleitlager GmbH; KS Kolbenschmidt Czech Republic a.s.; KS Kolbenschmidt France S.A.S.; KS Kolbenschmidt GmbH; KS Pistões Ltda. (Brazil); MS Motor Service International GmbH; Nitrochemie Aschau GmbH; Oerlikon Contraves AG (Switzerland); Pierburg GmbH; Pierburg Inc. (U.S.A.); Pierburg S.A. (Spain); Pierburg S.à.r.l. (France); Pierburg S.p.A. (Italy); Rheinmetall Canada Inc.; Rheinmetall Defense Electronics GmbH; Rheinmetall Italia S.p.A. (Italy); Rheinmetall Landsysteme GmbH; Rheinmetall Waffe Munition GmbH; RWM Schweiz AG.

PRINCIPAL COMPETITORS

Defense: General Dynamics Corp.; ThyssenKrupp Technologies AG; Titran Joint Stock Co.; Smiths Group PLC; Iveco Magirus AG; Heil Co.; Znamya Engineering Works Joint Stock Co.; RUAG Holding; Automotive: Faurecia S.A.; Mahle GmbH; TRW Automotive GmbH; Bosch Corp.; Keihin Corp.; Sauer-Danfoss Inc.; SFS Holding AG; Siemens VDO Automotive S.A.S.; Walbro Corp.

FURTHER READING

"Ausbau zivile Aktivitäten," *Frankfurter-Allgemaine,* April 2, 1992, p. 21.

Donberg, Deborah, "Diversified Rheinmetall Prepares Debut, Analysts See Credit Stable," *Euroweek,* October 27, 2000, p. 2.

Ehrhardt, Heinrich, *Hammerschläge: 70 Jahre Deutsher Arbeiter under Erfinder,* Leipzig: K.F. Koehler, 1923.

Haig, Simonian, "Joining the Big League," *Financial Times,* May 11, 1998, p. FTS2.

Marsh, Peter, "A Conglomerate Forced to Sharpen Up Its Act," *Financial Times,* October 26, 2001, p. 14.

Marsh, Peter, Alexander Nicoll, and Haid Simonian, "Broad Is Beautiful for the Chairman of Rheinmetall," *Financial Times,* May 4, 1998, p. 21.

Milne, Richard, "Lead Stake in Rheinmetall up for Sale," *Financial Times,* November 25, 2004, p. 28.

Rheinmetall -eine Technologie-Gruppe, Düsseldorf: Rheinmetall Berlin AG, 1993.

"Rheinmetall Has Acquired 100% of Zaugg Elektronic of Switzerland, a Manufacturer of Military Fuse Systems for the European and North American Markets," *Armada International,* August–September 2007, p. 4.

"Rheinmetall Has Taken Over Operations of Stork PWV from Its Parent Company Stork NV in the Netherlands," *Armada International,* April–May 2008, p. 4.

"Rheinmetall kauft Heimann," *Frankfurter-Allgemaine,* April 2, 1993, p. 20.

"Rheinmetall Sells Hirschmann to HgCapital," *Control Engineering,* April 2004, p. 17.

Zeittafel 1889–1989, Düsseldorf: Rheinmetall Berlin AG, April 1989.

St. Jude Medical, Inc.

One Lillehei Plaza
St. Paul, Minnesota 55117-9983
U.S.A.
Telephone: (651) 483-2000
Toll Free: (800) 328-9634
Fax: (651) 490-4310
Web site: http://www.sjm.com

Public Company
Incorporated: 1976
Employees: 12,000
Sales: $3.78 billion (2007)
Stock Exchanges: New York
Ticker Symbol: STJ
NAICS: 334510 Electromedical and Electrotherapeutic Apparatus Manufacturing; 339112 Surgical and Medical Instrument Manufacturing; 339113 Surgical Appliance and Supplies Manufacturing

■ ■ ■

From its beginnings in mechanical heart valves, St. Jude Medical, Inc. (SJM), has evolved into one of the world's leading producers of cardiovascular medical devices. Cardiac rhythm management products, a sector in which SJM ranks number two in the world behind Medtronic, Inc., account for more than 60 percent of the firm's revenues. Products in this area include implantable cardioverter defibrillators, which are used to treat hearts that beat too fast; cardiac resynchronization therapy devices, used to treat patients suffering from heart failure; and pacemakers, used to treat hearts that beat too slowly or beat irregularly. SJM's remaining revenues are derived from three other market segments: cardiovascular products, such as mechanical and tissue-replacement heart valves and heart-valve repair devices; devices to treat atrial fibrillation, a rapid and inconsistent heart rhythm occurring in the organ's upper chambers; and neuromodulation systems, consisting of implantable devices used to treat chronic pain and other conditions by delivering either electrical current or drugs directly to targeted nerves. Based in St. Paul, Minnesota, the company maintains manufacturing operations in Arizona, California, Minnesota, New Jersey, Oregon, South Carolina, Texas, Puerto Rico, Canada, Brazil, and Sweden. SJM sells its products in more than 100 countries worldwide.

MECHANICAL HEART VALVE ORIGINS

In 1972 the bileaflet mechanical heart valve was developed at the University of Minnesota. This new valve was made of pyrolytic carbon, a hard, shiny material that did not cause blood clots and could last for years in the human body. St. Jude Medical, Inc., was formed and incorporated in 1976 to further develop, market, and manufacture this valve. The company was founded by Manuel A. Villafana, a businessman who began his career at the helm of Cardiac Pacemakers, Inc., revolutionizing the industry with the innovation of long-lasting lithium batteries. Two years before selling his company to Eli Lilly for $127 million, Villafana formed SJM. (He named the company after the patron saint of lost causes and hospital workers.)

COMPANY PERSPECTIVES

It is our mission to develop medical technology and services that put more control into the hands of those who treat cardiac, neurological and chronic pain patients, worldwide. We do this because we are dedicated to advancing the practice of medicine by reducing risk wherever possible and contributing to successful outcomes for every patient.

In February 1977, SJM made an initial stock offering at $3.50 per share. In October, the first human implant of the SJM mechanical heart valve took place. Dr. Demetre Nicoloff performed the operation on Helen Heikkinen, a 69-year-old heart patient, at the University of Minnesota Hospital in Minneapolis.

A superb salesman, Villafana convinced so many heart surgeons to try the SJM heart valve that the company was criticized for the emphasis placed on sales in what was supposedly a clinical trial program. The Food and Drug Administration (FDA) became involved, prompting Villafana's departure from the company in 1981. Villafana went on to establish Helix BioCore, Inc., later ATS Medical, Inc., a competitor company.

In 1982 SJM received approval from the FDA to market its mechanical heart valve in the United States. SJM's profits began to ascend rapidly, rising from $2.3 million in 1982 to $4.3 million in 1983. By 1984, SJM had achieved revenues of almost $35 million and profits of $5.3 million, solely from sales of its mechanical heart valve. Twenty-five percent of the 100,000 artificial valves implanted in diseased hearts that year were SJM valves. As a one-product company with a market value of $41 million, SJM could not afford any threat to the successful manufacturing of that vital product.

PROLONGED LEGAL BATTLE WITH CARBOMEDICS

A threat did come in 1984, however. The distinctiveness of SJM's heart valve was found in the marriage of a bileaflet design, created by St. Jude engineers, and its anti-blood-clotting carbon skin coating, produced and supplied by CarboMedics, a subsidiary of Intermedics, Inc., a cardiac-pacemaker company. In March 1984 the two companies were unable to reach an agreement on a long-term supply contract and filed countersuits.

The dispute had actually begun shortly after CarboMedics was purchased by Intermedics in 1979. Intermedics's reputation in the field was that of a tough player, and SJM executives began to quietly look for a second-source supplier of the valve's carbon coating. In addition, Villafana had launched a pacemaker-development project, in hopes of diversifying the company. G. Russell Chambers, Intermedics's director, threatened to raise the price of the carbon coating when he learned of the pacemaker project. Pacemaker sales accounted for the majority of Intermedics's profits. Chambers's threat worked; Villafana dropped the pacemaker project.

At the same time, a company called Hemex was formed in 1979, selling a heart valve that was similar to SJM's. Observing that Intermedics officers and directors owned stakes in Hemex and that Chambers's son, Rusty Chambers, was Hemex's chairman, SJM inferred that Intermedics was behind this new competitor in the valve business.

Although Chambers denied any connection between the companies, SJM's new CEO, LaVerne Rees, was unconvinced. In 1981 Rees directed the company to take the necessary steps toward development of its own carbon coating. When this costly and ambitious project was announced in SJM's 1983 annual report, Chambers was outraged and demanded that SJM halt all research efforts. According to *Business Week,* an SJM consultant then attempted to purchase the carbon formula from an employee of CarboMedics. In 1983 Chambers directed his company to stop supplying SJM with carbon components. The dispute became heated, and court depositions alleged that CarboMedics hired detectives to search SJM garbage cans for stolen trade secrets.

CarboMedics charged SJM with patent infringement, while SJM responded with breach of contract, antitrust, and restraint-of-trade claims. Essentially, SJM alleged that Intermedics sought to achieve a monopoly and to restrain trade in the heart-valve business. Each company accused the other of theft of trade secrets and contract violation. In the fall of 1984 SJM's board let Rees go, leaving Chairman William Hendrickson in command, with Thomas M. Garrett III (the attorney who drafted SJM's articles of incorporation) playing a greater role in advising the company.

The legal battle continued for two years and involved court cases in the United States as well as in Europe. Because CarboMedics refused to supply SJM during this period, SJM ran out of completed valves to sell, forcing doctors and patients to look elsewhere for supplies, and eroding the sales and stock market earnings of both companies. According to *Business Week,* in 1985 SJM produced only about one-third of the 25,000 heart valves it had produced in 1984. Intermedics lost approximately $20 million on an annual basis, and SJM

KEY DATES

1976: Manuel A. Villafana founds St. Jude Medical, Inc. (SJM), to develop, market, and make the bileaflet mechanical heart valve.
1977: Company goes public and begins a clinical trial of the heart valve.
1982: FDA grants approval to SJM for the marketing of the mechanical heart valve.
1994: SJM purchases the cardiac pacing device businesses of Siemens AG.
1996: Daig Corporation, a maker of specialized cardiovascular catheters, is acquired, as are the assets of Telectronics Pacing Systems, Inc., and Medtel.
1997: SJM acquires Ventritex, maker of implantable cardioverter defibrillators.
1999: SJM acquires the Angio-Seal unit of Tyco International Ltd. and Vascular Science, Inc.
2000: FDA approves the Photon DR, SJM's first dual-chamber defibrillator.
2004: Company introduces its first cardiac resynchronization therapy devices, used to treat patients suffering from heart failure.
2005: SJM expands outside cardiovascular devices for the first time via the $1.35 billion acquisition of Advanced Neuromodulation Systems, Inc.

sank from record revenues of $35 million in 1984 to $26 million in 1985. SJM's stock, which had previously been a high-rated investment, plummeted, as did that of CarboMedics. Meanwhile, competitors in the heart-valve industry had a field day, as their sales and their share of the market increased.

In February 1985 SJM named Lawrence A. Lehmkuhl as its new president and CEO. Lehmkuhl, who had previously served as divisional president at American Hospital Supply Corporation, made it his first priority to end the supplier boycott of SJM, which threatened to destroy the company's ability to produce and market its only product. Lehmkuhl was selected not only on the basis of his potential to resolve the dispute but also as a leader who might broaden the company's product line, eliminating the vulnerability associated with being a one-product company. In September 1985 an agreement was signed by the two companies, allowing SJM to continue its carbon manufacturing research and development efforts and to produce limited quantities of pyrolytic carbon.

A RETURN TO GROWTH

In 1986 the first SJM mechanical heart valve produced with the company's own pyrolytic carbon-coated components was implanted in a patient in Germany. SJM augmented its mechanical heart-valve business in 1986 when it acquired BioImplant, expanding into tissue heart valves. For several years, however, the company sold the tissue valves only outside of the United States. SJM implemented a two-for-one stock split, tripling its authorized common shares to 30 million. Revenues for 1986 rose to $60.5 million.

Once again, the company demonstrated consistent growth and stock market value. By 1988, SJM was again a favorite pick for investment specialists. Fiscal 1987 had closed with a net profit of $17 million and $1.55 a share, with net income rising 44 percent over the prior year to $71.8 million and sales climbing 19 percent. Furthermore, the company had no debt. In fact, SJM's cash balance was an astonishing $65 million. In an article in *Barron's,* investment specialist Bing Carlin selected SJM as his favorite investment, citing competitor Baxter Travenol Laboratories, Inc.'s suspension of its heart valves (because of possible malfunction) and the FDA's approval of SJM's new low-cost plant in Puerto Rico as optimistic factors for SJM. Another competitor, Pfizer Inc., also experienced failure with its heart valve. In addition, SJM's decision to sell directly to hospitals, rather than working through distributors, meant that the company would retain more profits. The company achieved revenues of $114 million and $148 million in 1988 and 1989, respectively.

In 1990 SJM established its International Division, headquartered in Brussels, Belgium. SJM was still a top-rated pick for investors, and the company's stock was selling at 20 times earnings. Other than the decline in profits in 1985, SJM had demonstrated revenue growth of 30 percent or more each year, with revenues of $175.2 million in 1990, and the company possessed over $150 million in cash. More than 300,000 SJM mechanical heart valves had been put to use.

One reason for SJM's success was that the average age of heart-valve recipients had declined. Older patients favored nonmechanical heart valves, which were made of pig tissue and did not require anticlotting medication. Such tissue valves had an average age of five years, and as the age of heart patients declined, the life expectancy after implant increased. This increased life expectancy created a greater demand for mechanical valves, because tissue valves would have to be replaced through open-heart surgery after five years.

In addition, SJM had reached an agreement with CarboMedics, giving SJM the right to make increasing quantities of components until 1998 and to make all parts in-house beginning in 1998. The pricing structure contained within the agreement significantly reduced SJM's costs, in exchange for SJM's commitment to purchase decreasing percentages of carbon components over the next five years. Since the revelation of Baxter Travenol's design flaw, SJM had faced virtually no serious competition. The heart-valve market was not large enough to attract major pharmaceutical companies as competitors.

Under the leadership of Lehmkuhl, SJM had begun to make cautious acquisitions. Those acquisitions included a Canadian company that manufactured porcine valves that were sold internationally (while awaiting U.S. FDA approval), a company that made intra-aortic balloon pumps, and a centrifugal pump system. In addition, SJM had expanded its research department, funding vascular graft research. The core of SJM's operations, however, remained its heart-valve business. In 1991 SJM received FDA approval for two internally developed products: the BiFlex annuloplasty ring and the sterile aortic valved graft. SJM became the only heart-valve manufacturer with two sources for pyrolytic carbon-coated components. Revenues rose again, to $209.8 million in 1991.

1992 DOWNTURN AND ITS AFTERMATH

After five years with annual earnings growth of 59 percent and an 84 percent rise in shares in 1991, SJM's stock suddenly took another downturn in the summer of 1992. The catalyst was the company's disclosure, on July 1, that second-quarter sales and earnings had fallen short of analysts' projections. On July 2, investors pulled $285 million out of SJM, 16 percent of the company's market capitalization.

Lehmkuhl attributed the shortfall to aggressive promotion of tissue valves by two competitors, Medtronic, Inc., and the newly named Baxter International Inc. (the former Baxter Travenol). *Barron's* magazine also cited a decline in open-heart surgeries in Los Angeles, one of SJM's largest markets, as a negative factor, along with an "inventory adjustment" by a Japanese customer and decreased sales in Poland. The shortfall was estimated to be only 2 percent of the domestic market (SJM controlled more than 45 percent of the international market and 60 percent of the U.S. market). Nevertheless, because 95 percent of the company's sales continued to be generated by the heart valve, even that small setback was enough to scare off investors who were wary of the risks of a one-product company.

The result was that SJM's shares, which had been priced at $55.50 in January 1992, dropped dangerously to $27.50. Ironically, sales climbed 3.5 percent over the previous year's second quarter to $57 million, and earnings per share rose from 45 cents to 52 cents. Moreover, the company closed 1992 with another dramatic increase, achieving $239.5 million in revenues.

Seeing competition from tissue-valve companies as a major challenge, SJM began to work toward sales of tissue valves in the United States. The company sold both tissue and mechanical valves in Europe, and in 1992 it formed a partnership with Hancock Jaffe Laboratories to design and market a new bioprosthetic tissue valve in the United States. Also during this time, SJM began construction of a new 65,000-square-foot facility for manufacturing pyrolytic carbon–coated components. The facility would undergo FDA qualifications in 1994 and 1995.

Taking a long anticipated step toward long-term stability, Lehmkuhl made his first aggressive maneuver toward an acquisition strategy when he hired John Alexander as vice-president for corporate development in July 1992. Alexander had previously spearheaded business development and strategy for Baxter International's diagnostics division. SJM had been criticized for being too conservative with its $300 million cash supply by observers who could not understand why the company did not diversify through acquisitions earlier. Lehmkuhl had been cautious, in part, because any acquisition would initially dilute SJM's tremendous earning power. Healthcare company prices had dropped significantly since the beginning of 1992, and the time was seen as ripe for the beginning of an acquisition strategy.

Ronald Matricaria, formerly an executive with Eli Lilly and Company, replaced Lehmkuhl as president and CEO in 1993, while Lehmkuhl remained as company chairman. Matricaria was known as an aggressive competitor, having built Lilly's cardiac pacemakers unit from a failing business to a world leader. Matricaria breathed new life into the acquisition hunt, giving it the code name "Project Runner" and involving the company's top management in a process of self-examination and assessment. This process focused on identifying SJM's business strengths—the manufacture of implant devices and an intricate knowledge of blood flow and clotting—and applying those strengths to potential areas of acquisition. The company studied 16 medical specialties fields in order to make its decision.

In the spring of 1993, the company signed an exclusive license and supply agreement with Telios Pharmaceuticals, Inc., to utilize Telios's proprietary cell adhesion technology. In August, SJM bought a large minority stake in InControl Inc., a company developing an implantable machine to stop atrial fibrillation (rapid pulsing of the heart's upper chambers). In December, SJM acquired Electromedics, a Colorado maker of blood management and blood conservation equipment and related disposable devices, in a $90 million deal. Yet the industry, according to the *Wall Street Journal,* was "on the rocks"; as a consequence, SJM's stock suffered.

The decline in market value was attributed to two primary factors: cost-cutting by corporations and insurance companies and a looming uncertainty, due to President Bill Clinton's proposed healthcare plan, about the future of medical care. SJM faced other problems as well. The company's tax rate went up almost five percentage points through the loss of tax benefits from manufacturing in Puerto Rico. Moreover, in September 1993 CarboMedics received approval to sell heart valves in the United States. SJM was not yet ready to promote the improved tissue valve being developed. Instead, the company continued its acquisition strategy, hoping to renew growth through diversification. Revenues continued to rise, with sales of $252.6 million at the end of 1993.

THREE MAJOR ACQUISITIONS, 1994–96

In June 1994 SJM announced that it was prepared to make a major acquisition. Project Runner had arrived at its conclusion: SJM would enter the expanding market for cardiac rhythm management. SJM would purchase the cardiac pacing device businesses of Siemens AG, the world's number two maker of pacemakers for slow heartbeats (behind Medtronic), for more than $500 million. The acquisition, which was completed in September 1994 at a cost of $525 million, launched SJM as a top-tier company in the realm of pacing device manufacturers. Further, SJM more than doubled its sales and tripled its workforce. In 1993 Siemens's cardiac rhythm management business (called Siemens Pacesetter, Inc., renamed Pacesetter, Inc.) had generated more than $350 million in sales with a 1,300-strong workforce.

The year 1994 brought several new developments in existing products as well. SJM announced the first U.S. implants of its stentless tissue heart valve, previously marketed internationally. It also received FDA approval to market its new collagen-impregnated aortic-valved graft in the United States. In addition, the company launched an alliance with Advanced Tissue Sciences to pursue the joint development of tissue-engineered heart valves and, under the auspices of The Heart Valve Company (the joint venture between SJM and Hancock Jaffe Laboratories), made its first implant of the new bioprosthetic heart valve at Glenfield Hospital in Leicester, England. Finally, the company made a $12 million equity investment in Endo Vascular Technologies, Inc., a leading company in the development of products to less invasively repair damaged or diseased blood vessels.

Net revenues jumped to $848.1 million by 1995, while net profits stood at $117.1 million, resulting in a 13.8 percent profit margin. The following year the company continued its program of diversification through acquisition. In May 1996 SJM acquired Minnetonka, Minnesota-based Daig Corporation, a maker of specialized cardiovascular catheters, for more than $400 million. During medical procedures, surgeons used Daig catheters as high-tech probes able to maneuver through blood vessels to the heart. One line of Daig catheters were known as electrophysiology catheters and were used, for example, to deliver precise doses of radiofrequency energy into the heart to correct an irregular heartbeat.

In April, St. Jude Medical announced that it would pay about $72 million for Cyberonics Inc., which was based in Webster, Texas, and was developing a pacemaker-like device for the treatment of epilepsy. SJM pulled out of this deal in October 1996, however, just prior to announcing the purchases of Ventritex, Inc., and the cardiac rhythm management assets of Telectronics Pacing Systems, Inc., and Medtel for a total of more than $500 million. In November SJM completed the acquisition of the assets of Telectronics and Medtel from Pacific Dunlop Ltd., an Australian conglomerate, while the purchase of Ventritex closed in May 1997. Ventritex brought St. Jude Medical a significant position in another segment of the cardiovascular device market, implantable cardioverter defibrillators (ICDs).

Similar to pacemakers, which generally treat slow heart rates, ICDs are used to correct extremely rapid heart rates. Following completion of the Ventritex acquisition, SJM created a new division, the Cardiac Rhythm Management Division, to encompass the firm's pacemaker operations and those of Ventritex, Telectronics, and Medtel. Also in 1997, the FDA granted approval to SJM's Toronto SPV pig-tissue heart value, which was notable as the first U.S.-approved stentless valve (a valve that does not require plastic or metal frames, called stents, to hold it in place). The valve had been approved for sale in Europe in 1995. These approvals were important because valves made from tissue were gaining in popularity based on studies finding them to be more durable than originally thought, a trend that ran counter to SJM's strength in mechanical valves.

DIFFICULTIES, LITIGATION, MANAGEMENT SHAKEUP

St. Jude Medical had some difficulty digesting the acquisitions of Ventritex and Telectronics. This led to slower than expected revenue growth and reduced profits, the latter stemming in part from special acquisition-related charges of $52.9 million in 1996 and $58.7 million in 1997. By 1998, revenues had surpassed the $1 billion mark for the first time, specifically totaling $1.02 billion, while the net profit figure of $129.1 million translated into a 12.7 percent profit margin. Most of the profits, however, were being generated by the mainstay heart-valve operations, which accounted for only about 30 percent of overall revenues.

The company also had to contend with a lawsuit filed by rival heart device maker Guidant Corporation, which had been spun off from Eli Lilly earlier in the decade. Guidant had sued SJM in November 1996, alleging patent infringement in regard to ICD patents licensed by Guidant to Telectronics in 1994. Essentially, Guidant disputed SJM's claim that it had obtained access to the patents when it acquired Telectronics. In August 2000 an arbitrator ruled that SJM had failed to purchase enough assets from Pacific Dunlop for the patent licenses to be transferred, thereby reviving Guidant's original patent infringement lawsuit against St. Jude Medical. In July 2001 a federal jury delivered a verdict favoring Guidant, awarding $140 million in damages. A federal judge early the next year, however, overturned the verdict, and the matter remained in the court system deep into the decade.

Meanwhile, management changes were taking place at the company, which was feeling pressure from shareholders because of its poor performance compared to such rivals as Medtronic and Guidant. In January 1998 Fred Parks was named president and chief operating officer and appeared headed for the CEO position. However, Parks, who had been hired away from EG&G Inc., a Massachusetts-based electronics company, left SJM in March 1999 when Terry L. Shepherd was named president and CEO. Shepherd, who had worked alongside Matricaria at Eli Lilly, had headed SJM's Heart Valve Division. Matricaria remained St. Jude Medical's chairman.

In Shepherd's first year at the helm, St. Jude Medical made two significant acquisitions. In March 1999 the company spent $167 million in cash for the Angio-Seal unit of Tyco International Ltd. Angio-Seal, which was integrated into the Daig Division, produced vascular sealing devices used to help seal the punctures in leg arteries that are created by catheters during angioplasty, a procedure used to clear blockages in heart arteries. SJM in September 1999 acquired Vascular Science Inc. for $80 million in cash and $20 million in milestone payments tied to product development goals. A privately held firm based in St. Paul, Vascular Science was developing a device designed to enable surgeons to perform coronary-artery-bypass surgery without using sutures. In connection with these acquisitions, St. Jude Medical in 1999 took charges totaling $115.2 million for purchased in-process research and development and an additional $9.8 million for a restructuring of European operations.

SILZONE RECALL AND LITIGATION

SJM got off to a rough start in 2000. In January the company voluntarily recalled some of its mechanical heart valves, after finding that ones which had been coated with an infection-preventing substance called Silzone had a high frequency of blood leakage. About 36,000 of the valves had been implanted since the coating was introduced in 1997, and St. Jude Medical announced that it would no longer use the Silzone coating. Lawsuits were quickly filed in connection with the potentially defective device, and eventually a number of U.S.-based suits seeking class-action status were consolidated into one case. Although SJM was well protected by product-liability insurance, the quantity of Silzone cases was such that it was forced to set aside tens of millions of dollars for costs not covered by this insurance. As was the case with the Guidant litigation, a number of Silzone cases, including the U.S. class-action suit, were still pending as the end of the first decade of the 21st century neared.

Later in 2000, meanwhile, SJM alerted doctors worldwide about possible problems with several of its pacemaker models. The problems were believed to affect a small number of the pacemakers and involved electronic and mechanical malfunctions. On the brighter side, in late 2000 St. Jude Medical won FDA approval for its first dual-chamber defibrillator, the Photon DR. Dual-chamber ICDs, which worked on both the lower and upper chambers of the heart, were gaining popularity among doctors at the expense of single-chamber models, and SJM had been beaten to market in this burgeoning sector by archrivals Medtronic and Guidant. Also in late 2000 came FDA approval of SJM's Integrity Micro AutoCapture Pacing System, which was noteworthy for being the world's smallest dual-chamber pacemaker. In January 2001 Daniel J. Starks was named president and COO of St. Jude Medical, having previously headed the Cardiac Rhythm Management Division and thereby playing a key role in the development of the newly approved Photon and Integrity products.

In 2001 and 2002 SJM leveraged a rapidly growing market for ICDs to spectacular effect, registering record net income of $276.3 million by 2002 on revenues of $1.59 billion, also an all-time high. By this time the company's cardiac rhythm management products were responsible for about 80 percent of sales. Unfortunately, both Medtronic and Guidant had beaten SJM to the market with cardiac resynchronization therapy (CRT) devices, used to treat patients suffering from heart failure. At the time, this was the fastest-growing segment of the cardiac rhythm management device market. In 2004 SJM gained FDA approval for and brought to market its first CRT devices.

A top management handover also occurred in 2004. Shepherd retired, having led St. Jude Medical through a five-year period of stellar growth highlighted by a doubling of revenues and a more than fourfold increase in the firm's stock price. Starks succeeded Shepherd as chairman, president, and CEO. Among other developments in 2004, Starks substantially bolstered SJM's atrial fibrillation business through a series of acquisitions and investments and then combined these ventures within an Atrial Fibrillation Division, which began operations in January 2005. A Cardiology Division was created at this time to concentrate the further development of the company's vascular closure business, the market leader. Later in 2005 SJM acquired Velocimed, LLC, a maker of heart-surgery devices headquartered in Maple Grove, Minnesota. Velocimed's product lineup included the Venture catheter and Premere, a device for closing a small hole in the heart.

2005: EXPANDING INTO NEUROMODULATION SYSTEMS

In November 2005 St. Jude Medical expanded outside the cardiovascular device market for the first time through the $1.35 billion acquisition of Advanced Neuromodulation Systems, Inc. (ANS). Based in Plano, Texas, ANS specialized in the nascent area of neuromodulation systems, implantable devices used to treat chronic pain or other conditions by delivering electrical current directly to targeted nerves. At the time of the acquisition, ANS had already brought to market a system to treat chronic back and leg pain called Eon and was investigating the use of neuromodulation for the treatment of such maladies as Parkinson's, migraines, depression, obsessive-compulsive disorder, and obesity. In a market in which overall annual sales were estimated at $1 billion, ANS had held the number two position behind Medtronic.

Also in 2005, SJM took advantage of a wounded Guidant to push its share of the cardiac defibrillator market up from around 12 percent to more than 20 percent. Guidant was the subject of a takeover battle between Johnson & Johnson and Boston Scientific Corporation (eventually won by the latter), and it had also been forced into a huge recall of its ICDs because of potential safety problems. In 2006, however, SJM felt the effects of a weak market for ICDs in the United States as the Guidant recall and another by Medtronic led many doctors and patients to shy away from the devices. Strong growth for its atrial fibrillation and neuromodulation devices enabled SJM to nevertheless post a 13.3 percent gain in revenues, to $3.3 billion. The company also benefited from its strong commitment to research and development. SJM's 2006 R&D budget amounted to 13 percent of net sales. Among the new products introduced that year was the Merlin Patient Care System, a portable computer designed to help physicians more easily program and analyze data from their patients' ICDs and pacemakers.

St. Jude Medical maintained its torrid pace of new product introductions in 2007, debuting more than 20 new ICD and pacemaker products. Among these were the Current and Promote ICDs, which were embedded with radio-frequency wireless capability to more easily and securely "communicate" with the computers physicians used to program the devices and download data from them. Current and Promote were also built on SJM's new Unity platform, a consolidated hardware and software platform that was to be used for many of the company's subsequent ICDs, pacemakers, and heart-failure devices. By using this single platform, SJM hoped to speed up the introduction of both new products and new features in existing products.

Despite a still sluggish ICD market, SJM enjoyed across-the-board growth in all of the major segments of its business in 2007, with overall net sales up 14.4 percent, to $3.78 billion. The net earnings of $559 million, however, represented a gain of only 2 percent over the previous year thanks in part to a variety of special charges adding up to an after-tax total of $92.9 million. Seeking further growth outside ICDs, St. Jude Medical in early 2008 received FDA approval to launch its first clinical trial of a neuromodulation device to treat depression. In July 2008 SJM ventured deeper into the atrial fibrillation market by acquiring EP MedSystems, Inc., of West Berlin, New Jersey, for roughly $91 million in cash and stock. The deal marked SJM's entry into the rapidly growing market for intracardiac ultrasound echocardiography (ICE) devices. EP MedSystems' ICE products were used to provide live visualization of devices and anatomy during catheter-based procedures in electrophysiology and interventional cardiology procedures. Going forward, St. Jude Medical was likely to seek additional acquisitions to broaden its position in its core markets while maintaining a strong commitment to developing new products internally.

Heidi Feldman
Updated, David E. Salamie

PRINCIPAL SUBSIDIARIES

Pacesetter, Inc.; St. Jude Medical S.C., Inc.; St. Jude Medical Europe, Inc.; St. Jude Medical Canada, Inc.; St. Jude Medical (Shanghai) Co., Ltd.; St. Jude Medical Australia Pty., Ltd.; St. Jude Medical Brasil, Ltda. (Brazil); St. Jude Medical, Atrial Fibrillation Division, Inc.; St. Jude Medical Colombia, Ltda.; St. Jude Medical ATG, Inc.; St. Jude Medical (Thailand) Co., Ltd.; Irvine Biomedical, Inc.; St. Jude Medical, Cardiology Division, Inc.; St. Jude Medical Argentina S.A.; Advanced Neuromodulation Systems, Inc.; SJM International, Inc.; St. Jude Medical Luxembourg S.à r.l.; St. Jude Medical Nederland B.V. (Netherlands); St. Jude Medical AB (Sweden); SJM Coordination Center BVBA (Belgium); St. Jude Medical Holdings B.V. (Netherlands); St. Jude Medical Japan Co., Ltd.; St. Jude Medical India Private Limited; St. Jude Medical (Singapore) Pte. Ltd.; St. Jude Medical (Malaysia) Sdn Bhd; St. Jude Medical Taiwan Co.; St. Jude Medical Korea YH; St. Jude Medical (Hong Kong) Limited; St. Jude Medical Sweden AB; St. Jude Medical Danmark A/S (Denmark); St. Jude Medical (Portugal) - Distribuição de Produtos Médicos, Lda.; St. Jude Medical Export Ges.m.b.H. (Austria); St. Jude Medical Medizintechnik Ges.m.b.H. (Austria); St. Jude Medical Italia S.p.A. (Italy); St. Jude Medical Belgium; St. Jude Medical España S.A. (Spain); St. Jude Medical France S.A.S.; St. Jude Medical Finland Oy; St. Jude Medical Sp.zo.o. (Poland); St. Jude Medical GmbH (Germany); St. Jude Medical Kft (Hungary); St. Jude Medical UK Limited; St. Jude Medical (Schweiz) AG (Switzerland); UAB "St. Jude Medical Baltic" (Lithuania); St. Jude Medical Norway AS.

PRINCIPAL DIVISIONS

ANS Division; Atrial Fibrillation Division; Cardiac Rhythm Management Division; Cardiovascular Division; International Division; U.S. Division.

PRINCIPAL COMPETITORS

Medtronic, Inc.; Boston Scientific Corporation; Abbott Laboratories; CarboMedics Inc.; ATS Medical, Inc.; Edwards Lifesciences Corporation.

FURTHER READING

Alexander, Steve, "St. Jude to Buy Houston Company: First Will Spend $84 Million for Cyberonics," *Minneapolis Star Tribune,* April 9, 1996, p. 1D.

———, "The Wait Is Over: St. Jude Announces Big Acquisition," *Minneapolis Star Tribune,* June 29, 1994, p. 1D.

Barker, Robert, "All Heart: Examining a Bitter Corporate Feud," *Barron's,* February 11, 1985, pp. 14–30.

Burton, Thomas M., "St. Jude Medical Agrees to Acquire Ventritex," *Wall Street Journal,* October 24, 1996, p. B4.

———, "St. Jude Medical's CEO to Step Down in the Wake of Disappointing Results," *Wall Street Journal,* March 3, 1999, p. B17.

———, "St. Jude to Buy Siemens Cardiac Pacemaker Lines," *Wall Street Journal,* June 28, 1994, pp. A3, A8.

———, "St. Jude to Diversify with Acquisition," *Wall Street Journal,* October 17, 2005, p. A9.

———, "Some Pacemakers Are Defective, St. Jude Says in Letter to Doctors," *Wall Street Journal,* February 16, 2000, p. B7.

Cochran, Thomas N., "Heartening Prospects," *Barron's,* June 6, 1988, p. 60.

David, Gregory E., "Heart to Heart: Crosstown Rivals Medtronic and St. Jude Fight to Keep the World's Blood Flowing," *Financial World,* September 1, 1994, pp. 22–24.

Dorfman, John R., "St. Jude Medical Shares Will Reap Rewards for Long Term Investors, Some Managers Say," *Wall Street Journal,* January 17, 1994, p. C2.

Feder, Barnaby J., "Defibrillator Maker Props Up Stress Test Company," *New York Times,* March 22, 2007, p. C9.

———, "With the Spotlight on a Rival, St. Jude Medical Shines," *New York Times,* January 13, 2006, p. C1.

Fiedler, Terry, "Approval for Defibrillator Puts St. Jude in Big Market," *Minneapolis Star Tribune,* October 31, 2000, p. 1D.

———, "Fast Seal, Faster Healing," *Minneapolis Star Tribune,* May 6, 2002, p. 1D.

———, "A Perfectible Heart," *Minneapolis Star Tribune,* October 3, 2002, p. 1D.

———, "St. Jude Buys Local Firm with New Product," *Minneapolis Star Tribune,* September 10, 1999, p. 1D.

———, "St. Jude Buys Vascular-Seal Company," *Minneapolis Star Tribune,* February 6, 1999, p. 1D.

———, "St. Jude Issues Second Product Warning in Month," *Minneapolis Star Tribune,* February 17, 2000, p. 3D.

———, "St. Jude Makes Some Deals," *Minneapolis Star Tribune,* October 24, 1996, p. 1D.

———, "St. Jude Recalls Valves That Pose Risk of Leak," *Minneapolis Star Tribune,* January 25, 2000, p. 1D.

———, "St. Jude to Restructure, Hire President, COO," *Minneapolis Star Tribune,* May 17, 1997, p. 1D.

Forsyth, Randall W., "Too Good to Last?" *Barron's,* January 6, 1992, p. 35.

Gianturco, Michael, "Go with the Greats," *Forbes,* July 19, 1993.

Matricaria, Ronald A., "Diversification Process Developed at St. Jude," *Minneapolis Star Tribune,* December 26, 1994, p. 3D.

Metzler, Melissa, "One-Time Charges Hurt St. Jude's Bottom Line," *Minneapolis–St. Paul CityBusiness,* July 7, 2000, p. S39.

Miller, James P., "St. Jude Medical to Acquire Daig for $427 Million," *Wall Street Journal,* January 31, 1996, p. B3.

Moore, Janet, "The Fast Track to Being No. 2: The New Head of St. Jude's Defibrillator Business Hopes to Overtake Boston Scientific in the $5.7 Billion Market," *Minneapolis Star Tribune,* August 27, 2007, p. 1D.

———, "St. Jude Earnings Fall, but Sales Rise," *Minneapolis Star Tribune,* January 24, 2008, p. 2D.

———, "St. Jude to Test Antidepressant," *Minneapolis Star Tribune,* February 8, 2008, p. 2D.

———, "A Steady Pulse: St. Jude Medical's CEO Is Retiring, but All Bets Are on a Smooth Transition," *Minneapolis Star Tribune,* December 11, 2003, p. 1D.

Netzer, Baie, "These Health-Care Stocks Can Prosper Even in the Face of Cost-Cutting," *Money,* July 1990, pp. 55, 58.

Pitzer, Mary J., "The Bad Blood over a Heart Valve," *Business Week,* May 13, 1985, pp. 141, 144.

St. Anthony, Neal, "Diversification Starting to Pay Off for St. Jude Medical," *Minneapolis Star Tribune,* October 30, 1998, p. 1D.

"St. Jude Agrees to Buy Electromedics in $90 Million Deal," *Wall Street Journal,* December 8, 1993, p. C14.

"St. Jude Medical Picks Lawrence Lehmkuhl As President and Chief," *Wall Street Journal,* February 12, 1985, p. 47.

Twitchell, Evelyn Ellison, "Heartfelt Gains: But Is St. Jude Medical Fully Priced?" *Barron's,* November 20, 2000, p. 56.

Wyatt, Edward A., "The Mugging of St. Jude," *Barron's,* August 31, 1992, pp. 17, 25.

Zipser, Andy, "Heart's Content," *Barron's,* September 3, 1990, p. 34.

———, "Twelve Winning Months," *Barron's,* January 6, 1992, p. 34.

Salem Communications Corporation

4880 Santa Rosa Road
Camarillo, California 93012
U.S.A.
Telephone: (805) 987-0400
Fax: (805) 384-4520
Web site: http://www.salem.cc

Public Company
Incorporated: 1986
Employees: 1,177
Sales: $231.72 million (2007)
Stock Exchanges: NASDAQ
Ticker Symbol: SALM
NAICS: 515112 Radio Stations; 511120 Periodical Publishers

■ ■ ■

Salem Communications Corporation is a multimedia company catering to Christian audiences. Salem's core business is its network of radio stations. The company owns 96 stations in 38 markets that feature one of three formats: Christian teaching and talk, contemporary Christian music, and conservative news talk. The company owns the Salem Radio Network, a national syndicator of programming that serves approximately 2,000 affiliated radio stations. Salem operates Salem Radio Representatives, a national radio advertising sales firm with offices in a dozen U.S. cities. Apart from its radio assets, Salem owns Salem Web Network, a provider of online Christian content; Salem Publishing, a publisher of Christian magazines; and Xulon Press, a digital publisher of books written for Christian audiences.

THE TWO FOUNDERS

When Edward G. Atsinger III and Stuart W. Epperson decided to dedicate their careers to spreading Christian beliefs, Salem, from the Hebrew "shalom," or peace, became the vehicle for executing their plan. More than two decades separated the partners' start in the broadcasting business and their decision to form Salem, but the years were significant, nonetheless. Atsinger and Epperson met each other during the period, and each spent the time learning the nuances of the radio business.

For Atsinger, in particular, the years before Salem's formation provided invaluable training. In 1969, the 29-year-old took a sabbatical from Los Angeles City College where he worked as an associate professor of speech. He used the time and his personal savings to build a country-and-western radio station, WKBQ-AM, in Garner, North Carolina, a small community just outside Raleigh. The project proved to be a great test of his ability to attract listeners with the most modest of resources. Just before Atsinger secured his first radio license, the Federal Communications Commission (FCC) had passed what was informally known as the *suburban rule,* a piece of legislation that made Atsinger's first attempt at broadcasting exceptionally difficult. The FCC declared that if a suburban operator penetrated the corporate limits of an adjacent city with a five-millivolt signal or stronger, the suburban operator would have to meet the technical qualifications of serving the city. For

COMPANY PERSPECTIVES

Through the strength of our Christian Teaching and Talk format, the influence of our News Talk format and the growing popularity of our Contemporary Christian Music format, we are well-positioned to improve upon our leadership position in Christian and family-themed radio.

Atsinger, the suburban rule meant building a station with a relatively weak signal, forcing him to build a three-tower directional instead of a non-directional so that WKBQ-AM would serve fewer people. "This was a great training ground," Atsinger recalled in an October 1, 1994, interview with *Billboard.* "I had to build this thing myself. And when you can make it with a three-tower directional, 250-watt daytimer licensed to Garner, North Carolina, you can make it anywhere."

Epperson got his start in radio in 1946. His brother had built a radio station in the family farmhouse in Virginia, which the ten-year-old Epperson used to broadcast Bible verses he read. Roughly two decades later, he was building his own radio stations while Atsinger was teaching at Los Angeles City College. The two men met at Bob Jones University, a Christian college based in Greenville, South Carolina, and "did a lot of chatting about the radio business," Atsinger said in his October 1994 *Billboard* interview.

ACQUISITION OF FIRST PROPERTY: 1972

The discussions between Epperson, who married Atsinger's sister, and Atsinger led to a business partnership in 1972. They decided to buy a radio station together in Bakersfield, California. While they were in the process of negotiating the deal, an FM license in Oxnard, California, became available, which the partners also purchased. "FM was not the king of the road in 1973," Atsinger said in a December 27, 1999, interview with *Forbes.* "And Oxnard was not the center of the world." Within four years, Atsinger and Epperson decided to focus their existing properties and all future radio station purchases on religious programming. "I made up my mind early on that I would like to do a religious format," Atsinger told *Billboard.* "I felt there was a need there that wasn't being satisfied. I have always been active in the conservative evangelical community. I made a commitment that I was going to do it." The pair set out with a consistent and simple approach: "We identify this niche and target primarily the conservative Christian community, both Catholic and Protestant, and then we superserve that segment," Atsinger explained.

A DIFFERENT WAY OF DOING BUSINESS AND THE FORMATION OF SALEM

By committing themselves to a religious format, Atsinger and Epperson chased financial success in a way that differed from the goals pursued by traditional radio companies. Traditional radio companies generated nearly all their revenue from advertising sales; Atsinger and Epperson collected the bulk of their revenue from selling blocks of airtime to religious groups, operating in a manner similar to a television station that sells airtime to producers of infomercials. A need not being satisfied in the early 1970s would lead Atsinger to his primary customer: block-programming ministries, religious groups who could never find a steady way to proselytize and to evangelize. Radio stations frequently changed their formats, limiting the ability of religious groups to build an audience large enough to pay for airtime, which forced them to restrict their programming to small towns and to broadcast at the far ends of the AM band. Atsinger believed he could acquire radio properties in large markets and provide block-programming ministries with a consistent, on-air pulpit for spreading their message.

Such was the strategy underpinning Salem, which was formed in 1986, basing its operations in Camarillo, California. With Epperson serving as chairman and Atsinger serving as chief executive officer, Salem was created to become the corporate entity that would control the partners' radio acquisitions and their diversification into other media. The foray into non-broadcasting properties began not long after Salem was founded. In 1992, when Salem operated nearly two dozen radio stations, Salem Radio Representatives was formed, a company created to cultivate national spot advertising business for Christian radio. The following year, the company launched Salem Radio Network, an entity that produced Christian programming to be distributed to Salem-owned stations and to other religious stations.

PUBLIC OFFERING IN 1999

Salem's diversification would turn it into a multimedia company, but before the company blossomed in a variety of directions, its mainstay business benefited from two major impetuses of growth. The Telecommunications Act of 1996 allowed the company to own

KEY DATES

1986: Edward G. Atsinger III and Stuart W. Epperson form Salem to operate their Christian-oriented radio stations.
1992: Company begins diversifying into non-radio businesses.
1993: Salem Radio Network is formed.
1999: Salem completes its initial public offering of stock.
2002: After spending $300 million during the previous two-and-a-half years, Salem operates 83 radio stations.
2005: Salem acquires Christianity.com, its sixth, non-radio web site.
2006: Salem celebrates its 20th anniversary.
2007: Stagnant sales growth combined with a 50 percent decrease in net income undermines the company's reputation on Wall Street.

up to eight radio stations in a single market, freeing it to develop and to implement an aggressive acquisition strategy. The second driving force propelling expansion occurred in July 1999, when Salem completed its initial public offering (IPO) of stock, a roughly $200 million offering that gave the company a war chest to embark on a buying spree.

Salem owned 48 radio stations when it completed its IPO. The total was enough to rank the company as the largest religious radio broadcaster in the United States and as the nation's eighth largest radio broadcaster, regardless of format. In contrast to the small-town beginnings of Atsinger's and Epperson's radio acquisitions, Salem operated as a primarily metropolitan broadcaster, owning stations in nine of the ten largest markets and 14 of the 20 largest markets. Revenues for the company totaled nearly $90 million, more than half of which was collected from the approximately 100 religious groups that purchased block programming time from Salem, paying fees for a 26-minute slot that ranged from $30 for the Oxnard station to $800 for company-owned stations in Los Angeles and New York City.

DIVERSIFICATION WITH THE NEW MILLENNIUM

To its expanding network of radio properties, Salem added other ways to disseminate Christian-related content, further penetrating a market valued at $3.5 billion. In January 1999, the company purchased OnePlace.com, a Christian web site that became the foundation for its Internet company, OnePlace Ltd. Concurrently, Salem jumped into the publishing business with the purchase of CCM Communications, publisher of *CCM Magazine, CCM Update, Christian Research Report, Youthworker,* and *Worship Leader.* To these assets, Salem added Reach Satellite Network in February 2000. For $3.1 million, the company gained control of the Solid Gospel Radio Network, a satellite-delivered programming service with more than 115 affiliates throughout the country; Nashville, Tennessee, radio stations WVRY-FM and WBOZ-FM; and solidgospel.com, a web site. Significantly, the acquisition also marked the arrival of a new executive. Jim Cumbee, principal owner of Reach Satellite Network, was given responsibility for managing OnePlace Ltd. and the family of CCM Communication publications, later renamed Salem Publishing.

NEW FORMAT, "THE FISH": 2000

While Atsinger and Epperson shaped Salem into a multimedia company, they managed to keep their focus on the company's core business. The company's radio assets experienced tremendous growth in the very early 2000s, swelling in size following the IPO. Salem operated approximately 52 radio stations when it went public, a number that would nearly double within the next two years. As the number of Salem radio stations increased, the company began favoring a new format, contemporary Christian music, which was rising in popularity nationwide. In 2001, there were 163 radio stations programming contemporary Christian music, double the number of five years earlier. Of the 163 radio stations, 115 carried Salem Radio Network's syndicated, 24-hour format called *Today's Christian Music.* Salem also introduced a new format dubbed "The Fish," a live, localized version of the syndicated format aired on its own stations. In August 2000, KFSH-FM in Los Angeles was the first station to be re-branded as The Fish; a dozen more were converted during the ensuing two years.

The substantial increase in radio stations and the increasing use of the contemporary Christian music format began to change the way Salem made its living. The company became more reliant on advertisers for its revenue, as sales to block-programming ministries diminished. "Our advertising sales will gradually increase over the next few years because we have launched a number of music and talk stations that are 100 percent driven by advertising," a Salem executive explained in the January 29, 2001, issue of the *Los Angeles Business Journal.*

Salem was becoming more like a conventional radio station operator, a function of the rising mainstream popularity of Christian programming and a cause for some financial concern by the company. Although sales to block-programming ministries tended to generate less revenue than sales to advertisers, the relationship had shielded Salem from fluctuations in the economy. As advertising sales became increasingly important to the company, accounting for 55 percent of its revenue by 2001, Salem found itself suffering from the same problem affecting conventional radio station operators: a slumping advertising market.

PROBLEMS WITH WALL STREET

In the years leading up to its 20th anniversary in 2006, Salem's progress was highlighted by strong financial performance coupled with frustration over the company's image on Wall Street. Expansion of the company's radio network flattened out after 2003, hovering around 100 properties during the succeeding years, but it continued to expand in other areas. The company purchased its sixth, non-radio web site, Christianity.com, in 2005 for $3.4 million. Financial growth during the period would have seemed a source of confidence in the company, but its stock performance did not reflect a company in favor among investors. Between 2003 and 2006, Salem's revenue increased from $167 million to $206 million, while net income increased from a loss of $677,000 to a gain of nearly $19 million. The company's stock price cascaded downward, however, falling from more than $30 per share in 2004 to less than $19 a year later. "They've had an exorbitant number of start-up properties purchased over the past six months," an analyst noted in the May 30, 2005, issue of the *Los Angeles Business Journal*. "At this point they have more properties in start-up mode than I've seen in a long time."

As Salem celebrated its 20th anniversary in 2006, it continued to fret over its declining value on the market. During the first nine months of the year, its stock dropped 31 percent, dipping below $12 per share. The company held sway as the unrivaled leader in religious broadcasting, possessed an impressive portfolio of non-radio assets, but there were reservations about its ability to win over the investment community consistently in the years ahead. Flat sales growth in 2007 combined with a drop in net income from $18.9 million to $8.1 million only added to the skepticism on Wall Street. "The religious audience is large and growing," an analyst commented in the September 4, 2006, issue of the *Los Angeles Business Journal*, summing up the perception of Salem and its target market. "As the undisputed leader in religious radio broadcasting, Salem stands uniquely positioned for sustainable, industry-leading growth. But Salem's growth remains temporarily impaired. Until evidence of its recovery is uncovered, we fear, the stock will be stalled."

Jeffrey L. Covell

PRINCIPAL SUBSIDIARIES

Bison Media, Inc.; Caron Broadcasting, Inc.; CCM Communications, Inc.; Common Ground Broadcasting, Inc.; Inspiration Media, Inc.; Inspiration Media of Texas, LLC; New Inspiration Broadcasting Company, Inc.; NI Acquisition Corp.; OnePlace, LLC; Pennsylvania Media Associates, Inc.; Reach Satellite Network, Inc.; Salem Consumer Products; Salem Communications Acquisition Corporation; Salem Communications Holding Corporation; Salem Media Corporation; Salem Media of Colorado, Inc.; Salem Media of Hawaii, Inc.; Salem Media of Illinois, LLC; Salem Media of Kentucky, Inc.; Salem Media of New York, LLC; Salem Media of Ohio, Inc.; Salem Media of Oregon, Inc.; Salem Media of Texas, Inc.; Salem Media of Virginia, Inc.; Salem Music Network, Inc.; Salem Radio Network Incorporation; Salem Radio Operations, LLC; Salem Radio Properties, Inc.; Salem Radio Representatives, Inc.; Salem Satellite Media, LLC; SCA License Corporation; SCA–Palo Alto, LLC; SCHC Lubbock Application, Inc.; South Texas Broadcasting, Inc.; SRN News Network, Inc.

PRINCIPAL COMPETITORS

Clear Channel Communications, Inc.; CBS Radio Inc.; Radio One, Inc.

FURTHER READING

Bachman, Katy, "Christian Music Fans Tuning in to Salem," *MEDIAWEEK*, June 4, 2001, p. 13.

Boehlert, Eric, "Salem Builds Christian Radio Empire," *Billboard*, October 1, 1994, p. 73.

"Camarillo, Calif.-based Salem Communications Loses Revenue Following Attacks," *Ventura County Star*, October 8, 2001.

Crowe, Deborah, "Slowdown in Salem's Growth Means Downturn in Share Price," *Los Angeles Business Journal*, March 20, 2006, p. 39.

Freedman, Michael, "Articles of Faith: What Does It Take to Run a Religious Radio Empire?" *Forbes*, December 27, 1999, p. 281.

Hart, Mickey, "Getting Religion on the Radio," *San Fernando Valley Business Journal*, December 9, 2002, p. 6.

———, "Investors See Promise in Salem's Acquisition Strategy," *San Fernando Valley Business Journal*, June 10, 2002, p. 7.

Lowry, Tom, "Religion Rocks—So Sayeth Investors," *Business Week,* June 10, 2002, p. 122.

Maio, Pat, "Religious Broadcaster Hits Static in Plans to Continue Expansion," *Los Angeles Business Journal,* March 22, 2004, p. 35.

Nash, James, "Christian Broadcaster Runs into Some Skepticism," *Los Angeles Business Journal,* May 30, 2005, p. 32.

Price, Deborah Evans, "Salem Acquires Reach in Nashville," *Billboard,* February 26, 2000, p. 8.

Rathbun, Elizabeth A., "Salem Renders unto Caesar," *Broadcasting & Cable,* June 14, 1999, p. 91.

Riley-Katz, Anne, "Salem Radio Seeking Christian Music Stars," *Los Angeles Business Journal,* May 1, 2006, p. 15.

Russell, Joel, "Which Salem?" *Los Angeles Business Journal,* September 4, 2006, p. 15.

Sieroty, Chris, "Christian Media Company Targeting Growing Market," *Los Angeles Business Journal,* January 29, 2001, p. 51.

Weiss, Jeff, "Salem Beats Industry Rivals with Diversification," *San Fernando Valley Business,* February 28, 2005, p. 5.

Sapporo Holdings Limited

4-20-1 Ebisu
Shibuya-ku
Tokyo, 150-8522
Japan
Telephone: (+81 3) 5423-2111
Fax: (+81 3) 5423-2057
Web site: http://www.sapporoholdings.jp/english/

Public Company
Incorporated: 1949 as Nippon Breweries, Ltd.
Employees: 4,075
Sales: ¥449.01 billion ($3.93 billion) (2007)
Stock Exchanges: Tokyo
Ticker Symbol: 2501
NAICS: 312120 Breweries; 424810 Beer and Ale Merchant Wholesalers; 312130 Wineries; 312140 Distilleries; 312111 Soft Drink Manufacturing; 312112 Bottled Water Manufacturing; 531120 Lessors of Nonresidential Buildings (Except Miniwarehouses); 722110 Full-Service Restaurants; 722410 Drinking Places (Alcoholic Beverages)

■ ■ ■

Over the course of its more than 130-year history, Sapporo Holdings Limited has evolved from a government-owned beer maker into a multinational brewer with additional interests in wines and spirits, soft drinks, restaurants, and real estate. Along with Asahi Breweries, Ltd., Kirin Holdings Company, Limited, and Suntory Ltd., Sapporo ranks among Japan's "Big Four" breweries; it holds about 13 percent of the country's beer market, placing it neck-and-neck with Suntory for third place behind Kirin and Asahi. Among its brands in the Japanese beer market are the flagship Black Label and premium Yebisu Beer, and Sapporo also has entries in *happoshu* (a low-malt beerlike beverage) and so-called third-category beer, which contains no malt. As part of its partnership with the British firm Diageo plc, Sapporo Breweries also imports Guinness Irish stout into Japan. Overseas, the Sapporo brand is the best-selling Japanese beer in North America, where the company also gained a beachhead in the premium sector via the 2006 acquisition of Canada-based Sleeman Breweries Ltd.

LATE 19TH-CENTURY FOUNDING

Beer was introduced to Japan in the mid-1800s. The American primarily responsible for renewing trade relations with Japan, Commodore Matthew Perry, brought several cases of beer to Japan as a gift for the Tokugawa Shogunate. The beverage was so well liked that the Japanese government soon decided to establish a brewing industry. After an extensive search for a suitable area, wild hops were found growing on the island of Hokkaido, the northernmost island in the Japanese archipelago. As a result, in 1876 the commissioner-general for the development of Hokkaido founded Japan's first brewery in the town of Sapporo. (Coincidentally, the global beer capitals of Munich, Milwaukee, and Sapporo are all located along the 45 degrees north latitude.)

The original government facility was designed by the brewmaster Seibei Nakagawa, who had returned to Japan after studying beer-making techniques in

COMPANY PERSPECTIVES

The Sapporo Group's management philosophy is "to make people's lives richer and more enjoyable," and we strive to increase stakeholder satisfaction by maintaining integrity in corporate conduct that reinforces stakeholder trust and by aiming to achieve continuous growth in corporate value.

We recently announced the Sapporo Group's New Management Framework which sets its sights on 2016, our 140th anniversary. In the past, plans have been grounded on the conditions current at the time the plan is conceived. In contrast, the New Management Framework envisions the company in the year 2016 and outlines the policies needed to make the changes required to achieve that vision.

Germany. The first product brewed in the factory was called Sapporo cold beer or German beer, and even some of the early labels were printed in German as well as in Japanese.

In 1886 the brewery was sold by the government to Okura-Gumi, a private trading company. One year later, Okura-Gumi itself was purchased by a group of Japanese businessmen, who then reorganized the brewing operations under the name Sapporo Brewery Ltd. A number of other breweries, which would soon figure prominently in Sapporo's development, also were started during this time, including Nippon Brewing Company Ltd., Osaka Brewery, Kirin Brewery Company, and Nippon Beer Kosen Brewery.

1906–49: THE DAI NIPPON ERA

In 1906 Sapporo Brewery, Nippon Brewing Company, and Osaka Brewery were amalgamated as Dai Nippon Brewery Co., Ltd. This process of amalgamation and consolidation continued for 20 years until, in 1933, Nippon Beer Kosen Brewery also was absorbed by Dai Nippon.

During the 1920s and 1930s Japanese militarists, implementing their plan to make Japan the dominant economic power in Asia, began to centralize the brewing industry. By 1943, the merger of all Japanese breweries was virtually complete: Dai Nippon and Kirin were the only two brewing companies left in Japan. In fact, the militarists were powerful enough to force the Sapporo division of Dai Nippon to establish joint ventures in the occupied territories of Korea and Manchuria.

At this stage, local markets were dominated by particular brands. Dai Nippon sold Sapporo beer in the region north of the Kanto district, primarily in Hokkaido. The company also manufactured Yebisu and Asahi brand beers; the former was popular in the Tokyo area and the latter in the Kansai area. Not surprisingly, because of the increased demand for beer (it was rapidly superseding sake, the traditional drink), its production continued throughout the war.

POSTWAR REVIVAL OF SAPPORO

The current structure of Japan's brewing industry originated after World War II during the U.S. occupation. In 1949 Dai Nippon Brewery, which had cornered nearly 70 percent of the beer market in Japan, was divided into Nippon Breweries, Ltd., and Asahi Breweries, Ltd. Initially, Nippon Breweries marketed beer exclusively under its own brand name; it was not until 1956 that beer displaying the Sapporo label was reintroduced.

Nippon's growth during the postwar period, primarily because of an expanding product line, was impressive; from 1951 to 1981 production at the company's facilities increased by a factor of 15. During that same period, the brewery's sales increased from ¥20 billion to ¥330 billion, and its capitalization from ¥100 million to more than ¥14.1 billion. Supporting this growth was the construction of new breweries, in Osaka, in 1961; in Sendai, in 1971; and in Shizuoka, in 1980.

It was not until 1964 that Nippon Breweries changed its name to Sapporo Breweries Limited. Shortly thereafter, arrangements were made to merge the Sapporo and Asahi breweries. By this time they had become the second and third largest breweries, respectively, in Japan. (Kirin had captured the largest share of the domestic beer market.) The merger never materialized, however.

The formation of a joint venture with Guinness plc, called Sapporo-Guinness, also took place in 1964. This agreement led to the sale of Irish stout in Japan. By 1976 the consumption of stout beer had risen dramatically and a sales war ensued with the Kirin brewery, which had its own version of the beverage. Even though the cost of Guinness's product was twice that of Kirin's, Sapporo managed to maintain about 45 percent of the domestic stout market by relying heavily on Guinness's quality image.

In 1971 Sapporo reintroduced Yebisu Beer to the market as a premium 100 percent barley beer. That same year Sapporo entered the wine market when it formed a joint venture with Mitsui and Company Ltd. to import both wine and liquor. Sapporo Liquor

KEY DATES

1876: Japan's first brewery is built in Sapporo by the government.
1886: Government sells the brewery to a private trading company.
1887: Group of Japanese businessmen buy the brewery and reorganize it as Sapporo Brewery Ltd.
1906: Sapporo Brewery, Nippon Brewing Company, and Osaka Brewery are amalgamated as Dai Nippon Brewery Co., Ltd.
1949: Dai Nippon is divided into Nippon Breweries, Ltd., and Asahi Breweries, Ltd.; Nippon Breweries is the successor to Sapporo Brewery but initially markets only Nippon Beer.
1956: Sapporo Beer is reintroduced into the Japanese market.
1964: Nippon Breweries changes its name to Sapporo Breweries Limited; through a joint venture with Guinness plc, the company begins selling Guinness Irish stout in Japan.
1971: Yebisu Beer is reintroduced as a premium, all-barley beer; company enters the wine market as an importer.
1976: Production of wine begins at the Katsunuma Winery, west of Tokyo.
1977: Company introduces the first draft beer, Sapporo Black Label.
1984: The company's first foreign subsidiary is established in the United States.
1994: Sapporo-developed Yebisu Garden Place, a downtown Tokyo office complex featuring retail outlets and condominiums, opens and becomes the company's new headquarters.
1995: Guinness (later Diageo plc) begins contract production of Sapporo Premium Lager for European distribution.
2003: Company reorganizes into a holding company as Sapporo Holdings Limited.
2004: Sapporo introduces Draft One, the first entrant in third-category beer.
2006: Canadian premium beer maker Sleeman Breweries Ltd. is acquired.

Company Ltd. first began to import Nicolas, Hoch, and Melini wines. The company then started to produce its own wines at the Katsunuma Winery west of Tokyo in 1976; its Polaire brand of wine eventually would include the top five best-sellers in Japan. After the Okayama Winery was established in 1984, a wine cooler, a sparkling wine, and Hyosai, a white brandy, also were added to the growing domestically produced beverage line. In addition, the Sapporo Liquor Company imported Bailey's Irish Cream, Bombay Gin, Green Island Rum, and several scotches, including J&B Rare, Dunhill, Knockando, and Spay Royal.

First established in 1908, Sapporo's research and development division was created to breed varieties of barley and hops especially suited to Japan's climate. In the mid-1970s the Sapporo laboratory developed a technique for the ceramic filtration of beer. Since the introduction of pasteurization in the early part of the 20th century, beer had been sterilized by means of a heating process. This was necessary because the yeast residue in beer rendered it unsuitable for extended storage or long-distance transportation. However, the problem with heating beer was that the high temperature affected its flavor. Sapporo's unique ceramic filtration method removed the yeast residue from beer without having to heat it. The beer was filtered at a constant temperature of zero to one degree centigrade through a long ceramic cylinder; a thin coating of diatomaceous earth in the tube trapped the yeast residue. The first draft beer made with this new process went on the market in 1977 ("Sapporo Black Label"), and in 1985 the filtration technology was exported to South Korea and to Miller Brewing Company in the United States. Even so, Sapporo continued to pasteurize many of its products.

Throughout its history, rising prices for raw materials cut into company profits. Sapporo's supply of yeast came from a strain originally developed at the Sapporo laboratory. Although Sapporo brand beer was brewed exclusively in Japan, much of the barley and hops used in its manufacture was, historically, imported from Canada, Australia, West Germany, and Czechoslovakia. During the 1970s the Japanese government raised the brewery's already high costs by requiring them to purchase domestically grown barley; this accounted for 20 to 25 percent of the barley used in the entire industry. Originally intended to protect farmers who had switched from the cultivation of rice (which was in surplus) to barley, the domestic strain cost brewers 3.7 times as much as imported ones.

In spite of such roadblocks, Sapporo grew consistently. In fact, from 1985 to 1987 the company enjoyed record sales and earnings. Sapporo attributed its success to reduced materials costs, a decreasing interest payment burden, and effective management of surplus funds. Furthermore, the appreciation of the yen and the consequent lower price of foreign malt also helped boost results.

NEW MARKETS AND PRODUCTS, DIVERSIFICATION

As the Japanese beer market fast approached saturation in the mid-1980s, however, Sapporo sought new markets through geographic and product diversification. Having established distributorships in more than 30 countries around the world, the company founded its first full-fledged foreign subsidiary in the United States in 1984. The Sapporo brand quickly became the number one Japanese beer in the very large U.S. beer market.

While striving to maintain a premium image for its flagship beers, Sapporo catered to both ends of the Japanese beer market in the late 1980s and early 1990s. The company introduced the gold-labeled Yebisu Beer and the ultra-dry Kissui ale for the upscale market. Around the same time, it inked a contract with the U.S.-based Stroh Brewing Company to import a bargain-priced beer into the country. After five years of research and development, the company also launched "Drafty," a sparkling alcoholic drink that the company was able to offer at a low price, because of the product's low malt content, which incurred less tax.

In 1988 Sapporo's research and development department expanded into the propagation of rare orchids for sale in the United States, Europe, and domestically. In addition, the Sapporo laboratory conducted research in fields such as soft drinks as well as the application of beer yeast to the development of food seasonings and health food products. Sapporo scientists also investigated the utilization of recent discoveries in biotechnology to develop agricultural chemicals and pharmaceuticals.

The seeds of Sapporo's burgeoning restaurant empire were planted with the establishment of the brewery's first beer hall in 1899. By 1994, a beer hall division had grown to become Sapporo Lion Limited, a 180-location chain that contributed about 5 percent of the company's annual revenues and an incalculable amount to Sapporo's brand cachet. Echoing an American trend, the company began to develop several "brew-pubs" featuring boutique beers brewed onsite.

Having put its first soft drink, Ribbon Citron, on the market as early as 1909, Sapporo placed ever increasing emphasis on its nonalcoholic beverage line. By the late 1980s, this product segment included traditional and medicinal teas, Beans-brand canned coffees, and a variety of carbonated sodas and mineral waters. The company concentrated on introducing all-natural, wholesome drinks with fruit flavors and light carbonation in the early 1990s.

Although real estate still contributed only 6.5 percent of Sapporo's total annual revenues in the early 1990s, this segment was considered the cornerstone of the company's diversification strategy. Development activities took center stage with the 1994 opening of the Yebisu Garden Place, a downtown Tokyo office complex that featured retail outlets and upscale condominiums that cost the company ¥295 billion and took ten years to complete. The brewer proudly moved its headquarters to the new facility that same year. Yet far from abandoning its historical birthplace, the company redeveloped its first brewery into what it referred to as a "cultural mall," incorporating public services, retail, and leisure centers.

SEEKING OVERSEAS GROWTH LATE IN THE CENTURY

The second half of the 1990s were marked by expansionary moves overseas. In 1995 the company began exporting the Black Label draft beer to Taiwan. By 1997 sales had exceeded one million cases. In October 1995 the alliance between Sapporo and Guinness expanded. That month, Guinness (later Diageo plc) began contract production in Ireland of a beer called Sapporo Premium Lager. Sapporo contracted with Marubeni Corporation, a Japanese trading firm, to distribute Sapporo Premium in several countries in Western Europe. In 1997 distribution was expanded to Russia, Poland, and Sweden. In the U.S. market, the long successful Sapporo Draft brand was joined by Yebisu and Sapporo Black beer in 1996. Another key country targeted for growth was China. In December 1996 Sapporo established a joint venture with two of the leading breweries in Jiangsu Province, Jiangsu Brewery and Nangton Five Stars Brewery. The joint venture began producing Sapporo Premium Lager for local consumption in May 1998.

Back in Japan, the company's beer lineup underwent some changes. Black Label and Yebisu were steady performers, but Drafty was replaced first in January 1998 by Drafty Special and then in October 1998 by Bräu. The latter, like its predecessors, was part of a rapidly growing category called *happoshu,* or sparkling low-malt beverage. In producing *happoshu,* Japanese brewers were taking advantage of a quirk in the Japanese tax system, which taxed beer according to malt content. The tax on low-malt beers was significantly lower, resulting in a retail price about two-thirds that of a regular beer. Budget-conscious consumers, wracked by the lengthy Japanese recession, snapped up the lower-priced beer in increasing numbers, so that by 2000 the *happoshu* segment accounted for 22 percent of the overall beer market. (To maintain a beerlike taste, producers of *happoshu* used various types of malt substitutes.) Bräu, which was touted for its hops that were grown without the use of chemicals, found more success than either version of Drafty.

Sapporo's more aggressive approach to developing new brands could be traced to the heightened competition that characterized the Japanese brewing industry in the late 1990s. The beer market in Japan was maturing, Japanese consumers were developing more diverse beverage tastes, and the appreciation of the yen provided a pricing advantage to what quickly became an onslaught of imported beers from the United States and Europe. Sapporo's revenues declined in both 1996 and 1997; in 1997 the company posted its first net loss since its emergence out of Dai Nippon. This development was tied not to the company's struggling beer operations, but rather to an extraordinary loss of ¥29.4 billion from its securities holdings. In September 1998 Sapporo announced that it would reduce its workforce by about 1,000 by the end of 2001, in a cost-cutting and profit-enhancing move. The cuts were slated to be made through attrition, accelerated retirement, and a hiring freeze. Sapporo also planned to close two of its breweries in 2000 and a third in 2002. A further extraordinary loss tied to the slumping Japanese stock market led to a second straight net loss in 1998. Sapporo suffered another decline in sales in 1999, a 5.4 percent drop, but returned to the black, posting net income of ¥4.43 billion ($43.3 million).

EARLY 21ST-CENTURY INITIATIVES

The first years of the 21st century saw the Japanese beer market remain stagnant, with *happoshu* gaining a steadily larger share of the sector's sales, eventually as high as 40 percent. A price war in 2002 among *happoshu* producers was a key factor in a 73 percent plunge in Sapporo's net income that year, to ¥1.17 billion ($9.7 million). This poor showing prompted the company to close two more breweries, a plant in Sapporo with operations dating back more than a century and one in Kawaguchi in the Saitama prefecture. Sapporo also reorganized into a holding company structure in July 2003 as the parent company, under the name Sapporo Holdings Limited, assumed responsibility for four main operating subsidiaries: the beer-focused Sapporo Breweries Limited, soft-drink specialist Sapporo Beverage Co., Ltd., restaurant operator Sapporo Lion Limited, and Sapporo's real estate arm, Yebisu Garden Place Co., Ltd. Sapporo Lion's stock had been publicly traded on the Tokyo Stock Exchange, but Sapporo turned that firm into a wholly owned subsidiary via a stock swap as part of the reorganization. The subsidiaries gained more autonomy within the new structure.

During 2003 sales growth for *happoshu* products slowed as a tax increase on the low-malt beverages eroded but did not eliminate their price advantage over regular beer. Sapporo responded to this new market reality by creating the first entrant of what came to be called third-category beer. Draft One, a beerlike alcoholic beverage that made its Japanese national debut in February 2004, was produced from hops, protein from peas, and other ingredients. Because it contained no malt, it was taxed at a rate even lower than that of *happoshu*. Also in 2004, Sapporo centered its *happoshu* offerings on its flagship Namashibori brand. Brisk sales of Draft One helped Sapporo in 2004 post its first increase in net sales in several years as well as record profits of ¥4.64 billion ($44.6 million).

As competitors rushed into third-category beer and the overall beer market in Japan remained flat, Sapporo continued its drive into overseas markets, particularly North America, which accounted for around 70 percent of the company's foreign beer sales. By 2004 Sapporo had completed a switch from importation to local production of its beers for the North American market through a partnership with the Canadian beer company Sleeman Breweries Ltd. In October 2006 Sapporo significantly stepped up its North American penetration by acquiring Sleeman for approximately $260 million. Based in Guelph, Ontario, with a history dating back to 1834, Sleeman was the leading producer and distributor of premium beer in Canada. Overall, it ranked a distant third in its home market to the Canadian giants Labatt Breweries of Canada and Molson Companies Limited. The importance of Sapporo's international expansion became apparent in 2007 when the company created a fifth main subsidiary, Sapporo International Inc., to oversee further development of its overseas brewery business.

In March 2005 Takao Murakami was named Sapporo president and group CEO, succeeding Tatshusi Iwama. A veteran of the company's beer division, Murakami had played a key role in the development of Draft One. The new leader further diversified Sapporo's domestic product lineup via the April 2006 acquisition of the *shochu* distilled-spirit business of Kikkoman Corporation. Sales of *shochu,* a local spirit similar to vodka but specially distilled to remove all harsh flavors, had been on the rise since 1999. Also in 2006, Sapporo launched a new business plan that called for ¥10 billion in cost cuts and ¥70 billion in investments in research and development, acquisitions, and plant and equipment upgrades through the end of 2008.

FENDING OFF AN UNSOLICITED TAKEOVER OFFER

By 2006 Steel Partners, a New York-based activist investment fund led by Warren G. Lichtenstein, had become Sapporo's largest shareholder with a stake of around 18 percent. That same year, Sapporo adopted anti-takeover measures intended to thwart would-be acquirers. Nevertheless, in February 2007 Steel Partners made a proposal to take control of Sapporo by increasing its stake to 66.6 percent, offering ¥825 per share, which translated into a total price of ¥157.3 billion ($1.3 billion). Sapporo eventually rejected this proposal as well as a revised one set forth by Steel Partners in March 2008. In the revised deal, Steel Partners boosted its per share offer to ¥875 and also sought to increase its stake to only 33.3 percent. In the wake of the second rejection, Steel Partners expressed its lack of confidence in the abilities of the managers then running Sapporo and also recommended that Sapporo hire an investment banker to explore a possible sale of all or part of the company.

In the meantime, Sapporo in 2007 entered into an alliance with New York-based investment bank Morgan Stanley to attempt to maximize the value of its vast property holdings and expand its real estate business. For the year, Sapporo's real estate unit was its strongest business, thanks to strong demand for office space and rising rents amid solid economic growth in Japan. The real estate unit contributed more than half of the company's operating income and helped push net income to a record ¥5.51 billion ($48.3 million) on revenues of ¥449.01 billion ($3.93 billion). Early the next year, Sapporo shut down its oldest remaining brewery, located in Osaka and built in 1961. With the shutdown, the company aimed to increase the capacity utilization of its five remaining breweries in Japan at a time when its share of the stagnant domestic beer market was shrinking. During the first half of 2008, in fact, Sapporo managed to capture a market share of just 12.1 percent. This enabled Suntory and its 13 percent share to seize the number three position in the Japanese market for the first time since entering the field in 1963. Coming at a time when it remained under pressure from Steel Partners, this bad news on the market share front served to deal Sapporo a further psychological blow.

April Dougal Gasbarre
Updated, David E. Salamie

PRINCIPAL SUBSIDIARIES

Sapporo Breweries Limited; Sapporo International Inc.; Sleeman Breweries Ltd. (Canada); Sapporo U.S.A., Inc.; Sapporo Beverage Co., Ltd.; Sapporo Lion Limited; Yebisu Garden Place Co., Ltd.

PRINCIPAL COMPETITORS

Asahi Breweries, Ltd.; Kirin Holdings Company, Limited; Suntory Ltd.

FURTHER READING

Hall, Kenji, "Changes Brewing at Sapporo," *Business Week Online,* February 26, 2007, http://www.businessweek.com/globalbiz/content/feb2007/gb20070216_322024.htm.

Harney, Alexandra, "Sapporo to Cut Staff by 30 Percent," *Financial Times,* September 3, 1998, p. 33.

Kachi, Hiroyuki, "Sapporo Adopts Takeover Defense," *Wall Street Journal Asia,* March 30, 2007, p. 25.

———, "Sapporo in Tokyo Tie-Up with Morgan Stanley," *Wall Street Journal Asia,* October 31, 2007, p. 27.

Kachi, Hiroyuki, and Jamie Miyazaki, "Steel Partners Seeks Control of Sapporo," *Wall Street Journal,* February 16, 2007, p. A10.

Kanabayashi, Masayoshi, "Top Japan Breweries Expand Quickly to Tap China's Beer Market," *Asian Wall Street Journal,* March 27, 1997, p. 4.

Sanchanta, Mariko, "Bulging Property Portfolio Whets Steel Partners' Thirst for Sapporo," *Financial Times,* February 28, 2007, p. 28.

———, "Sapporo Reinforces Defences After Steel Partners' Move," *Financial Times,* December 1, 2006, p. 18.

———, "Steel Partners Sets Sights on Sapporo," *Financial Times,* February 16, 2007, p. 23.

———, "Steel Partners Sweetens Bid for Sapporo Stake," *Financial Times,* March 11, 2008, p. 22.

"Sapporo Beer Wants to Set New Challenges," *Yomiuri Report from Japan,* May 19, 1995, p. 3.

"Sapporo Unit to Buy Sleeman, Canadian Brewer," *Wall Street Journal Asia,* August 14, 2006, p. 3.

Segawa, Daisuke, "Sapporo Drafts More Customers with Draft One," *Daily Yomiuri,* December 20, 2004, p. 8.

Tanaka, Kazuo, *The History of Sapporo Breweries Ltd.,* Sapporo-shi: Hokkaido Shinbunsha, 1993, 226 p.

Selecta AG

Postfach
Murten, CH-3280
Switzerland
Telephone: (+41 026) 678 74 74
Fax: (+41 026) 678 74 44
Web site: http://www.selecta.com

Private Company
Incorporated: 1957
Employees: 5,000
Sales: EUR 700 million ($900 million) (2007 est.)
NAICS: 333311 Automatic Vending Machine Manufacturing; 423440 Other Commercial Equipment Merchant Wholesalers

■ ■ ■

Selecta AG is Europe's undisputed vending machine champion. The Murten, Switzerland-based company manages more than 150,000 vending machines, serving more than five million customers across 24 countries. Selecta does not manufacture the machines—which come from suppliers in Italy, China, and elsewhere—but instead purchases the machines and places them at the client's location. The company then services the machines, including money collection, restocking, and carrying out maintenance and repair. These services are handled by more than 5,000 employees from a network of more than 250 branches offices. Selecta supplies a variety of machines, ranging from smaller table-top vending machines to large-scale machines found in public places. The group's machines offer cold and hot drinks, snack foods, and merchandise. Machines are found at businesses and workplaces in the private sector, as well as in public areas, such as subway and train stations and schools, as well as in service stations. In response to growing criticism of the poor nutritional quality of many snack foods and soft drinks, Selecta has been forced to remove many of its machines from public schools. The company has also developed machine formats with more healthful food selections, such as the Vitalité line, rolled out in the Paris Metro and elsewhere, and featuring fruit juices, fruit salads and fresh fruits, and fruit purees. Other machines replace soft drinks with a selection of bottled waters. Selecta was acquired by German investment group Allianz Capital Partners in 2007. The company is led by CEO Justin Tydeman. In 2007, Selecta's total revenues topped EUR 700 million ($900 million).

AMERICAN SNACK FOOD INSPIRATION IN THE FIFTIES

Joseph Jeger was an employee at a company in Basel, Switzerland, when he was sent to the United States on a business trip in 1950. During the trip, Jeger encountered the automatic vending machine for the first time. Jeger quickly understood the potential of this new type of snack food dispenser, and obtained permission from his employer to install several of the machines at the company's factory. Jeger returned to Basel with five machines, paid for with his savings.

The machines were an instant success, and due to their constant use by the factory's employees, often required servicing. In particular, the machines' American

> **COMPANY PERSPECTIVES**
>
> Our goal is simple: to serve consumers and clients well. We do the most to give our consumers and clients the best experience, continually improving our services, developing new concepts and solutions and working hard.

origins meant that parts were difficult to come by, and needed to be refitted to European standards. Into the middle of the 1950s, Jeger opened a small shop in a garage in Murten, and hired an employee to help service the machines.

Before long, Jeger began refining the American-made machines' design, adapting them to Swiss standards, but also to Swiss snacking habits. This led to Jeger's first self-designed model, the Selecta, introduced in 1957. Jeger then incorporated the company under the Selecta name, and set out to expand the business throughout Switzerland. The success of the first hand-built Selecta design led Jeger to develop the company's own manufacturing capabilities and in 1959 Selecta acquired Schweizerische Automatengesellschaft, to produce the machines on a larger scale.

By 1960, Selecta had opened its first branch office, Basel, providing restocking and maintenance services to a growing list of clients in that Swiss city and the surrounding region. The success of the vending machine concept in the meantime had begun to inspire others to enter the market as well. A growing number of vending machine manufacturers appeared in Europe, accompanied by large numbers of vending machine services companies. Among these was the Compagnie Suisse de Distribution Automatique, which Selecta acquired in 1969, extending the company's reach into Switzerland's French-speaking region.

Selecta crossed the border for the first time in 1971, when it launched a subsidiary in Germany. At the time, the European vending market remained highly fragmented, with most companies focused on their individual markets. This began to change in the 1980s, particularly with the buildup to the creation of the European Union in the early 1990s. Selecta recognized the need to join with a larger partner in order to fund its own international expansion effort. In 1985, therefore, Selecta was acquired by fellow Swiss group Merkur AG (later Valora). That company, founded in Olten in 1905 as Schweizer Chocoladen & Colonialhaus, had grown into one of the country's leading restaurant and food groups, especially in the coffee segment. The acquisition not only provided Selecta with strong financial backing, but also with an impressive array of food brands to stock in an ever-growing network of vending machines.

CONSOLIDATING MARKETS IN THE EIGHTIES AND NINETIES

As part of Merkur, Selecta launched its European expansion drive starting in 1986. The company's initial target was the German market, where it led the consolidation of the highly fragmented vending machine sector. The company completed a bold string of acquisitions, buying nearly two dozen primarily local and regional businesses between 1986 and 1993, and achieving national scale in Europe's largest single domestic market. In 1994, the company restructured and merged all of its German operations. These were then reorganized into four regional divisions.

Selecta carried out a similar consolidation in Switzerland into the early 1990s. The company first bought Swiss-O-Mat in 1989. Following that purchase, Selecta added a second Swiss firm, Avag Betriebsverpflegungs, based in Zürich. By the middle of the 1990s, Selecta had solidified its position as Switzerland's vending machine leader.

By then, the company was also on its way toward becoming the European leader as well. Selecta's next stop was France, where it gained instant leadership of the vending machine market with its acquisition of that country's SAFAA in 1989. The following year, Selecta entered the Scandinavian markets as well, focusing especially on the Swedish market, where it acquired market leader Canteen in 1990. By 1994, Selecta had extended into Iceland, through a franchising partnership.

Selecta targeted growth in the Central European region at the middle of the 1990s. In 1995, the company established a new subsidiary for the Austrian market, then added operations in the Czech Republic and Slovakia starting in 1999. The group expanded its Nordic region operations as well. Selecta entered Finland in 1996, through the acquisition of a local company, then also extended its reach into the Baltic region. In that year, also, Selecta added operations in Belgium, creating a new subsidiary for that market.

PUBLIC OFFERING AND COMPASS TAKEOVER

With the growing expansion of its vending machine services operations, which accounted for nearly 80

KEY DATES

1950: Joseph Jeger returns from U.S. business trip with five vending machines.
1957: After modifying U.S. machines, Jeger establishes Selecta machine and company.
1969: First international expansion takes place in Germany.
1985: Company is acquired by Merkur (later Valora).
1989: Company acquires French leader SAFAA.
1997: Public offering allows Compass Plc to acquire 20 percent of shares.
2001: Company acquires 100 percent of Selecta; Selecta acquires Vendepac in the United Kingdom.
2007: Compass sells Selecta to Allianz Capital Partners for $1.5 billion.

percent of group sales into the late 1990s, Selecta had begun phasing out parts of its original Trade business. The company had ended its own production of vending machinery, instead sourcing machines from a variety of manufacturers, including Wittenborg, Wurlitzer, Electrolux-Zanussi, and others. Through the end of the 1990s, Selecta moved toward exiting the purchase and sale of vending machines, as its services offerings replaced these as the major part of the company's operations.

Selecta also developed new vending machine formats, including specialized machines first installed as part of a contract with the Paris Metro. The success of the Metro format then encouraged the company to introduce it into other markets. By the end of the 1990s, the company had gained contracts with subway systems in ten major European cities. Among these were Madrid, starting in 1998. That contract provided the springboard for Selecta's wider entry into the Spanish market, with the creation of a dedicated subsidiary that year. Two years later, Selecta entered Turkey, forming a joint venture there.

In the meantime, Selecta had taken on a major partner. In 1997, Merkur changed its name to Valora, then spun off Selecta in a public offering on the Swiss Stock Exchange. The offering enabled the newly formed European catering giant Compass PLC to enter the group's shareholding structure, with a 20 percent stake. While Compass, engaged in a highly aggressive acquisition drive to build its core catering and restaurant operations, initially denied its intention to take over Selecta, by the end of the decade it had purchased a further 13 percent stake in Selecta. Finally, in March 2001 Compass moved to take full control of Selecta, and the company removed its listing from the stock exchange.

Under Compass, Selecta's own growth accelerated into the middle of the decade. Already in August 2001, Selecta's new financial muscle enabled it to fill an important gap in its European network, through the acquisition of the United Kingdom's Vendepac Ltd. That acquisition gave Selecta control of the leading vending machine operator in the United Kingdom and Ireland. In 2003, Vendepac changed its name, becoming Selecta UK.

NEW OWNERS IN 2007

In the meantime, Selecta had continued to expand its European reach in its bid to become the region's outright leader. By the end of 2001, the company acquired vending machine companies and established its own operations in several new markets, including the Netherlands, Denmark, Norway, and Hungary. Through the middle of the decade, Selecta continued to add on to its network. In 2004, for example, the company acquired the Netherlands' number four vending machine operator, Koninglijke Olland BV.

A few gaps remained in Selecta's European network. In 2007, the company at least filled one of the largest of these, as it entered Italy through its purchase of that country's leader, GoExpress. In this way, Selecta expanded its total network to 24 countries, and the total number of machines under its control to more than 150,000.

The end of 2007 also represented another turning point for the company, as Compass Plc restructured its own holdings around its core catering and support services operations. This led Compass to sell its entire stake in Selecta, to German investment group Allianz Capital Partners. That deal was worth nearly $1.5 billion. With new owners, Selecta looked forward to its further expansion.

M. L. Cohen

PRINCIPAL SUBSIDIARIES

Selecta Deutschland GmbH; Selecta France SA; Selecta Sweden AB; Selecta UK Ltd.

PRINCIPAL COMPETITORS

Enodis PLC; Autobar S.p.A.; N and W Global Vending S.p.A.; Illy Caffè S.p.A.; Azkoyen S.A.; NSM-

LOEWEN Entertainment GmbH; Aimia Foods Ltd.; Sielaff GmbH; N and W Global Technology GmbH; Jede AB; Fountain S.A./NV.

FURTHER READING

Blackwell, David Harold, "Compass Fills Gap with £84m Vendepac Buy," *Financial Times,* July 24, 2001, p. 24.

Bourguignon, A., "Selecta, le Leader de la Distribution Automatique en Europe," *Distripedia,* November 12, 2007.

"Compass Attempts to Swallow Selecta," *Daily Mail,* February 13, 2001, p. 69.

"Compass Buys Top UK Vending Chain for $12M," *Nation's Restaurant News,* August 6, 2001, p. 50.

Muspratt, Caroline, "Compass Sells off Selecta and Returns £500m to Investors," *Daily Telegraph,* May 14, 2007.

"Selecta Posts 69% Turnover Rise," *Neue Zuercher Zeitung,* February 2, 2000, p. 13.

"Selecta Tests 'Healthier Fare' Vending Machines," *just-food.com,* October 19, 2005.

Walsh, Dominic, "Compass to Pay £374m for Control of Selecta," *Times,* February 13, 2001, p. 30.

skinnyCorp, LLC

4043 North Ravenswood Avenue, Suite 106
Chicago, Illinois 60613
U.S.A.
Telephone: (773) 878-3557
Fax: (888) 595-3258
Web site: http://www.skinnycorp.com

Private Company
Incorporated: 2000
Employees: 50
Sales: $30 million (2007 est.)
NAICS: 315999 Other Apparel Accessories and Other Apparel Manufacturing; 448190 Other Clothing Stores

■ ■ ■

SkinnyCorp, LLC, was created to house online projects launched by the founders of Threadless.com. The umbrella company controls ExtraTasty.com, a community web site that provides recipes for mixed drinks based on the alcohol, mixers, and garnishes the user has at home. YayHooray.com, another social network, provides forums that allow members to discuss how to create other community-driven web sites. Nakedandangry.com offers weekly contests in which users submit fabric patterns. Members vote on the designs and the winning pattern is used to manufacture a variety of items, such as sweaters, belts, pillows, and socks. SkinnyCorp's most successful project is Threadless.com, a web site that allows users to submit designs for T-shirts. After the winning design is selected by the Threadless community, the design is printed on T-shirts and sold to the public. Threadless also operates a retail store in Chicago, the first of a small chain of outlets planned by the company.

JAKE NICKELL AND THE GENESIS OF THREADLESS

When Jake Nickell was 20 years old, he could be found at one of three locations. During the day, he worked at CompUSA, selling computers and related items at one of the retailer's stores in Chicago. In the evenings, he was on the campus of the Illinois Institute of Art, where he was studying multimedia on a part-time basis. When not at work or school, Nickell usually was in his small Chicago apartment, sitting in front of his computer. There, he would spend hours on Dreamless.org, home of an online community for illustrators and programmers. The hours at CompUSA paid Nickell's bills, the hours at the Illinois Institute of Art promised the start of a career, but the time spent on the Dreamless web site proved most valuable, serving as the inspiration for Threadless.com.

Nickell chatted online with other Dreamless members, discussing ideas about web design on the web site's forums and playing what became known as "Photoshop tennis." The "serve" was the submission of an image, which two designers would manipulate with Photoshop software, passing their distortions back and forth, challenging each other to create the most intriguing image possible. Dreamless was an online haven for digital artists between 1999 and 2001, the period when Nickell religiously frequented the forums and the period when the idea for Threadless crystallized in his mind.

COMPANY PERSPECTIVES

This all started out as a hobby. We love coming up with ideas that turn into awesome communities that people can enjoy and benefit from using.

Fittingly, the concept for Threadless sprang from a T-shirt design contest. In 2000, Nickell was working on a design for a T-shirt he intended to submit in an online contest run by New Media Underground, an informal group of web designers based in London, England. Members of the Dreamless community voted for the best design, and they chose one of their own, Nickell. His design, three lines of gray text, was patterned after the layout of the Dreamless web site, which struck a chord among the Dreamless faithful who voted. For his efforts, Nickell won nothing—no prize money, not even a copy of his shirt—but the experience did enrich him in one, immensely valuable way. The contest planted the seed that grew into Threadless, an idea that soon led him to quit his job at CompUSA and abandon his studies at the Illinois Institute of Art. Within a few short years, he was giving interviews to *CNN, Business Week,* and *Inc.,* presiding as chief executive officer of one of the most fawned over businesses of his era.

A PLAN PUT INTO ACTION IN 2000

Nickell's idea was straightforward, but it sparked a phenomenal amount of interest from the titans of the corporate world and the sages of business theory. He thought about giving designers the opportunity to submit their T-shirt designs online, have members vote for the best design, and give the winner a small cash prize. More coveted than the prize money, as numerous winners would testify, the artist's winning design would be printed in limited-edition runs and sold to the public. Nickell discussed the idea with one of his friends on Dreamless, Jacob DeHart, a 19-year-old engineering student at Purdue University. DeHart loved the idea, matched Nickell's start-up capital of $500, and the pair hired a lawyer to establish their business, skinnyCorp LLC. They had enough money left over to print two dozen shirts.

Threadless.com, initially the sole asset of skinnyCorp LLC, held its first design contest in November 2000. Nickell and DeHart offered the winner two free shirts, production of a small batch of the winning design that would be sold online, and a promise that the proceeds from the sale of the shirts would be used to fund future contests. Tapping into the Dreamless community, they received nearly 100 submissions. After the voting concluded, Threadless offered the shirts for sale in January 2001, charging $12 per shirt. Orders flowed in, exhausting supply within days.

The response was encouraging, but not enough for Nickell or DeHart to commit all their time to their fledgling business. "It was just a hobby, a way for people to get their artwork out," Nickell said in an interview published in the June 2008 issue of *Inc.* Nickell and DeHart made their living as freelance web designers while the Threadless concept incubated in the online world, hosting regular contests that provided users with an automated rating system to score designs on a scale of one to five. "We had no idea what it would become," Nickell said in an interview published in the November 26, 2007, issue of *Business Week.*

FROM HOBBY TO FULL-TIME PURSUIT

Although Nickell and DeHart did not consider Threadless a full-time job, they did not only administer contests on their web site. They worked hard to spread the word of what their concept was about, using their contacts within the Dreamless community to create Threadless' own community. They developed the idea of "StreetTeams," which counted every Threadless member as one of its constituents. StreetTeam members helped promote the web site by helping themselves: If a member wore a Threadless shirt, photographed it, and uploaded the image on the Threadless web site, the member earned $1.50 for future purchases; for referring someone else who bought a Threadless shirt, the member received $3 in credit. Individuals in the community were encouraged to place a hyperlink on other web sites to connect to Threadless.com; members were given a unique StreetTeam Uniform Resource Locator (URL) to inform friends via email. The Threadless community responded enthusiastically. By 2008 a Threadless member, "Captain Oblivious," headed the pack, earning nearly $50,000 in credit toward purchases.

By 2002, Nickell and DeHart had more than an inkling that Threadless represented something beyond a hobby. They quit their jobs and devoted all their time to managing the electric growth of their business. At the end of 2003, Threadless generated $600,000 in revenue, counted more than 10,000 individuals as registered members, and enjoyed a profit margin that would have confounded any other marketer of printed T-shirts. The cash prize for the winning design in a contest, originally $100, shot up, reflecting the skyrocketing growth of

KEY DATES

2000: Jake Nickell and Jacob DeHart host their first design contest on Threadless.com.
2003: Membership in Threadless.com exceeds 10,000, pushing revenues to $600,000.
2004: Threadless.com boasts 70,000 registered users.
2006: A New York-based venture capital firm, Insight Venture Partners, acquires a minority stake in skinnyCorp.
2007: Threadless opens its first retail location, a 1,700-square-foot store in Chicago.
2008: More than 700,000 registered users form the Threadless community.

Threadless. Contest winners began collecting $2,500 for their efforts, but, for many, the real prize was exposure. "It wasn't so much the money," one contest winner explained in the June 2008 issue of *Inc.,* "It was how cool it was to get your shirts printed."

ATTRACTING THE ATTENTION OF MAINSTREAM RETAILERS

The popularity of Threadless mushroomed, becoming an Internet phenomenon. By the end of 2004, the Threadless community counted 70,000 members. In 2005, Nickell was courted by massive, mainstream retailers. Urban Outfitters, Inc., approached Threadless, asking to carry the company's shirts in the retailer's chain of 150 stores. Target Corporation sent Nickell a contract, several hundred pages in length, offering to sell tens of thousands of Threadless shirts in its stores and on its web site. Nickell shied away from both deals, fearing the spirit of the Threadless philosophy would be lost in the hands of major retailers. He did accept one offer in 2005, however, an invitation that showed Threadless had become something more profound than a wildly successful Internet company.

NICKELL IN THE IVORY TOWER

Nickell was invited to the campus of the Massachusetts Institute of Technology (MIT), asked to speak at a gathering at the university's Sloan School of Management. The invitation came from Eric von Hippel, a noted economist and head of the innovation and entrepreneurship group at the Sloan School of Management. In attendance, sitting in front of a somewhat bewildered Nickell, were a dozen executives from corporations such as General Mills, Pitney Bowes, Clorox, and Google, as well as a group of MIT researchers. During the late 1970s, von Hippel developed the theory of "user innovation," that the majority of product innovations were developed by the people who used the product, not by corporate research and development laboratories. Von Hippel argued that the conventional process of product development (market research, focus groups, testing, redesign, and retesting) was ineffective, a costly approach that largely failed to incorporate the needs and desires of customers. In Threadless, von Hippel found a prime example of user innovation in action. "They're the beginning of a new wave," he declared in the June 2008 issue of *Inc.* Nickell, in the same issue of *Inc.,* offered his perspective. "I think of it as common sense," he said, before asking, "Why wouldn't you want to make the products that people want you to make?"

Nickell had little time to reflect on whether Threadless stood on the vanguard of a new type of consumerism. Managing the company's frenetic growth was a more pressing matter, necessitating a substantial increase in his payroll, the establishment of a new main office, and responding to the wishes of his rapidly growing community of Threadless members. In 2006, he sold a minority stake in his business to a New York-based venture capital firm, Insight Venture Partners. Threadless ended the year with $18 million in sales, from which it earned a handsome return of roughly $6 million. Not long after Insight Venture acquired its stake, DeHart left Threadless, unwilling to expand the concept any further.

THREADLESS GETS PHYSICAL

Growth continued at a more than 200 percent pace in 2007, the year Nickell decided to establish the first Threadless retail store. "We really had no good reason to open a store," he said in an interview published in the November 26, 2007, issue of *Business Week.* "It just seemed like a fun thing to do." Despite his nonchalant attitude, Nickell did have at least one reason for opening the store, envisioning it as a promotional tool for the Threadless web site.

The store, like the company's business model, bucked convention. Located in Chicago's Lakeview neighborhood, the two-story, 1,700-square-foot shop, which opened in September, featured zinc panels, hardwood accents, and 20 flat-screen television monitors, the norm for any upscale retail outlet. What set the store apart from other retail establishments was the lack of inventory. A typical apparel outlet housed piles of clothing and racks of garments, offering customers a plethora of ways to spend their money. In the Threadless' Chicago store, apparel was conspicuous by its absence: There were roughly 20 shirt designs for sale on the lower level. The top floor was used exclusively to display artwork. Before opening the store, Nickell presumed it would lose money, but within six months the shop was generating a profit. Nickell, surprised not for the first time by the success of Threadless, began hatching plans for further physical expansion. He began arranging for a second Chicago store, Threadless Kids. He looked beyond Chicago, revealing his intention to open a store in Boulder, Colorado. Other cities were included in his expansion plans, promising the debut of Threadless stores in Austin, Seattle, and Minneapolis.

THE THREADLESS COMMUNITY IN CONTROL

As Nickell drew up his plans for the future, the popularity of Threadless continued its meteoric rise. From the beginning of 2005 to 2008, the number of registered Threadless members increased at a fantastic rate, leaping from 70,000 to more than 700,000. An apparel company with no designers, no photographers or models, no sales force, and no distributor, was recording jaw-dropping financial success. Profit margins exceeded 30 percent, revenues climbed exponentially, and nearly every product made by the company sold out: Threadless never printed a shirt that failed commercially because its customers had essentially ordered its production. "Threadless completely blurs that line of who is a producer and who is a consumer," Karim Lakhani, a professor at Harvard Business School, said in an interview published in the June 2008 issue of *Inc.* "The customers end up playing a critical role across all its operations: idea generation, marketing, sales forecasting." The arrangement worked in Nickell's favor, enabling him to look to the future with a degree of confidence few other chief executive officers enjoyed. His customers would lead Threadless in the direction they wanted, leaving Nickell at the helm to enjoy the ride.

Jeffrey L. Covell

PRINCIPAL SUBSIDIARIES

Threadless.com; ExtraTasty.com; YayHoorray.com; Nakedandangry.com.

PRINCIPAL COMPETITORS

The Gap Inc.; American Eagle Outfitters, Inc.; Pacific Sunwear of California, Inc.

FURTHER READING

Chafkin, Max, "The Customer Is the Company," *Inc.*, June 2008, p. 88.

"Consumer Driven Design: 'Threadless' Dot Com Is Inspired Ecommerce," *Internet Wire,* January 11, 2006.

Copple, Brandon, "Jake Nickell, 26, and Jacob DeHart, 24," *Crain's Chicago Business,* October 23, 2006, p. 74.

Gilmour, Maggie, "Threadless: From Clicks to Bricks," *Business Week,* November 26, 2007, p. 84.

"Insight Backs skinnyCorp to Aid in Growth of Threadless.com, the Highly Trafficked Apparel Design Community," *Internet Wire,* November 3, 2006.

Sonae SGPS, S.A.

Lugar do Espido Via Norte
Apartado 1011
Maia, 4471-909
Portugal
Telephone: (351 22) 948 75 22
Fax: (351 22) 948 77 22
Web site: http://www.sonae.pt

Public Company
Incorporated: 1959 as Sociedade Nacional de Aglomerados e Estratificados
Employees: 34,628
Sales: EUR 4.63 billion ($7.12 billion) (2007)
Stock Exchanges: Euronext Lisbon
Ticker Symbols: SOVT F; SONPL; SONP.IN
NAICS: 443111 Household Appliance Stores; 443112 Radio, Television, and Other Electronics Stores; 443120 Computer and Software Stores; 444110 Home Centers; 445110 Supermarkets and Other Grocery (Except Convenience) Stores; 448130 Children's and Infants' Clothing Stores; 451110 Sporting Goods Stores; 511110 Newspaper Publishers; 517110 Wired Telecommunications Carriers; 517212 Cellular and Other Wireless Telecommunications; 518111 Internet Service Providers; 531120 Lessors of Nonresidential Buildings (Except Miniwarehouses); 531312 Nonresidential Property Managers; 551112 Offices of Other Holding Companies

Sonae SGPS, S.A., is the largest private employer in Portugal. A holding company, it owns both food and nonfood retail chains in Portugal and a half-share in one of the nation's leading telecommunications companies. Sonae also has a half-share in a real estate development company that owns and manages shopping centers in several European countries. Sonae's chairman, the dynamic entrepreneur Belmiro Mendes de Azevedo, owns more than half of the company's shares and is Portugal's richest individual.

FROM MANUFACTURING TO RETAIL: 1959–90

Sociedade Nacional de Aglomerados e Estratificados, or Sonae, was founded by Afonso Pinto de Magalhães in 1959 in Maia, Portugal, a suburb of Oporto. Azevedo, the son of a carpenter in a nearby village, joined the firm in 1965, two years after earning a degree in chemical engineering. He had made a name for himself as a handball player at the sports club where Magalhães was president. Sonae was engaged in making high-pressure decorative laminate wood products but had fewer than 60 employees and was technically bankrupt. Within three years of becoming its general manager, Azevedo was able to make it profitable. Over the next two decades the company expanded not only into the manufacture and export of wood-based panels but to related areas such as chemicals and resins.

When Banco Pinto de Magalhães was formed in 1972, Azevedo became its administrator. In spite of his gifts and ambition, he might not have risen much further except for the socialist revolution of 1974 and its

KEY DATES

1959: Sonae is founded as a small firm that manufactures decorative laminated wood products.
1982: Sonae enters food retailing by purchasing a supermarket chain.
1984: Belmiro de Azevedo takes effective control of the company.
1988: Sonae has become Portugal's largest private enterprise.
1991: Sonae launches what becomes an international shopping center and parking lot operator.
1998: Sonae introduces Optimus, a mobile phone company.
2001: Sonae's shares have lost four-fifths of their value as the dot-com boom ends.
2005: Company's wood-panel business, biggest in the world, is spun off.
2007: Company spins off Sonae Capital, its subholding for miscellaneous enterprises.

consequent upheaval of the Portuguese economy. Magalhães fled to Brazil in 1975 and did not return until at least five years later. His bank was nationalized, his heirs proved incapable of dealing with the situation, and somehow Azevedo came to the fore, in what a profile of the entrepreneur called a complicated story, full of intrigue and suspense.

Azevedo bought his first few shares of Sonae in 1980. Magalhães, regarding him as indispensable, sold him 16 percent of the shares in 1983. Following the death of Magalhães the following year and by means of negotiations with his heirs, Azevedo raised his stake to 35 percent, effectively taking control of Sonae. By the end of 1988 Sonae was the biggest private enterprise in Portugal. Its revenues had grown more than fiftyfold in six years. It employed 8,000 workers in 70 enterprises. The company, Sonae Investimentos, SGPS, was majority-owned by Azevedo. He remained in control of the enterprise notwithstanding a legal dispute with the Pinto de Magalhães family, which in 1994 still held a 7 percent stake and at one point succeeded in suspending Azevedo's own shares.

Azevedo wanted to make Sonae a major European company, which he regarded as impossible within the confined wood-products area, but most of Portugal's industries were under government control at the time. He saw an opportunity, however, in the retail segment, which was divided into thousands of small stores, often family-owned. The fragmentation of the market meant high prices, which Sonae was about to undercut decisively. Azevedo established a subholding, Sonae Distribuição, which purchased the Modelo chain of supermarkets in 1982. Forming a joint venture with a French retailer, Promodès, S.A., Modelo opened Portugal's first hypermarket in 1986.

According to one of its executives, Modelo was extremely disorganized and suffered from high labor costs. Sonae, availing itself of Promodès' expertise, marketed the chain's products aggressively, with an emphasis on fresh produce. By 1990 there were 40 Modelo stores throughout Portugal, some of them franchised outlets. Four were hypermarkets: three under the Modelo Continente name, plus a Modelo Prisunic. Partly to ease supply problems, Sonae established a service company called Modis that transported the goods needed by the chain from three warehouses in major cities. Another joint venture with a French firm established Sodiscol, which furnished consumer products to hotels and restaurants. Mordomo was founded to offer such products directly to the home. Still another joint venture with a French enterprise brought Modelo into the field of selling furniture and electric appliances. In addition, Modelo took a minority stake in a Brazilian chain with 60 supermarkets in four states.

BRANCHING OUT: 1990–2000

Sonae Distribuição continued to grow during the next decade, outstripping all other retail food chains. However, in 1991 Azevedo decided to sell the Modelo supermarkets and concentrate on a new chain of Modelo Hiper mini-hypermarkets. Two years later, the government, deciding that the Hiper units would be too big, blocked Sonae's plan for these outlets, which were to be 2,000 to 4,600 square meters in size. Sonae adjusted: instead of opening an initial five mini-hypermarkets of over 2,000 square meters, it inaugurated 12 with selling space of 1,999 square meters.

Beginning in 1997, Sonae Distribuçāo acquired a Brazilian hypermarket chain and two supermarket chains. It also took part in such specialty retail ventures as Worten (electronics and home appliances), Maxmat (hardware), Modalfo (clothing), Sportzone (sports equipment), and Vobis (computer equipment). By 1998 it had over 200 retail units in Portugal and more than 100 in Brazil.

The entry of Sonae into real estate was logical for a conglomerate with a growing need for space, especially for its retail outlets. Accordingly, Sonae Imobiliária was created in 1991 to build shopping centers. As a pioneer in the field, it was able to open in choice locations, and within a decade owned or co-owned nine commercial centers, three malls, and a retail park. These facilities were intended not only to accommodate Sonae's Modelo units but also future retail activities of the group.

The first of these was CascaiShopping, a joint venture with the Brazilian enterprise Multiplan that was the first regional shopping center in Portugal. This was followed in 1992 by the smaller Coimbra Shopping. Between 1994 and 1996 Sonae Imobiliária introduced Via Catarina with a Dutch partner, Colombo with a Portuguese bank, and also launched Gala Shopping. The Sonae subholding also expanded into parking lot management and a series of shopping center projects in other European countries and Brazil.

Meanwhile, Sonae Indústria was making its mark internationally for its high-quality but inexpensive products. By the end of the 1980s it was the largest nonfinancial private company in Portugal. Then it began manufacturing in other countries, including Spain, Great Britain, and Canada. In 1993 this division took a quarter-share of Tafisa, S.A., which was Spain's second largest producer of wood-based derivatives. Seeking diversity, it also formed an association with Japan's Sumitomo Forestry to supply wood products of medium-density fibers. By 1995 Sonae Indústria ranked second in the world in the manufacture of wood-based panels, and by 2000 it had some 50-odd plants in 15 countries. By then Sonae was the world's leading producer of wood panels.

As if Sonae was not diverse enough, it also encompassed an array of miscellaneous businesses that were placed under a subholding named Pargeste, SGPS. These enterprises, which were to be held only until ready for sale, included Interlog, SGPS, engaged in communications and information technologies; Público, S.A., publisher of a daily newspaper; SIRS, for Radio Nova; Prosa, a computer-selling business in which Apple, Inc., held a share; and several others engaged in engineering or tourism, travel, and leisure. Of the former, the most important was Contacto, which was voted best in the construction and public works field in 1995 by the business magazine *Exame*. Contacto, which had the English firm Wilmott Dixon as its minority partner, had as its main customer Sonae itself, for which it was building commercial centers. The latter enterprises included vacation properties, hotels, fitness centers, and travel agencies.

To manage his far-flung enterprises, which were exporting to more than 60 countries, Azevedo hired young business-school graduates and moved them around from one unit to another. In this way they received exposure to a range of functional and operational roles. "I believe that good management should leave room for a little bit of chaos," he told Peter Collis for an article that appeared in *International Management* in 1988. "If everything is too organized, innovation and creativity disappear." Azevedo urged his managers to upgrade their skills and teach others to do so. He himself spent as much as three months a year traveling to other countries and attending business-school classes and conferences abroad. One result was that Sonae's supermarkets were the first in Europe to have a scanner at every checkout counter.

Sonae Indústria and Pargeste were spun off from Sonae Investimentos in 1996 into a new holding called Imparsa. However, in 1999 Imparsa and Pargeste were reincorporated into Sonae SGPS, S.A. (the former Sonae Investimentos). Azevedo said that the parent company would be the portfolio manager, while the subholdings would manage the businesses. "Most of the companies in Portugal are either our partners or our customers or our suppliers," Azevedo told David Lanchner for *Institutional Investor* in 2001. "That network helps all of our businesses."

SONAE IN THE 21ST CENTURY

Sonae's next move was into telecommunications. The holding company fielded three start-up enterprises in the late 1990s: Novis, a fixed-line telephone company; Optimus, a mobile phone company; and Clix, a free Internet service provider. These companies were placed in a new subholding named Sonaecom. Launched over Christmas 1998, Optimus had France Télécom SA as a partner with a 23.7 percent stake. An Optimus promotional campaign that invited people to be "pioneers" and wooed them with the promise of low-cost rates succeeded in signing up 285,000 customers in the face of two well-established rivals. Optimus had a market share of 16 percent a year later and 22 percent by late 2001. Like some other Sonae subholdings, Sonaecom had its own listing on the Lisbon stock exchange.

Sonae's revenues reached EUR 5.75 billion (about $5.18 billion) in 2000, with a net profit of EUR 255 million (about $230 million). Its share price more than doubled between late 1999 and early 2000. However, the dot-com boom was ending in Europe as well as the United States. The subsequent U.S. recession affected the global economy, leaving Sonae Indústria especially exposed to flagging sales. The share price of Modelo Continente (now the name of the retailing and distribution business) was affected by fears over its Brazil investments. The reorganized Sonae Turismo subholding of hotels, resorts, travel, leisure, fitness, and sports was continuing to lose money. By late 2001 parent Sonae's stock was worth only one-fifth of its peak value.

Sonae recovered from these problems in the following years. Sonae Immobilária became Sonae Sierra, and Sonae Turismo was absorbed into Sonae Capital, which was also engaged in construction, engineering, residential development, transport and logistics, insurance, brokerage, the auto sector, and other services. Sonae Indústria was spun off from the parent company in 2005, and Sonae Capital in 2007. In 2005 Modelo Continente sold its retail operations in Brazil but acquired 26 Carrefour stores in Portugal. Sonae Sierra opened shopping centers in Spain, Germany, Romania, and Brazil but sold half of its Brazil subsidiary. Modelo Continente became Sonae Distribução in 2007.

In mid-2007 Sonae owned 91 percent of Sonae Distribução, 52 percent of Sonaecom, and 50 percent of Sonae Sierra. Of its revenue of EUR 4.63 billion ($7.12 billion) in 2007, distribution accounted for 73 percent, telecommunications for 19 percent, and shopping centers for 6 percent. The year ended with 646 stores, including 124 Continente, Modelo, and Modelo Bonjour food stores in Portugal and 356 nonfood stores overall. Sonae Sierra owned 47 shopping centers in seven countries.

Fifty-three percent of Sonae's share capital belonged to Efanor Investments SGPS SA, a private holding company belonging to Azevedo, and 40 percent was in the hands of private individuals and institutional investors. Azevedo was chairman of the board of directors. He resigned as chief executive officer in 2007 and was succeeded by his son Duarte Paulo Teixeira de Azevedo.

Robert Halasz

PRINCIPAL SUBSIDIARIES

Sonae Distribução (91%); Sonae Sierra (50%); Sonaecom (50.1%).

PRINCIPAL COMPETITORS

Jerónimo Martins, SGPS, SA; Portugal Telecom, SA; Vodafone Group plc.

FURTHER READING

Anderson, Jamie, and Rob Goffee, "From Wood Panels to Mobile Phones: Strategic Diversification at Sonae Group," *Business Strategy Review,* Winter 2001, pp. 57–70.

"Big Fish in Small Ponds," *Economist,* December 2, 2000, Portugal supplement, p. 13.

Bryan-Low, Cassell, and Erik Burns, "Audacious Deal in Portugal," *Wall Street Journal,* February 8, 2006, p. C16.

Canha, Isabel, "Novo modelo vai chegar á província," *Exame,* July 1990, pp. 88–90.

Collis, Peter, "Portugal's Odd Man In," *International Management,* November 1988, pp. 50–51, 53.

"Europe's Most Powerful Families," *Euromoney,* May 1994, p. 78.

Guttman, Robert J., "Sonae: Portuguese Firm Discovers New Worlds of Profit," *Europe,* December 1999/January 2000, p. 27.

Lanchner, David, "Empire Unbuilder?" *Institutional Investor* (International Edition), August 2001, pp. 14+.

Mónica, Maria Filomena, *Os grandes patrões da indústria portuguesa,* Lisbon: Publicações Dom Quixote, 1990, pp. 109–34.

"The Portuguese Professor," *Economist,* May 11, 1996, p. 65.

Vasco, Rute Sousa, "Por Dentro do Império Sonae," *Exame,* December 1994, pp. 37–40, 42, 44, 46–48, and "De Candidato a Líder," pp. 50, 52.

Wise, Peter, "Dreaming at the Top," *Financial Times,* August 24, 1994, p. 9.

Sterilite Corporation

30 Scales Lane
Townsend, Massachusetts 01469
U.S.A.
Telephone: (978) 597-8702
Fax: (978) 597-0686
Web site: http://www.sterilite.com

Private Company
Incorporated: 1939 as UnitedPlastics
Sales: $200 million (2007 est.)
NAICS: 326190 Other Plastics Product Manufacturing

■ ■ ■

A private company based in Townsend, Massachusetts, Sterilite Corporation is the world's largest independent manufacturer of plastics housewares, relying mostly on injection molding technology. In the general storage category, Sterilite offers totes, lockers, storage boxes in a variety of sizes, underbed storage boxes, storage drawers, drawer carts, storage crates, and storage trays. Household products include laundry baskets, pails, and hampers. Sterilite's kitchenware products include food storage containers in a myriad of shapes and sizes, sink sets, dish pans, organizer trays, ice cube trays, bowls, pitchers, and tumblers. In the hardware category Sterilite manufactures shelving, cabinets, and other organizing products for use in the garage, basement, utility room, or attic. Seasonal items include storage boxes suitable for garden supplies or holiday decorations.

Sterilite products are widely distributed, available in supermarkets, drugstores, mass merchants, discounters, hardware stores, and home centers. In addition to its Townsend plant, Sterilite maintains operations in Birmingham, Alabama; Lake Havasu City, Arizona; Massillon, Ohio; Clinton, South Carolina; and Ennis, Texas. Sterilite is owned and managed by the third generation of the Stone family. Albert Stone serves as chairman, while his brother, David Stone, is Sterilite's president.

DEPRESSION-ERA ROOTS

Sterilite was founded as UnitedPlastics in Fitchburg, Massachusetts, as a partnership in 1939 by brothers Saul and Edward Stone, who had originally been in the business of manufacturing wooden heels for women's shoes, and Earl Tupper of Tupperware fame. Tupper was a former tree surgeon whose business had failed during the Great Depression. He became fascinated by plastics and went to work for Du Pont Corporation in Leominster, Massachusetts, and in 1938 he formed his own company to design and engineer industrial plastics. Tupper also developed injection-molding machines to create shaped objects, such as shoe heels, the initial purpose of Sterilite. Plastic shoe heels produced by the Stones and Tupper were not practical, however, due to the limitations of the plastics of the time, which did not offer enough heat resistance to offset the debilitating effects of hot weather. While Tupper and his company made gas masks and signal lamps for the military during World War II, and after the war became famous for plastic food storage containers, the Stone brothers and UnitedPlastics used their injection molding equipment to turn out personal items for the military as part of the war effort, including combs and toothbrush holders.

COMPANY PERSPECTIVES

For 70 years, Sterilite products have helped make life easier and more organized in millions of homes, schools and offices. We produce a wide range of innovative solutions that include food containers, dish drainers, laundry baskets, wastebaskets, storage boxes, drawer carts, cabinets and shelving. Sterilite is one of the most desired and trusted brands for houseware and storage products today, making quality and attractive products consumers need.

During the postwar period, just like Tupper and other manufacturers, they turned their attention to consumer products, producing an array of plastic goods, including tumblers, tableware, decorative giftware, toys, and household containers. Increasingly UnitedPlastics focused on the housewares business, especially promotional plastic storage containers. The styrene material the company used was brittle, however, and not until the introduction of clarified polypropylene was the company able to graduate beyond promotional containers to offer higher quality items. Not only was clarified polypropylene heat resistant, it was clearer, an important quality because consumers liked to see what was inside a food storage container. In the 1960s Sterilite introduced a wide variety of food storage bowls as well as an early version of the storage bin.

MOVE TO TOWNSEND, MASSACHUSETTS: 1968

Around 1964 the second generation took charge of UnitedPlastics. Albert Stone, the son of Edward Stone, became president, and cousin Conrad Stone became vice-president. In 1968 the company moved out of its three-story plant in Fitchburg, relocating its headquarters to Townsend, Massachusetts. It was not until the 1970s that UnitedPlastics changed its name to Sterilite Corporation.

While Sterilite was an innovative company in the storage field, it faced stiff competition from Rubbermaid Inc., an Ohio-based company that had made its mark with rubber household products, such as bath mats, but also turned its attention to plastic products. A public company since 1955, Rubbermaid had more clout and better brand recognition than Sterilite, relegating the latter to secondary status in the market. Nevertheless, Sterilite prospered on its own terms, proving to be an innovator that steadily expanded its product lines. In the late 1970s the company kept pace with consumer tastes by introducing a wide variety of new colors. The company also benefited from a lean management staff. Free of layers of bureaucracy, Sterilite was able to more quickly fill customer needs. In addition, the company forged strong relationships with suppliers to achieve and maintain its competitive edge.

Sterilite began to shift its focus to home organization products in the 1980s while expanding its distribution to include mass merchants, such as Bradlees, Caldo, Dollar General, Fred Meyer, Target, and Wal-Mart. A third generation of the Stone family also became involved in the business. Albert Stone's sons, David and Steven, took on increasing levels of responsibility in the organization during this period. David became vice-president of marketing and later the company's general counsel. Steven rose to the post of vice-president of manufacturing by the start of the 1990s, overseeing factories in Massachusetts; Birmingham, Alabama; and Lake Havasu City, Arizona. Few family companies were able to make the transition to a third generation, but "fortunately, for me," Albert Stone told the *Weekly Home Furnishings Newspaper,* "I had sons who were more interested in the business than I was." They were also highly competitive individuals, both of them high school and college hockey players who would compete in men's leagues after completing their schooling. They also complemented one another because David was interested in the business side, especially sales and marketing, and Steve was attracted to the manufacturing side.

Sterilite completed an acquisition in 1991, adding the RecyclEase Inc.'s brand name and that company's in-home recycling product. Sterilite had entered the in-home sorting market in the late 1980s through its Recycling Solutions line of products that included different sizes of bins and barrels and the Waste Sorting System, which contained three different colored stacking bins to allow consumers to separate plastic, glass, and metal with space on top for newsprint. Sterilite did especially well marketing its recycling bins and barrels to municipalities, and the addition of the RecyclEase product was intended to strengthen the consumer portion of the business.

ALABAMA PLANT OPENS: 1992

From the mid-1980s into the 1990s Sterilite enjoyed an annual growth rate of 15 percent. To keep pace with demand as well as a growing number of products, the company decided in 1991 to invest $15 million to open a new Alabama plant and warehouse, which served 22

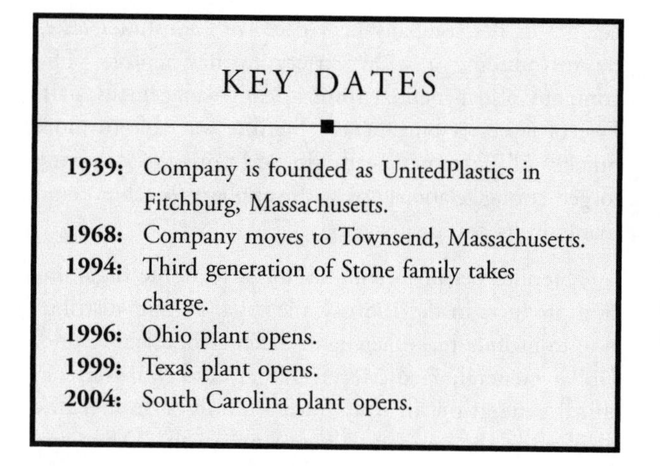

KEY DATES

1939: Company is founded as UnitedPlastics in Fitchburg, Massachusetts.
1968: Company moves to Townsend, Massachusetts.
1994: Third generation of Stone family takes charge.
1996: Ohio plant opens.
1999: Texas plant opens.
2004: South Carolina plant opens.

southern and central states. Opening a year later, at 625,000 square feet, the facility was twice the size of its predecessor and the largest plant Sterilite operated. At the same time, the company acquired 140,000 square feet of warehouse space to complement the 270,000-square-foot facility in Townsend, and the Arizona facility was doubled in size to 400,000 square feet. Sterilite also expanded its research and design and marketing departments to stimulate the steady flow of new products. Twenty new products, or about 10 percent of the more than 175 items the company had to offer, were introduced in 1991, and given that the new products provided the strongest sales it was not surprising that Sterilite planned to continue the trend. In 1993 the company introduced its Ultra line of household containers, offering heavy-duty construction combined with contemporary styling and user-friendly features. One of the most popular items in the line was a laundry basket, a common item that Sterilite essentially reinvented, adding a stronger body, ergonomic handles on all four sides, and a more stylish look.

The early 1990s also brought some changes to the top ranks at Sterilite. Although in his early 50s, Conrad Stone retired in 1993. A year later Albert Stone stepped down as president, turning over the post and day-to-day control to his son, David, while staying on as chairman of the board. Steven Stone was also named executive vice-president, remaining the head of manufacturing. By this stage Sterilite was generating an estimated $180 million in annual sales, making it the second largest plastic storage company, trailing only Rubbermaid. The company refused to become complacent, however, continuing to keep tabs on trends and developing products to match. Realizing that it had given short shrift to its food container business, Sterilite in 1995 unveiled the UltraSeal product line. UltraSeal containers included transparent side windows and a "thumb-print tab" for easing opening and closing.

FIRST MAJOR ADVERTISING CAMPAIGN: 1995

The addition of UltraSeal rounded out Sterilite's product lines—home organization, household containers, and food storage—and prompted the Stones to launch their first consumer advertising campaign to build brand awareness and identify Sterilite with high-quality products and reasonable prices. Using the "Sterilite Keeps You Together" tag, the print and television campaign broke in 1995. As Sterilite was gaining momentum, it also benefited from missteps made by its chief rival, Rubbermaid, in the mid-1990s.

Sterilite made nonresin products while Rubbermaid relied on resins. When the price of the raw material tripled between 1994 and 1996, Rubbermaid steadily increased prices, forcing many retailers to reduce their own margins to keep customers satisfied. One of the most important customers, Wal-Mart, was reluctant to pay the high prices, and when Rubbermaid would not budge, the retail giant responded by relegating Rubbermaid products to less desirable shelf locations and began promoting Sterilite products. Other mass merchants followed suit to the benefit of Sterilite and other Rubbermaid rivals, who began aggressively introducing new houseware products, some of which were innovative and others that were essentially copies of Rubbermaid products but less expensive. Sterilite, for example, brought to market a version of Rubbermaid's upscale contoured trash can. As a result of the industry shakeup, Rubbermaid was acquired by Newell Company in 1998 and began to revamp its operation.

To keep up with increasing demand, Sterilite opened its fourth plant, located in Massillon, Ohio, in 1996. Almost immediately the company outgrew the facility. Two expansions soon followed, and a third, costing $17 million, was begun in 1999 and completed in 2000, bringing the amount of manufacturing space to 430,000 square feet. A fifth plant came on line in Ennis, Texas, in September 1999 at the cost of more than $50 million. One million square feet in size, it was easily the largest plant Sterilite owned and had the potential to grow to 1.7 million square feet.

Further growth followed in the new century, so that by 2003 plans were made to build a sixth manufacturing facility on 240 acres of farmland near Clinton, South Carolina. The site was close to Interstate 26 and well situated to serve the southeastern United States. At a cost of $65 million the new plant would be even larger than that in Ennis, slated to comprise two million square feet. The first phase of the plant opened in mid-2004.

TOWNSEND BENEFITS FROM COMPANY'S GENEROSITY

Sterilite and the Stone family enjoyed prosperity in the first decade of the 2000s. In 2007 and 2008 the company made headlines for its generosity, rather than its business success. Sterilite agreed to construct two new buildings for Townsend: a new facility for the town's Highway Department and a combination senior center and library, both fully furnished. They were projects that the community had wanted for years but lacked the funds to proceed with. As a result of the Stone family's generosity, Townsend could revamp its capital improvements budget and allow for the immediate construction of other needed municipal facilities, including a new police station. The Highway Department building opened in June 2008 and the library–senior center was scheduled for completion in the fall of 2009.

Ed Dinger

PRINCIPAL COMPETITORS

Home Products International, Inc.; Newell Rubbermaid Inc.; Tupperware Brands Corporation.

FURTHER READING

Esposito, Frank, "S.C. to Gain 600 Jobs from Sterilite Plant," *Plastics News,* November 24, 2003, p. 1.

Hill, Dawn, "A Higher Standing: 'Reinvented' Sterilite Climbs in Plastic Organization," *HFN,* September 11, 1995, p. 31.

Ledson, Shannon, "Sterilite Opens Plant, May Expand Another," *Plastics News,* September 6, 1999, p. 10.

Owen, Paula J., "Sterilite to Erect 2 Buildings," *Telegram & Gazette* (Worcester, Mass.), May 9, 2008, p. B1.

Troy, Terry, "New Sterilite Plant to Open," *HFD,* January 27, 1992, p. 80.

———, "Rolling Stones," *HFD,* November 23, 1992, p. 42.

Sub Pop Ltd.

2013 Fourth Avenue, Third Floor
Seattle, Washington 98121
U.S.A.
Telephone: (206) 441-8441
Fax: (206) 441-8245
Web site: http://www.subpop.com

Private Company
Incorporated: 1988
Employees: 25
Sales: $4.2 million (2007 est.)
NAICS: 711320 Promoters of Performing Arts, Sports, and Similar Events Without Facilities

■ ■ ■

Sub Pop Ltd., an independent rock record label, promotes artists such as The Shins, The Postal Service, and Iron and Wine, distributing compact discs, digital audio and video media, and vinyl records. Famous for the role it played in the widespread popularity of music emanating from Seattle during the early 1990s, Sub Pop is regarded as one of the most influential independent labels in the United States. Its diverse roster of artists has progressed past Mudhoney and Nirvana to include Wolf Eyes, No Age, and The Thermals. Warner Music Group owns 49 percent of Sub Pop.

FIRST THE NEWSLETTER: *SUBTERRANEAN POP*

In 1971, when Seattle-based Boeing Co. laid off 60,000 workers, a billboard near the airport read: "Will the Last Person Leaving Seattle Please Turn Out the Lights." Once the hub of bustling activity related to shipping, logging, and the mad rush for gold to the north in Alaska, the city was watching itself die a slow death. People were leaving: The city's population was on a steady decline, dropping from 565,000 in 1965 to under a half million by 1980. Tucked away in a corner geographically, Seattle seemed to be receding from view, but its stature swelled in a phenomenal fashion roughly two decades after the billboard appeared on the way to Seattle-Tacoma International Airport.

Arguably the most important impetus for the city's resurgence came not from the software made by Microsoft, nor from the espresso-coffee craze that became the lifeblood of Starbucks. Music, perhaps more than any other factor, wrenched Seattle from its retreat into the backwaters and set it on a course of vibrancy, growth, and international fame. "Grunge," a term coined by a member of the British press for the "Seattle sound," turned the city into a phenomenon in the 1990s, attracting legions to the new mecca of music and creating exceptionally fertile ground for the small, unassuming music industry that resided in the city before it catapulted onto the global stage.

Two native midwesterners were in place to capitalize on the extraordinary times, the founders of Sub Pop Ltd. Bruce Pavitt, born in Chicago, moved to the Pacific Northwest in 1980. He enrolled at Evergreen State College, an experimental college in Olympia, Washington, 60 miles south of Seattle. "It was the only place I could major in punk rock," Pavitt remarked in an August 31, 1992, interview with *Forbes*. While he was at Evergreen, Pavitt created the first incarnation of Sub Pop, a

COMPANY PERSPECTIVES

"Sub Pop was the grunge label, right?" That's right—the original home to Nirvana, Soundgarden and Mudhoney, incredible bands all. Bands whose members even, on occasion, wore flannel shirts. And 15 years after the rest of America draped itself in fashionable, grungy flannels (and then promptly took them to the thrift stores where they always belonged), Sub Pop is again one of the top music companies in the land, with artists racking up *Saturday Night Live* appearances and Grammy nominations.

In fact, while much of the music industry has been desperately trying to put the brakes on declining sales, Sub Pop has been giving away music by top-sellers and working with unorthodox business models.

Seriously, who'd've thought it? Other than the humble founders of Sub Pop, that is?

newsletter he published titled *Subterranean Pop.* Dedicated to covering the alternative music happenings in the United States, *Subterranean Pop* became the first vehicle through which Pavitt distributed music. Between 1980 and 1986, he released three cassettes and one album as part of handing out his newsletter, each a compilation of little-known artists and each bearing the name "Sub Pop."

After earning his degree from Evergreen State, Pavitt moved to Seattle and got a job cooking in a restaurant. During his off-hours, he began writing a column for the *Rocket,* a free publication covering the Seattle music scene. The name of his column, "Sub Pop," represented the second incarnation of the company he later would lead.

PAVITT AND PONEMAN

The third incarnation of Sub Pop occurred after Pavitt met a native of Toledo, Ohio, Jonathan Poneman. Poneman moved to Seattle in 1979 to enroll at the University of Washington, where he majored in broadcast journalism. While Pavitt spent his hours out of class producing *Subterranean Pop,* Poneman worked as a disc jockey and booked local bands. Reports differ as to how the two first met, either working together in the tape duplication room at Muzak, Inc., the preeminent supplier of "elevator" music, or in a mattress store, but once they did meet, the conversation turned to combining their efforts.

Pavitt and Poneman recorded their first band in 1987, Green River, a local band that contained four members who would lead the incubating Grunge movement, Stone Gossard, Steve Turner, Jeff Ament, and Mark Arm. The following year, they backed the efforts of another Seattle band, Soundgarden, whose album recorded nominal commercial success. Nominal was a relative term for two aspiring entrepreneurs, however: Pavitt and Poneman decided to jump headlong and full-time into running a label after the Soundgarden experience. They pooled their finances, using $19,000 to start what would become known as Sub Pop Ltd.

SUB POP AND MUDHONEY

Financial duress beset Sub Pop within weeks. Start-up capital, meager to start with, was consumed within three months. The label owed people money, and the small staff at Sub Pop headquarters were reminded of the demands for money by the insistent knocks on their office door by creditors. All seemed lost until the Seattle music scene produced the first glimmer of the power that would attract the attention of the world. Green River split up, sending its members in different directions: Stone Gossard and Jeff Ament later became the heart of Pearl Jam; Steve Turner and Mark Arm formed Mudhoney, one of the principal agents of the Grunge movement and the salvation of Sub Pop at its darkest hour.

Mudhoney, signed by Sub Pop, showed perhaps the first hint of the seductive force gathering strength in Seattle. The band, in an inexplicable instant, became the darling of fans in England right at the time Sub Pop was being besieged by creditors. The label responded to the overseas interest by quickly producing a Mudhoney record that remained on the British music charts for more than a year.

The salvation offered by Mudhoney occurred roughly at the same time Sub Pop learned a stinging, defining lesson. The first Seattle band of the era bolted out of the gate, but only after it had severed its ties to Sub Pop. Soundgarden left Sub Pop and signed with the far larger A&M Records, which produced *Badmotorfinger,* an album that sold more than two million copies worldwide. "We were basically naive record collectors and music aficionados," Poneman was quoted as saying in the August 31, 1992, issue of *Forbes.* Much later, in a June 28, 2008, interview with *Billboard,* he would look back on his career and share what he thought was his best decision as a business owner: "Not to be too cynical," he said, "but I would say hiring a good attorney has been one of the [best]."

KEY DATES

1980: While in college, Bruce Pavitt begins publishing a newsletter, *Subterranean Pop.*
1987: Pavitt and Jonathan Poneman record their first band, Green River.
1988: Sub Pop signs its second band, Soundgarden.
1992: Nirvana, a former Sub Pop band, releases *Nevermind,* for which Sub Pop receives royalty payments.
1995: Warner Music Group acquires a 49 percent interest in Sub Pop.
1996: Bruce Pavitt resigns.
2008: Sub Pop celebrates its 20th anniversary.

SUB POP AND NIRVANA

In the wake of the Soundgarden experience, Sub Pop's contracts became more sophisticated. Rising bands in the future would have a much harder time leaving the independent label without paying heavily for their exit, a strategy that paid off almost immediately after Pavitt and Poneman watched Soundgarden slip out of their grasp. One of their bands, Nirvana, was beginning to break out, on its way toward immense commercial success that would confirm Seattle as the epicenter of the rock-and-roll universe during the early 1990s. The band was fast on the rise, requiring more support than Sub Pop could hope to offer, which sent the band's attorney into action. He reached an agreement with David Geffen's DGC label to represent his clients, but Sub Pop was not going to make the exit easy. Sub Pop did let Nirvana go, enabling DGC to produce *Nevermind,* an album that jumped to the top of the charts in the spring of 1992, selling seven million copies worldwide. However, the deal that was struck entitled Sub Pop to receive a more than 2 percent royalty on Nirvana's future record sales and the rights to songs Nirvana recorded before it switched to DGC.

SUB POP AND WARNER MUSIC GROUP

The legal front included another chapter in Sub Pop's development, one that eventually saw it sign an ownership deal with a much larger label. Sub Pop signed a distribution agreement with Caroline Records in July 1991, but the alliance turned combative within two years. The Seattle-based label sued its New York-based distributor in mid-1993, unilaterally declaring its contract void because of Caroline Records' failure to pay monies it allegedly misappropriated. The $12 million lawsuit was settled out of court for an undisclosed sum later in the year, freeing Sub Pop to sign a distribution agreement with Warner Music Group's Alternative Distribution Alliance (ADA). "I feel that ADA's got a very proactive policy toward fulfilling what our needs are," Poneman said in an October 23, 1993, interview with *Billboard.* "It's a new company, and with newness, there are new opportunities," he said, before adding, "We remain autonomous; nobody at ADA is telling us what to do."

Sub Pop's relationship with Warner Music soon grew deeper. In 1995, Warner Music paid $20 million for a 49 percent stake in Sub Pop, a deal that provided a measure of financial security to the much smaller label. It also marked the end of an era: In April 1996, Pavitt resigned from Sub Pop, believing he had accomplished all he could hope to accomplish in running a record company. Pavitt's departure left Poneman alone at the helm. There, the 36-year-old faced the daunting task of spiriting Sub Pop's success in a post-Grunge world.

INDESTRUCTIBLE SUB POP

"Going out of business since 1988," Sub Pop's web site declared during its 20th anniversary year. The label, on numerous occasions during its first two decades of business, was deemed to be on the verge of collapse, but it did more than persevere. Sub Pop thrived as Seattle's popularity faded in the music world, asserting itself as one of the most respected independent labels in the world. The label developed new revenue streams—a store, a catalog, a monthly subscription service—but in a broader sense its longevity stemmed from the promotion of the Sub Pop name as a brand. A rarity in the music industry, the Sub Pop name on a recording was as important as the name of the artist in the minds of some consumers, which gave the label a unique identity that transcended any particular genre of music.

Sub Pop celebrated its 20th anniversary in 2008, reckoning its age from the date Pavitt and Poneman leased their first office space in April 1988. For Poneman, there was much to celebrate, as Sub Pop enjoyed one of its most successful years in 2007. The popularity of Sub Pop bands such as The Shins, The Postal Service, and Iron and Wine kept the label at the forefront of a market notorious for the fickle tastes of its target audience. It had withstood the test of time, evolving past the halcyon days of the "Seattle sound" to represent the peripheral, dynamic music scene its larger competitors either did not see or chose to overlook. "I don't think they've been known as a grunge label for a very long time," a *Billboard* senior editor said in the January 27, 2008, edition of the *Seattle Times.* "Sub Pop remains one of the most important indie-rock labels, regardless of its history with that particular type of music. They're very in touch with the pulse of the underground scene, while simultaneously building bands that are selling as many records as some major-label acts."

Jeffrey L. Covell

PRINCIPAL SUBSIDIARIES

Sub Pop Records.

PRINCIPAL COMPETITORS

Matador Records, Inc.; Victory Records, Inc.; Wind-Up Entertainment, Inc.

FURTHER READING

Davies, Barbara, "Dirt on Mudhoney," *Billboard,* November 21, 1992, p. 20.

Harding, Cortney, "Jonathan Poneman: Sub Pop Founder Takes Stock of the Last 20 Years and Plans for the Future," *Billboard,* June 28, 2008, p. 25.

———, "Such Great Heights: Sub Pop, Merge Honchos Reflect on a Banner 2007," *Billboard,* December 22, 2007, p. 38.

Kugiya, Hugo, "Beyond Grunge at Sub Pop," *Seattle Times,* August 11, 1996, p. 14.

Martens, Todd, "Shades of Indie Grey: For Smaller Labels, File Sharing Isn't Black and White," *Billboard,* July 9, 2005, p. 30.

Morris, Chris, "Sub Pop's Commercial Resurgence," *Billboard,* April 10, 2004, p. 11.

———, "Sub Pop Sues to End Caroline Distrib Deal," *Billboard,* July 31, 1993, p. 9.

———, "Sub Pop to Be Distributed by ADA: Seattle Indie Settles Caroline Dispute," *Billboard,* October 23, 1993, p. 12.

Newcomb, Peter, "From Toledo to Nirvana," *Forbes,* August 31, 1992, p. 61.

Scanlon, Tom, "Sub Pop's Got Some Kind of Record," *Seattle Times,* January 27, 2008.

Wolk, Douglas, "The Shins Change Their Life," *Billboard,* February 3, 2007, p. 28.

SUEZ-TRACTEBEL S.A.

Pl. du Trone 1
Brussels, B-1000
Belgium
Telephone: (+32 02) 510 71 11
Fax: (+32 02) 510 73 30
Web site: http://www.tractebel.be

Wholly Owned Subsidiary of GDF SUEZ
Incorporated: 2003
Employees: 7,916
Sales: EUR 6.91billion ($8.5 billion) (2007)
NAICS: 221122 Electric Power Distribution; 221210 Natural Gas Distribution; 221310 Water Supply and Irrigation Systems

■ ■ ■

SUEZ-TRACTEBEL S.A. (Suez-Tractebel), part of France's GDF SUEZ (Suez), is the holding company for two primary operations: Suez Energy International and Tractebel Engineering. Suez Energy International (SEI) is the group's larger business, accounting for 95 percent of its turnover. SEI oversees the Suez group's international energy operations outside of Europe. The company's is a leading power producer in Brazil and Thailand, with generating capacity reaching the North, South, and Central American markets, as well as the Asian, Middle East, and African markets. Altogether SEI's power generation capacity reached 30,000 megawatts (MW) per year in 2007. In addition, SEI is active in the liquefied natural gas (LNG) sector in both the Atlantic and Pacific markets, with a particularly strong presence in the North American LNG market. SEI also operates gas transportation and distribution businesses in North and South America and in Asia, distributing both to third parties and directly to customers. SEI's operations include more than 3,500 kilometers of high-voltage transmission lines and nearly 15,500 kilometers of natural gas pipelines.

The second, smaller part of Suez-Tractebel is Tractebel Engineering. That company is one of the leading energy sector engineering firms in Europe. The company provides consulting, design, and engineering services for the construction and operation of electrical power generation plants, natural gas plants, nuclear power facilities, and infrastructure projects on an international basis. Suez-Tractebel was formed in 2003, following the merger of Tractebel with Société Générale de Belgique. Suez-Tractebel then became a 100 percent subsidiary of Suez. In 2007, the company's combined sales topped EUR 6.9 billion ($8.5 billion).

ROOTS IN THE 19TH CENTURY

Tractebel celebrated its 100th anniversary in 1995, tracing its history back to the creation of two companies, Compagnie Mutuelle des Tramways and Société Générale Belge d'Entreprises Electriques in 1895 by longtime controlling shareholder Société Générale de Belgique (SGB), the Belgium holding company powerhouse. SGB's own history traced back to 1822 and before the official creation of the Belgian state, when it was established by William I of Orange. Charged with fostering the economic and industrial development of the southern provinces of the Low

COMPANY PERSPECTIVES

Our mission is to establish long-term partnerships with our customers in order to help them meet their objectives of competitiveness, reliability and safety. Our multi-skilled teams therefore develop innovative technological solutions that combine economic and technical performance. Clearly, our multidisciplinary approach and our experience of operational support play a decisive role.

Countries, which had only recently emerged from under the rulership of the Austro-Hungarian empire, Société Générale de Pays Bas, as it was then called, was given the authority to issue bank notes and act as the state cashier, a role it continued to play after Belgium's independence from the Netherlands in 1830.

After Banque Nationale de Belgique was formally established in 1850, SGB concentrated on its role as Belgium's primary joint-venture capital and development concern, playing a key role in developing the country's infrastructure. In this capacity, SGB provided capital for the building of Belgium rail and road infrastructure, major construction projects, coal and other mining activities, and the development of the country's gas and electrical utilities, as well as other industrial projects. In 1895, SGB established subsidiary companies for two of its primary activities, tram (streetcar) construction and operation, and electricity gas distribution. Both Compagnie Mutuelle des Tramways and Société Générale d'Entreprises Electriques were active internationally, with the subsidiaries of the former supplying streetcar lines to cities around the world, and the latter becoming through its subsidiaries a global utility operator. By the start of World War I, these international efforts represented as much as 70 percent of both companies' activities.

The social and political upheaval following World War I, however, and the rise of new nation states, particularly with the breakup of Austria-Hungary, saw the nationalization of many of the companies' foreign subsidiaries. In October 1929, the two companies were combined, forming Tractebel. The newly named company continued to lose its foreign utility and tramway concessions, especially during the Depression of the 1930s and the buildup to World War II. By 1945, Tractebel had been forced to give up its international operations entirely. For the next 40 years, the company would concentrate almost solely on its home market.

Following the Depression and World War II, SGB began consolidating the related activities of its many subsidiaries, giving rise to Electrobel, which served as Belgium's primary utility supplier, and Tractionel, which provided industrial engineering services, including playing a role in establishing the company's nuclear power industry. Electrobel and Tractionel also began operating a joint-venture subsidiary, Tractionel Electrobel Engineering, which grew to become the sixth largest international engineering design firm. Both Tractionel and Electrobel evolved into major Belgian holding companies, with Tractionel's holdings extending beyond its energy portfolio into the foods, chemicals, cable television, and property sectors. SGB remained principal shareholder of both companies.

SUEZ AS WHITE NIGHT IN 1986

In 1986, Tractionel and Electrobel agreed to merge operations, forming the modern-day Tractebel. Several factors were behind this move: the growing internationalization of the world industry, with the resulting heightening of international competition; the coming unification of the European market; and a rising trend toward the deregulation of many state-controlled industries. The newly combined companies' operations boasted a 1985 portfolio worth some BEF 56 billion, with combined net profits of BEF 5.7 billion. One year later, Tractebel's portfolio had grown to BEF 67.8 billion and the company's net profit reached BEF 6.15 billion (worth nearly $164 million). Tractebel itself, however, remained a largely passive holding company. More than 90 percent of the company's business came from its utility holdings.

In 1987, with the breakup of Imperial Continental Gas into two companies, the Calor Group and Contibel, Tractebel and partner Groupe Bruxelles Lambert, launched a successful takeover bid for Contibel, which contained a strong portfolio of investments in Belgium's utilities. The bid, which cost the two holding companies nearly $740 million, gave Tractebel tighter control of the Belgian utility sector. Yet the "Black Monday" stock market crash in October of that year cost the company dearly, and exposed it and parent SGB to new vulnerabilities.

These became particularly evident the following year, as parent SGB faced a new upheaval: In 1988 Carlo De Benedetti, the Italian industrialist, launched a hostile takeover bid for SGB. The company resisted for several months, and finally turned to the French Compagnie Financière de Suez as a "white knight." Suez's holding in SGB rose to 63 percent, while SGB's

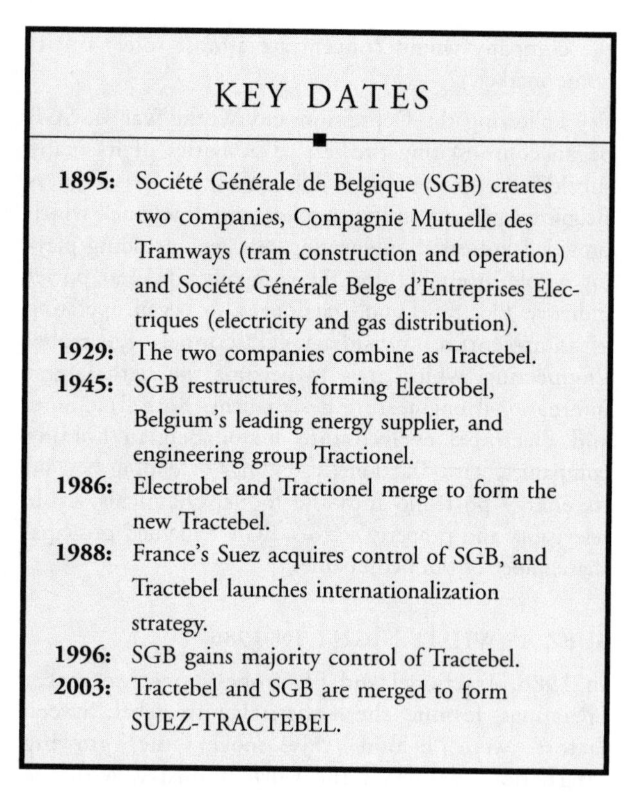

KEY DATES

1895: Société Générale de Belgique (SGB) creates two companies, Compagnie Mutuelle des Tramways (tram construction and operation) and Société Générale Belge d'Entreprises Electriques (electricity and gas distribution).
1929: The two companies combine as Tractebel.
1945: SGB restructures, forming Electrobel, Belgium's leading energy supplier, and engineering group Tractionel.
1986: Electrobel and Tractionel merge to form the new Tractebel.
1988: France's Suez acquires control of SGB, and Tractebel launches internationalization strategy.
1996: SGB gains majority control of Tractebel.
2003: Tractebel and SGB are merged to form SUEZ-TRACTEBEL.

own holdings, previously spread out over a variety of industries, tightened to focus on several major Belgian players, including Tractebel. One year later, SGB increased its hold on Tractebel, after swapping part of its shares in Belgian oil and petrochemicals group Petrofina, the country's largest company, for a large part of the Tractebel shares held by rival Groupe Bruxelles Lambert, led by Albert Frere. The deal boosted SGB's participation in Tractebel to more than 40 percent. By then, Tractebel's net profits had risen to BEF 9.5 billion ($271 million). More than 85 percent of the company's profits, however, continued to come from the Belgian energy market.

The attempted takeover of SGB and its subsequent rescue by Suez spurred Tractebel to make its own transformation. In 1989, faced with the inevitable loss of its near-monopoly on Belgium's utility sector with the looming unification of the European market, Tractebel adopted a new strategy calling for the company to return to the global industrial market of its early history. Leading the company's transformation was Baron Philippe Bodson, who had earned his title of nobility as the head of the Belgium Industrial Federation prior to joining Tractebel.

RETURN TO GLOBAL FOCUS IN THE NINETIES

The U.S. market, where deregulation had progressed rapidly, became one of Tractebel's primary expansion targets. Tractebel at first eyed building a media portfolio, beginning in 1989 with the $30 million purchase of a 20 percent stake in Act III Communications, based in Los Angeles. The company's communications arm would increase its U.S. presence during the first half of the 1990s, adding, through its Coditel subsidiary and its financial and management participation in the Prime Cable Group, cable television operations in the Houston, Las Vegas, and other large U.S. city markets. Next, the company began building its U.S. energy portfolio, adding, through its American Tractebel Corporation subsidiary, 50 percent ownership of the construction and operation of an electrical plant in Quebec. The company also returned to Argentina's energy market, where the company had been active early in the century, after that country abandoned state control of the utility sector. In Europe, Tractebel, through its Fabricom subsidiary, purchased 70 percent of Hungary's PVV, focused on that country's electrical utility market. On the home front, the company's Electrabel and Distrigas subsidiaries reached agreement to build an electricity generating facility in Zeebrugge.

Posting a net profit of BEF 29.4 billion ($835 million) in 1994, Tractebel's international expansion would continue into the mid-1990s. As Bodson explained to the *Houston Chronicle,* "The Belgian market is almost saturated and that is why we have decided to go abroad." The company's expansion drive was helped by its strong war chest, Bodson continued: "I think an acquisition of half a billion dollars would definitely be possible for us, even tomorrow." In May 1995, Tractebel, through its Powerfin subsidiary, paid $206 million for the friendly takeover of CRSS, based in Houston. This move gave Tractebel access to the U.S. utility market, with several electric power generating stations, principally located in Vermont. Meanwhile, the company's energy utility interests had spread to include locations in Ireland, Hungary, Portugal, Oman, Italy, Chile, and other countries. After taking over the utility management of Kazakhstan, formed after the breakup of the Soviet Union, Tractebel company would also move into the Asian market, adding Thailand, Singapore, and India, among others. In the United States, Tractebel increased its energy capacity, when it announced a $500 million joint-venture with Phillips Coal Co. to build a 400 MW lignite-burning power plant in Mississippi.

In September 1996, SGB reached agreement with Electrafina and Royale Belge, both controlled by Groupe Bruxelles Lambert, to buy those companies' combined 25 percent share of Tractebel. The purchase, worth some BEF 49 billion ($1.6 billion), raised SGB's ownership position to more than 65 percent. Several months later, however, SGB prompted the merger between Tractebel and another subsidiary, Powerfin, in which Tractebel already had a strong interest. The merger, which involved a shares flotation in Tractebel, and the dissolving of Powerfin's shares into Tractebel, decreased SGB's direct participation in Tractebel to 50.3 percent. This move came in the light of major development in SGB's control: the merger of parent company Suez into French water company Lyonnaise des Eaux, a move that effectively placed the Belgian utility sector under a foreign utility operator's control for the first time.

EXPANDING INTO THE NEW CENTURY

Tractebel's total power generating capacity reached 32,000 MW by 1996, and the company's operations by then spanned more than 100 countries. Tractebel continued to seek further growth, leading the company to acquire a 50 percent stake in H-Power Company of Thailand. In that year, also, Tractebel became the first European group to found an energy trading company in the United States, creating Tractebel Energy Marketing in Houston in 1997. Tractebel also continued its push to develop its power sector engineering operations into a global force, securing a number of high-profile contracts through the 1990s. These included a stake in the construction of the Al Manah Power Station starting in 1994, the first privately built and operated power plant in the United Arab Emirates; and the construction of a 600 MW plant to be built in Syria, starting from 1998.

In 2000, Tractebel added to its European presence through the purchase of a 25 percent share of Poland's Tadeusza Kosciuszki SA, which operated a power plant in Polaniec. The following year, the company paid $189 million to acquire 80 percent of a natural gas-based power plant in Nuevo León, Mexico. This led Tractebel to step up its Latin American operations, launching a $200 million investment to increase its position in the Mexican energy market, including the construction of a new natural gas–fired power plant in Nuevo León, completed in 2003. The company also acquired Edelnor, a power generator based in Chile, in 2002.

Parent company Suez in the meantime launched a major reorganization of its holdings. This led to the merger of Tractebel and the remaining components of Société Générale de Belgique, forming a new holding company, Suez-Tractebel. The new company, 100 percent controlled by Suez, was then organized into two primary businesses. The first, and larger, regrouped all of the Suez group's power generation, natural gas transport and distribution, and related energy sector operations outside of Europe into a single company, Suez Energy International. The new company boasted a power plant network producing more than 30,000 MW of power, more than 3,500 kilometers of high-voltage transmission lines, and nearly 15,500 kilometers of natural gas pipelines. The second part of the new group, Tractebel Engineering, regrouped the company's globally operating energy sector engineering operations.

Suez-Tractebel boasted a number of strengths, such as positions as the leading private power generators for the Brazil and Thai markets, as well as a major position in the Persian Gulf region as well. The company had also grown into one of the largest suppliers of LNG to the North American market. This position was reinforced in 2005, when the company launched the development of a $900 million LNG port near Gloucester, Massachusetts.

At the same time, the company's engineering wing continued to develop its position in the world, gaining a contract to develop a plan to link the Saudi Arabian and Egyptian power grids in 2006. In 2007, Tractebel Engineering gained a major new contract, when the Libyan government hired the firm to develop its strategic gas master plan for the development of its national gas network into 2025. With total revenues of more than EUR 6.9 billion in 2007, Suez-Tractebel remained one of the four main pillars of the giant Suez group.

M. L. Cohen

PRINCIPAL SUBSIDIARIES

Suez Energy International S.A.; Tractebel Engineering S.A.

PRINCIPAL COMPETITORS

Electricité de France; ENI S.p.A.; E.ON AG; Energy Future Holdings Corp.; National Grid PLC; ENEL S.p.A.; RWE AG; ENDESA S.A.; E.ON Energie AG; Veolia Environnement; Vivendi S.A.

FURTHER READING

Banks, Howard, "Counterattack," *Forbes,* February 24, 1997, p. 70.

Buckley, Neil, "Alarm Sounds over Tractebel," *Financial Times,* April 4, 1997, p. 26.

———, "Tractebel and Powerfin Set for $8 Billion Merger," *Financial Times,* March 18, 1997, p. 33.

George, Alan, "Tractebel Makes Its Middle East Mark," *Petroleum Times Energy Report,* April 24, 1998, p. 9.

Gottschalk, Arthur, "Belgium's Tractebel Wants to Light Up the US," *Journal of Commerce,* April 10, 1997, p. 7B.

Javetski, John, "Tractebel, Belgium's Centenarian, Takes up Globetrotting—Again," *Electrical World,* March 1996, p. 26.

Minder, Ralph, "CRSS Suitor Still Searching," *Houston Chronicle,* May 28, 1995, p. 7.

"Tractebel Plant Begins Power Production," *South American Business Information,* February 21, 2003.

"Tractebel Sells US Unit," *Oil Daily,* February 16, 2005.

"Tractebel to Draw Up Gas Masterplan," *Middle East Economic Digest,* February 8, 2008, p. 12.

The Swiss Colony®
FAMILY OWNED SINCE 1926

The Swiss Colony, Inc.

1112 7th Avenue
Monroe, Wisconsin 53566
U.S.A.
Telephone: (608) 328-8400
Fax: (608) 328-8457
Web site: http://www.swisscolony.com

Private Company
Incorporated: 1954
Employees: 1,200
Sales: $600 million (2007 est.)
NAICS: 453220 Gift, Novelty, and Souvenir Stores

■ ■ ■

As one of the largest direct-marketing firms in the United States, The Swiss Colony, Inc., has a gift for virtually every season and occasion. From cookies, pastries, nuts, and candies to chocolates, cheese spreads, sausages, and smoked salmon, the Monroe, Wisconsin-based retailer is best known for its food gifts. Employing approximately 1,200 permanent and 6,000 temporary workers, The Swiss Colony operates a bakery that makes literally thousands of different types of baked goods. In 2007 alone, the bakery made 51.6 million petits fours (frosted cakelike cubes) and used almost two million pounds of chocolate to make a range of delicious treats.

For those in search of nonfood items, the company sells home décor, apparel, and more. By 2008, sales of food items accounted for only 20 percent of the company's business, with the strongest growth occurring in its range of nonfood gift catalogs. In addition to a handful of outlet stores, where items are sold at a discount, and an established e-commerce operation, the company's specialty gift catalogs include Tender Filet, Seventh Avenue, Midnight Velvet, Ginny's, Through the Country Door, Monroe and Main, and ASHRO. Specialized catalogs such as these are helping the company distribute its revenue more evenly throughout the year; about 85 percent of orders still fall within the holiday season.

PART-TIME ENTERPRISE: 1926–60

The idea that led to The Swiss Colony originated as a class project during the 1920s at the University of Wisconsin, Madison. During his senior year, a student named Ray Kubly Sr. and two classmates developed an advertising campaign for a company that sold cheese by mail. Following graduation, Kubly's marketing project materialized into a real home-based business, called The Swiss Colony, which would remain a part-time concern for some 35 years.

Operating from the basement of his Monroe, Wisconsin, home, in 1926 Kubly secured large wheels of Wisconsin cheese and sold hand-cut portions via mail, promoting the goods with mimeographed handbills. A local Railway Express agent helped him spread the word to potential customers, and after one year of operation Kubly's enterprise had sold 50 packages of cheese.

Born on September 3, 1901, on a dairy farm in Clarno Township, Wisconsin, Kubly attended Lawrence College in Appleton, before heading to the University of Wisconsin, Madison, where he was a star athlete on the

COMPANY PERSPECTIVES

Loyal customers have made us enormously successful because we deliver what they want—quality products, affordable prices, and friendly service.

track team. He is recognized for helping to spread the popularity of Baby Swiss cheese, which Swiss settlers had been making in Wisconsin since their arrival in Green County many years before, throughout the nation.

The Swiss Colony successfully weathered the economic turmoil of the Great Depression, and by 1938 growth caused Kubly to move his part-time enterprise to rented space. That year, the company shipped between two and three tons of cheese in December alone, relying on Rail Express to send approximately 400 packages to customers across the country.

Employment during the 1941 Christmas season totaled 100 people, with a payroll of $19,000. In 1947 the company acquired the Chalet Cheese Co. from Karl Schwager, which later became Enchanted Cheese before it was assimilated into The Swiss Colony.

In time, Kubly's business began setting a variety of records. These included a mail-handling record for the town of Monroe in 1948. The volume of cheese sold by The Swiss Colony was so great that the Milwaukee Railroad added an entire boxcar to accommodate the extra parcel post items between December 9 and the Christmas holiday. In addition, a temporary supplemental post office space was established to handle the extra mail volume. In all, The Swiss Colony sold approximately one million pounds of cheese that year. In 1950, the company's package volume helped set a daily cancellations record (48,900) at the Monroe Post Office.

A number of important developments occurred at The Swiss Colony during the 1950s. After the company was incorporated in 1954, Raymond R. "Pat" Kubly Jr. rejoined The Swiss Colony after serving in the Air Force. Kubly, who majored in physics and mathematics in college, had planned to become a scientist, but instead chose to work alongside his father in the family business. Pat and his brother, Mike, had worked a variety of jobs at The Swiss Colony during their high school and college years. At the decade's end, the company established its first bakery in downtown Monroe, at a location that eventually became home to the company's first retail store.

In 1958 The Swiss Colony's mascot, Chris Mouse, was born. In addition gracing the covers of the company's holiday catalogs, chocolate likenesses of the festive mascot eventually became a favorite with children everywhere.

By the late 1950s technology had become an important part of The Swiss Colony's burgeoning direct-mail operations. The company relied on computers and punch cards to produce mailing lists and labels, invoices, and shipping orders.

EXPANSION AND MODERNIZATION: 1961–78

In 1961 Ray Kubly Sr. decided to give up his job as vice-president and general manager of Borden Co.'s Lakeshire-Marty division and make The Swiss Colony a full-time endeavor. Unfortunately, he was only able to devote all of his time to The Swiss Colony for a few short years. In February 1968 he died of a heart attack. Pat Kubly, who had been named president the previous year, assumed leadership of the company. He provided both the guidance and creativity needed to ensure the company's continued growth.

Technological advancements enabled The Swiss Colony to maximize the efficiency of its operations during the 1960s. By 1967 the company was using tape-driven computers. Two years later, the SC Data Center was established to serve businesses of The Swiss Colony, as well as other companies located within a 150-mile radius.

During the 1970s, advancements in technology and automation also made bakery operation easier and more efficient for The Swiss Colony. Instead of melting down ten-pound blocks of chocolate and tempering them before use, for example, the company began buying tanker loads of melted chocolate. Heated storage tanks were installed, which could hold thousands of gallons of chocolate. This new approach enabled the company to coat petit fours with chocolate at a daily rate of 70,000 by the late 1970s. When this process was done by hand, the company had coated 60,000 petit fours for the entire year in 1961.

BEYOND THE CHEESE: 1979–2008

The introduction of the Gift Collection in 1979 marked The Swiss Colony's initial foray into nonfood catalogs, which would become big business in the coming decades. A noteworthy milestone was reached in 1982, when The Swiss Colony introduced Seventh Avenue, its first full-fledged nonfood catalog. Seventh Avenue, which had its roots in the Gift Collection, evolved into

KEY DATES

1926: Ray Kubly Sr. begins selling hand-cut portions of Wisconsin cheese by mail.
1954: The Swiss Colony is officially incorporated.
1959: The company establishes its first bakery in downtown Monroe.
1961: Ray Kubly Sr. gives up his job as vice-president and general manager of the Borden Co.'s Lakeshire-Marty division and works at The Swiss Colony full-time.
1968: Ray Kubly Sr. dies; Pat Kubly, who had been named president the previous year, assumes leadership of the company.
1979: The Swiss Colony begins offering catalogs with nonfood items.
1995: John Baumann is the first nonfamily member to serve as president.

an affiliated company in 1986. The operation paved the way for other new catalogs, including Midnight Velvet in 1987.

While catalog sales were rising, tremendous growth also had occurred on the retail front. By 1980 The Swiss Colony had 225 retail locations in place at shopping malls throughout the nation.

Behind the company's success were many loyal employees. In 1987 The Swiss Colony's very first employee, John Chambers, who had started working for the company in 1932, finally retired. Chambers was later recognized by The Swiss Colony with a Lifetime Achievement Award in 1996.

During the early 1990s, The Swiss Colony opened a combination café and cheese store in Madison, Wisconsin's Highland Gale Mall. In addition to soups and sandwiches, the store offered The Swiss Colony's cheeses, cheese spreads, beef logs, and crackers. The café was meant to be a prototype for a national chain of similar stores.

Several noteworthy developments took place during the mid-1990s. In 1995 John Baumann became the third person, and the first nonfamily member, to sit in the president's seat at The Swiss Colony, succeeding Pat Kubly. A Monroe native, Baumann was a former sportswriter for the *Wisconsin State Journal* who went on to earn an M.B.A. from Northwestern University.

In 1995 The Swiss Colony brought its DeWitt facility online to handle shipping for some of its nonfood operations. This was a growing category for The Swiss Colony, which was made evident by the 1995 debut of its Honey Creek Marketplace catalog, offering jewelry, housewares, and other gift items in addition to food.

While growth was occurring in the nonfood arena, food items continued to be The Swiss Colony's bread and butter. For example, in 1995 alone the company sold 77 million petit fours. Handling this level of production volume would become a challenge the following decade, when a tight job market made large numbers of temporary workers harder to come by. By this time The Swiss Colony relied upon a workforce of about 5,000 temporary workers, some 4,000 of whom were needed in Monroe and another 1,000 in Madison. About 60 percent of these employees returned each year.

When the World Wide Web made its public debut during the mid-1990s, it opened the doors of e-commerce to businesses small and large. The Swiss Colony was no exception. The company unveiled its first web site, www.swisscolony.com, in 1997. Evergreen Internet, which had built e-commerce sites for Spiegel and Nabisco, was chosen to build the new site, which offered all of the items from The Swiss Colony's print catalog.

As of 1998, The Swiss Colony continued to be a very seasonal operation, with approximately 95 percent of sales occurring in the seven weeks before the Christmas holiday. By this time, rising shopping mall rents and heightened cheese and sausage competition from supermarkets had prompted the company to scale back its base of retail locations. A small retail presence was maintained in shopping malls with approximately 80 kiosks, some of which were franchised.

By the end of the 1990s, The Swiss Colony had estimated sales of about $300 million. Ranked as one of the nation's leading catalog companies, the company employed about 1,000 regular employees and 4,800 seasonal workers at this time. In order to keep regular workers busy during the off-season, The Swiss Colony handled ordering and shipping and performed data entry tasks for other companies.

By the early 2000s, The Swiss Colony's call center operations had become very sophisticated. In all, the company operated a total of six contact centers and handled approximately four million calls annually. Difficult economic conditions prompted the closure of The Swiss Colony's Cassville call center in 2002, leading to the loss of about ten full-time jobs and 100 temporary positions. The company contact centers remained in Monroe and Dickeyville, Wisconsin, as well as Hannibal, Missouri, and Clinton, Iowa.

The Swiss Colony's estimated annual revenues stood at $500 million by 2005, about 20 percent of which came from online orders. Around this time, challenges ranged from stronger competition in the Internet and catalog arenas to consumers' fickle low-carbohydrate dietary habits. In this climate, The Swiss Colony scaled back the size of its production staff in Monroe and shuttered operations in Mauston and Danville, Illinois.

Within two years, The Swiss Colony was generating an estimated $600 million from its catalogs, of which 100 million were mailed annually. The company's sales mix had changed considerably since it began offering nonfood items during the late 1970s. In fact, only 20 percent of sales came from food items by 2008.

Heading into the 21st century's second decade, The Swiss Colony continued to operate under the Kubly family's ownership, with Pat Kubly (Ray's son) serving as chairman and Ryan Kubly (Ray's grandson) as director of strategic planning.

From its humble start as a part-time basement enterprise, the company's operations had grown to 1.8 million square feet of owned or leased space in 12 communities throughout the Midwest. The company relied on 1,200 regular employees and approximately 6,000 temporary workers to meet the demands of its customers.

With decades of direct-marketing know-how and insight into consumer gift-giving, The Swiss Colony seemed well prepared for success as the company moved toward its 100th anniversary.

Paul R. Greenland

PRINCIPAL SUBSIDIARIES

Ginny's Inc.; Monroe & Main Inc.; Seventh Avenue Inc.; The Tender Filet Inc.; Through the Country Door Inc.

PRINCIPAL COMPETITORS

Harry and David Direct Marketing; Omaha Steaks International Inc.; Spiegel Brands Inc.

FURTHER READING

Balousek, Marv, "More Than Cheese; Swiss Colony Turns Over a New Page in Its Storied History by Stocking Its Product Cupboard with Catalogs," *Wisconsin State Journal,* April 15, 2007.

Glessner, Jim, *The Swiss Colony,* Charleston, S.C.: Arcadia Publishing, 2006.

Hajewski, Ris, "Swiss Colony's Success More Than Sweets and Cheese; Monroe Catalog Company Looks to New Areas for Growth, Year-Round Sales," *Milwaukee Journal Sentinel,* December 14, 1998.

Oncken, John, "Swiss Colony Is a Big Cheese in a Small Town," *Capital Times,* December 2, 1994.

———, "There's More Than Cheese to Swiss Colony," *Capital Times,* December 23, 2004.

Syniverse Holdings Inc.

8125 Highwoods Palm Way
Tampa, Florida 33647-1776
U.S.A.
Telephone: (813) 637-5000
Toll Free: (888) 724-3579
Web site: http://www.syniverse.com

Public Company
Incorporated: 1987 as GTE Telecommunication Services Inc.
Employees: 1,128
Sales: $377.5 million (2007)
Stock Exchanges: New York
Ticker Symbol: SVR
NAICS: 517212 Cellular and Other Wireless Telecommunications

■ ■ ■

Syniverse Holdings Inc., doing business as Syniverse Technologies Inc., provides a variety of services to over 600 wireless telecommunications companies in more than 120 countries, including most of the largest wireless carriers in the United States and overseas. For a fee, Syniverse facilitates roaming, allowing calls from wireless subscribers to be seamlessly transmitted across the networks of rival wireless and wireline carriers. Syniverse also offers roaming settlement and fraud management services, and data roaming services. Other offerings include enterprise network solutions for business customers, the secure delivery of next generation and Wi-Fi services, and number porting, allowing customers to keep their phone number when changing carriers. Syniverse maintains offices around the world. Corporate headquarters are in Tampa, Florida, with regional headquarters in Argentina, the Netherlands, and Hong Kong. Syniverse is a public company listed on the New York Stock Exchange.

GTE ORIGINS: 1987

Syniverse was formed in 1987 by GTE Corporation as GTE Telecommunication Services Inc., one of seven businesses that comprised the newly created GTE Information Services division based in Tampa. GTE Telecommunication Services quickly found its niche filling the need for an inter-carrier wireless roaming telephone service, acquiring the ACCESS, PVS, and Cell-U-Rator technologies from Bell Atlantic in 1987 to provide roaming services. A year later the company introduced Follow Me Roaming, its first automatic call delivery product.

The wireless telephone industry was still in its infancy as the 1990s dawned, and GTE Telecommunication Services kept pace with the growth of the industry by adding new products and services for wireless carriers. It became involved in the fraud management field in 1991 with the introduction of the Fraud-Manager product to support the new IS-41 technology, a standard that allowed for the linking of cellular networks. In 1993 the company unveiled a fraud profiler to detect cloning, and developed the industry's first intelligent network services for Signaling System 7 (SS7), a system that separated the channel carrying the

COMPANY PERSPECTIVES

Syniverse Technologies makes it possible for over 500 communications companies in more than 100 countries to address market changes and demands as they deliver everything from voice calls to sophisticated data and video services.

call from the information that set up and managed it, thereby increasing both efficiency and security. Ameritech became the first customer for GTE Telecommunication Services' INLink service, which coupled SS7 transport with IS-41 to also provide wireless telephone subscribers with custom calling features such as call waiting when roaming. INLink also allowed the carriers to better manage roaming traffic, by supplying daily reports on traffic in individual markets.

Other products introduced by GTE Telecommunication Services in the mid-1990s included RoamerXchange in 1994, to support roaming and provide clearing services. A year later the company launched another industry first, GlobalRoam, which facilitated international roaming. GTE Telecommunication Services offered the first prepaid wireless solution to support roaming in 1997 and the following year introduced the first wireless user authentication system to bolster security further and deter fraud. In addition, GTE Telecommunication Services sought to help wireless carriers deal with the problem of "churn," customer attrition, by offering the ChurnManager system, which helped carriers to better maintain customer relationships and retain subscribers.

In the final years of the century, GTE Telecommunication Services introduced another fraud prevention measure, a wireless user authentication system. It also signed major carriers in Asia to provide the first international roaming service in the Far East, and began serving the Mercosul region (the common market of Argentina, Brazil, Paraguay, and Uruguay) through a partnership with Embratel—Empresa Brasileira de Telecomunicações S.A., a Brazilian telecommunications company. In addition, GTE Telecommunication Services began tailoring its services for competitive local exchange carriers (CLECs), local exchange carriers (LECs), long-distance telephone companies (IntereXchange Carriers or IXCs), paging companies, and Internet service providers (ISPs).

MERGER LEADS TO NAME CHANGE: 2000

The early 2000s brought major changes to GTE Telecommunication Services. Early in the year the parent company folded its GTE Intelligent Network Services operation into the division, allowing it to offer a wider range of services to its customers. Next, in June 2000, GTE Corporation merged with Bell Atlantic to create Verizon Communications, which became the new parent company. A year later it became a subsidiary of Verizon Information Services Inc. and assumed a new name: TSI Telecommunication Services Inc. In the meantime, the company introduced the industry's first voice-activated location-based services and added a clearinghouse for wireless service providers. In 2001 it also entered the European market, offering a number of mobile data services.

In late 2001 Verizon agreed to sell TSI to Chicago private equity firm GTCR Golder Rauner for $775 million; the deal was completed in February 2002. Edward Evans, former president and COO of wireless-service company Dobson Communications, was named CEO. The new management team began investing in improvements to the company's network, redesigning it, upgrading hardware, and expanding geographic coverage. TSI also restructured the sales organization which became more oriented towards customer service in order to drive new sales opportunities. Sales offices were established in key markets, staffed with local professionals familiar with the industry and the market.

In 2002 a sales and support office was opened in London. A year later a European headquarters was opened in Utrecht, the Netherlands. This spadework led to the first roaming clearinghouse contracts with major European wireless carriers. In addition to Europe, TSI Telecommunication Services BV served the Middle East and Africa. TSI also opened an Asia Pacific headquarters in Hong Kong. Furthermore, Evans and his team placed an emphasis on developing services that catered to emerging technologies. For example, TSI developed a wireless local number portability solution, allowing subscribers to keep their phone numbers when switching carriers as mandated by the federal government. Five of the top six wireless carriers in the United States became customers of the number portability services.

In addition to organic growth, TSI looked to expand externally, making strategic acquisitions another point of emphasis. In July 2003 TSI acquired Brience Inc. for 100,000 shares of stock. Brience developed information access and integration for mobile communications applications. Late in 2003 TSI completed a second acquisition, paying $800,000 and assuming $1.3 million in debt to add London, England-based Soft-

KEY DATES

1987: GTE Telecommunication Services Inc. is formed.
1994: RoamerXchange is introduced.
2001: Company changes name to TSI Telecommunication Services Inc.
2002: Investment firm GTCR Golder Rauner acquires TSI.
2004: Company is taken public as Syniverse Holdings Inc.
2007: Billing Services Group is acquired for $290 million.

wright Solutions Ltd., a major European provider of mobile number portability services as well as other software products and services for wireless carriers and enterprise customers, which included Accenture, American Express, Orange, and Vodafone. In 2004 the company paid about $55 million for the EDS Interoperator Services North America, a wireless clearinghouse service company whose business was folded into existing operations.

SYNIVERSE NAME ADOPTED: 2004

TSI elected to change its name in March 2004, a move that was not surprising given that there were other companies known as TSI. Moreover, the company was limited to the telecommunications sector and wanted its name to reflect a broader appeal. Syniverse Technologies was the choice, the word *Syniverse* a blend of "synergy" and "universe," meant to connote the company's intent to act as global catalyst for "meaningful connections." The new brand was also expected to help the company move into new markets and improve its position in Europe. Moreover, the name change prepared the ground for an initial public offering (IPO) of stock that was announced in November 2004 and completed in February 2005. The company also looked to take advantage of an improving balance sheet. Total revenues increased 22 percent to $332.4 million in 2004, resulting in net income of $15 million. Underwriters of the offering included Lehman Brothers Inc., Goldman Sachs & Co., Bear Stearns & Co, Inc., Deutsche Bank Securities Inc., Robert W. Baird & Co. Inc., Friedman Billings Ramsey & Co. Inc., and Raymond James & Associates Inc. Syniverse hoped to raise about $425 million, earmarked to pay off debt, but in the end had to lower its asking price of $22 per share to $16. As a result, the IPO raised $281.6 million. Shares then began trading on the New York Stock Exchange.

NEW HEADQUARTERS: 2005

Syniverse won a global Vodafone contract in 2005, the additional business helping to improve revenues to $341.8 million in 2005 and $9.8 million in net income. The results did not meet the expectations of investors, however, and the price of Syniverse stock fell to about $10 a share before mounting a recovery. Also of note in 2005, Syniverse moved its headquarters from downtown Tampa after 11 years to a corporate campus in the New Tampa area. The move was prompted by that year's hurricanes, which raised concerns about the security of the company's servers and switches, the heart of the business. The new 189,000-square-foot, six-floor facility was located outside of a flood evacuation zone. It also offered an improved electrical infrastructure.

The chief operating officer left in 2005 to return to his native Northwest and Evans assumed those responsibilities in addition to his own. Early in 2006 Evans then stepped aside and Tony Holcombe took over as president and chief executive officer. Holcombe had been the president at Emdeon Corp. and a member of the Syniverse board of directors since 2003. Evans agreed to stay on as chairman, focusing on strategy and mergers and acquisitions, until the 2007 annual meeting. At the end of 2006, however, Evans elected to leave to pursue other opportunities in the wireless broadband services industry. A non-executive chairman of the board was elected, Robert J. Marino, a member of the board for the previous two years and a man with 20 years of executive experience in telecommunications.

Under new leadership, Syniverse continued to pursue a strategy of internal and external growth. In June 2006 Hong Kong-based Interactive Technologies Holdings Limited, serving wireless carriers in the Asia Pacific market, was acquired for $38 million. In addition to growing its presence in the Far East, Syniverse gained a development team and new mobile-data-oriented products. Asian expansion continued in 2007 when Syniverse signed a multiyear agreement with SmarTone-Vodafone of Hong Kong to provide data clearing services, including roamer billing records.

PURCHASE OF BILLING SERVICES GROUP: 2007

Syniverse strengthened its presence in other markets as well in 2007. A regional headquarters was opened in Buenos Aires, Argentina, to cover Central America and the Caribbean, and a regional office was opened in São Paulo, Brazil. A new regional office also was opened in Dubai, United Arab Emirates, for the company's expanding customer base in the Middle East and Africa. Later in the year, Syniverse expanded its footprint in Eastern Europe, reaching a deal with VimpelCom Group to provide mobile communications clearinghouse services in Armenia, Kazakhstan, Russia, Tajikistan, Ukraine, and Uzbekistan. Syniverse closed 2007 with a major acquisition, the $290 million purchase of U.K. rival Billing Services Group, a deal that created an industry powerhouse and required several months to close because the European Union made sure the combination did not violate antimonopoly laws. Not only did the addition of BSG Wireless expand Syniverse's global footprint it also offered the promise of improved operating efficiencies that could have a positive impact on the company's bottom line.

Syniverse improved revenues to $377.5 million in 2007, resulting in net income of $52.4 million. Sales continued to grow in the first quarter of 2008, prompting management to estimate year-end revenues as high as $465 million and net income of about $60 million.

Ed Dinger

PRINCIPAL SUBSIDIARIES

Billing Services Group; Syniverse Technologies, Inc.; Syniverse Technologies, BV; Syniverse Brience, LLC.

PRINCIPAL COMPETITORS

Electronic Data Systems Corporation; VeriSign, Inc.; XIUS-bcgi.

FURTHER READING

Bora, Madahusmita, "Syniverse Star Rises in Stock Universe," *St. Petersburg Times,* May 8, 2008, p. 1D.

Goldstein, Alan, "GTE Wants to Make Money with Its Wealth of Information," *St. Petersburg Times,* May 6, 1990, p. 1I.

Hau, Louis, "Planned Syniverse IPO Dwarfs Neighbors,'" *St. Petersburg Times,* November 24, 2004, p. 1D.

Helgeson, Baird, "Syniverse Set to Issue Stock," *Tampa Tribune,* November 23, 2004, p. 1.

Hinman, Michael, "Syniverse Shares Fall on News of Alltel Acquisition," *Tampa Bay Business Journal,* June 5, 2008.

McElligott, Tim, "TSI's New Global Syniverse," *Telephony,* March 8, 2004, p. 16.

Mullins, Richard, "Syniverse Promotes Technology Exec. to President," *Tampa Tribune,* January 10, 2006, p. 1.

———, "Syniverse to Buy Competitor," *Tampa Tribune,* April 3, 2007, p. 4.

Whitaker-Moore, Aja, "Syniverse to Raise $425.5M," *Tampa Bay Business Journal,* November 23, 2004.

Taylor Devices, Inc.

90 Taylor Drive
North Tonawanda, New York 14120
U.S.A.
Telephone: (716) 694-0800
Fax: (716) 695-6015
Web site: http://www.taylordevices.com

Public Company
Incorporated: 1955
Employees: 92
Sales: $16.5 million (2007)
Stock Exchanges: NASDAQ
Ticker Symbol: TAYD
NAICS: 332312 Fabricated Structural Metal Manufacturing; 333298 All Other Industrial Machinery Manufacturing; 336399 All Other Motor Vehicle Parts Manufacturing; 333999 All Other General Purpose Machinery Manufacturing

■ ■ ■

Taylor Devices, Inc., designs and manufactures shock absorption, rate control, and energy storage devices that are used in machinery, equipment, and structures. The company's products—shock absorbers, fluid dampers, liquid springs, crane buffers, acoustic mountings—mitigate the effects of earthquake tremors, high winds, and the vibrations inherent in industrial machinery and equipment. Taylor Devices sells its products primarily in North America, serving industrial, heavy construction, aerospace, defense, and automotive customers.

EARLY YEARS

Taylor Devices' 36th anniversary marked a momentous year in its development, a year in which the spectacle of a father-and-son clash determined control over two companies founded by the patriarch of the family, Paul Taylor. Familial battles within a company's management often served as only a distraction, giving industry observers a salacious sideshow that provided little toward the company's benefit. In the case of the fight for Taylor Devices, however, the heated battle determined much, with the victor's vision for the company leading to an immediate improvement in the health of the company. Taylor Devices benefited in the end from the familial squabble at the beginning of the 1990s, but it also owed much to the architect of its early years, Paul Taylor.

Taylor formed Taylor Devices in 1955 when he was 40 years old. He established the company in North Tonawanda, New York, a small town located midway between Buffalo and Niagara Falls. From his facilities in North Tonawanda, Taylor began serving industrial and military customers, leading a small staff that designed and manufactured tension control, energy storage, and shock absorption devices to be used in various types of machinery and equipment. Not long after founding Taylor Devices, Taylor formed another, smaller company, Tayco Developments, which he took public in 1963. Although a separate company from publicly traded Taylor Devices, Tayco Developments served as the research-and-development arm of his efforts to produce tension control, energy storage, and shock absorption devices.

COMPANY PERSPECTIVES

In general, all of our products are used to absorb, control, or mitigate the motion of masses. This motion may be transient, such as caused by earthquakes or explosions, or steady state, such as caused by vibration or controlled power excitation.

DOUGLAS TAYLOR ENTERS THE COMPANY

Paul Taylor's son, Douglas Taylor, joined Taylor Devices in 1968, more than 20 years before the pair would square off in the company's boardroom. Before hostilities broke out, father and son worked together amicably, building a small yet vertically integrated business presence in North Tonawanda. Tayco Realty Corp. was formed in 1977, a company majority owned by Taylor Devices. The subsidiary owned and leased office and manufacturing space to Taylor Devices. In 1984, another subsidiary was formed, a company that served as a source of controversy between Paul Taylor and Douglas Taylor. Tayco Technology Inc. was formed to manufacture inexpensive plastic shock absorbers for use in equipment such as exercise machines.

When Tayco Technology was formed, Taylor Devices was generating $4.7 million in annual sales. The company relied heavily on defense and aerospace related business, deriving 63 percent of its revenue from such work. The nature of the company's business, most of which was classified, made it impossible in many instances to inform investors of the types of projects it was involved in, creating a veil of secrecy over the North Tonawanda operations. What shareholders did know was that the company recorded flat sales growth during much of the 1980s. By the end of the decade, Taylor Devices continued to generate less than $5 million in annual revenue, posting modest net income of roughly $30,000.

Taylor Devices enjoyed an uptick in business at the start of the 1990s when the United States launched Operation Desert Storm. The company, which had worked on the U.S. Air Force's B-2 Stealth Bomber, supplied sophisticated, hydraulic shock absorbers to the U.S. military during the Gulf War. Specifically, the company supplied highly engineered shock absorbers for the U.S. Navy's Tomahawk missiles, which required eight Taylor Devices-designed shock absorbers for support.

FATHER AND SON FIGHT FOR CONTROL

One month after cease-fire was declared in the Persian Gulf, hostilities in North Tonawanda erupted, touching off what Paul Taylor, in a December 2, 1991, interview with *Business First of Buffalo,* referred to as the "April Massacre." Although there was no evidence of discord between 76-year-old Paul Taylor and 43-year-old Douglas Taylor before 1991, Douglas Taylor clearly had been unhappy with the financial performance of the family businesses for some time. Stagnant revenue growth and meager profits at Taylor Devices during the 1980s represented the bright spot among the four businesses. Tayco Developments, Tayco Realty, and Tayco Technology had been losing money for years. Tayco Developments, a company with only two employees, generated $43,894 in revenue in 1991, a year in which it posted a $61,000 loss. As badly as Tayco Developments performed, Tayco Technology performed even worse. The subsidiary never made any money, racked up more than $1 million in losses, and defaulted on several loans.

Taylor Devices' board of directors was not aware Tayco Technology had defaulted on any loans. When the directors learned of the delinquent payments, they confronted Paul Taylor at the company's annual meeting in April 1991. After Paul Taylor refused to answer their questions, the board held a vote and named Douglas Taylor president of Taylor Devices. "At that meeting," Paul Taylor explained in the November 11, 1991, edition of *Business First of Buffalo,* "I was fired from my position as president and barred from future entry. My son demanded that I return my company car, and if I refused he said he would call the police."

Immediately after being elected president, Douglas Taylor shut down Tayco Technology. Paul Taylor responded by filing a lawsuit in May 1991 against his son and two other Taylor Devices executives. Concurrently, he launched a proxy battle to regain control of Tayco Developments, in which he held a 36 percent stake, and Taylor Devices. Douglas Taylor offered his riposte, filing a countersuit that alleged his father had mismanaged the company, had entered into an agreement with an investment banking company without the approval of Taylor Devices' directors, and had commandeered more than $145,000 from his other businesses without board approval to keep Tayco Technology afloat.

The fight for control of the two public companies founded by Paul Taylor became a public dispute covered by the business press and watched closely by the residents of North Tonawanda. Paul Taylor showed little hesitation in expressing his anger at the turn of events, leaving no question that he deeply resented his ouster.

KEY DATES

1955: Paul Taylor establishes Taylor Devices.
1968: Paul Taylor's son, Douglas Taylor, joins Taylor Devices.
1991: Paul Taylor is fired as president and is replaced by Douglas Taylor.
1999: Taylor Devices designs shock absorbers used on the retractable roof at Safeco Field in Seattle, Washington.
2005: Taylor Devices celebrates its 50th anniversary.

Douglas Taylor, in contrast, used a different tone in public. "This really isn't a family feud," he claimed in the November 11, 1991, edition of *Business First of Buffalo.* "This has not had any effect one way or another on our personal relationship. This is strictly business." Whether or not Douglas Taylor truly believed his words, there was no doubt about Paul Taylor's feelings when the proxy vote took place in November 1991.

Father and son each offered a slate of directors for shareholders to approve, an election that would decide which generation of the Taylor family would lead Taylor Devices and Tayco Developments forward. The results gave an overwhelming victory to one side. Paul Taylor received 1,635 votes for his list of directors. Douglas Taylor's roster of directors received 1,093,811 votes. The defeat left Paul Taylor fuming. "I'll fight this to my last dime and dying breath," he said in a December 2, 1991, interview with *Business First of Buffalo.* "What he's done is wrong. Some people will answer upstairs for this nonsense." His next comment confirmed irreparable harm had been done to the relationship with his son. "What he's doing is wrong," Paul Taylor said, "and the only place I want to see him is in the courtroom or at a shareholders' meeting. That excludes the funeral parlor when I kick the bucket."

A NEW ERA IN LEADERSHIP

Although Paul Taylor vowed to continue his fight, the proxy battle in November essentially ended the battle. He began developing an auxiliary jet engine for boats. "It can go 200 miles-per-hour and weighs only about 150 pounds," he declared in his December 2, 1991, interview with *Business First of Buffalo.* Soon afterward, he formed another North Tonawanda company, Kinarrest, which developed commercial plastic and compound products. Meanwhile, Taylor Devices shareholders were witnessing the start of the Douglas Taylor era, and they liked what they saw.

One year after gaining control of the family businesses, Douglas Taylor could point to tangible evidence of success. Sales at Taylor Devices jumped 37 percent, surpassing the $6 million mark, while net income soared from $51,986 to $233,965. At Tayco Developments, which increased its payroll from two to three employees during the year, the results were more heartening. The company's revenue increased from $43,894 to $311,228 and a $61,610 loss was transformed into a $127,491 profit. "I've taken the chains off," Taylor declared in a September 21, 1992, interview with *Business First of Buffalo,* referring to his treatment of Taylor Devices employees. "This is what we expect, what the company expects, and they've tried their darnedest to meet those goals." A director of the company offered his view on the contrasting managerial styles of Paul Taylor and Douglas Taylor in the same interview. "I thought we had some good people and thought they could do better without the rigid discipline of the past," he said. "Rather than having Paul Taylor having control and stifling everyone, it's now more of a team effort than a paternal effort. Before it was P.T.'s invention and he had say over everything from garbage can liners to production to engineering."

With the defining event of its first 40 years in business behind it, Taylor Devices pressed ahead under the leadership of Douglas Taylor. By the end of the 1990s, the company had eclipsed the $10 million mark in sales, generating $11.1 million in revenue. The total was derived from its six major product lines: seismic dampers; fluidicshoks; crane and industrial buffers; self-adjusting shock absorbers; liquid die springs; and vibration dampers.

TAYLOR DEVICES IN THE NEW CENTURY

One of the most high-profile projects in Taylor Device's history reached completion by the end of the 1990s. Taylor Devices was called in for its expertise in the construction of Seattle, Washington's Safeco Field, the new stadium for Major League Baseball's Seattle Mariners. For the $517 million project, completed in 1999, Taylor Devices designed and made its largest shock absorbers ever, eight, 24-foot-long dampers that weighed 4.5 tons each. The shock absorbers were developed to serve as a buffer between Safeco Field's side columns and the 13,000-ton retractable roof that the columns supported.

Taylor Devices would have preferred a more robust construction market in the United States during the first years of the 21st century. Construction activity, particularly heavy construction, was on the wane as Douglas Taylor guided his company toward its 50th anniversary. Some of the sting from the declining construction-related sales was lessened, however, by bustling activity overseas. At Taylor Devices' annual meeting during its 50th anniversary year, five of the six projects presented to shareholders were taking place outside the United States, with four of the projects centered in Asia. China was an area of particular interest to the company. "Everywhere you look in Shanghai, there's construction projects everywhere," a Taylor Devices executive said in the November 14, 2005, edition of *Buffalo News.* New bridge construction, industrial construction, and the erection of multistory buildings in Shanghai and elsewhere in China benefited Taylor Devices, creating a need for its products.

Financially, the years surrounding the company's 50th anniversary inspired both optimism and pessimism. Sales in 2003 reached $13.8 million before slipping to $11.2 million in 2005. Revenues began to climb during the ensuing period, reaching $14.7 million in 2006 and $16.5 million in 2007. Most encouraging, profits climbed strongly after a $60,000 loss in 2004. Taylor Devices posted gains of $202,107 in 2005, $485,793 in 2006, and $619, 271 in 2007. Looking ahead, with Douglas Taylor at the helm, Taylor Devices hoped the pattern of rising financial totals would continue in the future.

Jeffrey L. Covell

PRINCIPAL SUBSIDIARIES

Tayco Realty Corporation (58%).

PRINCIPAL COMPETITORS

Cleveland Pneumatic Tool Company; Menasco Manufacturing Company; Kaydon Corporation; ZF Zachs Automotive of America; ITT Corporation.

FURTHER READING

Baker, M. Sharon, "Father Loses to Son in Proxy Battle," *Business First of Buffalo,* December 2, 1991, p. 1.

———, "Father, Son Do Battle over Taylor Firms," *Business First of Buffalo,* November 11, 1991, p. 1.

———, "Left to His Own Devices, Douglas Taylor Turns a Profit at His Father's Old Company," *Business First of Buffalo,* September 21, 1992, p. 1.

———, "New Government Contract Makes Taylor Brass Bullish on Future," *Business First of Buffalo,* September 30, 1991, p. 16.

Glynn, Matt, "Taylor Devices Is Keeping Busy with Projects Overseas," *Buffalo News,* November 14, 2005.

Lewis, John, "Super-Size Shocks Stop Stadium Shakes," *Design News,* January 22, 2001, p. 39.

McMeekin, Bill, "Investor Buys 5.86 Percent of Taylor Devices' Stock," *Business First of Buffalo,* October 16, 1989, p. 5.

"Taylor Devices Inc.," *Business First of Buffalo,* January 2, 1989, p. 14.

Teknor Apex Company

505 Central Avenue
Pawtucket, Rhode Island 02861
U.S.A.
Telephone: (401) 725-8000
Toll Free: (800) 556-3864
Fax: (401) 722-9511
Web site: http://www.teknorapex.com

Private Company
Incorporated: 1924 as Apex Tire
Employees: 2,240
Sales: $680 million (2006 est.)
NAICS: 325991 Custom Compounding of Purchased Resin; 325188 All Other Inorganic Chemical Manufacturing; 326220 Rubber and Plastics Hoses and Belting Manufacturing

■ ■ ■

Teknor Apex Company is a privately held, Pawtucket, Rhode Island-based international manufacturer of advanced polymer materials, operating facilities in nine United States locations as well as units in the United Kingdom, China, and Singapore. The company divides its business among seven divisions. The Vinyl division specializes in polyvinyl chloride (PVC) compounds, used in wire and cable, automotive, appliance, medical, furniture, housewares, and building and construction products. The Thermoplastic Elastomer Compounds (TPE) division serves the wire and cable, packaging, transportation, sporting goods, writing instruments, medical, and building and construction markets. Teknor's Engineered Thermoplastics division is comprised of subsidiaries Chem Polymer Corporation and Singapore-based Singapore Polymer. These units produce a variety of grades of nylon as well as other compounds used in the automotive, building and construction, electrical, steel wire coating, and consumer products markets. The Teknor Color Company division supplies colorants to the international plastics industry, covering the full spectrum of polymers.

Manufacturing out of a plant in Brownsville, Tennessee, Teknor's Chemical division is a custom producer of a wide variety of ethers used by major multinational customers, and plasticizers and additives used by other Teknor divisions. The Specialty Compounding division provides blending services, producing thermoplastic compounds and additive blends to produce such products as flame retardants, antioxidants, UV light stabilizers, heat stabilizers, and antistats. Finally, Teknor's Lawn & Garden division is a major U.S. producer of widely distributed vinyl hoses, including commercial hoses, reel hoses, sprinkler hoses, soaker hoses, as well as farm and boat-camper hoses. Teknor also sells the NeverKink brand of garden hose. Teknor is headed by the third generation of the Fain family.

TIRE STORE ORIGINS: 1924

Teknor Apex was founded in Providence, Rhode Island, in 1924 as Apex Tire, a tire recapper and retailer, by Alfred A. Fain and his son-in-law, Albert Plavin. A retired wholesale grocery executive, Fain was new to the tire trade but fared well enough to grow the business into a chain of 16 stores spread across the East Coast. In 1936

COMPANY PERSPECTIVES

Teknor Apex is dedicated to providing our customers quality products with superior service and value.

he was joined by his 22-year-old son, Norman M. Fain, after he graduated from the University of Rhode Island. The younger Fain was well familiar with the business, having spent his summers working in the Providence store. Apex moved its headquarters to Pawtucket, Rhode Island, in the wake of a hurricane in 1938 that destroyed the Providence location.

It was during World War II that Apex branched beyond tire recapping and retailing. Like most of U.S. industry, Apex served the military in the first half of the 1940s, recapping tires for Navy airplanes. Because the company had such a high demand for rubber, the U.S. government allowed Apex to acquire rubber mixing equipment. The equipment became operational in the final year of the war, 1945, prompting the company to change its name to Apex Tire and Rubber Company.

In the postwar years, Apex phased out tire recapping in favor of producing rubber compounds to serve the growing industrial needs of New England during the economic boom that followed the end of the conflict. The company also grew through acquisitions, purchasing Thompson Chemical Company. Norman Fain then recruited a fellow University of Rhode Island alumnus, Victor J. Baxt, a chemist, to take charge of the business in 1946. It was around this time that Apex also became involved in vinyl to keep pace with a switch in the wire and cable industry from rubber to vinyl. What began as the fulfillment of a request to mix vinyl compounds for nearby American Insulated Wire became a focus in 1949 when Apex began to produce its own vinyl resins and plasticizers. The company was among the first to develop UL-approved compounds for the wire and cable industry.

POSTWAR EXPANSION

The postwar era brought the rise of the suburbs where much of the baby boom generation was raised, lawns were maintained, and gardens planted. It was not surprising that Apex would take advantage of its vinyl capabilities in the late 1950s to begin producing vinyl garden hoses. It was a sidelight that over the years grew into a significant portion of the company's business. The product started out as a non-reinforced hose, but that would change over the years. Apex took advantage of its experience in the tire business to produce radial-belted garden hoses, and as women became the primary buyers, the company added colors. The company's colorant business had its origins during the 1950s as well, when in 1959 Apex began offering colorants for plastic to its vinyl compounds customers. In addition, Apex's extrusion technology that produced hoses was put to use to manufacture one of the 1950s' biggest fads: the hula-hoop.

The decade of the 1950s also saw Apex expand its production capacity and reach across the United States. In 1956 a new plant was opened in Hebronville, Massachusetts, to produce chemicals, PVC resin, and phthalic anhydride, an industrial chemical used in the large-scale production of plasticizers. Three years later Apex opened a plant in Aberdeen, Mississippi, to produce PVC resins and compounds, and plasticizers. Garden hose production was added in 1961.

The Fain family decided to sell Apex and Thompson Chemical in 1964 to Continental Oil Company. The operations were bundled into a subsidiary called Thompson Apex, which would have a short tenure under Conoco's ownership. Conoco ran afoul of the Federal Trade Commission because of further acquisitions in chemicals and was forced to resolve the restraint of trade charges by divesting some of its assets. Thus, in 1968 the Fain family and others repurchased Thompson Apex. During Conoco's brief ownership, the company opened a PVC resin plant in Assonet, Massachusetts, as well as a facility in the United Kingdom.

Norman Fain was joined in the purchase of Thompson Apex by the Baxt family and other investors. Fain served as chairman of the company that had taken the name Teknor Apex. Conoco had created a distinctive diamond logo around the initials T and A, and in order to keep using it, Fain concocted the Teknor Apex name. He took over as chairman of Teknor, and held the same post at another family enterprise, Apex Inc., a regional discount department-store chain. In addition to Victor Baxt, another key partner was Herbert Malin, a former Dow Chemical engineer who had come to Apex in 1956.

ENTRY OF JONATHAN FAIN: 1972

A third generation of the Fain family joined the company in 1972 when Norman's son, Jonathan D. Fain, became a full-time employee. The 1970s also brought further expansion to Teknor. A new plant was opened in Brownsville, Tennessee, in 1971. City of Industry, California-based Maclin Company was then acquired in 1977 to provide Teknor with a West Coast

KEY DATES

1924: Alfred Fain founds Apex Tire.
1945: Name is changed to Apex Tire and Rubber Company.
1964: Continental Oil Company acquires Apex.
1968: Fain family buys back company, which is renamed Teknor Apex.
1972: Third generation, represented by Jonathan D. Fain, joins company.
1993: Jonathan Fain is named chief executive.
2001: Singapore Polymer Corp. Ltd. is acquired.
2005: Chem Polymer is acquired.
2006: Rubber division is phased out.

presence and complete its national footprint. In addition, Teknor in 1974 renovated its Pawtucket facility, which had once housed a retail operation, to expand the company's manufacturing capacity. The colorant business also expanded through acquisitions. In 1981 the Teknor Color Company was formed to house these units as a Teknor subsidiary. Diversity became the watchword for Teknor, allowing it to weather difficult economic conditions in the early 1980s and early 1990s. Among the product lines the company unveiled were geomarine tubing, mats, telephone cord plastics, and automobile steering wheels and dashboards. To support the garden hose business and provide vinyl compounding, Teknor opened a new plant in Fountain Inn, South Carolina, in 1992.

In 1993 Jonathan Fain replaced his father as president, but Norman Fain did not retire. In fact, he continued to come into the office almost every day until six weeks before he died in November 2003 at the age of 89. A pair of companies were acquired in the 1990s to bolster Teknor's colorant business. Lodi, Ohio-based Accurate Color and Compounding was purchased in 1995, and Jacksonville, Texas-based Progressive Polymers was added a year later. Teknor also acquired St. Albans, Vermont-based QST, a compounder of thermoplastic elastomers.

Expansion continued for Teknor in the new century. A new plant built in Henderson, Kentucky, in 2000 bolstered the company's thermoplastic elastomers business. A year later Teknor turned its attention overseas, acquiring Singapore Polymer Corp. Ltd. (SPC), a step taken to remain close to the petrochemical industry that had migrated to Southeast Asia. The most diversified compounding company in the region, SPC produced polyolefin, styrenic polymer, thermoplastic elastomer, and PVC compounds, serving the wire and cable, bottle, medical, footwear, and automotive markets. A 100,000-square-foot PVC compounding plant was on the verge of opening, and construction on another 100,000-square-foot headquarters and manufacturing complex was already underway, but was early enough along that Teknor was still able to make sure the lines were set up in a manner consistent with its North American operations, thus providing global customers with a consistent product. When the new plant opened in late 2003 it produced thermoplastic elastomers, black and white masterbatches, and engineering resin compounds.

EUROPEAN ASPIRATIONS: 2002

A few months after the SPC purchase, Teknor, in April 2002, turned its attention to Europe. An agreement was made with a German firm, PRS Plastic Technologie Service GmbH, to produce Teknor's thermoplastic vulcanisate materials for sale in the European Union. Teknor grew its European presence later in 2004 with the acquisition of a U.K. company, Chem Polymer, an engineering thermoplastics company, providing Teknor with its first manufacturing operations in Europe. Teknor gained plants in the British West Midlands, in Oldbury and Cinderford, as well as a plant in Fort Myers, Florida. Not only did the location of Chem Polymer's plants allow Teknor to better serve the global needs of customers by making it more of a single source, Teknor's and Chem Polymer's product lines complemented one another nicely. "In general," according to the *Providence Journal,* Teknor "makes the softer materials used by manufacturers of plastic items; Chem Polymer makes the harder materials, such as reinforced and structural plastics." As an example, "Chem Polymer makes materials that are used for the housing on many electric drills and other hand tools, and Teknor Apex materials make up the softer hand grips for the tools."

While most of Teknor's product lines were thriving, the rubber division, which had provided the foundation for the company, had become a money-losing operation, due in large measure to the high cost of oil. An increasing number of consumers were opting for smaller cars, which used smaller tires and lowered the demand for rubber. In August 2007, Teknor announced that the division was being eliminated, thereby cutting 150 jobs at the Pawtucket and Brownsville, Tennessee, plants where the rubber compounds were produced. Another 40 employees were slated to take early retirement. Also affected by the move was Teknor's Blocks and Mats division. A buyer was lined up and the business was divested at the start of 2007.

MANUFACTURING IN CHINA: 2007

Teknor opened a new plant in the Suzhou Industrial Park in Jiangsu, China, in October 2007. A new subsidiary operated the facility under the name of Teknor Apex (Suzhou) Advanced Polymer Compounds Co. Pte. Ltd. The plant manufactured rigid and flexible vinyl, thermoplastic elastomers, engineering thermoplastics, and other specialty compounds needed in the appliance, automotive, building, electronics, medical device, wire and cable, and other markets. Again, this initiative was part of an overarching goal of becoming a single-source provider to global customers. In keeping with this strategy, Teknor in 2008 established Teknor Apex UK Holdings Ltd. to serve as a holding company for its European units and coordinate the company's expansion in this important market.

Ed Dinger

PRINCIPAL SUBSIDIARIES

Carolina Company; Haywood Company; Maclin Company; Singapore Polymer Corp. Ltd.; Teknor Apex (Suzhou) Advanced Polymer Compounds Co. Pte Ltd.; Teknor Apex U.K. Ltd.; Teknor Color Company.

PRINCIPAL COMPETITORS

GLS Corporation; RB Rubber Products, Inc.; Tekni-Plex, Inc.

FURTHER READING

Downing, Neil, "Pawtucket, R.I. Raw Materials Maker Buys British Company," *Providence Journal,* January 4, 2005.

Esposito, Frank, "Teknor Apex Wrapping Up Asia Expansion," *Plastics News,* July 28, 2003, p. 10.

———, "Teknor Sets Own Pace Through Downturn," *Plastics News,* May 7, 2001, p. 13.

———, "Teknor Sheds Rubber Division," *Plastics News,* September 18, 2006, p. 16.

———, "Teknor's Norman Fain, 89, Dies," *Plastics News,* November 17, 2003, p. 22.

Needham, Cynthia, "Apex Chief, Philanthropist Norman Fain Dies at 89," *Providence Journal,* November 2, 2003, p. B1.

"Teknor Apex," *Chilton's Hardware Age,* May 1988, p. 62.

Tesoro Corporation

300 Concord Plaza Drive
San Antonio, Texas 78216-6999
U.S.A.
Telephone: (210) 283-2000
Fax: (210) 283-2045
Web site: http://www.tsocorp.com

Public Company
Incorporated: 1964 as Tesoro Petroleum Corporation
Employees: 5,500
Sales: $21.92 billion (2007)
Stock Exchanges: New York
Ticker Symbol: TSO
NAICS: 324110 Petroleum Refineries; 424710 Petroleum Bulk Stations and Terminals; 424720 Petroleum and Petroleum Products Merchant Wholesalers (Except Bulk Stations and Terminals); 447110 Gasoline Stations with Convenience Stores; 447190 Other Gasoline Stations; 486110 Pipeline Transportation of Crude Oil; 486910 Pipeline Transportation of Refined Petroleum Products

■ ■ ■

Tesoro Corporation is an independent energy company concentrating on refining, distributing, and marketing petroleum products. With seven refineries in Alaska, Hawaii, North Dakota, Utah, California, and Washington state having a combined capacity of 660,000 barrels per day, Tesoro is one of the largest independent refining and marketing firms in the western United States. In connection with its refining operations, Tesoro sells refined products, including gasoline, jet fuel, diesel fuel, and heavy fuel oils, in the bulk and wholesale markets and also owns and operates 900 miles of crude oil and refined petroleum product pipelines. On the marketing side, the company distributes its products in 17 western and mid-continental states through more than 900 branded retail stations, 445 of which are owned by the company and operated under the Tesoro, Shell, Mirastar, and USA Gasoline brands. Through an agreement with Wal-Mart Stores, Inc., Tesoro sells its gasoline at selected Wal-Mart locations in 13 western states, with these stations operating under the Mirastar brand, which was developed by the company exclusively for the retailing giant.

In its early years Tesoro grew rapidly through the acquisition of a wide spectrum of energy businesses. This growth weakened the company's financial status, however, and it was later forced to shed many of its subsidiaries and devote a large amount of its attention to avoiding takeover, both internal and external, and battling with dissident shareholders. Later, by the late 1990s, the company appeared to have found a formula for success by abandoning its upstream operations and beefing up its core downstream activities. Key acquisitions of refineries and gas stations in 2001, 2002, and 2007 secured Tesoro's position as a leader in its sector among U.S. independents.

OFFSHOOT OF TEXSTAR

Tesoro was founded by Robert V. West, Jr., in 1964. West had earned a doctorate in chemical engineering and then spent his entire career in the petroleum industry,

> **COMPANY PERSPECTIVES**
>
> Our strategy is to create a value-added refining and marketing business that has economies of scale, a competitive cost structure, effective management information systems and outstanding employees focused on achieving operational excellence in a global market while providing stockholders competitive returns in any economic environment. Our goals are focused on operating our facilities in a safe, reliable and environmentally responsible way, improving our profitability by achieving greater operational and administrative efficiencies and using excess cash flows from operations in a balanced way to create shareholder value.

rising to become president of Texstar Petroleum Company, a subsidiary of a larger company, Texstar Corporation, that was controlled by Texas wildcatter Tom Slick. After Slick's death in a plane crash, West persuaded the executors of Slick's estate to sell the company West ran, with its oil-producing properties, to him. West borrowed $6.5 million to purchase the stock of Texstar Petroleum from its parent company and merged Texstar into the new company he had set up, Tesoro Petroleum Corporation, *Tesoro* meaning "treasure" in Spanish.

In its previous incarnation, Tesoro had been a small but profitable oil and gas company. In its new form, however, the company carried such a high debt burden that it was difficult for Tesoro to save the money necessary to expand. West embarked on an effort to financially stabilize his company by joining it with another, stronger entity. After three years of searching, West found two publicly owned companies that suited his needs, and in a complicated series of transactions, the three merged. With funding from Chicago's Continental Illinois bank, the Intex Oil Company (which had been founded in California in 1939 as the Exploration and Development Company) was joined with the Sioux Oil Company and with Tesoro. The new entity took the name of Tesoro in December 1968.

With this transformation, Tesoro became a company possessing a pool of stockholders, solid financial standing, a listing on the American Stock Exchange, and workable arrangements with investment banking houses, allowing it to raise capital for further expansion. West embarked on a ten-year spree of acquisitions in the energy business, picking up a mixed bag of companies at bargain-basement prices. The first step in this direction was taken when Tesoro sold $25 million worth of stock in late 1968. With this money, the company paid off its bank debt entirely, leaving $18 million in cash for investment.

SPATE OF ACQUISITIONS

Among Tesoro's first acquisitions were Clymore Petroleum Corporation and Trident Offshore Company, Ltd., in which Tesoro purchased a 55 percent interest. Tesoro's most important new venture involved the island government of Trinidad and Tobago. The company discovered that the British Petroleum Company (BP) planned to divest itself of its oil-producing operations in Trinidad and that the country's government intended to buy them. Because the Trinidadian government had no experience in the petroleum business, Tesoro was able to persuade it to enter into joint ownership of the properties, forming Trinidad-Tesoro Petroleum Company Limited. Incorporated in Trinidad in 1969, the company was 50.1 percent owned by the island's government, with the remainder owned by Tesoro. Both partners contributed $50,000 to the venture, which subsequently purchased BP's holdings, including properties, equipment, and remaining oil products for $28 million. The rest of the money necessary for this purchase was raised through loans from banks and a deferred payment plan with BP. Once it had taken over BP's operations in Trinidad, Tesoro was able to restore them to profit-making status by renovating existing wells and making production less wasteful.

In addition to its operations in Trinidad, Tesoro also commenced construction of a refinery for crude oil on the west coast of Alaska at Kenai in early 1969. Building this facility took more than a year, and when it was completed, Tesoro experienced difficulty in operating it profitably. The problem of bringing crude oil to the refinery and transporting finished products to market had yet to be resolved in an economical fashion. In addition, the company faced stiff competition from the much larger Standard Oil Company (California), later Chevron Corporation, which owned the only other refinery in Alaska, producing a difficult competitive marketplace. "We held our noses and went underwater for a while," West told *Forbes* magazine in 1973, explaining the refinery's money-losing operations. Eventually, however, prices for refined petroleum products did rise, and the Alaskan refinery became profitable.

Tesoro also continued to purchase companies with a broad range of functions in the petroleum industry, including truck and pipeline transportation, petroleum

KEY DATES

1964: Robert V. West Jr. founds Tesoro Petroleum Corporation as a spinoff of Texstar Corporation.
1968: Via merger with Intex Oil Company and Sioux Oil Company, Tesoro becomes a publicly traded firm.
1969: Company acquires half-interest in British Petroleum's oil-producing operations in Trinidad and Tobago, with the island nation's government holding the other half; Tesoro begins construction of an oil refinery on the west coast of Alaska.
1971: Company enters the marketing sector through the purchase of S&N Investment Company and Digas Company, operator of gasoline service stations.
1974: Following the purchase of two sizable exploratory tracts in Bolivia, Tesoro Inter-American Production Company is formed and takes responsibility for Caribbean and Latin American operations.
1975: Company spends $83 million for a 36.7 percent interest in the Puerto Rican firm Commonwealth Oil Refining Company (Corco).
1977: Tesoro writes off $59 million of its investment in Corco, which soon files for bankruptcy.
1980: Company fends off the first of several takeover attempts by Diamond Shamrock Corporation.
1985: Company sells its share of Trinidad-Tesoro to the island nation's government.
1988: Tesoro sells its domestic oil and gas producing properties to American Exploration.
1995: Company sells some of its oil and gas production properties in Texas to Coastal Corporation for $74 million.
1998: Company acquires two refineries in Hawaii and Washington state, as well as 32 retail gas stations in Hawaii.
1999: Company's exit from exploration and production is completed by selling domestic operations to EEX Corporation and the Bolivian-based activities to BG PLC.
2000: An agreement is reached with Wal-Mart Stores, Inc., to open and operate filling stations at Wal-Mart outlets under the name Mirastar.
2001: Tesoro acquires refineries in Utah and North Dakota and 45 gas stations in a $677 million deal with BP p.l.c.
2002: Golden Eagle refinery in Martinez, California, is acquired.
2003: Sale of marine services unit leaves Tesoro a pure refiner and marketer of petroleum products.
2004: Company name is changed to Tesoro Corporation.
2007: In a $1.82 billion deal, Tesoro acquires a refinery located near Los Angeles and 276 Shell-branded, southern California gas stations.

equipment manufacturing and rental, and crude oil production. In looking for acquisitions, the company sought properties that not only were profitable but also showed promise of continuing to return profits over the long term. Accordingly, Tesoro purchased Cardinal Transports, Inc., in early 1969. In March of the following year, the company added a Texas firm called Petroleum Distributing Company as well as the Land & Marine Rental Company and the Louisiana Barreling Company. Later that year, Tesoro invested in the Arnold Pipe Rental Company, Ltd., D&W Investments, Inc., and certain portions of Spira Chek, Inc. In early 1971 Tesoro continued its vertical integration when it took on the operation of gasoline service stations by buying the S&N Investment Company and the Digas Company, both located in southern California. These chains were subsequently expanded into many areas of the United States.

NYSE LISTING

With its diverse operations, and activities in both Trinidad and Alaska running smoothly, Tesoro readied itself for further expansion with another sale of stock. In a symbolic move, the company switched its listing from the American Stock Exchange to the New York Stock Exchange, becoming the only San Antonio-based firm to be listed on the so-called Big Board. In August 1971 Tesoro raised $32.2 million in an equity offering. With these funds, the company increased its geographical reach once again, buying Redco, a subsidiary of Asamera Oil, which owned land on Borneo in Indonesia that could be explored for oil, as well as the rights to any oil found.

West also began negotiations with an Arab ruler to refine and market crude oil produced in his country. With the expectation that these talks would bear fruit, Tesoro established in September 1972 a wholly owned European subsidiary, Tesoro-Europe Petroleum B.V., to market petroleum products. In addition, the company bought the Dutch firm DeHumber Handelmaatschappij B.V. and four associated companies for $4 million. These companies handled wholesale and retail marketing operations. Tesoro's European interests were subsequently further expanded when the company acquired an interest in the rights to explore for petroleum in the Dutch sector of the North Sea oilfield.

During this time, Tesoro continued to expand its American holdings, purchasing the Charles Wheatley Company in February 1972. This privately owned firm manufactured valves for use in the oil industry. In May 1973 Tesoro bought FWI, Inc., from Falcon Seaboard, Inc., in Houston. During the next year Eagle Transport Company and Turner Drill Pipe, two petroleum industry services located in Texas, also were brought onboard. By the end of 1973 Tesoro was able to report that its steady pace of acquisitions in all sectors of the petroleum industry had allowed it to quintuple its earnings in just five years in business.

In 1973 the Organization of Petroleum Exporting Countries (OPEC) oil embargo caused an energy crisis in the United States, raising awareness of the importance of alternative energy sources to petroleum. Accordingly, Tesoro moved for the first time to incorporate other forms of fossil fuels in its operations. In September 1974 the company formed Tesoro Coal Company. Four months later it increased its coal holdings when it bought the Buckhorn Hazard Coal Company.

Geographically, Tesoro moved onto another continent when it acquired two sizable exploratory tracts in Bolivia. This led to the formation in 1974 of Tesoro Inter-American Production Company, which took over the company's holdings in Trinidad and also took responsibility for future operations in the Caribbean and Latin America. By the end of the 1974 fiscal year, Tesoro had gross revenues exceeding $500 million and earnings of about $60 million. The company had operations in 30 states and five foreign countries.

SOURING OF CORCO INVESTMENT

Operating from this position of strength, Tesoro made a serious error in June 1975, when it paid $83 million for 36.7 percent of the stock of the Commonwealth Oil Refining Company (Corco), a Puerto Rican oil refiner and petrochemical processor that was one and a half times as large as Tesoro. Corco had been caught short by the sharp rise in petroleum prices in 1974, and its profitability had fallen, bringing the cost of its stock down as well. Tesoro sent out a team of new managers to try to turn around the fortunes of its new subsidiary.

Despite the fact that Tesoro's debt had grown in size to 1.3 times its equity, the company continued its pace of acquisitions, purchasing the GO Drilling Company of Texas, which owned three oil drilling rigs. In the following year, the company expanded its Alaskan operations when it bought the Nikiski Alaska Pipeline Company. Tesoro diversified into a third area of the energy industry, forming Tesoro Natural Gas Company in April 1977 to purchase and transport natural gas.

By this time, however, Tesoro's financial position had become perilous, and the company's era of rapid expansion through haphazard acquisition came to a close. In 1977 Tesoro was forced to write off $59 million in Corco investments and lost $58 million overall. This bad news prompted a suit by shareholders against the company, alleging that Tesoro's Corco investment constituted mismanagement. It was clear that the company had bitten off more than it could chew.

Tesoro's lenders, concerned about the company's level of past borrowing, forced the company to liquidate many of its properties to earn cash to pay off some of its debt. Tesoro sold its North Sea oil interests as well as an equipment manufacturer. The company also was forced to sell all but five of its American oil and gas properties, including refineries in Montana and Wyoming. This divestiture program continued throughout 1978, which was capped by Corco's declaration of Chapter 11 bankruptcy. Tesoro subsequently reduced its interest in this subsidiary, surrendering its stock in 1981 and selling its final ownership of Corco for $2.8 million in 1983. Overall, Tesoro had sacrificed a vast amount of capital in its bid to make Corco succeed.

Further difficulties arose in December 1978 when various investigations by the Internal Revenue Service (IRS), the Securities and Exchange Commission, and the U.S. Justice Department resulted in the company having to pay tax penalties. It also had to disclose that it had paid more than $1.3 million in bribes to officials in Bolivia and other foreign countries over a six-year period. This commenced a five-year federal investigation of Tesoro by a grand jury, which was not closed until February 1984.

In an effort to rebuild, Tesoro brought in management consultants in 1979 to help it create a plan for future growth. West told *Business Week* that Tesoro had undergone "a general change in philosophy" that would result in a more careful, integrated, and planned program of expansion and acquisition. As part of its new strategy, the company invested $45 million to upgrade its Alaskan refining facility, confident that the facility's remote location and ready source of raw materials in the Alaska oilfields would continue to make it a profitable enterprise.

FENDING OFF TAKEOVER BIDS

By 1980 Tesoro had reduced its debt load to 20 percent of equity from 80 percent and was once again in the black. Belying his vow to stick to sensible investment in the petroleum industry, West made an abortive attempt to purchase Gulfstream American, a manufacturer of corporate jets, early in the year. After this was abandoned, Tesoro itself became the object of a potential corporate takeover in August when the Diamond Shamrock Corporation, a chemicals and natural resources producer, purchased 4.5 percent of the company's stock and announced that it would buy the company in an effort to move into the petroleum industry. Tesoro quickly filed two lawsuits to block this attempt. When Trinidad's government announced that it would not work with Diamond Shamrock, the attempt was dropped.

Tesoro remained in danger of corporate takeover, however. Its debt-ridden coal operation as well as new tax laws in Trinidad that penalized Trinidad-Tesoro kept earnings and the company's stock value low. Amid the disorder, speculators on Wall Street began to buy up the company's stock, anticipating its takeover or its split into several parts.

In June 1982 this speculation bore fruit when Tesoro announced a plan to sell its domestic oil, gas, and coal properties, as well as its interest in the Trinidadian company, and split its remaining holdings into two companies. The proposal, however, was subject to approval by the company's board. Ultimately, only the company's money-losing coal operations were sold, for $4.35 million, to Shamrock Coal Company.

Despite the sale, Tesoro's persistently poor performance and low stock price continued to anger some investors, causing dissent among the ranks of the company's stockholders. When some began to agitate for replacement of Tesoro's management team through a proxy fight, West sold a large chunk of stock in the company to a subsidiary of Charter Company, an oil and insurance concern that was run by a friend. Subsequently, Tesoro tried to take over another small oil company, Enstar Corporation, and failed when it was sold to other suitors. The company instead purchased a 50 percent interest in offshore exploratory oil and gas properties owned by the Pel-Tex Oil Company.

In 1985 Tesoro further restructured its stock offerings to prevent any corporate takeover attempts. In addition, after years of proposals to do so, the company sold its nearly one-half share in Trinidad-Tesoro Petroleum to the island nation's government. The company announced plans to take over another oil producer but canceled them when, later in the year, its bond ratings were lowered, reflecting a loss of confidence in Tesoro's financial health. The company reported a loss of $87 million at the end of 1985.

Matters continued to worsen in 1986, as Tesoro wrote off $44.3 million on an attempt to find oil in Trinidad and also gave up the value of its Indonesian reserves. Exploration in other areas of the world fared no better; wells in Turkey also turned up dry. In Bolivia, the country's government proved unable to pay Tesoro for its services and then announced that it would reimburse the company not in cash but in goods. Tesoro's $30 million joint venture with Pel-Tex also yielded little.

The one bright spot in the company's portfolio was its Alaskan refinery. Tesoro announced that it would upgrade the facility, which turned a profit providing fuel for the Alaska market, including substantial military operations. Nevertheless, Tesoro's 1986 balance sheet showed losses of $124.8 million, and the company continued to fend off takeover attempts. In April 1986 Cavalcade Oil made an offer to buy the company but was rejected.

In 1987 two more suitors had arrived: Oakville, a Hong Kong investment concern, and Pentane Partners, formed specifically to take over the company. Tesoro's problems had grown to include an $800 million shareholder suit, filed in July 1987 against the company's management for corruption and securities fraud, as well as other legal difficulties. Tesoro won its court case but not without suffering the embarrassing revelation that it had hired prostitutes for foreign officials. In addition, a Federal Bureau of Investigation probe into jury tampering was initiated, and the IRS demanded more than $50 million in back taxes.

By the end of 1987, Pentane Partners owned 9.74 percent of the company, and Oakville held 6.2 percent of Tesoro's stock. The company reported losses of $1.7 million and joined the list of *Forbes*'s 500 poorest performing firms in sales growth. In May 1988 Tesoro's board rejected a bid by Pentane for the remainder of the company. In the next few months, the company reached an agreement with the IRS to pay only $20.6 million in back taxes and sold its domestic oil and gas producing properties to American Exploration Company for $21 million in an effort to shore up its financial standing. By August 1988 the company was also 5.3 percent owned by the chairman of another oil company, Stone Petroleum Corporation.

In 1988 Pentane made two additional attempts to acquire Tesoro, and the company also saw a $190 million offer by Harken Oil and Gas, Inc., made and dropped. After a $56 million fine from the federal government for violating regulations on petroleum pricing and allocation, Tesoro reported a $30.5 million loss for the 1989 fiscal year.

By the following year, the company was back in the black with earnings of $22.7 million, but 1991 proved a disappointment, as the war in the Persian Gulf drove up prices for crude oil, while prices for refined products remained stable. This meant that profits on Tesoro's principal money-earning property, its Alaska refinery, were held down. The company earned only $3.9 million in 1991 and omitted its fourth quarterly dividend payment. Difficulties continued in 1992, as the company laid off 60 employees and closed offices in an effort to reduce costs. For 1992, Tesoro posted a net loss of $65.8 million on revenues of $946.4 million.

FIGHTS WITH DISSIDENT SHAREHOLDERS

By the early 1990s, Metropolitan Life Insurance Company had gained a 28 percent stake in Tesoro after Charter Company went bankrupt and Metropolitan Life acquired the stake that Charter had held. With three members on the Tesoro board, Metropolitan was able to use its considerable leverage to force the ouster of West. In 1993 Metropolitan reached an agreement with Tesoro on a recapitalization plan in which Tesoro would buy back the stake over the course of several years. Tesoro began doing so in 1994, leading to the resignation of the Metropolitan representatives from the Tesoro board.

With Michael D. Burke leading the company as president and CEO, Tesoro faced additional disgruntled shareholders in the mid-1990s. At the annual meetings of both 1994 and 1995, a group of dissident shareholders led by Kevin Flannery, head of Whelan Management Group, attempted but failed to oust the firm's board of directors. The dissidents were unhappy with the way that the board was managing the company and specifically sought to sell Tesoro's refinery in Alaska to focus on exploration and production. The company actually moved in the opposite direction in September 1995 when it sold some of its oil and gas production properties in Texas to Coastal Corporation for $74 million. That same month, Burke resigned from the company and was succeeded by Bruce A. Smith, who was promoted from his position as chief operating officer.

Smith was able to put an end to the shareholder revolt in early 1996. After Flannery and company launched a third bid to oust the company board, negotiations led to an agreement in April 1996. Tesoro agreed to increase the size of the board to nine members by naming three new directors, including a member of the dissident shareholders, Alan Kaufman. In addition, the shareholder group agreed to drop all pending legal action and to not seek control of the company or support any effort to do so for three years.

FOCUSING ON DOWNSTREAM OPERATIONS

Freed from the distractions of takeover battles and disgruntled shareholders, Tesoro was able to focus on developing a longer range plan to secure the company's future. Eventually, near the end of the century, the company decided to focus on its downstream operations. To that end, Tesoro in May 1998 completed the acquisition of a refinery and retail outlets in Hawaii that had been owned by Broken Hill Proprietary Company Ltd. The $252.2 million deal included a 95,000-barrel-per-day refinery, located about 22 miles west of Honolulu at Kapolei, and 32 retail gasoline service stations. Tesoro then gained its third refinery in August 1998 when it acquired a 108,000-barrel-per-day refinery in Anacortes, Washington, from Shell Oil Company for $280.1 million. The acquisitions increased the company's revenues to $1.49 billion for 1998, a significant increase over the $937.9 million figure of the preceding year.

This expansion also increased the company's debt load from $148 million to $520 million, which highlighted the need for a paring down of operations. In early 1999, then, the company announced that it would seek to sell or spin off its exploration and production operations. The divestment of the upstream side of the company was completed in December 1999 through two transactions. The domestic assets were sold to EEX Corporation for $215 million, while the Bolivian exploration and production operations were sold to U.K.-based BG PLC for $100 million. The divestments enabled Tesoro to reduce its debt to less than $400 million.

In addition to its newly bolstered refining operations, Tesoro in early 2000 also had a retail network consisting of about 245 stations, 64 of which were company owned and operated. In January 2000 the company moved to expand its retail side by entering into an agreement with Wal-Mart Stores, Inc., to build and operate filling stations at Wal-Mart stores in 11 western states, which was later expanded to 17 states. The companies later agreed to use a new brand, Mirastar, for the stations. By the end of 2000, there were 20 Mirastar outlets in operation, with plans for an additional 80 to 90 units to be opened each year from 2001 to 2003. Tesoro reported 2000 earnings of $73.3 million on revenues of $5.1 billion.

2001–02 ACQUISITION SPREE

In September 2001 Tesoro further expanded both its refining and retailing operations through a $677 million deal with BP p.l.c. Acquired thereby were a refinery in Salt Lake City with a capacity of 55,000 barrels a day and a 60,000-barrel-per-day refinery in Mandan, North Dakota. This brought Tesoro's total refinery capacity to 390,000 barrels per day. Also included in the deal were 45 retail gasoline stations, contracts to supply 300 Amoco-branded stations, as well as associated pipelines, bulk storage facilities, and product distribution terminals. Around this same time, Tesoro announced that it would spend more than $85 million on a major upgrade of its refinery in Washington. The company also said that it was exploring its options regarding its marine services unit. A divestment of the unit would enable Tesoro to be fully focused on refining and retailing and perhaps to pay down some of its debt, which had increased to more than $1 billion following the BP deal. In November 2001 Tesoro acquired 37 retail gas stations with convenience stores from Gull Industries, Inc. The stations were located in Washington, Oregon, and Idaho.

Tesoro secured its sixth refinery in May 2002 when it spent approximately $923 million for the Golden Eagle refinery in Martinez, California, in the San Francisco Bay area plus 70 northern California gasoline stations. The 168,000-barrel-per-day facility was purchased from Valero Energy Corporation, which was forced to sell the refinery to gain regulatory approval for its purchase of Ultramar Diamond Shamrock Corporation. The purchase of Golden Eagle filled a geographic void in Tesoro's western U.S. refining network, and it marked the culmination of a remarkable nine months during which the company more than doubled its refining capacity, from 275,000 to nearly 560,000 barrels per day.

This latest acquisition spree also, however, pushed Tesoro's debt load from a little more than $350 million to $2 billion. In danger of drifting toward defaulting on its bank loans, the company in June 2002 announced plans to slash its debt by $500 million by the end of 2003 through selling assets, cutting costs, and reducing capital spending. Divestments completed during 2002 included the 70 stations purchased with the Golden Eagle refinery and the product pipeline system in North Dakota and Minnesota acquired with the Mandan refinery. The latter was sold to Kaneb Pipe Line Partners, L.P. for $100 million. In 2003 Tesoro sold its marine services unit for $32 million, leaving it a pure refiner and marketer of petroleum products. The deal also marked the successful completion of the debt-reduction effort.

Strong results for 2004, including record net income of $328 million on record revenues of $12.26 billion, enabled Tesoro to reduce its debt load by a further $400 million to $1.22 billion. The company marked its newfound status as a pure refiner and marketer by simplifying its name to Tesoro Corporation in November of that year. Tesoro's momentum continued through 2006, another record-breaking year, with net income of $801 million on sales of $18.1 billion. The record results were fueled in part by unprecedentedly high refining margins, a key industry metric that measures the difference between the price refiners pay for crude oil and the prices of the products they make from the crude.

By this time, the company had embarked on a major capital project at its flagship Golden Eagle refinery to modify the facility's coker, a unit designed to turn heavy petroleum into refinable material. The upgrade was in part prompted by a $1.1 million fine Tesoro had agreed to pay to governmental entities in northern California for air pollution that had been released from the refinery in early 2005 when a boiler feeding the coker malfunctioned. The modification of the coker, completed in the spring of 2008, was designed to not only reduce the plant's air emissions but also increase the refinery's reliability and cut costs by enabling the refinery to process more heavy, and cheaper, grades of crude oil. The project ended up costing roughly $610 million.

RESUMPTION OF ACQUISITIONS IN 2007

In the meantime, sitting on nearly $1 billion in cash, Tesoro returned to acquisition mode in 2007. In a $1.82 billion deal completed that May, Tesoro picked up a 100,000-barrel-per-day refinery located near Los Angeles, its seventh refinery and one that once again fit in quite well geographically with the other six. Also gained in the purchase from Shell Oil Products US, a unit of Royal Dutch Shell plc, were a 42,000-barrel-per-day refined products terminal and a network of 276 Shell-branded gas stations located throughout southern California, 128 of which were company owned. In a second deal also finalized in May 2007, Tesoro expanded further on the retail side in a buyout of 138 USA Gasoline stations located mainly in California. The stations, purchased from USA Petroleum Corp. for $286 million, continued to operate under the USA Gasoline name.

Hard on the heels of these acquisitions, Tesoro was once again facing a possible takeover bid. In late October 2007 billionaire investor Kirk Kerkorian, who already owned a 4 percent stake in the company, announced plans to spend $1.4 billion to purchase an additional 16 percent of Tesoro's common stock at $64 a share, which at the time represented a 12 percent premium over the stock's trading price. Less than a month later, Tesoro's board adopted a so-called poison pill that was intended to ward off a hostile takeover. Kerkorian quickly withdrew his offer.

By this time, refining margins were being squeezed as crude oil prices rapidly soared to record levels while prices at the pump rose but not nearly as quickly. Tesoro responded late in 2007 with an announced shift in its growth strategy. The firm intended to hold off on making further acquisitions and instead invest in its existing facilities. An effort was launched to generate as much as $1 billion in operating cash during 2008 through cost cutting and reductions in capital expenditures and working capital. At the same time, plans were made to spend billions of dollars in capital expenditures from 2008 through 2012 to improve the refineries' reliability and enable them to process a wider variety of crude oils, including cheaper grades. A new approach was clearly needed as Tesoro posted net losses for both the fourth quarter of 2007 and the first quarter of 2008. In the volatile environment of 2008, investors had soured on the company, pushing the stock down below $19 a share by early July, a 70 percent drop from its October 2007 record high of nearly $66. Although the new initiatives in place had the potential to spark a longer term turnaround, Tesoro was likely to struggle in the shorter term without a halt in the historic upsurge in crude oil prices.

Elizabeth Rourke
Updated, David E. Salamie

PRINCIPAL SUBSIDIARIES

Tesoro Alaska Company; Tesoro Refining and Marketing Company.

PRINCIPAL COMPETITORS

Chevron Corporation; Exxon Mobil Corporation; Shell Oil Company; BP p.l.c.; ConocoPhillips; Valero Energy Corporation; Arctic Slope Regional Corporation; Sunoco, Inc.; Suncor Energy, Inc.; Frontier Oil Corporation.

FURTHER READING

Aldridge, James, "Tesoro Eyes Western U.S. for Expanded Retail, Refining," *San Antonio Business Journal,* September 28, 2001, p. 4.

———, "Tesoro Petroleum Planning Major Upgrade for Refinery," *San Antonio Business Journal,* August 25, 2000, p. 6.

Baltimore, Chris, "Texas Supreme Court Hands Tenneco Loss in Take-or-Pay Suit," *Oil Daily,* August 19, 1996, pp. 1+.

Barrionuevo, Alexei, "Tesoro Expands to California in Agreeing to Buy Valero Refinery for $945 Million," *Wall Street Journal,* February 5, 2002, p. B11.

———, "Tesoro Petroleum Sells Its Operations in Bolivia to BG," *Wall Street Journal,* December 31, 1999, p. B5.

Brammer, Rhonda, "Bargain Hunter," *Barron's,* March 14, 1994, pp. 20–21.

Burrough, Bryan, "Collapse of an Old-Boy Oil Network Places Tesoro in Vulnerable Position for Takeover," *Wall Street Journal,* June 12, 1984.

Campoy, Ana, "Crude Conversation: Tesoro's CEO Talks About the Refining Industry's Future—and His Company's Place in It," *Wall Street Journal,* August 27, 2007, p. R6.

———, "Refiners Cash in on High Gasoline Prices," *Wall Street Journal,* May 18, 2007, p. A10.

"EEX to Buy Tesoro's Upstream Holdings," *Oil Daily,* October 12, 1999.

Fan, Aliza, "Spring Finally Breaks for Tesoro Petroleum As Chill of Shareholder Battle, Lawsuit Pass," *Oil Daily,* May 31, 1996, pp. 3+.

———, "Tesoro Fires Back at Dissidents, Wins Order Blocking Vote on Board, Bylaws," *Oil Daily,* January 11, 1996, p. 3.

———, "Unhappy Tesoro Shareholders Try Takeover of Board to Improve Company's Standing," *Oil Daily,* May 10, 1995, pp. 1+.

Fletcher, Sam, and Peter Eisen, "Tesoro to Sell Bolivian Upstream to BG, Focus on Downstream," *Oil Daily,* November 23, 1999.

Jefferson, Greg, "Tesoro Follows a Long Rainbow," *San Antonio Express-News,* June 16, 2002, p. 1K.

———, "Tesoro's Pipeline Finds a Buyer," *San Antonio Express-News,* November 23, 2002, p. 1D.

Kovski, Alan, "Tesoro Agrees to Buy Hawaii Refinery from BHP for $275 Million," *Oil Daily,* March 20, 1998, p. 5.

Lorek, Laura, "Tesoro Looking at Ways to Change Refinery Product Mix," *Oil Daily,* May 6, 1992, p. 4.

Monroe, Melissa S., "Tesoro Altering Company Name," *San Antonio Express-News,* November 10, 2004, p. 3E.

"Opportunity Talks," *Forbes,* November 15, 1973.

Phalon, Richard, "'Tis a Far, Far Better Thing," *Forbes,* March 1, 1982.

"Tesoro Petroleum Corporation: An Address by Dr. Robert V. West, Jr., Chairman of the Board and Chief Executive Officer, at the Harvard Business School, February 19, 1975," San Antonio: Tesoro Petroleum Corporation, 1975.

"Tesoro Petroleum: The Irony of Becoming a Takeover Target," *Business Week,* October 6, 1980.

Vaughan, Vicki, "Restructured Tesoro Is Riding High," *San Antonio Express-News,* April 16, 2006, p. 1K.

———, "Tesoro Buying on West Coast," *San Antonio Express-News,* January 30, 2007, p. 1E.

———, "Tesoro Modifies Its Growth Policy," *San Antonio Express-News,* December 6, 2007, p. 3E.

———, "Tesoro Posts $40 Million Loss in 4Q," *San Antonio Express-News,* February 1, 2008, p. 1C.

Vogel, Todd, "Why Is Tesoro So Popular?" *Business Week,* December 21, 1987.

Teton Energy Corporation

410 Seventeenth Street, Suite 1850
Denver, Colorado 80202
U.S.A.
Telephone: (303) 565-4600
Fax: (303) 565-4606
Web site: http://www.teton-energy.com

Public Private Company
Incorporated: 1998 as Teton Petroleum Company
Employees: 8
Sales: $23.69 million (2007)
Stock Exchanges: American
Ticker Symbol: TEC
NAICS: 211111 Crude Petroleum and Natural Gas Extraction

■ ■ ■

Teton Energy Corporation is an independent energy company that develops, produces, and markets oil and natural gas. The company operates in four basins in the Rocky Mountain and midwest regions of the United States: Denver-Julesburg Basin; Piceance Basin; Williston Basin; and Big Horn Basin. Formerly a company with all its operations in Russia, Teton Energy is committed to expanding its presence in North America, preferably in the United States, through the acquisition of oil and gas holdings. Annual revenues collected by the company increased from $797,000 in 2005 to $23.6 million in 2007.

ORIGINS

Teton Energy celebrated its tenth anniversary in 2008 as a substantially different company than the similarly named Teton Petroleum Company that came into existence a decade earlier. Teton Petroleum traced its roots to an Ontario, Canada, company named Mangesite Mines Limited, which was incorporated in 1962. Mangesite Mines changed its name to EQ Resources Ltd. in 1989. Roughly a decade later, EQ Resources reincorporated in Delaware, shedding its Canadian heritage just before merging with American Tyumen Exploration Company in November 1998. According to the way the merger was structured, EQ Resources emerged as the surviving entity, an event that prompted EQ Resources to change its name to Teton Petroleum.

After the merger, Teton Petroleum's management had some thinking to do. The company's assets at the time of its birth consisted of licenses to explore for gold in Ghana, licenses for oil and gas production in Dagestan, Russia, and licenses to produce oil and gas in western Siberia, Russia. Executives had to decide which of the three holdings would become the lifeblood of the new company. After debating the matter, Teton Petroleum officials disposed of their gold licenses and, fearing political instability in Dagestan, a region embroiled in the Chechen conflict, they disposed of a subsidiary, Teton Oil, Inc., that held oil and gas licenses there. The moves left the company solely focused on oil and gas exploration, development, and production in western Siberia through what was known as the Goloil license

> ## COMPANY PERSPECTIVES
>
> Teton's objective is to expand its natural gas and oil reserves, production and revenues through a strategy that includes growth through the acquisition and development of high repeatability resource play acreage, acquisition of operated properties to control the level and timing of capital spending and the pursuit of strategic acquisitions that expand or complement existing operations and provide consolidation opportunities.

Teton Petroleum's involvement in western Siberia was conducted through Goltech Petroleum LLC, a company organized under the laws of Texas that owned 70.59 percent of Goloil. Teton Petroleum owned 50 percent of Goltech, splitting ownership with Petromed Oil Limited, a company that assumed day-to-day responsibility for operating Goltech. The arrangement gave Teton Petroleum an indirect ownership stake of 35.29 percent in Goloil.

EXPANSION IN RUSSIA

Activity in the license area increased after Teton Petroleum staked its future on the western Siberian holdings. New wells were drilled, including four in 2001, which gave the area a total of seven producing wells. The most significant addition of 2001 was the completion of a 25-mile pipeline in June. Before the pipeline was completed, production at the wells was suspended at certain times of the year because of transportation difficulties related to the region's severe weather. Capable of transporting and producing oil year-round for the first time, Goloil produced 425,459 barrels of oil in 2001, substantially more than the 133,887 barrels produced in 1999, the first year Teton Petroleum was involved in the area.

Expansion in western Siberia continued for the next several years. In 2002, six additional wells were drilled, a year in which Teton Petroleum became the sole owner of Goltech. The following year, seven new wells were drilled, giving the Goloil license a total of 21 producing wells. Production exploded as a result of the investment in expansion, reaching 2.5 million barrels of oil in 2003, or nearly six times the total produced two years earlier.

NEW LEADERSHIP IN 2003

The end of 2003 marked the last full year Teton Petroleum was involved in western Siberia. A number of new directors and executives joined the company between 2002 and 2003, including Teton Petroleum's new president and chief executive officer, Karl F. Arleth. Arleth brought a wealth of experience with him when he joined Teton Petroleum, having held numerous senior management positions after earning degrees in geology from the University of California at Riverside and San Diego State University. Beginning in 1977, Arleth spent 15 years working for Amoco Corporation as an exploration and development geologist, project supervisor, and manager. Next, he served as president of Amoco Poland Ltd. for four years and as president of Amoco Caspian Sea Petroleum Ltd. in Azerbaijan for two years, before leaving Amoco at the end of the 1990s. After more than two decades at Amoco, Arleth served as a director of Big Horn Resources, a Calgary, Canada-based oil and gas company, and as chief operating officer of Sefton Resources, Inc., another oil and gas exploration company. Arleth joined Teton Petroleum as a director in 2002 and was named president and chief executive officer in May 2003.

A FUTURE IN NORTH AMERICA

Arleth and Teton Petroleum's new slate of directors who joined the company between 2002 and 2003 decided to lead the company in an entirely new direction. Teton Petroleum entered 2004 as a Russian oil producer, but it would exit the year looking for business thousands of miles away from the Goloil's area of influence. In mid-2004, Arleth sold Teton Petroleum's interest in Goloil, gaining $13 million from the transaction, and set the company's sights on oil and gas exploration and development in North America.

After searching for opportunities in North America, Teton Petroleum made its first move in December 2004. The company reached an agreement to acquire 180,000 acres of oil and gas leases in the eastern Denver-Julesburg (DJ) Basin, a geologic depression extending across eastern Colorado, southwestern Wyoming, northwestern Kansas, and western Nebraska. Next, in February 2005, Teton Petroleum purchased a 25 percent membership interest in Piceance Gas Resources, LLC, a company with oil and gas rights to 6,300 acres in the Piceance Basin in western Colorado.

The first two deals, completed in early 2005, gave Teton Petroleum the foundation it would build on in the coming years. Between April and July 2005, the company added to its interests in the DJ Basin by acquiring roughly 182,000 acres on the eastern flank of the basin, a swath of property known as "Noble AMI." By the time the company filed its annual financial

KEY DATES

1998: EQ Resources Ltd. and American Tyumen Exploration Company merge, creating Teton Petroleum Company.
2001: Construction of a 25-mile pipeline is completed, enabling year-round production at Teton Petroleum's properties in western Siberia.
2003: Karl F. Arleth is named president and chief executive officer of Teton Petroleum.
2004: Company leaves Russia and begins searching for opportunities in North America.
2005: Company changes its name to Teton Energy Corporation and acquires oil and gas properties in Denver-Julesburg Basin and Piceance Basin.
2006: Teton Energy enters Williston Basin.
2007: Company acquires acreage in Big Horn Basin.
2008: Assets are acquired in Central Kansas Uplift, nearly doubling the company's net proved reserves.

report for 2005 with the Securities and Exchange Commission, it had changed its name to Teton Energy Corporation.

Revenues, which totaled less than $800,000 in 2005, would increase by leaps in succeeding years as Teton Energy ventured into new basins. A third basin was added to the company's operating portfolio in May 2006, when Teton Energy purchased a 25 percent working interest in the Williston Basin located in North Dakota. The transaction covered more than 85,000 acres Teton Energy purchased from American Oil and Gas, Inc., which held a 50 percent working interest in the acreage. Teton Energy, American Oil and Gas, and several other partners in the project were targeting an oil formation called Mississippian Bakken and the natural gas within the Red River formation. Teton Energy estimated it could drill 135 wells in the oil formation and ten wells in the Red River formation.

While Teton Energy secured a position in a third basin, it deepened its involvement where it already had a presence. The company drilled 18 wells in Piceance Basin in 2006. In DJ Basin, the company drilled 20 wells. The investment in expansion led to a banner year for a company in the early stages of establishing itself in the North American energy market. Net production soared 719 percent in 2006. The company's proved reserves increased 77 percent. A 399 percent increase in gas sales was recorded during the year, lifting the company's total revenues from $797,000 in 2005 to $4.02 million in 2006. Arleth, pleased by the results, wrote to shareholders in the 2006 annual report, explaining the goals for the coming year. "As we look forward, we know that what worked for us last year may not next year. Our goal in 2007 is to achieve continued strong drillbit results, while turning our focus toward operated property acquisitions that will increasingly allow us to control and focus our future growth. The opportunities and challenges we face may be different every year," he concluded, "yet the goal is the same: seek opportunities, acquire assets, and execute for our shareholders."

BIG HORN BASIN ACQUISITION IN 2007

Arleth's three objectives guided his actions in 2007, a year that saw Teton Energy live up to expectations created after its fruitful 2006. In May, the company added a fourth basin to its portfolio by securing a position on more than 16,000 acres in the Big Horn Basin, a geologic depression located in Wyoming. Unlike the company's other holdings, in which its working interest ranged from 12.5 percent to 73 percent, the Big Horn Basin investment gave Teton Energy a 100 percent working interest in the acreage. Drilling at Big Horn Basin was expected to begin in 2008.

Although the highlight of 2007, the Big Horn Basin acquisition represented only part of the progress achieved during the year. In the DJ Basin, 81 new wells either were drilled or acquired. The company moved into two directions at Piceance Basin. In October, Teton Energy sold 50 percent of its assets in the basin for $38 million, roughly 12 times what it paid for the properties on a per acre basis. The divestiture cut the company's working interest in Piceance Basin from 25 percent to 12.5 percent. Expansion also occurred in the Grand Valley Field located in the basin, with 41 wells drilled during the year. Acquisitions and new wells (one new well was drilled in Williston Basin) fueled growth at Teton Energy. The company's net proved reserves increased 99 percent, its net production increased 66 percent, and its revenues skyrocketed, more than quintupling to $23.6 million.

CENTRAL KANSAS UPLIFT IN 2008

A decade after Teton Energy began operating as Teton Petroleum, it stood as an aggressive player in the North American energy market. The company was looking to expand, having spent $35 million on capital expenditures in 2007 and having earmarked $36 million for capital expenditures during 2008. The money set aside for 2008 excluded acquisitions, which promised to play a significant role in the company's growth plans. In February 2008, Arleth demonstrated his penchant for acquiring assets when he struck a deal to acquire reserves, production, and acreage in an area in Kansas known as the Central Kansas Uplift. Teton Energy paid Shelby Resources, LLC, and more than a dozen other working-interest owners $53.4 million for the assets. The acquisition was completed in April 2008, nearly doubling Teton Energy's net proved reserves and daily net production.

"The United States' demand for energy continues to increase and we intend to be a meaningful participant in delivering domestic supplies to the American energy markets," Arleth wrote to shareholders in the company's 2007 annual report. During his first five years in charge of the company, Arleth had engineered profound changes, shepherding Teton Energy out of the Russian oil patch and guiding it to a new destiny in North America. His expanding portfolio of properties was beginning to drive exponential financial growth as the company concluded its first decade of business and prepared for the coming years. In the future, further acquisitions were expected in the company's existing regions of influence and perhaps into new, promising regions of oil and gas exploration and development.

Jeffrey L. Covell

PRINCIPAL SUBSIDIARIES

Goltech Petroleum, LLC.

PRINCIPAL COMPETITORS

Delta Petroleum Corporation; Encore Acquisition Company; Bill Barrett Corporation.

FURTHER READING

"Teton Begins Production Testing on N.D. Goliath Well," *Gas Processors Report,* November 20, 2007.

"Teton Completes Piceance Wells," *Oil Daily,* April 13, 2006.

"Teton Energy Announces First Well Spud in the Williston Basin," *CNW Group,* September 27, 2006.

"Teton Energy Corp.," *Oil and Gas Investor,* September 2005, p. SS110.

"Teton Energy Corp.," *Oil and Gas Investor,* September 2006, p. S123.

"United States: Teton Energy Signs Exploration Agreement with Unit Petroleum for Big Horn Basin Project," *TendersInfo,* June 26, 2008.

TouchTunes Music Corporation

740 Broadway, Suite 1102
New York, New York 10003
U.S.A.
Telephone: (212) 991-6540
Toll Free: (888) 338-5853
Fax: (646) 365-0011
Web site: http://www.touchtunes.com

Private Company
Incorporated: 1993 as TouchTunes Digital Jukebox, Inc.
Employees: 215
Sales: $68 million (2006 est.)
NAICS: 334310 Audio and Video Equipment Manufacturing

■ ■ ■

TouchTunes Music Corporation is the leading producer of digital downloading jukeboxes, which have been installed in more than 30,000 bars, restaurants, pool halls, and similar venues in North America. The firm's devices use the MP3 audio format and can be updated instantly via a secure Internet connection from a central library of over two million songs, which are licensed from all of the major record companies and many large independents. TouchTunes jukeboxes accept both cash and credit cards and can be networked with portable game-playing devices, including the company's own PlayPorTT, as well as social networking web sites. Controlling interest in the firm is held by VantagePoint Venture Partners of California.

BEGINNINGS

TouchTunes traces its origins to 1993, when Canadian entrepreneur and self-described "gadget freak" Tony Mastronardi invested in a digital compression technology that he thought had potential for use with music. Unable to attract backers, Mastronardi hit on the idea of applying it to jukeboxes, which generated annual revenues of about $1.8 billion in the United States and Canada. To fund the new approach, Mastronardi mortgaged his home and formed a partnership with French inventor Guy Nathan and European businessman Tonino Lattanzi to found TouchTunes Digital Jukebox, Inc., which would be based in Montreal.

In December 1994 the company engineered a reverse merger with Technical Maintenance Corp. (TMC), which was traded over the counter on the NASDAQ. Mastronardi was named president, with Lattanzi as vice-president and Nathan as secretary. TouchTunes Digital Jukebox would be a subsidiary of Las Vegas-based TMC.

Over the next two years the firm continued working to develop its system, in July 1996 announcing it had received the first performing rights license for a digital jukebox. TMC's machine would use MP3 music files downloaded from a central server via telephone lines and would offer distinct advantages over traditional disc-based jukeboxes, including minimal maintenance due to few moving parts; a potentially unlimited number of songs and rapid addition of new hit recordings; no waiting time between selections; and accurate, instant calculations of play totals and other tracking data.

COMPANY PERSPECTIVES

TouchTunes is the largest out-of-home interactive entertainment network, providing innovative solutions to over 30,000 bars, restaurants, retailers and other businesses in North America. TouchTunes introduced the world's first digital-downloading, pay-per-play commercial jukebox in 1998 and now operates the largest network of interactive entertainment systems, playing over 1.5 million songs per day. TouchTunes maintains a digital music library covering more than two million licensed tracks from every major record label, plus independent music distributors and a host of independent labels.

In early 1997 performance trials of the jukebox began at 20 locations in cities such as Chicago, New York, and Los Angeles. The firm was in the process of signing deals with record companies and music publishers and reached an agreement to use the phone lines of MCI for downloading content.

Mastronardi and Nathan were officially hired by the company in March 1997 at salaries of $125,000 each, having previously received no pay. TouchTunes, which had raised about $3.3 million from outside investors, also issued 35 million shares of new common and preferred stock and added three board members. The company was actively seeking patents for its technology, which it would soon begin to win.

After completion of a successful trial run, TouchTunes began hiring a sales team headed by jukebox industry veterans. In late 1997 the firm opened a marketing and technical support office near Chicago in preparation for a 1998 product launch. Installations would be performed by established coin-operated machine suppliers around the United States. TouchTunes' New Age Digital Jukeboxes, as they were initially called, featured proprietary software running on an Intel processor, housed in audio units designed and built in Quebec by respected American audio manufacturer Bose Corporation.

DIGITAL JUKEBOX INSTALLATIONS

In the early fall of 1998 TouchTunes jukeboxes began appearing around the United States, and over 100 were in place by November. More than $10 million in fresh capital was invested during the year, much of which came from subsidiaries of pension fund manager Caisse de Dépôt et Placement du Québec, which had previously put $2.4 million into the firm. Although based in Canada, TouchTunes concentrated on the U.S. market where there were some 320,000 jukeboxes, far more than the 10,000 in its home country.

The efforts of the upstart company with the new technology were not welcomed by established jukebox makers, who over the years had seen 78 rpm discs replaced by 45s and later CDs; there was considerable industry opposition to the firm's efforts. Support came from music companies, however, who liked the greatly improved data collection and royalty payments, as well as the public, who enjoyed the enhanced music selection and sound quality.

In the past, jukeboxes were generally purchased by the owner of a bar or restaurant, who would also buy records or CDs, cover the cost of maintenance, and pay performance fees to rights organizations ASCAP and BMI, earning about 60 percent of the cash deposited after overhead. Regional coin-op companies typically kept them stocked with music and performed repairs. TouchTunes' initial plan was to supply, but not sell, its units through such firms, taking 45 percent of the money deposited with a $69 weekly minimum. The venue owner's only responsibilities were emptying the cashbox, controlling the playback volume, and adjusting the playlist. It typically cost 50 cents to play one song, with a jukebox in a popular spot taking in several hundred dollars per week.

New songs could be downloaded while the device was in use (taking about 15 minutes each over a phone line), with removal of unpopular titles done instantly. Each machine uploaded play totals and detailed tracking information to the company, which disseminated it to record labels for payment of royalties and for use in their research on consumer trends. The machines could also be programmed to promote new acts by playing their music between purchased plays.

By late 1998 the firm had signed license agreements with recording industry giants Universal and BMG, and soon added two of the other three major players in the industry, Warner Music and Capitol/EMI, as well as independents such as Zomba, Jive, Beggars Banquet, Epitaph, and Fantasy. The fifth major player, Sony Music, would hold out for several years, however. Separate deals were worked out with music publishers, who represented the interests of songwriters.

In December 1998 Technical Maintenance Corp. changed its name to TouchTunes Music Corporation. Its Canadian subsidiary would continue to bear the name TouchTunes Digital Jukebox, Inc.

KEY DATES

1993: TouchTunes Digital Jukebox, Inc., is founded in Montreal.
1994: Reverse merger is arranged with publicly traded Technical Maintenance Corp. of Las Vegas.
1998: Company rolls out world's first downloading digital jukebox; Technical Maintenance changes its name to TouchTunes Music Corporation.
2000: Partnership is formed with Merit Industries to co-market electronic bar games.
2001: New wall-mounted Maestro jukebox debuts.
2003: Tune Central virtual music library, offering access to 100,000 songs, is introduced.
2005: VantagePoint Venture Partners buys control of firm and takes it private.
2007: Credit card processing capabilities are added, and White Rabbit Games are acquired.

REACHING ONE MILLION WEEKLY PLAYS IN MID-2000

By April 1999, some 350 jukeboxes had been installed, and 100,000 songs were being played per week. That month a loan for $10.4 million was secured from the National Bank of Canada, and by August 2000 the firm's Genesis jukebox (as it was called) was in more than 2,000 locations. Over one million songs were being played each week on the devices.

Although it was still far from recording a profit, TouchTunes had received more than $46 million from investors, with subsidiaries of Caisse de Dépôt et Placement du Québec and Société Innovatech du grand Montreal holding the largest stakes. The company had 120 employees, with most working in Montreal and others located in Chicago, Los Angeles, and Philadelphia.

Seeking to enhance its offerings, TouchTunes formed a partnership with U.S. coin-operated game maker Merit Industries to develop and co-market new devices. The company was also working to secure Canadian and British music rights, while looking to add advertising to the jukeboxes' touch-screens and explore other markets such as hotels, stores, and airlines.

In the fall of 2000 TouchTunes announced it had signed exclusive distribution agreements with a number of regional coin machine operators to further boost market penetration. Its jukeboxes were available for sale or lease, costing about $6,000 to purchase. The company's server had more than 70,000 songs available for download, which typically included 80 to 90 percent of the songs on the *Billboard* Hot 100 list of hits, and each jukebox could store 750 songs. Competitors were working on similar products, however, with older jukebox firms, such as Rowe International, trying to regain ground lost to TouchTunes. For 2000 the company had sales of $17.1 million and a loss of $10.2 million.

In February 2001 François Plamondon was named company president, with Tony Mastronardi remaining CEO and adding the title of chairman of the board. Plamondon had served as chief operating officer and chief financial officer for more than a year, having previously been an executive vice-president at digital video effects company Discreet Logic. In August the company received a $5 million loan guarantee from two of its major shareholders, and in September 2001 the new Maestro wall-mounted jukebox was unveiled.

Despite the increasing number of jukeboxes installed and growing revenue figures, TouchTunes was continuing to lose money, and in the latter half of 2001 a restructuring was effected that included the layoff of 30 percent of its workforce. At year's end President François Plamondon left the company and cofounder Mastronardi took back the title of president.

In early 2002 the firm's losses narrowed, and in June publishing and music industry veteran John Perrachon was named president and CEO. Mastronardi would remain on board as executive vice-president and vice-chairman, with cofounder Guy Nathan continuing to work on research and development. For the year TouchTunes' revenues increased by more than 20 percent to $23.8 million, and it reported a net loss of $1.2 million, much improved over the $9.1 million lost in 2001.

TouchTunes donated six jukeboxes to troops serving in Iraq in May 2003. Its devices had already been placed at many other military installations in the United States. In June the company restructured $16 million in debt and unpaid dividends owed its principal shareholders by issuing them stock worth $12.5 million.

INTRODUCTION OF TUNE CENTRAL

In the fall of 2003 the company introduced Tune Central, a new interactive feature that gave jukebox customers access to its 100,000-song library for double the usual price per song. Although still hampered by a reliance on slow dial-up phone lines, the firm had software that improved transmission speed.

During the same period, TouchTunes signed a long-sought licensing agreement with Sony Music, and in early 2004 it cut deals with music rights organizations ASCAP and BMI. This greatly simplified the process of paying songwriters, which had heretofore required working directly with copyright owners.

In April a long-simmering dispute with rival digital jukebox maker Ecast was settled, with the firms agreeing to cross-license patents each had claimed were infringed. In June, cofounder Tony Mastronardi resigned as executive vice-president and vice-chairman, though he would remain a member of the firm's board, and in August Chairman Pierre Desjardins and another board member quit. William Meder was subsequently appointed chair.

In December 2004 TouchTunes announced the installation of its 10,000th jukebox. The year was the company's first in the black, with a profit of $1.6 million recorded on sales of $38.9 million.

By the spring of 2005 California-based VantagePoint Venture Partners had bought the ownership stakes held by the Caisse de Dépôt et Placement du Québec and taken controlling interest in TouchTunes. The firm's new owner had sizable financial resources to help grow its business.

PRIVATE IN DECEMBER 2005

In December 2005 TouchTunes declared a 1-to-2,000 reverse stock split which took it private, fractional shareholders being paid off in cash. The firm also opened a new 21,000-square-foot sales and service headquarters in Lake Zurich, Illinois, near Chicago, and unveiled the Allegro floor model jukebox. The new device had improved reliability features and styling reminiscent of a 1950s jukebox, with an arched top and neon-like light strips. Sales for 2005 were close to $52 million and the firm was taking in about $40 million from music service fees, paying back $15 million to copyright holders. In January 2006 the one-billionth song was played on a TouchTunes jukebox.

The coin-op industry was embracing digital jukeboxes, finding that they increased revenues over CD versions due to the greater music variety offered. Manufacturers, seeking to boost the fees they received for providing music, sold them at a discount, with TouchTunes taking a loss of about $1,000 per unit. Sales consisted of 60 percent floor models, 35 percent wall units, and the rest conversion kits for Rowe and NSM CD players, which were produced under the company's brand name by Miele, Inc., of Pennsylvania.

There were new threats on the horizon, however, including satellite music networks and portable MP3 players, which brought free music of seemingly infinite variety to nightspots with minimal effort. Coin-op firms were fighting back by inserting clauses in contracts that required jukebox owners to ban outside music, as events such as "iPod Nights" were reported growing in popularity from coast to coast.

In July 2006 TouchTunes announced a pact with AT&T that would provide high-speed Internet connections to its jukeboxes where available, allowing faster access to the popular Tune Central library and other features such as live concert feeds. In a nod to the popularity of social networking web sites, another new offering allowed customers to log on to mytouchtunes.com, create a playlist of songs, email it to friends with a get-together invitation, and then call it up at a jukebox to hear. Those using the feature could also receive free bonus plays.

In October, the company's jukeboxes began to display the *Billboard* music charts on-screen, with users able to select tunes directly from the lists. During the month the 20,000th TouchTunes jukebox was also installed. The machines were owned by nearly 1,800 regional operators in the United States, Canada, and Latin America, and the firm claimed 70 percent of the digital downloading jukebox market. The newest models stored 2,000 songs, with more than 600,000 others available from TuneCentral. Almost 90 percent of boxes had broadband connections.

CREDIT CARD OPTION IN LATE 2006

In December 2006 TouchTunes selected Optimal Payments, Inc., to process credit card transactions on its jukeboxes, which had previously only accepted cash. The machines were subsequently modified to include card readers.

In January 2007 the company named computer industry executive Art Matin president and CEO, replacing John Perrachon, who would remain on the firm's board. TouchTunes resolved a potential problem with tabletop game partner Merit in July, announcing that the forthcoming Generation 3 version of its jukebox software would be made backward-compatible with Merit's Gamelink program. A new program, Connect-TT, was slated to be added, which unlike Gamelink could accept credit cards. When networked with TouchTunes jukeboxes, game devices had up to 15 percent greater revenue than stand-alone units.

In October, the firm acquired White Rabbit Games Studio LLC, a maker of bar games. It became part of a new division, TouchTunes Games Studio, which would market PlayPorTT, an interactive touch-screen device that could play games and connect wirelessly to identical units or a jukebox. The player could be moved around the venue, staying in a docking station/charging tower with up to eight others when not in use. Swiping a credit card on the tower would start a play session and provide a security deposit if the device were removed from the premises.

During 2007 TouchTunes also reached deals to supply hundreds of jukeboxes to AMF bowling alleys and Bennigan's restaurants and offered a week-early preview of a new album by Columbia artist Wyclef Jean. At year's end an ad campaign for Absolut Vodka ran on 10,000 of its devices, while the firm traded patent infringement charges with Merit Entertainment and rival Rowe International. TouchTunes had new executive offices in New York, although it continued to maintain significant operations in Montreal and Chicago.

In January 2008 the 30,000th TouchTunes jukebox was installed, and in April the company introduced an updated version of its popular Allegro model, which had sold 10,000 units in just two years. The firm also announced its devices had been enhanced to interact with cell phones and web-based social networks. A new ad campaign for Durex condoms, as well as a jukebox-based poll for Rock the Vote, were begun as well.

A decade after it created the first digital downloading jukebox, TouchTunes Music had moved to the front ranks of the industry, with more than 30,000 units installed in North America. The company's state-of-the-art devices had many advantages over older record- and compact disc-based systems, and also generated a steady revenue stream from licensed music plays downloaded from the Tune Central library. TouchTunes was continuing to innovate with new Internet, credit card, and game-playing features, and backed by deep-pocketed VantagePoint Venture Partners, it appeared solidly positioned for further growth.

Frank Uhle

PRINCIPAL SUBSIDIARIES

TouchTunes Digital Jukebox, Inc. (Canada).

PRINCIPAL COMPETITORS

Rowe International; Rock-Ola Manufacturing Corporation; NSM Music Group Limited; Ecast, Inc.

FURTHER READING

Kukec, Anna Marie, "AT&T Dabbles in Music," *Chicago Daily Herald,* July 6, 2006, p. 1.

Leger, Kathryn, "Going for the Jukebox Jackpot," *National Post,* December 28, 1998, p. C2.

Maney, Kevin, "New Jukebox Tunes in Off-Site Digitized Music," *USA Today,* January 22, 1997, p. 1D.

McLaughlin, Hillary, "Singing a Different Tune—The Jukebox Goes Digital," *Hamilton Spectator,* June 5, 1998, p. C4.

Montano, Nick, "TouchTunes Acquires White Rabbit Games," *Vending Times,* October 2007.

"Taking (Legal) Advantage of MP3 Technologies," *Toronto Star,* October 23, 2000, p. BU4.

"TouchTunes Premieres the TouchTunes PlayPorTT," *Wireless News,* October 3, 2007.

"TouchTunes Reports Progress Modifying Gen3 Jukebox Platform to Interoperate with Existing Technology Supporting Merit Links," *Vending Times,* August, 2007.

Traiman, Steve, "TouchTunes Music Brings Digital Downloading to the Jukebox," *Billboard,* February 10, 2001, p. 66.

Webb, Marcus, "Industry Pros Identify Latest Trends Reshaping the Coin-Op Music Sector," *Vending Times,* November, 2006.

———, "TouchTunes Split Will Privatize Firm," *Vending Times,* January, 2006.

Trend Micro Inc.

Shinjuku Maynds Tower
2-1-Yoyogi
Shibaya-ku
Tokyo, 151-0053
Japan
Telephone: (+81 3) 5334 3600
Fax: (+81 3) 5334 3651
Web site: http://www.trendmicro.com

Public Company
Incorporated: 1988
Employees: 3,000
Sales: ¥99.8 billion ($848.8 million) (2007)
Stock Exchanges: Tokyo NASDAQ
Ticker Symbols: 4704; TMIC
NAICS: 511210 Software Publishers

■ ■ ■

Trend Micro Inc. is one of the world's leading developers of antivirus and computer security applications and hardware. The Tokyo-based company is an industry innovator and ranks number three globally, behind Symantec and McAfee, and continues to dominate many markets in which it operates. Trend Micro's products include the Network VirusWall family, with hardware and software solutions to block computer viruses and other malware from entering corporate and other networks. The company's product strategy, Total Web Threat Protection, features web site reputation analysis to head off attacks from viruses and other threats. Trend Micro targets businesses and Internet service providers, telecommunications companies, and network systems developers to identify and destroy viruses before they reach end consumers. The company also produces software and services for the home office and consumer markets, including Internet Security Pro and Internet Security 2008. Headquartered in Japan, Trend Micro operates research, engineering, and development centers in Taiwan, the United States, Germany, and elsewhere, and provides 24/7 virus-alert services from its Philippines operation. Listed on the Tokyo Stock Exchange and the NASDAQ, Trend Micro is led by cofounders Steven Chang, chairman, and Eva Chen, CEO. In 2007, the company's revenues topped ¥99.8 billion ($849 million).

STRIKING BACK AT PIRATES IN 1988

Taipei, Taiwan-born Steven Chang's family operated a bowling alley, and Chang's first work experience was at the family business. Yet Chang's own career lay in the nascent computer software industry of the early 1980s. After earning a bachelor's degree in applied mathematics from Taiwan's Fu Jen Catholic University, Chang came to the United States, where he earned a master's degree in computer science at Lehigh University in Pennsylvania. In 1981, Chang began marketing software for Hewlett-Packard.

In 1984, Chang raised $50,000 to buy the Chinese-language rights to a U.S.-developed database management application. Together with two friends, Chang returned to Taiwan and founded AsiaTek in 1985. The company set to work translating and adapting the

COMPANY PERSPECTIVES

Vision: A world where it is absolutely safe to exchange digital information. Mission: Develop, deliver and support the most flexible and customizable internet security solutions to address the ever-changing threats on the Web.

database program for the Chinese-speaking population. One of the first Chinese-specific database programs to be introduced, the product was highly successful, so successful that the program was quickly copied. As Chang recalled to *New Media Age:* "We were so naive, everyone copied it and we lost all our money."

The experience led Chang to recognize the need for computer security. Chang and his engineering team developed a copy-protection device, resulting in one of the first dongles, a device that plugs into the computer's serial port. The dongle contains a code needed to run the program. At the same time, the software added code that detected a pirated copy of the software and reportedly destroyed the computer's hard drive. Instead of attempting to market the product itself, however, AsiaTek tried to sell it. As Chang recalled to *Fortune:* "We were purely a technology company and didn't know much about marketing then." By 1986, AsiaTek had sold the rights to the dongle to U.S.-based Rainbow Technology, which paid $125,000.

That might have been the end of Chang's career, if one of the engineers on his staff had not introduced him to the concept of the computer virus. Into the second half of the 1980s, viruses remained quite rare; the industry had identified only ten at the end of the decade. The original viruses were boot sector viruses, written to attack the computer's BIOS, rather than the actual operating system. Motherboard manufacturers quickly began incorporating antivirus code into their BIOS software. The appearance of the first viruses, coupled with his own experience with software piracy, led Chang to recognize that computer security would remain an important part of the computer industry into the 2000s.

Chang decided to start again, this time focused on computer security. With the money generated from the sale of the AsiaTek dongle, Chang and wife Jenny Chen moved to Los Angeles and established a new company, Trend Micro. The couple was joined by Chen's sister, Eva Chen, who soon emerged as one of the driving forces behind the company's growth. Chen had originally launched her studies as a philosophy major in Taiwan. Nonetheless, the need to find a job drove Chen to begin studying international management. The new direction brought her in contact with computers, and Chen quickly discovered a natural affinity for computer technology. Before long, Chen had changed direction again, this time earning a degree in information systems management.

The trio behind Trend Micro proved highly complementary. Chang's interest leaned toward the business side, whereas Jenny Chen became responsible for the family company's communications. Eva Chen's technological training prepared her to become the company's chief technology officer. While Chang built the company's U.S. base, Chen established the company's product development operations in Taiwan. In this way, Trend Micro tapped the large pool of trained software engineers in Taiwan, where wages were still half of what the company would have had to pay in the United States. Chen herself drew no salary during the company's early years and instead supported herself as a sports journalist and science fiction writer.

Trend Micro initially focused on developing a new generation of copy protection software. Then a client came to Chen complaining of a bug that was preventing the application from running. The company quickly identified a virus, reported by Chen as C-Brain, considered the first true computer virus, as a source of the malfunction and added a tool to its copy protection software to remove the virus. That tool quickly became a major selling point for Trend Micro's software, while C-Brain notoriety spawned an ever increasing number of new viruses. By the end of the 1980s the company had decided to focus on the antivirus market.

BIG IN JAPAN IN THE NINETIES

In 1991 Trend Micro reached an exclusive agreement to supply its antivirus software on an OEM basis to Intel Corporation. That agreement, however, meant that Trend Micro could no longer market its own products in the U.S. and European markets. Instead, Trend Micro turned its target to the Asian region especially the fast-growing computer market in Japan. The company became one of the first antivirus players to enter the Japanese market, adapting its software to the current Japanese operating systems. Also in 1991, the company launched its first successful product there, Virus Buster. In addition, the company adapted its software to the Chinese and other Asian markets. While other antivirus developers struggled to accommodate many different operating systems in the region, Trend Micro flourished. In Taiwan, for example, the company grew into one of

KEY DATES

1988: Steve Chang and Eva Chen found Trend Micro in United States and develop first antivirus software.
1991: Trend Micro reaches OEM agreement with Intel and launches Virus Buster in Japan.
1998: After moving to Japan, Trend Micro goes public on Tokyo Stock Exchange.
2004: Eva Chen becomes company CEO and launches new computer security strategy.
2005: Trend Micro acquires anti-spyware software developer InterLude and reputation analysis developer Kelkea.
2007: Trend Micro acquires HijackThis anti-spyware tool and Provilla, producer of data-leak prevention software.

the most well-known brands in the computer software sector.

By the early 1990s, however, Japan had become the company's primary market. In response, Chang moved the company's headquarters to Tokyo, while Chen moved to the United States to take over as head of the U.S. office. The company also stayed ahead of its competition (in the early 1990s there were more than 200 antivirus programs on the market) through a consistent string of innovative products. In particular, the company was among the first to recognize the need to extend virus protection beyond the consumer market, and it began developing tools for the corporate and IT infrastructure sectors. Leading this charge was Eva Chen, who became the group's chief technology officer in 1995.

In 1995, the company launched ServerProtect, the first program designed to provide antivirus protection for LAN servers, rather than for the individual workstations. The company also recognized the growing importance of the Internet as a transmission vector for computer viruses. This awareness led to the launch of the industry's first Internet Gateway Server-based antivirus program, Interscan VirusWall. Similarly, the boom in email use, which for much of the late 1990s remained the most highly used Internet feature, led Trend Micro to introduce the first email server scanning tool, ScanMail. By 1998, Trend Micro had bundled its antivirus technology into a new centralized management package, the Virus Control System.

Trend Micro's market dominance in Japan and much of Asia brought new investor interest in the second half of the decade. In 1997, Softbank acquired a 35 percent stake in the company. By 1998, Trend Micro had gone public, listing its shares on the Tokyo Stock Exchange. A year later, the company added a listing on the NASDAQ. Trend Micro had also innovated in another way, adapting the U.S.-style stock option packages for its Japanese and other staff. The company was said to have created more than 200 millionaires with its stock listings.

BRAND BUILDING

The rising use of and growing dependence on the Internet in the early 2000s played a role in Trend Micro's continued growth. Indeed, from 1998 on the company blossomed, registering double-digit revenue growth for most of the following decade. From revenues of just $67 million in 1997, Trend Micro grew into an industry heavyweight, posting nearly $850 million in sales by 2008.

A number of factors contributed to this success. For one, the company remained highly focused on its antivirus software through the late 1990s, despite its major competitors, including Symantec and McAfee, which had begun developing bundled suites of computer and security services. Chang reckoned that its customers, especially its corporate and IT infrastructure customers, would prefer its singleminded focus.

That focus was highlighted by the outbreaks of the first truly global virus attacks, including the Good Times, Michelangelo, and Melissa viruses. Trend Micro, which had established a 24/7 virus tracking service in the Philippines, proved itself the quickest to respond to these new threats. In addition, the company posted free virus-removal tools, even for users who were not Trend Micro customers. Thus the company generated strong publicity and a new generation of large-scale orders. After the Melissa virus attack, for example, General Electric enlisted Trend Micro's software and services in a $1 million contract, the company's largest to date.

Not all of Trend Micro's efforts were effective, however. In 2001, a new virus, the Nimda worm, wreaked havoc on the world's servers, including Trend Micro's own systems. Yet the event inspired Chen to lead Trend Micro into new territory: hardware development. As Chen told it, inspiration for the new direction came one night at dinner with her two children. Realizing that she often solved disputes between them by physically separating them, Chen came up with an idea to develop a similar method for networks. Working with a team of engineers, Chen led the development of a new hardware device, called the Network VirusWall, positioned in front of the network to scan incoming packets before they entered the actual network. Launched in 2004, the new device was a major success, helping to solidify Trend Micro's reputation at the cutting edge of the virus market.

CHANGING COURSE, PURSUING ACQUISITIONS

In 2004, Steve Chang, who had served as both chairman and CEO of the company, decided to separate the two functions, turning over the CEO spot to cofounder Eva Chen. By then, the computer security market itself had been undergoing a significant change as new threats, including spyware, malware, pharming (the creation of fake web sites), and phishing (methods for encouraging users to divulge sensitive information) became more prevalent.

Chen abandoned the group's former antivirus focus as it began incorporating new anti-spyware, botnet-detection, and other protective measures into its software. In order to accomplish this enhancement, the company launched a series of acquisitions through the middle of the first decade of the 2000s. In 2005, for example, the company acquired anti-spyware developer InterMute Inc. The company then purchased Kelkea Inc., a company that specialized in IP (Internet protocol) filtering and reputation services (verifying the authenticity of web sites). These moves led the company to launch its own Network Reputation Services in 2005, followed by its botnet protection platform, Intercloud Security Services, in 2006.

By 2007, the company had bought the highly popular anti-spyware freeware program HijackThis, which enabled users to build log files in order to spot increasingly sophisticated spyware and malware in their systems. Trend Micro also sought to develop its proactive technologies and in October 2007 reached an agreement to acquire Provilla. The company, founded in 2005, had been developing its LeakProof data-leak prevention software, designed to block the transmission of sensitive data. As a pioneer in the computer protection market, Trend Micro had become an industry leader with a proven track record of innovation.

M. L. Cohen

PRINCIPAL SUBSIDIARIES

Servicentro TMLA S.A.B. de C.V. (Mexico); Trend Micro (China) Incorporated; Trend Micro (EMEA) Limited (Ireland); Trend Micro (NZ) Limited; Trend Micro (Singapore) Private Limited; Trend Micro (Thailand) Limited; Trend Micro (UK) Limited; Trend Micro Australia Pty. Ltd.; Trend Micro Deutschland Gmbh (Germany); Trend Micro do Brasil Ltda.; Trend Micro France; Trend Micro Hong Kong Limited; Trend Micro Inc. (U.S.A.); Trend Micro Incorporated (Taiwan); Trend Micro India Private Limited; Trend Micro Italy S.r.l.; Trend Micro Korea Inc. (South Korea); Trend Micro Latinoamerica S.A.B. de C.V. (Mexico); Trend Micro Malaysia Sdn. Bhd.

PRINCIPAL COMPETITORS

Symantec Inc.; McAfee Inc.; AVG Technologies.

FURTHER READING

Carroll, Mark, "Color Me Global, Says Trend Micro CTO," *Electronic Engineering Times,* April 3, 2000, p. 163.

"Dell to Preload Trend Micro Software on PCs," *eWeek,* October 28, 2005.

Dempsey, Michael, "With a Pragmatic and Practical Approach, Trend Micro of the US Has Gone from Strength to Strength, Regularly Winning Plaudits in the Anti-Virus Industry," *Financial Times,* June 7, 2000, p. 8.

Hatlestad, Luc, "Crafting a Secure Vision," *VARBusiness,* June 27, 2005, p. 37.

Kraar, Louis, Richard Evans, and Sheree R. Curry, "A World of Cool Companies, *Fortune,* October 28, 1996, p. 162.

Lewis, Elen, "Keeping the Big Boys Safe," *New Media Age,* April 13, 2000, p. 28.

Mackie, Jeff, "Tales from the Frontline," *Computer Dealer News,* May 20, 2005, p. 30.

Messmer, Ellen, "Trend Micro Buys Data-Leak Specialist Provilla," *Network World,* October 25, 2007.

"Staying One Step Ahead of the Worms," *Business Week,* November 12, 2001, p. 26.

"Trend Micro Acquires Security Tool," *Computerworld,* March 19, 2007, p. 11.

"Trend Micro Seeks Cure in Virus Battle," *eWeek,* May 28, 2001, p. 16.

Tripwire, Inc.

326 Southwest Broadway, 3rd Floor
Portland, Oregon 97205
U.S.A.
Telephone: (503) 276-7500
Toll Free: (800) 874-7947
Fax: (503) 223-0182
Web site: http://www.tripwire.com

Private Company
Incorporated: 1997 as Tripwire Security Systems, Inc.
Employees: 226
Sales: $48 million (2007 est.)
NAICS: 511210 Software Publishers

■ ■ ■

Tripwire, Inc., is one of the leading developers of configuration audit and control software, supplying products that help companies maintain the integrity of their critical system files. Tripwire's software monitors corporate networks and data files, alerting system administrators to changes occurring across the information technology infrastructure. The company's products monitor servers, routers, switches, web pages, and other network devices. Investors in Tripwire include Bessemer Venture Partners, Advanced Technology Ventures, and Sun Microsystems, which have provided the company with more than $50 million in funding.

ORIGINS

Nearly 2,000 miles to the east of company headquarters in Portland, Oregon, Tripwire, the product, was developed five years before the formation of its eponymous company. In 1992, at the West Lafayette, Indiana, campus of Purdue University, the software code underpinning Tripwire was written, the pioneering work of Gene Kim and Eugene Spafford.

The relationship of Kim and Spafford exemplified the rapid technological advances pushing computer science forward during the early 1990s. Expertise one year became obsolete knowledge the next year, creating the dynamics that explained the collaboration of Spafford, professor and head of the computer science department at Purdue, with Gene Kim, undergraduate student. In 1992 Spafford and Kim wrote the code for software they christened Tripwire, a product designed to guard against intruders attempting to hack into a computer system open to the Internet. The malicious threat present in 1992 grew enormously in gravity in succeeding years, as nearly every company established a presence on the Internet and used the revolutionary network to conduct its business, thus making their data vulnerable to attacks from outsiders.

The capabilities written into the code coauthored by Spafford and Kim held promise in 1992, but, for commercial gain, the pair left Tripwire alone. The software was offered as "freeware," a product free to be used, copied, and disseminated to anyone who wanted to use it. Network administrators interested in the offerings from the nascent, so-called Internet security market leaped at the chance to insert Tripwire into their computer systems, taking advantage of the software's configuration audit and control capabilities that alerted users whenever pernicious changes occurred in their

COMPANY PERSPECTIVES

Tripwire configuration audit and control solutions are designed to help effectively control change by detecting it whenever and wherever it happens. Our solutions become even more automated and effective when used as part of the change management capabilities required for self-healing or organic IT computing initiatives. In these solutions, Tripwire plays the key role of detecting the change, checking its validity, and if unwanted, activating the self-healing (remediation) process.

critical system files. Kim moved on after earning his degree at Purdue and enrolled at the University of Arizona, where he earned his master's degree in computer science. Tripwire, meanwhile, was downloaded one million times during the first five years of its creation, according to Purdue's calculations.

THE LURE OF PROFITS

Academic innovation was not looked upon as an opportunity for commercial gain until Kim met Wyatt Starnes. Unlike Kim, Starnes did not sprout from academia. Starnes never earned a degree, but he made up for his lack of technical expertise in a technological industry with an indefatigable drive, managerial shrewdness, and an ability to woo audiences with a passionate sales pitch. Early in his professional career, Starnes learned the nuances of semiconductor test applications, experience he put to use working for a variety of technology companies such as Data General Corporation, Monolithic Memories Inc., and Maruman Integrated Circuits. With such experience, Starnes built a résumé that enabled him to win an executive position at a small start-up concern, Megatest Corporation.

At Megatest, Starnes excelled. The company, with Starnes serving as its vice-president of sales and marketing, blossomed from an unknown into one of the leading semiconductor test companies in the world, thanks largely to its role as the premier supplier of test equipment to the largest semiconductor manufacturer in the world, Intel Corporation. Starnes, after spearheading the company's marketing efforts during its dramatic transformation, spent two years serving as president of Megatest Japan. After Megatest, Starnes served as president of Trisys before launching his entrepreneurial career with Eclipse Technologies. Soon after helping start the company, Starnes sold his interest in the start-up and joined Infinite Pictures Inc. Infinite Pictures was a three-dimensional graphics company that counted Gene Kim as one of its employees.

After Kim and Starnes met in the offices of Infinite Pictures, Kim presumably at some point told Starnes about his development of Tripwire. For Starnes, the adept marketer with an executive's sense of business opportunity, Kim's revelation of Tripwire served as a call to action. Together, the pair began hatching plans to start their own company. They left Infinite Pictures and in May 1997 founded Tripwire, which initially operated under the name Tripwire Security Systems, Inc. Negotiations with Purdue resulted in an exclusive licensing agreement for the Tripwire technology in exchange for a 2.5 percent interest in the company Kim and Starnes established in Portland.

THE WYATT SHOW BEGINNING IN 1997

Kim coauthored Tripwire and was more versed in the technical aspects of the start-up's business than Starnes, but Starnes, president and chief executive officer of the company, was the dominant personality of the two founders. Tripwire, as employees characterized the company in a February 22, 2004, interview with the *ORian,* was "The Wyatt Show." The basis for the technology was in place, having circulated among network administrators for five years at the time of the company's formation, but selling the idea to investors was another matter. Tripwire needed capital to get up and running. For that vital supply to cash, the company relied on its pitchman, Starnes.

Tripwire software was made commercially available in 1998, the year Starnes and Kim headed south to Silicon Valley to spark investor interest in their fledgling concern. Starnes became the face of Tripwire, explaining to institutional investors how Tripwire's approach differed from other products on the market. Conventional security products built a "firewall" around an Internet server that attempted to parry attacks from outside, but, as Starnes later remarked in a May 19, 2000, interview with *Business Journal–Portland,* "You'll never be able to build the security perimeter high enough and wide enough." A more effective defense, Starnes argued, was realized using Tripwire, which monitored a system by taking periodic snapshots of data and files to determine when an anomaly occurred. "We focus on whether your data is the same as it was yesterday," Starnes explained in his *Business Journal–Portland* interview.

KEY DATES

1992: Gene Kim and Eugene Spafford coauthor detection-intrusion software they name Tripwire.

1997: Kim and Wyatt Starnes form Tripwire to sell Tripwire software.

1999: Tripwire software exceeds $1 million in sales.

2003: Starnes, Tripwire's chief executive officer, is diagnosed with cancer.

2004: Starnes resigns from Tripwire and is replaced by Intel veteran Jim Johnson.

2005: Tripwire introduces Tripwire Enterprise, which extends the application of the company's software beyond the server and desktop level.

2007: During its tenth anniversary, the company records its third straight year of profits.

VENTURE CAPITAL FUELS EXPANSION

Starnes's efforts succeeded in giving Tripwire the funds to fuel its development. Starnes was able to secure $2.4 million in capital from the company's first investors. More money followed, as Starnes and Kim enjoyed an encouraging start to their partnership. A turning point in the development of their company occurred in 1999: Tripwire entered the year with a couple customers and 17 employees, and by the end of 1999, the company boasted 450 customers, which necessitated increasing the payroll to 70 employees. Sales by the end of the year reached $1.3 million, a 435 percent increase from the $250,390 collected at the end of the company's first year in business.

A second round of financing at the start of 2000, giving Tripwire $9 million, helped the two founders maintain their momentum. Tripwire's main concern, according to the May 19, 2000, edition of *Business Journal–Portland,* was "tripping over its feet as it tries to manage fast growth while balancing business fundamentals." The company pressed ahead, establishing sales offices in California, Tokyo, Munich, Germany, and Paris, using $24 million in funding received at the start of 2001 to finance its expansion. Tripwire forged distribution relationships that opened up sales channels in 17 countries. Its payroll swelled to 172 employees, as customers such as AT&T Corp., Ernst & Young, and the U.S. House of Representatives, turned to the burgeoning Portland company for help in protecting their computer systems.

THE PUSH TO ENTER A BIGGER MARKET

Tripwire was doing well, but not well enough to satisfy the investors who had contributed nearly $50 million to the company. Starnes needed to orchestrate another turning point in the company's development. The goal was to transform the company's business model by increasing the average price of its software and the number of copies each customer purchased. Instead of selling a customer $500 worth of software utilities, Starnes wanted to market a more comprehensive product, one that a company would buy to install on thousands of computers at a time. The strategy meant moving into the more populated enterprise security market, an area crowded with competitors who were larger and more established than Tripwire.

Starnes struggled to guide Tripwire out of its initial niche, a task made exceedingly hard after tragedy struck. In September 2003, the 48-year-old chief executive officer learned he had a malignant tumor the size of a large marble on the back of his tongue. Starnes underwent chemotherapy treatments, lost 40 pounds, and endured nearly constant nausea, yet continued to correspond with Tripwire staff via e-mail during his battle with cancer. "Shielding Wyatt from the business doesn't really work," Kim said in a February 22, 2004, interview with the *ORian.* "The absence of information simply triggers more questions and e-mail."

Starnes returned to Tripwire's offices at the start of 2004 when his doctors informed him his cancer was in remission. Carrying a feeding tube inserted into his stomach, Starnes made a valiant effort to resume his full duties at the company, but when his doctors, concerned about his slow pace of recovery, advised rest, Starnes relented. In April 2004, amid rumors that Tripwire's board of directors was seeking to replace him, Starnes announced his resignation. Despite the urgings of his doctors, Starnes took only a short break after leaving Tripwire. Before the end of the year, he started another company devoted to ensuring the integrity of data, SignaCert, Inc., which occupied offices not far from Tripwire's headquarters in Portland.

NEW LEADERSHIP IN 2004

The end of "The Wyatt Show" marked the beginning of the Johnson era. In May 2004, Jim Johnson was hired as Tripwire's new president and chief executive officer. Johnson had spent 27 years working for Intel, serving as the site manager for the company's operations in Oregon. He promised a seamless transition in leadership, while also declaring his intention to lead Tripwire into the crowded yet lucrative enterprise market. "Wyatt set the company on a path," Johnson said in a May 15, 2004, interview with the *ORian.* "The fundamental strategy of the company remains unchanged. We have a plan in place, and my marching orders are to go execute the plan. I'm here to keep pushing, keep focusing, and keep driving toward being wildly successful."

Tripwire fell short of becoming "wildly" successful during the first years of Johnson's tenure, but the new chief executive officer did succeed in steering the company toward a promising future. The company introduced Tripwire Enterprise in 2005, a product that extended its change detection and auditing capabilities beyond the server level. The long-awaited product release enabled customers to track, manage, and report changes across the entire information-technology infrastructure, injecting financial vitality into the Portland company. After years of posting annual losses, Tripwire began to generate a profit. By the time it celebrated its tenth anniversary in 2007, the company had posted profits for three straight years, generating its best ever quarter in terms of profits and sales during the fourth quarter of its anniversary year.

ANTICIPATED WALL STREET DEBUT

Orders, distinct from revenues, grew to $52 million during 2007, which positioned the company for a possible initial public offering (IPO) of stock. Johnson, in a January 23, 2008, interview with the *Business Journal–Portland,* said Tripwire was expected to be large enough within 12 to 18 months to consider filing for an IPO. A public debut offered a way for the company's institutional investors to earn a return on the $53 million they had invested in Tripwire. It also offered a way for individual investors to acquire a stake in Tripwire and reap the potential financial rewards of the company's growth in the future. With Johnson at the helm and consistent profitability on display, Tripwire appeared to be headed toward the most successful period in its history.

Jeffrey L. Covell

PRINCIPAL COMPETITORS

Symantec Corporation; McAfee, Inc.; Internet Security Systems, Inc.; Solidcore Systems, Inc.

FURTHER READING

Bermant, Charles, "Tripwire Explored Ways to Build a Corporate Culture," *Investor's Business Daily,* May 30, 2001, p. A6.

Earnshaw, Aliza, "Network Security Firms See More Awareness," *Business Journal–Portland,* November 2, 2001, p. 29.

"Finalist, Product of the Year: Tripwire Inc.," *Business Journal–Portland,* November 30, 2001, p. S31.

Giegerich, Andy, "E-Commerce Risks Work for Tripwire," *Business Journal–Portland,* October 13, 2000, p. 14.

Hunsberger, Brent, "Founder of Portland, Ore., Security Software Firm Resigns Due to Cancer," *ORian,* April 24, 2004.

McMillan, Dan, "Good Timing Helps Tripwire Land $9M in Venture Capital," *Business Journal–Portland,* February 25, 2000, p. 8.

———, "Tripwire Security Systems Tripping Toward Profits," *Business Journal–Portland,* May 19, 2000, p. 16.

Pace, Mark, "Tripwire: Last Defense Before Checkmate," *InfoWorld,* June 14, 1999, p. 37.

Schurr, Amy, "Buttressing the Corporate Firewall," *PC Week,* January 23, 1995, p. N17.

"Shaking the Money Tree, Tripwire Catches $24M," *Business Journal–Portland,* January 19, 2001, p. 4.

Sickinger, Ted, "Former Intel Manager Takes Over at Portland, Ore., Software Firm Tripwire," *ORian,* May 15, 2004.

———, "Tripwire CEO Beats Cancer, Shifts Priorities at Portland, Ore., Software Firm," *ORian,* February 22, 2004.

"Signaling an Increased Commitment to the Japanese Market," *Japan-U.S. Business Report,* March 2000, p. 32.

Strom, Shelly, "Tripwire Partners Up with Lloyd's of London," *Business Journal–Portland,* March 2, 2001, p. 21.

"Tripwire Aims to Find Needle in IT Haystack," *eWeek,* February 5, 2007.

"Tripwire Celebrates 10 Years of Innovation," *Internet Wire,* May 7, 2007.

"Tripwire Considers an I.P.O.," *Business Journal–Portland,* January 23, 2008.

USA Mobility Inc.

6677 Richmond Highway
Alexandria, Virginia 22306
U.S.A.
Telephone: (866) 662-3049
Fax: (866) 379-5861
Web site: http://www.usamobility.com

Public Company
Incorporated: 1986 as Arch Communications Group Inc.
Employees: 978
Sales: $424.6 million (2007)
Stock Exchanges: NASDAQ
Ticker Symbol: USMO
NAICS: 513321 Paging

■ ■ ■

Alexandria, Virginia-based USA Mobility Inc. is a leading player in the market for paging products and wireless services. It serves up both one- and two-way paging solutions to a wide range of customers. In addition to government and healthcare, the company has an especially strong presence in the business sector, counting more than two-thirds of the *Fortune* 1000 among its client base. In addition to offering paging, USA Mobility is a mobile voice and data services provider through Sprint Nextel. The company claims that its paging networks reach 90 percent of all U.S. residents. Its services extend into Mexican and Canadian markets via relationships with roaming partners.

ORIGINS: 1986–89

USA Mobility Inc. was officially established as a holding company to facilitate acquisition of Metrocall Holdings Inc. on November 16, 2004, by Arch Wireless Inc. The company was formed originally as Arch Communications Group Inc. in January 1986. In early 1989 the company snapped up SDM Communications Inc. In May of that year, C. Edward Baker Jr. was named chairman and CEO, beginning a long period of senior leadership.

RAPID GROWTH THROUGH ACQUISITIONS: 1990–99

Arch Wireless grew rapidly during the 1990s via a string of acquisitions. In 1993 the company secured a geographic foothold on the East Coast by acquiring in a series of cash deals a number of privately owned paging firms. At that time, new businesses were obtained in New Hampshire, New York, and Maine.

More activity in this region followed in 1994, when Arch Wireless acquired firms in Massachusetts and Rhode Island. AD-VU Systems Inc. was acquired midway through the year, paving the way for a flurry of activity in December. At that time Arch Wireless shelled out $500,000 for paging system assets owned by BellSouth Telecommunications Inc. A $14.9 million cash deal for the stock of Becker Beeper Inc. quickly followed. Arch Wireless capped off the year by acquiring paging businesses operating in the Wisconsin/Illinois and Florida markets in deals collectively worth about $31 million.

COMPANY PERSPECTIVES

USA Mobility serves over 70% of the *Fortune* 1000 companies, government agencies at all levels and many of the largest healthcare organizations across the country. We also provide network services to leaders in the telecommunications industry as well as the wireless reseller community.

In 1995 Arch Wireless continued along the acquisition path. The company bolstered its Arch Southeast Communications Inc. business early in the year via the purchase of Metairie, Louisiana-based Groome Enterprises Inc. for $7.7 million, followed by the acquisition of Data Transmission Inc. for $8.6 million. Other deals that year included the acquisition of Professional Paging & Radio Inc. ($3.0 million) and Beta Tele-Page Inc. ($8.8 million). Arch Wireless also negotiated a stock deal for USA Mobile Communications Holdings Inc. in 1995.

After acquiring Westlink Holdings Inc. for $325.4 million in 1996, Arch Wireless sold its site management arm to OmniAmerica Inc. for about $38 million in late 1998. The company then capped off the 1990s with a $671.1 million deal for MobileMedia Communications Inc.

DIFFICULT TIMES: 2000–03

By the new millennium, Arch Wireless owned one of the nation's largest and most reliable wireless networks. This position was bolstered by a major $985 million deal in November 2000, when the company acquired Dallas, Texas-based Paging Network Inc. (PageNet), which had filed for Chapter 11 bankruptcy. Both companies provided services throughout the United States and the District of Columbia. PageNet's reach extended to Canada, the U.S. Virgin Islands, and Puerto Rico, while Arch Wireless also served the Caribbean market.

The merger with PageNet, which was the 35th acquisition for Arch Wireless, created the nation's largest paging business, with roughly 13 million customers. At this time the company marketed its services via a network of company-owned stores and a direct sales force of approximately 1,600 people. Integrating the two firms, which employed some 9,000 people, was a sizable task, and was expected to take as long as 18 months. Following the deal, Arch Wireless continued operations from Westborough, Massachusetts, and C. Edward Baker Jr. continued as chairman and CEO.

During the early 2000s Arch Wireless operated in a climate characterized by growing demand for cell phones and falling demand for traditional paging services. In order to stay competitive with such players as Skytel and WebLink, the company began selling two-way wireless Internet and email services and devices.

In 2001 the company began selling its Arch Webster wireless two-way messaging and email service at hundreds of Wireless Retail kiosks across the country, which were located at stores such as Wal-Mart, Sam's Club, and Super Kmart. The company also forged a partnership with Motorola Inc. and MSN to offer MSN Hotmail, MSN instant messaging services, and MSN Mobile content via Motorola's Talkabout T900.

Despite efforts such as these, the loss of traditional one-way paging customers was substantial, totaling two million pagers in 2000 and roughly 2.6 million in 2001. The addition of new two-way customers was not enough to offset these hefty losses. Arch Wireless saw its stock price plummet, and the company was delisted from the NASDAQ National Market in April. In December, the company filed for Chapter 11 bankruptcy.

Arch Wireless filed a joint plan of reorganization in January 2002 and continued to focus on new revenue streams. A new product called Arch Wireless Enterprise Solution was introduced around this time, giving corporate customers the ability to access email, calendar, and other enterprise applications via a wireless connection.

By midyear the financial picture was improving. The company emerged from bankruptcy on May 29, eliminating $1.8 billion of its $2.1 billion debt load. Of the 9,000-plus employees on the company's roster at the time of the PageNet deal, 5,000 had been let go.

A flurry of stock exchange-related developments occurred in 2003. In April the company's common stock began trading on the Boston Stock Exchange under the symbol AWL. New transfer restrictions on the company's stock prompted the NASDAQ to assign it a new trading symbol (AWIAV) on June 18. Then, on July 23 the company's Class A common stock began trading on the NASDAQ National Market under the symbol AWIN.

Arch Wireless continued to operate in a difficult climate in 2003, losing some 477,000 subscribers in the first quarter alone, 460,000 of which were one-way paging customers. In all, the company's subscriber base totaled about 5.1 million midway through the year.

KEY DATES

1986: Company is formed as Arch Communications Group Inc. and eventually adopts the name Arch Wireless.
1989: C. Edward Baker Jr. is named chairman and CEO.
2000: Arch Wireless acquires Dallas, Texas-based Paging Network Inc. (PageNet) for $985 million.
2001: Company files for Chapter 11 bankruptcy.
2002: Arch Wireless emerges from bankruptcy.
2004: Arch Wireless merges with Alexandria, Virginia-based competitor Metrocall Holdings Inc. in a cash and stock deal worth approximately $326 million; deal marks the departure of Arch Wireless CEO C. Edward Baker Jr.; newly named USA Mobility Inc. begins trading on the NASDAQ National Market under the symbol USMO.

NEW INDUSTRY LEADER: 2004–08

A major development unfolded in March 2004, when Arch Wireless announced plans to acquire Alexandria, Virginia-based competitor Metrocall Holdings Inc. in a cash and stock merger worth approximately $326 million. Like Arch Wireless, Metrocall had grown through a series of acquisitions over the years. The company had experienced its share of hard times, filing for bankruptcy in June 2002 and emerging that October. By this time the number of paging customers in the United States had plummeted to 12 million, down from 40 million in 1999.

In merging, the industry's two leading firms hoped to achieve $200 million in savings over a four-year period by streamlining operations and reducing staff rosters. The proposed merger prompted a probe by the U.S. Department of Justice, which sought to determine if hindered competition would have a negative impact on paging services for the healthcare industry and other customers not able to use alternative services such as cellular phones.

In November 2004 the Department of Justice indicated it would not challenge the Arch Wireless merger with Metrocall and closed its investigation. The Federal Communications Commission granted its consent, and despite opposition from some of Metrocall's largest shareholders, the deal received shareholder approval and was completed on November 16. The completion of the merger, which created a new paging industry leader, brought Arch Wireless and Metrocall Holdings together as a holding company named USA Mobility Inc., which began trading on the NASDAQ National Market on November 17, under the symbol USMO.

Significantly, the deal marked the departure of longtime Arch Wireless CEO C. Edward Baker Jr. In addition, Arch Wireless COO Lyndon Daniels and CFO J. Roy Pottle also left the company. Metrocall President and CEO Vincent D. Kelly was named as the new president and CEO of USA Mobility. The company's headquarters were relocated to Alexandria, Virginia.

The integration of operations quickly began as the company moved to reduce its costs in an ever challenging climate. USA Mobility lost 979,000 messaging units in 2004, leaving the company with about 6.2 million subscribers, nearly 5.7 million of whom had traditional one-way paging service.

In May 2005, USA Mobility reduced its three operating divisions, each of which contained five regions, into two six-region divisions. A number of executive changes also occurred, including the departure of COO Stan Sech, who was succeeded by Peter C. Barnett. Some nine months after the merger, USA Mobility announced that the company had repaid its $140 million in bank debt. It ended the year by returning $41 million to shareholders in the form of a special distribution.

USA Mobility ushered in 2006 by becoming a member of a national trade association called the American Association of Paging Carriers. By this time the company had partnered with Cingular Wireless and Sprint Nextel to offer mobile and data services, including GPS location. The company provided customers with everything from pagers and phones to GPS and wireless data applications, including wireless asset tracking.

In April, USA Mobility unveiled a new corporate logo and the tagline, "One Source for Wireless," which attempted to better reflect the company's position as a comprehensive wireless provider. Midway through 2006, USA Mobility made another special distribution to its shareholders, returning $3 per share for a total of about $82 million.

In the fall of 2006 a successful pilot project was carried out with Amcom Software Inc., in which an integrated communications system was developed for Durham, North Carolina-based Duke University Medical Center. In early 2007 the two companies formed a sales and marketing alliance that allowed them to offer complete, integrated wireless solutions that other healthcare organizations could use to automate both routine and emergency communications throughout multifacility networks.

In mid-2007 USA Mobility introduced its Coaster Pager, which allowed healthcare providers to equip patients in waiting rooms with pagers that notified them when they were ready to be seen by a provider. Operating like pagers in busy restaurants, the devices gave patients faced with long wait times the freedom to move beyond waiting rooms and visit cafeterias, gift shops, and local retailers.

Developments continued to unfold in 2007 as USA Mobility partnered with weather information provider Weatherbug to offer severe weather alerts to government and enterprise customers, including hospitals in hurricane-prone areas. The partnership combined National Weather Service alerts with alerts from Weatherbug's 8,000 tracking stations and delivered them to USA Mobility customers with pagers and Sprint GPS-enabled devices.

USA Mobility made a number of changes to its executive lineup in 2007. These included the departure of COO Peter Barnett, who was succeeded by CFO Thomas L. Schilling in October. In addition to the new COO position, Schilling retained his role as CFO. The company concluded its 2007 fiscal year with revenues of $424.6 million, down from $497.7 million in 2006.

USA Mobility was strongly focused on marketing to large corporations, government agencies, and the healthcare sector. These segments had grown to represent 77.6 percent of the company's subscribers at the conclusion of fiscal 2007, compared to 67.7 percent a year before. In particular, healthcare had become an especially strong niche, accounting for 42.1 percent of subscribers.

Looking ahead, USA Mobility seemed well prepared to maintain its position as a leading wireless firm. The company had survived the industry's difficult transition from one-way paging by offering a broader array of products and services suited to the changing needs of organizations in a variety of industries.

Paul R. Greenland

PRINCIPAL SUBSIDIARIES

Arch Canada Inc.; Arch Wireless Communications Inc.; Arch Wireless Holdings Inc.; Arch Wireless Inc.; Arch Wireless License Co. LLC; Arch Wireless Operating Company Inc.; GTES LLC; Metrocall Holdings Inc.; Metrocall Inc.; Metrocall Ventures Inc.; MobileMedia Communications Inc.; Paging Network Canadian Holdings Inc.

PRINCIPAL COMPETITORS

AT&T Mobility LLC; Skytel Corp.; Verizon Wireless Messaging, LLC; American Messaging Service, Inc.

FURTHER READING

"Arch Wireless Completes Merger with PageNet, Becomes Leading Provider of Two-Way Internet Messaging," *PR Newswire,* November 10, 2000.

Bajaj, Vikas, "Paging Companies Struggle to Stay Viable, Pin Hopes on New Devices," *Knight-Ridder/Tribune Business News,* April 10, 2001.

Bray, Hiawatha, "Paging Company Arch Wireless in Massachusetts Files for Bankruptcy," *Boston Globe,* December 7, 2001.

Howe, Peter J., "Westborough, Mass., Paging Company Attempts Tough Corporate Makeover," *Boston Globe,* June 22, 2002.

"Metrocall/Arch Merger Completed," *PR Newswire,* November 16, 2004.

"PageNet Stakeholders Vote Overwhelmingly to Accept Plan of Reorganization and Merger with Arch Wireless," *Business Wire,* October 23, 2000.

"USA Mobility Completes Repayment of Bank Debt," *PR Newswire,* August 22, 2005.

Vector Aerospace Corporation

105 Bedford Road, Suite 300
Toronto, Ontario M5R 2K4
Canada
Telephone: (416) 925-1143
Fax: (416) 925-7214
Web site: http://www.vectoraerospace.com

Public Company
Incorporated: 1998
Employees: 3,000
Sales: CAD 339.1 million (2007)
Stock Exchanges: Toronto
Ticker Symbol: RNO
NAICS: 488190 Other Support Activities for Air Transportation

■ ■ ■

Vector Aerospace Corporation is a maintenance, repair, and overhaul (MRO) organization serving fixed-wing aircraft, helicopters, and industrial turbines. It was formed in a 1998 spinoff of CHC Helicopter Corporation, a leading operator of rotorcraft to support the offshore oil industry. The company was originally led by Mark Dobbin, son of CHC founder Craig Dobbin, but after a few years a shareholder group led by Northstar Aerospace Chairman Donald Jackson won control in a proxy fight. Vector's headquarters were subsequently relocated from Newfoundland to Northstar's home base of Toronto.

Vector performs MRO services for a variety of commercial and military customers in Canada, the United States, the United Kingdom, and South Africa. In 2008 it greatly augmented its European operations with the controversial purchase of the helicopter maintenance unit of Great Britain's Defence Aviation and Repair Agency (DARA).

CHC'S MRO

Vector Aerospace Corporation was formed from the maintenance, repair, and overhaul (MRO) operations of CHC Helicopter Corporation. In two decades Newfoundland entrepreneur Craig Dobbin had fashioned CHC into a leading global provider of helicopters for the offshore oil industry. Along the way, it had picked up some MRO facilities, most notably Atlantic Turbines Inc., which specialized in fixed-wing aircraft, on Prince Edward Island, and the ACRO Aerospace Division on the other side of the country, in British Columbia.

Finding that the repair business was less susceptible to the severe cycles that affected the oil industry, CHC built its MRO segment in 1998 by adding southern England's Hunting Airmotive, later called SIGMA Aerospace. This operation specialized in fixed-wing aircraft rather than helicopters.

SPINOFF AND EARLY ACQUISITIONS

In June 1998 CHC Corporation spun off its MRO unit as Vector Aerospace Corporation in an initial public offering (IPO). The stock (actually a combination of shares and warrants) was listed on the Toronto Stock Exchange at CAD 8.75 a share (ticker symbol: RNO).

COMPANY PERSPECTIVES

At Vector Aerospace, we are committed to being the benchmark against which maintenance, repair and overhaul businesses are measured. We aim to set the standard of customer service, continuously challenging ourselves to do better, and to deliver on our promises.

CHC reaped proceeds of CAD 192.5 million ($127 million) in the IPO while holding on to a one-fifth interest. CHC divested its final 20 percent stake in Vector Aerospace in September 1999.

Vector hopped on the acquisition trail soon after its spinoff. In early 1999 it agreed to acquire Helipro, an MRO company based in Vancouver, for CAD 39 million. Helipro had annual revenues of CAD 25 million. After the acquisition, Helipro's engine business was joined with the existing ACRO Aerospace unit, leaving the rest of Helipro to specialize in structural work.

In June 1999 Vector bought California's Tower Aviation Services and Advanced Turbine Technology out of bankruptcy for CAD 10 million. These became the Alameda Aerospace unit at the Navy base at Alameda, which specialized in engine and avionics repairs for fixed-wing aircraft, a segment that accounted for more than half of Vector's total business.

RESILIENT BUSINESS MODEL

The businesses that made up Vector had sales of CAD 225 million in 1998, rising to CAD 268 million in its first full year as an independent company. Revenues approached CAD 300 million by 2000, and the company was consistently profitable. Vector then had 1,300 employees in several divisions: Sigma Aerospace, Atlantic Turbines, ACRO Aerospace, Helipro, Alameda Aerospace, and a software business called Pathix.

Increasingly airlines and military operators were outsourcing maintenance. However, MROs such as Vector were facing new competition from original equipment manufacturers who were seeking a piece of the market.

By 2001 a global economic downturn was further vindicating Vector's business model. Operators were more interested in mending old aircraft than investing in new ones. This was particularly true in the case of helicopters used in the offshore oil industry. With oil prices relatively low, there was little incentive for energy companies to make large capital purchases.

After the September 11, 2001, terrorist attacks on the United States, however, airlines retired many older planes in favor of more efficient newer models. This would remain a theme for several years as fuel prices reached unprecedented levels. The Alameda unit was most affected by this change, Mark Dobbin told the *Canadian Press.* Another trend was an increasing percentage of business from military customers, particularly in helicopters. Vector provided services to the armed forces of a number of countries, including Canada, the United States, the United Kingdom, Colombia, and Saudi Arabia.

POWER STRUGGLES

Military conflict overseas, SARS, and other factors combined to make the aviation industry a difficult place in which to turn a profit. As Vector's shares fell to a fraction of their offering price, the company became a takeover target.

Donald Jackson, chairman of Northstar Aerospace Inc., held a less than 10 percent stake in Vector and led a proxy fight against its management team then led by Mark Dobbin. Although Northstar was already involved in aircraft maintenance, Jackson said he was not interested in merging the companies. Kenneth Rowe, CEO of another rival, Halifax-based IMP Group Inc., joined Jackson in his takeover efforts, which succeeded after several months in November 2003. Jackson took over as chairman after his successful proxy struggle. He soon relocated Vector's headquarters to Northstar's base of Toronto.

Mark Dobbin and two other top-level executives had provisions in their contracts mandating a payout estimated at $24 million in the event the board of directors was replaced. A number of observers classified this as a poison pill; Dobbin countered that the obligations had been in place since Vector was formed and represented service that predated the company itself. The day before they were replaced, the old board fired these executives in an attempt to lessen this liability on the company. A lawsuit by Dobbins and the others followed; Vector had these cases settled for a cumulative $12 million by 2008.

The company again appeared a takeover target in 2005 as a number of players amassed small holdings in it. In January an investment group controlled by ousted CEO Mark Dobbin had lifted its holdings in Vector to nearly an 11 percent stake.

Meanwhile former corporate parent CHC Helicopter Corporation had begun to acquire helicopter overhaul and repair companies again. A Vector acquisition could have made sense for Northstar Aerospace and

KEY DATES

1998: CHC Helicopter Corporation spins off its maintenance, repair, and overhaul unit as Vector Aerospace Corporation.
1999: Vector acquires Helipro and Tower Aviation companies.
2003: Northstar Aerospace Chairman Donald Jackson leads successful proxy battle for control of Vector.
2008: Declan O'Shea becomes CEO; Vector buys U.K. government's DARA helicopter maintenance unit.

the IMP Group, which owned 28 percent of shares, as well.

There was a consensus that the industry was due for consolidation, reported the *Globe and Mail,* yet there was reluctance to be the first to start a bidding war. IMP Group Chairman Kenneth Rowe sued Vector Chairman Donald Jackson, claiming he had improperly acquired the shares that Craig Dobbin had first offered IMP.

In March 2008 Declan O'Shea took over the duties of president and CEO from Donald Jackson, who remained chairman. O'Shea had previously worked for SR Technics.

BIG IN BRITAIN

In 2008 Vector bought the helicopter repair and spare parts operations of the United Kingdom's Defence Aviation and Repair Agency (DARA) for £17 million (CAD 33 million). There were reportedly more than two dozen other bidders for the business.

The privatization was controversial and prompted an outcry from politicians and labor unions over concerns about job security and national defense implications. A Vector official pointed out that the company already repaired Royal Air Force transports through its Sigma Aerospace unit.

The DARA operations had annual turnover of about £80 million (CAD 160 million) and 1,300 employees. This was a huge addition to Vector's existing workforce of 3,000, and a strategic investment in the future of the European helicopter industry.

Vector dubbed the new units Vector Aerospace Helicopter Services Fleetlands and Vector Aerospace Component Services Almondbank. It was also changing the names of its existing Engine Services (Atlantic Turbines International and Sigma Aerospace) and Helicopter Services (ACROHELIPRO) businesses to emphasize the Vector Aerospace name.

Frederick C. Ingram

PRINCIPAL DIVISIONS

Helicopter; Fixed-Wing.

PRINCIPAL OPERATING UNITS

Helicopter Services; Component Services; Engine Services.

PRINCIPAL SUBSIDIARIES

Vector Aerospace Holdings Limited; Sigma Aerospace Holdings Limited (U.K.).

PRINCIPAL COMPETITORS

TIMCO Aviation Services, Inc.; Barnes Group Inc.; Teleflex Incorporated; IMP Group Inc.; Fairchild Corporation; AAR Corp.; Banner Aerospace, Inc.

FURTHER READING

"CEO Interview: Mark Dobbin—Vector Aerospace Corporation," *Wall Street Transcript,* June 12, 2000.

"CEO Interview: Mark Dobbin—Vector Aerospace Corporation," *Wall Street Transcript Digest,* June 24, 2002.

Dabrowski, Wojtek, "Avoid Vector Until Parachutes Have Opened: Beacon's Jonathan Norwood," *National Post's Financial Post & FP Investing,* November 26, 2003, p. IN01.

———, "Dissidents Win Vector Power Struggle: New Directors Installed," *National Post's Financial Post & FP Investing,* November 29, 2003, p. FP3.

———, "Northstar Concedes Vector May Be Target: Aerospace Rival in Acquisition Mode," *National Post,* Financial Post Sec., May 23, 2003, p. FP5.

———, "Vector Rival Denies Merger Plans: Boardroom Moves Aim 'to Create Shareholder Value,'" *National Post's Financial Post & FP Investing,* May 21, 2003, p. FP5.

Fitzpatrick, Peter, "$35-Million Executive Package Too Rich for Tiny Vector; Board: For Severance, Pensions," *National Post's Financial Post & FP Investing,* November 15, 2003, p. FP01.

———, "Vector Stretches Its Wings: For Mark Dobbin, the Takeoff for CHC Helicopter's Repair Unit Was a Lot Bumpier Than Expected—But the Flight Is Beginning to Smooth Out," *National Post,* Financial Post Sec., March 8, 1999, p. C6.

Gutschi, Monica, "Once a Target, Vector Aerospace Is Now a Buyer," *Globe and Mail* (Canada), February 20, 2008, p. B13.

———, "Vector Aero Good Takeover Target, but Where's the Bid?" *Dow Jones News Service,* February 2, 2005.

———, "Vector Aero Outlook Better Despite Industry Challenges," *Dow Jones News Service,* April 11, 2003.

Ingram, Frederick C., "CHC Helicopter Corporation," in *International Directory of Company Histories,* Vol. 67, edited by Jay P. Pederson. Detroit: Gale Group, 2005, pp.101–03.

Jasper, Chris, "Ambitious Vector Homes In on Fresh Round of MRO Take-Overs," *Flight International,* January 30, 2001, p. 30.

McGregor, Glen, "Canadian Firm Helps Military in Columbia: Federal Government Gives OK Despite Country's Rights Record," *Ottawa Citizen,* February 21, 2001, p. A4.

Middlemiss, Jim, "$16-Million Vector Lawsuit to Begin; Share Sales at Issue," *National Post's Financial Post & FP Investing,* May 29, 2008, p. FP6.

"No Job Cuts Included in Vector Aerospace's $29.5M Restructuring Charge," *Canadian Press,* December 14, 2001.

Norton-Taylor, Richard, "Uproar Over Sale of Helicopter Repair Agency to Canadian Firm," *Guardian* (London), Financial Sec., January 12, 2008, p. 43.

Paddon, David, "Vector Aerospace Shareholders Install New CEO After Old Board Concedes Defeat," *Canadian Press,* November 28, 2003.

Pitts, Gordon, "Aviation Heavyweights Circling Vector; East Coast-based CHC Helicopter, IMP Group Are Jockeying for a Takeover Position of the Toronto Aircraft Repair Firm," *Globe and Mail* (Canada), February 8, 2005, p. B8.

Tedesco, Theresa, "The Pill at Vector Is Tough to Swallow: Peterson Could Be Unclear on the Director Concept," *National Post's Financial Post & FP Investing,* November 15, 2003, p. FP02.

Vueling Airlines S.A.

Parque de Negocios Mas Blau II
Plaza Pla de l'Estany, 5
El Prat de Llobregat
Barcelona, 08820
Spain
Telephone: (+34 93) 378 78 78
Fax: (+34 93) 378 78 79
Web site: http://www.vueling.com

Public Company
Incorporated: 2004
Employees: 1,100
Sales: EUR 362.67 million (2007)
Stock Exchanges: Bolsa de Madrid
Ticker Symbol: VLG
NAICS: 481110 Scheduled Passenger Air Transportation

■ ■ ■

Vueling Airlines S.A. is a leading Spanish low-cost carrier, or as the company puts it, a "next generation airline." Its reach extends from its base in Barcelona to Spain's major vacation spots and several of Europe's major cities. It competes with both legacy carriers and other European discount airlines. More than six million people fly Vueling every year. Vueling operates somewhat differently from the typical low-cost carrier model in that it flies from major, rather than secondary, airports.

BASED IN BARCELONA

The idea for Barcelona's Vueling Airlines reportedly sprang from a conversation a few airline personnel had with company cofounder Carlos Muñoz in an airport in November 2002, according to Cathy Buyck in *Air Transport World.* Muñoz was a veteran of his family's company AMC and had earned an M.B.A. degree in the United States. He tapped Lazaro Ros to be the new airline's chief operating officer. The aim was to introduce a low-cost carrier (LCC) to the Spanish skies.

Southwest Airlines of the United States is generally considered the originator of the widely imitated LCC concept. Under this model, airlines reduced operating costs by flying a single type of aircraft, and keeping them in the sky making money as many hours as possible every day. There was usually but a single class of seating. Frills were kept to a minimum and online sales simplified the distribution of tickets. These techniques allowed LCCs to drastically undercut the fares charged by legacy airlines.

By the time of Vueling's launch in 2004, several new airlines had been quite successful with the model elsewhere in Europe, most notably Ireland's RyanAir Holdings plc and easyJet plc of the United Kingdom. However, Vueling's founders claimed inspiration from JetBlue, a U.S. upstart that operated a low-cost model but promised a higher level of service. For example, it had a policy of not intentionally overbooking flights or canceling flights due to lack of ticket sales, unlike some local rivals who were notorious for such practices.

Early financial backing came from foreigners familiar with the success of the LCC concept, including

COMPANY PERSPECTIVES

Our aim was to create an airline with which flying became a genuine pleasure, with which paying less was not equivalent to lowering standards in terms of service or comfort and which was open, sincere and user-friendly. So if we tell you there are extremely cheap flights up for grabs then we wish to do so because it is the truth. We wanted an airline with kindly staff who placed no barriers between themselves and the customer, we wanted to operate with new aircraft, to fly to major airports and to neither delay flights nor overbook them. It's as simple as that. And it's all happening so spread the word.

JetBlue President Dave Barger, and London venture capital firm Apax Partners, which became the largest shareholder with a 39 percent stake. Spain's Grupo Planeta, a conglomerate controlled by the Lara family, took the next largest slice, 30 percent, through a subsidiary called Inversiones Hemisferio. Vueling management held 23 percent. Total startup capital was EUR 30 million.

The carrier was incorporated in February 2004 as Vueling Airlines S.A. There were about 120 employees when it began commercial operations. Commercial service commenced on July 1 with a single Airbus A320 connecting Barcelona, Ibiza, Valencia, and Paris. The plane was full; Vueling had offered tickets at just EUR 10, less than a typical cab fare. It added Brussels and Ibiza to the network with the arrival of another A320 a couple weeks later. The A320s had a capacity of 180 passengers each.

The Mediterranean city of Barcelona was a unique launching pad. Until then, most of Spain's aviation industry had been centered on either the capital of Madrid or the vacation island of Majorca. Yet Barcelona boasted a number of advantages, the foremost being little low-fare competition. In addition, El Prat Airport was adequate and relatively inexpensive, and would be part of Spain's ambitious expansion program to double its total airport capacity.

From the beginning, Vueling had employed wordplay to project a hip, friendly attitude. In fact, the company name is a kind of anglicization of the Spanish word for "flying." The company's first planes were dubbed *Barceloning* and *Born to Be Vueling*. The tradition continued as the carrier applied such whimsical names as *Vueling the Sky; Veni, Vidi, Vueling; Vueling the World;* and *The Joy of Vueling* to its brand-new, multimillion-dollar aircraft. The airline's seventh plane, which entered service in October 2005 was dubbed *Eloy Fructuoso* after the airline's one-millionth passenger, a tradition that continued with the 12th plane, named after the two-millionth passenger, Connie Baraja.

RAPID GROWTH

Vueling carried more than two million passengers in 2005, when revenues were about EUR 115 million. Ancillary sales, including snacks, and travel reservations, accounted for an impressive one-fifth of the total. By the end of the year, the airline was operating nine aircraft, all of them Airbus A320s. There were about 360 employees.

Vueling opened a second hub in Madrid in November 2005. It was a gutsy move, admitted Muñoz in *Air Transport World*, as this was the home base of flag carrier Iberia, Lineas Aéreas de España, S.A. However, the two operated at different price points, and at least one of Europe's largest LCCs, Ryanair, was neglecting the market due to its lack of interest in Spain's domestic routes.

Vueling and JetBlue instituted an exchange program for cabin crew in February 2006. The former was an outspoken admirer of the latter, and hoped to learn more about its customer service practices. For its part, JetBlue was interested in Vueling's creativity in marketing and ancillary sales, Muñoz told *Air Transport World*.

Vueling lost EUR 10.7 million in 2006 on revenues of EUR 235.5 million. The airline carried 3.5 million passengers during the year and the fleet grew to 16 aircraft. Vueling became a public company on December 1, 2006, when it floated 43 percent of shares in a EUR 191 million ($253 million) initial public offering (IPO) on the Bolsa de Madrid. The market was receptive; Air Berlin and Aer Lingus had had successful IPOs earlier in the year, and Vueling shares climbed 16 percent at the end of their first day of trading. Proceeds were earmarked for buying new planes and opening a new base outside Spain.

INTENSE COMPETITION

Vueling did not have the discount traveler to itself for long. Not only did established LCCs Ryanair and easyJet multiply their excursions to Spain, a favorite holiday destination from Britain, but state airline Iberia backed a new budget airline called Clickair, S.A., which was launched in 2006 and was also based in Barcelona. Muñoz told *Airline Business* that Iberia's move seemed

KEY DATES

2002: Carlos Muñoz and Lázaro Ros prepare to launch a new budget airline for the underserved southwestern Europe market.
2004: Vueling Airlines S.A. begins flight operations.
2006: Company floats a EUR 191 million ($253 million) IPO.
2007: Management is replaced as company struggles with onslaught of low-cost competitors.
2008: Carrier considers merger with new local rival Clickair S.A.

to confuse its own customers, leading many to make the switch to Vueling. Because Clickair operated on many routes transferred from Iberia, this seemed to result in a net decrease in business for the flag carrier.

In the liberalized European aviation market, Vueling also had to contend with legacy carriers from other countries, such as SAS, which had an offshoot called Spanair S.A. based in Majorca. The market was getting crowded, drawing some speculation of forthcoming consolidation activity.

Vueling opened a base in Paris in 2007, an expensive gambit. Relentless competition was also blamed for faltering finances. Vueling cut fares by a fifth as it tangled in a vicious fare war with its domestic rivals. At the same time, fuel prices were rising to unprecedented levels. The carrier posted a loss of EUR 63.2 million for the year on revenues of EUR 362.7 million. (As usual, ancillary sales accounted for one-third of the total.)

The board dismissed company founders Carlos Muñoz and Lazaro Ros in November 2007. A recently appointed chairperson was also replaced, as were some other board members. These moves reportedly came at the urging of Grupo Planeta investment unit Inversiones Hemisferio, which remained the largest shareholder after the IPO and was increasing its stake. (Apax Partners had sold the last of its shares in June 2006.)

Vueling's passenger count rose to more than six million in 2007. The airline then employed about 1,100 people and operated two-dozen aircraft at year-end. It was fielding 150 flights a day on 57 daily routes, a dramatic increase within just three years. A new hub opened in Seville, Spain, in July 2007.

In spite of the increase in traffic, the airline was plainly in a crisis. Vueling urged its passengers to "fly cheap, fly well," but apparently they were getting too sweet a deal. The problem, according to one official, was that fares were not meeting the carrier's flight expenses. It was hoped the airline could attract more business passengers, allowing it to raise rates.

Cost-cutting measures included leasing out planes and deferring deliveries of 40 aircraft on order. The airline reportedly also hired an investment bank to study "strategic alternatives," a phrase that usually included the possibility of a merger or sale. One company with whom Vueling was considering a combination was Clickair. According to *Aviation Daily*, this would have created Spain's third largest airline behind Iberia and Spanair.

Lars Nygaard, formerly managing director of rival Spanair S.A., stepped up as CEO in this challenging environment at the end of 2007. The company did not expect to be able to break even until 2009. With no one making any money, the aviation industry seemed ripe as ever for some kind of consolidation.

Frederick C. Ingram

PRINCIPAL COMPETITORS

Iberia, Lineas Aéreas de España, S.A.; Spanair S.A.; easyJet plc; Ryanair Holdings plc; Air Madrid Lineas Aéreas S.A.; Air Europa Líneas Aéreas, S.A.; Clickair, S.A.

FURTHER READING

Baker, Colin, "Iberia Low-Cost Arm Takes on Vueling," *Airline Business,* June 20, 2006.

Braude, Jonathan, "Apax Leads $36M Investment," *Daily Deal,* May 20, 2004.

Buyck, Cathy, "¿Hablas LCC?" *Air Transport World,* February 2006, pp. 47–49.

Ezard, Kerry, "Local Conflict," *Airline Business,* November 21, 2006.

———, "Vueling Ousts Managers," *Airline Business,* November 20, 2007.

Flottau, Jens, "Peninsula Push; European Network and Low-Cost Carriers Head for Spain in Fight for Supremacy," *Aviation Week & Space Technology,* October 2, 2006, p. 59.

Harding, Ben, "Dogfight for Survival in the Spanish Skies," *Birmingham Post,* August 15, 2007, p. 22.

Hetz, Robert, "Vueling Shares Hit Low After Apax Stake Sale," *Reuters News,* June 6, 2007.

McGee, Brian, "Rivals Put Squeeze on Profit at Vueling," *International Herald Tribune,* October 19, 2007.

Ranson, Lori, "Vueling Not Concerned About LCCs Flooding Spanish Market," *Aviation Daily,* October 12, 2006, p. 3.

"Saffron Brand for Vueling Airlines," *Design Week,* June 24, 2004, p. 3.

Sinclair, Jason, "Hemisferio Still Talking with Clickair Hldrs," *Dow Jones International News,* March 31, 2008.

"Spain's Vueling Takes Off," *Flight International,* August 1, 2004, p. 19.

Tardy, Martial, "Spain: Vueling Shareholder Admits Talks with Clickair," *Aviation Daily,* January 30, 2008, p. 5.

"Vueling Airlines Completes EUR 191 Million IPO," *Airfinance Journal,* December 2006.

"Vueling CEO Says Air Price War Can't Last," *Reuters News,* September 18, 2007.

Webasto Roof Systems Inc.

1757 Northfield Drive
Rochester Hills, Michigan 48309
U.S.A.
Telephone: (248) 997-5100
Fax: (248) 997-5581
Web site: http://www.webasto.us

Wholly Owned Subsidiary of Webasto AG
Incorporated: 1974
Employees: 1,100
Sales: $400 million (2007 est.)
NAICS: 336370 Motor Vehicle Metal Stamping; 336399 All Other Motor Vehicle Parts Manufacturing

■ ■ ■

Webasto Roof Systems Inc. is a leading manufacturer of products for the transportation industry. In addition to sunroofs, the company makes convertible roof systems, tailgates, and heaters for automobiles. Since 2000, the company has operated as a wholly owned subsidiary of Webasto AG, founded in 1901 and headquartered in Stockdorf, Germany.

ORIGINS: 1974–89

Webasto Roof Systems dates to 1974, when Germany's Webasto AG established Webasto Sunroofs Inc. as its first foreign subsidiary. During its early years, the company operated as a joint venture between Webasto AG and the Cosma Division of Canada's Magna International, with operations based in Rochester Hills, Michigan, just north of Detroit.

Webasto AG got its start in 1901 as a sheet metal goods manufacturer formed by Wilhelm Baier. The company's expertise included the development of folding roofs for coaches (1932) and passenger cars (1936), steel sunroofs for passenger cars (1956), and the first sliding sunroof (1969). Magna International had been formed in 1961 as Magna Electronics Corporation Ltd. and adopted the Magna International nameplate in 1973. Webasto counted the development of the first sliding glass sunroof (1979) among its early accomplishments.

SUNROOF LEADER: 1990–99

Webasto Sunroofs quickly established itself as a leading supplier to U.S. automotive manufacturers and was chosen to supply sunroofs for the 1991 Ford Explorer. The following year, Webasto Sunroofs supplied what at the time were some of the largest original equipment, single-piece glass roofs when it provided parts for the 1993 Nissan Quest and Mercury Villager.

Heading into the mid-1990s, Webasto Sunroofs unveiled an innovative, solar-powered sunroof. The unit included solar-powered exhaust fans that replaced hot air inside of a car with cooler outside air when the vehicle's interior exceeded 85 degrees. This was accomplished through the use of a vented roof, which special rain sensors closed in the event of inclement weather.

By early 1995 Webasto Sunroofs had become the largest automotive sunroof supplier in the world. In

COMPANY PERSPECTIVES

Our statement "Feel the drive" is more than a promise; it's a requirement. Webasto has addressed every aspect of vehicle usage with solutions to increase comfort every step of the way.

North America alone, the company held about 50 percent of the market. That year, the company's sales reached the $120 million mark. Progress continued in mid-1995 when Toyota Motor Manufacturing USA Inc. chose Webasto Sunroofs as the supplier for the Toyota Camry. The contract, which called for a high production volume, came after the company passed a demanding qualification and bidding process.

The 1990s were not without challenges for Webasto Sunroofs. For example, in 1996 the company was forced to lay off one-third of its workforce (about 80 employees) due to a strike by the United Auto Workers Local 696 in Dayton, Ohio, which affected production at General Motors. On the upside, the company secured a contract to equip roughly 33 percent of all 1997 Ford Expeditions with electric tilt-slide sunroofs that year.

As the World Wide Web made its public debut during the mid-1990s, Webasto Sunroofs was quick to develop an online presence. In late 1996 the company created a site that supplied information to aftermarket installers and distributors, automobile dealers, consumers, and original equipment manufacturers. The site also became an important channel from which Webasto Sunroofs garnered feedback from these key audiences.

Webasto Sunroofs sales climbed to $177 million in 1997, and the company's workforce grew to 770, up from 592 in 1996. When ASC Inc., which had introduced sunroofs to the U.S. automotive industry and supplied them to Chrysler since the mid-1970s, lost a contract to equip Chrysler's Cirrus and Stratus models with sunroofs, Webasto was chosen as ASC's replacement.

In September 1997, Webasto Sunroofs made several key changes to its executive staff. At that time Fred Olson, an executive with Magna International's Atoma Division, was named to lead the business as general manager. In addition, Webasto AG executive Peter Holbach was named to a newly created position of general manager of operations. At the same time, the company began searching for an additional location in the southern United States, part of a strategy to be closer to automotive manufacturers such as Toyota and General Motors, which were positioning operations in the region.

Developed in 1996, Webasto's Lamella sunroof became available in Europe on the 1998 Mercedes Class A and was slated for introduction in the United States on sport-utility vehicles (SUVs) by 1999. The Lamella comprised a series of slats or louvers, which lay flat when the roof was closed.

Innovations continued at Webasto Sunroofs during the late 1990s. In 1999 the company developed the Starlite 7-B, a sunroof for the Volkswagen Beetle that was specially designed to fit the car's curved roof. In September the company unveiled the new SolAire product line. Drawing its name from the words "sun," and "air," the new brand sought to more accurately reflect a driver's experience when using a sunroof. The SolAire line replaced virtually all of Webasto Sunroofs' Starlite products. The company concluded the decade with a 42 percent share of the global automotive sunroof market.

GROWTH AND CHANGE IN THE NEW CENTURY

A major development occurred following the dawn of the new millennium when Magna International sold its 50 percent stake in Webasto Sunroofs to Webasto AG in July 2000. At that time, Webasto Sunroofs maintained its headquarters in Rochester Hills, Michigan. In addition, the company had grown to include seven engineering and manufacturing sites in Michigan, California, and Kentucky. The company's workforce had risen to 1,000 employees, and sales exceeded $250 million.

During the early 2000s Webasto Sunroofs provided sunroof systems for more than 40 different model vehicles from Chrysler (PT Cruiser); Ford (Expedition, F-150 Super Crew, Lincoln Navigator, Mercury Sable, and Taurus); General Motors (Blazer, Grand Prix, Grand Am, and Jimmy); and Toyota (Camry). In 2000 alone, the company estimated its sunroof production would exceed one million systems.

In July 2000 Webasto strengthened its market leadership position by acquiring Hollandia Sunroofs Inc., another industry leader that was the North American distribution arm of Netherlands-based Vermuelen Hollandia Sunroofs. By November Webasto Sunroofs had changed its name to Webasto Roof Systems Inc., which remained a wholly owned subsidiary of Webasto AG. That month, Fred Olson was officially named the company's first president and CEO.

In 2001 Webasto Roof Systems opened a new North American technical center in Rochester Hills,

KEY DATES

1974: Webasto AG establishes Webasto Sunroofs Inc. as a joint venture with the Cosma Division of Canada's Magna International.
2000: Magna International sells its 50 percent stake in Webasto Sunroofs to Webasto AG; Webasto acquires Hollandia Sunroofs Inc.; Webasto Sunroofs changes its name to Webasto Roof Systems Inc.; Fred Olson is named the company's first president and CEO.
2008: Brett Healy succeeds Fred Olson as president and CEO.

Michigan. That year, the company partnered with Indianapolis, Indiana-based Oxford Consulting Group to streamline interactions with its suppliers. Specifically, Oxford helped Webasto move from cumbersome transactions conducted via Electronic Data Interchange, the standardized, electronic exchange of business information such as inventory data and invoices, to implement a new e-business transaction processing solution from Sterling Commerce named GENTRAN: Server.

Progress continued at Webasto Roof Systems in 2002. In a pioneering effort, the company introduced the first retractable hardtop roof that year. In March, Webasto moved forward with plans to expand its presence in Lexington, Kentucky, by breaking ground on a $28 million, 200,000-square-foot plant there. Located on an 18-acre site across from the company's existing 115,000-square-foot facility, the new plant allowed Webasto to produce complex roof systems involving large glass assemblies. These included panorama-style roofs that the company was producing in Europe for the Mercedes C-Class sports coupe. The new plant eventually led to business deals with Nissan, Subaru, and Honda.

Making panorama-style glass sunroofs even better, Webasto Roof Systems allowed owners of the high-end Maybach 62 sedan from DaimlerChrysler to have greater control over lighting conditions inside the car through the use of a new electro-transparent glass system. Among the most challenging developments in its history, the system enabled passengers to quickly change the properties of the glass from transparent to opaque. Additionally, they were able to choose from 16 different levels of soft lighting to control brightness within the rear part of the car.

POSITIVE PRODUCT AND FACILITY CHANGES

Webasto's innovative products began catching on with automotive manufacturers for use on niche vehicles. The company's UltraView panoramic glass roof offered passengers in the 2004 Cadillac SRX sport wagon almost a half square meter of sky, while a vented glass panel provided comfort for passengers in the vehicle's third row.

Another noteworthy development unfolded in November 2003 when Webasto began construction of an Aftermarket Competence Center in Fenton, Michigan. The new center's focus included sunroofs and other products such as auxiliary heaters that ran independently of the engine, allowing vehicles to stay warm when idling in cold environments.

Webasto Roof Systems continued to make progress. In April 2004, plans were announced for the construction of a 105,000-square-foot plant in Murray, Kentucky. The $14 million facility was located in the Murray-Calloway County Industrial Park and was slated to open in the summer of 2005 and employ approximately 150 people. It was around this same time that the company's new Lexington plant came online, opening its doors on May 17. Between the two new facilities, Kentucky gained about 575 new jobs.

A BROADER FOCUS: 2006–08

As Webasto moved forward into the second half of the decade, it continued to introduce innovative new products, such as the first modular roof. By this time the company was focusing on more profitable convertible roof systems, as well as the emerging North American market for automotive heaters.

Porsche was the first manufacturer to offer Webasto's preheating systems, making the devices available in its Cayenne model. However, Webasto hoped to eventually offer preheaters for the SUV and minivan segments. Among the advantages of preheaters was a reduced risk of theft while warming up cold vehicles, which was a concern to insurance companies, and reduced environmental impact from emissions.

In 2006 Webasto introduced six new types of convertible roofs. However, drastic production cuts by Chrysler, Ford, and General Motors had a negative impact on sales, leading parent Webasto AG to record the first operating loss in its 105-year history. This dip prompted the company to lay off approximately 450 people, about 280 of whom worked in Germany.

Despite the difficult industry climate in 2006, Webasto Roof Systems was in a good position on the marketing front. The company rounded out the year with news that four of the Car and Truck of the Year finalists (the Saturn Aura, Ford Edge, Chevrolet Silverado, and Mazda CX-7) were equipped with Webasto sunroof systems.

The next few years brought more developments at Webasto Roof Systems. In 2007 the company unveiled the world's largest polycarbonate panorama roof. In December of that year, Vice-President of Business Development Brett Healy was named president and CEO. Healy took the helm from Fred Olson on January 1, 2008, following the latter's retirement. However, Olson remained on the Webasto Roof Systems board.

In a December 11, 2007, *PR Newswire* release, Franz-Josef Kortuem, chairman of Webasto AG's management board, said: "Fred has successfully led WRSI through a period of unprecedented profitable growth. We are very grateful for his leadership in the last ten years. During Mr. Olson's tenure WRSI has opened five new facilities, become the market leader in roof systems in North America and our revenue has grown from $150 million to over $400 million."

Although Olson had held the top job at Webasto Roof Systems for roughly a decade, he left the company in experienced hands; Healy had been employed by Webasto Roof Systems since 1984. Under his watch, the company could be expected to reinforce its position of global leadership in the automobile roof and temperature management systems markets.

Paul R. Greenland

PRINCIPAL COMPETITORS

DuPont Automotive; Magna International Inc.; Visteon Climate Control Systems Ltd.

FURTHER READING

Feth, Gerd Gregor, and Georg Küffner, *100 Years of Webasto,* Stockdorf, Germany: Webasto AG, 2001.

Sherefkin, Robert, "Webasto Sunroofs Shuffles Leaders, Looks to Expand," *Automotive News,* September 15, 1997.

Strong, Michael, "Merger Puts Webasto, Hollandia in Sunny Spot," *Crain's Detroit Business,* September 11, 2000.

"Sunroof Giant Webasto AG Completes Purchase of North American Unit from Magna," *PR Newswire,* July 17, 2000.

"Webasto Roof Systems Inc. Appoints New President and CEO," *PR Newswire,* December 11, 2007.

"Webasto Roof Systems Inc. to Open Second Facility in Lexington, Kentucky," *PR Newswire,* March 26, 2002.

Wells Fargo & Company

420 Montgomery Street
San Francisco, California 94104-1207
U.S.A.
Telephone: (415) 396-4000
Toll Free: (866) 878-5865
Fax: (415) 397-2987
Web site: http://www.wellsfargo.com

Public Company
Incorporated: 1968 as Wells Fargo Bank, N.A.
Employees: 160,900
Total Assets: $575.44 billion (2007)
Stock Exchanges: New York
Ticker Symbol: WFC
NAICS: 522110 Commercial Banking; 522210 Credit Card Issuing; 522220 Sales Financing; 522291 Consumer Lending; 522292 Real Estate Credit; 522298 All Other Nondepository Credit Intermediation; 523110 Investment Banking and Securities Dealing; 523120 Securities Brokerage; 523920 Portfolio Management; 523930 Investment Advice; 523991 Trust, Fiduciary, and Custody Activities; 524210 Insurance Agencies and Brokerages; 551111 Offices of Bank Holding Companies

■ ■ ■

Wells Fargo & Company is a diversified financial services company, ranking as the fifth largest bank holding company in the United States in total assets as of early 2008. The company's community banking operations serve more than 11 million customers through more than 3,300 bank branches (or what the company calls "stores") in 23 states, most of which are in the western United States—Ohio being the easternmost state of operation. Wells Fargo is the nation's second largest home mortgage lender, serving all 50 states through more than 2,400 mortgage offices, including standalone "stores" and departments within the bank branches. The company is one of the top "cross-sellers" of financial services in the country, offering credit cards, debit cards, personal and home-equity loans and lines of credit, wealth management services, and insurance (the firm is the nation's largest crop insurer). Business-oriented services include commercial banking services, lending, investment banking, venture capital, and equipment leasing. Wells Fargo is one of the leaders in the realm of online banking, having become the first major financial services firm to offer Internet banking in 1995.

The Wells Fargo of the early 21st century is the product of more than 2,000 mergers over a history spanning more than a century and a half. The bank has three main predecessors, however. In 1998 Norwest Corporation acquired the original Wells Fargo & Company and adopted the acquiree's name. Norwest's history originates in 1929 when several midwest banks joined forces within a banking cooperative called Northwest Bancorporation, which was known as Banco. During the 1980s, Banco diversified into other areas of financial services, its affiliates reorganized, and Banco changed its name in 1983 to Norwest. Fifteen years later it acquired the original Wells Fargo. Wells traces its origins to a banking and express business formed in 1852 to exploit the economic opportunities created by the California gold rush. The banking operation split off

COMPANY PERSPECTIVES

Our vision: We want to satisfy all our customers' financial needs, help them succeed financially, be the premier provider of financial services in every one of our markets, and be known as one of America's great companies.

from the express business in 1905. Throughout its colorful history, the company provided innovative services to its customers and demonstrated an ability to weather economic conditions that ruined its competitors. In 1996 Wells Fargo acquired Los Angeles-based First Interstate Bancorp in a major takeover. First Interstate first emerged as a separate company in 1957 as a spinoff of the banking interests of Transamerica Corporation called Firstamerica Bancorporation. Four years later the company was renamed Western Bancorporation, and in 1981 it adopted the First Interstate name. As it traced its origins to Transamerica, First Interstate had a lineage dating to 1904, when A. P. Giannini opened the Bank of Italy in San Francisco.

NORWEST'S EARLY HISTORY

During the generally prosperous 1920s, the nation's agricultural sector did not share in the good times. Many smaller banks that had overextended credit to farmers ran into serious trouble. In the Upper Midwest alone, 1,500 banks became insolvent from 1920 to 1929. It was with this backdrop that in early 1929, just months before the stock market crash, two banking associations were formed in the Twin Cities of Minnesota: Northwest Bancorporation and First Bank Stock (later known as First Bank System Inc. and then U.S. Bancorp). The Northwest cooperative, known more simply as Banco, initially included Northwestern National Bank of Minneapolis and several other midwestern banks. Banco acquired stock in the affiliated banks and served as a mutual protection association for the beleaguered banks. Another 90 banks joined Banco in its first year of operation and by 1932 there were 139 affiliates.

During the Great Depression, numerous additional banks failed, another 700 in the Upper Midwest by 1932. None of the Banco members went under, and no depositor lost any savings, because the group was able to move liquidity around the system and in some cases, inject new capital into troubled banks. The number of members did decline, however, as some units in the group merged while others were sold. Membership fell to 83 by 1940 then to 70 by 1952.

One of Banco's strategic advantages in the long run was its ability to operate in multiple states. The McFadden Act of 1927 had prohibited banks from operating branches across state lines. Banco was one of three major banks (the others being First Bank System and First Interstate Bancorp) that was allowed to conduct interstate banking under a grandfather clause in the 1927 act. This advantage was tempered somewhat by the emergence of bank holding companies in the late 1960s, but under the holding company arrangement, a subsidiary bank in one state was a separate entity from a subsidiary bank in another state. Prior to the 1970s, the affiliated members of Banco were largely autonomous. During that decade, however, Banco began adopting a more unified structure in terms of systemwide planning, marketing, data processing, funds management, and loan syndication. By the end of the decade, Banco consisted of 85 affiliates in seven states: Minnesota, Wisconsin, Iowa, Nebraska, South Dakota, North Dakota, and Montana. Total assets had reached $11 billion, ranking Banco as the 20th largest bank in the United States. Banco was also active on the international banking scene through its lead bank, Northwestern National, which controlled Canadian American Bank, a merchant bank with offices in Winnipeg, London, Nassau, and Luxembourg.

DECLINING FORTUNES, THEN TURNAROUND

Banco was beset by a series of major setbacks in the early 1980s. The troubles actually began in late 1979 when Richard H. Vaughan, the president and CEO, died by electrocution when he touched an electrical wire that had fallen during a storm. This set off a management crisis. Chester Lind stepped in as a caretaker leader until a more permanent successor could be found. In October 1981 John W. Morrison was named chairman and CEO. The new leader began centralizing the still loosely knit confederation. In 1982 the 80-odd affiliates began to be grouped into eight regions reporting to a corporate vice-chairman. Plans were also laid to unify all the affiliates and Banco itself under a new name. The change occurred in 1983, when Northwest Bancorporation became Norwest Corporation. Tellingly, the new name did not include "bank" or some variant thereof because Morrison aimed to create a diversified financial services company. To that end he had engineered the acquisition of Dial Corporation in September 1982 for $252 million. Based in Des Moines, Iowa, Dial had more than 460 offices in 38 states offering consumer loans for everything from cars to sailboats. It was

KEY DATES

1852: Henry Wells and William G. Fargo form Wells, Fargo & Company to provide express and banking services to California.
1860: Wells Fargo gains control of Overland Mail Company, leading to operation of the western portion of the Pony Express.
1866: "Grand consolidation" unites Wells Fargo, Holladay, and Overland Mail stage lines under the Wells Fargo name.
1904: A. P. Giannini creates the Bank of Italy in San Francisco.
1905: Wells Fargo separates its banking and express operations; Wells Fargo's bank merges with the Nevada National Bank to form the Wells Fargo Nevada National Bank.
1923: Wells Fargo Nevada merges with the Union Trust Company to form the Wells Fargo Bank & Union Trust Company.
1928: Giannini forms Transamerica Corporation as a holding company for his banking and other interests.
1929: Northwest Bancorporation, or Banco, is formed as a banking association.
1954: Wells shortens its name to Wells Fargo Bank.
1957: Transamerica spins off its banking operations, including 23 banks in 11 western states, as Firstamerica Corporation.
1960: Wells Fargo merges with American Trust Company to form the Wells Fargo Bank American Trust Company.
1961: Firstamerica changes its name to Western Bancorporation.
1962: Wells again shortens its name to Wells Fargo Bank.
1968: Wells converts to a federal banking charter, becoming Wells Fargo Bank, N.A.
1969: Wells Fargo & Company holding company is formed, with Wells Fargo Bank as its main subsidiary.
1981: Western Bancorporation changes its name to First Interstate Bancorp.
1982: Banco acquires consumer finance firm Dial Corporation, which is renamed Norwest Financial Service the following year.
1983: Banco is renamed Norwest Corporation.
1986: Wells Fargo acquires Crocker National Corporation.
1988: Wells Fargo acquires Barclays Bank of California.
1995: Wells Fargo becomes the first major financial services firm to offer Internet banking.
1996: Wells Fargo acquires First Interstate for $11.3 billion.
1998: Norwest acquires Wells Fargo for $31.7 billion and adopts the Wells Fargo name.
2000: Wells Fargo acquires First Security Corporation.

considered one of the top consumer finance firms in the country and had a $1 billion consumer loan operation. Dial was renamed Norwest Financial Services Inc. in 1983.

While these restructuring initiatives were being carried out, the bank suffered another blow during the 1982 Thanksgiving weekend when the downtown Minneapolis headquarters burned to the ground. It would be six years before Norwest would be able to move into its new quarters at the Norwest Center, during which time the corporate staff was scattered around 26 different sites in the city, leading to numerous logistical difficulties. Meanwhile, with the farm economy going into a tailspin starting in 1981, Norwest began feeling the effects because it had a heavy farm loan portfolio: $1.2 billion, or 7 percent of its overall loan portfolio. Norwest had another $1.2 billion in loans in foreign markets, which caused additional problems in the early 1980s as Norwest, like most U.S. banks, had made many bad loans overseas. As a result, Norwest saw its nonperforming loans increase 500 percent from 1983 to 1984, to more than $500 million. Further trouble came from the bank's mortgage unit, Norwest Mortgage Inc., which had been quickly built into the second largest holder of mortgages in the United States. In the summer of 1984 Norwest Mortgage lost nearly $100 million from an unsuccessful effort to hedge its mounting interest-rate risk on adjustable-rate mortgages. The loan losses and the mortgage debacle led to a drop in net income from $125.2 million in 1983 to $69.5 million in 1984.

In August 1984 the head of Norwest Mortgage was fired because of the hedging losses. By early 1995 substantial portions of Norwest Mortgage were divested, including operations involved in servicing mortgages and buying mortgages from other lenders for resale. The unit focused strictly on originating mortgages. In the wake of Norwest's poor performance in 1984, Morrison resigned and was replaced by Lloyd P. Johnson, former vice-chairman of Security Pacific Corporation. Johnson soon brought onboard Richard M. Kovacevich, who was hired away from Citicorp to become vice-chairman and CEO of Norwest's banking group in early 1996 (he was named to the additional posts of president and COO of Norwest Corp. in January 1989). The new managers began slashing away at Norwest's bloated bureaucracy. They drastically curtailed the bank's agricultural and international loan portfolios, the former being reduced to $400 million by early 1989, the latter to $10 million. By December 1988, the nonperforming loan total stood at just $150 million. To help prevent future calamities, Norwest instituted tighter lending criteria.

On the banking side, Kovacevich (pronounced Koe-VAH-suh-vitch) continued the process of standardizing the operating methods of the various Norwest banks, increased marketing efforts, and expanded the services offered. He also began seeking acquisitions, particularly aiming to bolster Norwest's presence in key cities; in 1986, for example, Norwest acquired Toy National Bank of Sioux City, Iowa, which had assets of $145 million. At the same time came the pruning of some rural operations, including eight banks in southern Minnesota and seven branches in South Dakota. Later in the decade, opportunities to expand outside the group's traditional seven-state banking region began to arise as the barriers to interstate banking began to be dismantled. In 1988 Norwest entered rapidly growing Arizona for the first time through the purchase of a small bank near Phoenix. Norwest ended the 1980s fully recovered from its early-decade travails and ranking as one of the nation's most profitable regional banking companies and the 30th largest bank overall, with assets in excess of $25 billion. Net income stood at $237 million for 1989.

NORWEST'S LATE-CENTURY ACQUISITION SPREE

Acquisitions continued in the early 1990s. By early 1991 Norwest had 291 bank branches in 11 states, having moved into Indiana, Illinois, and Wyoming. In April 1990 Norwest paid $173 million for Sheboygan-based First Interstate of Wisconsin, a $2 billion concern. Also acquired was a troubled savings and loan association in Norwest's home state, First Minnesota Savings Bank. The largest purchase to that time came in 1992 when Norwest paid about $420 million in stock for United Banks of Colorado Inc., a bank based in Denver with total assets of $6.3 billion. Norwest Financial grew through acquisition as well, with the 1992 purchase of Trans Canada Credit, the second largest consumer finance firm in Canada. By the end of 1992 Norwest had total assets of $44.56 billion, more than double the figure of 1988. At the beginning of 1993, Johnson handed over his CEO position to Kovacevich.

Expansion of the banking operation into New Mexico and Texas came in 1993 through the acquisition of First United Bank Group Inc. of Albuquerque for about $490 million. First United had assets of $3.8 billion. Between January 1994 and June 1995, Norwest made an additional 25 acquisitions, including several in Texas, making it the most active acquirer among bank holding companies. In 1995 Norwest Mortgage became the nation's leading originator of home mortgages following the acquisition of Directors Mortgage Loan Corp., a Riverside, California-based lender with a residential mortgage portfolio of $13.1 billion. The following year Norwest Mortgage became the biggest home-mortgage servicer as well through the $600 million purchase of the bulk of the mortgage unit of the Prudential Insurance Co. of America. Meanwhile, in May 1996 Norwest Financial completed the purchase of $1-billion-asset ITT Island Finance, a consumer finance company based in San Juan, Puerto Rico. About one-quarter of Norwest Corp.'s earnings were generated by Norwest Financial in the mid-1990s, with another 12 percent coming from Norwest Mortgage. The traditional community banking operations, which extended to 16 states by 1995, accounted for only about 37 percent of the total. By year-end 1995, Norwest had total assets of $72.13 billion, making it the 13th largest bank holding company in the nation. Net income, which was nearing the $1 billion mark, had grown at a compounded annual rate of 25 percent over the previous eight years.

One of the keys to Norwest's success in the retail banking sector following the arrival of Kovacevich was the emphasis on relationship banking. His focus was on smaller customers, checking account depositors and small businesses, and he aimed to build relationships with them that would lead to cross-selling of other financial services: an auto loan, a mortgage, insurance, a mutual fund, and so on. To do so required the maintenance of an extensive network of bank branches staffed by well-trained tellers and bankers. This ran counter to the mid-1990s trend in the industry away from expensive branch banking and toward impersonal automated teller machines (ATMs) and Internet banking, the latter of course making cross-selling difficult. It was also in this cross-selling that the main units of Norwest—the retail bank, the finance company, and the mortgage company—fit and worked together. Another key to Norwest's success was its focus on these three key areas. Although it did have other operations, such as a successful venture capital unit, the bank was not moving into such areas as investment banking, unlike numerous other banks, and it was not attempting to compete with large New York securities firms.

By the end of 1997, Norwest had become the 11th largest bank in the United States with total assets of $88.54 billion. With bank branches in 16 states, Norwest had the largest contiguous bank franchise in the nation. Its strongest markets were in Minnesota, Texas, Colorado, and Iowa. Having entered the Texas market only a few years earlier, Norwest had built up a $10 billion presence there by buying 33 bank and trust outfits. Norwest Mortgage was national in scope, while Norwest Financial covered all 50 states, with additional operations in Canada, the Caribbean, and Central America. Net income had reached $1.35 billion by 1997. Norwest had grown into this position of strength without completing any of the blockbuster mergers that shook up the banking industry in the 1990s, but in June 1998 the bank joined in the consolidation frenzy when it agreed to acquire Wells Fargo & Company.

WELLS FARGO'S 1852 FOUNDING AS BANKING AND EXPRESS BUSINESS

Soon after gold was discovered in early 1848 at Sutter's Mill near Coloma, California, financiers and entrepreneurs from all over North America and the world flocked to California, drawn by the promise of huge profits. Vermont native Henry Wells and New Yorker William G. Fargo watched the California boom economy with keen interest. Before either Wells or Fargo could pursue opportunities offered in the West, however, they had business to attend to in the East. Wells, founder of Wells and Company, and Fargo, a partner in Livingston, Fargo and Company, were major figures in the young and fiercely competitive express industry. In 1849 a new rival, John Butterfield, founder of Butterfield, Wasson & Company, entered the express business. Butterfield, Wells, and Fargo soon realized that their competition was destructive and wasteful, and in 1850 they decided to join forces to form the American Express Company.

Soon after the new company was formed, Wells, the first president of American Express, and Fargo, its vice-president, proposed expanding their business to California. Fearing that American Express's most powerful rival, Adams and Company (later renamed Adams Express Company), would acquire a monopoly in the West, the majority of the American Express Company's directors balked. Undaunted, Wells and Fargo decided to start their own business while continuing to fulfill their responsibilities as officers and directors of American Express.

On March 18, 1852, they organized Wells, Fargo & Company, a joint-stock association with an initial capitalization of $300,000, to provide express and banking services to California. Financier Edwin B. Morgan was appointed Wells Fargo's first president. The company opened its first office, in San Francisco, in July 1852. The immediate challenge facing Morgan and Danforth N. Barney, who became president in 1853, was to establish the company in two highly competitive fields under conditions of rapid growth and unpredictable change. At the time, California regulated neither the banking nor the express industry, so both fields were wide open. Anyone with a wagon and team of horses could open an express company, and all it took to open a bank was a safe and a room to keep it in. Because of its late entry into the California market, Wells Fargo faced well-established competition in both fields.

From the beginning, the fledgling company offered diverse and mutually supportive services: general forwarding and commissions; buying and selling of gold dust, bullion, and specie (or coin); and freight service between New York and California. Under Morgan's and Barney's direction, express and banking offices were quickly established in key communities bordering the goldfields and a network of freight and messenger routes was soon in place throughout California. Barney's policy of subcontracting express services to established companies, rather than duplicating existing services, was a key factor in Wells Fargo's early success.

In 1855, Wells Fargo faced its first crisis when the California banking system collapsed as a result of overspeculation. A run on Page, Bacon & Company, a San Francisco bank, began when the collapse of its St. Louis, Missouri, parent was made public. The run soon spread to other major financial institutions, all of which, including Wells Fargo, were forced to close their doors. The following Tuesday Wells Fargo reopened in sound condition, despite a loss of one-third of its net worth. Wells Fargo was one of the few financial and express companies to survive the panic, partly because it kept sufficient assets on hand to meet customers' demands rather than transferring all its assets to New York.

STAGECOACHING, OVERLAND EXPRESS, AND THE PONY EXPRESS

Surviving the Panic of 1855 gave Wells Fargo two advantages. First, it faced virtually no competition in the banking and express business in California after the crisis; second, Wells Fargo attained a reputation for dependability and soundness. From 1855 through 1866, Wells Fargo expanded rapidly, becoming the West's all-purpose business, communications, and transportation agent. Under Barney's direction, the company developed its own stagecoach business, helped start and then took over the Overland Mail Company, and participated in the Pony Express. This period culminated with the "grand consolidation" of 1866 when Wells Fargo consolidated under its own name the ownership and operation of the entire overland mail route from the Missouri River to the Pacific Ocean and many stagecoach lines in the western states.

In its early days, Wells Fargo participated in the staging business to support its banking and express businesses. The character of Wells Fargo's participation changed when it helped start the Overland Mail Company. Overland Mail was organized in 1857 by men with substantial interests in four of the leading express companies: American Express, United States Express, Adams Express, and Wells Fargo. John Butterfield, the third founder of American Express, was made Overland Mail's president. In 1858 Overland Mail was awarded a government contract to carry the U.S. mail over the southern overland route from St. Louis to California. From the beginning, Wells Fargo was Overland Mail's banker and primary lender.

In 1859 there was a crisis when Congress failed to pass the annual post office appropriation bill and left the post office with no way to pay for the Overland Mail Company's services. As Overland Mail's indebtedness to Wells Fargo climbed, Wells Fargo became increasingly disenchanted with Butterfield's management strategy. In March 1860 Wells Fargo threatened to foreclose. As a compromise, Butterfield resigned as president of Overland Mail and control of the company passed to Wells Fargo. Wells Fargo, however, did not acquire ownership of the company until the consolidation of 1866.

Wells Fargo's involvement in Overland Mail led to its participation in the Pony Express in the last six of the express's 18 months of existence. Russell, Majors & Waddell launched the privately owned and operated Pony Express. By the end of 1860, the Pony Express was in deep financial trouble; its fees did not cover its costs and, without government subsidies and lucrative mail contracts, it could not make up the difference. After Overland Mail, by then controlled by Wells Fargo, was awarded a $1 million government contract in early 1861 to provide daily mail service over a central route (the Civil War had forced the discontinuation of the southern line), Wells Fargo took over the western portion of the Pony Express route from Salt Lake City to San Francisco. Russell, Majors & Waddell continued to operate the eastern leg from Salt Lake City to St. Joseph, Missouri, under subcontract.

The Pony Express ended when transcontinental telegraph lines were completed in late 1861. Overland mail and express services were continued, however, by the coordinated efforts of several companies. From 1862 to 1865 Wells Fargo operated a private express line between San Francisco and Virginia City, Nevada; Overland Mail stagecoaches covered the route from Carson City, Nevada, to Salt Lake City; and Ben Holladay, who had acquired Russell, Majors & Waddell, ran a stagecoach line from Salt Lake City to Missouri.

THE 1866 "GRAND CONSOLIDATION"

By 1866, Holladay had built a staging empire with lines in eight western states and was challenging Wells Fargo's supremacy in the West. A showdown between the two transportation giants in late 1866 resulted in Wells Fargo's purchase of Holladay's operations. The "grand consolidation" spawned a new enterprise that operated under the Wells Fargo name and combined the Wells Fargo, Holladay, and Overland Mail lines and became the undisputed stagecoach leader. Barney resigned as president of Wells Fargo to devote more time to his own business, the United States Express Company; Louis McLane Jr., Wells Fargo's general manager in California, replaced him.

The Wells Fargo stagecoach empire was short-lived. McLane had reached an agreement with a railroad group that failed. Although the Central Pacific Railroad, already operating over the Sierra Mountains to Reno, Nevada, carried Wells Fargo's express, the company did not have an exclusive contract. Moreover, the Union Pacific Railroad was encroaching on the territory served by Wells Fargo stagelines. Ashbel H. Barney, Danforth Barney's brother and cofounder of United States Express Company, replaced McLane as president in 1868. The transcontinental railroad was completed in the following year, causing the stage business to dwindle and Wells Fargo's stock to fall.

Central Pacific promoters, led by Lloyd Tevis, organized the Pacific Express Company to compete with Wells Fargo. The Tevis group also started buying Wells Fargo stock at its sharply reduced price. In October

1869 William Fargo, his brother Charles, and Ashbel Barney traveled to Omaha, Nebraska, to confer with Tevis and his associates. There Wells Fargo agreed to buy the Pacific Express Company at a much-inflated price and received exclusive express rights for ten years on the Central Pacific Railroad and a much needed infusion of capital. All of this, however, came at a price: control of Wells Fargo shifted to Tevis.

Ashbel Barney resigned in 1870 and was replaced as president by William Fargo. In 1872 William Fargo also resigned to devote full-time to his duties as president of American Express. Lloyd Tevis replaced Fargo as president of Wells Fargo, and the company expanded rapidly under his management. The number of banking and express offices grew from 436 in 1871 to 3,500 by 1900. During this period, Wells Fargo also established the first transcontinental express line, using more than a dozen railroads. The company first gained access to the lucrative East Coast markets beginning in 1888; successfully promoted the use of refrigerated freight cars in California; had opened branch banks in Virginia City, Carson City, and Salt Lake City by 1876; and expanded its express services to Japan, Australia, Hong Kong, South America, Mexico, and Europe. In 1885 Wells Fargo also began selling money orders.

EARLY 20TH CENTURY: INDEPENDENTLY RUN WELLS FARGO BANK

In 1905 Wells Fargo separated its banking and express operations. Edward H. Harriman, a prominent financier and dominant figure in the Southern Pacific and Union Pacific railroads, had gained control of Wells Fargo. Harriman reached an agreement with Isaias W. Hellman, a Los Angeles banker, to merge Wells Fargo's bank with the Nevada National Bank, founded in 1875 by the Nevada silver moguls James G. Fair, James Flood, John Mackay, and William O'Brien, to form the Wells Fargo Nevada National Bank.

Wells Fargo & Company Express had moved to New York City in 1904. In 1918 the government forced Wells Fargo Express to consolidate its domestic operations with those of the other major express companies. This wartime measure resulted in the formation of American Railway Express (later Railway Express Agency). Wells Fargo continued some overseas express operations until the 1960s.

The two years following the merger tested the newly reorganized bank's, and Hellman's, capacities. In April 1906 the San Francisco earthquake and fire destroyed most of the city's business district, including the Wells Fargo Nevada National Bank building. The bank's vaults and credit were left intact, however, and the bank committed its resources to restoring San Francisco. Money flowed into San Francisco from around the country to support rapid reconstruction of the city. As a result, the bank's deposits increased dramatically, from $16 million to $35 million in 18 months.

The Panic of 1907, begun in New York in October, followed on the heels of this frenetic reconstruction period. The stock market had crashed in March. Several New York banks, deeply involved in efforts to manipulate the market after the crash, experienced a run when speculators were unable to pay for stock they had purchased. The run quickly spread to other New York banks, which were forced to suspend payment, and then to Chicago and the rest of the country. Wells Fargo lost $1 million in deposits weekly for six weeks in a row. The years following the panic were committed to a slow and painstaking recovery.

In 1920 Hellman was very briefly succeeded as president by his son, I. W. Hellman Jr., who was followed by Frederick L. Lipman. Lipman's management strategy included both expansion and the conservative banking practices of his predecessors. In late 1923, Wells Fargo Nevada National Bank merged with the Union Trust Company, founded in 1893 by I. W. Hellman, to form the Wells Fargo Bank & Union Trust Company. The bank prospered during the 1920s, and Lipman's careful reinvestment of the bank's earnings placed the bank in a good position to survive the Great Depression. Following the collapse of the banking system in 1933, the company was able to extend immediate and substantial help to its troubled correspondents. The war years were prosperous and uneventful for Wells Fargo.

POST–WORLD WAR II ERA: EXPANDING OVERSEAS AND IN CALIFORNIA

In the 1950s, Wells Fargo President I. W. Hellman III, grandson of Isaias Hellman, began a modest expansion program, acquiring two San Francisco Bay–area banks and opening a small branch network around San Francisco. In 1954 the name of the bank was shortened to Wells Fargo Bank, to capitalize on frontier imagery and in preparation for further expansion.

In 1960 Hellman engineered the merger of Wells Fargo Bank with American Trust Company, a large northern California retail-banking system and the second oldest financial institution in California, to form the Wells Fargo Bank American Trust Company, renamed Wells Fargo Bank again in 1962. This merger of California's two oldest banks created the 11th largest banking institution in the United States. Following the merger, Wells Fargo's involvement in international banking greatly accelerated. The company opened a Tokyo representative office and, eventually, additional branch offices in Seoul, Hong Kong, and Nassau, as well as representative offices in Mexico City, São Paulo, Caracas, Buenos Aires, and Singapore.

In November 1966 Wells Fargo's board of directors elected Richard P. Cooley president and CEO. At 42, Cooley was one of the youngest men to head a major bank. Stephen Chase, who planned to retire in January 1968, became chairman. Cooley's rise to the top had been a quick one. From a branch manager in 1960 he rose to become a senior vice-president in 1964, an executive vice-president in 1965, and in April 1966 a director of the company. A year later Cooley enticed Ernest C. Arbuckle, the former dean of Stanford's business school, to join Wells Fargo's board as chairman.

In 1967 Wells Fargo, with three other California banks, introduced a Master Charge card (subsequently called MasterCard) to its customers as part of its plan to challenge Bank of America in the consumer lending business. Initially 30,000 merchants participated in the plan. Credit cards would later prove to be a particularly profitable operation.

Cooley's early strategic initiatives were in the direction of making Wells Fargo's branch network statewide. The Federal Reserve had blocked the bank's earlier attempts to acquire an established bank in southern California. As a result, Wells Fargo had to build its own branch system. This expansion was costly and depressed the bank's earnings in the later 1960s. In 1968 Wells Fargo changed from a state to a federal banking charter, in part so that it could set up subsidiaries for businesses such as equipment leasing and credit cards rather than having to create special divisions within the bank. The charter conversion was completed August 15, 1968, with the bank renamed Wells Fargo Bank, N.A. The bank successfully completed a number of acquisitions during 1968 as well. The Bank of Pasadena, First National Bank of Azusa, Azusa Valley Savings Bank, and Sonoma Mortgage Corporation were all integrated into Wells Fargo's operations.

In 1969 Wells Fargo formed a holding company, Wells Fargo & Company, and purchased the rights to its own name from the American Express Corporation. Although the bank always had the right to use the name for banking, American Express had retained the right to use it for other financial services. Wells Fargo could use its name in any area of financial services it chose (except the armored car trade; those rights had been sold to another company two years earlier).

RAPID GROWTH IN THE SEVENTIES

Between 1970 and 1975 Wells Fargo's domestic profits rose faster than those of any other U.S. bank. Wells Fargo's loans to businesses increased dramatically after 1971. To meet the demand for credit, the bank frequently borrowed short-term from the Federal Reserve to lend at higher rates of interest to businesses and individuals.

In 1973 a tighter monetary policy made this arrangement less profitable, but Wells Fargo saw an opportunity in the new interest limits on passbook savings. When the allowable rate increased to 5 percent, Wells Fargo was the first to begin paying the higher rate. The bank attracted many new customers as a result, and within two years its market share of the retail savings trade increased more than two points, a substantial increase in California's competitive banking climate. With its increased deposits, Wells Fargo was able to reduce its borrowings from the Federal Reserve, and the one-half percent premium it paid for deposits was more than made up for by the savings in interest payments. In 1975 the rest of the California banks instituted a 5 percent passbook savings rate, but they failed to recapture their market share.

In 1973 the bank made a number of key policy changes. Wells Fargo decided to go after the medium-sized corporate and consumer loan businesses, where interest rates were higher. Slowly Wells Fargo eliminated its excess debt, and by 1974 its balance sheet showed a much healthier bank. Under Carl Reichardt, who later became president of the bank, Wells Fargo's real estate lending bolstered the bottom line. The bank focused on California's flourishing home and apartment mortgage business and left risky commercial developments to other banks.

While Wells Fargo's domestic operations were making it the envy of competitors in the early 1970s, its international operations were less secure. The bank's 25 percent holding in Allgemeine Deutsche Credit-Anstalt, a West German bank, cost Wells Fargo $4 million because of bad real estate loans. Another joint banking venture, the Western American Bank, which was formed in London in 1968 with several other American banks, was hard hit by the recession of 1974 and failed. Unfavorable exchange rates hit Wells Fargo for another $2 million in 1975. In response, the bank slowed its overseas expansion program and concentrated on developing overseas branches of its own rather than tying itself to the fortunes of other banks.

Wells Fargo's investment services became a leader during the late 1970s. According to *Institutional Investor,* Wells Fargo garnered more new accounts from the 350 largest pension funds between 1975 and 1980 than any other money manager. The bank's aggressive marketing of its services included seminars explaining modern portfolio theory. Wells Fargo's early success, particularly with indexing (weighting investments to match the weightings of the Standard and Poor's 500) brought many new clients aboard.

By the end of the 1970s Wells Fargo's overall growth had slowed somewhat. Earnings were only up 12 percent in 1979 compared with an average of 19 percent between 1973 and 1978. In 1980 Richard Cooley, chairman of the holding company, told *Fortune,* "It's time to slow down. The last five years have created too great a strain on our capital, liquidity, and people."

CONCENTRATING ON CALIFORNIA IN THE EIGHTIES

In 1981 the banking community was shocked by the news of a $21.3 million embezzlement scheme by a Wells Fargo employee, one of the largest embezzlements ever. L. Ben Lewis, an operations officer at Wells Fargo's Beverly Drive branch, pleaded guilty to the charges. Lewis had routinely written phony debit and credit receipts to pad the accounts of his cronies and received a $300,000 cut in return.

The early 1980s saw a sharp decline in Wells Fargo's performance. Richard Cooley announced the bank's plan to scale down its operations overseas and concentrate on the California market. In January 1983, Carl Reichardt became chairman and CEO of the holding company and of Wells Fargo Bank. Cooley, who had led the bank since the late 1960s, left to revive a troubled rival. Reichardt relentlessly attacked costs, eliminating 100 branches and cutting 3,000 jobs. He also closed down the bank's European offices at a time when most banks were expanding their overseas networks.

Rather than taking advantage of banking deregulation, which was enticing other banks into all sorts of new financial ventures, Reichardt and Wells Fargo President Paul Hazen kept things simple and focused on California. Reichardt and Hazen beefed up Wells Fargo's retail network through improved services such as an extensive ATM network, and through active marketing of those services.

In 1986 Wells Fargo purchased rival Crocker National Corporation from Britain's Midland Bank for about $1.1 billion. The acquisition was touted as a brilliant maneuver by Wells Fargo. Not only did Wells Fargo double its branch network in southern California and increase its consumer loan portfolio by 85 percent, but the bank did it at an unheard of price, paying about 127 percent of book value at a time when American banks were generally going for 190 percent. In addition, Midland kept about $3.5 billion in loans of dubious value.

Crocker doubled the strength of Wells Fargo's primary market, making Wells Fargo the tenth largest bank in the United States. Furthermore, the integration of Crocker's operations into Wells Fargo's went considerably smoother than expected. In the 18 months after the acquisition, 5,700 jobs were trimmed from the banks' combined staff and costs were cut considerably.

Before and after the acquisition, Reichardt and Hazen aggressively cut costs and eliminated unprofitable portions of Wells Fargo's business. During the three years before the acquisition, Wells Fargo sold its realty-services subsidiary, its residential-mortgage service operation, and its corporate trust and agency businesses. Over 70 domestic bank branches and 15 foreign branches were also closed during this period. In 1987 Wells Fargo set aside large reserves to cover potential losses on its Latin American loans, most notably to Brazil and Mexico. This caused its net income to drop sharply, but by mid-1989 the bank had sold or written off all of its medium- and long-term Third World debt.

Concentrating on California was a very successful strategy for Wells Fargo. After its acquisition of Barclays Bank of California in May 1988, few targets remained. One region Wells Fargo considered expanding into in the late 1980s was Texas, where it made an unsuccessful bid for Dallas's FirstRepublic Corporation in 1988. In early 1989 Wells Fargo expanded into full-service brokerage and launched a joint venture with the Japanese company Nikko Securities called Wells Fargo Nikko Investment Advisors. Also in 1989, the company divested itself of its last international offices, further tightening its focus on domestic commercial and consumer banking activities.

Wells Fargo & Company's major subsidiary, Wells Fargo Bank, was still loaded with debt, including relatively risky real estate loans, in the late 1980s. The bank, however, had greatly improved its loan-loss ratio since the early 1980s. Furthermore, Wells continued to improve its health and to thrive during the early 1990s under the direction of Reichardt and Hazen. Much of that growth was attributable to gains in the California market. Indeed, despite an ailing regional economy during the early 1990s, Wells Fargo posted healthy gains in that core market. Wells slashed its labor force, by more than 500 workers in 1993 alone, and boosted cash flow with technical innovations. The bank began selling stamps through its ATMs, for example, and in 1995 was partnering with CyberCash, a software start-up company, to begin offering its services over the Internet.

After dipping in 1991, Wells's net income surged to $283 million in 1992 before climbing briskly to $841 million in 1994. At the end of 1994, after 12 years of service during which Wells Fargo & Co. investors enjoyed a 1,781 percent return, Reichardt stepped aside as head of the company. He was succeeded by Hazen. Wells Fargo Bank entered 1995 as the second largest bank in California and the seventh largest in the United States, with $51 billion in assets. Under Hazen, the bank continued to improve its loan portfolio, boost service offerings, and cut operating costs. During 1995 Wells Fargo Nikko Investment Advisors was sold to Barclays PLC for $440 million.

1996 TAKEOVER OF FIRST INTERSTATE

Late in 1995 Wells Fargo began pursuing a hostile takeover of First Interstate Bancorp, a Los Angeles-based bank holding company with $58 billion in assets and 1,133 offices in California and 12 other western states. Wells Fargo had long been interested in acquiring First Interstate, whose origins began with the founding in 1904 of the Bank of Italy in San Francisco by A. P. Giannini. After expanding his empire to the financial center of New York but being blocked from consolidating his various financial ventures, Giannini in 1928 formed a holding company, the Transamerica Corporation, which began business with $1.1 billion in assets and both banking and nonbanking activities. From the 1930s through the mid-1950s, Transamerica made a number of acquisitions of banks and other financial corporations throughout the western United States, creating the framework for the later First Interstate system.

The Bank Holding Company Act of 1956 placed new restrictions on companies such as Transamerica. Therefore, in 1957, Transamerica's banking operations, which included 23 banks in 11 western states, were spun off as Firstamerica Corporation. Transamerica pursued its insurance and other operations. Firstamerica changed its name to Western Bancorporation in 1961. Western expanded steadily in the 1960s, both domestically and overseas, ending the decade with assets of more than $10 billion. The bank's financial services network grew through the 1974 founding of the Western Bancorporation Mortgage Company and the 1979 formation of Western Bancorp Venture Capital Company.

In June 1981 the company changed its name to First Interstate Bancorp. The First Interstate name became a systemwide brand for most of the company's banks, thus promoting greater public recognition of the company and internal consistency. During the 1980s, in addition to acquiring more banks, First Interstate jumped into new areas of financial services as the deregulation of the banking industry progressed. In 1983 the First Interstate Discount Brokerage was set up to provide bank customers with securities and commodities support. In 1984 the bank branched into merchant banking with the purchase of Continental Illinois Ltd. and equipment leasing with the acquisition of the Commercial Alliance Corporation of New York; and broadened its mortgage banking activities by acquiring the Republic Realty Mortgage Corporation. In 1986 and 1987, First Interstate made a bold $3.2 billion attempt to hostilely take over the ailing Bank of America, but the bid was successfully defeated.

First Interstate ran into its own troubles in the late 1980s and early 1990s stemming from bad real estate loans and the severe recession in California. The bank posted losses in the hundreds of millions for 1987, 1989, and 1991. Consequently, First Interstate concentrated on rebuilding and rejuvenating its existing operations rather than acquiring new ones. A number of noncore unprofitable subsidiaries were jettisoned, including the equipment leasing unit, a government securities operation, and most of the wholesale banking unit. Rumors of a takeover of First Interstate were rife in the early 1990s before the bank recovered fully by mid-decade under the leadership of Joe Pinola and William Siart.

Despite First Interstate's healthier condition, and with the banking industry consolidation in full swing, Wells Fargo made a hostile bid for First Interstate in October 1995 initially valued at $10.8 billion. Other banks came forward as potential "white knights," including Norwest, Bank One Corporation, and First Bank System. The latter made a serious bid for First Interstate, with the two banks reaching a formal merger agreement in November valued initially at $10.3 billion. However, First Bank ran into regulatory difficulties with the way it had structured its offer and was forced to bow out of the takeover battle in mid-January 1996. Talks between Wells Fargo and First Interstate then led within days to a merger agreement. When completed in April 1996, following an antitrust review that stipulated the selling of 61 bank branches in California, the acquisition was valued at $11.3 billion. The newly enlarged Wells Fargo had assets of about $116 billion, loans of $72 billion, and deposits of $89 billion. It ranked as the ninth largest bank in the United States.

Wells Fargo aimed to generate $800 million in annual operational savings out of the combined bank within 18 months, and immediately upon completion of the takeover announced a workforce reduction of 16 percent, or 7,200 positions, by the end of 1996. The merger, however, quickly turned disastrous as efforts to consolidate operations, which were placed on an ambitious timetable, led to major problems. Computer system glitches led to lost customer deposits and bounced checks. Branch closures led to long lines at the remaining branches. There was also a culture clash with the two banks and their customers. Wells Fargo had been at the forefront of high-tech banking, emphasizing ATMs and online banking, as well as the small-staffed supermarket "branches," at the expense of traditional branch banking. By contrast, First Interstate had emphasized personalized relationship banking, and its customers were used to dealing with tellers and bankers not machines. This led to a mass exodus of First Interstate management talent and to the alienation of numerous customers, many of whom took their banking business elsewhere.

1998: EMERGENCE OF THE NEW WELLS FARGO FROM COMBINATION OF WELLS FARGO AND NORWEST

The financial performance of Wells Fargo, as well as its stock price, suffered from this botched merger, leaving the bank vulnerable to being taken over itself as banking consolidation continued unabated. This time, Wells Fargo entered into a friendly merger agreement with Norwest, which was announced in June 1998. The deal was completed in November of that year and was valued at $31.7 billion, with Norwest acquiring Wells Fargo and then changing its own name to Wells Fargo & Company because of the latter's greater public recognition and the former's regional connotations. Norwest also agreed to relocate the headquarters of the new Wells Fargo to San Francisco based on the bank's $54 billion in deposits in California versus $13 billion in Minnesota. The head of Wells Fargo, Paul Hazen, was named chairman of the new company, while the head of Norwest, Richard Kovacevich, became president and CEO.

The new Wells Fargo started off as the nation's seventh largest bank with $196 billion in assets, $130 billion in deposits, and 15 million retail banking, finance, and mortgage customers. The banking operation included more than 2,850 branches in 21 states from Ohio to California. Norwest Mortgage (later Wells Fargo Home Mortgage) had 824 offices in 50 states, while Norwest Financial (later Wells Fargo Financial) had nearly 1,350 offices in 47 states, ten provinces of Canada, the Caribbean, Latin America, and elsewhere.

The integration of Norwest and Wells Fargo proceeded much more smoothly than the combination of Wells Fargo and First Interstate. A key reason was that the process was allowed to progress at a much slower and more manageable pace than that of the earlier merger. The plan allowed for two to three years to complete the integration, while the cost-cutting goal was a more modest $650 million in annual savings within three years. Rather than the mass layoffs that were typical of many mergers, Wells Fargo announced a workforce reduction of only 4,000 to 5,000 employees over a two-year period.

Continuing the Norwest tradition of making numerous smaller acquisitions each year, Wells Fargo acquired 13 companies during 1999 with total assets of $2.4 billion. The largest of these was the February purchase of Brownsville, Texas-based Mercantile Financial Enterprises, Inc., which had $779 million in assets. The acquisition pace picked up in 2000 with Wells Fargo expanding its retail banking into two more states: Michigan, through the buyout of Michigan Financial Corporation ($975 million in assets), and Alaska, through the purchase of National Bancorp of Alaska Inc. ($3 billion in assets). Wells Fargo also acquired First Commerce Bancshares, Inc., of Lincoln, Nebraska, which had $2.9 billion in assets, and a Seattle-based regional brokerage firm, Ragen MacKenzie Group Incorporated, which had more than $11 billion in assets under management.

FIRST SECURITY AND OTHER EARLY 21ST-CENTURY DEALS

In October 2000 Wells Fargo made its largest deal since the Norwest–Wells Fargo merger when it paid nearly $3 billion in stock for First Security Corporation, a $23 billion bank holding company based in Salt Lake City, Utah, and operating in seven western states. Wells Fargo thereby became the largest banking franchise in terms of deposits in New Mexico, Nevada, Idaho, and Utah, as well as the largest banking franchise in the West overall. Also gained in the deal was the Van Kesper investment firm, which increased Wells Fargo's brokerage sales force by 15 percent.

Following completion of the First Security acquisition, Wells Fargo had total assets of $263 billion. Its strategy echoed that of the old Norwest: making selective acquisitions and pursuing cross-selling of an ever-wider array of credit and investment products to its vast customer base. Under Kovacevich's leadership, Wells Fargo was posting smart growth in revenues and profits and was the envy of the banking industry for the smooth way in which it had completed the Norwest–Wells Fargo merger as well as its knack for integrating smaller banks.

Speculation arose at this time that the next "stage" for Wells Fargo might involve a major merger with an eastern bank that would create a nationwide retail bank or a merger that would bring the bank one of the two other things it did not have, a global presence and a large investment banking arm, but Kovacevich seemed content concentrating on western U.S. banking and the broader finance and mortgage operations. Wells Fargo was more profitable than most of the "megabanks" that had formed in the 1990s, with the reason perhaps lying in its more modest ambitions.

In the spring of 2001, Hazen retired and Kovacevich took on the chairmanship as well. That year, Wells Fargo continued to pursue one of Kovacevich's prime goals: substantially bolstering the company's investment, trust, brokerage, and insurance businesses, toward the ultimate aim of increasing earnings from these businesses from 16 percent of overall earnings to 25 percent. Following up on the additions of Ragen Mackenzie and Van Kesper, Wells Fargo purchased ACO Brokerage Holdings Corporation, parent of the Acordia group of insurance companies, based in Chicago. This acquisition more than tripled Wells Fargo's insurance sales force and boosted its insurance business to more than 170 sales locations in 38 states. Wells Fargo moved into the number five position among the nation's insurance brokers and also ranked as the largest bank-owned insurance brokerage in the United States. Also in 2001, the company acquired Irving, Texas-based H.D. Vest, Inc., a provider of comprehensive financial planning services through a network of approximately 6,000 independent tax professionals and financial advisers.

MAINTAINING STELLAR REPUTATION IN TURBULENT TIMES

Despite the turbulent economic climate at the start of the 21st century, Wells Fargo performed admirably well, maintaining its reputation as one of the best-run banks in the United States. The company suffered a slight setback in 2001 when it was forced to take a $1.1 billion charge principally to write down the value of venture capital investments made in technology companies whose stock plunged after the dot-com bubble burst. Wells Fargo bounced back in 2002, its 150th anniversary year, as earnings soared 43 percent to $5.71 billion and total assets grew 14 percent to nearly $350 billion. Part of the asset growth stemmed from the February 2002 purchase of several banks and other businesses from Marquette Bancshares, Inc., and Texas Financial Bancorporation, Inc. Wells Fargo gained 117 bank and financial offices located in Minnesota, South Dakota, Iowa, Illinois, Wisconsin, Texas, and New Mexico. These operations had assets of roughly $6 billion.

Between 2003 and 2006 net earnings at Wells Fargo grew at an annual compounded rate of nearly 12 percent, reaching $8.48 billion by 2006, when total assets were approaching $500 billion. These stellar results were partly attributable to the company's success at cross-selling. By 2006 Wells Fargo was averaging 5.2 financial products per retail banking customer, up from 3.2 in 1998, and six per wholesale banking customer. At this time, many competitors managed to average only around two products per customer, and Kovacevich had set a lofty goal of eventually reaching eight products per customer.

As one of the largest consumer lenders in the United States, Wells Fargo also benefited from the booming housing market of the first years of the 21st century, which was fueled by historically low interest rates. In this environment, the mortgage industry thrived from the frenzied activity in home buying and refinancing. During this period, Wells Fargo was the nation's largest residential mortgage originator, writing nearly $400 billion in mortgages in 2006 alone. The firm was also active on the home-equity loan front, building up a portfolio that reached $79 billion by the end of 2006.

This period also saw Wells Fargo complete some important acquisitions. In October 2003 Seattle-based Pacific Northwest Bancorp was acquired. This deal strengthened Wells Fargo's position in western and central Washington, adding 57 banking locations and $2.9 billion in assets. At the end of the following year, the company paid a bargain price to acquire $29 billion in assets under management from the financially troubled Strong Financial Corporation, based in Menomonee Falls, Wisconsin. The purchase pushed Wells Fargo's mutual fund assets under management to more than $100 billion, placing it among the top 20 mutual fund companies in the nation.

In June 2007 Kovacevich stepped down as CEO after a remarkable period at the helm highlighted by consistent double-digit percentage growth in revenues and profits. His successor, John G. Stumpf, was promoted from the position of president and COO, having joined Norwest in 1982 as a loan administrator and eventually working his way up to head of Wells Fargo's community banking unit in 2002. Kovacevich remained chairman.

This management transition occurred at a time of turmoil in the U.S. banking industry. The housing market had rapidly deteriorated from what had clearly been another financial bubble, precipitating an implosion in the subprime mortgage market and an ensuing wider credit crunch. Wells Fargo seemed particularly vulnerable given its leading position among mortgage originators, and its stock took a hit during the second half of 2007 because of this exposure, but the firm fared much better than many of its peers, for a number of reasons: it did not have a large number of subprime loans on its books; it had steered clear of most of the more exotic, and risky, types of mortgage loans that had been written during the boom times; and it did not have on its books a great deal of mortgages written by outside brokers, some of whom had used sloppy underwriting practices. Wells Fargo was also aided by a particularly strong balance sheet; it was in fact the only U.S. bank with triple-A ratings from both of the major credit agencies.

Wells Fargo did end up taking a $1.4 billion special loan-loss provision for the fourth quarter of 2007, but this charge covered losses from its portfolio of home-equity loans. In this area, the company had strayed from its conservative lending policies by buying prime home-equity loans from brokers, a practice it had since discontinued, and these loans were turning sour at an accelerated rate. The $1.4 billion charge pushed net income for 2007 down 4 percent.

Further problems with its home-equity loans were certainly possible, and Wells Fargo was also seeing rising delinquencies in its portfolio of auto loans. In the first quarter of 2008, the company added an additional $500 million to its reserves to cover future loan losses. Nevertheless, Wells Fargo seemed better positioned than a number of rivals who had incurred much larger loan losses and/or were forced to seek large outside infusions of capital to repair their damaged balance sheets. Its own strong balance sheet and confidence in its strategies made Wells Fargo one of the few major banks pursuing acquisitions during this crisis period. During 2007 the company bought two California banks, Placer Sierra Bancshares of Sacramento and Greater Bay Bancorp of East Palo Alto, with a combined $10.85 billion in assets. In May 2008 Wells Fargo bolstered its growing insurance unit by acquiring Denver-based Flatiron Credit Company, Inc., one of the nation's largest insurance premium finance companies. Wells Fargo intended to continue pursuing similar acquisitions, taking advantage of the difficult economic environment to bolster its diversified array of financial services operations.

Dave Mote
Updated, David E. Salamie

PRINCIPAL SUBSIDIARIES

Wells Fargo Bank, N.A.

PRINCIPAL COMPETITORS

Bank of America Corporation; JPMorgan Chase & Co.; U.S. Bancorp; Citigroup Inc.; KeyCorp; Washington Mutual, Inc.; UnionBanCal Corporation; BancWest Corporation; Zions Bancorporation.

FURTHER READING

Acello, Richard, "The Boy Wonder Banker Relaxes—Just Briefly," *San Diego Daily Transcript,* January 6, 1995, p. 1.

Asher, Joseph, "Golden Jubilee for Two Holding Companies in Twin Cities," *ABA Banking Journal,* June 1979, pp. 102–04.

Bailey, Jeff, and Richard Gibson, "Branching Out: Two Minnesota Banks Illustrate the Pitfalls of Interstate Networks," *Wall Street Journal,* July 26, 1985.

Bayot, Jennifer, "Wells Fargo Adds Strong Financial's Assets," *New York Times,* May 27, 2004, p. C6.

Beebe, Lucius M., and Charles M. Clegg, *U.S. West: The Saga of Wells Fargo,* New York: E.P. Dutton, 1949, 320 p.

Bennett, Robert A., "The Banker Who Would Be Scrooge," *New York Times Magazine,* Business World suppl., pp. 16–18, 36.

Bradford, Stacey L., "Norwest Passage," *Financial World,* January 21, 1997, pp. 41–43.

Bryan, Robert, "First Interstate: California's Restless Giant," *Bankers Monthly,* October 1986, pp. 23+.

Byrne, Harlan S., "Norwest Corp.: Earnings Surge at Bank Company's Consumer, Mortgage Operations," *Barron's,* October 26, 1992, pp. 31–32.

———, "On the Money: Norwest Corp. Has Been Making the Right Moves," *Barron's,* January 5, 1987.

Carlsen, Clifford, "Wells Fargo Hitches Wagon to Commerce on the Net," *San Francisco Business Times,* December 16, 1994, p. 6.

Carlton, Jim, "Wells Fargo Discovers Getting Together Is Hard to Do: Efforts to Merge Operations with First Interstate Result in Alienated Customers," *Wall Street Journal,* July 21, 1997, p. B4.

Carrns, Ann, "Not Yet Circling Wagons: Wells Fargo Shares Hit a Subprime Rut, but Wheels Stay On," *Wall Street Journal,* April 11, 2007, p. C1.

———, "Reining in Risky Bets: Even Steady Wells Fargo Didn't Say 'Whoa' amid Housing Frenzy; Are More Losses Ahead?" *Wall Street Journal,* December 27, 2007, pp. C1, C3.

———, "Stumpf Succeeds Kovacevich atop Wells Fargo," *Wall Street Journal,* June 28, 2007, p. B6.

Carson, Teresa, et al., "Wells Fargo May Have Bagged a Bargain in Crocker," *Business Week,* February 24, 1986, p. 35.

Chandler, Robert J., *Wells Fargo* (Images of America series), Charleston, S.C.: Arcadia Publishing, 2006, 127 p.

Chucker, Harold, *Banco at Fifty: A History of Northwest Bancorporation, 1929–1979,* Minneapolis: Northwest Bancorporation, 1979, 71 p.

———, *Norwest at Sixty: A History of Norwest Corporation, 1929–1989,* Minneapolis: Norwest, 1989, 59 p.

DePass, Dee, "Norwest Goes West: $31.4 Billion Buys New Name, Home," *Minneapolis Star Tribune,* June 9, 1998, p. 1A.

———, "Norwest Officially Acquires Wells Fargo," *Minneapolis Star Tribune,* November 3, 1998, p. 1D.

———, "Norwest Scouts Carefully Looking for the Right Deal," *Minneapolis Star Tribune,* December 22, 1997, p. 1D.

———, "U.S. Bancorp, Norwest Grow in Different Ways," *Minneapolis Star Tribune,* December 22, 1997, p. 1D.

Dobbs, Kevin, "Wells Execs Look Outward—and See Opportunities," *American Banker,* March 10, 2008, p. 1.

Eisenstein, Paul A., "Turnaround at Norwest," *United States Banker,* January 1989, pp. 38+.

Ellis, James E., "It's Not Sexy, but It's Sure," *Business Week,* April 2, 1990, pp. 96–97.

Engen, John R., "The Acquiring Mind of Richard Kovacevich," *Corporate Report-Minnesota,* October 1995, pp. 28–30+.

"First Interstate Breathes Again," *United States Banker,* February 1993, pp. 34+.

Fradkin, Philip L., and Andy Anderson, *Stagecoach,* Book One: *Wells Fargo and the American West* and Book Two: *Wells Fargo and the Rise of the American Financial Services Industry,* New York: Simon and Schuster Source, 2002, 461 p.

Glater, Jonathan D., "The Big Bank That Thinks Small: Norwest Targets 'Little Guys,'" *Washington Post,* January 8, 1995, p. H1.

Gold, Jacqueline S., "Bank to the Future," *Institutional Investor,* September 2001, pp. 54–56+.

Hallinan, Joseph T., "Wells Fargo May Need New System for Success," *Wall Street Journal,* January 7, 2003, p. C1.

Himelstein, Linda, and Kathleen Morris, "Why Wells Fargo Is Circling the Wagons," *Business Week,* June 9, 1997, pp. 92–93.

Hungerford, Edward, *Wells Fargo: Advancing the American Frontier,* New York: Random House, 1949, 274 p.

Hyman, Sidney, *Challenge and Response: The First Security Corporation, First Fifty Years, 1928–1978,* Salt Lake City: University of Utah, Graduate School of Business, 1978, 462 p.

Iwata, Edward, "How to Make a Merger Work: Dick Kovacevich Is Successfully Piloting the New Wells Fargo," *San Francisco Examiner,* August 10, 1999, p. C1.

Kibbie, Daniel C., *Their Bank, Our Bank, the Quality Bank: A History of the First Interstate Bank of California,* Costa Mesa, Calif.: Professional Publications, 1982, 328 p.

King, Ralph T., Jr., and Steven Lipin, "Wells Fargo Sets Big Cuts in California After Merger: Pact with First Interstate Could Take Heavy Toll in Branches, Personnel," *Wall Street Journal,* January 24, 1996, p. A3.

King, Ralph T., Jr., Timothy L. O'Brien, and Steven L. Lipin, "California Dream: A Chance to Cut Costs Drives Wells Fargo Bid for First Interstate," *Wall Street Journal,* October 19, 1995, pp. A1+.

Knecht, G. Bruce, "Banking Maverick: Norwest Corp. Relies on Branches, Pushes Service—and Prospers," *Wall Street Journal,* August 17, 1995, pp. A1+.

Kover, Amy, "Dick Kovacevich Does It His Way," *Fortune,* May 15, 2000, pp. 299–300+.

Levine, Thomas B., et al., "Two California Banks Riding Different Waves," *Business Week,* May 9, 1988, p. 127.

Loomis, Noel M., *Wells Fargo: An Illustrated History,* New York: Clarkson N. Potter, 1968, 340 p.

Mandaro, Laura, "How Kovacevich Kept Wells Ahead," *American Banker,* December 4, 2003, p. 2A.

Milligan, John W., "The Fight for First Interstate," *United States Banker,* March 1996, pp. 32–36, 38–40.

Moody, Ralph, *Wells Fargo,* Boston: Houghton Mifflin, 1961, 184 p.

Mullen, Liz, "Banking on Independence," *Los Angeles Business Journal,* March 14, 1994, pp. 14+.

Murray, Matt, "Norwest, Wells Fargo Agree to a Merger," *Wall Street Journal,* June 9, 1998, p. A2.

"Norwest: Hurtling into Innovative Services," *Business Week,* May 28, 1984, pp. 78–79.

O'Donnell, Thomas C., "A 'Loyal Number Two' Takes Charge," *Forbes,* September 29, 1980, pp. 46+.

Prince, C. J., "Cool Hand Kovacevich," *Chief Executive,* May 2001, pp. 22–28.

Racine, John, "How First Interstate Beats the California Blues," *American Banker,* January 11, 1995, pp. 4+.

Reid, Joe, *100 Proud Years: State to Dial to Norwest Financial,* Des Moines, Iowa: Norwest Financial, 1997, 154 p.

Roosevelt, Phil, "King of the Cross-Sell: Richard Kovacevich Wants to Turn Wells Fargo into a Perpetual-Motion Machine," *Barron's,* October 11, 1999, pp. 20, 23.

Rose, Sanford, "They're Still Pioneering at Wells Fargo Bank," *Fortune,* July 1976, p. 122.

St. Anthony, Neal, "From Go-Go to Cut-Cut: Norwest, Growing Fast but Spending a Lot, Now Focuses on Controlling Costs," *Minneapolis Star Tribune,* August 5, 1994, p. 1D.

———, "Norwest Corp. Knows How to Grow," *Minneapolis Star Tribune,* August 13, 1990, p. 1D.

Schafer, Lee, "Executive of the Year: Lloyd P. Johnson," *Corporate Report-Minnesota,* January 1991, pp. 28+.

Sinton, Peter, "Bungles Bruise Wells Fargo: Merger Woes Hurt Once Sterling Reputation," *San Francisco Chronicle,* June 26, 1997, p. D1.

———, "Wells Fargo Wagon Rolls On," *San Francisco Chronicle,* March 25, 1996, p. B2.

Somasundarum, Meera, "Norwest, Banking Giant, Seeks Gains by Stressing Services for Customers," *Wall Street Journal,* December 10, 1996, p. B11A.

Timmons, Heather, "Can the Wells Fargo Wagon Roll Alone?" *Business Week,* October 23, 2000, p. 144.

Veverka, Mark, "Bank on Them," *Barron's,* February 18, 2008, pp. 21–23.

"Waving Good-bye to Wells Fargo," *Business Week,* August 1, 1994, p. 36.

Weiner, Steve, "The Wal-Mart of Banking," *Forbes,* March 4, 1991, pp. 62, 65.

"Wells Fargo's Fight to Hold the West," *Business Week,* June 14, 1982, pp. 90+.

Wells Fargo Since 1852, San Francisco: Wells Fargo & Company, 2000.

Wilson, Neill C., *Treasure Express: Epic Days of the Wells Fargo,* New York: Macmillan, 1936, 322 p.

Winther, Oscar O., *Via Western Express and Stagecoach,* Stanford, Calif.: Stanford University Press, 1945, 158 p.

Zuckerman, Sam, "A New Stage for Wells' Hazen," *San Francisco Chronicle,* November 4, 1998, p. D2.

Whitbread PLC

Whitbread Court
Houghton Hall Business Park
Porz Avenue
Dunstable, LU5 5XE
United Kingdom
Telephone: (+44 1582) 424200
Fax: (+44 207) 806 5497
Web site: http://www.whitbread.co.uk

Public Company
Founded: 1742
Incorporated: 1889 as Whitbread and Company PLC
Employees: 33,000
Sales: £1.22 billion ($2.42 billion) (2008)
Stock Exchanges: London
Ticker Symbol: WTB
NAICS: 721110 Hotels (Except Casino Hotels) and Motels; 722110 Full-Service Restaurants; 722213 Snack and Nonalcoholic Beverage Bars

■ ■ ■

Whitbread PLC is one of the leading players in the U.K. leisure industry, concentrating in the early 21st century on hotels, pub restaurants, and coffee shops. Whitbread's roots, however, were in brewing. Founded as a single brewery, the company grew to become one of the most prestigious of London's older breweries, with its history closely paralleling that of the Whitbread family, which retained continuous control of the company from 1742 to 1992. Whitbread began to diversify in the early 1960s. Its long involvement in the pub industry led to a deeper delving into the restaurant sector, with a key development being the 1974 launch of the Beefeater casual dining chain. The company later, in 1995, acquired the Costa Coffee chain. Whitbread entered the lodging industry during this same period, by creating the Travel Inn budget chain in 1987.

At the beginning of the 21st century, Whitbread shifted its focus to these newer areas of operations, breaking with its history by selling its brewery operations in 2000 and then its pubs in 2001. In 2004 the company bolstered its budget hotel business by purchasing Premier Lodge, which was merged with Travel Inn to form Premier Travel Inn. By 2007 Whitbread's lodging business, operating simply as Premier Inn, was the largest in the United Kingdom, with more than 36,000 rooms in 500-plus hotels. By this same time, Whitbread was operating more than 400 pub restaurants under the names Beefeater, Brewers Fayre, and Table Table. The majority of these were located on the same site as a Premier Inn. Costa, meantime, had become the largest and fastest-growing coffee-shop chain in the United Kingdom. In addition to having opened more than 700 Costa outlets in the United Kingdom, Whitbread was also expanding the brand overseas, where more than 300 additional Costa units were operating in more than 20 countries, with China and Russia two of the key growth markets.

FORMATION OF GOAT BREWHOUSE BY SAMUEL WHITBREAD: 1742

Samuel Whitbread, at the age of 14, was sent to London by his mother in 1734 to become an apprentice to a

COMPANY PERSPECTIVES

Our vision is to be the best hospitality company that there is—a family of related hotel and restaurant brands recognised by our people, guests and investors as leaders in each market in which we operate. Our business is focused on growth sectors of hotels, restaurants and coffee stores. Our priorities, on behalf of our shareholders, are to grow our business and to achieve annual improvements in the return on their capital. We are doing this by: growing the profitability, scale and market share of our leading brands; developing new brands that have the potential to reach significant scale; managing our business so that shareholder value is added by each of our activities; ensuring that each of our brands is a leader in its field for customer service; becoming the employer of choice in the UK hotels and restaurants sector; working to meet our responsibilities to the wider stakeholders in our business, including commercial partners and the communities in which our brands operate.

brewer. Whitbread, raised as a Puritan, proved to be an extremely hard worker. In 1742, eight years after coming to London, he established his own brewery, the Goat Brewhouse, with a £2,000 inheritance and additional underwriting from John Howard, the renowned prison reformer. As the brewery became successful, Howard's investment became more lucrative; it even led to a reciprocation of financial support by Whitbread for Howard's reform movement.

By 1750 Whitbread had acquired an additional brewery located on Chiswell Street. At this time there were more than 50 breweries in London, but, despite intense competition, the Whitbread brewery expanded rapidly. By 1760 its annual output had reached 64,000 barrels, second only to Calvert and Company.

Whitbread was enthusiastic about new brewing methods. He employed several well-known engineers who helped to improve the quality and increase the production volume of the company's stout and porter (a sweeter, weaker stout).

The Whitbread family had a long history of involvement in English politics. Samuel Whitbread's forefathers fought with Oliver Cromwell's Roundheads during the English Civil War and later developed a connection with the Bedfordshire preacher and author John Bunyan. Samuel Whitbread himself was elected to Parliament in 1768 as a representative of Bedford. His son, Samuel II, succeeded him in Parliament in 1790, and Whitbread descendants served in Parliament almost continuously until 1910.

Samuel Whitbread died in 1796, by which time his company stood as the largest brewery in the United Kingdom, having become the first to attain annual production of 200,000 barrels. Samuel II assumed control of the brewery, but was so preoccupied with Parliament that by 1799 he was compelled to take on a partner. The partnership, however, was short-lived. The brewery entered into seven more partnerships over the next 70 years, only two of which were successful. Most notably, Whitbread's 1812 partnership with the Martineau and Bland brewery resulted in a full merger of the two companies' brewing operations. The Martineau and Bland facility at Lambeth, however, was later closed and its equipment was moved to Chiswell Street.

During the early 19th century the bulk of Whitbread's business was conducted with "free houses," public houses (or pubs) neither owned by, nor bound to sell only the products of one brewer. These pubs numbered several hundred, and their business remained fairly stable. However, when the Drury Lane Theatre burned down in 1809, Samuel II saw an opportunity to profit from its renovation. He led a committee to restore the theater, invested heavily in the project, and persuaded several friends to join him. The venture yielded only a small dividend when the theater was reopened, and cost Whitbread the friendship of many of his fellow investors. In Parliament, Whitbread opposed the resumption of war with Napoleon, a position that made him even more unpopular. In July 1815, shortly after the battle of Waterloo, Samuel Whitbread II committed suicide.

Whitbread's sons, William Henry and Samuel Charles, inherited their father's interest in the brewery. Whitbread family control, however, had been greatly diminished by the company's nine partners. It was not until 1819 that the Whitbread brothers were able to reestablish direct family control over the operation. The number of partners was reduced, and the brewery remained under Whitbread control for many years.

In 1834 Whitbread introduced ale to its product line. The ale gained immediate popularity and resulted in a substantial increase in turnover for the brewery. Whitbread expanded even more dramatically after 1869, when the family established its last partnership. One year earlier, the company had begun producing bottled beer.

KEY DATES

1742: After working as an apprentice, Samuel Whitbread establishes his own brewery in London.
1750: Whitbread opens a second brewery on Chiswell Street.
1796: The annual output of the company's stout and porter reaches 200,000 barrels, a first among U.K. brewers.
1834: Ale is added to the product line.
1868: Production of bottled beer begins.
1889: The company goes public.
1955: Whitbread begins expanding through the acquisition of smaller brewers.
1968: The company gains the right to brew Heineken lager under license.
1974: The first Beefeater restaurant opens.
1979: Family-friendly pub food chain Brewers Fayre is established.
1987: The Travel Inn budget hotel chain is launched.
1989: Boddingtons brewery is acquired; a decision to focus principally on hotels and restaurants, while retaining brewery operations, leads to the sale of the wine and spirits division to Allied-Lyons.
1990: The Monopolies and Mergers Commission issues an order related to its investigation of the U.K. system of tied houses, leading Whitbread to sell 1,300 of its pubs and lease another 1,000 by 1992.
1992: Involvement of Whitbread family in company management ends.
1995: Whitbread purchases 16 Marriott hotels and signs an agreement with Marriott International to develop the brand in the United Kingdom; company acquires the David Lloyd Leisure chain of sports and fitness clubs and the Costa Coffee chain of coffee shops.
1999: Whitbread's bid to acquire the U.K. retailing operations of Allied Domecq, including 3,500 pubs, fails.
2000: Whitbread Beer Company is sold to Interbrew S.A.
2001: Company's pub operations are sold to Morgan Grenfell Private Equity.
2004: Premier Lodge is acquired and merged with Travel Inn to form Premier Travel Inn, the clear U.K. budget lodging leader.
2005: Whitbread's Marriott hotel assets are placed into a joint venture, which is later sold.
2007: David Lloyd Leisure is divested; Premier Travel Inn is rebranded as Premier Inn.
2008: The 1,000th Costa Coffee shop opens in Moscow.

GOING PUBLIC IN 1889

During the 1880s, a sudden and significant decline in demand for beer caused many "free houses" to sell their leases to breweries (and thereby become "tied houses"). Breweries such as Whitbread, which had established numerous tied houses, were forced to extend loans to public house operators so that they could remain in business. The capital required to purchase free house leases and to extend loans could be satisfied only by the public through share flotations. Therefore, when Whitbread's partnership agreement expired in 1889, the partners decided to transform the brewery into a public company.

An attempt by brewers to raise the profitability of tied houses by reducing beer prices backfired; their tenants competed on price and went even further into debt. A recession in 1900 forced Whitbread to write down the value of its tied house properties, a move that may have saved the company. Demand for beer recovered steadily and permitted Whitbread to increase its production every year from 1899 to 1912. Accordingly, the value of tied houses recovered as they became profitable. Just prior to World War I, however, the government raised its license duty on tied houses, rendering many of them financial liabilities. Whitbread stopped buying tied houses, and instead concentrated on expanding its bottled beer trade.

Although Whitbread weathered this difficult period virtually intact, many competitors were forced to close. Whitbread's ability to survive was attributed to three factors: the maintenance of a harmonious relationship between the brewer and the publican (public house operator), sustaining a good public image of the brand, and keeping influence in government.

Francis Pelham Whitbread, the director of the brewery at the time, devoted his energies to maintaining a stable atmosphere for profitable brewing; as chairman of the Brewers Society, he promoted better brewer-vendor relations. Later, as chairman and treasurer of the politically active National Trade Defence Association, he lobbied against the temperance movement in Parliament. After World War I he played a major role in the formation of policies within the brewing industry and was particularly opposed to the proliferation of tied houses.

During the interwar period Whitbread took over the Jude Hanbury brewery. As its situation with vendors remained unsettled, Whitbread concentrated further on the expansion of bottled beer sales. Whitbread beer had become available throughout the world. Francis Whitbread, however, became increasingly divorced from the everyday operation of the brewery; his position as a spokesman for the industry and his dedication to philanthropic activities occupied most of his time.

On December 29, 1940, German incendiary bombs landed in five separate areas of the brewery. Each of the fires was put out by the company fire brigade, with the exception of a malt fire, which, like burning coal dust, is very difficult to extinguish. It was finally doused a week later. Damage to the brewery and the surrounding area was great. Nevertheless, Whitbread resumed brewing almost immediately.

Francis Pelham Whitbread died in 1941. His leadership of the brewery was highly conservative, especially when compared with the policies of his successors. Francis was in many ways a popular figurehead for the company. Much of the actual burden of management fell on the shoulders of Samuel Howard Whitbread, who served with the company from 1915 until his death in 1944. William Henry Whitbread assumed leadership of the company that year but was forced to postpone his plans for the rehabilitation of the brewery until after the war.

WAVE OF AMALGAMATIONS IN THE POSTWAR ERA

Although the war ended less than a year later, the British economy continued to suffer from aftereffects for many years. Conditions were so grave that Whitbread was unable to begin its modernization until 1950. At that time Whitbread undertook a sweeping rationalization program, which included the concentration of human resources and retooling of machinery.

Other smaller breweries were in less stable condition, and many were threatened with bankruptcy. Whitbread, however, offered an amalgamation scheme to these breweries. Under this formula, called the "Whitbread Umbrella," failing breweries agreed to coordinate their operations and distribution networks with Whitbread. Many of these arrangements resulted in Whitbread's eventual acquisition of the smaller brewers. In the period from 1955 to 1971, Whitbread took over 26 breweries and expanded its number of tied houses from less than 100 to 10,000.

Some of the breweries acquired by Whitbread were large well-established companies. Beginning with the Dutton brewery in 1964, Whitbread took over Rhymney in 1966, Threlfall and Fremlin in 1967, Strong in 1968, and Brickwood in 1971. These additions to Whitbread also gave the company greater geographical coverage: Threlfall's was located in the northwest port of Liverpool, and Brickwood's was in Portsmouth, on the south coast.

STREAMLINING AND BEGINNINGS OF DIVERSIFICATION

The 1970s were characterized as a period of streamlining for Whitbread and also saw the beginning of a move toward diversification. The company disposed of many of its marginally profitable or outdated operations; even the Chiswell Street brewery was closed in 1976. Still, Whitbread suffered from the aftereffects of a serious economic recession during the mid-1970s, and the company came close to bankruptcy. A gradual economic recovery led to improvements in the market that greatly strengthened Whitbread's financial position.

Meanwhile, however, as popular demand shifted from ale to lager, total beer consumption began to fall. Whitbread started to de-emphasize certain brewing assets and began to diversify outside brewing. The company had gained a chain of wine retail outlets when it acquired Thresher in 1962. Along the way, Whitbread built up a wines and spirits division that included Beefeater Gin, Long John Scotch Whisky, and Cutty Sark Scotch Whisky. Food was added in 1974 with the opening of the first Beefeater Restaurant & Pub, which was in the casual dining sector, and with the 1979 debut of Brewers Fayre, a family-friendly chain of pub food outlets.

Notwithstanding these nonbeer ventures, Whitbread did not abandon the brewing industry but in fact became more active in licensing non-U.K. brewer's brands. In 1968 the company gained the right to brew Heineken lager under a license agreement and in 1976 the Stella Artois brand began production by Whitbread under a similar agreement. The Belgian beer soon became the best-selling premium lager in the United Kingdom.

FURTHER EXPANSION INTO RESTAURANTEURING AND ENTRANCE INTO LODGING

Whitbread continued to diversify in the 1980s under the guidance of new leadership. William Henry Whitbread had given up day-to-day control of the company during the 1970s, whereupon Samuel Whitbread (a fifth-generation descendant of the company's founder) became chief executive and, eventually, chairman in 1984. He initially sought to bolster his company's restaurant holdings. In 1982 a 50-50 joint venture with PepsiCo, Inc., began, which went on to build a significant chain of Pizza Hut restaurants in the United Kingdom. T.G.I. Friday's joined the company's restaurant fold three years later, when Whitbread signed a franchise agreement to develop U.K.-based outlets of this chain, also in the casual dining sector. By the 1996 fiscal year, beer operations accounted for only 43 percent of profits, with wine and spirits accounting for 20 percent and retail operations 37 percent.

Next, Whitbread entered the hotel industry. The year 1987 marked the debut of the Travel Inn chain, budget hotels that were usually located next to another Whitbread property such as a Brewers Fayre, Beefeater, or T.G.I. Friday's. Whitbread's diversification program gained further momentum in 1989 when management announced that the company would focus on the leisure retailing industries in general, with a particular emphasis on areas, such as travel and eating out, that were projected to grow rapidly through the end of the century. Brewing was still to be included in the mix but would continue to account for smaller percentages of company profits, notwithstanding the 1989 acquisition of Boddingtons brewery. Another sector to be retained was the Thresher unit, which specialized in retail outlets for alcoholic beverages; Thresher was subsequently bolstered with the opening of the first Wine Rack in 1989 and the 1991 acquisition of Bottoms Up, a chain of wine superstores. On the divestment side was the company's wine and spirits division, which included a distiller of such brands as Beefeater Gin and a U.S.-based importer and distributor of wines and spirits. The division was sold late in 1989 to Allied-Lyons PLC for £545 million ($880.2 million).

COMPLIANCE WITH 1990 MMC ORDERS

The year 1989 was also important because it was the year that Whitbread began to plan for its compliance with new rules on tied houses set down by the British government's Monopolies and Mergers Commission (MMC). After an investigation into the system of tied houses that had been created from the numerous mergers in the brewing industry in the 1960s and 1970s, in early 1990 the MMC ordered brewers with more than 2,000 pubs to sell or lease half of the number greater than 2,000, meaning that Whitbread would have to do so with about 2,300 pubs. The MMC gave brewers a November 1, 1992, deadline to comply. Meanwhile, Peter Jarvis, who had joined Whitbread from Unilever in 1976, took over as chief executive in 1990. Later, in August 1992, Michael Angus, chairman of The Boots Company PLC and former chairman of Unilever, became chairman of Whitbread as well, taking over from Samuel Whitbread, who remained on the board as a nonexecutive director. This management team, noticeably minus a Whitbread for the first time in the company's 250-year history, led the company through the MMC compliance process.

Following the issue of the MMC orders, Whitbread first pulled its pubs out of its brewery division. It then sold about 1,300 of them by the deadline, and leased the remaining 1,000 on a short-term basis. At the time the United Kingdom had too many pubs, and property values had fallen sharply since the boom years of the early 1980s. Consequently, Whitbread's profits took a large hit from the forced sales and squeezed its plans to expand its retail activities. A plan for Whitbread to take the Pizza Hut chain into continental Europe fell apart when the company could not afford to commit the initial £100 million needed.

A further consequence of the MMC orders was that Whitbread had to untangle itself from its complicated system of cross-holdings in regional brewers, held through Whitbread Investment Company, that it had developed during its acquisition spree. In November 1993 Whitbread acquired Whitbread Investment Company, then in March 1994 sold nearly all its regional brewery stakes, raising about £300 million in the process.

RENEWED SPENDING SPREE IN LEISURE SECTORS

Whitbread thus emerged from the MMC orders with some cash to spend on its leisure businesses. A new wave of activity began in 1994 with the acquisition of the Maredo steak restaurant chain located in Germany. In August 1995 Whitbread paid Canada-based Scott's Hospitality Inc. £180 million ($288.2 million) for 16 Marriott hotels and also signed an agreement with Marriott International, Inc., to develop the brand name in the United Kingdom. That same month, the company acquired David Lloyd Leisure (DLL) for £200.7 million ($321.3 million). DLL, named after tennis champion David Lloyd, operated 20 private sports and fitness clubs as well as 24 nursery schools through its Gatehouse Nursery Services subsidiary. In March 1997 DLL bought Curzon Management Associates and its five London gym sites.

Whitbread's restaurant holdings received further boosts in 1995 and 1996. The Costa Coffee chain of coffee shops was acquired in October 1995. The chain had been founded in 1978 by Bruno and Sergio Costa as an outgrowth of the brothers' wholesale coffee roasting business. In July 1996, £133 million ($208.8 million) was spent to purchase Pelican Group and its 110 restaurants spread throughout several chains, most notably Café Rouge, a French bistro/café; Dôme, a bar/café emphasizing beer, drinks, coffee, and café-style food; and Mamma Amalfi, a family-style Italian restaurant. In November 1996 Whitbread bought the BrightReasons group for £46 million ($72.2 million). The key chain acquired therein was Bella Pasta, with 55 outlets, while the Pizza Piazza chain was subsequently sold to Passion For Food for £11.25 million and 102 Pizzaland restaurants were converted to Pizza Huts and other Whitbread restaurant brands. The acquired pizza chains were jettisoned to avoid a conflict with Pizza Hut.

In the summer of 1997 Jarvis stepped down as chief executive and was replaced by David Thomas, who had joined Whitbread in 1984 as a regional director of the Inns division. Thomas took over a company that had seen sales and profits rise throughout the 1990s, thanks in large part to Whitbread's increasing emphasis on nonbeer activities.

FAILED ALLIED DOMECQ BID IN LATE NINETIES

By fiscal 1999 the evolution of the company away from its roots was increasingly obvious. Less than 12 percent of operating profits were generated by the brewing operations that year. The continuing lackluster beer sales led Whitbread to close one of its breweries and to sell another, leaving it with three breweries capable of producing more than one million barrels a year. Also during the year, the company sold 253 of its leased pubs, 40 Beefeater outlets, and the Gatehouse Nursery unit. In August 1998 Whitbread merged its wine and alcohol retail outlets—Thresher, Wine Rack, and others—with those of Allied Domecq PLC, forming a 50-50 joint venture called First Quench Retailing Ltd.

At this point, Whitbread's core operations in brewing and pubs were in mature industries with little prospect for future growth. Thomas saw one opportunity in this area, consolidating the group's collection of pubs with those of another company, thereby gaining the cost savings of economies of scale. When Allied Domecq placed its U.K. retailing operations up for sale, including 3,500 pubs and its stakes in soft drink maker Britvic and in First Quench, Thomas aggressively pursued a deal. In May 1999, after lengthy negotiations that eventually turned hostile, Whitbread and Allied reached an agreement on a £2.36 billion offer, later raised to £2.85 billion under pressure from a rival bid by Punch Taverns. In July 1999 the Office of Fair Trading (OFT) referred Whitbread's bid to the Competition Commission, a development that killed the bid because it had been made conditional on OFT approval. Whitbread declined to make an unconditional offer, ending its bid for control of the Allied properties, which were subsequently purchased by Punch Taverns. Whitbread also shelved a planned spinoff of its beer unit, the Whitbread Beer Company. Had its takeover of the Allied pubs gone through, Whitbread would have had to divest its brewery operations to comply with the 1989 beer orders of the MMC.

NEW ERA IN 21ST CENTURY, MINUS BEER AND PUBS

In the wake of this failed bid, Whitbread embarked on a remarkable two-year period of transformation that launched the company into a new era. The company first completed two smaller but telling acquisitions, indicating the future direction. In September 1999 Whitbread spent £78.3 million for Racquets & Healthtrack Group Ltd., cementing its position as the largest operator of health and fitness clubs in the United Kingdom. The six Racquets & Healthtrack clubs were later rebranded under the David Lloyd Leisure name, increasing the size of that chain to 47 outlets and 170,000 members. Then in January 2000 Whitbread took over Swallow Group plc in a £730 million deal. Swallow operated 36 upscale hotels in the United Kingdom; under Whitbread they would be converted to the Marriott brand, nearly doubling the size of that chain from 5,700 rooms to almost 11,000.

Shortly after completion of the Swallow buy, Whitbread made the historic decision to sell both its brewing and pubs operations. Whitbread Beer Company was the first to go and was purchased by Interbrew S.A. in May 2000 for £400 million. Then in May 2001 the pubs were offloaded to Morgan Grenfell Private Equity, a unit of Deutsche Bank AG, for £1.63 billion. The sale did not include the so-called food-led pubs, or pub restaurants, namely, Brewers Fayre, Brewsters, and Beefeater. Part of the proceeds from the sale of the pubs, £1.1 billion worth, was returned to shareholders at the equivalent of £2.30 per share; most of the remainder went to reduce debt. In between these two transactions, in October 2000, Whitbread also disposed of its 50 percent interest in First Quench. By mid-2001, then, a new Whitbread had emerged, focused on upscale and budget hotels, restaurants, and health and fitness clubs. While this transformation was taking place, a new chairman came onboard in June 2000; succeeding Angus was John Banham, who was serving as chairman of two other U.K. firms: aggregates producer Tarmac plc and retailer Kingfisher plc.

In the months that followed the sale of the pub estate, Whitbread began repositioning its remaining operations to secure the company's future. In August 2001 Whitbread announced that it would spend more than £500 million over the following five years to double the number of David Lloyd Leisure outlets to 100. At the same time the Curzon health club chain, which served the budget end of the market, was slated for divestment to further the company's focus on the upscale market served by the David Lloyd clubs. Curzon was subsequently sold in 2002.

The restaurant portfolio was also in need of an overhaul, as several of the Whitbread chains were not performing satisfactorily. In May 2002 Whitbread sold its Pelican and BrightReasons restaurant groups to Tragus Holdings Limited for £25 million in a management-led buyout. Included in the deal were 153 restaurants under the Café Rouge, Bella Pasta, Mamma Amalfi, Abbaye, Leadenhall Wine Bar, and Oriel names. This left Whitbread with its Pizza Hut, Costa Coffee, and T.G.I. Friday's restaurants in addition to the Brewers Fayre, Brewsters, and Beefeater pub restaurants.

The restaurant sell-off completed, in large part, Whitbread's disposal program, leading the company to focus on organically growing the remaining core. In addition to the planned expansion of David Lloyd Leisure, there were plans to increase the number of Costa Coffee outlets from 300 to 500 by 2004. At the same time, Whitbread in 2003 launched an overhaul of the underperforming Beefeater chain. After the sale of about 50 of the less desirable locations, the remaining 150 Beefeaters gradually had their drab, dusky interiors replaced with a lighter design featuring American diner-style booth seating, while their traditional limited menu was replaced by one featuring a wider range of more contemporary food options. This makeover was one of the last initiatives of the Thomas era as the chief executive stepped down in June 2004, having shepherded Whitbread through its most significant shift in focus in its 250-plus-year history.

FURTHER NARROWING TO HANDFUL OF OWNED BRANDS

The new chief executive, Alan Parker, had a strong background in the hospitality industry and had served as head of Whitbread's hotel operations. In July 2004, shortly after assuming the top spot, Parker bolstered the firm's position in budget hotels by engineering the acquisition of Premier Lodge from Spirit Group for £505 million ($920 million). The 132-unit Premier, which had been the number three budget hotel chain in the United Kingdom, was merged with Travel Inn to form Premier Travel Inn, the clear U.K. budget lodging leader. By the end of the 2005 fiscal year, Premier Travel Inn boasted of 28,400 rooms in more than 450 hotels across the United Kingdom.

A comprehensive review of Whitbread's operations led to another round of divestments as Parker attempted to improve the firm's financial performance. Among the assets sold in 2005 were the Maredo restaurant chain in Germany and the company's 23.5 percent stake in the soft-drink maker Britvic. Whitbread moved its headquarters from London to Luton in a cost-saving action and sold off its historic Chiswell brewery, which had been used as a conferencing and banqueting site. The company's pub restaurant businesses were placed under one management team, and the underperforming Brewsters locations were converted into Brewers Fayre outlets, reducing Whitbread's operations in this area to two chains, the other being Beefeater.

Finally, Whitbread also announced plans to sell its Marriott hotel holdings and relinquish its U.K. license to the Marriott name. In 2005 Whitbread and Marriott International formed a joint venture that took control of the U.K. Marriotts as they were placed up for sale. The following April the Marriott properties were purchased by Royal Bank of Scotland Group plc for £951 million ($1.7 billion). Jettisoning its upscale hotel assets was designed to enable Whitbread to concentrate on its Premier Travel Inn budget brand. During fiscal 2006 Whitbread used part of the proceeds from the asset sales to pay out £410 million to its shareholders through a combination of special dividends and stock repurchases. In the midst of this hectic year, Banham retired from his position as Whitbread chairman and was succeeded by Anthony Habgood, who was also the chairman of distributor Bunzl plc, where he had previously served as chief executive. The following year Whitbread returned another £400 million to shareholders in the form of stock repurchases.

The divestment of Marriott was part of a larger shift at Whitbread, away from ventures involving brands licensed from other companies and toward the building of a more focused portfolio of businesses operating under company-owned brands. Thus, in September 2006 Whitbread sold its 50 percent interest in the U.K. Pizza Hut venture to its partner, YUM! Brands, Inc., garnering net proceeds of £99 million. The following

March, Whitbread sold off its T.G.I. Friday's restaurants in a £70.4 million deal. After these deals were completed, Whitbread owned all of the brands of the companies it operated.

Significant changes also refigured the company's pub restaurant holdings. Whitbread elected to focus its pub restaurant business on those sites located adjacent to a Premier Travel Inn because such dual sites had proven to provide superior returns. In July 2006, 239 standalone Beefeater and Brewers Fayre locations were therefore sold to Mitchells & Butlers plc for £497 million ($920 million). The divestment of David Lloyd Leisure enabled Whitbread to pay greater attention to its businesses with higher growth potential, particularly Premier Travel Inn and Costa Coffee. The fitness chain was sold to London & Regional Holdings Limited and Bank of Scotland for £925 million ($1.88 billion). During fiscal 2008, proceeds from the latest divestments were used to pay down debt and for another £338 million in stock buybacks.

The latest disposals had also slimmed Whitbread down to a handful of core businesses: the Premier Travel Inn budget hotels, the Beefeater and Brewers Fayre pub restaurants, and the Costa Coffee chain. In mid-2007 the company launched an effort to rebrand its budget hotel chain as simply Premier Inn. The move was designed in part to end confusion in the marketplace between the old name and the rival Travelodge chain. At the time, Premier Inn was in the midst of a major expansion aimed at doubling the chain to more than 45,000 rooms in the United Kingdom by 2010. In advance of the 2012 Summer Olympics in London, Whitbread also budgeted £100 million to open six new Premier Inns in the U.K. capital and add 1,200 rooms toward its ultimate goal of having more than 8,500 London rooms by 2012. Planning was also advancing on the first overseas Premier Inns. Whitbread had entered into joint ventures with local partners in Dubai and India to expand the chain into the Gulf region and India, respectively. The first overseas Premier Inn opened in Dubai in April 2008.

Costa, in the meantime, was the subject of accelerating growth. Between early 2006 and early 2008, the chain nearly doubled in size, from 550 units to more than 1,000. The 1,000th outlet opened in Moscow's Pushkin Square in March 2008 and was the first in Russia. The push into Russia was part of an aggressive overseas expansion that had included the debut of more than 300 Costa shops in 22 nations, including countries throughout Europe and the Middle East as well as China and India. Whitbread also attempted to revitalize its pub restaurants by converting more than 100 Brewers Fayre locations into a new concept called Table Table, officially launched in May 2008. The typical Table Table outlet, which was more upmarket than Whitbread's other restaurants and was aimed at 30- to 45-year-olds, featured a number of different styles of dining spaces under one roof to provide more choices to its customers. Whitbread thus had growth initiatives underway across its three operating sectors, having achieved a strong revenue jump of more than 11 percent in fiscal 2008, to £1.22 billion ($2.42 billion).

Updated, David E. Salamie

PRINCIPAL SUBSIDIARIES

Whitbread Group PLC; Premier Inn Hotels Limited; Whitbread Restaurants Limited; Premier Inn Limited; Whitbread Hotel Company Limited; Costa Limited.

PRINCIPAL COMPETITORS

Travelodge Hotels Ltd.; InterContinental Hotels Group PLC; Hilton Hotels Corporation; The Restaurant Group plc; Starbucks Corporation; Caffè Nero Group Ltd.

FURTHER READING

Aspden, Peter, "Whitbread Closes Book on Awards," *Financial Times,* December 13, 2005, p. 4.

Barker, Alex, "Whitbread's Diet Is 'Good for Shareholders,'" *Financial Times,* August 8, 2006, p. 18.

Barrow, Martin, "Brewer to Spend £300m on Retail to Offset Decline," *Times* (London), November 2, 1995, p. 27.

Blitz, Roger, "Whitbread Takes Coffee Shops to China," *Financial Times,* November 28, 2007, p. 22.

———, "Whitbread to Spend £22m Rebranding Premier Chain," *Financial Times,* June 20, 2007, p. 21.

Blitz, Roger, and Maggie Urry, "Buoyant Whitbread Seeks Growth," *Financial Times,* April 29, 2008, p. 18.

Britton, Noelle, "Whitbread Brews Up a Potent Mix," *Marketing,* December 4, 1986, pp. 26+.

Buckley, Neil, "A New Brew for Whitbread," *Financial Times,* August 12, 1995, p. WFT5.

Choueke, Mark, "Who Will Slice Up Whitbread, Parker or Private Equity?" *Sunday Telegraph* (London), April 1, 2007.

"A Conundrum That Could Have Whitbread Crying in Its Beer," *Times* (London), May 13, 1992, p. 21.

Craig, Malcolm, "What's Next for Whitbread?" *Leisure and Hospitality Business,* April 5, 2001, p. 10.

Daneshkhu, Scheherazade, "Whitbread to Sell Pelican Restaurants," *Financial Times,* October 15, 2001, p. 30.

Friedman, Amanda Moslé, "Having Words with Alan Parker," *Nation's Restaurant News,* October 22, 2007, p. 106.

Garrahan, Matthew, "Tired Beefeater Gets a 'B2' Wake-Up Call," *Financial Times,* October 27, 2003, p. 25.

———, "Whitbread Adamant No Break-up Is Planned," *Financial Times,* October 26, 2005, p. 21.

———, "Whitbread Plans to Sell Up to 260 Pubs," *Financial Times,* April 26, 2006, p. 18.

———, "Whitbread to Return £400m to Shareholders," *Financial Times,* March 15, 2005, p. 22.

Gwyther, Matthew, "Whitbread on the Wagon," *Management Today,* September 2001, pp. 74–75, 77, 79.

Hearn, Louisa, "Whitbread Appoints Parker As New Leader," *Financial Times,* December 17, 2003, p. 27.

Holstein, William J., and Richard A. Melcher, "Whitbread Wakes Up with a Headache," *Business Week,* April 29, 1985, pp. 44+.

Hore, Andrew, "Vultures Hungrily Eye Up Whitbread," *Express on Sunday* (London), May 29, 2005.

John, Peter, "Moving from a Siberia of the Hotel Industry to an Executive Hot Spot," *Financial Times,* October 29, 2004, p. 23.

———, "Whitbread Wins Battle for Premier Lodge Chain," *Financial Times,* July 24, 2004, p. 4.

———, "Whitbread's £800m Sell-Off Cuts Historic City Ties," *Financial Times,* October 29, 2004, p. 23.

Jones, Adam, "Whitbread Exits Bistros and Pasta Cafes," *Financial Times,* June 1, 2002, p. 12.

Killgren, Lucy, "Whitbread Investors to Get £350m," *Financial Times,* October 25, 2006, p. 20.

"Losing a Beer Belly," *Economist,* August 12, 1995, p. 54.

McLaughlin, John, "Too Close for Comfort: French Marriage a Failure for Whitbread and Pizza Hut," *Restaurant Business,* September 1, 1992, p. 30.

Morgan, David, *Whitbread's Entire,* London: Whitbread, 1978, 54 p.

Murray, Alasdair, "Whitbread to Seek Links with Regionals," *Times* (London), August 12, 1996, p. 40.

Osborne, Alistair, "Gentleman of Leisure Who Weaned Whitbread off the Bottle," *Daily Telegraph* (London), May 3, 2003.

Parker-Pope, Tara, "Whitbread PLC Expands into Leisure As Traditional Beer Market Contracts," *Wall Street Journal,* August 9, 1995, p. A6.

Ritchie, Berry, *An Uncommon Brewer: The Story of Whitbread, 1742–1992,* London: James and James, 1992, 144 p.

Saigol, Lina, "Whitbread Returns £1.1bn to Shareholders," *Financial Times,* March 21, 2001, p. 26.

Saigol, Lina, and John Thornhill, "Future Whitbread Butterfly Emerges from Its Chrysalis," *Financial Times,* October 20, 2000, p. 26.

Simms, Jane, "Doubting Thomas," *Director,* September 2001, pp. 60–64.

The Story of Whitbread's, 3rd ed., London: Whitbread, 1964, 54 p.

Walsh, Dominic, "Fewer Doubts About Thomas," *Leisure and Hospitality Business,* January 10, 2002, p. 8.

Warwick-Ching, Lucy, "Whitbread Set to Sell TGI Friday's Restaurants for £70.4m," *Financial Times,* January 18, 2007, p. 21.

Wiggins, Jenny, "Whitbread Sells Fitness Chain," *Financial Times,* June 4, 2007, p. 20.

Willman, John, "All Eyes Focus on Whitbread's Plans to Rebuild Its Life," *Financial Times,* October 22, 1999, p. 28.

Yates, Andrew, "They're Not Only Here for the Beer," *Independent* (London), May 19, 1999, p. BR3.

Wilton Products, Inc.

2240 West 75th Street
Woodridge, Illinois 60517
U.S.A.
Telephone: (630) 963-1818
Toll Free: (800) 794-5866
Fax: (630) 963-7196
Web site: http://www.wilton.com

Private Company
Incorporated: 1954 as Wilton Enterprises
Employees: 670
Sales: $325 million (2005 est.)
NAICS: 423990 Other Miscellaneous Durable Goods Merchant Wholesalers

■ ■ ■

Wilton Products, Inc., is a private company based in the Chicago suburb of Woodridge, Illinois, comprised of four primary subsidiaries. The flagship unit is Wilton Enterprises, which carries on the tradition that made the Wilton name synonymous with cake decorating. Although the company continues to run The Wilton School of Cake Decorating, the focus is now on consumer products: Performance Pans bakeware, including novelty shapes; Candy Melts confectionery coating and other toppings and molded candy; dessert stands sold under the Cupcakes 'N More brand; wedding cake accessories and other wedding and bridal shower accessories; and baby shower accessories. Wilton also sells books and videos on cake decorating and baking (including the popular *Wilton Yearbook,* containing hundreds of decorating ideas, recipes, and product listings); cookie cutters, presses, and pans; candy-making tools, molds, and ingredients; and party goods, including a wide variety of birthday candles and theme party items. Many of the birthday theme products are licensed properties, such as Care Bears, Sesame Street, SpongeBob SquarePants, Spiderman, Scooby-Doo, NASCAR, Strawberry Shortcake, and several Disney characters. Wilton's Copco division offers designer tea kettles and upscale kitchenware, while the Weston Gallery division offers a wide selection of upscale picture frames.

The second major subsidiary of Wilton Products is Carlstadt, New Jersey-based EK Success LTD, involved in the popular scrapbooking supply sector as well as other paper crafts, offering albums, paper, stickers, stamps, adhesives, punches, tools, and other related products. Also participating in the scrapbooking market is another Wilton subsidiary, Kansas City, Missouri-based K & Company, LLC. Finally, Dimensions Holdings LLC is a Reading, Pennsylvania-based crafts company, involved in such categories as cross-stitching, crewel, needlepoint, and fabric crafts. Wilton Products is owned by the Chicago private equity firm GTCR Golder Rauner, LLC.

DEPRESSION-ERA ORIGINS

The man behind the founding of Wilton was Dewey McKinley Wilton, his name a tribute to the heroes of the Spanish-American War of 1898. Having worked in a candy factory while growing up in Chicago, Wilton first learned the craft of pulled sugar, knowledge that he then shared with French and German pastry chefs, who in

COMPANY PERSPECTIVES

Wilton Products, Inc., a family of four distinct companies with one vision—to be the industry leader in celebration, crafts and specialty housewares, where great people deliver innovative products and exceptional customer service.

turn taught him the art of cake decorating. He then combined candymaking with European cake decorating techniques to develop his own unique approach. He worked in Chicago hotel bakeries and began producing specialty cakes for area caterers. In 1929 he started the Wilton Company by opening a cake decorating and candymaking school, with classes initially conducted in the dining room of his home. His students, bakers and chefs, each paid $25 a lesson.

With a growing reputation, Wilton began taking his classes on the road in 1933, touring the United States and conducting one-day classes with groups of five students, who were generally professional chefs or bakers. It was not until 1946 that Wilton began advertising, placing his first notice in *Bakers Helper* magazine for classes conducted at his home. As a result, seven students enrolled for a two-week course at a cost of $150. Demand for the course outgrew Wilton's home and soon he began operating out of a lodge hall, but it too proved inadequate, prompting Wilton to move into a 6,000-square-foot location that could accommodate 18 students. With the availability of funding for schooling from the GI Bill of Rights, many former servicemen were eager to enroll in Wilton's school to become professional bakers and candymakers. Enrollment swelled to as many as 50, with Wilton teaching in both Chicago and around the country in baker supply houses.

POSTWAR PUBLISHING EFFORTS

Wilton also trained his children, including Norman, Martha, and Wesley, in the art of cake decorating, and they too became instructors. When enrollment fell off at the start of the 1950s, the Wilton family used their expertise to establish a bridal cake shop. The Wiltons also began work on a cake decorating book. When no major publisher was willing to take a chance on the book, the family opted in 1953 to self-publish *Modern Cake Decorating: Pulled Sugar and Candy Making,* credited to McKinley Wilton and Norman Wilton. A year later they coauthored and self-published *The Homemaker's Pictorial Encyclopedia of Modern Cake Decorating,* which in its first printing sold an impressive 10,000 copies and over the course of its life netted 500,000 copies, a major publishing success by any standard.

The books spurred interest in cake decorating in the general public, but it proved difficult for enthusiasts of the "Wilton Method" to find decorating supply vendors that catered to the public. Hence, to make available the decorating bags, paste colors, parchment paper, and turntables required to turn out stylized cakes, the Wiltons launched a mail-order business in 1959. It was so popular that it moved from the basement of the Wiltons' home to a 12,000-square-foot facility. The family also expanded beyond distribution and became a manufacturer with its first product, the Tuk-N-Ruffle, which laid a ruffling around the base of a cake. By 1962 Wilton products became available in retail stores as well.

The Wiltons also continued to publish books in the 1960s. *Wilton's Wonderland of Cake Decorating* was issued in 1960, co-published with Bailey & Swinfen. Further editions of the encyclopedia were also offered, as well as a $1 cake decorating book published in 1964 to stimulate business and *Cake and Food Decorating Ideas,* released in 1967, followed two years later by *Your Personal Guide to Cake and Food Decorating Ideas.* The *Wilton Yearbook* made its debut in 1970. After being published every other year, it became an annual product starting in 1976.

DEATH OF FOUNDER: 1965

In April 1965 Dewey McKinley Wilton died at the age of 66 in Scottsdale, Arizona. The Wiltons continued to own the business until 1973 when it was sold to Pillsbury Company, although some of the Wiltons remained involved, continuing to teach the techniques developed by the founder. In 1977 Vincent A. Naccarato became president of the Wilton Enterprises Inc. Pillsbury division. He had joined Wilton in 1969 and would play a key role in the history of the company. It was also in 1977 that Wilton moved its headquarters to Woodridge, Illinois.

As part of a corporate giant like Pillsbury, Wilton was placed in a dominant position in the cake-decorating field. The company was able to advertise its wares on Pillsbury cake mixes and flours, and take advantage of Pillsbury's marketing might to distribute press kits at major baking contests and offer decorating demonstrations and baking classes at department stores. Not everyone was happy with the arrangements, however. Los Angeles-based Parrish's Cake Decorating Supplies Inc. sued Pillsbury and Wilton, charging

KEY DATES

1929: Dewey McKinley Wilton founds company by giving cake decorating lessons.
1946: Company begins advertising.
1953: Wilton publishes first book.
1959: Wilton launches mail-order business.
1965: McKinley Wilton dies.
1973: Pillsbury Company acquires Wilton Enterprises.
1981: Management team acquires Wilton in leveraged buyout.
1984: Company is taken public.
1988: Wilton returns to private status.
1991: Rowoco is acquired.
2007: GTCR Golder Rauner, LLC, acquires Wilton, merges it with other assets.

antitrust conduct. In May 1981 Parrish won and received a $5.5 million judgment. A few months later Pillsbury sold Wilton Enterprises to a group of investors led by Naccarato in a $21 million leveraged buyout.

Naccarato looked to expand Wilton in the houseware category in 1984 through the acquisition of Copco, maker of teakettles and cast-iron cookware founded in 1960. He then took Wilton public in January 1984, making an initial public offering (IPO) of stock priced at $10 a share. Business quickly took a turn for the worse, however, leading to problems for both Wilton and Naccarato. Some of the reasons for a decline in revenues were cultural: Americans were too busy to bake cakes and pies from scratch, relying increasingly on prepackaged products. In addition, there were growing health concerns over baked goods in general, as consumers became more aware of cholesterol levels and also looked to lose weight. As revenues fell, some buyers of Wilton stock were not pleased with this performance and in December 1985 a group of shareholders filed a $13 million class-action lawsuit, contending that Wilton had misled them by reporting incorrect financial information prior to the IPO.

Naccarato fell out of favor with the Wilton board of directors, and a week after the company reported a loss of $2.64 million on revenues of $47.94 million (a 6 percent decline over the prior year), Naccarato was ousted, although his departure was portrayed as a resignation to "pursue other interests." He was replaced as chief executive officer by Chairman William G. Hendrickson until Douglas E. Pease, a former Sara Lee Corp. executive, was named the permanent replacement, along with James Bentz, a General Mills Inc. executive, who took over as president. "Permanent" was a relative term, however. Naccarato retained a significant stake in the company and less than a year later he returned to the helm. Pease and Bentz had cut about one-third of Wilton's 2,500 products, but sales continued to slide, totaling $44.5 million in fiscal 1986 and resulting in a further loss of $1.4 million. The shareholder suit continued to weigh on Wilton as did a $10 million revolving credit agreement in which the company lapsed into violation. The company was forced to be put on the block, easing the way for Naccarato to return. In August 1986, following another boardroom showdown, Pease and Bentz resigned and Naccarato was named vice-chairman and CEO. In addition, a new financing agreement was put in place to restore Wilton's creditworthiness, and a settlement was soon reached in the class-action lawsuit, Wilton agreeing to pay the plaintiffs $1.3 million.

Naccarato brought in some new executive talent and began to quickly return Wilton to profitability, although the company remained up for sale until late 1987. To generate more revenue the company turned to the retail bakery business, opening Cake & Party Works Shop in Arlington Heights, Illinois, followed by a store in Woodridge. Because of Wilton's problems, the price of its stock did not reflect its rebound, prompting Naccarato and some of his senior executives to make a bid to again take the company private. The initial offer was $6 a share, an improvement over the $4 a share level the stock was trading at, but the $24 million total offer did not win over the board of directors. The bid was then improved to $7.38 a share, or $29 million, and accepted in October 1988.

LAUNCH OF WESTON GALLERY: 1988

As a private company once again, Wilton continued to pursue expansion. In 1988 Weston Gallery was formed to design, manufacture, and distribute a line of picture frames, and in October 1989 Wilton acquired a half-interest in Let Them Eat Cake, Inc., a Chicago-based retail baker. A year later Wilton Enterprises was renamed Wilton Industries, Inc., which included three divisions: Wilton Enterprises, Copco, and Weston Gallery. In 1991 a fourth division was formed with the acquisition of Rowoco, maker of kitchen gadgets. The Wilton subsidiaries operated independently, responsible for their own product development, manufacturing, sales, marketing, and other operations; the goal was to allow the divisions to better respond to their particular markets. Areas such as accounting, billing, and credit were handled at the corporate level, an arrangement which proved beneficial because customers could more easily do business with any of the four divisions. A further acquisition was completed in 1996 when Wilton added a Canadian bakery distributor, establishing a platform for a Canadian operation.

Home baking continued to experience sluggish growth in the 1990s, as the pace of family life remained hectic, leaving little time for cooking, let alone baking. In the bakeware category, companies looked to market higher-profit products, such as hard-anodized bakeware and specialty shapes. In keeping with this trend Wilton introduced the Wonderform line of specialty shape pans. The company was also able to deal with poor business conditions through the diversity provided by its four divisions.

While the bakeware market continued to erode in the twenty-first century, Wilton's overall business was strong enough that a new state-of-the-art 441,000-square-foot distribution center was opened in Romeoville, Illinois, in April 2002. The demand for cake decoration instruction also remained solid within a certain market, and Wilton continued to leverage and build its name in this area in 2006 with the launch of a Public Television show, *Bake Decorate Celebrate!*, featuring baking and decorating tips.

SALE OF COMPANY: 2007

In fiscal 2005 Wilton generated sales of $325 million, according to industry estimates. Naccarato decided the time had come to sell Wilton, and in August 2007, private equity firm GTCR Golder Rauner, LLC, acquired the business. Several months earlier GTCR had acquired scrapbooking company EK Success; GTCR also owned scrapbooking firm K & Company. At the same time it bought Wilton, GTCR also added Dimensions Holdings LLC, a hobby products manufacturer. Wilton, EK Success, Dimensions, and K & Company were then merged together under Wilton Products, Inc. CEO Steven Fraser was chosen to lead the enterprise.

Ed Dinger

PRINCIPAL SUBSIDIARIES

Wilton Enterprises; EK Success LTD; K & Company, LLC; Dimensions Holdings LLC.

PRINCIPAL COMPETITORS

Lifetime Brands, Inc.; Mrs. Grossman's Paper Company Inc.; Newell Rubbermaid Inc.; The Pampered Chef, Ltd.

FURTHER READING

Chavez, Donna, "Learning Is Just Frosting on the Cake," *Chicago Tribune,* June 9, 1991, p. 1.

"Equity Firm Acquires Wilton Industries," *Naperville Sun,* August 2, 2007, p. 17.

"McKinley Wilton," *Chicago Tribune,* April 10, 1962, p. A14.

Murphy, H. Lee, "Revived Wilton Cooks Up Growth," *Crain's Chicago Business,* December 21, 1987, p. 14.

———, "Wilton Execs Offer $24-Million LBO," *Crain's Chicago Business,* July 11, 1988, p. 4.

———, "Wilton's Rocky Public Life Set to End in LBO," *Crain's Chicago Business,* October 3, 1988, p. 63.

Paul, Cynthia A., "Wilton's Family; 4 Distinctive Siblings," *HFN—The Weekly Newspaper for the Home Furnishing Network,* January 16, 1995, p. 106.

Snyder, David, "Facing Impatient Lenders, Wilton Posts 'For Sale' Sign," *Crain's Chicago Business,* April 14, 1986, p. 86.

Taylor, Susan, "Wilton Products Celebrates 80th Anniversary," *Chicago Tribune,* May 14, 2008.

Worldwide Pants Inc.

1697 Broadway, Suite 805
New York, New York 10019
U.S.A.
Telephone: (212) 975-5300
Fax: (212) 975-4780
Web site: http://www.cbs.com/latenight/lateshow

Private Company
Incorporated: 1993
Employees: 70
Sales: $15 million (2008 est.)
NAICS: 711510 Independent Artists, Writers, and Performers; 512110 Motion Picture and Video Production

■ ■ ■

Worldwide Pants Inc. is the corporate entity responsible for Stupid Pet and Human Tricks and virtually all other creative, production, and marketing aspects of the *Late Show with David Letterman,* the after-primetime home of funnyman David Letterman. Letterman created his own production company, Worldwide Pants Inc., in 1993 after he joined CBS (Columbia Broadcasting Company). Letterman serves as Worldwide's chairman and chief source of inspiration, although the daily operations are overseen by Rob Burnett, who joined Letterman's writing team in 1988. In addition to producing the high profile *Late Show,* Worldwide has brought several award-winning series to television, including *Everybody Loves Raymond, Ed,* and the *Late Late Show.* When Letterman signed a new contract in 2006 to stay at CBS for five more years, Worldwide's success and longevity were ensured at least through the end of 2010.

EARLY YEARS: 1960–82

Without David Letterman, there would be no Worldwide Pants, Inc. Letterman was born in Indianapolis, Indiana, to Harry, a florist, and Dorothy, a homemaker. Dave was the middle of three children (one older sister, one younger) in a solidly middle-class neighborhood near the famed Indianapolis Speedway. His father was a funny, hardworking man who began having health problems when Dave was a boy. Harry Letterman's first heart attack was at age 36; a second fatal attack occurred in 1973. Dave was devastated by his death and later found a father figure in the legendary Johnny Carson.

Letterman attended Broad Ripple High School, graduated, and headed to Ball State University in Muncie, Indiana. He graduated with a degree in radio and television in 1969, and had stints on Ball State's student-run WBST and WAGO. He also worked at Indianapolis radio stations where his often irreverent behavior gained the ire of his supervisors. Letterman moved to Los Angeles in 1975, hoping to be a comedy writer. He managed to write bits for a few sitcoms and began doing standup at the now well-known Comedy Store. In 1977 Letterman scored an appearance on the *Starland Vocal Band's* short-lived variety show, then appeared on Mary Tyler Moore's CBS variety series, *Mary,* in 1978. Although he was not heralded as the next big thing, Letterman held his own and a few months later appeared on *The Tonight Show.* Johnny Carson, the top-

KEY DATES

1969: David Letterman graduates from Ball State University with a degree in radio and television.

1975: Letterman moves to Los Angeles, begins doing standup comedy.

1977: Letterman makes his first television appearance on the *Starland Vocal Band*'s variety show.

1978: Letterman appears on *The Tonight Show* for the first time.

1980: *The David Letterman Show* debuts on NBC as a morning comedy-variety show.

1982: *Late Night with David Letterman* debuts on NBC.

1985: Letterman introduces the "Top 10 List" on *Late Night.*

1991: Jay Leno is selected to succeed *Tonight Show*'s retiring Johnny Carson.

1993: Worldwide Pants Inc. is formed as Letterman's production company and the *Late Show with David Letterman* debuts on CBS.

1995: Worldwide begins producing the *Late Late Show* with Tom Snyder as host.

1996: *Everybody Loves Raymond,* starring Ray Romano, becomes a huge hit for Worldwide and CBS.

2000: Worldwide-produced *Ed,* a comedy-drama starring Tom Cavanaugh, premieres on NBC.

2002: A network bidding war erupts as Letterman's contract with CBS nears its end.

2005: Worldwide Pants produces its first feature film, *Strangers with Candy,* starring Amy Sedaris.

2006: Letterman re-signs with CBS to host *Late Show* until 2010.

2007: Worldwide Pants negotiates its own contract with the striking Writers Guild of America, bringing the show back on the air.

2008: The *Late Show with David Letterman* celebrates 15 years of success on CBS.

rated show's host, liked Letterman and booked the up-and-comer for frequent appearances over the next decade.

By 1980 Letterman had parlayed his comedic skills into hosting his own morning comedy-variety show for NBC. Although *The David Letterman Show* lasted only a few months, it nonetheless introduced the gawky comedian to the Academy of Television Arts and Sciences, which awarded Letterman his first Emmy. Letterman soon began working on a late-night variety show for NBC appropriately named *Late Night with David Letterman.* The new show was slated to run after Carson's *Tonight Show,* a time slot often considered the wasteland of TV viewing, since most viewers hit the sack after Carson. Letterman was not worried, late-late night was fertile ground for his zany, skewed sense of humor. *Late Night with David Letterman* debuted in February 1982 and ushered in a new era of irreverent talk show antics. Much like the network's *Saturday Night Live,* Letterman attracted a far younger audience than Carson and other late night programming.

LETTERMAN CONQUERS THE UNIVERSE: 1983–92

For the next decade, *Late Night* enjoyed success and became a cultural phenomenon. Letterman was always innovative and creative, sometimes absurd, sometimes acerbic, but perennially funny. As *Late Night*'s ratings climbed, Letterman garnered respect and clout in the entertainment industry. He had a knack for taking seemingly ordinary folks, like Calvert DeForest, who became Larry "Bud" Melman and performed goofy stunts on the show and outside it, in venues across the nation. The immensely funny Top 10 Lists debuted in 1985 and the caliber of Letterman's guests climbed to include award-winning entertainers, newsmakers, sports stars, politicians, and "normal" people who had gained attention or notoriety.

Year after year, Letterman's antics were honored with numerous Emmy nominations and several wins. A practice that served Letterman and his show well was hiring interns. One in particular, Rob Burnett, came on board in 1986 as a writer and would play a pivotal role in Letterman's *Late Night* success, as well as future endeavors. As *Late Night*'s popularity grew, Letterman still returned to *The Tonight Show* to crack jokes with his mentor, Johnny Carson. He also guest-hosted and many believed Letterman would be Carson's successor when the King of Late Night retired. Unfortunately, NBC's network brass wanted to own the entire evening with comedian Jay Leno in Johnny's seat and Letterman continuing to dominate the 12:30 A.M. Eastern time slot. Letterman, however, saw himself as heir apparent to Johnny's throne and wanted to exit the late-late night time slot. Although he never stated it publicly, Carson reportedly considered Letterman his successor as well.

In the end NBC executives chose Leno over Letterman, believing Leno appealed to a wider audience, including the older, more sophisticated viewers who had watched Johnny Carson for decades. Letterman was caustic, edgy, and too unpredictable for Carson's longtime fans. Leno was a kinder, gentler version of Letterman; to NBC it was a no-brainer: Leno at 11:30 P.M. and Letterman at 12:30 A.M.

When the line-up was formally announced in 1991, Letterman made no secret of his feelings: once his contract with NBC expired, he would leave the network. Despite his anger over the *Tonight Show* imbroglio, all was not gloom and doom. In 1992 Letterman was honored with the prestigious George Foster Peabody Award for taking one of television's most conventional formats and "infusing it with freshness and imagination."

SOUR GRAPES AND BRIGHT SUNSHINE: 1993–99

Letterman may have lamented NBC's decision, but his cloud truly had a silver lining. Once it was known Letterman planned to leave NBC, both CBS and ABC offered the comedian his own show opposite Leno and *The Tonight Show.* The wrangling soon began with NBC trying to hold on, barring him from negotiating with other sources. In the end, Letterman agreed to extend his contract through the end of June 1993 and NBC would allow him to look into "opportunities" elsewhere without crying foul.

Despite a lucrative offer from ABC, Letterman accepted CBS's offer of $16 million a year and the 11:30 P.M. time slot. With his decision came the founding of his own production company, Worldwide Pants, Inc. Not only would Letterman be in the driver's seat as host of his new show, but his company would own and produce it, charging CBS a licensing fee to broadcast it.

On August 30, 1993, the *Late Show with David Letterman* premiered on CBS and clobbered Leno in the ratings. The show routinely beat *The Tonight Show* for more than a year, but then lost its lead by its second full year on the air. Yet despite lower Nielsen ratings, the *Late Show with David Letterman* consistently ranked higher in polls, People's Choice awards, and Emmy nominations. The *Late Show* won the Emmy for Outstanding Variety, Music or Comedy show in 1994, which turned out to be the first of many. The year had also marked one of Letterman's most inspired stunts: sending his mother, Dorothy, to Lillehammer, Norway, to cover the Olympics.

As the *Late Show* found its audience and won awards, Worldwide Pants branched out. The production company's first non-Letterman show was a new sitcom starring Letterman's friend Bonnie Hunt. *The Building* premiered in 1993, but did not fare well and was canceled. Worldwide and Hunt teamed up again for 1995's *The Bonnie Hunt Show* (later renamed *Bonnie*), and it too failed to find sufficient audience. In addition to primetime offerings, Worldwide also tackled the time slot following *Late Show* by producing the *Late Late Show.* The talk fest's first host was Tom Snyder, former host of *Tomorrow* on NBC, the time slot Letterman took with *Late Night* in 1982. Letterman was a fan of Snyder and happy to bring him back to late night in 1995.

Worldwide's next project, backing a new CBS comedy called *Everybody Loves Raymond,* would put the company and Rob Burnett, *Late Show*'s executive producer and Worldwide's president, firmly on the map. Starring comedian Ray Romano, the show debuted in September 1996 and became a huge hit. Letterman, Burnett, and Worldwide's staff continued to look for programming with the same potential as *Raymond.* They created a comedy/drama ("dramedy") called *Ed* in 1998, but CBS passed on the show. The next year, 1999, found the Worldwide-produced *Late Late Show* without a host with the imminent departure of Snyder. He was replaced with Craig Kilborn of Comedy Central's comedy-news *The Daily Show,* who brought a fresh approach and hipper attitude to the late-late night program.

EVERYTHING OLD BECOMES NEW AGAIN: 2000–07

The new millennium brought Worldwide Pants and its chairman new highs and lows. In January Letterman underwent quintuple bypass surgery, taking the host away from his show for an extended period. *Late Show,* however, suffered little during his absence. Reruns were introduced by a host of friends, celebrities, and comedians including favorites Drew Barrymore, Steve Martin, Regis Philbin, Julia Roberts, Ray Romano, and Robin Williams; next came actual guest hosts including Bill Cosby and Janeane Garofalo. When Letterman returned in February, he trounced Leno in the ratings.

While the host was getting back to his regular routine, Worldwide Pants had not slowed down. Executive Producer and CEO Rob Burnett backed several new shows, including *Welcome to New York,* a short-lived comedy starring Christine Baranski and Jim Gaffigan, and found a home for *Ed* starring Tom Cavanaugh. The latter enjoyed cult status until 2004 but was a milestone for Letterman as it marked his return to working with NBC after their "spat" years before. During *Ed*'s successful run, Letterman and Worldwide were in talks with CBS to sign a new contract; the deal was sealed with a new $150 million contract to stay on the air until 2007. The *Late Late Show* underwent its own shakeup when Craig Kilborn stepped down and was replaced by Craig Ferguson (of the *Drew Carey Show*) in January 2005. Soon after, Johnny Carson, who had reportedly been writing jokes for Letterman to do on-air, died of emphysema. Letterman dedicated an entire episode to Johnny Carson and his jokes; it was a somber yet fitting tribute.

The year 2005 also marked Worldwide's segue into major feature films with a prequel to Comedy Central's popular *Strangers with Candy* series. Worldwide premiered the film at Cannes and sold the rights to Warner International for $3 million. Starring Amy Sedaris, the film became mired in legal issues and was finally released in 2006. Sedaris had been a longtime favorite of Letterman and a recurring *Late Show* guest.

Worldwide produced another quirky comedy series, *The Knights of Prosperity,* in 2007 starring Donal Logue of *Grounded for Life* fame. The premise, about a group of burglars who planned to rob a celebrity, was unusual but had a strong cast. Unfortunately, the show did not attract a significant audience and the Writers Guild of America (WGA) strike hit TV land. Although Letterman continued to pay his writers at the beginning of the strike, it was soon apparent the walkout could be long-term. Worldwide Pants scored a major coup in December 2007 by negotiating its own contract, allowing writers for both the *Late Show* and *Late Late Show* to return to work while others languished. Letterman celebrated his 25th year of late-night comedy in 2007 with few signs of slowing down. He and Worldwide Pants had signed a new contract with CBS to keep *Late Show* on the air until 2010, and the company continued to develop shows for television while exploring feature film properties. Throughout the formation and continued success of Worldwide Pants, David Letterman had unequivocally demonstrated he was far more than just a late-night funnyman. He had proven himself a shrewd businessman and powerful creative force within the entertainment industry; his enormous staying power seemed to suggest that he would rank among the few celebrities to dictate when and how his long run in the spotlight would end.

Nelson Rhodes

PRINCIPAL COMPETITORS

Carsey-Warner LLC; Sony Pictures Television; Warner Bros. Television Production.

FURTHER READING

Adalian, Josef, "Dave Still the Eye's Guy: Letterman Reups with CBS in 5-Year, $150-Million Deal," *Daily Variety,* March 12, 2002, p. 1.

———, "Letterman Sweet on *Candy* Pic," *Daily Variety,* July 13, 2004, p. 1.

Andreeva, Nellie, "WGA May Okay *Letterman* Return," *ADWEEK Online,* December 16, 2007.

Bernstein, Paula, "Letterman Late Rates Top Leno's," *Variety,* March 6, 2000, p. 56.

Coe, Steve, "Clearances Are the Big Issue As CBS Tries to Get Letterman into the Eye," *Broadcasting,* December 14, 1992, p. 11.

———, "Letterman Jumps to CBS," *Broadcasting,* January 18, 1993, p. 4.

Freeman, Mike, "NBC's Late-Night Lament: Leno or Letterman," *Broadcasting,* January 4, 1993, p. 26.

Kafka, Peter, "The Producer," *Forbes,* July 8, 2002, p. 136.

Mandese, Joe, "Letterman Bolting, and Dominos Falling," *Advertising Age,* August 31, 1992, p. 1.

McClellan, Steve, "Letterman Adds Latest Late-Night Wrinkle," *Broadcasting,* December 14, 1992, p. 35.

———, "Letterman's Rapid Recovery," *Broadcasting & Cable,* February 7, 2000, p. 72.

McGowan, William G., "Selling Out with a Smirk," *Washington Monthly,* March 1986, pp. 38.

Sachs, Andrea, "*Late Night with David Letterman* Book of Top Ten Lists," *Time,* October 8, 1990, p. 18.

Salter, Chuck, "Who Ever Said Comedy Had to Be Fun?" *Fast Company,* May 2003, p. 96.

Schumuckler, Eric, "A Snyder Side of Letterman," *MediaWeek,* April 18, 1994, p. 3.

Song, Sora, "Tonight on Letterman: H-E-E-E-E-E-E-R-E's JOHNNY," *Time,* January 31, 2005, p. 77.

Zoglin, Richard, "He's No Johnny Carson," *Time,* February 6, 1989, p. 66.

———, "Politics, Late-Night Style," *Time,* June 12, 1989, p. 66.

Xantrex Technology Inc.

8999 Nelson Way
Burnaby, British Columbia V5A 4B5
Canada
Telephone: (604) 422-8595
Fax: (604) 420-1591
Web site: http://www.xantrex.com

Public Company
Incorporated: 1983
Employees: 739
Sales: $234.23 million (2007)
Stock Exchanges: Toronto
Ticker Symbol: XTX
NAICS: 334419 Other Electronic Component Manufacturing

■ ■ ■

Xantrex Technology Inc. designs and manufactures advanced power electronic products that convert raw electrical energy into usable power. The company's products are able to convert power from a number of sources, such as solar photovoltaic panels, wind turbines, batteries, or directly from the electricity grid, producing the type of high-quality power demanded by most electronic and electrical appliances and devices. Xantrex's systems also monitor, manage, and control the flow of electricity. Ranging from handheld to luggage-sized systems, the company's products are integrated with equipment made by other manufacturers or used as stand-alone systems to provide independent power solutions. Xantrex maintains facilities in Vancouver, British Columbia; Arlington, Washington; Livermore, California; Elkhart, Indiana; Barcelona, Spain; and Reading, England.

ORIGINS

Xantrex's prominence in the marketplace took years to develop. The company, a global leader in advanced power electronics in the early 21st century, labored in relative anonymity during its first phase of development. The years, a roughly 15-year span stretching from 1983 to the late 1990s, were spent honing its skills, searching for its identity, and waiting for the maturation of the technology that would underpin its competitive strength in the global marketplace.

The company initially developed power electronic equipment to serve the test and measurement market, a pursuit that led it to acquire technically advanced skills it would put to use serving industrial, commercial, and consumer customers, not the industrial customers it served exclusively during the 1980s. The turning point in the company's market orientation occurred in 1998, by which point the technology involved in a key component of its devices had evolved sufficiently to enable introduction into the mainstream market.

TECHNOLOGICAL ADVANCES

Xantrex, in its later guise, made products that functioned as the intelligent interface between power sources and end users for power levels less than one megawatt. The company's advanced technology converted raw electrical power into the high-quality, reli-

COMPANY PERSPECTIVES

Xantrex is a world leader in advanced power electronics, enabling delivery of electricity anytime anywhere.

able power demanded by most electronic and electrical equipment. The technology involved power semiconductor chips, compact and efficient high-frequency power switching circuits, and proprietary software. One of the principal attributes that distinguished Xantrex's power electronics products from traditional power conversion equipment was size. The company's systems were small and lightweight, possessing qualities that only could be achieved once technology had advanced beyond a certain point. Raw power was converted by passing it through power semiconductor switches within a converter, switches that were based on the same silicon chip technology as the integrated circuits in personal computers. Accordingly, the same technological leaps that made personal computers smaller and more powerful during the 1990s could be likened to the technological advances that enabled Xantrex's products to become smaller and more powerful, setting the stage for the company's transformation at the end of the decade.

Advanced power electronic converters such as those made by Xantrex used high-frequency power conversion. The semiconductor switches were operated at high switching frequencies, generally above 20,000 cycles per second. The high frequencies enabled the capacitors, transformers, and other electrical components in the power electronic converter to be much smaller than the components in converters based on low-frequency technology. The smaller components resulted in substantial gains in power density, which, in turn, enabled the development of compact power supply systems that were one-tenth the size and weight of systems using low-frequency technology.

NEW STRATEGY IN 1998

The capability to make small, efficient, and reliable power converters opened up a wealth of business opportunities Xantrex hoped to exploit. In 1998 the company directed its energies toward three segments of the advanced power electronics market: distributed power, programmable power, and mobile power.

The company's efforts in distributed power focused on designing and producing power electronics capable of converting power from sources such as solar, wind, fuel cells, microturbines, advanced batteries, and flywheels. Once converted, the electrical power was intended to be used as a primary or backup power source for homes and small businesses, as well as for industrial and utility applications. Xantrex's programmable power forays were related to its early efforts during the 1980s. The company developed and manufactured programmable power supplies tailored for industrial customers to use to test products during manufacturing processes and to help them develop electrical equipment for research-and-development activities. Xantrex's mobile power products essentially functioned as sophisticated generators, providing reliable sources of electrical power in instances when appliances and other electronic devices were disconnected from utility power. The company's inverter/chargers turned direct current (DC) into alternating current (AC), enabling built-in or external battery sources to provide the type of electrical current used to power equipment and devices found in the home, office, and in vehicles and boats.

Xantrex's revamped strategy fueled energetic financial growth for the first time in the company's history. During its first 15 years of existence, the company never reached the $10-million-in-sales mark in a single year. During the next ten years, as the company focused on the distributed power, programmable power, and mobile power market segments, annual revenues leaped from $10 million to $234 million.

UMEDALY JOINS XANTREX IN 1999

Presiding over the exponential increase in revenues was Mossadiq S. Umedaly, who was appointed chief executive officer and chairman in 1999. Umedaly earned undergraduate and graduate degrees in business administration from McMaster University in Hamilton, Ontario. After earning his degrees, he spent five years working for the accounting firm Pricewaterhouse. Next, he joined the Aga Khan Development Network, holding a number of senior-level positions that gave him considerable responsibility for planning, building, commissioning, and managing a $300 million medical university and teaching hospital in Karachi, Pakistan. Umedaly returned to Canada once his work in Pakistan was completed, joining a Burnaby, British Columbia-based company named Ballard Power Systems Inc. Ballard Power, Xantrex's neighbor and future partner, developed fuel-cell technology for use in vehicles. Umedaly served as Ballard Power's vice-president and chief financial officer from 1990 to 1998.

Umedaly orchestrated a series of acquisitions as he set out to implement Xantrex's plan of attack. The

KEY DATES

1983: Xantrex is founded.
1998: Company decides to concentrate on distributed power, programmable power, and mobile power products.
1999: Mossadiq S. Umedaly is appointed chairman and chief executive officer of Xantrex.
2000: Xantrex acquires Trace Holdings, LLC, Heart Interface Corp., and Cruising Equipment Co.
2004: Company completes its initial public offering of stock.
2005: John Wallace is named chief executive officer.
2007: Xantrex acquires Elgar Electronics Corp.

acquisitions accelerated the company's development in its three areas of concentration, giving it recognized brand names with the stroke of a pen. In October 1999, Umedaly signed a purchase agreement for Statpower Technologies Corporation, a Burnaby-based manufacturer of DC-to-AC power inverters, smart microprocessor controlled battery chargers, and battery packs. He also succeeded in raising $35 million from investors during the year, roughly the same total he raised in 2000, when part of the funds went to pay for three acquisitions. Early in the year, Umedaly acquired Arlington, Washington-based Trace Holdings, LLC, and its two operating divisions, Trace Engineering and Trace Technologies, strengthening Xantrex's mobile power capabilities. Heart Interface Corporation was acquired during the year as well as Cruising Equipment Company. Both companies were based in Seattle, Washington, competing as major suppliers of power inverters and instrumentation tailored for the recreational vehicle and marine markets.

By the time Xantrex's acquisition spree was completed in April 2000, the company touted itself as the world's leading provider of advanced power electronics and controls. The company, with operations in British Columbia, Washington, and California, was marketing products under the Trace, Statpower, Heart, Cruising, and Xantrex brand names, serving commercial, consumer, recreational, and residential markets. Revenues, which reached $45 million at the end of 1999, jumped to $95 million by the end of 2000, ignited by the numerous applications for the company's power electronics technologies.

In 2000, Trace Engineering sponsored a meeting during the annual International Trucking Show in Las Vegas to promote using AC power instead of idling truck engines to run truckers' auxiliary devices. Tom Boyle, president of Boyle Transportation, became one of the first fleet owners to take advantage of AC infrastructure, purchasing 40 Freightliner Century Class S/T systems equipped with Xantrex's TRUCKPOWER inverter/chargers. The TRUCKPOWER inverter/chargers converted DC power to AC power, enabling a truck's batteries to be recharged while running all the AC and DC loads. "First and foremost," Boyle said in a November 2000 interview with *Fleet Equipment,* "it's for our drivers. Our newest trucks feature components that will make their life easier and safer on the road—AC power will allow them to cook in the trucks, plus have the comforts of home. Our driver turnover rate is near zero, and we'd like to keep it that way."

NEW PRODUCT INTRODUCTIONS IN 2001

In 2001, the company's presence in the mainstream consumer market was bolstered with the release of its "power-in-the box" systems. The xPower family of products included the xPower 300, the xPower 600, and the xPower 1500, which retailed for $149.95, $249.95, and $379.95, respectively. The products were compact systems that provided unplugged electricity, converting power obtained from batteries into a source of household power that could be used to power tools, refrigerators, lights, fans, television sets, computers, and other appliances. The systems, ranging in size from the handheld xPower 300 to the luggage-sized xPower 1500, were promoted as a cleaner and quieter alternative to generators.

"When the power goes out," Umedaly said in an August 10, 2001, interview with *Canadian Corporate News,* "people worry about becoming disconnected with the outside world. They feel the need to stay connected by being able to power communications equipment like phones, televisions, and computers. People also worry," he continued, "about food and medication spoiling in the fridge, safety and security without lights, or lost productivity if they have a home office or small business. Our xPower 1500 is an ideal short-term source of electricity to help people overcome these types of inconveniences during a blackout."

Strategic alliances, leadership changes, and a public debut highlighted Xantrex's progress as it neared its 25th anniversary. In mid-2003, the company collaborated with Umedaly's former employer, Ballard Power, to demonstrate a fuel-cell-based auxiliary power unit (APU) to be used in commercial trucking. "It shows the potential for generating low-noise, low-emission, on-board electrical power to meet all the needs of a long-haul trucker," a Xantrex executive said in a May 1, 2003, interview with *Modern Bulk Transporter.* The APU, using an electrical management system built by Xantrex, created power by extracting hydrogen from a methanol fuel source and converting it into electricity.

Roughly a year later, Xantrex formed an alliance with Sacramento, California-based Atlantis Energy Systems that opened up a promising revenue stream. Atlantis made Sunslates, a photovoltaic, fiber-cement roofing product, while Xantrex made solar grid tie converters that turned the energy collected by Sunslates into utility-grade, AC electricity. The two companies began offering their products as a single package, which made it easier and more affordable for homebuilders to install solar power systems.

XANTREX GOES PUBLIC, ACQUIRES ELGAR ELECTRONICS

Xantrex completed its initial public offering (IPO) of stock in 2004, a CAD 67 million offering that marked the company's debut on the Toronto Stock Exchange. With the proceeds from the IPO, the company pressed ahead with its three-pronged attack, recording steady increases in its business volume. In 2005, Umedaly appointed a new chief executive officer, John Wallace, who had spent more than a decade working on alternative fuel vehicles for Ford Motor Company.

Umedaly, who continued to serve as chairman, and Wallace completed two important deals on the eve of Xantrex's 25th anniversary. In early 2007, the pair strengthened the company's programmable power business by agreeing to acquire Elgar Electronics Corporation for $108 million. Based in San Diego, California, Elgar ranked as a leading manufacturer of programmable power products, boasting the most extensive product portfolio in the industry. "The acquisition of Elgar is a strategically compelling transaction for Xantrex," Umedaly explained in a January 29, 2007, interview with *CNW Group.* "Elgar is highly complementary to Xantrex's portfolio of businesses and growth strategies," he added. The acquisition, which added Elgar's nearly $65 million in revenue, was completed in March, the same month Umedaly and Wallace signed a joint-venture agreement with Shanghai Power Transmission & Distribution Co., Ltd. The agreement called for Xantrex to design and to produce solar and wind power electronics products for the renewable energy market in China. The company was slated to perform its work at a facility to be built in Shanghai. In the future, similar accords, as well as the company's independent efforts to expand, promised to deliver continued financial growth to Xantrex.

Jeffrey L. Covell

PRINCIPAL SUBSIDIARIES

Xantrex US; Xantrex International (Barbados).

PRINCIPAL COMPETITORS

Sharp Corporation; Siemens AG; Agilent Technologies, Inc.; Charles Industries, Ltd.

FURTHER READING

"Boyle Transportation Orders 40 Trucks Equipped with AC Power," *Fleet Equipment,* November 2000, p. 68.

"Fuel Cell APUs for Trucks," *Diesel Progress North American Edition,* May 2003, p. 8.

Maynard, Nigel F., "Power Play: New National Program Makes Solar Power Cheaper and Easier," *Builder,* April 2004, p. 44.

Rhodes, Nikki, "Partnership Generates Heat," *Professional Builder (1993),* March 2004, p. S10.

Wilhelm, Steve, "Solar Power Firm Gets $38.5 Million Infusion," *Puget Sound Business Journal,* July 13, 2001, p. 17.

"Xantrex and Shanghai Electric Sign Joint Venture Agreement for China Renewable Energy Market," *CNW Group,* March 15, 2007.

"Xantrex Announces Closing of Acquisition of Elgar Electronics," *CNW Group,* March 12, 2007.

"Xantrex Appoints John Wallace As Chief Executive Officer," *CNW Group,* November 1, 2005.

"Xantrex Expands Its Solar Technology to European Market," *Wireless News,* February 23, 2005.

"Xantrex Expands Solar Grid Tie Inverter Line in Europe," *CNW Group,* October 6, 2005.

"Xantrex xPower Products Provide Portable Household Electricity," *Canadian Corporate News,* August 10, 2001.

Cumulative Index to Companies

Listings in this index are arranged in alphabetical order under the company name. Company names beginning with a letter or proper name such as Eli Lilly & Co. will be found under the first letter of the company name. Definite articles (The, Le, La) are ignored for alphabetical purposes as are forms of incorporation that precede the company name (AB, NV). Company names printed in **bold** *type have full, historical essays on the page numbers appearing in bold. Updates to entries that appeared in earlier volumes are signified by the notation* **(upd.)**. *This index is cumulative with volume numbers printed in bold type.*

A

A&E Television Networks, 32 3–7
A&P *see* The Great Atlantic & Pacific Tea Company, Inc.
A & W Brands, Inc., 25 3–5 *see also* Cadbury Schweppes PLC.
A-dec, Inc., 53 3–5
A-Mark Financial Corporation, 71 3–6
A.B. Chance Industries Co., Inc. *see* Hubbell Inc.
A.B.Dick Company, 28 6–8
A.B. Watley Group Inc., 45 3–5
A.C. Moore Arts & Crafts, Inc., 30 3–5
A.C. Nielsen Company, 13 3–5 *see also* ACNielsen Corp.
A. Duda & Sons, Inc., 88 1–4
A. F. Blakemore & Son Ltd., 90 1–4
A.G. Edwards, Inc., 8 3–5; 32 17–21 (upd.)
A.H. Belo Corporation, 10 3–5; 30 13–17 (upd.)
A.L. Pharma Inc., 12 3–5 *see also* Alpharma Inc.
A.M. Castle & Co., 25 6–8
A. Moksel AG, 59 3–6
A. Nelson & Co. Ltd., 75 3–6
A. O. Smith Corporation, 11 3–6; 40 3–8 (upd.); 93 1–9 (upd.)
A.P. Møller - Maersk A/S, 57 3–6
A.S. Watson & Company Ltd., 84 1–4
A.S. Yakovlev Design Bureau, 15 3–6
A. Schulman, Inc., 8 6–8; 49 3–7 (upd.)
A.T. Cross Company, 17 3–5; 49 8–12 (upd.)
A.W. Faber-Castell Unternehmensverwaltung GmbH & Co., 51 3–6
AAF-McQuay Incorporated, 26 3–5
Aalborg Industries A/S, 90 5–8
AAON, Inc., 22 3–6
AAR Corp., 28 3–5
Aardman Animations Ltd., 61 3–5
Aarhus United A/S, 68 3–5
Aaron Brothers Holdings, Inc. *see* Michaels Stores, Inc.
Aaron Rents, Inc., 14 3–5; 35 3–6 (upd.)
AARP, 27 3–5
Aavid Thermal Technologies, Inc., 29 3–6
Abar Corporation *see* Ipsen International Inc.
Abaxis, Inc., 83 1-4
Abatix Corp., 57 7–9
ABB Asea Brown Boveri Ltd. *see* ABB Ltd.
ABB Ltd., II 1–4; 22 7–12 (upd.); 65 3–10 (upd.)
Abbey National plc, 10 6–8; 39 3–6 (upd.)
Abbott Laboratories, I 619–21; 11 7–9 (upd.); 40 9–13 (upd.); 93 10–18 (upd.)
ABC Appliance, Inc., 10 9–11
ABC Carpet & Home Co. Inc., 26 6–8
ABC Family Worldwide, Inc., 52 3–6
ABC, Inc. *see* Capital Cities/ABC Inc.
ABC Learning Centres Ltd., 93 19–22
ABC Rail Products Corporation, 18 3–5
ABC Stores *see* MNS, Ltd.
ABC Supply Co., Inc., 22 13–16
Abengoa S.A., 73 3–5
Abercrombie & Fitch Company, 15 7–9; 35 7–10 (upd.); 75 7–11 (upd.)
Abertis Infraestructuras, S.A., 65 11–13
ABF *see* Associated British Foods plc.
Abigail Adams National Bancorp, Inc., 23 3–5
Abiomed, Inc., 47 3–6
Abitibi-Consolidated, Inc., IV 245–47; 25 9–13 (upd.)
ABM Industries Incorporated, 25 14–16 (upd.)
ABN *see* Algemene Bank Nederland N.V.
ABN AMRO Holding, N.V., 50 3–7
Abrams Industries Inc., 23 6–8
Abraxas Petroleum Corporation, 89 1–5
Abril S.A., 95 1–4
Abt Associates Inc., 95 5–9
Abu Dhabi National Oil Company, IV 363–64; 45 6–9 (upd.)
Academic Press *see* Reed Elsevier plc.
Academy of Television Arts & Sciences, Inc., 55 3–5
Academy Sports & Outdoors, 27 6–8
Acadian Ambulance & Air Med Services, Inc., 39 7–10

Access Business Group *see* Alticor Inc.
ACCION International, 87 1–4
Acciona S.A., 81 1–4
Acclaim Entertainment Inc., 24 3–8
ACCO World Corporation, 7 3–5; 51 7–10 (upd.)
Accor S.A., 10 12–14; 27 9–12 (upd.); 69 3–8 (upd.)
Accredited Home Lenders Holding Co., 91 1–4
Accubuilt, Inc., 74 3–5
Accuray Incorporated, 95 10–13
AccuWeather, Inc., 73 6–8
ACE Cash Express, Inc., 33 3–6
Ace Hardware Corporation, 12 6–8; 35 11–14 (upd.)
Acer Incorporated, 16 3–6; 73 9–13 (upd.)
Acergy SA, 97 1–4
Aceros Fortuna S.A. de C.V. *see* Carpenter Technology Corp.
Aceto Corp., 38 3–5
AchieveGlobal Inc., 90 9–12
Acindar Industria Argentina de Aceros S.A., 87 5–8
Ackerley Communications, Inc., 9 3–5
Ackermans & van Haaren N.V., 97 5–8
ACLU *see* American Civil Liberties Union (ACLU).
Acme-Cleveland Corp., 13 6–8
Acme United Corporation, 70 3–6
ACNielsen Corporation, 38 6–9 (upd.)
Acorn Products, Inc., 55 6–9
Acosta Sales and Marketing Company,Inc., 77 1–4
ACS *see* Affiliated Computer Services, Inc.; Alaska Communications Systems Group, Inc.
Acsys, Inc., 44 3–5
Actelion Ltd., 83 5-8
Action Performance Companies, Inc., 27 13–15
Activision, Inc., 32 8–11; 89 6–11 (upd.)
Actuant Corporation, 94 1–8 (upd.)
Acuity Brands, Inc., 90 13–16
Acushnet Company, 64 3–5
Acuson Corporation, 10 15–17; 36 3–6 (upd.)
Acxiom Corporation, 35 15–18
Adam Opel AG, 7 6–8; 21 3–7 (upd.); 61 6–11 (upd.)
Adams Childrenswear Ltd., 95 14–19
The Adams Express Company, 86 1–5
Adams Golf, Inc., 37 3–5
Adams Media Corporation *see* F&W Publications, Inc.
Adani Enterprises Ltd., 97 9–12
Adaptec, Inc., 31 3–6
ADC Telecommunications, Inc., 10 18–21; 30 6–9 (upd.); 89 12–17 (upd.)
Adecco S.A., 36 7–11 (upd.)
Adelphia Communications Corporation, 17 6–8; 52 7–10 (upd.)
ADESA, Inc., 71 7–10
Adia S.A., 6 9–11 *see also* Adecco S.A.
adidas Group AG, 14 6–9; 33 7–11 (upd.); 75 12–17 (upd.)
Aditya Birla Group, 79 1–5
ADM *see* Archer Daniels Midland Co.
Administaff, Inc., 52 11–13
Administración Nacional de Combustibles, Alcohol y Pórtland, 93 23–27
Admiral Co. *see* Maytag Corp.
ADNOC *see* Abu Dhabi National Oil Co.
Adobe Systems Incorporated, 10 22–24; 33 12–16 (upd.)
Adolf Würth GmbH & Co. KG, 49 13–15
Adolfo Dominguez S.A., 72 3–5
Adolph Coors Company, I 236–38; 13 9–11 (upd.); 36 12–16 (upd.) *see also* Molson Coors Brewing Co.
Adolphe Lafont *see* Vivarte SA.
ADP *see* Automatic Data Processing, Inc.
ADT Security Services, Inc., 12 9–11; 44 6–9 (upd.)
Adtran Inc., 22 17–20
Advance Auto Parts, Inc., 57 10–12
Advance Publications Inc., IV 581–84; 19 3–7 (upd.); 96 1–7 (upd.)
Advanced Circuits Inc., 67 3–5
Advanced Fibre Communications, Inc., 63 3–5
Advanced Marketing Services, Inc., 34 3–6
Advanced Medical Optics, Inc., 79 6–9
Advanced Micro Devices, Inc., 6 215–17; 30 10–12 (upd.)
Advanced Neuromodulation Systems, Inc., 73 14–17
Advanced Technology Laboratories, Inc., 9 6–8
Advanced Web Technologies *see* Miner Group Int.
Advanstar Communications, Inc., 57 13–17
Advanta Corporation, 8 9–11; 38 10–14 (upd.)
Advantica Restaurant Group, Inc., 27 16–19 (upd.)
Adventist Health, 53 6–8
The Advertising Council, Inc., 76 3–6
The Advisory Board Company, 80 1–4 *see also* The Corporate Executive Board Co.
Advo, Inc., 6 12–14; 53 9–13 (upd.)
Advocat Inc., 46 3–5
AECOM Technology Corporation, 79 10–13
AEG A.G., I 409–11
Aegean Marine Petroleum Network Inc., 89 18–21
Aegek S.A., 64 6–8
Aegis Group plc, 6 15–16
AEGON N.V., III 177–79; 50 8–12 (upd.) *see also* Transamerica–An AEGON Company
AEI Music Network Inc., 35 19–21
AEON Co., Ltd., V 96–99; **68 6–10 (upd.)**
AEP *see* American Electric Power Co.
AEP Industries, Inc., 36 17–19
Aer Lingus Group plc, 34 7–10; 89 22–27 (upd.)
Aero Mayflower Transit Company *see* Mayflower Group Inc.
Aeroflot - Russian Airlines JSC, 6 57–59; 29 7–10 (upd.); 89 28–34 (upd.)
AeroGrow International, Inc., 95 20–23
Aerojet-General Corp., 63 6–9
Aerolíneas Argentinas S.A., 33 17–19; 69 9–12 (upd.)
Aeronca Inc., 46 6–8
Aéroports de Paris, 33 20–22
Aéropostale, Inc., 89 35–38
Aeroquip Corporation, 16 7–9 *see also* Eaton Corp.
Aerosonic Corporation, 69 13–15
The Aérospatiale Group, 7 9–12; 21 8–11 (upd.) *see also* European Aeronautic Defence and Space Company EADS N.V.
AeroVironment, Inc., 97 13–16
The AES Corporation, 10 25–27; 13 12–15 (upd.); 53 14–18 (upd.)
Aetna, Inc., III 180–82; 21 12–16 (upd.); 63 10–16 (upd.)
Aetna Insulated Wire *see* The Marmon Group, Inc.
AFC Enterprises, Inc., 32 12–16 (upd.); 83 9-15 (upd.)
Affiliated Computer Services, Inc., 61 12–16
Affiliated Foods Inc., 53 19–21
Affiliated Managers Group, Inc., 79 14–17
Affiliated Publications, Inc., 7 13–16
Affinity Group Holding Inc., 56 3–6
AFLAC Incorporated, 10 28–30 (upd.); 38 15–19 (upd.)
African Rainbow Minerals Ltd., 97 17–20
Africare, 59 7–10
After Hours Formalwear Inc., 60 3–5
Aftermarket Technology Corp., 83 16-19
AG Barr plc, 64 9–12
Ag-Chem Equipment Company, Inc., 17 9–11 *see also* AGCO Corp.
Ag Services of America, Inc., 59 11–13
Aga Foodservice Group PLC, 73 18–20
AGCO Corp., 13 16–18; 67 6–10 (upd.)
Agence France-Presse, 34 11–14
Agere Systems Inc., 61 17–19
Agfa Gevaert Group N.V., 59 14–16
Aggregate Industries plc, 36 20–22
Aggreko Plc, 45 10–13
Agilent Technologies Inc., 38 20–23; 93 28–32 (upd.)
Agilysys Inc., 76 7–11 (upd.)
Agnico-Eagle Mines Limited, 71 11–14
Agora S.A. Group, 77 5–8
AGRANA *see* Südzucker AG.
Agri Beef Company, 81 5–9
Agrigenetics, Inc. *see* Mycogen Corp.
Agrium Inc., 73 21–23
AgustaWestland N.V., 75 18–20

Agway, Inc., 7 17–18; 21 17–19 (upd.) *see also* Cargill Inc.
AHL Services, Inc., 27 20–23
Ahlstrom Corporation, 53 22–25
Ahmanson *see* H.F. Ahmanson & Co.
AHMSA *see* Altos Hornos de México, S.A. de C.V.
Ahold *see* Koninklijke Ahold NV.
AHP *see* American Home Products Corp.
AICPA *see* The American Institute of Certified Public Accountants.
AIG *see* American International Group, Inc.
AIMCO *see* Apartment Investment and Management Co.
Air & Water Technologies Corporation, 6 441–42 *see also* Aqua Alliance Inc.
Air Berlin GmbH & Co. Luftverkehrs KG, 71 15–17
Air Canada, 6 60–62; 23 9–12 (upd.); 59 17–22 (upd.)
Air China, 46 9–11
Air Express International Corporation, 13 19–20
Air France *see* Societe Air France.
Air-India Limited, 6 63–64; 27 24–26 (upd.)
Air Jamaica Limited, 54 3–6
Air Liquide *see* L'Air Liquide SA.
Air Mauritius Ltd., 63 17–19
Air Methods Corporation, 53 26–29
Air Midwest, Inc. *see* Mesa Air Group, Inc.
Air New Zealand Limited, 14 10–12; 38 24–27 (upd.)
Air Pacific Ltd., 70 7–9
Air Partner PLC, 93 33–36
Air Products and Chemicals, Inc., I 297–99; 10 31–33 (upd.); 74 6–9 (upd.)
Air Sahara Limited, 65 14–16
Air T, Inc., 86 6–9
Air Wisconsin Airlines Corporation, 55 10–12
Air Zimbabwe (Private) Limited, 91 5–8
AirAsia Berhad, 93 37–40
Airborne Freight Corporation, 6 345–47; 34 15–18 (upd.) *see also* DHL Worldwide Network S.A./N.V.
Airborne Systems Group, 89 39–42
Airbus Industrie *see* G.I.E. Airbus Industrie.
Airgas, Inc., 54 7–10
Airguard Industries, Inc. *see* CLARCOR Inc.
Airlink Pty Ltd *see* Qantas Airways Ltd.
Airstream *see* Thor Industries, Inc.
AirTouch Communications, 11 10–12 *see also* Vodafone Group PLC.
Airtours Plc, 27 27–29, 90, 92
AirTran Holdings, Inc., 22 21–23
Aisin Seiki Co., Ltd., III 415–16; 48 3–5 (upd.)
Aitchison & Colegrave *see* Bradford & Bingley PLC.
Aiwa Co., Ltd., 30 18–20
Ajegroup S.A, 92 1–4
Ajinomoto Co., Inc., II 463–64; 28 9–11 (upd.)
AK Steel Holding Corporation, 19 8–9; 41 3–6 (upd.)
Akamai Technologies, Inc., 71 18–21
Akbank TAS, 79 18–21
Akerys S.A., 90 17–20
AKG Acoustics GmbH, 62 3–6
Akin, Gump, Strauss, Hauer & Feld, L.L.P., 33 23–25
Akorn, Inc., 32 22–24
Akro-Mills Inc. *see* Myers Industries, Inc.
Aktiebolaget SKF, III 622–25; 38 28–33 (upd.); 89 401–09 (upd.)
Akzo Nobel N.V., 13 21–23; 41 7–10 (upd.)
Al Habtoor Group L.L.C., 87 9–12
Al-Tawfeek Co. For Investment Funds Ltd. *see* Dallah Albaraka Group.
Alabama Farmers Cooperative, Inc., 63 20–22
Alabama National BanCorporation, 75 21–23
Alain Afflelou SA, 53 30–32
Alain Manoukian *see* Groupe Alain Manoukian.
Alamo Group Inc., 32 25–28
Alamo Rent A Car, 6 348–50; 24 9–12 (upd.); 84 5–11 (upd.)
ALARIS Medical Systems, Inc., 65 17–20
Alascom, Inc. *see* AT&T Corp.
Alaska Air Group, Inc., 6 65–67; 29 11–14 (upd.)
Alaska Communications Systems Group, Inc., 89 43–46
Alaska Railroad Corporation, 60 6–9
Alba-Waldensian, Inc., 30 21–23 *see also* E.I. du Pont de Nemours and Co.
Albany International Corporation, 8 12–14; 51 11–14 (upd.)
Albany Molecular Research, Inc., 77 9–12
Albemarle Corporation, 59 23–25
Alberici Corporation, 76 12–14
The Albert Fisher Group plc, 41 11–13
Albert Heijn NV *see* Koninklijke Ahold N.V. (Royal Ahold).
Albert's Organics, Inc. *see* United Natural Foods, Inc.
Alberta Energy Company Ltd., 16 10–12; 43 3–6 (upd.)
Alberto-Culver Company, 8 15–17; 36 23–27 (upd.); 91 9–15 (upd.)
Albertson's, Inc., II 601–03; 7 19–22 (upd.); 30 24–28 (upd.); 65 21–26 (upd.)
Alcan Aluminium Limited, IV 9–13; 31 7–12 (upd.)
Alcatel S.A., 9 9–11; 36 28–31 (upd.)
Alco Health Services Corporation, III 9–10 *see also* AmeriSource Health Corp.
Alco Standard Corporation, I 412–13
Alcoa Inc., 56 7–11 (upd.)
Alderwoods Group, Inc., 68 11–15 (upd.)
Aldi Einkauf GmbH & Co. OHG, 13 24–26; 86 10–14 (upd.)
Aldila Inc., 46 12–14
Aldus Corporation, 10 34–36 *see also* Adobe Systems Inc.
Alès Groupe, 81 10–13
Alex Lee Inc., 18 6–9; 44 10–14 (upd.)
Alexander & Alexander Services Inc., 10 37–39 *see also* Aon Corp.
Alexander & Baldwin, Inc., 10 40–42; 40 14–19 (upd.)
Alexander's, Inc., 45 14–16
Alexandra plc, 88 5–8
Alfa Corporation, 60 10–12
Alfa-Laval AB, III 417–21; 64 13–18 (upd.)
Alfa Romeo, 13 27–29; 36 32–35 (upd.)
Alfa, S.A. de C.V., 19 10–12
Alfesca hf, 82 1–4
Alfred A. Knopf, Inc. *see* Random House, Inc.
Alfred Dunhill Limited *see* Vendôme Luxury Group plc.
Alfred Kärcher GmbH & Co KG, 94 9–14
Alfred Ritter GmbH & Co. KG, 58 3–7
Alga *see* BRIO AB.
Algemene Bank Nederland N.V., II 183–84
Algerian Saudi Leasing Holding Co. *see* Dallah Albaraka Group.
Algo Group Inc., 24 13–15
Alico, Inc., 63 23–25
Alienware Corporation, 81 14–17
Align Technology, Inc., 94 15–18
Alimentation Couche-Tard Inc., 77 13–16
Alitalia–Linee Aeree Italiane, S.p.A., 6 68–69; 29 15–17 (upd.); 97 21–27 (upd.)
Aljazeera Satellite Channel, 79 22–25
All American Communications Inc., 20 3–7
The All England Lawn Tennis & Croquet Club, 54 11–13
All Nippon Airways Co., Ltd., 6 70–71; 38 34–37 (upd.); 91 16–20 (upd.)
Alldays plc, 49 16–19
Allders plc, 37 6–8
Alleanza Assicurazioni S.p.A., 65 27–29
Alleghany Corporation, 10 43–45; 60 13–16 (upd.)
Allegheny Energy, Inc., 38 38–41 (upd.)
Allegheny Ludlum Corporation, 8 18–20
Allegheny Power System, Inc., V 543–45 *see also* Allegheny Energy, Inc.
Allegheny Steel Distributors, Inc. *see* Reliance Steel & Aluminum Co.
Allegiance Life Insurance Company *see* Horace Mann Educators Corp.
Allegiant Travel Company, 97 28–31
Allegis Group, Inc., 95 24–27
Allen-Bradley Co. *see* Rockwell Automation.
Allen Canning Company, 76 15–17
Allen-Edmonds Shoe Corporation, 61 20–23

Allen Foods, Inc., 60 17–19
Allen Organ Company, 33 26–29
Allen Systems Group, Inc., 59 26–28
Allerderm *see* Virbac Corp.
Allergan, Inc., 10 46–49; 30 29–33 (upd.); 77 17–24 (upd.)
Allgemeine Elektricitäts-Gesellschaft *see* AEG A.G.
Allgemeine Handelsgesellschaft der Verbraucher AG *see* AVA AG.
Alliance and Leicester plc, 88 9–12
Alliance Assurance Company *see* Royal & Sun Alliance Insurance Group plc.
Alliance Atlantis Communications Inc., 39 11–14
Alliance Boots plc, 83 20-28 (upd.)
Alliance Capital Management Holding L.P., 63 26–28
Alliance Entertainment Corp., 17 12–14 *see also* Source Interlink Companies, Inc.
Alliance Resource Partners, L.P., 81 18–21
Alliance UniChem Plc *see* Alliance Boots plc.
Alliant Techsystems Inc., 8 21–23; 30 34–37 (upd.); 77 25–31 (upd.)
Allianz AG, III 183–86; 15 10–14 (upd.); 57 18–24 (upd.)
Allied Corporation *see* AlliedSignal Inc.
The Allied Defense Group, Inc., 65 30–33
Allied Domecq PLC, 29 18–20
Allied Healthcare Products, Inc., 24 16–19
Allied Irish Banks, plc, 16 13–15; 43 7–10 (upd.); 94 19–24 (upd.)
Allied-Lyons plc, I 215–16 *see also* Carlsberg A/S.
Allied Plywood Corporation *see* Ply Gem Industries Inc.
Allied Products Corporation, 21 20–22
Allied-Signal Corp., I 414–16 *see also* AlliedSignal, Inc.
Allied Signal Engines, 9 12–15
Allied Waste Industries, Inc., 50 13–16
Allied Worldwide, Inc., 49 20–23
AlliedSignal Inc., 22 29–32 (upd.) *see also* Honeywell Inc.
Allison Gas Turbine Division, 9 16–19
Allmerica Financial Corporation, 63 29–31
Allou Health & Beauty Care, Inc., 28 12–14
Alloy, Inc., 55 13–15
The Allstate Corporation, 10 50–52; 27 30–33 (upd.)
ALLTEL Corporation, 6 299–301; 46 15–19 (upd.)
Alltrista Corporation, 30 38–41 *see also* Jarden Corp.
Allwaste, Inc., 18 10–13
Almacenes Exito S.A., 89 47–50
Almaden Vineyards *see* Canandaigua Brands, Inc.
Almanij NV, 44 15–18 *see also* Algemeene Maatschappij voor Nijverheidskrediet.
Almay, Inc. *see* Revlon Inc.
Almost Family, Inc., 93 41–44
Aloha Airlines, Incorporated, 24 20–22
Alpargatas S.A.I.C., 87 13–17
Alpha Airports Group PLC, 77 32–35
Alpharma Inc., 35 22–26 (upd.)
Alpine Confections, Inc., 71 22–24
Alpine Electronics, Inc., 13 30–31
Alpine Lace Brands, Inc., 18 14–16 *see also* Land O'Lakes, Inc.
Alps Electric Co., Ltd., II 5–6; 44 19–21 (upd.)
Alrosa Company Ltd., 62 7–11
Alsco *see* Steiner Corp.
Alside Inc., 94 25–29
Altadis S.A., 72 6–13 (upd.)
ALTANA AG, 87 18–22
AltaVista Company, 43 11–13
Altera Corporation, 18 17–20; 43 14–18 (upd.)
Alternative Living Services *see* Alterra Healthcare Corp.
Alternative Tentacles Records, 66 3–6
Alternative Youth Services, Inc. *see* Res-Care, Inc.
Alterra Healthcare Corporation, 42 3–5
Alticor Inc., 71 25–30 (upd.)
Altiris, Inc., 65 34–36
Altos Hornos de México, S.A. de C.V., 42 6–8
Altran Technologies, 51 15–18
Altron Incorporated, 20 8–10
Aluar Aluminio Argentino S.A.I.C., 74 10–12
Alumalsa *see* Aluminoy y Aleaciones S.A.
Aluminum Company of America, IV 14–16; 20 11–14 (upd.) *see also* Alcoa Inc.
Alvin Ailey Dance Foundation, Inc., 52 14–17
Alvis Plc, 47 7–9
ALZA Corporation, 10 53–55; 36 36–39 (upd.)
Amalgamated Bank, 60 20–22
AMAX Inc., IV 17–19 *see also* Cyprus Amex.
Amazon.com, Inc., 25 17–19; 56 12–15 (upd.)
AMB Generali Holding AG, 51 19–23
AMB Property Corporation, 57 25–27
Ambac Financial Group, Inc., 65 37–39
Ambassadors International, Inc., 68 16–18 (upd.)
AmBev *see* Companhia de Bebidas das Américas.
Amblin Entertainment, 21 23–27
AMC Entertainment Inc., 12 12–14; 35 27–29 (upd.)
AMCC *see* Applied Micro Circuits Corp.
AMCOL International Corporation, 59 29–33 (upd.)
Amcor Ltd., IV 248–50; 19 13–16 (upd.); 78 1–6 (upd.)
AMCORE Financial Inc., 44 22–26
AMD *see* Advanced Micro Devices, Inc.
Amdahl Corporation, III 109–11; 14 13–16 (upd.); 40 20–25 (upd.) *see also* Fujitsu Ltd.
Amdocs Ltd., 47 10–12
Amec Spie S.A., 57 28–31
Amedysis, Inc., 53 33–36
Amer Group plc, 41 14–16
Amerada Hess Corporation, IV 365–67; 21 28–31 (upd.); 55 16–20 (upd.)
Amerchol Corporation *see* Union Carbide Corp.
AMERCO, 6 351–52; 67 11–14 (upd.)
Ameren Corporation, 60 23–27 (upd.)
Ameri-Kart Corp. *see* Myers Industries, Inc.
America Online, Inc., 10 56–58; 26 16–20 (upd.) *see also* CompuServe Interactive Services, Inc.; AOL Time Warner Inc.
America West Holdings Corporation, 6 72–74; 34 22–26 (upd.)
America's Car-Mart, Inc., 64 19–21
America's Favorite Chicken Company, Inc., 7 26–28 *see also* AFC Enterprises, Inc.
American & Efird, Inc., 82 5-9
American Airlines, I 89–91; 6 75–77 (upd.) *see also* AMR Corp.
American Apparel, Inc., 90 21–24
American Association of Retired Persons *see* AARP.
American Axle & Manufacturing Holdings, Inc., 67 15–17
American Banknote Corporation, 30 42–45
American Bar Association, 35 30–33
American Biltrite Inc., 16 16–18; 43 19–22 (upd.)
American Brands, Inc., V 395–97 *see also* Fortune Brands, Inc.
American Builders & Contractors Supply Co. *see* ABC Supply Co., Inc.
American Building Maintenance Industries, Inc., 6 17–19 *see also* ABM Industries Inc.
American Business Information, Inc., 18 21–25
American Business Interiors *see* American Furniture Company, Inc.
American Business Products, Inc., 20 15–17
American Campus Communities, Inc., 85 1–5
American Can Co. *see* Primerica Corp.
The American Cancer Society, 24 23–25
American Capital Strategies, Ltd., 91 21–24
American Cast Iron Pipe Company, 50 17–20
American Civil Liberties Union (ACLU), 60 28–31
American Classic Voyages Company, 27 34–37
American Coin Merchandising, Inc., 28 15–17; 74 13–16 (upd.)
American Colloid Co., 13 32–35 *see* AMCOL International Corp.
American Commercial Lines Inc. *see* CSX Corp.
American Cotton Growers Association *see* Plains Cotton Cooperative Association.

American Crystal Sugar Company, 11 13–15; 32 29–33 (upd.)
American Cyanamid, I 300–02; 8 24–26 (upd.)
American Eagle Outfitters, Inc., 24 26–28; 55 21–24 (upd.)
American Ecology Corporation, 77 36–39
American Electric Power Company, V 546–49; 45 17–21 (upd.)
American Express Company, II 395–99; 10 59–64 (upd.); 38 42–48 (upd.)
American Family Corporation, III 187–89 *see also* AFLAC Inc.
American Financial Group Inc., III 190–92; 48 6–10 (upd.)
American Foods Group, 43 23–27
American Furniture Company, Inc., 21 32–34
American General Corporation, III 193–94; 10 65–67 (upd.); 46 20–23 (upd.)
American General Finance Corp., 11 16–17
American Girl, Inc., 69 16–19 (upd)
American Golf Corporation, 45 22–24
American Gramaphone LLC, 52 18–20
American Greetings Corporation, 7 23–25; 22 33–36 (upd.); 59 34–39 (upd.)
American Healthways, Inc., 65 40–42
American Home Mortgage Holdings, Inc., 46 24–26
American Home Products, I 622–24; 10 68–70 (upd.) *see also* Wyeth.
American Homestar Corporation, 18 26–29; 41 17–20 (upd.)
American Institute of Certified Public Accountants (AICPA), 44 27–30
American International Group, Inc., III 195–98; 15 15–19 (upd.); 47 13–19 (upd.)
American Italian Pasta Company, 27 38–40; 76 18–21 (upd.)
American Kennel Club, Inc., 74 17–19
American Lawyer Media Holdings, Inc., 32 34–37
American Library Association, 86 15–19
American Licorice Company, 86 20–23
American Locker Group Incorporated, 34 19–21
American Lung Association, 48 11–14
American Machine and Metals *see* AMETEK, Inc.
American Maize-Products Co., 14 17–20
American Management Association, 76 22–25
American Management Systems, Inc., 11 18–20
American Media, Inc., 27 41–44; 82 10–15 (upd.)
American Medical Association, 39 15–18
American Medical International, Inc., III 73–75
American Medical Response, Inc., 39 19–22
American Metals Corporation *see* Reliance Steel & Aluminum Co.
American Modern Insurance Group *see* The Midland Co.
American Motors Corp., I 135–37 *see also* DaimlerChrysler AG.
América Móvil, S.A. de C.V., 80 5–8
American MSI Corporation *see* Moldflow Corp.
American National Insurance Company, 8 27–29; 27 45–48 (upd.)
American Olean Tile Company *see* Armstrong Holdings, Inc.
American Oriental Bioengineering Inc., 93 45–48
American Pad & Paper Company, 20 18–21
American Pfauter *see* Gleason Corp.
American Pharmaceutical Partners, Inc., 69 20–22
American Pop Corn Company, 59 40–43
American Power Conversion Corporation, 24 29–31; 67 18–20 (upd.)
American Premier Underwriters, Inc., 10 71–74
American President Companies Ltd., 6 353–55 *see also* APL Ltd.
American Printing House for the Blind, 26 13–15
American Re Corporation, 10 75–77; 35 34–37 (upd.)
American Red Cross, 40 26–29
American Reprographics Company, 75 24–26
American Residential Mortgage Corporation, 8 30–31
American Restaurant Partners, L.P., 93 49–52
American Retirement Corporation, 42 9–12 *see also* Brookdale Senior Living.
American Rice, Inc., 33 30–33
American Rug Craftsmen *see* Mohawk Industries, Inc.
American Safety Razor Company, 20 22–24
American Savings Bank *see* Hawaiian Electric Industries, Inc.
American Science & Engineering, Inc., 81 22–25
American Seating Company, 78 7–11
American Skiing Company, 28 18–21
American Society for the Prevention of Cruelty to Animals (ASPCA), 68 19–22
The American Society of Composers, Authors and Publishers (ASCAP), 29 21–24
American Software Inc., 22 214; **25 20–22**
American Standard Companies Inc., III 663–65; 30 46–50 (upd.)
American States Water Company, 46 27–30
American Steamship Company *see* GATX.
American Stores Company, II 604–06; 22 37–40 (upd.) *see also* Albertson's, Inc.
American Superconductor Corporation, 97 32–36
American Technical Ceramics Corp., 67 21–23
American Telephone and Telegraph Company *see* AT&T.
American Tobacco Co. *see* B.A.T. Industries PLC.; Fortune Brands, Inc.
American Tourister, Inc., 16 19–21 *see also* Samsonite Corp.
American Tower Corporation, 33 34–38
American Vanguard Corporation, 47 20–22
American Water Works Company, Inc., 6 443–45; 38 49–52 (upd.)
American Woodmark Corporation, 31 13–16
American Yearbook Company *see* Jostens, Inc.
AmeriCares Foundation, Inc., 87 23–28
Amerigon Incorporated, 97 37–40
AMERIGROUP Corporation, 69 23–26
Amerihost Properties, Inc., 30 51–53
AmeriSource Health Corporation, 37 9–11 (upd.)
AmerisourceBergen Corporation, 64 22–28 (upd.)
Ameristar Casinos, Inc., 33 39–42; 69 27–31 (upd.)
Ameritech Corporation, V 265–68; 18 30–34 (upd.) *see also* AT&T Corp.
Ameritrade Holding Corporation, 34 27–30
Ameriwood Industries International Corp., 17 15–17 *see also* Dorel Industries Inc.
Amerock Corporation, 53 37–40
Ameron International Corporation, 67 24–26
Amersham PLC, 50 21–25
Ames Department Stores, Inc., 9 20–22; 30 54–57 (upd.)
AMETEK, Inc., 9 23–25
N.V. Amev, III 199–202 *see also* Fortis, Inc.
Amey Plc, 47 23–25
AMF Bowling, Inc., 40 30–33
Amfac/JMB Hawaii L.L.C., I 417–18; 24 32–35 (upd.)
Amgen, Inc., 10 78–81; 30 58–61 (upd.); 89 51–57 (upd.)
AMI Metals, Inc. *see* Reliance Steel & Aluminum Co.
AMICAS, Inc., 69 32–34
Amkor Technology, Inc., 69 35–37
Ammirati Puris Lintas *see* Interpublic Group of Companies, Inc.
Amnesty International, 50 26–29
Amoco Corporation, IV 368–71; 14 21–25 (upd.) *see also* BP p.l.c.
Amoskeag Company, 8 32–33 *see also* Fieldcrest Cannon, Inc.
AMP, Inc., II 7–8; 14 26–28 (upd.)
Ampacet Corporation, 67 27–29

Ampco-Pittsburgh Corporation, 79 26–29
Ampex Corporation, 17 18–20
Amphenol Corporation, 40 34–37
AMR *see* American Medical Response, Inc.
AMR Corporation, 28 22–26 (upd.); 52 21–26 (upd.)
AMREP Corporation, 21 35–37
AMS *see* Advanced Marketing Services, Inc.
Amscan Holdings, Inc., 61 24–26
AmSouth Bancorporation, 12 15–17; 48 15–18 (upd.)
Amsted Industries Incorporated, 7 29–31
Amsterdam-Rotterdam Bank N.V., II 185–86
Amstrad plc, III 112–14; 48 19–23 (upd.)
AmSurg Corporation, 48 24–27
Amtech *see* American Building Maintenance Industries, Inc.; ABM Industries Inc.
Amtrak *see* The National Railroad Passenger Corp.
Amtran, Inc., 34 31–33
AMVESCAP PLC, 65 43–45
Amway Corporation, III 11–14; 13 36–39 (upd.); 30 62–66 (upd.) *see also* Alticor Inc.
Amy's Kitchen Inc., 76 26–28
Amylin Pharmaceuticals, Inc., 67 30–32
ANA *see* All Nippon Airways Co., Ltd.
Anacomp, Inc., 94 30–34
Anadarko Petroleum Corporation, 10 82–84; 52 27–30 (upd.)
Anadolu Efes Biracilik ve Malt Sanayii A.S., 95 28–31
Anaheim Angels Baseball Club, Inc., 53 41–44
Analex Corporation, 74 20–22
Analog Devices, Inc., 10 85–87
Analogic Corporation, 23 13–16
Analysts International Corporation, 36 40–42
Analytic Sciences Corporation, 10 88–90
Analytical Surveys, Inc., 33 43–45
Anam Group, 23 17–19
Anaren Microwave, Inc., 33 46–48
Anchor Bancorp, Inc., 10 91–93
Anchor Brewing Company, 47 26–28
Anchor Gaming, 24 36–39
Anchor Hocking Glassware, 13 40–42
Andersen, 10 94–95; 29 25–28 (upd.); 68 23–27 (upd.)
The Anderson-DuBose Company, 60 32–34
Anderson Trucking Service, Inc., 75 27–29
The Andersons, Inc., 31 17–21
Andis Company, Inc., 85 6–9
Andreas Stihl AG & Co. KG, 16 22–24; 59 44–47 (upd.)
Andrew Corporation, 10 96–98; 32 38–41 (upd.)
Andrews Kurth, LLP, 71 31–34
Andrews McMeel Universal, 40 38–41
Andritz AG, 51 24–26
Andronico's Market, 70 10–13
Andrx Corporation, 55 25–27
Angelica Corporation, 15 20–22; 43 28–31 (upd.)
AngioDynamics, Inc., 81 26–29
Angliss International Group *see* Vestey Group Ltd.
Anglo-Abrasives Ltd. *see* Carbo PLC.
Anglo American PLC, IV 20–23; 16 25–30 (upd.); 50 30–36 (upd.)
Anheuser-Busch Companies, Inc., I 217–19; 10 99–101 (upd.); 34 34–37 (upd.)
Anixter International Inc., 88 13–16
Anker BV, 53 45–47
Annie's Homegrown, Inc., 59 48–50
AnnTaylor Stores Corporation, 13 43–45; 37 12–15 (upd.); 67 33–37 (upd.)
ANR Pipeline Co., 17 21–23
Anritsu Corporation, 68 28–30
The Anschutz Company, 12 18–20; 36 43–47 (upd.); 73 24–30 (upd.)
Ansell Ltd., 60 35–38 (upd.)
Ansoft Corporation, 63 32–34
Anteon Corporation, 57 32–34
Anthem Electronics, Inc., 13 46–47
Anthony & Sylvan Pools Corporation, 56 16–18
Anthracite Industries, Inc. *see* Asbury Carbons, Inc.
Anthropologie, Inc. *see* Urban Outfitters, Inc.
Antinori *see* Marchesi Antinori SRL.
The Antioch Company, 40 42–45
ANTK Tupolev *see* Aviacionny Nauchno-Tehnicheskii Komplex im. A.N. Tupoleva.
Antofagasta plc, 65 46–49
Antonov Design Bureau, 53 48–51
AOK-Bundesverband (Federation of the AOK), 78 12–16
AOL Time Warner Inc., 57 35–44 (upd.)
Aon Corporation, III 203–05; 45 25–28 (upd.)
AP *see* The Associated Press.
Apache Corporation, 10 102–04; 32 42–46 (upd.); 89 58–65 (upd.)
Apartment Investment and Management Company, 49 24–26
Apasco S.A. de C.V., 51 27–29
Apax Partners Worldwide LLP, 89 66–69
Apex Digital, Inc., 63 35–37
APH *see* American Printing House for the Blind.
APi Group, Inc., 64 29–32
APL Limited, 61 27–30 (upd.)
APLIX S.A. *see* Velcro Industries N.V.
Apogee Enterprises, Inc., 8 34–36
Apollo Group, Inc., 24 40–42
Applause Inc., 24 43–46 *see also* Russ Berrie and Co., Inc.
Apple & Eve L.L.C., 92 5–8
Apple Bank for Savings, 59 51–53
Apple Computer, Inc., III 115–16; 6 218–20 (upd.); 36 48–51 (upd.); 77 40–45 (upd.)
Apple Corps Ltd., 87 29–34
Applebee's International Inc., 14 29–31; 35 38–41 (upd.)
Appliance Recycling Centers of America, Inc., 42 13–16
Applica Incorporated, 43 32–36 (upd.)
Applied Bioscience International, Inc., 10 105–07
Applied Films Corporation, 48 28–31
Applied Materials, Inc., 10 108–09; 46 31–34 (upd.)
Applied Micro Circuits Corporation, 38 53–55
Applied Power Inc., 9 26–28; 32 47–51 (upd.) *see also* Actuant Corp.
Applied Signal Technology, Inc., 87 35–38
Applied Technology Solutions *see* RWD Technologies, Inc.
Aprilia SpA, 17 24–26
AptarGroup, Inc., 69 38–41
Aqua Alliance Inc., 32 52–54 (upd.)
aQuantive, Inc., 81 30–33
Aquarion Company, 84 12–16
Aquarius Platinum Ltd., 63 38–40
Aquent, 96 8–11
Aquila, Inc., 50 37–40 (upd.)
AR Accessories Group, Inc., 23 20–22
ARA *see* Consorcio ARA, S.A. de C.V.
ARA Services, II 607–08 *see also* Aramark.
Arab Potash Company, 85 10–13
Arabian Gulf Oil Company *see* National Oil Corp.
Aracruz Celulose S.A., 57 45–47
Aral AG, 62 12–15
ARAMARK Corporation, 13 48–50; 41 21–24 (upd.)
Arandell Corporation, 37 16–18
Arapuã *see* Lojas Arapuã S.A.
ARBED S.A., IV 24–27; 22 41–45 (upd.) *see also* Arcelor Gent.
Arbeitsgemeinschaft der öffentlich-rechtlichen Rundfunkanstalten der Bundesrepublick *see* ARD.
The Arbitron Company, 38 56–61
Arbor Drugs Inc., 12 21–23 *see also* CVS Corp.
Arby's Inc., 14 32–34
Arc International, 76 29–31
ARCA *see* Appliance Recycling Centers of America, Inc.
Arcadia Group plc, 28 27–30 (upd.)
Arcadis NV, 26 21–24
Arcelor Gent, 80 9–12
Arch Chemicals, Inc., 78 17–20
Arch Mineral Corporation, 7 32–34
Arch Wireless, Inc., 39 23–26
Archer Daniels Midland Company, I 419–21; 11 21–23 (upd.); 32 55–59 (upd.); 75 30–35 (upd.)
Archie Comics Publications, Inc., 63 41–44
Archon Corporation, 74 23–26 (upd.)

Archstone-Smith Trust, **49** 27–30
Archway Cookies, Inc., **29** 29–31
ARCO *see* Atlantic Richfield Co.
ARCO Chemical Company, **10** 110–11 *see also* Lyondell Chemical Co.
Arcor S.A.I.C., **66** 7–9
Arctco, Inc., **16** 31–34
Arctic Cat Inc., **40** 46–50 (upd.); **96** 12–19 (upd.)
Arctic Slope Regional Corporation, **38** 62–65
ARD, **41** 25–29
Arden Group, Inc., **29** 32–35
Arena Resources, Inc., **97** 41–44
AREVA NP, **90** 25–30 (upd.)
Argentaria Caja Postal y Banco Hipotecario S.A. *see* Banco Bilbao Vizcaya Argentaria S.A.
Argon ST, Inc., **81** 34–37
Argos S.A. *see* Cementos Argos S.A.
Argosy Gaming Company, **21** 38–41 *see also* Penn National Gaming, Inc.
Argyll Group PLC, **II** 609–10 *see also* Safeway PLC.
Arianespace S.A., **89** 70–73
Ariba, Inc., **57** 48–51
Ariens Company, **48** 32–34
Aris Industries, Inc., **16** 35–38
Aristocrat Leisure Limited, **54** 14–16
Aristokraft Inc. *see* MasterBrand Cabinets, Inc.
The Aristotle Corporation, **62** 16–18
AriZona Beverages *see* Ferolito, Vultaggio & Sons.
Arjo Wiggins Appleton p.l.c., **34** 38–40
Ark Restaurants Corp., **20** 25–27
Arkansas Best Corporation, **16** 39–41; **94** 35–40 (upd.)
Arkla, Inc., **V** 550–51
Arla Foods amba, **48** 35–38
Armani *see* Giorgio Armani S.p.A.
Armco Inc., **IV** 28–30 *see also* AK Steel.
Armor All Products Corp., **16** 42–44
Armor Holdings, Inc., **27** 49–51
Armour *see* Tommy Armour Golf Co.
Armstrong Air Conditioning Inc. *see* Lennox International Inc.
Armstrong Holdings, Inc., **III** 422–24; **22** 46–50 (upd.); **81** 38–44 (upd.)
Army and Air Force Exchange Service, **39** 27–29
Arnhold and S. Bleichroeder Advisers, LLC, **97** 45–49
Arnold & Porter, **35** 42–44
Arnold Clark Automobiles Ltd., **60** 39–41
Arnoldo Mondadori Editore S.p.A., **IV** 585–88; **19** 17–21 (upd.); **54** 17–23 (upd.)
Arnott's Ltd., **66** 10–12
Aro Corp. *see* Ingersoll-Rand Company Ltd.
Arotech Corporation, **93** 53–56
ArQule, Inc., **68** 31–34
ARRIS Group, Inc., **89** 74–77
Arriva PLC, **69** 42–44
Arrow Air Holdings Corporation, **55** 28–30
Arrow Electronics, Inc., **10** 112–14; **50** 41–44 (upd.)
Arsenal Holdings PLC, **79** 30–33
The Art Institute of Chicago, **29** 36–38
Art Van Furniture, Inc., **28** 31–33
Artesyn Technologies Inc., **46** 35–38 (upd.)
ArthroCare Corporation, **73** 31–33
Arthur Andersen & Company, Société Coopérative, **10** 115–17 *see also* Andersen.
The Arthur C. Clarke Foundation, **92** 9–12
Arthur D. Little, Inc., **35** 45–48
Arthur J. Gallagher & Co., **73** 34–36
Arthur Murray International, Inc., **32** 60–62
Artisan Entertainment Inc., **32** 63–66 (upd.)
Arts and Entertainment Network *see* A&E Television Networks.
Artsana SpA, **92** 13–16
Arval *see* PHH Arval.
Arvin Industries, Inc., **8** 37–40 *see also* ArvinMeritor, Inc.
ArvinMeritor, Inc., **54** 24–28 (upd.)
A/S Air Baltic Corporation, **71** 35–37
AS Estonian Air, **71** 38–40
Asahi Breweries, Ltd., **I** 220–21; **20** 28–30 (upd.); **52** 31–34 (upd.)
Asahi Denka Kogyo KK, **64** 33–35
Asahi Glass Company, Ltd., **III** 666–68; **48** 39–42 (upd.)
Asahi Komag Co., Ltd. *see* Komag, Inc.
Asahi National Broadcasting Company, Ltd., **9** 29–31
Asahi Shimbun, **9** 29–30
Asanté Technologies, Inc., **20** 31–33
ASARCO Incorporated, **IV** 31–34; **40** 220–22, 411
Asatsu-DK Inc, **82** 16–20
Asbury Automotive Group Inc., **60** 42–44
Asbury Carbons, Inc., **68** 35–37
ASC, Inc., **55** 31–34
ASCAP *see* The American Society of Composers, Authors and Publishers.
Ascend Communications, Inc., **24** 47–51 *see also* Lucent Technologies Inc.
Ascendia Brands, Inc., **97** 50–53
Ascential Software Corporation, **59** 54–57
Ascom AG, **9** 32–34
ASDA Group Ltd., **II** 611–12; **28** 34–36 (upd.); **64** 36–38 (upd.)
ASEA AB *see* ABB Ltd.
ASG *see* Allen Systems Group, Inc.
Ash Grove Cement Company, **94** 41–44
Ashanti Goldfields Company Limited, **43** 37–40
Ashdown *see* Repco Corporation Ltd.
Ashland Inc., **19** 22–25; **50** 45–50 (upd.)
Ashland Oil, Inc., **IV** 372–74 *see also* Marathon.
Ashley Furniture Industries, Inc., **35** 49–51
Ashtead Group plc, **34** 41–43
Ashworth, Inc., **26** 25–28
Asia Pacific Breweries Limited, **59** 58–60
AsiaInfo Holdings, Inc., **43** 41–44
Asiana Airlines, Inc., **46** 39–42
ASIX Inc. *see* Manatron, Inc.
ASICS Corporation, **57** 52–55
ASK Group, Inc., **9** 35–37
Ask Jeeves, Inc., **65** 50–52
ASML Holding N.V., **50** 51–54
ASPCA *see* American Society for the Prevention of Cruelty to Animals (ASPCA).
Aspect Telecommunications Corporation, **22** 51–53
Aspen Publishers *see* Wolters Kluwer NV.
Aspen Skiing Company, **15** 23–26
Asplundh Tree Expert Co., **20** 34–36; **59** 61–65 (upd.)
Assicurazioni Generali SpA, **III** 206–09; **15** 27–31 (upd.)
Assisted Living Concepts, Inc., **43** 45–47
Associated British Foods plc, **II** 465–66; **13** 51–53 (upd.); **41** 30–33 (upd.)
Associated British Ports Holdings Plc, **45** 29–32
Associated Estates Realty Corporation, **25** 23–25
Associated Grocers, Incorporated, **9** 38–40; **31** 22–26 (upd.)
Associated International Insurance Co. *see* Gryphon Holdings, Inc.
Associated Milk Producers, Inc., **11** 24–26; **48** 43–46 (upd.)
Associated Natural Gas Corporation, **11** 27–28
Associated Newspapers Holdings P.L.C. *see* Daily Mail and General Trust plc.
The Associated Press, **13** 54–56; **31** 27–30 (upd.); **73** 37–41 (upd.)
Association des Centres Distributeurs E. Leclerc, **37** 19–21
Association of Junior Leagues International Inc., **60** 45–47
Assurances Générales de France, **63** 45–48
Assured Guaranty Ltd., **93** 57–60
AST Research, Inc., **9** 41–43
Astec Industries, Inc., **79** 34–37
Astellas Pharma Inc., **97** 54–58 (upd.)
AstenJohnson Inc., **90** 31–34
Aston Villa plc, **41** 34–36
Astoria Financial Corporation, **44** 31–34
Astra *see* PT Astra International Tbk.
AstraZeneca PLC, **I** 625–26; **20** 37–40 (upd.); **50** 55–60 (upd.)
Astronics Corporation, **35** 52–54
Asur *see* Grupo Aeropuerto del Sureste, S.A. de C.V.
Asurion Corporation, **83** 29-32
ASV, Inc., **34** 44–47; **66** 13–15 (upd.)
AT&T Bell Laboratories, Inc., **13** 57–59 *see also* Lucent Technologies Inc.
AT&T Corporation, **V** 259–64; **29** 39–45 (upd.); **61 68** 38–45 (upd.)
AT&T Istel Ltd., **14** 35–36

AT&T Wireless Services, Inc., 54 29–32 (upd.)
At Home Corporation, 43 48–51
ATA Holdings Corporation, 82 21–25
Atanor S.A., 62 19–22
Atari Corporation, 9 44–47; 23 23–26 (upd.); 66 16–20 (upd.)
ATC Healthcare Inc., 64 39–42
Atchison Casting Corporation, 39 30–32
ATE Investment *see* Atlantic Energy, Inc.
The Athlete's Foot Brands LLC, 84 17–20
The Athletics Investment Group, 62 23–26
ATI Technologies Inc., 79 38–41
Atkins Nutritionals, Inc., 58 8–10
Atkinson Candy Company, 87 39–42
Atlanta Bread Company International, Inc., 70 14–16
Atlanta Gas Light Company, 6 446–48; 23 27–30 (upd.)
Atlanta National League Baseball Club, Inc., 43 52–55
Atlantic & Pacific Tea Company (A&P) *see* The Great Atlantic & Pacific Tea Company, Inc.
Atlantic American Corporation, 44 35–37
Atlantic Coast Airlines Holdings, Inc., 55 35–37
Atlantic Coast Carton Company *see* Caraustar Industries, Inc.
Atlantic Energy, Inc., 6 449–50
The Atlantic Group, 23 31–33
Atlantic Premium Brands, Ltd., 57 56–58
Atlantic Richfield Company, IV 375–77; 31 31–34 (upd.)
Atlantic Southeast Airlines, Inc., 47 29–31
Atlantis Plastics, Inc., 85 14–17
Atlas Air, Inc., 39 33–35
Atlas Bolt & Screw Company *see* The Marmon Group, Inc.
Atlas Copco AB, III 425–27; 28 37–41 (upd.); 85 18–24 (upd.)
Atlas Tag & Label *see* BISSELL, Inc.
Atlas Van Lines, Inc., 14 37–39
Atmel Corporation, 17 32–34
ATMI, Inc., 93 61–64
Atmos Energy Corporation, 43 56–58
Atochem S.A., I 303–04, 676 *see also* Total-Fina-Elf.
Atos Origin S.A., 69 45–47
Atrix Laboratories, Inc. *see* QLT Inc.
Attachmate Corporation, 56 19–21
Attica Enterprises S.A., 64 43–45
Atwood Mobil Products, 53 52–55
Au Bon Pain Co., Inc., 18 35–38
AU Optronics Corporation, 67 38–40
Au Printemps S.A., V 9–11 *see also* Pinault-Printemps-Redoute S.A.
Aubert & Duval Holding *see* Eramet.
Auchan, 37 22–24
The Auchter Company, 78 21–24
Audible Inc., 79 42–45
Audio King Corporation, 24 52–54
Audiovox Corporation, 34 48–50; 90 35–39 (upd.)
August Schell Brewing Company Inc., 59 66–69
August Storck KG, 66 21–23
Ault Incorporated, 34 51–54
Auntie Anne's, Inc., 35 55–57
Aurea Concesiones de Infraestructuras SA *see* Abertis Infraestructuras, S.A.
Aurora Casket Company, Inc., 56 22–24
Aurora Foods Inc., 32 67–69
Austal Limited, 75 36–39
The Austin Company, 8 41–44; 72 14–18 (upd.)
Austin Nichols *see* Pernod Ricard S.A.
Austin Powder Company, 76 32–35
Australia and New Zealand Banking Group Limited, II 187–90; 52 35–40 (upd.)
Australian Wheat Board *see* AWB Ltd.
Austrian Airlines AG (Österreichische Luftverkehrs AG), 33 49–52
Authentic Fitness Corp., 20 41–43; 51 30–33 (upd.)
Auto Value Associates, Inc., 25 26–28
Autobacs Seven Company Ltd., 76 36–38
Autobytel Inc., 47 32–34
Autocam Corporation, 51 34–36
Autodesk, Inc., 10 118–20; 89 78–82 (upd.)
Autogrill SpA, 49 31–33
Autoliv, Inc., 65 53–55
Autologic Information International, Inc., 20 44–46
Automated Sciences Group, Inc. *see* CACI International Inc.
Automatic Data Processing, Inc., III 117–19; 9 48–51 (upd.); 47 35–39 (upd.)
Automobiles Citroën, 7 35–38
Automobili Lamborghini Holding S.p.A., 13 60–62; 34 55–58 (upd.); 91 25–30 (upd.)
AutoNation, Inc., 50 61–64
Autoridad del Canal de Panamá, 94 45–48
Autoroutes du Sud de la France SA, 55 38–40
Autotote Corporation, 20 47–49 *see also* Scientific Games Corp.
AutoTrader.com, L.L.C., 91 31–34
AutoZone, Inc., 9 52–54; 31 35–38 (upd.)
Auvil Fruit Company, Inc., 95 32–35
AVA AG (Allgemeine Handelsgesellschaft der Verbraucher AG), 33 53–56
Avado Brands, Inc., 31 39–42
Avalon Correctional Services, Inc., 75 40–43
AvalonBay Communities, Inc., 58 11–13
Avantium Technologies BV, 79 46–49
Avco Financial Services Inc., 13 63–65 *see also* Citigroup Inc.
Avecia Group PLC, 63 49–51
Aveda Corporation, 24 55–57
Avedis Zildjian Co., 38 66–68
Avendt Group, Inc. *see* Marmon Group, Inc.
Aventine Renewable Energy Holdings, Inc., 89 83–86
Avery Dennison Corporation, IV 251–54; 17 27–31 (upd.); 49 34–40 (upd.)
Aviacionny Nauchno-Tehnicheskii Komplex im. A.N. Tupoleva, 24 58–60
Aviacsa *see* Consorcio Aviacsa, S.A. de C.V.
Aviall, Inc., 73 42–45
Avianca Aerovías Nacionales de Colombia SA, 36 52–55
Aviation Sales Company, 41 37–39
Avid Technology Inc., 38 69–73
Avionics Specialties Inc. *see* Aerosonic Corp.
Avions Marcel Dassault-Breguet Aviation, I 44–46 *see also* Groupe Dassault Aviation SA.
Avis Group Holdings, Inc., 6 356–58; 22 54–57 (upd.); 75 44–49 (upd.)
Avista Corporation, 69 48–50 (upd.)
Aviva PLC, 50 65–68 (upd.)
Avnet Inc., 9 55–57
Avocent Corporation, 65 56–58
Avon Products, Inc., III 15–16; 19 26–29 (upd.); 46 43–46 (upd.)
Avondale Industries, Inc., 7 39–41; 41 40–43 (upd.)
AVTOVAZ Joint Stock Company, 65 59–62
AVX Corporation, 67 41–43
AWA *see* America West Holdings Corp.
AWB Ltd., 56 25–27
Awrey Bakeries, Inc., 56 28–30
AXA Colonia Konzern AG, III 210–12; 49 41–45 (upd.)
Axcan Pharma Inc., 85 25–28
Axcelis Technologies, Inc., 95 36–39
Axel Johnson Group, I 553–55
Axel Springer Verlag AG, IV 589–91; 20 50–53 (upd.)
Axsys Technologies, Inc., 93 65–68
Aydin Corp., 19 30–32
Aynsley China Ltd. *see* Belleek Pottery Ltd.
Azcon Corporation, 23 34–36
Azerbaijan Airlines, 77 46–49
Azienda Generale Italiana Petroli *see* ENI S.p.A.
Aztar Corporation, 13 66–68; 71 41–45 (upd.)
AZZ Incorporated, 93 69–72

B

B&D *see* Barker & Dobson.
B&G Foods, Inc., 40 51–54
B&J Music Ltd. *see* Kaman Music Corp.
B&Q plc *see* Kingfisher plc.
B.A.T. Industries PLC, 22 70–73 (upd.) *see also* Brown and Williamson Tobacco Corporation
B. Dalton Bookseller Inc., 25 29–31 *see also* Barnes & Noble, Inc.

B/E Aerospace, Inc., **30 72–74**
B.F. Goodrich Co. *see* The BFGoodrich Co.
B.J. Alan Co., Inc., **67 44–46**
The B. Manischewitz Company, LLC, **31 43–46**
B.R. Guest Inc., **87 43–46**
B.W. Rogers Company, **94 49–52**
BA *see* British Airways plc.
BAA plc, **10 121–23; 33 57–61 (upd.)**
Baan Company, **25 32–34**
Babbage's, Inc., **10 124–25** *see also* GameStop Corp.
The Babcock & Wilcox Company, **82 26–30**
Babcock International Group PLC, **69 51–54**
Babolat VS, S.A., **97 63–66**
Baby Lock USA *see* Tacony Corp.
Baby Superstore, Inc., **15 32–34** *see also* Toys 'R Us, Inc.
Bacardi & Company Ltd., **18 39–42; 82 31–36 (upd.)**
Baccarat, **24 61–63**
Bachman's Inc., **22 58–60**
Bachoco *see* Industrias Bachoco, S.A. de C.V.
Back Bay Restaurant Group, Inc., **20 54–56**
Back Yard Burgers, Inc., **45 33–36**
Backus y Johnston *see* Unión de Cervecerias Peruanas Backus y Johnston S.A.A.
Bad Boy Worldwide Entertainment Group, **58 14–17**
Badger Meter, Inc., **22 61–65**
Badger Paper Mills, Inc., **15 35–37**
Badger State Ethanol, LLC, **83 33-37**
BAE Systems Ship Repair, **73 46–48**
Bahamas Air Holdings Ltd., **66 24–26**
Bahlsen GmbH & Co. KG, **44 38–41**
Baidu.com Inc., **95 40–43**
Bailey Nurseries, Inc., **57 59–61**
Bain & Company, **55 41–43**
Baird & Warner Holding Company, **87 47–50**
Bairnco Corporation, **28 42–45**
Bajaj Auto Limited, **39 36–38**
Baker *see* Michael Baker Corp.
Baker and Botts, L.L.P., **28 46–49**
Baker & Daniels LLP, **88 17–20**
Baker & Hostetler LLP, **40 55–58**
Baker & McKenzie, **10 126–28; 42 17–20 (upd.)**
Baker & Taylor Corporation, **16 45–47; 43 59–62 (upd.)**
Baker Hughes Incorporated, **III 428–29; 22 66–69 (upd.); 57 62–66 (upd.)**
Bakkavör Group hf., **91 35–39**
Balance Bar Company, **32 70–72**
Balchem Corporation, **42 21–23**
Baldor Electric Company, **21 42–44; 97 63–67 (upd.)**
Baldwin & Lyons, Inc., **51 37–39**
Baldwin Piano & Organ Company, **18 43–46** *see also* Gibson Guitar Corp.
Baldwin Technology Company, Inc., **25 35–39**
Balfour Beatty Construction Ltd., **36 56–60 (upd.)**
Ball Corporation, **I 597–98; 10 129–31 (upd.); 78 25–29 (upd.)**
Ball Horticultural Company, **78 30–33**
Ballantine Books *see* Random House, Inc.
Ballantyne of Omaha, Inc., **27 56–58**
Ballard Medical Products, **21 45–48** *see also* Kimberly-Clark Corp.
Ballard Power Systems Inc., **73 49–52**
Ballistic Recovery Systems, Inc., **87 51–54**
Bally Manufacturing Corporation, **III 430–32**
Bally Total Fitness Corporation, **25 40–42; 94 53–57 (upd.)**
Balmac International, Inc., **94 58–61**
Bâloise-Holding, **40 59–62**
Baltek Corporation, **34 59–61**
Baltika Brewery Joint Stock Company, **65 63–66**
Baltimore & Ohio Railroad *see* CSX Corp.
Baltimore Aircoil Company, Inc., **66 27–29**
Baltimore Gas and Electric Company, **V 552–54; 25 43–46 (upd.)**
Baltimore Orioles L.P., **66 30–33**
Baltimore Technologies Plc, **42 24–26**
The Bama Companies, Inc., **80 13–16**
Banamex *see* Grupo Financiero Banamex S.A.
Banana Republic Inc., **25 47–49** *see also* Gap, Inc.
Banc One Corporation, **10 132–34** *see also* JPMorgan Chase & Co.
Banca Commerciale Italiana SpA, **II 191–93**
Banca Fideuram SpA, **63 52–54**
Banca Intesa SpA, **65 67–70**
Banca Monte dei Paschi di Siena SpA, **65 71–73**
Banca Nazionale del Lavoro SpA, **72 19–21**
Banca Serfin *see* Grupo Financiero Serfin, S.A.
Banco Bilbao Vizcaya Argentaria S.A., **II 194–96; 48 47–51 (upd.)**
Banco Bradesco S.A., **13 69–71**
Banco Central, **II 197–98; 56 65** *see also* Banco Santander Central Hispano S.A.
Banco de Crédito del Perú, **9273–76**
Banco Comercial Português, SA, **50 69–72**
Banco de Chile, **69 55–57**
Banco de Comercio, S.A. *see* Grupo Financiero BBVA Bancomer S.A.
Banco do Brasil S.A., **II 199–200**
Banco Espírito Santo e Comercial de Lisboa S.A., **15 38–40** *see also* Espírito Santo Financial Group S.A.
Banco Itaú S.A., **19 33–35**
Banco Popular *see* Popular, Inc.
Banco Santander Central Hispano S.A., **36 61–64 (upd.)**
Banco Serfin *see* Grupo Financiero Serfin, S.A.
Bancomer S.A. *see* Grupo Financiero BBVA Bancomer S.A.
Bandag, Inc., **19 36–38**
Bandai Co., Ltd., **55 44–48**
Banfi Products Corp., **36 65–67**
Banfield, The Pet Hospital *see* Medical Management International, Inc.
Bang & Olufsen Holding A/S, **37 25–28; 86 24–29 (upd.)**
Bank Austria AG, **23 37–39**
Bank Brussels Lambert, **II 201–03**
Bank Hapoalim B.M., **II 204–06; 54 33–37 (upd.)**
Bank Leumi le-Israel B.M., **60 48–51**
Bank of America Corporation, **46 47–54 (upd.)**
Bank of Boston Corporation, **II 207–09** *see also* FleetBoston Financial Corp.
Bank of China, **63 55–57**
Bank of Cyprus Group, **91 40–43**
Bank of East Asia Ltd., **63 58–60**
Bank of Granite Corporation, **89 87–91**
Bank of Hawaii Corporation, **73 53–56**
Bank of Ireland, **50 73–76**
Bank of Mississippi, Inc., **14 40–41**
Bank of Montreal, **II 210–12; 46 55–58 (upd.)**
Bank of New England Corporation, **II 213–15**
Bank of New York Company, Inc., **II 216–19; 46 59–63 (upd.)**
The Bank of Nova Scotia, **II 220–23; 59 70–76 (upd.)**
The Bank of Scotland *see* The Governor and Company of the Bank of Scotland.
Bank of the Ozarks, Inc., **91 44–47**
Bank of the Philippine Islands, **58 18–20**
Bank of Tokyo-Mitsubishi Ltd., **II 224–25; 15 41–43 (upd.)**
Bank One Corporation, **36 68–75 (upd.)** *see also* JPMorgan Chase & Co.
BankAmerica Corporation, **II 226–28** *see also* Bank of America.
Bankers Trust New York Corporation, **II 229–31**
Banknorth Group, Inc., **55 49–53**
Bankrate, Inc., **83 38-41**
Banner Aerospace, Inc., **14 42–44; 37 29–32 (upd.)**
Banorte *see* Grupo Financiero Banorte, S.A. de C.V.
Banque Nationale de Paris S.A., **II 232–34** *see also* BNP Paribas Group.
Banta Corporation, **12 24–26; 32 73–77 (upd.); 79 50–56 (upd.)**
Banyan Systems Inc., **25 50–52**
Baptist Health Care Corporation, **82 37–40**
Bar-S Foods Company, **76 39–41**
Barbara's Bakery Inc., **88 21–24**
Barclay Furniture Co. *see* LADD Furniture, Inc.
Barclays PLC, **II 235–37; 20 57–60 (upd.); 64 46–50 (upd.)**
BarclaysAmerican Mortgage Corporation, **11 29–30**
Barco NV, **44 42–45**

Barden Companies, Inc., 76 42–45
Bare Escentuals, Inc., 91 48–52
Barilla G. e R. Fratelli S.p.A., 17 35–37; 50 77–80 (upd.)
Barings PLC, 14 45–47
Barlow Rand Ltd., I 422–24
Barmag AG, 39 39–42
Barnes & Noble, Inc., 10 135–37; 30 67–71 (upd.); 75 50–55 (upd.)
Barnes Group, Inc., 13 72–74; 69 58–62 (upd.)
Barnett Banks, Inc., 9 58–60 *see also* Bank of America Corp.
Barnett Inc., 28 50–52
Barney's, Inc., 28 53–55
Baron de Ley S.A., 74 27–29
Baron Philippe de Rothschild S.A., 39 43–46
Barr *see* AG Barr plc.
Barr Pharmaceuticals, Inc., 26 29–31; 68 46–49 (upd.)
Barratt Developments plc, I 556–57; 56 31–33 (upd.)
Barrett Business Services, Inc., 16 48–50
Barrett-Jackson Auction Company L.L.C., 88 25–28
Barrick Gold Corporation, 34 62–65
Barry Callebaut AG, 29 46–48; 71 46–49 (upd.)
Barry-Wehmiller Companies, Inc., 90 40–43
The Bartell Drug Company, 94 62–65
Barton Malow Company, 51 40–43
Barton Protective Services Inc., 53 56–58
The Baseball Club of Seattle, LP, 50 81–85
BASF Aktiengesellschaft, I 305–08; 18 47–51 (upd.); 50 86–92 (upd.)
Bashas' Inc., 33 62–64; 80 17–21 (upd.)
The Basketball Club of Seattle, LLC, 50 93–97
Bass PLC, I 222–24; 15 44–47 (upd.); 38 74–78 (upd.)
Bass Pro Shops, Inc., 42 27–30
Bassett Furniture Industries, Inc., 18 52–55; 95 44–50 (upd.)
BAT Industries plc, I 425–27 *see also* British American Tobacco PLC.
Bata Ltd., 62 27–30
Bates Worldwide, Inc., 14 48–51; 33 65–69 (upd.)
Bath Iron Works Corporation, 12 27–29; 36 76–79 (upd.)
Battelle Memorial Institute, Inc., 10 138–40
Batten Barton Durstine & Osborn *see* Omnicom Group Inc.
Battle Mountain Gold Company, 23 40–42 *see also* Newmont Mining Corp.
Bauer Publishing Group, 7 42–43
Bauerly Companies, 61 31–33
Baugur Group hf, 81 45–49
Baumax AG, 75 56–58
Bausch & Lomb Inc., 7 44–47; 25 53–57 (upd.); 96 20–26 (upd.)
Bavaria S.A., 90 44–47
Baxi Group Ltd., 96 27–30
Baxter International Inc., I 627–29; 10 141–43 (upd.)
The Bay *see* The Hudson's Bay Co.
Bay State Gas Company, 38 79–82
Bayard SA, 49 46–49
BayBanks, Inc., 12 30–32
Bayer A.G., I 309–11; 13 75–77 (upd.); 41 44–48 (upd.)
Bayerische Hypotheken- und Wechsel-Bank AG, II 238–40 *see also* HVB Group.
Bayerische Motoren Werke A.G., I 138–40; 11 31–33 (upd.); 38 83–87 (upd.)
Bayerische Vereinsbank A.G., II 241–43 *see also* HVB Group.
Bayernwerk AG, V 555–58; 23 43–47 (upd.) *see also* E.On AG.
Bayou Steel Corporation, 31 47–49
BB&T Corporation, 79 57–61
BB Holdings Limited, 77 50–53
BBA *see* Bush Boake Allen Inc.
BBA Aviation plc, 90 48–52
BBAG Osterreichische Brau-Beteiligungs-AG, 38 88–90
BBC *see* British Broadcasting Corp.
BBDO Worldwide *see* Omnicom Group Inc.
BBGI *see* Beasley Broadcast Group, Inc.
BBN Corp., 19 39–42
BBVA *see* Banco Bilbao Vizcaya Argentaria S.A.
BCE, Inc., V 269–71; 44 46–50 (upd.)
BCI *see* Banca Commerciale Italiana SpA.
BDO Seidman LLP, 96 31–34
BE&K, Inc., 73 57–59
BEA *see* Bank of East Asia Ltd.
BEA Systems, Inc., 36 80–83
Beacon Roofing Supply, Inc., 75 59–61
Bear Creek Corporation, 38 91–94
Bear Stearns Companies, Inc., II 400–01; 10 144–45 (upd.); 52 41–44 (upd.)
Bearings, Inc., 13 78–80
Beasley Broadcast Group, Inc., 51 44–46
Beate Uhse AG, 96 35–39
Beatrice Company, II 467–69 *see also* TLC Beatrice International Holdings, Inc.
BeautiControl Cosmetics, Inc., 21 49–52
Beazer Homes USA, Inc., 17 38–41
bebe stores, inc., 31 50–52
Bechtel Group, Inc., I 558–59; 24 64–67 (upd.)
Beckett Papers, 23 48–50
Beckman Coulter, Inc., 22 74–77
Beckman Instruments, Inc., 14 52–54
Becton, Dickinson & Company, I 630–31; 11 34–36 (upd.); 36 84–89 (upd.)
Bed Bath & Beyond Inc., 13 81–83; 41 49–52 (upd.)
Beech Aircraft Corporation, 8 49–52 *see also* Raytheon Aircraft Holdings Inc.
Beech-Nut Nutrition Corporation, 21 53–56; 51 47–51 (upd.)
Beer Nuts, Inc., 86 30–33
Behr GmbH & Co. KG, 72 22–25
Behring Diagnostics *see* Dade Behring Holdings Inc.
BEI Technologies, Inc., 65 74–76
Beiersdorf AG, 29 49–53
Bekaert S.A./N.V., 90 53–57
Bekins Company, 15 48–50
Bel *see* Fromageries Bel.
Bel Fuse, Inc., 53 59–62
Bel/Kaukauna USA, 76 46–48
Belco Oil & Gas Corp., 40 63–65
Belden CDT Inc., 19 43–45; 76 49–52 (upd.)
Belgacom, 6 302–04
Belk, Inc., V 12–13; 19 46–48 (upd.); 72 26–29 (upd.)
Bell and Howell Company, 9 61–64; 29 54–58 (upd.)
Bell Atlantic Corporation, V 272–74; 25 58–62 (upd.) *see also* Verizon Communications.
Bell Canada Enterprises Inc. *see* BCE, Inc.
Bell Canada International, Inc., 6 305–08
Bell Helicopter Textron Inc., 46 64–67
Bell Industries, Inc., 47 40–43
Bell Resources *see* TPG NV.
Bell Sports Corporation, 16 51–53; 44 51–54 (upd.)
Bellcore *see* Telcordia Technologies, Inc.
Belleek Pottery Ltd., 71 50–53
Belleville Shoe Manufacturing Company, 92 17–20
Bellisio Foods, Inc., 95 51–54
BellSouth Corporation, V 276–78; 29 59–62 (upd.) *see also* AT&T Corp.
Bellway Plc, 45 37–39
Belo Corporation *see* A.H. Belo Corporation
Beloit Corporation, 14 55–57 *see also* Metso Corp.
Belron International Ltd., 76 53–56
Belvedere S.A., 93 77–81
Bemis Company, Inc., 8 53–55; 91 53–60 (upd.)
Ben & Jerry's Homemade, Inc., 10 146–48; 35 58–62 (upd.); 80 22–28 (upd.)
Ben Bridge Jeweler, Inc., 60 52–54
Ben E. Keith Company, 76 57–59
Benchmark Capital, 49 50–52
Benchmark Electronics, Inc., 40 66–69
Benckiser N.V. *see* Reckitt Benckiser plc.
Bendix Corporation, I 141–43
Beneficial Corporation, 8 56–58
Benesse Corporation, 76 60–62
Bénéteau SA, 55 54–56
Benetton Group S.p.A., 10 149–52; 67 47–51 (upd.)
Benfield Greig Group plc, 53 63–65
Benguet Corporation, 58 21–24
Benihana, Inc., 18 56–59; 76 63–66 (upd.)
Benjamin Moore and Co., 13 84–87; 38 95–99 (upd.)

BenQ Corporation, **67** 52–54
Benton Oil and Gas Company, **47** 44–46
Berean Christian Stores, **96** 40–43
Beretta *see* Fabbrica D' Armi Pietro Beretta S.p.A.
Bergdorf Goodman Inc., **52** 45–48
Bergen Brunswig Corporation, **V** 14–16; **13** 88–90 (upd.) *see also* AmerisourceBergen Corp.
Berger Bros Company, **62** 31–33
Beringer Blass Wine Estates Ltd., **22** 78–81; **66** 34–37 (upd.)
Berjaya Group Bhd., **67** 55–57
Berkeley Farms, Inc., **46** 68–70
Berkshire Hathaway Inc., **III** 213–15; **18** 60–63 (upd.); **42** 31–36 (upd.); **89** 92–99 (upd.)
Berkshire Realty Holdings, L.P., **49** 53–55
Berlex Laboratories, Inc., **66** 38–40
Berliner Stadtreinigungsbetriebe, **58** 25–28
Berliner Verkehrsbetriebe (BVG), **58** 29–31
Berlinwasser Holding AG, **90** 58–62
Berlitz International, Inc., **13** 91–93; **39** 47–50 (upd.)
Bernard C. Harris Publishing Company, Inc., **39** 51–53
Bernard Chaus, Inc., **27** 59–61
Bernard Hodes Group Inc., **86** 34–37
Bernard Matthews Ltd., **89** 100–04
The Bernick Companies, **75** 62–65
Bernina Holding AG, **47** 47–50
Bernstein-Rein,**92** 21–24
The Berry Company *see* L. M. Berry and Company
Berry Petroleum Company, **47** 51–53
Berry Plastics Corporation, **21** 57–59
Bertelsmann A.G., **IV** 592–94; **43** 63–67 (upd.); **91** 61–68 (upd.)
Bertucci's Corporation, **16** 54–56; **64** 51–54 (upd.)
Berwick Offray, LLC, **70** 17–19
Besix Group S.A./NV, **94** 66–69
Besnier SA, **19** 49–51 *see also* Groupe Lactalis
Best Kosher Foods Corporation, **82** 41–44
Best Buy Co., Inc., **9** 65–66; **23** 51–53 (upd.); **63** 61–66 (upd.)
Bestfoods, **22** 82–86 (upd.)
Bestseller A/S, **90** 63–66
Bestway Transportation *see* TNT Freightways Corp.
BET Holdings, Inc., **18** 64–66
Beth Abraham Family of Health Services, **94** 70–74
Beth Israel Medical Center *see* Continuum Health Partners, Inc.
Bethlehem Steel Corporation, **IV** 35–37; **7** 48–51 (upd.); **27** 62–66 (upd.)
Better Made Snack Foods, Inc., **90** 67–69
Bettys & Taylors of Harrogate Ltd., **72** 30–32
Betz Laboratories, Inc., **I** 312–13; **10** 153–55 (upd.)
Beverly Enterprises, Inc., **III** 76–77; **16** 57–59 (upd.)
Bewag AG, **39** 54–57
BFC Construction Corporation, **25** 63–65
The BFGoodrich Company, **V** 231–33; **19** 52–55 (upd.) *see also* Goodrich Corp.
BFI *see* The British Film Institute; Browning-Ferris Industries, Inc.
BFP Holdings Corp. *see* Big Flower Press Holdings, Inc.
BG Products Inc., **96** 44–47
BG&E *see* Baltimore Gas and Electric Co.
Bharti Tele-Ventures Limited, **75** 66–68
BHC Communications, Inc., **26** 32–34
BHP Billiton, **67** 58–64 (upd.)
Bhs plc, **17** 42–44
Bianchi International (d/b/a Gregory Mountain Products), **76** 67–69
Bibliographisches Institut & F.A. Brockhaus AG, **74** 30–34
BIC Corporation, **8** 59–61; **23** 54–57 (upd.)
BICC PLC, **III** 433–34 *see also* Balfour Beatty plc.
Bicoastal Corporation, **II** 9–11
Biffa plc, **92** 25–28
Big A Drug Stores Inc., **79** 62–65
Big B, Inc., **17** 45–47
Big Bear Stores Co., **13** 94–96
Big Brothers Big Sisters of America, **85** 29–33
Big Dog Holdings, Inc., **45** 40–42
Big 5 Sporting Goods Corporation, **55** 57–59
Big Flower Press Holdings, Inc., **21** 60–62 *see also* Vertis Communications.
The Big Food Group plc, **68** 50–53 (upd.)
Big Idea Productions, Inc., **49** 56–59
Big Lots, Inc., **50** 98–101
Big O Tires, Inc., **20** 61–63
Big Rivers Electric Corporation, **11** 37–39
Big V Supermarkets, Inc., **25** 66–68
Big Y Foods, Inc., **53** 66–68
Bigard *see* Groupe Bigard S.A.
BigBen Interactive S.A., **72** 33–35
Bilfinger & Berger AG, **I** 560–61; **55** 60–63 (upd.)
Bill & Melinda Gates Foundation, **41** 53–55
Bill Barrett Corporation, **71** 54–56
Bill Blass Ltd., **32** 78–80
Billabong International Ltd., **44** 55–58
Billing Concepts, Inc., **26** 35–38; **72** 36–39 (upd.)
Bimbo *see* Grupo Industrial Bimbo.
Bindley Western Industries, Inc., **9** 67–69 *see also* Cardinal Health, Inc.
The Bing Group, **60** 55–58
Bingham Dana LLP, **43** 68–71
Binks Sames Corporation, **21** 63–66
Binney & Smith Inc., **25** 69–72
Bio-Rad Laboratories, Inc., **93** 82–86
Biogen Idec Inc., **14** 58–60; **36** 90–93 (upd.); **71** 57–59 (upd.)
Bioindustrias *see* Valores Industriales S.A.
Biokyowa *see* Kyowa Hakko Kogyo Co., Ltd.
Biolase Technology, Inc., **87** 55–58
bioMérieux S.A., **75** 69–71
Biomet, Inc., **10** 156–58; **93** 87–94 (upd.)
Biosite Incorporated, **73** 60–62
Biovail Corporation, **47** 54–56
BioWare Corporation, **81** 50–53
Bird Corporation, **19** 56–58
Birds Eye Foods, Inc., **69** 66–72 (upd.)
Birkenstock Footprint Sandals, Inc., **12** 33–35; **42** 37–40 (upd.)
Birmingham Steel Corporation, **13** 97–98; **40** 70–73 (upd.) *see also* Nucor Corporation
Birse Group PLC, **77** 54–58
Birthdays Ltd., **70** 20–22
BISSELL, Inc., **9** 70–72; **30** 75–78 (upd.)
The BISYS Group, Inc., **73** 63–65
BIW *see* Bath Iron Works.
BJ Services Company, **25** 73–75
BJ's Wholesale Club, Inc., **94** 75–78
BKD LLP, **96** 48–51
The Black & Decker Corporation, **III** 435–37; **20** 64–68 (upd.); **67** 65–70 (upd.)
Black & Veatch LLP, **22** 87–90
Black Box Corporation, **20** 69–71; **96** 52–56 (upd.)
Black Diamond Equipment, Ltd., **62** 34–37
Black Entertainment Television *see* BET Holdings, Inc.
Black Hills Corporation, **20** 72–74
Blackbaud, Inc., **85** 34–37
BlackBerry *see* Research in Motion Ltd.
Blackboard Inc., **89** 105–10
Blackfoot Telecommunications Group, **60** 59–62
BlackRock, Inc., **79** 66–69
Blacks Leisure Group plc, **39** 58–60
Blackwater USA, **76** 70–73
Blackwell Publishing (Holdings) Ltd., **78** 34–37
Blair Corporation, **25** 76–78; **31** 53–55
Blessings Corp., **19** 59–61
Blimpie International, Inc., **15** 55–57; **49** 60–64 (upd.)
Blish-Mize Co., **95** 55–58
Blizzard Entertainment, **78** 38–42
Block Communications, Inc., **81** 54–58
Block Drug Company, Inc., **8** 62–64; **27** 67–70 (upd.) *see also* GlaxoSmithKline plc.
Blockbuster Inc., **9** 73–75; **31** 56–60 (upd.); **76** 74–78 (upd.)
Blodgett Holdings, Inc., **61** 34–37 (upd.)
Blokker Holding B.V., **84** 21–24
Blonder Tongue Laboratories, Inc., **48** 52–55
Bloomberg L.P., **21** 67–71
Bloomingdale's Inc., **12** 36–38

Blount International, Inc., 12 39–41; 48 56–60 (upd.)
BLP Group Companies *see* Boron, LePore & Associates, Inc.
Blue Bell Creameries L.P., 30 79–81
Blue Bird Corporation, 35 63–66
Blue Circle Industries PLC, III 669–71 *see also* Lafarge Cement UK.
Blue Coat Systems, Inc., 83 42-45
Blue Cross and Blue Shield Association, 10 159–61
Blue Diamond Growers, 28 56–58
Blue Heron Paper Company, 90 70–73
Blue Martini Software, Inc., 59 77–80
Blue Mountain Arts, Inc., 29 63–66
Blue Nile Inc., 61 38–40
Blue Rhino Corporation, 56 34–37
Blue Ridge Beverage Company Inc., 82 45–48
Blue Square Israel Ltd., 41 56–58
Bluefly, Inc., 60 63–65
Bluegreen Corporation, 80 29–32
BlueLinx Holdings Inc., 97 68–72
Blundstone Pty Ltd., 76 79–81
Blyth, Inc., 18 67–69; 74 35–38 (upd.)
BMC Industries, Inc., 17 48–51; 59 81–86 (upd.)
BMC Software, Inc., 55 64–67
BMG/Music *see* Bertelsmann AG.
BMHC *see* Building Materials Holding Corp.
BMI *see* Broadcast Music Inc.
BMW *see* Bayerische Motoren Werke.
BNA *see* Bureau of National Affairs, Inc.
BNE *see* Bank of New England Corp.
BNL *see* Banca Nazionale del Lavoro S.p.A.
BNP Paribas Group, 36 94–97 (upd.)
Boardwalk Pipeline Partners, LP, 87 59–62
Boart Longyear Company, 26 39–42
Boatmen's Bancshares Inc., 15 58–60 *see also* Bank of America Corp.
Bob Evans Farms, Inc., 9 76–79; 63 67–72 (upd.)
Bob's Red Mill Natural Foods, Inc., 63 73–75
Bobit Publishing Company, 55 68–70
Bobs Candies, Inc., 70 23–25
BOC Group plc, I 314–16; 25 79–82 (upd.); 78 43–49 (upd.)
Boca Resorts, Inc., 37 33–36
Boddie-Noell Enterprises, Inc., 68 54–56
Bodum Design Group AG, 47 57–59
Body Glove International LLC, 88 29–32
The Body Shop International plc, 11 40–42; 53 69–72 (upd.)
Bodycote International PLC, 63 76–78
Boehringer Ingelheim GmbH *see* C.H. Boehringer Sohn.
The Boeing Company, I 47–49; 10 162–65 (upd.); 32 81–87 (upd.)
Bogen Communications International, Inc., 62 38–41
Bohemia, Inc., 13 99–101
BÖHLER-UDDEHOLM AG, 73 66–69
Boiron S.A., 73 70–72
Boise Cascade Corporation, IV 255–56; 8 65–67 (upd.); 32 88–92 (upd.); 95 59–66 (upd.)
Boizel Chanoine Champagne S.A., 94 79–82
Boliden AB, 80 33–36
Bojangles Restaurants Inc., 97 73–77
Bollinger Shipyards, Inc., 61 41–43
Bols Distilleries NV, 74 39–42
Bolsa Mexicana de Valores, S.A. de C.V., 80 37–40
Bolton Group B.V., 86 38–41
Bombardier Inc., 42 41–46 (upd.); 87 63–71 (upd.)
The Bombay Company, Inc., 10 166–68; 71 60–64 (upd.)
Bon Appetit Holding AG, 48 61–63
The Bon Marché, Inc., 23 58–60 *see also* Federated Department Stores Inc.
Bon Secours Health System, Inc., 24 68–71
The Bon-Ton Stores, Inc., 16 60–62; 50 106–10 (upd.)
Bond Corporation Holdings Limited, 10 169–71
Bonduelle SA, 51 52–54
Bongard *see* Aga Foodservice Group PLC.
Bongrain SA, 25 83–85
Bonhams 1793 Ltd., 72 40–42
Bonneville International Corporation, 29 67–70
Bonneville Power Administration, 50 102–05
Bonnier AB, 52 49–52
Book-of-the-Month Club, Inc., 13 105–07
Booker plc, 13 102–04; 31 61–64 (upd.)
Booker Cash & Carry Ltd., 68 57–61 (upd.)
Books-A-Million, Inc., 14 61–62; 41 59–62 (upd.); 96 57–61 (upd.)
Books Are Fun, Ltd. *see* The Reader's Digest Association, Inc.
Bookspan, 86 42–46
Boole & Babbage, Inc., 25 86–88 *see also* BMC Software, Inc.
Booth Creek Ski Holdings, Inc., 31 65–67
The Boots Company PLC, V 17–19; 24 72–76 (upd.) *see also* Alliance Boots plc.
Boots & Coots International Well Control, Inc., 79 70–73
Booz Allen & Hamilton Inc., 10 172–75
Boral Limited, III 672–74; 43 72–76 (upd.)
Borden, Inc., II 470–73; 22 91–96 (upd.)
Borders Group, Inc., 15 61–62; 43 77–79 (upd.)
Borealis AG, 94 83–86
Borg-Warner Automotive, Inc., 14 63–66; 32 93–97 (upd.)
Borg-Warner Corporation, III 438–41 *see also* Burns International.
BorgWarner Inc., 85 38–44 (upd.)
Borland International, Inc., 9 80–82
Boron, LePore & Associates, Inc., 45 43–45
Bosch *see* Robert Bosch GmbH.
Boscov's Department Store, Inc., 31 68–70
Bose Corporation, 13 108–10; 36 98–101 (upd.)
Boss Holdings, Inc., 97 78–81
Boston Acoustics, Inc., 22 97–99
The Boston Beer Company, Inc., 18 70–73; 50 111–15 (upd.)
Boston Celtics Limited Partnership, 14 67–69
Boston Chicken, Inc., 12 42–44 *see also* Boston Market Corp.
The Boston Consulting Group, 58 32–35
Boston Edison Company, 12 45–47
Boston Market Corporation, 48 64–67 (upd.)
Boston Pizza International Inc., 88 33–38
Boston Professional Hockey Association Inc., 39 61–63
Boston Properties, Inc., 22 100–02
Boston Scientific Corporation, 37 37–40; 77 58–63 (upd.)
The Boston Symphony Orchestra Inc., 93 95–99
Bou-Matic, 62 42–44
Bourbon *see* Groupe Bourbon S.A.
Bourbon Corporation, 82 49-52
Bouygues S.A., I 562–64; 24 77–80 (upd.); 97 82–87 (upd.)
Bovis *see* Peninsular and Oriental Steam Navigation Company (Bovis Division)
Bowater PLC, IV 257–59
Bowne & Co., Inc., 23 61–64; 79 74–80 (upd.)
Bowthorpe plc, 33 70–72
The Boy Scouts of America, 34 66–69
Boyd Bros. Transportation Inc., 39 64–66
Boyd Coffee Company, 53 73–75
Boyd Gaming Corporation, 43 80–82
The Boyds Collection, Ltd., 29 71–73
Boyne USA Resorts, 71 65–68
Boys & Girls Clubs of America, 69 73–75
Bozell Worldwide Inc., 25 89–91
Bozzuto's, Inc., 13 111–12
BP p.l.c., 45 46–56 (upd.)
BPB plc, 83 46-49
Braathens ASA, 47 60–62
Brach's Confections, Inc., 15 63–65; 74 43–46 (upd.)
Bradford & Bingley PLC, 65 77–80
Bradlees Discount Department Store Company, 12 48–50
Bradley Air Services Ltd., 56 38–40
Brady Corporation, 78 50–55 (upd.)
Brake Bros plc, 45 57–59
Bramalea Ltd., 9 83–85
Brambles Industries Limited, 42 47–50
Brammer PLC, 77 64–67
The Branch Group, Inc., 72 43–45

BrandPartners Group, Inc., 58 36–38
Brannock Device Company, 48 68–70
Brascan Corporation, 67 71–73
Brasfield & Gorrie LLC, 87 72–75
Brasil Telecom Participaçoes S.A., 57 67–70
Brass Eagle Inc., 34 70–72
Brauerei Beck & Co., 9 86–87; 33 73–76 (upd.)
Braun GmbH, 51 55–58
Brazil Fast Food Corporation, 74 47–49
Brazos Sportswear, Inc., 23 65–67
Breeze-Eastern Corporation, 95 67–70
Bremer Financial Corp., 45 60–63
Brenntag AG, 8 68–69; 23 68–70 (upd.)
Briazz, Inc., 53 76–79
The Brickman Group, Ltd., 87 76–79
Bricorama S.A., 68 62–64
Bridgeport Machines, Inc., 17 52–54
Bridgestone Corporation, V 234–35; 21 72–75 (upd.); 59 87–92 (upd.)
Bridgford Foods Corporation, 27 71–73
Briggs & Stratton Corporation, 8 70–73; 27 74–78 (upd.)
Brigham Exploration Company, 75 72–74
Brigham's Inc., 72 46–48
Bright Horizons Family Solutions, Inc., 31 71–73
Brightpoint, Inc., 18 74–77
Brillstein-Grey Entertainment, 80 41–45
The Brink's Company, 58 39–43 (upd.)
Brinker International, Inc., 10 176–78; 38 100–03 (upd.); 75 75–79 (upd.)
BRIO AB, 24 81–83
Brioche Pasquier S.A., 58 44–46
Brioni Roman Style S.p.A., 67 74–76
BRISA Auto-estradas de Portugal S.A., 64 55–58
Bristol Hotel Company, 23 71–73
Bristol-Myers Squibb Company, III 17–19; 9 88–91 (upd.); 37 41–45 (upd.)
Bristow Helicopters Ltd., 70 26–28
Britannia Soft Drinks Ltd. (Britvic), 71 69–71
Britannica.com *see* Encyclopaedia Britannica, Inc.
Brite Voice Systems, Inc., 20 75–78
British Aerospace plc, I 50–53; 24 84–90 (upd.)
British Airways plc, I 92–95; 14 70–74 (upd.); 43 83–88 (upd.)
British American Tobacco PLC, 50 116–19 (upd.)
British-Borneo Oil & Gas PLC, 34 73–75
British Broadcasting Corporation Ltd., 7 52–55; 21 76–79 (upd.); 89 111–17 (upd.)
British Coal Corporation, IV 38–40
British Columbia Telephone Company, 6 309–11
British Energy Plc, 49 65–68 *see also* British Nuclear Fuels PLC.
The British Film Institute, 80 46–50
British Gas plc, V 559–63 *see also* Centrica plc.
British Land Plc, 54 38–41
British Midland plc, 38 104–06
The British Museum, 71 72–74
British Nuclear Fuels PLC, 6 451–54
British Oxygen Co *see* BOC Group.
The British Petroleum Company plc, IV 378–80; 7 56–59 (upd.); 21 80–84 (upd.) *see also* BP p.l.c.
British Railways Board, V 421–24
British Sky Broadcasting Group plc, 20 79–81; 60 66–69 (upd.)
British Steel plc, IV 41–43; 19 62–65 (upd.)
British Sugar plc, 84 25–29
British Telecommunications plc, V 279–82; 15 66–70 (upd.) *see also* BT Group plc.
The British United Provident Association Limited, 79 81–84
British Vita plc, 9 92–93; 33 77–79 (upd.)
British World Airlines Ltd., 18 78–80
Britvic Soft Drinks Limited *see* Britannia Soft Drinks Ltd. (Britvic)
Broadcast Music Inc., 23 74–77; 90 74–79 (upd.)
Broadcom Corporation, 34 76–79; 90 80–85 (upd.)
The Broadmoor Hotel, 30 82–85
Broadwing Corporation, 70 29–32
Brobeck, Phleger & Harrison, LLP, 31 74–76
Brockhaus *see* Bibliographisches Institut & F.A. Brockhaus AG.
Brodart Company, 84 30–33
Broder Bros. Co., 38 107–09
Broderbund Software, Inc., 13 113–16; 29 74–78 (upd.)
Broken Hill Proprietary Company Ltd., IV 44–47; 22 103–08 (upd.) *see also* BHP Billiton.
Bronco Drilling Company, Inc., 89 118–21
Bronner Brothers Inc., 92 29–32
Bronner Display & Sign Advertising, Inc., 82 53-57
Brookdale Senior Living, 91 69–73
Brooke Group Ltd., 15 71–73 *see also* Vector Group Ltd.
Brookfield Properties Corporation, 89 122–25
Brooklyn Union Gas, 6 455–57 *see also* KeySpan Energy Co.
Brooks Brothers Inc., 22 109–12
Brooks Sports Inc., 32 98–101
Brookshire Grocery Company, 16 63–66; 74 50–53 (upd.)
Brookstone, Inc., 18 81–83
Brose Fahrzeugteile GmbH & Company KG, 84 34–38
Brother Industries, Ltd., 14 75–76
Brother's Brother Foundation, 93 100–04
Brothers Gourmet Coffees, Inc., 20 82–85 *see also* The Procter & Gamble Co.
Broughton Foods Co., 17 55–57 *see also* Suiza Foods Corp.
Brouwerijen Alken-Maes N.V., 86 47–51
Brown & Brown, Inc., 41 63–66
Brown & Haley, 23 78–80
Brown & Root, Inc., 13 117–19 *see also* Kellogg Brown & Root Inc.
Brown & Sharpe Manufacturing Co., 23 81–84
Brown and Williamson Tobacco Corporation, 14 77–79; 33 80–83 (upd.)
Brown Brothers Harriman & Co., 45 64–67
Brown-Forman Corporation, I 225–27; 10 179–82 (upd.); 38 110–14 (upd.)
Brown Group, Inc., V 351–53; 20 86–89 (upd.) *see also* Brown Shoe Company, Inc.
Brown Jordan International Inc., 74 54–57 (upd.)
Brown Printing Company, 26 43–45
Brown Shoe Company, Inc., 68 65–69 (upd.)
Browning-Ferris Industries, Inc., V 749–53; 20 90–93 (upd.)
Broyhill Furniture Industries, Inc., 10 183–85
Bruce Foods Corporation, 39 67–69
Bruegger's Corporation, 63 79–82
Bruno's Supermarkets, Inc., 7 60–62; 26 46–48 (upd.); 68 70–73 (upd.)
Brunschwig & Fils Inc., 96 62–65
Brunswick Corporation, III 442–44; 22 113–17 (upd.); 77 68–75 (upd.)
Brush Engineered Materials Inc., 67 77–79
Brush Wellman Inc., 14 80–82
Bruster's Real Ice Cream, Inc., 80 51–54
BSA *see* The Boy Scouts of America.
BSC *see* Birmingham Steel Corporation
BSH Bosch und Siemens Hausgeräte GmbH, 67 80–84
BSN Groupe S.A., II 474–75 *see also* Groupe Danone
BT Group plc, 49 69–74 (upd.)
BTG, Inc., 45 68–70
BTG Plc, 87 80–83
BTR plc, I 428–30
BTR Siebe plc, 27 79–81 *see also* Invensys PLC.
Buca, Inc., 38 115–17
Buck Consultants, Inc., 55 71–73
Buck Knives Inc., 48 71–74
Buckeye Partners, L.P., 70 33–36
Buckeye Technologies, Inc., 42 51–54
The Buckle, Inc., 18 84–86
Bucyrus International, Inc., 17 58–61
The Budd Company, 8 74–76 *see also* ThyssenKrupp AG.
Buderus AG, 37 46–49
Budgens Ltd., 59 93–96
Budget Group, Inc., 25 92–94 *see also* Cendant Corp.
Budget Rent a Car Corporation, 9 94–95
Budweiser Budvar, National Corporation, 59 97–100

Buena Vista Home Video *see* The Walt Disney Co.
Bufete Industrial, S.A. de C.V., 34 80–82
Buffalo Grill S.A., 94 87–90
Buffalo Wild Wings, Inc., 56 41–43
Buffets Holdings, Inc., 10 186–87; 32 102–04 (upd.); 93 105–09 (upd.)
Bugatti Automobiles S.A.S., 94 91–94
Bugle Boy Industries, Inc., 18 87–88
Buhrmann NV, 41 67–69
Buick Motor Co. *see* General Motors Corp.
Build-A-Bear Workshop Inc., 62 45–48
Building Materials Holding Corporation, 52 53–55
Bulgari S.p.A., 20 94–97
Bull *see* Compagnie des Machines Bull S.A.
Bull S.A., 43 89–91 (upd.)
Bulley & Andrews, LLC, 55 74–76
Bulova Corporation, 13 120–22; 41 70–73 (upd.)
Bumble Bee Seafoods L.L.C., 64 59–61
Bundy Corporation, 17 62–65
Bunge Ltd., 62 49–51
Bunzl plc, IV 260–62; 31 77–80 (upd.)
Burberry Group plc, 17 66–68; 41 74–76 (upd.); 92 33–37 (upd.)
Burda Holding GmbH. & Co., 23 85–89
Burdines, Inc., 60 70–73
The Bureau of National Affairs, Inc., 23 90–93
Bureau Veritas SA, 55 77–79
Burelle S.A., 23 94–96
Burger King Corporation, II 613–15; 17 69–72 (upd.); 56 44–48 (upd.)
Burgett, Inc., 97 88–91
Burke, Inc., 88 39–42
Burke Mills, Inc., 66 41–43
Burlington Coat Factory Warehouse Corporation, 10 188–89; 60 74–76 (upd.)
Burlington Industries, Inc., V 354–55; 17 73–76 (upd.)
Burlington Northern Santa Fe Corporation, V 425–28; 27 82–89 (upd.)
Burlington Resources Inc., 10 190–92 *see also* ConocoPhillips.
Burmah Castrol PLC, IV 381–84; 30 86–91 (upd.) *see also* BP p.l.c.
Burns International Security Services, 13 123–25 *see also* Securitas AB.
Burns International Services Corporation, 41 77–80 (upd.)
Burns, Philp & Company Ltd., 63 83–86
Burpee & Co. *see* W. Atlee Burpee & Co.
Burr-Brown Corporation, 19 66–68
Burroughs & Chapin Company, Inc., 86 52–55
Burt's Bees, Inc., 58 47–50
The Burton Corporation, V 20–22; 94 95–100 (upd.)
The Burton Group plc, *see also* Arcadia Group plc.
Burton Snowboards Inc., 22 118–20, 460
Busch Entertainment Corporation, 73 73–75
Bush Boake Allen Inc., 30 92–94 *see also* International Flavors & Fragrances Inc.
Bush Brothers & Company, 45 71–73
Bush Industries, Inc., 20 98–100
Business Men's Assurance Company of America, 14 83–85
Business Objects S.A., 25 95–97
Business Post Group plc, 46 71–73
Butler Manufacturing Company, 12 51–53; 62 52–56 (upd.)
Butterick Co., Inc., 23 97–99
Buttrey Food & Drug Stores Co., 18 89–91
buy.com, Inc., 46 74–77
Buzztime Entertainment, Inc. *see* NTN Buzztime, Inc.
BVR Systems (1998) Ltd., 93 110–13
BWAY Corporation, 24 91–93

C

C&A, 40 74–77 (upd.)
C&A Brenninkmeyer KG, V 23–24
C&G *see* Cheltenham & Gloucester PLC.
C&J Clark International Ltd., 52 56–59
C&K Market, Inc., 81 59–61
C & S Wholesale Grocers, Inc., 55 80–83
C-COR.net Corp., 38 118–21
C-Cube Microsystems, Inc., 37 50–54
C. Bechstein Pianofortefabrik AG, 96 66–71
C.F. Martin & Co., Inc., 42 55–58
The C.F. Sauer Company, 90 86–89
C. Hoare & Co., 77 76–79
C.H. Boehringer Sohn, 39 70–73
C.H. Guenther & Son, Inc., 84 39–42
C.H. Heist Corporation, 24 111–13
C.H. Robinson Worldwide, Inc., 11 43–44; 40 78–81 (upd.)
C.I. Traders Limited, 61 44–46
C. Itoh & Co., I 431–33 *see also* ITOCHU Corp.
C.R. Bard, Inc., 9 96–98; 65 81–85 (upd.)
C.R. Meyer and Sons Company, 74 58–60
C-Tech Industries Inc., 90 90–93
CAA *see* Creative Artists Agency LLC.
Cabela's Inc., 26 49–51; 68 74–77 (upd.)
Cable & Wireless HKT, 30 95–98 (upd.)
Cable and Wireless plc, V 283–86; 25 98–102 (upd.)
Cabletron Systems, Inc., 10 193–94
Cablevision Electronic Instruments, Inc., 32 105–07
Cablevision Systems Corporation, 7 63–65; 30 99–103 (upd.)
Cabot Corporation, 8 77–79; 29 79–82 (upd.); 91 74–80 (upd.)
Cache Incorporated, 30 104–06
CACI International Inc., 21 85–87; 72 49–53 (upd.)
Cactus Feeders, Inc., 91 81–84
Cactus S.A., 90 94–97
Cadbury Schweppes PLC, II 476–78; 49 75–79 (upd.)
Cadence Design Systems, Inc., 11 45–48; 48 75–79 (upd.)
Cadmus Communications Corporation, 23 100–03 *see also* Cenveo Inc.
CAE USA Inc., 48 80–82
Caere Corporation, 20 101–03
Caesars World, Inc., 6 199–202
Caffè Nero Group PLC, 63 87–89
Cagle's, Inc., 20 104–07
Cahners Business Information, 43 92–95
Caisse des Dépôts et Consignations, 90 98–101
CAL *see* China Airlines.
Cal-Maine Foods, Inc., 69 76–78
CalAmp Corp., 87 84–87
Calavo Growers, Inc., 47 63–66
CalComp Inc., 13 126–29
Calcot Ltd., 33 84–87
Caldor Inc., 12 54–56
Calgon Carbon Corporation, 73 76–79
California Cedar Products Company, 58 51–53
California Pizza Kitchen Inc., 15 74–76; 74 61–63 (upd.)
California Sports, Inc., 56 49–52
California Steel Industries, Inc., 67 85–87
California Water Service Group, 79 85–88
Caliper Life Sciences, Inc., 70 37–40
Callanan Industries, Inc., 60 77–79
Callard and Bowser-Suchard Inc., 84 43–46
Callaway Golf Company, 15 77–79; 45 74–77 (upd.)
Callon Petroleum Company, 47 67–69
Calloway's Nursery, Inc., 51 59–61
CalMat Co., 19 69–72 *see also* Vulcan Materials Co.
Calpine Corporation, 36 102–04
Caltex Petroleum Corporation, 19 73–75 *see also* ChevronTexaco Corp.
Calvin Klein, Inc., 22 121–24; 55 84–88 (upd.)
Camaïeu S.A., 72 54–56
Camargo Corrêa S.A., 93 114–18
CamBar *see* Cameron & Barkley Co.
Cambrex Corporation, 16 67–69; 44 59–62 (upd.)
Cambridge SoundWorks, Inc., 48 83–86
Cambridge Technology Partners, Inc., 36 105–08
Camden Property Trust, 77 80–83
Cameco Corporation, 77 84–87
Camelot Music, Inc., 26 52–54
Cameron & Barkley Company, 28 59–61 *see also* Hagemeyer North America.
Campbell-Ewald Advertising, 86 56–60
Campbell-Mithun-Esty, Inc., 16 70–72 *see also* Interpublic Group of Companies, Inc.
Campbell Scientific, Inc., 51 62–65

Campbell Soup Company, II 479–81; 7 66–69 (upd.); 26 55–59 (upd.); 71 75–81 (upd.)
Campeau Corporation, V 25–28
The Campina Group, 78 61–64
Campo Electronics, Appliances & Computers, Inc., 16 73–75
Campofrío Alimentación S.A, 59 101–03
Canada Packers Inc., II 482–85
Canada Trust *see* CT Financial Services Inc.
Canadair, Inc., 16 76–78 *see also* Bombardier Inc.
The Canadian Broadcasting Corporation (CBC), 37 55–58
Canadian Imperial Bank of Commerce, II 244–46; 61 47–51 (upd.)
Canadian National Railway Company, 6 359–62; 71 82–88 (upd.)
Canadian Pacific Railway Limited, V 429–31; 45 78–83 (upd.); 95 71–80 (upd.)
Canadian Tire Corporation, Limited, 71 89–93 (upd.)
Canadian Utilities Limited, 13 130–32; 56 53–56 (upd.)
Canal Plus, 10 195–97; 34 83–86 (upd.)
Canandaigua Brands, Inc., 13 133–35; 34 87–91 (upd.) *see also* Constellation Brands, Inc.
Canary Wharf Group Plc, 30 107–09
Cancer Treatment Centers of America, Inc., 85 45–48
Candela Corporation, 48 87–89
Candie's, Inc., 31 81–84
Candle Corporation, 64 62–65
Candlewood Hotel Company, Inc., 41 81–83
Canfor Corporation, 42 59–61
Cannon Design, 63 90–92
Cannon Express, Inc., 53 80–82
Cannondale Corporation, 21 88–90
Cano Petroleum Inc., 97 92–95
Canon Inc., III 120–21; 18 92–95 (upd.); ; 79 89–95 (upd.)
Canstar Sports Inc., 16 79–81 *see also* NIKE, Inc.
Cantel Medical Corporation, 80 55–58
Canterbury Park Holding Corporation, 42 62–65
Cantine Giorgio Lungarotti S.R.L., 67 88–90
Cantor Fitzgerald, L.P., 92 38–42
CanWest Global Communications Corporation, 35 67–703
Cap Gemini Ernst & Young, 37 59–61
Cap Rock Energy Corporation, 46 78–81
Caparo Group Ltd., 90 102–06
Capcom Company Ltd., 83 50-53
Cape Cod Potato Chip Company, 90 107–10
Capel Incorporated, 45 84–86
Capezio/Ballet Makers Inc., 62 57–59
Capita Group PLC, 69 79–81
Capital Cities/ABC Inc., II 129–31
Capital Holding Corporation, III 216–19 *see also* Providian Financial Corp.
Capital One Financial Corporation, 52 60–63
Capital Radio plc, 35 71–73
Capital Senior Living Corporation, 75 80–82
Capitalia S.p.A., 65 86–89
Capitol Records, Inc., 90 111–16
CapStar Hotel Company, 21 91–93
Capstone Turbine Corporation, 75 83–85
Captain D's, LLC, 59 104–06
Captaris, Inc., 89 126–29
The Carphone Warehouse Group PLC, 83 54-57
Car Toys, Inc., 67 91–93
Caradon plc, 20 108–12 (upd.) *see also* Novar plc.
Carus Publishing Company, 93 128–32
Caraustar Industries, Inc., 19 76–78; 44 63–67 (upd.)
The Carbide/Graphite Group, Inc., 40 82–84
Carbo PLC, 67 94–96 (upd.)
Carbone Lorraine S.A., 33 88–90
Carborundum Company, 15 80–82 *see also* Carbo PLC.
Cardinal Health, Inc., 18 96–98; 50 120–23 (upd.)
Cardo AB, 53 83–85
Cardone Industries Inc., 92 43–47
Cardtronics, Inc., 93 119–23
Career Education Corporation, 45 87–89
CareerBuilder, Inc., 93 124–27
Caremark Rx, Inc., 10 198–200; 54 42–45 (upd.)
Carey International, Inc., 26 60–63
Cargill, Incorporated, II 616–18; 13 136–38 (upd.); 40 85–90 (upd.); 89 130–39 (upd.)
Cargolux Airlines International S.A., 49 80–82
Carhartt, Inc., 30 110–12; 77 88–92 (upd.)
Caribiner International, Inc., 24 94–97
Caribou Coffee Company, Inc., 28 62–65; 97 96–102 (upd.)
Caritas Internationalis, 72 57–59
Carl Allers Etablissement A/S, 72 60–62
Carl Kühne KG (GmbH & Co.), 94 101–05
Carl Zeiss AG, III 445–47; 34 92–97 (upd.); 91 85–92 (upd.)
Carl's Jr. *see* CKE Restaurants, Inc.
Carlisle Companies Inc., 8 80–82; 82 58-62 (upd.)
Carlsberg A/S, 9 99–101; 29 83–85 (upd.)
Carlson Companies, Inc., 6 363–66; 22 125–29 (upd.); 87 88–95 (upd.)
Carlson Restaurants Worldwide, 69 82–85
Carlson Wagonlit Travel, 55 89–92
Carlton and United Breweries Ltd., I 228–29 *see also* Foster's Group Limited
Carlton Communications plc, 15 83–85; 50 124–27 (upd.)
Carma Laboratories, Inc., 60 80–82
CarMax, Inc., 55 93–95
Carmichael Lynch Inc., 28 66–68
Carmike Cinemas, Inc., 14 86–88; 37 62–65 (upd.); 74 64–67 (upd.)
Carnation Company, II 486–89 *see also* Nestlé S.A.
Carnegie Corporation of New York, 35 74–77
Carnival Corporation, 6 367–68; 27 90–92 (upd.); 78 65–69 (upd.)
Carolina First Corporation, 31 85–87
Carolina Freight Corporation, 6 369–72
Carolina Power & Light Company, V 564–66; 23 104–07 (upd.) *see also* Progress Energy, Inc.
Carolina Telephone and Telegraph Company, 10 201–03
Carpenter Technology Corporation, 13 139–41; 95 81–86 (upd.)
CARQUEST Corporation, 29 86–89
Carr-Gottstein Foods Co., 17 77–80
Carrabba's Italian Grill *see* Outback Steakhouse, Inc.
CarrAmerica Realty Corporation, 56 57–59
Carrefour SA, 10 204–06; 27 93–96 (upd.); 64 66–69 (upd.)
The Carriage House Companies, Inc., 55 96–98
Carriage Services, Inc., 37 66–68
Carrier Access Corporation, 44 68–73
Carrier Corporation, 7 70–73; 69 86–91 (upd.)
Carrizo Oil & Gas, Inc., 97 103–06
Carroll's Foods, Inc., 46 82–85
Carrols Restaurant Group, Inc., 92 48–51
The Carsey-Werner Company, L.L.C., 37 69–72
Carson, Inc., 31 88–90
Carson Pirie Scott & Company, 15 86–88
CART *see* Championship Auto Racing Teams, Inc.
Carter Hawley Hale Stores, V 29–32
Carter Holt Harvey Ltd., 70 41–44
Carter Lumber Company, 45 90–92
Carter-Wallace, Inc., 8 83–86; 38 122–26 (upd.)
Cartier Monde, 29 90–92
Carvel Corporation, 35 78–81
Carver Bancorp, Inc., 94 106–10
Carver Boat Corporation LLC, 88 43–46
Carvin Corp., 89 140–43
Casa Bancária Almeida e Companhia *see* Banco Bradesco S.A.
Casa Cuervo, S.A. de C.V., 31 91–93
Casa Herradura *see* Grupo Industrial Herradura, S.A. de C.V.
Casa Saba *see* Grupo Casa Saba, S.A. de C.V.
Casas Bahia Comercial Ltda., 75 86–89
Cascade Corporation, 65 90–92
Cascade General, Inc., 65 93–95

Cascade Natural Gas Corporation, 9 102–04
Cascades Inc., 71 94–96
Casco Northern Bank, 14 89–91
Casey's General Stores, Inc., 19 79–81; 83 58-63 (upd.)
Cash America International, Inc., 20 113–15; 61 52–55 (upd.)
Cash Systems, Inc., 93 133–36
Casino Guichard-Perrachon S.A., 59 107–10 (upd.)
CASIO Computer Co., Ltd., III 448–49; 16 82–84 (upd.); 40 91–95 (upd.)
Castle & Cooke, Inc., II 490–92; 20 116–19 (upd.) *see also* Dole Food Company, Inc.
Castorama S.A. *see* Groupe Castorama-Dubois Investissements.
Castro Model Ltd., 86 61–64
Casual Corner Group, Inc., 43 96–98
Casual Male Retail Group, Inc., 52 64–66
Caswell-Massey Co. Ltd., 51 66–69
Catalina Lighting, Inc., 43 99–102 (upd.)
Catalina Marketing Corporation, 18 99–102
Catalytica Energy Systems, Inc., 44 74–77
Catellus Development Corporation, 24 98–101
Caterpillar Inc., III 450–53; 15 89–93 (upd.); 63 93–99 (upd.)
Cathay Pacific Airways Limited, 6 78–80; 34 98–102 (upd.)
Catherines Stores Corporation, 15 94–97
Catholic Charities USA, 76 82–84
Catholic Health Initiatives, 91 93–98
Catholic Order of Foresters, 24 102–05; 97 107–11 (upd.)
Cato Corporation, 14 92–94
Cattleman's, Inc., 20 120–22
Cattles plc, 58 54–56
Cavco Industries, Inc., 65 96–99
Cazenove Group plc, 72 63–65
CB&I *see* Chicago Bridge & Iron Company N.V.
CB Commercial Real Estate Services Group, Inc., 21 94–98
CB Richard Ellis Group, Inc., 70 45–50 (upd.)
CBI Industries, Inc., 7 74–77 *see also* Chicago Bridge & Iron Company N.V.
CBN *see* The Christian Broadcasting Network, Inc.
CBOT *see* Chicago Board of Trade.
CBP *see* Corporation for Public Broadcasting.
CBRL Group, Inc., 35 82–85 (upd.); 86 65–70 (upd.)
CBS Corporation, II 132–34; 6 157–60 (upd.); 28 69–73 (upd.) *see also* CBS Television Network.
CBS Television Network, 66 44–48 (upd.)
CBSI *see* Complete Business Solutions, Inc.
CCA *see* Corrections Corporation of America.
CCA Industries, Inc., 53 86–89
CCC Information Services Group Inc., 74 68–70
CCG *see* The Clark Construction Group, Inc.
CCH Inc., 14 95–97
CCM Inc. *see* The Hockey Co.
CDC *see* Control Data Corp.
CDC Corporation, 71 97–99
CDI Corporation, 6 139–41; 54 46–49 (upd.)
CDL *see* City Developments Ltd.
CDW Computer Centers, Inc., 16 85–87; 52 67–70 (upd.)
CEC Entertainment, Inc., 31 94–98 (upd.)
CECAB *see* Groupe CECAB S.C.A.
Cedar Fair, L.P., 22 130–32
CEDC *see* Central European Distribution Corp.
Celadon Group Inc., 30 113–16
Celanese Corp., I 317–19 *see also* Hoechst Celanese Corp.
Celanese Mexicana, S.A. de C.V., 54 50–52
Celebrate Express, Inc., 70 51–53
Celebrity, Inc., 22 133–35
Celera Genomics, 74 71–74
Celestial Seasonings, Inc., 16 88–91 *see also* The Hain Celestial Group, Inc.
Celestica Inc., 80 59–62
Celgene Corporation, 67 97–100
CellStar Corporation, 83 64-67
Cementos Argos S.A., 91 99–101
CEMEX S.A. de C.V., 20 123–26; 59 111–16 (upd.)
CEMIG *see* Companhia Energética De Minas Gerais S.A.
Cencosud S.A., 69 92–94
Cendant Corporation, 44 78–84 (upd.)
Centel Corporation, 6 312–15 *see also* EMBARQ Corp.
Centennial Communications Corporation, 39 74–76
Centerior Energy Corporation, V 567–68
Centerplate, Inc., 79 96–100
Centex Corporation, 8 87–89; 29 93–96 (upd.)
Centocor Inc., 14 98–100
Central and South West Corporation, V 569–70
Central European Distribution Corporation, 75 90–92
Central European Media Enterprises Ltd., 61 56–59
Central Florida Investments, Inc., 93 137–40
Central Garden & Pet Company, 23 108–10; 58 57–60 (upd.)
Central Hudson Gas And Electricity Corporation, 6 458–60
Central Independent Television, 7 78–80; 23 111–14 (upd.)
Central Japan Railway Company, 43 103–06
Central Maine Power, 6 461–64
Central National-Gottesman Inc., 95 87–90
Central Newspapers, Inc., 10 207–09 *see also* Gannett Company, Inc.
Central Parking Corporation, 18 103–05
Central Soya Company, Inc., 7 81–83
Central Sprinkler Corporation, 29 97–99
Central Vermont Public Service Corporation, 54 53–56
Centrica plc, 29 100–05 (upd.)
Centuri Corporation, 54 57–59
Century Aluminum Company, 52 71–74
Century Business Services, Inc., 52 75–78
Century Casinos, Inc., 53 90–93
Century Communications Corp., 10 210–12
Century Telephone Enterprises, Inc., 9 105–07; 54 60–63 (upd.)
Century Theatres, Inc., 31 99–101
Cenveo Inc., 71 100–04 (upd.)
CEPCO *see* Chugoku Electric Power Company Inc.
Cephalon, Inc., 45 93–96
Cepheid, 77 93–96
Ceradyne, Inc., 65 100–02
Cerner Corporation, 16 92–94; 94 111–16 (upd.)
CertainTeed Corporation, 35 86–89
Certegy, Inc., 63 100–03
Cerveceria Polar, I 230–31 *see also* Empresas Polar SA.
Ceské aerolinie, a.s., 66 49–51
Cesky Telecom, a.s., 64 70–73
Cessna Aircraft Company, 8 90–93; 27 97–101 (upd.)
Cetelem S.A., 21 99–102
CeWe Color Holding AG, 76 85–88
ČEZ a. s., 97 112–15
CG&E *see* Cincinnati Gas & Electric Co.
CGM *see* Compagnie Générale Maritime.
Chadbourne & Parke, 36 109–12
Chadwick's of Boston, Ltd., 29 106–08
Chalk's Ocean Airways *see* Flying Boat, Inc.
The Chalone Wine Group, Ltd., 36 113–16
Champion Enterprises, Inc., 17 81–84
Champion Industries, Inc., 28 74–76
Champion International Corporation, IV 263–65; 20 127–30 (upd.) *see also* International Paper Co.
Championship Auto Racing Teams, Inc., 37 73–75
Chancellor Beacon Academies, Inc., 53 94–97
Chancellor Media Corporation, 24 106–10
Chanel SA, 12 57–59; 49 83–86 (upd.)
Channel Four Television Corporation, 93 141–44
Chantiers Jeanneau S.A., 96 78–81

Chaoda Modern Agriculture (Holdings) Ltd., 87 96–99
Chaparral Steel Co., 13 142–44
Charal S.A., 90 117–20
Chargeurs International, 6 373–75; 21 103–06 (upd.)
Charisma Brands LLC, 74 75–78
The Charles Machine Works, Inc., 64 74–76
Charles River Laboratories International, Inc., 42 66–69
The Charles Schwab Corporation, 8 94–96; 26 64–67 (upd.); 81 62–68 (upd.)
The Charles Stark Draper Laboratory, Inc., 35 90–92
Charles Vögele Holding AG, 82 63-66
Charlotte Russe Holding, Inc., 35 93–96; 90 121–25 (upd.)
The Charmer Sunbelt Group, 95 91–94
Charming Shoppes, Inc., 8 97–98; 38 127–29 (upd.)
Charoen Pokphand Group, 62 60–63
Chart House Enterprises, Inc., 17 85–88; 96 82–86 (upd.)
Chart Industries, Inc., 21 107–09
Charter Communications, Inc., 33 91–94
ChartHouse International Learning Corporation, 49 87–89
Chas. Levy Company LLC, 60 83–85
Chase General Corporation, 91 102–05
The Chase Manhattan Corporation, II 247–49; 13 145–48 (upd.) *see also* JPMorgan Chase & Co.
Chateau Communities, Inc., 37 76–79
Chattanooga Bakery, Inc., 86 75–78
Chattem, Inc., 17 89–92; 88 47–52 (upd.)
Chautauqua Airlines, Inc., 38 130–32
CHC Helicopter Corporation, 67 101–03
Checker Motors Corp., 89 144–48
Checkers Drive-In Restaurants, Inc., 16 95–98; 74 79–83 (upd.)
CheckFree Corporation, 81 69–72
Checkpoint Systems, Inc., 39 77–80
Chedraui *see* Grupo Comercial Chedraui S.A. de C.V.
The Cheesecake Factory Inc., 17 93–96
Chef Solutions, Inc., 89 149–52
Chello Zone Ltd., 93 145–48
Chelsea Milling Company, 29 109–11
Chelsea Piers Management Inc., 86 79–82
Chelsfield PLC, 67 104–06
Cheltenham & Gloucester PLC, 61 60–62
Chemcentral Corporation, 8 99–101
Chemed Corporation, 13 149–50
Chemfab Corporation, 35 97–101
Chemi-Trol Chemical Co., 16 99–101
Chemical Banking Corporation, II 250–52; 14 101–04 (upd.)
Chemical Waste Management, Inc., 9 108–10
Chemtura Corporation, 91 106–20 (upd.)
CHEP Pty. Ltd., 80 63–66
Cherokee Inc., 18 106–09
Cherry Lane Music Publishing Company, Inc., 62 64–67
Chesapeake Corporation, 8 102–04; 30 117–20 (upd.); 93 149–55 (upd.)
Chesapeake Utilities Corporation, 56 60–62
Cheshire Building Society, 74 84–87
Chesebrough-Pond's USA, Inc., 8 105–07
Cheung Kong (Holdings) Ltd., IV 693–95; 20 131–34 (upd.); 94 117–24 (upd.)
ChevronTexaco Corporation, IV 385–87;19 82–85 (upd.); 47 70–76 (upd.)
Cheyenne Software, Inc., 12 60–62
CHF Industries, Inc., 84 47–50
Chi-Chi's Inc., 13 151–53; 51 70–73 (upd.)
Chi Mei Optoelectronics Corporation, 75 93–95
Chiasso Inc., 53 98–100
Chiat/Day Inc. Advertising, 11 49–52 *see also* TBWA/Chiat/Day.
Chibu Electric Power Company, Incorporated, V 571–73
Chic by H.I.S, Inc., 20 135–37 *see also* VF Corp.
Chicago and North Western Holdings Corporation, 6 376–78 *see also* Union Pacific Corp.
Chicago Bears Football Club, Inc., 33 95–97
Chicago Blackhawk Hockey Team, Inc. *see* Wirtz Corp.
Chicago Board of Trade, 41 84–87
Chicago Bridge & Iron Company N.V., 82 67-73 (upd.)
Chicago Mercantile Exchange Holdings Inc., 75 96–99
Chicago National League Ball Club, Inc., 66 52–55
Chicago Pizza & Brewery, Inc., 44 85–88
Chicago Review Press Inc., 84 51–54
Chicago Tribune *see* Tribune Co.
Chick-fil-A Inc., 23 115–18; 90 126–31 (upd.)
Chicken of the Sea International, 24 114–16 (upd.)
Chico's FAS, Inc., 45 97–99
Children's Comprehensive Services, Inc., 42 70–72
Children's Hospitals and Clinics, Inc., 54 64–67
The Children's Place Retail Stores, Inc., 37 80–82; 86 83–87 (upd.)
ChildrenFirst, Inc., 59 117–20
Childtime Learning Centers, Inc., 34 103–06 *see also* Learning Care Group, Inc.
Chiles Offshore Corporation, 9 111–13
China Airlines, 34 107–10
China Automotive Systems Inc., 87 100–103
China Construction Bank Corp., 79 101–04
China Eastern Airlines Co. Ltd., 31 102–04
China Life Insurance Company Limited, 65 103–05
China Merchants International Holdings Co., Ltd., 52 79–82
China National Cereals, Oils and Foodstuffs Import and Export Corporation (COFCO), 76 89–91
China National Petroleum Corporation, 46 86–89
China Nepstar Chain Drugstore Ltd., 97 116–19
China Netcom Group Corporation (Hong Kong) Limited, 73 80–83
China Shenhua Energy Company Limited, 83 68-71
China Southern Airlines Company Ltd., 33 98–100
China Telecom, 50 128–32
Chinese Petroleum Corporation, IV 388–90; 31 105–08 (upd.)
Chipotle Mexican Grill, Inc., 67 107–10
CHIPS and Technologies, Inc., 9 114–17
Chiquita Brands International, Inc., 7 84–86; 21 110–13 (upd.); 83 72-79 (upd.)
Chiron Corporation, 10 213–14; 36 117–20 (upd.)
Chisholm-Mingo Group, Inc., 41 88–90
Chittenden & Eastman Company, 58 61–64
Chock Full o'Nuts Corp., 17 97–100
Chocoladefabriken Lindt & Sprüngli AG, 27 102–05
Choice Hotels International, Inc., 14 105–07; 83 80-83 (upd.)
ChoicePoint Inc., 65 106–08
Chorus Line Corporation, 30 121–23
Chr. Hansen Group A/S, 70 54–57
Chris-Craft Corporation, 9 118–19; 31 109–12 (upd.); 80 67–71 (upd.)
Christensen Boyles Corporation, 26 68–71
The Christian Broadcasting Network, Inc., 52 83–85
Christian Dalloz SA, 40 96–98
Christian Dior S.A., 19 86–88; 49 90–93 (upd.)
Christian Salvesen Plc, 45 100–03
The Christian Science Publishing Society, 55 99–102
Christie's International plc, 15 98–101; 39 81–85 (upd.)
Christofle SA, 40 99–102
Christopher & Banks Corporation, 42 73–75
Chromcraft Revington, Inc., 15 102–05
The Chronicle Publishing Company, Inc., 23 119–22
Chronimed Inc., 26 72–75
Chrysalis Group plc, 40 103–06
Chrysler Corporation, I 144–45; 11 53–55 (upd.) *see also* DaimlerChrysler AG

CHS Inc., 60 86–89
CH2M HILL Companies Ltd., 22 136–38; 96 72–77 (upd.)
Chubb Corporation, III 220–22; 14 108–10 (upd.); 37 83–87 (upd.)
Chubb, PLC, 50 133–36
Chubu Electric Power Company, Inc., V 571–73; 46 90–93 (upd.)
Chuck E. Cheese *see* CEC Entertainment, Inc.
Chugach Alaska Corporation, 60 90–93
Chugai Pharmaceutical Co., Ltd., 50 137–40
Chugoku Electric Power Company Inc., V 574–76; 53 101–04 (upd.)
Chunghwa Picture Tubes, Ltd., 75 100–02
Chupa Chups S.A., 38 133–35
Church & Dwight Co., Inc., 29 112–15; 68 78–82 (upd.)
Church's Chicken, 66 56–59
Churchill Downs Incorporated, 29 116–19
Cia Hering, 72 66–68
Cianbro Corporation, 14 111–13
Ciba-Geigy Ltd., I 632–34; 8 108–11 (upd.) *see also* Novartis AG.
CIBC *see* Canadian Imperial Bank of Commerce.
Ciber, Inc., 18 110–12
CIENA Corporation, 54 68–71
Cifra, S.A. de C.V., 12 63–65 *see also* Wal-Mart de Mexico, S.A. de C.V.
CIGNA Corporation, III 223–27; 22 139–44 (upd.); 45 104–10 (upd.)
Cimarex Energy Co., 81 73–76
Cimentos de Portugal SGPS S.A. (Cimpor), 76 92–94
Ciments Français, 40 107–10
Cimpor *see* Cimentos de Portugal SGPS S.A.
Cinar Corporation, 40 111–14
Cincinnati Bell, Inc., 6 316–18
Cincinnati Financial Corporation, 16 102–04; 44 89–92 (upd.)
Cincinnati Gas & Electric Company, 6 465–68 *see also* Duke Energy Corp.
Cincinnati Lamb Inc., 72 69–71
Cincinnati Milacron Inc., 12 66–69 *see also* Milacron, Inc.
Cincom Systems Inc., 15 106–08
Cinemark Holdings, Inc., 95 95–99
Cinemas de la República, S.A. de C.V., 83 84-86
Cinemeccanica S.p.A., 78 70–73
Cineplex Odeon Corporation, 6 161–63; 23 123–26 (upd.)
Cinnabon, Inc., 23 127–29; 90 132–36 (upd.)
Cinram International, Inc., 43 107–10
Cintas Corporation, 21 114–16; 51 74–77 (upd.)
CIPSA *see* Compañia Industrial de Parras, S.A. de C.V. (CIPSA).
CIPSCO Inc., 6 469–72 *see also* Ameren Corp.
The Circle K Company, II 619–20; 20 138–40 (upd.)
Circon Corporation, 21 117–20
Circuit City Stores, Inc., 9 120–22; 29 120–24 (upd.); 65 109–14 (upd.)
Circus Circus Enterprises, Inc., 6 203–05
Cirque du Soleil Inc., 29 125–28
Cirrus Design Corporation, 44 93–95
Cirrus Logic, Inc., 11 56–57; 48 90–93 (upd.)
Cisco-Linksys LLC, 86 88–91
Cisco Systems, Inc., 11 58–60; 34 111–15 (upd.); 77 97–103 (upd.)
Cisneros Group of Companies, 54 72–75
CIT Group Inc., 76 95–98
Citadel Communications Corporation, 35 102–05
CitFed Bancorp, Inc., 16 105–07 *see also* Fifth Third Bancorp.
CITGO Petroleum Corporation, IV 391–93; 31 113–17 (upd.)
Citi Trends, Inc., 80 72–75
Citibank *see* Citigroup Inc
CITIC Pacific Ltd., 18 113–15
Citicorp, II 253–55; 9 123–26 (upd.) *see also* Citigroup Inc.
Citicorp Diners Club, Inc., 90 137–40
Citigroup Inc., 30 124–28 (upd.); 59 121–27 (upd.)
Citizen Watch Co., Ltd., III 454–56; 21 121–24 (upd.); 81 77–82 (upd.)
Citizens Communications Company, 79 105–08 (upd.)
Citizens Financial Group, Inc., 42 76–80; 87 104–112 (upd.)
Citizens Utilities Company, 7 87–89 *see also* Citizens Communications Company
Citrix Systems, Inc., 44 96–99
Citroën *see* PSA Peugeot Citroen S.A.
City Brewing Company LLC, 73 84–87
City Developments Limited, 89 153–56
City Public Service, 6 473–75
CJ Banks *see* Christopher & Banks Corp.
CJ Corporation, 62 68–70
CJSC Transmash Holding, 93 446–49
CKE Restaurants, Inc., 19 89–93; 46 94–99 (upd.)
Claire's Stores, Inc., 17 101–03; 94 125–29 (upd.)
CLARCOR Inc., 17 104–07; 61 63–67 (upd.)
Clare Rose Inc., 68 83–85
Clarion Company Ltd., 64 77–79
The Clark Construction Group, Inc., 8 112–13
Clark Equipment Company, 8 114–16
Classic Vacation Group, Inc., 46 100–03
Clayton Homes Incorporated, 13 154–55; 54 76–79 (upd.)
Clayton Williams Energy, Inc., 87 113–116
Clean Harbors, Inc., 73 88–91
Clear Channel Communications, Inc., 23 130–32 *see also* Live Nation, Inc.
Clearly Canadian Beverage Corporation, 48 94–97
Clearwire, Inc., 69 95–97
Cleary, Gottlieb, Steen & Hamilton, 35 106–09
Cleco Corporation, 37 88–91
The Clemens Family Corporation, 93 156–59
Clement Pappas & Company, Inc., 92 52–55
Cleveland-Cliffs Inc., 13 156–58; 62 71–75 (upd.)
Cleveland Indians Baseball Company, Inc., 37 92–94
Click Wine Group, 68 86–88
Clif Bar Inc., 50 141–43
Clifford Chance LLP, 38 136–39
Clinton Cards plc, 39 86–88
Cloetta Fazer AB, 70 58–60
The Clorox Company, III 20–22; 22 145–48 (upd.); 81 83–90 (upd.)
Close Brothers Group plc, 39 89–92
The Clothestime, Inc., 20 141–44
Clougherty Packing Company, 72 72–74
Club Méditerranée S.A., 6 206–08; 21 125–28 (upd.); 91 121–27 (upd.)
ClubCorp, Inc., 33 101–04
CMC *see* Commercial Metals Co.
CME *see* Campbell-Mithun-Esty, Inc.; Central European Media Enterprises Ltd.; Chicago Mercantile Exchange Inc.
CMG Worldwide, Inc., 89 157–60
CMGI, Inc., 76 99–101
CMIH *see* China Merchants International Holdings Co., Ltd.
CML Group, Inc., 10 215–18
CMO *see* Chi Mei Optoelectronics Corp.
CMP Media Inc., 26 76–80
CMS Energy Corporation, V 577–79; 14 114–16 (upd.)
CN *see* Canadian National Railway Co.
CNA Financial Corporation, III 228–32; 38 140–46 (upd.)
CNET Networks, Inc., 47 77–80
CNG *see* Consolidated Natural Gas Co.
CNH Global N.V., 38 147–56 (upd.)
CNP *see* Compagnie Nationale à Portefeuille.
CNPC *see* China National Petroleum Corp.
CNS, Inc., 20 145–47 *see also* GlaxoSmithKline plc.
Co-operative Group (CWS) Ltd., 51 86–89
Coach, Inc., 10 219–21; 45 111–15 (upd.)
Coach USA, Inc., 24 117–19; 55 103–06 (upd.)
Coachmen Industries, Inc., 77 104–07
Coal India Ltd., IV 48–50; 44 100–03 (upd.)
Coastal Corporation, IV 394–95; 31 118–21 (upd.)
Coats plc, V 356–58; 44 104–07 (upd.)
COBE Cardiovascular, Inc., 61 68–72
COBE Laboratories, Inc., 13 159–61
Coberco *see* Friesland Coberco Dairy Foods Holding N.V.
Cobham plc, 30 129–32
Coborn's, Inc., 30 133–35

Cobra Electronics Corporation, 14 117–19
Cobra Golf Inc., 16 108–10
Coca-Cola Bottling Co. Consolidated, 10 222–24
The Coca-Cola Company, I 232–35; 10 225–28 (upd.); 32 111–16 (upd.); 67 111–17 (upd.)
Coca-Cola Enterprises, Inc., 13 162–64
Cochlear Ltd., 77 108–11
Cockerill Sambre Group, IV 51–53; 26 81–84 (upd.) *see also* Arcelor Gent.
Codelco *see* Corporacion Nacional del Cobre de Chile.
Coeur d'Alene Mines Corporation, 20 148–51
COFCO *see* China National Cereals, Oils and Foodstuffs Import and Export Corp.
The Coffee Beanery, Ltd., 95 100–05
Coffee Holding Co., Inc., 95 106–09
Coflexip S.A., 25 103–05 *see also* Technip.
Cogent Communications Group, Inc., 55 107–10
Cogentrix Energy, Inc., 10 229–31
Cognex Corporation, 76 102–06
Cognizant Technology Solutions Corporation, 59 128–30
Cognos Inc., 44 108–11
Coherent, Inc., 31 122–25
Cohu, Inc., 32 117–19
Coinmach Laundry Corporation, 20 152–54
Coinstar, Inc., 44 112–14
Colas S.A., 31 126–29
Cold Spring Granite Company, 16 111–14; 67 118–22 (upd.)
Cold Stone Creamery, 69 98–100
Coldwater Creek Inc., 21 129–31; 74 88–91 (upd.)
Coldwell Banker Co. *see* CB Richard Ellis Group, Inc.
Cole National Corporation, 13 165–67; 76 107–10 (upd.)
Cole's Quality Foods, Inc., 68 92–94
The Coleman Company, Inc., 9 127–29; 30 136–39 (upd.)
Coleman Natural Products, Inc., 68 89–91
Coles Express Inc., 15 109–11
Coles Group Limited, V 33–35; 20 155–58 (upd.); 85 49–56 (upd.)
Colfax Corporation, 58 65–67
Colgate-Palmolive Company, III 23–26; 14 120–23 (upd.); 35 110–15 (upd.); 71 105–10 (upd.)
Collectors Universe, Inc., 48 98–100
Colliers International Property Consultants Inc., 92 56–59
Collins & Aikman Corporation, 13 168–70; 41 91–95 (upd.)
Collins Industries, Inc., 33 105–07
Colonial Properties Trust, 65 115–17
Colonial Williamsburg Foundation, 53 105–07
Color Kinetics Incorporated, 85 57–60
Colorado Baseball Management, Inc., 72 75–78
Colorado MEDtech, Inc., 48 101–05
Colt Industries Inc., I 434–36
COLT Telecom Group plc, 41 96–99
Colt's Manufacturing Company, Inc., 12 70–72
Columbia Forest Products Inc., 78 74–77
The Columbia Gas System, Inc., V 580–82; 16 115–18 (upd.)
Columbia/HCA Healthcare Corporation, 15 112–14
Columbia House Company, 69 101–03
Columbia Sportswear Company, 19 94–96; 41 100–03 (upd.)
Columbia TriStar Motion Pictures Companies, II 135–37; 12 73–76 (upd.)
Columbus McKinnon Corporation, 37 95–98
Com Ed *see* Commonwealth Edison.
Comair Holdings Inc., 13 171–73; 34 116–20 (upd.)
Combe Inc., 72 79–82
Comcast Corporation, 7 90–92; 24 120–24 (upd.)
Comdial Corporation, 21 132–35
Comdisco, Inc., 9 130–32
Comerci *see* Controladora Comercial Mexicana, S.A. de C.V.
Comerica Incorporated, 40 115–17
COMFORCE Corporation, 40 118–20
Cominco Ltd., 37 99–102
Command Security Corporation, 57 71–73
Commerce Clearing House, Inc., 7 93–94 *see also* CCH Inc.
Commercial Credit Company, 8 117–19 *see also* Citigroup Inc.
Commercial Federal Corporation, 12 77–79; 62 76–80 (upd.)
Commercial Financial Services, Inc., 26 85–89
Commercial Metals Company, 15 115–17; 42 81–84(upd.)
Commercial Union plc, III 233–35 *see also* Aviva PLC.
Commercial Vehicle Group, Inc., 81 91–94
Commerzbank A.G., II 256–58; 47 81–84 (upd.)
Commodore International, Ltd., 7 95–97
Commonwealth Edison, V 583–85
Commonwealth Energy System, 14 124–26
Commonwealth Telephone Enterprises, Inc., 25 106–08
CommScope, Inc., 77 112–15
Community Coffee Co. L.L.C., 53 108–10
Community Health Systems, Inc., 71 111–13
Community Newspaper Holdings, Inc., 91 128–31
Community Psychiatric Centers, 15 118–20
Compagnia Italiana dei Jolly Hotels S.p.A., 71 114–16
Compagnie de Saint-Gobain, III 675–78; 16 119–23 (upd.); 64 80–84 (upd.)
Compagnie des Alpes, 48 106–08
Compagnie des Cristalleries de Baccarat *see* Baccarat.
Compagnie des Machines Bull S.A., III 122–23 *see also* Bull S.A.; Groupe Bull.
Compagnie Financière de Paribas, II 259–60 *see also* BNP Paribas Group.
Compagnie Financière Richemont AG, 50 144–47
Compagnie Financière Sucres et Denrées S.A., 60 94–96
Compagnie Générale d'Électricité, II 12–13
Compagnie Générale des Établissements Michelin, V 236–39; 42 85–89 (upd.)
Compagnie Générale Maritime et Financière, 6 379–81
Compagnie Maritime Belge S.A., 95 110–13
Compagnie Nationale à Portefeuille, 84 55–58
Companhia Brasileira de Distribuiçao, 76 111–13
Companhia de Bebidas das Américas, 57 74–77
Companhia de Tecidos Norte de Minas - Coteminas, 77 116–19
Companhia Energética de Minas Gerais S.A., 65 118–20
Companhia Siderúrgica Nacional, 76 114–17
Companhia Suzano de Papel e Celulose S.A., 94 130–33
Companhia Vale do Rio Doce, IV 54–57; 43 111–14 (upd.)
Compania Cervecerias Unidas S.A., 70 61–63
Compañia de Minas BuenaventuraS.A.A., 92160–63
Compañia Española de Petróleos S.A. (Cepsa), IV 396–98; 56 63–66 (upd.)
Compañia Industrial de Parras, S.A. de C.V. (CIPSA), 84 59–62
Compaq Computer Corporation, III 124–25; 6 221–23 (upd.); 26 90–93 (upd.) *see also* Hewlett-Packard Co.
Compass Bancshares, Inc., 73 92–94
Compass Group PLC, 34 121–24
Compass Minerals International, Inc., 79 109–12
CompDent Corporation, 22 149–51
CompHealth Inc., 25 109–12
Complete Business Solutions, Inc., 31 130–33
Comprehensive Care Corporation, 15 121–23
Comptoirs Modernes S.A., 19 97–99 *see also* Carrefour SA.
CompuAdd Computer Corporation, 11 61–63
CompuCom Systems, Inc., 10 232–34
CompuDyne Corporation, 51 78–81

CompUSA, Inc., 10 235–36; 35 116–18 (upd.)
CompuServe Interactive Services, Inc., 10 237–39; 27 106–08 (upd.) *see also* AOL Time Warner Inc.
Computer Associates International, Inc., 6 224–26; 49 94–97 (upd.)
Computer Data Systems, Inc., 14 127–29
Computer Learning Centers, Inc., 26 94–96
Computer Sciences Corporation, 6 227–29
ComputerLand Corp., 13 174–76
Computervision Corporation, 10 240–42
Compuware Corporation, 10 243–45; 30 140–43 (upd.); 66 60–64 (upd.)
Comsat Corporation, 23 133–36 *see also* Lockheed Martin Corp.
Comshare Inc., 23 137–39
Comstock Resources, Inc., 47 85–87
Comtech Telecommunications Corp., 75 103–05
Comverse Technology, Inc., 15 124–26; 43 115–18 (upd.)
Con Ed *see* Consolidated Edison, Inc.
ConAgra Foods, Inc., II 493–95; 12 80–82 (upd.); 42 90–94 (upd.); 85 61–68 (upd.)
Conair Corporation, 17 108–10; 69 104–08 (upd.)
Conaprole *see* Cooperativa Nacional de Productores de Leche S.A. (Conaprole).
Concentra Inc., 71 117–19
Concepts Direct, Inc., 39 93–96
Concha y Toro *see* Viña Concha y Toro S.A.
Concord Camera Corporation, 41 104–07
Concord EFS, Inc., 52 86–88
Concord Fabrics, Inc., 16 124–26
Concurrent Computer Corporation, 75 106–08
Condé Nast Publications, Inc., 13 177–81; 59 131–34 (upd.)
Cone Mills LLC, 8 120–22; 67 123–27 (upd.)
Conexant Systems, Inc., 36 121–25
Confluence Holdings Corporation, 76 118–20
Congoleum Corp., 18 116–19
CONMED Corporation, 87 117–120
Conn-Selmer, Inc., 55 111–14
Conn's, Inc., 67 128–30
Connecticut Light and Power Co., 13 182–84
Connecticut Mutual Life Insurance Company, III 236–38
The Connell Company, 29 129–31
Conner Peripherals, Inc., 6 230–32
Connetics Corporation, 70 64–66
Connors Bros. Income Fund *see* George Weston Ltd.
ConocoPhillips, IV 399–402; 16 127–32 (upd.); 63 104–15 (upd.)
Conrad Industries, Inc., 58 68–70
Conseco Inc., 10 246–48; 33 108–12 (upd.)
Conso International Corporation, 29 132–34
CONSOL Energy Inc., 59 135–37
Consolidated Delivery & Logistics, Inc., 24 125–28 *see also* Velocity Express Corp.
Consolidated Edison, Inc., V 586–89; 45 116–20 (upd.)
Consolidated Freightways Corporation, V 432–34; 21 136–39 (upd.); 48 109–13 (upd.)
Consolidated Graphics, Inc., 70 67–69
Consolidated Natural Gas Company, V 590–91; 19 100–02 (upd.) *see also* Dominion Resources, Inc.
Consolidated Papers, Inc., 8 123–25; 36 126–30 (upd.)
Consolidated Products, Inc., 14 130–32
Consolidated Rail Corporation, V 435–37
Consorcio ARA, S.A. de C.V., 79 113–16
Consorcio Aviacsa, S.A. de C.V., 85 69–72
Consorcio G Grupo Dina, S.A. de C.V., 36 131–33
Constar International Inc., 64 85–88
Constellation Brands, Inc., 68 95–100 (upd.)
The Consumers Gas Company Ltd., 6 476–79; 43 154 *see also* Enbridge Inc.
Consumers Power Co., 14 133–36
Consumers Union, 26 97–99
Consumers Water Company, 14 137–39
The Container Store, 36 134–36
ContiGroup Companies, Inc., 43 119–22 (upd.)
Continental AG, V 240–43; 56 67–72 (upd.)
Continental Airlines, Inc., I 96–98; 21 140–43 (upd.); 52 89–94 (upd.)
Continental Bank Corporation, II 261–63 *see also* Bank of America.
Continental Cablevision, Inc., 7 98–100
Continental Can Co., Inc., 15 127–30
Continental Corporation, III 239–44
Continental General Tire Corp., 23 140–42
Continental Grain Company, 10 249–51; 13 185–87 (upd.) *see also* ContiGroup Companies, Inc.
Continental Group Co., I 599–600
Continental Medical Systems, Inc., 10 252–54
Continental Resources, Inc., 89 161–65
Continuum Health Partners, Inc., 60 97–99
Control Data Corporation, III 126–28 *see also* Seagate Technology, Inc.
Control Data Systems, Inc., 10 255–57
Controladora Comercial Mexicana, S.A. de C.V., 36 137–39
Controladora Mabe, S.A. de C.V., 82 74-77
Converse Inc., 9 133–36; 31 134–38 (upd.)
Conzzeta Holding, 80 76–79
Cooker Restaurant Corporation, 20 159–61; 51 82–85 (upd.)
Cookson Group plc, III 679–82; 44 115–20 (upd.)
CoolBrands International Inc., 35 119–22
CoolSavings, Inc., 77 120–24
Coop Schweiz Genossenschaftsverband, 48 114–16
Coopagri Bretagne, 88 53–56
Cooper Cameron Corporation, 20 162–66 (upd.); 58 71–75 (upd.)
The Cooper Companies, Inc., 39 97–100
Cooper Industries, Inc., II 14–17; 44 121–25 (upd.)
Cooper Tire & Rubber Company, 8 126–28; 23 143–46 (upd.)
Cooperativa Nacional de Productores de Leche S.A. (Conaprole),92 60–63
Coopers & Lybrand, 9 137–38 *see also* PricewaterhouseCoopers.
Coors Company *see* Adolph Coors Co.
Copa Holdings, S.A., 93 164–67
Copart Inc., 23 147–49
Copec *see* Empresas Copec S.A.
The Copley Press, Inc., 23 150–52
Coppel, S.A. de C.V., 82 78-81
The Copps Corporation, 32 120–22
Cora S.A./NV, 94 134–37
Corbis Corporation, 31 139–42
Corby Distilleries Limited, 14 140–42
The Corcoran Group, Inc., 58 76–78
Cordis Corporation, 19 103–05; 46 104–07 (upd.)
Cordon Bleu *see* Le Cordon Bleu S.A.
Corel Corporation, 15 131–33; 33 113–16 (upd.); 76 121–24 (upd.)
Corelio S.A./N.V., 96 87–90
CoreStates Financial Corp, 16 111–15 *see also* Wachovia Corp.
Corinthian Colleges, Inc., 39 101–04; 92 64–69 (upd.)
Cornelsen Verlagsholding GmbH & Co., 90 141–46
Corning Inc., III 683–85; 44 126–30 (upd.); 90 147–53 (upd.)
Corporación Geo, S.A. de C.V., 81 95–98
Corporación Interamericana de Entretenimiento, S.A. de C.V., 83 87-90
Corporación Internacional de Aviación, S.A. de C.V. (Cintra), 20 167–69
Corporación José R. Lindley S.A., 92 70–73
Corporación Multi-Inversiones, 94 138–42
Corporacion Nacional del Cobre de Chile, 40 121–23
The Corporate Executive Board Company, 89 166–69
Corporate Express, Inc., 22 152–55; 47 88–92 (upd.)
Corporate Software Inc., 9 139–41
Corporation for Public Broadcasting, 14 143–45; 89 170–75 (upd.)

Correctional Services Corporation, 30 144–46
Corrections Corporation of America, 23 153–55
Correos y Telegrafos S.A., 80 80–83
Corrpro Companies, Inc., 20 170–73
CORT Business Services Corporation, 26 100–02
El Corte Inglés Group, 26 128–31 (upd.)
Cortefiel S.A., 64 89–91
Corticeira Amorim, Sociedade Gestora de Participaço es Sociais, S.A., 48 117–20
Corus Bankshares, Inc., 75 109–11
Corus Group plc, 49 98–105 (upd.)
Corvi *see* Grupo Corvi S.A. de C.V.
Cosi, Inc., 53 111–13
Cosmair Inc., 8 129–32 *see also* L'Oreal.
The Cosmetic Center, Inc., 22 156–58
Cosmo Oil Co., Ltd., IV 403–04; 53 114–16 (upd.)
Cosmolab Inc., 96 91–94
Cost Plus, Inc., 27 109–11
Cost-U-Less, Inc., 51 90–93
CoStar Group, Inc., 73 95–98
Costco Wholesale Corporation, 43 123–25 (upd.)
Coto Centro Integral de Comercializacion S.A., 66 65–67
Cott Corporation, 52 95–98
Cotter & Company, V 37–38 *see also* TruServ Corp.
Cotton Incorporated, 46 108–11
Coty, Inc., 36 140–42
Coudert Brothers, 30 147–50
Council on International Educational Exchange Inc., 81 99–102
Country Kitchen International, Inc., 76 125–27
Countrywide Credit Industries, Inc., 16 133–36
County Seat Stores Inc., 9 142–43
Courier Corporation, 41 108–12
Courtaulds plc, V 359–61; 17 116–19 (upd.) *see also* Akzo Nobel N.V.
Courts Plc, 45 121–24
Cousins Properties Incorporated, 65 121–23
Covance Inc., 30 151–53
Covanta Energy Corporation, 64 92–95 (upd.)
Coventry Health Care, Inc., 59 138–40
Covidien Ltd., 91 132–35
Covington & Burling, 40 124–27
Cowen Group, Inc., 92 74–77
Cowles Media Company, 23 156–58 *see also* Primedia Inc.
Cox Enterprises, Inc., IV 595–97; 22 159–63 (upd.); 67 131–35 (upd.)
Cox Radio, Inc., 89 176–80
CP *see* Canadian Pacific Railway Ltd.
CPAC, Inc., 86 92–95
CPC International Inc., II 496–98 *see also* Bestfoods.
CPI Aerostructures, Inc., 75 112–14
CPI Corp., 38 157–60
CPL *see* Carolina Power & Light Co.
CPT *see* Chunghwa Picture Tubes, Ltd.
CR England, Inc., 63 116–18
CRA International, Inc., 93 168–71
CRA Limited, IV 58–61 *see also* Rio Tinto plc.
Cracker Barrel Old Country Store, Inc., 10 258–59 *see also* CBRL Group, Inc.
Craftmade International, Inc., 44 131–33
craigslist, inc., 89 181–84
Crain Communications, Inc., 12 83–86; 35 123–27 (upd.)
Cram Company *see* The George F. Cram Company, Inc.
Cramer, Berkowitz & Co., 34 125–27
Crane & Co., Inc., 26 103–06; 30 42
Crane Co., 8 133–36; 30 154–58 (upd.)
Cranium, Inc., 69 109–11
Cranswick plc, 40 128–30
Crate and Barrel, 9 144–46 *see also* Euromarket Designs Inc.
Cravath, Swaine & Moore, 43 126–28
Crawford & Company, 87 121–126
Cray Inc., III 129–31; 16 137–40 (upd.); 75 115–21 (upd.)
Creative Artists Agency LLC, 38 161–64
Creative Technology Ltd., 57 78–81
Credence Systems Corporation, 90 154–57
Credit Acceptance Corporation, 18 120–22
Crédit Agricole Group, II 264–66; 84 63–68 (upd.)
Crédit Lyonnais, 9 147–49; 33 117–21 (upd.)
Crédit National S.A., 9 150–52
Crédit Suisse Group, II 267–69; 21 144–47 (upd.); 59 141–47 (upd.) *see also* Schweizerische Kreditanstalt.
Credito Italiano, II 270–72
Cree Inc., 53 117–20
Cremonini S.p.A., 57 82–84
Creo Inc., 48 121–24
Cresud S.A.C.I.F. y A., 63 119–21
Crete Carrier Corporation, 95 114–17
CRH plc, 64 96–99
Crispin Porter + Bogusky, 83 91-94
Cristalerias de Chile S.A., 67 136–38
Crit *see* Groupe Crit S.A.
Crocs, Inc., 80 84–87
Croda International Plc, 45 125–28
Crompton Corporation, 9 153–55; 36 143–50 (upd.) *see also* Chemtura Corp.
Croscill, Inc., 42 95–97
Crosman Corporation, 62 81–83
Cross Company *see* A.T. Cross Co.
CROSSMARK, 79 117–20
Crowley Maritime Corporation, 6 382–84; 28 77–80 (upd.)
Crowley, Milner & Company, 19 106–08
Crown Books Corporation, 21 148–50 *see also* Random House, Inc.
Crown Central Petroleum Corporation, 7 101–03
Crown, Cork & Seal Company, Inc., I 601–03; 13 188–90 (upd.); 32 123–27 (upd.) *see also* Crown Holdings, Inc.
Crown Crafts, Inc., 16 141–43
Crown Equipment Corporation, 15 134–36; 93 172–76 (upd.)
Crown Holdings, Inc., 83 95-102 (upd.)
Crown Media Holdings, Inc., 45 129–32
Crown Vantage Inc., 29 135–37
CRSS Inc., 6 142–44; 23 491
Cruise America Inc., 21 151–53
CryoLife, Inc., 46 112–14
Crystal Brands, Inc., 9 156–58
CS First Boston Inc., II 402–04
CSA *see* China Southern Airlines Company Ltd.
CSC *see* Computer Sciences Corp.
CSG Systems International, Inc., 75 122–24
CSK Auto Corporation, 38 165–67
CSM N.V., 65 124–27
CSR Limited, III 686–88; 28 81–84 (upd.); 85 73–80 (upd.)
CSS Industries, Inc., 35 128–31
CSX Corporation, V 438–40; 22 164–68 (upd.); 79 121–27 (upd.)
CT&T *see* Carolina Telephone and Telegraph Co.
CTB International Corporation, 43 129–31 (upd.)
CTG, Inc., 11 64–66
Ctrip.com International Ltd., 97 120–24
CTS Corporation, 39 105–08
Cubic Corporation, 19 109–11
CUC International Inc., 16 144–46 *see also* Cendant Corp.
Cuisinart Corporation, 24 129–32
Cuisine Solutions Inc., 84 69–72
Culbro Corporation, 15 137–39 *see also* General Cigar Holdings, Inc.
CulinArt, Inc., 92 78–81
Cullen/Frost Bankers, Inc., 25 113–16
Culligan Water Technologies, Inc., 12 87–88; 38 168–70 (upd.)
Culp, Inc., 29 138–40
Culver Franchising System, Inc., 58 79–81
Cumberland Farms, Inc., 17 120–22; 84 73–77 (upd.)
Cumberland Packing Corporation, 26 107–09
Cummins Engine Co., Inc., I 146–48; 12 89–92 (upd.); 40 131–35 (upd.)
Cumulus Media Inc., 37 103–05
CUNA Mutual Group, 62 84–87
Cunard Line Ltd., 23 159–62
CUNO Incorporated, 57 85–89
Current, Inc., 37 106–09
Curtice-Burns Foods, Inc., 7 104–06; 21 154–57 (upd.) *see also* Birds Eye Foods, Inc.
Curtiss-Wright Corporation, 10 260–63; 35 132–37 (upd.)
Curves International, Inc., 54 80–82
Cushman & Wakefield, Inc., 86 96–100

Custom Chrome, Inc., 16 147–49; 74 92–95 (upd.)
Cutera, Inc., 84 78–81
Cutter & Buck Inc., 27 112–14
CVPS *see* Central Vermont Public Service Corp.
CVRD *see* Companhia Vale do Rio Doce Ltd.
CVS Corporation, 45 133–38 (upd.)
CWM *see* Chemical Waste Management, Inc.
Cybermedia, Inc., 25 117–19
Cyberonics, Inc., 79 128–31
Cybex International, Inc., 49 106–09
Cydsa *see* Grupo Cydsa, S.A. de C.V.
Cygne Designs, Inc., 25 120–23
Cygnus Business Media, Inc., 56 73–77
Cymer, Inc., 77 125–28
Cypress Semiconductor Corporation, 20 174–76; 48 125–29 (upd.)
Cyprus Airways Public Limited, 81 103–06
Cyprus Amax Minerals Company, 21 158–61
Cyprus Minerals Company, 7 107–09
Cyrk Inc., 19 112–14
Cystic Fibrosis Foundation, 93 177–80
Cytec Industries Inc., 27 115–17
Cytyc Corporation, 69 112–14
Czarnikow-Rionda Company, Inc., 32 128–30

D

D&B *see* Dun & Bradstreet Corp.
D&H Distributing Co., 95 118–21
D&K Wholesale Drug, Inc., 14 146–48
D-Link Corporation, 83 103-106
D.F. Stauffer Biscuit Company, 82 82-85
D.G. Yuengling & Son, Inc., 38 171–73
D.R. Horton, Inc., 58 82–84
Dachser GmbH & Co. KG, 88 57–61
D'Addario & Company, Inc. *see* J. D'Addario & Company, Inc.
Dade Behring Holdings Inc., 71 120–22
Daesang Corporation, 84 82–85
Daewoo Group, III 457–59; 18 123–27 (upd.); 57 90–94 (upd.)
Daffy's Inc., 26 110–12
D'Agostino Supermarkets Inc., 19 115–17
DAH *see* DeCrane Aircraft Holdings Inc.
Dai-Ichi Kangyo Bank Ltd., II 273–75
Dai Nippon *see also* listings under Dainippon.
Dai Nippon Printing Co., Ltd., IV 598–600; 57 95–99 (upd.)
Daido Steel Co., Ltd., IV 62–63
The Daiei, Inc., V 39–40; 17 123–25 (upd.); 41 113–16 (upd.)
Daihatsu Motor Company, Ltd., 7 110–12; 21 162–64 (upd.)
Daiichikosho Company Ltd., 86 101–04
Daikin Industries, Ltd., III 460–61
Daiko Advertising Inc., 79 132–35
Daily Mail and General Trust plc, 19 118–20
The Daimaru, Inc., V 41–42; 42 98–100 (upd.)
Daimler-Benz Aerospace AG, 16 150–52
Daimler-Benz AG, I 149–51; 15 140–44 (upd.)
DaimlerChrysler AG, 34 128–37 (upd.); 64 100–07 (upd.)
Dain Rauscher Corporation, 35 138–41 (upd.)
Daio Paper Corporation, IV 266–67; 84 86–89 (upd.)
Dairy Crest Group plc, 32 131–33
Dairy Farm International Holdings Ltd., 97 125–28
Dairy Farmers of America, Inc., 94 143–46
Dairy Mart Convenience Stores, Inc., 7 113–15; 25 124–27 (upd.) *see also* Alimentation Couche-Tard Inc.
Dairy Queen *see* International Dairy Queen, Inc.
Dairyland Healthcare Solutions, 73 99–101
Daishowa Paper Manufacturing Co., Ltd., IV 268–70; 57 100–03 (upd.)
Daisy Outdoor Products Inc., 58 85–88
Daisytek International Corporation, 18 128–30
Daiwa Bank, Ltd., II 276–77; 39 109–11 (upd.)
Daiwa Securities Company, Limited, II 405–06
Daiwa Securities Group Inc., 55 115–18 (upd.)
Daktronics, Inc., 32 134–37
Dal-Tile International Inc., 22 169–71
Dale Carnegie & Associates Inc., 28 85–87; 78 78–82 (upd.)
Dalgety PLC, II 499–500 *see also* PIC International Group PLC
Dalhoff Larsen & Horneman A/S, 96 95–99
Dalian Shide Group, 91 136–39
Dalkia Holding, 66 68–70
Dallah Albaraka Group, 72 83–86
Dallas Cowboys Football Club, Ltd., 33 122–25
Dallas Semiconductor Corporation, 13 191–93; 31 143–46 (upd.)
Dalli-Werke GmbH & Co. KG, 86 105–10
Dallis Coffee, Inc., 86 111–14
Damark International, Inc., 18 131–34 *see also* Provell Inc.
Dames & Moore, Inc., 25 128–31 *see also* URS Corp.
Dan River Inc., 35 142–46; 86 115–20 (upd.)
Dana Corporation, I 152–53; 10 264–66 (upd.)
Danaher Corporation, 7 116–17; 77 129–33 (upd.)
Danaos Corporation, 91 140–43
Daniel Measurement and Control, Inc., 16 153–55; 74 96–99 (upd.)
Daniel Thwaites Plc, 95 122–25
Danisco A/S, 44 134–37
Dannon Co., Inc., 14 149–51
Danone Group *see* Groupe Danone.
Danske Bank Aktieselskab, 50 148–51
Danskin, Inc., 12 93–95; 62 88–92 (upd.)
Danzas Group, V 441–43; 40 136–39 (upd.)
D'Arcy Masius Benton & Bowles, Inc., 6 20–22; 32 138–43 (upd.)
Darden Restaurants, Inc., 16 156–58; 44 138–42 (upd.)
Darigold, Inc., 9 159–61
Darling International Inc., 85 81–84
Dart Group PLC, 16 159–62; 77 134–37 (upd.)
Darty S.A., 27 118–20
DASA *see* Daimler-Benz Aerospace AG.
Dassault-Breguet *see* Avions Marcel Dassault-Breguet Aviation.
Dassault Systèmes S.A., 25 132–34 *see also* Groupe Dassault Aviation SA.
Data Broadcasting Corporation, 31 147–50
Data General Corporation, 8 137–40 *see also* EMC Corp.
Datapoint Corporation, 11 67–70
Datascope Corporation, 39 112–14
Datek Online Holdings Corp., 32 144–46
Dauphin Deposit Corporation, 14 152–54
Dave & Buster's, Inc., 33 126–29
The Davey Tree Expert Company, 11 71–73
The David and Lucile Packard Foundation, 41 117–19
The David J. Joseph Company, 14 155–56; 76 128–30 (upd.)
David Jones Ltd., 60 100–02
David's Bridal, Inc., 33 130–32
Davide Campari-Milano S.p.A., 57 104–06
Davis Polk & Wardwell, 36 151–54
Davis Service Group PLC, 45 139–41
DaVita Inc., 73 102–05
DAW Technologies, Inc., 25 135–37
Dawn Food Products, Inc., 17 126–28
Dawson Holdings PLC, 43 132–34
Day & Zimmermann Inc., 9 162–64; 31 151–55 (upd.)
Day International, Inc., 84 90–93
Day Runner, Inc., 14 157–58; 41 120–23 (upd.)
Dayton Hudson Corporation, V 43–44; 18 135–37 (upd.) *see also* Target Corp.
DB *see* Deutsche Bundesbahn.
dba Luftfahrtgesellschaft mbH, 76 131–33
DC Comics Inc., 25 138–41
DC Shoes, Inc., 60 103–05
DCN S.A., 75 125–27
DDB Worldwide Communications, 14 159–61 *see also* Omnicom Group Inc.
DDi Corp., 7 118–20; 97 129–32 (upd.)
De Beers Consolidated Mines Limited / De Beers Centenary AG, IV 64–68; 7 121–26 (upd.); 28 88–94 (upd.)
De Dietrich & Cie., 31 156–59

De La Rue plc, **10** 267–69; **34** 138–43 (upd.); **46** 251
Dean & DeLuca, Inc., **36** 155–57
Dean Foods Company, **7** 127–29; **21** 165–68 (upd.); **73** 106–15 (upd.)
Dean Witter, Discover & Co., **12** 96–98 *see also* Morgan Stanley Dean Witter & Co.
Dearborn Mid-West Conveyor Company, **56** 78–80
Death Row Records, **27** 121–23 *see also* Tha Row Records.
Deb Shops, Inc., **16** 163–65; **76** 134–37 (upd.)
Debeka Krankenversicherungsverein auf Gegenseitigkeit, **72** 87–90
Debenhams Plc, **28** 95–97
Debevoise & Plimpton, **39** 115–17
DEC *see* Digital Equipment Corp.
Deceuninck N.V., **84** 94–97
Dechert, **43** 135–38
Deckers Outdoor Corporation, **22** 172–74
Decora Industries, Inc., **31** 160–62
Decorator Industries Inc., **68** 101–04
DeCrane Aircraft Holdings Inc., **36** 158–60
DeepTech International Inc., **21** 169–71
Deere & Company, **III** 462–64; **21** 172–76 (upd.); **42** 101–06 (upd.)
Defiance, Inc., **22** 175–78
Degussa-Hüls AG, **IV** 69–72; **32** 147–53 (upd.)
DeKalb Genetics Corporation, **17** 129–31 *see also* Monsanto Co.
Del Laboratories, Inc., **28** 98–100
Del Monte Foods Company, **7** 130–32; **23** 163–66 (upd.)
Del Taco, Inc., **58** 89–92
Del Webb Corporation, **14** 162–64 *see also* Pulte Homes, Inc.
Delachaux S.A., **76** 138–40
Delaware North Companies Inc., **7** 133–36; **96** 100–05 (upd.)
Delco Electronics Corporation *see* GM Hughes Electronics Corp.
Delhaize "Le Lion" S.A., **44** 143–46
Deli Universal NV, **66** 71–74
dELiA*s Inc., **29** 141–44
Delicato Vineyards, Inc., **50** 152–55
Dell Computer Corporation, **9** 165–66; **31** 163–66 (upd.); **63** 122–26 (upd.)
Deloitte Touche Tohmatsu International, **9** 167–69; **29** 145–48 (upd.)
De'Longhi S.p.A., **66** 75–77
DeLorme Publishing Company, Inc., **53** 121–23
Delphax Technologies Inc., **94** 147–50
Delphi Automotive Systems Corporation, **45** 142–44
Delta and Pine Land Company, **33** 133–37; **59** 148–50
Delta Air Lines, Inc., **I** 99–100; **6** 81–83 (upd.); **39** 118–21 (upd.); **92** 82–87 (upd.)
Delta Woodside Industries, Inc., **8** 141–43; **30** 159–61 (upd.)
Deltec, Inc., **56** 81–83
Deltic Timber Corporation, **46** 115–17
Deluxe Corporation, **7** 137–39; **22** 179–82 (upd.); **73** 116–20 (upd.)
DEMCO, Inc., **60** 106–09
DeMoulas / Market Basket Inc., **23** 167–69
Den Norske Stats Oljeselskap AS, **IV** 405–07 *see also* Statoil ASA.
DenAmerica Corporation, **29** 149–51
Denbury Resources, Inc., **67** 139–41
Denby Group plc, **44** 147–50
Dendrite International, Inc., **70** 70–73
Denison International plc, **46** 118–20
Denner AG, **88** 62–65
Dennis Publishing Ltd., **62** 93–95
Dennison Manufacturing Company *see* Avery Dennison Corp.
DENSO Corporation, **46** 121–26 (upd.)
Dentsply International Inc., **10** 270–72
Dentsu Inc., **I** 9–11; **16** 166–69 (upd.); **40** 140–44 (upd.)
Denver Nuggets, **51** 94–97
DEP Corporation, **20** 177–80
Department 56, Inc., **14** 165–67; **34** 144–47 (upd.)
DEPFA BANK PLC, **69** 115–17
Deposit Guaranty Corporation, **17** 132–35
DePuy, Inc., **30** 162–65; **37** 110–13 (upd.)
Desarrolladora Homex, S.A. de C.V., **87** 127–130
Desc, S.A. de C.V., **23** 170–72
Deschutes Brewery, Inc., **57** 107–09
Designer Holdings Ltd., **20** 181–84
Desnoes and Geddes Limited, **79** 136–39
Destec Energy, Inc., **12** 99–101
Detroit Diesel Corporation, **10** 273–75; **74** 100–03 (upd.)
The Detroit Edison Company, **V** 592–95 *see also* DTE Energy Co.
The Detroit Lions, Inc., **55** 119–21
The Detroit Pistons Basketball Company, **41** 124–27
Detroit Red Wings, **74** 104–06
Detroit Tigers Baseball Club, Inc., **46** 127–30
Deutsch, Inc., **42** 107–10
Deutsche Babcock AG, **III** 465–66
Deutsche Bahn AG, **46** 131–35 (upd.)
Deutsche Bank AG, **II** 278–80; **40** 145–51 (upd.)
Deutsche Börse AG, **59** 151–55
Deutsche BP Aktiengesellschaft, **7** 140–43
Deutsche Bundepost Telekom, **V** 287–90 *see also* Deutsche Telekom AG
Deutsche Bundesbahn, **V** 444–47
Deutsche Lufthansa AG, **I** 110–11; **26** 113–16 (upd.); **68** 105–09 (upd.)
Deutsche Post AG, **29** 152–58
Deutsche Steinzeug Cremer & Breuer Aktiengesellschaft, **91** 144–48
Deutsche Telekom AG, **48** 130–35 (upd.)
Deutscher Sparkassen- und Giroverband (DSGV), **84** 98–102
Deutz AG, **39** 122–26
Deveaux S.A., **41** 128–30
Developers Diversified Realty Corporation, **69** 118–20
DeVito/Verdi, **85** 85–88
Devon Energy Corporation, **61** 73–75
Devoteam S.A., **94** 151–54
Devro plc, **55** 122–24
DeVry Inc., **29** 159–61; **82** 86-90 (upd.)
Devtek Corporation *see* Héroux-Devtek Inc.
Dewberry, **78** 83–86
Dewey Ballantine LLP, **48** 136–39
Dex Media, Inc., **65** 128–30
Dexia NV/SA, **42** 111–13; **88** 66–69 (upd.)
The Dexter Corporation, **I** 320–22; **12** 102–04 (upd.) *see also* Invitrogen Corp.
DFS Group Ltd., **66** 78–80
DH Technology, Inc., **18** 138–40
DHB Industries Inc., **85** 89–92
DHL Worldwide Network S.A./N.V., **6** 385–87; **24** 133–36 (upd.); **69** 121–25 (upd.)
Di Giorgio Corp., **12** 105–07
Diadora SpA, **86** 121–24
Diageo plc, **24** 137–41 (upd.); **79** 140–48 (upd.)
Diagnostic Products Corporation, **73** 121–24
Diagnostic Ventures Inc. *see* DVI, Inc.
Dial-A-Mattress Operating Corporation, **46** 136–39
The Dial Corporation, **8** 144–46; **23** 173–75 (upd.)
Dialogic Corporation, **18** 141–43
Diamond of California, **64** 108–11 (upd.)
Diamond Shamrock Corporation , **IV** 408–11 *see also* Ultramar Diamond Shamrock Corp.
DiamondCluster International, Inc., **51** 98–101
Diana Shipping Inc., **95** 126–29
Diavik Diamond Mines Inc., **85** 93–96
Dibrell Brothers, Incorporated, **12** 108–10
dick clark productions, inc., **16** 170–73
Dick Corporation, **64** 112–14
Dick's Sporting Goods, Inc., **59** 156–59
Dickten Masch Plastics LLC, **90** 158–61
Dictaphone Healthcare Solutions, **78** 87–92
Diebold, Incorporated, **7** 144–46; **22** 183–87 (upd.)
Diedrich Coffee, Inc., **40** 152–54
Diehl Stiftung & Co. KG, **79** 149–53
Dierbergs Markets Inc., **63** 127–29
Diesel SpA, **40** 155–57
Dietrich & Cie *see* De Dietrich & Cie.
Dietz and Watson, Inc., **92** 88–92
Digex, Inc., **46** 140–43
Digi International Inc., **9** 170–72

Digital Equipment Corporation, III 132–35; 6 233–36 (upd.) *see also* Compaq Computer Corp.
Digital River, Inc., 50 156–59
Digitas Inc., 81 107–10
Dillard Paper Company, 11 74–76 *see also* International Paper Co.
Dillard's Inc., V 45–47; 16 174–77 (upd.); 68 110–14 (upd.)
Dillingham Construction Corporation, 44 151–54 (upd.)
Dillingham Corp., I 565–66
Dillon Companies Inc., 12 111–13
Dime Savings Bank of New York, F.S.B., 9 173–74 *see also* Washington Mutual, Inc.
Dimension Data Holdings PLC, 69 126–28
DIMON Inc., 27 124–27
Dina *see* Consorcio G Grupo Dina, S.A. de C.V.
Diodes Incorporated, 81 111–14
Dionex Corporation, 46 144–46
Dior *see* Christian Dior S.A.
Dippin' Dots, Inc., 56 84–86
Direct Focus, Inc., 47 93–95
Direct Wines Ltd., 84 103–106
Directed Electronics, Inc., 87 131–135
Directorate General of Telecommunications, 7 147–49
DIRECTV, Inc., 38 174–77; 75 128–32 (upd.)
Dirk Rossmann GmbH, 94 155–59
Discount Auto Parts, Inc., 18 144–46
Discount Drug Mart, Inc., 14 172–73
Discount Tire Company Inc., 84 107–110
Discovery Communications, Inc., 42 114–17
Discovery Partners International, Inc., 58 93–95
Discreet Logic Inc., 20 185–87 *see also* Autodesk, Inc.
Disney *see* The Walt Disney Co.
Distillers Co. plc, I 239–41 *see also* Diageo PLC.
Distribución y Servicio D&S S.A., 71 123–26
Distrigaz S.A., 82 91-94
ditech.com, 93 181–84
The Dixie Group, Inc., 20 188–90; 80 88–92 (upd.)
Dixon Industries, Inc., 26 117–19
Dixon Ticonderoga Company, 12 114–16; 69 129–33 (upd.)
Dixons Group plc, V 48–50; 19 121–24 (upd.); 49 110–13 (upd.)
Djarum PT, 62 96–98
DKB *see* Dai-Ichi Kangyo Bank Ltd.
DKNY *see* Donna Karan International Inc.
DLJ *see* Donaldson, Lufkin & Jenrette.
DMB&B *see* D'Arcy Masius Benton & Bowles.
DMGT *see* Daily Mail and General Trust.
DMI Furniture, Inc., 46 147–50
Do it Best Corporation, 30 166–70
Dobrogea Grup S.A., 82 95-98
Dobson Communications Corporation, 63 130–32
Doctor's Associates Inc., 67 142–45 (upd.)
The Doctors' Company, 55 125–28
Doctors Without Borders *see* Médecins Sans Frontières.
Documentum, Inc., 46 151–53
Dofasco Inc., IV 73–74; 24 142–44 (upd.)
Dogan Sirketler Grubu Holding A.S., 83 107-110
Dogi International Fabrics S.A., 52 99–102
Dolan Media Company, 94 160–63
Dolby Laboratories Inc., 20 191–93
Dolce & Gabbana SpA, 62 99–101
Dole Food Company, Inc., 9 175–76; 31 167–70 (upd.); 68 115–19 (upd.)
Dollar Thrifty Automotive Group, Inc., 25 142–45
Dollar Tree Stores, Inc., 23 176–78; 62 102–05 (upd.)
Dollywood Corporation *see* Herschend Family Entertainment Corp.
Doman Industries Limited, 59 160–62
Dominick & Dominick LLC, 92 93–96
Dominick's Finer Foods, Inc., 56 87–89
Dominion Homes, Inc., 19 125–27
Dominion Resources, Inc., V 596–99; 54 83–87 (upd.)
Dominion Textile Inc., 12 117–19
Domino Printing Sciences PLC, 87 136–139
Domino Sugar Corporation, 26 120–22
Domino's, Inc., 7 150–53; 21 177–81 (upd.); 63 133–39 (upd.)
Domtar Corporation, IV 271–73; 89 185–91 (upd.)
Don Massey Cadillac, Inc., 37 114–16
Donaldson Company, Inc., 16 178–81; 49 114–18 (upd.)
Donaldson, Lufkin & Jenrette, Inc., 22 188–91
Donatos Pizzeria Corporation, 58 96–98
Donna Karan International Inc., 15 145–47; 56 90–93 (upd.)
Donnelly Corporation, 12 120–22; 35 147–50 (upd.)
Donnkenny, Inc., 17 136–38
Donruss Playoff L.P., 66 81–84
Dooney & Bourke Inc., 84 111–114
Dorel Industries Inc., 59 163–65
Dorian Drake International Inc., 96 106–09
Dorling Kindersley Holdings plc, 20 194–96 *see also* Pearson plc.
Dorsey & Whitney LLP, 47 96–99
Doskocil Companies, Inc., 12 123–25 *see also* Foodbrands America, Inc.
Dot Foods, Inc., 69 134–37
Dot Hill Systems Corp., 93 185–88
Double-Cola Co.-USA, 70 74–76
DoubleClick Inc., 46 154–57
Doubletree Corporation, 21 182–85
Douglas & Lomason Company, 16 182–85
Doux S.A., 80 93–96
Dover Corporation, III 467–69; 28 101–05 (upd.); 90 162–67 (upd.)
Dover Downs Entertainment, Inc., 43 139–41
Dover Publications Inc., 34 148–50
The Dow Chemical Company, I 323–25; 8 147–50 (upd.); 50 160–64 (upd.)
Dow Jones & Company, Inc., IV 601–03; 19 128–31 (upd.); 47 100–04 (upd.)
Dow Jones Telerate, Inc., 10 276–78 *see also* Reuters Group PLC.
DP World, 81 115–18
DPL Inc., 6 480–82; 96 110–15 (upd.)
DQE, 6 483–85; 38 40
Dr. August Oetker KG, 51 102–06
Dr Pepper/Seven Up, Inc., 9 177–78; 32 154–57 (upd.)
Dr. Reddy's Laboratories Ltd., 59 166–69
Drackett Professional Products, 12 126–28 *see also* S.C. Johnson & Son, Inc.
Draftfcb, 94 164–68
Dragados y Construcciones *see* Grupo Dragados SA.
Drägerwerk AG, 83 111-114
Drake Beam Morin, Inc., 44 155–57
Draper and Kramer Inc., 96 116–19
Draper Fisher Jurvetson, 91 149–52
Dräxlmaier Group, 90 168–72
Dreams Inc., 97 133–3
DreamWorks SKG, 43 142–46
The Drees Company, Inc., 41 131–33
Dresdner Bank A.G., II 281–83; 57 110–14 (upd.)
Dresdner Kleinwort Wasserstein, 60 110–13 (upd.)
The Dress Barn, Inc., 24 145–46
Dresser Industries, Inc., III 470–73; 55 129–31 (upd.)
Drew Industries Inc., 28 106–08
Drexel Burnham Lambert Incorporated, II 407–09 *see also* New Street Capital Inc.
Drexel Heritage Furnishings Inc., 12 129–31
Dreyer's Grand Ice Cream, Inc., 17 139–41 *see also* Nestlé S.A.
The Dreyfus Corporation, 70 77–80
DRI *see* Dominion Resources, Inc.
Dril-Quip, Inc., 81 119–21
Drinker, Biddle and Reath L.L.P., 92 97–101
DriveTime Automotive Group Inc., 68 120–24 (upd.)
Drs. Foster & Smith, Inc., 62 106–08
DRS Technologies, Inc., 58 99–101
Drug Emporium, Inc., 12 132–34 *see also* Big A Drug Stores Inc.
Drypers Corporation, 18 147–49
DryShips Inc., 95 130–33
DS Smith Plc, 61 76–79
DSC Communications Corporation, 12 135–37 *see also* Alcatel S.A.

DSGV *see* Deutscher Sparkassen- und Giroverband (DSGV).
DSM N.V., I 326–27; 56 94–96 (upd.)
DSW Inc., 73 125–27
DTAG *see* Dollar Thrifty Automotive Group, Inc.
DTE Energy Company, 20 197–201 (upd.); 94 169–76 (upd.)
DTS, Inc., 80 97–101
Du Pareil au Même, 43 147–49
Du Pont *see* E.I. du Pont de Nemours & Co.
Dualstar Entertainment Group LLC, 76 141–43
Duane Reade Holding Corp., 21 186–88
Ducati Motor Holding SpA, 30 171–73; 86 125–29 (upd.)
Duck Head Apparel Company, Inc., 42 118–21
Ducks Unlimited, Inc., 87 140–143
Duckwall-ALCO Stores, Inc., 24 147–49
Ducommun Incorporated, 30 174–76
Duferco Group, 94 177–80
Duke Energy Corporation, V 600–02; 27 128–31 (upd.)
Duke Realty Corporation, 57 115–17
The Dun & Bradstreet Corporation, IV 604–05; 19 132–34 (upd.); 61 80–84 (upd.)
Dun & Bradstreet Software Services Inc., 11 77–79
Dunavant Enterprises, Inc., 54 88–90
Duncan Aviation, Inc., 94 181–84
Duncan Toys Company, 55 132–35
Dunn-Edwards Corporation, 56 97–99
Dunn Industries, Inc. *see* JE Dunn Construction Group, Inc.
Dunnes Stores Ltd., 58 102–04
Duplex Products, Inc., 17 142–44
Dupont *see* E.I. du Pont de Nemours & Co.
Duracell International Inc., 9 179–81; 71 127–31 (upd.)
Durametallic, 21 189–91 *see also* Duriron Company Inc.
Duriron Company Inc., 17 145–47 *see also* Flowserve Corp.
Dürkopp Adler AG, 65 131–34
Duron Inc., 72 91–93 *see also* The Sherwin-Williams Co.
Dürr AG, 44 158–61
Duty Free International, Inc., 11 80–82 *see also* World Duty Free Americas, Inc.
DVI, Inc., 51 107–09
Duvernay Oil Corp., 83 115-118
Dyax Corp., 89 192–95
Dyckerhoff AG, 35 151–54
Dycom Industries, Inc., 57 118–20
Dyersburg Corporation, 21 192–95
Dylex Limited, 29 162–65
Dynatec Corporation, 87 144–147
Dynaction S.A., 67 146–48
Dynamic Materials Corporation, 81 122–25
Dynatech Corporation, 13 194–96
DynCorp, 45 145–47
Dynea, 68 125–27
Dynegy Inc., 49 119–22 (upd.)
Dyson Group PLC, 71 132–34

E

E. & J. Gallo Winery, I 242–44; 7 154–56 (upd.); 28 109–11 (upd.)
E! Entertainment Television Inc., 17 148–50
E-Systems, Inc., 9 182–85
E*Trade Financial Corporation, 20 206–08; 60 114–17 (upd.)
E-Z Serve Corporation, 17 169–71
E-Z-EM Inc., 89 196–99
E H Booth & Company Ltd., 90 173–76
E.I. du Pont de Nemours and Company, I 328–30; 8 151–54 (upd.); 26 123–27 (upd.); 73 128–33 (upd.)
E.On AG, 50 165–73 (upd.)
E.piphany, Inc., 49 123–25
E.W. Howell Co., Inc., 72 94–96 *see also* Obayashi Corporation
The E.W. Scripps Company, IV 606–09; 7 157–59 (upd.); 28 122–26 (upd.); 66 85–89 (upd.)
EADS N.V. *see* European Aeronautic Defence and Space Company EADS N.V.
EADS SOCATA, 54 91–94
Eagle Hardware & Garden, Inc., 16 186–89 *see also* Lowe's Companies, Inc.
Eagle-Picher Industries, Inc., 8 155–58; 23 179–83 (upd.) *see also* PerkinElmer Inc.
Eagle-Tribune Publishing Co., 91 153–57
Earl Scheib, Inc., 32 158–61
Earle M. Jorgensen Company, 82 99–102
The Earthgrains Company, 36 161–65
EarthLink, Inc., 36 166–68
East Japan Railway Company, V 448–50; 66 90–94 (upd.)
East Penn Manufacturing Co., Inc., 79 154–57
Easter Seals, Inc., 58 105–07
Eastern Airlines, I 101–03
The Eastern Company, 48 140–43
Eastern Enterprises, 6 486–88
EastGroup Properties, Inc., 67 149–51
Eastland Shoe Corporation, 82 103–106
Eastman Chemical Company, 14 174–75; 38 178–81 (upd.)
Eastman Kodak Company, III 474–77; 7 160–64 (upd.); 36 169–76 (upd.); 91 158–69 (upd.)
Easton Sports, Inc., 66 95–97
easyJet Airline Company Limited, 39 127–29; 52 330
Eateries, Inc., 33 138–40
Eaton Corporation, I 154–55; 10 279–80 (upd.); 67 152–56 (upd.)
Eaton Vance Corporation, 18 150–53
eBay Inc., 32 162–65; 67 157–61 (upd.)
Ebara Corporation, 83 119-122
EBSCO Industries, Inc., 17 151–53; 40 158–61 (upd.)
ECC Group plc, III 689–91 *see also* English China Clays plc.
ECC International Corp., 42 122–24
Ecco Sko A/S, 62 109–11
Echlin Inc., I 156–57; 11 83–85 (upd.) *see also* Dana Corp.
Echo Bay Mines Ltd., IV 75–77; 38 182–85 (upd.)
The Echo Design Group, Inc., 68 128–30
EchoStar Communications Corporation, 35 155–59
ECI Telecom Ltd., 18 154–56
Eckerd Corporation, 9 186–87 *see also* J.C. Penney Company, Inc.
Eckes AG, 56 100–03
Eclipse Aviation Corporation, 87 148–151
Ecolab Inc., I 331–33; 13 197–200 (upd.); 34 151–56 (upd.); 85 97–105 (upd.)
eCollege.com, 85 106–09
Ecology and Environment, Inc., 39 130–33
The Economist Group Ltd., 67 162–65
Ecopetrol *see* Empresa Colombiana de Petróleos.
ECS S.A, 12 138–40
Ed S.A.S., 88 70–73
Edasa *see* Embotelladoras del Atlántico, S.A.
Eddie Bauer Holdings, Inc., 9 188–90; 36 177–81 (upd.); 87 152–159 (upd.)
Edeka Zentrale A.G., II 621–23; 47 105–07 (upd.)
edel music AG, 44 162–65
Edelbrock Corporation, 37 117–19
Edelman, 62 112–15
EDF *see* Electricité de France.
EDGAR Online, Inc., 91 170–73
Edgars Consolidated Stores Ltd., 66 98–100
Edge Petroleum Corporation, 67 166–68
Edipresse S.A., 82 107–110
Edison Brothers Stores, Inc., 9 191–93
Edison International, 56 104–07 (upd.)
Edison Schools Inc., 37 120–23
Éditions Gallimard, 72 97–101
Editis S.A., 78 93–97
Editora Abril S.A *see* Abril S.A.
Editorial Television, S.A. de C.V., 57 121–23
EdK *see* Edeka Zentrale A.G.
Edmark Corporation, 14 176–78; 41 134–37 (upd.)
EDO Corporation, 46 158–61
EDP Group *see* Electricidade de Portugal, S.A.
The Edrington Group Ltd., 88 74–78
EDS *see* Electronic Data Systems Corp.
Educate Inc., 86 130–35 (upd.)
Education Management Corporation, 35 160–63
Educational Broadcasting Corporation, 48 144–47
Educational Testing Service, 12 141–43; 62 116–20 (upd.)

Edw. C. Levy Co., 42 125–27
Edward D. Jones & Company L.P., 30 177–79; 66 101–04 (upd.)
Edward Hines Lumber Company, 68 131–33
Edward J. DeBartolo Corporation, 8 159–62
Edwards and Kelcey, 70 81–83
Edwards Brothers, Inc., 92 102–06
Edwards Theatres Circuit, Inc., 31 171–73
EFJ, Inc., 81 126–29
EG&G Incorporated, 8 163–65; 29 166–69 (upd.)
Egan Companies, Inc., 94 185–88
EGAT *see* Electricity Generating Authority of Thailand (EGAT).
Egghead.com, Inc., 9 194–95; 31 174–77 (upd.)
EGL, Inc., 59 170–73
Egmont Group, 93 189–93
EgyptAir, 6 84–86; 27 132–35 (upd.)
Egyptian General Petroleum Corporation, IV 412–14; 51 110–14 (upd.)
eHarmony.com Inc., 71 135–38
Eiffage, 27 136–38
8x8, Inc., 94 189–92
800-JR Cigar, Inc., 27 139–41
84 Lumber Company, 9 196–97; 39 134–36 (upd.)
Eileen Fisher Inc., 61 85–87
Einstein/Noah Bagel Corporation, 29 170–73
eircom plc, 31 178–81 (upd.)
Eka Chemicals AB, 92 107–10
Ekco Group, Inc., 16 190–93
El Al Israel Airlines Ltd., 23 184–87
El Camino Resources International, Inc., 11 86–88
El Chico Restaurants, Inc., 19 135–38; 36 162–63
El Corte Inglés, S.A., V 51–53; 26 128–31 (upd.)
El Paso Corporation, 66 105–08 (upd.)
El Paso Electric Company, 21 196–98
El Paso Natural Gas Company, 12 144–46 *see also* El Paso Corp.
El Pollo Loco, Inc., 69 138–40
El Puerto de Liverpool, S.A.B. de C.V., 97 137–40
Elamex, S.A. de C.V., 51 115–17
Elan Corporation PLC, 63 140–43
Elano Corporation, 14 179–81
The Elder-Beerman Stores Corp., 10 281–83; 63 144–48 (upd.)
Elders IXL Ltd., I 437–39
Electrabel N.V., 67 169–71
Electric Boat Corporation, 86 136–39
Electric Lightwave, Inc., 37 124–27
Electricidade de Portugal, S.A., 47 108–11
Electricité de France, V 603–05; 41 138–41 (upd.)
Electricity Generating Authority of Thailand (EGAT), 56 108–10
Electro Rent Corporation, 58 108–10
Electrocomponents PLC, 50 174–77
Electrolux AB, 22 24–28 (upd.); 53 124–29 (upd.)
Electrolux Group, III 478–81
Electromagnetic Sciences Inc., 21 199–201
Electronic Arts Inc., 10 284–86; 85 110–15 (upd.)
Electronic Data Systems Corporation, III 136–38; 28 112–16 (upd.) *see also* Perot Systems Corp.
Electronics Boutique Holdings Corporation, 72 102–05
Electronics for Imaging, Inc., 15 148–50; 43 150–53 (upd.)
Elektra *see* Grupo Elektra, S.A. de C.V.
Elektra Entertainment Group, 64 115–18
Elektrowatt AG, 6 489–91 *see also* Siemens AG.
Element K Corporation, 94 193–96
Elementis plc, 40 162–68 (upd.)
Elephant Pharmacy, Inc., 83 123-126
Elf Aquitaine SA, 21 202–06 (upd.) *see also* Société Nationale Elf Aquitaine.
Eli Lilly and Company, I 645–47; 11 89–91 (upd.); 47 112–16 (upd.)
Elior SA, 49 126–28
Elite World S.A., 94 197–201
Elizabeth Arden, Inc., 8 166–68; 40 169–72 (upd.)
Eljer Industries, Inc., 24 150–52
Elkay Manufacturing Company, 73 134–36
ElkCorp, 52 103–05
Ellen Tracy, Inc., 55 136–38
Ellerbe Becket, 41 142–45
Ellett Brothers, Inc., 17 154–56
Elma Electronic AG, 83 127-130
Elmer Candy Corporation, 88 79–82
Elmer's Restaurants, Inc., 42 128–30
Elpida Memory, Inc., 83 131-134
Elscint Ltd., 20 202–05
Elsevier NV, IV 610–11 *see also* Reed Elsevier.
Elsinore Corporation, 48 148–51
Elvis Presley Enterprises, Inc., 61 88–90
EMAP plc, 35 164–66
EMBARQ Corporation, 83 135-138
Embers America Restaurants, 30 180–82
Embotelladora Andina S.A., 71 139–41
Embraer *see* Empresa Brasileira de Aeronáutica S.A.
Embrex, Inc., 72 106–08
EMC Corporation, 12 147–49; 46 162–66 (upd.)
EMCOR Group Inc., 60 118–21
EMCORE Corporation, 97 141–44
Emerson, 46 167–71 (upd.)
Emerson Electric Co., II 18–21
Emerson Radio Corp., 30 183–86
Emery Worldwide Airlines, Inc., 6 388–91; 25 146–50 (upd.)
Emge Packing Co., Inc., 11 92–93
EMI Group plc, 22 192–95 (upd.); 81 130–37 (upd.)
Emigrant Savings Bank, 59 174–76
The Emirates Group, 39 137–39; 81 138–42 (upd.)
Emmis Communications Corporation, 47 117–21
Empi, Inc., 27 132–35
Empire Blue Cross and Blue Shield, III 245–46 *see also* WellChoice, Inc.
The Empire District Electric Company, 77 138–41
Empire Resorts, Inc., 72 109–12
Empire Resources, Inc., 81 143–46
Employee Solutions, Inc., 18 157–60
Empresa Brasileira de Aeronáutica S.A. (Embraer), 36 182–84
Empresa Colombiana de Petróleos, IV 415–18
Empresas Almacenes Paris S.A., 71 142–44
Empresas CMPC S.A., 70 84–87
Empresas Copec S.A., 69 141–44
Empresas ICA Sociedad Controladora, S.A. de C.V., 41 146–49
Empresas Polar SA, 55 139–41 (upd.)
Empresas Públicas de Medellín S.A.E.S.P., 91 174–77
Enbridge Inc., 43 154–58
ENCAD, Incorporated, 25 151–53 *see also* Eastman Kodak Co.
Encompass Services Corporation, 33 141–44
Encore Acquisition Company, 73 137–39
Encore Computer Corporation, 13 201–02; 74 107–10 (upd.)
Encore Wire Corporation, 81 147–50
Encyclopedia Britannica, Inc., 7 165–68; 39 140–44 (upd.)
Endemol Entertainment Holding NV, 46 172–74; 53 154
ENDESA S.A., V 606–08; 46 175–79 (upd.)
Endo Pharmaceuticals Holdings Inc., 71 145–47
Endurance Specialty Holdings Ltd., 85 116–19
Energen Corporation, 21 207–09; 97 145–49 (upd.)
Energis plc, 44 363; **47 122–25**
Energizer Holdings, Inc., 32 171–74
Energy Brands Inc., 88 83–86
Energy Conversion Devices, Inc., 75 133–36
Enersis S.A., 73 140–43
Enesco Corporation, 11 94–96
Engelhard Corporation, IV 78–80; 21 210–14 (upd.); 72 113–18 (upd.)
Engineered Support Systems, Inc., 59 177–80
Engle Homes, Inc., 46 180–82
English China Clays Ltd., 15 151–54 (upd.); 40 173–77 (upd.)
Engraph, Inc., 12 150–51 *see also* Sonoco Products Co.
ENI S.p.A., 69 145–50 (upd.)
ENMAX Corporation, 83 139-142
Ennis, Inc., 21 215–17; 97 150–54 (upd.)
Enodis plc, 68 134–37
EnPro Industries, Inc., 93 194–98

Enquirer/Star Group, Inc., 10 287–88 *see also* American Media, Inc.
Enrich International, Inc., 33 145–48
Enron Corporation, V 609–10; 19 139–41; 46 183–86 (upd.)
ENSCO International Incorporated, 57 124–26
Enserch Corp., V 611–13 *see also* Texas Utilities.
Enskilda S.A. *see* Skandinaviska Enskilda Banken AB.
Enso-Gutzeit Oy, IV 274–77 *see also* Stora Enso Oyj.
Ente Nazionale Idrocarburi, IV 419–22 *see also* ENI S.p.A.
Ente Nazionale per l'Energia Elettrica, V 614–17
Entercom Communications Corporation, 58 111–12
Entergy Corporation, V 618–20; 45 148–51 (upd.)
Enterprise Inns plc, 59 181–83
Enterprise Oil plc, 11 97–99; 50 178–82 (upd.)
Enterprise Rent-A-Car Company, 6 392–93; 69 151–54 (upd.)
Entertainment Distribution Company, 89 200–03
Entravision Communications Corporation, 41 150–52
Entreprise Nationale Sonatrach, IV 423–25 *see also* Sonatrach.
Envirodyne Industries, Inc., 17 157–60
Environmental Industries, Inc., 31 182–85
Environmental Power Corporation, 68 138–40
Environmental Systems Research Institute Inc. (ESRI), 62 121–24
Enzo Biochem, Inc., 41 153–55
Eon Labs, Inc., 67 172–74
EPAM Systems Inc., 96 120–23
EPCOR Utilities Inc., 81 151–54
Epic Systems Corporation, 62 125–28
EPIQ Systems, Inc., 56 111–13
Equant N.V., 52 106–08
Equifax, Inc., 6 23–25; 28 117–21 (upd.); 90 177–83 (upd.)
Equistar Chemicals, LP, 71 148–50
Equitable Life Assurance Society of the United States, III 247–49
Equitable Resources, Inc., 6 492–94; 54 95–98 (upd.)
Equity Marketing, Inc., 26 136–38
Equity Office Properties Trust, 54 99–102
Equity Residential, 49 129–32
Equus Computer Systems, Inc., 49 133–35
Eram SA, 51 118–20
Eramet, 73 144–47
Ercros S.A., 80 102–05
ERGO Versicherungsgruppe AG, 44 166–69
Ergon, Inc., 95 134–37
Erickson Retirement Communities, 57 127–30
Ericsson *see* Telefonaktiebolaget LM Ericsson.
Eridania Béghin-Say S.A., 36 185–88
Erie Indemnity Company, 35 167–69
ERLY Industries Inc., 17 161–62
Ermenegildo Zegna SpA, 63 149–52
Ernie Ball, Inc., 56 114–16
Ernst & Young, 9 198–200; 29 174–77 (upd.)
Eroski *see* Grupo Eroski
Erste Bank der Osterreichischen Sparkassen AG, 69 155–57
ESCADA AG, 71 151–53
Escalade, Incorporated, 19 142–44
Eschelon Telecom, Inc., 72 119–22
ESCO Technologies Inc., 87 160–163
Eskimo Pie Corporation, 21 218–20
Espírito Santo Financial Group S.A., 79 158–63 (upd.)
ESPN, Inc., 56 117–22
Esporta plc, 35 170–72
Esprit de Corp., 8 169–72; 29 178–82 (upd.)
ESS Technology, Inc., 22 196–98
Essar Group Ltd., 79 164–67
Essef Corporation, 18 161–63 *see also* Pentair, Inc.
Esselte, 64 119–21
Esselte Leitz GmbH & Co. KG, 48 152–55
Esselte Pendaflex Corporation, 11 100–01
Essence Communications, Inc., 24 153–55
Essex Corporation, 85 120–23
Essilor International, 21 221–23
The Estée Lauder Companies Inc., 9 201–04; 30 187–91 (upd.); 92199–207 (upd.)
Esterline Technologies Corp., 15 155–57
Estes Express Lines, Inc., 86 140–43
Etablissements Economiques du Casino Guichard, Perrachon et ie, S.C.A., 12 152–54 *see also* Casino Guichard-Perrachon S.A.
Etablissements Franz Colruyt N.V., 68 141–43
Établissements Jacquot and Cie S.A.S., 92 111–14
Etam Developpement SA, 44 170–72
ETBD *see* Europe Through the Back Door.
Eternal Word Television Network, Inc., 57 131–34
Ethan Allen Interiors, Inc., 12 155–57; 39 145–48 (upd.)
Ethicon, Inc., 23 188–90
Ethiopian Airlines, 81 155–58
Ethyl Corp., I 334–36; 10 289–91 (upd.)
Etienne Aigner AG, 52 109–12
Etihad Airways PJSC, 89 204–07
EToys, Inc., 37 128–30
ETS *see* Educational Testing Service.
Euralis *see* Groupe Euralis.
Eurazeo, 80 106–09
The Eureka Company, 12 158–60 *see also* White Consolidated Industries Inc.
Euro Disney S.C.A., 20 209–12; 58 113–16 (upd.)
Euro RSCG Worldwide S.A., 13 203–05
Eurocopter S.A., 80 110–13
Eurofins Scientific S.A., 70 88–90
Euromarket Designs Inc., 31 186–89 (upd.)
Euronet Worldwide, Inc., 83 143-146
Euronext N.V., 37 131–33; 89 208–11 (upd.)
Europe Through the Back Door Inc., 65 135–38
European Aeronautic Defence and Space Company EADS N.V., 52 113–16 (upd.)
European Investment Bank, 66 109–11
Eurotunnel Group, 13 206–08; 37 134–38 (upd.)
EVA Airways Corporation, 51 121–23
Evans & Sutherland Computer Corporation, 19 145–49; 78 98–103 (upd.)
Evans, Inc., 30 192–94
Everex Systems, Inc., 16 194–96
Evergreen Energy, Inc., 97 155–59
Evergreen International Aviation, Inc., 53 130–33
Evergreen Marine Corporation (Taiwan) Ltd., 13 209–11; 50 183–89 (upd.)
Everlast Worldwide Inc., 47 126–29
Evraz Group S.A., 97 160–63
EWTN *see* Eternal Word Television Network, Inc.
Exabyte Corporation, 12 161–63; 40 178–81 (upd.)
Exar Corp., 14 182–84
EXCEL Communications Inc., 18 164–67
Excel Technology, Inc., 65 139–42
Executive Jet, Inc., 36 189–91 *see also* NetJets Inc.
Executone Information Systems, Inc., 13 212–14; 15 195
Exel plc, 51 124–30 (upd.)
Exelon Corporation, 48 156–63 (upd.); 49 65
Exide Electronics Group, Inc., 20 213–15
Exito *see* Almacenes Exito S.A.
Expand SA, 48 164–66
Expedia, Inc., 58 117–21
Expeditors International of Washington Inc., 17 163–65; 78 104–08 (upd.)
Experian Information Solutions Inc., 45 152–55
Exponent, Inc., 95 138–41
Exportadora Bananera Noboa, S.A., 91 178–81
Express Scripts Inc., 17 166–68; 44 173–76 (upd.)
Extended Stay America, Inc., 41 156–58
Extendicare Health Services, Inc., 6 181–83
Extreme Pizza *see* OOC Inc.
EXX Inc., 65 143–45

Exxon Mobil Corporation, IV 426–30; 7 169–73 (upd.); 32 175–82 (upd.); 67 175–86 (upd.)
Eye Care Centers of America, Inc., 69 158–60
Ezaki Glico Company Ltd., 72 123–25
EZCORP Inc., 43 159–61

F

F&W Publications, Inc., 71 154–56
F.A.O. Schwarz *see* FAO Schwarz
The F. Dohmen Co., 77 142–45
F. Hoffmann-La Roche & Co. A.G., I 642–44; 50 190–93 (upd.)
F. Korbel & Bros. Inc., 68 144–46
F.W. Webb Company, 95 142–45
Fab Industries, Inc., 27 142–44
Fabbrica D' Armi Pietro Beretta S.p.A., 39 149–51
Faber-Castell *see* A.W. Faber-Castell Unternehmensverwaltung GmbH & Co.
Fabri-Centers of America Inc., 16 197–99 *see also* Jo-Ann Stores, Inc.
Facebook, Inc., 90 184–87
Facom S.A., 32 183–85
FactSet Research Systems Inc., 73 148–50
Faegre & Benson LLP, 97 164–67
FAG—Kugelfischer Georg Schäfer AG, 62 129–32
Fair Grounds Corporation, 44 177–80
Fair, Isaac and Company, 18 168–71
Fairchild Dornier GmbH, 9 205–08; 48 167–71 (upd.)
Fairclough Construction Group plc, I 567–68
Fairfax Financial Holdings Limited, 57 135–37
Fairfax Media Ltd., 94 202–08 (upd.)
Fairfield Communities, Inc., 36 192–95
Fairmont Hotels & Resorts Inc., 69 161–63
Faiveley S.A., 39 152–54
Falcon Products, Inc., 33 149–51
Falconbridge Limited, 49 136–39
Fallon Worldwide, 22 199–201; 71 157–61 (upd.)
Family Christian Stores, Inc., 51 131–34
Family Dollar Stores, Inc., 13 215–17; 62 133–36 (upd.)
Family Golf Centers, Inc., 29 183–85
Famous Brands Ltd., 86 144–47
Famous Dave's of America, Inc., 40 182–84
Fannie Mae, 45 156–59 (upd.)
Fannie May Confections Brands, Inc., 80 114–18
Fansteel Inc., 19 150–52
Fanuc Ltd., III 482–83; 17 172–74 (upd.); 75 137–40 (upd.)
FAO Schwarz, 46 187–90
Farah Incorporated, 24 156–58
Faribault Foods, Inc., 89 212–15
Farley Northwest Industries Inc., I 440–41
Farley's & Sathers Candy Company, Inc., 62 137–39
Farm Family Holdings, Inc., 39 155–58
Farm Journal Corporation, 42 131–34
Farmacias Ahumada S.A., 72 126–28
Farmer Bros. Co., 52 117–19
Farmer Jack Supermarkets, 78 109–13
Farmer Mac *see* Federal Agricultural Mortgage Corp.
Farmers Insurance Group of Companies, 25 154–56
Farmland Foods, Inc., 7 174–75
Farmland Industries, Inc., 48 172–75
FARO Technologies, Inc., 87 164–167
Farouk Systems, Inc., 78 114–17
Farrar, Straus and Giroux Inc., 15 158–60
Fastenal Company, 14 185–87; 42 135–38 (upd.)
FASTWEB S.p.A., 83 147-150
Fat Face Ltd., 68 147–49
Fatburger Corporation, 64 122–24
FATS, Inc. *see* Firearms Training Systems, Inc.
Faultless Starch/Bon Ami Company, 55 142–45
Faurecia S.A., 70 91–93
FAvS *see* First Aviation Services Inc.
Faygo Beverages Inc., 55 146–48
Fazoli's Management, Inc., 27 145–47; 76 144–47 (upd.)
Featherlite Inc., 28 127–29
Fedders Corporation, 18 172–75; 43 162–67 (upd.)
Federal Agricultural Mortgage Corporation, 75 141–43
Federal Deposit Insurance Corporation, 93 208–12
Federal Express Corporation, V 451–53 *see also* FedEx Corp.
Federal Home Loan Mortgage Corp. *see* Freddie Mac.
Federal-Mogul Corporation, I 158–60; 10 292–94 (upd.); 26 139–43 (upd.)
Federal National Mortgage Association, II 410–11 *see also* Fannie Mae.
Federal Paper Board Company, Inc., 8 173–75
Federal Prison Industries, Inc., 34 157–60
Federal Signal Corp., 10 295–97
Federated Department Stores Inc., 9 209–12; 31 190–94 (upd.) *see also* Macy's, Inc.
Fédération Internationale de Football Association, 27 148–51
Federation Nationale d'Achats des Cadres *see* FNAC.
Federico Paternina S.A., 69 164–66
FedEx Corporation, 18 176–79 (upd.); 42 139–44 (upd.)
Feed The Children, Inc., 68 150–52
FEI Company, 79 168–71
Feld Entertainment, Inc., 32 186–89 (upd.)
Feldmühle Nobel AG, III 692–95 *see also* Metallgesellschaft.
Fellowes Manufacturing Company, 28 130–32
Fenaco, 86 148–51
Fender Musical Instruments Company, 16 200–02; 43 168–72 (upd.)
Fenwick & West LLP, 34 161–63
Ferolito, Vultaggio & Sons, 27 152–55
Ferrara Fire Apparatus, Inc., 84 115–118
Ferrara Pan Candy Company, 90 188–91
Ferrari S.p.A., 13 218–20; 36 196–200 (upd.)
Ferrellgas Partners, L.P., 35 173–75
Ferrero SpA, 54 103–05
Ferretti Group SpA, 90 192–96
Ferro Corporation, 8 176–79; 56 123–28 (upd.)
Ferrovial *see* Grupo Ferrovial
F5 Networks, Inc., 72 129–31
FHP International Corporation, 6 184–86
Fiat SpA, I 161–63; 11 102–04 (upd.); 50 194–98 (upd.)
FiberMark, Inc., 37 139–42; 53 24
Fibreboard Corporation, 16 203–05 *see also* Owens Corning Corp.
Ficosa *see* Grupo Ficosa International.
Fidelity Investments Inc., II 412–13; 14 188–90 (upd.) *see also* FMR Corp.
Fidelity National Financial Inc., 54 106–08
Fidelity Southern Corporation, 85 124–27
Fieldale Farms Corporation, 23 191–93
Fieldcrest Cannon, Inc., 9 213–17; 31 195–200 (upd.)
Fielmann AG, 31 201–03
FIFA *see* Fédération Internationale de Football Association.
Fifth Third Bancorp, 13 221–23; 31 204–08 (upd.)
Le Figaro *see* Société du Figaro S.A.
Figgie International Inc., 7 176–78
Fiji Water LLC, 74 111–13
Fila Holding S.p.A., 20 216–18; 52 120–24 (upd.)
FileNet Corporation, 62 140–43
Fili Enterprises, Inc., 70 94–96
Filipacchi Medias S.A. *see* Hachette Filipacchi Medias S.A.
Film Roman, Inc., 58 122–24
Filtrona plc, 88 87–91
Fimalac S.A., 37 143–45
FINA, Inc., 7 179–81 *see also* Total Fina Elf S.A.
Finarte Casa d'Aste S.p.A., 93 213–16
Findel plc, 60 122–24
Findorff *see* J.H. Findorff and Son, Inc.
Fingerhut Companies, Inc., 9 218–20; 36 201–05 (upd.)
Finisar Corporation, 92 115–18
The Finish Line, Inc., 29 186–88; 68 153–56 (upd.)
FinishMaster, Inc., 24 159–61
Finlay Enterprises, Inc., 16 206–08; 76 148–51 (upd.)
Finmeccanica S.p.A., 84 119–123

Finnair Oy, 6 87–89; 25 157–60 (upd.); 61 91–95 (upd.)
Finning International Inc., 69 167–69
Fired Up, Inc., 82 111–14
Firearms Training Systems, Inc., 27 156–58
Fireman's Fund Insurance Company, III 250–52
Firmenich International S.A., 60 125–27
First Albany Companies Inc., 37 146–48
First Alert, Inc., 28 133–35
The First American Corporation, 52 125–27
First Aviation Services Inc., 49 140–42
First Bank System Inc., 12 164–66 *see also* U.S. Bancorp
First Brands Corporation, 8 180–82
First Cash Financial Services, Inc., 57 138–40
First Chicago Corporation, II 284–87 *see also* Bank One Corp.
First Choice Holidays PLC, 40 185–87
First Colony Coffee & Tea Company, 84 124–126
First Commerce Bancshares, Inc., 15 161–63 *see also* Wells Fargo & Co.
First Commerce Corporation, 11 105–07 *see also* JPMorgan Chase & Co.
First Data Corporation, 30 195–98 (upd.)
First Empire State Corporation, 11 108–10
First Executive Corporation, III 253–55
First Fidelity Bank, N.A., New Jersey, 9 221–23
First Financial Management Corporation, 11 111–13
First Hawaiian, Inc., 11 114–16
First Industrial Realty Trust, Inc., 65 146–48
First International Computer, Inc., 56 129–31
First Interstate Bancorp, II 288–90 *see also* Wells Fargo & Co.
The First Marblehead Corporation, 87 168–171
First Mississippi Corporation, 8 183–86 *see also* ChemFirst, Inc.
First Nationwide Bank, 14 191–93 see also Citigroup Inc.
First of America Bank Corporation, 8 187–89
First Pacific Company Limited, 18 180–82
First Security Corporation, 11 117–19 see also Wells Fargo & Co.
First Solar, Inc., 95 146–50
First Team Sports, Inc., 22 202–04
First Tennessee National Corporation, 11 120–21; 48 176–79 (upd.)
First Union Corporation, 10 298–300 *see also* Wachovia Corp.
First USA, Inc., 11 122–24
First Virginia Banks, Inc., 11 125–26 see also BB&T Corp.
The First Years Inc., 46 191–94
Firstar Corporation, 11 127–29; 33 152–55 (upd.)
FirstGroup plc, 89 216–19
Fiserv Inc., 11 130–32; 33 156–60 (upd.)
Fish & Neave, 54 109–12
Fisher Companies, Inc., 15 164–66
Fisher Controls International, LLC, 13 224–26; 61 96–99 (upd.)
Fisher-Price Inc., 12 167–69; 32 190–94 (upd.)
Fisher Scientific International Inc., 24 162–66
Fisk Corporation, 72 132–34
Fiskars Corporation, 33 161–64
Fisons plc, 9 224–27; 23 194–97 (upd.)
5 & Diner Franchise Corporation, 72 135–37
FKI Plc, 57 141–44
Flagstar Companies, Inc., 10 301–03 *see also* Advantica Restaurant Group, Inc.
Flanders Corporation, 65 149–51
Flanigan's Enterprises, Inc., 60 128–30
Flatiron Construction Corporation, 92 119–22
Fleer Corporation, 15 167–69
FleetBoston Financial Corporation, 9 228–30; 36 206–14 (upd.)
Fleetwood Enterprises, Inc., III 484–85; 22 205–08 (upd.); 81 159–64 (upd.)
Fleming Companies, Inc., II 624–25; 17 178–81 (upd.)
Fletcher Challenge Ltd., IV 278–80; 19 153–57 (upd.)
Fleury Michon S.A., 39 159–61
Flexsteel Industries Inc., 15 170–72; 41 159–62 (upd.)
Flextronics International Ltd., 38 186–89
Flight Options, LLC, 75 144–46
FlightSafety International, Inc., 9 231–33; 29 189–92 (upd.)
Flint Ink Corporation, 13 227–29; 41 163–66 (upd.)
FLIR Systems, Inc., 69 170–73
Floc'h & Marchand, 80 119–21
Florida Crystals Inc., 35 176–78
Florida East Coast Industries, Inc., 59 184–86
Florida Gaming Corporation, 47 130–33
Florida Progress Corp., V 621–22; 23 198–200 (upd.) *see also* Progress Energy, Inc.
Florida Public Utilities Company, 69 174–76
Florida Rock Industries, Inc., 46 195–97 *see also* Patriot Transportation Holding, Inc.
Florida's Natural Growers, 45 160–62
Florists' Transworld Delivery, Inc., 28 136–38
Florsheim Shoe Group Inc., 9 234–36; 31 209–12 (upd.)
Flotek Industries Inc., 93 217–20
Flour City International, Inc., 44 181–83
Flow International Corporation, 56 132–34
Flowers Industries, Inc., 12 170–71; 35 179–82 (upd.) *see also* Keebler Foods Co.
Flowserve Corporation, 33 165–68; 77 146–51 (upd.)
FLSmidth & Co. A/S, 72 138–40
Fluke Corporation, 15 173–75
Fluor Corporation, I 569–71; 8 190–93 (upd.); 34 164–69 (upd.)
FlyBE *see* Jersey European Airways (UK) Ltd.
Flying Boat, Inc. (Chalk's Ocean Airways), 56 135–37
Flying J Inc., 19 158–60
Flying Pigeon Bicycle Co. *see* Tianjin Flying Pigeon Bicycle Co., Ltd.
FMC Corp., I 442–44; 11 133–35 (upd.); 89 220–27 (upd.)
FMR Corp., 8 194–96; 32 195–200 (upd.)
FNAC, 21 224–26
FNMA *see* Federal National Mortgage Association.
Foamex International Inc., 17 182–85
Focus Features, 78 118–22
Fokker *see* N.V. Koninklijke Nederlandse Vliegtuigenfabriek Fokker.
Foley & Lardner, 28 139–42
Follett Corporation, 12 172–74; 39 162–65 (upd.)
Fonterra Co-Operative Group Ltd., 58 125–27
Food Circus Super Markets, Inc., 88 92–96
The Food Emporium, 64 125–27
Food For The Poor, Inc., 77 152–55
Food Lion LLC, II 626–27; 15 176–78 (upd.); 66 112–15 (upd.)
Foodarama Supermarkets, Inc., 28 143–45 *see also* Wakefern Food Corp.
FoodBrands America, Inc., 23 201–04 *see also* Doskocil Companies, Inc.; Tyson Foods, Inc.
Foodmaker, Inc., 14 194–96 *see also* Jack in the Box Inc.
Foot Locker, Inc., 68 157–62 (upd.)
Foot Petals L.L.C., 95 151–54
Foote, Cone & Belding Worldwide, I 12–15; 66 116–20 (upd.)
Footstar, Incorporated, 24 167–69 *see also* Foot Locker, Inc.
Forbes Inc., 30 199–201; 82 115–20 (upd.)
Force Protection Inc., 95 155–58
The Ford Foundation, 34 170–72
Ford Motor Company, I 164–68; 11 136–40 (upd.); 36 215–21 (upd.); 64 128–34 (upd.)
Ford Motor Company, S.A. de C.V., 20 219–21
FORE Systems, Inc., 25 161–63 *see also* Telefonaktiebolaget LM Ericsson.
FöreningsSparbanken AB, 69 177–80
Forest City Enterprises, Inc., 16 209–11; 52 128–31 (upd.)

Forest Laboratories, Inc., 11 141–43; 52 132–36 (upd.)
Forest Oil Corporation, 19 161–63; 91 182–87 (upd.)
Forever Living Products International Inc., 17 186–88
Forever 21, Inc., 84 127–129
FormFactor, Inc., 85 128–31
Formica Corporation, 13 230–32
Formosa Plastics Corporation, 14 197–99; 58 128–31 (upd.)
Forrester Research, Inc., 54 113–15
Forstmann Little & Co., 38 190–92
Fort Howard Corporation, 8 197–99 *see also* Fort James Corp.
Fort James Corporation, 22 209–12 (upd.) *see also* Georgia-Pacific Corp.
Fortis, Inc., 15 179–82; 47 134–37 (upd.); 50 4–6
Fortum Corporation, 30 202–07 (upd.) *see also* Neste Oil Corp.
Fortune Brands, Inc., 29 193–97 (upd.); 68 163–67 (upd.)
Fortunoff Fine Jewelry and Silverware Inc., 26 144–46
Forward Air Corporation, 75 147–49
Forward Industries, Inc., 86 152–55
The Forzani Group Ltd., 79 172–76
Fossil, Inc., 17 189–91
Foster Poultry Farms, 32 201–04
Foster Wheeler Corporation, 6 145–47; 23 205–08 (upd.); 76 152–56 (upd.)
Foster's Group Limited, 7 182–84; 21 227–30 (upd.); 50 199–203 (upd.)
FosterGrant, Inc., 60 131–34
Foundation Health Corporation, 12 175–77
Fountain Powerboats Industries, Inc., 28 146–48
Four Seasons Hotels Inc., 9 237–38; 29 198–200 (upd.)
Four Winns Boats LLC, 96 124–27
4Kids Entertainment Inc., 59 187–89
Fourth Financial Corporation, 11 144–46
Fox Entertainment Group, Inc., 43 173–76
Fox Family Worldwide, Inc., 24 170–72 *see also* ABC Family Worldwide, Inc.
Fox, Inc. *see* Twentieth Century Fox Film Corp.
Foxboro Company, 13 233–35
FoxHollow Technologies, Inc., 85 132–35
FoxMeyer Health Corporation, 16 212–14 see also McKesson Corp.
Foxworth-Galbraith Lumber Company, 91 188–91
FPL Group, Inc., V 623–25; 49 143–46 (upd.)
Framatome SA, 19 164–67 aee also Alcatel S.A.; AREVA.
France Télécom Group, V 291–93; 21 231–34 (upd.)
Francotyp-Postalia Holding AG, 92 123–27
Frank J. Zamboni & Co., Inc., 34 173–76
Frank Russell Company, 46 198–200
Frank's Nursery & Crafts, Inc., 12 178–79
Franke Holding AG, 76 157–59
Frankel & Co., 39 166–69
Frankfurter Allgemeine Zeitung GmbH, 66 121–24
Franklin Covey Company, 11 147–49; 37 149–52 (upd.)
Franklin Electric Company, Inc., 43 177–80
Franklin Electronic Publishers, Inc., 23 209–13
The Franklin Mint, 69 181–84
Franklin Resources, Inc., 9 239–40
Franz Inc., 80 122–25
Fraport AG Frankfurt Airport Services Worldwide, 90 197–202
Fraser & Neave Ltd., 54 116–18
Fred Alger Management, Inc., 97 168–72
Fred Meyer Stores, Inc., V 54–56; 20 222–25 (upd.); 64 135–39 (upd.)
Fred Usinger Inc., 54 119–21
The Fred W. Albrecht Grocery Co., 13 236–38
Fred Weber, Inc., 61 100–02
Fred's, Inc., 23 214–16; 62 144–47 (upd.)
Freddie Mac, 54 122–25
Frederick Atkins Inc., 16 215–17
Frederick's of Hollywood Inc., 16 218–20; 59 190–93 (upd.)
Freedom Communications, Inc., 36 222–25
Freeport-McMoRan Copper & Gold, Inc., IV 81–84; 7 185–89 (upd.); 57 145–50 (upd.)
Freescale Semiconductor, Inc., 83 151-154
Freeze.com LLC, 77 156–59
Freixenet S.A., 71 162–64
French Connection Group plc, 41 167–69
French Fragrances, Inc., 22 213–15 *see also* Elizabeth Arden, Inc.
Frequency Electronics, Inc., 61 103–05
Fresenius AG, 56 138–42
Fresh America Corporation, 20 226–28
Fresh Choice, Inc., 20 229–32
Fresh Enterprises, Inc., 66 125–27
Fresh Express Inc., 88 97–100
Fresh Foods, Inc., 29 201–03
FreshDirect, LLC, 84 130–133
Fretter, Inc., 10 304–06
Freudenberg & Co., 41 170–73
Fried, Frank, Harris, Shriver & Jacobson, 35 183–86
Fried. Krupp GmbH, IV 85–89 *see also* ThyssenKrupp AG.
Friedman, Billings, Ramsey Group, Inc., 53 134–37
Friedman's Inc., 29 204–06
Friedrich Grohe AG & Co. KG, 53 138–41
Friendly Ice Cream Corporation, 30 208–10; 72 141–44 (upd.)
Friesland Coberco Dairy Foods Holding N.V., 59 194–96
Frigidaire Home Products, 22 216–18
Frisch's Restaurants, Inc., 35 187–89; 92 128–32 (upd.)
Frito-Lay North America, 32 205–10; 73 151–58 (upd.)
Fritz Companies, Inc., 12 180–82
Fromageries Bel, 23 217–19; 25 83–84
Frontier Airlines Holdings Inc., 22 219–21; 84 134–138 (upd.)
Frontier Corp., 16 221–23
Frontier Natural Products Co-Op, 82 121–24
Frontline Ltd., 45 163–65
Frost & Sullivan, Inc., 53 142–44
Frozen Food Express Industries, Inc., 20 233–35
Frucor Beverages Group Ltd., 96 128–31
Fruehauf Corp., I 169–70
Fruit of the Loom, Inc., 8 200–02; 25 164–67 (upd.)
Fruth Pharmacy, Inc., 66 128–30
Fry's Electronics, Inc., 68 168–70
Frymaster Corporation, 27 159–62
FSI International, Inc., 17 192–94 *see also* FlightSafety International, Inc.
FTI Consulting, Inc., 77 160–63
FTP Software, Inc., 20 236–38
Fubu, 29 207–09
Fuel Tech, Inc., 85 136–40
Fuel Systems Solutions, Inc., 97 173–77
FuelCell Energy, Inc., 75 150–53
Fuji Bank, Ltd., II 291–93
Fuji Electric Co., Ltd., II 22–23; 48 180–82 (upd.)
Fuji Photo Film Co., Ltd., III 486–89; 18 183–87 (upd.); 79 177–84 (upd.)
Fuji Television Network Inc., 91 192–95
Fujisawa Pharmaceutical Company, Ltd., I 635–36; 58 132–34 (upd.) *see also* Astellas Pharma Inc.
Fujitsu-ICL Systems Inc., 11 150–51
Fujitsu Limited, III 139–41; 16 224–27 (upd.); 40 145–50 (upd.)
Fulbright & Jaworski L.L.P., 47 138–41
Fuller Smith & Turner P.L.C., 38 193–95
Funai Electric Company Ltd., 62 148–50
Funco, Inc., 20 239–41 *see also* GameStop Corp.
Fuqua Enterprises, Inc., 17 195–98
Fuqua Industries Inc., I 445–47
Furmanite Corporation, 92 133–36
Furniture Brands International, Inc., 39 170–75 (upd.)
Furon Company, 28 149–51 *see also* Compagnie de Saint-Gobain.
Furr's Restaurant Group, Inc., 53 145–48
Furr's Supermarkets, Inc., 28 152–54
Furukawa Electric Co., Ltd., III 490–92
Future Now, Inc., 12 183–85
Future Shop Ltd., 62 151–53

Fyffes Plc, **38** 196–99

G

G&K Holding S.A., **95** 159–62
G&K Services, Inc., **16** 228–30
G A Pindar & Son Ltd., **88** 101–04
G.D. Searle & Co., **I** 686–89; **12** 186–89 (upd.); **34** 177–82 (upd.)
G. Heileman Brewing Co., **I** 253–55 *see also* Stroh Brewery Co.
G.I.E. Airbus Industrie, **I** 41–43; **12** 190–92 (upd.)
G.I. Joe's, Inc., **30** 221–23
G-III Apparel Group, Ltd., **22** 222–24
G. Leblanc Corporation, **55** 149–52
G.S. Blodgett Corporation, **15** 183–85 *see also* Blodgett Holdings, Inc.
Gabelli Asset Management Inc., **30** 211–14 *see also* Lynch Corp.
Gables Residential Trust, **49** 147–49
Gadzooks, Inc., **18** 188–90
GAF, **I** 337–40; **22** 225–29 (upd.)
Gage Marketing Group, **26** 147–49
Gaiam, Inc., **41** 174–77
Gainsco, Inc., **22** 230–32
Galardi Group, Inc., **72** 145–47
Galaxy Investors, Inc., **97** 178–81
Galaxy Nutritional Foods, Inc., **58** 135–37
Gale International LLC, **93** 221–24
Galenica AG, **84** 139–142
Galeries Lafayette S.A., **V** 57–59; **23** 220–23 (upd.)
Galey & Lord, Inc., **20** 242–45; **66** 131–34 (upd.)
Gallaher Group Plc, **49** 150–54 (upd.)
Gallaher Limited, **V** 398–400; **19** 168–71 (upd.)
Gallo Winery *see* E. & J. Gallo Winery.
The Gallup Organization, **37** 153–56
Galoob Toys *see* Lewis Galoob Toys Inc.
Galyan's Trading Company, Inc., **47** 142–44
The Gambrinus Company, **40** 188–90
Gambro AB, **49** 155–57
The GAME Group plc, **80** 126–29
GameStop Corp., **69** 185–89 (upd.)
GAMI *see* Great American Management and Investment, Inc.
Gaming Partners InternationalCorporation, **92225**–28
Gander Mountain Company, **20** 246–48; **90** 203–08 (upd.)
Gannett Company, Inc., **IV** 612–13; **7** 190–92 (upd.); **30** 215–17 (upd.); **66** 135–38 (upd.)
Gano Excel Enterprise Sdn. Bhd., **89** 228–31
Gantos, Inc., **17** 199–201
GAP *see* Grupo Aeroportuario del Pacífico, S.A. de C.V.
The Gap, Inc., **V** 60–62; **18** 191–94 (upd.); **55** 153–57 (upd.)
Garan, Inc., **16** 231–33; **64** 140–43 (upd.)
The Garden Company Ltd., **82** 125–28
Garden Fresh Restaurant Corporation, **31** 213–15
Garden Ridge Corporation, **27** 163–65
Gardenburger, Inc., **33** 169–71; **76** 160–63 (upd.)
Gardner Denver, Inc., **49** 158–60
Garmin Ltd., **60** 135–37
Garst Seed Company, Inc., **86** 156–59
Gart Sports Company, **24** 173–75 *see also* Sports Authority, Inc.
Gartner, Inc., **21** 235–37; **94** 209–13 (upd.)
Garuda Indonesia, **6** 90–91; **58** 138–41 (upd.)
Gas Natural SDG S.A., **69** 190–93
GASS *see* Grupo Ángeles Servicios de Salud, S.A. de C.V.
Gasunie *see* N.V. Nederlandse Gasunie.
Gate Gourmet International AG, **70** 97–100
GateHouse Media, Inc., **91** 196–99
The Gates Corporation, **9** 241–43
Gateway Corporation Ltd., **II** 628–30 *see also* Somerfield plc.
Gateway, Inc., **10** 307–09; **27** 166–69 (upd.); **63** 153–58 (upd.)
The Gatorade Company, **82** 129–32
Gatti's Pizza, Inc. *see* Mr. Gatti's, LP.
GATX, **6** 394–96; **25** 168–71 (upd.)
Gaumont S.A., **25** 172–75; **91** 200–05 (upd.)
Gaylord Container Corporation, **8** 203–05
Gaylord Entertainment Company, **11** 152–54; **36** 226–29 (upd.)
Gaz de France, **V** 626–28; **40** 191–95 (upd.)
Gazprom *see* OAO Gazprom.
GBC *see* General Binding Corp.
GC Companies, Inc., **25** 176–78 *see also* AMC Entertainment Inc.
GE *see* General Electric Co.
GE Aircraft Engines, **9** 244–46
GE Capital Aviation Services, **36** 230–33
GEA AG, **27** 170–74
GEAC Computer Corporation Ltd., **43** 181–85
Geberit AG, **49** 161–64
Gecina SA, **42** 151–53
Gedney *see* M.A. Gedney Co.
Geerlings & Wade, Inc., **45** 166–68
Geest Plc, **38** 200–02 *see also* Bakkavör Group hf.
Gefco SA, **54** 126–28
Geffen Records Inc., **26** 150–52
GEHE AG, **27** 175–78
Gehl Company, **19** 172–74
GEICO Corporation, **10** 310–12; **40** 196–99 (upd.)
Geiger Bros., **60** 138–41
Gelita AG, **74** 114–18
GEMA (Gesellschaft für musikalische Aufführungs- und mechanische Vervielfältigungsrechte), **70** 101–05
Gemini Sound Products Corporation, **58** 142–44
Gemplus International S.A., **64** 144–47
Gen-Probe Incorporated, **79** 185–88
Gencor Ltd., **IV** 90–93; **22** 233–37 (upd.) *see also* Gold Fields Ltd.
GenCorp Inc., **9** 247–49
Genentech, Inc., **I** 637–38; **8** 209–11 (upd.); **32** 211–15 (upd.); **75** 154–58 (upd.)
General Accident plc, **III** 256–57 *see also* Aviva PLC.
General Atomics, **57** 151–54
General Bearing Corporation, **45** 169–71
General Binding Corporation, **10** 313–14; **73** 159–62 (upd.)
General Cable Corporation, **40** 200–03
The General Chemical Group Inc., **37** 157–60
General Cigar Holdings, Inc., **66** 139–42 (upd.)
General Cinema Corporation, **I** 245–46 *see also* GC Companies, Inc.
General DataComm Industries, Inc., **14** 200–02
General Dynamics Corporation, **I** 57–60; **10** 315–18 (upd.); **40** 204–10 (upd.); **88** 105–13 (upd.)
General Electric Company, **II** 27–31; **12** 193–97 (upd.); **34** 183–90 (upd.); **63** 159–68 (upd.)
General Electric Company, PLC, **II** 24–26 *see also* Marconi plc.
General Employment Enterprises, Inc., **87** 172–175
General Growth Properties, Inc., **57** 155–57
General Host Corporation, **12** 198–200
General Housewares Corporation, **16** 234–36
General Instrument Corporation, **10** 319–21 *see also* Motorola, Inc.
General Maritime Corporation, **59** 197–99
General Mills, Inc., **II** 501–03; **10** 322–24 (upd.); **36** 234–39 (upd.); **85** 141–49 (upd.)
General Motors Corporation, **I** 171–73; **10** 325–27 (upd.); **36** 240–44 (upd.); **64** 148–53 (upd.)
General Nutrition Companies, Inc., **11** 155–57; **29** 210–14 (upd.)
General Public Utilities Corporation, **V** 629–31 *see also* GPU, Inc.
General Re Corporation, **III** 258–59; **24** 176–78 (upd.)
General Sekiyu K.K., **IV** 431–33 *see also* TonenGeneral Sekiyu K.K.
General Signal Corporation, **9** 250–52 *see also* SPX Corp.
General Tire, Inc., **8** 212–14
Generale Bank, **II** 294–95 *see also* Fortis, Inc.
Générale des Eaux Group, **V** 632–34 *see* Vivendi Universal S.A.
Generali *see* Assicurazioni Generali.
Genesco Inc., **17** 202–06; **84** 143–149 (upd.)
Genesee & Wyoming Inc., **27** 179–81
Genesis Health Ventures, Inc., **18** 195–97 *see also* NeighborCare,Inc.

Genesis Microchip Inc., 82 133–37
Genetics Institute, Inc., 8 215–18
Geneva Steel, 7 193–95
Genmar Holdings, Inc., 45 172–75
Genovese Drug Stores, Inc., 18 198–200
Genoyer *see* Groupe Genoyer.
GenRad, Inc., 24 179–83
Gentex Corporation, 26 153–57
Genting Bhd., 65 152–55
Gentiva Health Services, Inc., 79 189–92
Genuardi's Family Markets, Inc., 35 190–92
Genuine Parts Company, 9 253–55; 45 176–79 (upd.)
Genzyme Corporation, 13 239–42; 38 203–07 (upd.); 77 164–70 (upd.)
geobra Brandstätter GmbH & Co. KG, 48 183–86
Geodis S.A., 67 187–90
The Geon Company, 11 158–61
Georg Fischer AG Schaffhausen, 61 106–09
George A. Hormel and Company, II 504–06 *see also* Hormel Foods Corp.
The George F. Cram Company, Inc., 55 158–60
George P. Johnson Company, 60 142–44
George S. May International Company, 55 161–63
George Weston Ltd., II 631–32; 36 245–48 (upd.); 88 114–19 (upd.)
George Wimpey plc, 12 201–03; 51 135–38 (upd.)
Georgia Gulf Corporation, 9 256–58; 61 110–13 (upd.)
Georgia-Pacific Corporation, IV 281–83; 9 259–62 (upd.); 47 145–51 (upd.)
Geotek Communications Inc., 21 238–40
Gerald Stevens, Inc., 37 161–63
Gerber Products Company, 7 196–98; 21 241–44 (upd)
Gerber Scientific, Inc., 12 204–06; 84 150–154 (upd.)
Gerdau S.A., 59 200–03
Gerhard D. Wempe KG, 88 120–25
Gericom AG, 47 152–54
Gerling-Konzern Versicherungs-Beteiligungs-Aktiengesellschaft, 51 139–43
German American Bancorp, 41 178–80
Gerresheimer Glas AG, 43 186–89
Gerry Weber International AG, 63 169–72
Gesellschaft für musikalische Aufführungs- und mechanische Vervielfältigungsrechte *see* GEMA.
Getrag Corporate Group, 92 137–42
Getronics NV, 39 176–78
Getty Images, Inc., 31 216–18
Gevaert *see* Agfa Gevaert Group N.V.
Gévelot S.A., 96 132–35
Gevity HR, Inc., 63 173–77
GF Health Products, Inc., 82 138–41
GFI Informatique SA, 49 165–68
GfK Aktiengesellschaft, 49 169–72
GFS *see* Gordon Food Service Inc.
Ghirardelli Chocolate Company, 30 218–20
Gianni Versace SpA, 22 238–40
Giant Cement Holding, Inc., 23 224–26
Giant Eagle, Inc., 86 160–64
Giant Food LLC, II 633–35; 22 241–44 (upd.); 83 155-161 (upd.)
Giant Industries, Inc., 19 175–77; 61 114–18 (upd.)
Giant Manufacturing Company, Ltd., 85 150–54
GIB Group, V 63–66; 26 158–62 (upd.)
Gibbs and Dandy plc, 74 119–21
Gibraltar Steel Corporation, 37 164–67
Gibson, Dunn & Crutcher LLP, 36 249–52
Gibson Greetings, Inc., 12 207–10 *see also* American Greetings Corp.
Gibson Guitar Corp., 16 237–40
Giddings & Lewis, Inc., 10 328–30
GiFi S.A., 74 122–24
Gilbane, Inc., 34 191–93
Gildan Activewear, Inc., 81 165–68
Gildemeister AG, 79 193–97
Gilead Sciences, Inc., 54 129–31
Gillett Holdings, Inc., 7 199–201
The Gillette Company, III 27–30; 20 249–53 (upd.); 68 171–76 (upd.)
Gilman & Ciocia, Inc., 72 148–50
Ginnie Mae *see* Government National Mortgage Association.
Giorgio Armani S.p.A., 45 180–83
Girl Scouts of the USA, 35 193–96
Giesecke & Devrient GmbH, 83 162-166
The Gitano Group, Inc., 8 219–21
GIV *see* Granite Industries of Vermont, Inc.
Givaudan SA, 43 190–93
Given Imaging Ltd., 83 167-170
GKN plc, III 493–96; 38 208–13 (upd.); 89 232–41 (upd.)
Glaces Thiriet S.A., 76 164–66
Glacier Bancorp, Inc., 35 197–200
Glacier Water Services, Inc., 47 155–58
Glamis Gold, Ltd., 54 132–35
Glanbia plc, 59 204–07, 364
Glatfelter Wood Pulp Company *see* P.H. Glatfelter Company
Glaverbel Group, 80 130–33
Glaxo Holdings plc, I 639–41; 9 263–65 (upd.)
GlaxoSmithKline plc, 46 201–08 (upd.)
Glazer's Wholesale Drug Company, Inc., 82 142–45
Gleason Corporation, 24 184–87
Glen Dimplex, 78 123–27
Glico *see* Ezaki Glico Company Ltd.
The Glidden Company, 8 222–24
Global Berry Farms LLC, 62 154–56
Global Crossing Ltd., 32 216–19
Global Hyatt Corporation, 75 159–63 (upd.)
Global Imaging Systems, Inc., 73 163–65
Global Industries, Ltd., 37 168–72
Global Marine Inc., 9 266–67
Global Outdoors, Inc., 49 173–76
Global Payments Inc., 91 206–10
Global Power Equipment Group Inc., 52 137–39
GlobalSantaFe Corporation, 48 187–92 (upd.)
Globo Comunicação e Participações S.A., 80 134–38
Glock Ges.m.b.H., 42 154–56
Glon *see* Groupe Glon.
Glotel plc, 53 149–51
Glu Mobile Inc., 95 163–66
Gluek Brewing Company, 75 164–66
GM *see* General Motors Corp.
GM Hughes Electronics Corporation, II 32–36 *see also* Hughes Electronics Corp.
GMH Communities Trust, 87 176–178
GNC *see* General Nutrition Companies, Inc.
GNMA *see* Government National Mortgage Association.
The Go-Ahead Group Plc, 28 155–57
Go Sport *see* Groupe Go Sport S.A.
Go-Video, Inc. *see* Sensory Science Corp.
Godfather's Pizza Incorporated, 25 179–81
Godiva Chocolatier, Inc., 64 154–57
Goetze's Candy Company, Inc., 87 179–182
Gol Linhas Aéreas Inteligentes S.A., 73 166–68
Gold Fields Ltd., IV 94–97; 62 157–64 (upd.)
Gold Kist Inc., 17 207–09; 26 166–68 (upd.) *see also* Pilgrim's Pride Corp.
Gold'n Plump Poultry, 54 136–38
Gold's Gym International, Inc., 71 165–68
Goldcorp Inc., 87 183–186
Golden Belt Manufacturing Co., 16 241–43
Golden Books Family Entertainment, Inc., 28 158–61 *see also* Random House, Inc.
Golden Corral Corporation, 10 331–33; 66 143–46 (upd.)
Golden Enterprises, Inc., 26 163–65
Golden Krust Caribbean Bakery, Inc., 68 177–79
Golden State Foods Corporation, 32 220–22
Golden State Vintners, Inc., 33 172–74
Golden Telecom, Inc., 59 208–11
Golden West Financial Corporation, 47 159–61
The Goldman Sachs Group Inc., II 414–16; 20 254–57 (upd.); 51 144–48 (upd.)
Goldstar Co., Ltd., 12 211–13 *see also* LG Corp.
Golin/Harris International, Inc., 88 126–30
Golub Corporation, 26 169–71; 96 136–39 (upd.)
GOME Electrical Appliances Holding Ltd., 87 187–191

Gonnella Baking Company, 40 211–13
The Good Guys!, Inc., 10 334–35; 30 224–27 (upd.)
The Good Humor-Breyers Ice Cream Company, 14 203–05 *see also* Unilever PLC.
Goodby Silverstein & Partners, Inc., 75 167–69
Goodman Fielder Ltd., 52 140–43
Goodman Holding Company, 42 157–60
GoodMark Foods, Inc., 26 172–74
Goodrich Corporation, 46 209–13 (upd.)
GoodTimes Entertainment Ltd., 48 193–95
Goodwill Industries International, Inc., 16 244–46; 66 147–50 (upd.)
Goody Products, Inc., 12 214–16
Goody's Family Clothing, Inc., 20 265–67; 64 158–61 (upd.)
The Goodyear Tire & Rubber Company, V 244–48; 20 259–64 (upd.); 75 170–78 (upd.)
Google, Inc., 50 204–07
Gordmans, Inc., 74 125–27
Gordon Biersch Brewery Restaurant Group,Inc., 92229–32
Gordon Food Service Inc., 8 225–27; 39 179–82 (upd.)
The Gorman-Rupp Company, 18 201–03; 57 158–61 (upd.)
Gorton's, 13 243–44
Gosling Brothers Ltd., 82 146–49
Goss Holdings, Inc., 43 194–97
Gottschalks, Inc., 18 204–06; 91 211–15 (upd.)
Gould Electronics, Inc., 14 206–08
Gould Paper Corporation, 82 150–53
Goulds Pumps Inc., 24 188–91
The Governor and Company of the Bank of Scotland, 10 336–38
Goya Foods Inc., 22 245–47; 91 216–21 (upd.)
GP Strategies Corporation, 64 162–66 (upd.)
GPS Industries, Inc., 81 169–72
GPU *see* General Public Utilities Corp.
GPU, Inc., 27 182–85 (upd.)
Grace *see* W.R. Grace & Co.
GraceKennedy Ltd., 92 143–47
Graco Inc., 19 178–80; 67 191–95 (upd.)
Gradall Industries, Inc., 96 140–43
Graeter's Manufacturing Company, 86 165–68
Graham Corporation, 62 165–67
Graham Packaging Holdings Company, 87 192–196
Grampian Country Food Group, Ltd., 85 155–59
Grameen Bank, 31 219–22
Granada Group PLC, II 138–40; 24 192–95 (upd.)
Granaria Holdings B.V., 66 151–53
GranCare, Inc., 14 209–11
Grand Casinos, Inc., 20 268–70
Grand Hotel Krasnapolsky N.V., 23 227–29
Grand Metropolitan plc, I 247–49; 14 212–15 (upd.) *see also* Diageo plc.
Grand Piano & Furniture Company, 72 151–53
Grand Union Company, 7 202–04; 28 162–65 (upd.)
GrandVision S.A., 43 198–200
Granite Broadcasting Corporation, 42 161–64
Granite City Food & Brewery Ltd., 94 214–17
Granite Construction Incorporated, 61 119–21
Granite Industries of Vermont, Inc., 73 169–72
Granite Rock Company, 26 175–78
Granite State Bankshares, Inc., 37 173–75
Grant Prideco, Inc., 57 162–64
Grant Thornton International, 57 165–67
Graphic Industries Inc., 25 182–84
Graphic Packaging Holding Company, 96 144–50 (upd.)
Gray Communications Systems, Inc., 24 196–200
Graybar Electric Company, Inc., 54 139–42
Great American Management and Investment, Inc., 8 228–31
The Great Atlantic & Pacific Tea Company, Inc., II 636–38; 16 247–50 (upd.); 55 164–69 (upd.)
Great Harvest Bread Company, 44 184–86
Great Lakes Bancorp, 8 232–33
Great Lakes Chemical Corp., I 341–42; 14 216–18 (upd.) *see also* Chemtura Corp.
Great Lakes Dredge & Dock Company, 69 194–97
Great Plains Energy Incorporated, 65 156–60 (upd.)
The Great Universal Stores plc, V 67–69; 19 181–84 (upd.) *see also* GUS plc.
Great-West Lifeco Inc., III 260–61 *see also* Power Corporation of Canada.
Great Western Financial Corporation, 10 339–41 *see also* Washington Mutual, Inc.
Great White Shark Enterprises, Inc., 89 242–45
Great Wolf Resorts, Inc., 91 222–26
Greatbatch Inc., 72 154–56
Grede Foundries, Inc., 38 214–17
Greek Organization of Football Prognostics S.A. (OPAP), 97 182–85
The Green Bay Packers, Inc., 32 223–26
Green Mountain Coffee, Inc., 31 227–30
Green Tree Financial Corporation, 11 162–63 *see also* Conseco, Inc.
The Greenalls Group PLC, 21 245–47
Greenberg Traurig, LLP, 65 161–63
The Greenbrier Companies, 19 185–87
Greene King plc, 31 223–26
Greene, Tweed & Company, 55 170–72
Greenpeace International, 74 128–30
GreenPoint Financial Corp., 28 166–68
Greenwood Mills, Inc., 14 219–21
Greg Manning Auctions, Inc., 60 145–46
Greggs PLC, 65 164–66
Greif Inc., 15 186–88; 66 154–56 (upd.)
Grévin & Compagnie SA, 56 143–45
Grey Global Group Inc., 6 26–28; 66 157–61 (upd.)
Grey Wolf, Inc., 43 201–03
Greyhound Lines, Inc., I 448–50; 32 227–31 (upd.)
Griffin Industries, Inc., 70 106–09
Griffin Land & Nurseries, Inc., 43 204–06
Griffon Corporation, 34 194–96
Grill Concepts, Inc., 74 131–33
Grinnell Corp., 13 245–47
Grist Mill Company, 15 189–91
Gristede's Foods Inc., 68 31 231–33; 180–83 (upd.)
Grohe *see* Friedrich Grohe AG & Co. KG.
Grolier Inc., 16 251–54; 43 207–11 (upd.)
Grolsch *see* Royal Grolsch NV.
Grossman's Inc., 13 248–50
Ground Round, Inc., 21 248–51
Group 4 Falck A/S, 42 165–68
Group Health Cooperative, 41 181–84
Group 1 Automotive, Inc., 52 144–46
Groupama S.A., 76 167–70
Groupe Air France, 6 92–94 *see also* Societe Air France.
Groupe Alain Manoukian, 55 173–75
Groupe André, 17 210–12 *see also* Vivarte SA.
Groupe Bolloré, 67 196–99
Groupe Bourbon S.A., 60 147–49
Groupe Bigard S.A., 96 151–54
Groupe Bull *see* Compagnie des Machines Bull.
Groupe Casino *see* Casino Guichard-Perrachon S.A.
Groupe Castorama-Dubois Investissements, 23 230–32 *see also* Kingfisher plc.
Groupe CECAB S.C.A., 88 131–34
Groupe Crit S.A., 74 134–36
Groupe Danone, 32 232–36 (upd.); 93 233–40 (upd.)
Groupe Dassault Aviation SA, 26 179–82 (upd.)
Groupe de la Cité, IV 614–16
Groupe DMC (Dollfus Mieg & Cie), 27 186–88
Groupe Euralis, 86 169–72
Groupe Fournier SA, 44 187–89
Groupe Genoyer, 96 155–58
Groupe Glon, 84 155–158
Groupe Go Sport S.A., 39 183–85
Groupe Guillin SA, 40 214–16
Groupe Herstal S.A., 58 145–48
Groupe Jean-Claude Darmon, 44 190–92

Groupe Lactalis, 78 128–32 (upd.)
Groupe Lapeyre S.A., 33 175–77
Groupe LDC *see* L.D.C. S.A.
Groupe Le Duff S.A., 84 159–162
Groupe Léa Nature, 88 135–38
Groupe Legris Industries, 23 233–35
Groupe Les Echos, 25 283–85
Groupe Limagrain, 74 137–40
Groupe Louis Dreyfus S.A., 60 150–53
Groupe Monnoyeur, 72 157–59
Groupe Open, 74 141–43
Groupe Partouche SA, 48 196–99
Groupe Pinault-Printemps-Redoute *see* Pinault-Printemps-Redoute S.A.
Groupe Promodès S.A., 19 326–28
Groupe Rougier SA, 21 438–40
Groupe SEB, 35 201–03
Groupe Sidel S.A., 21 252–55
Groupe Soufflet SA, 55 176–78
Groupe Vidéotron Ltée., 20 271–73
Groupe Yves Saint Laurent, 23 236–39 *see also* Gucci Group N.V.
Groupe Zannier S.A., 35 204–07
Grow Biz International, Inc., 18 207–10 *see also* Winmark Corp.
Grow Group Inc., 12 217–19
GROWMARK, Inc., 88 139–42
Groz-Beckert Group, 68 184–86
Grubb & Ellis Company, 21 256–58
Gruma, S.A. de C.V., 31 234–36
Grumman Corp., I 61–63; 11 164–67 (upd.) *see aslo* Northrop Grumman Corp.
Grunau Company Inc., 90 209–12
Grundfos Group, 83 171-174
Grundig AG, 27 189–92
Gruntal & Co., L.L.C., 20 274–76
Grupo Aeroportuario del Centro Norte, S.A.B. de C.V., 97 186–89
Grupo Aeroportuario del Pacífico, S.A. de C.V., 85 160–63
Grupo Aeropuerto del Sureste, S.A. de C.V., 48 200–02
Grupo Ángeles Servicios de Salud, S.A. de C.V., 84 163–166
Grupo Bufete *see* Bufete Industrial, S.A. de C.V.
Grupo Carso, S.A. de C.V., 21 259–61
Grupo Casa Saba, S.A. de C.V., 39 186–89
Grupo Clarín S.A., 67 200–03
Grupo Comercial Chedraui S.A. de C.V., 86 173–76
Grupo Corvi S.A. de C.V., 86 177–80
Grupo Cydsa, S.A. de C.V., 39 190–93
Grupo Dina *see* Consorcio G Grupo Dina, S.A. de C.V.
Grupo Dragados SA, 55 179–82
Grupo Elektra, S.A. de C.V., 39 194–97
Grupo Eroski, 64 167–70
Grupo Ferrovial, S.A., 40 217–19
Grupo Ficosa International, 90 213–16
Grupo Financiero Banamex S.A., 54 143–46
Grupo Financiero Banorte, S.A. de C.V., 51 149–51
Grupo Financiero BBVA Bancomer S.A., 54 147–50
Grupo Financiero Galicia S.A., 63 178–81
Grupo Financiero Serfin, S.A., 19 188–90
Grupo Gigante, S.A. de C.V., 34 197–99
Grupo Herdez, S.A. de C.V., 35 208–10
Grupo IMSA, S.A. de C.V., 44 193–96
Grupo Industrial Bimbo, 19 191–93
Grupo Industrial Durango, S.A. de C.V., 37 176–78
Grupo Industrial Herradura, S.A. de C.V., 83 175-178
Grupo Industrial Lala, S.A. de C.V., 82 154–57
Grupo Industrial Saltillo, S.A. de C.V., 54 151–54
Grupo Leche Pascual S.A., 59 212–14
Grupo Lladró S.A., 52 147–49
Grupo Mexico, S.A. de C.V., 40 220–23
Grupo Modelo, S.A. de C.V., 29 218–20
Grupo Omnilife S.A. de C.V., 88 143–46
Grupo Planeta, 94 218–22
Grupo Portucel Soporcel, 60 154–56
Grupo Posadas, S.A. de C.V., 57 168–70
Grupo TACA, 38 218–20
Grupo Televisa, S.A., 18 211–14; 54 155–58 (upd.)
Grupo TMM, S.A. de C.V., 50 208–11
Grupo Transportación Ferroviaria Mexicana, S.A. de C.V., 47 162–64
Grupo Viz, S.A. de C.V., 84 167–170
Gruppo Coin S.p.A., 41 185–87
Gruppo Riva Fire SpA, 88 147–50
Gryphon Holdings, Inc., 21 262–64
GSC Enterprises, Inc., 86 181–84
GSD&M Advertising, 44 197–200
GSD&M's Idea City, 90 217–21
GSG&T, Inc. *see* Gulf States Utilities Co.
GSI Commerce, Inc., 67 204–06
GSU *see* Gulf States Utilities Co.
GT Bicycles, 26 183–85
GT Interactive Software, 31 237–41 *see also* Infogrames Entertainment S.A.
GTE Corporation, V 294–98; 15 192–97 (upd.) *see also* British Columbia Telephone Company; Verizon Communications.
GTSI Corp., 57 171–73
Guangzhou Pearl River Piano Group Ltd., 49 177–79
Guangzhou R&F Properties Co., Ltd., 95 167–69
Guardian Financial Services, 11 168–70; 64 171–74 (upd.)
Guardian Industries Corp., 87 197–204
Guardian Media Group plc, 53 152–55
Guardsmark, L.L.C., 77 171–74
Gucci Group N.V., 15 198–200; 50 212–16 (upd.)
Guenther *see* C.H. Guenther & Son, Inc.
Guerbet Group, 46 214–16
Guerlain, 23 240–42
Guess, Inc., 15 201–03; 68 187–91 (upd.)
Guest Supply, Inc., 18 215–17
Guida-Seibert Dairy Company, 84 171–174
Guidant Corporation, 58 149–51
Guilbert S.A., 42 169–71
Guilford Mills Inc., 8 234–36; 40 224–27 (upd.)
Guillemot Corporation, 41 188–91, 407, 409
Guillin *see* Groupe Guillin SA
Guinness/UDV, I 250–52; 43 212–16 (upd.) *see also* Diageo plc.
Guinot Paris S.A., 82 158–61
Guitar Center, Inc., 29 221–23; 68 192–95 (upd.)
Guittard Chocolate Company, 55 183–85
Gulf + Western Inc., I 451–53 *see also* Paramount Communications; Viacom Inc.
Gulf Air Company, 56 146–48
Gulf Agency Company Ltd., 78 133–36
Gulf Island Fabrication, Inc., 44 201–03
Gulf States Utilities Company, 6 495–97 *see also* Entergy Corp.
GulfMark Offshore, Inc., 49 180–82
Gulfstream Aerospace Corporation, 7 205–06; 28 169–72 (upd.)
Gund, Inc., 96 159–62
Gunite Corporation, 51 152–55
The Gunlocke Company, 23 243–45
Gunnebo AB, 53 156–58
GUS plc, 47 165–70 (upd.)
Guthy-Renker Corporation, 32 237–40
Guttenplan's Frozen Dough Inc., 88 151–54
Guy Degrenne SA, 44 204–07
Guyenne et Gascogne, 23 246–48
Gwathmey Siegel & Associates Architects LLC, 26 186–88
GWR Group plc, 39 198–200
Gymboree Corporation, 15 204–06; 69 198–201 (upd.)

H

H&R Block, Inc., 9 268–70; 29 224–28 (upd.); 82 162–69 (upd.)
H.B. Fuller Company, 8 237–40; 32 254–58 (upd.); 75 179–84 (upd.)
H. Betti Industries Inc., 88 155–58
H.D. Vest, Inc., 46 217–19
H. E. Butt Grocery Company, 13 251–53; 32 259–62 (upd.); 85 164–70 (upd.)
H.F. Ahmanson & Company, II 181–82; 10 342–44 (upd.) *see also* Washington Mutual, Inc.
H.J. Heinz Company, II 507–09; 11 171–73 (upd.); 36 253–57 (upd.)
H.J. Russell & Company, 66 162–65
H. Lundbeck A/S, 44 208–11
H.M. Payson & Co., 69 202–04
H.O. Penn Machinery Company, Inc., 96 163–66
H-P *see* Hewlett-Packard Co.
The H.W. Wilson Company, 66 166–68
Ha-Lo Industries, Inc., 27 193–95
The Haartz Corporation, 94 223–26
Habersham Bancorp, 25 185–87

Habitat for Humanity International, 36 258–61
Hach Co., 18 218–21
Hachette Filipacchi Medias S.A., 21 265–67
Hachette S.A., IV 617–19 *see also* Matra-Hachette S.A.
Haci Omer Sabanci Holdings A.S., 55 186–89 *see also* Akbank TAS
Hackman Oyj Adp, 44 212–15
Hadco Corporation, 24 201–03
Haeger Industries Inc., 88 159–62
Haemonetics Corporation, 20 277–79
Haftpflichtverband der Deutschen Industrie Versicherung auf Gegenseitigkeit V.a.G. *see* HDI (Haftpflichtverband der Deutschen Industrie Versicherung auf Gegenseitigkeit V.a.G.).
Hagemeyer N.V., 39 201–04
Haggar Corporation, 19 194–96; 78 137–41 (upd.)
Haggen Inc., 38 221–23
Hagoromo Foods Corporation, 84 175–178
Hahn Automotive Warehouse, Inc., 24 204–06
Haier Group Corporation, 65 167–70
Haights Cross Communications, Inc., 84 179–182
The Hain Celestial Group, Inc., 27 196–98; 43 217–20 (upd.)
Hair Club For Men Ltd., 90 222–25
Hakuhodo, Inc., 6 29–31; 42 172–75 (upd.)
HAL Inc., 9 271–73 *see also* Hawaiian Airlines, Inc.
Hal Leonard Corporation, 96 167–71
Hale-Halsell Company, 60 157–60
Half Price Books, Records, Magazines Inc., 37 179–82
Hall, Kinion & Associates, Inc., 52 150–52
Halliburton Company, III 497–500; 25 188–92 (upd.); 55 190–95 (upd.)
Hallmark Cards, Inc., IV 620–21; 16 255–57 (upd.); 40 228–32 (upd.); 87 205–212 (upd.)
Hamilton Beach/Proctor-Silex Inc., 17 213–15
Hammacher Schlemmer & Company Inc., 21 268–70; 72 160–62 (upd.)
Hammerson plc, IV 696–98; 40 233–35 (upd.)
Hammond Manufacturing Company Limited, 83 179-182
Hamon & Cie (International) S.A., 97 190–94
Hamot Health Foundation, 91 227–32
Hampton Affiliates, Inc., 77 175–79
Hampton Industries, Inc., 20 280–82
Hampshire Group Ltd., 82 170–73
Hancock Fabrics, Inc., 18 222–24
Hancock Holding Company, 15 207–09
Handleman Company, 15 210–12; 86 185–89 (upd.)
Handspring Inc., 49 183–86
Handy & Harman, 23 249–52
Hang Seng Bank Ltd., 60 161–63
Hanger Orthopedic Group, Inc., 41 192–95
Hanjin Shipping Co., Ltd., 50 217–21
Hankyu Corporation, V 454–56; 23 253–56 (upd.)
Hankyu Department Stores, Inc., V 70–71; 62 168–71 (upd.)
Hanmi Financial Corporation, 66 169–71
Hanna Andersson Corp., 49 187–90
Hanna-Barbera Cartoons Inc., 23 257–59, 387
Hannaford Bros. Co., 12 220–22
Hanover Compressor Company, 59 215–17
Hanover Direct, Inc., 36 262–65
Hanover Foods Corporation, 35 211–14
Hansen Natural Corporation, 31 242–45; 76 171–74 (upd.)
Hansgrohe AG, 56 149–52
Hanson Building Materials America Inc., 60 164–66
Hanson PLC, III 501–03; 7 207–10 (upd.); 30 228–32 (upd.)
Hanwha Group, 62 172–75
Hapag-Lloyd AG, 6 397–99; 97 195–203 (upd.)
Happy Kids Inc., 30 233–35
Harbert Corporation, 14 222–23
Harbison-Walker Refractories Company, 24 207–09
Harbour Group Industries, Inc., 90 226–29
Harcourt Brace and Co., 12 223–26
Harcourt Brace Jovanovich, Inc., IV 622–24
Harcourt General, Inc., 20 283–87 (upd.)
Hard Rock Cafe International, Inc., 12 227–29; 32 241–45 (upd.)
Harding Lawson Associates Group, Inc., 16 258–60
Hardinge Inc., 25 193–95
HARIBO GmbH & Co. KG, 44 216–19
Harkins Amusement Enterprises, Inc., 94 227–31
Harland and Wolff Holdings plc, 19 197–200
Harland Clarke Holdings Corporation, 94 232–35 (upd.)
Harlem Globetrotters International, Inc., 61 122–24
Harlequin Enterprises Limited, 52 153–56
Harley-Davidson, Inc., 7 211–14; 25 196–200 (upd.)
Harleysville Group Inc., 37 183–86
Harman International Industries Inc., 15 213–15
Harmon Industries, Inc., 25 201–04 *see also* General Electric Co.
Harmonic Inc., 43 221–23
Harmony Gold Mining Company Limited, 63 182–85
Harnischfeger Industries, Inc., 8 241–44; 38 224–28 (upd.)
Harold's Stores, Inc., 22 248–50
Harper Group Inc., 17 216–19
HarperCollins Publishers, 15 216–18
Harpo Inc., 28 173–75; 66 172–75 (upd.)
Harrah's Entertainment, Inc., 16 261–63; 43 224–28 (upd.)
Harris Corporation, II 37–39; 20 288–92 (upd.); 78 142–48 (upd.)
Harris Interactive Inc., 41 196–99; 92 148–53 (upd.)
Harris Publishing *see* Bernard C. Harris Publishing Company, Inc.
The Harris Soup Company (Harry's Fresh Foods),92 154–157
Harris Teeter Inc., 23 260–62; 72 163–66 (upd.)
Harrisons & Crosfield plc, III 696–700 *see also* Elementis plc.
Harrods Holdings, 47 171–74
Harry London Candies, Inc., 70 110–12
Harry N. Abrams, Inc., 58 152–55
Harry Winston Inc., 45 184–87
Harry's Farmers Market Inc., 23 263–66 *see also* Whole Foods Market, Inc.
Harry's Fresh Foods *see* The Harris Soup Company (Harry's Fresh Foods)
Harsco Corporation, 8 245–47 *see also* United Defense Industries, Inc.
Harte-Hanks Communications, Inc., 17 220–22; 63 186–89 (upd.)
Hartmann Inc., 96 172–76
Hartmarx Corporation, 8 248–50; 32 246–50 (upd.)
The Hartstone Group plc, 14 224–26
The Hartz Mountain Corporation, 12 230–32; 46 220–23 (upd.)
Harvey Norman Holdings Ltd., 56 153–55
Harveys Casino Resorts, 27 199–201 *see also* Harrah's Entertainment, Inc.
Harza Engineering Company, 14 227–28
Hasbro, Inc., III 504–06; 16 264–68 (upd.); 43 229–34 (upd.)
Haskel International, Inc., 59 218–20
Hastings Entertainment, Inc., 29 229–31
Hastings Manufacturing Company, 56 156–58
Hauser, Inc., 46 224–27
Havas, SA, 10 345–48; 33 178–82 (upd.) *see also* Vivendi Universal Publishing
Haverty Furniture Companies, Inc., 31 246–49
Hawaiian Airlines Inc., 22 251–53 (upd.) *see also* HAL Inc.
Hawaiian Electric Industries, Inc., 9 274–77
Hawaiian Holdings, Inc., 96 177–81 (upd.)
Hawk Corporation, 59 221–23
Hawker Siddeley Group Public Limited Company, III 507–10
Hawkeye Holdings LLC, 86 246–49
Hawkins Chemical, Inc., 16 269–72

Haworth Inc., 8 251–52; 39 205–08 (upd.)
Hay House, Inc., 93 241–45
Hayel Saeed Anam Group of Cos., 92 158–61
Hayes Corporation, 24 210–14
Hayes Lemmerz International, Inc., 27 202–04
Haynes International, Inc., 88 163–66
Haynes Publishing Group P.L.C., 71 169–71
Hays plc, 27 205–07; 78 149–53 (upd.)
Hazelden Foundation, 28 176–79
Hazlewood Foods plc, 32 251–53
HBO *see* Home Box Office Inc.
HCA—The Healthcare Company, 35 215–18 (upd.)
HCI Direct, Inc., 55 196–98
HDI (Haftpflichtverband der Deutschen Industrie Versicherung auf Gegenseitigkeit V.a.G.), 53 159–63
HDOS Enterprises, 72 167–69
HDR Inc., 48 203–05
Head N.V., 55 199–201
Headlam Group plc, 95 170–73
Headwaters Incorporated, 56 159–62
Headway Corporate Resources, Inc., 40 236–38
Health Care & Retirement Corporation, 22 254–56
Health Communications, Inc., 72 170–73
Health Management Associates, Inc., 56 163–65
Health O Meter Products Inc., 14 229–31
Health Risk Management, Inc., 24 215–17
Health Systems International, Inc., 11 174–76
HealthExtras, Inc., 75 185–87
HealthMarkets, Inc., 88 167–72 (upd.)
HealthSouth Corporation, 14 232–34; 33 183–86 (upd.)
Healthtex, Inc., 17 223–25 *see also* VF Corp.
The Hearst Corporation, IV 625–27; 19 201–04 (upd.); 46 228–32 (upd.)
Heartland Express, Inc., 18 225–27
The Heat Group, 53 164–66
Hechinger Company, 12 233–36
Hecla Mining Company, 20 293–96
Heekin Can Inc., 13 254–56 *see also* Ball Corp.
Heelys, Inc., 87 213–216
Heery International, Inc., 58 156–59
HEICO Corporation, 30 236–38
Heidelberger Druckmaschinen AG, 40 239–41
Heidelberger Zement AG, 31 250–53
Heidrick & Struggles International, Inc., 28 180–82
Heijmans N.V., 66 176–78
Heileman Brewing Co *see* G. Heileman Brewing Co.
Heilig-Meyers Company, 14 235–37; 40 242–46 (upd.)
Heineken N.V., I 256–58; 13 257–59 (upd.); 34 200–04 (upd.); 90 230–36 (upd.)
Heinrich Deichmann-Schuhe GmbH & Co. KG, 88 173–77
Heinz Co *see* H.J. Heinz Co.
Helen of Troy Corporation, 18 228–30
Helene Curtis Industries, Inc., 8 253–54; 28 183–85 (upd.) *see also* Unilever PLC.
Helix Energy Solutions Group, Inc., 81 173–77
Hella KGaA Hueck & Co., 66 179–83
Hellenic Petroleum SA, 64 175–77
Heller, Ehrman, White & McAuliffe, 41 200–02
Helly Hansen ASA, 25 205–07
Helmerich & Payne, Inc., 18 231–33
Helmsley Enterprises, Inc., 9 278–80; 39 209–12 (upd.)
Helzberg Diamonds, 40 247–49
Hemlo Gold Mines Inc., 9 281–82 *see also* Newmont Mining Corp.
Henderson Land Development Company Ltd., 70 113–15
Hendrick Motorsports, Inc., 89 250–53
Henkel KGaA, III 31–34; 34 205–10 (upd.); 95 174–83 (upd.)
Henkel Manco Inc., 22 257–59
The Henley Group, Inc., III 511–12
Hennes & Mauritz AB, 29 232–34
Henry Boot plc, 76 175–77
Henry Crown and Company, 91 233–36
Henry Dreyfuss Associates LLC, 88 178–82
Henry Ford Health System, 84 183–187
Henry Modell & Company Inc., 32 263–65
Henry Schein, Inc., 31 254–56; 70 116–19 (upd.)
Hensel Phelps Construction Company, 72 174–77
Hensley & Company, 64 178–80
HEPCO *see* Hokkaido Electric Power Company Inc.
Her Majesty's Stationery Office, 7 215–18
Heraeus Holding GmbH, IV 98–100; 54 159–63 (upd.)
Herald Media, Inc., 91 237–41
Herbalife Ltd., 17 226–29; 41 203–06 (upd.); 92 162–67 (upd.)
Hercules Inc., I 343–45; 22 260–63 (upd.); 66 184–88 (upd.)
Hercules Technology Growth Capital, Inc., 87 217–220
Herley Industries, Inc., 33 187–89
Herman Goelitz, Inc., 28 186–88 *see also* Jelly Belly Candy Co.
Herman Miller, Inc., 8 255–57; 77 180–86 (upd.)
Hermès International S.A., 14 238–40; 34 211–14 (upd.)
Héroux-Devtek Inc., 69 205–07
Herr Foods Inc., 84 188–191
Herradura *see* Grupo Industrial Herradura, S.A. de C.V.
Herschend Family Entertainment Corporation, 73 173–76
Hershey Foods Corporation, II 510–12; 15 219–22 (upd.); 51 156–60 (upd.)
Herstal *see* Groupe Herstal S.A.
Hertie Waren- und Kaufhaus GmbH, V 72–74
The Hertz Corporation, 9 283–85; 33 190–93 (upd.)
Heska Corporation, 39 213–16
Heublein Inc., I 259–61
Heuer *see* TAG Heuer International SA.
Hewitt Associates, Inc., 77 187–90
Hewlett-Packard Company, III 142–43; 6 237–39 (upd.); 28 189–92 (upd.); 50 222–30 (upd.)
Hexal AG, 69 208–10
Hexagon AB, 78 154–57
Hexcel Corporation, 28 193–95
HI *see* Houston Industries Inc.
Hibbett Sporting Goods, Inc., 26 189–91; 70 120–23 (upd.)
Hibernia Corporation, 37 187–90
Hickory Farms, Inc., 17 230–32
HickoryTech Corporation, 92 168–71
High Falls Brewing Company LLC, 74 144–47
High Tech Computer Corporation, 81 178–81
Highland Gold Mining Limited, 95 184–87
Highlights for Children, Inc., 95 188–91
Highmark Inc., 27 208–11
Highsmith Inc., 60 167–70
Highveld Steel and Vanadium Corporation Limited, 59 224–27
Hilo Hattie *see* Pomare Ltd.
Hilb, Rogal & Hobbs Company, 77 191–94
Hildebrandt International, 29 235–38
Hill's Pet Nutrition, Inc., 27 212–14
Hillenbrand Industries, Inc., 10 349–51; 75 188–92 (upd.)
Hillerich & Bradsby Company, Inc., 51 161–64
The Hillhaven Corporation, 14 241–43 *see also* Vencor, Inc.
Hills Stores Company, 13 260–61
Hillsdown Holdings, PLC, II 513–14; 24 218–21 (upd.)
Hilti AG, 53 167–69
Hilton Group plc, III 91–93; 19 205–08 (upd.); 62 176–79 (upd.); 49 191–95 (upd.)
Hindustan Lever Limited, 79 198–201
Hines Horticulture, Inc., 49 196–98
Hino Motors, Ltd., 7 219–21; 21 271–74 (upd.)
HiPP GmbH & Co. Vertrieb KG, 88 183–88
Hiram Walker Resources Ltd., I 262–64
Hispanic Broadcasting Corporation, 35 219–22
HIT Entertainment PLC, 40 250–52
Hitachi, Ltd., I 454–55; 12 237–39 (upd.); 40 253–57 (upd.)
Hitachi Metals, Ltd., IV 101–02

Hitachi Zosen Corporation, III 513–14; 53 170–73 (upd.)
Hitchiner Manufacturing Co., Inc., 23 267–70
Hite Brewery Company Ltd., 97 204–07
HMI Industries, Inc., 17 233–35
HMV Group plc, 59 228–30
HNI Corporation, 74 148–52 (upd.)
Ho-Chunk Inc., 61 125–28
HOB Entertainment, Inc., 37 191–94
Hobby Lobby Stores Inc., 80 139–42
Hobie Cat Company, 94 236–39
Hochtief AG, 33 194–97; 88 189–94 (upd.)
The Hockey Company, 34 215–18; 70 124–26 (upd.)
Hodes *see* Bernard Hodes Group Inc.
Hodgson Mill, Inc., 88 195–98
Hoechst AG, I 346–48; 18 234–37 (upd.)
Hoechst Celanese Corporation, 13 262–65
Hoenig Group Inc., 41 207–09
Hoesch AG, IV 103–06
Hoffman Corporation, 78 158–12
Hoffmann-La Roche & Co *see* F. Hoffmann-La Roche & Co.
Hogan & Hartson L.L.P., 44 220–23
Hohner *see* Matth. Hohner AG.
HOK Group, Inc., 59 231–33
Hokkaido Electric Power Company Inc. (HEPCO), V 635–37; 58 160–63 (upd.)
Hokuriku Electric Power Company, V 638–40
Holberg Industries, Inc., 36 266–69
Holden Ltd., 62 180–83
Holderbank Financière Glaris Ltd., III 701–02 *see also* Holnam Inc
N.V. Holdingmaatschappij De Telegraaf, 23 271–73
Holiday Inns, Inc., III 94–95 *see also* Promus Companies, Inc.
Holiday Retirement Corp., 87 221–223
Holiday RV Superstores, Incorporated, 26 192–95
Holidaybreak plc, 96 182–86
Holland & Knight LLP, 60 171–74
Holland Burgerville USA, 44 224–26
The Holland Group, Inc., 82 174–77
Hollander Home Fashions Corp., 67 207–09
Holley Performance Products Inc., 52 157–60
Hollinger International Inc., 24 222–25; 62 184–88 (upd.)
Holly Corporation, 12 240–42
Hollywood Casino Corporation, 21 275–77
Hollywood Entertainment Corporation, 25 208–10
Hollywood Media Corporation, 58 164–68
Hollywood Park, Inc., 20 297–300
Holme Roberts & Owen LLP, 28 196–99
Holmen AB, 52 161–65 (upd.)
Holnam Inc., 8 258–60; 39 217–20 (upd.)
Holophane Corporation, 19 209–12
Holson Burnes Group, Inc., 14 244–45
Holt and Bugbee Company, 66 189–91
Holt's Cigar Holdings, Inc., 42 176–78
Holtzbrinck *see* Verlagsgruppe Georg von Holtzbrinck.
Homasote Company, 72 178–81
Home Box Office Inc., 7 222–24; 23 274–77 (upd.); 76 178–82 (upd.)
The Home Depot, Inc., V 75–76; 18 238–40 (upd.); 97 208–13 (upd.)
Home Hardware Stores Ltd., 62 189–91
Home Inns & Hotels Management Inc., 95 195–95
Home Insurance Company, III 262–64
Home Interiors & Gifts, Inc., 55 202–04
Home Products International, Inc., 55 205–07
Home Properties of New York, Inc., 42 179–81
Home Retail Group plc, 91 242–46
Home Shopping Network, Inc., V 77–78; 25 211–15 (upd.) *see also* HSN.
HomeBase, Inc., 33 198–201 (upd.)
Homestake Mining Company, 12 243–45; 38 229–32 (upd.)
Hometown Auto Retailers, Inc., 44 227–29
HomeVestors of America, Inc., 77 195–98
Homex *see* Desarrolladora Homex, S.A. de C.V.
Hon Hai Precision Industry Co., Ltd., 59 234–36
HON Industries Inc., 13 266–69 *see* HNI Corp.
Honda Motor Company Ltd., I 174–76; 10 352–54 (upd.); 29 239–42 (upd.); 96 187–93 (upd.)
Honeywell Inc., II 40–43; 12 246–49 (upd.); 50 231–35 (upd.)
Hong Kong and China Gas Company Ltd., 73 177–79
Hong Kong Dragon Airlines Ltd., 66 192–94
Hong Kong Telecommunications Ltd., 6 319–21 *see also* Cable & Wireless HKT.
Hongkong and Shanghai Banking Corporation Limited, II 296–99 *see also* HSBC Holdings plc.
Hongkong Electric Holdings Ltd., 6 498–500; 23 278–81 (upd.)
Hongkong Land Holdings Ltd., IV 699–701; 47 175–78 (upd.)
Honshu Paper Co., Ltd., IV 284–85 *see also* Oji Paper Co., Ltd.
Hoogovens *see* Koninklijke Nederlandsche Hoogovens en Staalfabricken NV.
Hooker Furniture Corporation, 80 143–46
Hooper Holmes, Inc., 22 264–67
Hooters of America, Inc., 18 241–43; 69 211–14 (upd.)
The Hoover Company, 12 250–52; 40 258–62 (upd.)
HOP, LLC, 80 147–50
Hops Restaurant Bar and Brewery, 46 233–36
Hopson Development Holdings Ltd., 87 224–227
Horace Mann Educators Corporation, 22 268–70; 90 237–40 (upd.)
Horizon Organic Holding Corporation, 37 195–99
Hormel Foods Corporation, 18 244–47 (upd.); 54 164–69 (upd.)
Horsehead Industries, Inc., 51 165–67
Horseshoe Gaming Holding Corporation, 62 192–95
Horton Homes, Inc., 25 216–18
Horween Leather Company, 83 183-186
Hoshino Gakki Co. Ltd., 55 208–11
Hospira, Inc., 71 172–74
Hospital Central Services, Inc., 56 166–68
Hospital Corporation of America, III 78–80 *see also* HCA - The Healthcare Co.
Hospitality Franchise Systems, Inc., 11 177–79 *see also* Cendant Corp.
Hospitality Worldwide Services, Inc., 26 196–98
Hoss's Steak and Sea House Inc., 68 196–98
Host America Corporation, 79 202–06
Hot Dog on a Stick *see* HDOS Enterprises.
Hot Stuff Foods, 85 171–74
Hot Topic Inc., 33 202–04; 86 190–94 (upd.)
Hotel Properties Ltd., 71 175–77
Houchens Industries Inc., 51 168–70
Houghton Mifflin Company, 10 355–57; 36 270–74 (upd.)
House of Fabrics, Inc., 21 278–80 *see also* Jo-Ann Stores, Inc.
House of Fraser PLC, 45 188–91 *see also* Harrods Holdings.
House of Prince A/S, 80 151–54
Household International, Inc., II 417–20; 21 281–86 (upd.) *see also* HSBC Holdings plc.
Houston Industries Incorporated, V 641–44 *see also* Reliant Energy Inc.
Houston Wire & Cable Company, 97 214–17
Hovnanian Enterprises, Inc., 29 243–45; 89 254–59 (upd.)
Howard Hughes Medical Institute, 39 221–24
Howard Johnson International, Inc., 17 236–39; 72 182–86 (upd.)
Howmet Corporation, 12 253–55 *see also* Alcoa Inc.
HP *see* Hewlett-Packard Co.
HSBC Holdings plc, 12 256–58; 26 199–204 (upd.); 80 155–63 (upd.)
HSN, 64 181–85 (upd.)
Huawei Technologies Company Ltd., 87 228–231

Hub Group, Inc., 38 233–35
Hub International Limited, 89 260–64
Hubbard Broadcasting Inc., 24 226–28; 79 207–12 (upd.)
Hubbell Inc., 9 286–87; 31 257–59 (upd.); 76 183–86 (upd.)
The Hudson Bay Mining and Smelting Company, Limited, 12 259–61
Hudson Foods Inc., 13 270–72 *see also* Tyson Foods, Inc.
Hudson River Bancorp, Inc., 41 210–13
Hudson's Bay Company, V 79–81; 25 219–22 (upd.); 83 187-194 (upd.)
Huffy Corporation, 7 225–27; 30 239–42 (upd.)
Hughes Electronics Corporation, 25 223–25
Hughes Hubbard & Reed LLP, 44 230–32
Hughes Markets, Inc., 22 271–73 *see also* Kroger Co.
Hughes Supply, Inc., 14 246–47
Hugo Boss AG, 48 206–09
Huhtamäki Oyj, 64 186–88
HUK-Coburg, 58 169–73
Hulman & Company, 44 233–36
Hüls A.G., I 349–50 *see also* Degussa-Hüls AG.
Humana Inc., III 81–83; 24 229–32 (upd.)
The Humane Society of the United States, 54 170–73
Hummel International A/S, 68 199–201
Hummer Winblad Venture Partners, 97 218–21
Hungarian Telephone and Cable Corp., 75 193–95
Hungry Howie's Pizza and Subs, Inc., 25 226–28
Hunt Consolidated, Inc., 7 228–30; 27 215–18 (upd.)
Hunt Manufacturing Company, 12 262–64
Hunt-Wesson, Inc., 17 240–42 *see also* ConAgra Foods, Inc.
Hunter Fan Company, 13 273–75
Hunting plc, 78 163–16
Huntingdon Life Sciences Group plc, 42 182–85
Huntington Bancshares Incorporated, 11 180–82; 87 232–238 (upd.)
Huntington Learning Centers, Inc., 55 212–14
Huntleigh Technology PLC, 77 199–202
Hunton & Williams, 35 223–26
Huntsman Chemical Corporation, 8 261–63
Huron Consulting Group Inc., 87 239–243
Hurricane Hydrocarbons Ltd., 54 174–77
Husky Energy Inc., 47 179–82
Hutchinson Technology Incorporated, 18 248–51; 63 190–94 (upd.)
Hutchison Whampoa Limited, 18 252–55; 49 199–204 (upd.)
Huttig Building Products, Inc., 73 180–83
HVB Group, 59 237–44 (upd.)
Hvide Marine Incorporated, 22 274–76
Hy-Vee, Inc., 36 275–78
Hyatt Corporation, III 96–97; 16 273–75 (upd.) *see* Global Hyatt Corp.
Hyde Athletic Industries, Inc., 17 243–45 *see also* Saucony Inc.
Hyder plc, 34 219–21
Hydril Company, 46 237–39
Hydro-Quebéc, 6 501–03; 32 266–69 (upd.)
Hylsamex, S.A. de C.V., 39 225–27
Hypercom Corporation, 27 219–21
Hyperion Software Corporation, 22 277–79
Hyperion Solutions Corporation, 76 187–91
Hyster Company, 17 246–48
Hyundai Group, III 515–17; 7 231–34 (upd.); 56 169–73 (upd.)

I

I.C. Isaacs & Company, 31 260–62
I.M. Pei & Associates *see* Pei Cobb Freed & Partners Architects LLP.
IAC Group, 96 194–98
Iams Company, 26 205–07
IAWS Group plc, 49 205–08
Iberdrola, S.A., 49 209–12
Iberia Líneas Aéreas De España S.A., 6 95–97; 36 279–83 (upd.); 91 247–54 (upd.)
IBERIABANK Corporation, 37 200–02
IBJ *see* The Industrial Bank of Japan Ltd.
IBM *see* International Business Machines Corp.
IBP, Inc., II 515–17; 21 287–90 (upd.)
Ibstock Brick Ltd., 37 203–06 (upd.)
Ibstock plc, 14 248–50
IC Industries Inc., I 456–58 *see also* Whitman Corp.
ICA AB, II 639–40
ICEE-USA *see* J & J Snack Foods Corp.
Iceland Group plc, 33 205–07 *see also* The Big Food Group plc.
Icelandair, 52 166–69
Icelandic Group hf, 81 182–85
ICF International, Inc., 28 200–04; 94 240–47 (upd.)
ICI *see* Imperial Chemical Industries plc.
ICL plc, 6 240–42
ICN Pharmaceuticals, Inc., 52 170–73
Icon Health & Fitness, Inc., 38 236–39
Idaho Power Company, 12 265–67
IDB Communications Group, Inc., 11 183–85
IDB Holding Corporation Ltd., 97 222–25
Idearc Inc., 90 241–44
Idemitsu Kosan Co., Ltd., IV 434–36; 49 213–16 (upd.)
Identix Inc., 44 237–40
IDEO Inc., 65 171–73
IDEXX Laboratories, Inc., 23 282–84
IDG Books Worldwide, Inc., 27 222–24 *see also* International Data Group, Inc.
IDG Communications, Inc *see* International Data Group, Inc.
IdraPrince, Inc., 76 192–94
IDT Corporation, 34 222–24
IDX Systems Corporation, 64 189–92
IEC Electronics Corp., 42 186–88
IFF *see* International Flavors & Fragrances Inc.
IG Group Holdings plc, 97 226–29
Igloo Products Corp., 21 291–93
IGT *see* International Game Technology.
IHC Caland N.V., 71 178–80
IHI *see* Ishikawajima-Harima Heavy Industries Co., Ltd.
IHOP Corporation, 17 249–51; 58 174–77 (upd.)
Ihr Platz GmbH + Company KG, 77 203–06
IHS Inc., 78 167–70
IKEA Group, V 82–84; 26 208–11 (upd.); 94 248–53 (upd.)
IKON Office Solutions, Inc., 50 236–39
Il Fornaio (America) Corporation, 27 225–28
ILFC *see* International Lease Finance Corp.
Ilitch Holdings Inc., 37 207–210; 86 195–200 (upd.)
Illinois Bell Telephone Company, 14 251–53
Illinois Central Corporation, 11 186–89
Illinois Power Company, 6 504–07 *see also* Ameren Corp.
Illinois Tool Works Inc., III 518–20; 22 280–83 (upd.); 81 186–91 (upd.)
Illumina, Inc., 93 246–49
illycaffè SpA, 50 240–44
ILX Resorts Incorporated, 65 174–76
Image Entertainment, Inc., 94 254–57
Imagine Entertainment, 91 255–58
Imagine Foods, Inc., 50 245–47
Imasco Limited, V 401–02
Imation Corporation, 20 301–04 *see also* 3M Co.
Imatra Steel Oy Ab, 55 215–17
IMAX Corporation, 28 205–08; 78 171–76 (upd.)
IMC Fertilizer Group, Inc., 8 264–66
ImClone Systems Inc., 58 178–81
IMCO Recycling, Incorporated, 32 270–73
Imerys S.A., 40 176, **263–66 (upd.)**
Imetal S.A., IV 107–09
IMG, 78 177–80
IMI plc, 9 288–89; 29 364
Immucor, Inc., 81 192–96
Immunex Corporation, 14 254–56; 50 248–53 (upd.)
Imo Industries Inc., 7 235–37; 27 229–32 (upd.)
IMPATH Inc., 45 192–94
Imperial Chemical Industries plc, I 351–53; 50 254–58 (upd.)
Imperial Holly Corporation, 12 268–70 *see also* Imperial Sugar Co.
Imperial Industries, Inc., 81 197–200
Imperial Oil Limited, IV 437–39; 25 229–33 (upd.); 95 196–203 (upd.)

Imperial Parking Corporation, 58 182–84
Imperial Sugar Company, 32 274–78 (upd.)
Imperial Tobacco Group PLC, 50 259–63
IMS Health, Inc., 57 174–78
In Focus Systems, Inc., 22 287–90
In-N-Out Burgers Inc., 19 213–15; 74 153–56 (upd.)
In-Sink-Erator, 66 195–98
InaCom Corporation, 13 276–78
Inamed Corporation, 79 213–16
Inchcape PLC, III 521–24; 16 276–80 (upd.); 50 264–68 (upd.)
Inco Limited, IV 110–12; 45 195–99 (upd.)
Incyte Genomics, Inc., 52 174–77
Indel, Inc., 78 181–84
Independent News & Media PLC, 61 129–31
Indian Airlines Ltd., 46 240–42
Indian Oil Corporation Ltd., IV 440–41; 48 210–13 (upd.)
Indiana Bell Telephone Company, Incorporated, 14 257–61
Indiana Energy, Inc., 27 233–36
Indianapolis Motor Speedway Corporation, 46 243–46
Indigo Books & Music Inc., 58 185–87
Indigo NV, 26 212–14 *see also* Hewlett-Packard Co.
Indosat *see* PT Indosat Tbk.
Indus International Inc., 70 127–30
Industria de Diseño Textil S.A. (Inditex), 64 193–95
Industrial Bank of Japan, Ltd., II 300–01
Industrial Light & Magic *see* Lucasfilm Ltd.
Industrial Services of America, Inc., 46 247–49
Industrias Bachoco, S.A. de C.V., 39 228–31
Industrias Penoles, S.A. de C.V., 22 284–86
Industrie Natuzzi S.p.A., 18 256–58
Industrie Zignago Santa Margherita S.p.A., 67 210–12
Infineon Technologies AG, 50 269–73
Infinity Broadcasting Corporation, 11 190–92; 48 214–17 (upd.)
InFocus Corporation, 92 172–75
Infogrames Entertainment S.A., 35 227–30
Informa Group plc, 58 188–91
Information Access Company, 17 252–55
Information Builders, Inc., 22 291–93
Information Holdings Inc., 47 183–86
Information Resources, Inc., 10 358–60
Informix Corporation, 10 361–64; 30 243–46 (upd.) *see also* International Business Machines Corp.
InfoSonics Corporation, 81 201–04
InfoSpace, Inc., 91 259–62
Infosys Technologies Ltd., 38 240–43
Ing. C. Olivetti & C., S.p.A., III 144–46 *see also* Olivetti S.p.A
Ingalls Shipbuilding, Inc., 12 271–73
Ingenico—Compagnie Industrielle et Financière d'Ingénierie, 46 250–52
Ingersoll-Rand Company, III 525–27; 15 223–26 (upd.); 55 218–22 (upd.)
Ingles Markets, Inc., 20 305–08
Ingram Industries, Inc., 11 193–95; 49 217–20 (upd.)
Ingram Micro Inc., 52 178–81
INI *see* Instituto Nacional de Industria.
Initial Security, 64 196–98
Inktomi Corporation, 45 200–04
Inland Container Corporation, 8 267–69 *see also* Temple-Inland Inc.
Inland Steel Industries, Inc., IV 113–16; 19 216–20 (upd.)
Innovative Solutions & Support, Inc., 85 175–78
Innovo Group Inc., 83 195-199
INPEX Holdings Inc., 97 230–33
Input/Output, Inc., 73 184–87
Inserra Supermarkets, 25 234–36
Insight Enterprises, Inc., 18 259–61
Insilco Corporation, 16 281–83
Inso Corporation, 26 215–19
Instinet Corporation, 34 225–27
Insituform Technologies, Inc., 83 200-203
Instituto Nacional de Industria, I 459–61
Insurance Auto Auctions, Inc., 23 285–87
Integra LifeSciences Holdings Corporation, 87 244–247
Integrated BioPharma, Inc., 83 204-207
Integrated Defense Technologies, Inc., 54 178–80
Integrity Inc., 44 241–43
Intel Corporation, II 44–46; 10 365–67 (upd.); 36 284–88 (upd.); 75 196–201 (upd.)
IntelliCorp, Inc., 45 205–07
Intelligent Electronics, Inc., 6 243–45
Inter Link Foods PLC, 61 132–34
Inter Parfums Inc., 35 235–38; 86 201–06 (upd.)
Inter-Regional Financial Group, Inc., 15 231–33 *see also* Dain Rauscher Corp.
Interbrand Corporation, 70 131–33
Interbrew S.A., 17 256–58; 50 274–79 (upd.)
Interceramic *see* Internacional de Ceramica, S.A. de C.V.
Interco Incorporated, III 528–31 *see also* Furniture Brands International, Inc.
IntercontinentalExchange, Inc., 95 204–07
Intercorp Excelle Foods Inc., 64 199–201
InterDigital Communications Corporation, 61 135–37
Interep National Radio Sales Inc., 35 231–34
Interface, Inc., 8 270–72; 29 246–49 (upd.); 76 195–99 (upd.)
Interfax News Agency, 86 207–10
Intergraph Corporation, 6 246–49; 24 233–36 (upd.)
The Interlake Corporation, 8 273–75
Intermec Technologies Corporation, 72 187–91
INTERMET Corporation, 32 279–82; 77 207–12 (upd.)
Intermix Media, Inc., 83 208-211
Intermountain Health Care, Inc., 27 237–40
Internacional de Ceramica, S.A. de C.V., 53 174–76
International Airline Support Group, Inc., 55 223–25
International Brotherhood of Teamsters, 37 211–14
International Business Machines Corporation, III 147–49; 6 250–53 (upd.); 30 247–51 (upd.); 63 195–201 (upd.)
International Controls Corporation, 10 368–70
International Creative Management, Inc., 43 235–37
International Dairy Queen, Inc., 10 371–74; 39 232–36 (upd.)
International Data Group, Inc., 7 238–40; 25 237–40 (upd.)
International Family Entertainment Inc., 13 279–81 *see also* ABC Family Worldwide, Inc.
International Flavors & Fragrances Inc., 9 290–92; 38 244–48 (upd.)
International Game Technology, 10 375–76; 41 214–16 (upd.)
International House of Pancakes *see* IHOP Corp.
International Lease Finance Corporation, 48 218–20
International Management Group, 18 262–65 *see also* IMG.
International Multifoods Corporation, 7 241–43; 25 241–44 (upd.) *see also* The J. M. Smucker Co.
International Olympic Committee, 44 244–47
International Paper Company, IV 286–88; 15 227–30 (upd.); 47 187–92 (upd.); 97 234–43 (upd.)
International Power PLC, 50 280–85 (upd.)
International Profit Associates, Inc., 87 248–251
International Rectifier Corporation, 31 263–66; 71 181–84 (upd.)
International Shipbreaking Ltd. L.L.C., 67 213–15
International Shipholding Corporation, Inc., 27 241–44
International Speedway Corporation, 19 221–23; 74 157–60 (upd.)
International Telephone & Telegraph Corporation, I 462–64; 11 196–99 (upd.)
International Total Services, Inc., 37 215–18
Interpool, Inc., 92 176–79

The Interpublic Group of Companies, Inc., I 16–18; 22 294–97 (upd.); 75 202–05 (upd.)
Interscope Music Group, 31 267–69
Intersil Corporation, 93 250–54
Interstate Bakeries Corporation, 12 274–76; 38 249–52 (upd.)
Interstate Hotels & Resorts Inc., 58 192–94
Intertek Group plc, 95 208–11
InterVideo, Inc., 85 179–82
Intevac, Inc., 92 180–83
Intimate Brands, Inc., 24 237–39
Intrado Inc., 63 202–04
Intrawest Corporation, 15 234–36; 84 192–196 (upd.)
Intres B.V., 82 178–81
Intuit Inc., 14 262–64; 33 208–11 (upd.); 73 188–92 (upd.)
Intuitive Surgical, Inc., 79 217–20
Invacare Corporation, 11 200–02; 47 193–98 (upd.)
Invensys PLC, 50 286–90 (upd.)
inVentiv Health, Inc., 81 205–08
The Inventure Group, Inc., 96 199–202 (upd.)
Inverness Medical Innovations, Inc., 63 205–07
Inversiones Nacional de Chocolates S.A., 88 199–202
Investcorp SA, 57 179–82
Investor AB, 63 208–11
Invitrogen Corporation, 52 182–84
Invivo Corporation, 52 185–87
Iogen Corporation, 81 209–13
Iomega Corporation, 21 294–97
IONA Technologies plc, 43 238–41
Ionatron, Inc., 85 183–86
Ionics, Incorporated, 52 188–90
Iowa Beef Processors *see* IBP, Inc.
Iowa Telecommunications Services, Inc., 85 187–90
Ipalco Enterprises, Inc., 6 508–09
IPC Magazines Limited, 7 244–47
Ipiranga S.A., 67 216–18
Ipsen International Inc., 72 192–95
Ipsos SA, 48 221–24
IranAir, 81 214–17
Irex Contracting Group, 90 245–48
Irish Distillers Group, 96 203–07
Irish Life & Permanent Plc, 59 245–47
Irkut Corporation, 68 202–04
iRobot Corporation, 83 212-215
Iron Mountain, Inc., 33 212–14
IRSA Inversiones y Representaciones S.A., 63 212–15
Irvin Feld & Kenneth Feld Productions, Inc., 15 237–39 *see also* Feld Entertainment, Inc.
Irwin Financial Corporation, 77 213–16
Irwin Toy Limited, 14 265–67
Isbank *see* Turkiye Is Bankasi A.S.
Iscor Limited, 57 183–86
Isetan Company Limited, V 85–87; 36 289–93 (upd.)
Ishikawajima-Harima Heavy Industries Company, Ltd., III 532–33; 86 211–15 (upd.)
The Island ECN, Inc., 48 225–29
Isle of Capri Casinos, Inc., 41 217–19
Ispat Inland Inc., 30 252–54; 40 267–72 (upd.)
Israel Aircraft Industries Ltd., 69 215–17
Israel Chemicals Ltd., 55 226–29
ISS A/S, 49 221–23
Istituto per la Ricostruzione Industriale S.p.A., I 465–67; 11 203–06 (upd.)
Isuzu Motors, Ltd., 9 293–95; 23 288–91 (upd.); 57 187–91 (upd.)
Itaú *see* Banco Itaú S.A.
ITC Holdings Corp., 75 206–08
Itel Corporation, 9 296–99
Items International Airwalk Inc., 17 259–61
ITM Entreprises SA, 36 294–97
Ito-Yokado Co., Ltd., V 88–89; 42 189–92 (upd.)
ITOCHU Corporation, 32 283–87 (upd.)
Itoh *see* C. Itoh & Co.
Itoham Foods Inc., II 518–19; 61 138–40 (upd.)
Itron, Inc., 64 202–05
ITT Educational Services, Inc., 33 215–17; 76 200–03 (upd.)
ITT Sheraton Corporation, III 98–101 *see also* Starwood Hotels & Resorts Worldwide, Inc.
ITW *see* Illinois Tool Works Inc.
i2 Technologies, Inc., 87 252–257
Ivar's, Inc., 86 216–19
IVAX Corporation, 11 207–09; 55 230–33 (upd.)
IVC Industries, Inc., 45 208–11
iVillage Inc., 46 253–56
Iwerks Entertainment, Inc., 34 228–30
IXC Communications, Inc., 29 250–52

J

J & J Snack Foods Corporation, 24 240–42
J&R Electronics Inc., 26 224–26
J. & W. Seligman & Co. Inc., 61 141–43
J.A. Jones, Inc., 16 284–86
J. Alexander's Corporation, 65 177–79
J.B. Hunt Transport Services Inc., 12 277–79
J. Baker, Inc., 31 270–73
J C Bamford Excavators Ltd., 83 216-222
J. C. Penney Company, Inc., V 90–92; 18 269–73 (upd.); 43 245–50 (upd.); 91 263–72 (upd.)
J. Crew Group, Inc., 12 280–82; 34 231–34 (upd.); 88 203–08
J.D. Edwards & Company, 14 268–70 *see also* Oracle Corp.
J.D. Power and Associates, 32 297–301
J. D'Addario & Company, Inc., 48 230–33
J.F. Shea Co., Inc., 55 234–36
J.H. Findorff and Son, Inc., 60 175–78
J.I. Case Company, 10 377–81 *see also* CNH Global N.V.
J.J. Darboven GmbH & Co. KG, 96 208–12
J.J. Keller & Associates, Inc., 81 2180–21
The J. Jill Group, Inc., 35 239–41; 90 249–53 (upd.)
J.L. Hammett Company, 72 196–99
J Lauritzen A/S, 90 254–57
The J. M. Smucker Company, 11 210–12; 87 258–265 (upd.)
J.M. Voith AG, 33 222–25
J.P. Morgan Chase & Co., II 329–32; 30 261–65 (upd.); 38 253–59 (upd.)
J.R. Simplot Company, 16 287–89; 60 179–82 (upd.)
J Sainsbury plc, II 657–59; 13 282–84 (upd.); 38 260–65 (upd.); 95 212–20 (upd.)
J. W. Pepper and Son Inc., 86 220–23
J. Walter Thompson Co. *see* JWT Group Inc.
Jabil Circuit, Inc., 36 298–301; 88 209–14
Jack Henry and Associates, Inc., 17 262–65; 94 258–63 (upd.)
Jack in the Box Inc., 89 265–71 (upd.)
Jack Morton Worldwide, 88 215–18
Jack Schwartz Shoes, Inc., 18 266–68
Jackpot Enterprises Inc., 21 298–300
Jackson Hewitt, Inc., 48 234–36
Jackson National Life Insurance Company, 8 276–77
Jacmar Companies, 87 266–269
Jaco Electronics, Inc., 30 255–57
Jacob Leinenkugel Brewing Company, 28 209–11
Jacobs Engineering Group Inc., 6 148–50; 26 220–23 (upd.)
Jacobs Suchard (AG), II 520–22 *see also* Kraft Jacobs Suchard AG.
Jacobson Stores Inc., 21 301–03
Jacor Communications, Inc., 23 292–95
Jacques Whitford, 92 184–87
Jacquot *see* Établissements Jacquot and Cie S.A.S.
Jacuzzi Brands Inc., 23 296–98; 76 204–07 (upd.)
JAFCO Co. Ltd., 79 221–24
Jaguar Cars, Ltd., 13 285–87
JAKKS Pacific, Inc., 52 191–94
JAL *see* Japan Airlines Company, Ltd.
Jalate Inc., 25 245–47
Jamba Juice Company, 47 199–202
James Avery Craftsman, Inc., 76 208–10
James Beattie plc, 43 242–44
James Hardie Industries N.V., 56 174–76
James Original Coney Island Inc., 84 197–200
James Purdey & Sons Limited, 87 270–275
James River Corporation of Virginia, IV 289–91 *see also* Fort James Corp.
Jani-King International, Inc., 85 191–94
Janssen Pharmaceutica N.V., 80 164–67
JanSport, Inc., 70 134–36
Janus Capital Group Inc., 57 192–94

Japan Airlines Company, Ltd., I 104–06; 32 288–92 (upd.)
Japan Broadcasting Corporation, 7 248–50
Japan Leasing Corporation, 8 278–80
Japan Pulp and Paper Company Limited, IV 292–93
Japan Tobacco Inc., V 403–04; 46 257–60 (upd.)
Jarden Corporation, 93 255–61 (upd.)
Jardine Cycle & Carriage Ltd., 73 193–95
Jardine Matheson Holdings Limited, I 468–71; 20 309–14 (upd.); 93 262–71 (upd.)
Jarvis plc, 39 237–39
Jason Incorporated, 23 299–301
Jay Jacobs, Inc., 15 243–45
Jayco Inc., 13 288–90
Jays Foods, Inc., 90 258–61
Jazz Basketball Investors, Inc., 55 237–39
Jazzercise, Inc., 45 212–14
JB Oxford Holdings, Inc., 32 293–96
JCDecaux S.A., 76 211–13
JD Wetherspoon plc, 30 258–60
JDS Uniphase Corporation, 34 235–37
JE Dunn Construction Group, Inc., 85 195–98
The Jean Coutu Group (PJC) Inc., 46 261–65
Jean-Georges Enterprises L.L.C., 75 209–11
Jeanneau *see* Chantiers Jeanneau S.A.
Jefferies Group, Inc., 25 248–51
Jefferson-Pilot Corporation, 11 213–15; 29 253–56 (upd.)
Jefferson Properties, Inc. *see* JPI.
Jefferson Smurfit Group plc, IV 294–96; 19 224–27 (upd.); 49 224–29 (upd.) *see also* Smurfit-Stone Container Corp.
Jel Sert Company, 90 262–65
Jeld-Wen, Inc., 45 215–17
Jelly Belly Candy Company, 76 214–16
Jenkens & Gilchrist, P.C., 65 180–82
Jennie-O Turkey Store, Inc., 76 217–19
Jennifer Convertibles, Inc., 31 274–76
Jenny Craig, Inc., 10 382–84; 29 257–60 (upd.); 92 188–93 (upd.)
Jenoptik AG, 33 218–21
Jeppesen Sanderson, Inc., 92 194–97
Jerónimo Martins SGPS S.A., 96 213–16
Jerry's Famous Deli Inc., 24 243–45
Jersey European Airways (UK) Ltd., 61 144–46
Jersey Mike's Franchise Systems, Inc., 83 223-226
Jervis B. Webb Company, 24 246–49
Jet Airways (India) Private Limited, 65 183–85
JetBlue Airways Corporation, 44 248–50
Jetro Cash & Carry Enterprises Inc., 38 266–68
Jewett-Cameron Trading Company, Ltd., 89 272–76
JFE Shoji Holdings Inc., 88 219–22
JG Industries, Inc., 15 240–42
Jillian's Entertainment Holdings, Inc., 40 273–75
Jim Beam Brands Worldwide, Inc., 14 271–73; 58 194–96 (upd.)
The Jim Henson Company, 23 302–04
The Jim Pattison Group, 37 219–22
Jimmy Carter Work Project *see* Habitat for Humanity International.
Jitney-Jungle Stores of America, Inc., 27 245–48
JJB Sports plc, 32 302–04
JLA Credit *see* Japan Leasing Corp.
JLG Industries, Inc., 52 195–97
JLL *see* Jones Lang LaSalle Inc.
JLM Couture, Inc., 64 206–08
JMB Realty Corporation, IV 702–03 *see also* Amfac/JMB Hawaii L.L.C.
Jo-Ann Stores, Inc., 72 200–03 (upd.)
Jockey International, Inc., 12 283–85; 34 238–42 (upd.); 77 217–23 (upd.)
The Joffrey Ballet of Chicago, 52 198–202
John B. Sanfilippo & Son, Inc., 14 274–76
John Brown plc, I 572–74
The John D. and Catherine T. MacArthur Foundation, 34 243–46
John D. Brush Company Inc., 94 264–67
The John David Group plc, 90 266–69
John Deere *see* Deere & Co.
John Dewar & Sons, Ltd., 82 182–86
John Fairfax Holdings Limited, 7 251–54 *see also* Fairfax Media Ltd.
John Frieda Professional Hair Care Inc., 70 137–39
John H. Harland Company, 17 266–69
John Hancock Financial Services, Inc., III 265–68; 42 193–98 (upd.)
John Laing plc, I 575–76; 51 171–73 (upd.) *see also* Laing O'Rourke PLC.
John Lewis Partnership plc, V 93–95; 42 199–203 (upd.)
John Menzies plc, 39 240–43
The John Nuveen Company, 21 304–065
John Paul Mitchell Systems, 24 250–52
John Q. Hammons Hotels, Inc., 24 253–55
John W. Danforth Company, 48 237–39
John Wiley & Sons, Inc., 17 270–72; 65 186–90 (upd.)
Johnny Rockets Group, Inc., 31 277–81; 76 220–24 (upd.)
Johns Manville Corporation, 64 209–14 (upd.)
Johnson *see* Axel Johnson Group.
Johnson & Higgins, 14 277–80 *see also* Marsh & McLennan Companies, Inc.
Johnson & Johnson, III 35–37; 8 281–83 (upd.); 36 302–07 (upd.); 75 212–18 (upd.)
Johnson Controls, Inc., III 534–37; 26 227–32 (upd.); 59 248–54 (upd.)
Johnson Matthey PLC, IV 117–20; 16 290–94 (upd.); 49 230–35 (upd.)
Johnson Outdoors Inc., 84 201–205 (upd.)
Johnson Publishing Company, Inc., 28 212–14; 72 204–07 (upd.)
Johnson Wax *see* S.C. Johnson & Son, Inc.
Johnson Worldwide Associates, Inc., 28 215–17 *see also* Johnson Outdoors Inc.
Johnsonville Sausage L.L.C., 63 216–19
Johnston Industries, Inc., 15 246–48
Johnston Press plc, 35 242–44
Johnstown America Industries, Inc., 23 305–07
Jolly Hotels *see* Compagnia Italiana dei Jolly Hotels S.p.A.
Jones Apparel Group, Inc., 11 216–18; 39 244–47 (upd.)
Jones, Day, Reavis & Pogue, 33 226–29
Jones Intercable, Inc., 21 307–09
Jones Knowledge Group, Inc., 97 244–48
Jones Lang LaSalle Incorporated, 49 236–38
Jones Medical Industries, Inc., 24 256–58
Jones Soda Co., 69 218–21
Jongleurs Comedy Club *see* Regent Inns plc.
Jordache Enterprises, Inc., 23 308–10
The Jordan Company LP, 70 140–42
Jordan Industries, Inc., 36 308–10
Jordan-Kitt Music Inc., 86 224–27
Jos. A. Bank Clothiers, Inc., 31 282–85
José de Mello SGPS S.A., 96 217–20
Joseph T. Ryerson & Son, Inc., 15 249–51 *see also* Ryerson Tull, Inc.
Jostens, Inc., 7 255–57; 25 252–55 (upd.); 73 196–200 (upd.)
Jotun A/S, 80 168–71
JOULÉ Inc., 58 197–200
Journal Communications, Inc., 86 228–32
Journal Register Company, 29 261–63
JPI, 49 239–41
JPMorgan Chase & Co., 91 273–84 (upd.)
JPS Textile Group, Inc., 28 218–20
JSC MMC Norilsk Nickel, 48 300–02
JSP Corporation, 74 161–64
j2 Global Communications, Inc., 75 219–21
The Judge Group, Inc., 51 174–76
Jugos del Valle, S.A. de C.V., 85 199–202
Juicy Couture, Inc., 80 172–74
Jujo Paper Co., Ltd., IV 297–98
Julius Baer Holding AG, 52 203–05
Julius Blüthner Pianofortefabric GmbH, 78 185–88
Julius Meinl International AG, 53 177–80
Jumbo S.A., 96 221–24
Jumeirah Group, 83 227-230
Jungheinrich AG, 96 225–30
Juniper Networks, Inc., 43 251–55
Juno Lighting, Inc., 30 266–68
Juno Online Services, Inc., 38 269–72 *see also* United Online, Inc.

Jupitermedia Corporation, 75 222–24
Jurys Doyle Hotel Group plc, 64 215–17
JUSCO Co., Ltd., V 96–99 *see also* AEON Co., Ltd.
Just Bagels Manufacturing, Inc., 94 268–71
Just Born, Inc., 32 305–07
Just For Feet, Inc., 19 228–30
Justin Industries, Inc., 19 231–33 *see also* Berkshire Hathaway Inc.
Juventus F.C. S.p.A, 53 181–83
JVC *see* Victor Company of Japan, Ltd.
JWP Inc., 9 300–02 *see also* EMCOR Group Inc.
JWT Group Inc., I 19–21 *see also* WPP Group plc.

K

K&B Inc., 12 286–88
K & G Men's Center, Inc., 21 310–12
K-Swiss Inc., 33 243–45; 89 277–81 (upd.)
K-tel International, Inc., 21 325–28
Kadant Inc., 96 231–34 (upd.)
Kaiser Aluminum Corporation, IV 121–23; 84 212–217 (upd.)
Kaiser Foundation Health Plan, Inc., 53 184–86
Kajima Corporation, I 577–78; 51 177–79 (upd.)
Kal Kan Foods, Inc., 22 298–300
Kaman Corporation, 12 289–92; 42 204–08 (upd.)
Kaman Music Corporation, 68 205–07
Kampgrounds of America, Inc., 33 230–33
Kamps AG, 44 251–54
Kana Software, Inc., 51 180–83
Kanebo, Ltd., 53 187–91
Kanematsu Corporation, IV 442–44; 24 259–62 (upd.)
Kansai Paint Company Ltd., 80 175–78
The Kansai Electric Power Company, Inc., V 645–48; 62 196–200 (upd.)
Kansallis-Osake-Pankki, II 302–03
Kansas City Power & Light Company, 6 510–12 *see also* Great Plains Energy Inc.
Kansas City Southern Industries, Inc., 6 400–02; 26 233–36 (upd.)
The Kansas City Southern Railway Company, 92 198–202
Kao Corporation, III 38–39; 20 315–17 (upd.); 79 225–30 (upd.)
Kaplan, Inc., 42 209–12; 90 270–75 (upd.)
Kar Nut Products Company, 86 233–36
Karan Co. *see* Donna Karan Co.
Karl Kani Infinity, Inc., 49 242–45
Karlsberg Brauerei GmbH & Co KG, 41 220–23
Karmann *see* Wilhelm Karmann GmbH.
Karstadt Aktiengesellschaft, V 100–02; 19 234–37 (upd.)
Karstadt Quelle AG, 57 195–201 (upd.)
Karsten Manufacturing Corporation, 51 184–86
Kash n' Karry Food Stores, Inc., 20 318–20
Kashi Company, 89 282–85
Kasper A.S.L., Ltd., 40 276–79
kate spade LLC, 68 208–11
Katokichi Company Ltd., 82 187–90
Katy Industries Inc., I 472–74; 51 187–90 (upd.)
Katz Communications, Inc., 6 32–34 *see also* Clear Channel Communications, Inc.
Katz Media Group, Inc., 35 245–48
Kaufhof Warenhaus AG, V 103–05; 23 311–14 (upd.)
Kaufman and Broad Home Corporation, 8 284–86 *see also* KB Home.
Kaufring AG, 35 249–52
Kawai Musical Instruments Manufacturing Co.,Ltd., 78 189–92
Kawasaki Heavy Industries, Ltd., III 538–40; 63 220–23 (upd.)
Kawasaki Kisen Kaisha, Ltd., V 457–60; 56 177–81 (upd.)
Kawasaki Steel Corporation, IV 124–25
Kay-Bee Toy Stores, 15 252–53 *see also* KB Toys.
Kaydon Corporation, 18 274–76
KB Home, 45 218–22 (upd.)
KB Toys, Inc., 35 253–55 (upd.); 86 237–42 (upd.)
KC *see* Kenneth Cole Productions, Inc.
KCPL *see* Kansas City Power & Light Co.
KCSI *see* Kansas City Southern Industries, Inc.
KCSR *see* The Kansas City Southern Railway.
Keane, Inc., 56 182–86
Keebler Foods Company, 36 311–13
Keio Corporation, V 461–62; 96 235–39 (upd.)
The Keith Companies Inc., 54 181–84
Keithley Instruments Inc., 16 299–301
Kelda Group plc, 45 223–26
Kelley Blue Book Company, Inc., 84 218–221
Keller Group PLC, 95 221–24
Kelley Drye & Warren LLP, 40 280–83
Kellogg Brown & Root, Inc., 62 201–05 (upd.)
Kellogg Company, II 523–26; 13 291–94 (upd.); 50 291–96 (upd.)
Kellwood Company, 8 287–89; 85 203–08 (upd.)
Kelly-Moore Paint Company, Inc., 56 187–89
Kelly Services, Inc., 6 35–37; 26 237–40 (upd.)
The Kelly-Springfield Tire Company, 8 290–92
Kelsey-Hayes Group of Companies, 7 258–60; 27 249–52 (upd.)
Kemet Corp., 14 281–83
Kemira Oyj, 70 143–46
Kemper Corporation, III 269–71; 15 254–58 (upd.)
Ken's Foods, Inc., 88 223–26
Kendall International, Inc., 11 219–21 *see also* Tyco International Ltd.
Kendall-Jackson Winery, Ltd., 28 221–23
Kendle International Inc., 87 276–279
Kenetech Corporation, 11 222–24
Kenexa Corporation, 87 280–284
Kenmore Air Harbor Inc., 65 191–93
Kennametal, Inc., 13 295–97; 68 212–16 (upd.)
Kennecott Corporation, 7 261–64; 27 253–57 (upd.) *see also* Rio Tinto PLC.
Kennedy-Wilson, Inc., 60 183–85
Kenneth Cole Productions, Inc., 25 256–58
Kensey Nash Corporation, 71 185–87
Kensington Publishing Corporation, 84 222–225
Kent Electronics Corporation, 17 273–76
Kentucky Electric Steel, Inc., 31 286–88
Kentucky Fried Chicken *see* KFC Corp.
Kentucky Utilities Company, 6 513–15
Kenwood Corporation, 31 289–91
Kenya Airways Limited, 89 286–89
Keolis SA, 51 191–93
Kepco *see* Korea Electric Power Corporation; Kyushu Electric Power Company Inc.
Keppel Corporation Ltd., 73 201–03
Keramik Holding AG Laufen, 51 194–96
Kerasotes ShowPlace Theaters LLC, 80 179–83
Kerr Group Inc., 24 263–65
Kerr-McGee Corporation, IV 445–47; 22 301–04 (upd.); 68 217–21 (upd.)
Kerry Group plc, 27 258–60; 87 285–291 (upd.)
Kerry Properties Limited, 22 305–08
Kerzner International Limited, 69 222–24 (upd.)
Kesa Electricals plc, 91 285–90
Kesko Ltd (Kesko Oy), 8 293–94; 27 261–63 (upd.)
Ketchum Communications Inc., 6 38–40
Kettle Foods Inc., 48 240–42
Kewaunee Scientific Corporation, 25 259–62
Kewpie Kabushiki Kaisha, 57 202–05
Key Safety Systems, Inc., 63 224–26
Key Tronic Corporation, 14 284–86
KeyCorp, 8 295–97; 92272–81 (upd.)
Keyes Fibre Company, 9 303–05
Keys Fitness Products, LP, 83 231-234
KeySpan Energy Co., 27 264–66
Keystone International, Inc., 11 225–27 *see also* Tyco International Ltd.
KFC Corporation, 7 265–68; 21 313–17 (upd.); 89 290–96 (upd.)
Kforce Inc., 71 188–90
KHD Konzern, III 541–44
KI, 57 206–09
Kia Motors Corporation, 12 293–95; 29 264–67 (upd.); 56 173
Kiabi Europe, 66 199–201
Kidde plc, I 475–76; 44 255–59 (upd.)

Kiehl's Since 1851, Inc., 52 209–12
Kikkoman Corporation, 14 287–89; 47 203–06 (upd.)
Kimball International, Inc., 12 296–98; 48 243–47 (upd.)
Kimberly-Clark Corporation, III 40–41; 16 302–05 (upd.); 43 256–60 (upd.)
Kimberly-Clark de México, S.A. de C.V., 54 185–87
Kimco Realty Corporation, 11 228–30
Kinder Morgan, Inc., 45 227–30
KinderCare Learning Centers, Inc., 13 298–300
Kinetic Concepts, Inc., 20 321–23
King & Spalding, 23 315–18
The King Arthur Flour Company, 31 292–95
King Kullen Grocery Co., Inc., 15 259–61
King Nut Company, 74 165–67
King Pharmaceuticals, Inc., 54 188–90
King Ranch, Inc., 14 290–92; 60 186–89 (upd.)
King World Productions, Inc., 9 306–08; 30 269–72 (upd.)
Kingfisher plc, V 106–09; 24 266–71 (upd.); 83 235-242 (upd.)
Kingston Technology Corporation, 20 324–26
Kinki Nippon Railway Company Ltd., V 463–65
Kinko's Inc., 16 306–08; 43 261–64 (upd.)
Kinney Shoe Corp., 14 293–95
Kinray Inc., 85 209–12
Kinross Gold Corporation, 36 314–16
Kintera, Inc., 75 225–27
Kirby Corporation, 18 277–79; 66 202–04 (upd.)
Kirin Brewery Company, Limited, I 265–66; 21 318–21 (upd.); 63 227–31 (upd.)
Kirkland & Ellis LLP, 65 194–96
Kirshenbaum Bond + Partners, Inc., 57 210–12
Kit Manufacturing Co., 18 280–82
Kitchell Corporation, 14 296–98
KitchenAid, 8 298–99
Kitty Hawk, Inc., 22 309–11
Kiva, 95 225–29
Kiwi International Airlines Inc., 20 327–29
KKR *see* Kohlberg Kravis Roberts & Co.
KLA-Tencor Corporation, 11 231–33; 45 231–34 (upd.)
Klabin S.A., 73 204–06
Klasky Csupo, Inc., 78 193–97
Klaus Steilmann GmbH & Co. KG, 53 192–95
Klein Tools, Inc., 95 230–34
Kleiner, Perkins, Caufield & Byers, 53 196–98
Kleinwort Benson Group PLC, II 421–23; 22 55 *see also* Dresdner Kleinwort Wasserstein.
Klement's Sausage Company, 61 147–49
KLM Royal Dutch Airlines *see* Koninklijke Luftvaart Maatschappij N.V.
Klöckner-Werke AG, IV 126–28; 58 201–05 (upd.)
Kluwer Publishers *see* Wolters Kluwer NV.
Kmart Corporation, V 110–12; 18 283–87 (upd.); 47 207–12 (upd.)
KN *see* Kühne & Nagel Group.
Knape & Vogt Manufacturing Company, 17 277–79
K'Nex Industries, Inc., 52 206–08
Knight-Ridder, Inc., IV 628–30; 15 262–66 (upd.); 67 219–23 (upd.)
Knight Trading Group, Inc., 70 147–49
Knight Transportation, Inc., 64 218–21
Knoll, Inc., 14 299–301; 80 184–88 (upd.)
Knorr-Bremse AG, 84 226–231
Knorr Co. *see* C.H. Knorr Co.
The Knot, Inc., 74 168–71
Knott's Berry Farm, 18 288–90
Knowledge Learning Corporation, 51 197–99; 54 191
Knowledge Universe, Inc., 54 191–94
KnowledgeWare Inc., 9 309–11; 31 296–98 (upd.)
KOA *see* Kampgrounds of America, Inc.
Koala Corporation, 44 260–62
Kobe Steel, Ltd., IV 129–31; 19 238–41 (upd.)
Kobrand Corporation, 82 191–94
Koç Holding A.S., I 478–80; 54 195–98 (upd.)
Koch Enterprises, Inc., 29 215–17
Koch Industries, Inc., IV 448–49; 20 330–32 (upd.); 77 224–30 (upd.)
Kodak *see* Eastman Kodak Co.
Kodansha Ltd., IV 631–33; 38 273–76 (upd.)
Koenig & Bauer AG, 64 222–26
Kohl's Corporation, 9 312–13; 30 273–75 (upd.); 77 231–35 (upd.)
Kohlberg Kravis Roberts & Co., 24 272–74; 56 190–94 (upd.)
Kohler Company, 7 269–71; 32 308–12 (upd.)
Kohn Pedersen Fox Associates P.C., 57 213–16
Kolbenschmidt Pierburg AG, 97 249–53
The Koll Company, 8 300–02
Kollmorgen Corporation, 18 291–94
Kolmar Laboratories Group, 96 240–43
Komag, Inc., 11 234–35
Komatsu Ltd., III 545–46; 16 309–11 (upd.); 52 213–17 (upd.)
Konami Corporation, 96 244–47
KONE Corporation, 27 267–70; 76 225–28 (upd.)
Konica Corporation, III 547–50; 30 276–81 (upd.)
König Brauerei GmbH & Co. KG, 35 256–58 (upd.)
Koninklijke Ahold N.V., II 641–42; 16 312–14 (upd.)
Koninklijke Grolsch BV *see* Royal Grolsch NV.
Koninklijke Houthandel G Wijma & Zonen BV, 96 248–51
Koninklijke KPN N.V. *see* Royal KPN N.V.
Koninklijke Luchtvaart Maatschappij N.V., I 107–09; 28 224–27 (upd.)
Koninklijke Nederlandsche Hoogovens en Staalfabrieken NV, IV 132–34
N.V. Koninklijke Nederlandse Vliegtuigenfabriek Fokker, I 54–56; 28 327–30 (upd.)
Koninklijke Nedlloyd N.V., 6 403–05; 26 241–44 (upd.)
Koninklijke Numico N.V. *see* Royal Numico N.V.
Koninklijke Philips Electronics N.V., 50 297–302 (upd.)
Koninklijke PTT Nederland NV, V 299–301 *see also* Royal KPN NV.
Koninklijke Vendex KBB N.V. (Royal Vendex KBB N.V.), 62 206–09 (upd.)
Koninklijke Wessanen nv, II 527–29; 54 199–204 (upd.)
Koo Koo Roo, Inc., 25 263–65
Kookmin Bank, 58 206–08
Koor Industries Ltd., II 47–49; 25 266–68 (upd.); 68 222–25 (upd.)
Kopin Corporation, 80 189–92
Koppers Industries, Inc., I 354–56; 26 245–48 (upd.)
Korbel Champagne Cellers *see* F. Korbel & Bros. Inc.
Körber AG, 60 190–94
Korea Electric Power Corporation (Kepco), 56 195–98
Korean Air Lines Co. Ltd., 6 98–99; 27 271–73 (upd.)
Koret of California, Inc., 62 210–13
Korn/Ferry International, 34 247–49
Kos Pharmaceuticals, Inc., 63 232–35
Koss Corporation, 38 277–79
Kotobukiya Co., Ltd., V 113–14; 56 199–202 (upd.)
KPMG International, 10 385–87; 33 234–38 (upd.)
KPN *see* Koninklijke PTT Nederland N.V.
Kraft Foods Inc., II 530–34; 7 272–77 (upd.); 45 235–44 (upd.); 91 291–306 (upd.)
Kraft Jacobs Suchard AG, 26 249–52 (upd.)
KraftMaid Cabinetry, Inc., 72 208–10
Kraus-Anderson Companies, Inc., 36 317–20; 83 243-248 (upd.)
Krause Publications, Inc., 35 259–61
Krause's Furniture, Inc., 27 274–77
Kredietbank N.V., II 304–056
Kreditanstalt für Wiederaufbau, 29 268–72
Kreisler Manufacturing Corporation, 97 254–57
Krispy Kreme Doughnut Corporation, 21 322–24; 61 150–54 (upd.)
The Kroger Company, II 643–45; 15 267–70 (upd.); 65 197–202 (upd.)
Kroll Inc., 57 217–20
Kronos, Inc., 18 295–97; 19 468

Kruger Inc., 17 280–82
Krung Thai Bank Public Company Ltd., 69 225–27
Krupp AG *see* Fried. Krupp GmbH; ThyssenKrupp AG.
Kruse International, 88 227–30
The Krystal Company, 33 239–42
KSB AG, 62 214–18
KT&G Corporation, 62 219–21
K2 Inc., 16 295–98; 84 206–211 (upd.)
KU Energy Corporation, 11 236–38 *see also* LG&E Energy Corp.
Kubota Corporation, III 551–53
Kudelski Group SA, 44 263–66
Kuehne & Nagel International AG, V 466–69; 53 199–203 (upd.)
Kuhlman Corporation, 20 333–35
Kühne *see* Carl Kühne KG (GmbH & Co.).
Kühne & Nagel International AG, V 466–69
Kulicke and Soffa Industries, Inc., 33 246–48; 76 229–31 (upd.)
Kumagai Gumi Company, Ltd., I 579–80
Kumon Institute of Education Co., Ltd., 72 211–14
Kuoni Travel Holding Ltd., 40 284–86
Kurzweil Technologies, Inc., 51 200–04
The Kushner-Locke Company, 25 269–71
Kuwait Airways Corporation, 68 226–28
Kuwait Flour Mills & Bakeries Company, 84 232–234
Kuwait Petroleum Corporation, IV 450–52; 55 240–43 (upd.)
Kvaerner ASA, 36 321–23
Kwang Yang Motor Company Ltd., 80 193–96
Kwik-Fit Holdings plc, 54 205–07
Kwik Save Group plc, 11 239–41
Kymmene Corporation, IV 299–303 *see also* UPM-Kymmene Corp.
Kyocera Corporation, II 50–52; 21 329–32 (upd.); 79 231–36 (upd.)
Kyokuyo Company Ltd., 75 228–30
Kyowa Hakko Kogyo Co., Ltd., III 42–43; 48 248–50 (upd.)
Kyphon Inc., 87 292–295
Kyushu Electric Power Company Inc., V 649–51

L

L. and J.G. Stickley, Inc., 50 303–05
L-3 Communications Holdings, Inc., 48 251–53
L.A. Darling Company, 92 203–06
L.A. Gear, Inc., 8 303–06; 32 313–17 (upd.)
L.A. T Sportswear, Inc., 26 257–59
L.B. Foster Company, 33 255–58
L.D.C. SA, 61 155–57
L.L. Bean, Inc., 10 388–90; 38 280–83 (upd.); 91 307–13 (upd.)
The L.L. Knickerbocker Co., Inc., 25 272–75
L. Luria & Son, Inc., 19 242–44
L. M. Berry and Company, 80 197–200
L.S. Starrett Company, 13 301–03; 64 227–30 (upd.)
La Choy Food Products Inc., 25 276–78
La Madeleine French Bakery & Café, 33 249–51
La Poste, V 270–72; 47 213–16 (upd.)
The La Quinta Companies, 11 242–44; 42 213–16 (upd.)
La Reina Inc., 96 252–55
La Senza Corporation, 66 205–07
La-Z-Boy Incorporated, 14 302–04; 50 309–13 (upd.)
LAB *see* Lloyd Aéreo Boliviano S.A
LaBarge Inc., 41 224–26
Labatt Brewing Company Limited, I 267–68; 25 279–82 (upd.)
Labeyrie SAS, 80 201–04
LabOne, Inc., 48 254–57
Labor Ready, Inc., 29 273–75; 88 231–36 (upd.)
Laboratoires Arkopharma S.A., 75 231–34
Laboratoires de Biologie Végétale Yves Rocher, 35 262–65
Laboratory Corporation of America Holdings, 42 217–20 (upd.)
LaBranche & Co. Inc., 37 223–25
LaCie Group S.A., 76 232–34
Lacks Enterprises Inc., 61 158–60
Laclede Steel Company, 15 271–73
LaCrosse Footwear, Inc., 18 298–301; 61 161–65 (upd.)
Ladbroke Group PLC, II 141–42; 21 333–36 (upd.) *see also* Hilton Group plc.
LADD Furniture, Inc., 12 299–301 *see also* La-Z-Boy Inc.
Ladish Co., Inc., 30 282–84
Lafarge Cement UK, 54 208–11 (upd.)
Lafarge Coppée S.A., III 703–05
Lafarge Corporation, 28 228–31
Lafuma S.A., 39 248–50
Laidlaw International, Inc., 80 205–08
Laing O'Rourke PLC, 93 282–85 (upd.)
L'Air Liquide SA, I 357–59; 47 217–20 (upd.)
Lakeland Industries, Inc., 45 245–48
Lakes Entertainment, Inc., 51 205–07
Lakeside Foods, Inc., 89 297–301
Lala *see* Grupo Industrial Lala, S.A. de C.V.
Lam Research Corporation, 11 245–47; 31 299–302 (upd.)
Lam Son Sugar Joint Stock Corporation (Lasuco), 60 195–97
Lamar Advertising Company, 27 278–80; 70 150–53 (upd.)
The Lamaur Corporation, 41 227–29
Lamb Weston, Inc., 23 319–21
Lamborghini *see* Automobili Lamborghini S.p.A.
Lamonts Apparel, Inc., 15 274–76
The Lamson & Sessions Co., 13 304–06; 61 166–70 (upd.)
Lan Chile S.A., 31 303–06
Lancair International, Inc., 67 224–26
Lancaster Colony Corporation, 8 307–09; 61 171–74 (upd.)
Lance, Inc., 14 305–07; 41 230–33 (upd.)
Lancer Corporation, 21 337–39
Land O'Lakes, Inc., II 535–37; 21 340–43 (upd.); 81 222–27 (upd.)
Land Securities PLC, IV 704–06; 49 246–50 (upd.)
LandAmerica Financial Group, Inc., 85 213–16
Landauer, Inc., 51 208–10
Landec Corporation, 95 235–38
Landmark Communications, Inc., 12 302–05; 55 244–49 (upd.)
Landmark Theatre Corporation, 70 154–56
Landor Associates, 81 228–31
Landry's Restaurants, Inc., 15 277–79; 65 203–07 (upd.)
Lands' End, Inc., 9 314–16; 29 276–79 (upd.); 82 195–200 (upd.)
Landsbanki Islands hf, 81 232–35
Landstar System, Inc., 63 236–38
Lane Bryant, Inc., 64 231–33
The Lane Co., Inc., 12 306–08
Lanier Worldwide, Inc., 75 235–38
Lanoga Corporation, 62 222–24 *see also* Pro-Build Holdings Inc.
Lapeyre S.A. *see* Groupe Lapeyre S.A.
Larry Flynt Publishing Inc., 31 307–10
Larry H. Miller Group, 29 280–83
Las Vegas Sands, Inc., 50 306–08
Laserscope, 67 227–29
LaSiDo Inc., 58 209–11
Lason, Inc., 31 311–13
Lassonde Industries Inc., 68 229–31
Lasuco *see* Lam Son Sugar Joint Stock Corp.
Latham & Watkins, 33 252–54
Latrobe Brewing Company, 54 212–14
Lattice Semiconductor Corp., 16 315–17
Lauda Air Luftfahrt AG, 48 258–60
Laura Ashley Holdings plc, 13 307–09; 37 226–29 (upd.)
The Laurel Pub Company Limited, 59 255–57
Laurent-Perrier SA, 42 221–23
Laurus N.V., 65 208–11
Lavoro Bank AG *see* Banca Nazionale del Lavoro SpA.
Lawson Software, 38 284–88
Lawter International Inc., 14 308–10 *see also* Eastman Chemical Co.
Layne Christensen Company, 19 245–47
Lazard LLC, 38 289–92
Lazare Kaplan International Inc., 21 344–47
Lazio *see* Società Sportiva Lazio SpA.
Lazy Days RV Center, Inc., 69 228–30
LCA-Vision, Inc, 85 217–20
LCC International, Inc., 84 235–238
LCI International, Inc., 16 318–20 *see also* Qwest Communications International, Inc.
LDB Corporation, 53 204–06

LDC, 68 232–34
LDC S.A.*see* L.D.C. S.A.
LDDS-Metro Communications, Inc., 8 310–12 *see also* MCI WorldCom, Inc.
LDI Ltd., LLC, 76 235–37
Le Bon Marché *see* The Bon Marché.
Le Chateau Inc., 63 239–41
Le Cordon Bleu S.A., 67 230–32
Le Duff *see* Groupe Le Duff S.A.
Le Monde S.A., 33 308–10
Léa Nature *see* Groupe Léa Nature.
Leap Wireless International, Inc., 69 231–33
LeapFrog Enterprises, Inc., 54 215–18
Lear Corporation, 16 321–23; 71 191–95 (upd.)
Lear Siegler Inc., I 481–83
Learjet Inc., 8 313–16; 27 281–85 (upd.)
Learning Care Group, Inc., 76 238–41 (upd.)
The Learning Company Inc., 24 275–78
Learning Tree International Inc., 24 279–82
LeaRonal, Inc., 23 322–24 *see also* Rohm and Haas Co.
Leaseway Transportation Corp., 12 309–11
Leatherman Tool Group, Inc., 51 211–13
Lebhar-Friedman, Inc., 55 250–52
Leblanc Corporation *see* G. Leblanc Corp.
LeBoeuf, Lamb, Greene & MacRae, L.L.P., 29 284–86
LECG Corporation, 93 286–89
Leche Pascual *see* Grupo Leche Pascual S.A.
Lechmere Inc., 10 391–93
Lechters, Inc., 11 248–50; 39 251–54 (upd.)
Leclerc *see* Association des Centres Distributeurs E. Leclerc.
LeCroy Corporation, 41 234–37
Ledcor Industries Limited, 46 266–69
Ledesma Sociedad Anónima Agrícola Industrial, 62 225–27
Lee Apparel Company, Inc., 8 317–19
Lee Enterprises, Incorporated, 11 251–53; 64 234–37 (upd.)
Leeann Chin, Inc., 30 285–88
Lefrak Organization Inc., 26 260–62
Legal & General Group plc, III 272–73; 24 283–85 (upd.)
The Legal Aid Society, 48 261–64
Legal Sea Foods Inc., 96 256–60
Legent Corporation, 10 394–96 *see also* Computer Associates International, Inc.
Legg Mason, Inc., 33 259–62
Leggett & Platt, Inc., 11 254–56; 48 265–68 (upd.)
Lego A/S, 13 310–13; 40 287–91 (upd.)
Legrand SA, 21 348–50
Lehigh Portland Cement Company, 23 325–27
Leica Camera AG, 35 266–69
Leica Microsystems Holdings GmbH, 35 270–73
Leidy's, Inc., 93 290–92
Leinenkugel Brewing Company *see* Jacob Leinenkugel Brewing Co.
Leiner Health Products Inc., 34 250–52
Lend Lease Corporation Limited, IV 707–09; 17 283–86 (upd.); 52 218–23 (upd.)
LendingTree, LLC, 93 293–96
Lennar Corporation, 11 257–59
Lennox International Inc., 8 320–22; 28 232–36 (upd.)
Lenovo Group Ltd., 80 209–12
Lenox, Inc., 12 312–13
LensCrafters Inc., 23 328–30; 76 242–45 (upd.)
L'Entreprise Jean Lefebvre, 23 331–33 *see also* Vinci.
Leo Burnett Company, Inc., I 22–24; 20 336–39 (upd.)
The Leona Group LLC, 84 239–242
Leprino Foods Company, 28 237–39
Leroux S.A.S., 65 212–14
Leroy Merlin SA, 54 219–21
Les Boutiques San Francisco, Inc., 62 228–30
Les Echos *see* Groupe Les Echos.
Les Schwab Tire Centers, 50 314–16
Lesaffre *see* Societe Industrielle Lesaffre.
Lesco Inc., 19 248–50
The Leslie Fay Company, Inc., 8 323–25; 39 255–58 (upd.)
Leslie's Poolmart, Inc., 18 302–04
Leucadia National Corporation, 11 260–62; 71 196–200 (upd.)
Leupold & Stevens, Inc., 52 224–26
Level 3 Communications, Inc., 67 233–35
Levenger Company, 63 242–45
Lever Brothers Company, 9 317–19 *see also* Unilever.
Levi, Ray & Shoup, Inc., 96 261–64
Levi Strauss & Co., V 362–65; 16 324–28 (upd.)
Levitz Furniture Inc., 15 280–82
Levy Restaurants L.P., 26 263–65
Lewis Drug Inc., 94 272–76
Lewis Galoob Toys Inc., 16 329–31
LEXIS-NEXIS Group, 33 263–67
Lexmark International, Inc., 18 305–07; 79 237–42 (upd.)
LG&E Energy Corporation, 6 516–18; 51 214–17 (upd.)
LG Corporation, 94 277–83 (upd.)
Li & Fung Limited, 59 258–61
Libbey Inc., 49 251–54
The Liberty Corporation, 22 312–14
Liberty Livewire Corporation, 42 224–27
Liberty Media Corporation, 50 317–19
Liberty Mutual Holding Company, 59 262–64
Liberty Orchards Co., Inc., 89 302–05
Liberty Property Trust, 57 221–23
Liberty Travel, Inc., 56 203–06
Libyan National Oil Corporation, IV 453–55 *see also* National Oil Corp.
Liebherr-International AG, 64 238–42
Life Care Centers of America Inc., 76 246–48
Life is good, Inc., 80 213–16
Life Technologies, Inc., 17 287–89
Life Time Fitness, Inc., 66 208–10
LifeCell Corporation, 77 236–39
Lifeline Systems, Inc., 32 374; 53 207–09
LifeLock, Inc., 91 314–17
LifePoint Hospitals, Inc., 69 234–36
Lifetime Brands, Inc., 27 286–89; 73 207–11 (upd.)
Lifetime Entertainment Services, 51 218–22
Lifetouch Inc., 86 243–47
Lifeway Foods, Inc., 65 215–17
LifeWise Health Plan of Oregon, Inc., 90 276–79
Ligand Pharmaceuticals Incorporated, 10 48; 47 221–23
LILCO *see* Long Island Lighting Co.
Lillian Vernon Corporation, 12 314–15; 35 274–77 (upd.); 92 207–12 (upd.)
Lilly & Co *see* Eli Lilly & Co.
Lilly Endowment Inc., 70 157–59
Limagrain *see* Groupe Limagrain.
The Limited, Inc., V 115–16; 20 340–43 (upd.)
LIN Broadcasting Corp., 9 320–22
Linamar Corporation, 18 308–10
Lincare Holdings Inc., 43 265–67
Lincoln Center for the Performing Arts, Inc., 69 237–41
Lincoln Electric Co., 13 314–16
Lincoln National Corporation, III 274–77; 25 286–90 (upd.)
Lincoln Property Company, 8 326–28; 54 222–26 (upd.)
Lincoln Snacks Company, 24 286–88
Lincoln Telephone & Telegraph Company, 14 311–13
Lindal Cedar Homes, Inc., 29 287–89
Linde AG, I 581–83; 67 236–39 (upd.)
Lindley *see* Corporación José R. Lindley S.A.
Lindsay Manufacturing Co., 20 344–46
Lindt & Sprüngli *see* Chocoladefabriken Lindt & Sprüngli AG.
Linear Technology, Inc., 16 332–34
Linens 'n Things, Inc., 24 289–92; 75 239–43 (upd.)
Lintas: Worldwide, 14 314–16
The Lion Brewery, Inc., 86 248–52
Lion Corporation, III 44–45; 51 223–26 (upd.)
Lion Nathan Limited, 54 227–30
Lionel L.L.C., 16 335–38
Lions Gate Entertainment Corporation, 35 278–81
Lipman Electronic Engineering Ltd., 81 236–39
Lipton *see* Thomas J. Lipton Co.
Liqui-Box Corporation, 16 339–41
Liquidnet, Inc., 79 243–46
LIRR *see* The Long Island Rail Road Co.
Litehouse Inc., 60 198–201
Lithia Motors, Inc., 41 238–40
Littelfuse, Inc., 26 266–69

Little Caesar Enterprises, Inc., 7 278–79; 24 293–96 (upd.) *see also* Ilitch Holdings Inc.
Little Switzerland, Inc., 60 202–04
Little Tikes Company, 13 317–19; 62 231–34 (upd.)
Littleton Coin Company Inc., 82 201–04
Littlewoods plc, V 117–19; 42 228–32 (upd.)
Litton Industries Inc., I 484–86; 11 263–65 (upd.) *see also* Avondale Industries; Northrop Grumman Corp.
LIVE Entertainment Inc., 20 347–49
Live Nation, Inc., 80 217–22 (upd.)
LivePerson, Inc., 91 318–21
Liz Claiborne, Inc., 8 329–31; 25 291–94 (upd.)
LKQ Corporation, 71 201–03
Lloyd Aéreo Boliviano S.A., 95 239–42
Lloyd's, III 278–81; 22 315–19 (upd.); 74 172–76 (upd.)
Lloyds TSB Group plc, II 306–09; 47 224–29 (upd.)
LM Ericsson *see* Telefonaktiebolaget LM Ericsson.
Loblaw Companies Limited, 43 268–72
Lockheed Martin Corporation, I 64–66; 11 266–69 (upd.); 15 283–86 (upd.); 89 306–11 (upd.)
Loctite Corporation, 8 332–34; 30 289–91 (upd.)
LodgeNet Entertainment Corporation, 28 240–42
Loehmann's Inc., 24 297–99
Loewe AG, 90 280–85
The Loewen Group, Inc., 16 342–44; 40 292–95 (upd.) *see also* Alderwoods Group Inc.
Loews Corporation, I 487–88; 12 316–18 (upd.); 36 324–28 (upd.); 93 297–304 (upd.)
Logan's Roadhouse, Inc., 29 290–92
Loganair Ltd., 68 235–37
Logica plc, 14 317–19; 37 230–33 (upd.)
Logicon Inc., 20 350–52 *see also* Northrop Grumman Corp.
Logitech International S.A., 28 243–45; 69 242–45 (upd.)
LoJack Corporation, 48 269–73
Lojas Americanas S.A., 77 240–43
Lojas Arapuã S.A., 22 320–22; 61 175–78 (upd.)
Loma Negra C.I.A.S.A., 95 243–46
London Drugs Ltd., 46 270–73
London Fog Industries, Inc., 29 293–96
London Regional Transport, 6 406–08
London Scottish Bank plc, 70 160–62
London Stock Exchange Limited, 34 253–56
Lone Star Steakhouse & Saloon, Inc., 51 227–29
Lonely Planet Publications Pty Ltd., 55 253–55
The Long & Foster Companies, Inc, 85 221–24
Long Island Bancorp, Inc., 16 345–47
Long Island Lighting Company, V 652–54
The Long Island Rail Road Company, 68 238–40
Long John Silver's, 13 320–22; 57 224–29 (upd.)
Long-Term Credit Bank of Japan, Ltd., II 310–11
The Longaberger Company, 12 319–21; 44 267–70 (upd.)
Longs Drug Stores Corporation, V 120; 25 295–97 (upd.); 83 249-253 (upd.)
Longview Fibre Company, 8 335–37; 37 234–37 (upd.)
Lonmin plc, 66 211–16 (upd.)
Lonrho Plc, 21 351–55 *see also* Lonmin plc.
Lonza Group Ltd., 73 212–14
Lookers plc, 71 204–06
Loral Space & Communications Ltd., 8 338–40; 54 231–35 (upd.)
L'Oréal, III 46–49; 8 341–44 (upd.); 46 274–79 (upd.)
Los Angeles Lakers *see* California Sports, Inc.
Lost Arrow Inc., 22 323–25
LOT Polish Airlines (Polskie Linie Lotnicze S.A.), 33 268–71
LOT$OFF Corporation, 24 300–01
Lotte Confectionery Company Ltd., 76 249–51
Lotus Cars Ltd., 14 320–22
Lotus Development Corporation, 6 254–56; 25 298–302 (upd.)
LOUD Technologies, Inc., 95 247–50 (upd.)
Louis Dreyfus *see* Groupe Louis Dreyfus S.A.
Louis Vuitton, 10 397–99 *see also* LVMH Moët Hennessy Louis Vuitton SA.
The Louisiana Land and Exploration Company, 7 280–83
Louisiana-Pacific Corporation, IV 304–05; 31 314–17 (upd.)
Love's Travel Stops & Country Stores, Inc., 71 207–09
Lowe's Companies, Inc., V 122–23; 21 356–58 (upd.); 81 240–44 (upd.)
Löwenbräu AG, 80 223–27
Lowrance Electronics, Inc., 18 311–14
LPA Holding Corporation, 81 245–48
LSB Industries, Inc., 77 244–47
LSI *see* Lear Siegler Inc.
LSI Logic Corporation, 13 323–25; 64 243–47
LTU Group Holding GmbH, 37 238–41
The LTV Corporation, I 489–91; 24 302–06 (upd.)
The Lubrizol Corporation, I 360–62; 30 292–95 (upd.); 83 254-259 (upd.)
Luby's, Inc., 17 290–93; 42 233–38 (upd.)
Lucas Industries Plc, III 554–57
Lucasfilm Ltd., 12 322–24; 50 320–23 (upd.)
Lucent Technologies Inc., 34 257–60
Lucille Farms, Inc., 45 249–51
Lucky-Goldstar, II 53–54 *see also* LG Corp.
Lucky Stores Inc., 27 290–93
Ludendo S.A., 88 237–40
Lufkin Industries, Inc., 78 198–202
Lufthansa *see* Deutsche Lufthansa AG.
Luigino's, Inc., 64 248–50
Lukens Inc., 14 323–25 *see also* Bethlehem Steel Corp.
LUKOIL *see* OAO LUKOIL.
Luminar Plc, 40 296–98
Lunar Corporation, 29 297–99
Lund Food Holdings, Inc., 22 326–28
Lund International Holdings, Inc., 40 299–301
Lush Ltd., 93 305–08
Lutheran Brotherhood, 31 318–21
Luxottica SpA, 17 294–96; 52 227–30 (upd.)
LVMH Moët Hennessy Louis Vuitton SA, 33 272–77 (upd.) *see also* Christian Dior S.A.
Lycos *see* Terra Lycos, Inc.
Lydall, Inc., 64 251–54
Lyfra-S.A./NV, 88 241–43
Lyman-Richey Corporation, 96 265–68
Lynch Corporation, 43 273–76
Lynden Incorporated, 91 322–25
Lyondell Chemical Company, IV 456–57; 45 252–55 (upd.)
Lyonnaise des Eaux-Dumez, V 655–57 *see also* Suez Lyonnaise des Eaux.

M

M&F Worldwide Corp., 38 293–95
M-real Oyj, 56 252–55 (upd.)
M.A. Bruder & Sons, Inc., 56 207–09
M.A. Gedney Co., 51 230–32
M.A. Hanna Company, 8 345–47 *see also* PolyOne Corp.
M. DuMont Schauberg GmbH & Co. KG, 92 213–17
M.E.P.C. Ltd. *see* MEPC plc.
M.H. Meyerson & Co., Inc., 46 280–83
M. Shanken Communications, Inc., 50 324–27
Maatschappij tot Exploitatie van de Onderneming Krasnapolsky *see* Grand Hotel Krasnapolsky N.V.
Mabe *see* Controladora Mabe, S.A. de C.V.
Mabuchi Motor Co. Ltd., 68 241–43
Mac Frugal's Bargains - Closeouts Inc., 17 297–99 *see also* Big Lots, Inc.
Mac-Gray Corporation, 44 271–73
The Macallan Distillers Ltd., 63 246–48
MacAndrews & Forbes Holdings Inc., 28 246–49; 86 253–59 (upd.)
MacArthur Foundation *see* The John D. and Catherine T. MacArthur Foundation.
Mace Security International, Inc., 57 230–32
The Macerich Company, 57 233–35
MacGregor Golf Company, 68 244–46
Mack-Cali Realty Corporation, 42 239–41

Mack Trucks, Inc., I 177–79; 22 329–32 (upd.); 61 179–83 (upd.)
Mackay Envelope Corporation, 45 256–59
Mackays Stores Group Ltd., 92 218–21
Mackie Designs Inc., 33 278–81 *see also* LOUD Technologies, Inc.
Macklowe Properties, Inc., 95 251–54
Maclean Hunter Publishing Limited, IV 638–40; 26 270–74 (upd.) *see also* Rogers Communications Inc.
MacMillan Bloedel Limited, IV 306–09 *see also* Weyerhaeuser Co.
Macmillan, Inc., 7 284–86
The MacNeal-Schwendler Corporation, 25 303–05
MacNeil/Lehrer Productions, 87 296–299
Macquarie Bank Ltd., 69 246–49
Macromedia, Inc., 50 328–31
Macy's, Inc., 94 284–93 (upd.)
MADD *see* Mothers Against Drunk Driving.
Madden's on Gull Lake, 52 231–34
Madeco S.A., 71 210–12
Madeira Wine Company, S.A., 49 255–57
Madge Networks N.V., 26 275–77
Madison Dearborn Partners, LLC, 97 258–61
Madison Gas and Electric Company, 39 259–62
Madison-Kipp Corporation, 58 213–16
Madrange SA, 58 217–19
Mag Instrument, Inc., 67 240–42
Magellan Aerospace Corporation, 48 274–76
MaggieMoo's International, 89 312–16
Magma Copper Company, 7 287–90 *see also* BHP Billiton.
Magma Design Automation Inc., 78 203–27
Magma Power Company, 11 270–72
MagneTek, Inc., 15 287–89; 41 241–44 (upd.)
Magneti Marelli Holding SpA, 90 286–89
Magyar Telekom Rt, 78 208–11
MAI Systems Corporation, 11 273–76
Maid-Rite Corporation, 62 235–38
Maidenform, Inc., 20 352–55; 59 265–69 (upd.)
Mail Boxes Etc., 18 315–17; 41 245–48 (upd.) *see also* U.S. Office Products Co.
Mail-Well, Inc., 28 250–52 *see also* Cenveo Inc.
MAIN *see* Makhteshim-Agan Industries Ltd.
Maine & Maritimes Corporation, 56 210–13
Maine Central Railroad Company, 16 348–50
Maines Paper & Food Service Inc., 71 213–15
Maison Louis Jadot, 24 307–09
Majesco Entertainment Company, 85 225–29
The Major Automotive Companies, Inc., 45 260–62
Make-A-Wish Foundation of America, 97 262–65
Makhteshim-Agan Industries Ltd., 85 230–34
Makita Corporation, 22 333–35; 59 270–73 (upd.)
Malayan Banking Berhad, 72 215–18
Malaysian Airline System Berhad, 6 100–02; 29 300–03 (upd.); 97 266–71 (upd.)
Malcolm Pirnie, Inc., 42 242–44
Malden Mills Industries, Inc., 16 351–53
Malév Plc, 24 310–12
Mallinckrodt Group Inc., 19 251–53
Malt-O-Meal Company, 22 336–38; 63 249–53 (upd.)
Mammoet Transport B.V., 26 278–80
Man Aktiengesellschaft, III 561–63
MAN Roland Druckmaschinen AG, 94 294–98
Management and Training Corporation, 28 253–56
Manatron, Inc., 86 260–63
Manchester United Football Club plc, 30 296–98
Mandalay Resort Group, 32 322–26 (upd.)
Mandom Corporation, 82 205–08
Manhattan Associates, Inc., 67 243–45
Manhattan Group, LLC, 80 228–31
Manheim, 88 244–48
Manila Electric Company (Meralco), 56 214–16
Manischewitz Company *see* B. Manischewitz Co.
Manitoba Telecom Services, Inc., 61 184–87
Manitou BF S.A., 27 294–96
The Manitowoc Company, Inc., 18 318–21; 59 274–79 (upd.)
Mannatech Inc., 33 282–85
Mannesmann AG, III 564–67; 14 326–29 (upd.); 38 296–301 (upd.) *see also* Vodafone Group PLC.
Mannheim Steamroller *see* American Gramophone LLC.
Manning Selvage & Lee (MS&L), 76 252–54
MannKind Corporation, 87 300–303
Manor Care, Inc., 6 187–90; 25 306–10 (upd.)
Manpower Inc., 9 326–27; 30 299–302 (upd.); 73 215–18 (upd.)
ManTech International Corporation, 97 272–75
Manufactured Home Communities, Inc., 22 339–41
Manufacturers Hanover Corporation, II 312–14 *see also* Chemical Bank.
Manulife Financial Corporation, 85 235–38
Manutan International S.A., 72 219–21
Manville Corporation, III 706–09; 7 291–95 (upd.) *see also* Johns Manville Corp.
MAPCO Inc., IV 458–59
MAPICS, Inc., 55 256–58
Maple Grove Farms of Vermont, 88 249–52
Maple Leaf Foods Inc., 41 249–53
Maple Leaf Sports & Entertainment Ltd., 61 188–90
Maples Industries, Inc., 83 260-263
Marble Slab Creamery, Inc., 87 304–307
March of Dimes, 31 322–25
Marchesi Antinori SRL, 42 245–48
Marchex, Inc., 72 222–24
marchFIRST, Inc., 34 261–64
Marco Business Products, Inc., 75 244–46
Marco's Franchising LLC, 86 264–67
Marcolin S.p.A., 61 191–94
Marconi plc, 33 286–90 (upd.)
Marcopolo S.A., 79 247–50
The Marcus Corporation, 21 359–63
Marelli *see* Magneti Marelli Holding SpA.
Marfin Popular Bank plc, 92 222–26
Margarete Steiff GmbH, 23 334–37
Marie Brizard et Roger International S.A.S., 22 342–44; 97 276–80 (upd.)
Marie Callender's Restaurant & Bakery, Inc., 28 257–59
Mariella Burani Fashion Group, 92 227–30
Marine Products Corporation, 75 247–49
MarineMax, Inc., 30 303–05
Marion Laboratories Inc., I 648–49
Marion Merrell Dow, Inc., 9 328–29 (upd.)
Marionnaud Parfumeries SA, 51 233–35
Marisa Christina, Inc., 15 290–92
Maritz Inc., 38 302–05
Mark IV Industries, Inc., 7 296–98; 28 260–64 (upd.)
Mark T. Wendell Tea Company, 94 299–302
The Mark Travel Corporation, 80 232–35
Märklin Holding GmbH, 70 163–66
Marks and Spencer p.l.c., V 124–26; 24 313–17 (upd.); 85 239–47 (upd.)
Marks Brothers Jewelers, Inc., 24 318–20 *see also* Whitehall Jewellers, Inc.
Marlin Business Services Corp., 89 317–19
The Marmon Group, Inc., IV 135–38; 16 354–57 (upd.); 70 167–72 (upd.)
Marquette Electronics, Inc., 13 326–28
Marriott International, Inc., III 102–03; 21 364–67 (upd.); 83 264-270 (upd.)
Mars, Incorporated, 7 299–301; 40 302–05 (upd.)
Mars Petcare US Inc., 96 269–72
Marsh & McLennan Companies, Inc., III 282–84; 45 263–67 (upd.)
Marsh Supermarkets, Inc., 17 300–02; 76 255–58 (upd.)
Marshall & Ilsley Corporation, 56 217–20
Marshall Amplification plc, 62 239–42

Marshall Field's, 63 254–63 *see also* Target Corp.
Marshalls Incorporated, 13 329–31
Martek Biosciences Corporation, 65 218–20
Martell and Company S.A., 82 213–16
Marten Transport, Ltd., 84 243–246
Martha Stewart Living Omnimedia, Inc., 24 321–23; 73 219–22 (upd.)
Martignetti Companies, 84 247–250
Martin-Baker Aircraft Company Limited, 61 195–97
Martin Franchises, Inc., 80 236–39
Martin Guitar Company *see* C.F. Martin & Co., Inc.
Martin Industries, Inc., 44 274–77
Martin Marietta Corporation, I 67–69 *see also* Lockheed Martin Corp.
MartinLogan, Ltd., 85 248–51
Martini & Rossi SpA, 63 264–66
Martz Group, 56 221–23
Marubeni Corporation, I 492–95; 24 324–27 (upd.)
Maruha Group Inc., 75 250–53 (upd.)
Marui Company Ltd., V 127; 62 243–45 (upd.)
Maruzen Co., Limited, 18 322–24
Marvel Entertainment, Inc., 10 400–02; 78 212–19 (upd.)
Marvin Lumber & Cedar Company, 22 345–47
Mary Kay Inc., 9 330–32; 30 306–09 (upd.); 84 251–256 (upd.)
Maryland & Virginia Milk Producers Cooperative Association, Inc., 80 240–43
Maryville Data Systems Inc., 96 273–76
Marzotto S.p.A., 20 356–58; 67 246–49 (upd.)
The Maschhoffs, Inc., 82 217–20
Masco Corporation, III 568–71; 20 359–63 (upd.); 39 263–68 (upd.)
Maserati *see* Officine Alfieri Maserati S.p.A.
Mashantucket Pequot Gaming Enterprise Inc., 35 282–85
Masland Corporation, 17 303–05 *see also* Lear Corp.
Masonite International Corporation, 63 267–69
Massachusetts Mutual Life Insurance Company, III 285–87; 53 210–13 (upd.)
Massey Energy Company, 57 236–38
MasTec, Inc., 55 259–63 (upd.)
Master Lock Company, 45 268–71
MasterBrand Cabinets, Inc., 71 216–18
MasterCard Worldwide, 9 333–35; 96 277–81 (upd.)
MasterCraft Boat Company, Inc., 90 290–93
Matalan PLC, 49 258–60
Match.com, LP, 87 308–311
Material Sciences Corporation, 63 270–73
The MathWorks, Inc., 80 244–47
Matra-Hachette S.A., 15 293–97 (upd.) *see also* European Aeronautic Defence and Space Company EADS N.V.
Matria Healthcare, Inc., 17 306–09
Matrix Essentials Inc., 90 294–97
Matrix Service Company, 65 221–23
Matrixx Initiatives, Inc., 74 177–79
Matsushita Electric Industrial Co., Ltd., II 55–56; 64 255–58 (upd.)
Matsushita Electric Works, Ltd., III 710–11; 7 302–03 (upd.)
Matsuzakaya Company Ltd., V 129–31; 64 259–62 (upd.)
Matt Prentice Restaurant Group, 70 173–76
Mattel, Inc., 7 304–07; 25 311–15 (upd.); 61 198–203 (upd.)
Matth. Hohner AG, 53 214–17
Matthews International Corporation, 29 304–06; 77 248–52 (upd.)
Matussière et Forest SA, 58 220–22
Maui Land & Pineapple Company, Inc., 29 307–09
Maui Wowi, Inc., 85 252–55
Mauna Loa Macadamia Nut Corporation, 64 263–65
Maurices Inc., 95 255–58
Maus Frères SA, 48 277–79
Maverick Ranch Association, Inc., 88 253–56
Maverick Tube Corporation, 59 280–83
Max & Erma's Restaurants Inc., 19 258–60
Maxco Inc., 17 310–11
Maxicare Health Plans, Inc., III 84–86; 25 316–19 (upd.)
The Maxim Group, 25 320–22
Maxim Integrated Products, Inc., 16 358–60
MAXIMUS, Inc., 43 277–80
Maxtor Corporation, 10 403–05 *see also* Seagate Technology, Inc.
Maxus Energy Corporation, 7 308–10
Maxwell Communication Corporation plc, IV 641–43; 7 311–13 (upd.)
Maxwell Shoe Company, Inc., 30 310–12 *see also* Jones Apparel Group, Inc.
MAXXAM Inc., 8 348–50
Maxxim Medical Inc., 12 325–27
The May Department Stores Company, V 132–35; 19 261–64 (upd.); 46 284–88 (upd.)
May Gurney Integrated Services PLC, 95 259–62
May International *see* George S. May International Co.
Mayer, Brown, Rowe & Maw, 47 230–32
Mayfield Dairy Farms, Inc., 74 180–82
Mayflower Group Inc., 6 409–11
Mayo Foundation, 9 336–39; 34 265–69 (upd.)
Mayor's Jewelers, Inc., 41 254–57
Maytag Corporation, III 572–73; 22 348–51 (upd.); 82 221–25 (upd.)
Mazda Motor Corporation, 9 340–42; 23 338–41 (upd.); 63 274–79 (upd.)
Mazel Stores, Inc., 29 310–12
Mazzio's Corporation, 76 259–61
MBB *see* Messerschmitt-Bölkow-Blohm.
MBC Holding Company, 40 306–09
MBE *see* Mail Boxes Etc.
MBIA Inc., 73 223–26
MBK Industrie S.A., 94 303–06
MBNA Corporation, 12 328–30; 33 291–94 (upd.)
MC Sporting Goods *see* Michigan Sporting Goods Distributors Inc.
MCA Inc., II 143–45 *see also* Universal Studios.
McAfee Inc., 94 307–10
McAlister's Corporation, 66 217–19
McBride plc, 82 226–30
MCC *see* Morris Communications Corp.
McCain Foods Limited, 77 253–56
McCarthy Building Companies, Inc., 48 280–82
McCaw Cellular Communications, Inc., 6 322–24 *see also* AT&T Wireless Services, Inc.
McClain Industries, Inc., 51 236–38
The McClatchy Company, 23 342–44; 92 231–35 (upd.)
McCormick & Company, Incorporated, 7 314–16; 27 297–300 (upd.)
McCormick & Schmick's Seafood Restaurants, Inc., 71 219–21
McCoy Corporation, 58 223–25
McDATA Corporation, 75 254–56
McDermott International, Inc., III 558–60; 37 242–46 (upd.)
McDonald's Corporation, II 646–48; 7 317–19 (upd.); 26 281–85 (upd.); 63 280–86 (upd.)
McDonnell Douglas Corporation, I 70–72; 11 277–80 (upd.) *see also* Boeing Co.
McGrath RentCorp, 91 326–29
The McGraw-Hill Companies, Inc., IV 634–37; 18 325–30 (upd.); 51 239–44 (upd.)
MCI *see* Melamine Chemicals, Inc.
MCI WorldCom, Inc., V 302–04; 27 301–08 (upd.) *see also* Verizon Communications Inc.
McIlhenny Company, 20 364–67
McJunkin Corporation, 63 287–89
McKechnie plc, 34 270–72
McKee Foods Corporation, 7 320–21; 27 309–11 (upd.)
McKesson Corporation, I 496–98; 12 331–33 (upd.); 47 233–37 (upd.)
McKinsey & Company, Inc., 9 343–45
McLane Company, Inc., 13 332–34
McLeodUSA Incorporated, 32 327–30
McMenamins Pubs and Breweries, 65 224–26
McMoRan *see* Freeport-McMoRan Copper & Gold, Inc.
MCN Corporation, 6 519–22
McNaughton Apparel Group, Inc., 92 236–41 (upd.)
McPherson's Ltd., 66 220–22
McQuay International *see* AAF-McQuay Inc.

MCSi, Inc., **41** 258–60
McWane Corporation, **55** 264–66
MDC Partners Inc., **63** 290–92
MDU Resources Group, Inc., **7** 322–25; **42** 249–53 (upd.)
The Mead Corporation, **IV** 310–13; **19** 265–69 (upd.) *see also* MeadWestvaco Corp.
Mead Data Central, Inc., **10** 406–08 *see also* LEXIS-NEXIS Group.
Mead Johnson & Company, **84** 257–262
Meade Instruments Corporation, **41** 261–64
Meadowcraft, Inc., **29** 313–15
MeadWestvaco Corporation, **76** 262–71 (upd.)
Measurement Specialties, Inc., **71** 222–25
MEC *see* Mitsubishi Estate Company, Ltd.
Mecalux S.A., **74** 183–85
Mecklermedia Corporation, **24** 328–30 *see also* Jupitermedia Corp.
Medarex, Inc., **85** 256–59
Medco Containment Services Inc., **9** 346–48 *see also* Merck & Co., Inc.
Médecins sans Frontières, **85** 260–63
MEDecision, Inc., **95** 263–67
Media Arts Group, Inc., **42** 254–57
Media General, Inc., **7** 326–28; **38** 306–09 (upd.)
Mediacom Communications Corporation, **69** 250–52
MediaNews Group, Inc., **70** 177–80
Mediaset SpA, **50** 332–34
Medical Information Technology Inc., **64** 266–69
Medical Management International, Inc., **65** 227–29
Medical Staffing Network Holdings, Inc., **89** 320–23
Medicis Pharmaceutical Corporation, **59** 284–86
Medifast, Inc., **97** 281–85
MedImmune, Inc., **35** 286–89
Mediolanum S.p.A., **65** 230–32
Medis Technologies Ltd., **77** 257–60
Meditrust, **11** 281–83
Medline Industries, Inc., **61** 204–06
Medtronic, Inc., **8** 351–54; **30** 313–17 (upd.); **67** 250–55 (upd.)
Medusa Corporation, **24** 331–33
Mega Bloks, Inc., **61** 207–09
Megafoods Stores Inc., **13** 335–37
Meggitt PLC, **34** 273–76
Meidensha Corporation, **92** 242–46
Meier & Frank Co., **23** 345–47 *see also* Macy's, Inc.
Meijer Incorporated, **7** 329–31; **27** 312–15 (upd.)
Meiji Dairies Corporation, **II** 538–39; **82** 231–34 (upd.)
Meiji Mutual Life Insurance Company, **III** 288–89
Meiji Seika Kaisha Ltd., **II** 540–41; **64** 270–72 (upd.)
Mel Farr Automotive Group, **20** 368–70
Melaleuca Inc., **31** 326–28
Melamine Chemicals, Inc., **27** 316–18 *see also* Mississippi Chemical Corp.
Melitta Unternehmensgruppe Bentz KG, **53** 218–21
Mello Smello *see* The Miner Group International.
Mellon Financial Corporation, **II** 315–17; **44** 278–82 (upd.)
Mellon-Stuart Co., **I** 584–85 *see also* Michael Baker Corp.
The Melting Pot Restaurants, Inc., **74** 186–88
Melville Corporation, **V** 136–38 *see also* CVS Corp.
Melvin Simon and Associates, Inc., **8** 355–57 *see also* Simon Property Group, Inc.
MEMC Electronic Materials, Inc., **81** 249–52
Memorial Sloan-Kettering Cancer Center, **57** 239–41
Memry Corporation, **72** 225–27
The Men's Wearhouse, Inc., **17** 312–15; **48** 283–87 (upd.)
Menasha Corporation, **8** 358–61; **59** 287–92 (upd.)
Mendocino Brewing Company, Inc., **60** 205–07
The Mentholatum Company Inc., **32** 331–33
Mentor Corporation, **26** 286–88
Mentor Graphics Corporation, **11** 284–86
MEPC plc, **IV** 710–12
Mercantile Bankshares Corp., **11** 287–88
Mercantile Stores Company, Inc., **V** 139; **19** 270–73 (upd.) *see also* Dillard's Inc.
Mercer International Inc., **64** 273–75
Mercian Corporation, **77** 261–64
Merck & Co., Inc., **I** 650–52; **11** 289–91 (upd.); **34** 280–85 (upd.); **95** 268–78 (upd.)
Mercury Air Group, Inc., **20** 371–73
Mercury Communications, Ltd., **7** 332–34 *see also* Cable and Wireless plc.
Mercury Drug Corporation, **70** 181–83
Mercury General Corporation, **25** 323–25
Mercury Interactive Corporation, **59** 293–95
Mercury Marine Group, **68** 247–51
Meredith Corporation, **11** 292–94; **29** 316–19 (upd.); **74** 189–93 (upd.)
Merge Healthcare, **85** 264–68
Meridian Bancorp, Inc., **11** 295–97
Meridian Gold, Incorporated, **47** 238–40
Merillat Industries, LLC, **13** 338–39; **69** 253–55 (upd.)
Merisant Worldwide, Inc., **70** 184–86
Merisel, Inc., **12** 334–36
Merit Medical Systems, Inc., **29** 320–22
MeritCare Health System, **88** 257–61
Meritage Corporation, **26** 289–92
Merix Corporation, **36** 329–31; **75** 257–60 (upd.)
Merriam-Webster Inc., **70** 187–91
Merrill Corporation, **18** 331–34; **47** 241–44 (upd.)
Merrill Lynch & Co., Inc., **II** 424–26; **13** 340–43 (upd.); **40** 310–15 (upd.)
Merry-Go-Round Enterprises, Inc., **8** 362–64
The Mersey Docks and Harbour Company, **30** 318–20
Mervyn's California, **10** 409–10; **39** 269–71 (upd.) *see also* Target Corp.
Merz Group, **81** 253–56
Mesa Air Group, Inc., **11** 298–300; **32** 334–37 (upd.); **77** 265–70 (upd.)
Mesaba Holdings, Inc., **28** 265–67
Messerschmitt-Bölkow-Blohm GmbH., **I** 73–75 *see also* European Aeronautic Defence and Space Company EADS N.V.
Mestek, Inc., **10** 411–13
Metal Box plc, **I** 604–06 *see also* Novar plc.
Metal Management, Inc., **92** 247–50
Metaleurop S.A., **21** 368–71
Metalico Inc., **97** 286–89
Metallgesellschaft AG, **IV** 139–42; **16** 361–66 (upd.)
Metalurgica Mexicana Penoles, S.A. *see* Industrias Penoles, S.A. de C.V.
Metatec International, Inc., **47** 245–48
Metcash Trading Ltd., **58** 226–28
Meteor Industries Inc., **33** 295–97
Methanex Corporation, **40** 316–19
Methode Electronics, Inc., **13** 344–46
MetLife *see* Metropolitan Life Insurance Co.
Metris Companies Inc., **56** 224–27
Metro AG, **50** 335–39
Metro-Goldwyn-Mayer Inc., **25** 326–30 (upd.); **84** 263–270 (upd.)
Métro Inc., **77** 271–75
Metro Information Services, Inc., **36** 332–34
Metro International S.A., **93** 309–12
Metrocall, Inc., **41** 265–68
Metromedia Company, **7** 335–37; **14** 298–300 (upd.); **61** 210–14 (upd.)
Métropole Télévision S.A., **76** 272–74 (upd.)
Metropolitan Baseball Club Inc., **39** 272–75
Metropolitan Financial Corporation, **13** 347–49
Metropolitan Life Insurance Company, **III** 290–94; **52** 235–41 (upd.)
The Metropolitan Museum of Art, **55** 267–70
Metropolitan Opera Association, Inc., **40** 320–23
Metropolitan Transportation Authority, **35** 290–92
Metsä-Serla Oy, **IV** 314–16 *see also* M-real Oyj.
Metso Corporation, **30** 321–25 (upd.); **85** 269–77 (upd.)
Mettler-Toledo International Inc., **30** 326–28
Mexican Restaurants, Inc., **41** 269–71

Meyer International Holdings, Ltd., 87 312–315
MFS Communications Company, Inc., 11 301–03 *see also* MCI WorldCom, Inc.
MG&E *see* Madison Gas and Electric.
MGA Entertainment, Inc., 95 279–82
MGIC Investment Corp., 52 242–44
MGM Grand Inc., 17 316–19
MGM/UA Communications Company, II 146–50 *see also* Metro-Goldwyn-Mayer Inc.
MGN *see* Mirror Group Newspapers Ltd.
Miami Herald Media Company, 92 251–55
Michael Anthony Jewelers, Inc., 24 334–36
Michael Baker Corporation, 14 333–35; 51 245–48 (upd.)
Michael C. Fina Co., Inc., 52 245–47
Michael Foods, Inc., 25 331–34
Michael Page International plc, 45 272–74
Michaels Stores, Inc., 17 320–22; 71 226–30 (upd.)
Michelin *see* Compagnie Générale des Établissements Michelin.
Michigan Bell Telephone Co., 14 336–38
Michigan National Corporation, 11 304–06 *see also* ABN AMRO Holding, N.V.
Michigan Sporting Goods Distributors, Inc., 72 228–30
Micrel, Incorporated, 77 276–79
Micro Warehouse, Inc., 16 371–73
MicroAge, Inc., 16 367–70
Microdot Inc., 8 365–68
Micron Technology, Inc., 11 307–09; 29 323–26 (upd.)
Micros Systems, Inc., 18 335–38
Microsemi Corporation, 94 311–14
Microsoft Corporation, 6 257–60; 27 319–23 (upd.); 63 293–97 (upd.)
MicroStrategy Incorporated, 87 316–320
Mid-America Apartment Communities, Inc., 85 278–81
Mid-America Dairymen, Inc., 7 338–40
Midas Inc., 10 414–15; 56 228–31 (upd.)
Middle East Airlines - Air Liban S.A.L., 79 251–54
The Middleby Corporation, 22 352–55
Middlesex Water Company, 45 275–78
The Middleton Doll Company, 53 222–25
Midland Bank plc, II 318–20; 17 323–26 (upd.) *see also* HSBC Holdings plc.
The Midland Company, 65 233–35
Midway Airlines Corporation, 33 301–03
Midway Games, Inc., 25 335–38
Midwest Air Group, Inc., 35 293–95; 85 282–86 (upd.)
Midwest Grain Products, Inc., 49 261–63
Midwest Resources Inc., 6 523–25
Miele & Cie. KG, 56 232–35
MiG *see* Russian Aircraft Corporation (MiG).
Migros-Genossenschafts-Bund, 68 252–55
MIH Limited, 31 329–32
Mikasa, Inc., 28 268–70
Mike-Sell's Inc., 15 298–300
Mikohn Gaming Corporation, 39 276–79
Milacron, Inc., 53 226–30 (upd.)
Milan AC S.p.A., 79 255–58
Milbank, Tweed, Hadley & McCloy, 27 324–27
Miles Laboratories, I 653–55 *see also* Bayer A.G.
Millea Holdings Inc., 64 276–81 (upd.)
Millennium & Copthorne Hotels plc, 71 231–33
Millennium Pharmaceuticals, Inc., 47 249–52
Miller Brewing Company, I 269–70; 12 337–39 (upd.) *see also* SABMiller plc.
Miller Industries, Inc., 26 293–95
Miller Publishing Group, LLC, 57 242–44
Milliken & Co., V 366–68; 17 327–30 (upd.); 82 235–39 (upd.)
Milliman USA, 66 223–26
Millipore Corporation, 25 339–43; 84 271–276 (upd.)
The Mills Corporation, 77 280–83
Milnot Company, 46 289–91
Milton Bradley Company, 21 372–75
Milton CAT, Inc., 86 268–71
Milwaukee Brewers Baseball Club, 37 247–49
Mine Safety Appliances Company, 31 333–35
Minebea Co., Ltd., 90 298–302
The Miner Group International, 22 356–58
Minerals & Metals Trading Corporation of India Ltd., IV 143–44
Minerals Technologies Inc., 11 310–12; 52 248–51 (upd.)
Minnesota Mining & Manufacturing Company, I 499–501; 8 369–71 (upd.); 26 296–99 (upd.) *see also* 3M Co.
Minnesota Power, Inc., 11 313–16; 34 286–91 (upd.)
Minntech Corporation, 22 359–61
Minolta Co., Ltd., III 574–76; 18 339–42 (upd.); 43 281–85 (upd.)
The Minute Maid Company, 28 271–74
Minuteman International Inc., 46 292–95
Minyard Food Stores, Inc., 33 304–07; 86 272–77 (upd.)
Miquel y Costas Miquel S.A., 68 256–58
Mirage Resorts, Incorporated, 6 209–12; 28 275–79 (upd.)
Miramax Film Corporation, 64 282–85
Miroglio SpA, 86 278–81
Mirror Group Newspapers plc, 7 341–43; 23 348–51 (upd.)
Misonix, Inc., 80 248–51
Mississippi Chemical Corporation, 39 280–83
Misys PLC, 45 279–81; 46 296–99
Mitchell Energy and Development Corporation, 7 344–46 *see also* Devon Energy Corp.
Mitchells & Butlers PLC, 59 296–99
Mitel Corporation, 18 343–46
MITRE Corporation, 26 300–02
MITROPA AG, 37 250–53
Mitsubishi Bank, Ltd., II 321–22 *see also* Bank of Tokyo-Mitsubishi Ltd.
Mitsubishi Chemical Corporation, I 363–64; 56 236–38 (upd.)
Mitsubishi Corporation, I 502–04; 12 340–43 (upd.)
Mitsubishi Electric Corporation, II 57–59; 44 283–87 (upd.)
Mitsubishi Estate Company, Limited, IV 713–14; 61 215–18 (upd.)
Mitsubishi Heavy Industries, Ltd., III 577–79; 7 347–50 (upd.); 40 324–28 (upd.)
Mitsubishi Materials Corporation, III 712–13
Mitsubishi Motors Corporation, 9 349–51; 23 352–55 (upd.); 57 245–49 (upd.)
Mitsubishi Oil Co., Ltd., IV 460–62 *see also* Nippon Mitsubishi Oil Corp.
Mitsubishi Rayon Co. Ltd., V 369–71
Mitsubishi Trust & Banking Corporation, II 323–24
Mitsui & Co., Ltd., I 505–08; 28 280–85 (upd.)
Mitsui Bank, Ltd., II 325–27 *see also* Sumitomo Mitsui Banking Corp.
Mitsui Marine and Fire Insurance Company, Limited, III 295–96
Mitsui Mining & Smelting Co., Ltd., IV 145–46
Mitsui Mining Company, Limited, IV 147–49
Mitsui Mutual Life Insurance Company, III 297–98; 39 284–86 (upd.)
Mitsui O.S.K. Lines Ltd., V 473–76; 96 282–87 (upd.)
Mitsui Petrochemical Industries, Ltd., 9 352–54
Mitsui Real Estate Development Co., Ltd., IV 715–16
Mitsui Trust & Banking Company, Ltd., II 328
Mitsukoshi Ltd., V 142–44; 56 239–42 (upd.)
Mity Enterprises, Inc., 38 310–12
MIVA, Inc., 83 271-275
Mizuho Financial Group Inc., 25 344–46; 58 229–36 (upd.)
MNS, Ltd., 65 236–38
Mo och Domsjö AB, IV 317–19 *see also* Holmen AB
Mobil Corporation, IV 463–65; 7 351–54 (upd.); 21 376–80 (upd.) *see also* Exxon Mobil Corp.

Mobile Mini, Inc., 58 237–39
Mobile Telecommunications Technologies Corp., 18 347–49
Mobile TeleSystems OJSC, 59 300–03
Mocon, Inc., 76 275–77
Modell's Sporting Goods *see* Henry Modell & Company Inc.
Modern Times Group AB, 36 335–38
Modern Woodmen of America, 66 227–29
Modine Manufacturing Company, 8 372–75; 56 243–47 (upd.)
MoDo *see* Mo och Domsjö AB.
Modtech Holdings, Inc., 77 284–87
Moen Incorporated, 12 344–45
Moët-Hennessy, I 271–72 *see also* LVMH Moët Hennessy Louis Vuitton SA.
Mohawk Industries, Inc., 19 274–76; 63 298–301 (upd.)
Mohegan Tribal Gaming Authority, 37 254–57
Moksel *see* A. Moksel AG.
MOL *see* Mitsui O.S.K. Lines, Ltd.
MOL Rt, 70 192–95
Moldflow Corporation, 73 227–30
Molex Incorporated, 11 317–19; 14 27; 54 236–41 (upd.)
Moliflor Loisirs, 80 252–55
Molinos Río de la Plata S.A., 61 219–21
Molins plc, 51 249–51
The Molson Companies Limited, I 273–75; 26 303–07 (upd.)
Molson Coors Brewing Company, 77 288–300 (upd.)
Monaco Coach Corporation, 31 336–38
Monadnock Paper Mills, Inc., 21 381–84
Monarch Casino & Resort, Inc., 65 239–41
The Monarch Cement Company, 72 231–33
Mondadori *see* Arnoldo Mondadori Editore S.p.A.
MoneyGram International, Inc., 94 315–18
Monfort, Inc., 13 350–52
Monnaie de Paris, 62 246–48
Monnoyeur Group *see* Groupe Monnoyeur.
Monoprix S.A., 86 282–85
Monro Muffler Brake, Inc., 24 337–40
Monrovia Nursery Company, 70 196–98
Monsanto Company, I 365–67; 9 355–57 (upd.); 29 327–31 (upd.); 77 301–07 (upd.)
Monsoon plc, 39 287–89
Monster Cable Products, Inc., 69 256–58
Monster Worldwide Inc., 74 194–97 (upd.)
Montana Coffee Traders, Inc., 60 208–10
The Montana Power Company, 11 320–22; 44 288–92 (upd.)
Montblanc International GmbH, 82 240–44
Montedison S.p.A., I 368–69; 24 341–44 (upd.)
Monterey Pasta Company, 58 240–43
Montgomery Ward & Co., Incorporated, V 145–48; 20 374–79 (upd.)
Montres Rolex S.A., 13 353–55; 34 292–95 (upd.)
Montupet S.A., 63 302–04
Moody's Corporation, 65 242–44
Moog Inc., 13 356–58
Moog Music, Inc., 75 261–64
Mooney Aerospace Group Ltd., 52 252–55
Moore Corporation Limited, IV 644–46 *see also* R.R. Donnelley & Sons Co.
Moore-Handley, Inc., 39 290–92
Moore Medical Corp., 17 331–33
Moran Towing Corporation, Inc., 15 301–03
The Morgan Crucible Company plc, 82 245–50
Morgan Grenfell Group PLC, II 427–29 *see also* Deutsche Bank AG.
The Morgan Group, Inc., 46 300–02
Morgan, Lewis & Bockius LLP, 29 332–34
Morgan Stanley Dean Witter & Company, II 430–32; 16 374–78 (upd.); 33 311–14 (upd.)
Morgans Hotel Group Company, 80 256–59
Morguard Corporation, 85 287–90
Morinaga & Co. Ltd., 61 222–25
Morinda Holdings, Inc., 82 251–54
Morningstar Inc., 68 259–62
Morris Communications Corporation, 36 339–42
Morris Travel Services L.L.C., 26 308–11
Morrison & Foerster LLP, 78 220–23
Morrison Knudsen Corporation, 7 355–58; 28 286–90 (upd.) *see also* The Washington Companies.
Morrison Restaurants Inc., 11 323–25
Morrow Equipment Co. L.L.C., 87 325–327
Morse Shoe Inc., 13 359–61
Morton International, Inc., 9 358–59 (upd.); 80 260–64 (upd.)
Morton Thiokol Inc., I 370–72 *see also* Thiokol Corp.
Morton's Restaurant Group, Inc., 30 329–31; 88 262–66 (upd.)
The Mosaic Company, 91 330–33
Mosinee Paper Corporation, 15 304–06 *see also* Wausau-Mosinee Paper Corp.
Moss Bros Group plc, 51 252–54
Mossimo, 27 328–30; 96 288–92 (upd.)
Mota-Engil, SGPS, S.A., 97 290–93
Motel 6, 13 362–64; 56 248–51 (upd.) *see also* Accor SA
Mothercare plc, 17 334–36; 78 224–27 (upd.)
Mothers Against Drunk Driving (MADD), 51 255–58
Mothers Work, Inc., 18 350–52
The Motley Fool, Inc., 40 329–31
Moto Photo, Inc., 45 282–84
Motor Cargo Industries, Inc., 35 296–99
Motorcar Parts & Accessories, Inc., 47 253–55
Motorola, Inc., II 60–62; 11 326–29 (upd.); 34 296–302 (upd.); 93 313–23 (upd.)
Motown Records Company L.P., 26 312–14
Mott's Inc., 57 250–53
Moulinex S.A., 22 362–65 *see also* Groupe SEB.
Mount *see also* Mt.
Mount Washington Hotel *see* MWH Preservation Limited Partnership.
Mountain States Mortgage Centers, Inc., 29 335–37
Mouvement des Caisses Desjardins, 48 288–91
Movado Group, Inc., 28 291–94
Movie Gallery, Inc., 31 339–41
Movie Star Inc., 17 337–39
Moy Park Ltd., 78 228–31
MPI *see* Michael Page International plc.
MPRG *see* Matt Prentice Restaurant Group.
MPS Group, Inc., 49 264–67
MPW Industrial Services Group, Inc., 53 231–33
Mr. Bricolage S.A., 37 258–60
Mr. Coffee, Inc., 15 307–09
Mr. Gasket Inc., 15 310–12
Mr. Gatti's, LP, 87 321–324
Mrs. Baird's Bakeries, 29 338–41
Mrs. Fields' Original Cookies, Inc., 27 331–35
Mrs. Grossman's Paper Company Inc., 84 277–280
MS&L *see* Manning Selvage & Lee.
MSC *see* Material Sciences Corp.
MSC Industrial Direct Co., Inc., 71 234–36
M6 *see* Métropole Télévision S.A..
Mt. *see also* Mount.
Mt. Olive Pickle Company, Inc., 44 293–95
MTA *see* Metropolitan Transportation Authority.
MTC *see* Management and Training Corp.
MTel *see* Mobile Telecommunications Technologies Corp.
MTG *see* Modern Times Group AB.
MTR Foods Ltd., 55 271–73
MTR Gaming Group, Inc., 75 265–67
MTS *see* Mobile TeleSystems.
MTS Inc., 37 261–64
Mueller Industries, Inc., 7 359–61; 52 256–60 (upd.)
Mulberry Group PLC, 71 237–39
Mullen Advertising Inc., 51 259–61
Multi-Color Corporation, 53 234–36
Multimedia Games, Inc., 41 272–76
Multimedia, Inc., 11 330–32
Munich Re (Münchener Rückversicherungs-Gesellschaft Aktiengesellschaft in München), III 299–301; 46 303–07 (upd.)

Murdock Madaus Schwabe, 26 315–19
Murphy Family Farms Inc., 22 366–68 *see also* Smithfield Foods, Inc.
Murphy Oil Corporation, 7 362–64; 32 338–41 (upd.); 95 283–89 (upd.)
Murphy's Pizza *see* Papa Murphy's International, Inc.
The Musco Family Olive Co., 91 334–37
Musco Lighting, 83 276-279
Musgrave Group Plc, 57 254–57
Music Corporation of America *see* MCA Inc.
Musicland Stores Corporation, 9 360–62; 38 313–17 (upd.)
Mutual Benefit Life Insurance Company, III 302–04
Mutual Life Insurance Company of New York, III 305–07
Muzak, Inc., 18 353–56
MWA *see* Modern Woodmen of America.
MWH Preservation Limited Partnership, 65 245–48
MWI Veterinary Supply, Inc., 80 265–68
Mycogen Corporation, 21 385–87 *see also* Dow Chemical Co.
Myers Industries, Inc., 19 277–79; 96 293–97 (upd.)
Mylan Laboratories Inc., I 656–57; 20 380–82 (upd.); 59 304–08 (upd.)
MYOB Ltd., 86 286–90
Myriad Genetics, Inc., 95 290–95
Myriad Restaurant Group, Inc., 87 328-331
MySpace.com *see* Intermix Media, Inc.

N

N.F. Smith & Associates LP, 70 199–202
N M Rothschild & Sons Limited, 39 293–95
N.V. *see under first word of company name*
Naamloze Vennootschap tot Exploitatie van het Café Krasnapolsky *see* Grand Hotel Krasnapolsky N.V.
Nabisco Brands, Inc., II 542–44 *see also* RJR Nabisco.
Nabisco Foods Group, 7 365–68 (upd.) *see also* Kraft Foods Inc.
Nabors Industries Ltd., 9 363–65; 91 338–44 (upd.)
NACCO Industries, Inc., 7 369–71; 78 232–36 (upd.)
Nadro S.A. de C.V., 86 291–94
Naf Naf SA, 44 296–98
Nagasakiya Co., Ltd., V 149–51; 69 259–62 (upd.)
Nagase & Co., Ltd., 8 376–78; 61 226–30 (upd.)
NAI *see* Natural Alternatives International, Inc.; Network Associates, Inc.
Nalco Holding Company, I 373–75; 12 346–48 (upd.); 89 324–30 (upd.)
Nam Tai Electronics, Inc., 61 231–34
Nantucket Allserve, Inc., 22 369–71
Napster, Inc., 69 263–66
NAS *see* National Audubon Society.
NASCAR *see* National Association for Stock Car Auto Racing.
NASD, 54 242–46 (upd.)
The NASDAQ Stock Market, Inc., 92 256–60
Nash Finch Company, 8 379–81; 23 356–58 (upd.); 65 249–53 (upd.)
Nashua Corporation, 8 382–84
Naspers Ltd., 66 230–32
Nastech Pharmaceutical Company Inc., 79 259–62
Nathan's Famous, Inc., 29 342–44
National Amusements Inc., 28 295–97
National Aquarium in Baltimore, Inc., 74 198–200
National Association for Stock Car Auto Racing, 32 342–44
National Association of Securities Dealers, Inc., 10 416–18 *see also* NASD.
National Audubon Society, 26 320–23
National Auto Credit, Inc., 16 379–81
National Bank of Canada, 85 291–94
National Bank of Greece, 41 277–79
The National Bank of South Carolina, 76 278–80
National Beverage Corporation, 26 324–26; 88 267–71 (upd.)
National Broadcasting Company, Inc., II 151–53; 6 164–66 (upd.); 28 298–301 (upd.) *see also* General Electric Co.
National Can Corp., I 607–08
National Car Rental System, Inc., 10 419–20 *see also* Republic Industries, Inc.
National City Corporation, 15 313–16; 97 294–302 (upd.)
National Collegiate Athletic Association, 96 298–302
National Convenience Stores Incorporated, 7 372–75
National Discount Brokers Group, Inc., 28 302–04 *see also* Deutsche Bank A.G.
National Distillers and Chemical Corporation, I 376–78 *see also* Quantum Chemical Corp.
National Educational Music Co. Ltd., 47 256–58
National Enquirer see American Media, Inc.
National Envelope Corporation, 32 345–47
National Equipment Services, Inc., 57 258–60
National Express Group PLC, 50 340–42
National Financial Partners Corp., 65 254–56
National Football League, 29 345–47 *see also* NFL.
National Frozen Foods Corporation, 94 319–22
National Fuel Gas Company, 6 526–28; 95 296–300 (upd.)
National Geographic Society, 9 366–68; 30 332–35 (upd.); 79 263–69 (upd.)
National Grape Co-operative Association, Inc., 20 383–85
National Grid USA, 51 262–66 (upd.)
National Gypsum Company, 10 421–24
National Health Laboratories Incorporated, 11 333–35 *see also* Laboratory Corporation of America Holdings.
National Heritage Academies, Inc., 60 211–13
National Hockey League, 35 300–03
National Home Centers, Inc., 44 299–301
National Instruments Corporation, 22 372–74
National Intergroup, Inc., V 152–53 *see also* FoxMeyer Health Corp.
National Iranian Oil Company, IV 466–68; 61 235–38 (upd.)
National Journal Group Inc., 67 256–58
National Media Corporation, 27 336–40
National Medical Enterprises, Inc., III 87–88 *see also* Tenet Healthcare Corp.
National Medical Health Card Systems, Inc., 79 270–73
National Oil Corporation, 66 233–37 (upd.)
National Oilwell, Inc., 54 247–50
National Organization for Women, Inc., 55 274–76
National Patent Development Corporation, 13 365–68 *see also* GP Strategies Corp.
National Picture & Frame Company, 24 345–47
National Power PLC, 12 349–51 *see also* International Power PLC.
National Presto Industries, Inc., 16 382–85; 43 286–90 (upd.)
National Public Radio, 19 280–82; 47 259–62 (upd.)
National R.V. Holdings, Inc., 32 348–51
National Railroad Passenger Corporation (Amtrak), 22 375–78; 66 238–42 (upd.)
National Record Mart, Inc., 29 348–50
National Research Corporation, 87 332-335
National Rifle Association of America, 37 265–68
National Sanitary Supply Co., 16 386–87
National Sea Products Ltd., 14 339–41
National Semiconductor Corporation, II 63–65; 6 261–63; 26 327–30 (upd.); 69 267–71 (upd.)
National Service Industries, Inc., 11 336–38; 54 251–55 (upd.)
National Standard Co., 13 369–71
National Starch and Chemical Company, 49 268–70
National Steel Corporation, 12 352–54 *see also* FoxMeyer Health Corp.
National TechTeam, Inc., 41 280–83
National Thoroughbred Racing Association, 58 244–47

National Transcommunications Ltd. *see* NTL Inc.
National Weather Service, 91 345–49
National Westminster Bank PLC, II 333–35
National Wine & Spirits, Inc., 49 271–74
Nationale-Nederlanden N.V., III 308–11
Nationale Portefeuille Maatschappij (NPM) *see* Compagnie Nationale à Portefeuille.
NationsBank Corporation, 10 425–27 *see also* Bank of America Corporation
Natrol, Inc., 49 275–78
Natura Cosméticos S.A., 75 268–71
Natural Alternatives International, Inc., 49 279–82
Natural Gas Clearinghouse *see* NGC Corp.
Natural Ovens Bakery, Inc., 72 234–36
Natural Selection Foods, 54 256–58
Natural Wonders Inc., 14 342–44
Naturally Fresh, Inc., 88 272–75
The Nature Conservancy, 28 305–07
Nature's Path Foods, Inc., 87 336–340
Nature's Sunshine Products, Inc., 15 317–19
Natuzzi Group *see* Industrie Natuzzi S.p.A.
NatWest Bank *see* National Westminster Bank PLC.
Naumes, Inc., 81 257–60
Nautica Enterprises, Inc., 18 357–60; 44 302–06 (upd.)
Navarre Corporation, 24 348–51
Navigant International, Inc., 47 263–66; 93 324–27 (upd.)
The Navigators Group, Inc., 92 261–64
Navistar International Corporation, I 180–82; 10 428–30 (upd.) *see also* International Harvester Co.
NAVTEQ Corporation, 69 272–75
Navy Exchange Service Command, 31 342–45
Navy Federal Credit Union, 33 315–17
NBC *see* National Broadcasting Company, Inc.
NBD Bancorp, Inc., 11 339–41 *see also* Bank One Corp.
NBGS International, Inc., 73 231–33
NBSC Corporation *see* National Bank of South Carolina.
NBTY, Inc., 31 346–48
NCAA *see* National Collegiate Athletic Assn.
NCH Corporation, 8 385–87
NCI Building Systems, Inc., 88 276–79
NCL Corporation, 79 274–77
NCNB Corporation, II 336–37 *see also* Bank of America Corp.
NCO Group, Inc., 42 258–60
NCR Corporation, III 150–53; 6 264–68 (upd.); 30 336–41 (upd.); 90 303–12 (upd.)
NDB *see* National Discount Brokers Group, Inc.
Nebraska Book Company, Inc., 65 257–59
Nebraska Furniture Mart, Inc., 94 323–26
Nebraska Public Power District, 29 351–54
NEBS *see* New England Business Services, Inc.
NEC Corporation, II 66–68; 21 388–91 (upd.); 57 261–67 (upd.)
N.V. Nederlandse Gasunie, V 658–61
Nedlloyd Group *see* Koninklijke Nedlloyd N.V.
Neenah Foundry Company, 68 263–66
Neff Corp., 32 352–53
NeighborCare, Inc., 67 259–63 (upd.)
The Neiman Marcus Group, Inc., 12 355–57; 49 283–87 (upd.)
Nektar Therapeutics, 91 350–53
Nelsons *see* A. Nelson & Co. Ltd.
Neogen Corporation, 94 327–30
Neopost S.A., 53 237–40
Neptune Orient Lines Limited, 47 267–70
NERCO, Inc., 7 376–79 *see also* Rio Tinto PLC.
NES *see* National Equipment Services, Inc.
Neste Oil Corporation, IV 469–71; 85 295–302 (upd.)
Nestlé S.A., II 545–49; 7 380–84 (upd.); 28 308–13 (upd.); 71 240–46 (upd.)
Nestlé Waters, 73 234–37
NetCom Systems AB, 26 331–33
Netezza Corporation, 69 276–78
Netflix, Inc., 58 248–51
NETGEAR, Inc., 81 261–64
NetIQ Corporation, 79 278–81
NetJets Inc., 96 303–07 (upd.)
Netscape Communications Corporation, 15 320–22; 35 304–07 (upd.)
Network Appliance, Inc., 58 252–54
Network Associates, Inc., 25 347–49
Network Equipment Technologies Inc., 92 265–68
Neuberger Berman Inc., 57 268–71
NeuStar, Inc., 81 265–68
Neutrogena Corporation, 17 340–44
Nevada Bell Telephone Company, 14 345–47 *see also* AT&T Corp.
Nevada Power Company, 11 342–44
Nevamar Company, 82 255–58
New Balance Athletic Shoe, Inc., 25 350–52; 68 267–70 (upd.)
New Belgium Brewing Company, Inc., 68 271–74
New Brunswick Scientific Co., Inc., 45 285–87
New Chapter Inc., 96 308–11
New Clicks Holdings Ltd., 86 295–98
New Dana Perfumes Company, 37 269–71
New England Business Service, Inc., 18 361–64; 78 237–42 (upd.)
New England Confectionery Co., 15 323–25
New England Electric System, V 662–64 *see also* National Grid USA.
New England Mutual Life Insurance Co., III 312–14 *see also* Metropolitan Life Insurance Co.
New Flyer Industries Inc., 78 243–46
New Holland N.V., 22 379–81 *see also* CNH Global N.V.
New Jersey Devils, 84 281–285
New Jersey Manufacturers Insurance Company, 96 312–16
New Jersey Resources Corporation, 54 259–61
New Line Cinema, Inc., 47 271–74
New Look Group plc, 35 308–10
New Orleans Saints LP, 58 255–57
The New Piper Aircraft, Inc., 44 307–10
New Plan Realty Trust, 11 345–47
New Seasons Market, 75 272–74
New Street Capital Inc., 8 388–90 (upd.) *see also* Drexel Burnham Lambert Inc.
New Times, Inc., 45 288–90
New Valley Corporation, 17 345–47
New World Development Company Limited, IV 717–19; 38 318–22 (upd.)
New World Pasta Company, 53 241–44
New World Restaurant Group, Inc., 44 311–14
New York City Health and Hospitals Corporation, 60 214–17
New York City Off-Track Betting Corporation, 51 267–70
New York Community Bancorp, Inc., 78 247–50
New York Daily News, 32 357–60
New York Eye and Ear Infirmary *see* Continuum Health Partners, Inc.
New York Health Care, Inc., 72 237–39
New York Life Insurance Company, III 315–17; 45 291–95 (upd.)
New York Philharmonic *see* Philharmonic-Symphony Society of New York, Inc.
New York Presbyterian Hospital *see* NewYork-Presbyterian Hospital.
New York Restaurant Group, Inc., 32 361–63
New York Shakespeare Festival Management, 92328–32
New York State Electric and Gas Corporation, 6 534–36
New York Stock Exchange, Inc., 9 369–72; 39 296–300 (upd.)
The New York Times Company, IV 647–49; 19 283–85 (upd.); 61 239–43 (upd.)
Neways, Inc., 78 251–54
Newcor, Inc., 40 332–35
Newell Rubbermaid Inc., 9 373–76; 52 261–71 (upd.)
Newfield Exploration Company, 65 260–62
Newhall Land and Farming Company, 14 348–50
Newly Weds Foods, Inc., 74 201–03
Newman's Own, Inc., 37 272–75

Newmont Mining Corporation, **7** 385–88; **94** 331–37 (upd.)
Newpark Resources, Inc., **63** 305–07
Newport Corporation, **71** 247–49
Newport News Shipbuilding Inc., **13** 372–75; **38** 323–27 (upd.)
News America Publishing Inc., **12** 358–60
News Corporation Limited, **IV** 650–53; **7** 389–93 (upd.); **46** 308–13 (upd.)
Newsquest plc, **32** 354–56
NewYork-Presbyterian Hospital, **59** 309–12
Nexans SA, **54** 262–64
NEXCOM *see* Navy Exchange Service Command.
Nexen Inc., **79** 282–85
Nexity S.A., **66** 243–45
Nexstar Broadcasting Group, Inc., **73** 238–41
Next Media Ltd., **61** 244–47
Next plc, **29** 355–57
Nextel Communications, Inc., **10** 431–33; **27** 341–45 (upd.)
Neyveli Lignite Corporation Ltd., **65** 263–65
NFC plc, **6** 412–14 *see also* Exel plc.
NFL *see* National Football League Inc.
NFL Films, **75** 275–78
NFO Worldwide, Inc., **24** 352–55
NGC Corporation, **18** 365–67 *see also* Dynegy Inc.
NGK Insulators Ltd., **67** 264–66
NH Hoteles S.A., **79** 286–89
NHK Spring Co., Ltd., **III** 580–82
Niagara Corporation, **28** 314–16
Niagara Mohawk Holdings Inc., **V** 665–67; **45** 296–99 (upd.)
NICE Systems Ltd., **83** 280-283
Nichii Co., Ltd., **V** 154–55
Nichimen Corporation, **IV** 150–52; **24** 356–59 (upd.) *see also* Sojitz Corp.
Nichirei Corporation, **70** 203–05
Nichiro Corporation, **86** 299–302
Nichols plc, **44** 315–18
Nichols Research Corporation, **18** 368–70
Nicklaus Companies, **45** 300–03
Nicor Inc., **6** 529–31; **86** 303–07 (upd.)
Nidec Corporation, **59** 313–16
Nielsen Marketing Research *see* AC Nielsen Co.
Nigerian National Petroleum Corporation, **IV** 472–74; **72** 240–43 (upd.)
Nihon Keizai Shimbun, Inc., **IV** 654–56
NII *see* National Intergroup, Inc.
NIKE, Inc., **V** 372–74; **8** 391–94 (upd.); **36** 343–48 (upd.); **75** 279–85 (upd.)
Nikken Global Inc., **32** 364–67
The Nikko Securities Company Limited, **II** 433–35; **9** 377–79 (upd.)
Nikon Corporation, **III** 583–85; **48** 292–95 (upd.)
Niman Ranch, Inc., **67** 267–69
Nimbus CD International, Inc., **20** 386–90
Nine West Group Inc., **11** 348–49; **39** 301–03 (upd.)
99¢ Only Stores, **25** 353–55
Nintendo Co., Ltd., **III** 586–88; **7** 394–96 (upd.); **28** 317–21 (upd.); **67** 270–76 (upd.)
NIOC *see* National Iranian Oil Co.
Nippon Credit Bank, **II** 338–39
Nippon Electric Glass Co. Ltd., **95** 301–05
Nippon Express Company, Ltd., **V** 477–80; **64** 286–90 (upd.)
Nippon Life Insurance Company, **III** 318–20; **60** 218–21 (upd.)
Nippon Light Metal Company, Ltd., **IV** 153–55
Nippon Meat Packers, Inc., **II** 550–51; **78** 255–57 (upd.)
Nippon Mining Co., Ltd., **IV** 475–77
Nippon Oil Corporation, **IV** 478–79; **63** 308–13 (upd.)
Nippon Seiko K.K., **III** 589–90
Nippon Sheet Glass Company, Limited, **III** 714–16
Nippon Shinpan Co., Ltd., **II** 436–37; **61** 248–50 (upd.)
Nippon Soda Co., Ltd., **85** 303–06
Nippon Steel Corporation, **IV** 156–58; **17** 348–51 (upd.); **96** 317–23 (upd.)
Nippon Suisan Kaisha, Limited, **II** 552–53; **92** 269–72 (upd.)
Nippon Telegraph and Telephone Corporation, **V** 305–07; **51** 271–75 (upd.)
Nippon Yusen Kabushiki Kaisha (NYK), **V** 481–83; **72** 244–48 (upd.)
Nippondenso Co., Ltd., **III** 591–94 *see also* DENSO Corp.
NIPSCO Industries, Inc., **6** 532–33
Nissan Motor Company Ltd., **I** 183–84; **11** 350–52 (upd.); **34** 303–07 (upd.); **92** 273–79 (upd.)
Nisshin Seifun Group Inc., **II** 554; **66** 246–48 (upd.)
Nisshin Steel Co., Ltd., **IV** 159–60
Nissho Iwai K.K., **I** 509–11
Nissin Food Products Company Ltd., **75** 286–88
Nitches, Inc., **53** 245–47
Nixdorf Computer AG, **III** 154–55 *see also* Wincor Nixdorf Holding GmbH.
NKK Corporation, **IV** 161–63; **28** 322–26 (upd.)
NL Industries, Inc., **10** 434–36
Noah Education Holdings Ltd., **97** 303–06
Noah's New York Bagels *see* Einstein/Noah Bagel Corp.
Nobel Industries AB, **9** 380–82 *see also* Akzo Nobel N.V.
Nobel Learning Communities, Inc., **37** 276–79; **76** 281–85 (upd.)
Noble Affiliates, Inc., **11** 353–55
Noble Roman's Inc., **14** 351–53
Nobleza Piccardo SAICF, **64** 291–93
Noboa *see also* Exportadora Bananera Noboa, S.A.
Nocibé SA, **54** 265–68
NOF Corporation, **72** 249–51
Nokia Corporation, **II** 69–71; **17** 352–54 (upd.); **38** 328–31 (upd.); **77** 308–13 (upd.)
NOL Group *see* Neptune Orient Lines Ltd.
Noland Company, **35** 311–14
Nolo.com, Inc., **49** 288–91
Nomura Securities Company, Limited, **II** 438–41; **9** 383–86 (upd.)
Noodle Kidoodle, **16** 388–91
Noodles & Company, Inc., **55** 277–79
Nooter Corporation, **61** 251–53
Noranda Inc., **IV** 164–66; **7** 397–99 (upd.); **64** 294–98 (upd.)
Norcal Waste Systems, Inc., **60** 222–24
Norddeutsche Affinerie AG, **62** 249–53
Nordea AB, **40** 336–39
NordicTrack, **22** 382–84 *see also* Icon Health & Fitness, Inc.
Nordisk Film A/S, **80** 269–73
Nordson Corporation, **11** 356–58; **48** 296–99 (upd.)
Nordstrom, Inc., **V** 156–58; **18** 371–74 (upd.); **67** 277–81 (upd.)
Norelco Consumer Products Co., **26** 334–36
Norfolk Southern Corporation, **V** 484–86; **29** 358–61 (upd.); **75** 289–93 (upd.)
Norinchukin Bank, **II** 340–41
Norm Thompson Outfitters, Inc., **47** 275–77
Norrell Corporation, **25** 356–59
Norsk Hydro ASA, **10** 437–40; **35** 315–19 (upd.)
Norske Skogindustrier ASA, **63** 314–16
Norstan, Inc., **16** 392–94
Nortek, Inc., **34** 308–12
Nortel Networks Corporation, **36** 349–54 (upd.)
North Atlantic Trading Company Inc., **65** 266–68
North Carolina National Bank Corporation *see* NCNB Corp.
The North Face, Inc., **18** 375–77; **78** 258–61 (upd.)
North Fork Bancorporation, Inc., **46** 314–17
North Pacific Group, Inc., **61** 254–57
North Star Steel Company, **18** 378–81
The North West Company, Inc., **12** 361–63
North West Water Group plc, **11** 359–62 *see also* United Utilities PLC.
Northeast Utilities, **V** 668–69; **48** 303–06 (upd.)
Northern and Shell Network plc, **87** 341–344
Northern Foods plc, **10** 441–43; **61** 258–62 (upd.)
Northern Rock plc, **33** 318–21
Northern States Power Company, **V** 670–72; **20** 391–95 (upd.) *see also* Xcel Energy Inc.
Northern Telecom Limited, **V** 308–10 *see also* Nortel Networks Corp.
Northern Trust Company, **9** 387–89

Northland Cranberries, Inc., 38 332–34
Northrop Grumman Corporation, I 76–77; 11 363–65 (upd.); 45 304–12 (upd.)
Northwest Airlines Corporation, I 112–14; 6 103–05 (upd.); 26 337–40 (upd.); 74 204–08 (upd.)
Northwest Natural Gas Company, 45 313–15
NorthWestern Corporation, 37 280–83
Northwestern Mutual Life Insurance Company, III 321–24; 45 316–21 (upd.)
Norton Company, 8 395–97
Norton McNaughton, Inc., 27 346–49 *see also* Jones Apparel Group, Inc.
Norwegian Cruise Lines *see* NCL Corporation
Norwich & Peterborough Building Society, 55 280–82
Norwood Promotional Products, Inc., 26 341–43
Nova Corporation of Alberta, V 673–75
NovaCare, Inc., 11 366–68
Novacor Chemicals Ltd., 12 364–66
Novar plc, 49 292–96 (upd.)
Novartis AG, 39 304–10 (upd.)
NovaStar Financial, Inc., 91 354–58
Novell, Inc., 6 269–71; 23 359–62 (upd.)
Novellus Systems, Inc., 18 382–85
Noven Pharmaceuticals, Inc., 55 283–85
Novo Nordisk A/S, I 658–60; 61 263–66 (upd.)
NOW *see* National Organization for Women, Inc.
NPC International, Inc., 40 340–42
The NPD Group, Inc., 68 275–77
NPM (Nationale Portefeuille Maatschappij) *see* Compagnie Nationale à Portefeuille.
NPR *see* National Public Radio, Inc.
NRG Energy, Inc., 79 290–93
NRT Incorporated, 61 267–69
NS *see* Norfolk Southern Corp.
NSF International, 72 252–55
NSK *see* Nippon Seiko K.K.
NSP *see* Northern States Power Co.
NSS Enterprises, Inc., 78 262–65
NTCL *see* Northern Telecom Ltd.
NTL Inc., 65 269–72
NTN Buzztime, Inc., 86 308–11
NTN Corporation, III 595–96; 47 278–81 (upd.)
NTTPC *see* Nippon Telegraph and Telephone Public Corp.
NU *see* Northeast Utilities.
Nu-kote Holding, Inc., 18 386–89
Nu Skin Enterprises, Inc., 27 350–53; 31 386–89; 76 286–90 (upd.)
Nucor Corporation, 7 400–02; 21 392–95 (upd.); 79 294–300 (upd.)
Nufarm Ltd., 87 345–348
Nuplex Industries Ltd., 92 280–83
Nutraceutical International Corporation, 37 284–86
NutraSweet Company, 8 398–400
Nutreco Holding N.V., 56 256–59
Nutrexpa S.A., 92 284–87
NutriSystem, Inc., 71 250–53
Nutrition for Life International Inc., 22 385–88
Nutrition 21 Inc., 97 307–11
Nuveen *see* John Nuveen Co.
NVIDIA Corporation, 54 269–73
NVR Inc., 8 401–03; 70 206–09 (upd.)
NWA, Inc. *see* Northwest Airlines Corp.
NYK *see* Nippon Yusen Kabushiki Kaisha (NYK).
NYMAGIC, Inc., 41 284–86
NYNEX Corporation, V 311–13 *see also* Verizon Communications.
NYRG *see* New York Restaurant Group, Inc.
NYSE *see* New York Stock Exchange.
NYSEG *see* New York State Electric and Gas Corp.

O

O&Y *see* Olympia & York Developments Ltd.
O.C. Tanner Co., 69 279–81
Oak Harbor Freight Lines, Inc., 53 248–51
Oak Industries Inc., 21 396–98 *see also* Corning Inc.
Oak Technology, Inc., 22 389–93 *see also* Zoran Corp.
Oakhurst Dairy, 60 225–28
Oakleaf Waste Management, LLC, 97 312–15
Oakley, Inc., 18 390–93; 49 297–302 (upd.)
Oaktree Capital Management, LLC, 71 254–56
Oakwood Homes Corporation, 13 155; 15 326–28
OAO AVTOVAZ *see* AVTOVAZ Joint Stock Co.
OAO Gazprom, 42 261–65
OAO LUKOIL, 40 343–46
OAO NK YUKOS, 47 282–85
OAO Severstal *see* Severstal Joint Stock Co.
OAO Siberian Oil Company (Sibneft), 49 303–06
OAO Tatneft, 45 322–26
Obayashi Corporation, 78 266–69 (upd.)
Oberto Sausage Company, Inc., 92 288–91
Obie Media Corporation, 56 260–62
Obrascon Huarte Lain S.A., 76 291–94
Observer AB, 55 286–89
Occidental Petroleum Corporation, IV 480–82; 25 360–63 (upd.); 71 257–61 (upd.)
Océ N.V., 24 360–63; 91 359–65 (upd.)
Ocean Beauty Seafoods, Inc., 74 209–11
Ocean Group plc, 6 415–17 *see also* Exel plc.
Ocean Spray Cranberries, Inc., 7 403–05; 25 364–67 (upd.); 83 284-290
Oceaneering International, Inc., 63 317–19
Ocesa *see* Corporación Interamericana de Entretenimiento, S.A. de C.V.
O'Charley's Inc., 19 286–88; 60 229–32 (upd.)
OCI *see* Orascom Construction Industries S.A.E.
OCLC Online Computer Library Center, Inc., 96 324–28
Octel Messaging, 14 354–56; 41 287–90 (upd.)
Ocular Sciences, Inc., 65 273–75
Odakyu Electric Railway Co., Ltd., V 487–89; 68 278–81 (upd.)
Odebrecht S.A., 73 242–44
Odetics Inc., 14 357–59
ODL, Inc., 55 290–92
Odwalla, Inc., 31 349–51
Odyssey Marine Exploration, Inc., 91 366–70
OEC Medical Systems, Inc., 27 354–56
OENEO S.A., 74 212–15 (upd.)
Office Depot, Inc., 8 404–05; 23 363–65 (upd.); 65 276–80 (upd.)
OfficeMax Inc., 15 329–31; 43 291–95 (upd.)
OfficeTiger, LLC, 75 294–96
Officine Alfieri Maserati S.p.A., 13 376–78
Offshore Logistics, Inc., 37 287–89
Obagi Medical Products, Inc., 95 310–13
Ogden Corporation, I 512–14; 6 151–53 *see also* Covanta Energy Corp.
Ogilvy Group Inc., I 25–27 *see also* WPP Group.
Oglebay Norton Company, 17 355–58
Oglethorpe Power Corporation, 6 537–38
Ohbayashi Corporation, I 586–87
The Ohio Art Company, 14 360–62; 59 317–20 (upd.)
Ohio Bell Telephone Company, 14 363–65; *see also* Ameritech Corp.
Ohio Casualty Corp., 11 369–70
Ohio Edison Company, V 676–78
Oil and Natural Gas Commission, IV 483–84; 90 313–17 (upd.)
Oil-Dri Corporation of America, 20 396–99; 89 331–36 (upd.)
Oil States International, Inc., 77 314–17
Oil Transporting Joint Stock Company Transneft, 92450–54
The Oilgear Company, 74 216–18
Oji Paper Co., Ltd., IV 320–22; 57 272–75 (upd.)
OJSC Wimm-Bill-Dann Foods, 48 436–39
Oki Electric Industry Company, Limited, II 72–74; 15 125; 21 390
Oklahoma Gas and Electric Company, 6 539–40
Okuma Holdings Inc., 74 219–21
Okura & Co., Ltd., IV 167–68
Olan Mills, Inc., 62 254–56
Old America Stores, Inc., 17 359–61
Old Dominion Freight Line, Inc., 57 276–79

Old Kent Financial Corp., 11 371–72 *see also* Fifth Third Bancorp.
Old Mutual PLC, IV 535; **61 270–72**
Old National Bancorp, 15 332–34
Old Navy, Inc., 70 210–12
Old Orchard Brands, LLC, 73 245–47
Old Republic International Corporation, 11 373–75; 58 258–61 (upd.)
Old Spaghetti Factory International Inc., 24 364–66
Old Town Canoe Company, 74 222–24
Olga's Kitchen, Inc., 80 274–76
Olin Corporation, I 379–81; 13 379–81 (upd.); 78 270–74 (upd.)
Olivetti S.p.A., 34 316–20 (upd.)
Olsten Corporation, 6 41–43; 29 362–65 (upd.) *see also* Adecco S.A.
Olympia & York Developments Ltd., IV 720–21; 9 390–92 (upd.)
OM Group, Inc., 17 362–64; 78 275–78 (upd.)
OMA *see* Grupo Aeroportuario del Centro Norte, S.A.B. de C.V.
Omaha Steaks International Inc., 62 257–59
O'Melveny & Myers, 37 290–93
Omni Hotels Corp., 12 367–69
Omnicare, Inc., 13 49 307–10
Omnicell, Inc., 89 337–40
Omnicom Group Inc., I 28–32; 22 394–99 (upd.); 77 318–25 (upd.)
Omnilife *see* Grupo Omnilife S.A. de C.V.
OmniSource Corporation, 14 366–67
OMNOVA Solutions Inc., 59 324–26
Omrix Biopharmaceuticals, Inc., 95 314–17
Omron Corporation, 28 331–35 (upd.); 53 46
Omron Tateisi Electronics Company, II 75–77
ÖMV Aktiengesellschaft, IV 485–87
On Assignment, Inc., 20 400–02
1-800-FLOWERS, Inc., 26 344–46
1-800-GOT-JUNK? LLC, 74 225–27
180s, L.L.C., 64 299–301
One Price Clothing Stores, Inc., 20 403–05
O'Neal Steel, Inc., 95 306–09
Oneida Ltd., 7 406–08; 31 352–55 (upd.); 88 280–85 (upd.)
ONEOK Inc., 7 409–12
Onet S.A., 92 292–95
Onex Corporation, 16 395–97; 65 281–85 (upd.)
Onion, Inc., 69 282–84
Onoda Cement Co., Ltd., III 717–19 *see also* Taiheiyo Cement Corp.
Ontario Hydro Services Company, 6 541–42; 32 368–71 (upd.)
Ontario Teachers' Pension Plan, 61 273–75
Onyx Acceptance Corporation, 59 327–29
Onyx Software Corporation, 53 252–55
OOC Inc., 97 316–19
OPAP S.A. *see* Greek Organization of Football Prognostics S.A. (OPAP)
Opel AG *see* Adam Opel AG.
Open *see* Groupe Open.
Open Text Corporation, 79 301–05
Openwave Systems Inc., 95 318–22
Operadora Mexicana de Aeropuertos *see* Grupo Aeroportuario del Centro Norte, S.A.B. de C.V.
Operation Smile, Inc., 75 297–99
Opinion Research Corporation, 46 318–22
The Oppenheimer Group, 76 295–98
Oppenheimer Wolff & Donnelly LLP, 71 262–64
Opsware Inc., 49 311–14
Option Care Inc., 48 307–10
Optische Werke G. Rodenstock, 44 319–23
Opus Group, 34 321–23
Oracle Corporation, 6 272–74; 24 367–71 (upd.); 67 282–87 (upd.)
Orange Glo International, 53 256–59
Orange S.A., 84 286–289
Orascom Construction Industries S.A.E., 87 349–352
OraSure Technologies, Inc., 75 300–03
Orbital Sciences Corporation, 22 400–03
Orbitz, Inc., 61 276–78
Orbotech Ltd., 75 304–06
Orchard Supply Hardware Stores Corporation, 17 365–67
Ore-Ida Foods Inc., 13 382–83; 78 279–82 (upd.)
Oregon Chai, Inc., 49 315–17
Oregon Dental Service Health Plan, Inc., 51 276–78
Oregon Freeze Dry, Inc., 74 228–30
Oregon Metallurgical Corporation, 20 406–08
Oregon Steel Mills, Inc., 14 368–70
O'Reilly Automotive, Inc., 26 347–49; 78 283–87 (upd.)
Organic Valley (Coulee Region Organic Produce Pool), 53 260–62
Organización Soriana, S.A. de C.V., 35 320–22
ORI *see* Old Republic International Corp.
Orion Oyj, 72 256–59
Orion Pictures Corporation, 6 167–70 *see also* Metro-Goldwyn-Mayer Inc.
ORIX Corporation, II 442–43; 44 324–26 (upd.)
Orkla ASA, 18 394–98; 82 259–64 (upd.)
Orleans Homebuilders, Inc., 62 260–62
Ormat Technologies, Inc., 87 353–358
Ormet Corporation, 82 265–68
Orrick, Herrington and Sutcliffe LLP, 76 299–301
Orszagos Takarekpenztar es Kereskedelmi Bank Rt. (OTP Bank), 78 288–91
Orthodontic Centers of America, Inc., 35 323–26
Orthofix International NV, 72 260–62
The Orvis Company, Inc., 28 336–39
Oryx Energy Company, 7 413–15
Osaka Gas Company, Ltd., V 679–81; 60 233–36 (upd.)
Oscar Mayer Foods Corp., 12 370–72 *see also* Kraft Foods Inc.
Oshawa Group Limited, II 649–50
OshKosh B'Gosh, Inc., 9 393–95; 42 266–70 (upd.)
Oshkosh Truck Corporation, 7 416–18
Oshman's Sporting Goods, Inc., 17 368–70 *see also* Gart Sports Co.
OSI Restaurant Partners, Inc., 88 286–91 (upd.)
Osmonics, Inc., 18 399–401
Osram GmbH, 86 312–16
Österreichische Bundesbahnen GmbH, 6 418–20
Österreichische Elektrizitätswirtschafts-AG, 85 307–10
Österreichische Post- und Telegraphenverwaltung, V 314–17
O'Sullivan Industries Holdings, Inc., 34 313–15
Otari Inc., 89 341–44
Otis Elevator Company, Inc., 13 384–86; 39 311–15 (upd.)
Otis Spunkmeyer, Inc., 28 340–42
Otor S.A., 77 326–29
OTP Bank *see* Orszagos Takarekpenztar es Kereskedelmi Bank Rt.
OTR Express, Inc., 25 368–70
Ottakar's plc, 64 302–04
Ottaway Newspapers, Inc., 15 335–37
Otter Tail Power Company, 18 402–05
Otto Bremer Foundation *see* Bremer Financial Corp.
Otto Versand GmbH & Co., V 159–61; 15 338–40 (upd.); 34 324–28 (upd.)
Outback Steakhouse, Inc., 12 373–75; 34 329–32 (upd.) *see also* OSI Restaurant Partners, Inc.
Outboard Marine Corporation, III 597–600; 20 409–12 (upd.) *see also* Bombardier Inc.
Outdoor Research, Incorporated, 67 288–90
Outdoor Systems, Inc., 25 371–73 *see also* Infinity Broadcasting Corp.
Outlook Group Corporation, 37 294–96
Outokumpu Oyj, 38 335–37
Outrigger Enterprises, Inc., 67 291–93
Overhead Door Corporation, 70 213–16
Overhill Corporation, 51 279–81
Overnite Corporation, 14 371–73; 58 262–65 (upd.)
Overseas Shipholding Group, Inc., 11 376–77
Overstock.com, Inc., 75 307–09
Owens & Minor, Inc., 16 398–401; 68 282–85 (upd.)
Owens Corning Corporation, III 720–23; 20 413–17 (upd.)
Owens-Illinois, Inc., I 609–11; 26 350–53 (upd.); 85 311–18 (upd.)
Owosso Corporation, 29 366–68
Oxfam GB, 87 359–362

Oxford Health Plans, Inc., **16** 402–04
Oxford Industries, Inc., **8** 406–08; **84** 290–296 (upd.)

P

P&C Foods Inc., **8** 409–11
P & F Industries, Inc., **45** 327–29
P&G *see* Procter & Gamble Co.
P.C. Richard & Son Corp., **23** 372–74
P.F. Chang's China Bistro, Inc., **37** 297–99; **86** 317–21 (upd.)
P.H. Glatfelter Company, **8** 412–14; **30** 349–52 (upd.); **83** 291-297 (upd.)
PACCAR Inc., **I** 185–86; **26** 354–56 (upd.)
Pacer International, Inc., **54** 274–76
Pacer Technology, **40** 347–49
Pacific Basin Shipping Ltd., **86** 322–26
Pacific Clay Products Inc., **88** 292–95
Pacific Coast Building Products, Inc., **94** 338–41
Pacific Coast Feather Company, **67** 294–96
Pacific Coast Restaurants, Inc., **90** 318–21
Pacific Dunlop Limited, **10** 444–46 *see also* Ansell Ltd.
Pacific Enterprises, **V** 682–84 *see also* Sempra Energy.
Pacific Ethanol, Inc., **81** 269–72
Pacific Gas and Electric Company, **V** 685–87 *see also* PG&E Corp.
Pacific Internet Limited, **87** 363–366
Pacific Sunwear of California, Inc., **28** 343–45; **47** 425
Pacific Telecom, Inc., **6** 325–28
Pacific Telesis Group, **V** 318–20 *see also* SBC Communications.
PacifiCare Health Systems, Inc., **11** 378–80
PacifiCorp, Inc., **V** 688–90; **26** 357–60 (upd.)
Packaging Corporation of America, **12** 376–78; **51** 282–85 (upd.)
Packard Bell Electronics, Inc., **13** 387–89
Packeteer, Inc., **81** 273–76
Paddock Publications, Inc., **53** 263–65
PagesJaunes Groupe SA, **79** 306–09
Paging Network Inc., **11** 381–83
Pagnossin S.p.A., **73** 248–50
PaineWebber Group Inc., **II** 444–46; **22** 404–07 (upd.) *see also* UBS AG.
Pakistan International Airlines Corporation, **46** 323–26
Pakistan State Oil Company Ltd., **81** 277–80
PAL *see* Philippine Airlines, Inc.
Palace Sports & Entertainment, Inc., **97** 320–25
PALIC *see* Pan-American Life Insurance Co.
Pall Corporation, **9** 396–98; **72** 263–66 (upd.)
Palm Harbor Homes, Inc., **39** 316–18
Palm, Inc., **36** 355–57; **75** 310–14 (upd.)
Palm Management Corporation, **71** 265–68
Palmer & Cay, Inc., **69** 285–87
Palmer Candy Company, **80** 277–81
Palmer Co. *see* R. M. Palmer Co.
Paloma Industries Ltd., **71** 269–71
Palomar Medical Technologies, Inc., **22** 408–10
Pamida Holdings Corporation, **15** 341–43
The Pampered Chef Ltd., **18** 406–08; **78** 292–96 (upd.)
Pamplin Corp. *see* R.B. Pamplin Corp.
Pan-American Life Insurance Company, **48** 311–13
Pan American World Airways, Inc., **I** 115–16; **12** 379–81 (upd.)
Panalpina World Transport (Holding) Ltd., **47** 286–88
Panamerican Beverages, Inc., **47** 289–91; **54** 74
PanAmSat Corporation, **46** 327–29
Panavision Inc., **24** 372–74
Pancho's Mexican Buffet, Inc., **46** 330–32
Panda Restaurant Group, Inc., **35** 327–29; **97** 326–30 (upd.)
Panera Bread Company, **44** 327–29
Panhandle Eastern Corporation, **V** 691–92 *see also* CMS Energy Corp.
Pantone Inc., **53** 266–69
The Pantry, Inc., **36** 358–60
Panzani, **84** 297–300
Papa Gino's Holdings Corporation, Inc., **86** 327–30
Papa John's International, Inc., **15** 344–46; **71** 272–76 (upd.)
Papa Murphy's International, Inc., **54** 277–79
Papeteries de Lancey, **23** 366–68
Papetti's Hygrade Egg Products, Inc., **39** 319–21
Pappas Restaurants, Inc., **76** 302–04
Par Pharmaceutical Companies, Inc., **65** 286–88
The Paradies Shops, Inc., **88** 296–99
Paradise Music & Entertainment, Inc., **42** 271–74
Paradores de Turismo de Espana S.A., **73** 251–53
Parametric Technology Corp., **16** 405–07
Paramount Pictures Corporation, **II** 154–56; **94** 342–47 (upd.)
Paramount Resources Ltd., **87** 367–370
PAREXEL International Corporation, **84** 301–304
Paribas *see* BNP Paribas Group.
Paris Corporation, **22** 411–13
Parisian, Inc., **14** 374–76 *see also* Belk, Inc.
Park Corp., **22** 414–16
Park-Ohio Holdings Corp., **17** 371–73; **85** 319–23 (upd.)
Parker Drilling Company, **28** 346–48
Parker-Hannifin Corporation, **III** 601–03; **24** 375–78 (upd.)
Parlex Corporation, **61** 279–81
Parmalat Finanziaria SpA, **50** 343–46
Parque Arauco S.A., **72** 267–69
Parras *see* Compañia Industrial de Parras, S.A. de C.V. (CIPSA).
Parsons Brinckerhoff, Inc., **34** 333–36
The Parsons Corporation, **8** 415–17; **56** 263–67 (upd.)
PartnerRe Ltd., **83** 298-301
Partouche SA *see* Groupe Partouche SA.
Party City Corporation, **54** 280–82
Pathé SA, **29** 369–71 *see also* Chargeurs International.
Pathmark Stores, Inc., **23** 369–71
Patina Oil & Gas Corporation, **24** 379–81
Patrick Industries, Inc., **30** 342–45
Patriot Transportation Holding, Inc., **91** 371–74
Patterson Dental Co., **19** 289–91
Patterson-UTI Energy, Inc., **55** 293–95
Patton Boggs LLP, **71** 277–79
Paul Harris Stores, Inc., **18** 409–12
Paul, Hastings, Janofsky & Walker LLP, **27** 357–59
Paul Mueller Company, **65** 289–91
Paul Reed Smith Guitar Company, **89** 345–48
The Paul Revere Corporation, **12** 382–83
Paul-Son Gaming Corporation, **66** 249–51
Paul, Weiss, Rifkind, Wharton & Garrison, **47** 292–94
Paulaner Brauerei GmbH & Co. KG, **35** 330–33
Paxson Communications Corporation, **33** 322–26
Pay 'N Pak Stores, Inc., **9** 399–401
Paychex, Inc., **15** 347–49; **46** 333–36 (upd.)
Payless Cashways, Inc., **11** 384–86; **44** 330–33 (upd.)
Payless ShoeSource, Inc., **18** 413–15; **69** 288–92 (upd.)
PayPal Inc., **58** 266–69
PBL *see* Publishing and Broadcasting Ltd.
PBS *see* Public Broadcasting Stations.
The PBSJ Corporation, **82** 269–73
PC Connection, Inc., **37** 300–04
PCA *see* Packaging Corporation of America.
PCA International, Inc., **62** 263–65
PCC *see* Companhia Suzano de Papel e Celulose S.A.
PCC Natural Markets, **94** 348–51
PCL Construction Group Inc., **50** 347–49
PCM Uitgevers NV, **53** 270–73
PCS *see* Potash Corp. of Saskatchewan Inc.
PDI, Inc., **52** 272–75
PDL BioPharma, Inc., **90** 322–25
PDO *see* Petroleum Development Oman.
PDQ Food Stores Inc., **79** 310–13
PDS Gaming Corporation, **44** 334–37
PDVSA *see* Petróleos de Venezuela S.A.
Peabody Energy Corporation, **10** 447–49; **45** 330–33 (upd.)

Peabody Holding Company, Inc., IV 169–72
Peace Arch Entertainment Group Inc., 51 286–88
The Peak Technologies Group, Inc., 14 377–80
Peapod, Inc., 30 346–48
Pearl Musical Instrument Company, 78 297–300
Pearle Vision, Inc., 13 390–92
Pearson plc, IV 657–59; 46 337–41 (upd.)
Peavey Electronics Corporation, 16 408–10; 94 352–56 (upd.)
Pechiney S.A., IV 173–75; 45 334–37 (upd.)
PECO Energy Company, 11 387–90 *see also* Exelon Corp.
Pediatric Services of America, Inc., 31 356–58
Pediatrix Medical Group, Inc., 61 282–85
Peebles Inc., 16 411–13; 43 296–99 (upd.)
Peek & Cloppenburg KG, 46 342–45
Peet's Coffee & Tea, Inc., 38 338–40
Peg Perego SpA, 88 300–03
Pegasus Solutions, Inc., 75 315–18
Pei Cobb Freed & Partners Architects LLP, 57 280–82
Pelican Products, Inc., 86 331–34
Pelikan Holding AG, 92 296–300
Pella Corporation, 12 384–86; 39 322–25 (upd.); 89 349–53 (upd.)
Pemco Aviation Group Inc., 54 283–86
Pemex *see* Petróleos Mexicanos.
Penaflor S.A., 66 252–54
Penauille Polyservices SA, 49 318–21
Pendleton Grain Growers Inc., 64 305–08
Pendleton Woolen Mills, Inc., 42 275–78
Penford Corporation, 55 296–99
Pengrowth Energy Trust, 95 323–26
The Peninsular and Oriental Steam Navigation Company, V 490–93; 38 341–46 (upd.)
Peninsular and Oriental Steam Navigation Company (Bovis Division), I 588–89 *see also* DP World.
Penn Engineering & Manufacturing Corp., 28 349–51
Penn National Gaming, Inc., 33 327–29
Penn Traffic Company, 13 393–95
Penn Virginia Corporation, 85 324–27
Penney's *see* J.C. Penney Company, Inc.
Pennon Group Plc, 45 338–41
Pennsylvania Blue Shield, III 325–27 *see also* Highmark Inc.
Pennsylvania Power & Light Company, V 693–94
Pennwalt Corporation, I 382–84
PennWell Corporation, 55 300–03
Pennzoil-Quaker State Company, IV 488–90; 20 418–22 (upd.); 50 350–55 (upd.)
Penske Corporation, V 494–95; 19 292–94 (upd.); 84 305–309 (upd.)
Pentair, Inc., 7 419–21; 26 361–64 (upd.); 81 281–87 (upd.)
Pentax Corporation, 78 301–05
Pentech International, Inc., 29 372–74
Pentland Group plc, 20 423–25
Penton Media, Inc., 27 360–62
Penzeys Spices, Inc., 79 314–16
People Express Airlines Inc., I 117–18
Peoples Energy Corporation, 6 543–44
PeopleSoft Inc., 14 381–83; 33 330–33 (upd.) *see also* Oracle Corp.
The Pep Boys—Manny, Moe & Jack, 11 391–93; 36 361–64 (upd.); 81 288–94 (upd.)
PEPCO *see* Potomac Electric Power Co.
Pepper *see* J. W. Pepper and Son Inc.
Pepper Hamilton LLP, 43 300–03
Pepperidge Farm, Incorporated, 81 295–300
The Pepsi Bottling Group, Inc., 40 350–53
PepsiAmericas, Inc., 67 297–300 (upd.)
PepsiCo, Inc., I 276–79; 10 450–54 (upd.); 38 347–54 (upd.); 93 333–44 (upd.)
Pequiven *see* Petroquímica de Venezuela S.A.
Perdigao SA, 52 276–79
Perdue Farms Inc., 7 422–24; 23 375–78 (upd.)
Perfetti Van Melle S.p.A., 72 270–73
Performance Food Group, 31 359–62; 96 329–34 (upd.)
Perini Corporation, 8 418–21; 82 274–79 (upd.)
PerkinElmer, Inc., 7 425–27; 78 306–10 (upd.)
Perkins Coie LLP, 56 268–70
Perkins Family Restaurants, L.P., 22 417–19
Perkins Foods Holdings Ltd., 87 371–374
Pernod Ricard S.A., I 280–81; 21 399–401 (upd.); 72 274–77 (upd.)
Perot Systems Corporation, 29 375–78
Perrigo Company, 12 387–89; 59 330–34 (upd.)
Perry Ellis International, Inc., 41 291–94
Perry's Ice Cream Company Inc., 90 326–29
The Perseus Books Group, 91 375–78
Perstorp AB, I 385–87; 51 289–92 (upd.)
Pertamina, IV 491–93; 56 271–74 (upd.)
Perusahaan Otomobil Nasional Bhd., 62 266–68
Pescanova S.A., 81 301–04
Pet Incorporated, 7 428–31
Petco Animal Supplies, Inc., 29 379–81; 74 231–34 (upd.)
Pete's Brewing Company, 22 420–22
Peter Kiewit Sons' Inc., 8 422–24
Peter Piper, Inc., 70 217–19
Peterbilt Motors Company, 89 354–57
Petersen Publishing Company, 21 402–04
Peterson American Corporation, 55 304–06
Petit Bateau, 95 327–31
PetMed Express, Inc., 81 305–08
Petrie Stores Corporation, 8 425–27
Petro-Canada Limited, IV 494–96
Petrobrás *see* Petróleo Brasileiro S.A.
Petrobras Energia Participaciones S.A., 72 278–81
Petroecuador *see* Petróleos del Ecuador.
Petrofac Ltd., 95 332–35
PetroFina S.A., IV 497–500; 26 365–69 (upd.)
Petrogal *see* Petróleos de Portugal.
Petrohawk Energy Corporation, 79 317–20
Petróleo Brasileiro S.A., IV 501–03
Petróleos de Portugal S.A., IV 504–06
Petróleos de Venezuela S.A., IV 507–09; 74 235–39 (upd.)
Petróleos del Ecuador, IV 510–11
Petróleos Mexicanos, IV 512–14; 19 295–98 (upd.)
Petroleum Development Oman LLC, IV 515–16
Petroleum Helicopters, Inc., 35 334–36
Petroliam Nasional Bhd (Petronas), 56 275–79 (upd.)
Petrolite Corporation, 15 350–52 *see also* Baker Hughes Inc.
Petromex *see* Petróleos de Mexico S.A.
Petron Corporation, 58 270–72
Petronas, IV 517–20 *see also* Petroliam Nasional Bhd.
Petrossian Inc., 54 287–89
PETsMART, Inc., 14 384–86; 41 295–98 (upd.)
Peugeot S.A., I 187–88 *see also* PSA Peugeot Citroen S.A.
The Pew Charitable Trusts, 35 337–40
Pez Candy, Inc., 38 355–57
The Pfaltzgraff Co. *see* Susquehanna Pfaltzgraff Co.
Pfizer Inc., I 661–63; 9 402–05 (upd.); 38 358–67 (upd.); 79 321–33 (upd.)
PFSweb, Inc., 73 254–56
PG&E Corporation, 26 370–73 (upd.)
PGA *see* The Professional Golfers' Association.
Phantom Fireworks *see* B.J. Alan Co., Inc.
Phar-Mor Inc., 12 390–92
Pharmacia & Upjohn Inc., I 664–65; 25 374–78 (upd.) *see also* Pfizer Inc.
Pharmion Corporation, 91 379–82
Phat Fashions LLC, 49 322–24
Phelps Dodge Corporation, IV 176–79; 28 352–57 (upd.); 75 319–25 (upd.)
PHH Arval, V 496–97; 53 274–76 (upd.)
PHI, Inc., 80 282–86 (upd.)
Philadelphia Eagles, 37 305–08
Philadelphia Electric Company, V 695–97 *see also* Exelon Corp.
Philadelphia Gas Works Company, 92 301–05

Philadelphia Media Holdings LLC, 92 306–10
Philadelphia Suburban Corporation, 39 326–29
Philharmonic-Symphony Society of New York, Inc. (New York Philharmonic), 69 293–97
Philip Environmental Inc., 16 414–16
Philip Morris Companies Inc., V 405–07; 18 416–19 (upd.); 44 338–43 (upd.) *see also* Kraft Foods Inc.
Philip Services Corp., 73 257–60
Philipp Holzmann AG, 17 374–77
Philippine Airlines, Inc., 6 106–08; 23 379–82 (upd.)
Philips Electronics N.V., 13 400–03 (upd.) *see also* Koninklijke Philips Electronics N.V.
Philips Electronics North America Corp., 13 396–99
N.V. Philips Gloeilampenfabriken, II 78–80 *see also* Philips Electronics N.V.
Phillips, de Pury & Luxembourg, 49 325–27
Phillips Foods, Inc., 63 320–22; 90 330–33 (upd.)
Phillips International, Inc., 78 311–14
Phillips Petroleum Company, IV 521–23; 40 354–59 (upd.) *see also* ConocoPhillips.
Phillips-Van Heusen Corporation, 24 382–85
Phoenix AG, 68 286–89
Phoenix Footwear Group, Inc., 70 220–22
Phoenix Mecano AG, 61 286–88
The Phoenix Media/Communications Group, 91 383–87
Phones 4u Ltd., 85 328–31
Photo-Me International Plc, 83 302-306
PHP Healthcare Corporation, 22 423–25
PhyCor, Inc., 36 365–69
Physician Sales & Service, Inc., 14 387–89
Physio-Control International Corp., 18 420–23
Piaggio & C. S.p.A., 20 426–29
PianoDisc *see* Burgett, Inc.
PIC International Group PLC, 24 386–88 (upd.)
Picanol N.V., 96 335–38
Picard Surgeles, 76 305–07
Piccadilly Cafeterias, Inc., 19 299–302
Pick 'n Pay Stores Ltd., 82 280–83
PictureTel Corp., 10 455–57; 27 363–66 (upd.)
Piedmont Natural Gas Company, Inc., 27 367–69
Pier 1 Imports, Inc., 12 393–95; 34 337–41 (upd.); 95 336–43 (upd.)
Pierce Leahy Corporation, 24 389–92 *see also* Iron Mountain Inc.
Piercing Pagoda, Inc., 29 382–84
Pierre & Vacances SA, 48 314–16
Piggly Wiggly Southern, Inc., 13 404–06
Pilgrim's Pride Corporation, 7 432–33; 23 383–85 (upd.); 90 334–38 (upd.)
Pilkington Group Limited, II 724–27; 34 342–47 (upd.); 87 375–383 (upd.)
Pillowtex Corporation, 19 303–05; 41 299–302 (upd.)
Pillsbury Company, II 555–57; 13 407–09 (upd.); 62 269–73 (upd.)
Pillsbury Madison & Sutro LLP, 29 385–88
Pilot Air Freight Corp., 67 301–03
Pilot Corporation, 49 328–30
Pilot Pen Corporation of America, 82 284–87
Pinault-Printemps-Redoute S.A., 19 306–09 (upd.) *see also* PPR S.A.
Pindar *see* G A Pindar & Son Ltd.
Pinguely-Haulotte SA, 51 293–95
Pinkerton's Inc., 9 406–09 *see also* Securitas AB.
Pinnacle Airlines Corp., 73 261–63
Pinnacle West Capital Corporation, 6 545–47; 54 290–94 (upd.)
Pioneer Electronic Corporation, III 604–06; 28 358–61 (upd.) *see also* Agilysys Inc.
Pioneer Hi-Bred International, Inc., 9 410–12; 41 303–06 (upd.)
Pioneer International Limited, III 728–30
Pioneer Natural Resources Company, 59 335–39
Pioneer-Standard Electronics Inc., 19 310–14 *see also* Agilysys Inc.
Piper Jaffray Companies Inc., 22 426–30 *see also* U.S. Bancorp.
Pirelli & C. S.p.A., V 249–51; 15 353–56 (upd.); 75 326–31 (upd.)
Piscines Desjoyaux S.A., 84 310–313
Pitman Company, 58 273–75
Pitney Bowes, Inc., III 156–58, 159; 19 315–18 (upd.); 47 295–99 (upd.)
Pittsburgh Brewing Company, 76 308–11
Pittsburgh Plate Glass Co. *see* PPG Industries, Inc.
Pittsburgh Steelers Sports, Inc., 66 255–57
The Pittston Company, IV 180–82; 19 319–22 (upd.) *see also* The Brink's Co.
Pittway Corporation, 9 413–15; 33 334–37 (upd.)
Pixar Animation Studios, 34 348–51
Pixelworks, Inc., 69 298–300
Pizza Hut Inc., 7 434–35; 21 405–07 (upd.)
Pizza Inn, Inc., 46 346–49
PKF International, 78 315–18
Placer Dome Inc., 20 430–33; 61 289–93 (upd.)
Plain Dealer Publishing Company, 92 311–14
Plains Cotton Cooperative Association, 57 283–86
Planar Systems, Inc., 61 294–97
Planet Hollywood International, Inc., 18 424–26; 41 307–10 (upd.)
Planeta *see* Grupo Planeta.
Plantation Pipe Line Company, 68 290–92
Plante & Moran, LLP, 71 280–83
Platinum Entertainment, Inc., 35 341–44
PLATINUM Technology, Inc., 14 390–92 *see also* Computer Associates International, Inc.
Plato Learning, Inc., 44 344–47
Play by Play Toys & Novelties, Inc., 26 374–76
Playboy Enterprises, Inc., 18 427–30
PlayCore, Inc., 27 370–72
Players International, Inc., 22 431–33
Playmates Toys, 23 386–88
Playskool, Inc., 25 379–81 *see also* Hasbro, Inc.
Playtex Products, Inc., 15 357–60
Pleasant Company, 27 373–75 *see also* American Girl, Inc.
Pleasant Holidays LLC, 62 274–76
Plessey Company, PLC, II 81–82 *see also* Marconi plc.
Plexus Corporation, 35 345–47; 80 287–91 (upd.)
PLIVA d.d., 70 223–25
Plum Creek Timber Company, Inc., 43 304–06
Pluma, Inc., 27 376–78
Ply Gem Industries Inc., 12 396–98
The PMI Group, Inc., 49 331–33
PMP Ltd., 72 282–84
PMT Services, Inc., 24 393–95
The PNC Financial Services Group Inc., II 342–43; 13 410–12 (upd.); 46 350–53 (upd.)
PNM Resources Inc., 51 296–300 (upd.)
Pochet SA, 55 307–09
Pogo Producing Company, 39 330–32
Pohang Iron and Steel Company Ltd., IV 183–85 *see also* POSCO.
Polar Air Cargo Inc., 60 237–39
Polaris Industries Inc., 12 399–402; 35 348–53 (upd.); 77 330–37 (upd.)
Polaroid Corporation, III 607–09; 7 436–39 (upd.); 28 362–66 (upd.); 93 345–53 (upd.)
Policy Management Systems Corporation, 11 394–95
Policy Studies, Inc., 62 277–80
Poliet S.A., 33 338–40
Polk Audio, Inc., 34 352–54
Polo/Ralph Lauren Corporation, 12 403–05; 62 281–85 (upd.)
Polski Koncern Naftowy ORLEN S.A., 77 338–41
PolyGram N.V., 23 389–92
PolyMedica Corporation, 77 342–45
PolyOne Corporation, 87 384–395 (upd.)
Pomare Ltd., 88 304–07
Pomeroy Computer Resources, Inc., 33 341–44
Ponderosa Steakhouse, 15 361–64
Poof-Slinky, Inc., 61 298–300
Poore Brothers, Inc., 44 348–50 *see also* The Inventure Group, Inc.

Pop Warner Little Scholars, Inc., 86 335–38
Pope & Talbot, Inc., 12 406–08; 61 301–05 (upd.)
Pope Cable and Wire B.V. *see* Belden CDT Inc.
Pope Resources LP, 74 240–43
Popular, Inc., 41 311–13
The Porcelain and Fine China Companies Ltd., 69 301–03
Porsche AG, 13 413–15; 31 363–66 (upd.)
The Port Authority of New York and New Jersey, 48 317–20
Port Imperial Ferry Corporation, 70 226–29
Portal Software, Inc., 47 300–03
Portillo's Restaurant Group, Inc., 71 284–86
Portland General Corporation, 6 548–51
Portland Trail Blazers, 50 356–60
Portmeirion Group plc, 88 308–11
Portucel *see* Grupo Portucel Soporcel.
Portugal Telecom SGPS S.A., 69 304–07
Posadas *see* Grupo Posadas, S.A. de C.V.
POSCO, 57 287–91 (upd.)
Post Office Group, V 498–501
Post Properties, Inc., 26 377–79
La Poste, V 470–72
Posterscope Worldwide, 70 230–32
Posti- Ja Telelaitos, 6 329–31
Potash Corporation of Saskatchewan Inc., 18 431–33
Potbelly Sandwich Works, Inc., 83 307-310
Potlatch Corporation, 8 428–30; 34 355–59 (upd.); 87 396–403 (upd.)
Potomac Electric Power Company, 6 552–54
Potter & Brumfield Inc., 11 396–98
Pou Chen Corporation, 81 309–12
Powell Duffryn plc, 31 367–70
Powell's Books, Inc., 40 360–63
Power Corporation of Canada, 36 370–74 (upd.); 85 332–39 (upd.)
Power-One, Inc., 79 334–37
PowerBar Inc., 44 351–53
Powergen PLC, 11 399–401; 50 361–64 (upd.)
Powerhouse Technologies, Inc., 27 379–81
POZEN Inc., 81 313–16
PP&L *see* Pennsylvania Power & Light Co.
PPB Group Berhad, 57 292–95
PPG Industries, Inc., III 731–33; 22 434–37 (upd.); 81 317–23 (upd.)
PPL Corporation, 41 314–17 (upd.)
PPR S.A., 74 244–48 (upd.)
PR Newswire, 35 354–56
PRS *see* Paul Reed Smith Guitar Co.
Prada Holding B.V., 45 342–45
Prairie Farms Dairy, Inc., 47 304–07
Pranda Jewelry plc, 70 233–35
Pratt & Whitney, 9 416–18
Praxair, Inc., 11 402–04; 48 321–24 (upd.)
Praxis Bookstore Group LLC, 90 339–42
Pre-Paid Legal Services, Inc., 20 434–37
Precision Castparts Corp., 15 365–67
Premark International, Inc., III 610–12 *see also* Illinois Tool Works Inc.
Premcor Inc., 37 309–11
Premier Industrial Corporation, 9 419–21
Premier Parks, Inc., 27 382–84 *see also* Six Flags, Inc.
Premium Standard Farms, Inc., 30 353–55
PremiumWear, Inc., 30 356–59
Preserver Group, Inc., 44 354–56
President Casinos, Inc., 22 438–40
Pressman Toy Corporation, 56 280–82
Presstek, Inc., 33 345–48
Preston Corporation, 6 421–23
Preussag AG, 17 378–82; 42 279–83 (upd.)
PreussenElektra Aktiengesellschaft, V 698–700 *see also* E.On AG.
PRG-Schultz International, Inc., 73 264–67
Price Communications Corporation, 42 284–86
The Price Company, V 162–64 *see also* Costco Wholesale Corp.
Price Pfister, Inc., 70 236–39
Price Waterhouse LLP, 9 422–24 *see also* PricewaterhouseCoopers
PriceCostco, Inc., 14 393–95 *see also* Costco Wholesale Corp.
Priceline.com Incorporated, 57 296–99
PriceSmart, Inc., 71 287–90
PricewaterhouseCoopers, 29 389–94 (upd.)
PRIDE Enterprises *see* Prison Rehabilitative Industries and Diversified Enterprises, Inc.
Pride International, Inc., 78 319–23
Primark Corp., 13 416–18 *see also* Thomson Corp.
Prime Hospitality Corporation, 52 280–83
Primedex Health Systems, Inc., 25 382–85
Primedia Inc., 22 441–43
Primerica Corporation, I 612–14
Prince Sports Group, Inc., 15 368–70
Princes Ltd., 76 312–14
Princess Cruise Lines, 22 444–46
The Princeton Review, Inc., 42 287–90
Principal Mutual Life Insurance Company, III 328–30
Printpack, Inc., 68 293–96
Printrak, A Motorola Company, 44 357–59
Printronix, Inc., 18 434–36
Prison Rehabilitative Industries and Diversified Enterprises, Inc. (PRIDE), 53 277–79
Pro-Build Holdings Inc., 95 344–48 (upd.)
The Procter & Gamble Company, III 50–53; 8 431–35 (upd.); 26 380–85 (upd.); 67 304–11 (upd.)
Prodigy Communications Corporation, 34 360–62
Proeza S.A. de C.V., 82 288–91
Professional Bull Riders Inc., 55 310–12
The Professional Golfers' Association of America, 41 318–21
Proffitt's, Inc., 19 323–25 *see also* Belk, Inc.
Programmer's Paradise, Inc., 81 324–27
Progress Energy, Inc., 74 249–52
Progress Software Corporation, 15 371–74
Progressive Corporation, 11 405–07; 29 395–98 (upd.)
Progressive Enterprises Ltd., 96 339–42
ProLogis, 57 300–02
Promus Companies, Inc., 9 425–27 *see also* Hilton Hotels Corp.
ProSiebenSat.1 Media AG, 54 295–98
Proskauer Rose LLP, 47 308–10
Protection One, Inc., 32 372–75
Provell Inc., 58 276–79 (upd.)
Providence Health System, 90 343–47
The Providence Journal Company, 28 367–69; 30 15
The Providence Service Corporation, 64 309–12
Provident Bankshares Corporation, 85 340–43
Provident Life and Accident Insurance Company of America, III 331–33 *see also* UnumProvident Corp.
Providian Financial Corporation, 52 284–90 (upd.)
Provigo Inc., II 651–53; 51 301–04 (upd.)
Provimi S.A., 80 292–95
Prudential Financial Inc., III 337–41; 30 360–64 (upd.); 82 292–98 (upd.)
Prudential plc, III 334–36; 48 325–29 (upd.)
PSA Peugeot Citroen S.A., 28 370–74 (upd.); 54 126
PSF *see* Premium Standard Farms, Inc.
PSI Resources, 6 555–57
Psion PLC, 45 346–49
Psychemedics Corporation, 89 358–61
Psychiatric Solutions, Inc., 68 297–300
PT Astra International Tbk, 56 283–86
PT Bank Buana Indonesia Tbk, 60 240–42
PT Indosat Tbk, 93 354–57
PTT Public Company Ltd., 56 287–90
Pubco Corporation, 17 383–85
Public Service Company of Colorado, 6 558–60
Public Service Company of New Hampshire, 21 408–12; 55 313–18 (upd.)
Public Service Company of New Mexico, 6 561–64 *see also* PNM Resources Inc.
Public Service Enterprise Group Inc., V 701–03; 44 360–63 (upd.)
Public Storage, Inc., 21 52 291–93
Publicis Groupe, 19 329–32; 77 346–50 (upd.)

Publishers Clearing House, **23 393–95; 64 313–16 (upd.)**
Publishers Group, Inc., **35 357–59**
Publishing and Broadcasting Limited, **54 299–302**
Publix Super Markets Inc., **7 440–42; 31 371–74 (upd.)**
Puck Lazaroff Inc. *see* The Wolfgang Puck Food Company, Inc.
Pueblo Xtra International, Inc., **47 311–13**
Puerto Rico Electric Power Authority, **47 314–16**
Puget Sound Energy Inc., **6 565–67; 50 365–68 (upd.)**
Puig Beauty and Fashion Group S.L., **60 243–46**
Pulaski Furniture Corporation, **33 349–52; 80 296–99 (upd.)**
Pulitzer Inc., **15 375–77; 58 280–83 (upd.)**
Pulsar Internacional S.A., **21 413–15**
Pulte Homes, Inc., **8 436–38; 42 291–94 (upd.)**
Puma AG Rudolf Dassler Sport, **35 360–63**
Pumpkin Masters, Inc., **48 330–32**
Punch International N.V., **66 258–60**
Punch Taverns plc, **70 240–42**
Puratos S.A./NV, **92 315–18**
Pure World, Inc., **72 285–87**
Purina Mills, Inc., **32 376–79**
Puritan-Bennett Corporation, **13 419–21**
Purolator Products Company, **21 416–18; 74 253–56 (upd.)**
Putt-Putt Golf Courses of America, Inc., **23 396–98**
PVC Container Corporation, **67 312–14**
PW Eagle, Inc., **48 333–36**
PWA Group, **IV 323–25** *see also* Svenska Cellulosa.
Pyramid Breweries Inc., **33 353–55**
Pyramid Companies, **54 303–05**
PZ Cussons plc, **72 288–90**

Q

Q.E.P. Co., Inc., **65 292–94**
Qantas Airways Ltd., **6 109–13; 24 396–401 (upd.); 68 301–07 (upd.)**
Qatar Airways Company Q.C.S.C., **87 404–407**
Qatar General Petroleum Corporation, **IV 524–26**
Qatar National Bank SAQ, **87 408–411**
Qatar Telecom QSA, **87 412–415**
Qdoba Restaurant Corporation, **93 358–62**
Qiagen N.V., **39 333–35**
QLT Inc., **71 291–94**
QRS Music Technologies, Inc., **95 349–53**
QSC Audio Products, Inc., **56 291–93**
Quad/Graphics, Inc., **19 333–36**
Quaker Chemical Corp., **91 388–91**
Quaker Fabric Corp., **19 337–39**
Quaker Foods North America, **II 558–60; 12 409–12 (upd.); 34 363–67 (upd.); 73 268–73 (upd.)**
Quaker State Corporation, **7 443–45; 21 419–22 (upd.)** *see also* Pennzoil-Quaker State Co.
QUALCOMM Incorporated, **20 438–41; 47 317–21 (upd.)**
Quality Chekd Dairies, Inc., **48 337–39**
Quality Dining, Inc., **18 437–40**
Quality Food Centers, Inc., **17 386–88** *see also* Kroger Co.
Quality Systems, Inc., **81 328–31**
Quanex Corporation, **13 422–24; 62 286–89 (upd.)**
Quanta Computer Inc., **47 322–24**
Quanta Services, Inc., **79 338–41**
Quantum Chemical Corporation, **8 439–41**
Quantum Corporation, **10 458–59; 62 290–93 (upd.)**
Quark, Inc., **36 375–79**
Quebéc Hydro-Electric Commission *see* Hydro-Quebéc.
Quebecor Inc., **12 412–14; 47 325–28 (upd.)**
Quelle Group, **V 165–67** *see also* Karstadt Quelle AG.
Quest Diagnostics Inc., **26 390–92**
Questar Corporation, **6 568–70; 26 386–89 (upd.)**
The Quick & Reilly Group, Inc., **20 442–44**
Quick Restaurants S.A., **94 357–60**
Quicken Loans, Inc., **93 363–67**
Quidel Corporation, **80 300–03**
The Quigley Corporation, **62 294–97**
Quiksilver, Inc., **18 441–43; 79 342–47 (upd.)**
QuikTrip Corporation, **36 380–83**
Quill Corporation, **28 375–77**
Quilmes Industrial (QUINSA) S.A., **67 315–17**
Quintiles Transnational Corporation, **21 423–25; 68 308–12 (upd.)**
Quixote Corporation, **15 378–80**
The Quizno's Corporation, **42 295–98**
Quovadx Inc., **70 243–46**
QVC Inc., **9 428–29; 58 284–87 (upd.)**
Qwest Communications International, Inc., **37 312–17**

R

R&B, Inc., **51 305–07**
R.B. Pamplin Corp., **45 350–52**
R.C. Bigelow, Inc., **49 334–36**
R.C. Willey Home Furnishings, **72 291–93**
R.G. Barry Corp., **17 389–91; 44 364–67 (upd.)**
R. Griggs Group Limited, **23 399–402; 31** 413–14
R.H. Macy & Co., Inc., **V 168–70; 8 442–45 (upd.); 30 379–83 (upd.)** *see also* Macy's, Inc.
R.J. Reynolds Tobacco Holdings, Inc., **30 384–87 (upd.)**
R. M. Palmer Co., **89 362–64**
R.P. Scherer Corporation, **I 678–80** *see also* Cardinal Health, Inc.
R.R. Donnelley & Sons Company, **IV 660–62; 38 368–71 (upd.)**
Rabobank Group, **26** 419; **33 356–58**
RAC *see* Roy Anderson Corp.
Racal-Datacom Inc., **11 408–10**
Racal Electronics PLC, **II 83–84** *see also* Thales S.A.
Racing Champions Corporation, **37 318–20**
Rack Room Shoes, Inc., **84 314–317**
Radeberger Gruppe AG, **75 332–35**
Radian Group Inc., **42 299–301** *see also* Onex Corp.
Radiation Therapy Services, Inc., **85 344–47**
Radio Flyer Inc., **34 368–70**
Radio One, Inc., **67 318–21**
RadioShack Corporation, **36 384–88 (upd.)**
Radius Inc., **16 417–19**
RAE Systems Inc., **83 311-314**
RAG AG, **35 364–67; 60 247–51 (upd.)**
Rag Shops, Inc., **30 365–67**
Ragdoll Productions Ltd., **51 308–11**
Raiffeisen Zentralbank Österreich AG, **85 348–52**
RailTex, Inc., **20 445–47**
Railtrack Group PLC, **50 369–72**
Rain Bird Corporation, **84 318–321**
Rainforest Café, Inc., **25 386–88; 88 312–16 (upd.)**
Rainier Brewing Company, **23 403–05**
Raleigh UK Ltd., **65 295–97**
Raley's Inc., **14 396–98; 58 288–91 (upd.)**
Rally's, **25 389–91; 68 313–16 (upd.)**
Rallye SA, **54 306–09**
Ralph Lauren *see* Polo/Ralph Lauren Corportion.
Ralphs Grocery Company, **35 368–70**
Ralston Purina Company, **II 561–63; 13 425–27 (upd.)** *see also* Ralcorp Holdings, Inc.; Nestlé S.A.
Ramsay Youth Services, Inc., **41 322–24**
Ramtron International Corporation, **89 365–68**
Ranbaxy Laboratories Ltd., **70 247–49**
Rand McNally & Company, **28 378–81; 53** 122
Randall's Food Markets, Inc., **40 364–67** *see also* Safeway Inc.
Random House, Inc., **13 428–30; 31 375–80 (upd.)**
Randon S.A. Implementos e Participações, **79 348–52**
Randstad Holding n.v., **16 420–22; 43 307–10 (upd.)**
Range Resources Corporation, **45 353–55**
The Rank Group plc, **II 157–59; 14 399–402 (upd.); 64 317–21 (upd.)**
Ranks Hovis McDougall Limited, **II 564–65; 28 382–85 (upd.)**
RAO Unified Energy System of Russia, **45 356–60**

Rapala-Normark Group, Ltd., 30 368–71
Rare Hospitality International Inc., 19 340–42
RAS *see* Riunione Adriatica di Sicurtà SpA.
Rascal House *see* Jerry's Famous Deli Inc.
Rathbone Brothers plc, 70 250–53
RathGibson Inc., 90 348–51
ratiopharm Group, 84 322–326
Ratner Companies, 72 294–96
Raven Industries, Inc., 33 359–61
Ravensburger AG, 64 322–26
Raving Brands, Inc., 64 327–29
Rawlings Sporting Goods Co., Inc., 24 402–04
Raychem Corporation, 8 446–47
Raymond James Financial Inc., 69 308–10
Raymond Ltd., 77 351–54
Rayonier Inc., 24 405–07
Rayovac Corporation, 13 431–34; 39 336–40 (upd.)
Raytech Corporation, 61 306–09
Raytheon Aircraft Holdings Inc., 46 354–57
Raytheon Company, II 85–87; 11 411–14 (upd.); 38 372–77 (upd.)
Razorfish, Inc., 37 321–24
RCA Corporation, II 88–90
RCM Technologies, Inc., 34 371–74
RCN Corporation, 70 254–57
RCS MediaGroup S.p.A., 96 343–46
RDO Equipment Company, 33 362–65
RE/MAX International, Inc., 59 344–46
Read-Rite Corp., 10 463–64
The Reader's Digest Association, Inc., IV 663–64; 17 392–95 (upd.); 71 295–99 (upd.)
Reading International Inc., 70 258–60
Real Madrid C.F., 73 274–76
Real Times, Inc., 66 261–65
Real Turismo, S.A. de C.V., 50 373–75
The Really Useful Group, 26 393–95
RealNetworks, Inc., 53 280–82
Reckitt Benckiser plc, II 566–67; 42 302–06 (upd.); 91 392–99 (upd.)
Reckson Associates Realty Corp., 47 329–31
Recording for the Blind & Dyslexic, 51 312–14
Recoton Corp., 15 381–83
Recovery Engineering, Inc., 25 392–94
Recreational Equipment, Inc., 18 444–47; 71 300–03 (upd.)
Recycled Paper Greetings, Inc., 21 426–28
Red Apple Group, Inc., 23 406–08
Red Bull GmbH, 60 252–54
Red McCombs Automotive Group, 91 400–03
Red Hat, Inc., 45 361–64
Red Robin Gourmet Burgers, Inc., 56 294–96
Red Roof Inns, Inc., 18 448–49 *see also* Accor S.A.
Red Spot Paint & Varnish Company, 55 319–22
Red Wing Pottery Sales, Inc., 52 294–96
Red Wing Shoe Company, Inc., 9 433–35; 30 372–75 (upd.); 83 315-321 (upd.)
Redback Networks, Inc., 92 319–22
Reddy Ice Holdings, Inc., 80 304–07
Redhook Ale Brewery, Inc., 31 381–84; 88 317–21 (upd.)
Redken Laboratories Inc., 84 327–330
Redland plc, III 734–36 *see also* Lafarge Cement UK.
Redlon & Johnson, Inc., 97 331–34
RedPeg Marketing, 73 277–79
RedPrairie Corporation, 74 257–60
Redrow Group plc, 31 385–87
Reebok International Ltd., V 375–77; 9 436–38 (upd.); 26 396–400 (upd.)
Reed & Barton Corporation, 67 322–24
Reed Elsevier plc, 31 388–94 (upd.)
Reed International PLC, IV 665–67; 17 396–99 (upd.)
Reeds Jewelers, Inc., 22 447–49
Regal-Beloit Corporation, 18 450–53; 97 335–42 (upd.)
Regal Entertainment Group, 59 340–43
The Regence Group, 74 261–63
Regency Centers Corporation, 71 304–07
Regent Communications, Inc., 87 416–420
Regent Inns plc, 95 354–57
Régie Nationale des Usines Renault, I 189–91 *see also* Renault S.A.
Regis Corporation, 18 454–56; 70 261–65 (upd.)
REI *see* Recreational Equipment, Inc.
Reichhold Chemicals, Inc., 10 465–67
Reiter Dairy, LLC, 94 361–64
Rejuvenation, Inc., 91 404–07
Reliance Electric Company, 9 439–42
Reliance Group Holdings, Inc., III 342–44
Reliance Industries Ltd., 81 332–36
Reliance Steel & Aluminum Company, 19 343–45; 70 266–70 (upd.)
Reliant Energy Inc., 44 368–73 (upd.)
Relìv International, Inc., 58 292–95
Remedy Corporation, 58 296–99
RemedyTemp, Inc., 20 448–50
Remington Arms Company, Inc., 12 415–17; 40 368–71 (upd.)
Remington Products Company, L.L.C., 42 307–10
Remington Rand *see* Unisys Corp.
Rémy Cointreau Group, 20 451–53; 80 308–12 (upd.)
Renaissance Learning Systems, Inc., 39 341–43
Renal Care Group, Inc., 72 297–99
Renault Argentina S.A., 67 325–27
Renault S.A., 26 401–04 (upd.); 74 264–68 (upd.)
Rengo Co., Ltd., IV 326
Renishaw plc, 46 358–60
RENK AG, 37 325–28
Renner Herrmann S.A., 79 353–56
Reno Air Inc., 23 409–11
Reno de Medici S.p.A., 41 325–27
Rent-A-Center, Inc., 45 365–67
Rent-Way, Inc., 33 366–68; 75 336–39 (upd.)
Rental Service Corporation, 28 386–88
Rentokil Initial Plc, 47 332–35
Rentrak Corporation, 35 371–74
Repco Corporation Ltd., 74 269–72
Repsol-YPF S.A., IV 527–29; 16 423–26 (upd.); 40 372–76 (upd.)
Republic Engineered Steels, Inc., 7 446–47; 26 405–08 (upd.)
Republic Industries, Inc., 26 409–11 *see also* AutoNation, Inc.
Republic New York Corporation, 11 415–19 *see also* HSBC Holdings plc.
Republic Services, Inc., 92 323–26
Res-Care, Inc., 29 399–402
Research in Motion Ltd., 54 310–14
Research Triangle Institute, 83 322-325
Réseau Ferré de France, 66 266–68
Reser's Fine Foods, Inc., 81 337–40
Resorts International, Inc., 12 418–20
Resource America, Inc., 42 311–14
Resources Connection, Inc., 81 341–44
Response Oncology, Inc., 27 385–87
Restaurant Associates Corporation, 66 269–72
Restaurants Unlimited, Inc., 13 435–37
Restoration Hardware, Inc., 30 376–78; 96 347–51 (upd.)
Retail Ventures, Inc., 82 299–03 (upd.)
Reuters Group PLC, IV 668–70; 22 450–53 (upd.); 63 323–27 (upd.)
Revco D.S., Inc., V 171–73 *see also* CVS Corp.
Revell-Monogram Inc., 16 427–29
Revere Electric Supply Company, 96 352–55
Revere Ware Corporation, 22 454–56
Revlon Inc., III 54–57; 17 400–04 (upd.); 64 330–35 (upd.)
Rewards Network Inc., 70 271–75 (upd.)
REX Stores Corp., 10 468–69
Rexam PLC, 32 380–85 (upd.); 85 353–61 (upd.)
Rexel, Inc., 15 384–87
Rexnord Corporation, 21 429–32; 76 315–19 (upd.)
The Reynolds and Reynolds Company, 50 376–79
Reynolds Metals Company, IV 186–88; 19 346–48 (upd.) *see also* Alcoa Inc.
RF Micro Devices, Inc., 43 311–13
RFC Franchising LLC, 68 317–19
RFF *see* Réseau Ferré de France.
RGI *see* Rockefeller Group International.
Rheinmetall AG, 9 443–46; 97 343–49 (upd.)
RHI AG, 53 283–86
Rhino Entertainment Company, 18 457–60; 70 276–80 (upd.)
RHM *see* Ranks Hovis McDougall.
Rhodes Inc., 23 412–14
Rhodia SA, 38 378–80
Rhône-Poulenc S.A., I 388–90; 10 470–72 (upd.)

Rica Foods, Inc., 41 328–30
Ricardo plc, 90 352–56
Rich Products Corporation, 7 448–49; 38 381–84 (upd.); 93 368–74 (upd.)
The Richards Group, Inc., 58 300–02
Richardson Electronics, Ltd., 17 405–07
Richardson Industries, Inc., 62 298–301
Richfood Holdings, Inc., 7 450–51; *see also* Supervalu Inc.
Richton International Corporation, 39 344–46
Richtree Inc., 63 328–30
Richwood Building Products, Inc. *see* Ply Gem Industries Inc.
Rickenbacker International Corp., 91 408–12
Ricoh Company, Ltd., III 159–61; 36 389–93 (upd.)
Ricola Ltd., 62 302–04
Riddell Sports Inc., 22 457–59; 23 449
Ride, Inc., 22 460–63
Ridley Corporation Ltd., 62 305–07
The Riese Organization, 38 385–88
Rieter Holding AG, 42 315–17
Riggs National Corporation, 13 438–40
Right Management Consultants, Inc., 42 318–21
Riklis Family Corp., 9 447–50
Rimage Corp., 89 369–72
Rinascente S.p.A., 71 308–10
Rinker Group Ltd., 65 298–301
Rio Tinto plc, 19 349–53 (upd.) 50 380–85 (upd.)
Ripley Entertainment, Inc., 74 273–76
Riser Foods, Inc., 9 451–54 *see also* Giant Eagle, Inc.
Ritchie Bros. Auctioneers Inc., 41 331–34
Rite Aid Corporation, V 174–76; 19 354–57 (upd.); 63 331–37 (upd.)
Ritter Sport *see* Alfred Ritter GmbH & Co. KG.
Ritter's Frozen Custard *see* RFC Franchising LLC.
Ritz Camera Centers, 34 375–77
The Ritz-Carlton Hotel Company, L.L.C., 9 455–57; 29 403–06 (upd.); 71 311–16 (upd.)
Ritz-Craft Corporation of Pennsylvania Inc., 94 365–68
Riunione Adriatica di Sicurtà SpA, III 345–48
Riva Fire *see* Gruppo Riva Fire SpA.
The Rival Company, 19 358–60
River Oaks Furniture, Inc., 43 314–16
River Ranch Fresh Foods LLC, 88 322–25
Riverwood International Corporation, 11 420–23; 48 340–44 (upd.) *see also* Graphic Packaging Holding Co.
Riviana Foods, 27 388–91
Riviera Holdings Corporation, 75 340–43
Riviera Tool Company, 89 373–76
RJR Nabisco Holdings Corp., V 408–10 *see also* R.J Reynolds Tobacco Holdings Inc., Nabisco Brands, Inc.; R.J. Reynolds Industries, Inc.
RM Auctions, Inc., 88 326–29
RMC Group p.l.c., III 737–40; 34 378–83 (upd.)
RMH Teleservices, Inc., 42 322–24
Roadhouse Grill, Inc., 22 464–66
Roadmaster Industries, Inc., 16 430–33
Roadway Express, Inc., V 502–03; 25 395–98 (upd.)
Roanoke Electric Steel Corporation, 45 368–70
Robbins & Myers Inc., 15 388–90
Roberds Inc., 19 361–63
Robert Bosch GmbH, I 392–93; 16 434–37 (upd.); 43 317–21 (upd.)
Robert Half International Inc., 18 461–63; 70 281–84 (upd.)
Robert Mondavi Corporation, 15 391–94; 50 386–90 (upd.)
Robert Talbott Inc., 88 330–33
Robert W. Baird & Co. Incorporated, 67 328–30
Robert Wood Johnson Foundation, 35 375–78
Robertet SA, 39 347–49
Roberts Pharmaceutical Corporation, 16 438–40
Robertson-Ceco Corporation, 19 364–66
Robins, Kaplan, Miller & Ciresi L.L.P., 89 377–81
Robinson Helicopter Company, 51 315–17
ROC *see* Royal Olympic Cruise Lines Inc.
Rocawear Apparel LLC, 77 355–58
Roche Biomedical Laboratories, Inc., 11 424–26 *see also* Laboratory Corporation of America Holdings.
Roche Bioscience, 14 403–06 (upd.)
Rochester Gas And Electric Corporation, 6 571–73
Rochester Telephone Corporation, 6 332–34
Röchling Gruppe, 94 369–74
Rock Bottom Restaurants, Inc., 25 399–401; 68 320–23 (upd.)
Rock-It Cargo USA, Inc., 86 339–42
Rock of Ages Corporation, 37 329–32
Rock-Tenn Company, 13 441–43; 59 347–51 (upd.)
The Rockefeller Foundation, 34 384–87
Rockefeller Group International Inc., 58 303–06
Rockford Corporation, 43 322–25
Rockford Products Corporation, 55 323–25
RockShox, Inc., 26 412–14
Rockwell Automation, 43 326–31 (upd.)
Rockwell International Corporation, I 78–80; 11 427–30 (upd.)
Rockwell Medical Technologies, Inc., 88 334–37
Rocky Mountain Chocolate Factory, Inc., 73 280–82
Rocky Shoes & Boots, Inc., 26 415–18
Rodale, Inc., 23 415–17; 47 336–39 (upd.)
Rodamco N.V., 26 419–21
Rodriguez Group S.A., 90 357–60
ROFIN-SINAR Technologies Inc, 81 345–48
Rogers Communications Inc., 30 388–92 (upd.) *see also* Maclean Hunter Publishing Ltd.
Rogers Corporation, 61 310–13; 80 313–17 (upd.)
Rohde & Schwarz GmbH & Co. KG, 39 350–53
Röhm and Haas Company, I 391–93; 26 422–26 (upd.); 77 359–66 (upd.)
ROHN Industries, Inc., 22 467–69
Rohr Incorporated, 9 458–60 *see also* Goodrich Corp.
Roland Berger & Partner GmbH, 37 333–36
Roland Corporation, 38 389–91
Roland Murten A.G., 7 452–53
Rolex *see* Montres Rolex S.A.
Roll International Corporation, 37 337–39
Rollerblade, Inc., 15 395–98; 34 388–92 (upd.)
Rollins, Inc., 11 431–34
Rolls-Royce Allison, 29 407–09 (upd.)
Rolls-Royce Group PLC, 67 331–36 (upd.)
Rolls-Royce Motors Ltd., I 194–96
Rolls-Royce plc, I 81–83; 7 454–57 (upd.); 21 433–37 (upd.)
Rolta India Ltd., 90 361–64
Roly Poly Franchise Systems LLC, 83 326-328
Romacorp, Inc., 58 307–11
Roman Meal Company, 84 331–334
Ron Tonkin Chevrolet Company, 55 326–28
RONA, Inc., 73 283–86
Ronco Corporation, 15 399–401; 80 318–23 (upd.)
Ronson PLC, 49 337–39
Rooms To Go Inc., 28 389–92
Rooney Brothers Co., 25 402–04
Roosevelt Hospital *see* Continuum Health Partners, Inc.
Roots Canada Ltd., 42 325–27
Roper Industries, Inc., 15 402–04; 50 391–95 (upd.)
Ropes & Gray, 40 377–80
Rorer Group, I 666–68
Rosauers Supermarkets, Inc., 90 365–68
Rose Acre Farms, Inc., 60 255–57
Rose Art Industries, 58 312–14
Rose's Stores, Inc., 13 444–46
Roseburg Forest Products Company, 58 315–17
Rosemount Inc., 15 405–08 *see also* Emerson.
Rosenbluth International Inc., 14 407–09 *see also* American Express Co.
Rosetta Stone Inc., 93 375–79
Ross Stores, Inc., 17 408–10; 43 332–35 (upd.)
Rossignol Ski Company, Inc. *see* Skis Rossignol S.A.
Rossmann *see* Dirk Rossmann GmbH.
Rostvertol plc, 62 308–10

Rosy Blue N.V., 84 335–338
Rotary International, 31 395–97
Rothmans UK Holdings Limited, V 411–13; 19 367–70 (upd.)
Roto-Rooter, Inc., 15 409–11; 61 314–19 (upd.)
Rotork plc, 46 361–64
The Rottlund Company, Inc., 28 393–95
Rouge Steel Company, 8 448–50
Rougier *see* Groupe Rougier, SA.
Roularta Media Group NV, 48 345–47
Rounder Records Corporation, 79 357–61
Roundy's Inc., 14 410–12; 58 318–21 (upd.)
The Rouse Company, 15 412–15; 63 338–41 (upd.)
Roussel Uclaf, I 669–70; 8 451–53 (upd.)
Rover Group Ltd., 7 458–60; 21 441–44 (upd.)
Rowan Companies, Inc., 43 336–39
Rowntree Mackintosh PLC, II 568–70 *see also* Nestlé S.A.
The Rowohlt Verlag GmbH, 96 356–61
Roy Anderson Corporation, 75 344–46
Roy F. Weston, Inc., 33 369–72
Royal & Sun Alliance Insurance Group plc, 55 329–39 (upd.)
Royal Ahold N.V. *see* Koninklijke Ahold N.V.
Royal Appliance Manufacturing Company, 15 416–18
The Royal Bank of Canada, II 344–46; 21 445–48 (upd.); 81 349–55 (upd.)
The Royal Bank of Scotland Group plc, 12 421–23; 38 392–99 (upd.)
Royal Canin S.A., 39 354–57
Royal Caribbean Cruises Ltd., 22 470–73; 74 277–81 (upd.)
Royal Crown Company, Inc., 23 418–20 *see also* Cott Corp.
Royal Doulton plc, 14 413–15; 38 400–04 (upd.)
Royal Dutch Petroleum Company, IV 530–32 *see also* Shell Transport and Trading Company p.l.c.
Royal Dutch/Shell Group, 49 340–44 (upd.)
Royal Grolsch NV, 54 315–18
Royal Group Technologies Limited, 73 287–89
Royal Insurance Holdings plc, III 349–51 *see also* Royal & Sun Alliance Insurance Group plc .
Royal KPN N.V., 30 393–95
Royal Nepal Airline Corporation, 41 335–38
Royal Numico N.V., 37 340–42
Royal Olympic Cruise Lines Inc., 52 297–99
Royal Packaging Industries Van Leer N.V., 30 396–98
Royal Ten Cate N.V., 68 324–26
Royal Vendex KBB N.V. *see* Koninklijke Vendex KBB N.V. (Royal Vendex KBB N.V.).
Royal Vopak NV, 41 339–41
RPC Group PLC, 81 356–59
RPC, Inc., 91 413–16
RPM International Inc., 8 454–57; 36 394–98 (upd.); 91 417–25 (upd.)
RSA Security Inc., 46 365–68
RSC *see* Rental Service Corp.
RTI Biologics, Inc., 96 362–65
RTL Group SA, 44 374–78
RTM Restaurant Group, 58 322–24
RTZ Corporation PLC, IV 189–92 *see also* Rio Tinto plc.
Rubbermaid Incorporated, III 613–15; 20 454–57 (upd.) *see also* Newell Rubbermaid Inc.
Rubio's Restaurants, Inc., 35 379–81
Ruby Tuesday, Inc., 18 464–66; 71 317–20 (upd.)
Rudolph Technologies Inc., 94 375–78
The Rugby Group plc, 31 398–400
Ruger Corporation *see* Sturm, Ruger & Co., Inc.
Ruhrgas AG, V 704–06; 38 405–09 (upd.)
Ruhrkohle AG, IV 193–95 *see also* RAG AG.
Ruiz Food Products, Inc., 53 287–89
Rural Cellular Corporation, 43 340–42
Rural/Metro Corporation, 28 396–98
Rural Press Ltd., 74 282–85
Rush Communications, 33 373–75 *see also* Phat Fashions LLC.
Rush Enterprises, Inc., 64 336–38
Russ Berrie and Company, Inc., 12 424–26; 82 304–08 (upd.)
Russell Corporation, 8 458–59; 30 399–401 (upd.); 82 309–13 (upd.)
Russell Reynolds Associates Inc., 38 410–12
Russell Stover Candies Inc., 12 427–29; 91 426–32 (upd.)
Russian Aircraft Corporation (MiG), 86 343–46
Russian Railways Joint Stock Co., 93 380–83
Rust International Inc., 11 435–36
Rusty, Inc., 95 358–61
Ruth's Chris Steak House, 28 399–401; 88 338–42 (upd.)
RWD Technologies, Inc., 76 320–22
RWE Group, V 707–10; 50 396–400 (upd.)
Ryan Beck & Co., Inc., 66 273–75
Ryan's Restaurant Group, Inc., 15 419–21; 68 327–30 (upd.)
Ryanair Holdings plc, 35 382–85
Ryder System, Inc., V 504–06; 24 408–11 (upd.)
Ryerson Tull, Inc., 40 381–84 (upd.)
Ryko Corporation, 83 329-333
The Ryland Group, Inc., 8 460–61; 37 343–45 (upd.)
Ryoshoku Ltd., 72 300–02
RZB *see* Raiffeisen Zentralbank Österreich AG.
RZD *see* Russian Railways Joint Stock Co.

S

S&C Electric Company, 15 422–24
S&D Coffee, Inc., 84 339–341
S&K Famous Brands, Inc., 23 421–23
S&P *see* Standard & Poor's Corp.
S.A.C.I. Falabella, 69 311–13
S.A. Cockerill Sambre *see* Cockerill Sambre Group.
s.a. GB-Inno-BM *see* GIB Group.
S.C. Johnson & Son, Inc., III 58–59; 28 409–12 (upd.); 89 382–89 (upd.)
S-K-I Limited, 15 457–59
SAA (Pty) Ltd., 28 402–04
Saab Automobile AB, 32 386–89 (upd.); 83 334-339 (upd.)
Saab-Scania A.B., I 197–98; 11 437–39 (upd.)
Saarberg-Konzern, IV 196–99 *see also* RAG AG.
Saatchi & Saatchi plc, I 33–35; 33 328–31 (upd.)
SAB *see* South African Breweries Ltd.
Sabanci Holdings *see* Haci Omer Sabanci Holdings A.S.
Sabaté Diosos SA, 48 348–50 *see also* OENEO S.A.
Sabena S.A./N.V., 33 376–79
SABIC *see* Saudi Basic Industries Corp.
SABMiller plc, 59 352–58 (upd.)
Sabratek Corporation, 29 410–12
Sabre Holdings Corporation, 26 427–30; 74 286–90 (upd.)
Sadia S.A., 59 359–62
Safe Flight Instrument Corporation, 71 321–23
SAFECO Corporation, III 352–54
Safeguard Scientifics, Inc., 10 473–75
Safelite Glass Corp., 19 371–73
Safeskin Corporation, 18 467–70 *see also* Kimberly-Clark Corp.
Safety Components International, Inc., 63 342–44
Safety 1st, Inc., 24 412–15
Safety-Kleen Systems Inc., 8 462–65; 82 314–20 (upd.)
Safeway Inc., II 654–56; 24 416–19 (upd.); 85 362–69 (upd.)
Safeway PLC, 50 401–06 (upd.)
Saffery Champness, 80 324–27
Safilo SpA, 40 155–56; **54 319–21**
Saga Communications, Inc., 27 392–94
The Sage Group, 43 343–46
SAGEM S.A., 37 346–48
SAIC *see* Science Applications International Corp.
Sainsbury's *see* J Sainsbury PLC.
Saint-Gobain *see* Compagnie de Saint Gobain S.A.
St Ives plc, 34 393–95
St. James's Place Capital, plc, 71 324–26
The St. Joe Company, 31 422–25
St. Joe Paper Company, 8 485–88
St. John Knits, Inc., 14 466–68
St. Jude Medical, Inc., 11 458–61; 43 347–52 (upd.); 97 350–58 (upd.)

St. Louis Music, Inc., 48 351–54
St. Luke's-Roosevelt Hospital Center *see* Continuum Health Partners, Inc.
St. Mary Land & Exploration Company, 63 345–47
St. Paul Bank for Cooperatives, 8 489–90
The St. Paul Travelers Companies, Inc., III 355–57; 22 492–95 (upd.); 79 362–69 (upd.)
Ste. Michelle Wine Estates Ltd., 96 408–11
Salem Communications Corporation, 97 359–63
salesforce.com, Inc., 79 370–73
Saks Inc., 24 420–23; 41 342–45 (upd.)
Salant Corporation, 12 430–32; 51 318–21 (upd.)
Salick Health Care, Inc., 53 290–92
Salix Pharmaceuticals, Ltd., 93 384–87
Sallie Mae *see* SLM Holding Corp.
Sally Beauty Company, Inc., 60 258–60
Salomon Inc., II 447–49; 13 447–50 (upd.) *see also* Citigroup Inc.
Salomon Worldwide, 20 458–60 *see also* adidas-Salomon AG.
Salt River Project, 19 374–76
Salton, Inc., 30 402–04; 88 343–48 (upd.)
The Salvation Army USA, 32 390–93
Salvatore Ferragamo Italia S.p.A., 62 311–13
Salzgitter AG, IV 200–01
Sam Ash Music Corporation, 30 405–07
Sam Levin Inc., 80 328–31
Sam's Club, 40 385–87
Sam's Wine & Spirits, 96 366–69
Samick Musical Instruments Co., Ltd., 56 297–300
Samsonite Corporation, 13 451–53; 43 353–57 (upd.)
Samsung Electronics Co., Ltd., 14 416–18; 41 346–49 (upd.)
Samsung Group, I 515–17
Samuel Cabot Inc., 53 293–95
Samuels Jewelers Incorporated, 30 408–10
San Diego Gas & Electric Company, V 711–14 *see also* Sempra Energy.
San Diego Padres Baseball Club L.P., 78 324–27
San Francisco Baseball Associates, L.P., 55 340–43
San Miguel Corporation, 15 428–30; 57 303–08 (upd.)
Sanborn Hermanos, S.A., 20 461–63
Sanborn Map Company Inc., 82 321–24
The Sanctuary Group PLC, 69 314–17
Sandals Resorts International, 65 302–05
Sanders Morris Harris Group Inc., 70 285–87
Sanderson Farms, Inc., 15 425–27
Sandia National Laboratories, 49 345–48
Sandoz Ltd., I 671–73 *see also* Novartis AG.
Sandvik AB, IV 202–04; 32 394–98 (upd.); 77 367–73 (upd.)
Sanford L.P., 82 325–29
Sanitec Corporation, 51 322–24
Sankyo Company, Ltd., I 674–75; 56 301–04 (upd.)
Sanlam Ltd., 68 331–34
SANLUIS Corporación, S.A.B. de C.V., 95 362–65
The Sanofi-Synthélabo Group, I 676–77; 49 349–51 (upd.)
SanomaWSOY Corporation, 51 325–28
Sanpaolo IMI S.p.A., 50 407–11
Sanrio Company, Ltd., 38 413–15
Santa Barbara Restaurant Group, Inc., 37 349–52
The Santa Cruz Operation, Inc., 38 416–21
Santa Fe Gaming Corporation, 19 377–79 *see also* Archon Corp.
Santa Fe International Corporation, 38 422–24
Santa Fe Pacific Corporation, V 507–09 *see also* Burlington Northern Santa Fe Corp.
Santa Margherita S.p.A. *see* Industrie Zignago Santa Margherita S.p.A.
Santos Ltd., 81 360–63
Sanwa Bank, Ltd., II 347–48; 15 431–33 (upd.)
SANYO Electric Co., Ltd., II 91–92; 36 399–403 (upd.); 95 366–73 (upd.)
Sanyo-Kokusaku Pulp Co., Ltd., IV 327–28
Sao Paulo Alpargatas S.A., 75 347–49
SAP AG, 16 441–44; 43 358–63 (upd.)
Sapa AB, 84 342–345
Sappi Limited, 49 352–55
Sapporo Holdings Limited, I 282–83; 13 454–56 (upd.); 36 404–07 (upd.); 97 364–69 (upd.)
Saputo Inc., 59 363–65
Sara Lee Corporation, II 571–73; 15 434–37 (upd.); 54 322–27 (upd.)
Sarnoff Corporation, 57 309–12
Sarris Candies Inc., 86 347–50
The SAS Group, 34 396–99 (upd.)
SAS Institute Inc., 10 476–78; 78 328–32 (upd.)
Sasol Limited, IV 533–35; 47 340–44 (upd.)
Saturn Corporation, 7 461–64; 21 449–53 (upd.); 80 332–38 (upd.)
Satyam Computer Services Ltd., 85 370–73
Saucony Inc., 35 386–89; 86 351–56 (upd.)
Sauder Woodworking Co., 12 433–34; 35 390–93 (upd.)
Saudi Arabian Airlines, 6 114–16; 27 395–98 (upd.)
Saudi Arabian Oil Company, IV 536–39; 17 411–15 (upd.); 50 412–17 (upd.)
Saudi Basic Industries Corporation (SABIC), 58 325–28
Sauer-Danfoss Inc., 61 320–22
Saul Ewing LLP, 74 291–94
Saur S.A.S., 92 327–30
Savannah Foods & Industries, Inc., 7 465–67 *see also* Imperial Sugar Co.
Sawtek Inc., 43 364–66 (upd.)
Sbarro, Inc., 16 445–47; 64 339–42 (upd.)
SBC Communications Inc., 32 399–403 (upd.)
SBC Warburg, 14 419–21 *see also* UBS AG.
Sberbank, 62 314–17
SBI *see* State Bank of India.
SBS Technologies, Inc., 25 405–07
SCA *see* Svenska Cellulosa AB.
SCANA Corporation, 6 574–76; 56 305–08 (upd.)
Scandinavian Airlines System, I 119–20 *see also* The SAS Group.
ScanSource, Inc., 29 413–15; 74 295–98 (upd.)
Scarborough Public Utilities Commission, 9 461–62
SCB Computer Technology, Inc., 29 416–18
SCEcorp, V 715–17 *see also* Edison International.
Schawk, Inc., 24 424–26
Scheels All Sports Inc., 63 348–50
Scheid Vineyards Inc., 66 276–78
Schell Brewing *see* August Schell Brewing Company Inc.
Schenck Business Solutions, 88 349–53
Schenker-Rhenus Ag, 6 424–26
Scherer *see* R.P. Scherer.
Scherer Brothers Lumber Company, 94 379–83
Schering A.G., I 681–82; 50 418–22 (upd.)
Schering-Plough Corporation, I 683–85; 14 422–25 (upd.); 49 356–62 (upd.)
Schibsted ASA, 31 401–05
Schieffelin & Somerset Co., 61 323–25
Schindler Holding AG, 29 419–22
Schlage Lock Company, 82 330–34
Schlotzsky's, Inc., 36 408–10
Schlumberger Limited, III 616–18; 17 416–19 (upd.); 59 366–71 (upd.)
Schmitt Music Company, 40 388–90
Schneider National, Inc., 36 411–13; 77 374–78 (upd.)
Schneider S.A., II 93–94; 18 471–74 (upd.)
Schneiderman's Furniture Inc., 28 405–08
Schnitzer Steel Industries, Inc., 19 380–82
Scholastic Corporation, 10 479–81; 29 423–27 (upd.)
Scholle Corporation, 96 370–73
School Specialty, Inc., 68 335–37
School-Tech, Inc., 62 318–20
Schott Brothers, Inc., 67 337–39
Schott Corporation, 53 296–98
Schottenstein Stores Corp., 14 426–28 *see also* Retail Ventures, Inc.
Schouw & Company A/S, 94 384–87
Schreiber Foods, Inc., 72 303–06

Schroders plc, 42 332–35
Schuff Steel Company, 26 431–34
Schultz Sav-O Stores, Inc., 21 454–56; 31 406–08 (upd.)
The Schwan Food Company, 7 468–70; 26 435–38 (upd.); 83 340-346 (upd.)
Schwebel Baking Company, 72 307–09
Schweitzer-Mauduit International, Inc., 52 300–02
Schweizerische Post-, Telefon- und Telegrafen-Betriebe, V 321–24
Schweppes Ltd. *see* Cadbury Schweppes PLC.
Schwinn Cycle and Fitness L.P., 19 383–85 *see also* Huffy Corp.
SCI *see* Service Corporation International.
SCI Systems, Inc., 9 463–64
Science Applications International Corporation, 15 438–40
Scientific-Atlanta, Inc., 6 335–37; 45 371–75 (upd.)
Scientific Games Corporation, 64 343–46 (upd.)
Scientific Learning Corporation, 95 374–77
Scitex Corporation Ltd., 24 427–32
SCO *see* Santa Cruz Operation, Inc.
The SCO Group Inc., 78 333–37
Scope Products, Inc., 94 388–91
SCOR S.A., 20 464–66
The Score Board, Inc., 19 386–88
Scotiabank *see* The Bank of Nova Scotia.
Scotsman Industries, Inc., 20 467–69
Scott Fetzer Company, 12 435–37; 80 339–43 (upd.)
Scott Paper Company, IV 329–31; 31 409–12 (upd.)
Scottish & Newcastle plc, 15 441–44; 35 394–97 (upd.)
Scottish and Southern Energy plc, 13 457–59; 66 279–84 (upd.)
Scottish Media Group plc, 32 404–06; 41 350–52
Scottish Power plc, 49 363–66 (upd.)
Scottish Radio Holding plc, 41 350–52
ScottishPower plc, 19 389–91
Scottrade, Inc., 85 374–77
The Scotts Company, 22 474–76
Scotty's, Inc., 22 477–80
The Scoular Company, 77 379–82
Scovill Fasteners Inc., 24 433–36
SCP Pool Corporation, 39 358–60
Screen Actors Guild, 72 310–13
The Scripps Research Institute, 76 323–25
SDGE *see* San Diego Gas & Electric Co.
SDL PLC, 67 340–42
Sea Containers Ltd., 29 428–31
Seaboard Corporation, 36 414–16; 85 378–82 (upd.)
SeaChange International, Inc., 79 374–78
SEACOR Holdings Inc., 83 347-350
Seagate Technology, Inc., 8 466–68; 34 400–04 (upd.)
The Seagram Company Ltd., I 284–86; 25 408–12 (upd.)
Seagull Energy Corporation, 11 440–42
Sealaska Corporation, 60 261–64
Sealed Air Corporation, 14 429–31; 57 313–17 (upd.)
Sealed Power Corporation, I 199–200 *see also* SPX Corp.
Sealright Co., Inc., 17 420–23
Sealy Inc., 12 438–40
Seaman Furniture Company, Inc., 32 407–09
Sean John Clothing, Inc., 70 288–90
SeaRay Boats Inc., 96 374–77
Sears plc, V 177–79
Sears, Roebuck and Co., V 180–83; 18 475–79 (upd.); 56 309–14 (upd.)
Sears Roebuck de México, S.A. de C.V., 20 470–72
Seat Pagine Gialle S.p.A., 47 345–47
Seattle City Light, 50 423–26
Seattle FilmWorks, Inc., 20 473–75
Seattle First National Bank Inc., 8 469–71 *see also* Bank of America Corp.
Seattle Lighting Fixture Company, 92 331–34
Seattle Pacific Industries, Inc., 92 335–38
Seattle Seahawks, Inc., 92 339–43
Seattle Times Company, 15 445–47
Seaway Food Town, Inc., 15 448–50 *see also* Spartan Stores Inc.
SEB Group *see* Skandinaviska Enskilda Banken AB.
SEB S.A. *see* Groupe SEB.
Sebastiani Vineyards, Inc., 28 413–15
The Second City, Inc., 88 354–58
Second Harvest, 29 432–34
Securicor Plc, 45 376–79
Securitas AB, 42 336–39
Security Capital Corporation, 17 424–27
Security Pacific Corporation, II 349–50
SED International Holdings, Inc., 43 367–69
Seddon Group Ltd., 67 343–45
SEGA Corporation, 73 290–93
Sega of America, Inc., 10 482–85
Segway LLC, 48 355–57
SEI Investments Company, 96 378–82
Seibu Department Stores, Ltd., V 184–86; 42 340–43 (upd.)
Seibu Railway Company Ltd., V 510–11; 74 299–301 (upd.)
Seigle's Home and Building Centers, Inc., 41 353–55
Seiko Corporation, III 619–21; 17 428–31 (upd.); 72 314–18 (upd.)
Seino Transportation Company, Ltd., 6 427–29
Seita, 23 424–27 *see also* Altadis S.A.
Seitel, Inc., 47 348–50
The Seiyu, Ltd., V 187–89; 36 417–21 (upd.)
Sekisui Chemical Co., Ltd., III 741–43; 72 319–22 (upd.)
Select Comfort Corporation, 34 405–08
Select Medical Corporation, 65 306–08
Selecta AG, 97 370–73
Selectour SA, 53 299–301
Selee Corporation, 88 359–62
Selfridges Plc, 34 409–11
The Selmer Company, Inc., 19 392–94
SEMCO Energy, Inc., 44 379–82
Seminis, Inc., 29 435–37
Semitool, Inc., 18 480–82; 79 379–82 (upd.)
Sempra Energy, 25 413–16 (upd.)
Semtech Corporation, 32 410–13
Seneca Foods Corporation, 17 432–34; 60 265–68 (upd.)
Sennheiser Electronic GmbH & Co. KG, 66 285–89
Senomyx, Inc., 83 351-354
Sensient Technologies Corporation, 52 303–08 (upd.)
Sensormatic Electronics Corp., 11 443–45
Sensory Science Corporation, 37 353–56
La Senza Corporation, 66 205–07
Sephora Holdings S.A., 82 335–39
Sepracor Inc., 45 380–83
Sequa Corporation, 13 460–63; 54 328–32 (upd.)
Sequana Capital, 78 338–42 (upd.)
Serco Group plc, 47 351–53
Serologicals Corporation, 63 351–53
Serono S.A., 47 354–57
Serta, Inc., 28 416–18
Servco Pacific Inc., 96 383–86
Service America Corp., 7 471–73
Service Corporation International, 6 293–95; 51 329–33 (upd.)
Service Merchandise Company, Inc., V 190–92; 19 395–99 (upd.)
The ServiceMaster Company, 6 44–46; 23 428–31 (upd.); 68 338–42 (upd.)
Servpro Industries, Inc., 85 383–86
7-Eleven, Inc., 32 414–18 (upd.)
Sevenson Environmental Services, Inc., 42 344–46
Seventh Generation, Inc., 73 294–96
Severn Trent PLC, 12 441–43; 38 425–29 (upd.)
Severstal Joint Stock Company, 65 309–12
Seyfarth Shaw LLP, 93 388–91
SFI Group plc, 51 334–36
SFX Entertainment, Inc., 36 422–25
SGI, 29 438–41 (upd.)
Shakespeare Company, 22 481–84
Shaklee Corporation, 12 444–46; 39 361–64 (upd.)
Shanghai Baosteel Group Corporation, 71 327–30
Shanghai Petrochemical Co., Ltd., 18 483–85
Shangri-La Asia Ltd., 71 331–33
Shanks Group plc, 45 384–87
Shannon Aerospace Ltd., 36 426–28
Shared Medical Systems Corporation, 14 432–34 *see also* Siemens AG.
Sharp Corporation, II 95–96; 12 447–49 (upd.); 40 391–95 (upd.)
The Sharper Image Corporation, 10 486–88; 62 321–24 (upd.)
The Shaw Group, Inc., 50 427–30

Shaw Industries, Inc., 9 465–67; 40 396–99 (upd.)
Shaw's Supermarkets, Inc., 56 315–18
Shea Homes *see* J.F. Shea Co., Inc.
Sheaffer Pen Corporation, 82 340–43
Shearer's Foods, Inc., 72 323–25
Shearman & Sterling, 32 419–22
Shearson Lehman Brothers Holdings Inc., II 450–52; 9 468–70 (upd.)
Shedd Aquarium Society, 73 297–99
Sheetz, Inc., 85 387–90
Shelby Williams Industries, Inc., 14 435–37
Sheldahl Inc., 23 432–35
Shell Oil Company, IV 540–41; 14 438–40 (upd.); 41 356–60 (upd.) *see also* Royal Dutch/Shell Group.
Shell Transport and Trading Company p.l.c., IV 530–32 *see also* Royal Dutch Petroleum Company; Royal Dutch/Shell.
Sheller-Globe Corporation, I 201–02 *see also* Lear Corp.
Shells Seafood Restaurants, Inc., 43 370–72
Shenandoah Telecommunications Company, 89 390–93
Shenhua Group *see* China Shenhua Energy Company Limited
Shepherd Neame Limited, 30 414–16
Sheplers, Inc., 96 387–90
The Sheridan Group, Inc., 86 357–60
Shermag, Inc., 93 392–97
The Sherwin-Williams Company, III 744–46; 13 469–71 (upd.); 89 394–400 (upd.)
Sherwood Brands, Inc., 53 302–04
Shikoku Electric Power Company, Inc., V 718–20; 60 269–72 (upd.)
Shimano Inc., 64 347–49
Shionogi & Co., Ltd., III 60–61; 17 435–37 (upd.)
Shiseido Company, Limited, III 62–64; 22 485–88 (upd.); 81 364–70 (upd.)
Shochiku Company Ltd., 74 302–04
Shoe Carnival Inc., 14 441–43; 72 326–29 (upd.)
Shoe Pavilion, Inc., 84 346–349
Shoney's, Inc., 7 474–76; 23 436–39 (upd.)
ShopKo Stores Inc., 21 457–59; 58 329–32 (upd.)
Shoppers Drug Mart Corporation, 49 367–70
Shoppers Food Warehouse Corporation, 66 290–92
Shorewood Packaging Corporation, 28 419–21
Showa Shell Sekiyu K.K., IV 542–43; 59 372–75 (upd.)
ShowBiz Pizza Time, Inc., 13 472–74 *see also* CEC Entertainment, Inc.
Showboat, Inc., 19 400–02 *see also* Harrah's Entertainment, Inc.
Showtime Networks, Inc., 78 343–47
Shred-It Canada Corporation, 56 319–21
Shriners Hospitals for Children, 69 318–20
Shubert Organization Inc., 24 437–39
Shuffle Master Inc., 51 337–40
Shure Inc., 60 273–76
Shurgard Storage Centers, Inc., 52 309–11
SHV Holdings N.V., 55 344–47
The Siam Cement Public Company Limited, 56 322–25
Sideco Americana S.A., 67 346–48
Sidel *see* Groupe Sidel S.A.
Siderar S.A.I.C., 66 293–95
Sidley Austin Brown & Wood, 40 400–03
Sidney Frank Importing Co., Inc., 69 321–23
Siebe plc *see* BTR Siebe plc.
Siebel Systems, Inc., 38 430–34
Siebert Financial Corp., 32 423–25
Siegel & Gale, 64 350–52
Siemens AG, II 97–100; 14 444–47 (upd.); 57 318–23 (upd.)
The Sierra Club, 28 422–24
Sierra Health Services, Inc., 15 451–53
Sierra Nevada Brewing Company, 70 291–93
Sierra On-Line, Inc., 15 454–56; 41 361–64 (upd.)
Sierra Pacific Industries, 22 489–91; 90 369–73 (upd.)
SIFCO Industries, Inc., 41
SIG plc, 71 334–36
Sigma-Aldrich Corporation, I 690–91; 36 429–32 (upd.); 93 398–404 (upd.)
Signet Banking Corporation, 11 446–48 *see also* Wachovia Corp.
Signet Group PLC, 61 326–28
Sikorsky Aircraft Corporation, 24 440–43
Silhouette Brands, Inc., 55 348–50
Silicon Graphics Inc., 9 471–73 *see also* SGI.
Siliconware Precision Industries Ltd., 73 300–02
Siltronic AG, 90 374–77
Silver Lake Cookie Company Inc., 95 378–81
Silver Wheaton Corp., 95 382–85
SilverPlatter Information Inc., 23 440–43
Silverstein Properties, Inc., 47 358–60
Simco S.A., 37 357–59
Sime Darby Berhad, 14 448–50; 36 433–36 (upd.)
Simmons Company, 47 361–64
Simon & Schuster Inc., IV 671–72; 19 403–05 (upd.)
Simon Property Group Inc., 27 399–402; 84 350–355 (upd.)
Simon Transportation Services Inc., 27 403–06
Simplex Technologies Inc., 21 460–63
Simplicity Manufacturing, Inc., 64 353–56
Simpson Investment Company, 17 438–41
Simpson Thacher & Bartlett, 39 365–68
Simula, Inc., 41 368–70
SINA Corporation, 69 324–27
Sinclair Broadcast Group, Inc., 25 417–19
Singapore Airlines Limited, 6 117–18; 27 407–09 (upd.); 83 355-359 (upd.)
Singapore Press Holdings Limited, 85 391–95
Singer & Friedlander Group plc, 41 371–73
The Singer Company N.V., 30 417–20 (upd.)
The Singing Machine Company, Inc., 60 277–80
Sir Speedy, Inc., 16 448–50
Sirius Satellite Radio, Inc., 69 328–31
Sirti S.p.A., 76 326–28
Siskin Steel & Supply Company, 70 294–96
Sistema JSFC, 73 303–05
Six Flags, Inc., 17 442–44; 54 333–40 (upd.)
Sixt AG, 39 369–72
SJW Corporation, 70 297–99
SK Group, 88 363–67
Skadden, Arps, Slate, Meagher & Flom, 18 486–88
Skalli Group, 67 349–51
Skandia Insurance Company, Ltd., 50 431–34
Skandinaviska Enskilda Banken AB, II 351–53; 56 326–29 (upd.)
Skanska AB, 38 435–38
Skechers U.S.A. Inc., 31 413–15; 88 368–72 (upd.)
Skeeter Products Inc., 96 391–94
SKF *see* Aktiebolaget SKF.
Skidmore, Owings & Merrill LLP, 13 475–76; 69 332–35 (upd.)
SkillSoft Public Limited Company, 81 371–74
skinnyCorp, LLC, 97 374–77
Skipton Building Society, 80 344–47
Skis Rossignol S.A., 15 460–62; 43 373–76 (upd.)
Skoda Auto a.s., 39 373–75
Skyline Chili, Inc., 62 325–28
Skyline Corporation, 30 421–23
SkyMall, Inc., 26 439–41
SkyWest, Inc., 25 420–24
Skyy Spirits LLC, 78 348–51
SL Green Realty Corporation, 44 383–85
SL Industries, Inc., 77 383–86
Sleeman Breweries Ltd., 74 305–08
Sleepy's Inc., 32 426–28
SLI, Inc., 48 358–61
Slim-Fast Foods Company, 18 489–91; 66 296–98 (upd.)
Slinky, Inc. *see* Poof-Slinky, Inc.
SLM Holding Corp., 25 425–28 (upd.)
Slough Estates PLC, IV 722–25; 50 435–40 (upd.)
Small Planet Foods, Inc., 89 410–14
Smart & Final LLC, 16 451–53; 94 392–96 (upd.)
SMART Modular Technologies, Inc., 86 361–64

SmartForce PLC, **43 377–80**
SMBC *see* Sumitomo Mitsui Banking Corp.
Smead Manufacturing Co., **17 445–48**
SMG *see* Scottish Media Group.
SMH *see* Sanders Morris Harris Group Inc.; The Swatch Group SA.
Smith & Hawken, Ltd., **68 343–45**
Smith & Nephew plc, **17 449–52; 41 374–78 (upd.)**
Smith & Wesson Corp., **30 424–27; 73 306–11 (upd.)**
Smith Barney Inc., **15 463–65** *see also* Citigroup Inc.
Smith Corona Corp., **13 477–80**
Smith International, Inc., **15 466–68; 59 376–80 (upd.)**
Smith-Midland Corporation, **56 330–32**
Smith's Food & Drug Centers, Inc., **8 472–74; 57 324–27 (upd.)**
Smithfield Foods, Inc., **7 477–78; 43 381–84 (upd.)**
SmithKline Beckman Corporation, **I 692–94** *see also* GlaxoSmithKline plc.
SmithKline Beecham plc, **III 65–67; 32 429–34 (upd.)** *see also* GlaxoSmithKline plc.
Smiths Industries PLC, **25 429–31**
Smithsonian Institution, **27 410–13**
Smithway Motor Xpress Corporation, **39 376–79**
Smoby International SA, **56 333–35**
Smorgon Steel Group Ltd., **62 329–32**
Smucker's *see* The J.M. Smucker Co.
Smurfit-Stone Container Corporation, **26 442–46 (upd.) ; 83 360-368 (upd.)**
Snap-On, Incorporated, **7 479–80; 27 414–16 (upd.)**
Snapfish, **83 369-372**
Snapple Beverage Corporation, **11 449–51**
SNC-Lavalin Group Inc., **72 330–33**
SNCF *see* Société Nationale des Chemins de Fer Français.
SNEA *see* Société Nationale Elf Aquitaine.
Snecma Group, **46 369–72**
Snell & Wilmer L.L.P., **28 425–28**
SNET *see* Southern New England Telecommunications Corp.
Snow Brand Milk Products Company, Ltd., **II 574–75; 48 362–65 (upd.)**
Soap Opera Magazine *see* American Media, Inc.
Sobeys Inc., **80 348–51**
Socata *see* EADS SOCATA.
Società Finanziaria Telefonica per Azioni, **V 325–27**
Società Sportiva Lazio SpA, **44 386–88**
Société Air France, **27 417–20 (upd.).**
Société BIC S.A., **73 312–15**
Société d'Exploitation AOM Air Liberté SA (AirLib), **53 305–07**
Societe des Produits Marnier-Lapostolle S.A., **88 373–76**
Société du Figaro S.A., **60 281–84**
Société du Louvre, **27 421–23**
Société Générale, **II 354–56; 42 347–51 (upd.)**
Société Industrielle Lesaffre, **84 356–359**
Société Luxembourgeoise de Navigation Aérienne S.A., **64 357–59**
Société Nationale des Chemins de Fer Français, **V 512–15; 57 328–32 (upd.)**
Société Nationale Elf Aquitaine, **IV 544–47; 7 481–85 (upd.)**
Société Norbert Dentressangle S.A., **67 352–54**
Société Tunisienne de l'Air-Tunisair, **49 371–73**
Society Corporation, **9 474–77**
Sodexho SA, **29 442–44; 91 433–36 (upd.)**
Sodiaal S.A., **19 50; 36 437–39 (upd.)**
SODIMA, **II 576–77** *see also* Sodiaal S.A.
Soft Sheen Products, Inc., **31 416–18**
Softbank Corporation, **13 481–83; 38 439–44 (upd.); 77 387–95 (upd.)**
Sojitz Corporation, **96 395–403 (upd.)**
Sol Meliá S.A., **71 337–39**
Sola International Inc., **71 340–42**
Sole Technology Inc., **93 405–09**
Solectron Corporation, **12 450–52; 48 366–70 (upd.)**
Solo Serve Corporation, **28 429–31**
Solutia Inc., **52 312–15**
Solvay & Cie S.A., **I 394–96; 21 464–67 (upd.)**
Solvay S.A., **61 329–34 (upd.)**
Somerfield plc, **47 365–69 (upd.)**
Sommer-Allibert S.A., **19 406–09** *see also* Tarkett Sommer AG.
Sonae SGPS, S.A., **97 378–81**
Sonat, Inc., **6 577–78** *see also* El Paso Corp.
Sonatrach, **65 313–17 (upd.)**
Sonera Corporation, **50 441–44** *see also* TeliaSonera AB.
Sonesta International Hotels Corporation, **44 389–91**
Sonic Automotive, Inc., **77 396–99**
Sonic Corp., **14 451–53; 37 360–63 (upd.)**
Sonic Innovations Inc., **56 336–38**
Sonic Solutions, Inc., **81 375–79**
SonicWALL, Inc., **87 421–424**
Sonoco Products Company, **8 475–77; 89 415–22 (upd.)**
SonoSite, Inc., **56 339–41**
Sony Corporation, **II 101–03; 12 453–56 (upd.); 40 404–10 (upd.)**
Sophus Berendsen A/S, **49 374–77**
Sorbee International Ltd., **74 309–11**
Soriana *see* Organización Soriana, S.A. de C.V.
Soros Fund Management LLC, **28 432–34**
Sorrento, Inc., **19 51; 24 444–46**
SOS Staffing Services, **25 432–35**
Sotheby's Holdings, Inc., **11 452–54; 29 445–48 (upd.); 84 360–365 (upd.)**
Soufflet SA *see* Groupe Soufflet SA.
Sound Advice, Inc., **41 379–82**
The Source Enterprises, Inc., **65 318–21**
Source Interlink Companies, Inc., **75 350–53**
The South African Breweries Limited, **I 287–89; 24 447–51 (upd.)** *see also* SABMiller plc.
South Beach Beverage Company, Inc., **73 316–19**
South Dakota Wheat Growers Association, **94 397–401**
South Jersey Industries, Inc., **42 352–55**
Southam Inc., **7 486–89** *see also* CanWest Global Communications Corp.
Southcorp Limited, **54 341–44**
Southdown, Inc., **14 454–56** *see also* CEMEX S.A. de C.V.
The Southern Company, **V 721–23; 38 445–49 (upd.)**
Southern Connecticut Gas Company, **84 366–370**
Southern Electric PLC, **13 484–86** *see also* Scottish and Southern Energy plc.
Southern Financial Bancorp, Inc., **56 342–44**
Southern Indiana Gas and Electric Company, **13 487–89**
Southern New England Telecommunications Corporation, **6 338–40**
Southern Pacific Transportation Company, **V 516–18** *see also* Union Pacific Corp.
Southern Peru Copper Corporation, **40 411–13**
Southern Poverty Law Center, Inc., **74 312–15**
Southern States Cooperative Incorporated, **36 440–42**
Southern Union Company, **27 424–26**
Southern Wine and Spirits of America, Inc., **84 371–375**
The Southland Corporation, **II 660–61; 7 490–92 (upd.)** *see also* 7-Eleven, Inc.
Southtrust Corporation, **11 455–57** *see also* Wachovia Corp.
Southwest Airlines Co., **6 119–21; 24 452–55 (upd.); 71 343–47 (upd.)**
Southwest Gas Corporation, **19 410–12**
Southwest Water Company, **47 370–73**
Southwestern Bell Corporation, **V 328–30** *see also* SBC Communications Inc.
Southwestern Electric Power Co., **21 468–70**
Southwestern Public Service Company, **6 579–81**
Southwire Company, Inc., **8 478–80; 23 444–47 (upd.)**
Souza Cruz S.A., **65 322–24**
Sovran Self Storage, Inc., **66 299–301**
SP Alpargatas *see* Sao Paulo Alpargatas S.A.
Spacehab, Inc., **37 364–66**
Spacelabs Medical, Inc., **71 348–50**
Spaghetti Warehouse, Inc., **25 436–38**
Spago *see* The Wolfgang Puck Food Company, Inc.

Spangler Candy Company, 44 392–95
Spanish Broadcasting System, Inc., 41 383–86
Spansion Inc., 80 352–55
Spanx, Inc., 89 423–27
Spar Aerospace Limited, 32 435–37
SPAR Handels AG, 35 398–401
Spark Networks, Inc., 91 437–40
Spartan Motors Inc., 14 457–59
Spartan Stores Inc., 8 481–82; 66 302–05 (upd.)
Spartech Corporation, 19 413–15; 76 329–32 (upd.)
Sparton Corporation, 18 492–95
Spear & Jackson, Inc., 73 320–23
Spear, Leeds & Kellogg, 66 306–09
Spec's Music, Inc., 19 416–18 *see also* Camelot Music, Inc.
Special Olympics, Inc., 93 410–14
Specialist Computer Holdings Ltd., 80 356–59
Specialized Bicycle Components Inc., 50 445–48
Specialty Coatings Inc., 8 483–84
Specialty Equipment Companies, Inc., 25 439–42
Specialty Products & Insulation Co., 59 381–83
Spector Photo Group N.V., 82 344–47
Spectrum Control, Inc., 67 355–57
Spectrum Organic Products, Inc., 68 346–49
Spee-Dee Delivery Service, Inc., 93 415–18
SpeeDee Oil Change and Tune-Up, 25 443–47
Speedway Motorsports, Inc., 32 438–41
Speedy Hire plc, 84 376–379
Speidel Inc., 96 404–07
Speizman Industries, Inc., 44 396–98
Spelling Entertainment, 14 460–62; 35 402–04 (upd.)
Spencer Stuart and Associates, Inc., 14 463–65
Spherion Corporation, 52 316–18
Spie *see* Amec Spie S.A.
Spiegel, Inc., 10 489–91; 27 427–31 (upd.)
SPIEGEL-Verlag Rudolf Augstein GmbH & Co. KG, 44 399–402
Spin Master, Ltd., 61 335–38
Spinnaker Exploration Company, 72 334–36
Spirax-Sarco Engineering plc, 59 384–86
Spirit Airlines, Inc., 31 419–21
Sport Chalet, Inc., 16 454–56; 94 402–06 (upd.)
Sport Supply Group, Inc., 23 448–50
Sportmart, Inc., 15 469–71 *see also* Gart Sports Co.
Sports & Recreation, Inc., 17 453–55
The Sports Authority, Inc., 16 457–59; 43 385–88 (upd.)
The Sports Club Company, 25 448–51
The Sportsman's Guide, Inc., 36 443–46
Springs Global US, Inc., V 378–79; 19 419–22 (upd.); 90 378–83 (upd.)
Sprint Communications Company, L.P., 9 478–80 *see also* Sprint Corporation; US Sprint Communications.
Sprint Corporation, 46 373–76 (upd.)
SPS Technologies, Inc., 30 428–30
SPSS Inc., 64 360–63
SPX Corporation, 10 492–95; 47 374–79 (upd.)
Spyglass Entertainment Group, LLC, 91 441–44
Square D, 90 384–89
Squibb Corporation, I 695–97 *see also* Bristol-Myers Squibb Co.
SR Teleperformance S.A., 86 365–68
SRA International, Inc., 77 400–03
SRAM Corporation, 65 325–27
SRC Holdings Corporation, 67 358–60
SRI International, Inc., 57 333–36
SSA *see* Stevedoring Services of America Inc.
SSAB Svenskt Stål AB, 89 428–31
Ssangyong Cement Industrial Co., Ltd., III 747–50; 61 339–43 (upd.)
SSL International plc, 49 378–81
SSOE Inc., 76 333–35
St. *see under* Saint
STAAR Surgical Company, 57 337–39
The Stabler Companies Inc., 78 352–55
Stage Stores, Inc., 24 456–59; 82 348–52 (upd.)
Stagecoach Holdings plc, 30 431–33
Stanadyne Automotive Corporation, 37 367–70
StanCorp Financial Group, Inc., 56 345–48
Standard Candy Company Inc., 86 369–72
Standard Chartered plc, II 357–59; 48 371–74 (upd.)
Standard Commercial Corporation, 13 490–92; 62 333–37 (upd.)
Standard Federal Bank, 9 481–83
Standard Life Assurance Company, III 358–61
Standard Microsystems Corporation, 11 462–64
Standard Motor Products, Inc., 40 414–17
Standard Pacific Corporation, 52 319–22
The Standard Register Company, 15 472–74; 93 419–25 (upd.)
Standex International Corporation, 17 456–59; 44 403–06 (upd.)
Stanhome Inc., 15 475–78
Stanley Furniture Company, Inc., 34 412–14
Stanley Leisure plc, 66 310–12
The Stanley Works, III 626–29; 20 476–80 (upd.); 79 383–91 (upd.)
Staple Cotton Cooperative Association (Staplcotn), 86 373–77
Staples, Inc., 10 496–98; 55 351–56 (upd.)
Star Banc Corporation, 11 465–67 *see also* Firstar Corp.
Star of the West Milling Co., 95 386–89
Starbucks Corporation, 13 493–94; 34 415–19 (upd.); 77 404–10 (upd.)
Starcraft Corporation, 30 434–36; 66 313–16 (upd.)
StarHub Ltd., 77 411–14
Starkey Laboratories, Inc., 52 323–25
Starrett *see* L.S. Starrett Co.
Starrett Corporation, 21 471–74
StarTek, Inc., 79 392–95
Starter Corp., 12 457–458
Starwood Hotels & Resorts Worldwide, Inc., 54 345–48
Starz LLC, 91 445–50
The Stash Tea Company, 50 449–52
State Auto Financial Corporation, 77 415–19
State Bank of India, 63 354–57
State Farm Mutual Automobile Insurance Company, III 362–64; 51 341–45 (upd.)
State Financial Services Corporation, 51 346–48
State Street Corporation, 8 491–93; 57 340–44 (upd.)
Staten Island Bancorp, Inc., 39 380–82
Stater Bros. Holdings Inc., 64 364–67
Station Casinos, Inc., 25 452–54; 90 390–95 (upd.)
Statoil ASA, 61 344–48 (upd.)
The Staubach Company, 62 338–41
STC PLC, III 162–64 *see also* Nortel Networks Corp.
The Steak n Shake Company, 41 387–90; 96 412–17 (upd.)
Steamships Trading Company Ltd., 82 353–56
Stearns, Inc., 43 389–91
Steel Authority of India Ltd., IV 205–07; 66 317–21 (upd.)
Steel Dynamics, Inc., 52 326–28
Steel Technologies Inc., 63 358–60
Steelcase Inc., 7 493–95; 27 432–35 (upd.)
Stefanel SpA, 63 361–63
Steiff *see* Margarete Steiff GmbH.
Steilmann Group *see* Klaus Steilmann GmbH & Co. KG.
Stein Mart Inc., 19 423–25; 72 337–39 (upd.)
Steinberg Incorporated, II 662–65
Steiner Corporation (Alsco), 53 308–11
Steinway Musical Properties, Inc., 19 426–29
Stelco Inc., IV 208–10; 51 349–52 (upd.)
Stelmar Shipping Ltd., 52 329–31
Stemilt Growers Inc., 94 407–10
Stepan Company, 30 437–39
The Stephan Company, 60 285–88
Stephens Inc., 92 344–48
Stephens Media, LLC, 91 451–54
Steria SA, 49 382–85
Stericycle, Inc., 33 380–82; 74 316–18 (upd.)
Sterilite Corporation, 97 382–85
STERIS Corporation, 29 449–52

Sterling Chemicals, Inc., 16 460–63; 78 356–61 (upd.)
Sterling Drug Inc., I 698–700
Sterling Electronics Corp., 18 496–98
Sterling European Airlines A/S, 70 300–02
Sterling Software, Inc., 11 468–70 *see also* Computer Associates International, Inc.
STET *see* Società Finanziaria Telefonica per Azioni.
Steuben Glass *see* Corning Inc.
Steve & Barry's LLC, 88 377–80
Stevedoring Services of America Inc., 28 435–37
Steven Madden, Ltd., 37 371–73
Stew Leonard's, 56 349–51
Stewart & Stevenson Services Inc., 11 471–73
Stewart Enterprises, Inc., 20 481–83
Stewart Information Services Corporation, 78 362–65
Stewart's Beverages, 39 383–86
Stewart's Shops Corporation, 80 360–63
Stickley *see* L. and J.G. Stickley, Inc.
Stiefel Laboratories, Inc., 90 396–99
Stihl *see* Andreas Stihl AG & Co. KG.
Stillwater Mining Company, 47 380–82
Stimson Lumber Company Inc., 78 366–69
Stinnes AG, 8 494–97; 23 451–54 (upd.); 59 387–92 (upd.)
Stirling Group plc, 62 342–44
STMicroelectronics NV, 52 332–35
Stock Yards Packing Co., Inc., 37 374–76
Stoddard International plc, 72 340–43
Stoll-Moss Theatres Ltd., 34 420–22
Stollwerck AG, 53 312–15
Stolt-Nielsen S.A., 42 356–59; 54 349–50
Stolt Sea Farm Holdings PLC, 54 349–51
Stone & Webster, Inc., 13 495–98; 64 368–72 (upd.)
Stone Container Corporation, IV 332–34 *see also* Smurfit-Stone Container Corp.
Stone Manufacturing Company, 14 469–71; 43 392–96 (upd.)
Stonyfield Farm, Inc., 55 357–60
The Stop & Shop Supermarket Company, II 666–67; 24 460–62 (upd.); 68 350–53 (upd.)
Stora Enso Oyj, IV 335–37; 36 447–55 (upd.); 85 396–408 (upd.)
Storage Technology Corporation, 6 275–77
Storage USA, Inc., 21 475–77
Storehouse PLC, 16 464–66 *see also* Mothercare plc.
Stouffer Corp., 8 498–501 *see also* Nestlé S.A.
StrataCom, Inc., 16 467–69
Stratagene Corporation, 70 303–06
Stratasys, Inc., 67 361–63
Strattec Security Corporation, 73 324–27
Stratus Computer, Inc., 10 499–501
Straumann Holding AG, 79 396–99
Strauss Discount Auto, 56 352–54
Strauss-Elite Group, 68 354–57
Strayer Education, Inc., 53 316–19
Stride Rite Corporation, 8 502–04; 37 377–80 (upd.); 86 378–84 (upd.)
Strine Printing Company Inc., 88 381–84
Strix Ltd., 51 353–55
The Strober Organization, Inc., 82 357–60 *see also* Pro-Build Holdings Inc.
The Stroh Brewery Company, I 290–92; 18 499–502 (upd.)
Strombecker Corporation, 60 289–91
Stroock & Stroock & Lavan LLP, 40 418–21
Strouds, Inc., 33 383–86
Stryker Corporation, 11 474–76; 29 453–55 (upd.); 79 400–05 (upd.)
Stuart C. Irby Company, 58 333–35
Stuart Entertainment Inc., 16 470–72
Student Loan Marketing Association, II 453–55 *see also* SLM Holding Corp.
Stuller Settings, Inc., 35 405–07
Sturm, Ruger & Company, Inc., 19 430–32
Stussy, Inc., 55 361–63
Sub Pop Ltd., 97 386–89
Sub-Zero Freezer Co., Inc., 31 426–28
Suburban Propane Partners, L.P., 30 440–42
Subway, 32 442–44 *see also* Doctor's Associates Inc.
Successories, Inc., 30 443–45
Sucden *see* Compagnie Financière Sucres et Denrées.
Suchard Co. *see* Jacobs Suchard.
Sudbury Inc., 16 473–75
Südzucker AG, 27 436–39
Suez Lyonnaise des Eaux, 36 456–59 (upd.)
SUEZ-TRACTEBEL S.A., 97 390–94 (upd.)
Suiza Foods Corporation, 26 447–50 *see also* Dean Foods Co.
Sukhoi Design Bureau Aviation Scientific-Industrial Complex, 24 463–65
Sullivan & Cromwell, 26 451–53
Sulzer Ltd., III 630–33; 68 358–62 (upd.)
Sumitomo Bank, Limited, II 360–62; 26 454–57 (upd.)
Sumitomo Chemical Company Ltd., I 397–98
Sumitomo Corporation, I 518–20; 11 477–80 (upd.)
Sumitomo Electric Industries, II 104–05
Sumitomo Heavy Industries, Ltd., III 634–35; 42 360–62 (upd.)
Sumitomo Life Insurance Company, III 365–66; 60 292–94 (upd.)
Sumitomo Metal Industries Ltd., IV 211–13; 82 361–66 (upd.)
Sumitomo Metal Mining Co., Ltd., IV 214–16
Sumitomo Mitsui Banking Corporation, 51 356–62 (upd.)
Sumitomo Realty & Development Co., Ltd., IV 726–27
Sumitomo Rubber Industries, Ltd., V 252–53
The Sumitomo Trust & Banking Company, Ltd., II 363–64; 53 320–22 (upd.)
The Summit Bancorporation, 14 472–74 *see also* FleetBoston Financial Corp.
Summit Family Restaurants Inc., 19 433–36
Sun Alliance Group PLC, III 369–74 *see also* Royal & Sun Alliance Insurance Group plc.
Sun Communities Inc., 46 377–79
Sun Company, Inc., IV 548–50 *see also* Sunoco, Inc.
Sun Country Airlines, I 30 446–49
Sun-Diamond Growers of California, 7 496–97 *see also* Diamond of California.
Sun Distributors L.P., 12 459–461
Sun Healthcare Group Inc., 25 455–58
Sun Hydraulics Corporation, 74 319–22
Sun International Hotels Limited, 26 462–65 *see also* Kerzner International Ltd.
Sun Life Financial Inc., 85 409–12
Sun-Maid Growers of California, 82 367–71
Sun Microsystems, Inc., 7 498–501; 30 450–54 (upd.); 91 455–62 (upd.)
Sun Pharmaceutical Industries Ltd., 57 345–47
Sun-Rype Products Ltd., 76 336–38
Sun Sportswear, Inc., 17 460–63
Sun Television & Appliances Inc., 10 502–03
Sun World International, LLC, 93 426–29
SunAmerica Inc., 11 481–83 *see also* American International Group, Inc.
Sunbeam-Oster Co., Inc., 9 484–86
Sunburst Hospitality Corporation, 26 458–61
Sunburst Shutters Corporation, 78 370–72
Suncor Energy Inc., 54 352–54
Suncorp-Metway Ltd., 91 463–66
Sundstrand Corporation, 7 502–04; 21 478–81 (upd.)
Sundt Corp., 24 466–69
SunGard Data Systems Inc., 11 484–85
Sunglass Hut International, Inc., 21 482–84; 74 323–26 (upd.)
Sunkist Growers, Inc., 26 466–69
Sunoco, Inc., 28 438–42 (upd.); 83 373-380 (upd.)
SunOpta Inc., 79 406–10
SunPower Corporation, 91 467–70
The Sunrider Corporation, 26 470–74
Sunrise Greetings, 88 385–88
Sunrise Medical Inc., 11 486–88
Sunrise Senior Living, Inc., 81 380–83

Sunsweet Growers *see* Diamond of California.
Suntech Power Holdings Company Ltd., 89 432–35
Sunterra Corporation, 75 354–56
Suntory Ltd., 65 328–31
SunTrust Banks Inc., 23 455–58
Super 8 Motels, Inc., 83 381-385
Super Food Services, Inc., 15 479–81
Supercuts Inc., 26 475–78
Superdrug Stores PLC, 95 390–93
Superior Energy Services, Inc., 65 332–34
Superior Essex Inc., 80 364–68
Superior Industries International, Inc., 8 505–07
Superior Uniform Group, Inc., 30 455–57
Supermarkets General Holdings Corporation, II 672–74 *see also* Pathmark Stores, Inc.
SUPERVALU INC., II 668–71; 18 503–08 (upd.); 50 453–59 (upd.)
Suprema Specialties, Inc., 27 440–42
Supreme International Corporation, 27 443–46
Suramericana de Inversiones S.A., 88 389–92
OAO Surgutneftegaz, 48 375–78
Surrey Satellite Technology Limited, 83 386-390
The Susan G. Komen Breast CancerFoundation, 78 373–76
Susquehanna Pfaltzgraff Company, 8 508–10
Sutter Home Winery Inc., 16 476–78
Suzano *see* Companhia Suzano de Papel e Celulose S.A.
Suzuki Motor Corporation, 9 487–89; 23 459–62 (upd.); 59 393–98 (upd.)
Sveaskog AB, 93 430–33
Svenska Cellulosa Aktiebolaget SCA, IV 338–40; 28 443–46 (upd.); 85 413–20 (upd.)
Svenska Handelsbanken AB, II 365–67; 50 460–63 (upd.)
Sverdrup Corporation, 14 475–78 *see also* Jacobs Engineering Group Inc.
Sveriges Riksbank, 96 418–22
SWA *see* Southwest Airlines.
SWALEC *see* Scottish and Southern Energy plc.
Swales & Associates, Inc., 69 336–38
Swank, Inc., 17 464–66; 84 380–384 (upd.)
Swarovski International Holding AG, 40 422–25
The Swatch Group SA, 26 479–81
Swedish Match AB, 12 462–64; 39 387–90 (upd.); 92 349–55 (upd.)
Swedish Telecom, V 331–33
SwedishAmerican Health System, 51 363–66
Sweet Candy Company, 60 295–97
Sweetheart Cup Company, Inc., 36 460–64
The Swett & Crawford Group Inc., 84 385–389
SWH Corporation, 70 307–09
Swift & Company, 55 364–67
Swift Energy Company, 63 364–66
Swift Transportation Co., Inc., 42 363–66
Swinerton Inc., 43 397–400
Swire Pacific Ltd., I 521–22; 16 479–81 (upd.); 57 348–53 (upd.)
Swisher International Group Inc., 23 463–65
Swiss Air Transport Company Ltd., I 121–22
Swiss Army Brands, Inc. *see* Victorinox AG.
Swiss Bank Corporation, II 368–70 *see also* UBS AG.
The Swiss Colony, Inc., 97 395–98
Swiss Federal Railways (Schweizerische Bundesbahnen), V 519–22
Swiss International Air Lines Ltd., 48 379–81
Swiss Reinsurance Company (Schweizerische Rückversicherungs-Gesellschaft), III 375–78; 46 380–84 (upd.)
Swiss Valley Farms Company, 90 400–03
Swisscom AG, 58 336–39
Swissport International Ltd., 70 310–12
Sybase, Inc., 10 504–06; 27 447–50 (upd.)
Sybron International Corp., 14 479–81
Sycamore Networks, Inc., 45 388–91
Sykes Enterprises, Inc., 45 392–95
Sylvan, Inc., 22 496–99
Sylvan Learning Systems, Inc., 35 408–11 *see also* Educate Inc.
Symantec Corporation, 10 507–09; 82 372–77 (upd.)
Symbol Technologies, Inc., 15 482–84 *see also* Motorola, Inc.
Symrise GmbH and Company KG, 89 436–40
Syms Corporation, 29 456–58; 74 327–30 (upd.)
Symyx Technologies, Inc., 77 420–23
Synaptics Incorporated, 95 394–98
Synchronoss Technologies, Inc., 95 399–402
Syneron Medical Ltd., 91 471–74
Syngenta International AG, 83 391-394
Syniverse Holdings Inc., 97 399–402
SYNNEX Corporation, 73 328–30
Synopsys, Inc., 11 489–92; 69 339–43 (upd.)
SynOptics Communications, Inc., 10 510–12
Synovus Financial Corp., 12 465–67; 52 336–40 (upd.)
Syntel, Inc., 92 356–60
Syntex Corporation, I 701–03
Synthes, Inc., 93 434–37
Sypris Solutions, Inc., 85 421–25
SyQuest Technology, Inc., 18 509–12
Syratech Corp., 14 482–84
SYSCO Corporation, II 675–76; 24 470–72 (upd.); 75 357–60 (upd.)
System Software Associates, Inc., 10 513–14
Systemax, Inc., 52 341–44
Systems & Computer Technology Corp., 19 437–39
Sytner Group plc, 45 396–98

T

T-Netix, Inc., 46 385–88
T-Online International AG, 61 349–51
T.J. Maxx *see* The TJX Companies, Inc.
T. Marzetti Company, 57 354–56
T. Rowe Price Associates, Inc., 11 493–96; 34 423–27 (upd.)
TA Triumph-Adler AG, 48 382–85
TAB Products Co., 17 467–69
Tabacalera, S.A., V 414–16; 17 470–73 (upd.) *see also* Altadis S.A.
TABCORP Holdings Limited, 44 407–10
TACA *see* Grupo TACA.
Taco Bell Corporation, 7 505–07; 21 485–88 (upd.); 74 331–34 (upd.)
Taco Cabana, Inc., 23 466–68; 72 344–47 (upd.)
Taco John's International Inc., 15 485–87; 63 367–70 (upd.)
Tacony Corporation, 70 313–15
TAG Heuer S.A., 25 459–61; 77 424–28 (upd.)
Tag-It Pacific, Inc., 85 426–29
Taiheiyo Cement Corporation, 60 298–301 (upd.)
Taittinger S.A., 43 401–05
Taiwan Semiconductor Manufacturing Company Ltd., 47 383–87
Taiwan Tobacco & Liquor Corporation, 75 361–63
Taiyo Fishery Company, Limited, II 578–79 *see also* Maruha Group Inc.
Taiyo Kobe Bank, Ltd., II 371–72
Takara Holdings Inc., 62 345–47
Takashimaya Company, Limited, V 193–96; 47 388–92 (upd.)
Take-Two Interactive Software, Inc., 46 389–91
Takeda Chemical Industries, Ltd., I 704–06; 46 392–95 (upd.)
The Talbots, Inc., 11 497–99; 31 429–32 (upd.); 88 393–98 (upd.)
Talisman Energy Inc., 9 490–93; 47 393–98 (upd.)
Talk America Holdings, Inc., 70 316–19
Talley Industries, Inc., 16 482–85
TALX Corporation, 92 361–64
TAM Linhas Aéreas S.A., 68 363–65
Tambrands Inc., 8 511–13 *see also* Procter & Gamble Co.
Tamedia AG, 53 323–26
Tamfelt Oyj Abp, 62 348–50
Tamron Company Ltd., 82 378–81
TAMSA *see* Tubos de Acero de Mexico, S.A.
Tandem Computers, Inc., 6 278–80 *see also* Hewlett-Packard Co.
Tandy Corporation, II 106–08; 12 468–70 (upd.) *see also* RadioShack Corp.

Tandycrafts, Inc., 31 433–37
Tanger Factory Outlet Centers, Inc., 49 386–89
Tanox, Inc., 77 429–32
TAP—Air Portugal Transportes Aéreos Portugueses S.A., 46 396–99 (upd.)
Tapemark Company Inc., 64 373–75
TAQA North Ltd., 95 403–06
Target Corporation, 10 515–17; 27 451–54 (upd.); 61 352–56 (upd.)
Tarkett Sommer AG, 25 462–64
Targetti Sankey SpA, 86 385–88
Tarmac Limited, III 751–54; 28 447–51 (upd.); 95 407–14 (upd.)
Taro Pharmaceutical Industries Ltd., 65 335–37
TAROM S.A., 64 376–78
Tarragon Realty Investors, Inc., 45 399–402
Tarrant Apparel Group, 62 351–53
Taser International, Inc., 62 354–57
Tasty Baking Company, 14 485–87; 35 412–16 (upd.)
Tata Iron & Steel Co. Ltd., IV 217–19; 44 411–15 (upd.)
Tata Tea Ltd., 76 339–41
Tate & Lyle PLC, II 580–83; 42 367–72 (upd.)
Tati SA, 25 465–67
Tatneft *see* OAO Tatneft.
Tattered Cover Book Store, 43 406–09
Tatung Co., 23 469–71
Taubman Centers, Inc., 75 364–66
TaurusHolding GmbH & Co. KG, 46 400–03
Taylor & Francis Group plc, 44 416–19
Taylor Corporation, 36 465–67
Taylor Devices, Inc., 97 403–06
Taylor Guitars, 48 386–89
Taylor Nelson Sofres plc, 34 428–30
Taylor Publishing Company, 12 471–73; 36 468–71 (upd.)
Taylor Woodrow plc, I 590–91; 38 450–53 (upd.)
TaylorMade-adidas Golf, 23 472–74; 96 423–28 (upd.)
TB Wood's Corporation, 56 355–58
TBS *see* Turner Broadcasting System, Inc.
TBWA/Chiat/Day, 6 47–49; 43 410–14 (upd.) *see also* Omnicom Group Inc.
TC Advertising *see* Treasure Chest Advertising, Inc.
TCBY Enterprises Inc., 17 474–76
TCF Financial Corporation, 47 399–402
Tchibo GmbH, 82 382–85
TCI *see* Tele-Communications, Inc.
TCO *see* Taubman Centers, Inc.
TD Bank *see* The Toronto-Dominion Bank.
TDC A/S, 63 371–74
TDK Corporation, II 109–11; 17 477–79 (upd.); 49 390–94 (upd.)
TDL Group Ltd., 46 404–06
TDS *see* Telephone and Data Systems, Inc.
TEAC Corporation, 78 377–80
Teachers Insurance and Annuity Association-College Retirement Equities Fund, III 379–82; 45 403–07 (upd.)
Teamsters Union *see* International Brotherhood of Teamsters.
TearDrop Golf Company, 32 445–48
Tech Data Corporation, 10 518–19; 74 335–38 (upd.)
Tech-Sym Corporation, 18 513–15; 44 420–23 (upd.)
TechBooks Inc., 84 390–393
TECHNE Corporation, 52 345–48
Technical Olympic USA, Inc., 75 367–69
Technip, 78 381–84
Technitrol, Inc., 29 459–62
Technology Research Corporation, 94 411–14
Technology Solutions Company, 94 415–19
Techtronic Industries Company Ltd., 73 331–34
Teck Corporation, 27 455–58
TECO Energy, Inc., 6 582–84
Tecumseh Products Company, 8 514–16; 71 351–55 (upd.)
Ted Baker plc, 86 389–92
Tee Vee Toons, Inc., 57 357–60
Teekay Shipping Corporation, 25 468–71; 82 386–91 (upd.)
Teijin Limited, V 380–82; 61 357–61 (upd.)
Tejon Ranch Company, 35 417–20
Tekelec, 83 395-399
Teknor Apex Company, 97 407–10
Tektronix, Inc., 8 517–21; 78 385–91 (upd.)
Telcordia Technologies, Inc., 59 399–401
Tele-Communications, Inc., II 160–62
Tele Norte Leste Participações S.A., 80 369–72
Telecom Argentina S.A., 63 375–77
Telecom Australia, 6 341–42 *see also* Telstra Corp. Ltd.
Telecom Corporation of New Zealand Limited, 54 355–58
Telecom Eireann, 7 508–10 *see also* eircom plc.
Telecom Italia Mobile S.p.A., 63 378–80
Telecom Italia S.p.A., 43 415–19
Teledyne Technologies Inc., I 523–25; 10 520–22 (upd.); 62 358–62 (upd.)
Telefonaktiebolaget LM Ericsson, V 334–36; 46 407–11 (upd.)
Telefónica de Argentina S.A., 61 362–64
Telefónica de España, S.A., V 337–40
Telefónica S.A., 46 412–17 (upd.)
Telefonos de Mexico S.A. de C.V., 14 488–90; 63 381–84 (upd.)
Telekom Malaysia Bhd, 76 342–44
Telekomunikacja Polska SA, 50 464–68
Telenor ASA, 69 344–46
Telephone and Data Systems, Inc., 9 494–96
TelePizza S.A., 33 387–89
Television de Mexico, S.A. *see* Grupo Televisa, S.A.
Television Española, S.A., 7 511–12
Télévision Française 1, 23 475–77
TeliaSonera AB, 57 361–65 (upd.)
Tellabs, Inc., 11 500–01; 40 426–29 (upd.)
Telsmith Inc., 96 429–33
Telstra Corporation Limited, 50 469–72
Telxon Corporation, 10 523–25
Tembec Inc., 66 322–24
Temple-Inland Inc., IV 341–43; 31 438–42 (upd.)
Tempur-Pedic Inc., 54 359–61
Ten Cate *see* Royal Ten Cate N.V.
Tenaris SA, 63 385–88
Tenet Healthcare Corporation, 55 368–71 (upd.)
TenFold Corporation, 35 421–23
Tengelmann Group, 27 459–62
Tennant Company, 13 499–501; 33 390–93 (upd.); 95 415–20 (upd.)
Tenneco Inc., I 526–28; 10 526–28 (upd.)
Tennessee Valley Authority, 50 473–77
TenneT B.V., 78 392–95
TEP *see* Tucson Electric Power Co.
TEPPCO Partners, L.P., 73 335–37
Tequila Herradura *see* Grupo Industrial Herradura, S.A. de C.V.
Teradyne, Inc., 11 502–04
Terex Corporation, 7 513–15; 40 430–34 (upd.); 91 475–82 (upd.)
The Terlato Wine Group, 48 390–92
Terra Industries, Inc., 13 502–04; 94 420–24 (upd.)
Terra Lycos, Inc., 43 420–25
Terrena L'Union CANA CAVAL, 70 320–22
Terumo Corporation, 48 393–95
Tesco plc, II 677–78; 24 473–76 (upd.); 68 366–70 (upd.)
Tesoro Corporation, 7 516–19; 45 408–13 (upd.); 97 411–19 (upd.)
Tessenderlo Group, 76 345–48
The Testor Corporation, 51 367–70
Tetley USA Inc., 88 399–402
Teton Energy Corporation, 97 420–23
Tetra Pak International SA, 53 327–29
Tetra Tech, Inc., 29 463–65
Teva Pharmaceutical Industries Ltd., 22 500–03; 54 362–65 (upd.)
Texaco Inc., IV 551–53; 14 491–94 (upd.); 41 391–96 (upd.) *see also* ChevronTexaco Corp.
Texas Air Corporation, I 123–24
Texas Industries, Inc., 8 522–24
Texas Instruments Incorporated, II 112–15; 11 505–08 (upd.); 46 418–23 (upd.)
Texas Pacific Group Inc., 36 472–74
Texas Rangers Baseball, 51 371–74
Texas Roadhouse, Inc., 69 347–49
Texas Utilities Company, V 724–25; 25 472–74 (upd.)
Textron Inc., I 529–30; 34 431–34 (upd.); 88 403–07 (upd.)

Textron Lycoming Turbine Engine, 9 497–99
TFM *see* Grupo Transportación Ferroviaria Mexicana, S.A. de C.V.
TF1 *see* Télévision Française 1
Tha Row Records, 69 350–52 (upd.)
Thai Airways International Public Company Limited, 6 122–24; 27 463–66 (upd.)
Thai Union Frozen Products PCL, 75 370–72
Thales S.A., 42 373–76
Thames Water plc, 11 509–11; 90 404–08 (upd.)
Thane International, Inc., 84 394–397
Thanulux Public Company Limited, 86 393–96
Thermadyne Holding Corporation, 19 440–43
Thermo BioAnalysis Corp., 25 475–78
Thermo Electron Corporation, 7 520–22
Thermo Fibertek, Inc., 24 477–79 *see also* Kadant Inc.
Thermo Instrument Systems Inc., 11 512–14
Thermo King Corporation, 13 505–07 *see also* Ingersoll-Rand Company Ltd.
Thermos Company, 16 486–88
Things Remembered, Inc., 84 398–401
Thiokol Corporation, 9 500–02 (upd.); 22 504–07 (upd.)
Thistle Hotels PLC, 54 366–69
Thomas & Betts Corporation, 11 515–17; 54 370–74 (upd.)
Thomas & Howard Company, Inc., 90 409–12
Thomas Cook Travel Inc., 9 503–05; 33 394–96 (upd.)
Thomas Crosbie Holdings Limited, 81 384–87
Thomas H. Lee Co., 24 480–83
Thomas Industries Inc., 29 466–69
Thomas J. Lipton Company, 14 495–97
Thomas Nelson Inc., 14 498–99; 38 454–57 (upd.)
Thomas Publishing Company, 26 482–85
Thomaston Mills, Inc., 27 467–70
Thomasville Furniture Industries, Inc., 12 474–76; 74 339–42 (upd.)
Thomsen Greenhouses and Garden Center, Incorporated, 65 338–40
The Thomson Corporation, 8 525–28; 34 435–40 (upd.); 77 433–39 (upd.)
THOMSON multimedia S.A., II 116–17; 42 377–80 (upd.)
Thor Industries Inc., 39 391–94; 92 365–370 (upd.)
Thorn Apple Valley, Inc., 7 523–25; 22 508–11 (upd.)
Thorn EMI plc, I 531–32 *see also* EMI plc; Thorn plc.
Thorn plc, 24 484–87
Thorntons plc, 46 424–26
ThoughtWorks Inc., 90 413–16
Thousand Trails, Inc., 33 397–99
THQ, Inc., 39 395–97; 92 371–375 (upd.)
Threadless.com *see* skinnyCorp, LLC.
The 3DO Company, 43 426–30
365 Media Group plc, 89 441–44
3Com Corporation, 11 518–21; 34 441–45 (upd.) *see also* Palm, Inc.
3i Group PLC, 73 338–40
3M Company, 61 365–70 (upd.)
Thrifty PayLess, Inc., 12 477–79 *see also* Rite Aid Corp.
ThyssenKrupp AG, IV 221–23; 28 452–60 (upd.); 87 425–438 (upd.)
TI Group plc, 17 480–83
TIAA-CREF *see* Teachers Insurance and Annuity Association-College Retirement Equities Fund.
Tianjin Flying Pigeon Bicycle Co., Ltd., 95 421–24
Tibbett & Britten Group plc, 32 449–52
TIBCO Software Inc., 79 411–14
TIC Holdings Inc., 92 376–379
Ticketmaster, 13 508–10; 37 381–84 (upd.); 76 349–53 (upd.)
Tidewater Inc., 11 522–24; 37 385–88 (upd.)
Tiffany & Co., 14 500–03; 78 396–401 (upd.)
TIG Holdings, Inc., 26 486–88
Tiger Aspect Productions Ltd., 72 348–50
Tilcon-Connecticut Inc., 80 373–76
Tilia Inc., 62 363–65
Tilley Endurables, Inc., 67 364–66
Tillotson Corp., 15 488–90
TIM *see* Telecom Italia Mobile S.p.A.
Timber Lodge Steakhouse, Inc., 73 341–43
The Timberland Company, 13 511–14; 54 375–79 (upd.)
Timberline Software Corporation, 15 491–93
Time Out Group Ltd., 68 371–73
Time Warner Inc., IV 673–76; 7 526–30 (upd.) *see also* AOL Time Warner Inc.
The Times Mirror Company, IV 677–78; 17 484–86 (upd.) *see also* Tribune Co.
TIMET *see* Titanium Metals Corp.
Timex Corporation, 7 531–33; 25 479–82 (upd.)
The Timken Company, 8 529–31; 42 381–85 (upd.)
Tiscali SpA, 48 396–99
TISCO *see* Tata Iron & Steel Company Ltd.
Tishman Speyer Properties, L.P., 47 403–06
Tissue Technologies, Inc. *see* Palomar Medical Technologies, Inc.
Titan Cement Company S.A., 64 379–81
The Titan Corporation, 36 475–78
Titan International, Inc., 89 445–49
Titanium Metals Corporation, 21 489–92
TiVo Inc., 75 373–75
TJ International, Inc., 19 444–47
The TJX Companies, Inc., V 197–98; 19 448–50 (upd.); 57 366–69 (upd.)
TLC Beatrice International Holdings, Inc., 22 512–15
TMP Worldwide Inc., 30 458–60 *see also* Monster Worldwide Inc.
TNT Freightways Corporation, 14 504–06
TNT Limited, V 523–25
TNT Post Group N.V., 27 471–76 (upd.); 30 461–63 (upd.) *see also* TPG N.V.
Tobu Railway Co Ltd, 6 430–32
Today's Man, Inc., 20 484–87
The Todd-AO Corporation, 33 400–04 *see also* Liberty Livewire Corp.
Todd Shipyards Corporation, 14 507–09
TODCO, 87 439–442
Todhunter International, Inc., 27 477–79
Tofutti Brands, Inc., 64 382–84
Tohan Corporation, 84 402–405
Toho Co., Ltd., 28 461–63
Tohuku Electric Power Company, Inc., V 726–28
The Tokai Bank, Limited, II 373–74; 15 494–96 (upd.)
Tokheim Corporation, 21 493–95
Tokio Marine and Fire Insurance Co., Ltd., III 383–86 *see also* Millea Holdings Inc.
Tokyo Electric Power Company, V 729–33; 74 343–48 (upd.)
Tokyo Gas Co., Ltd., V 734–36; 55 372–75 (upd.)
TOKYOPOP Inc., 79 415–18
Tokyu Corporation, V 526–28; 47 407–10 (upd.)
Tokyu Department Store Co., Ltd., V 199–202; 32 453–57 (upd.)
Tokyu Land Corporation, IV 728–29
Toll Brothers Inc., 15 497–99; 70 323–26 (upd.)
Tollgrade Communications, Inc., 44 424–27
Tom Brown, Inc., 37 389–91
Tom Doherty Associates Inc., 25 483–86
Tom's Foods Inc., 66 325–27
Tom's of Maine, Inc., 45 414–16
Tombstone Pizza Corporation, 13 515–17 *see also* Kraft Foods Inc.
Tomen Corporation, IV 224–25; 24 488–91 (upd.)
Tomkins plc, 11 525–27; 44 428–31 (upd.)
Tommy Hilfiger Corporation, 20 488–90; 53 330–33 (upd.)
TomTom N.V., 81 388–91
Tomy Company Ltd., 65 341–44
Tone Brothers, Inc., 21 496–98; 74 349–52 (upd.)
Tonen Corporation, IV 554–56; 16 489–92 (upd.)
TonenGeneral Sekiyu K.K., 54 380–86 (upd.)

Tong Yang Cement Corporation, **62 366–68**
Tonka Corporation, **25 487–89**
Too, Inc., **61 371–73**
Toolex International N.V., **26 489–91**
Tootsie Roll Industries, Inc., **12 480–82; 82 392–96 (upd.)**
The Topaz Group, Inc., **62 369–71**
Topco Associates LLC, **60 302–04**
Topcon Corporation, **84 406–409**
Toppan Printing Co., Ltd., **IV 679–81; 58 340–44 (upd.)**
The Topps Company, Inc., **13 518–20; 34 446–49 (upd.); 83 400-406 (upd.)**
Tops Appliance City, Inc., **17 487–89**
Tops Markets LLC, **60 305–07**
Toray Industries, Inc., **V 383–86; 51 375–79 (upd.)**
Torchmark Corporation, **9 506–08; 33 405–08 (upd.)**
Toresco Enterprises, Inc., **84 410–413**
The Toro Company, **7 534–36; 26 492–95 (upd.); 77 440–45 (upd.)**
Toromont Industries, Ltd., **21 499–501**
The Toronto-Dominion Bank, **II 375–77; 49 395–99 (upd.)**
Toronto Maple Leafs *see* Maple Leaf Sports & Entertainment Ltd.
Toronto Raptors *see* Maple Leaf Sports & Entertainment Ltd.
The Torrington Company, **13 521–24** *see also* Timken Co.
Torstar Corporation, **29 470–73** *see also* Harlequin Enterprises Ltd.
Tosco Corporation, **7 537–39** *see also* ConocoPhillips.
Toshiba Corporation, **I 533–35; 12 483–86 (upd.); 40 435–40 (upd.)**
Tosoh Corporation, **70 327–30**
Total Compagnie Française des Pétroles S.A., **IV 557–61** *see also* Total Fina Elf S.A.
Total Entertainment Restaurant Corporation, **46 427–29**
Total Fina Elf S.A., **50 478–86 (upd.)**
TOTAL S.A., **24 492–97 (upd.)**
Total System Services, Inc., **18 516–18**
Totem Resources Corporation, **9 509–11**
TOTO LTD., **III 755–56; 28 464–66 (upd.)**
Tottenham Hotspur PLC, **81 392–95**
Touchstone Films *see* The Walt Disney Co.
TouchTunes Music Corporation, **97 424–28**
Toupargel-Agrigel S.A., **76 354–56**
Touristik Union International GmbH. and Company K.G., **II 163–65** *see also* Preussag AG.
TOUSA *see* Technical Olympic USA, Inc.
Touton S.A., **92 380–383**
Tower Air, Inc., **28 467–69**
Tower Automotive, Inc., **24 498–500**
Towers Perrin, **32 458–60**
Town & Country Corporation, **19 451–53**
Town Sports International, Inc., **46 430–33**
Townsends, Inc., **64 385–87**
Toy Biz, Inc., **18 519–21** *see also* Marvel Entertainment, Inc.
Toymax International, Inc., **29 474–76**
Toyo Sash Co., Ltd., **III 757–58**
Toyo Seikan Kaisha Ltd., **I 615–16**
Toyoda Automatic Loom Works, Ltd., **III 636–39**
Toyota Motor Corporation, **I 203–05; 11 528–31 (upd.); 38 458–62 (upd.)**
Toys 'R Us, Inc., **V 203–06; 18 522–25 (upd.); 57 370–75 (upd.)**
TPG N.V., **64 388–91 (upd.)**
Tracor Inc., **17 490–92**
Tractebel S.A., **20 491–93** *see also* Suez Lyonnaise des Eaux; SUEZ-TRACTEBEL S.A.
Tractor Supply Company, **57 376–78**
Trader Classified Media N.V., **57 379–82**
Trader Joe's Company, **13 525–27; 50 487–90 (upd.)**
TradeStation Group, Inc., **83 407-410**
Traffix, Inc., **61 374–76**
Trailer Bridge, Inc., **41 397–99**
Trammell Crow Company, **8 532–34; 57 383–87 (upd.)**
Trane, **78 402–05**
Trans-Lux Corporation, **51 380–83**
Trans World Airlines, Inc., **I 125–27; 12 487–90 (upd.); 35 424–29 (upd.)**
Trans World Entertainment Corporation, **24 501–03; 68 374–77 (upd.)**
Transaction Systems Architects, Inc., **29 477–79; 82 397–402 (upd.)**
TransAlta Utilities Corporation, **6 585–87**
Transamerica—An AEGON Company, **I 536–38; 13 528–30 (upd.); 41 400–03 (upd.)**
Transammonia Group, **95 425–28**
Transatlantic Holdings, Inc., **11 532–33**
TransBrasil S/A Linhas Aéreas, **31 443–45**
TransCanada Corporation, **V 737–38; 93 438–45 (upd.)**
Transco Energy Company, **V 739–40** *see also* The Williams Companies.
Transiciel SA, **48 400–02**
Transitions Optical, Inc., **83 411-415**
CJSC Transmash Holding, **93 446–49**
Transmedia Network Inc., **20 494–97** *see also* Rewards Network Inc.
TransMontaigne Inc., **28 470–72**
Oil Transporting Joint Stock Company Transneft, **92450–54**
Transnet Ltd., **6 433–35**
Transocean Sedco Forex Inc., **45 417–19**
Transport Corporation of America, Inc., **49 400–03**
Transportes Aéreas Centro-Americanos *see* Grupo TACA.
Transportes Aereos Portugueses, S.A., **6 125–27** *see also* TAP—Air Portugal Transportes Aéreos Portugueses S.A.
TransPro, Inc., **71 356–59**
The Tranzonic Companies, **15 500–02; 37 392–95 (upd.)**
Travel Ports of America, Inc., **17 493–95**
Travelers Corporation, **III 387–90** *see also* Citigroup Inc.
Travelocity.com, Inc., **46 434–37**
Travelzoo Inc., **79 419–22**
Travis Boats & Motors, Inc., **37 396–98**
Travis Perkins plc, **34 450–52**
TRC Companies, Inc., **32 461–64**
Treadco, Inc., **19 454–56**
Treasure Chest Advertising Company, Inc., **32 465–67**
Tredegar Corporation, **52 349–51**
Tree of Life, Inc., **29 480–82**
Tree Top, Inc., **76 357–59**
TreeHouse Foods, Inc., **79 423–26**
Trek Bicycle Corporation, **16 493–95; 78 406–10 (upd.)**
Trelleborg AB, **93 455–64**
Trend Micro Inc., **97 429–32**
Trend-Lines, Inc., **22 516–18**
Trendwest Resorts, Inc., **33 409–11** *see also* Jeld-Wen, Inc.
Trex Company, Inc., **71 360–62**
Tri Valley Growers, **32 468–71**
Triarc Companies, Inc., **8 535–37; 34 453–57 (upd.)**
Tribune Company, **IV 682–84; 22 519–23 (upd.); 63 389–95 (upd.)**
Trico Marine Services, Inc., **89 450–53**
Trico Products Corporation, **15 503–05**
Tridel Enterprises Inc., **9 512–13**
Trident Seafoods Corporation, **56 359–61**
Trigen Energy Corporation, **42 386–89**
Trilon Financial Corporation, **II 456–57**
TriMas Corp., **11 534–36**
Trimble Navigation Limited, **40 441–43**
Třinecké Železárny A.S., **92 384–87**
Trinity Industries, Incorporated, **7 540–41**
Trinity Mirror plc, **49 404–10 (upd.)**
TRINOVA Corporation, **III 640–42**
TriPath Imaging, Inc., **77 446–49**
Triple Five Group Ltd., **49 411–15**
Triple P N.V., **26 496–99**
Tripwire, Inc., **97 433–36**
TriQuint Semiconductor, Inc., **63 396–99**
Trisko Jewelry Sculptures, Ltd., **57 388–90**
Triton Energy Corporation, **11 537–39**
Triumph-Adler *see* TA Triumph-Adler AG.
Triumph Group, Inc., **31 446–48**
Triumph Motorcycles Ltd., **53 334–37**
Trizec Corporation Ltd., **10 529–32**
The TriZetto Group, Inc., **83 416-419**
TRM Copy Centers Corporation, **18 526–28**
Tropicana Products, Inc., **28 473–77; 73 344–49 (upd.)**
Troutman Sanders L.L.P., **79 427–30**
True North Communications Inc., **23 478–80** *see also* Foote, Cone & Belding Worldwide.

True Religion Apparel, Inc., 79 431–34
True Temper Sports, Inc., 95 429–32
True Value Company, 74 353–57 (upd.)
Trump Organization, 23 481–84; 64 392–97 (upd.)
TRUMPF GmbH + Co. KG, 86 397–02
TruServ Corporation, 24 504–07 *see* True Value Co.
Trusthouse Forte PLC, III 104–06
TRW Automotive Holdings Corp., I 539–41; 11 540–42 (upd.); 14 510–13 (upd.); 75 376–82 (upd.)
TSA *see* Transaction Systems Architects, Inc.
Tsakos Energy Navigation Ltd., 91 483–86
TSB Group plc, 12 491–93
TSC *see* Tractor Supply Co.
Tsingtao Brewery Group, 49 416–20
TSMC *see* Taiwan Semiconductor Manufacturing Company Ltd.
TSYS *see* Total System Services, Inc.
TTL *see* Taiwan Tobacco & Liquor Corp.
TTX Company, 6 436–37; 66 328–30 (upd.)
Tubby's, Inc., 53 338–40
Tubos de Acero de Mexico, S.A. (TAMSA), 41 404–06
Tucows Inc., 78 411–14
Tucson Electric Power Company, 6 588–91
Tuesday Morning Corporation, 18 529–31; 70 331–33 (upd.)
TUF *see* Thai Union Frozen Products PCL.
TUI *see* Touristik Union International GmbH. and Company K.G.
TUI Group GmbH, 42 283; **44 432–35**
Tulip Ltd., 89 454–57
Tullow Oil plc, 83 420-423
Tully's Coffee Corporation, 51 384–86
Tultex Corporation, 13 531–33
Tumaro's Gourmet Tortillas, 85 430–33
Tumbleweed, Inc., 33 412–14; 80 377–81 (upd.)
Tunisair *see* Société Tunisienne de l'Air-Tunisair.
Tupolev Aviation and Scientific Technical Complex, 24 58–60
Tupperware Brands Corporation, 28 478–81; 78 415–20 (upd.)
TurboChef Technologies, Inc., 83 424-427
Turkish Airlines Inc. (Türk Hava Yollari A.O.), 72 351–53
Turkiye Is Bankasi A.S., 61 377–80
Türkiye Petrolleri Anonim Ortakliği, IV 562–64
Turner Broadcasting System, Inc., II 166–68; 6 171–73 (upd.); 66 331–34 (upd.)
Turner Construction Company, 66 335–38
The Turner Corporation, 8 538–40; 23 485–88 (upd.)
Turtle Wax, Inc., 15 506–09; 93 465–70 (upd.)
Tuscarora Inc., 29 483–85
The Tussauds Group, 55 376–78
Tutogen Medical, Inc., 68 378–80
Tuttle Publishing, 86 403–06
TV Azteca, S.A. de C.V., 39 398–401
TV Guide, Inc., 43 431–34 (upd.)
TVA *see* Tennessee Valley Authority.
TVE *see* Television Española, S.A.
TVI, Inc., 15 510–12
TW Services, Inc., II 679–80
TWA *see* Trans World Airlines.
TWC *see* The Weather Channel Cos.
Tweeter Home Entertainment Group, Inc., 30 464–66
Twentieth Century Fox Film Corporation, II 169–71; 25 490–94 (upd.)
24 Hour Fitness Worldwide, Inc., 71 363–65
24/7 Real Media, Inc., 49 421–24
Twin Disc, Inc., 21 502–04
Twinlab Corporation, 34 458–61
II-VI Incorporated, 69 353–55
Ty Inc., 33 415–17; 86 407–11 (upd.)
Tyco International Ltd., III 643–46; 28 482–87 (upd.); 63 400–06 (upd.)
Tyco Toys, Inc., 12 494–97 *see also* Mattel, Inc.
Tyler Corporation, 23 489–91
Tyndale House Publishers, Inc., 57 391–94
Tyson Foods, Inc., II 584–85; 14 514–16 (upd.); 50 491–95 (upd.)

U

U.S. *see also* US.
U.S. Aggregates, Inc., 42 390–92
U.S. Army Corps of Engineers, 91 491–95
U.S. Bancorp, 14 527–29; 36 489–95 (upd.)
U.S. Borax, Inc., 42 393–96
U.S. Can Corporation, 30 474–76
U.S. Cellular Corporation, 31 449–52 (upd.); 88 408–13 (upd.)
U.S. Delivery Systems, Inc., 22 531–33 *see also* Velocity Express Corp.
U.S. Foodservice, 26 503–06
U.S. Healthcare, Inc., 6 194–96
U.S. Home Corporation, 8 541–43; 78 421–26 (upd.)
U.S. News & World Report Inc., 30 477–80; 89 458–63 (upd.)
U.S. Office Products Company, 25 500–02
U.S. Physical Therapy, Inc., 65 345–48
U.S. Premium Beef LLC, 91 487–90
U.S. Robotics Corporation, 9 514–15; 66 339–41 (upd.)
U.S. Satellite Broadcasting Company, Inc., 20 505–07 *see also* DIRECTV, Inc.
U.S. Steel Corp *see* United States Steel Corp.
U.S. Timberlands Company, L.P., 42 397–400
U.S. Trust Corp., 17 496–98
U.S. Vision, Inc., 66 342–45
U S West, Inc., V 341–43; 25 495–99 (upd.)
UAL Corporation, 34 462–65 (upd.)
UAP *see* Union des Assurances de Paris.
UAW (International Union, United Automobile, Aerospace and Agricultural Implement Workers of America), 72 354–57
Ube Industries, Ltd., III 759–61; 38 463–67 (upd.)
Ubi Soft Entertainment S.A., 41 407–09
UBS AG, 52 352–59 (upd.)
UFA TV & Film Produktion GmbH, 80 382–87
UGI Corporation, 12 498–500
Ugine S.A., 20 498–500
Ugly Duckling Corporation, 22 524–27 *see also* DriveTime Automotive Group Inc.
UICI, 33 418–21 *see also* HealthMarkets, Inc.
Ukrop's Super Market's, Inc., 39 402–04
UL *see* Underwriters Laboratories, Inc.
Ulster Television PLC, 71 366–68
Ulta Salon, Cosmetics & Fragrance, Inc., 92471–73
Ultimate Electronics, Inc., 18 532–34; 69 356–59 (upd.)
Ultimate Leisure Group PLC, 75 383–85
Ultra Pac, Inc., 24 512–14
Ultra Petroleum Corporation, 71 369–71
Ultrak Inc., 24 508–11
Ultralife Batteries, Inc., 58 345–48
Ultramar Diamond Shamrock Corporation, IV 565–68; 31 453–57 (upd.)
ULVAC, Inc., 80 388–91
Umbro plc, 88 414–17
NV Umicore SA, 47 411–13
Umpqua Holdings Corporation, 87 443–446
Uncle Ben's Inc., 22 528–30
Uncle Ray's LLC, 90 417–19
Under Armour Performance Apparel, 61 381–83
Underberg AG, 92 388–393
Underwriters Laboratories, Inc., 30 467–70
UNG *see* United National Group, Ltd.
Uni-Marts, Inc., 17 499–502
Unibail SA, 40 444–46
Unibanco Holdings S.A., 73 350–53
Unica Corporation, 77 450–54
UNICEF *see* United Nations International Children's Emergency Fund (UNICEF).
Unicharm Corporation, 84 414–417
Unicom Corporation, 29 486–90 (upd.) *see also* Exelon Corp.
Unifi, Inc., 12 501–03; 62 372–76 (upd.)
Unified Grocers, Inc., 93 474–77
UniFirst Corporation, 21 505–07
Unigate PLC, II 586–87; 28 488–91 (upd.) *see also* Uniq Plc.

Unilever, II 588–91; 7 542–45 (upd.); 32 472–78 (upd.); 89 464–74 (upd.)
Unilog SA, 42 401–03
Union Bank of California, 16 496–98 *see also* UnionBanCal Corp.
Union Bank of Switzerland, II 378–79 *see also* UBS AG.
Union Camp Corporation, IV 344–46
Union Carbide Corporation, I 399–401; 9 516–20 (upd.); 74 358–63 (upd.)
Unión de Cervecerias Peruanas Backus y Johnston S.A.A.,92 394–397
Union des Assurances de Paris, III 391–94
Union Electric Company, V 741–43 *see also* Ameren Corp.
Unión Fenosa, S.A., 51 387–90
Union Financière de France Banque SA, 52 360–62
Union Pacific Corporation, V 529–32; 28 492–500 (upd.); 79 435–46 (upd.)
Union Planters Corporation, 54 387–90
Union Texas Petroleum Holdings, Inc., 9 521–23
UnionBanCal Corporation, 50 496–99 (upd.)
Uniq plc, 83 428-433 (upd.)
Unique Casual Restaurants, Inc., 27 480–82
Unison HealthCare Corporation, 25 503–05
Unisys Corporation, III 165–67; 6 281–83 (upd.); 36 479–84 (upd.)
Unit Corporation, 63 407–09
United Airlines, I 128–30; 6 128–30 (upd.) *see also* UAL Corp.
United Auto Group, Inc., 26 500–02; 68 381–84 (upd.)
United Biscuits (Holdings) plc, II 592–94; 42 404–09 (upd.)
United Brands Company, II 595–97
United Business Media plc, 52 363–68 (upd.)
United Dairy Farmers, Inc., 74 364–66
United Defense Industries, Inc., 30 471–73; 66 346–49 (upd.)
United Dominion Industries Limited, 8 544–46; 16 499–502 (upd.)
United Dominion Realty Trust, Inc., 52 369–71
United Farm Workers of America, 88 418–22
United Foods, Inc., 21 508–11
United HealthCare Corporation, 9 524–26 *see also* Humana Inc.
The United Illuminating Company, 21 512–14
United Industrial Corporation, 37 399–402
United Industries Corporation, 68 385–87
United Jewish Communities, 33 422–25
United Merchants & Manufacturers, Inc., 13 534–37
United National Group, Ltd., 63 410–13
United Nations International Children's Emergency Fund (UNICEF), 58 349–52
United Natural Foods, Inc., 32 479–82; 76 360–63 (upd.)
United Negro College Fund, Inc., 79 447–50
United News & Media plc, 28 501–05 (upd.) *see also* United Business Media plc.
United Newspapers plc, IV 685–87 *see also* United Business Media plc.
United Online, Inc., 71 372–77 (upd.)
United Overseas Bank Ltd., 56 362–64
United Pan-Europe Communications NV, 47 414–17
United Paper Mills Ltd., IV 347–50 *see also* UPM-Kymmene Corp.
United Parcel Service, Inc., V 533–35; 17 503–06 (upd.); 63 414–19; 94 425–30 (upd.)
United Press International, Inc., 25 506–09; 73 354–57 (upd.)
United Rentals, Inc., 34 466–69
United Retail Group Inc., 33 426–28
United Road Services, Inc., 69 360–62
United Service Organizations, 60 308–11
United States Cellular Corporation, 9 527–29 *see also* U.S. Cellular Corp.
United States Filter Corporation, 20 501–04 *see also* Siemens AG.
United States Health Care Systems, Inc. *see* U.S. Healthcare, Inc.
United States Pipe and Foundry Company, 62 377–80
United States Playing Card Company, 62 381–84
United States Postal Service, 14 517–20; 34 470–75 (upd.)
United States Shoe Corporation, V 207–08
United States Steel Corporation, 50 500–04 (upd.)
United States Surgical Corporation, 10 533–35; 34 476–80 (upd.)
United Stationers Inc., 14 521–23
United Talent Agency, Inc., 80 392–96
United Technologies Automotive Inc., 15 513–15
United Technologies Corporation, I 84–86; 10 536–38 (upd.); 34 481–85 (upd.)
United Telecommunications, Inc., V 344–47 *see also* Sprint Corp.
United Utilities PLC, 52 372–75 (upd.)
United Video Satellite Group, 18 535–37 *see also* TV Guide, Inc.
United Water Resources, Inc., 40 447–50; 45 277
United Way of America, 36 485–88
Unitika Ltd., V 387–89; 53 341–44 (upd.)
Unitil Corporation, 37 403–06
Unitog Co., 19 457–60 *see also* Cintas Corp.
Unitrin Inc., 16 503–05; 78 427–31 (upd.)
Univar Corporation, 9 530–32
Universal Compression, Inc., 59 402–04
Universal Corporation, V 417–18; 48 403–06 (upd.)
Universal Electronics Inc., 39 405–08
Universal Foods Corporation, 7 546–48 *see also* Sensient Technologies Corp.
Universal Forest Products, Inc., 10 539–40; 59 405–09 (upd.)
Universal Health Services, Inc., 6 191–93
Universal International, Inc., 25 510–11
Universal Manufacturing Company, 88 423–26
Universal Security Instruments, Inc., 96 434–37
Universal Stainless & Alloy Products, Inc., 75 386–88
Universal Studios, Inc., 33 429–33
Universal Technical Institute, Inc., 81 396–99
The University of Chicago Press, 79 451–55
University of Phoenix *see* Apollo Group, Inc.
Univision Communications Inc., 24 515–18; 83 434-439 (upd.)
UNM *see* United News & Media plc.
Uno Restaurant Holdings Corporation, 18 538–40; 70 334–37 (upd.)
Unocal Corporation, IV 569–71; 24 519–23 (upd.); 71 378–84 (upd.)
UNUM Corp., 13 538–40
UnumProvident Corporation, 52 376–83 (upd.)
Uny Co., Ltd., V 209–10; 49 425–28 (upd.)
UOB *see* United Overseas Bank Ltd.
UPC *see* United Pan-Europe Communications NV.
UPI *see* United Press International.
Upjohn Company, I 707–09; 8 547–49 (upd.) *see also* Pharmacia & Upjohn Inc.; Pfizer Inc.
UPM-Kymmene Corporation, 19 461–65; 50 505–11 (upd.)
UPS *see* United Parcel Service, Inc.
Uralita S.A., 96 438–41
Urban Outfitters, Inc., 14 524–26; 74 367–70 (upd.)
Urbi Desarrollos Urbanos, S.A. de C.V., 81 400–03
Urbium PLC, 75 389–91
URS Corporation, 45 420–23; 80 397–400 (upd.)
URSI *see* United Road Services, Inc.
US *see also* U.S.
US Airways Group, Inc., I 131–32; 6 131–32 (upd.); 28 506–09 (upd.); 52 384–88 (upd.)
US 1 Industries, Inc., 89 475–78
USA Interactive, Inc., 47 418–22 (upd.)
USA Mobility Inc., 97 437–40 (upd.)
USA Truck, Inc., 42 410–13
USAA, 10 541–43; 62 385–88 (upd.)
USANA, Inc., 29 491–93
USCC *see* United States Cellular Corp.

USF&G Corporation, III 395–98 *see also* The St. Paul Companies.
USG Corporation, III 762–64; 26 507–10 (upd.); 81 404–10 (upd.)
Ushio Inc., 91 496–99
Usinas Siderúrgicas de Minas Gerais S.A., 77 454–57
Usinger's Famous Sausage *see* Fred Usinger Inc.
Usinor SA, IV 226–28; 42 414–17 (upd.)
USO *see* United Service Organizations.
USPS *see* United States Postal Service.
USSC *see* United States Surgical Corp.
UST Inc., 9 533–35; 50 512–17 (upd.)
USX Corporation, IV 572–74; 7 549–52 (upd.) *see also* United States Steel Corp.
Utah Medical Products, Inc., 36 496–99
Utah Power and Light Company, 27 483–86 *see also* PacifiCorp.
Utilicorp United Inc., 6 592–94 *see also* Aquilla, Inc.
UTStarcom, Inc., 77 458–61
UTV *see* Ulster Television PLC.
Utz Quality Foods, Inc., 72 358–60
UUNET, 38 468–72
Uwajimaya, Inc., 60 312–14

V

V&S Vin & Sprit AB, 91 504–11 (upd.)
VA TECH ELIN EBG GmbH, 49 429–31
Vail Resorts, Inc., 11 543–46; 43 435–39 (upd.)
Vaillant GmbH, 44 436–39
Valassis Communications, Inc., 8 550–51; 37 407–10 (upd.); 76 364–67 (upd.)
Valeo, 23 492–94; 66 350–53 (upd.)
Valero Energy Corporation, 7 553–55; 71 385–90 (upd.)
Valhi, Inc., 19 466–68; 94 431–35 (upd.)
Vallen Corporation, 45 424–26
Valley Media Inc., 35 430–33
Valley National Gases, Inc., 85 434–37
Valley Proteins, Inc., 91 500–03
ValleyCrest Companies, 81 411–14 (upd.)
Vallourec SA, 54 391–94
Valmet Oy, III 647–49 *see also* Metso Corp.
Valmont Industries, Inc., 19 469–72
Valorem S.A., 88 427–30
Valores Industriales S.A., 19 473–75
The Valspar Corporation, 8 552–54; 32 483–86 (upd.); 77 462–68 (upd.)
Value City Department Stores, Inc., 38 473–75 *see also* Retail Ventures, Inc.
Value Line, Inc., 16 506–08; 73 358–61 (upd.)
Value Merchants Inc., 13 541–43
ValueClick, Inc., 49 432–34
ValueVision International, Inc., 22 534–36
Van Camp Seafood Company, Inc., 7 556–57 *see also* Chicken of the Sea International.
Van Hool S.A./NV, 96 442–45
Van Houtte Inc., 39 409–11
Van Lanschot NV, 79 456–59
Van Leer N.V. *see* Royal Packaging Industries Van Leer N.V.; Greif Inc.
Van's Aircraft, Inc., 65 349–51
Vance Publishing Corporation, 64 398–401
The Vanguard Group, Inc., 14 530–32; 34 486–89 (upd.)
Vanguard Health Systems Inc., 70 338–40
Vans, Inc., 16 509–11; 47 423–26 (upd.)
Varco International, Inc., 42 418–20
Vari-Lite International, Inc., 35 434–36
Varian Associates Inc., 12 504–06
Varian, Inc., 48 407–11 (upd.)
Variety Wholesalers, Inc., 73 362–64
Variflex, Inc., 51 391–93
VARIG S.A. (Viação Aérea Rio-Grandense), 6 133–35; 29 494–97 (upd.)
Varity Corporation, III 650–52 *see also* AGCO Corp.
Varlen Corporation, 16 512–14
Varsity Brands, Inc., 15 516–18; 94 436–40 (upd.)
Varta AG, 23 495–99
VASCO Data Security International, Inc., 79 460–63
Vastar Resources, Inc., 24 524–26
Vattenfall AB, 57 395–98
Vauxhall Motors Limited, 73 365–69
VBA - Bloemenveiling Aalsmeer, 88 431–34
VCA Antech, Inc., 58 353–55
Veba A.G., I 542–43; 15 519–21 (upd.) *see also* E.On AG.
Vebego International BV, 49 435–37
VECO International, Inc., 7 558–59 *see also* CH2M Hill Ltd.
Vector Aerospace Corporation, 97 441–44
Vector Group Ltd., 35 437–40 (upd.)
Vedior NV, 35 441–43
Veeco Instruments Inc., 32 487–90
Veit Companies, 43 440–42; 92 398–402 (upd.)
Velcro Industries N.V., 19 476–78; 72 361–64 (upd.)
Velocity Express Corporation, 49 438–41; 94 441–46 (upd.)
Velux A/S, 86 412–15
Venator Group Inc., 35 444–49 (upd.) *see also* Foot Locker Inc.
Vencor, Inc., 16 515–17
Vendex International N.V., 13 544–46 *see also* Koninklijke Vendex KBB N.V. (Royal Vendex KBB N.V.).
Vendôme Luxury Group plc, 27 487–89
Venetian Casino Resort, LLC, 47 427–29
Ventana Medical Systems, Inc., 75 392–94
Ventura Foods LLC, 90 420–23
Venture Stores Inc., 12 507–09
VeraSun Energy Corporation, 87 447–450
Verbatim Corporation, 14 533–35; 74 371–74 (upd.)
Vereinigte Elektrizitätswerke Westfalen AG, IV V 744–47
Veridian Corporation, 54 395–97
VeriFone, Inc., 18 541–44; 76 368–71 (upd.)
Verint Systems Inc., 73 370–72
VeriSign, Inc., 47 430–34
Veritas Software Corporation, 45 427–31
Verity Inc., 68 388–91
Verizon Communications Inc., 43 443–49 (upd.); 78 432–40 (upd.)
Verlagsgruppe Georg von Holtzbrinck GmbH, 35 450–53
Vermeer Manufacturing Company, 17 507–10
The Vermont Country Store, 93 478–82
Vermont Pure Holdings, Ltd., 51 394–96
The Vermont Teddy Bear Co., Inc., 36 500–02
Versace *see* Gianni Versace SpA.
Vertex Pharmaceuticals Incorporated, 83 440-443
Vertis Communications, 84 418–421
Vertrue Inc., 77 469–72
Vestas Wind Systems A/S, 73 373–75
Vestey Group Ltd., 95 433–37
VEW AG, 39 412–15
VF Corporation, V 390–92; 17 511–14 (upd.); 54 398–404 (upd.)
VHA Inc., 53 345–47
Viacom Inc., 7 560–62; 23 500–03 (upd.); 67 367–71 (upd.) *see also* Paramount Pictures Corp.
Viad Corp., 73 376–78
Viag AG, IV 229–32 *see also* E.On AG.
ViaSat, Inc., 54 405–08
Viasoft Inc., 27 490–93; 59 27
VIASYS Healthcare, Inc., 52 389–91
Viasystems Group, Inc., 67 372–74
Viatech Continental Can Company, Inc., 25 512–15 (upd.)
Vicat S.A., 70 341–43
Vickers plc, 27 494–97
Vicon Industries, Inc., 44 440–42
VICORP Restaurants, Inc., 12 510–12; 48 412–15 (upd.)
Victor Company of Japan, Limited, II 118–19; 26 511–13 (upd.); 83 444-449 (upd.)
Victoria Coach Station Ltd.*see* London Regional Transport.
Victoria Group, III 399–401; 44 443–46 (upd.)
Victorinox AG, 21 515–17; 74 375–78 (upd.)
Vicunha Têxtil S.A., 78 441–44
Victory Refrigeration, Inc., 82 403–06
Videojet Technologies, Inc., 90 424–27
Vidrala S.A., 67 375–77
Viel & Cie, 76 372–74
Vienna Sausage Manufacturing Co., 14 536–37

Viessmann Werke GmbH & Co., 37 411–14
Viewpoint International, Inc., 66 354–56
ViewSonic Corporation, 72 365–67
Viking Office Products, Inc., 10 544–46 *see also* Office Depot, Inc.
Viking Range Corporation, 66 357–59
Viking Yacht Company, 96 446–49
Village Roadshow Ltd., 58 356–59
Village Super Market, Inc., 7 563–64
Village Voice Media, Inc., 38 476–79
Villeroy & Boch AG, 37 415–18
Vilmorin Clause et Cie, 70 344–46
AO VimpelCom, 48 416–19
Vin & Spirit AB, 31 458–61 *see also* V&S Vin & Sprit AB.
Viña Concha y Toro S.A., 45 432–34
Vinci, 27 54; **43 450–52; 49** 44
Vincor International Inc., 50 518–21
Vinson & Elkins L.L.P., 30 481–83
Vintage Petroleum, Inc., 42 421–23
Vinton Studios, 63 420–22
Vion Food Group NV, 85 438–41
Virbac Corporation, 74 379–81
Virco Manufacturing Corporation, 17 515–17
Virgin Group Ltd., 12 513–15; 32 491–96 (upd.); 89 479–86 (upd.)
Virginia Dare Extract Company, Inc., 94 447–50
Viridian Group plc, 64 402–04
Visa International, 9 536–38; 26 514–17 (upd.)
Viscofan S.A., 70 347–49
Vishay Intertechnology, Inc., 21 518–21; 80 401–06 (upd.)
Vision Service Plan Inc., 77 473–76
Viskase Companies, Inc., 55 379–81
Vista Bakery, Inc., 56 365–68
Vista Chemical Company, I 402–03
Vistana, Inc., 22 537–39
VistaPrint Limited, 87 451–454
VISX, Incorporated, 30 484–86
Vita Plus Corporation, 60 315–17
Vital Images, Inc., 85 442–45
Vitalink Pharmacy Services, Inc., 15 522–24
Vitamin Shoppe Industries, Inc., 60 318–20
Vitasoy International Holdings Ltd., 94 451–54
Vitesse Semiconductor Corporation, 32 497–500
Vitro Corp., 10 547–48
Vitro Corporativo S.A. de C.V., 34 490–92
Vivarte SA, 54 409–12 (upd.)
Vivartia S.A., 82 407–10
Vivendi Universal S.A., 46 438–41 (upd.)
Vivra, Inc., 18 545–47 *see also* Gambro AB.
Vlasic Foods International Inc., 25 516–19
VLSI Technology, Inc., 16 518–20
VMware, Inc., 90 428–31
VNU N.V., 27 498–501
Vocento, 94 455–58
Vodafone Group Plc, 11 547–48; 36 503–06 (upd.); 75 395–99 (upd.)
voestalpine AG, IV 233–35; 57 399–403 (upd.)
Voith Sulzer Papiermaschinen GmbH *see* J.M. Voith AG.
Volcan Compañia Minera S.A.A., 92 403–06
Volcom, Inc., 77 477–80
Volga-Dnepr Group, 82 411–14
Volkswagen Aktiengesellschaft, I 206–08; 11 549–51 (upd.); 32 501–05 (upd.)
Volt Information Sciences Inc., 26 518–21
Volunteers of America, Inc., 66 360–62
AB Volvo, I 209–11; 7 565–68 (upd.); 26 9–12 (upd.); 67 378–83 (upd.)
Von Maur Inc., 64 405–08
Vonage Holdings Corp., 81 415–18
The Vons Companies, Incorporated, 7 569–71; 28 510–13 (upd.)
Vontobel Holding AG, 96 450–53
Vornado Realty Trust, 20 508–10
Vorwerk & Co., 27 502–04
Vosper Thornycroft Holding plc, 41 410–12
Vossloh AG, 53 348–52
Votorantim Participaçoes S.A., 76 375–78
Vought Aircraft Industries, Inc., 49 442–45
VSM *see* Village Super Market, Inc.
VTech Holdings Ltd., 77 481–84
Vueling Airlines S.A., 97 445–48
Vulcan Materials Company, 7 572–75; 52 392–96 (upd.)

W

W + K *see* Wieden + Kennedy.
W.A. Whitney Company, 53 353–56
W. Atlee Burpee & Co., 27 505–08
W.B Doner & Co., 56 369–72
W.C. Bradley Co., 69 363–65
W.H. Brady Co., 16 518–21 *see also* Brady Corp.
W. H. Braum, Inc., 80 407–10
W H Smith Group PLC, V 211–13
W Jordan (Cereals) Ltd., 74 382–84
W.L. Gore & Associates, Inc., 14 538–40; 60 321–24 (upd.)
W.P. Carey & Co. LLC, 49 446–48
W.R. Berkley Corporation, 15 525–27; 74 385–88 (upd.)
W.R. Grace & Company, I 547–50; 50 522–29 (upd.)
W.W. Grainger, Inc., V 214–15; 26 537–39 (upd.); 68 392–95 (upd.)
W.W. Norton & Company, Inc., 28 518–20
Waban Inc., 13 547–49 *see also* HomeBase, Inc.
Wabash National Corp., 13 550–52
Wabtec Corporation, 40 451–54
Wachovia Bank of Georgia, N.A., 16 521–23
Wachovia Bank of South Carolina, N.A., 16 524–26
Wachovia Corporation, 12 516–20; 46 442–49 (upd.)
Wachtell, Lipton, Rosen & Katz, 47 435–38
The Wackenhut Corporation, 14 541–43; 63 423–26 (upd.)
Wacker-Chemie GmbH, 35 454–58
Wacker Construction Equipment AG, 95 438–41
Wacoal Corp., 25 520–24
Waddell & Reed, Inc., 22 540–43
Waffle House Inc., 14 544–45; 60 325–27 (upd.)
Wagers Inc. (Idaho Candy Company), 86 416–19
Waggener Edstrom, 42 424–26
Wagon plc, 92 407–10
Wah Chang, 82 415–18
Wahl Clipper Corporation, 86 420–23
Wahoo's Fish Taco, 96 454–57
Wakefern Food Corporation, 33 434–37
Wal-Mart de Mexico, S.A. de C.V., 35 459–61 (upd.)
Wal-Mart Stores, Inc., V 216–17; 8 555–57 (upd.); 26 522–26 (upd.); 63 427–32 (upd.)
Walbridge Aldinger Co., 38 480–82
Walbro Corporation, 13 553–55
Waldbaum, Inc., 19 479–81
Waldenbooks, 17 522–24; 86 424–28 (upd.)
Walgreen Co., V 218–20; 20 511–13 (upd.); 65 352–56 (upd.)
Walker Manufacturing Company, 19 482–84
Walkers Shortbread Ltd., 79 464–67
Walkers Snack Foods Ltd., 70 350–52
Wall Drug Store, Inc., 40 455–57
Wall Street Deli, Inc., 33 438–41
Wallace Computer Services, Inc., 36 507–10
Walsworth Publishing Company, Inc., 78 445–48
The Walt Disney Company, II 172–74; 6 174–77 (upd.); 30 487–91 (upd.); 63 433–38 (upd.)
Walter Industries, Inc., III 765–67; 22 544–47 (upd.); 72 368–73 (upd.)
Walton Monroe Mills, Inc., 8 558–60 *see also* Avondale Industries.
WaMu *see* Washington Mutual, Inc.
Wanadoo S.A., 75 400–02
Wang Laboratories, Inc., III 168–70; 6 284–87 (upd.) *see also* Getronics NV.
Warburtons Ltd., 89 487–90
WARF *see* Wisconsin Alumni Research Foundation.
The Warnaco Group Inc., 12 521–23; 46 450–54 (upd.) *see also* Authentic Fitness Corp.
Warner Chilcott Limited, 85 446–49
Warner Communications Inc., II 175–77 *see also* AOL Time Warner Inc.
Warner-Lambert Co., I 710–12; 10 549–52 (upd.) *see also* Pfizer Inc.

Warner Music Group Corporation, 90 432–37 (upd.)
Warners' Stellian Inc., 67 384–87
Warrantech Corporation, 53 357–59
Warrell Corporation, 68 396–98
Warwick Valley Telephone Company, 55 382–84
Wascana Energy Inc., 13 556–58
The Washington Companies, 33 442–45
Washington Federal, Inc., 17 525–27
Washington Football, Inc., 35 462–65
Washington Gas Light Company, 19 485–88
Washington Mutual, Inc., 17 528–31; 93 483–89 (upd.)
Washington National Corporation, 12 524–26
Washington Natural Gas Company, 9 539–41 *see also* Puget Sound Energy Inc.
The Washington Post Company, IV 688–90; 20 515–18 (upd.)
Washington Scientific Industries, Inc., 17 532–34
Washington Water Power Company, 6 595–98 *see also* Avista Corp.
Wassall Plc, 18 548–50
Waste Connections, Inc., 46 455–57
Waste Holdings, Inc., 41 413–15
Waste Management, Inc., V 752–54
Water Pik Technologies, Inc., 34 498–501; 83 450-453 (upd.)
Waterford Wedgwood plc, 12 527–29; 34 493–97 (upd.)
Waterhouse Investor Services, Inc., 18 551–53
Waters Corporation, 43 453–57
Watkins-Johnson Company, 15 528–30
Watsco Inc., 52 397–400
Watson Pharmaceuticals Inc., 16 527–29; 56 373–76 (upd.)
Watson Wyatt Worldwide, 42 427–30
Wattie's Ltd., 7 576–78
Watts Industries, Inc., 19 489–91
Watts of Lydney Group Ltd., 71 391–93
Wausau-Mosinee Paper Corporation, 60 328–31 (upd.)
Waverly, Inc., 16 530–32
Wawa Inc., 17 535–37; 78 449–52 (upd.)
The Wawanesa Mutual Insurance Company, 68 399–401
Waxman Industries, Inc., 9 542–44
WAZ Media Group, 82 419–24
WB *see* Warner Communications Inc.
WD-40 Company, 18 554–57; 87 455–460 (upd.)
The Weather Channel Companies, 52 401–04 *see also* Landmark Communications, Inc.
Weatherford International, Inc., 39 416–18
Weaver Popcorn Company, Inc., 89 491–93
Webasto Roof Systems Inc., 97 449–52
Webber Oil Company, 61 384–86
Weber et Broutin France, 66 363–65
Weber-Stephen Products Co., 40 458–60
WebEx Communications, Inc., 81 419–23
WebMD Corporation, 65 357–60
Weeres Industries Corporation, 52 405–07
Weetabix Limited, 61 387–89
Weg S.A., 78 453–56
Wegener NV, 53 360–62
Wegmans Food Markets, Inc., 9 545–46; 41 416–18 (upd.)
Weider Nutrition International, Inc., 29 498–501
Weight Watchers International Inc., 12 530–32; 33 446–49 (upd.); 73 379–83 (upd.)
Weil, Gotshal & Manges LLP, 55 385–87
Weiner's Stores, Inc., 33 450–53
Wieden + Kennedy, 75 403–05
Wienerberger AG, 70 361–63
Weingarten Realty Investors, 95 442–45
The Weir Group PLC, 85 450–53
Weirton Steel Corporation, IV 236–38; 26 527–30 (upd.)
Weis Markets, Inc., 15 531–33; 84 422–426 (upd.)
The Weitz Company, Inc., 42 431–34
Welbilt Corp., 19 492–94; *see also* Enodis plc.
Welcome Wagon International Inc., 82 425–28
Weleda AG, 78 457–61
The Welk Group, Inc., 78 462–66
Wella AG, III 68–70; 48 420–23 (upd.)
WellChoice, Inc., 67 388–91 (upd.)
Wellco Enterprises, Inc., 84 427–430
Wellcome Foundation Ltd., I 713–15 *see also* GlaxoSmithKline plc.
Wellman, Inc., 8 561–62; 52 408–11 (upd.)
WellPoint Health Networks Inc., 25 525–29
Wells Fargo & Company, II 380–84; 12 533–37 (upd.); 38 483–92 (upd.); 97 453–67
Wells-Gardner Electronics Corporation, 43 458–61
Wells Rich Greene BDDP, 6 50–52
Wells' Dairy, Inc., 36 511–13
Wendell *see* Mark T. Wendell Tea Co.
Wendy's International, Inc., 8 563–65; 23 504–07 (upd.); 47 439–44 (upd.)
Wenner Bread Products Inc., 80 411–15
Wenner Media, Inc., 32 506–09
Werner Enterprises, Inc., 26 531–33
Weru Aktiengesellschaft, 18 558–61
Wessanen *see* Koninklijke Wessanen nv.
West Bend Co., 14 546–48
West Coast Entertainment Corporation, 29 502–04
West Corporation, 42 435–37
West Fraser Timber Co. Ltd., 17 538–40; 91 512–18 (upd.)
West Group, 34 502–06 (upd.)
West Linn Paper Company, 91 519–22
West Marine, Inc., 17 541–43; 90 438–42 (upd.)
West One Bancorp, 11 552–55 *see also* U.S. Bancorp.
West Pharmaceutical Services, Inc., 42 438–41
West Point-Pepperell, Inc., 8 566–69 *see also* WestPoint Stevens Inc.; JPS Textile Group, Inc.
West Publishing Co., 7 579–81
Westaff Inc., 33 454–57
Westamerica Bancorporation, 17 544–47
Westar Energy, Inc., 57 404–07 (upd.)
WestCoast Hospitality Corporation, 59 410–13
Westcon Group, Inc., 67 392–94
Westdeutsche Landesbank Girozentrale, II 385–87; 46 458–61 (upd.)
Westell Technologies, Inc., 57 408–10
Western Atlas Inc., 12 538–40
Western Beef, Inc., 22 548–50
Western Company of North America, 15 534–36
Western Digital Corporation, 25 530–32; 92 411–15 (upd.)
Western Gas Resources, Inc., 45 435–37
Western Oil Sands Inc., 85 454–57
Western Publishing Group, Inc., 13 559–61 *see also* Thomson Corp.
Western Resources, Inc., 12 541–43
The WesterN SizzliN Corporation, 60 335–37
Western Union Financial Services, Inc., 54 413–16
Western Wireless Corporation, 36 514–16
Westfield Group, 69 366–69
Westin Hotels and Resorts Worldwide, 9 547–49; 29 505–08 (upd.)
Westinghouse Electric Corporation, II 120–22; 12 544–47 (upd.) *see also* CBS Radio Group.
WestJet Airlines Ltd., 38 493–95
Westmoreland Coal Company, 7 582–85
Weston Foods Inc. *see* George Weston Ltd.
Westpac Banking Corporation, II 388–90; 48 424–27 (upd.)
WestPoint Stevens Inc., 16 533–36 *see also* JPS Textile Group, Inc.
Westport Resources Corporation, 63 439–41
Westvaco Corporation, IV 351–54; 19 495–99 (upd.) *see also* MeadWestvaco Corp.
Westwood One, Inc., 23 508–11
The Wet Seal, Inc., 18 562–64; 70 353–57 (upd.)
Wetterau Incorporated, II 681–82 *see also* Supervalu Inc.
Weyco Group, Incorporated, 32 510–13
Weyerhaeuser Company, IV 355–56; 9 550–52 (upd.); 28 514–17 (upd.); 83 454-461 (upd.)
WFS Financial Inc., 70 358–60
WFSC *see* World Fuel Services Corp.

WGBH Educational Foundation, 66 366–68
WH Smith PLC, 42 442–47 (upd.)
Wham-O, Inc., 61 390–93
Whatman plc, 46 462–65
Wheaton Industries, 8 570–73
Wheaton Science Products, 60 338–42 (upd.)
Wheelabrator Technologies, Inc., 6 599–600; 60 343–45 (upd.)
Wheeling-Pittsburgh Corporation, 7 586–88; 58 360–64 (upd.)
Wheels Inc., 96 458–61
Wherehouse Entertainment Incorporated, 11 556–58
Whirlpool Corporation, III 653–55; 12 548–50 (upd.); 59 414–19 (upd.)
Whitbread PLC, I 293–94; 20 519–22 (upd.); 52 412–17 (upd.); 97 468–76 (upd.)
White & Case LLP, 35 466–69
White Castle Management Company, 12 551–53; 36 517–20 (upd.); 85 458–64 (upd.)
White Consolidated Industries Inc., 13 562–64 *see also* Electrolux.
The White House, Inc., 60 346–48
White Lily Foods Company, 88 435–38
White Mountains Insurance Group, Ltd., 48 428–31
White Rose, Inc., 24 527–29
White Wave, 43 462–64
Whitehall Jewellers, Inc., 82 429–34 (upd.)
Whiting Petroleum Corporation, 81 424–27
Whiting-Turner Contracting Company, 95 446–49
Whitman Corporation, 10 553–55 (upd.) *see also* PepsiAmericas, Inc.
Whitman Education Group, Inc., 41 419–21
Whitney Holding Corporation, 21 522–24
Whittaker Corporation, I 544–46; 48 432–35 (upd.)
Whittard of Chelsea Plc, 61 394–97
Whole Foods Market, Inc., 20 523–27; 50 530–34 (upd.)
Wickes Inc., V 221–23; 25 533–36 (upd.)
Widmer Brothers Brewing Company, 76 379–82
Wikimedia Foundation, Inc., 91 523–26
Wilbert, Inc., 56 377–80
Wilbur Chocolate Company, 66 369–71
Wilco Farm Stores, 93 490–93
Wild Oats Markets, Inc., 19 500–02; 41 422–25 (upd.)
Wildlife Conservation Society, 31 462–64
Wilh. Wilhelmsen ASA, 94 459–62
Wilhelm Karmann GmbH, 94 463–68
Wilkinson Hardware Stores Ltd., 80 416–18
Wilkinson Sword Ltd., 60 349–52
Willamette Industries, Inc., IV 357–59; 31 465–68 (upd.) *see also* Weyerhaeuser Co.
Willamette Valley Vineyards, Inc., 85 465–69
Willbros Group, Inc., 56 381–83
William Grant & Sons Ltd., 60 353–55
William Hill Organization Limited, 49 449–52
William L. Bonnell Company, Inc., 66 372–74
William Lyon Homes, 59 420–22
William Morris Agency, Inc., 23 512–14
William Reed Publishing Ltd., 78 467–70
William Zinsser & Company, Inc., 58 365–67
Williams & Connolly LLP, 47 445–48
Williams Communications Group, Inc., 34 507–10
The Williams Companies, Inc., IV 575–76; 31 469–72 (upd.)
Williams Scotsman, Inc., 65 361–64
Williams-Sonoma, Inc., 17 548–50; 44 447–50 (upd.)
Williamson-Dickie Manufacturing Company, 14 549–50; 45 438–41 (upd.)
Willis Corroon Group plc, 25 537–39
Willkie Farr & Gallagher LLPLP, 95 450–53
Wilmington Trust Corporation, 25 540–43
Wilson Bowden Plc, 45 442–44
Wilson Sonsini Goodrich & Rosati, 34 511–13
Wilson Sporting Goods Company, 24 530–32; 84 431–436 (upd.)
Wilsons The Leather Experts Inc., 21 525–27; 58 368–71 (upd.)
Wilton Products, Inc., 97 477–80
Winbond Electronics Corporation, 74 389–91
Wincanton plc, 52 418–20
Winchell's Donut Houses Operating Company, L.P., 60 356–59
WinCo Foods Inc., 60 360–63
Wincor Nixdorf Holding GmbH, 69 370–73 (upd.)
Wind River Systems, Inc., 37 419–22
Windmere Corporation, 16 537–39 *see also* Applica Inc.
Windstream Corporation, 83 462-465
Windswept Environmental Group, Inc., 62 389–92
The Wine Group, Inc., 39 419–21
Winegard Company, 56 384–87
Winmark Corporation, 74 392–95
Winn-Dixie Stores, Inc., II 683–84; 21 528–30 (upd.); 59 423–27 (upd.)
Winnebago Industries, Inc., 7 589–91; 27 509–12 (upd.); 96 462–67 (upd.)
WinsLoew Furniture, Inc., 21 531–33 *see also* Brown Jordan International Inc.
Winston & Strawn, 35 470–73
Winterthur Group, III 402–04; 68 402–05 (upd.)
Wipro Limited, 43 465–68
The Wiremold Company, 81 428–34
Wirtz Corporation, 72 374–76
Wisconsin Alumni Research Foundation, 65 365–68
Wisconsin Bell, Inc., 14 551–53 *see also* AT&T Corp.
Wisconsin Central Transportation Corporation, 24 533–36
Wisconsin Dairies, 7 592–93
Wisconsin Energy Corporation, 6 601–03; 54 417–21 (upd.)
Wisconsin Public Service Corporation, 9 553–54 *see also* WPS Resources Corp.
Wise Foods, Inc., 79 468–71
Witco Corporation, I 404–06; 16 540–43 (upd.) *see also* Chemtura Corp.
Witness Systems, Inc., 87 461–465
Wizards of the Coast Inc., 24 537–40
WLR Foods, Inc., 21 534–36
Wm. B. Reily & Company Inc., 58 372–74
Wm. Morrison Supermarkets PLC, 38 496–98
Wm. Wrigley Jr. Company, 7 594–97; 58 375–79 (upd.)
WMC, Limited, 43 469–72
WMF *see* Württembergische Metallwarenfabrik AG (WMF).
WMS Industries, Inc., 15 537–39; 53 363–66 (upd.)
WMX Technologies Inc., 17 551–54
Wolfgang Puck Worldwide, Inc., 26 534–36; 70 364–67 (upd.)
Wolohan Lumber Co., 19 503–05 *see also* Lanoga Corp.
Wolseley plc, 64 409–12
Wolters Kluwer NV, 14 554–56; 33 458–61 (upd.)
The Wolverhampton & Dudley Breweries, PLC, 57 411–14
Wolverine Tube Inc., 23 515–17
Wolverine World Wide, Inc., 16 544–47; 59 428–33 (upd.)
Womble Carlyle Sandridge & Rice, PLLC, 52 421–24
Wood Hall Trust plc, I 592–93
Wood-Mode, Inc., 23 518–20
Woodcraft Industries Inc., 61 398–400
Woodward Governor Company, 13 565–68; 49 453–57 (upd.)
Woolrich Inc., 62 393–96
The Woolwich plc, 30 492–95
Woolworth Corporation, V 224–27; 20 528–32 (upd.) *see also* Kingfisher plc; Venator Group Inc.
Woolworths Group plc, 83 466-473
WordPerfect Corporation, 10 556–59 *see also* Corel Corp.
Workflow Management, Inc., 65 369–72
Working Assets Funding Service, 43 473–76
Workman Publishing Company, Inc., 70 368–71
World Acceptance Corporation, 57 415–18
World Bank Group, 33 462–65
World Book, Inc., 12 554–56

World Color Press Inc., 12 557–59 *see also* Quebecor Inc.
World Duty Free Americas, Inc., 29 509–12 (upd.)
World Fuel Services Corporation, 47 449–51
World Publications, LLC, 65 373–75
World Vision International, Inc., 93 494–97
World Wide Technology, Inc., 94 469–72
World Wrestling Federation Entertainment, Inc., 32 514–17
World's Finest Chocolate Inc., 39 422–24
WorldCorp, Inc., 10 560–62
Worldwide Pants Inc., 97 481–84
Worldwide Restaurant Concepts, Inc., 47 452–55
Worms et Cie, 27 513–15 *see also* Sequana Capital.
Worthington Foods, Inc., 14 557–59 *see also* Kellogg Co.
Worthington Industries, Inc., 7 598–600; 21 537–40 (upd.)
WPL Holdings, 6 604–06
WPP Group plc, 6 53–54; 48 440–42 (upd.) *see also* Ogilvy Group Inc.
WPS Resources Corporation, 53 367–70 (upd.)
WRG *see* Wells Rich Greene BDDP.
Wright Express Corporation, 80 419–22
Wright Medical Group, Inc., 61 401–05
Writers Guild of America, West, Inc., 92 416–20
WS Atkins Plc, 45 445–47
WTD Industries, Inc., 20 533–36
Wunderman, 86 429–32
Württembergische Metallwarenfabrik AG (WMF), 60 364–69
WVT Communications *see* Warwick Valley Telephone Co.
Wyant Corporation, 30 496–98
Wyeth, 50 535–39 (upd.)
Wyle Electronics, 14 560–62 *see also* Arrow Electronics, Inc.
Wyman-Gordon Company, 14 563–65
Wynn's International, Inc., 33 466–70
Wyse Technology, Inc., 15 540–42

X

X-Rite, Inc., 48 443–46
Xantrex Technology Inc., 97 485–88
Xcel Energy Inc., 73 384–89 (upd.)
Xeikon NV, 26 540–42
Xerium Technologies, Inc., 94 473–76
Xerox Corporation, III 171–73; 6 288–90 (upd.); 26 543–47 (upd.); 69 374–80 (upd.)
Xilinx, Inc., 16 548–50; 82 435–39 (upd.)
XM Satellite Radio Holdings, Inc., 69 381–84
Xstrata PLC, 73 390–93
XTO Energy Inc., 52 425–27

Y

Yageo Corporation, 16 551–53
Yahoo! Inc., 27 516–19; 70 372–75 (upd.)
Yamada Denki Co., Ltd., 85 470–73
Yamaha Corporation, III 656–59; 16 554–58 (upd.); 40 461–66 (upd.)
Yamaichi Securities Company, Limited, II 458–59
Yamato Transport Co. Ltd., V 536–38; 49 458–61 (upd.)
Yamazaki Baking Co., Ltd., 58 380–82
The Yankee Candle Company, Inc., 37 423–26; 38 192
YankeeNets LLC, 35 474–77
Yara International ASA, 94 477–81
Yarnell Ice Cream Company, Inc., 92 421–24
Yasuda Fire and Marine Insurance Company, Limited, III 405–07
Yasuda Mutual Life Insurance Company, III 408–09; 39 425–28 (upd.)
The Yasuda Trust and Banking Company, Limited, II 391–92; 17 555–57 (upd.)
The Yates Companies, Inc., 62 397–99
Yell Group PLC, 79 472–75
Yellow Corporation, 14 566–68; 45 448–51 (upd.) *see also* YRC Worldwide Inc.
Yellow Freight System, Inc. of Deleware, V 539–41
Yeo Hiap Seng Malaysia Bhd., 75 406–09
YES! Entertainment Corporation, 26 548–50
YMCA of the USA, 31 473–76
YOCREAM International, Inc., 47 456–58
Yokado Co. Ltd *see* Ito-Yokado Co. Ltd.
The Yokohama Rubber Company, Limited, V 254–56; 19 506–09 (upd.); 91 527–33 (upd.)
The York Group, Inc., 50 540–43
York International Corp., 13 569–71; *see also* Johnson Controls, Inc.
York Research Corporation, 35 478–80
Yoshinoya D & C Company Ltd., 88 439–42
Youbet.com, Inc., 77 485–88
Young & Co.'s Brewery, P.L.C., 38 499–502
Young & Rubicam, Inc., I 36–38; 22 551–54 (upd.); 66 375–78 (upd.)
Young Broadcasting Inc., 40 467–69
Young Innovations, Inc., 44 451–53
Young's Bluecrest Seafood Holdings Ltd., 81 435–39
Young's Market Company, LLC, 32 518–20
Younkers, 76 19 510–12; 383–86 (upd.)
Youth Services International, Inc., 21 541–43; 30 146
YouTube, Inc., 90 443–46
YPF Sociedad Anónima, IV 577–78 *see also* Repsol-YPF S.A.
YRC Worldwide Inc., 90 447–55 (upd.)
The Yucaipa Cos., 17 558–62
YUKOS *see* OAO NK YUKOS.
Yule Catto & Company plc, 54 422–25
Yum! Brands Inc., 58 383–85
Yves Rocher *see* Laboratoires de Biologie Végétale Yves Rocher.
YWCA of the U.S.A., 45 452–54

Z

Zachry Group, Inc., 95 454–57
Zacky Farms LLC, 74 396–98
Zale Corporation, 16 559–61; 40 470–74 (upd.); 91 534–41 (upd.)
Zambia Industrial and Mining Corporation Ltd., IV 239–41
Zamboni *see* Frank J. Zamboni & Co., Inc.
Zanett, Inc., 92 425–28
Zany Brainy, Inc., 31 477–79
Zapata Corporation, 25 544–46
Zapf Creation AG, 95 458–61
Zappos.com, Inc., 73 394–96
Zara International, Inc., 83 474-477
Zatarain's, Inc., 64 413–15
ZCMI *see* Zion's Cooperative Mercantile Institution.
Zebra Technologies Corporation, 14 569–71; 53 371–74 (upd.)
Zed Group, 93 498–501
Zeneca Group PLC, 21 544–46 *see also* AstraZeneca PLC.
Zenith Data Systems, Inc., 10 563–65
Zenith Electronics Corporation, II 123–25; 13 572–75 (upd.); 34 514–19 (upd.); 89 494–502 (upd.)
ZERO Corporation, 17 563–65; 88 443–47 (upd.)
ZF Friedrichshafen AG, 48 447–51
Ziebart International Corporation, 30 499–501; 66 379–82 (upd.)
The Ziegler Companies, Inc., 24 541–45; 63 442–48 (upd.)
Ziff Davis Media Inc., 12 560–63; 36 521–26 (upd.); 73 397–403 (upd.)
Zila, Inc., 46 466–69
Zildjian *see* Avedis Zildjian Co.
ZiLOG, Inc., 15 543–45; 72 377–80 (upd.)
Zimmer Holdings, Inc., 45 455–57
Zindart Ltd., 60 370–72
Zingerman's Community of Businesses, 68 406–08
Zinifex Ltd., 85 474–77
Zinsser *see* William Zinsser & Company, Inc.
Zion's Cooperative Mercantile Institution, 33 471–74
Zions Bancorporation, 12 564–66; 53 375–78 (upd.)
Zipcar, Inc., 92 429–32
Zippo Manufacturing Company, 18 565–68; 71 394–99 (upd.)
Zodiac S.A., 36 527–30
Zoltek Companies, Inc., 37 427–30
Zomba Records Ltd., 52 428–31
Zondervan Corporation, 24 546–49; 71 400–04 (upd.)
Zones, Inc., 67 395–97
Zoom Technologies, Inc., 18 569–71; 53 379–82 (upd.)

Zoran Corporation, 77 489–92
The Zubair Corporation L.L.C., 96 468–72
Zuffa L.L.C., 89 503–07
Zumiez, Inc., 77 493–96
Zumtobel AG, 50 544–48
Zurich Financial Services, III 410–12; 42 448–53 (upd.); 93 502–10 (upd.)
Zygo Corporation, 42 454–57
Zytec Corporation, 19 513–15 *see also* Artesyn Technologies Inc.

Index to Industries

Accounting

American Institute of Certified Public Accountants (AICPA), 44
Andersen, 29 (upd.); 68 (upd.)
Automatic Data Processing, Inc., III; 9 (upd.); 47 (upd.)
BDO Seidman LLP, 96
BKD LLP, 96
CROSSMARK, 79
Deloitte Touche Tohmatsu International, 9; 29 (upd.)
Ernst & Young, 9; 29 (upd.)
FTI Consulting, Inc., 77
Grant Thornton International, 57
Huron Consulting Group Inc., 87
KPMG International, 33 (upd.)
L.S. Starrett Co., 13
McLane Company, Inc., 13
NCO Group, Inc., 42
Paychex, Inc., 15; 46 (upd.)
PKF International 78
Plante & Moran, LLP, 71
PRG-Schultz International, Inc., 73
PricewaterhouseCoopers, 9; 29 (upd.)
Resources Connection, Inc., 81
Robert Wood Johnson Foundation, 35
Saffery Champness, 80
Schenck Business Solutions, 88
StarTek, Inc., 79
Travelzoo Inc., 79
Univision Communications Inc., 24; 83 (upd.)

Advertising & Other Business Services

ABM Industries Incorporated, 25 (upd.)
Abt Associates Inc., 95
AchieveGlobal Inc., 90
Ackerley Communications, Inc., 9
ACNielsen Corporation, 13; 38 (upd.)
Acosta Sales and Marketing Company, Inc., 77
Acsys, Inc., 44
Adecco S.A., 36 (upd.)
Adia S.A., 6
Administaff, Inc., 52
The Advertising Council, Inc., 76
The Advisory Board Company, 80
Advo, Inc., 6; 53 (upd.)
Aegis Group plc, 6
Affiliated Computer Services, Inc., 61
AHL Services, Inc., 27
Allegis Group, Inc., 95
Alloy, Inc., 55
Amdocs Ltd., 47
American Building Maintenance Industries, Inc., 6
American Library Association, 86
The American Society of Composers, Authors and Publishers (ASCAP), 29
Amey Plc, 47
Analysts International Corporation, 36
aQuantive, Inc., 81
The Arbitron Company, 38
Ariba, Inc., 57
Armor Holdings, Inc., 27
Asatsu-DK Inc., 82
Ashtead Group plc, 34
The Associated Press, 13
Avalon Correctional Services, Inc., 75
Bain & Company, 55
Barrett Business Services, Inc., 16
Barton Protective Services Inc., 53
Bates Worldwide, Inc., 14; 33 (upd.)
Bearings, Inc., 13
Berlitz International, Inc., 13
Bernard Hodes Group Inc., 86
Bernstein-Rein, 92
Big Flower Press Holdings, Inc., 21
Billing Concepts, Inc., 26; 72 (upd.)
The BISYS Group, Inc., 73
Boron, LePore & Associates, Inc., 45
The Boston Consulting Group, 58
Bozell Worldwide Inc., 25
BrandPartners Group, Inc., 58
Bright Horizons Family Solutions, Inc., 31
Broadcast Music Inc., 23; 90 (upd.)
Buck Consultants, Inc., 55
Bureau Veritas SA, 55
Burke, Inc., 88
Burns International Services Corporation, 13; 41 (upd.)
Cambridge Technology Partners, Inc., 36
Campbell-Ewald Advertising, 86
Campbell-Mithun-Esty, Inc., 16
Cannon Design, 63
Capita Group PLC, 69
Cardtronics, Inc., 93
Career Education Corporation, 45
Carmichael Lynch Inc., 28
Cash Systems, Inc., 93
Cazenove Group plc, 72
CCC Information Services Group Inc., 74
CDI Corporation, 6; 54 (upd.)
Central Parking Corporation, 18
Century Business Services, Inc., 52
Chancellor Beacon Academies, Inc., 53
ChartHouse International Learning Corporation, 49
Chiat/Day Inc. Advertising, 11
Chicago Board of Trade, 41
Chisholm-Mingo Group, Inc., 41
Christie's International plc, 15; 39 (upd.)
Cintas Corporation, 21
CMG Worldwide, Inc., 89
COMFORCE Corporation, 40

Command Security Corporation, 57
Computer Learning Centers, Inc., 26
Concentra Inc., 71
Corporate Express, Inc., 47 (upd.)
CoolSavings, Inc., 77
The Corporate Executive Board Company, 89
CORT Business Services Corporation, 26
Cox Enterprises, Inc., 22 (upd.)
CRA International, Inc., 93
craigslist, inc., 89
Creative Artists Agency LLC, 38
Crispin Porter + Bogusky, 83
CSG Systems International, Inc., 75
Cyrk Inc., 19
Daiko Advertising Inc., 79
Dale Carnegie & Associates Inc. 28; 78 (upd.)
D'Arcy Masius Benton & Bowles, Inc., 6; 32 (upd.)
Dawson Holdings PLC, 43
DDB Needham Worldwide, 14
Deluxe Corporation, 22 (upd.); 73 (upd.)
Dentsu Inc., I; 16 (upd.); 40 (upd.)
Deutsch, Inc., 42
Deutsche Post AG, 29
DeVito/Verdi, 85
Dewberry 78
DHL Worldwide Network S.A./N.V., 69 (upd.)
Digitas Inc., 81
DoubleClick Inc., 46
Draftfcb, 94
Drake Beam Morin, Inc., 44
The Dun & Bradstreet Corporation, 61 (upd.)
Earl Scheib, Inc., 32
eBay Inc., 67 (upd.)
EBSCO Industries, Inc., 17
Ecolab Inc., I; 13 (upd.); 34 (upd.); 85 (upd.)
Ecology and Environment, Inc., 39
Edelman, 62
Edison Schools Inc., 37
Educate Inc., 86 (upd.)
Education Management Corporation, 35
Electro Rent Corporation, 58
Employee Solutions, Inc., 18
Ennis, Inc., 21; 97 (upd.)
Equifax Inc., 6; 28 (upd.); 90 (upd.)
Equity Marketing, Inc., 26
ERLY Industries Inc., 17
Euro RSCG Worldwide S.A., 13
Expedia, Inc., 58
Fallon Worldwide, 22; 71 (upd.)
FileNet Corporation, 62
Finarte Casa d'Aste S.p.A., 93
Fiserv, Inc., 33 (upd.)
FlightSafety International, Inc., 29 (upd.)
Florists' Transworld Delivery, Inc., 28
Foote, Cone & Belding Worldwide, I; 66 (upd.)
Forrester Research, Inc., 54
Frankel & Co., 39
Franklin Covey Company, 37 (upd.)
Freeze.com LLC, 77
Frost & Sullivan, Inc., 53
FTI Consulting, Inc., 77
Gage Marketing Group, 26
The Gallup Organization, 37
Gartner, Inc., 21; 94 (upd.)
GEMA (Gesellschaft für musikalische Aufführungs- und mechanische Vervielfältigungsrechte), 70
General Employment Enterprises, Inc., 87
George P. Johnson Company, 60
George S. May International Company, 55
Gevity HR, Inc., 63
GfK Aktiengesellschaft, 49
Glotel plc, 53
Golin/Harris International, Inc., 88
Goodby Silverstein & Partners, Inc., 75
Grey Global Group Inc., 6; 66 (upd.)
Group 4 Falck A/S, 42
Groupe Crit S.A., 74
Groupe Jean-Claude Darmon, 44
GSD&M Advertising, 44
GSD&M's Idea City, 90
GSI Commerce, Inc., 67
Guardsmark, L.L.C., 77
Gwathmey Siegel & Associates Architects LLC, 26
Ha-Lo Industries, Inc., 27
Hakuhodo, Inc., 6; 42 (upd.)
Hall, Kinion & Associates, Inc., 52
Handleman Company, 15; 86 (upd.)
Harris Interactive Inc., 41; 92 (upd.)
Harte-Hanks, Inc., 63 (upd.)
Havas SA, 33 (upd.)
Hays plc, 27; 78 (upd.)
Headway Corporate Resources, Inc., 40
Heidrick & Struggles International, Inc., 28
Henry Dreyfuss Associates LLC, 88
Hewitt Associates, Inc., 77
Hildebrandt International, 29
Idearc Inc., 90
IKON Office Solutions, Inc., 50
IMS Health, Inc., 57
Interbrand Corporation, 70
Interep National Radio Sales Inc., 35
International Brotherhood of Teamsters, 37
International Management Group, 18
International Profit Associates, Inc., 87
International Total Services, Inc., 37
The Interpublic Group of Companies, Inc., I; 22 (upd.); 75 (upd.)
Intertek Group plc, 95
inVentiv Health, Inc., 81
Ipsos SA, 48
Iron Mountain, Inc., 33
ITT Educational Services, Inc., 39; 76 (upd.)
J.D. Power and Associates, 32
Jack Morton Worldwide, 88
Jackson Hewitt, Inc., 48
Jani-King International, Inc., 85
Japan Leasing Corporation, 8
JCDecaux S.A., 76
Jostens, Inc., 25 (upd.)
JOULÉ Inc., 58
JWT Group Inc., I
Katz Communications, Inc., 6
Katz Media Group, Inc., 35
Keane, Inc., 56
Kelly Services Inc., 6; 26 (upd.)
Ketchum Communications Inc., 6
Kforce Inc., 71
Kinko's Inc., 16; 43 (upd.)
Kirshenbaum Bond + Partners, Inc., 57
Kohn Pedersen Fox Associates P.C., 57
Korn/Ferry International, 34
Kroll Inc., 57
L. M. Berry and Company, 80
Labor Ready, Inc., 29; 88 (upd.)
Lamar Advertising Company, 27; 70 (upd.)
Landor Associates, 81
Le Cordon Bleu S.A., 67
Learning Care Group, Inc., 76 (upd.)
Learning Tree International Inc., 24
LECG Corporation, 93
Leo Burnett Company Inc., I; 20 (upd.)
The Leona Group LLC, 84
Lintas: Worldwide, 14
LivePerson, Inc., 91
Mail Boxes Etc., 18; 41 (upd.)
Manhattan Associates, Inc., 67
Manning Selvage & Lee (MS&L), 76
Manpower Inc., 30 (upd.); 73 (upd.)
Marchex, Inc., 72
marchFIRST, Inc., 34
Marco Business Products, Inc., 75
Maritz Inc., 38
Marlin Business Services Corp., 89
MAXIMUS, Inc., 43
MDC Partners Inc., 63
Mediaset SpA, 50
Milliman USA, 66
MIVA, Inc., 83
Monster Worldwide Inc., 74 (upd.)
Moody's Corporation, 65
MPS Group, Inc., 49
Mullen Advertising Inc., 51
Napster, Inc., 69
National Equipment Services, Inc., 57
National Media Corporation, 27
Navigant Consulting, Inc., 93
NAVTEQ Corporation, 69
Neopost S.A., 53
New England Business Services Inc., 18; 78 (upd.)
New Valley Corporation, 17
NFO Worldwide, Inc., 24
Nobel Learning Communities, Inc., 37; 76 (upd.)
Norrell Corporation, 25
Norwood Promotional Products, Inc., 26
The NPD Group, Inc., 68
O.C. Tanner Co., 69
Oakleaf Waste Management, LLC, 97
Obie Media Corporation, 56
Observer AB, 55
OfficeTiger, LLC, 75
The Ogilvy Group, Inc., I
Olsten Corporation, 6; 29 (upd.)
Omnicom Group, I; 22 (upd.); 77 (upd.)
On Assignment, Inc., 20
1-800-FLOWERS, Inc., 26
Opinion Research Corporation, 46
Oracle Corporation, 67 (upd.)
Orbitz, Inc., 61

Outdoor Systems, Inc., 25
Paris Corporation, 22
Paychex, Inc., 15; 46 (upd.)
PDI, Inc., 52
Pegasus Solutions, Inc., 75
Pei Cobb Freed & Partners Architects LLP, 57
Penauille Polyservices SA, 49
PFSweb, Inc., 73
Philip Services Corp., 73
Phillips, de Pury & Luxembourg, 49
Pierce Leahy Corporation, 24
Pinkerton's Inc., 9
Plante & Moran, LLP, 71
PMT Services, Inc., 24
Posterscope Worldwide, 70
Priceline.com Incorporated, 57
Publicis Groupe, 19; 77 (upd.)
Publishers Clearing House, 23; 64 (upd.)
Quintiles Transnational Corporation, 68 (upd.)
Quovadx Inc., 70
Randstad Holding n.v., 16; 43 (upd.)
RedPeg Marketing, 73
RedPrairie Corporation, 74
RemedyTemp, Inc., 20
Rental Service Corporation, 28
Rentokil Initial Plc, 47
Research Triangle Institute, 83
Resources Connection, Inc., 81
Rewards Network Inc., 70 (upd.)
The Richards Group, Inc., 58
Right Management Consultants, Inc., 42
Ritchie Bros. Auctioneers Inc., 41
Robert Half International Inc., 18
Roland Berger & Partner GmbH, 37
Ronco Corporation, 15; 80 (upd.)
Russell Reynolds Associates Inc., 38
Saatchi & Saatchi, I; 42 (upd.)
Schenck Business Solutions, 88
Securitas AB, 42
ServiceMaster Limited Partnership, 6
Servpro Industries, Inc., 85
Shared Medical Systems Corporation, 14
Sir Speedy, Inc., 16
Skidmore, Owings & Merrill LLP, 13; 69 (upd.)
SmartForce PLC, 43
SOS Staffing Services, 25
Sotheby's Holdings, Inc., 11; 29 (upd.); 84 (upd.)
Source Interlink Companies, Inc., 75
Spencer Stuart and Associates, Inc., 14
Spherion Corporation, 52
Steiner Corporation (Alsco), 53
Strayer Education, Inc., 53
Superior Uniform Group, Inc., 30
Sykes Enterprises, Inc., 45
Sylvan Learning Systems, Inc., 35
Synchronoss Technologies, Inc., 95
TA Triumph-Adler AG, 48
Taylor Nelson Sofres plc, 34
TBWA/Chiat/Day, 6; 43 (upd.)
Thomas Cook Travel Inc., 33 (upd.)
Ticketmaster, 76 (upd.)
Ticketmaster Group, Inc., 13; 37 (upd.)
TMP Worldwide Inc., 30
TNT Post Group N.V., 30
Towers Perrin, 32
Trader Classified Media N.V., 57
Traffix, Inc., 61
Transmedia Network Inc., 20
Treasure Chest Advertising Company, Inc., 32
TRM Copy Centers Corporation, 18
True North Communications Inc., 23
24/7 Real Media, Inc., 49
Tyler Corporation, 23
U.S. Office Products Company, 25
Unica Corporation, 77
UniFirst Corporation, 21
United Business Media plc, 52 (upd.)
United News & Media plc, 28 (upd.)
Unitog Co., 19
Valassis Communications, Inc., 37 (upd.); 76 (upd.)
ValleyCrest Companies, 81 (upd.)
ValueClick, Inc., 49
Vebego International BV, 49
Vedior NV, 35
Vertis Communications, 84
Vertrue Inc., 77
Viad Corp., 73
W.B Doner & Co., 56
The Wackenhut Corporation, 14; 63 (upd.)
Waggener Edstrom, 42
Warrantech Corporation, 53
WebEx Communications, Inc., 81
Welcome Wagon International Inc., 82
Wells Rich Greene BDDP, 6
Westaff Inc., 33
Whitman Education Group, Inc., 41
Wieden + Kennedy, 75
William Morris Agency, Inc., 23
Williams Scotsman, Inc., 65
Workflow Management, Inc., 65
WPP Group plc, 6; 48 (upd.)
Wunderman, 86
Xerox Corporation, III; 6 (upd.); 26 (upd.); 69 (upd.)
Young & Rubicam, Inc., I; 22 (upd.); 66 (upd.)

Aerospace

A.S. Yakovlev Design Bureau, 15
Aerojet-General Corp., 63
Aeronca Inc., 46
Aerosonic Corporation, 69
The Aerospatiale Group, 7; 21 (upd.)
AeroVironment, Inc., 97
AgustaWestland N.V., 75
Airborne Systems Group, 89
Alliant Techsystems Inc., 30 (upd.)
Antonov Design Bureau, 53
Arianespace S.A., 89
Aviacionny Nauchno-Tehnicheskii Komplex im. A.N. Tupoleva, 24
Aviall, Inc., 73
Avions Marcel Dassault-Breguet Aviation, I
B/E Aerospace, Inc., 30
Ballistic Recovery Systems, Inc., 87
Banner Aerospace, Inc., 14
BBA Aviation plc, 90
Beech Aircraft Corporation, 8
Bell Helicopter Textron Inc., 46
The Boeing Company, I; 10 (upd.); 32 (upd.)
Bombardier Inc., 42 (upd.); 87 (upd.)
British Aerospace plc, I; 24 (upd.)
CAE USA Inc., 48
Canadair, Inc., 16
Cessna Aircraft Company, 8
Cirrus Design Corporation, 44
Cobham plc, 30
CPI Aerostructures, Inc., 75
Daimler-Benz Aerospace AG, 16
DeCrane Aircraft Holdings Inc., 36
Diehl Stiftung & Co. KG, 79
Ducommun Incorporated, 30
Duncan Aviation, Inc., 94
EADS SOCATA, 54
Eclipse Aviation Corporation, 87
EGL, Inc., 59
Empresa Brasileira de Aeronáutica S.A. (Embraer), 36
European Aeronautic Defence and Space Company EADS N.V., 52 (upd.)
Fairchild Aircraft, Inc., 9
Fairchild Dornier GmbH, 48 (upd.)
Finmeccanica S.p.A., 84
First Aviation Services Inc., 49
G.I.E. Airbus Industrie, I; 12 (upd.)
General Dynamics Corporation, I; 10 (upd.); 40 (upd.); 88 (upd.
GKN plc, III; 38 (upd.); 89 (upd.)
Goodrich Corporation, 46 (upd.)
Groupe Dassault Aviation SA, 26 (upd.)
Grumman Corporation, I; 11 (upd.)
Grupo Aeropuerto del Sureste, S.A. de C.V., 48
Gulfstream Aerospace Corporation, 7; 28 (upd.)
HEICO Corporation, 30
International Lease Finance Corporation, 48
Irkut Corporation, 68
Israel Aircraft Industries Ltd., 69
Kolbenschmidt Pierburg AG, 97
N.V. Koninklijke Nederlandse Vliegtuigenfabriek Fokker, I; 28 (upd.)
Kreisler Manufacturing Corporation, 97
Lancair International, Inc., 67
Learjet Inc., 8; 27 (upd.)
Lockheed Martin Corporation, I; 11 (upd.); 15 (upd.); 89 (upd.)
Loral Space & Communications Ltd., 54 (upd.)
Magellan Aerospace Corporation, 48
Martin Marietta Corporation, I
Martin-Baker Aircraft Company Limited, 61
McDonnell Douglas Corporation, I; 11 (upd.)
Meggitt PLC, 34
Messerschmitt-Bölkow-Blohm GmbH., I
Moog Inc., 13
Mooney Aerospace Group Ltd., 52
The New Piper Aircraft, Inc., 44
Northrop Grumman Corporation, I; 11 (upd.); 45 (upd.)
Orbital Sciences Corporation, 22
Pemco Aviation Group Inc., 54

Pratt & Whitney, 9
Raytheon Aircraft Holdings Inc., 46
Robinson Helicopter Company, 51
Rockwell International Corporation, I; 11 (upd.)
Rolls-Royce Allison, 29 (upd.)
Rolls-Royce plc, I; 7 (upd.); 21 (upd.)
Rostvertol plc, 62
Russian Aircraft Corporation (MiG), 86
Safe Flight Instrument Corporation, 71
Sequa Corp., 13
Shannon Aerospace Ltd., 36
Sikorsky Aircraft Corporation, 24
Smiths Industries PLC, 25
Snecma Group, 46
Société Air France, 27 (upd.)
Spacehab, Inc., 37
Spar Aerospace Limited, 32
Sukhoi Design Bureau Aviation Scientific-Industrial Complex, 24
Sundstrand Corporation, 7; 21 (upd.)
Surrey Satellite Technology Limited, 83
Swales & Associates, Inc., 69
Teledyne Technologies Inc., 62 (upd.)
Textron Lycoming Turbine Engine, 9
Thales S.A., 42
Thiokol Corporation, 9; 22 (upd.)
United Technologies Corporation, I; 10 (upd.)
Van's Aircraft, Inc., 65
Vector Aerospace Corporation, 97
Vought Aircraft Industries, Inc., 49
Whittaker Corporation, 48 (upd.)
Woodward Governor Company, 49 (upd.)
Zodiac S.A., 36

Airlines

Aer Lingus Group plc, 34; 89 (upd.)
Aeroflot - Russian Airlines JSC, 6; 29 (upd.); 89 (upd.)
Aerolíneas Argentinas S.A., 33; 69 (upd.)
Air Berlin GmbH & Co. Luftverkehrs KG, 71
Air Canada, 6; 23 (upd.); 59 (upd.)
Air China, 46
Air Jamaica Limited, 54
Air Mauritius Ltd., 63
Air New Zealand Limited, 14; 38 (upd.)
Air Pacific Ltd., 70
Air Partner PLC, 93
Air Sahara Limited, 65
Air Wisconsin Airlines Corporation, 55
Air Zimbabwe (Private) Limited, 91
Air-India Limited, 6; 27 (upd.)
AirAsia Berhad, 93
AirTran Holdings, Inc., 22
Alaska Air Group, Inc., 6; 29 (upd.)
Alitalia-Linee Aeree Italiana, S.p.A., 6; 29 (upd.); 97 (upd.)
All Nippon Airways Co., Ltd., 6; 38 (upd.); 91 (upd.)
Allegiant Travel Company, 97
Aloha Airlines, Incorporated, 24
America West Holdings Corporation, 6; 34 (upd.)
American Airlines, I; 6 (upd.)
AMR Corporation, 28 (upd.); 52 (upd.)
Amtran, Inc., 34
Arrow Air Holdings Corporation, 55
A/S Air Baltic Corporation, 71
AS Estonian Air, 71
Asiana Airlines, Inc., 46
ATA Holdings Corporation, 82
Atlantic Coast Airlines Holdings, Inc., 55
Atlantic Southeast Airlines, Inc., 47
Atlas Air, Inc., 39
Austrian Airlines AG (Österreichische Luftverkehrs AG), 33
Aviacionny Nauchno-Tehnicheskii Komplex im. A.N. Tupoleva, 24
Avianca Aerovías Nacionales de Colombia SA, 36
Azerbaijan Airlines, 77
Bahamas Air Holdings Ltd., 66
Banner Aerospace, Inc., 37 (upd.)
Braathens ASA, 47
Bradley Air Services Ltd., 56
Bristow Helicopters Ltd., 70
British Airways PLC, I; 14 (upd.); 43 (upd.)
British Midland plc, 38
British World Airlines Ltd., 18
Cargolux Airlines International S.A., 49
Cathay Pacific Airways Limited, 6; 34 (upd.)
Ceské aerolinie, a.s., 66
Chautauqua Airlines, Inc., 38
China Airlines, 34
China Eastern Airlines Co. Ltd., 31
China Southern Airlines Company Ltd., 33
Comair Holdings Inc., 13; 34 (upd.)
Consorcio Aviacsa, S.A. de C.V., 85
Continental Airlines, Inc., I; 21 (upd.); 52 (upd.)
Copa Holdings, S.A., 93
Corporación Internacional de Aviación, S.A. de C.V. (Cintra), 20
Cyprus Airways Public Limited, 81
dba Luftfahrtgesellschaft mbH, 76
Delta Air Lines, Inc., I; 6 (upd.); 39 (upd.); 92 (upd.)
Deutsche Lufthansa AG, I; 26 (upd.); 68 (upd.)
Eastern Airlines, I
easyJet Airline Company Limited, 39
EgyptAir, 6; 27 (upd.)
El Al Israel Airlines Ltd., 23
The Emirates Group, 39; 81 (upd.)
Ethiopian Airlines, 81
Etihad Airways PJSC, 89
Eurocopter S.A., 80
EVA Airways Corporation, 51
Finnair Oyj, 6; 25 (upd.); 61 (upd.)
Flight Options, LLC, 75
Flying Boat, Inc. (Chalk's Ocean Airways), 56
Frontier Airlines Holdings Inc., 22; 84 (upd.)
Garuda Indonesia, 6
Gol Linhas Aéreas Inteligentes S.A., 73
Groupe Air France, 6
Grupo Aeroportuario del Pacífico, S.A. de C.V., 85
Grupo TACA, 38
Gulf Air Company, 56
Hawaiian Holdings, Inc., 9; 22 (upd.); 96 (upd.)
Hong Kong Dragon Airlines Ltd., 66
Iberia Líneas Aéreas de España S.A., 6; 36 (upd.); 91 (upd.)
Icelandair, 52
Indian Airlines Ltd., 46
IranAir, 81
Japan Air Lines Company Ltd., I; 32 (upd.)
Jersey European Airways (UK) Ltd., 61
Jet Airways (India) Private Limited, 65
JetBlue Airways Corporation, 44
Kenmore Air Harbor Inc., 65
Kenya Airways Limited, 89
Kitty Hawk, Inc., 22
Kiwi International Airlines Inc., 20
Koninklijke Luchtvaart Maatschappij, N.V. (KLM Royal Dutch Airlines), I; 28 (upd.)
Korean Air Lines Co., Ltd., 6; 27 (upd.)
Kuwait Airways Corporation, 68
Lan Chile S.A., 31
Lauda Air Luftfahrt AG, 48
Lloyd Aéreo Boliviano S.A., 95
Loganair Ltd., 68
LOT Polish Airlines (Polskie Linie Lotnicze S.A.), 33
LTU Group Holding GmbH, 37
Malév Plc, 24
Malaysian Airlines System Berhad, 6; 29 (upd.); 97 (upd.)
Mesa Air Group, Inc., 11; 32 (upd.); 77 (upd.)
Mesaba Holdings, Inc., 28
Middle East Airlines - Air Liban S.A.L., 79
Midway Airlines Corporation, 33
Midwest Air Group, Inc., 35; 85 (upd.)
NetJets Inc., 96 (upd.)
Northwest Airlines Corporation, I; 6 (upd.); 26 (upd.); 74 (upd.)
Offshore Logistics, Inc., 37
Pakistan International Airlines Corporation, 46
Pan American World Airways, Inc., I; 12 (upd.)
Panalpina World Transport (Holding) Ltd., 47
People Express Airlines, Inc., I
Petroleum Helicopters, Inc., 35
PHI, Inc., 80 (upd.)
Philippine Airlines, Inc., 6; 23 (upd.)
Pinnacle Airlines Corp., 73
Preussag AG, 42 (upd.)
Qantas Airways Ltd., 6; 24 (upd.); 68 (upd.)
Qatar Airways Company Q.C.S.C., 87
Reno Air Inc., 23
Royal Nepal Airline Corporation, 41
Ryanair Holdings plc, 35
SAA (Pty) Ltd., 28
Sabena S.A./N.V., 33
The SAS Group, 34 (upd.)
Saudi Arabian Airlines, 6; 27 (upd.)
Scandinavian Airlines System, I
Singapore Airlines Limited, 6; 27 (upd.); 83 (upd.)

SkyWest, Inc., 25
Société d'Exploitation AOM Air Liberté SA (AirLib), 53
Société Luxembourgeoise de Navigation Aérienne S.A., 64
Société Tunisienne de l'Air-Tunisair, 49
Southwest Airlines Co., 6; 24 (upd.); 71 (upd.)
Spirit Airlines, Inc., 31
Sterling European Airlines A/S, 70
Sun Country Airlines, 30
Swiss Air Transport Company, Ltd., I
Swiss International Air Lines Ltd., 48
TAM Linhas Aéreas S.A., 68
TAP—Air Portugal Transportes Aéreos Portugueses S.A., 46
TAROM S.A., 64
Texas Air Corporation, I
Thai Airways International Public Company Limited, 6; 27 (upd.)
Tower Air, Inc., 28
Trans World Airlines, Inc., I; 12 (upd.); 35 (upd.)
TransBrasil S/A Linhas Aéreas, 31
Transportes Aereos Portugueses, S.A., 6
Turkish Airlines Inc. (Türk Hava Yollari A.O.), 72
TV Guide, Inc., 43 (upd.)
UAL Corporation, 34 (upd.)
United Airlines, I; 6 (upd.)
US Airways Group, Inc., I; 6 (upd.); 28 (upd.); 52 (upd.)
VARIG S.A. (Viação Aérea Rio-Grandense), 6; 29 (upd.)
Virgin Group Ltd., 12; 32 (upd.); 89 (upd.)
Volga-Dnepr Group, 82
Vueling Airlines S.A., 97
WestJet Airlines Ltd., 38

Automotive

AB Volvo, I; 7 (upd.); 26 (upd.); 67 (upd.)
Accubuilt, Inc., 74
Adam Opel AG, 7; 21 (upd.); 61 (upd.)
ADESA, Inc., 71
Advance Auto Parts, Inc., 57
Aftermarket Technology Corp., 83
Aisin Seiki Co., Ltd., 48 (upd.)
Alamo Rent A Car, Inc., 6; 24 (upd.); 84 (upd.)
Alfa Romeo, 13; 36 (upd.)
Alvis Plc, 47
America's Car-Mart, Inc., 64
American Motors Corporation, I
Amerigon Incorporated, 97
Applied Power Inc., 32 (upd.)
Arnold Clark Automobiles Ltd., 60
ArvinMeritor, Inc., 8; 54 (upd.)
Asbury Automotive Group Inc., 60
ASC, Inc., 55
Autobacs Seven Company Ltd., 76
Autocam Corporation, 51
Autoliv, Inc., 65
Automobiles Citroen, 7
Automobili Lamborghini Holding S.p.A., 13; 34 (upd.); 91 (upd.)
AutoNation, Inc., 50
AutoTrader.com, L.L.C., 91
AVTOVAZ Joint Stock Company, 65
Bajaj Auto Limited, 39
Bayerische Motoren Werke AG, I; 11 (upd.); 38 (upd.)
Belron International Ltd., 76
Bendix Corporation, I
Blue Bird Corporation, 35
Bombardier Inc., 42 (upd.)
BorgWarner Inc., 14; 32 (upd.); 85 (upd.)
The Budd Company, 8
Bugatti Automobiles S.A.S., 94
Canadian Tire Corporation, Limited, 71 (upd.)
CarMax, Inc., 55
CARQUEST Corporation, 29
Caterpillar Inc., 63 (upd.)
Checker Motors Corp., 89
China Automotive Systems Inc., 87
Chrysler Corporation, I; 11 (upd.)
Commercial Vehicle Group, Inc., 81
CNH Global N.V., 38 (upd.)
Consorcio G Grupo Dina, S.A. de C.V., 36
Crown Equipment Corporation, 15; 93 (upd.)
CSK Auto Corporation, 38
Cummins Engine Company, Inc., I; 12 (upd.); 40 (upd.)
Custom Chrome, Inc., 16
Daihatsu Motor Company, Ltd., 7; 21 (upd.)
Daimler-Benz A.G., I; 15 (upd.)
DaimlerChrysler AG, 34 (upd.); 64 (upd.)
Dana Corporation, I; 10 (upd.)
Danaher Corporation, 77 (upd.)
Deere & Company, 42 (upd.)
Delphi Automotive Systems Corporation, 45
Directed Electronics, Inc., 87
Discount Tire Company Inc., 84
Don Massey Cadillac, Inc., 37
Donaldson Company, Inc., 49 (upd.)
Douglas & Lomason Company, 16
Dräxlmaier Group, 90
DriveTime Automotive Group Inc., 68 (upd.)
Ducati Motor Holding SpA, 30; 86 (upd.)
Eaton Corporation, I; 10 (upd.); 67 (upd.)
Echlin Inc., I; 11 (upd.)
Edelbrock Corporation, 37
Faurecia S.A., 70
Federal-Mogul Corporation, I; 10 (upd.); 26 (upd.)
Ferrara Fire Apparatus, Inc., 84
Ferrari S.p.A., 13; 36 (upd.)
Fiat SpA, I; 11 (upd.); 50 (upd.)
FinishMaster, Inc., 24
Force Protection Inc., 95
Ford Motor Company, I; 11 (upd.); 36 (upd.); 64 (upd.)
Ford Motor Company, S.A. de C.V., 20
Fruehauf Corporation, I
General Motors Corporation, I; 10 (upd.); 36 (upd.); 64 (upd.)
Gentex Corporation, 26
Genuine Parts Company, 9; 45 (upd.)
GKN plc, III; 38 (upd.); 89 (upd.)
Group 1 Automotive, Inc., 52
Grupo Ficosa International, 90
Guardian Industries Corp., 87
Harley-Davidson Inc., 7; 25 (upd.)
Hastings Manufacturing Company, 56
Hayes Lemmerz International, Inc., 27
Hendrick Motorsports, Inc., 89
The Hertz Corporation, 33 (upd.)
Hino Motors, Ltd., 7; 21 (upd.)
Holden Ltd., 62
Holley Performance Products Inc., 52
Hometown Auto Retailers, Inc., 44
Honda Motor Company Limited (Honda Giken Kogyo Kabushiki Kaisha), I; 10 (upd.); 29 (upd.); 96 (upd.)
Hyundai Group, III; 7 (upd.); 56 (upd.)
Insurance Auto Auctions, Inc., 23
Isuzu Motors, Ltd., 9; 23 (upd.); 57 (upd.)
INTERMET Corporation, 77 (upd.)
Jardine Cycle & Carriage Ltd., 73
Kawasaki Heavy Industries, Ltd., 63 (upd.)
Kelsey-Hayes Group of Companies, 7; 27 (upd.)
Key Safety Systems, Inc., 63
Kia Motors Corporation, 12; 29 (upd.)
Kolbenschmidt Pierburg AG, 97
Kwik-Fit Holdings plc, 54
Lazy Days RV Center, Inc., 69
Lear Corporation, 71 (upd.)
Lear Seating Corporation, 16
Les Schwab Tire Centers, 50
Lithia Motors, Inc., 41
LKQ Corporation, 71
Lookers plc, 71
Lotus Cars Ltd., 14
Lund International Holdings, Inc., 40
Mack Trucks, Inc., I; 22 (upd.); 61 (upd.)
The Major Automotive Companies, Inc., 45
Marcopolo S.A., 79
Masland Corporation, 17
Mazda Motor Corporation, 9; 23 (upd.); 63 (upd.)
Mel Farr Automotive Group, 20
Metso Corporation, 30 (upd.)
Midas Inc., 10; 56 (upd.)
Mitsubishi Motors Corporation, 9; 23 (upd.); 57 (upd.)
Monaco Coach Corporation, 31
Monro Muffler Brake, Inc., 24
Montupet S.A., 63
National R.V. Holdings, Inc., 32
Navistar International Corporation, I; 10 (upd.)
New Flyer Industries Inc. 78
Nissan Motor Company Ltd., I; 11 (upd.); 34 (upd.); 92 (upd.)
O'Reilly Automotive, Inc., 26; 78 (upd.)
Officine Alfieri Maserati S.p.A., 13
Oshkosh Truck Corporation, 7
Paccar Inc., I
PACCAR Inc., 26 (upd.)
Park-Ohio Holdings Corp., 17; 85 (upd.)
Pennzoil-Quaker State Company, IV; 20 (upd.); 50 (upd.)

Penske Corporation, V; 19 (upd.); 84 (upd.)
The Pep Boys—Manny, Moe & Jack, 11; 36 (upd.); 81 (upd.)
Perusahaan Otomobil Nasional Bhd., 62
Peterbilt Motors Company, 89
Peugeot S.A., I
Piaggio & C. S.p.A., 20
Pirelli & C. S.p.A., 75 (upd.)
Porsche AG, 13; 31 (upd.)
PSA Peugeot Citroen S.A., 28 (upd.)
R&B, Inc., 51
Randon S.A., 79
Red McCombs Automotive Group, 91
Regal-Beloit Corporation, 18; 97 (upd.)
Regie Nationale des Usines Renault, I
Renault Argentina S.A., 67
Renault S.A., 26 (upd.); 74 (upd.)
Repco Corporation Ltd., 74
Republic Industries, Inc., 26
The Reynolds and Reynolds Company, 50
Rheinmetall AG, 9; 97 (upd.)
Riviera Tool Company, 89
Robert Bosch GmbH., I; 16 (upd.); 43 (upd.)
RockShox, Inc., 26
Rockwell Automation, I; 11 (upd.); 43 (upd.)
Rolls-Royce plc, I; 21 (upd.)
Ron Tonkin Chevrolet Company, 55
Rover Group Ltd., 7; 21 (upd.)
Saab Automobile AB, I; 11 (upd.); 32 (upd.); 83 (upd.)
Safelite Glass Corp., 19
Safety Components International, Inc., 63
SANLUIS Corporación, S.A.B. de C.V., 95
Saturn Corporation, 7; 21 (upd.); 80 (upd.)
Sealed Power Corporation, I
Servco Pacific Inc., 96
Sheller-Globe Corporation, I
Sixt AG, 39
Skoda Auto a.s., 39
Sonic Automotive, Inc., 77
Spartan Motors Inc., 14
SpeeDee Oil Change and Tune-Up, 25
SPX Corporation, 10; 47 (upd.)
Standard Motor Products, Inc., 40
Strattec Security Corporation, 73
Superior Industries International, Inc., 8
Suzuki Motor Corporation, 9; 23 (upd.); 59 (upd.)
Sytner Group plc, 45
Titan International, Inc., 89
Toresco Enterprises, Inc., 84
Tower Automotive, Inc., 24
Toyota Motor Corporation, I; 11 (upd.); 38 (upd.)
CJSC Transmash Holding, 93
TransPro, Inc., 71
Triumph Motorcycles Ltd., 53
TRW Automotive Holdings Corp., 75 (upd.)
TRW Inc., 14 (upd.)
Ugly Duckling Corporation, 22
United Auto Group, Inc., 26; 68 (upd.)
United Technologies Automotive Inc., 15
Universal Technical Institute, Inc., 81
Valeo, 23; 66 (upd.)
Van Hool S.A./NV, 96
Vauxhall Motors Limited, 73
Volkswagen Aktiengesellschaft, I; 11 (upd.); 32 (upd.)
Wagon plc, 92
Walker Manufacturing Company, 19
Webasto Roof Systems Inc., 97
Wilhelm Karmann GmbH, 94
Winnebago Industries, Inc., 7; 27 (upd.); 96 (upd.)
Woodward Governor Company, 49 (upd.)
The Yokohama Rubber Company, Limited, V; 19 (upd.); 91 (upd.)
ZF Friedrichshafen AG, 48
Ziebart International Corporation, 30; 66 (upd.)

Beverages

A & W Brands, Inc., 25
Adolph Coors Company, I; 13 (upd.); 36 (upd.)
AG Barr plc, 64
Ajegroup S.A., 92
Allied Domecq PLC, 29
Allied-Lyons PLC, I
Anadolu Efes Biracilik ve Malt Sanayii A.S., 95
Anchor Brewing Company, 47
Anheuser-Busch Companies, Inc., I; 10 (upd.); 34 (upd.)
Apple & Eve L.L.C., 92
Asahi Breweries, Ltd., I; 20 (upd.); 52 (upd.)
Asia Pacific Breweries Limited, 59
August Schell Brewing Company Inc., 59
Bacardi & Company Ltd., 18; 82 (upd.)
Baltika Brewery Joint Stock Company, 65
Banfi Products Corp., 36
Baron de Ley S.A., 74
Baron Philippe de Rothschild S.A., 39
Bass PLC, I; 15 (upd.); 38 (upd.)
Bavaria S.A., 90
BBAG Osterreichische Brau-Beteiligungs-AG, 38
Belvedere S.A., 93
Beringer Blass Wine Estates Ltd., 22; 66 (upd.)
The Bernick Companies, 75
Blue Ridge Beverage Company Inc., 82
Boizel Chanoine Champagne S.A., 94
Bols Distilleries NV, 74
The Boston Beer Company, Inc., 18; 50 (upd.)
Brauerei Beck & Co., 9; 33 (upd.)
Britannia Soft Drinks Ltd. (Britvic), 71
Brown-Forman Corporation, I; 10 (upd.); 38 (upd.)
Brouwerijen Alken-Maes N.V., 86
Budweiser Budvar, National Corporation, 59
Cadbury Schweppes PLC, 49 (upd.)
Canandaigua Brands, Inc., 13; 34 (upd.)
Cantine Giorgio Lungarotti S.R.L., 67
Caribou Coffee Company, Inc., 28; 97 (upd.)
Carlsberg A/S, 9; 29 (upd.)
Carlton and United Breweries Ltd., I
Casa Cuervo, S.A. de C.V., 31
Central European Distribution Corporation, 75
Cerveceria Polar, I
The Chalone Wine Group, Ltd., 36
The Charmer Sunbelt Group, 95
City Brewing Company LLC, 73
Clearly Canadian Beverage Corporation, 48
Clement Pappas & Company, Inc., 92
Click Wine Group, 68
Coca Cola Bottling Co. Consolidated, 10
The Coca-Cola Company, I; 10 (upd.); 32 (upd.); 67 (upd.)
Coffee Holding Co., Inc., 95
Companhia de Bebidas das Américas, 57
Compania Cervecerias Unidas S.A., 70
Constellation Brands, Inc., 68 (upd.)
Corby Distilleries Limited, 14
Cott Corporation, 52
D.G. Yuengling & Son, Inc., 38
Dallis Coffee, Inc., 86
Daniel Thwaites Plc, 95
Davide Campari-Milano S.p.A., 57
Dean Foods Company, 21 (upd.)
Delicato Vineyards, Inc., 50
Deschutes Brewery, Inc., 57
Desnoes and Geddes Limited, 79
Diageo plc, 79 (upd.)
Direct Wines Ltd., 84
Distillers Company PLC, I
Double-Cola Co.-USA, 70
Dr Pepper/Seven Up, Inc., 9; 32 (upd.)
E. & J. Gallo Winery, I; 7 (upd.); 28 (upd.)
Eckes AG, 56
The Edrington Group Ltd., 88
Embotelladora Andina S.A., 71
Empresas Polar SA, 55 (upd.)
Energy Brands Inc., 88
F. Korbel & Bros. Inc., 68
Faygo Beverages Inc., 55
Federico Paternina S.A., 69
Ferolito, Vultaggio & Sons, 27
Fiji Water LLC, 74
Florida's Natural Growers, 45
Foster's Group Limited, 7; 21 (upd.); 50 (upd.)
Freixenet S.A., 71
Frucor Beverages Group Ltd., 96
Fuller Smith & Turner P.L.C., 38
G. Heileman Brewing Company Inc., I
The Gambrinus Company, 40
Gano Excel Enterprise Sdn. Bhd., 89
The Gatorade Company, 82
Geerlings & Wade, Inc., 45
General Cinema Corporation, I
Glazer's Wholesale Drug Company, Inc., 82
Gluek Brewing Company, 75
Golden State Vintners, Inc., 33
Gosling Brothers Ltd., 82
Grand Metropolitan PLC, I
Green Mountain Coffee, Inc., 31
The Greenalls Group PLC, 21
Greene King plc, 31
Groupe Danone, 32 (upd.); 93 (upd.)

Grupo Industrial Herradura, S.A. de C.V., 83
Grupo Modelo, S.A. de C.V., 29
Guinness/UDV, I; 43 (upd.)
The Hain Celestial Group, Inc., 43 (upd.)
Hansen Natural Corporation, 31; 76 (upd.)
Heineken N.V, I; 13 (upd.); 34 (upd.); 90 (upd.)
Heublein, Inc., I
High Falls Brewing Company LLC, 74
Hiram Walker Resources, Ltd., I
Hite Brewery Company Ltd., 97
illycaffè SpA, 50
Imagine Foods, Inc., 50
Interbrew S.A., 17; 50 (upd.)
Irish Distillers Group, 96
J.J. Darboven GmbH & Co. KG, 96
Jacob Leinenkugel Brewing Company, 28
JD Wetherspoon plc, 30
Jim Beam Brands Worldwide, Inc., 58 (upd.)
John Dewar & Sons, Ltd., 82
Jones Soda Co., 69
Jugos del Valle, S.A. de C.V., 85
Karlsberg Brauerei GmbH & Co KG, 41
Kendall-Jackson Winery, Ltd., 28
Kikkoman Corporation, 14
Kirin Brewery Company, Limited, I; 21 (upd.); 63 (upd.)
Kobrand Corporation, 82
König Brauerei GmbH & Co. KG, 35 (upd.)
Labatt Brewing Company Limited, I; 25 (upd.)
Latrobe Brewing Company, 54
Laurent-Perrier SA, 42
The Lion Brewery, Inc., 86
Lion Nathan Limited, 54
Löwenbräu AG, 80
The Macallan Distillers Ltd., 63
Madeira Wine Company, S.A., 49
Maison Louis Jadot, 24
Marchesi Antinori SRL, 42
Marie Brizard et Roger International S.A.S., 22; 97 (upd.)
Mark T. Wendell Tea Company, 94
Martell and Company S.A., 82
Martignetti Companies, 84
Martini & Rossi SpA, 63
Maui Wowi, Inc., 85
MBC Holding Company, 40
Mendocino Brewing Company, Inc., 60
Mercian Corporation, 77
Miller Brewing Company, I; 12 (upd.)
The Minute Maid Company, 28
Mitchells & Butlers PLC, 59
Moët-Hennessy, I
Molson Coors Brewing Company, I; 26 (upd.); 77 (upd.)
Montana Coffee Traders, Inc., 60
Mott's Inc., 57
National Beverage Corporation, 26; 88 (upd.)
National Grape Cooperative Association, Inc., 20
National Wine & Spirits, Inc., 49
Nestlé Waters, 73
New Belgium Brewing Company, Inc., 68
Nichols plc, 44
Ocean Spray Cranberries, Inc., 7; 25 (upd.); 83 (upd.)
Odwalla, Inc., 31
OENEO S.A., 74 (upd.)
Old Orchard Brands, LLC, 73
Oregon Chai, Inc., 49
Panamerican Beverages, Inc., 47
Parmalat Finanziaria SpA, 50
Paulaner Brauerei GmbH & Co. KG, 35
Peet's Coffee & Tea, Inc., 38
Penaflor S.A., 66
The Pepsi Bottling Group, Inc., 40
PepsiAmericas, Inc., 67 (upd.)
PepsiCo, Inc., I; 10 (upd.); 38 (upd.); 93 (upd.)
Pernod Ricard S.A., I; 21 (upd.); 72 (upd.)
Pete's Brewing Company, 22
Philip Morris Companies Inc., 18 (upd.)
Pittsburgh Brewing Company, 76
Pyramid Breweries Inc., 33
Quilmes Industrial (QUINSA) S.A., 67
R.C. Bigelow, Inc., 49
Radeberger Gruppe AG, 75
Rainier Brewing Company, 23
Red Bull GmbH, 60
Redhook Ale Brewery, Inc., 31; 88 (upd.)
Rémy Cointreau Group, 20; 80 (upd.)
Robert Mondavi Corporation, 15; 50 (upd.)
Royal Crown Company, Inc., 23
Royal Grolsch NV, 54
S&D Coffee, Inc., 84
SABMiller plc, 59 (upd.)
Sam's Wine & Spirits, 96
San Miguel Corporation, 57 (upd.)
Sapporo Holdings Limited, I; 13 (upd.); 36 (upd.); 97 (upd.)
Scheid Vineyards Inc., 66
Schieffelin & Somerset Co., 61
Scottish & Newcastle plc, 15; 35 (upd.)
The Seagram Company Ltd., I; 25 (upd.)
Sebastiani Vineyards, Inc., 28
Shepherd Neame Limited, 30
Sidney Frank Importing Co., Inc., 69
Sierra Nevada Brewing Company, 70
Skalli Group, 67
Skyy Spirits LLC 78
Sleeman Breweries Ltd., 74
Snapple Beverage Corporation, 11
Societe des Produits Marnier-Lapostolle S.A., 88
The South African Breweries Limited, I; 24 (upd.)
South Beach Beverage Company, Inc., 73
Southcorp Limited, 54
Southern Wine and Spirits of America, Inc., 84
Starbucks Corporation, 13; 34 (upd.); 77 (upd.)
The Stash Tea Company, 50
Ste. Michelle Wine Estates Ltd., 96
Stewart's Beverages, 39
The Stroh Brewery Company, I; 18 (upd.)
Suntory Ltd., 65
Sutter Home Winery Inc., 16
Taittinger S.A., 43
Taiwan Tobacco & Liquor Corporation, 75
Takara Holdings Inc., 62
Tata Tea Ltd., 76
The Terlato Wine Group, 48
Tetley USA Inc., 88
Todhunter International, Inc., 27
Triarc Companies, Inc., 34 (upd.)
Tropicana Products, Inc., 73 (upd.)
Tsingtao Brewery Group, 49
Tully's Coffee Corporation, 51
Underberg AG, 92
Unilever, II; 7 (upd.); 32 (upd.); 89 (upd.)
Unión de Cervecerias Peruanas Backus y Johnston S.A.A., 92
V&S Vin & Sprit AB, 91 (upd.)
Van Houtte Inc., 39
Vermont Pure Holdings, Ltd., 51
Vin & Spirit AB, 31
Viña Concha y Toro S.A., 45
Vincor International Inc., 50
Whitbread PLC, I; 20 (upd.); 52 (upd.); 97 (upd.)
Widmer Brothers Brewing Company, 76
Willamette Valley Vineyards, Inc., 85
William Grant & Sons Ltd., 60
The Wine Group, Inc., 39
The Wolverhampton & Dudley Breweries, PLC, 57
Young & Co.'s Brewery, P.L.C., 38

Bio-Technology

Actelion Ltd., 83
Amersham PLC, 50
Amgen, Inc., 10; 30 (upd.)
ArQule, Inc., 68
Bio-Rad Laboratories, Inc., 93
Biogen Idec Inc., 71 (upd.)
Biogen Inc., 14; 36 (upd.)
bioMérieux S.A., 75
BTG Plc, 87
Caliper Life Sciences, Inc., 70
Cambrex Corporation, 44 (upd.)
Celera Genomics, 74
Centocor Inc., 14
Charles River Laboratories International, Inc., 42
Chiron Corporation, 10; 36 (upd.)
Covance Inc., 30
CryoLife, Inc., 46
Cytyc Corporation, 69
Delta and Pine Land Company, 33
Dionex Corporation, 46
Dyax Corp., 89
Embrex, Inc., 72
Enzo Biochem, Inc., 41
Eurofins Scientific S.A., 70
Gen-Probe Incorporated, 79
Genentech, Inc., 32 (upd.)
Genzyme Corporation, 38 (upd.)
Gilead Sciences, Inc., 54
Howard Hughes Medical Institute, 39
Huntingdon Life Sciences Group plc, 42
IDEXX Laboratories, Inc., 23
ImClone Systems Inc., 58
Immunex Corporation, 14; 50 (upd.)

IMPATH Inc., 45
Incyte Genomics, Inc., 52
Inverness Medical Innovations, Inc., 63
Invitrogen Corporation, 52
The Judge Group, Inc., 51
Kendle International Inc., 87
Landec Corporation, 95
Life Technologies, Inc., 17
LifeCell Corporation, 77
Lonza Group Ltd., 73
Martek Biosciences Corporation, 65
Medarex, Inc., 85
Medtronic, Inc., 30 (upd.)
Millipore Corporation, 25; 84 (upd.)
Minntech Corporation, 22
Mycogen Corporation, 21
Nektar Therapeutics, 91
New Brunswick Scientific Co., Inc., 45
Omrix Biopharmaceuticals, Inc., 95
Pacific Ethanol, Inc., 81
Pharmion Corporation, 91
Qiagen N.V., 39
Quintiles Transnational Corporation, 21
Seminis, Inc., 29
Senomyx, Inc., 83
Serologicals Corporation, 63
Sigma-Aldrich Corporation, I; 36 (upd.); 93 (upd.)
Starkey Laboratories, Inc., 52
STERIS Corporation, 29
Stratagene Corporation, 70
Tanox, Inc., 77
TECHNE Corporation, 52
TriPath Imaging, Inc., 77
Waters Corporation, 43
Whatman plc, 46
Wisconsin Alumni Research Foundation, 65
Wyeth, 50 (upd.)

Chemicals

A. Schulman, Inc., 8
Aceto Corp., 38
Air Products and Chemicals, Inc., I; 10 (upd.); 74 (upd.)
Airgas, Inc., 54
Akzo Nobel N.V., 13; 41 (upd.)
Albemarle Corporation, 59
AlliedSignal Inc., 22 (upd.)
ALTANA AG, 87
American Cyanamid, I; 8 (upd.)
American Vanguard Corporation, 47
Arab Potash Company, 85
Arch Chemicals Inc. 78
ARCO Chemical Company, 10
Asahi Denka Kogyo KK, 64
Atanor S.A., 62
Atochem S.A., I
Avantium Technologies BV, 79
Avecia Group PLC, 63
Baker Hughes Incorporated, 22 (upd.); 57 (upd.)
Balchem Corporation, 42
BASF Aktiengesellschaft, I; 18 (upd.); 50 (upd.)
Bayer A.G., I; 13 (upd.); 41 (upd.)
Betz Laboratories, Inc., I; 10 (upd.)
The BFGoodrich Company, 19 (upd.)
BOC Group plc, I; 25 (upd.); 78 (upd.)
Brenntag AG, 8; 23 (upd.)
Burmah Castrol PLC, 30 (upd.)
Cabot Corporation, 8; 29 (upd.); 91 (upd.)
Calgon Carbon Corporation, 73
Caliper Life Sciences, Inc., 70
Cambrex Corporation, 16
Catalytica Energy Systems, Inc., 44
Celanese Corporation, I
Celanese Mexicana, S.A. de C.V., 54
Chemcentral Corporation, 8
Chemi-Trol Chemical Co., 16
Chemtura Corporation, 91 (upd.)
Church & Dwight Co., Inc., 29
Ciba-Geigy Ltd., I; 8 (upd.)
The Clorox Company, III; 22 (upd.); 81 (upd.)
Croda International Plc, 45
Crompton Corporation, 9; 36 (upd.)
Cytec Industries Inc., 27
Degussa-Hüls AG, 32 (upd.)
DeKalb Genetics Corporation, 17
The Dexter Corporation, I; 12 (upd.)
Dionex Corporation, 46
The Dow Chemical Company, I; 8 (upd.); 50 (upd.)
DSM N.V., I; 56 (upd.)
Dynaction S.A., 67
E.I. du Pont de Nemours & Company, I; 8 (upd.); 26 (upd.)
Eastman Chemical Company, 14; 38 (upd.)
Ecolab Inc., I; 13 (upd.); 34 (upd.); 85 (upd.)
Eka Chemicals AB, 92
Elementis plc, 40 (upd.)
Engelhard Corporation, 72 (upd.)
English China Clays Ltd., 15 (upd.); 40 (upd.)
Enterprise Rent-A-Car Company, 69 (upd.)
Equistar Chemicals, LP, 71
Ercros S.A., 80
ERLY Industries Inc., 17
Ethyl Corporation, I; 10 (upd.)
Ferro Corporation, 8; 56 (upd.)
Firmenich International S.A., 60
First Mississippi Corporation, 8
FMC Corporation, 89 (upd.)
Formosa Plastics Corporation, 14; 58 (upd.)
Fort James Corporation, 22 (upd.)
G.A.F., I
The General Chemical Group Inc., 37
Georgia Gulf Corporation, 9; 61 (upd.)
Givaudan SA, 43
Great Lakes Chemical Corporation, I; 14 (upd.)
GROWMARK, Inc., 88
Guerbet Group, 46
H.B. Fuller Company, 32 (upd.); 75 (upd.)
Hauser, Inc., 46
Hawkins Chemical, Inc., 16
Henkel KGaA, III; 34 (upd.); 95 (upd.)
Hercules Inc., I; 22 (upd.); 66 (upd.)
Hoechst A.G., I; 18 (upd.)
Hoechst Celanese Corporation, 13
Huls A.G., I
Huntsman Chemical Corporation, 8
IMC Fertilizer Group, Inc., 8
Imperial Chemical Industries PLC, I; 50 (upd.)
International Flavors & Fragrances Inc., 9; 38 (upd.)
Israel Chemicals Ltd., 55
Kemira Oyj, 70
Koppers Industries, Inc., I; 26 (upd.)
L'Air Liquide SA, I; 47 (upd.)
Lawter International Inc., 14
LeaRonal, Inc., 23
Loctite Corporation, 30 (upd.)
Lonza Group Ltd., 73
The Lubrizol Corporation, I; 30 (upd.); 83 (upd.)
Lyondell Chemical Company, 45 (upd.)
M.A. Hanna Company, 8
MacDermid Incorporated, 32
Makhteshim-Agan Industries Ltd., 85
Mallinckrodt Group Inc., 19
MBC Holding Company, 40
Melamine Chemicals, Inc., 27
Methanex Corporation, 40
Minerals Technologies Inc., 52 (upd.)
Mississippi Chemical Corporation, 39
Mitsubishi Chemical Corporation, I; 56 (upd.)
Mitsui Petrochemical Industries, Ltd., 9
Monsanto Company, I; 9 (upd.); 29 (upd.)
Montedison SpA, I
Morton International Inc., I; 9 (upd.); 80 (upd.)
The Mosaic Company, 91
Nagase & Company, Ltd., 8
Nalco Holding Company, I; 12 (upd.); 89 (upd.)
National Distillers and Chemical Corporation, I
National Sanitary Supply Co., 16
National Starch and Chemical Company, 49
NCH Corporation, 8
Nippon Soda Co., Ltd., 85
Nisshin Seifun Group Inc., 66 (upd.)
NL Industries, Inc., 10
Nobel Industries AB, 9
NOF Corporation, 72
Norsk Hydro ASA, 35 (upd.)
Novacor Chemicals Ltd., 12
Nufarm Ltd., 87
NutraSweet Company, 8
Occidental Petroleum Corporation, 71 (upd.)
Olin Corporation, I; 13 (upd.); 78 (upd.)
OM Group, Inc., 17; 78 (upd.)
OMNOVA Solutions Inc., 59
Penford Corporation, 55
Pennwalt Corporation, I
Perstorp AB, I; 51 (upd.)
Petrolite Corporation, 15
Pfizer Inc., 79 (upd.)
Pioneer Hi-Bred International, Inc., 41 (upd.)
PolyOne Corporation, 87 (upd.)

Praxair, Inc., 11
Quaker Chemical Corp., 91
Quantum Chemical Corporation, 8
Reichhold Chemicals, Inc., 10
Renner Herrmann S.A., 79
Rhodia SA, 38
Rhône-Poulenc S.A., I; 10 (upd.)
Robertet SA, 39
Rohm and Haas Company, I; 26 (upd.); 77 (upd.)
Roussel Uclaf, I; 8 (upd.)
RPM International Inc., 8; 36 (upd.); 91 (upd.)
RWE AG, 50 (upd.)
S.C. Johnson & Son, Inc., III; 28 (upd.); 89 (upd.)
The Scotts Company, 22
SCP Pool Corporation, 39
Sequa Corp., 13
Shanghai Petrochemical Co., Ltd., 18
Sigma-Aldrich Corporation, I; 36 (upd.); 93 (upd.)
Solutia Inc., 52
Solvay S.A., I; 21 (upd.); 61 (upd.)
Stepan Company, 30
Sterling Chemicals, Inc., 16; 78 (upd.)
Sumitomo Chemical Company Ltd., I
Takeda Chemical Industries, Ltd., 46 (upd.)
Teknor Apex Company, 97
Terra Industries, Inc., 13
Tessenderlo Group, 76
Teva Pharmaceutical Industries Ltd., 22
Tosoh Corporation, 70
Total Fina Elf S.A., 24 (upd.); 50 (upd.)
Transammonia Group, 95
Ube Industries, Ltd., 38 (upd.)
Union Carbide Corporation, I; 9 (upd.); 74 (upd.)
United Industries Corporation, 68
Univar Corporation, 9
The Valspar Corporation, 32 (upd.); 77 (upd.)
VeraSun Energy Corporation, 87
Vista Chemical Company, I
Witco Corporation, I; 16 (upd.)
Yule Catto & Company plc, 54
WD-40 Company, 87 (upd.)
Zeneca Group PLC, 21

Conglomerates

A.P. Møller - Maersk A/S, 57
Abengoa S.A., 73
Acciona S.A., 81
Accor SA, 10; 27 (upd.)
Ackermans & van Haaren N.V., 97
Adani Enterprises Ltd., 97
Aditya Birla Group, 79
Administración Nacional de Combustibles, Alcohol y Pórtland, 93
AEG A.G., I
Al Habtoor Group L.L.C., 87
Alcatel Alsthom Compagnie Générale d'Electricité, 9
Alco Standard Corporation, I
Alexander & Baldwin, Inc., 10, 40 (upd.)
Alfa, S.A. de C.V., 19
Alleghany Corporation, 60 (upd.)
Allied Domecq PLC, 29
Allied-Signal Inc., I
AMFAC Inc., I
The Anschutz Company, 73 (upd.)
The Anschutz Corporation, 36 (upd.)
Antofagasta plc, 65
Apax Partners Worldwide LLP, 89
APi Group, Inc., 64
Aramark Corporation, 13
ARAMARK Corporation, 41
Archer Daniels Midland Company, I; 11 (upd.); 75 (upd.)
Arkansas Best Corporation, 16
Associated British Ports Holdings Plc, 45
BAA plc, 33 (upd.)
Barlow Rand Ltd., I
Barratt Developments plc, 56 (upd.)
Bat Industries PLC, I
Baugur Group hf, 81
BB Holdings Limited, 77
Berjaya Group Bhd., 67
Berkshire Hathaway Inc., III; 18 (upd.); 42 (upd.); 89 (upd.)
Block Communications, Inc., 81
Bond Corporation Holdings Limited, 10
Brascan Corporation, 67
BTR PLC, I
Bunzl plc, 31 (upd.)
Burlington Northern Santa Fe Corporation, 27 (upd.)
Business Post Group plc, 46
C. Itoh & Company Ltd., I
C.I. Traders Limited, 61
Camargo Corrêa S.A., 93
Cargill, Incorporated, II; 13 (upd.); 40 (upd.); 89 (upd.)
CBI Industries, Inc., 7
Charoen Pokphand Group, 62
Chemed Corporation, 13
Chesebrough-Pond's USA, Inc., 8
China Merchants International Holdings Co., Ltd., 52
Cisneros Group of Companies, 54
CITIC Pacific Ltd., 18
CJ Corporation, 62
Colgate-Palmolive Company, 71 (upd.)
Colt Industries Inc., I
Compagnie Financiere Richemont AG, 50
The Connell Company, 29
Conzzeta Holding, 80
Cox Enterprises, Inc., 67 (upd.)
Cristalerias de Chile S.A., 67
CSR Limited, III; 28 (upd.); 85 (upd.)
Daewoo Group, 18 (upd.); 57 (upd.)
Dallah Albaraka Group, 72
De Dietrich & Cie., 31
Deere & Company, 21 (upd.)
Delaware North Companies Inc., 7; 96 (upd.)
Desc, S.A. de C.V., 23
The Dial Corp., 8
Dogan Sirketler Grubu Holding A.S., 83
Dr. August Oetker KG, 51
E.I. du Pont de Nemours and Company, 73 (upd.)
EBSCO Industries, Inc., 40 (upd.)
El Corte Inglés Group, 26 (upd.)
Elders IXL Ltd., I
Empresas Copec S.A., 69
Engelhard Corporation, 21 (upd.); 72 (upd.)
Essar Group Ltd., 79
Farley Northwest Industries, Inc., I
Fimalac S.A., 37
First Pacific Company Limited, 18
Fisher Companies, Inc., 15
Fletcher Challenge Ltd., 19 (upd.)
Florida East Coast Industries, Inc., 59
FMC Corporation, I; 11 (upd.)
Fortune Brands, Inc., 29 (upd.); 68 (upd.)
Fraser & Neave Ltd., 54
Fuqua Industries, Inc., I
General Electric Company, 34 (upd.); 63 (upd.)
Genting Bhd., 65
GIB Group, 26 (upd.)
Gillett Holdings, Inc., 7
The Gillette Company, 68 (upd.)
Granaria Holdings B.V., 66
Grand Metropolitan PLC, 14 (upd.)
Great American Management and Investment, Inc., 8
Greyhound Corporation, I
Groupe Bolloré, 67
Groupe Louis Dreyfus S.A., 60
Grupo Carso, S.A. de C.V., 21
Grupo Clarín S.A., 67
Grupo Industrial Bimbo, 19
Grupo Industrial Saltillo, S.A. de C.V., 54
Gulf & Western Inc., I
Haci Omer Sabanci Holdings A.S., 55
Hagemeyer N.V., 39
Hankyu Corporation, 23 (upd.)
Hanson PLC, III; 7 (upd.)
Hanwha Group, 62
Harbour Group Industries, Inc., 90
Hawk Corporation, 59
Henry Crown and Company, 91
Hitachi Zosen Corporation, 53 (upd.)
Hitachi, Ltd., I; 12 (upd.); 40 (upd.)
Ho-Chunk Inc., 61
Hutchison Whampoa Limited, 18; 49 (upd.)
Hyundai Group, III; 7 (upd.); 56 (upd.)
IC Industries, Inc., I
IDB Holding Corporation Ltd., 97
Ilitch Holdings Inc., 37; 86 (upd.)
Inchcape PLC, 16 (upd.); 50 (upd.)
Industria de Diseño Textil S.A. (Inditex), 64
Industrie Zignago Santa Margherita S.p.A., 67
Ingram Industries, Inc., 11; 49 (upd.)
Instituto Nacional de Industria, I
International Controls Corporation, 10
International Telephone & Telegraph Corporation, I; 11 (upd.)
Investor AB, 63
Ishikawajima-Harima Heavy Industries Company, Ltd., III; 86 (upd.)
Istituto per la Ricostruzione Industriale, I
ITOCHU Corporation, 32 (upd.)
J.R. Simplot Company, 60 (upd.)
Jardine Matheson Holdings Limited, I; 20 (upd.); 93 (upd.)
Jason Incorporated, 23

Jefferson Smurfit Group plc, 19 (upd.)
The Jim Pattison Group, 37
Jordan Industries, Inc., 36
José de Mello SGPS S.A., 96
Justin Industries, Inc., 19
Kanematsu Corporation, 24 (upd.)
Kao Corporation, 20 (upd.)
Katy Industries, Inc., I
Keppel Corporation Ltd., 73
Kesko Ltd. (Kesko Oy), 8; 27 (upd.)
Kidde plc, I; 44 (upd.)
King Ranch, Inc., 60 (upd.)
Knowledge Universe, Inc., 54
Koç Holding A.S., I; 54 (upd.)
Koch Industries, Inc., 77 (upd.)
Koninklijke Nedlloyd N.V., 26 (upd.)
Koor Industries Ltd., 25 (upd.); 68 (upd.)
Körber AG, 60
K2 Inc., 16; 84 (upd.)
The L.L. Knickerbocker Co., Inc., 25
Lancaster Colony Corporation, 8; 61 (upd.)
Larry H. Miller Group, 29
LDI Ltd., LLC, 76
Lear Siegler, Inc., I
Lefrak Organization Inc., 26
Leucadia National Corporation, 11; 71 (upd.)
Linde AG, 67 (upd.)
Litton Industries, Inc., I; 11 (upd.)
Loews Corporation, I; 12 (upd.); 36 (upd.); 93 (upd.)
Loral Corporation, 8
LTV Corporation, I; 24 (upd.)
LVMH Moët Hennessy Louis Vuitton SA, 33 (upd.)
The Marmon Group, Inc., 70 (upd.)
Marubeni Corporation, I; 24 (upd.)
MAXXAM Inc., 8
McKesson Corporation, I
McPherson's Ltd., 66
Melitta Unternehmensgruppe Bentz KG, 53
Menasha Corporation, 8
Metallgesellschaft AG, 16 (upd.)
Metromedia Company, 7; 61 (upd.)
Minnesota Mining & Manufacturing Company (3M), I; 8 (upd.); 26 (upd.)
Mitsubishi Corporation, I; 12 (upd.)
Mitsubishi Heavy Industries, Ltd., 40 (upd.)
Mitsui & Co., Ltd., I; 28 (upd.)
The Molson Companies Limited, I; 26 (upd.)
Montedison S.p.A., 24 (upd.)
NACCO Industries, Inc., 7; 78 (upd.)
Nagase & Co., Ltd., 61 (upd.)
National Service Industries, Inc., 11; 54 (upd.)
New Clicks Holdings Ltd., 86
New World Development Company Limited, 38 (upd.)
Nichimen Corporation, 24 (upd.)
Nichirei Corporation, 70
Nissho Iwai K.K., I
Norsk Hydro A.S., 10
Novar plc, 49 (upd.)
Ogden Corporation, I
Onex Corporation, 16; 65 (upd.)
Orkla ASA, 18; 82 (upd.)
Park-Ohio Holdings Corp., 17; 85 (upd.)
Pentair, Inc., 7; 26 (upd.); 81 (upd.)
Petrobras Energia Participaciones S.A., 72
Philip Morris Companies Inc., 44 (upd.)
Poliet S.A., 33
Powell Duffryn plc, 31
Power Corporation of Canada, 36 (upd.); 85 (upd.)
PPB Group Berhad, 57
Preussag AG, 17
The Procter & Gamble Company, III; 8 (upd.); 26 (upd.); 67 (upd.)
Proeza S.A. de C.V., 82
PT Astra International Tbk, 56
Pubco Corporation, 17
Pulsar Internacional S.A., 21
R.B. Pamplin Corp., 45
The Rank Organisation Plc, 14 (upd.)
Raymond Ltd., 77
Red Apple Group, Inc., 23
Roll International Corporation, 37
Rubbermaid Incorporated, 20 (upd.)
Samsung Group, I
San Miguel Corporation, 15
Sara Lee Corporation, 15 (upd.); 54 (upd.)
S.C. Johnson & Son, Inc., III; 28 (upd.); 89 (upd.)
Schindler Holding AG, 29
Scott Fetzer Company, 12; 80 (upd.)
Sea Containers Ltd., 29
Seaboard Corporation, 36; 85 (upd.)
Sealaska Corporation, 60
Sequa Corporation, 54 (upd.)
Sequana Capital, 78 (upd.)
ServiceMaster Inc., 23 (upd.)
SHV Holdings N.V., 55
Sideco Americana S.A., 67
Sime Darby Berhad, 14; 36 (upd.)
Sistema JSFC, 73
SK Group, 88
Société du Louvre, 27
Sojitz Corporation, 96 (upd.)
Sonae SGPS, S.A., 97
Standex International Corporation, 17; 44 (upd.)
Steamships Trading Company Ltd., 82
Stinnes AG, 23 (upd.)
Sudbury Inc., 16
Sumitomo Corporation, I; 11 (upd.)
Swire Pacific Limited, I; 16 (upd.); 57 (upd.)
Talley Industries, Inc., 16
Tandycrafts, Inc., 31
TaurusHolding GmbH & Co. KG, 46
Teijin Limited, 61 (upd.)
Teledyne, Inc., I; 10 (upd.)
Tenneco Inc., I; 10 (upd.)
Textron Inc., I; 34 (upd.); 88 (upd.)
Thomas H. Lee Co., 24
Thorn Emi PLC, I
Thorn plc, 24
TI Group plc, 17
Time Warner Inc., IV; 7 (upd.)
Tokyu Corporation, 47 (upd.)
Tomen Corporation, 24 (upd.)
Tomkins plc, 11; 44 (upd.)
Toshiba Corporation, I; 12 (upd.); 40 (upd.)
Tractebel S.A., 20
Transamerica–An AEGON Company, I; 13 (upd.); 41 (upd.)
The Tranzonic Cos., 15
Triarc Companies, Inc., 8
Triple Five Group Ltd., 49
TRW Inc., I; 11 (upd.)
Tyco International Ltd., 63 (upd.)
Unilever, II; 7 (upd.); 32 (upd.); 89 (upd.)
Unión Fenosa, S.A., 51
United Technologies Corporation, 34 (upd.)
Universal Studios, Inc., 33
Valhi, Inc., 19
Valorem S.A., 88
Valores Industriales S.A., 19
Veba A.G., I; 15 (upd.)
Vendôme Luxury Group plc, 27
Viacom Inc., 23 (upd.); 67 (upd.)
Virgin Group Ltd., 12; 32 (upd.); 89 (upd.)
Vivartia S.A., 82
Votorantim Participaçoes S.A., 76
W.R. Grace & Company, I; 50
Walter Industries, Inc., 72 (upd.)
The Washington Companies, 33
Watsco Inc., 52
Wheaton Industries, 8
Whitbread PLC, I; 20 (upd.); 52 (upd.); 97 (upd.)
Whitman Corporation, 10 (upd.)
Whittaker Corporation, I
Wirtz Corporation, 72
WorldCorp, Inc., 10
Worms et Cie, 27
Yamaha Corporation, 40 (upd.)

Construction

A. Johnson & Company H.B., I
ABC Supply Co., Inc., 22
Abertis Infraestructuras, S.A., 65
Abrams Industries Inc., 23
Acergy SA, 97
Aegek S.A., 64
Alberici Corporation, 76
Amec Spie S.A., 57
AMREP Corporation, 21
Anthony & Sylvan Pools Corporation, 56
Asplundh Tree Expert Co., 59 (upd.)
Astec Industries, Inc., 79
ASV, Inc., 34; 66 (upd.)
The Auchter Company, 78
The Austin Company, 8
Autoroutes du Sud de la France SA, 55
Balfour Beatty plc, 36 (upd.)
Baratt Developments PLC, I
Barton Malow Company, 51
Bauerly Companies, 61
BE&K, Inc., 73
Beazer Homes USA, Inc., 17
Bechtel Group, Inc., I; 24 (upd.)
Bellway Plc, 45
BFC Construction Corporation, 25
Bilfinger & Berger AG, I; 55 (upd.)

Bird Corporation, 19
Birse Group PLC, 77
Black & Veatch LLP, 22
Boral Limited, 43 (upd.)
Bouygues S.A., I; 24 (upd.); 97 (upd.)
The Branch Group, Inc., 72
Brasfield & Gorrie LLC, 87
BRISA Auto-estradas de Portugal S.A., 64
Brown & Root, Inc., 13
Bufete Industrial, S.A. de C.V., 34
Building Materials Holding Corporation, 52
Bulley & Andrews, LLC, 55
C.R. Meyer and Sons Company, 74
CalMat Co., 19
Cavco Industries, Inc., 65
Centex Corporation, 8; 29 (upd.)
Chugach Alaska Corporation, 60
Cianbro Corporation, 14
The Clark Construction Group, Inc., 8
Colas S.A., 31
Consorcio ARA, S.A. de C.V., 79
Corporación Geo, S.A. de C.V., 81
D.R. Horton, Inc., 58
Day & Zimmermann, Inc., 31 (upd.)
Desarrolladora Homex, S.A. de C.V., 87
Dick Corporation, 64
Dillingham Construction Corporation, I; 44 (upd.)
Dominion Homes, Inc., 19
The Drees Company, Inc., 41
Dycom Industries, Inc., 57
E.W. Howell Co., Inc., 72
Edw. C. Levy Co., 42
Eiffage, 27
Ellerbe Becket, 41
EMCOR Group Inc., 60
Empresas ICA Sociedad Controladora, S.A. de C.V., 41
Encompass Services Corporation, 33
Engle Homes, Inc., 46
Environmental Industries, Inc., 31
Eurotunnel PLC, 13
Fairclough Construction Group PLC, I
Flatiron Construction Corporation, 92
Fleetwood Enterprises, Inc., III: 22 (upd.); 81 (upd.)
Fluor Corporation, I; 8 (upd.); 34 (upd.)
Forest City Enterprises, Inc., 52 (upd.)
Fred Weber, Inc., 61
Furmanite Corporation, 92
George Wimpey plc, 12; 51 (upd.)
Gilbane, Inc., 34
Granite Construction Incorporated, 61
Granite Rock Company, 26
Great Lakes Dredge & Dock Company, 69
Grupo Dragados SA, 55
Grupo Ferrovial, S.A., 40
H.J. Russell & Company, 66
Habitat for Humanity International, 36
Heery International, Inc., 58
Heijmans N.V., 66
Henry Boot plc, 76
Hensel Phelps Construction Company, 72
Hillsdown Holdings plc, 24 (upd.)
Hochtief AG, 33; 88 (upd.)
Hoffman Corporation 78
Horton Homes, Inc., 25
Hospitality Worldwide Services, Inc., 26
Hovnanian Enterprises, Inc., 29; 89 (upd.)
IHC Caland N.V., 71
Irex Contracting Group, 90
J.A. Jones, Inc., 16
J C Bamford Excavators Ltd., 83
J.F. Shea Co., Inc., 55
J.H. Findorff and Son, Inc., 60
Jarvis plc, 39
JE Dunn Construction Group, Inc., 85
JLG Industries, Inc., 52
John Brown PLC, I
John Laing plc, I; 51 (upd.)
John W. Danforth Company, 48
Kajima Corporation, I; 51 (upd.)
Kaufman and Broad Home Corporation, 8
KB Home, 45 (upd.)
Kellogg Brown & Root, Inc., 62 (upd.)
Kitchell Corporation, 14
The Koll Company, 8
Komatsu Ltd., 16 (upd.)
Kraus-Anderson Companies, Inc., 36; 83 (upd.)
Kumagai Gumi Company, Ltd., I
L'Entreprise Jean Lefebvre, 23
Laing O'Rourke PLC, 93 (upd.)
Ledcor Industries Limited, 46
Lennar Corporation, 11
Lincoln Property Company, 8
Lindal Cedar Homes, Inc., 29
Linde A.G., I
MasTec, Inc., 55
Matrix Service Company, 65
May Gurney Integrated Services PLC, 95
McCarthy Building Companies, Inc., 48
Mellon-Stuart Company, I
Michael Baker Corp., 14
Modtech Holdings, Inc., 77
Mota-Engil, SGPS, S.A., 97
Morrison Knudsen Corporation, 7; 28 (upd.)
Morrow Equipment Co. L.L.C., 87
New Holland N.V., 22
Newpark Resources, Inc., 63
NVR Inc., 70 (upd.)
NVR L.P., 8
Obayashi Corporation 78
Obrascon Huarte Lain S.A., 76
Ohbayashi Corporation, I
Opus Group, 34
Orascom Construction Industries S.A.E., 87
Orleans Homebuilders, Inc., 62
The Parsons Corporation, 56 (upd.)
PCL Construction Group Inc., 50
The Peninsular & Oriental Steam Navigation Company (Bovis Division), I
Perini Corporation, 8; 82 (upd.)
Peter Kiewit Sons' Inc., 8
Philipp Holzmann AG, 17
Post Properties, Inc., 26
Pulte Homes, Inc., 8; 42 (upd.)
Pyramid Companies, 54
Redrow Group plc, 31
Rinker Group Ltd., 65
RMC Group p.l.c., 34 (upd.)
Rooney Brothers Co., 25
The Rottlund Company, Inc., 28
Roy Anderson Corporation, 75
The Ryland Group, Inc., 8; 37 (upd.)
Sandvik AB, 32 (upd.)
Schuff Steel Company, 26
Seddon Group Ltd., 67
Shorewood Packaging Corporation, 28
Simon Property Group Inc., 27; 84 (upd.)
Skanska AB, 38
Skidmore, Owings & Merrill LLP, 69 (upd.)
SNC-Lavalin Group Inc., 72
Speedy Hire plc, 84
Stabler Companies Inc. 78
Standard Pacific Corporation, 52
Stone & Webster, Inc., 64 (upd.)
Sundt Corp., 24
Swinerton Inc., 43
Tarmac Limited, III, 28 (upd.); 95 (upd.)
Taylor Woodrow plc, I; 38 (upd.)
Technical Olympic USA, Inc., 75
Terex Corporation, 7; 40 (upd.); 91 (upd.)
ThyssenKrupp AG, IV; 28 (upd.); 87 (upd.)
TIC Holdings Inc., 92
Toll Brothers Inc., 15; 70 (upd.)
Trammell Crow Company, 8
Tridel Enterprises Inc., 9
Turner Construction Company, 66
The Turner Corporation, 8; 23 (upd.)
U.S. Aggregates, Inc., 42
U.S. Home Corporation, 8; 78 (upd.)
Urbi Desarrollos Urbanos, S.A. de C.V., 81
VA TECH ELIN EBG GmbH, 49
Veit Companies, 43; 92 (upd.)
Wacker Construction Equipment AG, 95
Walbridge Aldinger Co., 38
Walter Industries, Inc., 22 (upd.)
The Weitz Company, Inc., 42
Whiting-Turner Contracting Company, 95
Willbros Group, Inc., 56
William Lyon Homes, 59
Wilson Bowden Plc, 45
Wood Hall Trust PLC, I
The Yates Companies, Inc., 62
Zachry Group, Inc., 95

Containers

Ball Corporation, I; 10 (upd.); 78 (upd.)
BWAY Corporation, 24
Chesapeake Corporation, 8; 30 (upd.); 93 (upd.)
Clarcor Inc., 17
Continental Can Co., Inc., 15
Continental Group Company, I
Crown Cork & Seal Company, Inc., I; 13 (upd.); 32 (upd.)
Crown Holdings, Inc., 83 (upd.)
Gaylord Container Corporation, 8
Golden Belt Manufacturing Co., 16
Graham Packaging Holdings Company, 87
Greif Inc., 15; 66 (upd.)

Grupo Industrial Durango, S.A. de C.V., 37
Hanjin Shipping Co., Ltd., 50
Inland Container Corporation, 8
Interpool, Inc., 92
Kerr Group Inc., 24
Keyes Fibre Company, 9
Libbey Inc., 49
Liqui-Box Corporation, 16
The Longaberger Company, 12
Longview Fibre Company, 8
The Mead Corporation, 19 (upd.)
Metal Box PLC, I
Molins plc, 51
National Can Corporation, I
Owens-Illinois, Inc., I; 26 (upd.); 85 (upd.)
Packaging Corporation of America, 51 (upd.)
Primerica Corporation, I
PVC Container Corporation, 67
Rexam PLC, 32 (upd.); 85 (upd.)
Reynolds Metals Company, 19 (upd.)
Royal Packaging Industries Van Leer N.V., 30
RPC Group PLC, 81
Sealright Co., Inc., 17
Shurgard Storage Centers, Inc., 52
Smurfit-Stone Container Corporation, 26 (upd.); 83 (upd.)
Sonoco Products Company, 8; 89 (upd.)
Thermos Company, 16
Toyo Seikan Kaisha, Ltd., I
U.S. Can Corporation, 30
Ultra Pac, Inc., 24
Viatech Continental Can Company, Inc., 25 (upd.)
Vidrala S.A., 67
Vitro Corporativo S.A. de C.V., 34

Drugs & Pharmaceuticals

A. Nelson & Co. Ltd., 75
A.L. Pharma Inc., 12
Abbott Laboratories, I; 11 (upd.); 40 (upd.); 93 (upd.)
Actelion Ltd., 83
Akorn, Inc., 32
Albany Molecular Research, Inc., 77
Allergan, Inc., 77 (upd.)
Alpharma Inc., 35 (upd.)
ALZA Corporation, 10; 36 (upd.)
American Home Products, I; 10 (upd.)
American Oriental Bioengineering Inc., 93
American Pharmaceutical Partners, Inc., 69
AmerisourceBergen Corporation, 64 (upd.)
Amersham PLC, 50
Amgen, Inc., 10; 89 (upd.)
Amylin Pharmaceuticals, Inc., 67
Andrx Corporation, 55
Astellas Pharma Inc., 97 (upd.)
AstraZeneca PLC, I; 20 (upd.); 50 (upd.)
Axcan Pharma Inc., 85
Barr Pharmaceuticals, Inc., 26; 68 (upd.)
Bayer A.G., I; 13 (upd.)
Berlex Laboratories, Inc., 66
Biovail Corporation, 47
Block Drug Company, Inc., 8
Boiron S.A., 73
Bristol-Myers Squibb Company, III; 9 (upd.); 37 (upd.)
BTG Plc, 87
C.H. Boehringer Sohn, 39
Caremark Rx, Inc., 10; 54 (upd.)
Carter-Wallace, Inc., 8; 38 (upd.)
Celgene Corporation, 67
Cephalon, Inc., 45
Chiron Corporation, 10
Chugai Pharmaceutical Co., Ltd., 50
Ciba-Geigy Ltd., I; 8 (upd.)
D&K Wholesale Drug, Inc., 14
Discovery Partners International, Inc., 58
Dr. Reddy's Laboratories Ltd., 59
Elan Corporation PLC, 63
Eli Lilly and Company, I; 11 (upd.); 47 (upd.)
Endo Pharmaceuticals Holdings Inc., 71
Eon Labs, Inc., 67
Express Scripts Inc., 44 (upd.)
F. Hoffmann-La Roche Ltd., I; 50 (upd.)
Fisons plc, 9; 23 (upd.)
Forest Laboratories, Inc., 52 (upd.)
FoxMeyer Health Corporation, 16
Fujisawa Pharmaceutical Company Ltd., I
G.D. Searle & Co., I; 12 (upd.); 34 (upd.)
Galenica AG, 84
GEHE AG, 27
Genentech, Inc., I; 8 (upd.); 75 (upd.)
Genetics Institute, Inc., 8
Genzyme Corporation, 13, 77 (upd.)
Glaxo Holdings PLC, I; 9 (upd.)
GlaxoSmithKline plc, 46 (upd.)
Groupe Fournier SA, 44
Groupe Léa Nature, 88
H. Lundbeck A/S, 44
Hauser, Inc., 46
Heska Corporation, 39
Hexal AG, 69
Hospira, Inc., 71
Huntingdon Life Sciences Group plc, 42
ICN Pharmaceuticals, Inc., 52
Immucor, Inc., 81
Integrated BioPharma, Inc., 83
IVAX Corporation, 55 (upd.)
Janssen Pharmaceutica N.V., 80
Johnson & Johnson, III; 8 (upd.)
Jones Medical Industries, Inc., 24
The Judge Group, Inc., 51
King Pharmaceuticals, Inc., 54
Kinray Inc., 85
Kos Pharmaceuticals, Inc., 63
Kyowa Hakko Kogyo Co., Ltd., 48 (upd.)
Laboratoires Arkopharma S.A., 75
Leiner Health Products Inc., 34
Ligand Pharmaceuticals Incorporated, 47
MannKind Corporation, 87
Marion Merrell Dow, Inc., I; 9 (upd.)
Matrixx Initiatives, Inc., 74
McKesson Corporation, 12; 47 (upd.)
Medicis Pharmaceutical Corporation, 59
MedImmune, Inc., 35
Merck & Co., Inc., I; 11 (upd.); 34 (upd.); 95 (upd.)
Merz Group, 81
Miles Laboratories, I
Millennium Pharmaceuticals, Inc., 47
Monsanto Company, 29 (upd.), 77 (upd.)
Moore Medical Corp., 17
Murdock Madaus Schwabe, 26
Mylan Laboratories Inc., I; 20 (upd.); 59 (upd.)
Myriad Genetics, Inc., 95
Nadro S.A. de C.V., 86
Nastech Pharmaceutical Company Inc., 79
National Patent Development Corporation, 13
Natrol, Inc., 49
Natural Alternatives International, Inc., 49
Nektar Therapeutics, 91
Novartis AG, 39 (upd.)
Noven Pharmaceuticals, Inc., 55
Novo Nordisk A/S, I; 61 (upd.)
Obagi Medical Products, Inc., 95
Omnicare, Inc., 49
Omrix Biopharmaceuticals, Inc., 95
Par Pharmaceutical Companies, Inc., 65
PDL BioPharma, Inc., 90
Perrigo Company, 59 (upd.)
Pfizer Inc., I; 9 (upd.); 38 (upd.); 79 (upd.)
Pharmacia & Upjohn Inc., I; 25 (upd.)
Pharmion Corporation, 91
PLIVA d.d., 70
PolyMedica Corporation, 77
POZEN Inc., 81
QLT Inc., 71
The Quigley Corporation, 62
Quintiles Transnational Corporation, 21
R.P. Scherer, I
Ranbaxy Laboratories Ltd., 70
ratiopharm Group, 84
Reckitt Benckiser plc, II; 42 (upd.); 91 (upd.)
Roberts Pharmaceutical Corporation, 16
Roche Bioscience, 14 (upd.)
Rorer Group, I
Roussel Uclaf, I; 8 (upd.)
Salix Pharmaceuticals, Ltd., 93
Sandoz Ltd., I
Sankyo Company, Ltd., I; 56 (upd.)
The Sanofi-Synthélabo Group, I; 49 (upd.)
Schering AG, I; 50 (upd.)
Schering-Plough Corporation, I; 14 (upd.); 49 (upd.)
Sepracor Inc., 45
Serono S.A., 47
Shionogi & Co., Ltd., 17 (upd.)
Sigma-Aldrich Corporation, I; 36 (upd.); 93 (upd.)
SmithKline Beecham plc, I; 32 (upd.)
Solvay S.A., 61 (upd.)
Squibb Corporation, I
Sterling Drug, Inc., I
Stiefel Laboratories, Inc., 90
Sun Pharmaceutical Industries Ltd., 57
The Sunrider Corporation, 26
Syntex Corporation, I
Takeda Chemical Industries, Ltd., I
Taro Pharmaceutical Industries Ltd., 65
Teva Pharmaceutical Industries Ltd., 22; 54 (upd.)

The Upjohn Company, I; 8 (upd.)
Vertex Pharmaceuticals Incorporated, 83
Virbac Corporation, 74
Vitalink Pharmacy Services, Inc., 15
Warner Chilcott Limited, 85
Warner-Lambert Co., I; 10 (upd.)
Watson Pharmaceuticals Inc., 16; 56 (upd.)
The Wellcome Foundation Ltd., I
Zila, Inc., 46

Electrical & Electronics

ABB ASEA Brown Boveri Ltd., II; 22 (upd.)
ABB Ltd., 65 (upd.)
Acer Incorporated, 16; 73 (upd.)
Acuson Corporation, 10; 36 (upd.)
ADC Telecommunications, Inc., 30 (upd.)
Adtran Inc., 22
Advanced Micro Devices, Inc., 30 (upd.)
Advanced Technology Laboratories, Inc., 9
Agere Systems Inc., 61
Agilent Technologies Inc., 38; 93 (upd.)
Agilysys Inc., 76 (upd.)
Aiwa Co., Ltd., 30
AKG Acoustics GmbH, 62
Akzo Nobel N.V., 13; 41 (upd.)
Alienware Corporation, 81
Alliant Techsystems Inc., 30 (upd.); 77 (upd.)
AlliedSignal Inc., 22 (upd.)
Alpine Electronics, Inc., 13
Alps Electric Co., Ltd., II
Altera Corporation, 18; 43 (upd.)
Altron Incorporated, 20
Amdahl Corporation, 40 (upd.)
American Power Conversion Corporation, 24; 67 (upd.)
American Superconductor Corporation, 97
American Technical Ceramics Corp., 67
Amerigon Incorporated, 97
Amkor Technology, Inc., 69
AMP Incorporated, II; 14 (upd.)
Amphenol Corporation, 40
Amstrad plc, 48 (upd.)
Analog Devices, Inc., 10
Analogic Corporation, 23
Anam Group, 23
Anaren Microwave, Inc., 33
Andrew Corporation, 10; 32 (upd.)
Anixter International Inc., 88
Anritsu Corporation, 68
Apex Digital, Inc., 63
Apple Computer, Inc., 36 (upd.); 77 (upd.)
Applied Power Inc., 32 (upd.)
Applied Signal Technology, Inc., 87
Argon ST, Inc., 81
Arotech Corporation, 93
ARRIS Group, Inc., 89
Arrow Electronics, Inc., 10; 50 (upd.)
Ascend Communications, Inc., 24
Astronics Corporation, 35
Atari Corporation, 9; 23 (upd.); 66 (upd.)
ATI Technologies Inc., 79
Atmel Corporation, 17
ATMI, Inc., 93
AU Optronics Corporation, 67
Audiovox Corporation, 34; 90 (upd.)
Ault Incorporated, 34
Autodesk, Inc., 10; 89 (upd.)
Avnet Inc., 9
AVX Corporation, 67
Axcelis Technologies, Inc., 95
Axsys Technologies, Inc., 93
Ballard Power Systems Inc., 73
Bang & Olufsen Holding A/S, 37; 86 (upd.)
Barco NV, 44
Bell Microproducts Inc., 69
Benchmark Electronics, Inc., 40
Bicoastal Corporation, II
Black Box Corporation, 20; 96 (upd.)
Blonder Tongue Laboratories, Inc., 48
Blue Coat Systems, Inc., 83
BMC Industries, Inc., 59 (upd.)
Bogen Communications International, Inc., 62
Bose Corporation, 13; 36 (upd.)
Boston Acoustics, Inc., 22
Bowthorpe plc, 33
Braun GmbH, 51
Broadcom Corporation, 34; 90 (upd.)
Bull S.A., 43 (upd.)
Burr-Brown Corporation, 19
BVR Systems (1998) Ltd., 93
C-COR.net Corp., 38
Cabletron Systems, Inc., 10
Cadence Design Systems, Inc., 48 (upd.)
Cambridge SoundWorks, Inc., 48
Canon Inc., 18 (upd.); 79 (upd.)
Carbone Lorraine S.A., 33
Cardtronics, Inc., 93
Carl Zeiss AG, III; 34 (upd.); 91 (upd.)
Cash Systems, Inc., 93
CASIO Computer Co., Ltd., 16 (upd.); 40 (upd.)
CDW Computer Centers, Inc., 52 (upd.)
Celestica Inc., 80
Checkpoint Systems, Inc., 39
Chi Mei Optoelectronics Corporation, 75
Chubb, PLC, 50
Chunghwa Picture Tubes, Ltd., 75
Cirrus Logic, Inc., 48 (upd.)
Cisco Systems, Inc., 34 (upd.); 77 (upd.)
Citizen Watch Co., Ltd., III; 21 (upd.); 81 (upd.)
Clarion Company Ltd., 64
Cobham plc, 30
Cobra Electronics Corporation, 14
Coherent, Inc., 31
Cohu, Inc., 32
Color Kinetics Incorporated, 85
Compagnie Générale d'Électricité, II
Concurrent Computer Corporation, 75
Conexant Systems, Inc., 36
Cooper Industries, Inc., II
Cray Inc., 75 (upd.)
Cray Research, Inc., 16 (upd.)
Cree Inc., 53
CTS Corporation, 39
Cubic Corporation, 19
Cypress Semiconductor Corporation, 20; 48 (upd.)
D&H Distributing Co., 95
D-Link Corporation, 83
Dai Nippon Printing Co., Ltd., 57 (upd.)
Daiichikosho Company Ltd., 86
Daktronics, Inc., 32
Dallas Semiconductor Corporation, 13; 31 (upd.)
DDi Corp., 97
De La Rue plc, 34 (upd.)
Dell Computer Corporation, 31 (upd.)
DH Technology, Inc., 18
Dictaphone Healthcare Solutions 78
Diehl Stiftung & Co. KG, 79
Digi International Inc., 9
Diodes Incorporated, 81
Directed Electronics, Inc., 87
Discreet Logic Inc., 20
Dixons Group plc, 19 (upd.)
Dolby Laboratories Inc., 20
Dot Hill Systems Corp., 93
DRS Technologies, Inc., 58
Dynatech Corporation, 13
E-Systems, Inc., 9
Electronics for Imaging, Inc., 15; 43 (upd.)
Elma Electronic AG, 83
Elpida Memory, Inc., 83
EMCORE Corporation, 97
Emerson, II; 46 (upd.)
Emerson Radio Corp., 30
ENCAD, Incorporated, 25
Equant N.V., 52
Equus Computer Systems, Inc., 49
ESS Technology, Inc., 22
Essex Corporation, 85
Everex Systems, Inc., 16
Exabyte Corporation, 40 (upd.)
Exar Corp., 14
Exide Electronics Group, Inc., 20
Finisar Corporation, 92
First Solar, Inc., 95
Fisk Corporation, 72
Flextronics International Ltd., 38
Fluke Corporation, 15
FormFactor, Inc., 85
Foxboro Company, 13
Freescale Semiconductor, Inc., 83
Frequency Electronics, Inc., 61
FuelCell Energy, Inc., 75
Fuji Electric Co., Ltd., II; 48 (upd.)
Fuji Photo Film Co., Ltd., 79 (upd.)
Fujitsu Limited, 16 (upd.); 42 (upd.)
Funai Electric Company Ltd., 62
Gateway, Inc., 63 (upd.)
General Atomics, 57
General Dynamics Corporation, I; 10 (upd.); 40 (upd.); 88 (upd.
General Electric Company, II; 12 (upd.)
General Electric Company, PLC, II
General Instrument Corporation, 10
General Signal Corporation, 9
Genesis Microchip Inc., 82
GenRad, Inc., 24
GM Hughes Electronics Corporation, II
Goldstar Co., Ltd., 12
Gould Electronics, Inc., 14
GPS Industries, Inc., 81
Grundig AG, 27
Guillemot Corporation, 41

Hadco Corporation, 24
Hamilton Beach/Proctor-Silex Inc., 17
Harman International Industries Inc., 15
Harris Corporation, II; 20 (upd.); 78 (upd.)
Hayes Corporation, 24
Herley Industries, Inc., 33
Hewlett-Packard Company, 28 (upd.); 50 (upd.)
Holophane Corporation, 19
Hon Hai Precision Industry Co., Ltd., 59
Honeywell Inc., II; 12 (upd.); 50 (upd.)
Hubbell Incorporated, 9; 31 (upd.)
Hughes Supply, Inc., 14
Hutchinson Technology Incorporated, 18; 63 (upd.)
Hypercom Corporation, 27
IDEO Inc., 65
IEC Electronics Corp., 42
Illumina, Inc., 93
Imax Corporation, 28
In Focus Systems, Inc., 22
Indigo NV, 26
InFocus Corporation, 92
Ingram Micro Inc., 52
Innovative Solutions & Support, Inc., 85
Integrated Defense Technologies, Inc., 54
Intel Corporation, II; 10 (upd.); 75 (upd.)
Intermec Technologies Corporation, 72
International Business Machines Corporation, III; 6 (upd.); 30 (upd.); 63 (upd.)
International Rectifier Corporation, 31; 71 (upd.)
Intersil Corporation, 93
Ionatron, Inc., 85
Itel Corporation, 9
Jabil Circuit, Inc., 36; 88 (upd.)
Jaco Electronics, Inc., 30
JDS Uniphase Corporation, 34
Johnson Controls, Inc., 59 (upd.)
Juno Lighting, Inc., 30
Katy Industries, Inc., 51 (upd.)
Keithley Instruments Inc., 16
Kemet Corp., 14
Kent Electronics Corporation, 17
Kenwood Corporation, 31
Kesa Electricals plc, 91
Kimball International, Inc., 48 (upd.)
Kingston Technology Corporation, 20
KitchenAid, 8
KLA-Tencor Corporation, 45 (upd.)
KnowledgeWare Inc., 9
Kollmorgen Corporation, 18
Konami Corporation, 96
Konica Corporation, III; 30 (upd.)
Koninklijke Philips Electronics N.V., 50 (upd.)
Koor Industries Ltd., II
Kopin Corporation, 80
Koss Corporation, 38
Kudelski Group SA, 44
Kulicke and Soffa Industries, Inc., 33; 76 (upd.)
Kyocera Corporation, II; 79 (upd.)
LaBarge Inc., 41
The Lamson & Sessions Co., 61 (upd.)
Lattice Semiconductor Corp., 16
LeCroy Corporation, 41
Legrand SA, 21
Lenovo Group Ltd., 80
Lexmark International, Inc., 79 (upd.)
Linear Technology, Inc., 16
Littelfuse, Inc., 26
Loewe AG, 90
Loral Corporation, 9
LOUD Technologies, Inc., 95 (upd.)
Lowrance Electronics, Inc., 18
LSI Logic Corporation, 13; 64
Lucent Technologies Inc., 34
Lucky-Goldstar, II
Lunar Corporation, 29
Mackie Designs Inc., 33
MagneTek, Inc., 15; 41 (upd.)
Magneti Marelli Holding SpA, 90
Marconi plc, 33 (upd.)
Marquette Electronics, Inc., 13
Matsushita Electric Industrial Co., Ltd., II
Maxim Integrated Products, Inc., 16
McDATA Corporation, 75
Measurement Specialties, Inc., 71
Medis Technologies Ltd., 77
Merix Corporation, 36; 75 (upd.)
Methode Electronics, Inc., 13
Mitel Corporation, 18
MITRE Corporation, 26
Mitsubishi Electric Corporation, II; 44 (upd.)
Molex Incorporated, 54 (upd.)
Monster Cable Products, Inc., 69
Motorola, Inc., II; 11 (upd.); 34 (upd.); 93 (upd.)
N.F. Smith & Associates LP, 70
Nam Tai Electronics, Inc., 61
National Instruments Corporation, 22
National Presto Industries, Inc., 16; 43 (upd.)
National Semiconductor Corporation, II; 26 (upd.); 69 (upd.)
NEC Corporation, II; 21 (upd.); 57 (upd.)
Network Equipment Technologies Inc., 92
Nexans SA, 54
Nintendo Co., Ltd., 28 (upd.)
Nokia Corporation, II; 17 (upd.); 38 (upd.); 77 (upd.)
Nortel Networks Corporation, 36 (upd.)
Northrop Grumman Corporation, 45 (upd.)
Oak Technology, Inc., 22
Océ N.V., 24; 91 (upd.)
Oki Electric Industry Company, Limited, II
Omnicell, Inc., 89
Omron Corporation, II; 28 (upd.)
Orbotech Ltd., 75
Otari Inc., 89
Otter Tail Power Company, 18
Palm, Inc., 36; 75 (upd.)
Palomar Medical Technologies, Inc., 22
Parlex Corporation, 61
The Peak Technologies Group, Inc., 14
Peavey Electronics Corporation, 16
Philips Electronics N.V., II; 13 (upd.)
Philips Electronics North America Corp., 13
Pioneer Electronic Corporation, 28 (upd.)
Pioneer-Standard Electronics Inc., 19
Pitney Bowes Inc., 47 (upd.)
Pittway Corporation, 9
Pixelworks, Inc., 69
Planar Systems, Inc., 61
The Plessey Company, PLC, II
Plexus Corporation, 35; 80 (upd.)
Polk Audio, Inc., 34
Polaroid Corporation, III; 7 (upd.); 28 (upd.); 93 (upd.)
Potter & Brumfield Inc., 11
Premier Industrial Corporation, 9
Protection One, Inc., 32
Quanta Computer Inc., 47; 79 (upd.)
Racal Electronics PLC, II
RadioShack Corporation, 36 (upd.)
Radius Inc., 16
RAE Systems Inc., 83
Ramtron International Corporation, 89
Raychem Corporation, 8
Rayovac Corporation, 13
Raytheon Company, II; 11 (upd.); 38 (upd.)
RCA Corporation, II
Read-Rite Corp., 10
Redback Networks, Inc., 92
Reliance Electric Company, 9
Research in Motion Ltd., 54
Rexel, Inc., 15
Richardson Electronics, Ltd., 17
Ricoh Company, Ltd., 36 (upd.)
Rimage Corp., 89
The Rival Company, 19
Rockford Corporation, 43
Rogers Corporation, 61
S&C Electric Company, 15
SAGEM S.A., 37
St. Louis Music, Inc., 48
Sam Ash Music Corporation, 30
Samsung Electronics Co., Ltd., 14; 41 (upd.)
SANYO Electric Co., Ltd., II; 36 (upd.); 95 (upd.)
Sarnoff Corporation, 57
ScanSource, Inc., 29; 74 (upd.)
Schneider S.A., II; 18 (upd.)
SCI Systems, Inc., 9
Scientific-Atlanta, Inc., 45 (upd.)
Scitex Corporation Ltd., 24
Seagate Technology, Inc., 34 (upd.)
SEGA Corporation, 73
Semitool, Inc., 79 (upd.)
Semtech Corporation, 32
Sennheiser Electronic GmbH & Co. KG, 66
Sensormatic Electronics Corp., 11
Sensory Science Corporation, 37
SGI, 29 (upd.)
Sharp Corporation, II; 12 (upd.); 40 (upd.)
Sheldahl Inc., 23
Shure Inc., 60
Siemens AG, II; 14 (upd.); 57 (upd.)
Silicon Graphics Incorporated, 9
Siltronic AG, 90
SL Industries, Inc., 77
SMART Modular Technologies, Inc., 86

Smiths Industries PLC, 25
Solectron Corporation, 12; 48 (upd.)
Sony Corporation, II; 12 (upd.); 40 (upd.)
Spansion Inc., 80
Spectrum Control, Inc., 67
SPX Corporation, 47 (upd.)
Square D, 90
Sterling Electronics Corp., 18
STMicroelectronics NV, 52
Strix Ltd., 51
Stuart C. Irby Company, 58
Sumitomo Electric Industries, Ltd., II
Sun Microsystems, Inc., 7; 30 (upd.); 91 (upd.)
Sunbeam-Oster Co., Inc., 9
SunPower Corporation, 91
Suntech Power Holdings Company Ltd., 89
Synaptics Incorporated, 95
Syneron Medical Ltd., 91
SYNNEX Corporation, 73
Synopsys, Inc., 69 (upd.)
Sypris Solutions, Inc., 85
SyQuest Technology, Inc., 18
Tandy Corporation, II; 12 (upd.)
Tatung Co., 23
TDK Corporation, II; 17 (upd.); 49 (upd.)
TEAC Corporation 78
Tech-Sym Corporation, 18
Technitrol, Inc., 29
Tektronix, Inc., 8
Teledyne Technologies Inc., 62 (upd.)
Telxon Corporation, 10
Teradyne, Inc., 11
Texas Instruments Inc., II; 11 (upd.); 46 (upd.)
Thales S.A., 42
Thomas & Betts Corporation, 11; 54 (upd.)
THOMSON multimedia S.A., II; 42 (upd.)
THQ, Inc., 92 (upd.)
The Titan Corporation, 36
TomTom N.V., 81
Tops Appliance City, Inc., 17
Toromont Industries, Ltd., 21
Trans-Lux Corporation, 51
Trimble Navigation Limited, 40
TriQuint Semiconductor, Inc., 63
Tweeter Home Entertainment Group, Inc., 30
Ultimate Electronics, Inc., 69 (upd.)
Ultrak Inc., 24
Universal Electronics Inc., 39
Universal Security Instruments, Inc., 96
Varian Associates Inc., 12
Veeco Instruments Inc., 32
VIASYS Healthcare, Inc., 52
Viasystems Group, Inc., 67
Vicon Industries, Inc., 44
Victor Company of Japan, Limited, II; 26 (upd.); 83 (upd.)
Vishay Intertechnology, Inc., 21; 80 (upd.)
Vitesse Semiconductor Corporation, 32
Vitro Corp., 10
VLSI Technology, Inc., 16
VTech Holdings Ltd., 77
Wells-Gardner Electronics Corporation, 43
Westinghouse Electric Corporation, II; 12 (upd.)
Winbond Electronics Corporation, 74
Wincor Nixdorf Holding GmbH, 69 (upd.)
Wyle Electronics, 14
Xantrex Technology Inc., 97
Xerox Corporation, III; 6 (upd.); 26 (upd.); 69 (upd.)
Yageo Corporation, 16
York Research Corporation, 35
Zenith Data Systems, Inc., 10
Zenith Electronics Corporation, II; 13 (upd.); 34 (upd.); 89 (upd.)
Zoom Telephonics, Inc., 18
Zoran Corporation, 77
Zumtobel AG, 50
Zytec Corporation, 19

Engineering & Management Services

AAON, Inc., 22
Aavid Thermal Technologies, Inc., 29
Acergy SA, 97
AECOM Technology Corporation, 79
Alliant Techsystems Inc., 30 (upd.)
Altran Technologies, 51
Amey Plc, 47
American Science & Engineering, Inc., 81
Analytic Sciences Corporation, 10
Arcadis NV, 26
Arthur D. Little, Inc., 35
The Austin Company, 8; 72 (upd.)
Babcock International Group PLC, 69
Balfour Beatty plc, 36 (upd.)
BE&K, Inc., 73
Birse Group PLC, 77
Brown & Root, Inc., 13
Bufete Industrial, S.A. de C.V., 34
C.H. Heist Corporation, 24
CDI Corporation, 6; 54 (upd.)
CH2M HILL Companies Ltd., 22; 96 (upd.)
The Charles Stark Draper Laboratory, Inc., 35
Coflexip S.A., 25
Corrections Corporation of America, 23
CRSS Inc., 6
Dames & Moore, Inc., 25
DAW Technologies, Inc., 25
Day & Zimmermann Inc., 9; 31 (upd.)
Donaldson Co. Inc., 16
Dycom Industries, Inc., 57
Edwards and Kelcey, 70
EG&G Incorporated, 8; 29 (upd.)
Eiffage, 27
Essef Corporation, 18
Exponent, Inc., 95
FKI Plc, 57
Fluor Corporation, 34 (upd.)
Forest City Enterprises, Inc., 52 (upd.)
Foster Wheeler Corporation, 6; 23 (upd.)
Foster Wheeler Ltd., 76 (upd.)
Framatome SA, 19
Fraport AG Frankfurt Airport Services Worldwide, 90
Gale International Llc, 93
Georg Fischer AG Schaffhausen, 61
Gilbane, Inc., 34
Great Lakes Dredge & Dock Company, 69
Grupo Dragados SA, 55
Halliburton Company, 25 (upd.)
Harding Lawson Associates Group, Inc., 16
Harza Engineering Company, 14
HDR Inc., 48
HOK Group, Inc., 59
ICF Kaiser International, Inc., 28
IHC Caland N.V., 71
Jacobs Engineering Group Inc., 6; 26 (upd.)
Jacques Whitford, 92
The Judge Group, Inc., 51
JWP Inc., 9
The Keith Companies Inc., 54
Keller Group PLC, 95
Klöckner-Werke AG, 58 (upd.)
Kvaerner ASA, 36
Layne Christensen Company, 19
The MacNeal-Schwendler Corporation, 25
Malcolm Pirnie, Inc., 42
McDermott International, Inc., 37 (upd.)
McKinsey & Company, Inc., 9
Michael Baker Corporation, 51 (upd.)
Mota-Engil, SGPS, S.A., 97
Nooter Corporation, 61
Oceaneering International, Inc., 63
Odebrecht S.A., 73
Ogden Corporation, 6
Opus Group, 34
PAREXEL International Corporation, 84
Parsons Brinckerhoff, Inc., 34
The Parsons Corporation, 8; 56 (upd.)
The PBSJ Corporation, 82
Petrofac Ltd., 95
Quanta Services, Inc., 79
RCM Technologies, Inc., 34
Renishaw plc, 46
Ricardo plc, 90
Rosemount Inc., 15
Roy F. Weston, Inc., 33
Royal Vopak NV, 41
Rust International Inc., 11
Sandia National Laboratories, 49
Sandvik AB, 32 (upd.)
Sarnoff Corporation, 57
Science Applications International Corporation, 15
Serco Group plc, 47
Siegel & Gale, 64
Siemens AG, 57 (upd.)
SRI International, Inc., 57
SSOE Inc., 76
Stone & Webster, Inc., 13; 64 (upd.)
Sulzer Ltd., 68 (upd.)
Susquehanna Pfaltzgraff Company, 8
Sverdrup Corporation, 14
Tech-Sym Corporation, 44 (upd.)
Technip 78
Tetra Tech, Inc., 29

ThyssenKrupp AG, IV; 28 (upd.); 87 (upd.)
Towers Perrin, 32
Tracor Inc., 17
TRC Companies, Inc., 32
Underwriters Laboratories, Inc., 30
United Dominion Industries Limited, 8; 16 (upd.)
URS Corporation, 45; 80 (upd.)
U.S. Army Corps of Engineers, 91
VA TECH ELIN EBG GmbH, 49
VECO International, Inc., 7
Vinci, 43
The Weir Group PLC, 85
Willbros Group, Inc., 56
WS Atkins Plc, 45

Entertainment & Leisure

A&E Television Networks, 32
Aardman Animations Ltd., 61
ABC Family Worldwide, Inc., 52
Academy of Television Arts & Sciences, Inc., 55
Acclaim Entertainment Inc., 24
Activision, Inc., 32; 89 (upd.)
AEI Music Network Inc., 35
Affinity Group Holding Inc., 56
Airtours Plc, 27
Alaska Railroad Corporation, 60
All American Communications Inc., 20
The All England Lawn Tennis & Croquet Club, 54
Alliance Entertainment Corp., 17
Alternative Tentacles Records, 66
Alvin Ailey Dance Foundation, Inc., 52
Amblin Entertainment, 21
AMC Entertainment Inc., 12; 35 (upd.)
American Golf Corporation, 45
American Gramaphone LLC, 52
American Kennel Club, Inc., 74
American Skiing Company, 28
Ameristar Casinos, Inc., 33; 69 (upd.)
AMF Bowling, Inc., 40
Anaheim Angels Baseball Club, Inc., 53
Anchor Gaming, 24
AOL Time Warner Inc., 57 (upd.)
Applause Inc., 24
Apple Corps Ltd., 87
Aprilia SpA, 17
Argosy Gaming Company, 21
Aristocrat Leisure Limited, 54
Arsenal Holdings PLC, 79
The Art Institute of Chicago, 29
The Arthur C. Clarke Foundation, 92
Artisan Entertainment Inc., 32 (upd.)
Asahi National Broadcasting Company, Ltd., 9
Aspen Skiing Company, 15
Aston Villa plc, 41
The Athletics Investment Group, 62
Atlanta National League Baseball Club, Inc., 43
The Atlantic Group, 23
Autotote Corporation, 20
Aztar Corporation, 13
Bad Boy Worldwide Entertainment Group, 58
Baker & Taylor Corporation, 16; 43 (upd.)
Bally Total Fitness Holding Corp., 25
Baltimore Orioles L.P., 66
Barden Companies, Inc., 76
The Baseball Club of Seattle, LP, 50
The Basketball Club of Seattle, LLC, 50
Bertelsmann A.G., IV; 15 (upd.); 43 (upd.); 91 (upd.)
Bertucci's Inc., 16
Big Idea Productions, Inc., 49
BigBen Interactive S.A., 72
BioWare Corporation, 81
Blockbuster Inc., 9; 31 (upd.); 76 (upd.)
Boca Resorts, Inc., 37
Bonneville International Corporation, 29
Booth Creek Ski Holdings, Inc., 31
Boston Celtics Limited Partnership, 14
Boston Professional Hockey Association Inc., 39
The Boston Symphony Orchestra Inc., 93
The Boy Scouts of America, 34
Boyne USA Resorts, 71
Brillstein-Grey Entertainment, 80
British Broadcasting Corporation Ltd., 7; 21 (upd.); 89 (upd.)
The British Film Institute, 80
The British Museum, 71
British Sky Broadcasting Group plc, 20; 60 (upd.)
Brunswick Corporation, III; 22 (upd.); 77 (upd.)
Busch Entertainment Corporation, 73
Cablevision Systems Corporation, 7
California Sports, Inc., 56
Callaway Golf Company, 45 (upd.)
Canterbury Park Holding Corporation, 42
Capcom Company Ltd., 83
Capital Cities/ABC Inc., II
Capitol Records, Inc., 90
Carlson Companies, Inc., 6; 22 (upd.); 87 (upd.)
Carlson Wagonlit Travel, 55
Carmike Cinemas, Inc., 14; 37 (upd.); 74 (upd.)
Carnival Corporation, 6; 27 (upd.); 78 (upd.)
The Carsey-Werner Company, L.L.C., 37
CBS Inc., II; 6 (upd.)
Cedar Fair, L.P., 22
Central European Media Enterprises Ltd., 61
Central Independent Television, 7; 23 (upd.)
Century Casinos, Inc., 53
Century Theatres, Inc., 31
Championship Auto Racing Teams, Inc., 37
Channel Four Television Corporation, 93
Chello Zone Ltd., 93
Chelsea Piers Management Inc., 86
Chicago Bears Football Club, Inc., 33
Chicago National League Ball Club, Inc., 66
Chris-Craft Corporation, 9, 31 (upd.); 80 (upd.)
Chrysalis Group plc, 40
Churchill Downs Incorporated, 29
Cinar Corporation, 40
Cinemark Holdings, Inc., 95
Cinemas de la República, S.A. de C.V., 83
Cineplex Odeon Corporation, 6; 23 (upd.)
Cinram International, Inc., 43
Cirque du Soleil Inc., 29
Classic Vacation Group, Inc., 46
Cleveland Indians Baseball Company, Inc., 37
Club Mediterranée S.A., 6; 21 (upd.); 91 (upd.)
ClubCorp, Inc., 33
CMG Worldwide, Inc., 89
Colonial Williamsburg Foundation, 53
Colorado Baseball Management, Inc., 72
Columbia Pictures Entertainment, Inc., II
Columbia TriStar Motion Pictures Companies, 12 (upd.)
Comcast Corporation, 7
Compagnie des Alpes, 48
Confluence Holdings Corporation, 76
Continental Cablevision, Inc., 7
Corporación Interamericana de Entretenimiento, S.A. de C.V., 83
Corporation for Public Broadcasting, 14; 89 (upd.)
Cox Enterprises, Inc., 22 (upd.)
Cranium, Inc., 69
Crown Media Holdings, Inc., 45
Cruise America Inc., 21
Cunard Line Ltd., 23
Dallas Cowboys Football Club, Ltd., 33
Dave & Buster's, Inc., 33
Death Row Records, 27
Denver Nuggets, 51
The Detroit Lions, Inc., 55
The Detroit Pistons Basketball Company, 41
Detroit Red Wings, 74
Detroit Tigers Baseball Club, Inc., 46
dick clark productions, inc., 16
DIRECTV, Inc., 38; 75 (upd.)
Dover Downs Entertainment, Inc., 43
DreamWorks SKG, 43
Dualstar Entertainment Group LLC, 76
E! Entertainment Television Inc., 17
edel music AG, 44
Educational Broadcasting Corporation, 48
Edwards Theatres Circuit, Inc., 31
Egmont Group, 93
Electronic Arts Inc., 10; 85 (upd.)
Elektra Entertainment Group, 64
Elsinore Corporation, 48
Elvis Presley Enterprises, Inc., 61
Empire Resorts, Inc., 72
Endemol Entertainment Holding NV, 46
Entertainment Distribution Company, 89
Equity Marketing, Inc., 26
ESPN, Inc., 56
Esporta plc, 35
Euro Disney S.C.A., 20; 58 (upd.)
Europe Through the Back Door Inc., 65
Fair Grounds Corporation, 44
Family Golf Centers, Inc., 29
FAO Schwarz, 46
Fédération Internationale de Football Association, 27

Feld Entertainment, Inc., 32 (upd.)
Film Roman, Inc., 58
First Choice Holidays PLC, 40
First Team Sports, Inc., 22
Fisher-Price Inc., 32 (upd.)
Florida Gaming Corporation, 47
Focus Features 78
4Kids Entertainment Inc., 59
Fox Entertainment Group, Inc., 43
Fox Family Worldwide, Inc., 24
Fuji Television Network Inc., 91
The GAME Group plc, 80
GameStop Corp., 69 (upd.)
Gaumont SA, 25; 91 (upd.)
Gaylord Entertainment Company, 11; 36 (upd.)
GC Companies, Inc., 25
Geffen Records Inc., 26
Gibson Guitar Corp., 16
Girl Scouts of the USA, 35
Global Outdoors, Inc., 49
Glu Mobile Inc., 95
GoodTimes Entertainment Ltd., 48
Granada Group PLC, II; 24 (upd.)
Grand Casinos, Inc., 20
Great Wolf Resorts, Inc., 91
Greek Organization of Football Prognostics S.A. (OPAP), 97
The Green Bay Packers, Inc., 32
Grévin & Compagnie SA, 56
Groupe Partouche SA, 48
Grupo Televisa, S.A., 54 (upd.)
H. Betti Industries Inc., 88
Hallmark Cards, Inc., IV; 16 (upd.); 40 (upd.); 87 (upd.)
Hanna-Barbera Cartoons Inc., 23
Hard Rock Cafe International, Inc., 32 (upd.)
Harlem Globetrotters International, Inc., 61
Harpo Inc., 28; 66 (upd.)
Harrah's Entertainment, Inc., 16; 43 (upd.)
Harveys Casino Resorts, 27
Hasbro, Inc., 43 (upd.)
Hastings Entertainment, Inc., 29
The Hearst Corporation, 46 (upd.)
The Heat Group, 53
Hendrick Motorsports, Inc., 89
Herschend Family Entertainment Corporation, 73
Hilton Group plc, III; 19 (upd.); 49 (upd.)
HIT Entertainment PLC, 40
HOB Entertainment, Inc., 37
Holidaybreak plc, 96
Hollywood Casino Corporation, 21
Hollywood Entertainment Corporation, 25
Hollywood Media Corporation, 58
Hollywood Park, Inc., 20
Home Box Office Inc., 7; 23 (upd.); 76 (upd.)
Horseshoe Gaming Holding Corporation, 62
IG Group Holdings plc, 97
Imagine Entertainment, 91
IMAX Corporation 28; 78 (upd.)
IMG 78
Indianapolis Motor Speedway Corporation, 46
Infinity Broadcasting Corporation, 48 (upd.)
Infogrames Entertainment S.A., 35
Integrity Inc., 44
International Creative Management, Inc., 43
International Family Entertainment Inc., 13
International Game Technology, 41 (upd.)
International Olympic Committee, 44
International Speedway Corporation, 19; 74 (upd.)
Interscope Music Group, 31
Intrawest Corporation, 15; 84 (upd.)
Irvin Feld & Kenneth Feld Productions, Inc., 15
Isle of Capri Casinos, Inc., 41
iVillage Inc., 46
Iwerks Entertainment, Inc., 34
Jackpot Enterprises Inc., 21
Japan Broadcasting Corporation, 7
Jazz Basketball Investors, Inc., 55
Jazzercise, Inc., 45
Jillian's Entertainment Holdings, Inc., 40
The Jim Henson Company, 23
The Joffrey Ballet of Chicago, 52
Jurys Doyle Hotel Group plc, 64
Juventus F.C. S.p.A, 53
K'Nex Industries, Inc., 52
Kampgrounds of America, Inc. (KOA), 33
Kerasotes ShowPlace Theaters LLC, 80
Kerzner International Limited, 69 (upd.)
King World Productions, Inc., 9; 30 (upd.)
Klasky Csupo Inc. 78
Knott's Berry Farm, 18
Kuoni Travel Holding Ltd., 40
The Kushner-Locke Company, 25
Ladbroke Group PLC, II; 21 (upd.)
Lakes Entertainment, Inc., 51
Landmark Theatre Corporation, 70
Las Vegas Sands, Inc., 50
Lego A/S, 13; 40 (upd.)
Liberty Livewire Corporation, 42
Liberty Media Corporation, 50
Liberty Travel, Inc., 56
Life Time Fitness, Inc., 66
Lifetime Entertainment Services, 51
Lincoln Center for the Performing Arts, Inc., 69
Lionel L.L.C., 16
Lions Gate Entertainment Corporation, 35
LIVE Entertainment Inc., 20
Live Nation, Inc., 80 (upd.)
LodgeNet Entertainment Corporation, 28
Lucasfilm Ltd., 12; 50 (upd.)
Luminar Plc, 40
Majesco Entertainment Company, 85
Manchester United Football Club plc, 30
Mandalay Resort Group, 32 (upd.)
Maple Leaf Sports & Entertainment Ltd., 61
The Marcus Corporation, 21
The Mark Travel Corporation, 80
Märklin Holding GmbH, 70
Martha Stewart Living Omnimedia, Inc., 73 (upd.)
Mashantucket Pequot Gaming Enterprise Inc., 35
MCA Inc., II
McMenamins Pubs and Breweries, 65
Media General, Inc., 7
Mediaset SpA, 50
Mega Bloks, Inc., 61
Metro-Goldwyn-Mayer Inc., 25 (upd.); 84 (upd.)
Metromedia Companies, 14
Métropole Télévision, 33
Métropole Télévision S.A., 76 (upd.)
Metropolitan Baseball Club Inc., 39
The Metropolitan Museum of Art, 55
Metropolitan Opera Association, Inc., 40
MGM Grand Inc., 17
MGM/UA Communications Company, II
Midway Games, Inc., 25
Mikohn Gaming Corporation, 39
Milan AC, S.p.A., 79
Milwaukee Brewers Baseball Club, 37
Miramax Film Corporation, 64
Mizuno Corporation, 25
Mohegan Tribal Gaming Authority, 37
Moliflor Loisirs, 80
Monarch Casino & Resort, Inc., 65
Motown Records Company L.P., 26
Movie Gallery, Inc., 31
Mr. Gatti's, LP, 87
MTR Gaming Group, Inc., 75
Multimedia Games, Inc., 41
Muzak, Inc., 18
National Amusements Inc., 28
National Aquarium in Baltimore, Inc., 74
National Association for Stock Car Auto Racing, 32
National Broadcasting Company, Inc., II; 6 (upd.)
National Collegiate Athletic Association, 96
National Football League, 29
National Hockey League, 35
National Public Radio, Inc., 19; 47 (upd.)
National Rifle Association of America, 37
National Thoroughbred Racing Association, 58
Navarre Corporation, 24
Navigant International, Inc., 47
NBGS International, Inc., 73
NCL Corporation, 79
New Jersey Devils, 84
New Line Cinema, Inc., 47
New Orleans Saints LP, 58
New York City Off-Track Betting Corporation, 51
New York Shakespeare Festival Management, 93
News Corporation Limited, 46 (upd.)
NFL Films, 75
Nicklaus Companies, 45
Nintendo Company, Ltd., 28 (upd.); 67 (upd.)
Nordisk Film A/S, 80
O'Charley's Inc., 19
Orion Pictures Corporation, 6

Outrigger Enterprises, Inc., 67
Palace Sports & Entertainment, Inc., 97
Paradise Music & Entertainment, Inc., 42
Paramount Pictures Corporation, II
Pathé SA, 29
Paul Reed Smith Guitar Company, 89
Paul-Son Gaming Corporation, 66
PDS Gaming Corporation, 44
Peace Arch Entertainment Group Inc., 51
Penn National Gaming, Inc., 33
Philadelphia Eagles, 37
Philharmonic-Symphony Society of New York, Inc. (New York Philharmonic), 69
Pierre & Vacances SA, 48
Pittsburgh Steelers Sports, Inc., 66
Pixar Animation Studios, 34
Platinum Entertainment, Inc., 35
Play by Play Toys & Novelties, Inc., 26
Players International, Inc., 22
Pleasant Holidays LLC, 62
PolyGram N.V., 23
Poof-Slinky, Inc., 61
Pop Warner Little Scholars, Inc., 86
Portland Trail Blazers, 50
Powerhouse Technologies, Inc., 27
Premier Parks, Inc., 27
President Casinos, Inc., 22
Preussag AG, 42 (upd.)
Princess Cruise Lines, 22
Professional Bull Riders Inc., 55
The Professional Golfers' Association of America, 41
Promus Companies, Inc., 9
ProSiebenSat.1 Media AG, 54
Publishing and Broadcasting Limited, 54
Putt-Putt Golf Courses of America, Inc., 23
Radio One, Inc., 67
Ragdoll Productions Ltd., 51
Rainforest Café, Inc., 25; 88 (upd.)
The Rank Group plc, II; 64 (upd.)
Rawlings Sporting Goods Co., Inc., 24
Real Madrid C.F., 73
The Really Useful Group, 26
Regal Entertainment Group, 59
Rentrak Corporation, 35
Rhino Entertainment Company, 18; 70 (upd.)
Ride, Inc., 22
Ripley Entertainment, Inc., 74
Riviera Holdings Corporation, 75
Rollerblade, Inc., 34 (upd.)
Roularta Media Group NV, 48
Rounder Records Corporation, 79
Royal Caribbean Cruises Ltd., 22; 74 (upd.)
Royal Olympic Cruise Lines Inc., 52
RTL Group SA, 44
Rush Communications, 33
Ryko Corporation, 83
S-K-I Limited, 15
Sabre Holdings Corporation, 74 (upd.)
Salomon Worldwide, 20
San Diego Padres Baseball Club LP 78
San Francisco Baseball Associates, L.P., 55
The Sanctuary Group PLC, 69
Santa Fe Gaming Corporation, 19
Schwinn Cycle and Fitness L.P., 19
Scientific Games Corporation, 64 (upd.)
Scottish Radio Holding plc, 41
Seattle FilmWorks, Inc., 20
Seattle Seahawks, Inc., 92
The Second City, Inc., 88
SEGA Corporation, 73
Sega of America, Inc., 10
Selectour SA, 53
SFX Entertainment, Inc., 36
Shedd Aquarium Society, 73
Shochiku Company Ltd., 74
Showboat, Inc., 19
Showtime Networks Inc. 78
Shubert Organization Inc., 24
Shuffle Master Inc., 51
The Singing Machine Company, Inc., 60
Sirius Satellite Radio, Inc., 69
Six Flags, Inc., 17; 54 (upd.)
Smithsonian Institution, 27
Società Sportiva Lazio SpA, 44
Sony Corporation, 40 (upd.)
Speedway Motorsports, Inc., 32
Spelling Entertainment Group, Inc., 14
Spin Master, Ltd., 61
The Sports Club Company, 25
Spyglass Entertainment Group, LLC, 91
Stanley Leisure plc, 66
Starz LLC, 91
Station Casinos, Inc., 25; 90 (upd.)
Stoll-Moss Theatres Ltd., 34
Stuart Entertainment Inc., 16
Sub Pop Ltd., 97
TABCORP Holdings Limited, 44
Take-Two Interactive Software, Inc., 46
TaylorMade-adidas Golf, 23; 96 (upd.)
Tee Vee Toons, Inc., 57
Tele-Communications, Inc., II
Television Española, S.A., 7
Texas Rangers Baseball, 51
Tha Row Records, 69 (upd.)
Thomas Cook Travel Inc., 9
The Thomson Corporation, 8
Thousand Trails, Inc., 33
THQ, Inc., 39
365 Media Group plc, 89
Ticketmaster Corp., 13
Tiger Aspect Productions Ltd., 72
The Todd-AO Corporation, 33
Toho Co., Ltd., 28
TOKYOPOP Inc., 79
Tomy Company Ltd., 65
The Topps Company, Inc., 13, 34 (upd.); 83 (upd.)
Tottenham Hotspur PLC, 81
Touristik Union International GmbH. and Company K.G., II
Town Sports International, Inc., 46
Toy Biz, Inc., 18
Trans World Entertainment Corporation, 24
Travelocity.com, Inc., 46
Tribune Company, 63 (upd.)
TUI Group GmbH, 44
Turner Broadcasting System, Inc., II; 6 (upd.); 66 (upd.)
The Tussauds Group, 55
Twentieth Century Fox Film Corporation, II; 25 (upd.)
24 Hour Fitness Worldwide, Inc., 71
Ubi Soft Entertainment S.A., 41
Ulster Television PLC, 71
Ultimate Leisure Group PLC, 75
United Pan-Europe Communications NV, 47
United States Playing Card Company, 62
United Talent Agency, Inc., 80
Universal Studios, Inc., 33
Univision Communications Inc., 24; 83 (upd.)
Urbium PLC, 75
USA Interactive, Inc., 47 (upd.)
Vail Resorts, Inc., 11; 43 (upd.)
Venetian Casino Resort, LLC, 47
Viacom Inc., 7; 23 (upd.)
Village Roadshow Ltd., 58
Vinton Studios, 63
Vivendi Universal S.A., 46 (upd.)
The Walt Disney Company, II; 6 (upd.); 30 (upd.); 63 (upd.)
Warner Communications Inc., II
Warner Music Group Corporation, 90 (upd.)
Washington Football, Inc., 35
The Welk Group Inc., 78
West Coast Entertainment Corporation, 29
WGBH Educational Foundation, 66
Wham-O, Inc., 61
Wherehouse Entertainment Incorporated, 11
Whitbread PLC, I; 20 (upd.); 52 (upd.); 97 (upd.)
Wildlife Conservation Society, 31
William Hill Organization Limited, 49
Wilson Sporting Goods Company, 24; 84 (upd.)
Wizards of the Coast Inc., 24
WMS Industries, Inc., 53 (upd.)
World Wrestling Federation Entertainment, Inc., 32
Worldwide Pants Inc., 97
Writers Guild of America, West, Inc., 92
XM Satellite Radio Holdings, Inc., 69
YankeeNets LLC, 35
YES! Entertainment Corporation, 26
YMCA of the USA, 31
Youbet.com, Inc., 77
Young Broadcasting Inc., 40
Zomba Records Ltd., 52
Zuffa L.L.C., 89

Financial Services: Banks

Abbey National plc, 10; 39 (upd.)
Abigail Adams National Bancorp, Inc., 23
ABN AMRO Holding, N.V., 50
Affiliated Managers Group, Inc., 79
Akbank TAS, 79
Alabama National BanCorporation, 75
Algemene Bank Nederland N.V., II
Alliance and Leicester plc, 88
Allianz AG, 57 (upd.)
Allied Irish Banks, plc, 16; 43 (upd.)
Almanij NV, 44
Amalgamated Bank, 60

AMCORE Financial Inc., 44
American Residential Mortgage Corporation, 8
AmSouth Bancorporation,12; 48 (upd.)
Amsterdam-Rotterdam Bank N.V., II
Anchor Bancorp, Inc., 10
Apple Bank for Savings, 59
Astoria Financial Corporation, 44
Australia and New Zealand Banking Group Limited, II; 52 (upd.)
Banca Commerciale Italiana SpA, II
Banca Fideuram SpA, 63
Banca Intesa SpA, 65
Banca Monte dei Paschi di Siena SpA, 65
Banca Nazionale del Lavoro SpA, 72
Banco Bilbao Vizcaya Argentaria S.A., II; 48 (upd.)
Banco Bradesco S.A., 13
Banco Central, II
Banco Comercial Português, SA, 50
Banco de Chile, 69
Banco de Crédito del Perú, 93
Banco do Brasil S.A., II
Banco Espírito Santo e Comercial de Lisboa S.A., 15
Banco Itaú S.A., 19
Banco Santander Central Hispano S.A., 36 (upd.)
Bank Austria AG, 23
Bank Brussels Lambert, II
Bank Hapoalim B.M., II; 54 (upd.)
Bank Leumi le-Israel B.M., 60
Bank of America Corporation, 46 (upd.)
Bank of Boston Corporation, II
Bank of China, 63
Bank of Cyprus Group, 91
Bank of East Asia Ltd., 63
Bank of Granite Corporation, 89
Bank of Hawaii Corporation, 73
Bank of Ireland, 50
Bank of Mississippi, Inc., 14
Bank of Montreal, II; 46 (upd.)
Bank of New England Corporation, II
The Bank of New York Company, Inc., II; 46 (upd.)
The Bank of Nova Scotia, II; 59 (upd.)
Bank of the Ozarks, Inc., 91
Bank of the Philippine Islands, 58
Bank of Tokyo-Mitsubishi Ltd., II; 15 (upd.)
Bank One Corporation, 10; 36 (upd.)
BankAmerica Corporation, II; 8 (upd.)
Bankers Trust New York Corporation, II
Banknorth Group, Inc., 55
Banque Nationale de Paris S.A., II
Barclays plc, II; 20 (upd.); 64 (upd.)
BarclaysAmerican Mortgage Corporation, 11
Barings PLC, 14
Barnett Banks, Inc., 9
BayBanks, Inc., 12
Bayerische Hypotheken- und Wechsel-Bank AG, II
Bayerische Vereinsbank A.G., II
BB&T Corporation, 79
Beneficial Corporation, 8
BNP Paribas Group, 36 (upd.)
Boatmen's Bancshares Inc., 15
Bremer Financial Corp., 45
Brown Brothers Harriman & Co., 45
C. Hoare & Co., 77
Caisse des Dépôts et Consignations, 90
Canadian Imperial Bank of Commerce, II; 61 (upd.)
Capitalia S.p.A., 65
Carolina First Corporation, 31
Casco Northern Bank, 14
The Chase Manhattan Corporation, II; 13 (upd.)
Cheltenham & Gloucester PLC, 61
Chemical Banking Corporation, II; 14 (upd.)
China Construction Bank Corp., 79
Citicorp, II; 9 (upd.)
Citigroup Inc., 30 (upd.); 59 (upd.)
Citizens Financial Group, Inc., 42; 87 (upd.)
Close Brothers Group plc, 39
Commercial Credit Company, 8
Commercial Federal Corporation, 12; 62 (upd.)
Commerzbank A.G., II; 47 (upd.)
Compagnie Financiere de Paribas, II
Compass Bancshares, Inc., 73
Continental Bank Corporation, II
CoreStates Financial Corp, 17
Corus Bankshares, Inc., 75
Countrywide Credit Industries, Inc., 16
Crédit Agricole Group, II; 84 (upd.)
Crédit Lyonnais, 9; 33 (upd.)
Crédit National S.A., 9
Credit Suisse Group, II; 21 (upd.); 59 (upd.)
Credito Italiano, II
Cullen/Frost Bankers, Inc., 25
CUNA Mutual Group, 62
The Dai-Ichi Kangyo Bank Ltd., II
The Daiwa Bank, Ltd., II; 39 (upd.)
Danske Bank Aktieselskab, 50
Dauphin Deposit Corporation, 14
DEPFA BANK PLC, 69
Deposit Guaranty Corporation, 17
Deutsche Bank AG, II; 14 (upd.); 40 (upd.)
Deutscher Sparkassen- und Giroverband (DSGV), 84
Dexia NV/SA, 42; 88 (upd.)
Dime Savings Bank of New York, F.S.B., 9
Donaldson, Lufkin & Jenrette, Inc., 22
Dresdner Bank A.G., II; 57 (upd.)
Emigrant Savings Bank, 59
Erste Bank der Osterreichischen Sparkassen AG, 69
Espèrito Santo Financial Group S.A., 79 (upd.)
European Investment Bank, 66
Fidelity Southern Corporation, 85
Fifth Third Bancorp, 13; 31 (upd.)
First Bank System Inc., 12
First Chicago Corporation, II
First Commerce Bancshares, Inc., 15
First Commerce Corporation, 11
First Empire State Corporation, 11
First Fidelity Bank, N.A., New Jersey, 9
First Hawaiian, Inc., 11
First Interstate Bancorp, II
First Nationwide Bank, 14
First of America Bank Corporation, 8
First Security Corporation, 11
First Tennessee National Corporation, 11; 48 (upd.)
First Union Corporation, 10
First Virginia Banks, Inc., 11
Firstar Corporation, 11; 33 (upd.)
Fleet Financial Group, Inc., 9
FleetBoston Financial Corporation, 36 (upd.)
FöreningsSparbanken AB, 69
Fourth Financial Corporation, 11
The Fuji Bank, Ltd., II
Generale Bank, II
German American Bancorp, 41
Glacier Bancorp, Inc., 35
Golden West Financial Corporation, 47
The Governor and Company of the Bank of Scotland, 10
Grameen Bank, 31
Granite State Bankshares, Inc., 37
Great Lakes Bancorp, 8
Great Western Financial Corporation, 10
GreenPoint Financial Corp., 28
Grupo Financiero Banamex S.A., 54
Grupo Financiero Banorte, S.A. de C.V., 51
Grupo Financiero BBVA Bancomer S.A., 54
Grupo Financiero Galicia S.A., 63
Grupo Financiero Serfin, S.A., 19
H.F. Ahmanson & Company, II; 10 (upd.)
Habersham Bancorp, 25
Hancock Holding Company, 15
Hang Seng Bank Ltd., 60
Hanmi Financial Corporation, 66
Hibernia Corporation, 37
The Hongkong and Shanghai Banking Corporation Limited, II
HSBC Holdings plc, 12; 26 (upd.); 80 (upd.)
Hudson River Bancorp, Inc., 41
Huntington Bancshares Incorporated, 11; 87 (upd.)
HVB Group, 59 (upd.)
IBERIABANK Corporation, 37
The Industrial Bank of Japan, Ltd., II
Irish Life & Permanent Plc, 59
Irwin Financial Corporation, 77
J Sainsbury plc, II; 13 (upd.); 38 (upd.); 95 (upd.)
J.P. Morgan & Co. Incorporated, II; 30 (upd.)
J.P. Morgan Chase & Co., 38 (upd.)
Japan Leasing Corporation, 8
JPMorgan Chase & Co., 91 (upd.)
Julius Baer Holding AG, 52
Kansallis-Osake-Pankki, II
KeyCorp, 8; 93 (upd.)
Kookmin Bank, 58
Kredietbank N.V., II
Kreditanstalt für Wiederaufbau, 29
Krung Thai Bank Public Company Ltd., 69
Landsbanki Islands hf, 81

Lloyds Bank PLC, II
Lloyds TSB Group plc, 47 (upd.)
Long Island Bancorp, Inc., 16
Long-Term Credit Bank of Japan, Ltd., II
Macquarie Bank Ltd., 69
Malayan Banking Berhad, 72
Manufacturers Hanover Corporation, II
Manulife Financial Corporation, 85
Marfin Popular Bank plc, 92
Marshall & Ilsley Corporation, 56
MBNA Corporation, 12
Mediolanum S.p.A., 65
Mellon Bank Corporation, II
Mellon Financial Corporation, 44 (upd.)
Mercantile Bankshares Corp., 11
Meridian Bancorp, Inc., 11
Metropolitan Financial Corporation, 13
Michigan National Corporation, 11
Midland Bank PLC, II; 17 (upd.)
The Mitsubishi Bank, Ltd., II
The Mitsubishi Trust & Banking Corporation, II
The Mitsui Bank, Ltd., II
The Mitsui Trust & Banking Company, Ltd., II
Mizuho Financial Group Inc., 58 (upd.)
Mouvement des Caisses Desjardins, 48
N M Rothschild & Sons Limited, 39
National Bank of Greece, 41
National Bank of Canada, 85
The National Bank of South Carolina, 76
National City Corporation, 15; 97 (upd.)
National Westminster Bank PLC, II
NationsBank Corporation, 10
NBD Bancorp, Inc., 11
NCNB Corporation, II
New York Community Bancorp Inc. 78
Nippon Credit Bank, II
Nordea AB, 40
Norinchukin Bank, II
North Fork Bancorporation, Inc., 46
Northern Rock plc, 33
Northern Trust Company, 9
NVR L.P., 8
Old Kent Financial Corp., 11
Old National Bancorp, 15
Orszagos Takarekpenztar es Kereskedelmi Bank Rt. (OTP Bank) 78
PNC Bank Corp., II; 13 (upd.)
The PNC Financial Services Group Inc., 46 (upd.)
Popular, Inc., 41
Provident Bankshares Corporation, 85
PT Bank Buana Indonesia Tbk, 60
Pulte Corporation, 8
Qatar National Bank SAQ, 87
Rabobank Group, 33
Raiffeisen Zentralbank Österreich AG, 85
Republic New York Corporation, 11
Riggs National Corporation, 13
Royal Bank of Canada, II; 21 (upd.); 81 (upd.)
The Royal Bank of Scotland Group plc, 12; 38 (upd.)
The Ryland Group, Inc., 8
St. Paul Bank for Cooperatives, 8
Sanpaolo IMI S.p.A., 50
The Sanwa Bank, Ltd., II; 15 (upd.)
SBC Warburg, 14
Sberbank, 62
Seattle First National Bank Inc., 8
Security Capital Corporation, 17
Security Pacific Corporation, II
Shawmut National Corporation, 13
Signet Banking Corporation, 11
Singer & Friedlander Group plc, 41
Skandinaviska Enskilda Banken AB, II; 56 (upd.)
Société Générale, II; 42 (upd.)
Society Corporation, 9
Southern Financial Bancorp, Inc., 56
Southtrust Corporation, 11
Standard Chartered plc, II; 48 (upd.)
Standard Federal Bank, 9
Star Banc Corporation, 11
State Bank of India, 63
State Financial Services Corporation, 51
State Street Corporation, 8; 57 (upd.)
Staten Island Bancorp, Inc., 39
The Sumitomo Bank, Limited, II; 26 (upd.)
Sumitomo Mitsui Banking Corporation, 51 (upd.)
The Sumitomo Trust & Banking Company, Ltd., II; 53 (upd.)
The Summit Bancorporation, 14
Suncorp-Metway Ltd., 91
SunTrust Banks Inc., 23
Svenska Handelsbanken AB, II; 50 (upd.)
Sveriges Riksbank, 96
Swiss Bank Corporation, II
Synovus Financial Corp., 12; 52 (upd.)
The Taiyo Kobe Bank, Ltd., II
TCF Financial Corporation, 47
The Tokai Bank, Limited, II; 15 (upd.)
The Toronto-Dominion Bank, II; 49 (upd.)
TSB Group plc, 12
Turkiye Is Bankasi A.S., 61
U.S. Bancorp, 14; 36 (upd.)
U.S. Trust Corp., 17
UBS AG, 52 (upd.)
Umpqua Holdings Corporation, 87
Unibanco Holdings S.A., 73
Union Bank of California, 16
Union Bank of Switzerland, II
Union Financière de France Banque SA, 52
Union Planters Corporation, 54
UnionBanCal Corporation, 50 (upd.)
United Overseas Bank Ltd., 56
USAA, 62 (upd.)
Van Lanschot NV, 79
Vontobel Holding AG, 96
Wachovia Bank of Georgia, N.A., 16
Wachovia Bank of South Carolina, N.A., 16
Washington Mutual, Inc., 17; 93 (upd.)
Wells Fargo & Company, II; 12 (upd.); 38 (upd.); 97 (upd.)
West One Bancorp, 11
Westamerica Bancorporation, 17
Westdeutsche Landesbank Girozentrale, II; 46 (upd.)
Westpac Banking Corporation, II; 48 (upd.)
Whitney Holding Corporation, 21
Wilmington Trust Corporation, 25
The Woolwich plc, 30
World Bank Group, 33
The Yasuda Trust and Banking Company, Ltd., II; 17 (upd.)
Zions Bancorporation, 12; 53 (upd.)

Financial Services: Excluding Banks

A.B. Watley Group Inc., 45
A.G. Edwards, Inc., 8; 32 (upd.)
ACCION International, 87
Accredited Home Lenders Holding Co., 91
ACE Cash Express, Inc., 33
Advanta Corporation, 8; 38 (upd.)
Ag Services of America, Inc., 59
Alliance Capital Management Holding L.P., 63
Allmerica Financial Corporation, 63
Ambac Financial Group, Inc., 65
America's Car-Mart, Inc., 64
American Capital Strategies, Ltd., 91
American Express Company, II; 10 (upd.); 38 (upd.)
American General Finance Corp., 11
American Home Mortgage Holdings, Inc., 46
Ameritrade Holding Corporation, 34
AMVESCAP PLC, 65
Apax Partners Worldwide LLP, 89
Arnhold and S. Bleichroeder Advisers, LLC, 97
Arthur Andersen & Company, Société Coopérative, 10
Avco Financial Services Inc., 13
Aviva PLC, 50 (upd.)
Bankrate, Inc., 83
Bear Stearns Companies, Inc., II; 10 (upd.); 52 (upd.)
Benchmark Capital, 49
Bill & Melinda Gates Foundation, 41
BlackRock, Inc., 79
Bolsa Mexicana de Valores, S.A. de C.V., 80
Bozzuto's, Inc., 13
Bradford & Bingley PLC, 65
Cantor Fitzgerald, L.P., 92
Capital One Financial Corporation, 52
Cardtronics, Inc., 93
Carnegie Corporation of New York, 35
Cash America International, Inc., 20; 61 (upd.)
Cash Systems, Inc., 93
Catholic Order of Foresters, 24; 97 (upd.)
Cattles plc, 58
Cendant Corporation, 44 (upd.)
Certegy, Inc., 63
Cetelem S.A., 21
The Charles Schwab Corporation, 8; 26 (upd.); 81 (upd.)
CheckFree Corporation, 81
Cheshire Building Society, 74
Chicago Mercantile Exchange Holdings Inc., 75
CIT Group Inc., 76
Citfed Bancorp, Inc., 16

Citicorp Diners Club, Inc., 90
Coinstar, Inc., 44
Comerica Incorporated, 40
Commercial Financial Services, Inc., 26
Compagnie Nationale à Portefeuille, 84
Concord EFS, Inc., 52
Coopers & Lybrand, 9
Cowen Group, Inc., 92
Cramer, Berkowitz & Co., 34
Credit Acceptance Corporation, 18
Cresud S.A.C.I.F. y A., 63
CS First Boston Inc., II
Dain Rauscher Corporation, 35 (upd.)
Daiwa Securities Group Inc., II; 55 (upd.)
Datek Online Holdings Corp., 32
The David and Lucile Packard Foundation, 41
Dean Witter, Discover & Co., 12
Deutsche Börse AG, 59
ditech.com, 93
Dominick & Dominick LLC, 92
Dow Jones Telerate, Inc., 10
Draper Fisher Jurvetson, 91
Dresdner Kleinwort Wasserstein, 60 (upd.)
Drexel Burnham Lambert Incorporated, II
The Dreyfus Corporation, 70
DVI, Inc., 51
E*Trade Financial Corporation, 20; 60 (upd.)
Eaton Vance Corporation, 18
Edward D. Jones & Company L.P., 66 (upd.)
Edward Jones, 30
Eurazeo, 80
Euronet Worldwide, Inc., 83
Euronext N.V., 37; 89 (upd.)
Experian Information Solutions Inc., 45
Fair, Isaac and Company, 18
Fannie Mae, 45 (upd.)
Federal Agricultural Mortgage Corporation, 75
Federal Deposit Insurance Corporation, 93
Federal National Mortgage Association, II
Fidelity Investments Inc., II; 14 (upd.)
First Albany Companies Inc., 37
First Data Corporation, 30 (upd.)
The First Marblehead Corporation, 87
First USA, Inc., 11
FMR Corp., 8; 32 (upd.)
Forstmann Little & Co., 38
Fortis, Inc., 15
Frank Russell Company, 46
Franklin Resources, Inc., 9
Fred Alger Management, Inc., 97
Freddie Mac, 54
Friedman, Billings, Ramsey Group, Inc., 53
Gabelli Asset Management Inc., 30
Gilman & Ciocia, Inc., 72
Global Payments Inc., 91
The Goldman Sachs Group Inc., II; 20 (upd.); 51 (upd.)
Grede Foundries, Inc., 38
Green Tree Financial Corporation, 11
Gruntal & Co., L.L.C., 20
Grupo Financiero Galicia S.A., 63
H&R Block, Inc., 9; 29 (upd.); 82 (upd.)
H.D. Vest, Inc., 46
H.M. Payson & Co., 69
Hercules Technology Growth Capital, Inc., 87
Hoenig Group Inc., 41
Household International, Inc., II; 21 (upd.)
Hummer Winblad Venture Partners, 97
Huron Consulting Group Inc., 87
IDB Holding Corporation Ltd., 97
Ingenico—Compagnie Industrielle et Financière d'Ingénierie, 46
Instinet Corporation, 34
Inter-Regional Financial Group, Inc., 15
IntercontinentalExchange, Inc., 95
Investcorp SA, 57
The Island ECN, Inc., 48
Istituto per la Ricostruzione Industriale S.p.A., 11
J. & W. Seligman & Co. Inc., 61
JAFCO Co. Ltd., 79
Janus Capital Group Inc., 57
JB Oxford Holdings, Inc., 32
Jefferies Group, Inc., 25
John Hancock Financial Services, Inc., 42 (upd.)
The John Nuveen Company, 21
Jones Lang LaSalle Incorporated, 49
The Jordan Company LP, 70
Kansas City Southern Industries, Inc., 26 (upd.)
Kleiner, Perkins, Caufield & Byers, 53
Kleinwort Benson Group PLC, II
Knight Trading Group, Inc., 70
Kohlberg Kravis Roberts & Co., 24; 56 (upd.)
KPMG Worldwide, 10
La Poste, 47 (upd.)
LaBranche & Co. Inc., 37
Lazard LLC, 38
Legg Mason, Inc., 33
LendingTree, LLC, 93
LifeLock, Inc., 91
Lilly Endowment Inc., 70
Liquidnet, Inc., 79
London Scottish Bank plc, 70
London Stock Exchange Limited, 34
M.H. Meyerson & Co., Inc., 46
MacAndrews & Forbes Holdings Inc., 28; 86 (upd.)
Madison Dearborn Partners, LLC, 97
MasterCard Worldwide, 9; 96 (upd.)
MBNA Corporation, 33 (upd.)
Merrill Lynch & Co., Inc., II; 13 (upd.); 40 (upd.)
Metris Companies Inc., 56
Morgan Grenfell Group PLC, II
Morgan Stanley Dean Witter & Company, II; 16 (upd.); 33 (upd.)
Mountain States Mortgage Centers, Inc., 29
NASD, 54 (upd.)
The NASDAQ Stock Market, Inc., 92
National Association of Securities Dealers, Inc., 10
National Auto Credit, Inc., 16
National Discount Brokers Group, Inc., 28
National Financial Partners Corp., 65
Navy Federal Credit Union, 33
Neuberger Berman Inc., 57
New Street Capital Inc., 8
New York Stock Exchange, Inc., 9; 39 (upd.)
The Nikko Securities Company Limited, II; 9 (upd.)
Nippon Shinpan Co., Ltd., II; 61 (upd.)
Nomura Securities Company, Limited, II; 9 (upd.)
Norwich & Peterborough Building Society, 55
NovaStar Financial, Inc., 91
Oaktree Capital Management, LLC, 71
Old Mutual PLC, 61
Ontario Teachers' Pension Plan, 61
Onyx Acceptance Corporation, 59
ORIX Corporation, II; 44 (upd.)
PaineWebber Group Inc., II; 22 (upd.)
PayPal Inc., 58
The Pew Charitable Trusts, 35
Piper Jaffray Companies Inc., 22
Pitney Bowes Inc., 47 (upd.)
Providian Financial Corporation, 52 (upd.)
Prudential Financial Inc., III; 30 (upd.); 82 (upd.)
The Quick & Reilly Group, Inc., 20
Quicken Loans, Inc., 93
Rathbone Brothers plc, 70
Raymond James Financial Inc., 69
Resource America, Inc., 42
Robert W. Baird & Co. Incorporated, 67
Ryan Beck & Co., Inc., 66
Safeguard Scientifics, Inc., 10
St. James's Place Capital, plc, 71
Salomon Inc., II; 13 (upd.)
Sanders Morris Harris Group Inc., 70
Sanlam Ltd., 68
SBC Warburg, 14
Schroders plc, 42
Scottrade, Inc., 85
SEI Investments Company, 96
Shearson Lehman Brothers Holdings Inc., II; 9 (upd.)
Siebert Financial Corp., 32
Skipton Building Society, 80
SLM Holding Corp., 25 (upd.)
Smith Barney Inc., 15
Soros Fund Management LLC, 28
Spear, Leeds & Kellogg, 66
State Street Boston Corporation, 8
Stephens Inc., 92
Student Loan Marketing Association, II
Sun Life Financial Inc., 85
T. Rowe Price Associates, Inc., 11; 34 (upd.)
Teachers Insurance and Annuity Association-College Retirement Equities Fund, 45 (upd.)
Texas Pacific Group Inc., 36
3i Group PLC, 73
Total System Services, Inc., 18
TradeStation Group, Inc., 83
Trilon Financial Corporation, II
United Jewish Communities, 33
The Vanguard Group, Inc., 14; 34 (upd.)

VeriFone Holdings, Inc., 18; 76 (upd.)
Viel & Cie, 76
Visa International, 9; 26 (upd.)
Wachovia Corporation, 12; 46 (upd.)
Waddell & Reed, Inc., 22
Washington Federal, Inc., 17
Waterhouse Investor Services, Inc., 18
Watson Wyatt Worldwide, 42
Western Union Financial Services, Inc., 54
WFS Financial Inc., 70
Working Assets Funding Service, 43
World Acceptance Corporation, 57
Yamaichi Securities Company, Limited, II
The Ziegler Companies, Inc., 24; 63 (upd.)
Zurich Financial Services, 42 (upd.); 93 (upd.)

Food Products

A. Duda & Sons, Inc., 88
A. Moksel AG, 59
Agri Beef Company, 81
Agway, Inc., 7
Ajinomoto Co., Inc., II; 28 (upd.)
Alabama Farmers Cooperative, Inc., 63
The Albert Fisher Group plc, 41
Alberto-Culver Company, 8; 36 (upd.); 91 (upd.)
Alfred Ritter GmbH & Co. KG, 58
Alfesca hf, 82
Allen Canning Company, 76
Alpine Confections, Inc., 71
Alpine Lace Brands, Inc., 18
American Crystal Sugar Company, 11; 32 (upd.)
American Foods Group, 43
American Italian Pasta Company, 27; 76 (upd.)
American Licorice Company, 86
American Maize-Products Co., 14
American Pop Corn Company, 59
American Rice, Inc., 33
Amfac/JMB Hawaii L.L.C., 24 (upd.)
Amy's Kitchen Inc., 76
Annie's Homegrown, Inc., 59
Archer-Daniels-Midland Company, 32 (upd.)
Archway Cookies, Inc., 29
Arcor S.A.I.C., 66
Arla Foods amba, 48
Arnott's Ltd., 66
Associated British Foods plc, II; 13 (upd.); 41 (upd.)
Associated Milk Producers, Inc., 11; 48 (upd.)
Atkinson Candy Company, 87
Atlantic Premium Brands, Ltd., 57
August Storck KG, 66
Aurora Foods Inc., 32
Auvil Fruit Company, Inc., 95
Awrey Bakeries, Inc., 56
B&G Foods, Inc., 40
The B. Manischewitz Company, LLC, 31
Bahlsen GmbH & Co. KG, 44
Bakkavör Group hf., 91
Balance Bar Company, 32
Baltek Corporation, 34
The Bama Companies, Inc., 80
Bar-S Foods Company, 76
Barbara's Bakery Inc., 88
Barilla G. e R. Fratelli S.p.A., 17; 50 (upd.)
Barry Callebaut AG, 71 (upd.)
Bear Creek Corporation, 38
Beatrice Company, II
Beech-Nut Nutrition Corporation, 21; 51 (upd.)
Beer Nuts, Inc., 86
Bel/Kaukauna USA, 76
Bellisio Foods, Inc., 95
Ben & Jerry's Homemade, Inc., 10; 35 (upd.); 80 (upd.)
Berkeley Farms, Inc., 46
Bernard Matthews Ltd., 89
Besnier SA, 19
Best Kosher Foods Corporation, 82
Bestfoods, 22 (upd.)
Better Made Snack Foods, Inc., 90
Bettys & Taylors of Harrogate Ltd., 72
Birds Eye Foods, Inc., 69 (upd.)
Blue Bell Creameries L.P., 30
Blue Diamond Growers, 28
Bob's Red Mill Natural Foods, Inc., 63
Bobs Candies, Inc., 70
Bolton Group B.V., 86
Bonduelle SA, 51
Bongrain SA, 25
Booker PLC, 13; 31 (upd.)
Borden, Inc., II; 22 (upd.)
Boyd Coffee Company, 53
Brach and Brock Confections, Inc., 15
Brake Bros plc, 45
Bridgford Foods Corporation, 27
Brigham's Inc., 72
Brioche Pasquier S.A., 58
British Sugar plc, 84
Brothers Gourmet Coffees, Inc., 20
Broughton Foods Co., 17
Brown & Haley, 23
Bruce Foods Corporation, 39
Bruegger's Corporation, 63
Bruster's Real Ice Cream, Inc., 80
BSN Groupe S.A., II
Bumble Bee Seafoods L.L.C., 64
Bunge Brasil S.A. 78
Bunge Ltd., 62
Bourbon Corporation, 82
Burns, Philp & Company Ltd., 63
Bush Boake Allen Inc., 30
Bush Brothers & Company, 45
The C.F. Sauer Company, 90
C.H. Robinson Worldwide, Inc., 40 (upd.)
C.H. Guenther & Son, Inc., 84
Cactus Feeders, Inc., 91
Cadbury Schweppes PLC, II; 49 (upd.)
Cagle's, Inc., 20
Cal-Maine Foods, Inc., 69
Calavo Growers, Inc., 47
Calcot Ltd., 33
Callard and Bowser-Suchard Inc., 84
Campbell Soup Company, II; 7 (upd.); 26 (upd.); 71 (upd.)
The Campina Group, 78
Campofrío Alimentación S.A, 59
Canada Packers Inc., II
Cape Cod Potato Chip Company, 90
Cargill, Incorporated, II; 13 (upd.); 40 (upd.); 89 (upd.)
Carnation Company, II
The Carriage House Companies, Inc., 55
Carroll's Foods, Inc., 46
Carvel Corporation, 35
Castle & Cooke, Inc., II; 20 (upd.)
Cattleman's, Inc., 20
Celestial Seasonings, Inc., 16
Cemoi S.A., 86
Central Soya Company, Inc., 7
Chaoda Modern Agriculture (Holdings) Ltd., 87
Charal S.A., 90
Chase General Corporation, 91
Chattanooga Bakery, Inc., 86
Chef Solutions, Inc., 89
Chelsea Milling Company, 29
Chicken of the Sea International, 24 (upd.)
China National Cereals, Oils and Foodstuffs Import and Export Corporation (COFCO), 76
Chiquita Brands International, Inc., 7; 21 (upd.); 83 (upd.)
Chock Full o'Nuts Corp., 17
Chocoladefabriken Lindt & Sprüngli AG, 27
Chr. Hansen Group A/S, 70
CHS Inc., 60
Chupa Chups S.A., 38
The Clemens Family Corporation, 93
Clif Bar Inc., 50
Cloetta Fazer AB, 70
The Clorox Company, III; 22 (upd.); 81 (upd.)
Clougherty Packing Company, 72
Coca-Cola Enterprises, Inc., 13
Coffee Holding Co., Inc., 95
Cold Stone Creamery, 69
Coleman Natural Products, Inc., 68
Community Coffee Co. L.L.C., 53
ConAgra Foods, Inc., II; 12 (upd.); 42 (upd.); 85 (upd.)
The Connell Company, 29
ContiGroup Companies, Inc., 43 (upd.)
Continental Grain Company, 10; 13 (upd.)
CoolBrands International Inc., 35
Coopagri Bretagne, 88
Cooperativa Nacional de Productores de Leche S.A. (Conaprole), 92
Corporación José R. Lindley S.A., 92
CPC International Inc., II
Cranswick plc, 40
CSM N.V., 65
Cuisine Solutions Inc., 84
Cumberland Packing Corporation, 26
Curtice-Burns Foods, Inc., 7; 21 (upd.)
Czarnikow-Rionda Company, Inc., 32
D.F. Stauffer Biscuit Company, 82
Daesang Corporation, 84
Dairy Crest Group plc, 32
Dalgery, PLC, II
Danisco A/S, 44
Dannon Co., Inc., 14
Darigold, Inc., 9

Dawn Food Products, Inc., 17
Dean Foods Company, 7; 21 (upd.); 73 (upd.)
DeKalb Genetics Corporation, 17
Del Monte Foods Company, 7; 23 (upd.)
Di Giorgio Corp., 12
Diageo plc, 24 (upd.)
Diamond of California, 64 (upd.)
Dietz and Watson, Inc., 92
Dippin' Dots, Inc., 56
Dobrogea Grup S.A., 82
Dole Food Company, Inc., 9; 31 (upd.); 68 (upd.)
Domino Sugar Corporation, 26
Doskocil Companies, Inc., 12
Dot Foods, Inc., 69
Doux S.A., 80
Dreyer's Grand Ice Cream, Inc., 17
The Earthgrains Company, 36
Elmer Candy Corporation, 88
Emge Packing Co., Inc., 11
Empresas Polar SA, 55 (upd.)
Eridania Béghin-Say S.A., 36
ERLY Industries Inc., 17
Eskimo Pie Corporation, 21
Établissements Jacquot and Cie S.A.S., 92
Exportadora Bananera Noboa, S.A., 91
Ezaki Glico Company Ltd., 72
Faribault Foods, Inc., 89
Farley's & Sathers Candy Company, Inc., 62
Farmland Foods, Inc., 7
Farmland Industries, Inc., 48
Ferrara Pan Candy Company, 90
Ferrero SpA, 54
Fieldale Farms Corporation, 23
First Colony Coffee & Tea Company, 84
Fleer Corporation, 15
Fleury Michon S.A., 39
Floc'h & Marchand, 80
Florida Crystals Inc., 35
Flowers Industries, Inc., 12; 35 (upd.)
Fonterra Co-Operative Group Ltd., 58
FoodBrands America, Inc., 23
Foster Poultry Farms, 32
Fred Usinger Inc., 54
Fresh America Corporation, 20
Fresh Express Inc., 88
Fresh Foods, Inc., 29
FreshDirect, LLC, 84
Friesland Coberco Dairy Foods Holding N.V., 59
Frito-Lay Company, 32
Frito-Lay North America, 73 (upd.)
Fromageries Bel, 23
Frontier Natural Products Co-Op, 82
Fyffes Plc, 38
Galaxy Nutritional Foods, Inc., 58
Gano Excel Enterprise Sdn. Bhd., 89
The Garden Company Ltd., 82
Gardenburger, Inc., 33; 76 (upd.)
Geest Plc, 38
General Mills, Inc., II; 10 (upd.); 36 (upd.); 85 (upd.)
George A. Hormel and Company, II
George Weston Ltd., II; 36 (upd.); 88 (upd.)
Gerber Products Company, 7; 21 (upd.)
Ghirardelli Chocolate Company, 30
Givaudan SA, 43
Glaces Thiriet S.A., 76
Glanbia plc, 59
Global Berry Farms LLC, 62
Godiva Chocolatier, Inc., 64
Goetze's Candy Company, Inc., 87
Gold Kist Inc., 17; 26 (upd.)
Gold'n Plump Poultry, 54
Golden Enterprises, Inc., 26
Gonnella Baking Company, 40
Good Humor-Breyers Ice Cream Company, 14
Goodman Fielder Ltd., 52
GoodMark Foods, Inc., 26
Gorton's, 13
Goya Foods Inc., 22; 91 (upd.)
Graeter's Manufacturing Company, 86
Grampian Country Food Group, Ltd., 85
Great Harvest Bread Company, 44
Grist Mill Company, 15
Groupe Bigard S.A., 96
Groupe CECAB S.C.A., 88
Groupe Danone, 32 (upd.); 93 (upd.)
Groupe Euralis, 86
Groupe Glon, 84
Groupe Lactalis, 78 (upd.)
Groupe Limagrain, 74
Groupe Soufflet SA, 55
Gruma, S.A. de C.V., 31
Grupo Comercial Chedraui S.A. de C.V., 86
Grupo Herdez, S.A. de C.V., 35
Grupo Industrial Lala, S.A. de C.V., 82
Grupo Leche Pascual S.A., 59
Grupo Viz, S.A. de C.V., 84
Guida-Seibert Dairy Company, 84
Guittard Chocolate Company, 55
Guttenplan's Frozen Dough Inc., 88
H.J. Heinz Company, II; 11 (upd.); 36 (upd.)
Hagoromo Foods Corporation, 84
The Hain Celestial Group, Inc., 27; 43 (upd.)
Hanover Foods Corporation, 35
HARIBO GmbH & Co. KG, 44
The Harris Soup Company (Harry's Fresh Foods), 92
Harry London Candies, Inc., 70
The Hartz Mountain Corporation, 12
Hayel Saeed Anam Group of Cos., 92
Hazlewood Foods plc, 32
Herman Goelitz, Inc., 28
Herr Foods Inc., 84
Hershey Foods Corporation, II; 15 (upd.); 51 (upd.)
Hill's Pet Nutrition, Inc., 27
Hillsdown Holdings plc, II; 24 (upd.)
HiPP GmbH & Co. Vertrieb KG, 88
Hodgson Mill, Inc., 88
Horizon Organic Holding Corporation, 37
Hormel Foods Corporation, 18 (upd.); 54 (upd.)
Hot Stuff Foods, 85
Hudson Foods Inc., 13
Hulman & Company, 44
Hunt-Wesson, Inc., 17
Iams Company, 26
IAWS Group plc, 49
IBP, Inc., II; 21 (upd.)
Iceland Group plc, 33
Icelandic Group hf, 81
Imagine Foods, Inc., 50
Imperial Holly Corporation, 12
Imperial Sugar Company, 32 (upd.)
Industrias Bachoco, S.A. de C.V., 39
Intercorp Excelle Foods Inc., 64
International Multifoods Corporation, 7; 25 (upd.)
Interstate Bakeries Corporation, 12; 38 (upd.)
The Inventure Group, Inc., 96 (upd.)
Inversiones Nacional de Chocolates S.A., 88
Itoham Foods Inc., II; 61 (upd.)
J & J Snack Foods Corporation, 24
The J. M. Smucker Company, 11; 87 (upd.)
J.R. Simplot Company, 16
Jacobs Suchard A.G., II
Jays Foods, Inc., 90
Jel Sert Company, 90
Jelly Belly Candy Company, 76
Jennie-O Turkey Store, Inc., 76
Jim Beam Brands Co., 14
John B. Sanfilippo & Son, Inc., 14
Johnsonville Sausage L.L.C., 63
Julius Meinl International AG, 53
Just Born, Inc., 32
Kal Kan Foods, Inc., 22
Kamps AG, 44
Kar Nut Products Company, 86
Kashi Company, 89
Katokichi Company Ltd., 82
Keebler Foods Company, 36
Kellogg Company, II; 13 (upd.); 50 (upd.)
Ken's Foods, Inc., 88
Kerry Group plc, 27; 87 (upd.)
Kettle Foods Inc., 48
Kewpie Kabushiki Kaisha, 57
Kikkoman Corporation, 14; 47 (upd.)
The King Arthur Flour Company, 31
King Nut Company, 74
King Ranch, Inc., 14
Klement's Sausage Company, 61
Koninklijke Wessanen nv, II; 54 (upd.)
Kraft Foods Inc., II; 7 (upd.); 45 (upd.); 91 (upd.)
Kraft Jacobs Suchard AG, 26 (upd.)
Krispy Kreme Doughnuts, Inc., 21; 61 (upd.)
Kuwait Flour Mills & Bakeries Company, 84
Kyokuyo Company Ltd., 75
L.D.C. SA, 61
La Choy Food Products Inc., 25
La Reina Inc., 96
Labeyrie SAS, 80
Lakeside Foods, Inc., 89
Lam Son Sugar Joint Stock Corporation (Lasuco), 60
Lamb Weston, Inc., 23
Lance, Inc., 14; 41 (upd.)

Land O'Lakes, Inc., II; 21 (upd.); 81 (upd.)
Lassonde Industries Inc., 68
LDC, 68
Ledesma Sociedad Anónima Agrícola Industrial, 62
Legal Sea Foods Inc., 96
Leidy's, Inc., 93
Leprino Foods Company, 28
Leroux S.A.S., 65
Lifeway Foods, Inc., 65
Liberty Orchards Co., Inc., 89
Lincoln Snacks Company, 24
Litehouse Inc., 60
Lotte Confectionery Company Ltd., 76
Lucille Farms, Inc., 45
Luigino's, Inc., 64
M.A. Gedney Co., 51
Madrange SA, 58
Malt-O-Meal Company, 22; 63 (upd.)
Maple Grove Farms of Vermont, 88
Maple Leaf Foods Inc., 41
Marble Slab Creamery, Inc., 87
Mars, Incorporated, 7; 40 (upd.)
Mars Petcare US Inc., 96
Maruha Group Inc., 75 (upd.)
Maryland & Virginia Milk Producers Cooperative Association, Inc., 80
The Maschhoffs, Inc., 82
Maui Land & Pineapple Company, Inc., 29
Mauna Loa Macadamia Nut Corporation, 64
Maverick Ranch Association, Inc., 88
McCain Foods Limited, 77
McCormick & Company, Incorporated, 7; 27 (upd.)
McIlhenny Company, 20
McKee Foods Corporation, 7; 27 (upd.)
Mead Johnson & Company, 84
Medifast, Inc., 97
Meiji Dairies Corporation, II; 82 (upd.)
Meiji Seika Kaisha, Ltd., II
Merisant Worldwide, Inc., 70
Michael Foods, Inc., 25
Mid-America Dairymen, Inc., 7
Midwest Grain Products, Inc., 49
Mike-Sell's Inc., 15
Milnot Company, 46
Molinos Río de la Plata S.A., 61
Monfort, Inc., 13
Morinda Holdings, Inc., 82
Morinaga & Co. Ltd., 61
Moy Park Ltd. 78
Mrs. Baird's Bakeries, 29
Mt. Olive Pickle Company, Inc., 44
MTR Foods Ltd., 55
Murphy Family Farms Inc., 22
The Musco Family Olive Co., 91
Nabisco Foods Group, II; 7 (upd.)
Nantucket Allserve, Inc., 22
Nathan's Famous, Inc., 29
National Presto Industries, Inc., 43 (upd.)
National Sea Products Ltd., 14
Natural Ovens Bakery, Inc., 72
Natural Selection Foods, 54
Naturally Fresh, Inc., 88
Nature's Path Foods, Inc., 87
Naumes, Inc., 81
Nestlé S.A., II; 7 (upd.); 28 (upd.); 71 (upd.)
New England Confectionery Co., 15
New World Pasta Company, 53
Newhall Land and Farming Company, 14
Newly Weds Foods, Inc., 74
Newman's Own, Inc., 37
Nichiro Corporation, 86
Niman Ranch, Inc., 67
Nippon Meat Packers, Inc., II; 78 (upd.)
Nippon Suisan Kaisha, Ltd., II; 92 (upd.)
Nisshin Seifun Group Inc., II; 66 (upd.)
Nissin Food Products Company Ltd., 75
Northern Foods plc, 10; 61 (upd.)
Northland Cranberries, Inc., 38
Nutraceutical International Corporation, 37
NutraSweet Company, 8
Nutreco Holding N.V., 56
Nutrexpa S.A., 92
NutriSystem, Inc., 71
Oakhurst Dairy, 60
Oberto Sausage Company, Inc., 92
Ocean Beauty Seafoods, Inc., 74
Ocean Spray Cranberries, Inc., 7; 25 (upd.); 83 (upd.)
OJSC Wimm-Bill-Dann Foods, 48
Olga's Kitchen, Inc., 80
Omaha Steaks International Inc., 62
Ore-Ida Foods Inc., 13; 78 (upd.)
Oregon Freeze Dry, Inc., 74
Organic Valley (Coulee Region Organic Produce Pool), 53
Orkla ASA, 18; 82 (upd.)
Oscar Mayer Foods Corp., 12
Otis Spunkmeyer, Inc., 28
Overhill Corporation, 51
Palmer Candy Company, 80
Panzani, 84
Papetti's Hygrade Egg Products, Inc., 39
Parmalat Finanziaria SpA, 50
Pendleton Grain Growers Inc., 64
Penford Corporation, 55
Penzeys Spices, Inc., 79
Pepperidge Farm, Incorporated, 81
PepsiCo, Inc., I; 10 (upd.); 38 (upd.); 93 (upd.)
Perdigao SA, 52
Perdue Farms Inc., 7; 23 (upd.)
Perfetti Van Melle S.p.A., 72
Performance Food Group, 96 (upd.)
Perkins Foods Holdings Ltd., 87
Perry's Ice Cream Company Inc., 90
Pescanova S.A., 81
Pet Incorporated, 7
Petrossian Inc., 54
Pez Candy, Inc., 38
Philip Morris Companies Inc., 18 (upd.)
Phillips Foods, Inc., 63
PIC International Group PLC, 24 (upd.)
Phillips Foods, Inc., 90 (upd.)
Pilgrim's Pride Corporation, 7; 23 (upd.); 90 (upd.)
The Pillsbury Company, II; 13 (upd.); 62 (upd.)
Pioneer Hi-Bred International, Inc., 9
Pizza Inn, Inc., 46
Poore Brothers, Inc., 44
PowerBar Inc., 44
Prairie Farms Dairy, Inc., 47
Premium Standard Farms, Inc., 30
Princes Ltd., 76
The Procter & Gamble Company, III; 8 (upd.); 26 (upd.); 67 (upd.)
Provimi S.A., 80
Punch Taverns plc, 70
Puratos S.A./NV, 92
Purina Mills, Inc., 32
Quaker Foods North America, 73 (upd.)
Quaker Oats Company, II; 12 (upd.); 34 (upd.)
Quality Chekd Dairies, Inc., 48
R. M. Palmer Co., 89
Ralston Purina Company, II; 13 (upd.)
Ranks Hovis McDougall Limited, II; 28 (upd.)
Reckitt Benckiser plc, II; 42 (upd.); 91 (upd.)
Reddy Ice Holdings, Inc., 80
Reser's Fine Foods, Inc., 81
Rica Foods, Inc., 41
Rich Products Corporation, 7; 38 (upd.); 93 (upd.)
Richtree Inc., 63
Ricola Ltd., 62
Ridley Corporation Ltd., 62
River Ranch Fresh Foods LLC, 88
Riviana Foods Inc., 27
Rocky Mountain Chocolate Factory, Inc., 73
Roland Murten A.G., 7
Roman Meal Company, 84
Rose Acre Farms, Inc., 60
Rowntree Mackintosh, II
Royal Numico N.V., 37
Ruiz Food Products, Inc., 53
Russell Stover Candies Inc., 12; 91 (upd.)
Sadia S.A., 59
Sanderson Farms, Inc., 15
Saputo Inc., 59
Sara Lee Corporation, II; 15 (upd.); 54 (upd.)
Sarris Candies Inc., 86
Savannah Foods & Industries, Inc., 7
Schlotzsky's, Inc., 36
Schreiber Foods, Inc., 72
The Schwan Food Company, 7; 26 (upd.); 83 (upd.)
Schwebel Baking Company, 72
Seaboard Corporation, 36; 85 (upd.)
See's Candies, Inc., 30
Seminis, Inc., 29
Seneca Foods Corporation, 60 (upd.)
Sensient Technologies Corporation, 52 (upd.)
Shearer's Foods, Inc., 72
Silhouette Brands, Inc., 55
Silver Lake Cookie Company Inc., 95
Skalli Group, 67
Slim-Fast Foods Company, 18; 66 (upd.)
Small Planet Foods, Inc., 89
Smithfield Foods, Inc., 7; 43 (upd.)
Snow Brand Milk Products Company, Ltd., II; 48 (upd.)
Société Industrielle Lesaffre, 84

Sodiaal S.A., 36 (upd.)
SODIMA, II
Sorbee International Ltd., 74
Sorrento, Inc., 24
Spangler Candy Company, 44
Spectrum Organic Products, Inc., 68
Standard Candy Company Inc., 86
Star of the West Milling Co., 95
Starbucks Corporation, 13; 34 (upd.); 77 (upd.)
Stock Yards Packing Co., Inc., 37
Stollwerck AG, 53
Stolt Sea Farm Holdings PLC, 54
Stolt-Nielsen S.A., 42
Stonyfield Farm, Inc., 55
Stouffer Corp., 8
Strauss-Elite Group, 68
Südzucker AG, 27
Suiza Foods Corporation, 26
Sun-Diamond Growers of California, 7
Sun-Maid Growers of California, 82
Sun-Rype Products Ltd., 76
Sun World International, LLC, 93
Sunkist Growers, Inc., 26
SunOpta Inc., 79
Supervalu Inc., 18 (upd.); 50 (upd.)
Suprema Specialties, Inc., 27
Sweet Candy Company, 60
Swift & Company, 55
The Swiss Colony, Inc., 97
Swiss Valley Farms Company, 90
Sylvan, Inc., 22
Symrise GmbH and Company KG, 89
Syngenta International AG, 83
T. Marzetti Company, 57
Taiyo Fishery Company, Limited, II
Tasty Baking Company, 14; 35 (upd.)
Tate & Lyle PLC, II; 42 (upd.)
TCBY Enterprises Inc., 17
TDL Group Ltd., 46
Terrena L'Union CANA CAVAL, 70
Thai Union Frozen Products PCL, 75
Thomas J. Lipton Company, 14
Thorn Apple Valley, Inc., 7; 22 (upd.)
Thorntons plc, 46
TLC Beatrice International Holdings, Inc., 22
Tofutti Brands, Inc., 64
Tom's Foods Inc., 66
Tombstone Pizza Corporation, 13
Tone Brothers, Inc., 21; 74 (upd.)
Tootsie Roll Industries, Inc., 12; 82 (upd.)
Touton S.A., 92
Townsends, Inc., 64
Tree Top, Inc., 76
TreeHouse Foods, Inc., 79
Tri Valley Growers, 32
Trident Seafoods Corporation, 56
Tropicana Products, Inc., 28
Tulip Ltd., 89
Tumaro's Gourmet Tortillas, 85
Tyson Foods, Inc., II; 14 (upd.); 50 (upd.)
U.S. Foodservice, 26
U.S. Premium Beef LLC, 91
Uncle Ben's Inc., 22
Uncle Ray's LLC, 90
Unigate PLC, II; 28 (upd.)
Unilever, II; 7 (upd.); 32 (upd.); 89 (upd.)
Uniq plc, 83 (upd.)
United Biscuits (Holdings) plc, II; 42 (upd.)
United Brands Company, II
United Farm Workers of America, 88
United Foods, Inc., 21
Universal Foods Corporation, 7
Utz Quality Foods, Inc., 72
Van Camp Seafood Company, Inc., 7
Ventura Foods LLC, 90
Vestey Group Ltd., 95
Vienna Sausage Manufacturing Co., 14
Vilmorin Clause et Cie, 70
Vion Food Group NV, 85
Vista Bakery, Inc., 56
Vlasic Foods International Inc., 25
W Jordan (Cereals) Ltd., 74
Wagers Inc. (Idaho Candy Company), 86
Walkers Shortbread Ltd., 79
Walkers Snack Foods Ltd., 70
Warburtons Ltd., 89
Warrell Corporation, 68
Wattie's Ltd., 7
Weaver Popcorn Company, Inc., 89
Weetabix Limited, 61
Weis Markets, Inc., 84 (upd.)
Wells' Dairy, Inc., 36
Wenner Bread Products Inc., 80
White Lily Foods Company, 88
White Wave, 43
Wilbur Chocolate Company, 66
Wimm-Bill-Dann Foods, 48
Wisconsin Dairies, 7
Wise Foods, Inc., 79
WLR Foods, Inc., 21
Wm. B. Reily & Company Inc., 58
Wm. Wrigley Jr. Company, 7; 58 (upd.)
World's Finest Chocolate Inc., 39
Worthington Foods, Inc., 14
Yamazaki Baking Co., Ltd., 58
Yarnell Ice Cream Company, Inc., 92
Yeo Hiap Seng Malaysia Bhd., 75
YOCREAM International, Inc., 47
Young's Bluecrest Seafood Holdings Ltd., 81
Zacky Farms LLC, 74
Zatarain's, Inc., 64

Food Services & Retailers

A. F. Blakemore & Son Ltd., 90
Advantica Restaurant Group, Inc., 27 (upd.)
AFC Enterprises, Inc., 32 (upd.); 83 (upd.)
Affiliated Foods Inc., 53
Albertson's, Inc., II; 7 (upd.); 30 (upd.); 65 (upd.)
Aldi Einkauf GmbH & Co. OHG, 13; 86 (upd.)
Alex Lee Inc., 18; 44 (upd.)
Allen Foods, Inc., 60
Almacenes Exito S.A., 89
Alpha Airports Group PLC, 77
America's Favorite Chicken Company, Inc., 7
American Restaurant Partners, L.P., 93
American Stores Company, II
Andronico's Market, 70
Applebee's International, Inc., 14; 35 (upd.)
ARA Services, II
Arby's Inc., 14
Arden Group, Inc., 29
Argyll Group PLC, II
Ark Restaurants Corp., 20
Asahi Breweries, Ltd., 20 (upd.)
ASDA Group Ltd., II; 28 (upd.); 64 (upd.)
Associated Grocers, Incorporated, 9; 31 (upd.)
Association des Centres Distributeurs E. Leclerc, 37
Atlanta Bread Company International, Inc., 70
Au Bon Pain Co., Inc., 18
Auchan, 37
Auntie Anne's, Inc., 35
Autogrill SpA, 49
Avado Brands, Inc., 31
B.R. Guest Inc., 87
Back Bay Restaurant Group, Inc., 20
Back Yard Burgers, Inc., 45
Bashas' Inc., 33; 80 (upd.)
Bear Creek Corporation, 38
Ben E. Keith Company, 76
Benihana, Inc., 18; 76 (upd.)
Bertucci's Corporation, 64 (upd.)
Bettys & Taylors of Harrogate Ltd., 72
Big Bear Stores Co., 13
The Big Food Group plc, 68 (upd.)
Big V Supermarkets, Inc., 25
Big Y Foods, Inc., 53
Blimpie International, Inc., 15; 49 (upd.)
Bob Evans Farms, Inc., 9; 63 (upd.)
Bob's Red Mill Natural Foods, Inc., 63
Boddie-Noell Enterprises, Inc., 68
Bojangles Restaurants Inc., 97
Bon Appetit Holding AG, 48
Boston Market Corporation, 12; 48 (upd.)
Boston Pizza International Inc., 88
Brazil Fast Food Corporation, 74
Briazz, Inc., 53
Brinker International, Inc., 10; 38 (upd.); 75 (upd.)
Brookshire Grocery Company, 16; 74 (upd.)
Bruegger's Corporation, 63
Bruno's Supermarkets, Inc., 7; 26 (upd.); 68 (upd.)
Buca, Inc., 38
Budgens Ltd., 59
Buffalo Wild Wings, Inc., 56
Buffets Holdings, Inc., 10; 32 (upd.); 93 (upd.)
Burger King Corporation, II; 17 (upd.); 56 (upd.)
Busch Entertainment Corporation, 73
C&K Market, Inc., 81
C & S Wholesale Grocers, Inc., 55
C.H. Robinson, Inc., 11
Caffè Nero Group PLC, 63
California Pizza Kitchen Inc., 15; 74 (upd.)

Captain D's, LLC, 59
Cargill, Incorporated, II; 13 (upd.); 40 (upd.); 89 (upd.)
Caribou Coffee Company, Inc., 28; 97 (upd.)
Carlson Companies, Inc., 6; 22 (upd.); 87 (upd.)
Carlson Restaurants Worldwide, 69
Carr-Gottstein Foods Co., 17
Carrols Restaurant Group, Inc., 92
Casey's General Stores, Inc., 19; 83 (upd.)
Casino Guichard-Perrachon S.A., 59 (upd.)
CBRL Group, Inc., 35 (upd.); 86 (upd.)
CEC Entertainment, Inc., 31 (upd.)
Centerplate, Inc., 79
Chart House Enterprises, Inc., 17
Checkers Drive-In Restaurants, Inc., 16; 74 (upd.)
The Cheesecake Factory Inc., 17
Chi-Chi's Inc., 13; 51 (upd.)
Chicago Pizza & Brewery, Inc., 44
Chick-fil-A Inc., 23; 90 (upd.)
Chipotle Mexican Grill, Inc., 67
Church's Chicken, 66
Cinnabon Inc., 23; 90 (upd.)
The Circle K Corporation, II
CKE Restaurants, Inc., 19; 46 (upd.)
Coborn's, Inc., 30
The Coffee Beanery, Ltd., 95
Coffee Holding Co., Inc., 95
Cold Stone Creamery, 69
Coles Group Limited, V; 20 (upd.); 85 (upd.)
Compass Group PLC, 34
Comptoirs Modernes S.A., 19
Consolidated Products Inc., 14
Controladora Comercial Mexicana, S.A. de C.V., 36
Cooker Restaurant Corporation, 20; 51 (upd.)
The Copps Corporation, 32
Cosi, Inc., 53
Cost-U-Less, Inc., 51
Coto Centro Integral de Comercializacion S.A., 66
Country Kitchen International, Inc., 76
Cracker Barrel Old Country Store, Inc., 10
Cremonini S.p.A., 57
CulinArt, Inc., 92
Culver Franchising System, Inc., 58
D'Agostino Supermarkets Inc., 19
Dairy Mart Convenience Stores, Inc., 7; 25 (upd.)
Daniel Thwaites Plc, 95
Darden Restaurants, Inc., 16; 44 (upd.)
Dean & DeLuca, Inc., 36
Del Taco, Inc., 58
Delhaize "Le Lion" S.A., 44
DeMoulas / Market Basket Inc., 23
DenAmerica Corporation, 29
Denner AG, 88
Deschutes Brewery, Inc., 57
Diedrich Coffee, Inc., 40
Dierbergs Markets Inc., 63
Distribución y Servicio D&S S.A., 71
Doctor's Associates Inc., 67 (upd.)
Dominick's Finer Foods, Inc., 56
Domino's, Inc., 7; 21 (upd.); 63 (upd.)
Donatos Pizzeria Corporation, 58
E H Booth & Company Ltd., 90
Eateries, Inc., 33
Ed S.A.S., 88
Edeka Zentrale A.G., II; 47 (upd.)
Einstein/Noah Bagel Corporation, 29
El Chico Restaurants, Inc., 19
El Pollo Loco, Inc., 69
Elior SA, 49
Elmer's Restaurants, Inc., 42
Embers America Restaurants, 30
Etablissements Economiques du Casino Guichard, Perrachon et Cie, S.C.A., 12
Famous Brands Ltd., 86
Famous Dave's of America, Inc., 40
Farmer Jack Supermarkets 78
Fatburger Corporation, 64
Fazoli's Management, Inc., 27; 76 (upd.)
Fili Enterprises, Inc., 70
Fired Up, Inc., 82
5 & Diner Franchise Corporation, 72
Flagstar Companies, Inc., 10
Flanigan's Enterprises, Inc., 60
Fleming Companies, Inc., II
Food Circus Super Markets, Inc., 88
The Food Emporium, 64
Food Lion LLC, II; 15 (upd.); 66 (upd.)
Foodarama Supermarkets, Inc., 28
Foodmaker, Inc., 14
The Fred W. Albrecht Grocery Co., 13
Fresh Choice, Inc., 20
Fresh Enterprises, Inc., 66
Fresh Foods, Inc., 29
Friendly Ice Cream Corporation, 30; 72 (upd.)
Frisch's Restaurants, Inc., 35; 92 (upd.)
Fuller Smith & Turner P.L.C., 38
Furr's Restaurant Group, Inc., 53
Furr's Supermarkets, Inc., 28
Galardi Group, Inc., 72
Galaxy Investors, Inc., 97
Garden Fresh Restaurant Corporation, 31
Gate Gourmet International AG, 70
The Gateway Corporation Ltd., II
Genuardi's Family Markets, Inc., 35
George Weston Ltd., II; 36 (upd.); 88 (upd.)
Ghirardelli Chocolate Company, 30
Giant Eagle, Inc., 86
Giant Food LLC, II; 22 (upd.); 83 (upd.)
Godfather's Pizza Incorporated, 25
Golden Corral Corporation, 10; 66 (upd.)
Golden Krust Caribbean Bakery, Inc., 68
Golden State Foods Corporation, 32
The Golub Corporation, 26; 96 (upd.)
Gordon Biersch Brewery Restaurant Group, Inc., 93
Gordon Food Service Inc., 8; 39 (upd.)
The Grand Union Company, 7; 28 (upd.)
The Great Atlantic & Pacific Tea Company, Inc., II; 16 (upd.); 55 (upd.)
Greggs PLC, 65
Grill Concepts, Inc., 74
Gristede's Foods Inc., 31; 68 (upd.)
Ground Round, Inc., 21
Groupe Le Duff S.A., 84
Groupe Promodès S.A., 19
Grupo Corvi S.A. de C.V., 86
Guyenne et Gascogne, 23
H.E. Butt Grocery Company, 13; 32 (upd.); 85 (upd.)
Haggen Inc., 38
Hannaford Bros. Co., 12
Hard Rock Cafe International, Inc., 12
Harris Teeter Inc., 23; 72 (upd.)
Harry's Farmers Market Inc., 23
HDOS Enterprises, 72
Hickory Farms, Inc., 17
Holberg Industries, Inc., 36
Holland Burgerville USA, 44
Hooters of America, Inc., 18; 69 (upd.)
Hops Restaurant Bar and Brewery, 46
Hoss's Steak and Sea House Inc., 68
Host America Corporation, 79
Hotel Properties Ltd., 71
Houchens Industries Inc., 51
Hughes Markets, Inc., 22
Hungry Howie's Pizza and Subs, Inc., 25
Hy-Vee, Inc., 36
ICA AB, II
Iceland Group plc, 33
IHOP Corporation, 17; 58 (upd.)
Il Fornaio (America) Corporation, 27
In-N-Out Burger, 19
In-N-Out Burgers Inc., 74 (upd.)
Ingles Markets, Inc., 20
Inserra Supermarkets, 25
Inter Link Foods PLC, 61
International Dairy Queen, Inc., 10; 39 (upd.)
ITM Entreprises SA, 36
Ito-Yokado Co., Ltd., 42 (upd.)
Ivar's, Inc., 86
J Sainsbury plc, II; 13 (upd.); 38 (upd.); 95 (upd.)
J. Alexander's Corporation, 65
Jack in the Box Inc., 89 (upd.)
Jacmar Companies, 87
Jamba Juice Company, 47
James Original Coney Island Inc., 84
JD Wetherspoon plc, 30
Jean-Georges Enterprises L.L.C., 75
Jerónimo Martins SGPS S.A., 96
Jerry's Famous Deli Inc., 24
Jersey Mike's Franchise Systems, Inc., 83
Jitney-Jungle Stores of America, Inc., 27
John Lewis Partnership plc, 42 (upd.)
Johnny Rockets Group, Inc., 31; 76 (upd.)
KFC Corporation, 7; 21 (upd.); 89 (upd.)
King Kullen Grocery Co., Inc., 15
Koninklijke Ahold N.V. (Royal Ahold), II; 16 (upd.)
Koo Koo Roo, Inc., 25
The Kroger Co., II; 15 (upd.); 65 (upd.)
The Krystal Company, 33
Kwik Save Group plc, 11
La Madeleine French Bakery & Café, 33
Landry's Restaurants, Inc., 15; 65 (upd.)
The Laurel Pub Company Limited, 59
Laurus N.V., 65
LDB Corporation, 53
Leeann Chin, Inc., 30
Levy Restaurants L.P., 26

Little Caesar Enterprises, Inc., 7; 24 (upd.)
Loblaw Companies Limited, 43
Logan's Roadhouse, Inc., 29
Lone Star Steakhouse & Saloon, Inc., 51
Long John Silver's, 13; 57 (upd.)
Luby's, Inc., 17; 42 (upd.)
Lucky Stores, Inc., 27
Lund Food Holdings, Inc., 22
Madden's on Gull Lake, 52
MaggieMoo's International, 89
Maid-Rite Corporation, 62
Maines Paper & Food Service Inc., 71
Marble Slab Creamery, Inc., 87
Marco's Franchising LLC, 86
Marie Callender's Restaurant & Bakery, Inc., 28
Marsh Supermarkets, Inc., 17; 76 (upd.)
Matt Prentice Restaurant Group, 70
Maui Wowi, Inc., 85
Max & Erma's Restaurants Inc., 19
Mayfield Dairy Farms, Inc., 74
Mazzio's Corporation, 76
McAlister's Corporation, 66
McCormick & Schmick's Seafood Restaurants, Inc., 71
McDonald's Corporation, II; 7 (upd.); 26 (upd.); 63 (upd.)
Megafoods Stores Inc., 13
Meijer Incorporated, 7
The Melting Pot Restaurants, Inc., 74
Metcash Trading Ltd., 58
Métro Inc., 77
Metromedia Companies, 14
Mexican Restaurants, Inc., 41
The Middleby Corporation, 22
Minyard Food Stores, Inc., 33; 86 (upd.)
MITROPA AG, 37
Monterey Pasta Company, 58
Morrison Restaurants Inc., 11
Morton's Restaurant Group, Inc., 30; 88 (upd.)
Mr. Gatti's, LP, 87
Mrs. Fields' Original Cookies, Inc., 27
Musgrave Group Plc, 57
Myriad Restaurant Group, Inc., 87
Nash Finch Company, 8; 23 (upd.); 65 (upd.)
Nathan's Famous, Inc., 29
National Convenience Stores Incorporated, 7
New Seasons Market, 75
New World Restaurant Group, Inc., 44
New York Restaurant Group, Inc., 32
Noble Roman's Inc., 14
Noodles & Company, Inc., 55
NPC International, Inc., 40
O'Charley's Inc., 19; 60 (upd.)
Old Spaghetti Factory International Inc., 24
OOC Inc., 97
The Oshawa Group Limited, II
OSI Restaurant Partners, Inc., 88 (upd.)
Outback Steakhouse, Inc., 12; 34 (upd.)
P&C Foods Inc., 8
P.F. Chang's China Bistro, Inc., 37; 86 (upd.)
Pacific Coast Restaurants, Inc., 90
Palm Management Corporation, 71
Pancho's Mexican Buffet, Inc., 46
Panda Restaurant Group, Inc., 35; 97 (upd.)
Panera Bread Company, 44
Papa Gino's Holdings Corporation, Inc., 86
Papa John's International, Inc., 15; 71 (upd.)
Papa Murphy's International, Inc., 54
Pappas Restaurants, Inc., 76
Pathmark Stores, Inc., 23
Peapod, Inc., 30
Penn Traffic Company, 13
Performance Food Group Company, 31
Perkins Family Restaurants, L.P., 22
Peter Piper, Inc., 70
Petrossian Inc., 54
Phillips Foods, Inc., 63
Picard Surgeles, 76
Piccadilly Cafeterias, Inc., 19
Piggly Wiggly Southern, Inc., 13
Pizza Hut Inc., 7; 21 (upd.)
Planet Hollywood International, Inc., 18; 41 (upd.)
Players International, Inc., 22
Ponderosa Steakhouse, 15
Portillo's Restaurant Group, Inc., 71
Potbelly Sandwich Works, Inc., 83
Progressive Enterprises Ltd., 96
Provigo Inc., II; 51 (upd.)
Publix Super Markets Inc., 7; 31 (upd.)
Pueblo Xtra International, Inc., 47
Qdoba Restaurant Corporation, 93
Quality Dining, Inc., 18
Quality Food Centers, Inc., 17
The Quizno's Corporation, 42
Rainforest Café, Inc., 25; 88 (upd.)
Rally's, 25; 68 (upd.)
Ralphs Grocery Company, 35
Randall's Food Markets, Inc., 40
Rare Hospitality International Inc., 19
Raving Brands, Inc., 64
Red Robin Gourmet Burgers, Inc., 56
Regent Inns plc, 95
Restaurant Associates Corporation, 66
Restaurants Unlimited, Inc., 13
RFC Franchising LLC, 68
Richfood Holdings, Inc., 7
Richtree Inc., 63
The Riese Organization, 38
Riser Foods, Inc., 9
Roadhouse Grill, Inc., 22
Rock Bottom Restaurants, Inc., 25; 68 (upd.)
Roly Poly Franchise Systems LLC, 83
Romacorp, Inc., 58
Rosauers Supermarkets, Inc., 90
Roundy's Inc., 58 (upd.)
RTM Restaurant Group, 58
Rubio's Restaurants, Inc., 35
Ruby Tuesday, Inc., 18; 71 (upd.)
Ruth's Chris Steak House, 28; 88 (upd.)
Ryan's Restaurant Group, Inc., 15; 68 (upd.)
Safeway Inc., II; 24 (upd.); 50 (upd.); 85 (upd.)
Santa Barbara Restaurant Group, Inc., 37
Sapporo Holdings Limited, I; 13 (upd.); 36 (upd.); 97 (upd.)
Sbarro, Inc., 16; 64 (upd.)
Schlotzsky's, Inc., 36
Schultz Sav-O Stores, Inc., 21
The Schwan Food Company, 26 (upd.); 83 (upd.)
Seaway Food Town, Inc., 15
Second Harvest, 29
See's Candies, Inc., 30
Selecta AG, 97
Seneca Foods Corporation, 17
Service America Corp., 7
SFI Group plc, 51
Shaw's Supermarkets, Inc., 56
Shells Seafood Restaurants, Inc., 43
Shoney's, Inc., 7; 23 (upd.)
ShowBiz Pizza Time, Inc., 13
Skyline Chili, Inc., 62
Smart & Final, Inc., 16
Smith's Food & Drug Centers, Inc., 8; 57 (upd.)
Sobeys Inc., 80
Sodexho SA, 29; 91 (upd.)
Somerfield plc, 47 (upd.)
Sonic Corporation, 14; 37 (upd.)
The Southland Corporation, II; 7 (upd.)
Spaghetti Warehouse, Inc., 25
SPAR Handels AG, 35
Spartan Stores Inc., 8
Starbucks Corporation, 13; 34 (upd.); 77 (upd.)
Stater Bros. Holdings Inc., 64
The Steak n Shake Company, 41; 96 (upd.)
Steinberg Incorporated, II
Stew Leonard's, 56
The Stop & Shop Supermarket Company, II; 68 (upd.)
Subway, 32
Super Food Services, Inc., 15
Supermarkets General Holdings Corporation, II
Supervalu Inc., II; 18 (upd.); 50 (upd.)
SWH Corporation, 70
SYSCO Corporation, II; 24 (upd.); 75 (upd.)
Taco Bell Corporation, 7; 21 (upd.); 74 (upd.)
Taco Cabana, Inc., 23; 72 (upd.)
Taco John's International, Inc., 15; 63 (upd.)
Tchibo GmbH, 82
TelePizza S.A., 33
Tesco PLC, II
Texas Roadhouse, Inc., 69
Thomas & Howard Company, Inc., 90
Timber Lodge Steakhouse, Inc., 73
Tops Markets LLC, 60
Total Entertainment Restaurant Corporation, 46
Toupargel-Agrigel S.A., 76
Trader Joe's Company, 13; 50 (upd.)
Travel Ports of America, Inc., 17
Tree of Life, Inc., 29
Triarc Companies, Inc., 34 (upd.)
Tubby's, Inc., 53
Tully's Coffee Corporation, 51

Tumbleweed, Inc., 33; 80 (upd.)
TW Services, Inc., II
Ukrop's Super Market's, Inc., 39
Unified Grocers, Inc., 93
Unique Casual Restaurants, Inc., 27
United Dairy Farmers, Inc., 74
United Natural Foods, Inc., 32; 76 (upd.)
Uno Restaurant Holdings Corporation, 18; 70 (upd.)
Uwajimaya, Inc., 60
Vail Resorts, Inc., 43 (upd.)
VICORP Restaurants, Inc., 12; 48 (upd.)
Victory Refrigeration, Inc., 82
Village Super Market, Inc., 7
The Vons Companies, Incorporated, 7; 28 (upd.)
W. H. Braum, Inc., 80
Waffle House Inc., 14; 60 (upd.)
Wahoo's Fish Taco, 96
Wakefern Food Corporation, 33
Waldbaum, Inc., 19
Wall Street Deli, Inc., 33
Wawa Inc., 17; 78 (upd.)
Wegmans Food Markets, Inc., 9; 41 (upd.)
Weis Markets, Inc., 15
Wendy's International, Inc., 8; 23 (upd.); 47 (upd.)
The WesterN SizzliN Corporation, 60
Wetterau Incorporated, II
Whitbread PLC, I; 20 (upd.); 52 (upd.); 97 (upd.)
White Castle Management Company, 12; 36 (upd.); 85 (upd.)
White Rose, Inc., 24
Whittard of Chelsea Plc, 61
Whole Foods Market, Inc., 50 (upd.)
Wild Oats Markets, Inc., 19; 41 (upd.)
Winchell's Donut Houses Operating Company, L.P., 60
WinCo Foods Inc., 60
Winn-Dixie Stores, Inc., II; 21 (upd.); 59 (upd.)
Wm. Morrison Supermarkets PLC, 38
Wolfgang Puck Worldwide, Inc., 26, 70 (upd.)
Worldwide Restaurant Concepts, Inc., 47
Yoshinoya D & C Company Ltd., 88
Young & Co.'s Brewery, P.L.C., 38
Yucaipa Cos., 17
Yum! Brands Inc., 58
Zingerman's Community of Businesses, 68

Health & Personal Care Products

Abaxis, Inc., 83
Abbott Laboratories, I; 11 (upd.); 40 (upd.); 93 (upd.)
Accuray Incorporated, 95
Advanced Medical Optics, Inc., 79
Advanced Neuromodulation Systems, Inc., 73
Akorn, Inc., 32
ALARIS Medical Systems, Inc., 65
Alberto-Culver Company, 8; 36 (upd.); 91 (upd.)
Alco Health Services Corporation, III
Alès Groupe, 81
Allergan, Inc., 10; 30 (upd.); 77 (upd.)
American Oriental Bioengineering Inc., 93
American Safety Razor Company, 20
American Stores Company, 22 (upd.)
Amway Corporation, III; 13 (upd.)
AngioDynamics, Inc., 81
ArthroCare Corporation, 73
Artsana SpA, 92
Ascendia Brands, Inc., 97
Atkins Nutritionals, Inc., 58
Aveda Corporation, 24
Avon Products, Inc., III; 19 (upd.); 46 (upd.)
Bally Total Fitness Holding Corp., 25
Bare Escentuals, Inc., 91
Bausch & Lomb Inc., 7; 25 (upd.); 96 (upd.)
Baxter International Inc., I; 10 (upd.)
BeautiControl Cosmetics, Inc., 21
Becton, Dickinson & Company, I; 11 (upd.)
Beiersdorf AG, 29
Big B, Inc., 17
Bindley Western Industries, Inc., 9
Biolase Technology, Inc., 87
Biomet, Inc., 10; 93 (upd.)
Biosite Incorporated, 73
Block Drug Company, Inc., 8; 27 (upd.)
The Body Shop International plc, 53 (upd.)
Boiron S.A., 73
Bolton Group B.V., 86
The Boots Company PLC, 24 (upd.)
Boston Scientific Corporation, 77 (upd.)
Bristol-Myers Squibb Company, III; 9 (upd.)
Bronner Brothers Inc., 92
C.R. Bard Inc., 9
Candela Corporation, 48
Cantel Medical Corporation, 80
Cardinal Health, Inc., 18; 50 (upd.)
Carl Zeiss AG, III; 34 (upd.); 91 (upd.)
Carson, Inc., 31
Carter-Wallace, Inc., 8
Caswell-Massey Co. Ltd., 51
CCA Industries, Inc., 53
Chattem, Inc., 17; 88 (upd.)
Chesebrough-Pond's USA, Inc., 8
Chronimed Inc., 26
Church & Dwight Co., Inc., 68 (upd.)
Cintas Corporation, 51 (upd.)
The Clorox Company, III; 22 (upd.); 81 (upd.)
CNS, Inc., 20
Colgate-Palmolive Company, III; 14 (upd.); 35 (upd.)
Combe Inc., 72
Conair Corp., 17
CONMED Corporation, 87
Connetics Corporation, 70
Cordis Corp., 19
Cosmair, Inc., 8
Cosmolab Inc., 96
Coty, Inc., 36
Covidien Ltd., 91
Cybex International, Inc., 49
Cytyc Corporation, 69
Dade Behring Holdings Inc., 71
Dalli-Werke GmbH & Co. KG, 86
Datascope Corporation, 39
Del Laboratories, Inc., 28
Deltec, Inc., 56
Dentsply International Inc., 10
DEP Corporation, 20
DePuy, Inc., 30
DHB Industries Inc., 85
Diagnostic Products Corporation, 73
The Dial Corp., 23 (upd.)
Direct Focus, Inc., 47
Drackett Professional Products, 12
Drägerwerk AG, 83
E-Z-EM Inc., 89
Elizabeth Arden, Inc., 8; 40 (upd.)
Empi, Inc., 26
Enrich International, Inc., 33
The Estée Lauder Companies Inc., 9; 30 (upd.); 93 (upd.)
Ethicon, Inc., 23
Farouk Systems Inc. 78
Forest Laboratories, Inc., 11
Forever Living Products International Inc., 17
FoxHollow Technologies, Inc., 85
French Fragrances, Inc., 22
G&K Holding S.A., 95
Gambro AB, 49
General Nutrition Companies, Inc., 11; 29 (upd.)
Genzyme Corporation, 13; 77 (upd.)
GF Health Products, Inc., 82
The Gillette Company, III; 20 (upd.)
Given Imaging Ltd., 83
Groupe Yves Saint Laurent, 23
Grupo Omnilife S.A. de C.V., 88
Guerlain, 23
Guest Supply, Inc., 18
Guidant Corporation, 58
Guinot Paris S.A., 82
Hanger Orthopedic Group, Inc., 41
Helen of Troy Corporation, 18
Helene Curtis Industries, Inc., 8; 28 (upd.)
Henkel KGaA, III; 34 (upd.); 95 (upd.)
Henry Schein, Inc., 31; 70 (upd.)
Herbalife Ltd., 17; 41 (upd.); 92 (upd.)
Huntleigh Technology PLC, 77
Immucor, Inc., 81
Inamed Corporation, 79
Integra LifeSciences Holdings Corporation, 87
Integrated BioPharma, Inc., 83
Inter Parfums Inc., 35; 86 (upd.)
Intuitive Surgical, Inc., 79
Invacare Corporation, 11
IVAX Corporation, 11
IVC Industries, Inc., 45
The Jean Coutu Group (PJC) Inc., 46
John Paul Mitchell Systems, 24
Johnson & Johnson, III; 8 (upd.); 36 (upd.); 75 (upd.)
Kanebo, Ltd., 53
Kao Corporation, III; 79 (upd.)
Kendall International, Inc., 11
Kensey Nash Corporation, 71
Keys Fitness Products, LP, 83

Kimberly-Clark Corporation, III; 16 (upd.); 43 (upd.)
Kolmar Laboratories Group, 96
Kyowa Hakko Kogyo Co., Ltd., III
Kyphon Inc., 87
L'Oréal SA, III; 8 (upd.); 46 (upd.)
Laboratoires de Biologie Végétale Yves Rocher, 35
The Lamaur Corporation, 41
Lever Brothers Company, 9
Lion Corporation, III; 51 (upd.)
Lush Ltd., 93
Luxottica SpA, 17; 52 (upd.)
Mandom Corporation, 82
Mannatech Inc., 33
Mary Kay Inc., 9; 30 (upd.); 84 (upd.)
Matrix Essentials Inc., 90
Maxxim Medical Inc., 12
Medco Containment Services Inc., 9
MEDecision, Inc., 95
Medifast, Inc., 97
Medline Industries, Inc., 61
Medtronic, Inc., 8; 67 (upd.)
Melaleuca Inc., 31
The Mentholatum Company Inc., 32
Mentor Corporation, 26
Merck & Co., Inc., I; 11 (upd.); 34 (upd.); 95 (upd.)
Merit Medical Systems, Inc., 29
Merz Group, 81
Natura Cosméticos S.A., 75
Nature's Sunshine Products, Inc., 15
NBTY, Inc., 31
NeighborCare, Inc., 67 (upd.)
Neutrogena Corporation, 17
New Dana Perfumes Company, 37
Neways Inc. 78
Nikken Global Inc., 32
NutriSystem, Inc., 71
Nutrition for Life International Inc., 22
Nutrition 21 Inc., 97
Ocular Sciences, Inc., 65
OEC Medical Systems, Inc., 27
Obagi Medical Products, Inc., 95
OraSure Technologies, Inc., 75
Orion Oyj, 72
Patterson Dental Co., 19
Perrigo Company, 12
Pfizer Inc., 79 (upd.)
Physician Sales & Service, Inc., 14
Playtex Products, Inc., 15
PolyMedica Corporation, 77
The Procter & Gamble Company, III; 8 (upd.); 26 (upd.); 67 (upd.)
PZ Cussons plc, 72
Quidel Corporation, 80
Reckitt Benckiser plc, II; 42 (upd.); 91 (upd.)
Redken Laboratories Inc., 84
Reliv International, Inc., 58
Revlon Inc., III; 17 (upd.)
Roche Biomedical Laboratories, Inc., 11
S.C. Johnson & Son, Inc., III; 28 (upd.); 89 (upd.)
Safety 1st, Inc., 24
St. Jude Medical, Inc., 11; 43 (upd.); 97 (upd.)
Schering-Plough Corporation, 14 (upd.)
Sephora Holdings S.A., 82
Shaklee Corporation, 39 (upd.)
Shionogi & Co., Ltd., III
Shiseido Company, Limited, III; 22 (upd.); 81 (upd.)
Slim-Fast Foods Company, 18; 66 (upd.)
Smith & Nephew plc, 17
SmithKline Beecham PLC, III
Soft Sheen Products, Inc., 31
Sola International Inc., 71
Spacelabs Medical, Inc., 71
STAAR Surgical Company, 57
Straumann Holding AG, 79
Stryker Corporation, 79 (upd.)
Sunrise Medical Inc., 11
Syneron Medical Ltd., 91
Synthes, Inc., 93
Tambrands Inc., 8
Terumo Corporation, 48
Thane International, Inc., 84
Tom's of Maine, Inc., 45
Transitions Optical, Inc., 83
The Tranzonic Companies, 37
Turtle Wax, Inc., 15; 93 (upd.)
Tutogen Medical, Inc., 68
Unicharm Corporation, 84
United States Surgical Corporation, 10; 34 (upd.)
USANA, Inc., 29
Utah Medical Products, Inc., 36
Ventana Medical Systems, Inc., 75
VHA Inc., 53
VIASYS Healthcare, Inc., 52
Vion Food Group NV, 85
VISX, Incorporated, 30
Vitamin Shoppe Industries, Inc., 60
Water Pik Technologies, Inc., 34; 83 (upd.)
Weider Nutrition International, Inc., 29
Weleda AG 78
Wella AG, III; 48 (upd.)
West Pharmaceutical Services, Inc., 42
Wright Medical Group, Inc., 61
Wyeth, 50 (upd.)
Zila, Inc., 46
Zimmer Holdings, Inc., 45

Health Care Services

Acadian Ambulance & Air Med Services, Inc., 39
Adventist Health, 53
Advocat Inc., 46
Almost Family, Inc., 93
Alterra Healthcare Corporation, 42
Amedysis, Inc., 53
The American Cancer Society, 24
American Healthways, Inc., 65
American Lung Association, 48
American Medical Association, 39
American Medical International, Inc., III
American Medical Response, Inc., 39
American Red Cross, 40
AMERIGROUP Corporation, 69
AmeriSource Health Corporation, 37 (upd.)
AmSurg Corporation, 48
Applied Bioscience International, Inc., 10
Assisted Living Concepts, Inc., 43
ATC Healthcare Inc., 64
Baptist Health Care Corporation, 82
Beverly Enterprises, Inc., III; 16 (upd.)
Bon Secours Health System, Inc., 24
Brookdale Senior Living, 91
C.R. Bard, Inc., 65 (upd.)
Cancer Treatment Centers of America, Inc., 85
Capital Senior Living Corporation, 75
Caremark Rx, Inc., 10; 54 (upd.)
Catholic Health Initiatives, 91
Children's Comprehensive Services, Inc., 42
Children's Hospitals and Clinics, Inc., 54
Chronimed Inc., 26
COBE Laboratories, Inc., 13
Columbia/HCA Healthcare Corporation, 15
Community Health Systems, Inc., 71
Community Psychiatric Centers, 15
CompDent Corporation, 22
CompHealth Inc., 25
Comprehensive Care Corporation, 15
Continental Medical Systems, Inc., 10
Continuum Health Partners, Inc., 60
Coventry Health Care, Inc., 59
Cystic Fibrosis Foundation, 93
DaVita Inc., 73
Easter Seals, Inc., 58
Erickson Retirement Communities, 57
Express Scripts Incorporated, 17
Extendicare Health Services, Inc., 6
Eye Care Centers of America, Inc., 69
FHP International Corporation, 6
Fresenius AG, 56
Genesis Health Ventures, Inc., 18
Gentiva Health Services, Inc., 79
GranCare, Inc., 14
Group Health Cooperative, 41
Grupo Ángeles Servicios de Salud, S.A. de C.V., 84
Hamot Health Foundation, 91
Hazelden Foundation, 28
HCA - The Healthcare Company, 35 (upd.)
Health Care & Retirement Corporation, 22
Health Management Associates, Inc., 56
Health Risk Management, Inc., 24
Health Systems International, Inc., 11
HealthSouth Corporation, 14; 33 (upd.)
Henry Ford Health System, 84
Highmark Inc., 27
The Hillhaven Corporation, 14
Holiday Retirement Corp., 87
Hooper Holmes, Inc., 22
Hospital Central Services, Inc., 56
Hospital Corporation of America, III
Howard Hughes Medical Institute, 39
Humana Inc., III; 24 (upd.)
Intermountain Health Care, Inc., 27
Jenny Craig, Inc., 10; 29 (upd.); 92 (upd.)
Kinetic Concepts, Inc. (KCI), 20
LabOne, Inc., 48
Laboratory Corporation of America Holdings, 42 (upd.)
LCA-Vision, Inc., 85

Life Care Centers of America Inc., 76
Lifeline Systems, Inc., 53
LifePoint Hospitals, Inc., 69
Lincare Holdings Inc., 43
Manor Care, Inc., 6; 25 (upd.)
March of Dimes, 31
Marshfield Clinic Inc., 82
Matria Healthcare, Inc., 17
Maxicare Health Plans, Inc., III; 25 (upd.)
Mayo Foundation, 9; 34 (upd.)
McBride plc, 82
Médecins sans Frontières, 85
Medical Management International, Inc., 65
Medical Staffing Network Holdings, Inc., 89
Memorial Sloan-Kettering Cancer Center, 57
Merge Healthcare, 85
Merit Medical Systems, Inc., 29
MeritCare Health System, 88
Myriad Genetics, Inc., 95
National Health Laboratories Incorporated, 11
National Medical Enterprises, Inc., III
National Research Corporation, 87
New York City Health and Hospitals Corporation, 60
New York Health Care, Inc., 72
NewYork-Presbyterian Hospital, 59
NovaCare, Inc., 11
NSF International, 72
Operation Smile, Inc., 75
Option Care Inc., 48
Orthodontic Centers of America, Inc., 35
Oxford Health Plans, Inc., 16
PacifiCare Health Systems, Inc., 11
Palomar Medical Technologies, Inc., 22
Pediatric Services of America, Inc., 31
Pediatrix Medical Group, Inc., 61
PHP Healthcare Corporation, 22
PhyCor, Inc., 36
PolyMedica Corporation, 77
Primedex Health Systems, Inc., 25
Providence Health System, 90
The Providence Service Corporation, 64
Psychemedics Corporation, 89
Psychiatric Solutions, Inc., 68
Quest Diagnostics Inc., 26
Radiation Therapy Services, Inc., 85
Ramsay Youth Services, Inc., 41
Renal Care Group, Inc., 72
Res-Care, Inc., 29
Response Oncology, Inc., 27
Rural/Metro Corporation, 28
Sabratek Corporation, 29
St. Jude Medical, Inc., 11; 43 (upd.); 97 (upd.)
Salick Health Care, Inc., 53
The Scripps Research Institute, 76
Select Medical Corporation, 65
Shriners Hospitals for Children, 69
Sierra Health Services, Inc., 15
Smith & Nephew plc, 41 (upd.)
Special Olympics, Inc., 93
The Sports Club Company, 25
SSL International plc, 49
Stericycle Inc., 33
Sun Healthcare Group Inc., 25
Sunrise Senior Living, Inc., 81
Susan G. Komen Breast Cancer Foundation 78
SwedishAmerican Health System, 51
Tenet Healthcare Corporation, 55 (upd.)
Twinlab Corporation, 34
U.S. Healthcare, Inc., 6
U.S. Physical Therapy, Inc., 65
Unison HealthCare Corporation, 25
United HealthCare Corporation, 9
United Nations International Children's Emergency Fund (UNICEF), 58
United Way of America, 36
Universal Health Services, Inc., 6
Vanguard Health Systems Inc., 70
VCA Antech, Inc., 58
Vencor, Inc., 16
VISX, Incorporated, 30
Vivra, Inc., 18
Volunteers of America, Inc., 66
WellPoint Health Networks Inc., 25
World Vision International, Inc., 93
YWCA of the U.S.A., 45

Hotels

Accor S.A., 69 (upd.)
Amerihost Properties, Inc., 30
Ameristar Casinos, Inc., 69 (upd.)
Archon Corporation, 74 (upd.)
Aztar Corporation, 13; 71 (upd.)
Bass PLC, 38 (upd.)
Boca Resorts, Inc., 37
Boyd Gaming Corporation, 43
Boyne USA Resorts, 71
Bristol Hotel Company, 23
The Broadmoor Hotel, 30
Caesars World, Inc., 6
Candlewood Hotel Company, Inc., 41
Carlson Companies, Inc., 6; 22 (upd.); 87 (upd.)
Castle & Cooke, Inc., 20 (upd.)
Cedar Fair, L.P., 22
Cendant Corporation, 44 (upd.)
Choice Hotels International, Inc., 14; 83 (upd.)
Circus Circus Enterprises, Inc., 6
City Developments Limited, 89
Club Mediterranée S.A., 6; 21 (upd.); 91 (upd.)
Compagnia Italiana dei Jolly Hotels S.p.A., 71
Daniel Thwaites Plc, 95
Doubletree Corporation, 21
Extended Stay America, Inc., 41
Fairmont Hotels & Resorts Inc., 69
Fibreboard Corporation, 16
Four Seasons Hotels Inc., 9; 29 (upd.)
Fuller Smith & Turner P.L.C., 38
Gables Residential Trust, 49
Gaylord Entertainment Company, 11; 36 (upd.)
Global Hyatt Corporation, 75 (upd.)
Granada Group PLC, 24 (upd.)
Grand Casinos, Inc., 20
Grand Hotel Krasnapolsky N.V., 23
Great Wolf Resorts, Inc., 91
Grupo Posadas, S.A. de C.V., 57
Helmsley Enterprises, Inc., 9
Hilton Hotels Corporation, III; 19 (upd.); 49 (upd.); 62 (upd.)
Holiday Inns, Inc., III
Home Inns & Hotels Management Inc., 95
Hospitality Franchise Systems, Inc., 11
Hotel Properties Ltd., 71
Howard Johnson International, Inc., 17; 72 (upd.)
Hyatt Corporation, III; 16 (upd.)
ILX Resorts Incorporated, 65
Interstate Hotels & Resorts Inc., 58
ITT Sheraton Corporation, III
JD Wetherspoon plc, 30
John Q. Hammons Hotels, Inc., 24
Jumeirah Group, 83
Kerzner International Limited, 69 (upd.)
The La Quinta Companies, 11; 42 (upd.)
Ladbroke Group PLC, 21 (upd.)
Landry's Restaurants, Inc., 65 (upd.)
Las Vegas Sands, Inc., 50
Madden's on Gull Lake, 52
Mandalay Resort Group, 32 (upd.)
Manor Care, Inc., 25 (upd.)
The Marcus Corporation, 21
Marriott International, Inc., III; 21 (upd.); 83 (upd.)
McMenamins Pubs and Breweries, 65
Millennium & Copthorne Hotels plc, 71
Mirage Resorts, Incorporated, 6; 28 (upd.)
Monarch Casino & Resort, Inc., 65
Morgans Hotel Group Company, 80
Motel 6, 13; 56 (upd.)
MTR Gaming Group, Inc., 75
MWH Preservation Limited Partnership, 65
NH Hoteles S.A., 79
Omni Hotels Corp., 12
Paradores de Turismo de Espana S.A., 73
Park Corp., 22
Players International, Inc., 22
Preussag AG, 42 (upd.)
Prime Hospitality Corporation, 52
Promus Companies, Inc., 9
Real Turismo, S.A. de C.V., 50
Red Roof Inns, Inc., 18
Regent Inns plc, 95
Resorts International, Inc., 12
The Ritz-Carlton Hotel Company, L.L.C., 9; 29 (upd.); 71 (upd.)
Riviera Holdings Corporation, 75
Sandals Resorts International, 65
Santa Fe Gaming Corporation, 19
The SAS Group, 34 (upd.)
SFI Group plc, 51
Shangri-La Asia Ltd., 71
Showboat, Inc., 19
Sol Meliá S.A., 71
Sonesta International Hotels Corporation, 44
Starwood Hotels & Resorts Worldwide, Inc., 54
Sun International Hotels Limited, 26
Sunburst Hospitality Corporation, 26
Super 8 Motels, Inc., 83
Thistle Hotels PLC, 54
Trusthouse Forte PLC, III

Vail Resorts, Inc., 43 (upd.)
WestCoast Hospitality Corporation, 59
Westin Hotels and Resorts Worldwide, 9; 29 (upd.)
Whitbread PLC, I; 20 (upd.); 52 (upd.); 97 (upd.)
Young & Co.'s Brewery, P.L.C., 38

Information Technology

A.B. Watley Group Inc., 45
AccuWeather, Inc., 73
Acxiom Corporation, 35
Adaptec, Inc., 31
Adobe Systems Incorporated, 10; 33 (upd.)
Advanced Micro Devices, Inc., 6
Agence France-Presse, 34
Agilent Technologies Inc., 38; 93 (upd.)
Akamai Technologies, Inc., 71
Aldus Corporation, 10
Allen Systems Group, Inc., 59
AltaVista Company, 43
Altiris, Inc., 65
Amdahl Corporation, III; 14 (upd.); 40 (upd.)
Amdocs Ltd., 47
America Online, Inc., 10; 26 (upd.)
American Business Information, Inc., 18
American Management Systems, Inc., 11
American Software Inc., 25
AMICAS, Inc., 69
Amstrad PLC, III
Analex Corporation, 74
Analytic Sciences Corporation, 10
Analytical Surveys, Inc., 33
Anker BV, 53
Ansoft Corporation, 63
Anteon Corporation, 57
AOL Time Warner Inc., 57 (upd.)
Apollo Group, Inc., 24
Apple Computer, Inc., III; 6 (upd.); 77 (upd.)
aQuantive, Inc., 81
The Arbitron Company, 38
Ariba, Inc., 57
Asanté Technologies, Inc., 20
Ascential Software Corporation, 59
AsiaInfo Holdings, Inc., 43
ASK Group, Inc., 9
Ask Jeeves, Inc., 65
ASML Holding N.V., 50
The Associated Press, 73 (upd.)
AST Research Inc., 9
At Home Corporation, 43
AT&T Bell Laboratories, Inc., 13
AT&T Corporation, 29 (upd.)
AT&T Istel Ltd., 14
Atos Origin S.A., 69
Attachmate Corporation, 56
Autodesk, Inc., 10; 89 (upd.)
Autologic Information International, Inc., 20
Automatic Data Processing, Inc., III; 9 (upd.); 47 (upd.)
Autotote Corporation, 20
Avantium Technologies BV, 79
Avid Technology Inc., 38
Avocent Corporation, 65
Aydin Corp., 19
Baan Company, 25
Baidu.com Inc., 95
Baltimore Technologies Plc, 42
Bankrate, Inc., 83
Banyan Systems Inc., 25
Battelle Memorial Institute, Inc., 10
BBN Corp., 19
BEA Systems, Inc., 36
Bell and Howell Company, 9; 29 (upd.)
Bell Industries, Inc., 47
Billing Concepts, Inc., 26; 72 (upd.)
Blackbaud, Inc., 85
Blackboard Inc., 89
Blizzard Entertainment 78
Bloomberg L.P., 21
Blue Martini Software, Inc., 59
BMC Software, Inc., 55
Boole & Babbage, Inc., 25
Booz Allen & Hamilton Inc., 10
Borland International, Inc., 9
Bowne & Co., Inc., 23
Brite Voice Systems, Inc., 20
Broderbund Software, 13; 29 (upd.)
BTG, Inc., 45
Bull S.A., 43 (upd.)
Business Objects S.A., 25
C-Cube Microsystems, Inc., 37
CACI International Inc., 21; 72 (upd.)
Cadence Design Systems, Inc., 11
Caere Corporation, 20
Cahners Business Information, 43
CalComp Inc., 13
Cambridge Technology Partners, Inc., 36
Candle Corporation, 64
Canon Inc., III
Cap Gemini Ernst & Young, 37
Captaris, Inc., 89
CareerBuilder, Inc., 93
Caribiner International, Inc., 24
Catalina Marketing Corporation, 18
CDC Corporation, 71
CDW Computer Centers, Inc., 16
Cerner Corporation, 16
CheckFree Corporation, 81
Cheyenne Software, Inc., 12
CHIPS and Technologies, Inc., 9
Ciber, Inc., 18
Cincom Systems Inc., 15
Cirrus Logic, Incorporated, 11
Cisco-Linksys LLC, 86
Cisco Systems, Inc., 11; 77 (upd.)
Citizen Watch Co., Ltd., III; 21 (upd.); 81 (upd.)
Citrix Systems, Inc., 44
CMGI, Inc., 76
CNET Networks, Inc., 47
Cogent Communications Group, Inc., 55
Cognizant Technology Solutions Corporation, 59
Cognos Inc., 44
Commodore International Ltd., 7
Compagnie des Machines Bull S.A., III
Compaq Computer Corporation, III; 6 (upd.); 26 (upd.)
Complete Business Solutions, Inc., 31
CompuAdd Computer Corporation, 11
CompuCom Systems, Inc., 10
CompUSA, Inc., 35 (upd.)
CompuServe Interactive Services, Inc., 10; 27 (upd.)
Computer Associates International, Inc., 6; 49 (upd.)
Computer Data Systems, Inc., 14
Computer Sciences Corporation, 6
Computervision Corporation, 10
Compuware Corporation, 10; 30 (upd.); 66 (upd.)
Comshare Inc., 23
Conner Peripherals, Inc., 6
Control Data Corporation, III
Control Data Systems, Inc., 10
Corbis Corporation, 31
Corel Corporation, 15; 33 (upd.); 76 (upd.)
Corporate Software Inc., 9
CoStar Group, Inc., 73
craigslist, inc., 89
Cray Research, Inc., III
Credence Systems Corporation, 90
CSX Corporation, 79 (upd.)
CTG, Inc., 11
Ctrip.com International Ltd., 97
Cybermedia, Inc., 25
Dairyland Healthcare Solutions, 73
Dassault Systèmes S.A., 25
Data Broadcasting Corporation, 31
Data General Corporation, 8
Datapoint Corporation, 11
Dell Computer Corp., 9
Dendrite International, Inc., 70
Deutsche Börse AG, 59
Dialogic Corporation, 18
DiamondCluster International, Inc., 51
Digex, Inc., 46
Digital Equipment Corporation, III; 6 (upd.)
Digital River, Inc., 50
Digitas Inc., 81
Dimension Data Holdings PLC, 69
ditech.com, 93
Documentum, Inc., 46
The Dun & Bradstreet Corporation, IV; 19 (upd.)
Dun & Bradstreet Software Services Inc., 11
DynCorp, 45
E.piphany, Inc., 49
EarthLink, Inc., 36
eCollege.com, 85
ECS S.A, 12
EDGAR Online, Inc., 91
Edmark Corporation, 14; 41 (upd.)
Egghead Inc., 9
El Camino Resources International, Inc., 11
Electronic Arts Inc., 10; 85 (upd.)
Electronic Data Systems Corporation, III; 28 (upd.)
Electronics for Imaging, Inc., 43 (upd.)
EMC Corporation, 12; 46 (upd.)
Encore Computer Corporation, 13; 74 (upd.)
Environmental Systems Research Institute Inc. (ESRI), 62
EPAM Systems Inc., 96

Epic Systems Corporation, 62
EPIQ Systems, Inc., 56
Evans and Sutherland Computer Company 19, 78 (upd.)
Exabyte Corporation, 12
Experian Information Solutions Inc., 45
Facebook, Inc., 90
FactSet Research Systems Inc., 73
FASTWEB S.p.A., 83
F5 Networks, Inc., 72
First Financial Management Corporation, 11
Fiserv Inc., 11
FlightSafety International, Inc., 9
FORE Systems, Inc., 25
Franklin Electronic Publishers, Inc., 23
Franz Inc., 80
FTP Software, Inc., 20
Fujitsu Limited, III; 42 (upd.)
Fujitsu-ICL Systems Inc., 11
Future Now, Inc., 12
Gartner, Inc., 21; 94 (upd.)
Gateway, Inc., 10; 27 (upd.)
GEAC Computer Corporation Ltd., 43
Gericom AG, 47
Getronics NV, 39
GFI Informatique SA, 49
Global Imaging Systems, Inc., 73
Google, Inc., 50
Groupe Open, 74
GSI Commerce, Inc., 67
GT Interactive Software, 31
Guthy-Renker Corporation, 32
Handspring Inc., 49
Hewlett-Packard Company, III; 6 (upd.)
Hyperion Software Corporation, 22
Hyperion Solutions Corporation, 76
ICL plc, 6
Identix Inc., 44
IDX Systems Corporation, 64
IKON Office Solutions, Inc., 50
Imation Corporation, 20
Indus International Inc., 70
Infineon Technologies AG, 50
Information Access Company, 17
Information Builders, Inc., 22
Information Resources, Inc., 10
Informix Corporation, 10; 30 (upd.)
InfoSpace, Inc., 91
Infosys Technologies Ltd., 38
Ing. C. Olivetti & C., S.p.a., III
Inktomi Corporation, 45
Input/Output, Inc., 73
Inso Corporation, 26
Intel Corporation, 36 (upd.)
IntelliCorp, Inc., 45
Intelligent Electronics, Inc., 6
Interfax News Agency, 86
Intergraph Corporation, 6; 24 (upd.)
Intermix Media, Inc., 83
International Business Machines Corporation, III; 6 (upd.); 30 (upd.); 63 (upd.)
InterVideo, Inc., 85
Intrado Inc., 63
Intuit Inc., 14; 33 (upd.); 73 (upd.)
Iomega Corporation, 21
IONA Technologies plc, 43
i2 Technologies, Inc., 87
J.D. Edwards & Company, 14
Jack Henry and Associates, Inc., 17
Janus Capital Group Inc., 57
Jones Knowledge Group, Inc., 97
The Judge Group, Inc., 51
Juniper Networks, Inc., 43
Juno Online Services, Inc., 38
Jupitermedia Corporation, 75
Kana Software, Inc., 51
Keane, Inc., 56
Kenexa Corporation, 87
Kintera, Inc., 75
KLA Instruments Corporation, 11
Knight Ridder, Inc., 67 (upd.)
KnowledgeWare Inc., 31 (upd.)
Komag, Inc., 11
Kronos, Inc., 18
Kurzweil Technologies, Inc., 51
LaCie Group S.A., 76
Lam Research Corporation, 11
Landauer, Inc., 51
Lason, Inc., 31
Lawson Software, 38
The Learning Company Inc., 24
Learning Tree International Inc., 24
Legent Corporation, 10
LendingTree, LLC, 93
Levi, Ray & Shoup, Inc., 96
LEXIS-NEXIS Group, 33
LifeLock, Inc., 91
Logica plc, 14; 37 (upd.)
Logicon Inc., 20
Logitech International S.A., 28; 69 (upd.)
LoJack Corporation, 48
Lotus Development Corporation, 6; 25 (upd.)
The MacNeal-Schwendler Corporation, 25
Macromedia, Inc., 50
Madge Networks N.V., 26
Magma Design Automation Inc. 78
MAI Systems Corporation, 11
Manatron, Inc., 86
ManTech International Corporation, 97
MAPICS, Inc., 55
Maryville Data Systems Inc., 96
Match.com, LP, 87
The MathWorks, Inc., 80
Maxtor Corporation, 10
Mead Data Central, Inc., 10
Mecklermedia Corporation, 24
MEDecision, Inc., 95
Medical Information Technology Inc., 64
Mentor Graphics Corporation, 11
Mercury Interactive Corporation, 59
Merge Healthcare, 85
Merisel, Inc., 12
Metatec International, Inc., 47
Metro Information Services, Inc., 36
Micro Warehouse, Inc., 16
Micron Technology, Inc., 11; 29 (upd.)
Micros Systems, Inc., 18
Microsoft Corporation, 6; 27 (upd.); 63 (upd.)
MicroStrategy Incorporated, 87
Misys plc, 45; 46
MITRE Corporation, 26
MIVA, Inc., 83
Moldflow Corporation, 73
Morningstar Inc., 68
The Motley Fool, Inc., 40
National Research Corporation, 87
National Semiconductor Corporation, 6
National TechTeam, Inc., 41
National Weather Service, 91
Navarre Corporation, 24
NAVTEQ Corporation, 69
NCR Corporation, III; 6 (upd.); 30 (upd.); 90 (upd.)
Netezza Corporation, 69
NetIQ Corporation, 79
Netscape Communications Corporation, 15; 35 (upd.)
Network Appliance, Inc., 58
Network Associates, Inc., 25
Nextel Communications, Inc., 10
NFO Worldwide, Inc., 24
NICE Systems Ltd., 83
Nichols Research Corporation, 18
Nimbus CD International, Inc., 20
Nixdorf Computer AG, III
Noah Education Holdings Ltd., 97
Novell, Inc., 6; 23 (upd.)
NVIDIA Corporation, 54
Océ N.V., 24; 91 (upd.)
OCLC Online Computer Library Center, Inc., 96
Odetics Inc., 14
Onyx Software Corporation, 53
Open Text Corporation, 79
Openwave Systems Inc., 95
Opsware Inc., 49
Oracle Corporation, 6; 24 (upd.); 67 (upd.)
Orbitz, Inc., 61
Packard Bell Electronics, Inc., 13
Packeteer, Inc., 81
Parametric Technology Corp., 16
PC Connection, Inc., 37
Pegasus Solutions, Inc., 75
PeopleSoft Inc., 14; 33 (upd.)
Perot Systems Corporation, 29
Phillips International Inc. 78
Pitney Bowes Inc., III
PLATINUM Technology, Inc., 14
Policy Management Systems Corporation, 11
Policy Studies, Inc., 62
Portal Software, Inc., 47
Primark Corp., 13
The Princeton Review, Inc., 42
Printrak, A Motorola Company, 44
Printronix, Inc., 18
Prodigy Communications Corporation, 34
Programmer's Paradise, Inc., 81
Progress Software Corporation, 15
Psion PLC, 45
Quality Systems, Inc., 81
Quantum Corporation, 10; 62 (upd.)
Quark, Inc., 36
Quicken Loans, Inc., 93
Racal-Datacom Inc., 11
Razorfish, Inc., 37
RCM Technologies, Inc., 34
RealNetworks, Inc., 53
Red Hat, Inc., 45

Remedy Corporation, 58
Renaissance Learning Systems, Inc., 39
Reuters Group PLC, 22 (upd.); 63 (upd.)
The Reynolds and Reynolds Company, 50
Ricoh Company, Ltd., III
Rocky Mountain Chocolate Factory, Inc., 73
Rolta India Ltd., 90
RSA Security Inc., 46
RWD Technologies, Inc., 76
SABRE Group Holdings, Inc., 26
The Sage Group, 43
salesforce.com, Inc., 79
The Santa Cruz Operation, Inc., 38
SAP AG, 16; 43 (upd.)
SAS Institute Inc., 10; 78 (upd.)
Satyam Computer Services Ltd., 85
SBS Technologies, Inc., 25
SCB Computer Technology, Inc., 29
Schawk, Inc., 24
Scientific Learning Corporation, 95
The SCO Group Inc., 78
SDL PLC, 67
Seagate Technology, Inc., 8
Siebel Systems, Inc., 38
Sierra On-Line, Inc., 15; 41 (upd.)
SilverPlatter Information Inc., 23
SINA Corporation, 69
SkillSoft Public Limited Company, 81
SmartForce PLC, 43
Softbank Corp., 13; 38 (upd.); 77 (upd.)
Sonic Solutions, Inc., 81
SonicWALL, Inc., 87
Spark Networks, Inc., 91
Specialist Computer Holdings Ltd., 80
SPSS Inc., 64
SRA International, Inc., 77
Standard Microsystems Corporation, 11
STC PLC, III
Steria SA, 49
Sterling Software, Inc., 11
Storage Technology Corporation, 6
Stratus Computer, Inc., 10
Sun Microsystems, Inc., 7; 30 (upd.); 91 (upd.)
SunGard Data Systems Inc., 11
Sybase, Inc., 10; 27 (upd.)
Sykes Enterprises, Inc., 45
Symantec Corporation, 10; 82 (upd.)
Symbol Technologies, Inc., 15
Synchronoss Technologies, Inc., 95
SYNNEX Corporation, 73
Synopsys, Inc., 11; 69 (upd.)
Syntel, Inc., 92
System Software Associates, Inc., 10
Systems & Computer Technology Corp., 19
T-Online International AG, 61
TALX Corporation, 92
Tandem Computers, Inc., 6
TenFold Corporation, 35
Terra Lycos, Inc., 43
The Thomson Corporation, 34 (upd.); 77 (upd.)
ThoughtWorks Inc., 90
3Com Corporation, 11; 34 (upd.)
The 3DO Company, 43
TIBCO Software Inc., 79
Timberline Software Corporation, 15
TomTom N.V., 81
TradeStation Group, Inc., 83
Traffix, Inc., 61
Transaction Systems Architects, Inc., 29; 82 (upd.)
Transiciel SA, 48
Trend Micro Inc., 97
Triple P N.V., 26
Tripwire, Inc., 97
The TriZetto Group, Inc., 83
Tucows Inc. 78
Ubi Soft Entertainment S.A., 41
Unica Corporation, 77
Unilog SA, 42
Unisys Corporation, III; 6 (upd.); 36 (upd.)
United Business Media plc, 52 (upd.)
United Online, Inc., 71 (upd.)
United Press International, Inc., 73 (upd.)
UUNET, 38
VASCO Data Security International, Inc., 79
Verbatim Corporation, 14
Veridian Corporation, 54
VeriFone Holdings, Inc., 18; 76 (upd.)
Verint Systems Inc., 73
VeriSign, Inc., 47
Veritas Software Corporation, 45
Verity Inc., 68
Viasoft Inc., 27
Vital Images, Inc., 85
VMware, Inc., 90
Volt Information Sciences Inc., 26
Wanadoo S.A., 75
Wang Laboratories, Inc., III; 6 (upd.)
WebMD Corporation, 65
WebEx Communications, Inc., 81
West Group, 34 (upd.)
Westcon Group, Inc., 67
Western Digital Corporation, 25; 92 (upd.)
Wikimedia Foundation, Inc., 91
Wind River Systems, Inc., 37
Wipro Limited, 43
Witness Systems, Inc., 87
Wolters Kluwer NV, 33 (upd.)
WordPerfect Corporation, 10
Wyse Technology, Inc., 15
Xerox Corporation, III; 6 (upd.); 26 (upd.); 69 (upd.)
Xilinx, Inc., 16; 82 (upd.)
Yahoo! Inc., 27; 70 (upd.)
YouTube, Inc., 90
Zanett, Inc., 92
Zapata Corporation, 25
Ziff Davis Media Inc., 36 (upd.)
Zilog, Inc., 15

Insurance

AEGON N.V., III; 50 (upd.)
Aetna Inc., III; 21 (upd.); 63 (upd.)
AFLAC Incorporated, 10 (upd.); 38 (upd.)
Alexander & Alexander Services Inc., 10
Alfa Corporation, 60
Alleanza Assicurazioni S.p.A., 65
Alleghany Corporation, 10
Allianz AG, III; 15 (upd.); 57 (upd.)
Allmerica Financial Corporation, 63
The Allstate Corporation, 10; 27 (upd.)
AMB Generali Holding AG, 51
American Family Corporation, III
American Financial Group Inc., III; 48 (upd.)
American General Corporation, III; 10 (upd.); 46 (upd.)
American International Group, Inc., III; 15 (upd.); 47 (upd.)
American National Insurance Company, 8; 27 (upd.)
American Premier Underwriters, Inc., 10
American Re Corporation, 10; 35 (upd.)
N.V. AMEV, III
AOK-Bundesverband (Federation of the AOK) 78
Aon Corporation, III; 45 (upd.)
Arthur J. Gallagher & Co., 73
Assicurazioni Generali SpA, III; 15 (upd.)
Assurances Générales de France, 63
Assured Guaranty Ltd., 93
Atlantic American Corporation, 44
Aviva PLC, 50 (upd.)
Axa, III
AXA Colonia Konzern AG, 27; 49 (upd.)
B.A.T. Industries PLC, 22 (upd.)
Baldwin & Lyons, Inc., 51
Bâloise-Holding, 40
Benfield Greig Group plc, 53
Berkshire Hathaway Inc., III; 18 (upd.); 42 (upd.); 89 (upd.)
Blue Cross and Blue Shield Association, 10
British United Provident Association Limited (BUPAL), 79
Brown & Brown, Inc., 41
Business Men's Assurance Company of America, 14
Capital Holding Corporation, III
Catholic Order of Foresters, 24; 97 (upd.)
China Life Insurance Company Limited, 65
ChoicePoint Inc., 65
The Chubb Corporation, III; 14 (upd.); 37 (upd.)
CIGNA Corporation, III; 22 (upd.); 45 (upd.)
Cincinnati Financial Corporation, 16; 44 (upd.)
CNA Financial Corporation, III; 38 (upd.)
Commercial Union PLC, III
Connecticut Mutual Life Insurance Company, III
Conseco Inc., 10; 33 (upd.)
The Continental Corporation, III
Crawford & Company, 87
Debeka Krankenversicherungsverein auf Gegenseitigkeit, 72
The Doctors' Company, 55
Empire Blue Cross and Blue Shield, III
Enbridge Inc., 43
Endurance Specialty Holdings Ltd., 85
Engle Homes, Inc., 46

The Equitable Life Assurance Society of the United States Fireman's Fund Insurance Company, III
ERGO Versicherungsgruppe AG, 44
Erie Indemnity Company, 35
Fairfax Financial Holdings Limited, 57
Farm Family Holdings, Inc., 39
Farmers Insurance Group of Companies, 25
Federal Deposit Insurance Corporation, 93
Fidelity National Financial Inc., 54
The First American Corporation, 52
First Executive Corporation, III
Foundation Health Corporation, 12
Gainsco, Inc., 22
GEICO Corporation, 10; 40 (upd.)
General Accident PLC, III
General Re Corporation, III; 24 (upd.)
Gerling-Konzern Versicherungs-Beteiligungs-Aktiengesellschaft, 51
GraceKennedy Ltd., 92
Great-West Lifeco Inc., III
Groupama S.A., 76
Gryphon Holdings, Inc., 21
Guardian Financial Services, 64 (upd.)
Guardian Royal Exchange Plc, 11
Harleysville Group Inc., 37
HDI (Haftpflichtverband der Deutschen Industrie Versicherung auf Gegenseitigkeit V.a.G.), 53
HealthExtras, Inc., 75
HealthMarkets, Inc., 88 (upd.)
Hilb, Rogal & Hobbs Company, 77
The Home Insurance Company, III
Horace Mann Educators Corporation, 22; 90 (upd.)
Household International, Inc., 21 (upd.)
Hub International Limited, 89
HUK-Coburg, 58
Irish Life & Permanent Plc, 59
Jackson National Life Insurance Company, 8
Jefferson-Pilot Corporation, 11; 29 (upd.)
John Hancock Financial Services, Inc., III; 42 (upd.)
Johnson & Higgins, 14
Kaiser Foundation Health Plan, Inc., 53
Kemper Corporation, III; 15 (upd.)
LandAmerica Financial Group, Inc., 85
Legal & General Group plc, III; 24 (upd.)
The Liberty Corporation, 22
Liberty Mutual Holding Company, 59
LifeWise Health Plan of Oregon, Inc., 90
Lincoln National Corporation, III; 25 (upd.)
Lloyd's, 74 (upd.)
Lloyd's of London, III; 22 (upd.)
The Loewen Group Inc., 40 (upd.)
Lutheran Brotherhood, 31
Manulife Financial Corporation, 85
Marsh & McLennan Companies, Inc., III; 45 (upd.)
Massachusetts Mutual Life Insurance Company, III; 53 (upd.)
MBIA Inc., 73
The Meiji Mutual Life Insurance Company, III
Mercury General Corporation, 25
Metropolitan Life Insurance Company, III; 52 (upd.)
MGIC Investment Corp., 52
The Midland Company, 65
Millea Holdings Inc., 64 (upd.)
Mitsui Marine and Fire Insurance Company, Limited, III
Mitsui Mutual Life Insurance Company, III; 39 (upd.)
Modern Woodmen of America, 66
Munich Re (Münchener Rückversicherungs-Gesellschaft Aktiengesellschaft in München), III; 46 (upd.)
The Mutual Benefit Life Insurance Company, III
The Mutual Life Insurance Company of New York, III
National Medical Health Card Systems, Inc., 79
Nationale-Nederlanden N.V., III
The Navigators Group, Inc., 92
New England Mutual Life Insurance Company, III
New Jersey Manufacturers Insurance Company, 96
New York Life Insurance Company, III; 45 (upd.)
Nippon Life Insurance Company, III; 60 (upd.)
Northwestern Mutual Life Insurance Company, III; 45 (upd.)
NYMAGIC, Inc., 41
Ohio Casualty Corp., 11
Old Republic International Corporation, 11; 58 (upd.)
Oregon Dental Service Health Plan, Inc., 51
Palmer & Cay, Inc., 69
Pan-American Life Insurance Company, 48
PartnerRe Ltd., 83
The Paul Revere Corporation, 12
Pennsylvania Blue Shield, III
The PMI Group, Inc., 49
Preserver Group, Inc., 44
Principal Mutual Life Insurance Company, III
The Progressive Corporation, 11; 29 (upd.)
Provident Life and Accident Insurance Company of America, III
Prudential Financial Inc., III; 30 (upd.); 82 (upd.)
Prudential plc, III; 48 (upd.)
Radian Group Inc., 42
The Regence Group, 74
Reliance Group Holdings, Inc., III
Riunione Adriatica di Sicurtà SpA, III
Royal & Sun Alliance Insurance Group plc, 55 (upd.)
Royal Insurance Holdings PLC, III
SAFECO Corporaton, III
The St. Paul Travelers Companies, Inc. III; 22 (upd.); 79 (upd.)
SCOR S.A., 20
Skandia Insurance Company, Ltd., 50
StanCorp Financial Group, Inc., 56
The Standard Life Assurance Company, III
State Auto Financial Corporation, 77
State Farm Mutual Automobile Insurance Company, III; 51 (upd.)
State Financial Services Corporation, 51
Stewart Information Services Corporation 78
Sumitomo Life Insurance Company, III; 60 (upd.)
The Sumitomo Marine and Fire Insurance Company, Limited, III
Sun Alliance Group PLC, III
Sun Life Financial Inc., 85
SunAmerica Inc., 11
Suncorp-Metway Ltd., 91
Suramericana de Inversiones S.A., 88
Svenska Handelsbanken AB, 50 (upd.)
The Swett & Crawford Group Inc., 84
Swiss Reinsurance Company (Schweizerische Rückversicherungs-Gesellschaft), III; 46 (upd.)
Teachers Insurance and Annuity Association-College Retirement Equities Fund, III; 45 (upd.)
Texas Industries, Inc., 8
TIG Holdings, Inc., 26
The Tokio Marine and Fire Insurance Co., Ltd., III
Torchmark Corporation, 9; 33 (upd.)
Transatlantic Holdings, Inc., 11
The Travelers Corporation, III
UICI, 33
Union des Assurances de Pans, III
United National Group, Ltd., 63
Unitrin Inc., 16; 78 (upd.)
UNUM Corp., 13
UnumProvident Corporation, 52 (upd.)
USAA, 10
USF&G Corporation, III
Victoria Group, 44 (upd.)
VICTORIA Holding AG, III
Vision Service Plan Inc., 77
W.R. Berkley Corporation, 15; 74 (upd.)
Washington National Corporation, 12
The Wawanesa Mutual Insurance Company, 68
WellChoice, Inc., 67 (upd.)
Westfield Group, 69
White Mountains Insurance Group, Ltd., 48
Willis Corroon Group plc, 25
Winterthur Group, III; 68 (upd.)
The Yasuda Fire and Marine Insurance Company, Limited, III
The Yasuda Mutual Life Insurance Company, III; 39 (upd.)
Zurich Financial Services, 42 (upd.); 93 (upd.)
Zürich Versicherungs-Gesellschaft, III

Legal Services

Akin, Gump, Strauss, Hauer & Feld, L.L.P., 33
American Bar Association, 35

American Lawyer Media Holdings, Inc., 32
Amnesty International, 50
Andrews Kurth, LLP, 71
Arnold & Porter, 35
Baker & Daniels LLP, 88
Baker & Hostetler LLP, 40
Baker & McKenzie, 10; 42 (upd.)
Baker and Botts, L.L.P., 28
Bingham Dana LLP, 43
Brobeck, Phleger & Harrison, LLP, 31
Cadwalader, Wickersham & Taft, 32
Chadbourne & Parke, 36
Cleary, Gottlieb, Steen & Hamilton, 35
Clifford Chance LLP, 38
Coudert Brothers, 30
Covington & Burling, 40
CRA International, Inc., 93
Cravath, Swaine & Moore, 43
Davis Polk & Wardwell, 36
Debevoise & Plimpton, 39
Dechert, 43
Dewey Ballantine LLP, 48
Dorsey & Whitney LLP, 47
Drinker, Biddle and Reath L.L.P., 92
Faegre & Benson LLP, 97
Fenwick & West LLP, 34
Fish & Neave, 54
Foley & Lardner, 28
Fried, Frank, Harris, Shriver & Jacobson, 35
Fulbright & Jaworski L.L.P., 47
Gibson, Dunn & Crutcher LLP, 36
Greenberg Traurig, LLP, 65
Heller, Ehrman, White & McAuliffe, 41
Hildebrandt International, 29
Hogan & Hartson L.L.P., 44
Holland & Knight LLP, 60
Holme Roberts & Owen LLP, 28
Hughes Hubbard & Reed LLP, 44
Hunton & Williams, 35
Jenkens & Gilchrist, P.C., 65
Jones, Day, Reavis & Pogue, 33
Kelley Drye & Warren LLP, 40
King & Spalding, 23
Kirkland & Ellis LLP, 65
Latham & Watkins, 33
LeBoeuf, Lamb, Greene & MacRae, L.L.P., 29
LECG Corporation, 93
The Legal Aid Society, 48
Mayer, Brown, Rowe & Maw, 47
Milbank, Tweed, Hadley & McCloy, 27
Morgan, Lewis & Bockius LLP, 29
Morrison & Foerster LLP 78
O'Melveny & Myers, 37
Oppenheimer Wolff & Donnelly LLP, 71
Orrick, Herrington and Sutcliffe LLP, 76
Patton Boggs LLP, 71
Paul, Hastings, Janofsky & Walker LLP, 27
Paul, Weiss, Rifkind, Wharton & Garrison, 47
Pepper Hamilton LLP, 43
Perkins Coie LLP, 56
Pillsbury Madison & Sutro LLP, 29
Pre-Paid Legal Services, Inc., 20
Proskauer Rose LLP, 47
Robins, Kaplan, Miller & Ciresi L.L.P., 89
Ropes & Gray, 40
Saul Ewing LLP, 74
Seyfarth Shaw LLP, 93
Shearman & Sterling, 32
Sidley Austin Brown & Wood, 40
Simpson Thacher & Bartlett, 39
Skadden, Arps, Slate, Meagher & Flom, 18
Snell & Wilmer L.L.P., 28
Southern Poverty Law Center, Inc., 74
Stroock & Stroock & Lavan LLP, 40
Sullivan & Cromwell, 26
Troutman Sanders L.L.P., 79
Vinson & Elkins L.L.P., 30
Wachtell, Lipton, Rosen & Katz, 47
Weil, Gotshal & Manges LLP, 55
White & Case LLP, 35
Williams & Connolly LLP, 47
Willkie Farr & Gallagher LLP, 95
Wilson Sonsini Goodrich & Rosati, 34
Winston & Strawn, 35
Womble Carlyle Sandridge & Rice, PLLC, 52

Manufacturing

A-dec, Inc., 53
A. Schulman, Inc., 49 (upd.)
A.B.Dick Company, 28
A.O. Smith Corporation, 11; 40 (upd.); 93 (upd.)
A.T. Cross Company, 17; 49 (upd.)
A.W. Faber-Castell Unternehmensverwaltung GmbH & Co., 51
AAF-McQuay Incorporated, 26
Aalborg Industries A/S, 90
AAON, Inc., 22
AAR Corp., 28
Aarhus United A/S, 68
ABB Ltd., 65 (upd.)
ABC Rail Products Corporation, 18
Abiomed, Inc., 47
ACCO World Corporation, 7; 51 (upd.)
Accubuilt, Inc., 74
Acindar Industria Argentina de Aceros S.A., 87
Acme United Corporation, 70
Acme-Cleveland Corp., 13
Acorn Products, Inc., 55
Acuity Brands, Inc., 90
Acushnet Company, 64
Acuson Corporation, 36 (upd.)
Adams Golf, Inc., 37
Adolf Würth GmbH & Co. KG, 49
Advanced Circuits Inc., 67
Advanced Neuromodulation Systems, Inc., 73
AEP Industries, Inc., 36
AeroGrow International, Inc., 95
Aftermarket Technology Corp., 83
Ag-Chem Equipment Company, Inc., 17
Aga Foodservice Group PLC, 73
AGCO Corporation, 13; 67 (upd.)
Agfa Gevaert Group N.V., 59
Agrium Inc., 73
Ahlstrom Corporation, 53
Airgas, Inc., 54
Aisin Seiki Co., Ltd., III
AK Steel Holding Corporation, 41 (upd.)
AKG Acoustics GmbH, 62
Aktiebolaget Electrolux, 22 (upd.)
Aktiebolaget SKF, III; 38 (upd.); 89 (upd.)
Alamo Group Inc., 32
ALARIS Medical Systems, Inc., 65
Alberto-Culver Company, 8; 36 (upd.); 91 (upd.)
Aldila Inc., 46
Alfa Laval AB, III; 64 (upd.)
Allen Organ Company, 33
Allen-Edmonds Shoe Corporation, 61
Alliant Techsystems Inc., 8; 30 (upd.); 77 (upd.)
The Allied Defense Group, Inc., 65
Allied Healthcare Products, Inc., 24
Allied Products Corporation, 21
Allied Signal Engines, 9
AlliedSignal Inc., 22 (upd.)
Allison Gas Turbine Division, 9
Alltrista Corporation, 30
Alps Electric Co., Ltd., 44 (upd.)
Alticor Inc., 71 (upd.)
Aluar Aluminio Argentino S.A.I.C., 74
Alvis Plc, 47
Amer Group plc, 41
American Axle & Manufacturing Holdings, Inc., 67
American Biltrite Inc., 43 (upd.)
American Business Products, Inc., 20
American Cast Iron Pipe Company, 50
American Greetings Corporation, 59 (upd.)
American Homestar Corporation, 18; 41 (upd.)
American Locker Group Incorporated, 34
American Power Conversion Corporation, 67 (upd.)
American Seating Company 78
American Standard Companies Inc., 30 (upd.)
American Technical Ceramics Corp., 67
American Tourister, Inc., 16
American Woodmark Corporation, 31
Ameriwood Industries International Corp., 17
Amerock Corporation, 53
Ameron International Corporation, 67
AMETEK, Inc., 9
AMF Bowling, Inc., 40
Ampacet Corporation, 67
Ampco-Pittsburgh Corporation, 79
Ampex Corporation, 17
Amway Corporation, 30 (upd.)
Analogic Corporation, 23
Anchor Hocking Glassware, 13
Andersen Corporation, 10
The Andersons, Inc., 31
Andis Company, Inc., 85
Andreas Stihl AG & Co. KG, 16; 59 (upd.)
Andritz AG, 51
Ansell Ltd., 60 (upd.)
Anthem Electronics, Inc., 13
Apasco S.A. de C.V., 51
Apex Digital, Inc., 63

Applica Incorporated, 43 (upd.)
Applied Films Corporation, 48
Applied Materials, Inc., 10; 46 (upd.)
Applied Micro Circuits Corporation, 38
Applied Power Inc., 9; 32 (upd.)
AptarGroup, Inc., 69
ARBED S.A., 22 (upd.)
Arc International, 76
Arctco, Inc., 16
Arctic Cat Inc., 40 (upd.); 96 (upd.)
AREVA NP, 90 (upd.)
Ariens Company, 48
The Aristotle Corporation, 62
Armor All Products Corp., 16
Armstrong Holdings, Inc., III; 22 (upd.); 81 (upd.)
Arotech Corporation, 93
Artesyn Technologies Inc., 46 (upd.)
ArthroCare Corporation, 73
ArvinMeritor, Inc., 54 (upd.)
Asahi Glass Company, Ltd., 48 (upd.)
Ashley Furniture Industries, Inc., 35
ASICS Corporation, 57
ASML Holding N.V., 50
Astec Industries, Inc., 79
Astronics Corporation, 35
ASV, Inc., 34; 66 (upd.)
Atlantis Plastics, Inc., 85
Atlas Copco AB, III; 28 (upd.); 85 (upd.)
ATMI, Inc., 93
Atwood Mobil Products, 53
AU Optronics Corporation, 67
Aurora Casket Company, Inc., 56
Austal Limited, 75
Austin Powder Company, 76
Avedis Zildjian Co., 38
Avery Dennison Corporation, 17 (upd.); 49 (upd.)
Avocent Corporation, 65
Avondale Industries, 7; 41 (upd.)
AVX Corporation, 67
AZZ Incorporated, 93
B.J. Alan Co., Inc., 67
The Babcock & Wilcox Company, 82
Badger Meter, Inc., 22
BAE Systems Ship Repair, 73
Baker Hughes Incorporated, III
Babolat VS, S.A., 97
Baldor Electric Company, 21; 97 (upd.)
Baldwin Piano & Organ Company, 18
Baldwin Technology Company, Inc., 25
Balfour Beatty plc, 36 (upd.)
Ballantyne of Omaha, Inc., 27
Ballard Medical Products, 21
Ballard Power Systems Inc., 73
Bally Manufacturing Corporation, III
Baltek Corporation, 34
Baltimore Aircoil Company, Inc., 66
Bandai Co., Ltd., 55
Barmag AG, 39
Barnes Group Inc., 13; 69 (upd.)
Barry Callebaut AG, 29
Barry-Wehmiller Companies, Inc., 90
Bassett Furniture Industries, Inc., 18; 95 (upd.)
Bath Iron Works, 12; 36 (upd.)
Baxi Group Ltd., 96
Beckman Coulter, Inc., 22
Beckman Instruments, Inc., 14
Becton, Dickinson & Company, 36 (upd.)
Behr GmbH & Co. KG, 72
BEI Technologies, Inc., 65
Beiersdorf AG, 29
Bekaert S.A./N.V., 90
Bel Fuse, Inc., 53
Belden CDT Inc., 76 (upd.)
Belden Inc., 19
Bell Sports Corporation, 16; 44 (upd.)
Belleek Pottery Ltd., 71
Belleville Shoe Manufacturing Company, 92
Beloit Corporation, 14
Bemis Company, Inc., 8; 91 (upd.)
Bénéteau SA, 55
Benjamin Moore & Co., 13; 38 (upd.)
BenQ Corporation, 67
Berger Bros Company, 62
Bernina Holding AG, 47
Berry Plastics Corporation, 21
Berwick Offray, LLC, 70
Bianchi International (d/b/a Gregory Mountain Products), 76
BIC Corporation, 8; 23 (upd.)
BICC PLC, III
Billabong International Ltd., 44
The Bing Group, 60
Binks Sames Corporation, 21
Binney & Smith Inc., 25
bioMérieux S.A., 75
Biomet, Inc., 10; 93 (upd.)
Biosite Incorporated, 73
BISSELL Inc., 9; 30 (upd.)
The Black & Decker Corporation, III; 20 (upd.); 67 (upd.)
Black Diamond Equipment, Ltd., 62
Blodgett Holdings, Inc., 61 (upd.)
Blount International, Inc., 12; 48 (upd.)
Blue Nile Inc., 61
Blundstone Pty Ltd., 76
Blyth Industries, Inc., 18
Blyth, Inc., 74 (upd.)
BMC Industries, Inc., 17; 59 (upd.)
Bodum Design Group AG, 47
BÖHLER-UDDEHOLM AG, 73
Boise Cascade Holdings, L.L.C., IV; 8 (upd.); 32 (upd.); 95 (upd.)
Bombardier Inc., 42 (upd.); 87 (upd.)
Boral Limited, 43 (upd.)
Borden, Inc., 22 (upd.)
Borg-Warner Corporation, III
BorgWarner Inc., 14; 32 (upd.); 85 (upd.)
Boston Scientific Corporation, 37; 77 (upd.)
Bou-Matic, 62
The Boyds Collection, Ltd., 29
BPB plc, 83
Brach's Confections, Inc., 74 (upd.)
Brady Corporation 78 (upd.)
Brammer PLC, 77
Brannock Device Company, 48
Brass Eagle Inc., 34
Breeze-Eastern Corporation, 95
Bridgeport Machines, Inc., 17
Briggs & Stratton Corporation, 8; 27 (upd.)
BRIO AB, 24
British Vita plc, 33 (upd.)
Brose Fahrzeugteile GmbH & Company KG, 84
Brother Industries, Ltd., 14
Brown & Sharpe Manufacturing Co., 23
Brown Jordan International Inc., 74 (upd.)
Brown-Forman Corporation, 38 (upd.)
Broyhill Furniture Industries, Inc., 10
Brunswick Corporation, III; 22 (upd.); 77 (upd.)
BSH Bosch und Siemens Hausgeräte GmbH, 67
BTR Siebe plc, 27
Buck Knives Inc., 48
Buckeye Technologies, Inc., 42
Bucyrus International, Inc., 17
Bugle Boy Industries, Inc., 18
Building Materials Holding Corporation, 52
Bulgari S.p.A., 20
Bulova Corporation, 13; 41 (upd.)
Bundy Corporation, 17
Burelle S.A., 23
Burgett, Inc., 97
Burton Snowboards Inc., 22
Bush Boake Allen Inc., 30
Bush Industries, Inc., 20
Butler Manufacturing Company, 12; 62 (upd.)
C&J Clark International Ltd., 52
C. Bechstein Pianofortefabrik AG, 96
C.F. Martin & Co., Inc., 42
C.R. Bard, Inc., 65 (upd.)
C-Tech Industries Inc., 90
California Cedar Products Company, 58
California Steel Industries, Inc., 67
Callaway Golf Company, 15; 45 (upd.)
Campbell Scientific, Inc., 51
Cannondale Corporation, 21
Canon Inc., 79 (upd.)
Capstone Turbine Corporation, 75
Caradon plc, 20 (upd.)
The Carbide/Graphite Group, Inc., 40
Carbo PLC, 67 (upd.)
Carbone Lorraine S.A., 33
Cardo AB, 53
Cardone Industries Inc., 92
Carhartt, Inc., 77 (upd.)
Carl Zeiss AG, III; 34 (upd.); 91 (upd.)
Carma Laboratories, Inc., 60
Carpenter Technology Corporation, 13; 95 (upd.)
Carrier Corporation, 7; 69 (upd.)
Carter Holt Harvey Ltd., 70
Carver Boat Corporation LLC, 88
Carvin Corp., 89
Cascade Corporation, 65
Cascade General, Inc., 65
CASIO Computer Co., Ltd., III; 40 (upd.)
Catalina Lighting, Inc., 43 (upd.)
Caterpillar Inc., III; 15 (upd.); 63 (upd.)
Cavco Industries, Inc., 65
Cementos Argos S.A., 91
CEMEX S.A. de C.V., 59 (upd.)
Central Garden & Pet Company, 58 (upd.)

Central Sprinkler Corporation, 29
Centuri Corporation, 54
Century Aluminum Company, 52
Cenveo Inc., 71 (upd.)
Cepheid, 77
Ceradyne, Inc., 65
Cessna Aircraft Company, 27 (upd.)
Champion Enterprises, Inc., 17
Chanel SA, 12; 49 (upd.)
Chantiers Jeanneau S.A., 96
Charisma Brands LLC, 74
The Charles Machine Works, Inc., 64
Chart Industries, Inc., 21; 96 (upd.)
Chicago Bridge & Iron Company N.V., 82 (upd.)
Chittenden & Eastman Company, 58
Chris-Craft Corporation, 9, 31 (upd.); 80 (upd.)
Christian Dalloz SA, 40
Christofle SA, 40
Chromcraft Revington, Inc., 15
Cinemeccanica SpA 78
Ciments Français, 40
Cincinnati Lamb Inc., 72
Cincinnati Milacron Inc., 12
Cinram International, Inc., 43
Circon Corporation, 21
Cirrus Design Corporation, 44
Citizen Watch Co., Ltd., III; 21 (upd.); 81 (upd.)
CLARCOR Inc., 17; 61 (upd.)
Clark Equipment Company, 8
Clayton Homes Incorporated, 13; 54 (upd.)
The Clorox Company, III; 22 (upd.); 81 (upd.)
CNH Global N.V., 38 (upd.)
Coach, Inc., 45 (upd.)
Coachmen Industries, Inc., 77
COBE Cardiovascular, Inc., 61
Cobra Golf Inc., 16
Cochlear Ltd., 77
Cockerill Sambre Group, 26 (upd.)
Cognex Corporation, 76
Cohu, Inc., 32
Colas S.A., 31
The Coleman Company, Inc., 30 (upd.)
Colfax Corporation, 58
Collins & Aikman Corporation, 41 (upd.)
Collins Industries, Inc., 33
Color Kinetics Incorporated, 85
Colorado MEDtech, Inc., 48
Colt's Manufacturing Company, Inc., 12
Columbia Sportswear Company, 19
Columbus McKinnon Corporation, 37
CommScope, Inc., 77
Compagnie de Saint-Gobain, 64 (upd.)
Compass Minerals International, Inc., 79
CompuDyne Corporation, 51
Conair Corporation, 69 (upd.)
Concord Camera Corporation, 41
Congoleum Corp., 18
Conn-Selmer, Inc., 55
Conrad Industries, Inc., 58
Conso International Corporation, 29
Consorcio G Grupo Dina, S.A. de C.V., 36
Constar International Inc., 64
Controladora Mabe, S.A. de C.V., 82
Converse Inc., 9
Cooper Cameron Corporation, 58 (upd.)
The Cooper Companies, Inc., 39
Cooper Industries, Inc., 44 (upd.)
Cordis Corporation, 46 (upd.)
Corning, Inc., III; 44 (upd.); 90 (upd.)
Corrpro Companies, Inc., 20
Corticeira Amorim, Sociedade Gestora de Participaço es Sociais, S.A., 48
CPAC, Inc., 86
Crane Co., 8; 30 (upd.)
Cranium, Inc., 69
Creative Technology Ltd., 57
Creo Inc., 48
CRH plc, 64
Crosman Corporation, 62
Crown Equipment Corporation, 15; 93 (upd.)
CTB International Corporation, 43 (upd.)
Cuisinart Corporation, 24
Culligan Water Technologies, Inc., 12; 38 (upd.)
Cummins Engine Company, Inc., 40 (upd.)
CUNO Incorporated, 57
Curtiss-Wright Corporation, 10; 35 (upd.)
Custom Chrome, Inc., 74 (upd.)
Cutera, Inc., 84
Cutter & Buck Inc., 27
Cyberonics, Inc., 79
Cybex International, Inc., 49
Cymer, Inc., 77
Dade Behring Holdings Inc., 71
Daewoo Group, III
Daikin Industries, Ltd., III
Daisy Outdoor Products Inc., 58
Dalhoff Larsen & Horneman A/S, 96
Dalian Shide Group, 91
Danaher Corporation, 7; 77 (upd.)
Daniel Industries, Inc., 16
Daniel Measurement and Control, Inc., 74 (upd.)
Danisco A/S, 44
Day Runner, Inc., 41 (upd.)
DC Shoes, Inc., 60
DCN S.A., 75
De'Longhi S.p.A., 66
Dearborn Mid-West Conveyor Company, 56
Deceuninck N.V., 84
Decora Industries, Inc., 31
Decorator Industries Inc., 68
DeCrane Aircraft Holdings Inc., 36
Deere & Company, III; 42 (upd.)
Defiance, Inc., 22
Delachaux S.A., 76
Dell Inc., 63 (upd.)
Deluxe Corporation, 73 (upd.)
DEMCO, Inc., 60
Denby Group plc, 44
Denison International plc, 46
DENSO Corporation, 46 (upd.)
Department 56, Inc., 14
DePuy Inc., 37 (upd.)
Detroit Diesel Corporation, 10; 74 (upd.)
Deutsche Babcock A.G., III
Deutsche Steinzeug Cremer & Breuer Aktiengesellschaft, 91
Deutz AG, 39
Devro plc, 55
DHB Industries Inc., 85
Dial-A-Mattress Operating Corporation, 46
Diadora SpA, 86
Diebold, Incorporated, 7; 22 (upd.)
Diehl Stiftung & Co. KG, 79
Diesel SpA, 40
Dixon Industries, Inc., 26
Dixon Ticonderoga Company, 12; 69 (upd.)
Djarum PT, 62
DMI Furniture, Inc., 46
Domino Printing Sciences PLC, 87
Donaldson Company, Inc., 49 (upd.)
Donnelly Corporation, 12; 35 (upd.)
Dorel Industries Inc., 59
Dot Hill Systems Corp., 93
Douglas & Lomason Company, 16
Dover Corporation, III; 28 (upd.); 90 (upd.)
Dresser Industries, Inc., III
Drew Industries Inc., 28
Drexel Heritage Furnishings Inc., 12
Dril-Quip, Inc., 81
Drypers Corporation, 18
DTS, Inc., 80
Ducommun Incorporated, 30
Duncan Toys Company, 55
Dunn-Edwards Corporation, 56
Duracell International Inc., 9; 71 (upd.)
Durametallic, 21
Duriron Company Inc., 17
Dürkopp Adler AG, 65
Duron Inc., 72
Dürr AG, 44
Dynea, 68
Dyson Group PLC, 71
E-Z-EM Inc., 89
EADS SOCATA, 54
Eagle-Picher Industries, Inc., 8; 23 (upd.)
East Penn Manufacturing Co., Inc., 79
The Eastern Company, 48
Eastman Kodak Company, III; 7 (upd.); 36 (upd.); 91 (upd.)
Easton Sports, Inc., 66
Eaton Corporation, I; 10 (upd.); 67 (upd.)
Ebara Corporation, 83
ECC International Corp., 42
Ecolab Inc., I; 13 (upd.); 34 (upd.); 85 (upd.)
Eddie Bauer Holdings, Inc., 9; 36 (upd.); 87 (upd.)
EDO Corporation, 46
EG&G Incorporated, 29 (upd.)
Ekco Group, Inc., 16
Elamex, S.A. de C.V., 51
Elano Corporation, 14
Electric Boat Corporation, 86
Electrolux AB, III; 53 (upd.)
Eljer Industries, Inc., 24
Elkay Manufacturing Company, 73
Elscint Ltd., 20
Empire Resources, Inc., 81

Encompass Services Corporation, 33
Encore Computer Corporation, 13; 74 (upd.)
Encore Wire Corporation, 81
Energizer Holdings, Inc., 32
Energy Conversion Devices, Inc., 75
Enesco Corporation, 11
Engineered Support Systems, Inc., 59
English China Clays Ltd., 40 (upd.)
Ennis, Inc., 21; 97 (upd.)
Enodis plc, 68
EnPro Industries, Inc., 93
Entertainment Distribution Company, 89
Ernie Ball, Inc., 56
Escalade, Incorporated, 19
ESCO Technologies Inc., 87
Esselte, 64
Esselte Leitz GmbH & Co. KG, 48
Essilor International, 21
Esterline Technologies Corp., 15
Ethan Allen Interiors, Inc., 12; 39 (upd.)
The Eureka Company, 12
Everlast Worldwide Inc., 47
Excel Technology, Inc., 65
EXX Inc., 65
Fabbrica D' Armi Pietro Beretta S.p.A., 39
Facom S.A., 32
FAG—Kugelfischer Georg Schäfer AG, 62
Faiveley S.A., 39
Falcon Products, Inc., 33
Fannie May Confections Brands, Inc., 80
Fanuc Ltd., III; 17 (upd.); 75 (upd.)
Farah Incorporated, 24
Farmer Bros. Co., 52
FARO Technologies, Inc., 87
Fastenal Company, 42 (upd.)
Faultless Starch/Bon Ami Company, 55
Featherlite Inc., 28
Fedders Corporation, 18; 43 (upd.)
Federal Prison Industries, Inc., 34
Federal Signal Corp., 10
FEI Company, 79
Fellowes Manufacturing Company, 28
Fender Musical Instruments Company, 16; 43 (upd.)
Ferretti Group SpA, 90
Ferro Corporation, 56 (upd.)
Figgie International Inc., 7
Firearms Training Systems, Inc., 27
First Alert, Inc., 28
First Brands Corporation, 8
First International Computer, Inc., 56
First Solar, Inc., 95
The First Years Inc., 46
Fisher Controls International, LLC, 13; 61 (upd.)
Fisher Scientific International Inc., 24
Fisher-Price Inc., 12; 32 (upd.)
Fiskars Corporation, 33
Fisons plc, 9
Flanders Corporation, 65
Fleetwood Enterprises, Inc., III; 22 (upd.); 81 (upd.)
Flexsteel Industries Inc., 15; 41 (upd.)
Flextronics International Ltd., 38
Flint Ink Corporation, 41 (upd.)
FLIR Systems, Inc., 69
Florsheim Shoe Company, 9
Flour City International, Inc., 44
Flow International Corporation, 56
Flowserve Corporation, 33; 77 (upd.)
FLSmidth & Co. A/S, 72
Force Protection Inc., 95
Fort James Corporation, 22 (upd.)
Forward Industries, Inc., 86
FosterGrant, Inc., 60
Fountain Powerboats Industries, Inc., 28
Four Winns Boats LLC, 96
Foxboro Company, 13
Framatome SA, 19
Francotyp-Postalia Holding AG, 92
Frank J. Zamboni & Co., Inc., 34
Franke Holding AG, 76
Franklin Electric Company, Inc., 43
The Franklin Mint, 69
Freudenberg & Co., 41
Friedrich Grohe AG & Co. KG, 53
Frigidaire Home Products, 22
Frymaster Corporation, 27
FSI International, Inc., 17
Fuel Systems Solutions, Inc., 97
Fuel Tech, Inc., 85
Fuji Photo Film Co., Ltd., III; 18 (upd.); 79 (upd.)
Fujisawa Pharmaceutical Company, Ltd., 58 (upd.)
Fuqua Enterprises, Inc., 17
Furniture Brands International, Inc., 39 (upd.)
Furon Company, 28
The Furukawa Electric Co., Ltd., III
G. Leblanc Corporation, 55
G.S. Blodgett Corporation, 15
Gaming Partners International Corporation, 93
Gardner Denver, Inc., 49
The Gates Corporation, 9
GE Aircraft Engines, 9
GEA AG, 27
Geberit AG, 49
Gehl Company, 19
Gelita AG, 74
Gemini Sound Products Corporation, 58
Gemplus International S.A., 64
Gen-Probe Incorporated, 79
GenCorp Inc., 8; 9 (upd.)
General Atomics, 57
General Bearing Corporation, 45
General Binding Corporation, 73 (upd.)
General Cable Corporation, 40
General Dynamics Corporation, I; 10 (upd.); 40 (upd.); 88 (upd.
General Housewares Corporation, 16
Genmar Holdings, Inc., 45
geobra Brandstätter GmbH & Co. KG, 48
Georg Fischer AG Schaffhausen, 61
The George F. Cram Company, Inc., 55
Georgia Gulf Corporation, 61 (upd.)
Gerber Scientific, Inc., 12; 84 (upd.)
Gerresheimer Glas AG, 43
Getrag Corporate Group, 92
Gévelot S.A., 96
Giant Manufacturing Company, Ltd., 85
Giddings & Lewis, Inc., 10
Gildemeister AG, 79
The Gillette Company, 20 (upd.)
GKN plc, III; 38 (upd.); 89 (upd.)
Glaverbel Group, 80
Gleason Corporation, 24
Glen Dimplex 78
The Glidden Company, 8
Global Power Equipment Group Inc., 52
Glock Ges.m.b.H., 42
Goodman Holding Company, 42
Goodrich Corporation, 46 (upd.)
Goody Products, Inc., 12
The Gorman-Rupp Company, 18; 57 (upd.)
Goss Holdings, Inc., 43
Goulds Pumps Inc., 24
Graco Inc., 19; 67 (upd.)
Gradall Industries, Inc., 96
Graham Corporation, 62
Granite Industries of Vermont, Inc., 73
Grant Prideco, Inc., 57
Greatbatch Inc., 72
Greene, Tweed & Company, 55
Greif Inc., 66 (upd.)
Griffin Industries, Inc., 70
Griffon Corporation, 34
Grinnell Corp., 13
Groupe André, 17
Groupe Genoyer, 96
Groupe Guillin SA, 40
Groupe Herstal S.A., 58
Groupe Legis Industries, 23
Groupe SEB, 35
Grow Group Inc., 12
Groz-Beckert Group, 68
Grunau Company Inc., 90
Grundfos Group, 83
Grupo Cydsa, S.A. de C.V., 39
Grupo IMSA, S.A. de C.V., 44
Grupo Industrial Saltillo, S.A. de C.V., 54
Grupo Lladró S.A., 52
Guangzhou Pearl River Piano Group Ltd., 49
Guardian Industries Corp., 87
Gulf Island Fabrication, Inc., 44
Gund, Inc., 96
Gunite Corporation, 51
The Gunlocke Company, 23
Guy Degrenne SA, 44
H.B. Fuller Company, 8; 32 (upd.); 75 (upd.)
H.O. Penn Machinery Company, Inc., 96
Hach Co., 18
Hackman Oyj Adp, 44
Haeger Industries Inc., 88
Haemonetics Corporation, 20
Haier Group Corporation, 65
Halliburton Company, III
Hallmark Cards, Inc., IV; 16 (upd.); 40 (upd.); 87 (upd.)
Hammond Manufacturing Company Limited, 83
Hamon & Cie (International) S.A., 97
Hansgrohe AG, 56
Hanson PLC, 30 (upd.)
Hardinge Inc., 25
Harland and Wolff Holdings plc, 19
Harmon Industries, Inc., 25

Harnischfeger Industries, Inc., 8; 38 (upd.)
Harsco Corporation, 8
Hartmann Inc., 96
Hartmarx Corporation, 32 (upd.)
The Hartz Mountain Corporation, 46 (upd.)
Hasbro, Inc., III; 16 (upd.)
Haskel International, Inc., 59
Hastings Manufacturing Company, 56
Hawker Siddeley Group Public Limited Company, III
Haworth Inc., 8; 39 (upd.)
Head N.V., 55
Headwaters Incorporated, 56
Health O Meter Products Inc., 14
Heekin Can Inc., 13
HEICO Corporation, 30
Heidelberger Druckmaschinen AG, 40
Hella KGaA Hueck & Co., 66
Henkel Manco Inc., 22
The Henley Group, Inc., III
Heraeus Holding GmbH, 54 (upd.)
Herman Miller, Inc., 8; 77 (upd.)
Hermès International S.A., 34 (upd.)
Héroux-Devtek Inc., 69
Hexagon AB 78
High Tech Computer Corporation, 81
Hillenbrand Industries, Inc., 10; 75 (upd.)
Hillerich & Bradsby Company, Inc., 51
Hillsdown Holdings plc, 24 (upd.)
Hilti AG, 53
Hindustan Lever Limited, 79
Hitachi Zosen Corporation, III
Hitchiner Manufacturing Co., Inc., 23
HMI Industries, Inc., 17
HNI Corporation, 74 (upd.)
The Hockey Company, 70
The Holland Group, Inc., 82
Hollander Home Fashions Corp., 67
Holnam Inc., 8
Holson Burnes Group, Inc., 14
Home Products International, Inc., 55
HON INDUSTRIES Inc., 13
Hooker Furniture Corporation, 80
The Hoover Company, 12; 40 (upd.)
Horween Leather Company, 83
Hoshino Gakki Co. Ltd., 55
Host America Corporation, 79
Hubbell Inc., 76 (upd.)
Huffy Corporation, 7; 30 (upd.)
Huhtamäki Oyj, 64
Hummel International A/S, 68
Hunt Manufacturing Company, 12
Hunter Fan Company, 13
Huntleigh Technology PLC, 77
Hydril Company, 46
Hyster Company, 17
Hyundai Group, III; 7 (upd.); 56 (upd.)
IAC Group, 96
Icon Health & Fitness, Inc., 38
IDEO Inc., 65
IdraPrince, Inc., 76
Igloo Products Corp., 21
Illinois Tool Works Inc., III; 22 (upd.); 81 (upd.)
Illumina, Inc., 93
Imatra Steel Oy Ab, 55
IMI plc, 9
Imo Industries Inc., 7; 27 (upd.)
In-Sink-Erator, 66
Inchcape PLC, III; 16 (upd.); 50 (upd.)
Indel Inc. 78
Industrie Natuzzi S.p.A., 18
Infineon Technologies AG, 50
Ingalls Shipbuilding, Inc., 12
Ingersoll-Rand Company Ltd., III; 15 (upd.); 55 (upd.)
Insilco Corporation, 16
Insituform Technologies, Inc., 83
Interco Incorporated, III
Interface, Inc., 8
The Interlake Corporation, 8
INTERMET Corporation, 77 (upd.)
Internacional de Ceramica, S.A. de C.V., 53
International Controls Corporation, 10
International Flavors & Fragrances Inc., 38 (upd.)
International Game Technology, 10
Intevac, Inc., 92
Intuitive Surgical, Inc., 79
Invacare Corporation, 47 (upd.)
Invensys PLC, 50 (upd.)
Invivo Corporation, 52
Ionatron, Inc., 85
Ionics, Incorporated, 52
Ipsen International Inc., 72
iRobot Corporation, 83
Irwin Toy Limited, 14
Ishikawajima-Harima Heavy Industries Co., Ltd., III; 86 (upd.)
Itron, Inc., 64
J C Bamford Excavators Ltd., 83
J. D'Addario & Company, Inc., 48
J.I. Case Company, 10
J.M. Voith AG, 33
Jabil Circuit, Inc., 36; 88 (upd.)
Jacuzzi Brands Inc., 76 (upd.)
Jacuzzi Inc., 23
JAKKS Pacific, Inc., 52
James Avery Craftsman, Inc., 76
James Hardie Industries N.V., 56
James Purdey & Sons Limited, 87
JanSport, Inc., 70
Japan Tobacco Inc., 46 (upd.)
Jarden Corporation, 93 (upd.)
Jayco Inc., 13
Jeld-Wen, Inc., 45
Jenoptik AG, 33
Jervis B. Webb Company, 24
JLG Industries, Inc., 52
John Frieda Professional Hair Care Inc., 70
Johns Manville Corporation, 64 (upd.)
Johnson Controls, Inc., III; 26 (upd.); 59 (upd.)
Johnson Matthey PLC, 49 (upd.)
Johnson Outdoors Inc., 28; 84 (upd.)
Johnstown America Industries, Inc., 23
Jones Apparel Group, Inc., 11
Jostens, Inc., 7; 25 (upd.); 73 (upd.)
Jotun A/S, 80
JSP Corporation, 74
Julius Blüthner Pianofortefabrik GmbH 78
Jungheinrich AG, 96
K'Nex Industries, Inc., 52
Kaman Corporation, 12; 42 (upd.)
Kaman Music Corporation, 68
Kansai Paint Company Ltd., 80
Karsten Manufacturing Corporation, 51
Kasper A.S.L., Ltd., 40
Katy Industries, Inc., 51 (upd.)
Kawai Musical Instruments Mfg Co. Ltd. 78
Kawasaki Heavy Industries, Ltd., III; 63 (upd.)
Kaydon Corporation, 18
KB Toys, Inc., 35 (upd.); 86 (upd.)
Kelly-Moore Paint Company, Inc., 56
Kenmore Air Harbor Inc., 65
Kennametal Inc., 68 (upd.)
Keramik Holding AG Laufen, 51
Kerr Group Inc., 24
Kewaunee Scientific Corporation, 25
Key Safety Systems, Inc., 63
Key Tronic Corporation, 14
Keystone International, Inc., 11
KHD Konzern, III
KI, 57
Kimball International, Inc., 12; 48 (upd.)
Kit Manufacturing Co., 18
Klein Tools, Inc., 95
Knape & Vogt Manufacturing Company, 17
Knoll Group Inc., 14; 80 (upd.)
Knorr-Bremse AG, 84
Koala Corporation, 44
Kobe Steel, Ltd., IV; 19 (upd.)
Koch Enterprises, Inc., 29
Koenig & Bauer AG, 64
Kohler Company, 7; 32 (upd.)
Komatsu Ltd., III; 16 (upd.); 52 (upd.)
KONE Corporation, 27; 76 (upd.)
Konica Corporation, III; 30 (upd.)
Kyocera Corporation, 79 (upd.)
KraftMaid Cabinetry, Inc., 72
Kreisler Manufacturing Corporation, 97
KSB AG, 62
Kubota Corporation, III; 26 (upd.)
Kuhlman Corporation, 20
Kwang Yang Motor Company Ltd., 80
Kyocera Corporation, 21 (upd.)
L-3 Communications Holdings, Inc., 48
L. and J.G. Stickley, Inc., 50
L.A. Darling Company, 92
L.B. Foster Company, 33
L.S. Starrett Company, 64 (upd.)
La-Z-Boy Incorporated, 14; 50 (upd.)
LaCie Group S.A., 76
Lacks Enterprises Inc., 61
LADD Furniture, Inc., 12
Ladish Co., Inc., 30
Lafarge Cement UK, 28; 54 (upd.)
Lafuma S.A., 39
Lakeland Industries, Inc., 45
Lam Research Corporation, 31 (upd.)
The Lamson & Sessions Co., 13; 61 (upd.)
Lancer Corporation, 21
The Lane Co., Inc., 12
Laserscope, 67
LaSiDo Inc., 58

LeapFrog Enterprises, Inc., 54
Lear Corporation, 71 (upd.)
Leatherman Tool Group, Inc., 51
Leggett & Platt, Inc., 11; 48 (upd.)
Leica Camera AG, 35
Leica Microsystems Holdings GmbH, 35
Lennox International Inc., 8; 28 (upd.)
Lenox, Inc., 12
Leupold & Stevens, Inc., 52
Lexmark International, Inc., 18; 79 (upd.)
Liebherr-International AG, 64
Lifetime Brands, Inc., 73 (upd.)
Linamar Corporation, 18
Lincoln Electric Co., 13
Lindal Cedar Homes, Inc., 29
Lindsay Manufacturing Co., 20
Lipman Electronic Engineering Ltd., 81
Little Tikes Company, 13; 62 (upd.)
Loctite Corporation, 8
Logitech International S.A., 28; 69 (upd.)
The Longaberger Company, 12; 44 (upd.)
LOUD Technologies, Inc., 95 (upd.)
Louis Vuitton, 10
LSB Industries, Inc., 77
Lucas Industries PLC, III
Lufkin Industries Inc. 78
Luxottica SpA, 17; 52 (upd.)
Lydall, Inc., 64
Lynch Corporation, 43
M&F Worldwide Corp., 38
M.A. Bruder & Sons, Inc., 56
Mabuchi Motor Co. Ltd., 68
MacAndrews & Forbes Holdings Inc., 28; 86 (upd.)
Mace Security International, Inc., 57
MacGregor Golf Company, 68
Mackay Envelope Corporation, 45
Madeco S.A., 71
Madison-Kipp Corporation, 58
Mag Instrument, Inc., 67
Maidenform, Inc., 59 (upd.)
Mail-Well, Inc., 28
Makita Corporation, 22; 59 (upd.)
MAN Aktiengesellschaft, III
Manhattan Group, LLC , 80
Manitou BF S.A., 27
The Manitowoc Company, Inc., 18; 59 (upd.)
Mannesmann AG, III; 14 (upd.)
Marcolin S.p.A., 61
Margarete Steiff GmbH, 23
Marine Products Corporation, 75
Marisa Christina, Inc., 15
Mark IV Industries, Inc., 7; 28 (upd.)
Märklin Holding GmbH, 70
The Marmon Group, 16 (upd.)
Marshall Amplification plc, 62
Martin-Baker Aircraft Company Limited, 61
Martin Industries, Inc., 44
MartinLogan, Ltd., 85
Marvin Lumber & Cedar Company, 22
Mary Kay Inc., 9; 30 (upd.); 84 (upd.)
Masco Corporation, III; 20 (upd.); 39 (upd.)
Masonite International Corporation, 63
Master Lock Company, 45
MasterBrand Cabinets, Inc., 71
MasterCraft Boat Company, Inc., 90
Material Sciences Corporation, 63
Matsushita Electric Industrial Co., Ltd., 64 (upd.)
Mattel, Inc., 7; 25 (upd.); 61 (upd.)
Matth. Hohner AG, 53
Matthews International Corporation, 29; 77 (upd.)
Maverick Tube Corporation, 59
Maxco Inc., 17
Maxwell Shoe Company, Inc., 30
Maytag Corporation, III; 22 (upd.); 82 (upd.)
McClain Industries, Inc., 51
McDermott International, Inc., III
McKechnie plc, 34
McWane Corporation, 55
Meade Instruments Corporation, 41
Meadowcraft, Inc., 29
Measurement Specialties, Inc., 71
Mecalux S.A., 74
Medtronic, Inc., 67 (upd.)
Meggitt PLC, 34
Meidensha Corporation, 92
Meiji Seika Kaisha Ltd., 64 (upd.)
MEMC Electronic Materials, Inc., 81
Memry Corporation, 72
Menasha Corporation, 59 (upd.)
Merck & Co., Inc., I; 11 (upd.); 34 (upd.); 95 (upd.)
Mercury Marine Group, 68
Merillat Industries Inc., 13
Merillat Industries, LLC, 69 (upd.)
Mestek Inc., 10
Metso Corporation, 30 (upd.); 85 (upd.)
Mettler-Toledo International Inc., 30
Meyer International Holdings, Ltd., 87
MGA Entertainment, Inc., 95
Michael Anthony Jewelers, Inc., 24
Micrel, Incorporated, 77
Microdot Inc., 8
The Middleton Doll Company, 53
Midwest Grain Products, Inc., 49
Miele & Cie. KG, 56
Mikasa, Inc., 28
Mikohn Gaming Corporation, 39
Milacron, Inc., 53 (upd.)
Miller Industries, Inc., 26
Millipore Corporation, 25; 84 (upd.)
Milton Bradley Company, 21
Mine Safety Appliances Company, 31
Minebea Co., Ltd., 90
Minolta Co., Ltd., III; 18 (upd.); 43 (upd.)
Minuteman International Inc., 46
Misonix, Inc., 80
Mitsubishi Heavy Industries, Ltd., III; 7 (upd.)
Mity Enterprises, Inc., 38
Mobile Mini, Inc., 58
Mocon, Inc., 76
Modine Manufacturing Company, 8; 56 (upd.)
Modtech Holdings, Inc., 77
Moen Incorporated, 12
Mohawk Industries, Inc., 19; 63 (upd.)
Molex Incorporated, 11
The Monarch Cement Company, 72
Monnaie de Paris, 62
Monster Cable Products, Inc., 69
Montblanc International GmbH, 82
Montres Rolex S.A., 13; 34 (upd.)
Montupet S.A., 63
Moog Music, Inc., 75
The Morgan Crucible Company plc, 82
Morrow Equipment Co. L.L.C., 87
Motorcar Parts & Accessories, Inc., 47
Moulinex S.A., 22
Movado Group, Inc., 28
Mr. Coffee, Inc., 15
Mr. Gasket Inc., 15
Mueller Industries, Inc., 7; 52 (upd.)
Multi-Color Corporation, 53
Musco Lighting, 83
Nashua Corporation, 8
National Envelope Corporation, 32
National Gypsum Company, 10
National Oilwell, Inc., 54
National Picture & Frame Company, 24
National Semiconductor Corporation, 69 (upd.)
National Standard Co., 13
National Starch and Chemical Company, 49
Natrol, Inc., 49
Natural Alternatives International, Inc., 49
NCI Building Systems, Inc., 88
NCR Corporation, III; 6 (upd.); 30 (upd.); 90 (upd.)
Neenah Foundry Company, 68
Neopost S.A., 53
NETGEAR, Inc., 81
New Balance Athletic Shoe, Inc., 25
New Holland N.V., 22
Newcor, Inc., 40
Newell Rubbermaid Inc., 9; 52 (upd.)
Newport Corporation, 71
Newport News Shipbuilding Inc., 13; 38 (upd.)
Nexans SA, 54
NGK Insulators Ltd., 67
NHK Spring Co., Ltd., III
Nidec Corporation, 59
NIKE, Inc., 36 (upd.)
Nikon Corporation, III; 48 (upd.)
Nintendo Company, Ltd., III; 7 (upd.); 67 (upd.)
Nippon Electric Glass Co. Ltd., 95
Nippon Seiko K.K., III
Nippondenso Co., Ltd., III
NKK Corporation, 28 (upd.)
NOF Corporation, 72
NordicTrack, 22
Nordson Corporation, 11; 48 (upd.)
Nortek, Inc., 34
Norton Company, 8
Norton McNaughton, Inc., 27
Novellus Systems, Inc., 18
NSS Enterprises Inc. 78
NTN Corporation, III; 47 (upd.)
Nu-kote Holding, Inc., 18
O'Sullivan Industries Holdings, Inc., 34
Oak Industries Inc., 21
Oakley, Inc., 49 (upd.)
Oakwood Homes Corporation, 15
ODL, Inc., 55

The Ohio Art Company,14; 59 (upd.)
Oil-Dri Corporation of America, 20; 89 (upd.)
The Oilgear Company, 74
Okuma Holdings Inc., 74
Old Town Canoe Company, 74
180s, L.L.C., 64
Oneida Ltd., 7; 31 (upd.); 88 (upd.)
Optische Werke G. Rodenstock, 44
Orange Glo International, 53
Orbotech Ltd., 75
Orthofix International NV, 72
Osmonics, Inc., 18
Osram GmbH, 86
Otis Elevator Company, Inc., 13; 39 (upd.)
Otor S.A., 77
Outboard Marine Corporation, III; 20 (upd.)
Outdoor Research, Incorporated, 67
Overhead Door Corporation, 70
Owens Corning Corporation, 20 (upd.)
Owosso Corporation, 29
P & F Industries, Inc., 45
Pacer Technology, 40
Pacific Coast Feather Company, 67
Pacific Dunlop Limited, 10
Pagnossin S.p.A., 73
Pall Corporation, 9; 72 (upd.)
Palm Harbor Homes, Inc., 39
Paloma Industries Ltd., 71
Panavision Inc., 24
Park Corp., 22
Park-Ohio Holdings Corp., 17; 85 (upd.)
Parker-Hannifin Corporation, III; 24 (upd.)
Parlex Corporation, 61
Patrick Industries, Inc., 30
Paul Mueller Company, 65
Pearl Corporation 78
Pechiney SA, IV; 45 (upd.)
Peg Perego SpA, 88
Pelican Products, Inc., 86
Pelikan Holding AG, 92
Pella Corporation, 12; 39 (upd.); 89 (upd.)
Penn Engineering & Manufacturing Corp., 28
Pentair, Inc., 7; 26 (upd.); 81 (upd.)
Pentax Corporation 78
Pentech International, Inc., 29
PerkinElmer Inc. 7; 78 (upd.)
Peterson American Corporation, 55
Phillips-Van Heusen Corporation, 24
Phoenix AG, 68
Phoenix Mecano AG, 61
Photo-Me International Plc, 83
Physio-Control International Corp., 18
Picanol N.V., 96
Pilkington Group Limited, III; 34 (upd.); 87 (upd.)
Pilot Pen Corporation of America, 82
Pinguely-Haulotte SA, 51
Pioneer Electronic Corporation, III
Pirelli & C. S.p.A., 75 (upd.)
Piscines Desjoyaux S.A., 84
Pitney Bowes, Inc., 19
Pittway Corporation, 33 (upd.)
Planar Systems, Inc., 61
PlayCore, Inc., 27
Playmates Toys, 23
Playskool, Inc., 25
Pleasant Company, 27
Ply Gem Industries Inc., 12
Pochet SA, 55
Polaris Industries Inc., 12; 35 (upd.); 77 (upd.)
Polaroid Corporation, III; 7 (upd.); 28 (upd.); 93 (upd.)
The Porcelain and Fine China Companies Ltd., 69
Portmeirion Group plc, 88
Pou Chen Corporation, 81
PPG Industries, Inc., III; 22 (upd.); 81 (upd.)
Prada Holding B.V., 45
Pranda Jewelry plc, 70
Praxair, Inc., 48 (upd.)
Precision Castparts Corp., 15
Premark International, Inc., III
Pressman Toy Corporation, 56
Presstek, Inc., 33
Price Pfister, Inc., 70
Prince Sports Group, Inc., 15
Printpack, Inc., 68
Printronix, Inc., 18
Puig Beauty and Fashion Group S.L., 60
Pulaski Furniture Corporation, 33; 80 (upd.)
Pumpkin Masters, Inc., 48
Punch International N.V., 66
Pure World, Inc., 72
Puritan-Bennett Corporation, 13
Purolator Products Company, 21; 74 (upd.)
PVC Container Corporation, 67
PW Eagle, Inc., 48
Q.E.P. Co., Inc., 65
QRS Music Technologies, Inc., 95
QSC Audio Products, Inc., 56
Quixote Corporation, 15
R. Griggs Group Limited, 23
Racing Champions Corporation, 37
Radio Flyer Inc., 34
Rain Bird Corporation, 84
Raleigh UK Ltd., 65
Rapala-Normark Group, Ltd., 30
RathGibson Inc., 90
Raven Industries, Inc., 33
Raychem Corporation, 8
Rayovac Corporation, 39 (upd.)
Raytech Corporation, 61
Recovery Engineering, Inc., 25
Red Spot Paint & Varnish Company, 55
Red Wing Pottery Sales, Inc., 52
Red Wing Shoe Company, Inc., 9; 30 (upd.); 83 (upd.)
Reed & Barton Corporation, 67
Regal-Beloit Corporation, 18; 97 (upd.)
Reichhold Chemicals, Inc., 10
Remington Arms Company, Inc., 12; 40 (upd.)
Remington Products Company, L.L.C., 42
RENK AG, 37
Renner Herrmann S.A., 79
Revell-Monogram Inc., 16
Revere Ware Corporation, 22
Revlon Inc., 64 (upd.)
Rexam PLC, 32 (upd.); 85 (upd.)
Rexnord Corporation, 21; 76 (upd.)
RF Micro Devices, Inc., 43
Rheinmetall AG, 9; 97 (upd.)
RHI AG, 53
Richardson Industries, Inc., 62
Rickenbacker International Corp., 91
Riddell Sports Inc., 22
Rieter Holding AG, 42
River Oaks Furniture, Inc., 43
Riviera Tool Company, 89
RMC Group p.l.c., 34 (upd.)
Roadmaster Industries, Inc., 16
Robbins & Myers Inc., 15
Robertson-Ceco Corporation, 19
Rock-Tenn Company, 59 (upd.)
Rockford Products Corporation, 55
RockShox, Inc., 26
Rockwell Automation, I; 11 (upd.); 43 (upd.)
Rockwell Medical Technologies, Inc., 88
Rodriguez Group S.A., 90
ROFIN-SINAR Technologies Inc., 81
Rogers Corporation, 61
Rohde & Schwarz GmbH & Co. KG, 39
Rohm and Haas Company, 77 (upd.)
ROHN Industries, Inc., 22
Rohr Incorporated, 9
Roland Corporation, 38
Rollerblade, Inc., 15; 34 (upd.)
Rolls-Royce Group PLC, 67 (upd.)
Ronson PLC, 49
Roper Industries, Inc., 15; 50 (upd.)
Rose Art Industries, 58
Roseburg Forest Products Company, 58
Rotork plc, 46
Royal Appliance Manufacturing Company, 15
Royal Canin S.A., 39
Royal Doulton plc, 14; 38 (upd.)
Royal Group Technologies Limited, 73
RPC Group PLC, 81
RPM International Inc., 8; 36 (upd.); 91 (upd.)
RTI Biologics, Inc., 96
Rubbermaid Incorporated, III
Russ Berrie and Company, Inc., 12; 82 (upd.)
Rusty, Inc., 95
S.C. Johnson & Son, Inc., III; 28 (upd.); 89 (upd.)
Sabaté Diosos SA, 48
Safe Flight Instrument Corporation, 71
Safeskin Corporation, 18
Safety Components International, Inc., 63
Safilo SpA, 54
St. Jude Medical, Inc., 11; 43 (upd.); 97 (upd.)
Salant Corporation, 12; 51 (upd.)
Salton, Inc., 30; 88 (upd.)
Samick Musical Instruments Co., Ltd., 56
Samsonite Corporation, 13; 43 (upd.)
Samuel Cabot Inc., 53
Sandvik AB, 32 (upd.); 77 (upd.)
Sanford L.P., 82
Sanitec Corporation, 51

SANLUIS Corporación, S.A.B. de C.V., 95
Sanrio Company, Ltd., 38
SANYO Electric Co., Ltd., II; 36 (upd.); 95 (upd.)
Sapa AB, 84
Sauder Woodworking Company, 12; 35 (upd.)
Sauer-Danfoss Inc., 61
Sawtek Inc., 43 (upd.)
Schindler Holding AG, 29
Schlage Lock Company, 82
Schlumberger Limited, III
School-Tech, Inc., 62
Schott Corporation, 53
Scotsman Industries, Inc., 20
Scott Fetzer Company, 12; 80 (upd.)
The Scotts Company, 22
Scovill Fasteners Inc., 24
Sea Ray Boats Inc., 96
SeaChange International, Inc., 79
Sealed Air Corporation, 14; 57 (upd.)
Sealy Inc., 12
Seattle Lighting Fixture Company, 92
Segway LLC, 48
Seiko Corporation, III; 17 (upd.); 72 (upd.)
Select Comfort Corporation, 34
Selee Corporation, 88
The Selmer Company, Inc., 19
Semitool, Inc., 18
Sequa Corp., 13
Serta, Inc., 28
Severstal Joint Stock Company, 65
Shakespeare Company, 22
Shanghai Baosteel Group Corporation, 71
The Shaw Group, Inc., 50
Sheaffer Pen Corporation, 82
Shelby Williams Industries, Inc., 14
Shermag, Inc., 93
The Sherwin-Williams Company, III; 13 (upd.); 89 (upd.)
Sherwood Brands, Inc., 53
Shimano Inc., 64
Shorewood Packaging Corporation, 28
Shuffle Master Inc., 51
Shurgard Storage Centers, Inc., 52
SIFCO Industries, Inc., 41
Siliconware Precision Industries Ltd., 73
Simmons Company, 47
Simplicity Manufacturing, Inc., 64
Simula, Inc., 41
The Singer Company N.V., 30 (upd.)
The Singing Machine Company, Inc., 60
Skeeter Products Inc., 96
Skis Rossignol S.A., 15; 43 (upd.)
Skyline Corporation, 30
SL Industries, Inc., 77
SLI, Inc., 48
Smead Manufacturing Co., 17
Smith & Wesson Corp., 30; 73 (upd.)
Smith Corona Corp., 13
Smith International, Inc., 15
Smith-Midland Corporation, 56
Smiths Industries PLC, 25
Smoby International SA, 56
Snap-On, Incorporated, 7; 27 (upd.)
Société BIC S.A., 73
Sola International Inc., 71
Sonic Innovations Inc., 56
Sonoco Products Company, 8; 89 (upd.)
SonoSite, Inc., 56
Spacelabs Medical, Inc., 71
Sparton Corporation, 18
Spear & Jackson, Inc., 73
Specialized Bicycle Components Inc., 50
Specialty Equipment Companies, Inc., 25
Specialty Products & Insulation Co., 59
Spectrum Control, Inc., 67
Speidel Inc., 96
Speizman Industries, Inc., 44
Spin Master, Ltd., 61
Spirax-Sarco Engineering plc, 59
SPS Technologies, Inc., 30
SPX Corporation, 47 (upd.)
SRAM Corporation, 65
SRC Holdings Corporation, 67
Stanadyne Automotive Corporation, 37
The Standard Register Company, 15; 93 (upd.)
Standex International Corporation, 17
Stanley Furniture Company, Inc., 34
The Stanley Works, III; 20 (upd.); 79 (upd.)
Starcraft Corporation, 66 (upd.)
Stearns, Inc., 43
Steel Authority of India Ltd., 66 (upd.)
Steel Dynamics, Inc., 52
Steel Technologies Inc., 63
Steelcase, Inc., 7; 27 (upd.)
Steinway Musical Properties, Inc., 19
Stelco Inc., 51 (upd.)
The Stephan Company, 60
Sterilite Corporation, 97
Stewart & Stevenson Services Inc., 11
STMicroelectronics NV, 52
Stratasys, Inc., 67
Strattec Security Corporation, 73
Straumann Holding AG, 79
Strombecker Corporation, 60
Stryker Corporation, 11; 29 (upd.); 79 (upd.)
Sturm, Ruger & Company, Inc., 19
Sub-Zero Freezer Co., Inc., 31
Sudbury Inc., 16
Sulzer Brothers Limited (Gebruder Sulzer Aktiengesellschaft), III
Sumitomo Heavy Industries, Ltd., III; 42 (upd.)
Sun Hydraulics Corporation, 74
Sunburst Shutter Corporation 78
Superior Essex Inc., 80
Susquehanna Pfaltzgraff Company, 8
Swank, Inc., 17; 84 (upd.)
Swarovski International Holding AG, 40
The Swatch Group SA, 26
Swedish Match AB, 12; 39 (upd.); 92 (upd.)
Sweetheart Cup Company, Inc., 36
Sybron International Corp., 14
Synthes, Inc., 93
Syratech Corp., 14
Systemax, Inc., 52
TAB Products Co., 17
Tacony Corporation, 70
TAG Heuer International SA, 25; 77 (upd.)
Tag-It Pacific, Inc., 85
Taiheiyo Cement Corporation, 60 (upd.)
Taiwan Semiconductor Manufacturing Company Ltd., 47
Tamron Company Ltd., 82
Targetti Sankey SpA, 86
Tarkett Sommer AG, 25
Taser International, Inc., 62
Taylor Devices, Inc., 97
Taylor Guitars, 48
TaylorMade-adidas Golf, 23; 96 (upd.)
TB Wood's Corporation, 56
TDK Corporation, 49 (upd.)
TearDrop Golf Company, 32
Techtronic Industries Company Ltd., 73
Tecumseh Products Company, 8; 71 (upd.)
Tektronix Inc., 8; 78 (upd.)
Telsmith Inc., 96
Tempur-Pedic Inc., 54
Tenaris SA, 63
Tennant Company, 13; 33 (upd.); 95 (upd.)
Terex Corporation, 7; 40 (upd.); 91 (upd.)
The Testor Corporation, 51
Tetra Pak International SA, 53
Thales S.A., 42
Thermadyne Holding Corporation, 19
Thermo BioAnalysis Corp., 25
Thermo Electron Corporation, 7
Thermo Fibertek, Inc., 24
Thermo Instrument Systems Inc., 11
Thermo King Corporation, 13
Thiokol Corporation, 22 (upd.)
Thomas & Betts Corp., 11; 54 (upd.)
Thomas Industries Inc., 29
Thomasville Furniture Industries, Inc., 12; 74 (upd.)
Thor Industries Inc., 39; 92 (upd.)
3M Company, 61 (upd.)
ThyssenKrupp AG, IV; 28 (upd.); 87 (upd.)
Tianjin Flying Pigeon Bicycle Co., Ltd., 95
Tilia Inc., 62
Timex Corporation, 7; 25 (upd.)
The Timken Company, 8; 42 (upd.)
Titan Cement Company S.A., 64
Titan International, Inc., 89
TiVo Inc., 75
TJ International, Inc., 19
Todd Shipyards Corporation, 14
Tokheim Corporation, 21
Tomy Company Ltd., 65
Tong Yang Cement Corporation, 62
Tonka Corporation, 25
Toolex International N.V., 26
The Topaz Group, Inc., 62
Topcon Corporation, 84
Topps Company, Inc., 13; 34 (upd.)
Toray Industries, Inc., 51 (upd.)
The Toro Company, 7; 26 (upd.); 77 (upd.)
The Torrington Company, 13
TOTO LTD., 28 (upd.)

TouchTunes Music Corporation, 97
Town & Country Corporation, 19
Toymax International, Inc., 29
Toyoda Automatic Loom Works, Ltd., III
Trane 78
CJSC Transmash Holding, 93
TransPro, Inc., 71
Tredegar Corporation, 52
Trek Bicycle Corporation, 16; 78 (upd.)
Trelleborg AB, 93
Trex Company, Inc., 71
Trico Products Corporation, 15
TriMas Corp., 11
Trinity Industries, Incorporated, 7
TRINOVA Corporation, III
TriPath Imaging, Inc., 77
TriQuint Semiconductor, Inc., 63
Trisko Jewelry Sculptures, Ltd., 57
Triumph Group, Inc., 31
True Temper Sports, Inc., 95
TRUMPF GmbH + Co. KG, 86
TRW Automotive Holdings Corp., 75 (upd.)
Tubos de Acero de Mexico, S.A. (TAMSA), 41
Tultex Corporation, 13
Tupperware Corporation, 28
TurboChef Technologies, Inc., 83
Turtle Wax, Inc., 15; 93 (upd.)
Twin Disc, Inc., 21
II-VI Incorporated, 69
Ty Inc., 33; 86 (upd.)
Tyco International Ltd., III; 28 (upd.)
Tyco Toys, Inc., 12
U.S. Robotics Corporation, 9; 66 (upd.)
Ube Industries, Ltd., 38 (upd.)
Ultralife Batteries, Inc., 58
ULVAC, Inc., 80
United Defense Industries, Inc., 30; 66 (upd.)
United Dominion Industries Limited, 8; 16 (upd.)
United Industrial Corporation, 37
United States Filter Corporation, 20
United States Pipe and Foundry Company, 62
Unitika Ltd., 53 (upd.)
Unitog Co., 19
Universal Manufacturing Company, 88
Ushio Inc., 91
Usinas Siderúrgicas de Minas Gerais S.A., 77
Utah Medical Products, Inc., 36
UTStarcom, Inc., 77
VA TECH ELIN EBG GmbH, 49
Vaillant GmbH, 44
Valley National Gases, Inc., 85
Vallourec SA, 54
Valmet Corporation (Valmet Oy), III
Valmont Industries, Inc., 19
The Valspar Corporation, 8
Vari-Lite International, Inc., 35
Varian, Inc., 48 (upd.)
Variflex, Inc., 51
Varity Corporation, III
Varlen Corporation, 16
Varta AG, 23
Velcro Industries N.V., 19; 72 (upd.)
Velux A/S, 86
Ventana Medical Systems, Inc., 75
Verbatim Corporation, 74 (upd.)
Vermeer Manufacturing Company, 17
Vestas Wind Systems A/S, 73
Viasystems Group, Inc., 67
Vickers plc, 27
Victor Company of Japan, Limited, II; 26 (upd.); 83 (upd.)
Victorinox AG, 21; 74 (upd.)
Videojet Technologies, Inc., 90
Vidrala S.A., 67
Viessmann Werke GmbH & Co., 37
ViewSonic Corporation, 72
Viking Range Corporation, 66
Viking Yacht Company, 96
Villeroy & Boch AG, 37
Virco Manufacturing Corporation, 17
Viscofan S.A., 70
Viskase Companies, Inc., 55
Vita Plus Corporation, 60
Vitro Corporativo S.A. de C.V., 34
voestalpine AG, 57 (upd.)
Vorwerk & Co., 27
Vosper Thornycroft Holding plc, 41
Vossloh AG, 53
VTech Holdings Ltd., 77
W.A. Whitney Company, 53
W.C. Bradley Co., 69
W.H. Brady Co., 17
W.L. Gore & Associates, Inc., 14; 60 (upd.)
W.W. Grainger, Inc., 26 (upd.); 68 (upd.)
Wabash National Corp., 13
Wabtec Corporation, 40
Wacker Construction Equipment AG, 95
Wahl Clipper Corporation, 86
Walbro Corporation, 13
Walter Industries, Inc., 72 (upd.)
Washington Scientific Industries, Inc., 17
Wassall Plc, 18
Waterford Wedgwood plc, 12; 34 (upd.)
Water Pik Technologies, Inc., 34; 83 (upd.)
Waters Corporation, 43
Watts Industries, Inc., 19
Watts of Lydney Group Ltd., 71
WD-40 Company, 18
Webasto Roof Systems Inc., 97
Weber-Stephen Products Co., 40
Weeres Industries Corporation, 52
Weg S.A. 78
The Weir Group PLC, 85
Welbilt Corp., 19
Wellman, Inc., 8; 52 (upd.)
Weru Aktiengesellschaft, 18
West Bend Co., 14
Westell Technologies, Inc., 57
Westerbeke Corporation, 60
Western Digital Corporation, 25; 92 (upd.)
Wheaton Science Products, 60 (upd.)
Wheeling-Pittsburgh Corporation, 58 (upd.)
Whirlpool Corporation, III; 12 (upd.); 59 (upd.)
White Consolidated Industries Inc., 13
Wilbert, Inc., 56
Wilkinson Sword Ltd., 60
William L. Bonnell Company, Inc., 66
William Zinsser & Company, Inc., 58
Williamson-Dickie Manufacturing Company, 45 (upd.)
Wilson Sporting Goods Company, 24; 84 (upd.)
Wilton Products, Inc., 97
Wincor Nixdorf Holding GmbH, 69 (upd.)
Windmere Corporation, 16
Winegard Company, 56
Winnebago Industries, Inc., 7; 27 (upd.); 96 (upd.)
WinsLoew Furniture, Inc., 21
The Wiremold Company, 81
WMS Industries, Inc., 15; 53 (upd.)
Wolverine Tube Inc., 23
Wood-Mode, Inc., 23
Woodcraft Industries Inc., 61
Woodward Governor Company, 13; 49 (upd.)
Wright Medical Group, Inc., 61
Württembergische Metallwarenfabrik AG (WMF), 60
Wyant Corporation, 30
Wyman-Gordon Company, 14
Wynn's International, Inc., 33
X-Rite, Inc., 48
Xerox Corporation, III; 6 (upd.); 26 (upd.); 69 (upd.)
Yamaha Corporation, III; 16 (upd.)
The Yokohama Rubber Company, Limited, V; 19 (upd.); 91 (upd.)
The York Group, Inc., 50
York International Corp., 13
Young Innovations, Inc., 44
Zapf Creation AG, 95
Zebra Technologies Corporation, 53 (upd.)
ZERO Corporation, 17; 88 (upd.)
ZiLOG, Inc., 72 (upd.)
Zindart Ltd., 60
Zippo Manufacturing Company, 18; 71 (upd.)
Zodiac S.A., 36
Zygo Corporation, 42

Materials

AK Steel Holding Corporation, 19
American Biltrite Inc., 16
American Colloid Co., 13
American Standard Inc., III
Ameriwood Industries International Corp., 17
Apasco S.A. de C.V., 51
Apogee Enterprises, Inc., 8
Asahi Glass Company, Limited, III
Asbury Carbons, Inc., 68
Bairnco Corporation, 28
Bayou Steel Corporation, 31
Blessings Corp., 19
Blue Circle Industries PLC, III
Bodycote International PLC, 63
Boral Limited, III
British Vita PLC, 9
Brush Engineered Materials Inc., 67
California Steel Industries, Inc., 67

Callanan Industries, Inc., 60
Cameron & Barkley Company, 28
Carborundum Company, 15
Carl Zeiss AG, III; 34 (upd.); 91 (upd.)
Carlisle Companies Inc., 8; 82 (upd.)
Carter Holt Harvey Ltd., 70
Cementos Argos S.A., 91
Cemex SA de CV, 20
Century Aluminum Company, 52
CertainTeed Corporation, 35
Chargeurs International, 6; 21 (upd.)
Chemfab Corporation, 35
Cimentos de Portugal SGPS S.A. (Cimpor), 76
Cold Spring Granite Company Inc., 16; 67 (upd.)
Columbia Forest Products Inc. 78
Compagnie de Saint-Gobain S.A., III; 16 (upd.)
Cookson Group plc, III; 44 (upd.)
Corning Inc., III; 44 (upd.); 90 (upd.)
CSR Limited, III; 28 (upd.); 85 (upd.)
Dal-Tile International Inc., 22
The David J. Joseph Company, 14; 76 (upd.)
The Dexter Corporation, 12 (upd.)
Dickten Masch Plastics LLC, 90
Dyckerhoff AG, 35
Dynamic Materials Corporation, 81
Dyson Group PLC, 71
ECC Group plc, III
Edw. C. Levy Co., 42
84 Lumber Company, 9; 39 (upd.)
ElkCorp, 52
Empire Resources, Inc., 81
English China Clays Ltd., 15 (upd.); 40 (upd.)
Envirodyne Industries, Inc., 17
Feldmuhle Nobel A.G., III
Fibreboard Corporation, 16
Filtrona plc, 88
Florida Rock Industries, Inc., 46
Foamex International Inc., 17
Formica Corporation, 13
GAF Corporation, 22 (upd.)
The Geon Company, 11
Giant Cement Holding, Inc., 23
Gibraltar Steel Corporation, 37
Granite Rock Company, 26
Groupe Sidel S.A., 21
Harbison-Walker Refractories Company, 24
Harrisons & Crosfield plc, III
Heidelberger Zement AG, 31
Hexcel Corporation, 28
Holderbank Financière Glaris Ltd., III
Holnam Inc., 39 (upd.)
Holt and Bugbee Company, 66
Homasote Company, 72
Howmet Corp., 12
Huttig Building Products, Inc., 73
Ibstock Brick Ltd., 14; 37 (upd.)
Imerys S.A., 40 (upd.)
Imperial Industries, Inc., 81
Internacional de Ceramica, S.A. de C.V., 53
International Shipbreaking Ltd. L.L.C., 67
Joseph T. Ryerson & Son, Inc., 15
Lafarge Coppée S.A., III
Lafarge Corporation, 28
Lehigh Portland Cement Company, 23
Loma Negra C.I.A.S.A., 95
Lyman-Richey Corporation, 96
Manville Corporation, III; 7 (upd.)
Material Sciences Corporation, 63
Matsushita Electric Works, Ltd., III; 7 (upd.)
McJunkin Corporation, 63
Medusa Corporation, 24
Mitsubishi Materials Corporation, III
Nevamar Company, 82
Nippon Sheet Glass Company, Limited, III
North Pacific Group, Inc., 61
Nuplex Industries Ltd., 92
OmniSource Corporation, 14
Onoda Cement Co., Ltd., III
Otor S.A., 77
Owens-Corning Fiberglass Corporation, III
Pacific Clay Products Inc., 88
Pilkington Group Limited, III; 34 (upd.); 87 (upd.)
Pioneer International Limited, III
PolyOne Corporation, 87 (upd.)
PPG Industries, Inc., III; 22 (upd.); 81 (upd.)
Redland plc, III
Rinker Group Ltd., 65
RMC Group p.l.c., III
Rock of Ages Corporation, 37
Rogers Corporation, 80 (upd.)
Royal Group Technologies Limited, 73
The Rugby Group plc, 31
Scholle Corporation, 96
Schuff Steel Company, 26
Sekisui Chemical Co., Ltd., III; 72 (upd.)
Severstal Joint Stock Company, 65
Shaw Industries, 9
The Sherwin-Williams Company, III; 13 (upd.); 89 (upd.)
The Siam Cement Public Company Limited, 56
SIG plc, 71
Simplex Technologies Inc., 21
Siskin Steel & Supply Company, 70
Solutia Inc., 52
Sommer-Allibert S.A., 19
Southdown, Inc., 14
Spartech Corporation, 19; 76 (upd.)
Ssangyong Cement Industrial Co., Ltd., III; 61 (upd.)
Steel Technologies Inc., 63
Sun Distributors L.P., 12
Symyx Technologies, Inc., 77
Tarmac Limited, III, 28 (upd.); 95 (upd.)
Tilcon-Connecticut Inc., 80
TOTO LTD., III; 28 (upd.)
Toyo Sash Co., Ltd., III
Tuscarora Inc., 29
U.S. Aggregates, Inc., 42
Ube Industries, Ltd., III
United States Steel Corporation, 50 (upd.)
USG Corporation, III; 26 (upd.); 81 (upd.)
Usinas Siderúrgicas de Minas Gerais S.A., 77
Vicat S.A., 70
voestalpine AG, 57 (upd.)
Vulcan Materials Company, 7; 52 (upd.)
Wacker-Chemie GmbH, 35
Walter Industries, Inc., III
Waxman Industries, Inc., 9
Weber et Broutin France, 66
Wienerberger AG, 70
Wolseley plc, 64
ZERO Corporation, 17; 88 (upd.)
Zoltek Companies, Inc., 37

Mining & Metals

A.M. Castle & Co., 25
Acindar Industria Argentina de Aceros S.A., 87
African Rainbow Minerals Ltd., 97
Aggregate Industries plc, 36
Agnico-Eagle Mines Limited, 71
Aktiebolaget SKF, III; 38 (upd.); 89 (upd.)
Alcan Aluminium Limited, IV; 31 (upd.)
Alcoa Inc., 56 (upd.)
Alleghany Corporation, 10
Allegheny Ludlum Corporation, 8
Alliance Resource Partners, L.P., 81
Alrosa Company Ltd., 62
Altos Hornos de México, S.A. de C.V., 42
Aluminum Company of America, IV; 20 (upd.)
AMAX Inc., IV
AMCOL International Corporation, 59 (upd.)
Amsted Industries Incorporated, 7
Anglo American Corporation of South Africa Limited, IV; 16 (upd.)
Anglo American PLC, 50 (upd.)
Aquarius Platinum Ltd., 63
ARBED S.A., IV, 22 (upd.)
Arcelor Gent, 80
Arch Mineral Corporation, 7
Armco Inc., IV
ASARCO Incorporated, IV
Ashanti Goldfields Company Limited, 43
Atchison Casting Corporation, 39
Barrick Gold Corporation, 34
Battle Mountain Gold Company, 23
Benguet Corporation, 58
Bethlehem Steel Corporation, IV; 7 (upd.); 27 (upd.)
BHP Billiton, 67 (upd.)
Birmingham Steel Corporation, 13; 40 (upd.)
Boart Longyear Company, 26
Bodycote International PLC, 63
Boliden AB, 80
Boral Limited, 43 (upd.)
British Coal Corporation, IV
British Steel plc, IV; 19 (upd.)
Broken Hill Proprietary Company Ltd., IV, 22 (upd.)
Brush Engineered Materials Inc., 67
Brush Wellman Inc., 14
Buderus AG, 37
Cameco Corporation, 77
Caparo Group Ltd., 90

Carpenter Technology Corporation, 13; 95 (upd.)
Chaparral Steel Co., 13
China Shenhua Energy Company Limited, 83
Christensen Boyles Corporation, 26
Cleveland-Cliffs Inc., 13; 62 (upd.)
Coal India Ltd., IV; 44 (upd.)
Cockerill Sambre Group, IV; 26 (upd.)
Coeur d'Alene Mines Corporation, 20
Cold Spring Granite Company Inc., 16; 67 (upd.)
Cominco Ltd., 37
Commercial Metals Company, 15; 42 (upd.)
Companhia Siderúrgica Nacional, 76
Companhia Vale do Rio Doce, IV; 43 (upd.)
Compañia de Minas Buenaventura S.A.A., 93
CONSOL Energy Inc., 59
Corporacion Nacional del Cobre de Chile, 40
Corus Group plc, 49 (upd.)
CRA Limited, IV
Cyprus Amax Minerals Company, 21
Cyprus Minerals Company, 7
Daido Steel Co., Ltd., IV
De Beers Consolidated Mines Limited/De Beers Centenary AG, IV; 7 (upd.); 28 (upd.)
Degussa Group, IV
Diavik Diamond Mines Inc., 85
Dofasco Inc., IV; 24 (upd.)
Dynatec Corporation, 87
Earle M. Jorgensen Company, 82
Echo Bay Mines Ltd., IV; 38 (upd.)
Engelhard Corporation, IV
Eramet, 73
Evergreen Energy, Inc., 97
Evraz Group S.A., 97
Falconbridge Limited, 49
Fansteel Inc., 19
Fluor Corporation, 34 (upd.)
Freeport-McMoRan Copper & Gold, Inc., IV; 7 (upd.); 57 (upd.)
Fried. Krupp GmbH, IV
Gencor Ltd., IV, 22 (upd.)
Geneva Steel, 7
Gerdau S.A., 59
Glamis Gold, Ltd., 54
Gold Fields Ltd., IV; 62 (upd.)
Goldcorp Inc., 87
Grupo Mexico, S.A. de C.V., 40
Gruppo Riva Fire SpA, 88
Handy & Harman, 23
Hanson Building Materials America Inc., 60
Hanson PLC, 30 (upd.)
Harmony Gold Mining Company Limited, 63
Haynes International, Inc., 88
Hecla Mining Company, 20
Hemlo Gold Mines Inc., 9
Heraeus Holding GmbH, IV
Highland Gold Mining Limited, 95
Highveld Steel and Vanadium Corporation Limited, 59
Hitachi Metals, Ltd., IV
Hoesch AG, IV
Homestake Mining Company, 12; 38 (upd.)
Horsehead Industries, Inc., 51
The Hudson Bay Mining and Smelting Company, Limited, 12
Hylsamex, S.A. de C.V., 39
IMCO Recycling, Incorporated, 32
Imerys S.A., 40 (upd.)
Imetal S.A., IV
Inco Limited, IV; 45 (upd.)
Industrias Penoles, S.A. de C.V., 22
Inland Steel Industries, Inc., IV; 19 (upd.)
Intermet Corporation, 32
Iscor Limited, 57
Ispat Inland Inc., 30; 40 (upd.)
JFE Shoji Holdings Inc., 88
Johnson Matthey PLC, IV; 16 (upd.)
JSC MMC Norilsk Nickel, 48
Kaiser Aluminum Corporation, IV; 84 (upd.)
Kawasaki Heavy Industries, Ltd., 63 (upd.)
Kawasaki Steel Corporation, IV
Kennecott Corporation, 7; 27 (upd.)
Kentucky Electric Steel, Inc., 31
Kerr-McGee Corporation, 22 (upd.)
Kinross Gold Corporation, 36
Klockner-Werke AG, IV
Kobe Steel, Ltd., IV; 19 (upd.)
Koninklijke Nederlandsche Hoogovens en Staalfabrieken NV, IV
Laclede Steel Company, 15
Layne Christensen Company, 19
Lonmin plc, 66 (upd.)
Lonrho Plc, 21
The LTV Corporation, I; 24 (upd.)
Lukens Inc., 14
Magma Copper Company, 7
The Marmon Group, IV; 16 (upd.)
Massey Energy Company, 57
MAXXAM Inc., 8
Meridian Gold, Incorporated, 47
Metaleurop S.A., 21
Metalico Inc., 97
Metallgesellschaft AG, IV
Minerals and Metals Trading Corporation of India Ltd., IV
Minerals Technologies Inc., 11; 52 (upd.)
Mitsui Mining & Smelting Co., Ltd., IV
Mitsui Mining Company, Limited, IV
Mueller Industries, Inc., 52 (upd.)
National Steel Corporation, 12
NERCO, Inc., 7
Newmont Mining Corporation, 7
Neyveli Lignite Corporation Ltd., 65
Niagara Corporation, 28
Nichimen Corporation, IV
Nippon Light Metal Company, Ltd., IV
Nippon Steel Corporation, IV; 17 (upd.); 96 (upd.)
Nisshin Steel Co., Ltd., IV
NKK Corporation, IV; 28 (upd.)
Noranda Inc., IV; 7 (upd.); 64 (upd.)
Norddeutsche Affinerie AG, 62
North Star Steel Company, 18
Nucor Corporation, 7; 21 (upd.); 79 (upd.)
Oglebay Norton Company, 17
Okura & Co., Ltd., IV
O'Neal Steel, Inc., 95
Oregon Metallurgical Corporation, 20
Oregon Steel Mills, Inc., 14
Ormet Corporation, 82
Outokumpu Oyj, 38
Park Corp., 22
Peabody Coal Company, 10
Peabody Energy Corporation, 45 (upd.)
Peabody Holding Company, Inc., IV
Pechiney SA, IV; 45 (upd.)
Peter Kiewit Sons' Inc., 8
Phelps Dodge Corporation, IV; 28 (upd.); 75 (upd.)
The Pittston Company, IV; 19 (upd.)
Placer Dome Inc., 20; 61 (upd.)
Pohang Iron and Steel Company Ltd., IV
POSCO, 57 (upd.)
Potash Corporation of Saskatchewan Inc., 18
Quanex Corporation, 13; 62 (upd.)
RAG AG, 35; 60 (upd.)
Reliance Steel & Aluminum Co., 19
Republic Engineered Steels, Inc., 7; 26 (upd.)
Reynolds Metals Company, IV
Rio Tinto PLC, 19 (upd.); 50 (upd.)
RMC Group p.l.c., 34 (upd.)
Roanoke Electric Steel Corporation, 45
Rouge Steel Company, 8
The RTZ Corporation PLC, IV
Ruhrkohle AG, IV
Ryerson Tull, Inc., 40 (upd.)
Saarberg-Konzern, IV
Salzgitter AG, IV
Sandvik AB, IV
Saudi Basic Industries Corporation (SABIC), 58
Schnitzer Steel Industries, Inc., 19
Severstal Joint Stock Company, 65
Shanghai Baosteel Group Corporation, 71
Siderar S.A.I.C., 66
Silver Wheaton Corp., 95
Smorgon Steel Group Ltd., 62
Southern Peru Copper Corporation, 40
Southwire Company, Inc., 8; 23 (upd.)
SSAB Svenskt Stål AB, 89
Steel Authority of India Ltd., IV
Stelco Inc., IV
Stillwater Mining Company, 47
Sumitomo Metal Industries Ltd., IV; 82 (upd.)
Sumitomo Metal Mining Co., Ltd., IV
Tata Iron & Steel Co. Ltd., IV; 44 (upd.)
Teck Corporation, 27
Tenaris SA, 63
Texas Industries, Inc., 8
ThyssenKrupp AG, IV; 28 (upd.); 87 (upd.)
The Timken Company, 8; 42 (upd.)
Titanium Metals Corporation, 21
Tomen Corporation, IV
Total Fina Elf S.A., 50 (upd.)
Třinecké Železárny A.S., 92
U.S. Borax, Inc., 42

Ugine S.A., 20
NV Umicore SA, 47
Universal Stainless & Alloy Products, Inc., 75
Uralita S.A., 96
Usinor SA, IV; 42 (upd.)
Usinor Sacilor, IV
VIAG Aktiengesellschaft, IV
Voest-Alpine Stahl AG, IV
Volcan Compañia Minera S.A.A., 92
Vulcan Materials Company, 52 (upd.)
Wah Chang, 82
Walter Industries, Inc., 22 (upd.)
Weirton Steel Corporation, IV; 26 (upd.)
Westmoreland Coal Company, 7
Wheeling-Pittsburgh Corp., 7
WMC, Limited, 43
Worthington Industries, Inc., 7; 21 (upd.)
Xstrata PLC, 73
Zambia Industrial and Mining Corporation Ltd., IV
Zinifex Ltd., 85

Paper & Forestry

Abitibi-Consolidated, Inc., IV; 25 (upd.)
Albany International Corporation, 51 (upd.)
Amcor Ltd, IV; 19 (upd.); 78 (upd.)
American Greetings Corporation, 59 (upd.)
American Pad & Paper Company, 20
Aracruz Celulose S.A., 57
Arjo Wiggins Appleton p.l.c., 34
Asplundh Tree Expert Co.,20; 59 (upd.)
Avery Dennison Corporation, IV
Badger Paper Mills, Inc., 15
Beckett Papers, 23
Bemis Company, Inc., 8; 91 (upd.)
Blue Heron Paper Company, 90
Bohemia, Inc., 13
Boise Cascade Holdings, L.L.C.,, IV; 8 (upd.); 32 (upd.); 95 (upd.)
Bowater PLC, IV
Bunzl plc, IV
Canfor Corporation, 42
Caraustar Industries, Inc., 19; 44 (upd.)
Carter Lumber Company, 45
Cascades Inc., 71
Central National-Gottesman Inc., 95
Champion International Corporation, IV; 20 (upd.)
Chesapeake Corporation, 8; 30 (upd.); 93 (upd.)
Consolidated Papers, Inc., 8; 36 (upd.)
Crane & Co., Inc., 26
Crown Vantage Inc., 29
CSS Industries, Inc., 35
Daio Paper Corporation, IV; 84 (upd.)
Daishowa Paper Manufacturing Co., Ltd., IV; 57 (upd.)
Deltic Timber Corporation, 46
Dillard Paper Company, 11
Doman Industries Limited, 59
Domtar Corporation, IV; 89 (upd.)
DS Smith Plc, 61
Empresas CMPC S.A., 70
Enso-Gutzeit Oy, IV
Esselte Pendaflex Corporation, 11
Federal Paper Board Company, Inc., 8
FiberMark, Inc., 37
Fletcher Challenge Ltd., IV
Fort Howard Corporation, 8
Fort James Corporation, 22 (upd.)
Georgia-Pacific Corporation, IV; 9 (upd.); 47 (upd.)
Gould Paper Corporation, 82
Graphic Packaging Holding Company, 96 (upd.)
Groupe Rougier SA, 21
Grupo Portucel Soporcel, 60
Guilbert S.A., 42
Hampton Affiliates, Inc., 77
Holmen AB, 52 (upd.)
Honshu Paper Co., Ltd., IV
International Paper Company, IV; 15 (upd.); 47 (upd.); 97 (upd.)
James River Corporation of Virginia, IV
Japan Pulp and Paper Company Limited, IV
Jefferson Smurfit Group plc, IV; 49 (upd.)
Jujo Paper Co., Ltd., IV
Kadant Inc., 96 (upd.)
Kimberly-Clark Corporation, 16 (upd.); 43 (upd.)
Kimberly-Clark de México, S.A. de C.V., 54
Klabin S.A., 73
Koninklijke Houthandel G Wijma & Zonen BV, 96
Kruger Inc., 17
Kymmene Corporation, IV
Longview Fibre Company, 8; 37 (upd.)
Louisiana-Pacific Corporation, IV; 31 (upd.)
M-real Oyj, 56 (upd.)
MacMillan Bloedel Limited, IV
Matussière et Forest SA, 58
The Mead Corporation, IV; 19 (upd.)
MeadWestvaco Corporation, 76 (upd.)
Mercer International Inc., 64
Metsa-Serla Oy, IV
Metso Corporation, 30 (upd.); 85 (upd.)
Miquel y Costas Miquel S.A., 68
Mo och Domsjö AB, IV
Monadnock Paper Mills, Inc., 21
Mosinee Paper Corporation, 15
Nashua Corporation, 8
National Envelope Corporation, 32
NCH Corporation, 8
Norske Skogindustrier ASA, 63
Oji Paper Co., Ltd., IV
P.H. Glatfelter Company, 8; 30 (upd.); 83 (upd.)
Packaging Corporation of America, 12
Papeteries de Lancey, 23
Plum Creek Timber Company, Inc., 43
Pope & Talbot, Inc., 12; 61 (upd.)
Pope Resources LP, 74
Potlatch Corporation, 8; 34 (upd.); 87 (upd.)
PWA Group, IV
Rayonier Inc., 24
Rengo Co., Ltd., IV
Reno de Medici S.p.A., 41
Rexam PLC, 32 (upd.); 85 (upd.)
Riverwood International Corporation, 11; 48 (upd.)
Rock-Tenn Company, 13; 59 (upd.)
Rogers Corporation, 61
St. Joe Paper Company, 8
Sanyo-Kokusaku Pulp Co., Ltd., IV
Sappi Limited, 49
Schweitzer-Mauduit International, Inc., 52
Scott Paper Company, IV; 31 (upd.)
Sealed Air Corporation, 14
Sierra Pacific Industries, 22; 90 (upd.)
Simpson Investment Company, 17
Smurfit-Stone Container Corporation, 83 (upd.)
Sonoco Products Company, 8; 89 (upd.)
Specialty Coatings Inc., 8
Stimson Lumber Company 78
Stone Container Corporation, IV
Stora Enso Oyj, IV; 36 (upd.); 85 (upd.)
Svenska Cellulosa Aktiebolaget SCA, IV; 28 (upd.); 85 (upd.)
Sveaskog AB, 93
Tapemark Company Inc., 64
Tembec Inc., 66
Temple-Inland Inc., IV; 31 (upd.)
Thomsen Greenhouses and Garden Center, Incorporated, 65
TJ International, Inc., 19
U.S. Timberlands Company, L.P., 42
Union Camp Corporation, IV
United Paper Mills Ltd. (Yhtyneet Paperitehtaat Oy), IV
Universal Forest Products, Inc., 10; 59 (upd.)
UPM-Kymmene Corporation, 19; 50 (upd.)
Wausau-Mosinee Paper Corporation, 60 (upd.)
West Fraser Timber Co. Ltd., 17; 91 (upd.)
West Linn Paper Company, 91
Westvaco Corporation, IV; 19 (upd.)
Weyerhaeuser Company, IV; 9 (upd.); 28 (upd.); 83 (upd.)
Wickes Inc., 25 (upd.)
Willamette Industries, Inc., IV; 31 (upd.)
WTD Industries, Inc., 20

Personal Services

AARP, 27
ABC Learning Centres Ltd., 93
ADT Security Services, Inc., 12; 44 (upd.)
Africare, 59
Alderwoods Group, Inc., 68 (upd.)
Ambassadors International, Inc., 68 (upd.)
American Civil Liberties Union (ACLU), 60
American Management Association, 76
American Retirement Corporation, 42
American Society for the Prevention of Cruelty to Animals (ASPCA), 68
AmeriCares Foundation, Inc., 87
Aquent, 96
Arthur Murray International, Inc., 32
Association of Junior Leagues International Inc., 60
Benesse Corporation, 76
Berlitz International, Inc., 39 (upd.)

Big Brothers Big Sisters of America, 85
Blackwater USA, 76
Bonhams 1793 Ltd., 72
Boys & Girls Clubs of America, 69
The Brickman Group, Ltd., 87
The Brink's Company, 58 (upd.)
Brother's Brother Foundation, 93
CareerBuilder, Inc., 93
Caritas Internationalis, 72
Carriage Services, Inc., 37
Catholic Charities USA, 76
CDI Corporation, 6; 54 (upd.)
CeWe Color Holding AG, 76
ChildrenFirst, Inc., 59
Childtime Learning Centers, Inc., 34
Chubb, PLC, 50
Corinthian Colleges, Inc., 39; 92 (upd.)
Correctional Services Corporation, 30
Correos y Telegrafos S.A., 80
Council on International Educational Exchange Inc., 81
CUC International Inc., 16
Curves International, Inc., 54
Cystic Fibrosis Foundation, 93
Davis Service Group PLC, 45
DeVry Inc., 29; 82 (upd.)
Educational Testing Service, 12; 62 (upd.)
eHarmony.com Inc., 71
Feed The Children, Inc., 68
Food For The Poor, Inc., 77
The Ford Foundation, 34
Franklin Quest Co., 11
Gold's Gym International, Inc., 71
Goodwill Industries International, Inc., 16; 66 (upd.)
GP Strategies Corporation, 64 (upd.)
Greenpeace International, 74
Greg Manning Auctions, Inc., 60
Gunnebo AB, 53
Hair Club For Men Ltd., 90
Herbalife Ltd., 17; 41 (upd.); 92 (upd.)
The Humane Society of the United States, 54
Huntington Learning Centers, Inc., 55
Imperial Parking Corporation, 58
Initial Security, 64
Jazzercise, Inc., 45
The John D. and Catherine T. MacArthur Foundation, 34
Jones Knowledge Group, Inc., 97
Kaplan, Inc., 42; 90 (upd.)
KinderCare Learning Centers, Inc., 13
Kiva, 95
Knowledge Learning Corporation, 51
Kumon Institute of Education Co., Ltd., 72
Labor Ready, Inc., 29; 88 (upd.)
Learning Care Group, Inc., 76 (upd.)
Lifetouch Inc., 86
The Loewen Group Inc., 16; 40 (upd.)
LPA Holding Corporation, 81
Mace Security International, Inc., 57
Make-A-Wish Foundation of America, 97
Management and Training Corporation, 28
Manpower, Inc., 9
Martin Franchises, Inc., 80
Match.com, LP, 87
Michael Page International plc, 45
Mothers Against Drunk Driving (MADD), 51
National Heritage Academies, Inc., 60
National Organization for Women, Inc., 55
Noah Education Holdings Ltd., 97
Nobel Learning Communities, Inc., 37; 76 (upd.)
Oxfam GB, 87
Prison Rehabilitative Industries and Diversified Enterprises, Inc. (PRIDE), 53
Recording for the Blind & Dyslexic, 51
Regis Corporation, 18; 70 (upd.)
Robert Half International Inc., 70 (upd.)
The Rockefeller Foundation, 34
Rollins, Inc., 11
Rosenbluth International Inc., 14
Rosetta Stone Inc., 93
Rotary International, 31
The Salvation Army USA, 32
Scientific Learning Corporation, 95
Screen Actors Guild, 72
Service Corporation International, 6; 51 (upd.)
The ServiceMaster Company, 68 (upd.)
SOS Staffing Services, 25
Spark Networks, Inc., 91
Special Olympics, Inc., 93
SR Teleperformance S.A., 86
Stewart Enterprises, Inc., 20
Supercuts Inc., 26
24 Hour Fitness Worldwide, Inc., 71
UAW (International Union, United Automobile, Aerospace and Agricultural Implement Workers of America), 72
United Negro College Fund, Inc., 79
United Service Organizations, 60
Weight Watchers International Inc., 12; 33 (upd.); 73 (upd.)
The York Group, Inc., 50
Youth Services International, Inc., 21
YWCA of the U.S.A., 45
World Vision International, Inc., 93

Petroleum

Abraxas Petroleum Corporation, 89
Abu Dhabi National Oil Company, IV; 45 (upd.)
Adani Enterprises Ltd., 97
Aegean Marine Petroleum Network Inc., 89
Agway, Inc., 21 (upd.)
Alberta Energy Company Ltd., 16; 43 (upd.)
Amerada Hess Corporation, IV; 21 (upd.); 55 (upd.)
Amoco Corporation, IV; 14 (upd.)
Anadarko Petroleum Corporation, 10; 52 (upd.)
ANR Pipeline Co., 17
Anschutz Corp., 12
Apache Corporation, 10; 32 (upd.); 89 (upd.)
Aral AG, 62
Arctic Slope Regional Corporation, 38
Arena Resources, Inc., 97
Ashland Inc., 19; 50 (upd.)
Ashland Oil, Inc., IV
Atlantic Richfield Company, IV; 31 (upd.)
Aventine Renewable Energy Holdings, Inc., 89
Badger State Ethanol, LLC, 83
Baker Hughes Incorporated, 22 (upd.); 57 (upd.)
Belco Oil & Gas Corp., 40
Benton Oil and Gas Company, 47
Berry Petroleum Company, 47
BG Products Inc., 96
BHP Billiton, 67 (upd.)
Bill Barrett Corporation, 71
BJ Services Company, 25
Blue Rhino Corporation, 56
Boardwalk Pipeline Partners, LP, 87
Boots & Coots International Well Control, Inc., 79
BP p.l.c., 45 (upd.)
Brigham Exploration Company, 75
The British Petroleum Company plc, IV; 7 (upd.); 21 (upd.)
British-Borneo Oil & Gas PLC, 34
Broken Hill Proprietary Company Ltd., 22 (upd.)
Bronco Drilling Company, Inc., 89
Burlington Resources Inc., 10
Burmah Castrol PLC, IV; 30 (upd.)
Callon Petroleum Company, 47
Caltex Petroleum Corporation, 19
Cano Petroleum Inc., 97
Carrizo Oil & Gas, Inc., 97
ChevronTexaco Corporation, IV; 19 (upd.); 47 (upd.)
Chiles Offshore Corporation, 9
Cimarex Energy Co., 81
China National Petroleum Corporation, 46
Chinese Petroleum Corporation, IV; 31 (upd.)
CITGO Petroleum Corporation, IV; 31 (upd.)
Clayton Williams Energy, Inc., 87
The Coastal Corporation, IV; 31 (upd.)
Compañia Española de Petróleos S.A. (Cepsa), IV; 56 (upd.)
Comstock Resources, Inc., 47
Conoco Inc., IV; 16 (upd.)
ConocoPhillips, 63 (upd.)
CONSOL Energy Inc., 59
Continental Resources, Inc., 89
Cooper Cameron Corporation, 20 (upd.)
Cosmo Oil Co., Ltd., IV; 53 (upd.)
Crown Central Petroleum Corporation, 7
DeepTech International Inc., 21
Den Norse Stats Oljeselskap AS, IV
Denbury Resources, Inc., 67
Deutsche BP Aktiengesellschaft, 7
Devon Energy Corporation, 61
Diamond Shamrock, Inc., IV
Distrigaz S.A., 82
Dril-Quip, Inc., 81
Duvernay Oil Corp., 83
Dynegy Inc., 49 (upd.)
E.On AG, 50 (upd.)
Edge Petroleum Corporation, 67

Egyptian General Petroleum Corporation, IV; 51 (upd.)
El Paso Corporation, 66 (upd.)
Elf Aquitaine SA, 21 (upd.)
Empresa Colombiana de Petróleos, IV
Enbridge Inc., 43
Encore Acquisition Company, 73
Energen Corporation, 21; 97 (upd.)
ENI S.p.A., 69 (upd.)
Enron Corporation, 19
ENSCO International Incorporated, 57
Ente Nazionale Idrocarburi, IV
Enterprise Oil PLC, 11; 50 (upd.)
Entreprise Nationale Sonatrach, IV
Equitable Resources, Inc., 54 (upd.)
Ergon, Inc., 95
Exxon Mobil Corporation, IV; 7 (upd.); 32 (upd.); 67 (upd.)
Ferrellgas Partners, L.P., 35
FINA, Inc., 7
Flying J Inc., 19
Flotek Industries Inc., 93
Forest Oil Corporation, 19; 91 (upd.)
OAO Gazprom, 42
General Sekiyu K.K., IV
Giant Industries, Inc., 19; 61 (upd.)
Global Industries, Ltd., 37
Global Marine Inc., 9
GlobalSantaFe Corporation, 48 (upd.)
Grey Wolf, Inc., 43
Halliburton Company, 25 (upd.); 55 (upd.)
Hanover Compressor Company, 59
Hawkeye Holdings LLC, 89
Helix Energy Solutions Group, Inc., 81
Hellenic Petroleum SA, 64
Helmerich & Payne, Inc., 18
Holly Corporation, 12
Hunt Consolidated, Inc., 7; 27 (upd.)
Hunting plc 78
Hurricane Hydrocarbons Ltd., 54
Husky Energy Inc., 47
Idemitsu Kosan Co., Ltd., 49 (upd.)
Idemitsu Kosan K.K., IV
Imperial Oil Limited, IV; 25 (upd.)
Indian Oil Corporation Ltd., IV; 48 (upd.); 95 (upd.)
INPEX Holdings Inc., 97
Input/Output, Inc., 73
Iogen Corporation, 81
Ipiranga S.A., 67
Kanematsu Corporation, IV
Kerr-McGee Corporation, IV; 22 (upd.); 68 (upd.)
Kinder Morgan, Inc., 45
King Ranch, Inc., 14
Koch Industries, Inc., IV; 20 (upd.), 77 (upd.)
Koppers Industries, Inc., 26 (upd.)
Kuwait Petroleum Corporation, IV; 55 (upd.)
Libyan National Oil Corporation, IV
The Louisiana Land and Exploration Company, 7
OAO LUKOIL, 40
Lyondell Petrochemical Company, IV
MAPCO Inc., IV
Maxus Energy Corporation, 7
McDermott International, Inc., 37 (upd.)
Meteor Industries Inc., 33
Mitchell Energy and Development Corporation, 7
Mitsubishi Oil Co., Ltd., IV
Mobil Corporation, IV; 7 (upd.); 21 (upd.)
MOL Rt, 70
Murphy Oil Corporation, 7; 32 (upd.); 95 (upd.)
Nabors Industries Ltd., 9; 91 (upd.)
National Fuel Gas Company, 6; 95 (upd.)
National Iranian Oil Company, IV; 61 (upd.)
National Oil Corporation, 66 (upd.)
Neste Oil Corporation, IV; 85 (upd.)
Newfield Exploration Company, 65
Nexen Inc., 79
NGC Corporation, 18
Nigerian National Petroleum Corporation, IV; 72 (upd.)
Nippon Oil Corporation, IV; 63 (upd.)
OAO NK YUKOS, 47
Noble Affiliates, Inc., 11
Occidental Petroleum Corporation, IV; 25 (upd.); 71 (upd.)
Odebrecht S.A., 73
Oil and Natural Gas Corporation Ltd., IV; 90 (upd.)
Oil States International, Inc., 77
ÖMV Aktiengesellschaft, IV
Oryx Energy Company, 7
Pacific Ethanol, Inc., 81
Pakistan State Oil Company Ltd., 81
Paramount Resources Ltd., 87
Parker Drilling Company, 28
Patina Oil & Gas Corporation, 24
Patterson-UTI Energy, Inc., 55
Pengrowth Energy Trust, 95
Penn Virginia Corporation, 85
Pennzoil-Quaker State Company, IV; 20 (upd.); 50 (upd.)
Pertamina, IV; 56 (upd.)
Petro-Canada Limited, IV
Petrobras Energia Participaciones S.A., 72
Petrofac Ltd., 95
PetroFina S.A., IV; 26 (upd.)
Petrohawk Energy Corporation, 79
Petróleo Brasileiro S.A., IV
Petróleos de Portugal S.A., IV
Petróleos de Venezuela S.A., IV; 74 (upd.)
Petróleos del Ecuador, IV
Petróleos Mexicanos, IV; 19 (upd.)
Petroleum Development Oman LLC, IV
Petroliam Nasional Bhd (Petronas), IV; 56 (upd.)
Petron Corporation, 58
Phillips Petroleum Company, IV; 40 (upd.)
Pioneer Natural Resources Company, 59
Pogo Producing Company, 39
Polski Koncern Naftowy ORLEN S.A., 77
Premcor Inc., 37
Pride International Inc. 78
PTT Public Company Ltd., 56
Qatar General Petroleum Corporation, IV
Quaker State Corporation, 7; 21 (upd.)
Range Resources Corporation, 45
Reliance Industries Ltd., 81
Repsol-YPF S.A., IV; 16 (upd.); 40 (upd.)
Resource America, Inc., 42
Rowan Companies, Inc., 43
Royal Dutch/Shell Group, IV; 49 (upd.)
RPC, Inc., 91
RWE AG, 50 (upd.)
St. Mary Land & Exploration Company, 63
Santa Fe International Corporation, 38
Santos Ltd., 81
Sasol Limited, IV; 47 (upd.)
Saudi Arabian Oil Company, IV; 17 (upd.); 50 (upd.)
Schlumberger Limited, 17 (upd.); 59 (upd.)
Seagull Energy Corporation, 11
Seitel, Inc., 47
Shanghai Petrochemical Co., Ltd., 18
Shell Oil Company, IV; 14 (upd.); 41 (upd.)
Showa Shell Sekiyu K.K., IV; 59 (upd.)
OAO Siberian Oil Company (Sibneft), 49
Smith International, Inc., 59 (upd.)
Société Nationale Elf Aquitaine, IV; 7 (upd.)
Sonatrach, 65 (upd.)
Spinnaker Exploration Company, 72
Statoil ASA, 61 (upd.)
Suburban Propane Partners, L.P., 30
SUEZ-TRACTEBEL S.A., 97 (upd.)
Sun Company, Inc., IV
Suncor Energy Inc., 54
Sunoco, Inc., 28 (upd.); 83 (upd.)
Superior Energy Services, Inc., 65
OAO Surgutneftegaz, 48
Swift Energy Company, 63
Talisman Energy Inc., 9; 47 (upd.)
TAQA North Ltd., 95
OAO Tatneft, 45
TEPPCO Partners, L.P., 73
Tesoro Corporation, 7; 45 (upd.); 97 (upd.)
Teton Energy Corporation, 97
Texaco Inc., IV; 14 (upd.); 41 (upd.)
Tidewater Inc., 37 (upd.)
TODCO, 87
Tom Brown, Inc., 37
Tonen Corporation, IV; 16 (upd.)
TonenGeneral Sekiyu K.K., 54 (upd.)
Tosco Corporation, 7
TOTAL S.A., IV; 24 (upd.)
Transammonia Group, 95
TransCanada Corporation, 93 (upd.)
TransMontaigne Inc., 28
Oil Transporting Joint Stock Company Transneft, 93
Transocean Sedco Forex Inc., 45
Travel Ports of America, Inc., 17
Triton Energy Corporation, 11
Tullow Oil plc, 83
Türkiye Petrolleri Anonim Ortakliği, IV
Ultra Petroleum Corporation, 71
Ultramar Diamond Shamrock Corporation, IV; 31 (upd.)
Union Texas Petroleum Holdings, Inc., 9
Unit Corporation, 63
Universal Compression, Inc., 59

Unocal Corporation, IV; 24 (upd.); 71 (upd.)
USX Corporation, IV; 7 (upd.)
Valero Energy Corporation, 7; 71 (upd.)
Valley National Gases, Inc., 85
Varco International, Inc., 42
Vastar Resources, Inc., 24
VeraSun Energy Corporation, 87
Vintage Petroleum, Inc., 42
Wascana Energy Inc., 13
Weatherford International, Inc., 39
Webber Oil Company, 61
Western Atlas Inc., 12
Western Company of North America, 15
Western Gas Resources, Inc., 45
Western Oil Sands Inc., 85
Westport Resources Corporation, 63
Whiting Petroleum Corporation, 81
The Williams Companies, Inc., IV; 31 (upd.)
World Fuel Services Corporation, 47
XTO Energy Inc., 52
YPF Sociedad Anonima, IV
The Zubair Corporation L.L.C., 96

Publishing & Printing

A.B.Dick Company, 28
A.H. Belo Corporation, 10; 30 (upd.)
Abril S.A., 95
AccuWeather, Inc., 73
Advance Publications Inc., IV; 19 (upd.); 96 (upd.)
Advanced Marketing Services, Inc., 34
Advanstar Communications, Inc., 57
Affiliated Publications, Inc., 7
Agence France-Presse, 34
Agora S.A. Group, 77
Aljazeera Satellite Channel, 79
American Banknote Corporation, 30
American Girl, Inc., 69
American Greetings Corporation, 7, 22 (upd.)
American Media, Inc., 27; 82 (upd.)
American Printing House for the Blind, 26
American Reprographics Company, 75
Andrews McMeel Universal, 40
The Antioch Company, 40
AOL Time Warner Inc., 57 (upd.)
Arandell Corporation, 37
Archie Comics Publications, Inc., 63
Arnoldo Mondadori Editore S.p.A., IV; 19 (upd.); 54 (upd.)
The Associated Press, 31 (upd.); 73 (upd.)
The Atlantic Group, 23
Audible Inc., 79
Axel Springer Verlag AG, IV; 20 (upd.)
Banta Corporation, 12; 32 (upd.); 79 (upd.)
Bauer Publishing Group, 7
Bayard SA, 49
Berlitz International, Inc., 13
Bernard C. Harris Publishing Company, Inc., 39
Bertelsmann A.G., IV; 15 (upd.); 43 (upd.); 91 (upd.)
Bibliographisches Institut & F.A. Brockhaus AG, 74
Big Flower Press Holdings, Inc., 21
Blackwell Publishing Ltd. 78
Blue Mountain Arts, Inc., 29
Bobit Publishing Company, 55
Bonnier AB, 52
Book-of-the-Month Club, Inc., 13
Bowne & Co., Inc., 23; 79 (upd.)
Broderbund Software, 13; 29 (upd.)
Brown Printing Company, 26
Burda Holding GmbH. & Co., 23
The Bureau of National Affairs, Inc., 23
Butterick Co., Inc., 23
Cadmus Communications Corporation, 23
Cahners Business Information, 43
Carl Allers Etablissement A/S, 72
Carus Publishing Company, 93
CCH Inc., 14
Central Newspapers, Inc., 10
Champion Industries, Inc., 28
Cherry Lane Music Publishing Company, Inc., 62
Chicago Review Press Inc., 84
ChoicePoint Inc., 65
The Christian Science Publishing Society, 55
The Chronicle Publishing Company, Inc., 23
Chrysalis Group plc, 40
CMP Media Inc., 26
Commerce Clearing House, Inc., 7
Community Newspaper Holdings, Inc., 91
Concepts Direct, Inc., 39
Condé Nast Publications, Inc., 13; 59 (upd.)
Consolidated Graphics, Inc., 70
Consumers Union, 26
The Copley Press, Inc., 23
Corelio S.A./N.V., 96
Cornelsen Verlagsholding GmbH & Co., 90
Courier Corporation, 41
Cowles Media Company, 23
Cox Enterprises, Inc., IV; 22 (upd.)
Crain Communications, Inc., 12; 35 (upd.)
Current, Inc., 37
Cygnus Business Media, Inc., 56
Dai Nippon Printing Co., Ltd., IV; 57 (upd.)
Daily Mail and General Trust plc, 19
Dawson Holdings PLC, 43
Day Runner, Inc., 14
DC Comics Inc., 25
De La Rue plc, 10; 34 (upd.)
DeLorme Publishing Company, Inc., 53
Deluxe Corporation, 7; 22 (upd.); 73 (upd.)
Dennis Publishing Ltd., 62
Dex Media, Inc., 65
Donruss Playoff L.P., 66
Dorling Kindersley Holdings plc, 20
Dover Publications Inc., 34
Dow Jones & Company, Inc., IV; 19 (upd.); 47 (upd.)
The Dun & Bradstreet Corporation, IV; 19 (upd.)
Duplex Products Inc., 17
The E.W. Scripps Company, IV; 7 (upd.); 28 (upd.); 66 (upd.)
Eagle-Tribune Publishing Co., 91
The Economist Group Ltd., 67
Edipresse S.A., 82
Éditions Gallimard, 72
Editis S.A. 78
Edmark Corporation, 14
Edwards Brothers, Inc., 92
Egmont Group, 93
Electronics for Imaging, Inc., 43 (upd.)
Elsevier N.V., IV
EMAP plc, 35
EMI Group plc, 22 (upd.); 81 (upd.)
Encyclopaedia Britannica, Inc., 7; 39 (upd.)
Engraph, Inc., 12
Enquirer/Star Group, Inc., 10
Entravision Communications Corporation, 41
Essence Communications, Inc., 24
F&W Publications, Inc., 71
Farm Journal Corporation, 42
Farrar, Straus and Giroux Inc., 15
Flint Ink Corporation, 13
Follett Corporation, 12; 39 (upd.)
Forbes Inc., 30; 82 (upd.)
Frankfurter Allgemeine Zeitung GmbH, 66
Franklin Electronic Publishers, Inc., 23
Freedom Communications, Inc., 36
G A Pindar & Son Ltd., 88
Gannett Company, Inc., IV; 7 (upd.); 30 (upd.); 66 (upd.)
GateHouse Media, Inc., 91
Geiger Bros., 60
Gibson Greetings, Inc., 12
Giesecke & Devrient GmbH, 83
Golden Books Family Entertainment, Inc., 28
Goss Holdings, Inc., 43
Graphic Industries Inc., 25
Gray Communications Systems, Inc., 24
Grolier Incorporated, 16; 43 (upd.)
Groupe de la Cite, IV
Groupe Les Echos, 25
Grupo Clarín S.A., 67
Grupo Televisa, S.A., 54 (upd.)
Guardian Media Group plc, 53
The H.W. Wilson Company, 66
Hachette, IV
Hachette Filipacchi Medias S.A., 21
Haights Cross Communications, Inc., 84
Hal Leonard Corporation, 96
Hallmark Cards, Inc., IV; 16 (upd.); 40 (upd.); 87 (upd.)
Harcourt Brace and Co., 12
Harcourt Brace Jovanovich, Inc., IV
Harcourt General, Inc., 20 (upd.)
Harlequin Enterprises Limited, 52
HarperCollins Publishers, 15
Harris Interactive Inc., 41; 92 (upd.)
Harry N. Abrams, Inc., 58
Harte-Hanks Communications, Inc., 17
Havas SA, 10; 33 (upd.)
Hay House, Inc., 93
Haynes Publishing Group P.L.C., 71

Hazelden Foundation, 28
Health Communications, Inc., 72
The Hearst Corporation, IV; 19 (upd.); 46 (upd.)
Her Majesty's Stationery Office, 7
Herald Media, Inc., 91
Highlights for Children, Inc., 95
N.V. Holdingmaatschappij De Telegraaf, 23
Hollinger International Inc., 24; 62 (upd.)
HOP, LLC, 80
Houghton Mifflin Company, 10; 36 (upd.)
IDG Books Worldwide, Inc., 27
IHS Inc. 78
Independent News & Media PLC, 61
Informa Group plc, 58
Information Holdings Inc., 47
International Data Group, Inc., 7; 25 (upd.)
IPC Magazines Limited, 7
J.J. Keller & Associates, Inc., 81
Jeppesen Sanderson, Inc., 92
John Fairfax Holdings Limited, 7
John H. Harland Company, 17
John Wiley & Sons, Inc., 17; 65 (upd.)
Johnson Publishing Company, Inc., 28; 72 (upd.)
Johnston Press plc, 35
Jostens, Inc., 25 (upd.); 73 (upd.)
Journal Communications, Inc., 86
Journal Register Company, 29
Jupitermedia Corporation, 75
Kaplan, Inc., 42
Kelley Blue Book Company, Inc., 84
Kensington Publishing Corporation, 84
Kinko's, Inc., 43 (upd.)
Knight Ridder, Inc., 67 (upd.)
Knight-Ridder, Inc., IV; 15 (upd.)
The Knot, Inc., 74
Kodansha Ltd., IV; 38 (upd.)
Krause Publications, Inc., 35
Landmark Communications, Inc., 12; 55 (upd.)
Larry Flynt Publishing Inc., 31
Le Monde S.A., 33
Lebhar-Friedman, Inc., 55
Lee Enterprises Inc., 11; 64 (upd.)
LEXIS-NEXIS Group, 33
Lonely Planet Publications Pty Ltd., 55
M. DuMont Schauberg GmbH & Co. KG, 92
M. Shanken Communications, Inc., 50
Maclean Hunter Publishing Limited, IV; 26 (upd.)
Macmillan, Inc., 7
Martha Stewart Living Omnimedia, Inc., 24; 73 (upd.)
Marvel Entertainment Inc., 10; 78 (upd.)
Matra-Hachette S.A., 15 (upd.)
Maxwell Communication Corporation plc, IV; 7 (upd.)
The McClatchy Company, 23; 92 (upd.)
The McGraw-Hill Companies, Inc., IV; 18 (upd.); 51 (upd.)
Mecklermedia Corporation, 24
Media General, Inc., 38 (upd.)
MediaNews Group, Inc., 70
Menasha Corporation, 59 (upd.)
Meredith Corporation, 11; 29 (upd.); 74 (upd.)
Merriam-Webster Inc., 70
Merrill Corporation, 18; 47 (upd.)
Metro International S.A., 93
Miami Herald Media Company, 92
Miller Publishing Group, LLC, 57
The Miner Group International, 22
Mirror Group Newspapers plc, 7; 23 (upd.)
Moore Corporation Limited, IV
Morris Communications Corporation, 36
Mrs. Grossman's Paper Company Inc., 84
Multimedia, Inc., 11
MYOB Ltd., 86
Naspers Ltd., 66
National Audubon Society, 26
National Geographic Society, 9; 30 (upd.); 79 (upd.)
National Journal Group Inc., 67
New Chapter Inc., 96
New Times, Inc., 45
New York Daily News, 32
The New York Times Company, IV; 19 (upd.); 61 (upd.)
News America Publishing Inc., 12
News Corporation Limited, IV; 7 (upd.)
Newsquest plc, 32
Next Media Ltd., 61
Nihon Keizai Shimbun, Inc., IV
Nolo.com, Inc., 49
Northern and Shell Network plc, 87
Oji Paper Co., Ltd., 57 (upd.)
Onion, Inc., 69
Ottaway Newspapers, Inc., 15
Outlook Group Corporation, 37
PagesJaunes Groupe SA, 79
Pantone Inc., 53
PCM Uitgevers NV, 53
Pearson plc, IV; 46 (upd.)
PennWell Corporation, 55
Penton Media, Inc., 27
The Perseus Books Group, 91
Petersen Publishing Company, 21
Philadelphia Media Holdings LLC, 92
The Phoenix Media/Communications Group, 91
Plain Dealer Publishing Company, 92
Plato Learning, Inc., 44
Playboy Enterprises, Inc., 18
Pleasant Company, 27
PMP Ltd., 72
PR Newswire, 35
Primedia Inc., 22
The Providence Journal Company, 28
Publishers Group, Inc., 35
Publishing and Broadcasting Limited, 54
Pulitzer Inc., 15; 58 (upd.)
Quad/Graphics, Inc., 19
Quebecor Inc., 12; 47 (upd.)
R.L. Polk & Co., 10
R.R. Donnelley & Sons Company, IV; 9 (upd.); 38 (upd.)
Rand McNally & Company, 28
Random House Inc., 13; 31 (upd.)
Ravensburger AG, 64
RCS MediaGroup S.p.A., 96
The Reader's Digest Association, Inc., IV; 17 (upd.); 71 (upd.)
Real Times, Inc., 66
Recycled Paper Greetings, Inc., 21
Reed Elsevier plc, IV; 17 (upd.); 31 (upd.)
Reuters Group PLC, IV; 22 (upd.); 63 (upd.)
Rodale, Inc., 23; 47 (upd.)
Rogers Communications Inc., 30 (upd.)
The Rowohlt Verlag GmbH, 96
Rural Press Ltd., 74
St Ives plc, 34
Salem Communications Corporation, 97
Sanborn Map Company Inc., 82
SanomaWSOY Corporation, 51
Schawk, Inc., 24
Schibsted ASA, 31
Scholastic Corporation, 10; 29 (upd.)
Scott Fetzer Company, 12; 80 (upd.)
Scottish Media Group plc, 32
Seat Pagine Gialle S.p.A., 47
Seattle Times Company, 15
The Sheridan Group, Inc., 86
The Sierra Club, 28
Simon & Schuster Inc., IV; 19 (upd.)
Singapore Press Holdings Limited, 85
Sir Speedy, Inc., 16
SkyMall, Inc., 26
Société du Figaro S.A., 60
Softbank Corp., 13
The Source Enterprises, Inc., 65
Southam Inc., 7
SPIEGEL-Verlag Rudolf Augstein GmbH & Co. KG, 44
The Standard Register Company, 15; 93 (upd.)
Stephens Media, LLC, 91
Strine Printing Company Inc., 88
Sunrise Greetings, 88
Tamedia AG, 53
Taylor & Francis Group plc, 44
Taylor Corporation, 36
Taylor Publishing Company, 12; 36 (upd.)
TechBooks Inc., 84
Thomas Crosbie Holdings Limited, 81
Thomas Nelson, Inc., 14; 38 (upd.)
Thomas Publishing Company, 26
The Thomson Corporation, 8; 34 (upd.); 77 (upd.)
Time Out Group Ltd., 68
The Times Mirror Company, IV; 17 (upd.)
Tohan Corporation, 84
TOKYOPOP Inc., 79
Tom Doherty Associates Inc., 25
Toppan Printing Co., Ltd., IV; 58 (upd.)
The Topps Company, Inc., 13; 34 (upd.); 83 (upd.)
Torstar Corporation, 29
Trader Classified Media N.V., 57
Tribune Company, IV, 22 (upd.); 63 (upd.)
Trinity Mirror plc, 49 (upd.)
Tuttle Publishing, 86
Tyndale House Publishers, Inc., 57
U.S. News & World Report Inc., 30; 89 (upd.)
United Business Media plc, 52 (upd.)

United News & Media plc, IV; 28 (upd.)
United Press International, Inc., 25; 73 (upd.)
The University of Chicago Press, 79
Valassis Communications, Inc., 8
Value Line, Inc., 16; 73 (upd.)
Vance Publishing Corporation, 64
Verlagsgruppe Georg von Holtzbrinck GmbH, 35
Village Voice Media, Inc., 38
VistaPrint Limited, 87
VNU N.V., 27
Volt Information Sciences Inc., 26
W.W. Norton & Company, Inc., 28
Wallace Computer Services, Inc., 36
Walsworth Publishing Co. 78
The Washington Post Company, IV; 20 (upd.)
Waverly, Inc., 16
WAZ Media Group, 82
Wegener NV, 53
Wenner Media, Inc., 32
West Group, 7; 34 (upd.)
Western Publishing Group, Inc., 13
WH Smith PLC, V; 42 (upd.)
William Reed Publishing Ltd. 78
Wolters Kluwer NV, 14; 33 (upd.)
Workman Publishing Company, Inc., 70
World Book, Inc., 12
World Color Press Inc., 12
World Publications, LLC, 65
Xeikon NV, 26
Yell Group PLC, 79
Zebra Technologies Corporation, 14
Ziff Davis Media Inc., 12; 36 (upd.); 73 (upd.)
Zondervan Corporation, 24; 71 (upd.)

Real Estate

Akerys S.A., 90
Alexander's, Inc., 45
Alico, Inc., 63
AMB Property Corporation, 57
American Campus Communities, Inc., 85
Amfac/JMB Hawaii L.L.C., 24 (upd.)
Apartment Investment and Management Company, 49
Archstone-Smith Trust, 49
Associated Estates Realty Corporation, 25
AvalonBay Communities, Inc., 58
Baird & Warner Holding Company, 87
Berkshire Realty Holdings, L.P., 49
Bluegreen Corporation, 80
Boston Properties, Inc., 22
Bouygues S.A., I; 24 (upd.); 97 (upd.)
Bramalea Ltd., 9
British Land Plc, 54
Brookfield Properties Corporation, 89
Burroughs & Chapin Company, Inc., 86
Camden Property Trust, 77
Canary Wharf Group Plc, 30
CapStar Hotel Company, 21
CarrAmerica Realty Corporation, 56
Castle & Cooke, Inc., 20 (upd.)
Catellus Development Corporation, 24
CB Commercial Real Estate Services Group, Inc., 21
CB Richard Ellis Group, Inc., 70 (upd.)
Central Florida Investments, Inc., 93
Chateau Communities, Inc., 37
Chelsfield PLC, 67
Cheung Kong (Holdings) Limited, IV; 20 (upd.)
City Developments Limited, 89
Clayton Homes Incorporated, 54 (upd.)
Colliers International Property Consultants Inc., 92
Colonial Properties Trust, 65
The Corcoran Group, Inc., 58
CoStar Group, Inc., 73
Cousins Properties Incorporated, 65
CSX Corporation 79 (upd.)
Cushman & Wakefield, Inc., 86
Del Webb Corporation, 14
Desarrolladora Homex, S.A. de C.V., 87
Developers Diversified Realty Corporation, 69
Draper and Kramer Inc., 96
Duke Realty Corporation, 57
Ducks Unlimited, Inc., 87
EastGroup Properties, Inc., 67
The Edward J. DeBartolo Corporation, 8
Enterprise Inns plc, 59
Equity Office Properties Trust, 54
Equity Residential, 49
Erickson Retirement Communities, 57
Fairfield Communities, Inc., 36
First Industrial Realty Trust, Inc., 65
Forest City Enterprises, Inc., 16; 52 (upd.)
Gale International Llc, 93
Gecina SA, 42
General Growth Properties, Inc., 57
GMH Communities Trust, 87
Great White Shark Enterprises, Inc., 89
Griffin Land & Nurseries, Inc., 43
Grubb & Ellis Company, 21
Guangzhou R&F Properties Co., Ltd., 95
The Haminerson Property Investment and Development Corporation plc, IV
Hammerson plc, 40
Harbert Corporation, 14
Helmsley Enterprises, Inc., 39 (upd.)
Henderson Land Development Company Ltd., 70
Home Properties of New York, Inc., 42
HomeVestors of America, Inc., 77
Hongkong Land Holdings Limited, IV; 47 (upd.)
Holiday Retirement Corp., 87
Hopson Development Holdings Ltd., 87
Hovnanian Enterprises, Inc., 29; 89 (upd.)
Hyatt Corporation, 16 (upd.)
ILX Resorts Incorporated, 65
IRSA Inversiones y Representaciones S.A., 63
J.F. Shea Co., Inc., 55
Jardine Cycle & Carriage Ltd., 73
JMB Realty Corporation, IV
Jones Lang LaSalle Incorporated, 49
JPI, 49
Kaufman and Broad Home Corporation, 8
Kennedy-Wilson, Inc., 60
Kerry Properties Limited, 22
Kimco Realty Corporation, 11
The Koll Company, 8
Land Securities PLC, IV; 49 (upd.)
Lefrak Organization Inc., 26
Lend Lease Corporation Limited, IV; 17 (upd.); 52 (upd.)
Liberty Property Trust, 57
Lincoln Property Company, 8; 54 (upd.)
The Loewen Group Inc., 40 (upd.)
The Long & Foster Companies, Inc., 85
The Macerich Company, 57
Mack-Cali Realty Corporation, 42
Macklowe Properties, Inc., 95
Manufactured Home Communities, Inc., 22
Maui Land & Pineapple Company, Inc., 29
Maxco Inc., 17
Meditrust, 11
Melvin Simon and Associates, Inc., 8
MEPC plc, IV
Meritage Corporation, 26
Mid-America Apartment Communities, Inc., 85
The Middleton Doll Company, 53
The Mills Corporation, 77
Mitsubishi Estate Company, Limited, IV; 61 (upd.)
Mitsui Real Estate Development Co., Ltd., IV
Morguard Corporation, 85
The Nature Conservancy, 28
New Plan Realty Trust, 11
New World Development Company Ltd., IV
Newhall Land and Farming Company, 14
Nexity S.A., 66
NRT Incorporated, 61
Olympia & York Developments Ltd., IV; 9 (upd.)
Park Corp., 22
Parque Arauco S.A., 72
Perini Corporation, 8
Pope Resources LP, 74
Post Properties, Inc., 26
Potlatch Corporation, 8; 34 (upd.); 87 (upd.)
ProLogis, 57
Public Storage, Inc., 52
Railtrack Group PLC, 50
RE/MAX International, Inc., 59
Reading International Inc., 70
Reckson Associates Realty Corp., 47
Regency Centers Corporation, 71
Rockefeller Group International Inc., 58
Rodamco N.V., 26
The Rouse Company, 15; 63 (upd.)
Sapporo Holdings Limited, I; 13 (upd.); 36 (upd.); 97 (upd.)
Shubert Organization Inc., 24
The Sierra Club, 28
Silverstein Properties, Inc., 47
Simco S.A., 37
SL Green Realty Corporation, 44
Slough Estates PLC, IV; 50 (upd.)
Sovran Self Storage, Inc., 66
Starrett Corporation, 21
The Staubach Company, 62
Storage USA, Inc., 21

Sumitomo Realty & Development Co., Ltd., IV
Sun Communities Inc., 46
Sunterra Corporation, 75
Tanger Factory Outlet Centers, Inc., 49
Tarragon Realty Investors, Inc., 45
Taubman Centers, Inc., 75
Taylor Woodrow plc, 38 (upd.)
Technical Olympic USA, Inc., 75
Tejon Ranch Company, 35
Tishman Speyer Properties, L.P., 47
Tokyu Land Corporation, IV
Trammell Crow Company, 8; 57 (upd.)
Trendwest Resorts, Inc., 33
Tridel Enterprises Inc., 9
Trizec Corporation Ltd., 10
The Trump Organization, 23; 64 (upd.)
Unibail SA, 40
United Dominion Realty Trust, Inc., 52
Vistana, Inc., 22
Vornado Realty Trust, 20
W.P. Carey & Co. LLC, 49
Weingarten Realty Investors, 95
William Lyon Homes, 59

Retail & Wholesale

A-Mark Financial Corporation, 71
A.C. Moore Arts & Crafts, Inc., 30
A.S. Watson & Company Ltd., 84
A.T. Cross Company, 49 (upd.)
Aaron Rents, Inc., 14; 35 (upd.)
Abatix Corp., 57
ABC Appliance, Inc., 10
ABC Carpet & Home Co. Inc., 26
Abercrombie & Fitch Company, 15; 75 (upd.)
Academy Sports & Outdoors, 27
Ace Hardware Corporation, 12; 35 (upd.)
Action Performance Companies, Inc., 27
Adams Childrenswear Ltd., 95
ADESA, Inc., 71
Adolfo Dominguez S.A., 72
AEON Co., Ltd., 68 (upd.)
Aéropostale, Inc., 89
After Hours Formalwear Inc., 60
Alabama Farmers Cooperative, Inc., 63
Alain Afflelou SA, 53
Alba-Waldensian, Inc., 30
Alberto-Culver Company, 8; 36 (upd.); 91 (upd.)
Albertson's, Inc., 65 (upd.)
Alimentation Couche-Tard Inc., 77
Alldays plc, 49
Allders plc, 37
Alliance Boots plc (updates Boots Group PLC), 83 (upd.)
Allou Health & Beauty Care, Inc., 28
Almacenes Exito S.A., 89
Alpha Airports Group PLC, 77
Alrosa Company Ltd., 62
Alticor Inc., 71 (upd.)
Amazon.com, Inc., 25; 56 (upd.)
AMERCO, 67 (upd.)
American Coin Merchandising, Inc., 28; 74 (upd.)
American Eagle Outfitters, Inc., 24; 55 (upd.)
American Furniture Company, Inc., 21
American Girl, Inc., 69 (upd.)
American Stores Company, 22 (upd.)
AmeriSource Health Corporation, 37 (upd.)
Ames Department Stores, Inc., 9; 30 (upd.)
Amscan Holdings, Inc., 61
Amway Corporation, 13; 30 (upd.)
The Anderson-DuBose Company, 60
The Andersons, Inc., 31
AnnTaylor Stores Corporation, 13; 37 (upd.); 67 (upd.)
Appliance Recycling Centers of America, Inc., 42
Arbor Drugs Inc., 12
Arcadia Group plc, 28 (upd.)
Army and Air Force Exchange Service, 39
Art Van Furniture, Inc., 28
ASDA Group plc, 28 (upd.)
Ashworth, Inc., 26
Au Printemps S.A., V
Audio King Corporation, 24
Authentic Fitness Corporation, 20; 51 (upd.)
Auto Value Associates, Inc., 25
Autobytel Inc., 47
AutoNation, Inc., 50
AutoTrader.com, L.L.C., 91
AutoZone, Inc., 9; 31 (upd.)
AVA AG (Allgemeine Handelsgesellschaft der Verbraucher AG), 33
Aveda Corporation, 24
Aviall, Inc., 73
Aviation Sales Company, 41
AWB Ltd., 56
B. Dalton Bookseller Inc., 25
Babbage's, Inc., 10
Baby Superstore, Inc., 15
Baccarat, 24
Bachman's Inc., 22
Bailey Nurseries, Inc., 57
Ball Horticultural Company 78
Banana Republic Inc., 25
Bare Escentuals, Inc., 91
Barnes & Noble, Inc., 10; 30 (upd.); 75 (upd.)
Barnett Inc., 28
Barney's, Inc., 28
Barrett-Jackson Auction Company L.L.C., 88
Bass Pro Shops, Inc., 42
Baumax AG, 75
Beacon Roofing Supply, Inc., 75
Bear Creek Corporation, 38
Bearings, Inc., 13
Beate Uhse AG, 96
bebe stores, inc., 31
Bed Bath & Beyond Inc., 13; 41 (upd.)
Belk Stores Services, Inc., V; 19 (upd.)
Belk, Inc., 72 (upd.)
Ben Bridge Jeweler, Inc., 60
Benetton Group S.p.A., 10; 67 (upd.)
Berean Christian Stores, 96
Bergdorf Goodman Inc., 52
Bergen Brunswig Corporation, V; 13 (upd.)
Bernard Chaus, Inc., 27
Best Buy Co., Inc., 9; 23 (upd.); 63 (upd.)
Bestseller A/S, 90
Bhs plc, 17
Big A Drug Stores Inc., 79
Big Dog Holdings, Inc., 45
Big 5 Sporting Goods Corporation, 55
The Big Food Group plc, 68 (upd.)
Big Lots, Inc., 50
Big O Tires, Inc., 20
Birkenstock Footprint Sandals, Inc., 42 (upd.)
Birthdays Ltd., 70
Black Box Corporation, 20; 96 (upd.)
Blacks Leisure Group plc, 39
Blair Corporation, 25; 31 (upd.)
Blish-Mize Co., 95
Blokker Holding B.V., 84
Bloomingdale's Inc., 12
Blue Nile Inc., 61
Blue Square Israel Ltd., 41
Bluefly, Inc., 60
BlueLinx Holdings Inc., 97
Blyth Industries, Inc., 18
The Body Shop International PLC, 11
The Bombay Company, Inc., 10; 71 (upd.)
The Bon Marché, Inc., 23
The Bon-Ton Stores, Inc., 16; 50 (upd.)
Booker Cash & Carry Ltd., 68 (upd.)
Books-A-Million, Inc., 14; 41 (upd.); 96 (upd.)
Bookspan, 86
The Boots Company PLC, V; 24 (upd.)
Borders Group, Inc., 15; 43 (upd.)
Boscov's Department Store, Inc., 31
Boss Holdings, Inc., 97
Bozzuto's, Inc., 13
Bradlees Discount Department Store Company, 12
Brambles Industries Limited, 42
Bricorama S.A., 68
Brioni Roman Style S.p.A., 67
Brodart Company, 84
Broder Bros. Co., 38
Bronner Display & Sign Advertising, Inc., 82
Brooks Brothers Inc., 22
Brookstone, Inc., 18
Brown Shoe Company, Inc., 68 (upd.)
Brunswick Corporation, 77 (upd.)
The Buckle, Inc., 18
Buhrmann NV, 41
Build-A-Bear Workshop Inc., 62
Building Materials Holding Corporation, 52
Burdines, Inc., 60
Burlington Coat Factory Warehouse Corporation, 10; 60 (upd.)
Burt's Bees, Inc., 58
The Burton Group plc, V
Buttrey Food & Drug Stores Co., 18
buy.com, Inc., 46
C&A, V; 40 (upd.)
C&J Clark International Ltd., 52
Cabela's Inc., 26; 68 (upd.)
Cablevision Electronic Instruments, Inc., 32

Cache Incorporated, 30
Cactus S.A., 90
Caldor Inc., 12
Calloway's Nursery, Inc., 51
Camaïeu S.A., 72
Camelot Music, Inc., 26
Campeau Corporation, V
Campo Electronics, Appliances & Computers, Inc., 16
Car Toys, Inc., 67
The Carphone Warehouse Group PLC, 83
Carrefour SA, 10; 27 (upd.); 64 (upd.)
Carson Pirie Scott & Company, 15
Carter Hawley Hale Stores, Inc., V
Carter Lumber Company, 45
Cartier Monde, 29
Casas Bahia Comercial Ltda., 75
Casey's General Stores, Inc., 19; 83 (upd.)
Castro Model Ltd., 86
Casual Corner Group, Inc., 43
Casual Male Retail Group, Inc., 52
Catherines Stores Corporation, 15
Cato Corporation, 14
CDW Computer Centers, Inc., 16
Celebrate Express, Inc., 70
Celebrity, Inc., 22
CellStar Corporation, 83
Cencosud S.A., 69
Central European Distribution Corporation, 75
Central Garden & Pet Company, 23
Cenveo Inc., 71 (upd.)
Chadwick's of Boston, Ltd., 29
Charlotte Russe Holding, Inc., 35; 90 (upd.)
Charming Shoppes, Inc., 38
Chas. Levy Company LLC, 60
ChevronTexaco Corporation, 47 (upd.)
Chiasso Inc., 53
The Children's Place Retail Stores, Inc., 37; 86 (upd.)
China Nepstar Chain Drugstore Ltd., 97
Christian Dior S.A., 49 (upd.)
Christopher & Banks Corporation, 42
Cifra, S.A. de C.V., 12
The Circle K Company, 20 (upd.)
Circuit City Stores, Inc., 9; 29 (upd.); 65 (upd.)
Clare Rose Inc., 68
Clinton Cards plc, 39
The Clothestime, Inc., 20
CML Group, Inc., 10
Co-operative Group (CWS) Ltd., 51
Coach, Inc., 45 (upd.)
Coborn's, Inc., 30
Coinmach Laundry Corporation, 20
Coldwater Creek Inc., 21; 74 (upd.)
Cole National Corporation, 13; 76 (upd.)
Cole's Quality Foods, Inc., 68
Coles Group Limited, V; 20 (upd.); 85 (upd.)
Collectors Universe, Inc., 48
Columbia House Company, 69
Comdisco, Inc., 9
Compagnie Financière Sucres et Denrées S.A., 60
Companhia Brasileira de Distribuiçao, 76
CompUSA, Inc., 10
Computerland Corp., 13
Concepts Direct, Inc., 39
Conn's, Inc., 67
The Container Store, 36
Controladora Comercial Mexicana, S.A. de C.V., 36
CoolSavings, Inc., 77
Coop Schweiz Genossenschaftsverband, 48
Coppel, S.A. de C.V., 82
Corby Distilleries Limited, 14
Corporate Express, Inc., 22; 47 (upd.)
Cortefiel S.A., 64
The Cosmetic Center, Inc., 22
Cost Plus, Inc., 27
Costco Wholesale Corporation, V; 43 (upd.)
Cotter & Company, V
County Seat Stores Inc., 9
Courts Plc, 45
CPI Corp., 38
Crate and Barrel, 9
Croscill, Inc., 42
CROSSMARK, 79
Crowley, Milner & Company, 19
Crown Books Corporation, 21
Cumberland Farms, Inc., 17; 84 (upd.)
CVS Corporation, 45 (upd.)
D&H Distributing Co., 95
Daffy's Inc., 26
The Daiei, Inc., V; 17 (upd.); 41 (upd.)
The Daimaru, Inc., V; 42 (upd.)
Dairy Farm International Holdings Ltd., 97
Dairy Mart Convenience Stores, Inc., 25 (upd.)
Daisytek International Corporation, 18
Damark International, Inc., 18
Dart Group Corporation, 16
Darty S.A., 27
David Jones Ltd., 60
David's Bridal, Inc., 33
Dayton Hudson Corporation, V; 18 (upd.)
Deb Shops, Inc., 16; 76 (upd.)
Debenhams Plc, 28
Deli Universal NV, 66
dELiA*s Inc., 29
Department 56, Inc., 34 (upd.)
Designer Holdings Ltd., 20
Deveaux S.A., 41
DFS Group Ltd., 66
Dick's Sporting Goods, Inc., 59
Diesel SpA, 40
Digital River, Inc., 50
Dillard Department Stores, Inc., V; 16 (upd.)
Dillard's Inc., 68 (upd.)
Dillon Companies Inc., 12
Discount Auto Parts, Inc., 18
Discount Drug Mart, Inc., 14
Dixons Group plc, V; 19 (upd.); 49 (upd.)
Do it Best Corporation, 30
Dollar Tree Stores, Inc., 23; 62 (upd.)
Donna Karan International Inc., 56 (upd.)
Dorian Drake International Inc., 96
Dreams Inc., 97
The Dress Barn, Inc., 24; 55 (upd.)
Drs. Foster & Smith, Inc., 62
Drug Emporium, Inc., 12
DSW Inc., 73
Du Pareil au Même, 43
Duane Reade Holding Corp., 21
Duckwall-ALCO Stores, Inc., 24
Dunnes Stores Ltd., 58
Duron Inc., 72
Duty Free International, Inc., 11
Dylex Limited, 29
E-Z Serve Corporation, 17
Eagle Hardware & Garden, Inc., 16
Eastman Kodak Company, III; 7 (upd.); 36 (upd.); 91 (upd.)
eBay Inc., 32
Eckerd Corporation, 9; 32 (upd.)
Eddie Bauer Holdings, Inc., 9; 36 (upd.); 87 (upd.)
Edgars Consolidated Stores Ltd., 66
Edward Hines Lumber Company, 68
Egghead.com, Inc., 31 (upd.)
Eileen Fisher Inc., 61
El Corte Inglés Group, V
El Puerto de Liverpool, S.A.B. de C.V., 97
The Elder-Beerman Stores Corp., 10; 63 (upd.)
Electrocomponents PLC, 50
Electronics Boutique Holdings Corporation, 72
Elephant Pharmacy, Inc., 83
Ellett Brothers, Inc., 17
EMI Group plc, 22 (upd.); 81 (upd.)
Empresas Almacenes Paris S.A., 71
Ermenegildo Zegna SpA, 63
ESCADA AG, 71
The Estée Lauder Companies Inc., 9; 30 (upd.); 93 (upd.)
Etablissements Franz Colruyt N.V., 68
Ethan Allen Interiors, Inc., 39 (upd.)
EToys, Inc., 37
Euromarket Designs Inc., 31 (upd.)
Evans, Inc., 30
Eye Care Centers of America, Inc., 69
EZCORP Inc., 43
F.W. Webb Company, 95
The F. Dohmen Co., 77
Family Christian Stores, Inc., 51
Family Dollar Stores, Inc., 13; 62 (upd.)
Fannie May Confections Brands, Inc., 80
Farmacias Ahumada S.A., 72
Fastenal Company, 14; 42 (upd.)
Faultless Starch/Bon Ami Company, 55
Fay's Inc., 17
Federated Department Stores, Inc., 9; 31 (upd.)
Fenaco, 86
Fielmann AG, 31
Fila Holding S.p.A., 20; 52 (upd.)
Finarte Casa d'Aste S.p.A., 93
Findel plc, 60
Fingerhut Companies, Inc., 9; 36 (upd.)
The Finish Line, Inc., 29; 68 (upd.)
Finlay Enterprises, Inc., 16; 76 (upd.)
Finning International Inc., 69
First Cash Financial Services, Inc., 57
Fleming Companies, Inc., 17 (upd.)
Florsheim Shoe Group Inc., 9; 31 (upd.)
FNAC, 21

Follett Corporation, 12
Foot Locker, Inc., 68 (upd.)
Footstar, Incorporated, 24
Forever 21, Inc., 84
Fortunoff Fine Jewelry and Silverware Inc., 26
The Forzani Group Ltd., 79
Foxworth-Galbraith Lumber Company, 91
Frank's Nursery & Crafts, Inc., 12
Fred Meyer Stores, Inc., V; 20 (upd.); 64 (upd.)
Fred's, Inc., 23; 62 (upd.)
Frederick Atkins Inc., 16
Frederick's of Hollywood, Inc., 59 (upd.)
Freeze.com LLC, 77
Fretter, Inc., 10
Friedman's Inc., 29
Fruth Pharmacy, Inc., 66
Fry's Electronics, Inc., 68
Funco, Inc., 20
Future Shop Ltd., 62
G&K Holding S.A., 95
G.I. Joe's, Inc., 30
Gadzooks, Inc., 18
Gaiam, Inc., 41
Galeries Lafayette S.A., V; 23 (upd.)
Galyan's Trading Company, Inc., 47
GameStop Corp., 69 (upd.)
Gander Mountain, Inc., 20; 90 (upd.)
Gantos, Inc., 17
The Gap, Inc., V; 18 (upd.); 55 (upd.)
Garden Ridge Corporation, 27
Garst Seed Company, Inc., 86
Gart Sports Company, 24
GEHE AG, 27
General Binding Corporation, 10
General Host Corporation, 12
Genesco Inc., 17; 84 (upd.)
Genovese Drug Stores, Inc., 18
Genuine Parts Company, 45 (upd.)
Gerald Stevens, Inc., 37
Gerhard D. Wempe KG, 88
Giant Food Inc., 22 (upd.)
GIB Group, V; 26 (upd.)
Gibbs and Dandy plc, 74
GiFi S.A., 74
Glacier Water Services, Inc., 47
Global Imaging Systems, Inc., 73
GOME Electrical Appliances Holding Ltd., 87
The Good Guys, Inc., 10; 30 (upd.)
Goodwill Industries International, Inc., 16
Goody's Family Clothing, Inc., 20; 64 (upd.)
Gordmans, Inc., 74
Gottschalks, Inc., 18; 91 (upd.)
Grand Piano & Furniture Company, 72
GrandVision S.A., 43
Graybar Electric Company, Inc., 54
The Great Universal Stores plc, V; 19 (upd.)
Griffin Land & Nurseries, Inc., 43
Grossman's Inc., 13
Groupe Alain Manoukian, 55
Groupe Castorama-Dubois Investissements, 23
Groupe DMC (Dollfus Mieg & Cie), 27
Groupe Go Sport S.A., 39
Groupe Lapeyre S.A., 33
Groupe Monnoyeur, 72
Groupe Zannier S.A., 35
Grow Biz International, Inc., 18
Grupo Casa Saba, S.A. de C.V., 39
Grupo Elektra, S.A. de C.V., 39
Grupo Eroski, 64
Grupo Gigante, S.A. de C.V., 34
Gruppo Coin S.p.A., 41
GSC Enterprises, Inc., 86
GT Bicycles, 26
GTSI Corp., 57
Gucci Group N.V., 15; 50 (upd.)
Guilbert S.A., 42
Guitar Center, Inc., 29; 68 (upd.)
GUS plc, 47 (upd.)
Gymboree Corporation, 69 (upd.)
Hahn Automotive Warehouse, Inc., 24
Hale-Halsell Company, 60
Half Price Books, Records, Magazines Inc., 37
Hallmark Cards, Inc., IV; 16 (upd.); 40 (upd.); 87 (upd.)
Hammacher Schlemmer & Company Inc., 21; 72 (upd.)
Hancock Fabrics, Inc., 18
Hankyu Department Stores, Inc., V; 62 (upd.)
Hanna Andersson Corp., 49
Hanover Compressor Company, 59
Hanover Direct, Inc., 36
Harold's Stores, Inc., 22
Harrods Holdings, 47
Harry Winston Inc., 45
Harvey Norman Holdings Ltd., 56
Hasbro, Inc., 43 (upd.)
Haverty Furniture Companies, Inc., 31
Headlam Group plc, 95
Hechinger Company, 12
Heilig-Meyers Company, 14; 40 (upd.)
Heinrich Deichmann-Schuhe GmbH & Co. KG, 88
Helzberg Diamonds, 40
Hennes & Mauritz AB, 29
Henry Modell & Company Inc., 32
Hensley & Company, 64
Hertie Waren- und Kaufhaus GmbH, V
Hibbett Sporting Goods, Inc., 26; 70 (upd.)
Highsmith Inc., 60
Hills Stores Company, 13
Hines Horticulture, Inc., 49
HMV Group plc, 59
Hobby Lobby Stores Inc., 80
The Hockey Company, 34
Holiday RV Superstores, Incorporated, 26
Holt's Cigar Holdings, Inc., 42
The Home Depot, Inc., V; 18 (upd.); 97 (upd.)
Home Hardware Stores Ltd., 62
Home Interiors & Gifts, Inc., 55
Home Retail Group plc, 91
Home Shopping Network, Inc., V; 25 (upd.)
HomeBase, Inc., 33 (upd.)
Hot Topic Inc., 33; 86 (upd.)
House of Fabrics, Inc., 21
House of Fraser PLC, 45
Houston Wire & Cable Company, 97
HSN, 64 (upd.)
Hudson's Bay Company, V; 25 (upd.); 83 (upd.)
Huttig Building Products, Inc., 73
Ihr Platz GmbH + Company KG, 77
IKEA International A/S, V; 26 (upd.)
InaCom Corporation, 13
Indigo Books & Music Inc., 58
Insight Enterprises, Inc., 18
Intermix Media, Inc., 83
International Airline Support Group, Inc., 55
Intimate Brands, Inc., 24
Intres B.V., 82
Isetan Company Limited, V; 36 (upd.)
Ito-Yokado Co., Ltd., V; 42 (upd.)
J&R Electronics Inc., 26
J. Baker, Inc., 31
The J. Jill Group Inc., 35; 90 (upd.)
J. C. Penney Company, Inc., V; 18 (upd.); 43 (upd.); 91 (upd.)
J.L. Hammett Company, 72
J. W. Pepper and Son Inc., 86
Jack Schwartz Shoes, Inc., 18
Jacobson Stores Inc., 21
Jalate Inc., 25
James Beattie plc, 43
Jay Jacobs, Inc., 15
Jennifer Convertibles, Inc., 31
Jetro Cash & Carry Enterprises Inc., 38
Jewett-Cameron Trading Company, Ltd., 89
JG Industries, Inc., 15
JJB Sports plc, 32
Jo-Ann Stores, Inc., 72 (upd.)
John Lewis Partnership plc, V; 42 (upd.)
Jordan-Kitt Music Inc., 86
Jumbo S.A., 96
JUSCO Co., Ltd., V
Just For Feet, Inc., 19
K & B Inc., 12
K & G Men's Center, Inc., 21
K-tel International, Inc., 21
Karstadt Aktiengesellschaft, V; 19 (upd.)
Kash n' Karry Food Stores, Inc., 20
Kasper A.S.L., Ltd., 40
kate spade LLC, 68
Kaufhof Warenhaus AG, V; 23 (upd.)
Kaufring AG, 35
Kay-Bee Toy Stores, 15
Keys Fitness Products, LP, 83
Kiabi Europe, 66
Kiehl's Since 1851, Inc., 52
Kingfisher plc, V; 24 (upd.); 83 (upd.)
Kinney Shoe Corp., 14
Kmart Corporation, V; 18 (upd.); 47 (upd.)
Knoll Group Inc., 14
Kohl's Corporation, 9; 30 (upd.); 77 (upd.)
Koninklijke Vendex KBB N.V. (Royal Vendex KBB N.V.), 62 (upd.)
Kotobukiya Co., Ltd., V; 56 (upd.)
Krause's Furniture, Inc., 27
Krispy Kreme Doughnuts, Inc., 21; 61 (upd.)
Kruse International, 88

L. and J.G. Stickley, Inc., 50
L. Luria & Son, Inc., 19
L.A. T Sportswear, Inc., 26
L.L. Bean, Inc., 10; 38 (upd.); 91 (upd.)
La Senza Corporation, 66
La-Z-Boy Incorporated, 14; 50 (upd.)
Lamonts Apparel, Inc., 15
Lands' End, Inc., 9; 29 (upd.); 82 (upd.)
Lane Bryant, Inc., 64
Lanier Worldwide, Inc., 75
Lanoga Corporation, 62
Laura Ashley Holdings plc, 37 (upd.)
Lazare Kaplan International Inc., 21
Le Chateau Inc., 63
Lechmere Inc., 10
Lechters, Inc., 11; 39 (upd.)
LensCrafters Inc., 23; 76 (upd.)
Leroy Merlin SA, 54
Les Boutiques San Francisco, Inc., 62
Lesco Inc., 19
Leslie's Poolmart, Inc., 18
Leupold & Stevens, Inc., 52
Levenger Company, 63
Levitz Furniture Inc., 15
Lewis Galoob Toys Inc., 16
Li & Fung Limited, 59
Liberty Orchards Co., Inc., 89
Life is Good, Inc., 80
Lifetime Brands, Inc., 27; 73 (upd.)
Lillian Vernon Corporation, 12; 35 (upd.); 92 (upd.)
The Limited, Inc., V; 20 (upd.)
Linens 'n Things, Inc., 24; 75 (upd.)
Little Switzerland, Inc., 60
Littleton Coin Company Inc., 82
Littlewoods plc, V; 42 (upd.)
LivePerson, Inc., 91
Liz Claiborne, Inc., 25 (upd.)
LKQ Corporation, 71
Loehmann's Inc., 24
Lojas Americanas S.A., 77
Lojas Arapuã S.A., 22; 61 (upd.)
London Drugs Ltd., 46
Longs Drug Stores Corporation, V; 25 (upd.); 83 (upd.)
Lookers plc, 71
Lost Arrow Inc., 22
LOT$OFF Corporation, 24
Love's Travel Stops & Country Stores, Inc., 71
Lowe's Companies, Inc., V; 21 (upd.); 81 (upd.)
Ludendo S.A., 88
Luxottica SpA, 17; 52 (upd.)
Lyfra-S.A./NV, 88
Mac Frugal's Bargains - Closeouts Inc., 17
Mac-Gray Corporation, 44
Mackays Stores Group Ltd., 92
Manheim, 88
Manutan International S.A., 72
Maples Industries, Inc., 83
MarineMax, Inc., 30
Marionnaud Parfumeries SA, 51
Marks and Spencer Group p.l.c., V; 24 (upd.); 85 (upd.)
Marks Brothers Jewelers, Inc., 24
Marlin Business Services Corp., 89
Marshall Field's, 63
Marshalls Incorporated, 13
Marui Company Ltd., V; 62 (upd.)
Maruzen Co., Limited, 18
Mary Kay Inc., 9; 30 (upd.); 84 (upd.)
Matalan PLC, 49
Matsuzakaya Company Ltd., V; 64 (upd.)
Maurices Inc., 95
Maus Frères SA, 48
The Maxim Group, 25
The May Department Stores Company, V; 19 (upd.); 46 (upd.)
Mayor's Jewelers, Inc., 41
Mazel Stores, Inc., 29
McCoy Corporation, 58
McGrath RentCorp, 91
McJunkin Corporation, 63
McKesson Corporation, 47 (upd.)
McLane Company, Inc., 13
McNaughton Apparel Group, Inc., 92 (upd.)
MCSi, Inc., 41
Media Arts Group, Inc., 42
Meier & Frank Co., 23
Meijer Incorporated, 27 (upd.)
Melville Corporation, V
The Men's Wearhouse, Inc., 17; 48 (upd.)
Menard, Inc., 34
Mercantile Stores Company, Inc., V; 19 (upd.)
Mercury Drug Corporation, 70
Merry-Go-Round Enterprises, Inc., 8
Mervyn's California, 10; 39 (upd.)
Metal Management, Inc., 92
Metro AG, 50
Michael C. Fina Co., Inc., 52
Michaels Stores, Inc., 17; 71 (upd.)
Michigan Sporting Goods Distributors, Inc., 72
Micro Warehouse, Inc., 16
MicroAge, Inc., 16
Migros-Genossenschafts-Bund, 68
Milton CAT, Inc., 86
Mitsukoshi Ltd., V; 56 (upd.)
MNS, Ltd., 65
Monoprix S.A., 86
Monrovia Nursery Company, 70
Monsoon plc, 39
Montgomery Ward & Co., Incorporated, V; 20 (upd.)
Moore-Handley, Inc., 39
Morrow Equipment Co. L.L.C., 87
Morse Shoe Inc., 13
Moss Bros Group plc, 51
Mothercare plc, 78 (upd.)
Mothers Work, Inc., 18
Moto Photo, Inc., 45
Mr. Bricolage S.A., 37
MSC Industrial Direct Co., Inc., 71
MTS Inc., 37
Mulberry Group PLC, 71
Musicland Stores Corporation, 9; 38 (upd.)
MWI Veterinary Supply, Inc., 80
Nagasakiya Co., Ltd., V; 69 (upd.)
Nash Finch Company, 65 (upd.)
National Educational Music Co. Ltd., 47
National Home Centers, Inc., 44
National Intergroup, Inc., V
National Record Mart, Inc., 29
National Wine & Spirits, Inc., 49
Natura Cosméticos S.A., 75
Natural Wonders Inc., 14
Navy Exchange Service Command, 31
Nebraska Book Company, Inc., 65
Neff Corp., 32
NeighborCare, Inc., 67 (upd.)
The Neiman Marcus Group, Inc., 12; 49 (upd.)
Netflix, Inc., 58
New Look Group plc, 35
Next plc, 29
Nichii Co., Ltd., V
NIKE, Inc., 36 (upd.)
Nine West Group Inc., 11
99;ct Only Stores, 25
Nocibé SA, 54
Noland Company, 35
Noodle Kidoodle, 16
Nordstrom, Inc., V; 18 (upd.); 67 (upd.)
Norelco Consumer Products Co., 26
Norm Thompson Outfitters, Inc., 47
North Pacific Group, Inc., 61
The North West Company, Inc., 12
Norton McNaughton, Inc., 27
Nu Skin Enterprises, Inc., 27; 76 (upd.)
Oakley, Inc., 49 (upd.)
Office Depot, Inc., 8; 23 (upd.); 65 (upd.)
OfficeMax, Inc., 15; 43 (upd.)
Olan Mills, Inc., 62
Old America Stores, Inc., 17
Old Navy, Inc., 70
One Price Clothing Stores, Inc., 20
O'Neal Steel, Inc., 95
The Oppenheimer Group, 76
Orchard Supply Hardware Stores Corporation, 17
Organización Soriana, S.A. de C.V., 35
The Orvis Company, Inc., 28
OshKosh B'Gosh, Inc., 42 (upd.)
Oshman's Sporting Goods, Inc., 17
Ottakar's plc, 64
Otto Versand (GmbH & Co.), V; 15 (upd.); 34 (upd.)
Overstock.com, Inc., 75
Owens & Minor, Inc., 16; 68 (upd.)
P.C. Richard & Son Corp., 23
Pamida Holdings Corporation, 15
The Pampered Chef, Ltd., 18; 78 (upd.)
The Pantry, Inc., 36
The Paradies Shops, Inc., 88
Parisian, Inc., 14
Party City Corporation, 54
Paul Harris Stores, Inc., 18
Pay 'N Pak Stores, Inc., 9
Payless Cashways, Inc., 11; 44 (upd.)
Payless ShoeSource, Inc., 18; 69 (upd.)
PCA International, Inc., 62
PDQ Food Stores, Inc., 79
Pearle Vision, Inc., 13
Peebles Inc., 16; 43 (upd.)
Peet's Coffee & Tea, Inc., 38
Penzeys Spices, Inc., 79
The Pep Boys—Manny, Moe & Jack, 11; 36 (upd.); 81 (upd.)
Petco Animal Supplies, Inc., 29; 74 (upd.)

Petit Bateau, 95
PetMed Express, Inc., 81
Petrie Stores Corporation, 8
PETsMART, Inc., 14; 41 (upd.)
PFSweb, Inc., 73
Phar-Mor Inc., 12
Phones 4u Ltd., 85
Photo-Me International Plc, 83
Pick 'n Pay Stores Ltd., 82
Pier 1 Imports, Inc., 12; 34 (upd.); 95 (upd.)
Piercing Pagoda, Inc., 29
Pilot Corporation, 49
Pinault-Printemps Redoute S.A., 19 (upd.)
Pitman Company, 58
Pomeroy Computer Resources, Inc., 33
Powell's Books, Inc., 40
PPR S.A., 74 (upd.)
Praxis Bookstore Group LLC, 90
The Price Company, V
PriceCostco, Inc., 14
PriceSmart, Inc., 71
Pro-Build Holdings Inc., 95 (upd.)
Proffitt's, Inc., 19
Provell Inc., 58 (upd.)
Provigo Inc., 51 (upd.)
Publishers Clearing House, 64 (upd.)
Puig Beauty and Fashion Group S.L., 60
Purina Mills, Inc., 32
Quelle Group, V
QuikTrip Corporation, 36
Quiksilver, Inc., 79 (upd.)
Quill Corporation, 28
QVC Inc., 58 (upd.)
R.C. Willey Home Furnishings, 72
R.H. Macy & Co., Inc., V; 8 (upd.); 30 (upd.)
RadioShack Corporation, 36 (upd.)
Rag Shops, Inc., 30
Raley's Inc., 14; 58 (upd.)
Rallye SA, 54
Rapala-Normark Group, Ltd., 30
Ratner Companies, 72
RDO Equipment Company, 33
Reckitt Benckiser plc, II; 42 (upd.); 91 (upd.)
Recoton Corp., 15
Recreational Equipment, Inc., 18; 71 (upd.)
Red McCombs Automotive Group, 91
Red Wing Shoe Company, Inc., 9; 30 (upd.); 83 (upd.)
Redlon & Johnson, Inc., 97
Reeds Jewelers, Inc., 22
Rejuvenation, Inc., 91
Reliance Steel & Aluminum Company, 70 (upd.)
Rent-A-Center, Inc., 45
Rent-Way, Inc., 33; 75 (upd.)
Restoration Hardware, Inc., 30; 96 (upd.)
Retail Ventures, Inc., 82 (upd.)
Revco D.S., Inc., V
REX Stores Corp., 10
Rhodes Inc., 23
Richton International Corporation, 39
Riklis Family Corp., 9
Rinascente S.p.A., 71
Rite Aid Corporation, V; 19 (upd.); 63 (upd.)
Ritz Camera Centers, 34
RM Auctions, Inc., 88
Roberds Inc., 19
Rocky Shoes & Boots, Inc., 26
Rogers Communications Inc., 30 (upd.)
RONA, Inc., 73
Ronco Corporation, 15; 80 (upd.)
Rooms To Go Inc., 28
Roots Canada Ltd., 42
Rose's Stores, Inc., 13
Ross Stores, Inc., 17; 43 (upd.)
Rosy Blue N.V., 84
Roundy's Inc., 14
Rush Enterprises, Inc., 64
Ryoshoku Ltd., 72
S&K Famous Brands, Inc., 23
S.A.C.I. Falabella, 69
Saks Inc., 24; 41 (upd.)
Sally Beauty Company, Inc., 60
Sam Ash Music Corporation, 30
Sam Levin Inc., 80
Sam's Club, 40
Samuels Jewelers Incorporated, 30
Sanborn Hermanos, S.A., 20
SanomaWSOY Corporation, 51
Scheels All Sports Inc., 63
Schmitt Music Company, 40
Schneiderman's Furniture Inc., 28
School Specialty, Inc., 68
Schottenstein Stores Corp., 14
Schultz Sav-O Stores, Inc., 31
The Score Board, Inc., 19
Scotty's, Inc., 22
The Scoular Company, 77
SCP Pool Corporation, 39
Seaman Furniture Company, Inc., 32
Sean John Clothing, Inc., 70
Sears plc, V
Sears Roebuck de México, S.A. de C.V., 20
Sears, Roebuck and Co., V; 18 (upd.); 56 (upd.)
SED International Holdings, Inc., 43
Seibu Department Stores, Ltd., V; 42 (upd.)
Seigle's Home and Building Centers, Inc., 41
The Seiyu, Ltd., V; 36 (upd.)
Selfridges Plc, 34
Service Merchandise Company, Inc., V; 19 (upd.)
7-Eleven, Inc., 32 (upd.)
Seventh Generation, Inc., 73
Shaklee Corporation, 12
The Sharper Image Corporation, 10; 62 (upd.)
Sheetz, Inc., 85
Sheplers, Inc., 96
The Sherwin-Williams Company, 89 (upd.)
Shoe Carnival Inc., 14; 72 (upd.)
ShopKo Stores Inc., 21; 58 (upd.)
Shoppers Drug Mart Corporation, 49
Shoppers Food Warehouse Corporation, 66
SIG plc, 71
Signet Group PLC, 61
skinnyCorp, LLC, 97
SkyMall, Inc., 26
Sleepy's Inc., 32
Smith & Hawken, Ltd., 68
Snapfish, 83
Solo Serve Corporation, 28
Sophus Berendsen A/S, 49
Sound Advice, Inc., 41
Source Interlink Companies, Inc., 75
Southern States Cooperative Incorporated, 36
Spartan Stores Inc., 66 (upd.)
Spec's Music, Inc., 19
Spector Photo Group N.V., 82
Spiegel, Inc., 10; 27 (upd.)
Sport Chalet, Inc., 16
Sport Supply Group, Inc., 23
Sportmart, Inc., 15
Sports & Recreation, Inc., 17
The Sports Authority, Inc., 16; 43 (upd.)
The Sportsman's Guide, Inc., 36
Stage Stores, Inc., 24; 82 (upd.)
Stanhome Inc., 15
Staple Cotton Cooperative Association (Staplcotn), 86
Staples, Inc., 10; 55 (upd.)
Starbucks Corporation, 13; 34 (upd.); 77 (upd.)
Starcraft Corporation, 30
Stefanel SpA, 63
Stein Mart Inc., 19; 72 (upd.)
Steve & Barry's LLC, 88
Stewart's Shops Corporation, 80
Stinnes AG, 8
The Stop & Shop Companies, Inc., 24 (upd.)
Storehouse PLC, 16
Strauss Discount Auto, 56
Stride Rite Corporation, 8
The Strober Organization, Inc., 82
Strouds, Inc., 33
Stuller Settings, Inc., 35
Successories, Inc., 30
Sun Television & Appliances Inc., 10
Sunglass Hut International, Inc., 21; 74 (upd.)
Superdrug Stores PLC, 95
Supreme International Corporation, 27
Swarovski International Holding AG, 40
The Swiss Colony, Inc., 97
Syms Corporation, 29; 74 (upd.)
Systemax, Inc., 52
Takashimaya Company, Limited, V; 47 (upd.)
The Talbots, Inc., 11; 31 (upd.); 88 (upd.)
Target Corporation, 61 (upd.)
Target Stores, 10; 27 (upd.)
Tati SA, 25
Tattered Cover Book Store, 43
Tech Data Corporation, 10; 74 (upd.)
Tengelmann Group, 27
Tesco plc, 24 (upd.); 68 (upd.)
Things Remembered, Inc., 84
Thomsen Greenhouses and Garden Center, Incorporated, 65
Thrifty PayLess, Inc., 12

Tiffany & Co., 14; 78 (upd.)
The Timberland Company, 54 (upd.)
The TJX Companies, Inc., V; 19 (upd.); 57 (upd.)
Today's Man, Inc., 20
Tokyu Department Store Co., Ltd., V; 32 (upd.)
Too, Inc., 61
Topco Associates LLC, 60
Tops Appliance City, Inc., 17
Total Fina Elf S.A., 50 (upd.)
Toys 'R' Us, Inc., V; 18 (upd.); 57 (upd.)
Tractor Supply Company, 57
Trans World Entertainment Corporation, 68 (upd.)
Travis Boats & Motors, Inc., 37
Travis Perkins plc, 34
Trend-Lines, Inc., 22
True Value Company, 74 (upd.)
TruServ Corporation, 24
Tuesday Morning Corporation, 18; 70 (upd.)
Tupperware Corporation, 28; 78 (upd.)
TVI, Inc., 15
Tweeter Home Entertainment Group, Inc., 30
U.S. Vision, Inc., 66
Ulta Salon, Cosmetics & Fragrance, Inc., 93
Ultimate Electronics, Inc., 18; 69 (upd.)
Ultramar Diamond Shamrock Corporation, 31 (upd.)
Uni-Marts, Inc., 17
United Rentals, Inc., 34
The United States Shoe Corporation, V
United Stationers Inc., 14
Universal International, Inc., 25
Uny Co., Ltd., V; 49 (upd.)
Urban Outfitters, Inc., 14; 74 (upd.)
Uwajimaya, Inc., 60
Vallen Corporation, 45
Valley Media Inc., 35
Value City Department Stores, Inc., 38
Value Merchants Inc., 13
ValueVision International, Inc., 22
Vans, Inc., 47 (upd.)
Variety Wholesalers, Inc., 73
VBA - Bloemenveiling Aalsmeer, 88
Venator Group Inc., 35 (upd.)
Vendex International N.V., 13
Venture Stores Inc., 12
The Vermont Country Store, 93
The Vermont Teddy Bear Co., Inc., 36
VF Corporation, 54 (upd.)
Viewpoint International, Inc., 66
Viking Office Products, Inc., 10
Vivarte SA, 54 (upd.)
Volcom, Inc., 77
Von Maur Inc., 64
Vorwerk & Co., 27
W. Atlee Burpee & Co., 27
W.W. Grainger, Inc., V
Waban Inc., 13
Wacoal Corp., 25
Wal-Mart de Mexico, S.A. de C.V., 35 (upd.)
Wal-Mart Stores, Inc., V; 8 (upd.); 26 (upd.); 63 (upd.)
Waldenbooks, 17; 86 (upd.)
Walgreen Co., V; 20 (upd.); 65 (upd.)
Wall Drug Store, Inc., 40
Warners' Stellian Inc., 67
Weiner's Stores, Inc., 33
West Marine, Inc., 17; 90 (upd.)
Western Beef, Inc., 22
The Wet Seal, Inc., 18; 70 (upd.)
Weyco Group, Incorporated, 32
WH Smith PLC, V; 42 (upd.)
The White House, Inc., 60
Whitehall Jewellers, Inc., 82 (upd.)
Whole Foods Market, Inc., 20
Wickes Inc., V; 25 (upd.)
Wilco Farm Stores, 93
Wilkinson Hardware Stores Ltd., 80
Williams Scotsman, Inc., 65
Williams-Sonoma, Inc., 17; 44 (upd.)
Wilsons The Leather Experts Inc., 21; 58 (upd.)
Wilton Products, Inc., 97
Windstream Corporation, 83
Winmark Corporation, 74
Wolohan Lumber Co., 19
Wolverine World Wide, Inc., 59 (upd.)
Woolworth Corporation, V; 20 (upd.)
Woolworths Group plc, 83
World Duty Free Americas, Inc., 29 (upd.)
Yamada Denki Co., Ltd., 85
The Yankee Candle Company, Inc., 37
Young's Market Company, LLC, 32
Younkers, 76 (upd.)
Younkers, Inc., 19
Zale Corporation, 16; 40 (upd.); 91 (upd.)
Zany Brainy, Inc., 31
Zappos.com, Inc., 73
Zara International, Inc., 83
Ziebart International Corporation, 30
Zion's Cooperative Mercantile Institution, 33
Zipcar, Inc., 92
Zones, Inc., 67
Zumiez, Inc., 77

Rubber & Tires

Aeroquip Corporation, 16
Bandag, Inc., 19
The BFGoodrich Company, V
Bridgestone Corporation, V; 21 (upd.); 59 (upd.)
Canadian Tire Corporation, Limited, 71 (upd.)
Carlisle Companies Incorporated, 8
Compagnie Générale des Établissements Michelin, V; 42 (upd.)
Continental AG, V; 56 (upd.)
Continental General Tire Corp., 23
Cooper Tire & Rubber Company, 8; 23 (upd.)
Day International, Inc., 84
Elementis plc, 40 (upd.)
General Tire, Inc., 8
The Goodyear Tire & Rubber Company, V; 20 (upd.); 75 (upd.)
The Kelly-Springfield Tire Company, 8
Les Schwab Tire Centers, 50
Myers Industries, Inc., 19; 96 (upd.)
Pirelli S.p.A., V; 15 (upd.)
Safeskin Corporation, 18
Sumitomo Rubber Industries, Ltd., V
Trelleborg AB, 93
Tillotson Corp., 15
Treadco, Inc., 19
Ube Industries, Ltd., 38 (upd.)
The Yokohama Rubber Company, Limited, V; 19 (upd.); 91 (upd.)

Telecommunications

A.H. Belo Corporation, 30 (upd.)
Abertis Infraestructuras, S.A., 65
Abril S.A., 95
Acme-Cleveland Corp., 13
ADC Telecommunications, Inc., 10; 89 (upd.)
Adelphia Communications Corporation, 17; 52 (upd.)
Adtran Inc., 22
Advanced Fibre Communications, Inc., 63
AEI Music Network Inc., 35
AirTouch Communications, 11
Alaska Communications Systems Group, Inc., 89
Alcatel S.A., 36 (upd.)
Alliance Atlantis Communications Inc., 39
ALLTEL Corporation, 6; 46 (upd.)
América Móvil, S.A. de C.V., 80
American Tower Corporation, 33
Ameritech Corporation, V; 18 (upd.)
Amstrad plc, 48 (upd.)
AO VimpelCom, 48
AOL Time Warner Inc., 57 (upd.)
Arch Wireless, Inc., 39
ARD, 41
ARRIS Group, Inc., 89
Ascom AG, 9
Aspect Telecommunications Corporation, 22
Asurion Corporation, 83
AT&T Bell Laboratories, Inc., 13
AT&T Corporation, V; 29 (upd.); 68 (upd.)
AT&T Wireless Services, Inc., 54 (upd.)
BCE Inc., V; 44 (upd.)
Beasley Broadcast Group, Inc., 51
Belgacom, 6
Bell Atlantic Corporation, V; 25 (upd.)
Bell Canada, 6
BellSouth Corporation, V; 29 (upd.)
Bertelsmann A.G., IV; 15 (upd.); 43 (upd.); 91 (upd.)
BET Holdings, Inc., 18
Bharti Tele-Ventures Limited, 75
BHC Communications, Inc., 26
Blackfoot Telecommunications Group, 60
Bonneville International Corporation, 29
Bouygues S.A., I; 24 (upd.); 97 (upd.)
Brasil Telecom Participaçoes S.A., 57
Brightpoint, Inc., 18
Brite Voice Systems, Inc., 20
British Broadcasting Corporation Ltd., 7; 21 (upd.); 89 (upd.)
British Columbia Telephone Company, 6
British Telecommunications plc, V; 15 (upd.)

Broadwing Corporation, 70
BT Group plc, 49 (upd.)
C-COR.net Corp., 38
Cable & Wireless HKT, 30 (upd.)
Cable and Wireless plc, V; 25 (upd.)
Cablevision Systems Corporation, 30 (upd.)
CalAmp Corp., 87
The Canadian Broadcasting Corporation (CBC), 37
Canal Plus, 10; 34 (upd.)
CanWest Global Communications Corporation, 35
Capital Radio plc, 35
Carlton Communications PLC, 15; 50 (upd.)
Carolina Telephone and Telegraph Company, 10
The Carphone Warehouse Group PLC, 83
Carrier Access Corporation, 44
CBS Corporation, 28 (upd.)
CBS Television Network, 66 (upd.)
Centel Corporation, 6
Centennial Communications Corporation, 39
Central European Media Enterprises Ltd., 61
Century Communications Corp., 10
Century Telephone Enterprises, Inc., 9; 54 (upd.)
Cesky Telecom, a.s., 64
Chancellor Media Corporation, 24
Channel Four Television Corporation, 93
Charter Communications, Inc., 33
Chello Zone Ltd., 93
China Netcom Group Corporation (Hong Kong) Limited, 73
China Telecom, 50
Chris-Craft Corporation, 9, 31 (upd.); 80 (upd.)
The Christian Broadcasting Network, Inc., 52
Chrysalis Group plc, 40
Chugach Alaska Corporation, 60
CIENA Corporation, 54
Cincinnati Bell, Inc., 6
Citadel Communications Corporation, 35
Citizens Communications Company, 79 (upd.)
Clear Channel Communications, Inc., 23
Clearwire, Inc., 69
Cogent Communications Group, Inc., 55
COLT Telecom Group plc, 41
Comcast Corporation, 24 (upd.)
Comdial Corporation, 21
Commonwealth Telephone Enterprises, Inc., 25
CommScope, Inc., 77
Comsat Corporation, 23
Comtech Telecommunications Corp., 75
Comverse Technology, Inc., 15; 43 (upd.)
Corning Inc., III; 44 (upd.); 90 (upd.)
Corporation for Public Broadcasting, 14; 89 (upd.)
Cox Radio, Inc., 89
Craftmade International, Inc., 44
Cumulus Media Inc., 37
DDI Corporation, 7
Deutsche Telekom AG, V; 48 (upd.)
Dialogic Corporation, 18
Directorate General of Telecommunications, 7
DIRECTV, Inc., 38; 75 (upd.)
Discovery Communications, Inc., 42
Dobson Communications Corporation, 63
DSC Communications Corporation, 12
EchoStar Communications Corporation, 35
ECI Telecom Ltd., 18
Egmont Group, 93
eircom plc, 31 (upd.)
Electric Lightwave, Inc., 37
Electromagnetic Sciences Inc., 21
EMBARQ Corporation, 83
Emmis Communications Corporation, 47
Empresas Públicas de Medellín S.A.E.S.P., 91
Energis plc, 47
Entercom Communications Corporation, 58
Entravision Communications Corporation, 41
Equant N.V., 52
Eschelon Telecom, Inc., 72
ESPN, Inc., 56
Eternal Word Television Network, Inc., 57
EXCEL Communications Inc., 18
Executone Information Systems, Inc., 13
Expand SA, 48
Facebook, Inc., 90
FASTWEB S.p.A., 83
4Kids Entertainment Inc., 59
Fox Family Worldwide, Inc., 24
France Télécom Group, V; 21 (upd.)
Frontier Corp., 16
Fuji Television Network Inc., 91
Gannett Co., Inc., 30 (upd.)
Garmin Ltd., 60
General DataComm Industries, Inc., 14
Geotek Communications Inc., 21
Getty Images, Inc., 31
Global Crossing Ltd., 32
Globo Comunicação e Participações S.A., 80
Glu Mobile Inc., 95
Golden Telecom, Inc., 59
Granite Broadcasting Corporation, 42
Gray Communications Systems, Inc., 24
Groupe Vidéotron Ltée., 20
Grupo Televisa, S.A., 18; 54 (upd.)
GTE Corporation, V; 15 (upd.)
Guthy-Renker Corporation, 32
GWR Group plc, 39
Harmonic Inc., 43
Havas, SA, 10
HickoryTech Corporation, 92
Hispanic Broadcasting Corporation, 35
Hong Kong Telecommunications Ltd., 6
Huawei Technologies Company Ltd., 87
Hubbard Broadcasting Inc., 24; 79 (upd.)
Hughes Electronics Corporation, 25
Hungarian Telephone and Cable Corp., 75
IDB Communications Group, Inc., 11
IDT Corporation, 34
Illinois Bell Telephone Company, 14
Indiana Bell Telephone Company, Incorporated, 14
PT Indosat Tbk, 93
Infineon Technologies AG, 50
Infinity Broadcasting Corporation, 11
InfoSonics Corporation, 81
InterDigital Communications Corporation, 61
Iowa Telecommunications Services, Inc., 85
IXC Communications, Inc., 29
Jacor Communications, Inc., 23
Jones Intercable, Inc., 21
j2 Global Communications, Inc., 75
Koninklijke PTT Nederland NV, V
Landmark Communications, Inc., 55 (upd.)
LCC International, Inc., 84
LCI International, Inc., 16
LDDS-Metro Communications, Inc., 8
Leap Wireless International, Inc., 69
Level 3 Communications, Inc., 67
LIN Broadcasting Corp., 9
Lincoln Telephone & Telegraph Company, 14
LodgeNet Entertainment Corporation, 28
Loral Space & Communications Ltd., 54 (upd.)
MacNeil/Lehrer Productions, 87
Magyar Telekom Rt. 78
Manitoba Telecom Services, Inc., 61
Mannesmann AG, 38
MasTec, Inc., 19; 55 (upd.)
McCaw Cellular Communications, Inc., 6
MCI WorldCom, Inc., V; 27 (upd.)
McLeodUSA Incorporated, 32
Mediacom Communications Corporation, 69
Mercury Communications, Ltd., 7
Metrocall, Inc., 41
Metromedia Companies, 14
Métropole Télévision, 33
Métropole Télévision S.A., 76 (upd.)
MFS Communications Company, Inc., 11
Michigan Bell Telephone Co., 14
MIH Limited, 31
MITRE Corporation, 26
Mobile Telecommunications Technologies Corp., 18
Mobile TeleSystems OJSC, 59
Modern Times Group AB, 36
The Montana Power Company, 44 (upd.)
Motorola, Inc., II; 11 (upd.); 34 (upd.); 93 (upd.)
Multimedia, Inc., 11
National Broadcasting Company, Inc., 28 (upd.)
National Grid USA, 51 (upd.)
National Weather Service, 91
NCR Corporation, III; 6 (upd.); 30 (upd.); 90 (upd.)
NetCom Systems AB, 26
NeuStar, Inc., 81
Nevada Bell Telephone Company, 14
New Valley Corporation, 17
Nexans SA, 54
Nexstar Broadcasting Group, Inc., 73
Nextel Communications, Inc., 27 (upd.)

Nippon Telegraph and Telephone Corporation, V; 51 (upd.)
Nokia Corporation, 77 (upd.)
Norstan, Inc., 16
Nortel Networks Corporation, 36 (upd.)
Northern Telecom Limited, V
NTL Inc., 65
NTN Buzztime, Inc., 86
NYNEX Corporation, V
Octel Messaging, 14; 41 (upd.)
Ohio Bell Telephone Company, 14
Olivetti S.p.A., 34 (upd.)
Orange S.A., 84
Österreichische Post- und Telegraphenverwaltung, V
Pacific Internet Limited, 87
Pacific Telecom, Inc., 6
Pacific Telesis Group, V
Paging Network Inc., 11
PanAmSat Corporation, 46
Paxson Communications Corporation, 33
The Phoenix Media/Communications Group, 91
PictureTel Corp., 10; 27 (upd.)
Portugal Telecom SGPS S.A., 69
Posti- ja Telelaitos, 6
Price Communications Corporation, 42
ProSiebenSat.1 Media AG, 54
Publishing and Broadcasting Limited, 54
Qatar Telecom QSA, 87
QUALCOMM Incorporated, 20; 47 (upd.)
QVC Network Inc., 9
Qwest Communications International, Inc., 37
RCN Corporation, 70
Regent Communications, Inc., 87
Research in Motion Ltd., 54
RMH Teleservices, Inc., 42
Rochester Telephone Corporation, 6
Rogers Communications Inc., 30 (upd.)
Royal KPN N.V., 30
Rural Cellular Corporation, 43
Saga Communications, Inc., 27
Salem Communications Corporation, 97
Sawtek Inc., 43 (upd.)
SBC Communications Inc., 32 (upd.)
Schweizerische Post-, Telefon- und Telegrafen-Betriebe, V
Scientific-Atlanta, Inc., 6; 45 (upd.)
Seat Pagine Gialle S.p.A., 47
Securicor Plc, 45
Shenandoah Telecommunications Company, 89
Sinclair Broadcast Group, Inc., 25
Sirius Satellite Radio, Inc., 69
Sirti S.p.A., 76
Società Finanziaria Telefonica per Azioni, V
Softbank Corporation, 77 (upd.)
Sonera Corporation, 50
Southern New England Telecommunications Corporation, 6
Southwestern Bell Corporation, V
Spanish Broadcasting System, Inc., 41
Spelling Entertainment, 35 (upd.)
Sprint Corporation, 9; 46 (upd.)
StarHub Ltd., 77
StrataCom, Inc., 16
Swedish Telecom, V
Swisscom AG, 58
Sycamore Networks, Inc., 45
Syniverse Holdings Inc., 97
SynOptics Communications, Inc., 10
T-Netix, Inc., 46
Talk America Holdings, Inc., 70
TDC A/S, 63
Tekelec, 83
Telcordia Technologies, Inc., 59
Tele Norte Leste Participações S.A., 80
Telecom Argentina S.A., 63
Telecom Australia, 6
Telecom Corporation of New Zealand Limited, 54
Telecom Eireann, 7
Telecom Italia Mobile S.p.A., 63
Telecom Italia S.p.A., 43
Telefonaktiebolaget LM Ericsson, V; 46 (upd.)
Telefónica de Argentina S.A., 61
Telefónica S.A., V; 46 (upd.)
Telefonos de Mexico S.A. de C.V., 14; 63 (upd.)
Telekom Malaysia Bhd, 76
Telekomunikacja Polska SA, 50
Telenor ASA, 69
Telephone and Data Systems, Inc., 9
Télévision Française 1, 23
TeliaSonera AB, 57 (upd.)
Tellabs, Inc., 11; 40 (upd.)
Telstra Corporation Limited, 50
Thomas Crosbie Holdings Limited, 81
Tiscali SpA, 48
The Titan Corporation, 36
Tollgrade Communications, Inc., 44
TV Azteca, S.A. de C.V., 39
U.S. Satellite Broadcasting Company, Inc., 20
U S West, Inc., V; 25 (upd.)
U.S. Cellular Corporation, 9; 31 (upd.); 88 (upd.)
UFA TV & Film Produktion GmbH, 80
United Pan-Europe Communications NV, 47
United Telecommunications, Inc., V
United Video Satellite Group, 18
Univision Communications Inc., 24; 83 (upd.)
USA Interactive, Inc., 47 (upd.)
USA Mobility Inc., 97 (upd.)
UTStarcom, Inc., 77
Verizon Communications Inc. 43 (upd.); 78 (upd.)
ViaSat, Inc., 54
Vivendi Universal S.A., 46 (upd.)
Vodafone Group Plc, 11; 36 (upd.); 75 (upd.)
Vonage Holdings Corp., 81
The Walt Disney Company, II; 6 (upd.); 30 (upd.); 63 (upd.)
Wanadoo S.A., 75
Watkins-Johnson Company, 15
The Weather Channel Companies, 52
West Corporation, 42
Western Union Financial Services, Inc., 54
Western Wireless Corporation, 36
Westwood One, Inc., 23
Williams Communications Group, Inc., 34
The Williams Companies, Inc., 31 (upd.)
Wipro Limited, 43
Wisconsin Bell, Inc., 14
Working Assets Funding Service, 43
Worldwide Pants Inc., 97
XM Satellite Radio Holdings, Inc., 69
Young Broadcasting Inc., 40
Zed Group, 93
Zoom Technologies, Inc., 53 (upd.)

Textiles & Apparel

Abercrombie & Fitch Company, 35 (upd.); 75 (upd.)
Adams Childrenswear Ltd., 95
adidas Group AG, 14; 33 (upd.); 75 (upd.)
Adolfo Dominguez S.A., 72
Aéropostale, Inc., 89
Alba-Waldensian, Inc., 30
Albany International Corp., 8
Alexandra plc, 88
Algo Group Inc., 24
Alpargatas S.A.I.C., 87
American & Efird, Inc., 82
American Apparel, Inc., 90
American Safety Razor Company, 20
Amoskeag Company, 8
Angelica Corporation, 15; 43 (upd.)
AR Accessories Group, Inc., 23
Aris Industries, Inc., 16
ASICS Corporation, 57
AstenJohnson Inc., 90
The Athlete's Foot Brands LLC, 84
Authentic Fitness Corporation, 20; 51 (upd.)
Babolat VS, S.A., 97
Banana Republic Inc., 25
Bata Ltd., 62
Benetton Group S.p.A., 10; 67 (upd.)
Bill Blass Ltd., 32
Birkenstock Footprint Sandals, Inc., 12
Blair Corporation, 25
Body Glove International LLC, 88
Boss Holdings, Inc., 97
Brazos Sportswear, Inc., 23
Brioni Roman Style S.p.A., 67
Brooks Brothers Inc., 22
Brooks Sports Inc., 32
Brown Group, Inc., V; 20 (upd.)
Brunschwig & Fils Inc., 96
Bugle Boy Industries, Inc., 18
Burberry Group plc, 17; 41 (upd.); 92 (upd.)
Burke Mills, Inc., 66
Burlington Industries, Inc., V; 17 (upd.)
Calcot Ltd., 33
Calvin Klein, Inc., 22; 55 (upd.)
Candie's, Inc., 31
Canstar Sports Inc., 16
Capel Incorporated, 45
Capezio/Ballet Makers Inc., 62
Carhartt, Inc., 30, 77 (upd.)
Cato Corporation, 14
Chargeurs International, 6; 21 (upd.)
Charles Vögele Holding AG, 82

Charming Shoppes, Inc., 8
Cherokee Inc., 18
CHF Industries, Inc., 84
Chic by H.I.S, Inc., 20
Chico's FAS, Inc., 45
Chorus Line Corporation, 30
Christian Dior S.A., 19; 49 (upd.)
Christopher & Banks Corporation, 42
Cia Hering, 72
Cintas Corporation, 51 (upd.)
Citi Trends, Inc., 80
Claire's Stores, Inc., 17
Coach Leatherware, 10
Coats plc, V; 44 (upd.)
Collins & Aikman Corporation, 13
Columbia Sportswear Company, 19; 41 (upd.)
Companhia de Tecidos Norte de Minas - Coteminas, 77
Compañia Industrial de Parras, S.A. de C.V. (CIPSA), 84
Concord Fabrics, Inc., 16
Cone Mills LLC, 8; 67 (upd.)
Converse Inc., 31 (upd.)
Cotton Incorporated, 46
Courtaulds plc, V; 17 (upd.)
Crocs, Inc., 80
Croscill, Inc., 42
Crown Crafts, Inc., 16
Crystal Brands, Inc., 9
Culp, Inc., 29
Cygne Designs, Inc., 25
Dan River Inc., 35; 86 (upd.)
Danskin, Inc., 12; 62 (upd.)
Deckers Outdoor Corporation, 22
Delta and Pine Land Company, 59
Delta Woodside Industries, Inc., 8; 30 (upd.)
Designer Holdings Ltd., 20
The Dixie Group, Inc., 20; 80 (upd.)
Dogi International Fabrics S.A., 52
Dolce & Gabbana SpA, 62
Dominion Textile Inc., 12
Donna Karan International Inc., 15; 56 (upd.)
Donnkenny, Inc., 17
Dooney & Bourke Inc., 84
Duck Head Apparel Company, Inc., 42
Dunavant Enterprises, Inc., 54
Dyersburg Corporation, 21
Eastland Shoe Corporation, 82
Ecco Sko A/S, 62
The Echo Design Group, Inc., 68
Edison Brothers Stores, Inc., 9
Eileen Fisher Inc., 61
Ellen Tracy, Inc., 55
Ennis, Inc., 21; 97 (upd.)
Eram SA, 51
Ermenegildo Zegna SpA, 63
ESCADA AG, 71
Esprit de Corp., 8; 29 (upd.)
Etam Developpement SA, 44
Etienne Aigner AG, 52
Evans, Inc., 30
Fab Industries, Inc., 27
Fabri-Centers of America Inc., 16
Fat Face Ltd., 68
Fieldcrest Cannon, Inc., 9; 31 (upd.)
Fila Holding S.p.A., 20
Florsheim Shoe Group Inc., 31 (upd.)
Foot Petals L.L.C., 95
Fossil, Inc., 17
Frederick's of Hollywood Inc., 16
French Connection Group plc, 41
Fruit of the Loom, Inc., 8; 25 (upd.)
Fubu, 29
G&K Services, Inc., 16
G-III Apparel Group, Ltd., 22
Galey & Lord, Inc., 20; 66 (upd.)
Garan, Inc., 16; 64 (upd.)
Gerry Weber International AG, 63
Gianni Versace SpA, 22
Gildan Activewear, Inc., 81
Giorgio Armani S.p.A., 45
The Gitano Group, Inc. 8
Gottschalks, Inc., 18; 91 (upd.)
Great White Shark Enterprises, Inc., 89
Greenwood Mills, Inc., 14
Groupe DMC (Dollfus Mieg & Cie), 27
Groupe Yves Saint Laurent, 23
Gucci Group N.V., 15; 50 (upd.)
Guess, Inc., 15; 68 (upd.)
Guilford Mills Inc., 8; 40 (upd.)
Gymboree Corporation, 15; 69 (upd.)
Haggar Corporation, 19; 78 (upd.)
Hampshire Group Ltd., 82
Hampton Industries, Inc., 20
Happy Kids Inc., 30
Hartmarx Corporation, 8
The Hartstone Group plc, 14
HCI Direct, Inc., 55
Healthtex, Inc., 17
Heelys, Inc., 87
Helly Hansen ASA, 25
Hermès S.A., 14
The Hockey Company, 34
Horween Leather Company, 83
Hugo Boss AG, 48
Hummel International A/S, 68
Hyde Athletic Industries, Inc., 17
I.C. Isaacs & Company, 31
Industria de Diseño Textil S.A., 64
Innovo Group Inc., 83
Interface, Inc., 8; 29 (upd.); 76 (upd.)
Irwin Toy Limited, 14
Items International Airwalk Inc., 17
J. Crew Group, Inc., 12; 34 (upd.); 88 (upd.)
JLM Couture, Inc., 64
Jockey International, Inc., 12; 34 (upd.); 77 (upd.)
The John David Group plc, 90
Johnston Industries, Inc., 15
Jones Apparel Group, Inc., 39 (upd.)
Jordache Enterprises, Inc., 23
Jos. A. Bank Clothiers, Inc., 31
JPS Textile Group, Inc., 28
Juicy Couture, Inc., 80
K-Swiss, Inc., 33; 89 (upd.)
Karl Kani Infinity, Inc., 49
Kellwood Company, 8; 85 (upd.)
Kenneth Cole Productions, Inc., 25
Kinney Shoe Corp., 14
Klaus Steilmann GmbH & Co. KG, 53
Koret of California, Inc., 62
L.A. Gear, Inc., 8; 32 (upd.)
L.L. Bean, Inc., 10; 38 (upd.); 91 (upd.)
LaCrosse Footwear, Inc., 18; 61 (upd.)
Laura Ashley Holdings plc, 13
Lee Apparel Company, Inc., 8
The Leslie Fay Company, Inc., 8; 39 (upd.)
Levi Strauss & Co., V; 16 (upd.)
Liz Claiborne, Inc., 8
London Fog Industries, Inc., 29
Lost Arrow Inc., 22
Maidenform, Inc., 20; 59 (upd.)
Malden Mills Industries, Inc., 16
Maples Industries, Inc., 83
Mariella Burani Fashion Group, 92
Marzotto S.p.A., 20; 67 (upd.)
Maurices Inc., 95
Milliken & Co., V; 17 (upd.); 82 (upd.)
Miroglio SpA, 86
Mitsubishi Rayon Co., Ltd., V
Mossimo, Inc., 27; 96 (upd.)
Mothercare plc, 17; 78 (upd.)
Movie Star Inc., 17
Mulberry Group PLC, 71
Naf Naf SA, 44
Nautica Enterprises, Inc., 18; 44 (upd.)
New Balance Athletic Shoe, Inc., 25; 68 (upd.)
NIKE, Inc., V; 8 (upd.); 75 (upd.)
Nine West Group, Inc., 39 (upd.)
Nitches, Inc., 53
The North Face Inc., 18; 78 (upd.)
Oakley, Inc., 18
Ormat Technologies, Inc., 87
OshKosh B'Gosh, Inc., 9; 42 (upd.)
Oxford Industries, Inc., 8; 84 (upd.)
Pacific Sunwear of California, Inc., 28
Peek & Cloppenburg KG, 46
Pendleton Woolen Mills, Inc., 42
Pentland Group plc, 20
Perry Ellis International, Inc., 41
Petit Bateau, 95
Phat Fashions LLC, 49
Phoenix Footwear Group, Inc., 70
Pillowtex Corporation, 19; 41 (upd.)
Plains Cotton Cooperative Association, 57
Pluma, Inc., 27
Polo/Ralph Lauren Corporation, 12; 62 (upd.)
Pomare Ltd., 88
Prada Holding B.V., 45
PremiumWear, Inc., 30
Puma AG Rudolf Dassler Sport, 35
Quaker Fabric Corp., 19
Quiksilver, Inc., 18; 79 (upd.)
R.G. Barry Corporation, 17; 44 (upd.)
Rack Room Shoes, Inc., 84
Raymond Ltd., 77
Recreational Equipment, Inc., 18
Red Wing Shoe Company, Inc., 9; 30 (upd.); 83 (upd.)
Reebok International Ltd., V; 9 (upd.); 26 (upd.)
Reliance Industries Ltd., 81
Rieter Holding AG, 42
Robert Talbott Inc., 88
Rocawear Apparel LLC, 77
Rollerblade, Inc., 15
Royal Ten Cate N.V., 68

Russell Corporation, 8; 30 (upd.); 82 (upd.)
Rusty, Inc., 95
St. John Knits, Inc., 14
Salant Corporation, 51 (upd.)
Salvatore Ferragamo Italia S.p.A., 62
Sao Paulo Alpargatas S.A., 75
Saucony Inc., 35; 86 (upd.)
Schott Brothers, Inc., 67
Seattle Pacific Industries, Inc., 92
Shaw Industries, Inc., 40 (upd.)
Shelby Williams Industries, Inc., 14
Shoe Pavilion, Inc., 84
Skechers U.S.A. Inc., 31; 88 (upd.)
skinnyCorp, LLC, 97
Sole Technology Inc., 93
Sophus Berendsen A/S, 49
Spanx, Inc., 89
Springs Global US, Inc., V; 19 (upd.); 90 (upd.)
Starter Corp., 12
Stefanel SpA, 63
Steiner Corporation (Alsco), 53
Steven Madden, Ltd., 37
Stirling Group plc, 62
Stoddard International plc, 72
Stone Manufacturing Company, 14; 43 (upd.)
Stride Rite Corporation, 8; 37 (upd.); 86 (upd.)
Stussy, Inc., 55
Sun Sportswear, Inc., 17
Superior Uniform Group, Inc., 30
Tag-It Pacific, Inc., 85
The Talbots, Inc., 11; 31 (upd.); 88 (upd.)
Tamfelt Oyj Abp, 62
Tarrant Apparel Group, 62
Ted Baker plc, 86
Teijin Limited, V
Thanulux Public Company Limited, 86
Thomaston Mills, Inc., 27
Tilley Endurables, Inc., 67
The Timberland Company, 13; 54 (upd.)
Tommy Hilfiger Corporation, 20; 53 (upd.)
Too, Inc., 61
Toray Industries, Inc., V
True Religion Apparel, Inc., 79
Tultex Corporation, 13
Under Armour Performance Apparel, 61
Unifi, Inc., 12; 62 (upd.)
United Merchants & Manufacturers, Inc., 13
United Retail Group Inc., 33
Unitika Ltd., V
Umbro plc, 88
Vans, Inc., 16; 47 (upd.)
Varsity Spirit Corp., 15
VF Corporation, V; 17 (upd.); 54 (upd.)
Vicunha Têxtil S.A. 78
Volcom, Inc., 77
Walton Monroe Mills, Inc., 8
The Warnaco Group Inc., 12; 46 (upd.)
Wellco Enterprises, Inc., 84
Wellman, Inc., 8; 52 (upd.)
West Point-Pepperell, Inc., 8
WestPoint Stevens Inc., 16
Weyco Group, Incorporated, 32
Williamson-Dickie Manufacturing Company, 14
Wolverine World Wide, Inc., 16; 59 (upd.)
Woolrich Inc., 62
Zara International, Inc., 83

Tobacco

Altadis S.A., 72 (upd.)
American Brands, Inc., V
B.A.T. Industries PLC, 22 (upd.)
British American Tobacco PLC, 50 (upd.)
Brooke Group Ltd., 15
Brown & Williamson Tobacco Corporation, 14; 33 (upd.)
Culbro Corporation, 15
Dibrell Brothers, Incorporated, 12
DIMON Inc., 27
800-JR Cigar, Inc., 27
Gallaher Group Plc, V; 19 (upd.); 49 (upd.)
General Cigar Holdings, Inc., 66 (upd.)
Holt's Cigar Holdings, Inc., 42
House of Prince A/S, 80
Imasco Limited, V
Imperial Tobacco Group PLC, 50
Japan Tobacco Incorporated, V
KT&G Corporation, 62
Nobleza Piccardo SAICF, 64
North Atlantic Trading Company Inc., 65
Philip Morris Companies Inc., V; 18 (upd.)
R.J. Reynolds Tobacco Holdings, Inc., 30 (upd.)
RJR Nabisco Holdings Corp., V
Rothmans UK Holdings Limited, V; 19 (upd.)
Seita, 23
Souza Cruz S.A., 65
Standard Commercial Corporation, 13; 62 (upd.)
Swedish Match AB, 12; 39 (upd.); 92 (upd.)
Swisher International Group Inc., 23
Tabacalera, S.A., V; 17 (upd.)
Taiwan Tobacco & Liquor Corporation, 75
Universal Corporation, V; 48 (upd.)
UST Inc., 9; 50 (upd.)
Vector Group Ltd., 35 (upd.)

Transport Services

Abertis Infraestructuras, S.A., 65
The Adams Express Company, 86
Aegean Marine Petroleum Network Inc., 89
Aéroports de Paris, 33
Air Express International Corporation, 13
Air Partner PLC, 93
Air T, Inc., 86
Airborne Freight Corporation, 6; 34 (upd.)
Alamo Rent A Car, Inc., 6; 24 (upd.); 84 (upd.)
Alaska Railroad Corporation, 60
Alexander & Baldwin, Inc., 10, 40 (upd.)
Allied Worldwide, Inc., 49
AMCOL International Corporation, 59 (upd.)
Amerco, 6
AMERCO, 67 (upd.)
American Classic Voyages Company, 27
American President Companies Ltd., 6
Anderson Trucking Service, Inc., 75
Anschutz Corp., 12
APL Limited, 61 (upd.)
Aqua Alliance Inc., 32 (upd.)
Arriva PLC, 69
Atlas Van Lines, Inc., 14
Attica Enterprises S.A., 64
Avis Group Holdings, Inc., 75 (upd.)
Avis Rent A Car, Inc., 6; 22 (upd.)
BAA plc, 10
Bekins Company, 15
Berliner Verkehrsbetriebe (BVG), 58
Bollinger Shipyards, Inc., 61
Boyd Bros. Transportation Inc., 39
Brambles Industries Limited, 42
The Brink's Company, 58 (upd.)
British Railways Board, V
Broken Hill Proprietary Company Ltd., 22 (upd.)
Buckeye Partners, L.P., 70
Budget Group, Inc., 25
Budget Rent a Car Corporation, 9
Burlington Northern Santa Fe Corporation, V; 27 (upd.)
C.H. Robinson Worldwide, Inc., 40 (upd.)
Canadian National Railway Company, 71 (upd.)
Canadian National Railway System, 6
Canadian Pacific Railway Limited, V; 45 (upd.); 95 (upd.)
Cannon Express, Inc., 53
Carey International, Inc., 26
Carlson Companies, Inc., 6; 22 (upd.); 87 (upd.)
Carolina Freight Corporation, 6
Celadon Group Inc., 30
Central Japan Railway Company, 43
Chargeurs International, 6; 21 (upd.)
CHC Helicopter Corporation, 67
CHEP Pty. Ltd., 80
Chicago and North Western Holdings Corporation, 6
Christian Salvesen Plc, 45
Coach USA, Inc., 24; 55 (upd.)
Coles Express Inc., 15
Compagnie Générale Maritime et Financière, 6
Compagnie Maritime Belge S.A., 95
Consolidated Delivery & Logistics, Inc., 24
Consolidated Freightways Corporation, V; 21 (upd.); 48 (upd.)
Consolidated Rail Corporation, V
CR England, Inc., 63
Crete Carrier Corporation, 95
Crowley Maritime Corporation, 6; 28 (upd.)
CSX Corporation, V; 22 (upd.); 79 (upd.)
Ctrip.com International Ltd., 97
Dachser GmbH & Co. KG, 88
Danaos Corporation, 91

Danzas Group, V; 40 (upd.)
Dart Group PLC, 77
Deutsche Bahn AG, V; 46 (upd.)
DHL Worldwide Network S.A./N.V., 6; 24 (upd.); 69 (upd.)
Diana Shipping Inc., 95
Dollar Thrifty Automotive Group, Inc., 25
Dot Foods, Inc., 69
DP World, 81
DryShips Inc., 95
East Japan Railway Company, V; 66 (upd.)
EGL, Inc., 59
Emery Air Freight Corporation, 6
Emery Worldwide Airlines, Inc., 25 (upd.)
Enterprise Rent-A-Car Company, 6
Estes Express Lines, Inc., 86
Eurotunnel Group, 37 (upd.)
EVA Airways Corporation, 51
Evergreen International Aviation, Inc., 53
Evergreen Marine Corporation (Taiwan) Ltd., 13; 50 (upd.)
Executive Jet, Inc., 36
Exel plc, 51 (upd.)
Expeditors International of Washington Inc., 17; 78 (upd.)
Federal Express Corporation, V
FedEx Corporation, 18 (upd.); 42 (upd.)
FirstGroup plc, 89
Forward Air Corporation, 75
Fritz Companies, Inc., 12
Frontline Ltd., 45
Frozen Food Express Industries, Inc., 20
Garuda Indonesia, 58 (upd.)
GATX Corporation, 6; 25 (upd.)
GE Capital Aviation Services, 36
Gefco SA, 54
General Maritime Corporation, 59
Genesee & Wyoming Inc., 27
Geodis S.A., 67
The Go-Ahead Group Plc, 28
The Greenbrier Companies, 19
Greyhound Lines, Inc., 32 (upd.)
Groupe Bourbon S.A., 60
Grupo Aeroportuario del Centro Norte, S.A.B. de C.V., 97
Grupo Aeroportuario del Pacífico, S.A. de C.V., 85
Grupo TMM, S.A. de C.V., 50
Grupo Transportación Ferroviaria Mexicana, S.A. de C.V., 47
Gulf Agency Company Ltd. 78
GulfMark Offshore, Inc., 49
Hanjin Shipping Co., Ltd., 50
Hankyu Corporation, V; 23 (upd.)
Hapag-Lloyd AG, 6; 97 (upd.)
Harland and Wolff Holdings plc, 19
Harper Group Inc., 17
Heartland Express, Inc., 18
The Hertz Corporation, 9
Holberg Industries, Inc., 36
Hospitality Worldwide Services, Inc., 26
Hub Group, Inc., 38
Hvide Marine Incorporated, 22
Illinois Central Corporation, 11
International Shipholding Corporation, Inc., 27
J.B. Hunt Transport Services Inc., 12
J Lauritzen A/S, 90
John Menzies plc, 39
Kansas City Southern Industries, Inc., 6; 26 (upd.)
The Kansas City Southern Railway Company, 92
Kawasaki Kisen Kaisha, Ltd., V; 56 (upd.)
Keio Corporation, V; 96 (upd.)
Keolis SA, 51
Kinki Nippon Railway Company Ltd., V
Kirby Corporation, 18; 66 (upd.)
Knight Transportation, Inc., 64
Koninklijke Nedlloyd Groep N.V., 6
Kuehne & Nagel International AG, V; 53 (upd.)
La Poste, V; 47 (upd.)
Laidlaw International, Inc., 80
Landstar System, Inc., 63
Leaseway Transportation Corp., 12
Loma Negra C.I.A.S.A., 95
London Regional Transport, 6
The Long Island Rail Road Company, 68
Lynden Incorporated, 91
Maine Central Railroad Company, 16
Mammoet Transport B.V., 26
Marten Transport, Ltd., 84
Martz Group, 56
Mayflower Group Inc., 6
Mercury Air Group, Inc., 20
The Mersey Docks and Harbour Company, 30
Metropolitan Transportation Authority, 35
Miller Industries, Inc., 26
Mitsui O.S.K. Lines Ltd., V; 96 (upd.)
Moran Towing Corporation, Inc., 15
The Morgan Group, Inc., 46
Morris Travel Services L.L.C., 26
Motor Cargo Industries, Inc., 35
National Car Rental System, Inc., 10
National Express Group PLC, 50
National Railroad Passenger Corporation (Amtrak), 22; 66 (upd.)
Neptune Orient Lines Limited, 47
NFC plc, 6
Nippon Express Company, Ltd., V; 64 (upd.)
Nippon Yusen Kabushiki Kaisha (NYK), V; 72 (upd.)
Norfolk Southern Corporation, V; 29 (upd.); 75 (upd.)
Oak Harbor Freight Lines, Inc., 53
Ocean Group plc, 6
Odakyu Electric Railway Co., Ltd., V; 68 (upd.)
Odyssey Marine Exploration, Inc., 91
Oglebay Norton Company, 17
Old Dominion Freight Line, Inc., 57
OMI Corporation, 59
The Oppenheimer Group, 76
Österreichische Bundesbahnen GmbH, 6
OTR Express, Inc., 25
Overnite Corporation, 14; 58 (upd.)
Overseas Shipholding Group, Inc., 11
Pacer International, Inc., 54
Pacific Basin Shipping Ltd., 86
Patriot Transportation Holding, Inc., 91
The Peninsular and Oriental Steam Navigation Company, V; 38 (upd.)
Penske Corporation, V; 19 (upd.); 84 (upd.)
PHH Arval, V; 53 (upd.)
Pilot Air Freight Corp., 67
Plantation Pipe Line Company, 68
Polar Air Cargo Inc., 60
The Port Authority of New York and New Jersey, 48
Port Imperial Ferry Corporation, 70
Post Office Group, V
Preston Corporation, 6
RailTex, Inc., 20
Railtrack Group PLC, 50
Réseau Ferré de France, 66
Roadway Express, Inc., V; 25 (upd.)
Rock-It Cargo USA, Inc., 86
Royal Olympic Cruise Lines Inc., 52
Royal Vopak NV, 41
Russian Railways Joint Stock Co., 93
Ryder System, Inc., V; 24 (upd.)
Santa Fe Pacific Corporation, V
Schenker-Rhenus AG, 6
Schneider National, Inc., 36; 77 (upd.)
Seaboard Corporation, 36; 85 (upd.)
SEACOR Holdings Inc., 83
Securicor Plc, 45
Seibu Railway Company Ltd., V; 74 (upd.)
Seino Transportation Company, Ltd., 6
Simon Transportation Services Inc., 27
Smithway Motor Xpress Corporation, 39
Société Nationale des Chemins de Fer Français, V; 57 (upd.)
Société Norbert Dentressangle S.A., 67
Southern Pacific Transportation Company, V
Spee-Dee Delivery Service, Inc., 93
Stagecoach Holdings plc, 30
Stelmar Shipping Ltd., 52
Stevedoring Services of America Inc., 28
Stinnes AG, 8; 59 (upd.)
Stolt-Nielsen S.A., 42
Sunoco, Inc., 28 (upd.); 83 (upd.)
Swift Transportation Co., Inc., 42
The Swiss Federal Railways (Schweizerische Bundesbahnen), V
Swissport International Ltd., 70
Teekay Shipping Corporation, 25; 82 (upd.)
Tibbett & Britten Group plc, 32
Tidewater Inc., 11; 37 (upd.)
TNT Freightways Corporation, 14
TNT Post Group N.V., V; 27 (upd.); 30 (upd.)
Tobu Railway Co Ltd, 6
Tokyu Corporation, V
Totem Resources Corporation, 9
TPG N.V., 64 (upd.)
Trailer Bridge, Inc., 41
Transnet Ltd., 6
Transport Corporation of America, Inc., 49
Trico Marine Services, Inc., 89
Tsakos Energy Navigation Ltd., 91
TTX Company, 6; 66 (upd.)
U.S. Delivery Systems, Inc., 22

Union Pacific Corporation, V; 28 (upd.); 79 (upd.)
United Parcel Service of America Inc., V; 17 (upd.)
United Parcel Service, Inc., 63
United Road Services, Inc., 69
United States Postal Service, 14; 34 (upd.)
US 1 Industries, Inc., 89
USA Truck, Inc., 42
Velocity Express Corporation, 49
Werner Enterprises, Inc., 26
Wheels Inc., 96
Wincanton plc, 52
Wisconsin Central Transportation Corporation, 24
Wright Express Corporation, 80
Yamato Transport Co. Ltd., V; 49 (upd.)
Yellow Corporation, 14; 45 (upd.)
Yellow Freight System, Inc. of Delaware, V
YRC Worldwide Inc., 90 (upd.)

Utilities

AES Corporation, 10; 13 (upd.); 53 (upd.)
Aggreko Plc, 45
Air & Water Technologies Corporation, 6
Alberta Energy Company Ltd., 16; 43 (upd.)
Allegheny Energy, Inc., V; 38 (upd.)
Ameren Corporation, 60 (upd.)
American Electric Power Company, Inc., V; 45 (upd.)
American States Water Company, 46
American Water Works Company, Inc., 6; 38 (upd.)
Aquarion Company, 84
Aquila, Inc., 50 (upd.)
Arkla, Inc., V
Associated Natural Gas Corporation, 11
Atlanta Gas Light Company, 6; 23 (upd.)
Atlantic Energy, Inc., 6
Atmos Energy Corporation, 43
Avista Corporation, 69 (upd.)
Baltimore Gas and Electric Company, V; 25 (upd.)
Bay State Gas Company, 38
Bayernwerk AG, V; 23 (upd.)
Berlinwasser Holding AG, 90
Bewag AG, 39
Big Rivers Electric Corporation, 11
Black Hills Corporation, 20
Bonneville Power Administration, 50
Boston Edison Company, 12
Bouygues S.A., I; 24 (upd.); 97 (upd.)
British Energy Plc, 49
British Gas plc, V
British Nuclear Fuels plc, 6
Brooklyn Union Gas, 6
California Water Service Group, 79
Calpine Corporation, 36
Canadian Utilities Limited, 13; 56 (upd.)
Cap Rock Energy Corporation, 46
Carolina Power & Light Company, V; 23 (upd.)
Cascade Natural Gas Corporation, 9
Centerior Energy Corporation, V
Central and South West Corporation, V
Central Hudson Gas and Electricity Corporation, 6
Central Maine Power, 6
Central Vermont Public Service Corporation, 54
Centrica plc, 29 (upd.)
ČEZ a. s., 97
Chesapeake Utilities Corporation, 56
China Shenhua Energy Company Limited, 83
Chubu Electric Power Company, Inc., V; 46 (upd.)
Chugoku Electric Power Company Inc., V; 53 (upd.)
Cincinnati Gas & Electric Company, 6
CIPSCO Inc., 6
Citizens Utilities Company, 7
City Public Service, 6
Cleco Corporation, 37
CMS Energy Corporation, V, 14
The Coastal Corporation, 31 (upd.)
Cogentrix Energy, Inc., 10
The Coleman Company, Inc., 9
The Columbia Gas System, Inc., V; 16 (upd.)
Commonwealth Edison Company, V
Commonwealth Energy System, 14
Companhia Energética de Minas Gerais S.A. CEMIG, 65
Compañia de Minas Buenaventura S.A.A., 93
Connecticut Light and Power Co., 13
Consolidated Edison, Inc., V; 45 (upd.)
Consolidated Natural Gas Company, V; 19 (upd.)
Consumers Power Co., 14
Consumers Water Company, 14
Consumers' Gas Company Ltd., 6
Covanta Energy Corporation, 64 (upd.)
Dalkia Holding, 66
Destec Energy, Inc., 12
The Detroit Edison Company, V
Dominion Resources, Inc., V; 54 (upd.)
DPL Inc., 6; 96 (upd.)
DQE, Inc., 6
DTE Energy Company, 20 (upd.)
Duke Energy Corporation, V; 27 (upd.)
E.On AG, 50 (upd.)
Eastern Enterprises, 6
Edison International, 56 (upd.)
El Paso Electric Company, 21
El Paso Natural Gas Company, 12
Electrabel N.V., 67
Electricidade de Portugal, S.A., 47
Electricité de France, V; 41 (upd.)
Electricity Generating Authority of Thailand (EGAT), 56
Elektrowatt AG, 6
The Empire District Electric Company, 77
Empresas Públicas de Medellín S.A.E.S.P., 91
Enbridge Inc., 43
ENDESA S.A., V; 46 (upd.)
Enersis S.A., 73
ENMAX Corporation, 83
Enron Corporation, V; 46 (upd.)
Enserch Corporation, V
Ente Nazionale per L'Energia Elettrica, V
Entergy Corporation, V; 45 (upd.)
Environmental Power Corporation, 68
EPCOR Utilities Inc., 81
Equitable Resources, Inc., 6; 54 (upd.)
Exelon Corporation, 48 (upd.)
Florida Progress Corporation, V; 23 (upd.)
Florida Public Utilities Company, 69
Fortis, Inc., 15; 47 (upd.)
Fortum Corporation, 30 (upd.)
FPL Group, Inc., V; 49 (upd.)
Gas Natural SDG S.A., 69
Gaz de France, V; 40 (upd.)
General Public Utilities Corporation, V
Générale des Eaux Group, V
GPU, Inc., 27 (upd.)
Great Plains Energy Incorporated, 65 (upd.)
Gulf States Utilities Company, 6
Hawaiian Electric Industries, Inc., 9
Hokkaido Electric Power Company Inc. (HEPCO), V; 58 (upd.)
Hokuriku Electric Power Company, V
Hong Kong and China Gas Company Ltd., 73
Hongkong Electric Holdings Ltd., 6; 23 (upd.)
Houston Industries Incorporated, V
Hyder plc, 34
Hydro-Québec, 6; 32 (upd.)
Iberdrola, S.A., 49
Idaho Power Company, 12
Illinois Bell Telephone Company, 14
Illinois Power Company, 6
Indiana Energy, Inc., 27
International Power PLC, 50 (upd.)
IPALCO Enterprises, Inc., 6
ITC Holdings Corp., 75
The Kansai Electric Power Company, Inc., V; 62 (upd.)
Kansas City Power & Light Company, 6
Kelda Group plc, 45
Kenetech Corporation, 11
Kentucky Utilities Company, 6
KeySpan Energy Co., 27
Korea Electric Power Corporation (Kepco), 56
KU Energy Corporation, 11
Kyushu Electric Power Company Inc., V
LG&E Energy Corporation, 6; 51 (upd.)
Long Island Lighting Company, V
Lyonnaise des Eaux-Dumez, V
Madison Gas and Electric Company, 39
Magma Power Company, 11
Maine & Maritimes Corporation, 56
Manila Electric Company (Meralco), 56
MCN Corporation, 6
MDU Resources Group, Inc., 7; 42 (upd.)
Middlesex Water Company, 45
Midwest Resources Inc., 6
Minnesota Power, Inc., 11; 34 (upd.)
The Montana Power Company, 11; 44 (upd.)
National Fuel Gas Company, 6; 95 (upd.)
National Grid USA, 51 (upd.)
National Power PLC, 12
Nebraska Public Power District, 29
N.V. Nederlandse Gasunie, V

Nevada Power Company, 11
New England Electric System, V
New Jersey Resources Corporation, 54
New York State Electric and Gas, 6
Neyveli Lignite Corporation Ltd., 65
Niagara Mohawk Holdings Inc., V; 45 (upd.)
Nicor Inc., 6; 86 (upd.)
NIPSCO Industries, Inc., 6
North West Water Group plc, 11
Northeast Utilities, V; 48 (upd.)
Northern States Power Company, V; 20 (upd.)
Northwest Natural Gas Company, 45
NorthWestern Corporation, 37
Nova Corporation of Alberta, V
NRG Energy, Inc., 79
Oglethorpe Power Corporation, 6
Ohio Edison Company, V
Oklahoma Gas and Electric Company, 6
ONEOK Inc., 7
Ontario Hydro Services Company, 6; 32 (upd.)
Osaka Gas Company, Ltd., V; 60 (upd.)
Österreichische Elektrizitätswirtschafts-AG, 85
Otter Tail Power Company, 18
Pacific Enterprises, V
Pacific Gas and Electric Company, V
PacifiCorp, V; 26 (upd.)
Panhandle Eastern Corporation, V
PECO Energy Company, 11
Pennon Group Plc, 45
Pennsylvania Power & Light Company, V
Peoples Energy Corporation, 6
PG&E Corporation, 26 (upd.)
Philadelphia Electric Company, V
Philadelphia Gas Works Company, 92
Philadelphia Suburban Corporation, 39
Piedmont Natural Gas Company, Inc., 27
Pinnacle West Capital Corporation, 6; 54 (upd.)
PNM Resources Inc., 51 (upd.)
Portland General Corporation, 6
Potomac Electric Power Company, 6
Power-One, Inc., 79
Powergen PLC, 11; 50 (upd.)
PPL Corporation, 41 (upd.)
PreussenElektra Aktiengesellschaft, V
Progress Energy, Inc., 74
PSI Resources, 6
Public Service Company of Colorado, 6
Public Service Company of New Hampshire, 21; 55 (upd.)
Public Service Company of New Mexico, 6
Public Service Enterprise Group Inc., V; 44 (upd.)
Puerto Rico Electric Power Authority, 47
Puget Sound Energy Inc., 6; 50 (upd.)
Questar Corporation, 6; 26 (upd.)
RAO Unified Energy System of Russia, 45
Reliant Energy Inc., 44 (upd.)
Revere Electric Supply Company, 96
Rochester Gas and Electric Corporation, 6
Ruhrgas AG, V; 38 (upd.)
RWE AG, V; 50 (upd.)
Salt River Project, 19
San Diego Gas & Electric Company, V
SCANA Corporation, 6; 56 (upd.)
Scarborough Public Utilities Commission, 9
SCEcorp, V
Scottish and Southern Energy plc, 66 (upd.)
Scottish Hydro-Electric PLC, 13
Scottish Power plc, 19; 49 (upd.)
Seattle City Light, 50
SEMCO Energy, Inc., 44
Sempra Energy, 25 (upd.)
Severn Trent PLC, 12; 38 (upd.)
Shikoku Electric Power Company, Inc., V; 60 (upd.)
SJW Corporation, 70
Sonat, Inc., 6
South Jersey Industries, Inc., 42
The Southern Company, V; 38 (upd.)
Southern Connecticut Gas Company, 84
Southern Electric PLC, 13
Southern Indiana Gas and Electric Company, 13
Southern Union Company, 27
Southwest Gas Corporation, 19
Southwest Water Company, 47
Southwestern Electric Power Co., 21
Southwestern Public Service Company, 6
Suez Lyonnaise des Eaux, 36 (upd.)
SUEZ-TRACTEBEL S.A., 97 (upd.)
TECO Energy, Inc., 6
Tennessee Valley Authority, 50
Tennet BV 78
Texas Utilities Company, V; 25 (upd.)
Thames Water plc, 11; 90 (upd.)
Tohoku Electric Power Company, Inc., V
The Tokyo Electric Power Company, 74 (upd.)
The Tokyo Electric Power Company, Incorporated, V
Tokyo Gas Co., Ltd., V; 55 (upd.)
TransAlta Utilities Corporation, 6
TransCanada PipeLines Limited, V
Transco Energy Company, V
Trigen Energy Corporation, 42
Tucson Electric Power Company, 6
UGI Corporation, 12
Unicom Corporation, 29 (upd.)
Union Electric Company, V
The United Illuminating Company, 21
United Utilities PLC, 52 (upd.)
United Water Resources, Inc., 40
Unitil Corporation, 37
Utah Power and Light Company, 27
UtiliCorp United Inc., 6
Vattenfall AB, 57
Vereinigte Elektrizitätswerke Westfalen AG, V
VEW AG, 39
Viridian Group plc, 64
Warwick Valley Telephone Company, 55
Washington Gas Light Company, 19
Washington Natural Gas Company, 9
Washington Water Power Company, 6
Westar Energy, Inc., 57 (upd.)
Western Resources, Inc., 12
Wheelabrator Technologies, Inc., 6
Wisconsin Energy Corporation, 6; 54 (upd.)
Wisconsin Public Service Corporation, 9
WPL Holdings, Inc., 6
WPS Resources Corporation, 53 (upd.)
Xcel Energy Inc., 73 (upd.)

Waste Services

Allied Waste Industries, Inc., 50
Allwaste, Inc., 18
American Ecology Corporation, 77
Appliance Recycling Centers of America, Inc., 42
Azcon Corporation, 23
Berliner Stadtreinigungsbetriebe, 58
Biffa plc, 92
Brambles Industries Limited, 42
Browning-Ferris Industries, Inc., V; 20 (upd.)
Chemical Waste Management, Inc., 9
Clean Harbors, Inc., 73
Copart Inc., 23
Darling International Inc., 85
E.On AG, 50 (upd.)
Ecolab Inc., I; 13 (upd.); 34 (upd.); 85 (upd.)
Ecology and Environment, Inc., 39
Empresas Públicas de Medellín S.A.E.S.P., 91
Fuel Tech, Inc., 85
Industrial Services of America, Inc., 46
Ionics, Incorporated, 52
ISS A/S, 49
Jani-King International, Inc., 85
Kelda Group plc, 45
MPW Industrial Services Group, Inc., 53
Newpark Resources, Inc., 63
Norcal Waste Systems, Inc., 60
Oakleaf Waste Management, LLC, 97
1-800-GOT-JUNK? LLC, 74
Onet S.A., 92
Pennon Group Plc, 45
Philip Environmental Inc., 16
Philip Services Corp., 73
Republic Services, Inc., 92
Roto-Rooter, Inc., 15; 61 (upd.)
Safety-Kleen Systems Inc., 8; 82 (upd.)
Saur S.A.S., 92
Sevenson Environmental Services, Inc., 42
Severn Trent PLC, 38 (upd.)
Servpro Industries, Inc., 85
Shanks Group plc, 45
Shred-It Canada Corporation, 56
Stericycle, Inc., 33; 74 (upd.)
TRC Companies, Inc., 32
Valley Proteins, Inc., 91
Veit Companies, 43; 92 (upd.)
Waste Connections, Inc., 46
Waste Holdings, Inc., 41
Waste Management, Inc., V
Wheelabrator Technologies, Inc., 60 (upd.)
Windswept Environmental Group, Inc., 62
WMX Technologies Inc., 17

Geographic Index

Algeria
Sonatrach, IV; 65 (upd.)

Argentina
Acindar Industria Argentina de Aceros S.A., 87
Aerolíneas Argentinas S.A., 33; 69 (upd.)
Alpargatas S.A.I.C., 87
Aluar Aluminio Argentino S.A.I.C., 74
Arcor S.A.I.C., 66
Atanor S.A., 62
Coto Centro Integral de Comercializacion S.A., 66
Cresud S.A.C.I.F. y A., 63
Grupo Clarín S.A., 67
Grupo Financiero Galicia S.A., 63
IRSA Inversiones y Representaciones S.A., 63
Ledesma Sociedad Anónima Agrícola Industrial, 62
Loma Negra C.I.A.S.A., 95
Molinos Río de la Plata S.A., 61
Nobleza Piccardo SAICF, 64
Penaflor S.A., 66
Petrobras Energia Participaciones S.A., 72
Quilmes Industrial (QUINSA) S.A., 67
Renault Argentina S.A., 67
Sideco Americana S.A., 67
Siderar S.A.I.C., 66
Telecom Argentina S.A., 63
Telefónica de Argentina S.A., 61
YPF Sociedad Anonima, IV

Australia
ABC Learning Centres Ltd., 93
Amcor Limited, IV; 19 (upd.), 78 (upd.)
Ansell Ltd., 60 (upd.)
Aquarius Platinum Ltd., 63
Aristocrat Leisure Limited, 54
Arnott's Ltd., 66
Austal Limited, 75
Australia and New Zealand Banking Group Limited, II; 52 (upd.)
AWB Ltd., 56
BHP Billiton, 67 (upd.)
Billabong International Ltd., 44
Blundstone Pty Ltd., 76
Bond Corporation Holdings Limited, 10
Boral Limited, III; 43 (upd.)
Brambles Industries Limited, 42
Broken Hill Proprietary Company Ltd., IV; 22 (upd.)
Burns, Philp & Company Ltd., 63
Carlton and United Breweries Ltd., I
Coles Group Limited, V; 20 (upd.); 85 (upd.)
Cochlear Ltd., 77
CRA Limited, IV; 85 (upd.)
CSR Limited, III; 28 (upd.)
David Jones Ltd., 60
Elders IXL Ltd., I
Fairfax Media Ltd., 94 (upd.)
Foster's Group Limited, 7; 21 (upd.); 50 (upd.)
Goodman Fielder Ltd., 52
Harvey Norman Holdings Ltd., 56
Holden Ltd., 62
James Hardie Industries N.V., 56
John Fairfax Holdings Limited, 7
Lend Lease Corporation Limited, IV; 17 (upd.); 52 (upd.)
Lion Nathan Limited, 54
Lonely Planet Publications Pty Ltd., 55
Macquarie Bank Ltd., 69
McPherson's Ltd., 66
Metcash Trading Ltd., 58
MYOB Ltd., 86
News Corporation Limited, IV; 7 (upd.); 46 (upd.)
Nufarm Ltd., 87
Pacific Dunlop Limited, 10
Pioneer International Limited, III
PMP Ltd., 72
Publishing and Broadcasting Limited, 54
Qantas Airways Ltd., 6; 24 (upd.); 68 (upd.)
Repco Corporation Ltd., 74
Ridley Corporation Ltd., 62
Rinker Group Ltd., 65
Rural Press Ltd., 74
Santos Ltd., 81
Smorgon Steel Group Ltd., 62
Southcorp Limited, 54
Suncorp-Metway Ltd., 91
TABCORP Holdings Limited, 44
Telecom Australia, 6
Telstra Corporation Limited, 50
Village Roadshow Ltd., 58
Westpac Banking Corporation, II; 48 (upd.)
WMC, Limited, 43
Zinifex Ltd., 85

Austria
AKG Acoustics GmbH, 62
Andritz AG, 51
Austrian Airlines AG (Österreichische Luftverkehrs AG), 33
Bank Austria AG, 23
Baumax AG, 75
BBAG Osterreichische Brau-Beteiligungs-AG, 38
BÖHLER-UDDEHOLM AG, 73
Borealis AG, 94
Erste Bank der Osterreichischen Sparkassen AG, 69

Gericom AG, 47
Glock Ges.m.b.H., 42
Julius Meinl International AG, 53
Lauda Air Luftfahrt AG, 48
ÖMV Aktiengesellschaft, IV
Österreichische Bundesbahnen GmbH, 6
Österreichische Elektrizitätswirtschafts-AG, 85
Österreichische Post- und Telegraphenverwaltung, V
Raiffeisen Zentralbank Österreich AG, 85
Red Bull GmbH, 60
RHI AG, 53
VA TECH ELIN EBG GmbH, 49
voestalpine AG, IV; 57 (upd.)
Wienerberger AG, 70
Zumtobel AG, 50

Azerbaijan

Azerbaijan Airlines, 77

Bahamas

Bahamas Air Holdings Ltd., 66
Kerzner International Limited, 69 (upd.)
Sun International Hotels Limited, 26
Teekay Shipping Corporation, 25; 82 (upd.)

Bahrain

Gulf Air Company, 56
Investcorp SA, 57

Bangladesh

Grameen Bank, 31

Belgium

Ackermans & van Haaren N.V., 97
Agfa Gevaert Group N.V., 59
Almanij NV, 44
Arcelor Gent, 80
Bank Brussels Lambert, II
Barco NV, 44
Bekaert S.A./N.V., 90
Belgacom, 6
Besix Group S.A./NV, 94
Brouwerijen Alken-Maes N.V., 86
C&A, 40 (upd.)
Cockerill Sambre Group, IV; 26 (upd.)
Compagnie Maritime Belge S.A., 95
Compagnie Nationale à Portefeuille, 84
Cora S.A./NV, 94
Corelio S.A./N.V., 96
Deceuninck N.V., 84
Delhaize "Le Lion" S.A., 44
Dexia NV/SA, 88 (upd.)
DHL Worldwide Network S.A./N.V., 69 (upd.)
Distrigaz S.A., 82
Electrabel N.V., 67
Etablissements Franz Colruyt N.V., 68
Generale Bank, II
GIB Group, V; 26 (upd.)
Glaverbel Group, 80
Groupe Herstal S.A., 58
Hamon & Cie (International) S.A., 97
Interbrew S.A., 17; 50 (upd.)
Janssen Pharmaceutica N.V., 80
Kredietbank N.V., II
Lyfra-S.A./NV, 88
PetroFina S.A., IV; 26 (upd.)
Picanol N.V., 96
Punch International N.V., 66
Puratos S.A./NV, 92
Quick Restaurants S.A., 94
Rosy Blue N.V., 84
Roularta Media Group NV, 48
Sabena S.A./N.V., 33
Solvay S.A., I; 21 (upd.); 61 (upd.)
Spector Photo Group N.V., 82
SUEZ-TRACTEBEL S.A., 97 (upd.)
Tessenderlo Group, 76
Tractebel S.A., 20
NV Umicore SA, 47
Van Hool S.A./NV, 96
Xeikon NV, 26

Belize

BB Holdings Limited, 77

Bermuda

Assured Guaranty Ltd., 93
Bacardi & Company Ltd., 18; 82 (upd.)
Central European Media Enterprises Ltd., 61
Covidien Ltd., 91
Endurance Specialty Holdings Ltd., 85
Frontline Ltd., 45
Gosling Brothers Ltd., 82
Jardine Matheson Holdings Limited, I; 20 (upd.); 93 (upd.)
Nabors Industries Ltd., 91 (upd.)
PartnerRe Ltd., 83
Sea Containers Ltd., 29
Tyco International Ltd., III; 28 (upd.); 63 (upd.)
VistaPrint Limited, 87
Warner Chilcott Limited, 85
White Mountains Insurance Group, Ltd., 48

Bolivia

Lloyd Aéreo Boliviano S.A., 95

Brazil

Abril S.A., 95
Aracruz Celulose S.A., 57
Banco Bradesco S.A., 13
Banco Itaú S.A., 19
Brasil Telecom Participaçoes S.A., 57
Brazil Fast Food Corporation, 74
Bunge Brasil S.A. 78
Camargo Corrêa S.A., 93
Casas Bahia Comercial Ltda., 75
Cia Hering, 72
Companhia Brasileira de Distribuiçao, 76
Companhia de Bebidas das Américas, 57
Companhia de Tecidos Norte de Minas - Coteminas, 77
Companhia Energética de Minas Gerais S.A. CEMIG, 65
Companhia Siderúrgica Nacional, 76
Companhia Suzano de Papel e Celulose S.A., 94
Companhia Vale do Rio Doce, IV; 43 (upd.)
Empresa Brasileira de Aeronáutica S.A. (Embraer), 36
G&K Holding S.A., 95
Gerdau S.A., 59
Globo Comunicação e Participações S.A., 80
Gol Linhas Aéreas Inteligentes S.A., 73
Ipiranga S.A., 67
Klabin S.A., 73
Lojas Americanas S.A., 77
Lojas Arapua S.A., 22; 61 (upd.)
Marcopolo S.A. 79
Natura Cosméticos S.A., 75
Odebrecht S.A., 73
Perdigao SA, 52
Petróleo Brasileiro S.A., IV
Randon S.A. 79
Renner Herrmann S.A. 79
Sadia S.A., 59
Sao Paulo Alpargatas S.A., 75
Souza Cruz S.A., 65
TAM Linhas Aéreas S.A., 68
Tele Norte Leste Participações S.A., 80
TransBrasil S/A Linhas Aéreas, 31
Unibanco Holdings S.A., 73
Usinas Siderúrgicas de Minas Gerais S.A., 77
VARIG S.A. (Viação Aérea Rio-Grandense), 6; 29 (upd.)
Vicunha Têxtil S.A. 78
Votorantim Participaçoes S.A., 76
Weg S.A. 78

Canada

Abitibi-Consolidated, Inc., V; 25 (upd.)
Abitibi-Price Inc., IV
Agnico-Eagle Mines Limited, 71
Agrium Inc., 73
Air Canada, 6; 23 (upd.); 59 (upd.)
Alberta Energy Company Ltd., 16; 43 (upd.)
Alcan Aluminium Limited, IV; 31 (upd.)
Alderwoods Group, Inc., 68 (upd.)
Algo Group Inc., 24
Alimentation Couche-Tard Inc., 77
Alliance Atlantis Communications Inc., 39
ATI Technologies Inc. 79
Axcan Pharma Inc., 85
Ballard Power Systems Inc., 73
Bank of Montreal, II; 46 (upd.)
The Bank of Nova Scotia, II; 59 (upd.)
Barrick Gold Corporation, 34
Bata Ltd., 62
BCE Inc., V; 44 (upd.)
Bell Canada, 6
BFC Construction Corporation, 25
BioWare Corporation, 81
Biovail Corporation, 47
Bombardier Inc., 42 (upd.); 87 (upd.)
Boston Pizza International Inc., 88
Bradley Air Services Ltd., 56
Bramalea Ltd., 9
Brascan Corporation, 67
British Columbia Telephone Company, 6
Brookfield Properties Corporation, 89
Cameco Corporation, 77
Campeau Corporation, V
Canada Packers Inc., II

Canadair, Inc., 16
The Canadian Broadcasting Corporation (CBC), 37
Canadian Imperial Bank of Commerce, II; 61 (upd.)
Canadian National Railway Company, 6, 71 (upd.)
Canadian Pacific Railway Limited, V; 45 (upd.); 95 (upd.)
Canadian Tire Corporation, Limited, 71 (upd.)
Canadian Utilities Limited, 13; 56 (upd.)
Canfor Corporation, 42
Canstar Sports Inc., 16
CanWest Global Communications Corporation, 35
Cascades Inc., 71
Celestica Inc., 80
CHC Helicopter Corporation, 67
Cinar Corporation, 40
Cineplex Odeon Corporation, 6; 23 (upd.)
Cinram International, Inc., 43
Cirque du Soleil Inc., 29
Clearly Canadian Beverage Corporation, 48
Cognos Inc., 44
Cominco Ltd., 37
Consumers' Gas Company Ltd., 6
CoolBrands International Inc., 35
Corby Distilleries Limited, 14
Corel Corporation, 15; 33 (upd.); 76 (upd.)
Cott Corporation, 52
Creo Inc., 48
Diavik Diamond Mines Inc., 85
Discreet Logic Inc., 20
Dofasco Inc., IV; 24 (upd.)
Doman Industries Limited, 59
Dominion Textile Inc., 12
Domtar Corporation, IV; 89 (upd.)
Dorel Industries Inc., 59
Duvernay Oil Corp., 83
Dynatec Corporation, 87
Dylex Limited, 29
Echo Bay Mines Ltd., IV; 38 (upd.)
Enbridge Inc., 43
ENMAX Corporation, 83
EPCOR Utilities Inc., 81
Extendicare Health Services, Inc., 6
Fairfax Financial Holdings Limited, 57
Fairmont Hotels & Resorts Inc., 69
Falconbridge Limited, 49
Finning International Inc., 69
Fortis, Inc., 15; 47 (upd.)
The Forzani Group Ltd. 79
Four Seasons Hotels Inc., 9; 29 (upd.)
Future Shop Ltd., 62
GEAC Computer Corporation Ltd., 43
George Weston Ltd, II; 36 (upd.); 88 (upd.)
Gildan Activewear, Inc., 81
Goldcorp Inc., 87
GPS Industries, Inc., 81
Great-West Lifeco Inc., III
Groupe Vidéotron Ltée., 20
Hammond Manufacturing Company Limited, 83
Harlequin Enterprises Limited, 52
Hemlo Gold Mines Inc., 9
Héroux-Devtek Inc., 69
Hiram Walker Resources, Ltd., I
The Hockey Company, 34; 70
Hollinger International Inc., 62 (upd.)
Home Hardware Stores Ltd., 62
The Hudson Bay Mining and Smelting Company, Limited, 12
Hudson's Bay Company, V; 25 (upd.); 83 (upd.)
Hurricane Hydrocarbons Ltd., 54
Husky Energy Inc., 47
Hydro-Québec, 6; 32 (upd.)
Imasco Limited, V
IMAX Corporation 28, 78 (upd.)
Imperial Oil Limited, IV; 25 (upd.); 95 (upd.)
Imperial Parking Corporation, 58
Inco Limited, IV; 45 (upd.)
Indigo Books & Music Inc., 58
Intercorp Excelle Foods Inc., 64
Intrawest Corporation, 15; 84 (upd.)
Iogen Corporation, 81
Irwin Toy Limited, 14
Jacques Whitford, 92
The Jean Coutu Group (PJC) Inc., 46
The Jim Pattison Group, 37
Kinross Gold Corporation, 36
Kruger Inc., 17
La Senza Corporation, 66
Labatt Brewing Company Limited, I; 25 (upd.)
LaSiDo Inc., 58
Lassonde Industries Inc., 68
Le Chateau Inc., 63
Ledcor Industries Limited, 46
Les Boutiques San Francisco, Inc., 62
Linamar Corporation, 18
Lions Gate Entertainment Corporation, 35
Loblaw Companies Limited, 43
The Loewen Group, Inc., 16; 40 (upd.)
London Drugs Ltd., 46
Maclean Hunter Publishing Limited, IV; 26 (upd.)
MacMillan Bloedel Limited, IV
Magellan Aerospace Corporation, 48
Manitoba Telecom Services, Inc., 61
Manulife Financial Corporation, 85
Maple Leaf Foods Inc., 41
Maple Leaf Sports & Entertainment Ltd., 61
Masonite International Corporation, 63
McCain Foods Limited, 77
MDC Partners Inc., 63
Mega Bloks, Inc., 61
Methanex Corporation, 40
Métro Inc., 77
Mitel Corporation, 18
The Molson Companies Limited, I; 26 (upd.)
Moore Corporation Limited, IV
Morguard Corporation, 85
Mouvement des Caisses Desjardins, 48
National Bank of Canada, 85
National Sea Products Ltd., 14
Nature's Path Foods, Inc., 87
New Flyer Industries Inc. 78
Nexen Inc. 79
Noranda Inc., IV; 7 (upd.); 64 (upd.)
Nortel Networks Corporation, 36 (upd.)
The North West Company, Inc., 12
Northern Telecom Limited, V
Nova Corporation of Alberta, V
Novacor Chemicals Ltd., 12
Olympia & York Developments Ltd., IV; 9 (upd.)
1-800-GOT-JUNK? LLC, 74
Onex Corporation, 16; 65 (upd.)
Ontario Hydro Services Company, 6; 32 (upd.)
Ontario Teachers' Pension Plan, 61
Open Text Corporation 79
The Oppenheimer Group, 76
The Oshawa Group Limited, II
Paramount Resources Ltd., 87
PCL Construction Group Inc., 50
Peace Arch Entertainment Group Inc., 51
Pengrowth Energy Trust, 95
Petro-Canada Limited, IV
Philip Environmental Inc., 16
Placer Dome Inc., 20; 61 (upd.)
Potash Corporation of Saskatchewan Inc., 18
Power Corporation of Canada, 36 (upd.); 85 (upd.)
Provigo Inc., II; 51 (upd.)
QLT Inc., 71
Quebecor Inc., 12; 47 (upd.)
Research in Motion Ltd., 54
Richtree Inc., 63
Ritchie Bros. Auctioneers Inc., 41
RM Auctions, Inc., 88
Rogers Communications Inc., 30 (upd.)
RONA, Inc., 73
Roots Canada Ltd., 42
Royal Bank of Canada, II; 21 (upd.), 81 (upd.)
Royal Group Technologies Limited, 73
Saputo Inc., 59
Scarborough Public Utilities Commission, 9
The Seagram Company Ltd., I; 25 (upd.)
Shermag, Inc., 93
Shoppers Drug Mart Corporation, 49
Shred-It Canada Corporation, 56
Silver Wheaton Corp., 95
Sleeman Breweries Ltd., 74
SNC-Lavalin Group Inc., 72
Sobeys Inc., 80
Southam Inc., 7
Spar Aerospace Limited, 32
Spin Master, Ltd., 61
Steinberg Incorporated, II
Stelco Inc., IV; 51 (upd.)
Sun Life Financial Inc., 85
Sun-Rype Products Ltd., 76
Suncor Energy Inc., 54
SunOpta Inc. 79
Talisman Energy Inc., 9; 47 (upd.)
TAQA North Ltd., 95
TDL Group Ltd., 46
Teck Corporation, 27
Tembec Inc., 66

The Thomson Corporation, 8; 34 (upd.); 77 (upd.)
Tilley Endurables, Inc., 67
Toromont Industries, Ltd., 21
The Toronto-Dominion Bank, II; 49 (upd.)
Torstar Corporation, 29
TransAlta Utilities Corporation, 6
TransCanada Corporation, V; 93 (upd.)
Tridel Enterprises Inc., 9
Trilon Financial Corporation, II
Triple Five Group Ltd., 49
Trizec Corporation Ltd., 10
Tucows Inc. 78
Van Houtte Inc., 39
Varity Corporation, III
Vector Aerospace Corporation, 97
Vincor International Inc., 50
Wascana Energy Inc., 13
The Wawanesa Mutual Insurance Company, 68
West Fraser Timber Co. Ltd., 17; 91 (upd.)
Western Oil Sands Inc., 85
WestJet Airlines Ltd., 38
Xantrex Technology Inc., 97

Cayman Islands

Garmin Ltd., 60
Herbalife Ltd., 92 (upd.)
United National Group, Ltd., 63

Chile

Banco de Chile, 69
Cencosud S.A., 69
Compania Cervecerias Unidas S.A., 70
Corporacion Nacional del Cobre de Chile, 40
Cristalerias de Chile S.A., 67
Distribución y Servicio D&S S.A., 71
Embotelladora Andina S.A., 71
Empresas Almacenes Paris S.A., 71
Empresas CMPC S.A., 70
Empresas Copec S.A., 69
Enersis S.A., 73
Farmacias Ahumada S.A., 72
Lan Chile S.A., 31
Madeco S.A., 71
Parque Arauco S.A., 72
S.A.C.I. Falabella, 69
Viña Concha y Toro S.A., 45

China

Air China, 46
American Oriental Bioengineering Inc., 93
Asia Info Holdings, Inc., 43
Baidu.com Inc., 95
Bank of China, 63
China Automotive Systems Inc., 87
China Construction Bank Corp. 79
China Eastern Airlines Co. Ltd., 31
China Life Insurance Company Limited, 65
China National Cereals, Oils and Foodstuffs Import and Export Corporation (COFCO), 76
China National Petroleum Corporation, 46
China Nepstar Chain Drugstore Ltd., 97
China Netcom Group Corporation (Hong Kong) Limited, 73
China Shenhua Energy Company Limited, 83
China Southern Airlines Company Ltd., 33
China Telecom, 50
Chinese Petroleum Corporation, IV; 31 (upd.)
Ctrip.com International Ltd., 97
Dalian Shide Group, 91
Egmont Group, 93
Guangzhou Pearl River Piano Group Ltd., 49
Haier Group Corporation, 65
Home Inns & Hotels Management Inc., 95
Huawei Technologies Company Ltd., 87
Li & Fung Limited, 59
Noah Education Holdings Ltd., 97
Shanghai Baosteel Group Corporation, 71
Shanghai Petrochemical Co., Ltd., 18
SINA Corporation, 69
Suntech Power Holdings Company Ltd., 89
Tianjin Flying Pigeon Bicycle Co., Ltd., 95
Tsingtao Brewery Group, 49
Zindart Ltd., 60

Colombia

Almacenes Exito S.A., 89
Avianca Aerovías Nacionales de Colombia SA, 36
Bavaria S.A., 90
Cementos Argos S.A., 91
Empresa Colombiana de Petróleos, IV
Empresas Públicas de Medellín S.A.E.S.P., 91
Inversiones Nacional de Chocolates S.A., 88
Suramericana de Inversiones S.A., 88
Valorem S.A., 88

Croatia

PLIVA d.d., 70

Cyprus

Bank of Cyprus Group, 91
Cyprus Airways Public Limited, 81
Marfin Popular Bank plc, 92

Czech Republic

Budweiser Budvar, National Corporation, 59
Ceské aerolinie, a.s., 66
Cesky Telecom, a.s., 64
ČEZ a. s., 97
Skoda Auto a.s., 39
Třinecké Železárny A.S., 92

Denmark

A.P. Møller - Maersk A/S, 57
Aalborg Industries A/S, 90
Aarhus United A/S, 68
Arla Foods amba, 48
Bang & Olufsen Holding A/S, 37; 86 (upd.)
Bestseller A/S, 90
Carl Allers Etablissement A/S, 72
Carlsberg A/S, 9; 29 (upd.)
Chr. Hansen Group A/S, 70
Dalhoff Larsen & Horneman A/S, 96
Danisco A/S, 44
Danske Bank Aktieselskab, 50
Ecco Sko A/S, 62
FLSmidth & Co. A/S, 72
Group 4 Falck A/S, 42
Grundfos Group, 83
H. Lundbeck A/S, 44
House of Prince A/S, 80
Hummel International A/S, 68
IKEA International A/S, V; 26 (upd.)
ISS A/S, 49
J Lauritzen A/S, 90
Lego A/S, 13; 40 (upd.)
Nordisk Film A/S, 80
Novo Nordisk A/S, I; 61 (upd.)
Schouw & Company A/S, 94
Sophus Berendsen A/S, 49
Sterling European Airlines A/S, 70
TDC A/S, 63
Velux A/S, 86
Vestas Wind Systems A/S, 73

Ecuador

Exportadora Bananera Noboa, S.A., 91
Petróleos del Ecuador, IV

Egypt

EgyptAir, 6; 27 (upd.)
Egyptian General Petroleum Corporation, IV; 51 (upd.)
Orascom Construction Industries S.A.E., 87

El Salvador

Grupo TACA, 38

Estonia

AS Estonian Air, 71

Ethiopia

Ethiopian Airlines, 81

Fiji

Air Pacific Ltd., 70

Finland

Ahlstrom Corporation, 53
Amer Group plc, 41
Dynea, 68
Enso-Gutzeit Oy, IV
Finnair Oyj, 6; 25 (upd.); 61 (upd.)
Fiskars Corporation, 33
Fortum Corporation, 30 (upd.)
Hackman Oyj Adp, 44
Huhtamäki Oyj, 64
Imatra Steel Oy Ab, 55
Kansallis-Osake-Pankki, II
Kemira Oyj, 70
Kesko Ltd. (Kesko Oy), 8; 27 (upd.)

KONE Corporation, 27; 76 (upd.)
Kymmene Corporation, IV
M-real Oyj, 56 (upd.)
Metsa-Serla Oy, IV
Metso Corporation, 30 (upd.); 85 (upd.)
Neste Oil Corporation, IV; 85 (upd.)
Nokia Corporation, II; 17 (upd.); 38 (upd.); 77 (upd.)
Orion Oyj, 72
Outokumpu Oyj, 38
Posti- ja Telelaitos, 6
Sanitec Corporation, 51
SanomaWSOY Corporation, 51
Sonera Corporation, 50
Stora Enso Oyj, 36 (upd.); 85 (upd.)
Tamfelt Oyj Abp, 62
United Paper Mills Ltd. (Yhtyneet Paperitehtaat Oy), IV
UPM-Kymmene Corporation, 19; 50 (upd.)
Valmet Corporation (Valmet Oy), III

France

Accor S.A., 10; 27 (upd.); 69 (upd.)
Aéroports de Paris, 33
The Aerospatiale Group, 7; 21 (upd.)
Agence France-Presse, 34
Akerys S.A., 90
Alain Afflelou SA, 53
Alcatel S.A., 9; 36 (upd.)
Alès Groupe, 81
Altran Technologies, 51
Amec Spie S.A., 57
Arc International, 76
AREVA NP, 90 (upd.)
Arianespace S.A., 89
Association des Centres Distributeurs E. Leclerc, 37
Assurances Générales de France, 63
Atochem S.A., I
Atos Origin S.A., 69
Au Printemps S.A., V
Auchan, 37
Automobiles Citroen, 7
Autoroutes du Sud de la France SA, 55
Avions Marcel Dassault-Breguet Aviation, I
Axa, III
Babolat VS, S.A., 97
Baccarat, 24
Banque Nationale de Paris S.A., II
Baron Philippe de Rothschild S.A., 39
Bayard SA, 49
Belvedere S.A., 93
Bénéteau SA, 55
Besnier SA, 19
BigBen Interactive S.A., 72
bioMérieux S.A., 75
BNP Paribas Group, 36 (upd.)
Boiron S.A., 73
Boizel Chanoine Champagne S.A., 94
Bonduelle SA, 51
Bongrain SA, 25
Bouygues S.A., I; 24 (upd.); 97 (upd.)
Bricorama S.A., 68
Brioche Pasquier S.A., 58
BSN Groupe S.A., II
Buffalo Grill S.A., 94
Bugatti Automobiles S.A.S., 94
Bull S.A., 43 (upd.)
Bureau Veritas SA, 55
Burelle S.A., 23
Business Objects S.A., 25
Camaïeu S.A., 72
Caisse des Dépôts et Consignations, 90
Canal Plus, 10; 34 (upd.)
Cap Gemini Ernst & Young, 37
Carbone Lorraine S.A., 33
Carrefour SA, 10; 27 (upd.); 64 (upd.)
Casino Guichard-Perrachon S.A., 59 (upd.)
Cemoi S.A., 86
Cetelem S.A., 21
Chanel SA, 12; 49 (upd.)
Chantiers Jeanneau S.A., 96
Charal S.A., 90
Chargeurs International, 6; 21 (upd.)
Christian Dalloz SA, 40
Christian Dior S.A., 19; 49 (upd.)
Christofle SA, 40
Ciments Français, 40
Club Mediterranée S.A., 6; 21 (upd.); 91 (upd.)
Coflexip S.A., 25
Colas S.A., 31
Compagnie de Saint-Gobain, III; 16 (upd.); 64 (upd.)
Compagnie des Alpes, 48
Compagnie des Machines Bull S.A., III
Compagnie Financiere de Paribas, II
Compagnie Financière Sucres et Denrées S.A., 60
Compagnie Générale d'Électricité, II
Compagnie Générale des Établissements Michelin, V; 42 (upd.)
Compagnie Générale Maritime et Financière, 6
Comptoirs Modernes S.A., 19
Coopagri Bretagne, 88
Crédit Agricole Group, II; 84 (upd.)
Crédit Lyonnais, 9; 33 (upd.)
Crédit National S.A., 9
Dalkia Holding, 66
Darty S.A., 27
Dassault Systèmes S.A., 25
DCN S.A., 75
De Dietrich & Cie., 31
Delachaux S.A., 76
Deveaux S.A., 41
Devoteam S.A., 94
Dexia Group, 42
Doux S.A., 80
Du Pareil au Même, 43
Dynaction S.A., 67
EADS SOCATA, 54
ECS S.A, 12
Ed S.A.S., 88
Éditions Gallimard, 72
Editis S.A. 78
Eiffage, 27
Electricité de France, V; 41 (upd.)
Elf Aquitaine SA, 21 (upd.)
Elior SA, 49
Eram SA, 51
Eramet, 73
Eridania Béghin-Say S.A., 36
Essilor International, 21
Etablissements Economiques du Casino Guichard, Perrachon et Cie, S.C.A., 12
Établissements Jacquot and Cie S.A.S., 92
Etam Developpement SA, 44
Eurazeo, 80
Euro Disney S.C.A., 20; 58 (upd.)
Euro RSCG Worldwide S.A., 13
Eurocopter S.A., 80
Eurofins Scientific S.A., 70
Euronext Paris S.A., 37
Expand SA, 48
Facom S.A., 32
Faiveley S.A., 39
Faurecia S.A., 70
Fimalac S.A., 37
Fleury Michon S.A., 39
Floc'h & Marchand, 80
FNAC, 21
Framatome SA, 19
France Télécom Group, V; 21 (upd.)
Fromageries Bel, 23
G.I.E. Airbus Industrie, I; 12 (upd.)
Galeries Lafayette S.A., V; 23 (upd.)
Gaumont S.A., 25; 91 (upd.)
Gaz de France, V; 40 (upd.)
Gecina SA, 42
Gefco SA, 54
Générale des Eaux Group, V
Geodis S.A., 67
Gévelot S.A., 96
GFI Informatique SA, 49
GiFi S.A., 74
Glaces Thiriet S.A., 76
GrandVision S.A., 43
Grévin & Compagnie SA, 56
Groupama S.A., 76
Groupe Air France, 6
Groupe Alain Manoukian, 55
Groupe André, 17
Groupe Bigard S.A., 96
Groupe Bolloré, 67
Groupe Bourbon S.A., 60
Groupe Castorama-Dubois Investissements, 23
Groupe CECAB S.C.A., 88
Groupe Crit S.A., 74
Groupe Danone, 32 (upd.); 93 (upd.)
Groupe Dassault Aviation SA, 26 (upd.)
Groupe de la Cite, IV
Groupe DMC (Dollfus Mieg & Cie), 27
Groupe Euralis, 86
Groupe Fournier SA, 44
Groupe Genoyer, 96
Groupe Glon, 84
Groupe Go Sport S.A., 39
Groupe Guillin SA, 40
Groupe Jean-Claude Darmon, 44
Groupe Lactalis 78 (upd.)
Groupe Lapeyre S.A., 33
Groupe Le Duff S.A., 84
Groupe Léa Nature, 88
Groupe Legris Industries, 23
Groupe Les Echos, 25
Groupe Limagrain, 74
Groupe Louis Dreyfus S.A., 60
Groupe Monnoyeur, 72
Groupe Monoprix S.A., 86

Groupe Open, 74
Groupe Partouche SA, 48
Groupe Promodès S.A., 19
Groupe Rougier SA, 21
Groupe SEB, 35
Groupe Sequana Capital 78 (upd.)
Groupe Sidel S.A., 21
Groupe Soufflet SA, 55
Groupe Yves Saint Laurent, 23
Groupe Zannier S.A., 35
Guerbet Group, 46
Guerlain, 23
Guilbert S.A., 42
Guillemot Corporation, 41
Guinot Paris S.A., 82
Guy Degrenne SA, 44
Guyenne et Gascogne, 23
Hachette, IV
Hachette Filipacchi Medias S.A., 21
Havas, SA, 10; 33 (upd.)
Hermès International S.A., 14; 34 (upd.)
Imerys S.A., 40 (upd.)
Imetal S.A., IV
Infogrames Entertainment S.A., 35
Ingenico—Compagnie Industrielle et Financière d'Ingénierie, 46
ITM Entreprises SA, 36
JCDecaux S.A., 76
Keolis SA, 51
Kiabi Europe, 66
L'Air Liquide SA, I; 47 (upd.)
L'Entreprise Jean Lefebvre, 23
L'Oréal SA, III; 8 (upd.); 46 (upd.)
L.D.C. SA, 61
La Poste, V; 47 (upd.)
Labeyrie SAS, 80
Laboratoires Arkopharma S.A., 75
Laboratoires de Biologie Végétale Yves Rocher, 35
LaCie Group S.A., 76
Lafarge Coppée S.A., III
Lafuma S.A., 39
Laurent-Perrier SA, 42
Lazard LLC, 38
LDC, 68
Le Cordon Bleu S.A., 67
Le Monde S.A., 33
Legrand SA, 21
Leroux S.A.S., 65
Leroy Merlin SA, 54
Ludendo S.A., 88
LVMH Möet Hennessy Louis Vuitton SA, I; 10; 33 (upd.)
Lyonnaise des Eaux-Dumez, V
Madrange SA, 58
Maison Louis Jadot, 24
Manitou BF S.A., 27
Manutan International S.A., 72
Marie Brizard & Roger International S.A.S., 22; 97 (upd.)
Marionnaud Parfumeries SA, 51
Martell and Company S.A., 82
Matra-Hachette S.A., 15 (upd.)
Matussière et Forest SA, 58
MBK Industrie S.A., 94
Metaleurop S.A., 21
Métropole Télévision, 33
Métropole Télévision S.A., 76 (upd.)
Moliflor Loisirs, 80
Monnaie de Paris, 62
Montupet S.A., 63
Moulinex S.A., 22
Mr. Bricolage S.A., 37
Naf Naf SA, 44
Neopost S.A., 53
Nestlé Waters, 73
Nexans SA, 54
Nexity S.A., 66
Nocibé SA, 54
OENEO S.A., 74 (upd.)
Onet S.A., 92
Otor S.A., 77
PagesJaunes Groupe SA 79
Panzani, 84
Papeteries de Lancey, 23
Pathé SA, 29
Pechiney SA, IV; 45 (upd.)
Penauille Polyservices SA, 49
Pernod Ricard S.A., I; 21 (upd.); 72 (upd.)
Petit Bateau, 95
Peugeot S.A., I
Picard Surgeles, 76
Pierre & Vacances SA, 48
Pinault-Printemps Redoute S.A., 19 (upd.)
Pinguely-Haulotte SA, 51
Piscines Desjoyaux S.A., 84
Pochet SA, 55
Poliet S.A., 33
PPR S.A., 74 (upd.)
Provimi S.A., 80
PSA Peugeot Citroen S.A., 28 (upd.)
Publicis S.A., 19; 77 (upd.)
Rallye SA, 54
Regie Nationale des Usines Renault, I
Rémy Cointreau Group, 20, 80 (upd.)
Renault S.A., 26 (upd.); 74 (upd.)
Réseau Ferré de France, 66
Rhodia SA, 38
Rhône-Poulenc S.A., I; 10 (upd.)
Robertet SA, 39
Rodriguez Group S.A., 90
Roussel Uclaf, I; 8 (upd.)
Royal Canin S.A., 39
Sabaté Diosos SA, 48
SAGEM S.A., 37
Salomon Worldwide, 20
The Sanofi-Synthélabo Group, I; 49 (upd.)
Saur S.A.S., 92
Schneider S.A., II; 18 (upd.)
SCOR S.A., 20
Seita, 23
Selectour SA, 53
Sephora Holdings S.A., 82
Simco S.A., 37
Skalli Group, 67
Skis Rossignol S.A., 15; 43 (upd.)
Smoby International SA, 56
Snecma Group, 46
Société Air France, 27 (upd.)
Société BIC S.A., 73
Société d'Exploitation AOM Air Liberté SA (AirLib), 53
Societe des Produits Marnier-Lapostolle S.A., 88
Société du Figaro S.A., 60
Société du Louvre, 27
Société Générale, II; 42 (upd.)
Société Industrielle Lesaffre, 84
Société Nationale des Chemins de Fer Français, V; 57 (upd.)
Société Nationale Elf Aquitaine, IV; 7 (upd.)
Société Norbert Dentressangle S.A., 67
Sodexho SA, 29; 91 (upd.)
Sodiaal S.A., 36 (upd.)
SODIMA, II
Sommer-Allibert S.A., 19
SR Teleperformance S.A., 86
Steria SA, 49
Suez Lyonnaise des Eaux, 36 (upd.)
Taittinger S.A., 43
Tati SA, 25
Technip 78
Télévision Française 1, 23
Terrena L'Union CANA CAVAL, 70
Thales S.A., 42
THOMSON multimedia S.A., II; 42 (upd.)
Total Fina Elf S.A., IV; 24 (upd.); 50 (upd.)
Toupargel-Agrigel S.A., 76
Touton S.A., 92
Transiciel SA, 48
Ubi Soft Entertainment S.A., 41
Ugine S.A., 20
Unibail SA, 40
Unilog SA, 42
Union des Assurances de Pans, III
Union Financière de France Banque SA, 52
Usinor SA, IV; 42 (upd.)
Valeo, 23; 66 (upd.)
Vallourec SA, 54
Vicat S.A., 70
Viel & Cie, 76
Vilmorin Clause et Cie, 70
Vinci, 43
Vivarte SA, 54 (upd.)
Vivendi Universal S.A., 46 (upd.)
Wanadoo S.A., 75
Weber et Broutin France, 66
Worms et Cie, 27
Zodiac S.A., 36

Germany

A. Moksel AG, 59
A.W. Faber-Castell Unternehmensverwaltung GmbH & Co., 51
Adam Opel AG, 7; 21 (upd.); 61 (upd.)
adidas Group AG, 14; 33 (upd.); 75 (upd.)
Adolf Würth GmbH & Co. KG, 49
AEG A.G., I
Air Berlin GmbH & Co. Luftverkehrs KG, 71
Aldi Einkauf GmbH & Co. OHG 13; 86 (upd.)
Alfred Kärcher GmbH & Co KG, 94
Alfred Ritter GmbH & Co. KG, 58
Allianz AG, III; 15 (upd.); 57 (upd.)
ALTANA AG, 87

AMB Generali Holding AG, 51
Andreas Stihl AG & Co. KG, 16; 59 (upd.)
AOK-Bundesverband (Federation of the AOK) 78
Aral AG, 62
ARD, 41
August Storck KG, 66
AVA AG (Allgemeine Handelsgesellschaft der Verbraucher AG), 33
AXA Colonia Konzern AG, 27; 49 (upd.)
Axel Springer Verlag AG, IV; 20 (upd.)
Bahlsen GmbH & Co. KG, 44
Barmag AG, 39
BASF Aktiengesellschaft, I; 18 (upd.); 50 (upd.)
Bauer Publishing Group, 7
Bayer A.G., I; 13 (upd.); 41 (upd.)
Bayerische Hypotheken- und Wechsel-Bank AG, II
Bayerische Motoren Werke AG, I; 11 (upd.); 38 (upd.)
Bayerische Vereinsbank A.G., II
Bayernwerk AG, V; 23 (upd.)
Beate Uhse AG, 96
Behr GmbH & Co. KG, 72
Beiersdorf AG, 29
Berliner Stadtreinigungsbetriebe, 58
Berliner Verkehrsbetriebe (BVG), 58
Berlinwasser Holding AG, 90
Bertelsmann A.G., IV; 15 (upd.); 43 (upd.); 91 (upd.)
Bewag AG, 39
Bibliographisches Institut & F.A. Brockhaus AG, 74
Bilfinger & Berger AG, I; 55 (upd.)
Brauerei Beck & Co., 9; 33 (upd.)
Braun GmbH, 51
Brenntag AG, 8; 23 (upd.)
Brose Fahrzeugteile GmbH & Company KG, 84
BSH Bosch und Siemens Hausgeräte GmbH, 67
Buderus AG, 37
Burda Holding GmbH. & Co., 23
C&A Brenninkmeyer KG, V
C. Bechstein Pianofortefabrik AG, 96
C.H. Boehringer Sohn, 39
Carl Kühne KG (GmbH & Co.), 94
Carl Zeiss AG, III; 34 (upd.); 91 (upd.)
CeWe Color Holding AG, 76
Commerzbank A.G., II; 47 (upd.)
Continental AG, V; 56 (upd.)
Cornelsen Verlagsholding GmbH & Co., 90
Dachser GmbH & Co. KG, 88
Daimler-Benz Aerospace AG, 16
DaimlerChrysler AG, I; 15 (upd.); 34 (upd.); 64 (upd.)
Dalli-Werke GmbH & Co. KG, 86
dba Luftfahrtgesellschaft mbH, 76
Debeka Krankenversicherungsverein auf Gegenseitigkeit, 72
Degussa Group, IV
Degussa-Huls AG, 32 (upd.)
Deutsche Babcock A.G., III
Deutsche Bahn AG, 46 (upd.)
Deutsche Bank AG, II; 14 (upd.); 40 (upd.)
Deutsche BP Aktiengesellschaft, 7
Deutsche Bundesbahn, V
Deutsche Bundespost TELEKOM, V
Deutsche Börse AG, 59
Deutsche Lufthansa AG, I; 26 (upd.); 68 (upd.)
Deutsche Post AG, 29
Deutsche Steinzeug Cremer & Breuer Aktiengesellschaft, 91
Deutsche Telekom AG, 48 (upd.)
Deutscher Sparkassen- und Giroverband (DSGV), 84
Deutz AG, 39
Diehl Stiftung & Co. KG 79
Dirk Rossmann GmbH, 94
Dr. August Oetker KG, 51
Drägerwerk AG, 83
Dräxlmaier Group, 90
Dresdner Bank A.G., II; 57 (upd.)
Dürkopp Adler AG, 65
Dürr AG, 44
Dyckerhoff AG, 35
E.On AG, 50 (upd.)
Eckes AG, 56
Edeka Zentrale A.G., II; 47 (upd.)
edel music AG, 44
ERGO Versicherungsgruppe AG, 44
ESCADA AG, 71
Esselte Leitz GmbH & Co. KG, 48
Etienne Aigner AG, 52
FAG—Kugelfischer Georg Schäfer AG, 62
Fairchild Dornier GmbH, 48 (upd.)
Feldmuhle Nobel A.G., III
Fielmann AG, 31
Francotyp-Postalia Holding AG, 92
Frankfurter Allgemeine Zeitung GmbH, 66
Fraport AG Frankfurt Airport Services Worldwide, 90
Fresenius AG, 56
Freudenberg & Co., 41
Fried. Krupp GmbH, IV
Friedrich Grohe AG & Co. KG, 53
GEA AG, 27
GEHE AG, 27
Gelita AG, 74
GEMA (Gesellschaft für musikalische Aufführungs- und mechanische Vervielfältigungsrechte), 70
geobra Brandstätter GmbH & Co. KG, 48
Gerhard D. Wempe KG, 88
Gerling-Konzern Versicherungs-Beteiligungs-Aktiengesellschaft, 51
Gerresheimer Glas AG, 43
Gerry Weber International AG, 63
Getrag Corporate Group, 92
GfK Aktiengesellschaft, 49
Giesecke & Devrient GmbH, 83
Gildemeister AG 79
Groz-Beckert Group, 68
Grundig AG, 27
Hansgrohe AG, 56
Hapag-Lloyd AG, 6; 97 (upd.)
HARIBO GmbH & Co. KG, 44
HDI (Haftpflichtverband der Deutschen Industrie Versicherung auf Gegenseitigkeit V.a.G.), 53
Heidelberger Druckmaschinen AG, 40
Heidelberger Zement AG, 31
Heinrich Deichmann-Schuhe GmbH & Co. KG, 88
Hella KGaA Hueck & Co., 66
Henkel KGaA, III; 34 (upd.); 95 (upd.)
Heraeus Holding GmbH, IV; 54 (upd.)
Hertie Waren- und Kaufhaus GmbH, V
Hexal AG, 69
HiPP GmbH & Co. Vertrieb KG, 88
Hochtief AG, 33; 88 (upd.)
Hoechst A.G., I; 18 (upd.)
Hoesch AG, IV
Hugo Boss AG, 48
HUK-Coburg, 58
Huls A.G., I
HVB Group, 59 (upd.)
Ihr Platz GmbH + Company KG, 77
Infineon Technologies AG, 50
J.J. Darboven GmbH & Co. KG, 96
J.M. Voith AG, 33
Jenoptik AG, 33
Julius Blüthner Pianofortefabrik GmbH 78
Jungheinrich AG, 96
Kamps AG, 44
Karlsberg Brauerei GmbH & Co KG, 41
Karstadt Quelle AG, V; 19 (upd.); 57 (upd.)
Kaufhof Warenhaus AG, V; 23 (upd.)
Kaufring AG, 35
KHD Konzern, III
Klaus Steilmann GmbH & Co. KG, 53
Klöckner-Werke AG, IV; 58 (upd.)
Knorr-Bremse AG, 84
Koenig & Bauer AG, 64
Kolbenschmidt Pierburg AG, 97
König Brauerei GmbH & Co. KG, 35 (upd.)
Körber AG, 60
Kreditanstalt für Wiederaufbau, 29
KSB AG, 62
Leica Camera AG, 35
Leica Microsystems Holdings GmbH, 35
Linde AG, I; 67 (upd.)
Loewe AG, 90
Löwenbräu AG, 80
LTU Group Holding GmbH, 37
M. DuMont Schauberg GmbH & Co. KG, 92
MAN Aktiengesellschaft, III
MAN Roland Druckmaschinen AG, 94
Mannesmann AG, III; 14 (upd.); 38 (upd.)
Margarete Steiff GmbH, 23
Märklin Holding GmbH, 70
Matth. Hohner AG, 53
Melitta Unternehmensgruppe Bentz KG, 53
Merz Group, 81
Messerschmitt-Bölkow-Blohm GmbH., I
Metallgesellschaft AG, IV; 16 (upd.)
Metro AG, 50
Miele & Cie. KG, 56
MITROPA AG, 37

Montblanc International GmbH, 82
Munich Re (Münchener Rückversicherungs-Gesellschaft Aktiengesellschaft in München), III; 46 (upd.)
Nixdorf Computer AG, III
Norddeutsche Affinerie AG, 62
Optische Werke G. Rodenstock, 44
Osram GmbH, 86
Otto Versand GmbH & Co., V; 15 (upd.); 34 (upd.)
Paulaner Brauerei GmbH & Co. KG, 35
Peek & Cloppenburg KG, 46
Philipp Holzmann AG, 17
Phoenix AG, 68
Porsche AG, 13; 31 (upd.)
Preussag AG, 17; 42 (upd.)
PreussenElektra Aktiengesellschaft, V
ProSiebenSat.1 Media AG, 54
Puma AG Rudolf Dassler Sport, 35
PWA Group, IV
Qiagen N.V., 39
Quelle Group, V
Radeberger Gruppe AG, 75
RAG AG, 35; 60 (upd.)
ratiopharm Group, 84
Ravensburger AG, 64
RENK AG, 37
Rheinmetall AG, 9; 97 (upd.)
Robert Bosch GmbH, I; 16 (upd.); 43 (upd.)
Röchling Gruppe, 94
Rohde & Schwarz GmbH & Co. KG, 39
Roland Berger & Partner GmbH, 37
The Rowohlt Verlag GmbH, 96
Ruhrgas AG, V; 38 (upd.)
Ruhrkohle AG, IV
RWE AG, V; 50 (upd.)
Saarberg-Konzern, IV
Salzgitter AG, IV
SAP AG, 16; 43 (upd.)
Schenker-Rhenus AG, 6
Schering AG, I; 50 (upd.)
Sennheiser Electronic GmbH & Co. KG, 66
Siemens AG, II; 14 (upd.); 57 (upd.)
Siltronic AG, 90
Sixt AG, 39
SPAR Handels AG, 35
SPIEGEL-Verlag Rudolf Augstein GmbH & Co. KG, 44
Stinnes AG, 8; 23 (upd.); 59 (upd.)
Stollwerck AG, 53
Südzucker AG, 27
Symrise GmbH and Company KG, 89
T-Online International AG, 61
TA Triumph-Adler AG, 48
Tarkett Sommer AG, 25
TaurusHolding GmbH & Co. KG, 46
Tchibo GmbH, 82
Tengelmann Group, 27
ThyssenKrupp AG, IV; 28 (upd.); 87 (upd.)
Touristik Union International GmbH. and Company K.G., II
TRUMPF GmbH + Co. KG, 86
TUI Group GmbH, 44
UFA TV & Film Produktion GmbH, 80
Vaillant GmbH, 44
Varta AG, 23
Veba A.G., I; 15 (upd.)
Vereinigte Elektrizitätswerke Westfalen AG, V
Verlagsgruppe Georg von Holtzbrinck GmbH, 35
VEW AG, 39
VIAG Aktiengesellschaft, IV
Victoria Group, III; 44 (upd.)
Viessmann Werke GmbH & Co., 37
Wilhelm Karmann GmbH, 94
Villeroy & Boch AG, 37
Volkswagen Aktiengesellschaft, I; 11 (upd.); 32 (upd.)
Vorwerk & Co., 27
Vossloh AG, 53
Wacker-Chemie GmbH, 35
Wacker Construction Equipment AG, 95
WAZ Media Group, 82
Wella AG, III; 48 (upd.)
Weru Aktiengesellschaft, 18
Westdeutsche Landesbank Girozentrale, II; 46 (upd.)
Wincor Nixdorf Holding GmbH, 69 (upd.)
Württembergische Metallwarenfabrik AG (WMF), 60
Zapf Creation AG, 95
ZF Friedrichshafen AG, 48

Ghana

Ashanti Goldfields Company Limited, 43

Greece

Aegean Marine Petroleum Network Inc., 89
Aegek S.A., 64
Attica Enterprises S.A., 64
Danaos Corporation, 91
Diana Shipping Inc., 95
DryShips Inc., 95
Greek Organization of Football Prognostics S.A. (OPAP), 97
Hellenic Petroleum SA, 64
Jumbo S.A., 96
National Bank of Greece, 41
Royal Olympic Cruise Lines Inc., 52
Stelmar Shipping Ltd., 52
Titan Cement Company S.A., 64
Tsakos Energy Navigation Ltd., 91
Vivartia S.A., 82

Guatemala

Corporación Multi-Inversiones, 94

Hong Kong

A.S. Watson & Company Ltd., 84
Bank of East Asia Ltd., 63
Cable & Wireless HKT, 30 (upd.)
Cathay Pacific Airways Limited, 6; 34 (upd.)
CDC Corporation, 71
Chaoda Modern Agriculture (Holdings) Ltd., 87
Cheung Kong (Holdings) Ltd., IV; 20 (upd.); 94 (upd.)
China Merchants International Holdings Co., Ltd., 52
CITIC Pacific Ltd., 18
Dairy Farm International Holdings Ltd., 97
First Pacific Company Limited, 18
The Garden Company Ltd., 82
GOME Electrical Appliances Holding Ltd., 87
Guangzhou R&F Properties Co., Ltd., 95
Hang Seng Bank Ltd., 60
Henderson Land Development Company Ltd., 70
Hong Kong and China Gas Company Ltd., 73
Hong Kong Dragon Airlines Ltd., 66
Hong Kong Telecommunications Ltd., 6
The Hongkong and Shanghai Banking Corporation Limited, II
Hongkong Electric Holdings Ltd., 6; 23 (upd.)
Hongkong Land Holdings Limited, IV; 47 (upd.)
Hopson Development Holdings Ltd., 87
Hutchison Whampoa Limited, 18; 49 (upd.)
Kerry Properties Limited, 22
Meyer International Holdings, Ltd., 87
Nam Tai Electronics, Inc., 61
New World Development Company Limited, IV; 38 (upd.)
Next Media Ltd., 61
Pacific Basin Shipping Ltd., 86
Playmates Toys, 23
Shangri-La Asia Ltd., 71
The Singer Company N.V., 30 (upd.)
Swire Pacific Limited, I; 16 (upd.); 57 (upd.)
Techtronic Industries Company Ltd., 73
Tommy Hilfiger Corporation, 20; 53 (upd.)
Vitasoy International Holdings Ltd., 94
VTech Holdings Ltd., 77

Hungary

Magyar Telekom Rt. 78
Malév Plc, 24
MOL Rt, 70
Orszagos Takarekpenztar es Kereskedelmi Bank Rt. (OTP Bank) 78

Iceland

Alfesca hf, 82
Bakkavör Group hf., 91
Baugur Group hf, 81
Icelandair, 52
Icelandic Group hf, 81
Landsbanki Islands hf, 81

India

Adani Enterprises Ltd., 97
Aditya Birla Group 79
Air Sahara Limited, 65
Air-India Limited, 6; 27 (upd.)
Bajaj Auto Limited, 39
Bharti Tele-Ventures Limited, 75
Coal India Limited, IV; 44 (upd.)
Dr. Reddy's Laboratories Ltd., 59

Essar Group Ltd. 79
Hindustan Lever Limited 79
Indian Airlines Ltd., 46
Indian Oil Corporation Ltd., IV; 48 (upd.)
Infosys Technologies Ltd., 38
Jet Airways (India) Private Limited, 65
Minerals and Metals Trading Corporation of India Ltd., IV
MTR Foods Ltd., 55
Neyveli Lignite Corporation Ltd., 65
Oil and Natural Gas Corporation Ltd., IV; 90 (upd.)
Ranbaxy Laboratories Ltd., 70
Raymond Ltd., 77
Reliance Industries Ltd., 81
Rolta India Ltd., 90
Satyam Computer Services Ltd., 85
State Bank of India, 63
Steel Authority of India Ltd., IV; 66 (upd.)
Sun Pharmaceutical Industries Ltd., 57
Tata Iron & Steel Co. Ltd., IV; 44 (upd.)
Tata Tea Ltd., 76
Wipro Limited, 43

Indonesia

Djarum PT, 62
Garuda Indonesia, 6; 58 (upd.)
PERTAMINA, IV
Pertamina, 56 (upd.)
PT Astra International Tbk, 56
PT Bank Buana Indonesia Tbk, 60
PT Indosat Tbk, 93

Iran

IranAir, 81
National Iranian Oil Company, IV; 61 (upd.)

Ireland

Aer Lingus Group plc, 34; 89 (upd.)
Allied Irish Banks, plc, 16; 43 (upd.); 94 (upd.)
Baltimore Technologies Plc, 42
Bank of Ireland, 50
CRH plc, 64
DEPFA BANK PLC, 69
Dunnes Stores Ltd., 58
eircom plc, 31 (upd.)
Elan Corporation PLC, 63
Fyffes Plc, 38
Glanbia plc, 59
Glen Dimplex 78
Harland and Wolff Holdings plc, 19
IAWS Group plc, 49
Independent News & Media PLC, 61
IONA Technologies plc, 43
Irish Distillers Group, 96
Irish Life & Permanent Plc, 59
Jefferson Smurfit Group plc, IV; 19 (upd.); 49 (upd.)
Jurys Doyle Hotel Group plc, 64
Kerry Group plc, 27; 87 (upd.)
Musgrave Group Plc, 57
Ryanair Holdings plc, 35
Shannon Aerospace Ltd., 36
SkillSoft Public Limited Company, 81
Telecom Eireann, 7
Thomas Crosbie Holdings Limited, 81
Waterford Wedgwood plc, 34 (upd.)

Israel

Amdocs Ltd., 47
Bank Hapoalim B.M., II; 54 (upd.)
Bank Leumi le-Israel B.M., 60
Blue Square Israel Ltd., 41
BVR Systems (1998) Ltd., 93
Castro Model Ltd., 86
ECI Telecom Ltd., 18
El Al Israel Airlines Ltd., 23
Elscint Ltd., 20
Given Imaging Ltd., 83
IDB Holding Corporation Ltd., 97
Israel Aircraft Industries Ltd., 69
Israel Chemicals Ltd., 55
Koor Industries Ltd., II; 25 (upd.); 68 (upd.)
Lipman Electronic Engineering Ltd., 81
Makhteshim-Agan Industries Ltd., 85
NICE Systems Ltd., 83
Orbotech Ltd., 75
Scitex Corporation Ltd., 24
Strauss-Elite Group, 68
Syneron Medical Ltd., 91
Taro Pharmaceutical Industries Ltd., 65
Teva Pharmaceutical Industries Ltd., 22; 54 (upd.)

Italy

AgustaWestland N.V., 75
Alfa Romeo, 13; 36 (upd.)
Alitalia—Linee Aeree Italiana, S.p.A., 6; 29 (upd.); 97 (upd.)
Alleanza Assicurazioni S.p.A., 65
Aprilia SpA, 17
Arnoldo Mondadori Editore S.p.A., IV; 19 (upd.); 54 (upd.)
Artsana SpA, 92
Assicurazioni Generali SpA, III; 15 (upd.)
Autogrill SpA, 49
Automobili Lamborghini Holding S.p.A., 13; 34 (upd.); 91 (upd.)
Banca Commerciale Italiana SpA, II
Banca Fideuram SpA, 63
Banca Intesa SpA, 65
Banca Monte dei Paschi di Siena SpA, 65
Banca Nazionale del Lavoro SpA, 72
Barilla G. e R. Fratelli S.p.A., 17; 50 (upd.)
Benetton Group S.p.A., 10; 67 (upd.)
Brioni Roman Style S.p.A., 67
Bulgari S.p.A., 20
Cantine Giorgio Lungarotti S.R.L., 67
Capitalia S.p.A., 65
Cinemeccanica SpA 78
Compagnia Italiana dei Jolly Hotels S.p.A., 71
Credito Italiano, II
Cremonini S.p.A., 57
Davide Campari-Milano S.p.A., 57
De'Longhi S.p.A., 66
Diadora SpA, 86
Diesel SpA, 40
Dolce & Gabbana SpA, 62
Ducati Motor Holding SpA, 30; 86 (upd.)
ENI S.p.A., 69 (upd.)
Ente Nazionale Idrocarburi, IV
Ente Nazionale per L'Energia Elettrica, V
Ermenegildo Zegna SpA, 63
Fabbrica D' Armi Pietro Beretta S.p.A., 39
FASTWEB S.p.A., 83
Ferrari S.p.A., 13; 36 (upd.)
Ferrero SpA, 54
Ferretti Group SpA, 90
Fiat SpA, I; 11 (upd.); 50 (upd.)
Fila Holding S.p.A., 20; 52 (upd.)
Finarte Casa d'Aste S.p.A., 93
Finmeccanica S.p.A., 84
Gianni Versace SpA, 22
Giorgio Armani S.p.A., 45
Gruppo Coin S.p.A., 41
Gruppo Riva Fire SpA, 88
Guccio Gucci, S.p.A., 15
illycaffè SpA, 50
Industrie Natuzzi S.p.A., 18
Industrie Zignago Santa Margherita S.p.A., 67
Ing. C. Olivetti & C., S.p.a., III
Istituto per la Ricostruzione Industriale S.p.A., I; 11
Juventus F.C. S.p.A, 53
Luxottica SpA, 17; 52 (upd.)
Magneti Marelli Holding SpA, 90
Marchesi Antinori SRL, 42
Marcolin S.p.A., 61
Mariella Burani Fashion Group, 92
Martini & Rossi SpA, 63
Marzotto S.p.A., 20; 67 (upd.)
Mediaset SpA, 50
Mediolanum S.p.A., 65
Milan AC, S.p.A. 79
Miroglio SpA, 86
Montedison SpA, I; 24 (upd.)
Officine Alfieri Maserati S.p.A., 13
Olivetti S.p.A., 34 (upd.)
Pagnossin S.p.A., 73
Parmalat Finanziaria SpA, 50
Peg Perego SpA, 88
Perfetti Van Melle S.p.A., 72
Piaggio & C. S.p.A., 20
Pirelli & C. S.p.A., 75 (upd.)
Pirelli S.p.A., V; 15 (upd.)
RCS MediaGroup S.p.A., 96
Reno de Medici S.p.A., 41
Rinascente S.p.A., 71
Riunione Adriatica di Sicurtè SpA, III
Safilo SpA, 54
Salvatore Ferragamo Italia S.p.A., 62
Sanpaolo IMI S.p.A., 50
Seat Pagine Gialle S.p.A., 47
Sirti S.p.A., 76
Società Finanziaria Telefonica per Azioni, V
Società Sportiva Lazio SpA, 44
Stefanel SpA, 63
Targetti Sankey SpA, 86
Telecom Italia Mobile S.p.A., 63
Telecom Italia S.p.A., 43
Tiscali SpA, 48

Jamaica

Air Jamaica Limited, 54
Desnoes and Geddes Limited 79
GraceKennedy Ltd., 92

Japan

AEON Co., Ltd., 68 (upd.)
Aisin Seiki Co., Ltd., III; 48 (upd.)
Aiwa Co., Ltd., 30
Ajinomoto Co., Inc., II; 28 (upd.)
All Nippon Airways Co., Ltd., 6; 38 (upd.); 91 (upd.)
Alpine Electronics, Inc., 13
Alps Electric Co., Ltd., II; 44 (upd.)
Anritsu Corporation, 68
Asahi Breweries, Ltd., I; 20 (upd.); 52 (upd.)
Asahi Denka Kogyo KK, 64
Asahi Glass Company, Ltd., III; 48 (upd.)
Asahi National Broadcasting Company, Ltd., 9
Asatsu-DK Inc., 82
ASICS Corporation, 57
Astellas Pharma Inc., 97 (upd.)
Autobacs Seven Company Ltd., 76
Bandai Co., Ltd., 55
Bank of Tokyo-Mitsubishi Ltd., II; 15 (upd.)
Benesse Corporation, 76
Bourbon Corporation, 82
Bridgestone Corporation, V; 21 (upd.); 59 (upd.)
Brother Industries, Ltd., 14
C. Itoh & Company Ltd., I
Canon Inc., III; 18 (upd.); 79 (upd.)
Capcom Company Ltd., 83
CASIO Computer Co., Ltd., III; 16 (upd.); 40 (upd.)
Central Japan Railway Company, 43
Chubu Electric Power Company, Inc., V; 46 (upd.)
Chugai Pharmaceutical Co., Ltd., 50
Chugoku Electric Power Company Inc., V; 53 (upd.)
Citizen Watch Co., Ltd., III; 21 (upd.); 81 (upd.)
Clarion Company Ltd., 64
Cosmo Oil Co., Ltd., IV; 53 (upd.)
Dai Nippon Printing Co., Ltd., IV; 57 (upd.)
The Dai-Ichi Kangyo Bank Ltd., II
Daido Steel Co., Ltd., IV
The Daiei, Inc., V; 17 (upd.); 41 (upd.)
Daihatsu Motor Company, Ltd., 7; 21 (upd.)
Daiichikosho Company Ltd., 86
Daikin Industries, Ltd., III
Daiko Advertising Inc. 79
The Daimaru, Inc., V; 42 (upd.)
Daio Paper Corporation, IV, 84 (upd.)
Daishowa Paper Manufacturing Co., Ltd., IV; 57 (upd.)
The Daiwa Bank, Ltd., II; 39 (upd.)
Daiwa Securities Group Inc., II; 55 (upd.)
DDI Corporation, 7
DENSO Corporation, 46 (upd.)
Dentsu Inc., I; 16 (upd.); 40 (upd.)
East Japan Railway Company, V; 66 (upd.)
Ebara Corporation, 83
Elpida Memory, Inc., 83
Ezaki Glico Company Ltd., 72
Fanuc Ltd., III; 17 (upd.); 75 (upd.)
The Fuji Bank, Ltd., II
Fuji Electric Co., Ltd., II; 48 (upd.)
Fuji Photo Film Co., Ltd., III; 18 (upd.); 79 (upd.)
Fuji Television Network Inc., 91
Fujisawa Pharmaceutical Company, Ltd., I; 58 (upd.)
Fujitsu Limited, III; 16 (upd.); 42 (upd.)
Funai Electric Company Ltd., 62
The Furukawa Electric Co., Ltd., III
General Sekiyu K.K., IV
Hakuhodo, Inc., 6; 42 (upd.)
Hankyu Department Stores, Inc., V; 23 (upd.); 62 (upd.)
Hagoromo Foods Corporation, 84
Hino Motors, Ltd., 7; 21 (upd.)
Hitachi, Ltd., I; 12 (upd.); 40 (upd.)
Hitachi Metals, Ltd., IV
Hitachi Zosen Corporation, III; 53 (upd.)
Hokkaido Electric Power Company Inc. (HEPCO), V; 58 (upd.)
Hokuriku Electric Power Company, V
Honda Motor Company Ltd., I; 10 (upd.); 29 (upd.); 96 (upd.)
Honshu Paper Co., Ltd., IV
Hoshino Gakki Co. Ltd., 55
Idemitsu Kosan Co., Ltd., IV; 49 (upd.)
The Industrial Bank of Japan, Ltd., II
INPEX Holdings Inc., 97
Isetan Company Limited, V; 36 (upd.)
Ishikawajima-Harima Heavy Industries Company, Ltd., III; 86 (upd.)
Isuzu Motors, Ltd., 9; 23 (upd.); 57 (upd.)
Ito-Yokado Co., Ltd., V; 42 (upd.)
ITOCHU Corporation, 32 (upd.)
Itoham Foods Inc., II; 61 (upd.)
Japan Airlines Company, Ltd., I; 32 (upd.)
JAFCO Co. Ltd. 79
Japan Broadcasting Corporation, 7
Japan Leasing Corporation, 8
Japan Pulp and Paper Company Limited, IV
Japan Tobacco Inc., V; 46 (upd.)
JFE Shoji Holdings Inc., 88
JSP Corporation, 74
Jujo Paper Co., Ltd., IV
JUSCO Co., Ltd., V
Kajima Corporation, I; 51 (upd.)
Kanebo, Ltd., 53
Kanematsu Corporation, IV; 24 (upd.)
The Kansai Electric Power Company, Inc., V; 62 (upd.)
Kansai Paint Company Ltd., 80
Kao Corporation, III; 20 (upd.); 79 (upd.)
Katokichi Company Ltd., 82
Kawai Musical Instruments Mfg Co. Ltd. 78
Kawasaki Heavy Industries, Ltd., III; 63 (upd.)
Kawasaki Kisen Kaisha, Ltd., V; 56 (upd.)
Kawasaki Steel Corporation, IV
Keio Corporation, V; 96 (upd.)
Kenwood Corporation, 31
Kewpie Kabushiki Kaisha, 57
Kikkoman Corporation, 14; 47 (upd.)
Kinki Nippon Railway Company Ltd., V
Kirin Brewery Company, Limited, I; 21 (upd.); 63 (upd.)
Kobe Steel, Ltd., IV; 19 (upd.)
Kodansha Ltd., IV; 38 (upd.)
Komatsu Ltd., III; 16 (upd.); 52 (upd.)
Konami Corporation, 96
Konica Corporation, III; 30 (upd.)
Kotobukiya Co., Ltd., V; 56 (upd.)
Kubota Corporation, III; 26 (upd.)
Kumagai Gumi Company, Ltd., I
Kumon Institute of Education Co., Ltd., 72
Kyocera Corporation, II; 21 (upd.); 79 (upd.)
Kyokuyo Company Ltd., 75
Kyowa Hakko Kogyo Co., Ltd., III; 48 (upd.)
Kyushu Electric Power Company Inc., V
Lion Corporation, III; 51 (upd.)
Long-Term Credit Bank of Japan, Ltd., II
Mabuchi Motor Co. Ltd., 68
Makita Corporation, 22; 59 (upd.)
Mandom Corporation, 82
Marubeni Corporation, I; 24 (upd.)
Maruha Group Inc., 75 (upd.)
Marui Company Ltd., V; 62 (upd.)
Maruzen Co., Limited, 18
Matsushita Electric Industrial Co., Ltd., II; 64 (upd.)
Matsushita Electric Works, Ltd., III; 7 (upd.)
Matsuzakaya Company Ltd., V; 64 (upd.)
Mazda Motor Corporation, 9; 23 (upd.); 63 (upd.)
Meidensha Corporation, 92
Meiji Dairies Corporation, II; 82 (upd.)
The Meiji Mutual Life Insurance Company, III
Meiji Seika Kaisha Ltd., II; 64 (upd.)
Mercian Corporation, 77
Millea Holdings Inc., 64 (upd.)
Minebea Co., Ltd., 90
Minolta Co., Ltd., III; 18 (upd.); 43 (upd.)
The Mitsubishi Bank, Ltd., II
Mitsubishi Chemical Corporation, I; 56 (upd.)
Mitsubishi Corporation, I; 12 (upd.)
Mitsubishi Electric Corporation, II; 44 (upd.)
Mitsubishi Estate Company, Limited, IV; 61 (upd.)
Mitsubishi Heavy Industries, Ltd., III; 7 (upd.); 40 (upd.)
Mitsubishi Materials Corporation, III
Mitsubishi Motors Corporation, 9; 23 (upd.); 57 (upd.)
Mitsubishi Oil Co., Ltd., IV
Mitsubishi Rayon Co., Ltd., V
The Mitsubishi Trust & Banking Corporation, II

Mitsui & Co., Ltd., 28 (upd.)
The Mitsui Bank, Ltd., II
Mitsui Bussan K.K., I
Mitsui Marine and Fire Insurance Company, Limited, III
Mitsui Mining & Smelting Co., Ltd., IV
Mitsui Mining Company, Limited, IV
Mitsui Mutual Life Insurance Company, III; 39 (upd.)
Mitsui O.S.K. Lines, Ltd., V; 96 (upd.)
Mitsui Petrochemical Industries, Ltd., 9
Mitsui Real Estate Development Co., Ltd., IV
The Mitsui Trust & Banking Company, Ltd., II
Mitsukoshi Ltd., V; 56 (upd.)
Mizuho Financial Group Inc., 58 (upd.)
Mizuno Corporation, 25
Morinaga & Co. Ltd., 61
Nagasakiya Co., Ltd., V; 69 (upd.)
Nagase & Co., Ltd., 8; 61 (upd.)
NEC Corporation, II; 21 (upd.); 57 (upd.)
NGK Insulators Ltd., 67
NHK Spring Co., Ltd., III
Nichii Co., Ltd., V
Nichimen Corporation, IV; 24 (upd.)
Nichirei Corporation, 70
Nichiro Corporation, 86
Nidec Corporation, 59
Nihon Keizai Shimbun, Inc., IV
The Nikko Securities Company Limited, II; 9 (upd.)
Nikon Corporation, III; 48 (upd.)
Nintendo Co., Ltd., III; 7 (upd.); 28 (upd.); 67 (upd.)
Nippon Credit Bank, II
Nippon Electric Glass Co. Ltd., 95
Nippon Express Company, Ltd., V; 64 (upd.)
Nippon Life Insurance Company, III; 60 (upd.)
Nippon Light Metal Company, Ltd., IV
Nippon Meat Packers Inc., II, 78 (upd.)
Nippon Oil Corporation, IV; 63 (upd.)
Nippon Seiko K.K., III
Nippon Sheet Glass Company, Limited, III
Nippon Shinpan Co., Ltd., II; 61 (upd.)
Nippon Soda Co., Ltd., 85
Nippon Steel Corporation, IV; 17 (upd.); 96 (upd.)
Nippon Suisan Kaisha, Ltd., II; 92 (upd.)
Nippon Telegraph and Telephone Corporation, V; 51 (upd.)
Nippon Yusen Kabushiki Kaisha (NYK), V; 72 (upd.)
Nippondenso Co., Ltd., III
Nissan Motor Company Ltd., I; 11 (upd.); 34 (upd.); 92 (upd.)
Nisshin Seifun Group Inc., II; 66 (upd.)
Nisshin Steel Co., Ltd., IV
Nissho Iwai K.K., I
Nissin Food Products Company Ltd., 75
NKK Corporation, IV; 28 (upd.)
NOF Corporation, 72
Nomura Securities Company, Limited, II; 9 (upd.)
Norinchukin Bank, II
NTN Corporation, III; 47 (upd.)
Obayashi Corporation 78
Odakyu Electric Railway Co., Ltd., V; 68 (upd.)
Ohbayashi Corporation, I
Oji Paper Co., Ltd., IV; 57 (upd.)
Oki Electric Industry Company, Limited, II
Okuma Holdings Inc., 74
Okura & Co., Ltd., IV
Omron Corporation, II; 28 (upd.)
Onoda Cement Co., Ltd., III
ORIX Corporation, II; 44 (upd.)
Osaka Gas Company, Ltd., V; 60 (upd.)
Otari Inc., 89
Paloma Industries Ltd., 71
Pearl Corporation 78
Pentax Corporation 78
Pioneer Electronic Corporation, III; 28 (upd.)
Rengo Co., Ltd., IV
Ricoh Company, Ltd., III; 36 (upd.)
Roland Corporation, 38
Ryoshoku Ltd., 72
Sankyo Company, Ltd., I; 56 (upd.)
Sanrio Company, Ltd., 38
The Sanwa Bank, Ltd., II; 15 (upd.)
SANYO Electric Co., Ltd., II; 36 (upd.); 95 (upd.)
Sanyo-Kokusaku Pulp Co., Ltd., IV
Sapporo Holdings Limited, I; 13 (upd.); 36 (upd.); 97 (upd.)
SEGA Corporation, 73
Seibu Department Stores, Ltd., V; 42 (upd.)
Seibu Railway Company Ltd., V; 74 (upd.)
Seiko Corporation, III; 17 (upd.); 72 (upd.)
Seino Transportation Company, Ltd., 6
The Seiyu, Ltd., V; 36 (upd.)
Sekisui Chemical Co., Ltd., III; 72 (upd.)
Sharp Corporation, II; 12 (upd.); 40 (upd.)
Shikoku Electric Power Company, Inc., V; 60 (upd.)
Shimano Inc., 64
Shionogi & Co., Ltd., III; 17 (upd.)
Shiseido Company, Limited, III; 22 (upd.), 81 (upd.)
Shochiku Company Ltd., 74
Showa Shell Sekiyu K.K., IV; 59 (upd.)
Snow Brand Milk Products Company, Ltd., II; 48 (upd.)
Softbank Corp., 13; 38 (upd.)
Sojitz Corporation, 96 (upd.)
Sony Corporation, II; 12 (upd.); 40 (upd.)
The Sumitomo Bank, Limited, II; 26 (upd.)
Sumitomo Chemical Company Ltd., I
Sumitomo Corporation, I; 11 (upd.)
Sumitomo Electric Industries, Ltd., II
Sumitomo Heavy Industries, Ltd., III; 42 (upd.)
Sumitomo Life Insurance Company, III; 60 (upd.)
The Sumitomo Marine and Fire Insurance Company, Limited, III
Sumitomo Metal Industries Ltd., IV; 82 (upd.)
Sumitomo Metal Mining Co., Ltd., IV
Sumitomo Mitsui Banking Corporation, 51 (upd.)
Sumitomo Realty & Development Co., Ltd., IV
Sumitomo Rubber Industries, Ltd., V
The Sumitomo Trust & Banking Company, Ltd., II; 53 (upd.)
Suntory Ltd., 65
Suzuki Motor Corporation, 9; 23 (upd.); 59 (upd.)
Taiheiyo Cement Corporation, 60 (upd.)
Taiyo Fishery Company, Limited, II
The Taiyo Kobe Bank, Ltd., II
Takara Holdings Inc., 62
Takashimaya Company, Limited, V; 47 (upd.)
Takeda Chemical Industries, Ltd., I; 46 (upd.)
Tamron Company Ltd., 82
TDK Corporation, II; 17 (upd.); 49 (upd.)
TEAC Corporation 78
Teijin Limited, V; 61 (upd.)
Terumo Corporation, 48
Tobu Railway Co Ltd, 6
Tohan Corporation, 84
Toho Co., Ltd., 28
Tohoku Electric Power Company, Inc., V
The Tokai Bank, Limited, II; 15 (upd.)
The Tokio Marine and Fire Insurance Co., Ltd., III
The Tokyo Electric Power Company, 74 (upd.)
The Tokyo Electric Power Company, Incorporated, V
Tokyo Gas Co., Ltd., V; 55 (upd.)
Tokyu Corporation, V; 47 (upd.)
Tokyu Department Store Co., Ltd., V; 32 (upd.)
Tokyu Land Corporation, IV
Tomen Corporation, IV; 24 (upd.)
Tomy Company Ltd., 65
TonenGeneral Sekiyu K.K., IV; 16 (upd.); 54 (upd.)
Topcon Corporation, 84
Toppan Printing Co., Ltd., IV; 58 (upd.)
Toray Industries, Inc., V; 51 (upd.)
Toshiba Corporation, I; 12 (upd.); 40 (upd.)
Tosoh Corporation, 70
TOTO LTD., III; 28 (upd.)
Toyo Sash Co., Ltd., III
Toyo Seikan Kaisha, Ltd., I
Toyoda Automatic Loom Works, Ltd., III
Toyota Motor Corporation, I; 11 (upd.); 38 (upd.)
Trend Micro Inc., 97
Ube Industries, Ltd., III; 38 (upd.)
ULVAC, Inc., 80
Unicharm Corporation, 84
Unitika Ltd., V; 53 (upd.)
Uny Co., Ltd., V; 49 (upd.)
Ushio Inc., 91

Victor Company of Japan, Limited, II; 26 (upd.); 83 (upd.)
Wacoal Corp., 25
Yamada Denki Co., Ltd., 85
Yamaha Corporation, III; 16 (upd.); 40 (upd.)
Yamaichi Securities Company, Limited, II
Yamato Transport Co. Ltd., V; 49 (upd.)
Yamazaki Baking Co., Ltd., 58
The Yasuda Fire and Marine Insurance Company, Limited, III
The Yasuda Mutual Life Insurance Company, III; 39 (upd.)
The Yasuda Trust and Banking Company, Ltd., II; 17 (upd.)
The Yokohama Rubber Company, Limited, V; 19 (upd.); 91 (upd.)
Yoshinoya D & C Company Ltd., 88

Jordan

Arab Potash Company, 85

Kenya

Kenya Airways Limited, 89

Kuwait

Kuwait Airways Corporation, 68
Kuwait Flour Mills & Bakeries Company, 84
Kuwait Petroleum Corporation, IV; 55 (upd.)

Latvia

A/S Air Baltic Corporation, 71

Lebanon

Middle East Airlines - Air Liban S.A.L. 79

Libya

National Oil Corporation, IV; 66 (upd.)

Liechtenstein

Hilti AG, 53

Luxembourg

ARBED S.A., IV; 22 (upd.)
Cactus S.A., 90
Cargolux Airlines International S.A., 49
Elite World S.A., 94
Espèrito Santo Financial Group S.A. 79 (upd.)
Gemplus International S.A., 64
Metro International S.A., 93
RTL Group SA, 44
Société Luxembourgeoise de Navigation Aérienne S.A., 64
Tenaris SA, 63

Malaysia

AirAsia Berhad, 93
Berjaya Group Bhd., 67
Gano Excel Enterprise Sdn. Bhd., 89
Genting Bhd., 65
Malayan Banking Berhad, 72
Malaysian Airlines System Berhad, 6; 29 (upd.); 97 (upd.)
Perusahaan Otomobil Nasional Bhd., 62
Petroliam Nasional Bhd (Petronas), IV; 56 (upd.)
PPB Group Berhad, 57
Sime Darby Berhad, 14; 36 (upd.)
Telekom Malaysia Bhd, 76
Yeo Hiap Seng Malaysia Bhd., 75

Mauritius

Air Mauritius Ltd., 63

Mexico

Alfa, S.A. de C.V., 19
Altos Hornos de México, S.A. de C.V., 42
América Móvil, S.A. de C.V., 80
Apasco S.A. de C.V., 51
Bolsa Mexicana de Valores, S.A. de C.V., 80
Bufete Industrial, S.A. de C.V., 34
Casa Cuervo, S.A. de C.V., 31
Celanese Mexicana, S.A. de C.V., 54
CEMEX S.A. de C.V., 20; 59 (upd.)
Cifra, S.A. de C.V., 12
Cinemas de la República, S.A. de C.V., 83
Compañia Industrial de Parras, S.A. de C.V. (CIPSA), 84
Consorcio ARA, S.A. de C.V. 79
Consorcio Aviacsa, S.A. de C.V., 85
Consorcio G Grupo Dina, S.A. de C.V., 36
Controladora Comercial Mexicana, S.A. de C.V., 36
Controladora Mabe, S.A. de C.V., 82
Coppel, S.A. de C.V., 82
Corporación Geo, S.A. de C.V., 81
Corporación Interamericana de Entretenimiento, S.A. de C.V., 83
Corporación Internacional de Aviación, S.A. de C.V. (Cintra), 20
Desarrolladora Homex, S.A. de C.V., 87
Desc, S.A. de C.V., 23
Editorial Television, S.A. de C.V., 57
Empresas ICA Sociedad Controladora, S.A. de C.V., 41
El Puerto de Liverpool, S.A.B. de C.V., 97
Ford Motor Company, S.A. de C.V., 20
Gruma, S.A. de C.V., 31
Grupo Aeroportuario del Centro Norte, S.A.B. de C.V., 97
Grupo Aeroportuario del Pacífico, S.A. de C.V., 85
Grupo Aeropuerto del Sureste, S.A. de C.V., 48
Grupo Ángeles Servicios de Salud, S.A. de C.V., 84
Grupo Carso, S.A. de C.V., 21
Grupo Casa Saba, S.A. de C.V., 39
Grupo Comercial Chedraui S.A. de C.V., 86
Grupo Corvi S.A. de C.V., 86
Grupo Cydsa, S.A. de C.V., 39
Grupo Elektra, S.A. de C.V., 39
Grupo Financiero Banamex S.A., 54
Grupo Financiero Banorte, S.A. de C.V., 51
Grupo Financiero BBVA Bancomer S.A., 54
Grupo Financiero Serfin, S.A., 19
Grupo Gigante, S.A. de C.V., 34
Grupo Herdez, S.A. de C.V., 35
Grupo IMSA, S.A. de C.V., 44
Grupo Industrial Bimbo, 19
Grupo Industrial Durango, S.A. de C.V., 37
Grupo Industrial Herradura, S.A. de C.V., 83
Grupo Industrial Lala, S.A. de C.V., 82
Grupo Industrial Saltillo, S.A. de C.V., 54
Grupo Mexico, S.A. de C.V., 40
Grupo Modelo, S.A. de C.V., 29
Grupo Omnilife S.A. de C.V., 88
Grupo Posadas, S.A. de C.V., 57
Grupo Televisa, S.A., 18; 54 (upd.)
Grupo TMM, S.A. de C.V., 50
Grupo Transportación Ferroviaria Mexicana, S.A. de C.V., 47
Grupo Viz, S.A. de C.V., 84
Hylsamex, S.A. de C.V., 39
Industrias Bachoco, S.A. de C.V., 39
Industrias Penoles, S.A. de C.V., 22
Internacional de Ceramica, S.A. de C.V., 53
Jugos del Valle, S.A. de C.V., 85
Kimberly-Clark de México, S.A. de C.V., 54
Nadro S.A. de C.V., 86
Organización Soriana, S.A. de C.V., 35
Petróleos Mexicanos, IV; 19 (upd.)
Proeza S.A. de C.V., 82
Pulsar Internacional S.A., 21
Real Turismo, S.A. de C.V., 50
Sanborn Hermanos, S.A., 20
SANLUIS Corporación, S.A.B. de C.V., 95
Sears Roebuck de México, S.A. de C.V., 20
Telefonos de Mexico S.A. de C.V., 14; 63 (upd.)
Tubos de Acero de Mexico, S.A. (TAMSA), 41
TV Azteca, S.A. de C.V., 39
Urbi Desarrollos Urbanos, S.A. de C.V., 81
Valores Industriales S.A., 19
Vitro Corporativo S.A. de C.V., 34
Wal-Mart de Mexico, S.A. de C.V., 35 (upd.)

Nepal

Royal Nepal Airline Corporation, 41

Netherlands

ABN AMRO Holding, N.V., 50
AEGON N.V., III; 50 (upd.)
Akzo Nobel N.V., 13; 41 (upd.)
Algemene Bank Nederland N.V., II
Amsterdam-Rotterdam Bank N.V., II
Arcadis NV, 26
ASML Holding N.V., 50
Avantium Technologies BV 79
Baan Company, 25
Blokker Holding B.V., 84
Bols Distilleries NV, 74
Bolton Group B.V., 86
Buhrmann NV, 41

The Campina Group, The 78
Chicago Bridge & Iron Company N.V., 82 (upd.)
CNH Global N.V., 38 (upd.)
CSM N.V., 65
Deli Universal NV, 66
DSM N.V., I; 56 (upd.)
Elsevier N.V., IV
Endemol Entertainment Holding NV, 46
Equant N.V., 52
Euronext N.V., 89 (upd.)
European Aeronautic Defence and Space Company EADS N.V., 52 (upd.)
Friesland Coberco Dairy Foods Holding N.V., 59
Getronics NV, 39
Granaria Holdings B.V., 66
Grand Hotel Krasnapolsky N.V., 23
Greenpeace International, 74
Gucci Group N.V., 50
Hagemeyer N.V., 39
Head N.V., 55
Heijmans N.V., 66
Heineken N.V., I; 13 (upd.); 34 (upd.); 90 (upd.)
IHC Caland N.V., 71
IKEA Group, 94 (upd.)
Indigo NV, 26
Intres B.V., 82
Ispat International N.V., 30
Koninklijke Ahold N.V. (Royal Ahold), II; 16 (upd.)
Koninklijke Houthandel G Wijma & Zonen BV, 96
Koninklijke Luchtvaart Maatschappij, N.V. (KLM Royal Dutch Airlines), I; 28 (upd.)
Koninklijke Nederlandsche Hoogovens en Staalfabrieken NV, IV
Koninklijke Nedlloyd N.V., 6; 26 (upd.)
Koninklijke Philips Electronics N.V., 50 (upd.)
Koninklijke PTT Nederland NV, V
Koninklijke Vendex KBB N.V. (Royal Vendex KBB N.V.), 62 (upd.)
Koninklijke Wessanen nv, II; 54 (upd.)
KPMG International, 10; 33 (upd.)
Laurus N.V., 65
Mammoet Transport B.V., 26
MIH Limited, 31
N.V. AMEV, III
N.V. Holdingmaatschappij De Telegraaf, 23
N.V. Koninklijke Nederlandse Vliegtuigenfabriek Fokker, I; 28 (upd.)
N.V. Nederlandse Gasunie, V
Nationale-Nederlanden N.V., III
New Holland N.V., 22
Nutreco Holding N.V., 56
Océ N.V., 24; 91 (upd.)
PCM Uitgevers NV, 53
Philips Electronics N.V., II; 13 (upd.)
PolyGram N.V., 23
Prada Holding B.V., 45
Qiagen N.V., 39
Rabobank Group, 33
Randstad Holding n.v., 16; 43 (upd.)
Rodamco N.V., 26
Royal Dutch/Shell Group, IV; 49 (upd.)
Royal Grolsch NV, 54
Royal KPN N.V., 30
Royal Numico N.V., 37
Royal Packaging Industries Van Leer N.V., 30
Royal Ten Cate N.V., 68
Royal Vopak NV, 41
SHV Holdings N.V., 55
Tennet BV 78
TNT Post Group N.V., V, 27 (upd.); 30 (upd.)
Toolex International N.V., 26
TomTom N.V., 81
TPG N.V., 64 (upd.)
Trader Classified Media N.V., 57
Triple P N.V., 26
Unilever N.V., II; 7 (upd.); 32 (upd.)
United Pan-Europe Communications NV, 47
Van Lanschot NV 79
VBA - Bloemenveiling Aalsmeer, 88
Vebego International BV, 49
Vedior NV, 35
Velcro Industries N.V., 19
Vendex International N.V., 13
Vion Food Group NV, 85
VNU N.V., 27
Wegener NV, 53
Wolters Kluwer NV, 14; 33 (upd.)

Netherlands Antilles

Orthofix International NV, 72
Velcro Industries N.V., 72

New Zealand

Air New Zealand Limited, 14; 38 (upd.)
Carter Holt Harvey Ltd., 70
Fletcher Challenge Ltd., IV; 19 (upd.)
Fonterra Co-Operative Group Ltd., 58
Frucor Beverages Group Ltd., 96
Nuplex Industries Ltd., 92
Progressive Enterprises Ltd., 96
Telecom Corporation of New Zealand Limited, 54
Wattie's Ltd., 7

Nigeria

Nigerian National Petroleum Corporation, IV; 72 (upd.)

Norway

Braathens ASA, 47
Den Norse Stats Oljeselskap AS, IV
Helly Hansen ASA, 25
Jotun A/S, 80
Kvaerner ASA, 36
Norsk Hydro ASA, 10; 35 (upd.)
Norske Skogindustrier ASA, 63
Orkla ASA, 18; 82 (upd.)
Schibsted ASA, 31
Statoil ASA, 61 (upd.)
Stolt Sea Farm Holdings PLC, 54
Telenor ASA, 69
Wilh. Wilhelmsen ASA, 94
Yara International ASA, 94

Oman

Petroleum Development Oman LLC, IV
The Zubair Corporation L.L.C., 96

Pakistan

Pakistan International Airlines Corporation, 46
Pakistan State Oil Company Ltd., 81

Panama

Autoridad del Canal de Panamá, 94
Copa Holdings, S.A., 93
Panamerican Beverages, Inc., 47
Willbros Group, Inc., 56

Papua New Guinea

Steamships Trading Company Ltd., 82

Peru

Ajegroup S.A., 92
Banco de Crédito del Perú, 93
Compañia de Minas Buenaventura S.A.A., 93
Corporación José R. Lindley S.A., 92
Southern Peru Copper Corporation, 40
Unión de Cervecerias Peruanas Backus y Johnston S.A.A., 92
Volcan Compañia Minera S.A.A., 92

Philippines

Bank of the Philippine Islands, 58
Benguet Corporation, 58
Manila Electric Company (Meralco), 56
Mercury Drug Corporation, 70
Petron Corporation, 58
Philippine Airlines, Inc., 6; 23 (upd.)
San Miguel Corporation, 15; 57 (upd.)

Poland

Agora S.A. Group, 77
LOT Polish Airlines (Polskie Linie Lotnicze S.A.), 33
Polski Koncern Naftowy ORLEN S.A., 77
Telekomunikacja Polska SA, 50

Portugal

Banco Comercial Português, SA, 50
Banco Espírito Santo e Comercial de Lisboa S.A., 15
BRISA Auto-estradas de Portugal S.A., 64
Cimentos de Portugal SGPS S.A. (Cimpor), 76
Corticeira Amorim, Sociedade Gestora de Participaço es Sociais, S.A., 48
Electricidade de Portugal, S.A., 47
Grupo Portucel Soporcel, 60
Jerónimo Martins SGPS S.A., 96
José de Mello SGPS S.A., 96
Madeira Wine Company, S.A., 49
Mota-Engil, SGPS, S.A., 97
Petróleos de Portugal S.A., IV
Portugal Telecom SGPS S.A., 69
Sonae SGPS, S.A., 97
TAP—Air Portugal Transportes Aéreos Portugueses S.A., 46
Transportes Aereos Portugueses, S.A., 6

Puerto Rico

Puerto Rico Electric Power Authority, 47

Qatar

Aljazeera Satellite Channel 79
Qatar Airways Company Q.C.S.C., 87
Qatar General Petroleum Corporation, IV
Qatar National Bank SAQ, 87
Qatar Telecom QSA, 87

Republic of Yemen

Hayel Saeed Anam Group of Cos., 92

Romania

Dobrogea Grup S.A., 82
TAROM S.A., 64

Russia

A.S. Yakovlev Design Bureau, 15
Aeroflot - Russian Airlines JSC, 6; 29 (upd.); 89 (upd.)
Alrosa Company Ltd., 62
AO VimpelCom, 48
Aviacionny Nauchno-Tehnicheskii Komplex im. A.N. Tupoleva, 24
AVTOVAZ Joint Stock Company, 65
Baltika Brewery Joint Stock Company, 65
Evraz Group S.A., 97
Golden Telecom, Inc., 59
Interfax News Agency, 86
Irkut Corporation, 68
JSC MMC Norilsk Nickel, 48
Mobile TeleSystems OJSC, 59
OAO Gazprom, 42
OAO LUKOIL, 40
OAO NK YUKOS, 47
OAO Siberian Oil Company (Sibneft), 49
OAO Surgutneftegaz, 48
OAO Tatneft, 45
OJSC Wimm-Bill-Dann Foods, 48
RAO Unified Energy System of Russia, 45
Rostvertol plc, 62
Russian Aircraft Corporation (MiG), 86
Russian Railways Joint Stock Co., 93
Sberbank, 62
Severstal Joint Stock Company, 65
Sistema JSFC, 73
Sukhoi Design Bureau Aviation Scientific-Industrial Complex, 24
CJSC Transmash Holding, 93
Oil Transporting Joint Stock Company Transneft, 93
Volga-Dnepr Group, 82

Saudi Arabia

Dallah Albaraka Group, 72
Saudi Arabian Airlines, 6; 27 (upd.)
Saudi Arabian Oil Company, IV; 17 (upd.); 50 (upd.)
Saudi Basic Industries Corporation (SABIC), 58

Scotland

Arnold Clark Automobiles Ltd., 60
Distillers Company PLC, I
General Accident PLC, III
The Governor and Company of the Bank of Scotland, 10
The Royal Bank of Scotland Group plc, 12
Scottish & Newcastle plc, 15
Scottish Hydro-Electric PLC, 13
Scottish Media Group plc, 32
ScottishPower plc, 19
Stagecoach Holdings plc, 30
The Standard Life Assurance Company, III

Singapore

Asia Pacific Breweries Limited, 59
City Developments Limited, 89
Creative Technology Ltd., 57
Flextronics International Ltd., 38
Fraser & Neave Ltd., 54
Hotel Properties Ltd., 71
Jardine Cycle & Carriage Ltd., 73
Keppel Corporation Ltd., 73
Neptune Orient Lines Limited, 47
Pacific Internet Limited, 87
Singapore Airlines Limited, 6; 27 (upd.); 83 (upd.)
Singapore Press Holdings Limited, 85
StarHub Ltd., 77
United Overseas Bank Ltd., 56

South Africa

African Rainbow Minerals Ltd., 97
Anglo American Corporation of South Africa Limited, IV; 16 (upd.)
Barlow Rand Ltd., I
De Beers Consolidated Mines Limited/De Beers Centenary AG, IV; 7 (upd.); 28 (upd.)
Dimension Data Holdings PLC, 69
Edgars Consolidated Stores Ltd., 66
Famous Brands Ltd., 86
Gencor Ltd., IV; 22 (upd.)
Gold Fields Ltd., IV; 62 (upd.)
Harmony Gold Mining Company Limited, 63
Highveld Steel and Vanadium Corporation Limited, 59
Iscor Limited, 57
Naspers Ltd., 66
New Clicks Holdings Ltd., 86
Pick 'n Pay Stores Ltd., 82
SAA (Pty) Ltd., 28
Sanlam Ltd., 68
Sappi Limited, 49
Sasol Limited, IV; 47 (upd.)
The South African Breweries Limited, I; 24 (upd.)
Transnet Ltd., 6

South Korea

Anam Group, 23
Asiana Airlines, Inc., 46
CJ Corporation, 62
Daesang Corporation, 84
Daewoo Group, III; 18 (upd.); 57 (upd.)
Electronics Co., Ltd., 14
Goldstar Co., Ltd., 12
Hanjin Shipping Co., Ltd., 50
Hanwha Group, 62
Hite Brewery Company Ltd., 97
Hyundai Group, III; 7 (upd.); 56 (upd.)
Kia Motors Corporation, 12; 29 (upd.)
Kookmin Bank, 58
Korea Electric Power Corporation (Kepco), 56
Korean Air Lines Co., Ltd., 6; 27 (upd.)
KT&G Corporation, 62
LG Corporation, 94 (upd.)
Lotte Confectionery Company Ltd., 76
Lucky-Goldstar, II
Pohang Iron and Steel Company Ltd., IV
POSCO, 57 (upd.)
Samick Musical Instruments Co., Ltd., 56
Samsung Electronics Co., Ltd., I; 41 (upd.)
SK Group, 88
Ssangyong Cement Industrial Co., Ltd., III; 61 (upd.)
Tong Yang Cement Corporation, 62

Spain

Abengoa S.A., 73
Abertis Infraestructuras, S.A., 65
Acciona S.A., 81
Adolfo Dominguez S.A., 72
Altadis S.A., 72 (upd.)
Banco Bilbao Vizcaya Argentaria S.A., II; 48 (upd.)
Banco Central, II
Banco do Brasil S.A., II
Banco Santander Central Hispano S.A., 36 (upd.)
Baron de Ley S.A., 74
Campofrío Alimentación S.A, 59
Chupa Chups S.A., 38
Compañia Española de Petróleos S.A. (Cepsa), IV; 56 (upd.)
Cortefiel S.A., 64
Correos y Telegrafos S.A., 80
Dogi International Fabrics S.A., 52
El Corte Inglés Group, V; 26 (upd.)
ENDESA S.A., V; 46 (upd.)
Ercros S.A., 80
Federico Paternina S.A., 69
Freixenet S.A., 71
Gas Natural SDG S.A., 69
Grupo Dragados SA, 55
Grupo Eroski, 64
Grupo Ferrovial, S.A., 40
Grupo Ficosa International, 90
Grupo Leche Pascual S.A., 59
Grupo Lladró S.A., 52
Grupo Planeta, 94
Iberdrola, S.A., 49
Iberia Líneas Aéreas de España S.A., 6; 36 (upd.); 91 (upd.)
Industria de Diseño Textil S.A., 64
Instituto Nacional de Industria, I
Mecalux S.A., 74
Miquel y Costas Miquel S.A., 68
NH Hoteles S.A. 79
Nutrexpa S.A., 92
Obrascon Huarte Lain S.A., 76
Paradores de Turismo de Espana S.A., 73
Pescanova S.A., 81
Puig Beauty and Fashion Group S.L., 60
Real Madrid C.F., 73
Repsol-YPF S.A., IV; 16 (upd.); 40 (upd.)
Sol Meliá S.A., 71
Tabacalera, S.A., V; 17 (upd.)

Telefónica S.A., V; 46 (upd.)
TelePizza S.A., 33
Television Española, S.A., 7
Terra Lycos, Inc., 43
Unión Fenosa, S.A., 51
Uralita S.A., 96
Vidrala S.A., 67
Viscofan S.A., 70
Vocento, 94
Vueling Airlines S.A., 97
Zara International, Inc., 83
Zed Group, 93

Sweden

A. Johnson & Company H.B., I
AB Volvo, I; 7 (upd.); 26 (upd.); 67 (upd.)
Aktiebolaget Electrolux, 22 (upd.)
Aktiebolaget SKF, III; 38 (upd.); 89 (upd.)
Alfa Laval AB, III; 64 (upd.)
Astra AB, I; 20 (upd.)
Atlas Copco AB, III; 28 (upd.); 85 (upd.)
Autoliv, Inc., 65
Boliden AB, 80
Bonnier AB, 52
BRIO AB, 24
Cardo AB, 53
Cloetta Fazer AB, 70
Electrolux AB, III; 53 (upd.)
Eka Chemicals AB, 92
FöreningsSparbanken AB, 69
Gambro AB, 49
Gunnebo AB, 53
Hennes & Mauritz AB, 29
Hexagon AB 78
Holmen AB, 52 (upd.)
ICA AB, II
Investor AB, 63
Mo och Domsjö AB, IV
Modern Times Group AB, 36
NetCom Systems AB, 26
Nobel Industries AB, 9
Nordea AB, 40
Observer AB, 55
Perstorp AB, I; 51 (upd.)
Saab Automobile AB, I; 11 (upd.); 32 (upd.); 83 (upd.)
Sandvik AB, IV; 32 (upd.); 77 (upd.)
Sapa AB, 84
The SAS Group, 34 (upd.)
Scandinavian Airlines System, I
Securitas AB, 42
Skandia Insurance Company, Ltd., 50
Skandinaviska Enskilda Banken AB, II; 56 (upd.)
Skanska AB, 38
SSAB Svenskt Stål AB, 89
Stora Kopparbergs Bergslags AB, IV
Sveaskog AB, 93
Svenska Cellulosa Aktiebolaget SCA, IV; 28 (upd.); 85 (upd.)
Svenska Handelsbanken AB, II; 50 (upd.)
Sveriges Riksbank, 96
Swedish Match AB, 12; 39 (upd.); 92 (upd.)
Swedish Telecom, V
Telefonaktiebolaget LM Ericsson, V; 46 (upd.)
TeliaSonera AB, 57 (upd.)
Trelleborg AB, 93
Vattenfall AB, 57
V&S Vin & Sprit AB, 91 (upd.)
Vin & Spirit AB, 31

Switzerland

ABB ASEA Brown Boveri Ltd., II; 22 (upd.)
ABB Ltd., 65 (upd.)
Actelion Ltd., 83
Adecco S.A., 36 (upd.)
Adia S.A., 6
Arthur Andersen & Company, Société Coopérative, 10
Ascom AG, 9
Bâloise-Holding, 40
Barry Callebaut AG, 29; 71 (upd.)
Bernina Holding AG, 47
Bodum Design Group AG, 47
Bon Appetit Holding AG, 48
Charles Vögele Holding AG, 82
Chocoladefabriken Lindt & Sprüngli AG, 27
Ciba-Geigy Ltd., I; 8 (upd.)
Compagnie Financiere Richemont AG, 50
Conzzeta Holding, 80
Coop Schweiz Genossenschaftsverband, 48
Credit Suisse Group, II; 21 (upd.); 59 (upd.)
Danzas Group, V; 40 (upd.)
De Beers Consolidated Mines Limited/De Beers Centenary AG, IV; 7 (upd.); 28 (upd.)
Denner AG, 88
Duferco Group, 94
Edipresse S.A., 82
Elektrowatt AG, 6
Elma Electronic AG, 83
F. Hoffmann-La Roche Ltd., I; 50 (upd.)
Fédération Internationale de Football Association, 27
Fenaco, 86
Firmenich International S.A., 60
Franke Holding AG, 76
Galenica AG, 84
Gate Gourmet International AG, 70
Geberit AG, 49
Georg Fischer AG Schaffhausen, 61
Givaudan SA, 43
Holderbank Financière Glaris Ltd., III
International Olympic Committee, 44
Jacobs Suchard A.G., II
Julius Baer Holding AG, 52
Keramik Holding AG Laufen, 51
Kraft Jacobs Suchard AG, 26 (upd.)
Kudelski Group SA, 44
Kuehne & Nagel International AG, V; 53 (upd.)
Kuoni Travel Holding Ltd., 40
Liebherr-International AG, 64
Logitech International S.A., 28; 69 (upd.)
Lonza Group Ltd., 73
Maus Frères SA, 48
Médecins sans Frontières, 85
Mettler-Toledo International Inc., 30
Migros-Genossenschafts-Bund, 68
Montres Rolex S.A., 13; 34 (upd.)
Nestlé S.A., II; 7 (upd.); 28 (upd.); 71 (upd.)
Novartis AG, 39 (upd.)
Panalpina World Transport (Holding) Ltd., 47
Pelikan Holding AG, 92
Phoenix Mecano AG, 61
Ricola Ltd., 62
Rieter Holding AG, 42
Roland Murten A.G., 7
Sandoz Ltd., I
Schindler Holding AG, 29
Schweizerische Post-, Telefon- und Telegrafen-Betriebe, V
Selecta AG, 97
Serono S.A., 47
STMicroelectronics NV, 52
Straumann Holding AG 79
Sulzer Ltd., III; 68 (upd.)
Swarovski International Holding AG, 40
The Swatch Group SA, 26
Swedish Match S.A., 12
Swiss Air Transport Company, Ltd., I
Swiss Bank Corporation, II
The Swiss Federal Railways (Schweizerische Bundesbahnen), V
Swiss International Air Lines Ltd., 48
Swiss Reinsurance Company (Schweizerische Rückversicherungs-Gesellschaft), III; 46 (upd.)
Swisscom AG, 58
Swissport International Ltd., 70
Syngenta International AG, 83
Synthes, Inc., 93
TAG Heuer International SA, 25; 77 (upd.)
Tamedia AG, 53
Tetra Pak International SA, 53
UBS AG, 52 (upd.)
Underberg AG, 92
Union Bank of Switzerland, II
Victorinox AG, 21; 74 (upd.)
Vontobel Holding AG, 96
Weleda AG 78
Winterthur Group, III; 68 (upd.)
Xstrata PLC, 73
Zurich Financial Services, 42 (upd.); 93 (upd.)
Zürich Versicherungs-Gesellschaft, III

Taiwan

Acer Incorporated, 16; 73 (upd.)
AU Optronics Corporation, 67
BenQ Corporation, 67
Chi Mei Optoelectronics Corporation, 75
China Airlines, 34
Chunghwa Picture Tubes, Ltd., 75
D-Link Corporation, 83
Directorate General of Telecommunications, 7
EVA Airways Corporation, 51
Evergreen Marine Corporation (Taiwan) Ltd., 13; 50 (upd.)
First International Computer, Inc., 56

Formosa Plastics Corporation, 14; 58 (upd.)
Giant Manufacturing Company, Ltd., 85
High Tech Computer Corporation, 81
Hon Hai Precision Industry Co., Ltd., 59
Kwang Yang Motor Company Ltd., 80
Pou Chen Corporation, 81
Quanta Computer Inc., 47
Siliconware Precision Industries Ltd., 73
Taiwan Semiconductor Manufacturing Company Ltd., 47
Taiwan Tobacco & Liquor Corporation, 75
Tatung Co., 23
Winbond Electronics Corporation, 74
Yageo Corporation, 16

Thailand

Charoen Pokphand Group, 62
Electricity Generating Authority of Thailand (EGAT), 56
Krung Thai Bank Public Company Ltd., 69
Pranda Jewelry plc, 70
PTT Public Company Ltd., 56
The Siam Cement Public Company Limited, 56
Thai Airways International Public Company Limited, 6; 27 (upd.)
Thai Union Frozen Products PCL, 75
Thanulux Public Company Limited, 86
The Topaz Group, Inc., 62

Tunisia

Société Tunisienne de l'Air-Tunisair, 49

Turkey

Akbank TAS 79
Anadolu Efes Biracilik ve Malt Sanayii A.S., 95
Dogan Sirketler Grubu Holding A.S., 83
Haci Omer Sabanci Holdings A.S., 55
Koç Holding A.S., I; 54 (upd.)
Turkish Airlines Inc. (Türk Hava Yollari A.O.), 72
Turkiye Is Bankasi A.S., 61
Türkiye Petrolleri Anonim Ortakliği, IV

Ukraine

Antonov Design Bureau, 53

United Arab Emirates

Abu Dhabi National Oil Company, IV; 45 (upd.)
Al Habtoor Group L.L.C., 87
DP World, 81
The Emirates Group, 39; 81 (upd.)
Etihad Airways PJSC, 89
Gulf Agency Company Ltd. 78
Jumeirah Group, 83

United Kingdom

A. F. Blakemore & Son Ltd., 90
A. Nelson & Co. Ltd., 75
Aardman Animations Ltd., 61
Abbey National plc, 10; 39 (upd.)
Acergy SA, 97
Adams Childrenswear Ltd., 95
Aegis Group plc, 6
AG Barr plc, 64
Aga Foodservice Group PLC, 73
Aggregate Industries plc, 36
Aggreko Plc, 45
AgustaWestland N.V., 75
Air Partner PLC, 93
Airtours Plc, 27
The Albert Fisher Group plc, 41
Alexandra plc, 88
The All England Lawn Tennis & Croquet Club, 54
Alldays plc, 49
Allders plc, 37
Alliance and Leicester plc, 88
Alliance Boots plc, 83 (upd.)
Allied Domecq PLC, 29
Allied-Lyons PLC, I
Alpha Airports Group PLC, 77
Alvis Plc, 47
Amersham PLC, 50
Amey Plc, 47
Amnesty International, 50
Amstrad plc, III; 48 (upd.)
AMVESCAP PLC, 65
Anglo American PLC, 50 (upd.)
Anker BV, 53
Antofagasta plc, 65
Apax Partners Worldwide LLP, 89
Apple Corps Ltd., 87
Arcadia Group plc, 28 (upd.)
Argyll Group PLC, II
Arjo Wiggins Appleton p.l.c., 34
Arriva PLC, 69
Arsenal Holdings PLC 79
ASDA Group Ltd., II; 28 (upd.); 64 (upd.)
Ashtead Group plc, 34
Associated British Foods plc, II; 13 (upd.); 41 (upd.)
Associated British Ports Holdings Plc, 45
Aston Villa plc, 41
AstraZeneca PLC, 50 (upd.)
AT&T Istel Ltd., 14
Avecia Group PLC, 63
Aviva PLC, 50 (upd.)
BAA plc, 10; 33 (upd.)
Babcock International Group PLC, 69
Balfour Beatty plc, 36 (upd.)
Barclays plc, II; 20 (upd.); 64 (upd.)
Barings PLC, 14
Barratt Developments plc, I; 56 (upd.)
Bass PLC, I; 15 (upd.); 38 (upd.)
Bat Industries PLC, I; 20 (upd.)
Baxi Group Ltd., 96
BBA Aviation plc, 90
Belleek Pottery Ltd., 71
Bellway Plc, 45
Belron International Ltd., 76
Benfield Greig Group plc, 53
Bernard Matthews Ltd., 89
Bettys & Taylors of Harrogate Ltd., 72
Bhs plc, 17
BICC PLC, III
Biffa plc, 92
The Big Food Group plc, 68 (upd.)
Birse Group PLC, 77
Birthdays Ltd., 70
Blacks Leisure Group plc, 39
Blackwell Publishing Ltd. 78
Blue Circle Industries PLC, III
BOC Group plc, I; 25 (upd.); 78 (upd.)
The Body Shop International plc, 11; 53 (upd.)
Bodycote International PLC, 63
Bonhams 1793 Ltd., 72
Booker Cash & Carry Ltd., 13; 31 (upd.); 68 (upd.)
The Boots Company PLC, V; 24 (upd.)
Bowater PLC, IV
Bowthorpe plc, 33
BP p.l.c., 45 (upd.)
BPB plc, 83
Bradford & Bingley PLC, 65
Brake Bros plc, 45
Brammer PLC, 77
Bristow Helicopters Ltd., 70
Britannia Soft Drinks Ltd. (Britvic), 71
British Aerospace plc, I; 24 (upd.)
British Airways PLC, I; 14 (upd.); 43 (upd.)
British American Tobacco PLC, 50 (upd.)
British Broadcasting Corporation Ltd., 7; 21 (upd.); 89 (upd.)
British Coal Corporation, IV
British Energy Plc, 49
The British Film Institute, 80
British Gas plc, V
British Land Plc, 54
British Midland plc, 38
The British Museum, 71
British Nuclear Fuels plc, 6
The British Petroleum Company plc, IV; 7 (upd.); 21 (upd.)
British Railways Board, V
British Sky Broadcasting Group plc, 20; 60 (upd.)
British Steel plc, IV; 19 (upd.)
British Sugar plc, 84
British Telecommunications plc, V; 15 (upd.)
British United Provident Association Limited (BUPA) 79
British Vita plc, 9; 33 (upd.)
British World Airlines Ltd., 18
British-Borneo Oil & Gas PLC, 34
BT Group plc, 49 (upd.)
BTG Plc, 87
BTR PLC, I
BTR Siebe plc, 27
Budgens Ltd., 59
Bunzl plc, IV; 31 (upd.)
Burberry Group plc, 17; 41 (upd.); 92 (upd.)
Burmah Castrol PLC, IV; 30 (upd.)
The Burton Group plc, V
Business Post Group plc, 46
C&J Clark International Ltd., 52
C. Hoare & Co., 77
C.I. Traders Limited, 61
Cable and Wireless plc, V; 25 (upd.)
Cadbury Schweppes PLC, II; 49 (upd.)
Caffè Nero Group PLC, 63
Canary Wharf Group Plc, 30
Caparo Group Ltd., 90

Capita Group PLC, 69
Capital Radio plc, 35
Caradon plc, 20 (upd.)
Carbo PLC, 67 (upd.)
Carlton Communications PLC, 15; 50 (upd.)
The Carphone Warehouse Group PLC, 83
Cartier Monde, 29
Cattles plc, 58
Cazenove Group plc, 72
Central Independent Television, 7; 23 (upd.)
Centrica plc, 29 (upd.)
Channel Four Television Corporation, 93
Chello Zone Ltd., 93
Chelsfield PLC, 67
Cheltenham & Gloucester PLC, 61
Cheshire Building Society, 74
Christian Salvesen Plc, 45
Christie's International plc, 15; 39 (upd.)
Chrysalis Group plc, 40
Chubb, PLC, 50
Clifford Chance LLP, 38
Clinton Cards plc, 39
Close Brothers Group plc, 39
Co-operative Group (CWS) Ltd., 51
Coats plc, V; 44 (upd.)
Cobham plc, 30
COLT Telecom Group plc, 41
Commercial Union PLC, III
Compass Group PLC, 34
Cookson Group plc, III; 44 (upd.)
Corus Group plc, 49 (upd.)
Courtaulds plc, V; 17 (upd.)
Courts Plc, 45
Cranswick plc, 40
Croda International Plc, 45
Daily Mail and General Trust plc, 19
Dairy Crest Group plc, 32
Dalgety, PLC, II
Daniel Thwaites Plc, 95
Dart Group PLC, 77
Davis Service Group PLC, 45
Dawson Holdings PLC, 43
De La Rue plc, 10; 34 (upd.)
Debenhams Plc, 28
Denby Group plc, 44
Denison International plc, 46
Dennis Publishing Ltd., 62
Devro plc, 55
Diageo plc, 24 (upd.); 79 (upd.)
Direct Wines Ltd., 84
Dixons Group plc, V; 19 (upd.); 49 (upd.)
Domino Printing Sciences PLC, 87
Dorling Kindersley Holdings plc, 20
Dresdner Kleinwort Wasserstein, 60 (upd.)
DS Smith Plc, 61
Dyson Group PLC, 71
E H Booth & Company Ltd., 90
easyJet Airline Company Limited, 39
ECC Group plc, III
The Economist Group Ltd., 67
The Edrington Group Ltd., 88
Electrocomponents PLC, 50
Elementis plc, 40 (upd.)
EMAP plc, 35
EMI Group plc, 22 (upd.); 81 (upd.)
Energis plc, 47
English China Clays Ltd., 15 (upd.); 40 (upd.)
Enodis plc, 68
Enterprise Inns plc, 59
Enterprise Oil PLC, 11; 50 (upd.)
Esporta plc, 35
Eurotunnel Group, 13; 37 (upd.)
Exel plc, 51 (upd.)
Fairclough Construction Group PLC, I
Fat Face Ltd., 68
Filtrona plc, 88
Findel plc, 60
First Choice Holidays PLC, 40
FirstGroup plc, 89
Fisons plc, 9; 23 (upd.)
FKI Plc, 57
French Connection Group plc, 41
Fuller Smith & Turner P.L.C., 38
G A Pindar & Son Ltd., 88
Gallaher Group Plc, 49 (upd.)
Gallaher Limited, V; 19 (upd.)
The GAME Group plc, 80
The Gateway Corporation Ltd., II
Geest Plc, 38
General Electric Company PLC, II
George Wimpey PLC, 12; 51 (upd.)
Gibbs and Dandy plc, 74
GKN plc, III; 38 (upd.); 89 (upd.)
GlaxoSmithKline plc, I; 9 (upd.); 46 (upd.)
Glotel plc, 53
The Go-Ahead Group Plc, 28
Grampian Country Food Group, Ltd., 85
Granada Group PLC, II; 24 (upd.)
Grand Metropolitan PLC, I; 14 (upd.)
The Great Universal Stores plc, V; 19 (upd.)
The Greenalls Group PLC, 21
Greene King plc, 31
Greggs PLC, 65
Guardian Financial Services, 64 (upd.)
Guardian Media Group plc, 53
Guardian Royal Exchange Plc, 11
Guinness/UDV, I; 43 (upd.)
GUS plc, 47 (upd.)
GWR Group plc, 39
Hammerson plc, 40
The Hammerson Property Investment and Development Corporation plc, IV
Hanson PLC, III; 7 (upd.); 30 (upd.)
Harrisons & Crosfield plc, III
Harrods Holdings, 47
The Hartstone Group plc, 14
Hawker Siddeley Group Public Limited Company, III
Haynes Publishing Group P.L.C., 71
Hays Plc, 27; 78 (upd.)
Hazlewood Foods plc, 32
Headlam Group plc, 95
Henry Boot plc, 76
Her Majesty's Stationery Office, 7
Highland Gold Mining Limited, 95
Hillsdown Holdings plc, II; 24 (upd.)
Hilton Group plc, 49 (upd.)
HIT Entertainment PLC, 40
HMV Group plc, 59
Holidaybreak plc, 96
Home Retail Group plc, 91
House of Fraser PLC, 45
HSBC Holdings plc, 12; 26 (upd.); 80 (upd.)
Hunting plc 78
Huntingdon Life Sciences Group plc, 42
Huntleigh Technology PLC, 77
IAC Group, 96
Ibstock Brick Ltd., 14; 37 (upd.)
ICL plc, 6
IG Group Holdings plc, 97
IMI plc, 9
Imperial Chemical Industries PLC, I; 50 (upd.)
Imperial Tobacco Group PLC, 50
Inchcape PLC, III; 16 (upd.); 50 (upd.)
Informa Group plc, 58
Inter Link Foods PLC, 61
International Power PLC, 50 (upd.)
Intertek Group plc, 95
Invensys PLC, 50 (upd.)
IPC Magazines Limited, 7
J C Bamford Excavators Ltd., 83
J Sainsbury plc, II; 13 (upd.); 38 (upd.); 95 (upd.)
James Beattie plc, 43
James Purdey & Sons Limited, 87
Jarvis plc, 39
JD Wetherspoon plc, 30
Jersey European Airways (UK) Ltd., 61
JJB Sports plc, 32
John Brown PLC, I
The John David Group plc, 90
John Dewar & Sons, Ltd., 82
John Laing plc, I; 51 (upd.)
John Lewis Partnership plc, V; 42 (upd.)
John Menzies plc, 39
Johnson Matthey PLC, IV; 16 (upd.); 49 (upd.)
Johnston Press plc, 35
Kelda Group plc, 45
Keller Group PLC, 95
Kennecott Corporation, 7; 27 (upd.)
Kesa Electricals plc, 91
Kidde plc, 44 (upd.)
Kingfisher plc, V; 24 (upd.); 83 (upd.)
Kleinwort Benson Group PLC, II
Kvaerner ASA, 36
Kwik-Fit Holdings plc, 54
Ladbroke Group PLC, II; 21 (upd.)
Lafarge Cement UK, 54 (upd.)
Land Securities PLC, IV; 49 (upd.)
Laing O'Rourke PLC, 93 (upd.)
Laura Ashley Holdings plc, 13; 37 (upd.)
The Laurel Pub Company Limited, 59
Legal & General Group plc, III; 24 (upd.)
Littlewoods plc, V; 42 (upd.)
Lloyd's, III; 22 (upd.); 74 (upd.)
Lloyds TSB Group plc, II; 47 (upd.)
Loganair Ltd., 68
Logica plc, 14; 37 (upd.)
London Regional Transport, 6
London Scottish Bank plc, 70
London Stock Exchange Limited, 34
Lonmin plc, 66 (upd.)
Lonrho Plc, 21
Lookers plc, 71
Lotus Cars Ltd., 14

Lucas Industries PLC, III
Luminar Plc, 40
Lush Ltd., 93
The Macallan Distillers Ltd., 63
Mackays Stores Group Ltd., 92
Madge Networks N.V., 26
Manchester United Football Club plc, 30
Marconi plc, 33 (upd.)
Marks and Spencer Group p.l.c., V; 24 (upd.); 85 (upd.)
Marshall Amplification plc, 62
Martin-Baker Aircraft Company Limited, 61
Matalan PLC, 49
Maxwell Communication Corporation plc, IV; 7 (upd.)
May Gurney Integrated Services PLC, 95
McBride plc, 82
McKechnie plc, 34
Meggitt PLC, 34
MEPC plc, IV
Mercury Communications, Ltd., 7
The Mersey Docks and Harbour Company, 30
Metal Box PLC, I
Michael Page International plc, 45
Midland Bank PLC, II; 17 (upd.)
Millennium & Copthorne Hotels plc, 71
Mirror Group Newspapers plc, 7; 23 (upd.)
Misys plc, 45; 46
Mitchells & Butlers PLC, 59
Molins plc, 51
Monsoon plc, 39
The Morgan Crucible Company plc, 82
Morgan Grenfell Group PLC, II
Moss Bros Group plc, 51
Mothercare plc, 17; 78 (upd.)
Moy Park Ltd. 78
Mulberry Group PLC, 71
N M Rothschild & Sons Limited, 39
National Express Group PLC, 50
National Power PLC, 12
National Westminster Bank PLC, II
New Look Group plc, 35
Newsquest plc, 32
Next plc, 29
NFC plc, 6
Nichols plc, 44
North West Water Group plc, 11
Northern and Shell Network plc, 87
Northern Foods plc, 10; 61 (upd.)
Northern Rock plc, 33
Norwich & Peterborough Building Society, 55
Novar plc, 49 (upd.)
NTL Inc., 65
Ocean Group plc, 6
Old Mutual PLC, 61
Orange S.A., 84
Ottakar's plc, 64
Oxfam GB, 87
Pearson plc, IV; 46 (upd.)
The Peninsular & Oriental Steam Navigation Company (Bovis Division), I
The Peninsular and Oriental Steam Navigation Company, V; 38 (upd.)
Pennon Group Plc, 45
Pentland Group plc, 20
Perkins Foods Holdings Ltd., 87
Petrofac Ltd., 95
Phones 4u Ltd., 85
Photo-Me International Plc, 83
PIC International Group PLC, 24 (upd.)
Pilkington Group Limited, III; 34 (upd.); 87 (upd.)
PKF International 78
The Plessey Company, PLC, II
The Porcelain and Fine China Companies Ltd., 69
Portmeirion Group plc, 88
Post Office Group, V
Posterscope Worldwide, 70
Powell Duffryn plc, 31
Powergen PLC, 11; 50 (upd.)
Princes Ltd., 76
Prudential plc, 48 (upd.)
Psion PLC, 45
Punch Taverns plc, 70
PZ Cussons plc, 72
R. Griggs Group Limited, 23
Racal Electronics PLC, II
Ragdoll Productions Ltd., 51
Railtrack Group PLC, 50
Raleigh UK Ltd., 65
The Rank Group plc, II; 14 (upd.); 64 (upd.)
Ranks Hovis McDougall Limited, II; 28 (upd.)
Rathbone Brothers plc, 70
The Really Useful Group, 26
Reckitt Benckiser plc, II; 42 (upd.); 91 (upd.)
Redland plc, III
Redrow Group plc, 31
Reed Elsevier plc, IV; 17 (upd.); 31 (upd.)
Regent Inns plc, 95
Renishaw plc, 46
Rentokil Initial Plc, 47
Reuters Group PLC, IV; 22 (upd.); 63 (upd.)
Rexam PLC, 32 (upd.); 85 (upd.)
Ricardo plc, 90
Rio Tinto PLC, 19 (upd.); 50 (upd.)
RMC Group p.l.c., III; 34 (upd.)
Rolls-Royce Group PLC, 67 (upd.)
Rolls-Royce plc, I; 7 (upd.); 21 (upd.)
Ronson PLC, 49
Rothmans UK Holdings Limited, V; 19 (upd.)
Rotork plc, 46
Rover Group Ltd., 7; 21 (upd.)
Rowntree Mackintosh, II
Royal & Sun Alliance Insurance Group plc, 55 (upd.)
The Royal Bank of Scotland Group plc, 38 (upd.)
Royal Doulton plc, 14; 38 (upd.)
Royal Dutch Petroleum Company/ The Shell Transport and Trading Company p.l.c., IV
Royal Insurance Holdings PLC, III
RPC Group PLC, 81
The RTZ Corporation PLC, IV
The Rugby Group plc, 31
Saatchi & Saatchi PLC, I
SABMiller plc, 59 (upd.)
Safeway PLC, 50 (upd.)
Saffery Champness, 80
The Sage Group, 43
St. James's Place Capital, plc, 71
The Sanctuary Group PLC, 69
SBC Warburg, 14
Schroders plc, 42
Scottish & Newcastle plc, 35 (upd.)
Scottish and Southern Energy plc, 66 (upd.)
Scottish Power plc, 49 (upd.)
Scottish Radio Holding plc, 41
SDL PLC, 67
Sea Containers Ltd., 29
Sears plc, V
Securicor Plc, 45
Seddon Group Ltd., 67
Selfridges Plc, 34
Serco Group plc, 47
Severn Trent PLC, 12; 38 (upd.)
SFI Group plc, 51
Shanks Group plc, 45
Shepherd Neame Limited, 30
SIG plc, 71
Signet Group PLC, 61
Singer & Friedlander Group plc, 41
Skipton Building Society, 80
Slough Estates PLC, IV; 50 (upd.)
Smith & Nephew plc, 17;41 (upd.)
SmithKline Beecham plc, III; 32 (upd.)
Smiths Industries PLC, 25
Somerfield plc, 47 (upd.)
Southern Electric PLC, 13
Specialist Computer Holdings Ltd., 80
Speedy Hire plc, 84
Spirax-Sarco Engineering plc, 59
SSL International plc, 49
St Ives plc, 34
Standard Chartered plc, II; 48 (upd.)
Stanley Leisure plc, 66
STC PLC, III
Stirling Group plc, 62
Stoddard International plc, 72
Stoll-Moss Theatres Ltd., 34
Stolt-Nielsen S.A., 42
Storehouse PLC, 16
Strix Ltd., 51
Superdrug Stores PLC, 95
Surrey Satellite Technology Limited, 83
Sun Alliance Group PLC, III
Sytner Group plc, 45
Tarmac Limited, III; 28 (upd.); 95 (upd.)
Tate & Lyle PLC, II; 42 (upd.)
Taylor & Francis Group plc, 44
Taylor Nelson Sofres plc, 34
Taylor Woodrow plc, I; 38 (upd.)
Ted Baker plc, 86
Tesco plc, II; 24 (upd.); 68 (upd.)
Thames Water plc, 11; 90 (upd.)
Thistle Hotels PLC, 54
Thorn Emi PLC, I
Thorn plc, 24
Thorntons plc, 46
3i Group PLC, 73
365 Media Group plc, 89
TI Group plc, 17

Tibbett & Britten Group plc, 32
Tiger Aspect Productions Ltd., 72
Time Out Group Ltd., 68
Tomkins plc, 11; 44 (upd.)
Tottenham Hotspur PLC, 81
Travis Perkins plc, 34
Trinity Mirror plc, 49 (upd.)
Triumph Motorcycles Ltd., 53
Trusthouse Forte PLC, III
TSB Group plc, 12
Tulip Ltd., 89
Tullow Oil plc, 83
The Tussauds Group, 55
Ulster Television PLC, 71
Ultimate Leisure Group PLC, 75
Ultramar PLC, IV
Umbro plc, 88
Unigate PLC, II; 28 (upd.)
Unilever, II; 7 (upd.); 32 (upd.); 89 (upd.)
Uniq plc, 83 (upd.)
United Biscuits (Holdings) plc, II; 42 (upd.)
United Business Media plc, 52 (upd.)
United News & Media plc, IV; 28 (upd.)
United Utilities PLC, 52 (upd.)
Urbium PLC, 75
Vauxhall Motors Limited, 73
Vendôme Luxury Group plc, 27
Vestey Group Ltd., 95
Vickers plc, 27
Virgin Group Ltd., 12; 32 (upd.); 89 (upd.)
Viridian Group plc, 64
Vodafone Group Plc, 11; 36 (upd.); 75 (upd.)
Vosper Thornycroft Holding plc, 41
W Jordan (Cereals) Ltd., 74
Wagon plc, 92
Walkers Shortbread Ltd. 79
Walkers Snack Foods Ltd., 70
Warburtons Ltd., 89
Wassall Plc, 18
Waterford Wedgwood Holdings PLC, 12
Watson Wyatt Worldwide, 42
Watts of Lydney Group Ltd., 71
Weetabix Limited, 61
The Weir Group PLC, 85
The Wellcome Foundation Ltd., I
WH Smith PLC, V, 42 (upd.)
Whatman plc, 46
Whitbread PLC, I; 20 (upd.); 52 (upd.); 97 (upd.)
Whittard of Chelsea Plc, 61
Wilkinson Hardware Stores Ltd., 80
Wilkinson Sword Ltd., 60
William Grant & Sons Ltd., 60
William Hill Organization Limited, 49
William Reed Publishing Ltd. 78
Willis Corroon Group plc, 25
Wilson Bowden Plc, 45
Wincanton plc, 52
Wm. Morrison Supermarkets PLC, 38
Wolseley plc, 64
The Wolverhampton & Dudley Breweries, PLC, 57
Wood Hall Trust PLC, I
The Woolwich plc, 30
Woolworths Group plc, 83
WPP Group plc, 6; 48 (upd.)
WS Atkins Plc, 45
Xstrata PLC, 73
Yell Group PLC 79
Young & Co.'s Brewery, P.L.C., 38
Young's Bluecrest Seafood Holdings Ltd., 81
Yule Catto & Company plc, 54
Zeneca Group PLC, 21
Zomba Records Ltd., 52

United States

A & E Television Networks, 32
A & W Brands, Inc., 25
A-dec, Inc., 53
A-Mark Financial Corporation, 71
A. Schulman, Inc., 8; 49 (upd.)
A.B. Watley Group Inc., 45
A.B.Dick Company, 28
A.C. Moore Arts & Crafts, Inc., 30
A. Duda & Sons, Inc., 88
A.G. Edwards, Inc., 8; 32
A.H. Belo Corporation, 10; 30 (upd.)
A.L. Pharma Inc., 12
A.M. Castle & Co., 25
A.O. Smith Corporation, 11; 40 (upd.); 93 (upd.)
A.T. Cross Company, 17; 49 (upd.)
AAF-McQuay Incorporated, 26
AAON, Inc., 22
AAR Corp., 28
Aaron Rents, Inc., 14; 35 (upd.)
AARP, 27
Aavid Thermal Technologies, Inc., 29
Abatix Corp., 57
Abaxis, Inc., 83
Abbott Laboratories, I; 11 (upd.); 40 (upd.); 93 (upd.)
ABC Appliance, Inc., 10
ABC Carpet & Home Co. Inc., 26
ABC Family Worldwide, Inc., 52
ABC Rail Products Corporation, 18
ABC Supply Co., Inc., 22
Abercrombie & Fitch Company, 15; 35 (upd.); 75 (upd.)
Abigail Adams National Bancorp, Inc., 23
Abiomed, Inc., 47
ABM Industries Incorporated, 25 (upd.)
Abrams Industries Inc., 23
Abraxas Petroleum Corporation, 89
Abt Associates Inc., 95
Academy of Television Arts & Sciences, Inc., 55
Academy Sports & Outdoors, 27
Acadian Ambulance & Air Med Services, Inc., 39
ACCION International, 87
Acclaim Entertainment Inc., 24
ACCO World Corporation, 7; 51 (upd.)
Accredited Home Lenders Holding Co., 91
Accubuilt, Inc., 74
Accuray Incorporated, 95
AccuWeather, Inc., 73
ACE Cash Express, Inc., 33
Ace Hardware Corporation, 12; 35 (upd.)
Aceto Corp., 38
AchieveGlobal Inc., 90
Ackerley Communications, Inc., 9
Acme United Corporation, 70
Acme-Cleveland Corp., 13
ACNielsen Corporation, 13; 38 (upd.)
Acorn Products, Inc., 55
Acosta Sales and Marketing Company, Inc., 77
Acsys, Inc., 44
Action Performance Companies, Inc., 27
Activision, Inc., 32; 89 (upd.)
Actuant Corporation, 94 (upd.)
Acuity Brands, Inc., 90
Acushnet Company, 64
Acuson Corporation, 10; 36 (upd.)
Acxiom Corporation, 35
The Adams Express Company, 86
Adams Golf, Inc., 37
Adaptec, Inc., 31
ADC Telecommunications, Inc., 10; 30 (upd.); 89 (upd.)
Adelphia Communications Corporation, 17; 52 (upd.)
ADESA, Inc., 71
Administaff, Inc., 52
Adobe Systems Inc., 10; 33 (upd.)
Adolph Coors Company, I; 13 (upd.); 36 (upd.)
ADT Security Services, Inc., 12; 44 (upd.)
Adtran Inc., 22
Advance Auto Parts, Inc., 57
Advance Publications Inc., IV; 19 (upd.); 96 (upd.)
Advanced Circuits Inc., 67
Advanced Fibre Communications, Inc., 63
Advanced Marketing Services, Inc., 34
Advanced Medical Optics, Inc. 79
Advanced Micro Devices, Inc., 6; 30 (upd.)
Advanced Neuromodulation Systems, Inc., 73
Advanced Technology Laboratories, Inc., 9
Advanstar Communications, Inc., 57
Advanta Corporation, 8; 38 (upd.)
Advantica Restaurant Group, Inc., 27 (upd.)
Adventist Health, 53
The Advertising Council, Inc., 76
The Advisory Board Company, 80
Advo, Inc., 6; 53 (upd.)
Advocat Inc., 46
AECOM Technology Corporation 79
AEI Music Network Inc., 35
AEP Industries, Inc., 36
AeroGrow International, Inc., 95
Aerojet-General Corp., 63
Aeronca Inc., 46
Aéropostale, Inc., 89
Aeroquip Corporation, 16
Aerosonic Corporation, 69
AeroVironment, Inc., 97
The AES Corporation, 10; 13 (upd.); 53 (upd.)
Aetna Inc., III; 21 (upd.); 63 (upd.)
AFC Enterprises, Inc., 32; 83 (upd.)
Affiliated Computer Services, Inc., 61
Affiliated Foods Inc., 53
Affiliated Managers Group, Inc. 79

Affiliated Publications, Inc., 7
Affinity Group Holding Inc., 56
AFLAC Incorporated, 10 (upd.); 38 (upd.)
Africare, 59
After Hours Formalwear Inc., 60
Aftermarket Technology Corp., 83
Ag Services of America, Inc., 59
Ag-Chem Equipment Company, Inc., 17
AGCO Corporation, 13; 67 (upd.)
Agere Systems Inc., 61
Agilent Technologies Inc., 38; 93 (upd.)
Agilysys Inc., 76 (upd.)
Agri Beef Company, 81
Agway, Inc., 7; 21 (upd.)
AHL Services, Inc., 27
Air & Water Technologies Corporation, 6
Air Express International Corporation, 13
Air Methods Corporation, 53
Air Products and Chemicals, Inc., I; 10 (upd.); 74 (upd.)
Air T, Inc., 86
Air Wisconsin Airlines Corporation, 55
Airborne Freight Corporation, 6; 34 (upd.)
Airborne Systems Group, 89
Airgas, Inc., 54
AirTouch Communications, 11
AirTran Holdings, Inc., 22
AK Steel Holding Corporation, 19; 41 (upd.)
Akamai Technologies, Inc., 71
Akin, Gump, Strauss, Hauer & Feld, L.L.P., 33
Akorn, Inc., 32
Alabama Farmers Cooperative, Inc., 63
Alabama National BanCorporation, 75
Alamo Group Inc., 32
Alamo Rent A Car, 6; 24 (upd.); 84 (upd.)
ALARIS Medical Systems, Inc., 65
Alaska Air Group, Inc., 6; 29 (upd.)
Alaska Communications Systems Group, Inc., 89
Alaska Railroad Corporation, 60
Alba-Waldensian, Inc., 30
Albany International Corporation, 8; 51 (upd.)
Albany Molecular Research, Inc., 77
Albemarle Corporation, 59
Alberici Corporation, 76
Alberto-Culver Company, 8; 36 (upd.); 91 (upd.)
Albertson's, Inc., II; 7 (upd.); 30 (upd.); 65 (upd.)
Alco Health Services Corporation, III
Alco Standard Corporation, I
Alcoa Inc., 56 (upd.)
Aldila Inc., 46
Aldus Corporation, 10
Alex Lee Inc., 18; 44 (upd.)
Alexander & Alexander Services Inc., 10
Alexander & Baldwin, Inc., 10; 40 (upd.)
Alexander's, Inc., 45
Alfa Corporation, 60
Alico, Inc., 63
Alienware Corporation, 81
Align Technology, Inc., 94
All American Communications Inc., 20
Alleghany Corporation, 10; 60 (upd.)
Allegheny Energy, Inc., 38 (upd.)
Allegheny Ludlum Corporation, 8
Allegheny Power System, Inc., V
Allegiant Travel Company, 97
Allegis Group, Inc., 95
Allen Canning Company, 76
Allen Foods, Inc., 60
Allen Organ Company, 33
Allen Systems Group, Inc., 59
Allen-Edmonds Shoe Corporation, 61
Allergan, Inc., 10; 30 (upd.); 77 (upd.)
Alliance Capital Management Holding L.P., 63
Alliance Entertainment Corp., 17
Alliance Resource Partners, L.P., 81
Alliant Techsystems Inc., 8; 30 (upd.); 77 (upd.)
The Allied Defense Group, Inc., 65
Allied Healthcare Products, Inc., 24
Allied Products Corporation, 21
Allied Signal Engines, 9
Allied Waste Industries, Inc., 50
Allied Worldwide, Inc., 49
AlliedSignal Inc., I; 22 (upd.)
Allison Gas Turbine Division, 9
Allmerica Financial Corporation, 63
Allou Health & Beauty Care, Inc., 28
Alloy, Inc., 55
The Allstate Corporation, 10; 27 (upd.)
ALLTEL Corporation, 6; 46 (upd.)
Alltrista Corporation, 30
Allwaste, Inc., 18
Almost Family, Inc., 93
Aloha Airlines, Incorporated, 24
Alpharma Inc., 35 (upd.)
Alpine Confections, Inc., 71
Alpine Lace Brands, Inc., 18
Alside Inc., 94
AltaVista Company, 43
Altera Corporation, 18; 43 (upd.)
Alternative Tentacles Records, 66
Alterra Healthcare Corporation, 42
Alticor Inc., 71 (upd.)
Altiris, Inc., 65
Altron Incorporated, 20
Aluminum Company of America, IV; 20 (upd.)
Alvin Ailey Dance Foundation, Inc., 52
ALZA Corporation, 10; 36 (upd.)
Amalgamated Bank, 60
AMAX Inc., IV
Amazon.com, Inc., 25; 56 (upd.)
AMB Property Corporation, 57
Ambac Financial Group, Inc., 65
Ambassadors International, Inc., 68 (upd.)
Amblin Entertainment, 21
AMC Entertainment Inc., 12; 35 (upd.)
AMCOL International Corporation, 59 (upd.)
AMCORE Financial Inc., 44
Amdahl Corporation, III; 14 (upd.); 40 (upd.)
Amdocs Ltd., 47
Amedysis, Inc., 53
Amerada Hess Corporation, IV; 21 (upd.); 55 (upd.)
Amerco, 6
AMERCO, 67 (upd.)
Ameren Corporation, 60 (upd.)
America Online, Inc., 10; 26 (upd.)
America West Holdings Corporation, 6; 34 (upd.)
America's Car-Mart, Inc., 64
America's Favorite Chicken Company, Inc., 7
AmeriCares Foundation, Inc., 87
American & Efird, Inc., 82
American Airlines, I; 6 (upd.)
American Apparel, Inc., 90
American Axle & Manufacturing Holdings, Inc., 67
American Banknote Corporation, 30
American Bar Association, 35
American Biltrite Inc., 16; 43 (upd.)
American Brands, Inc., V
American Building Maintenance Industries, Inc., 6
American Business Information, Inc., 18
American Business Products, Inc., 20
American Campus Communities, Inc., 85
The American Cancer Society, 24
American Capital Strategies, Ltd., 91
American Cast Iron Pipe Company, 50
American Civil Liberties Union (ACLU), 60
American Classic Voyages Company, 27
American Coin Merchandising, Inc., 28; 74 (upd.)
American Colloid Co., 13
American Crystal Sugar Company, 9; 32 (upd.)
American Cyanamid, I; 8 (upd.)
American Eagle Outfitters, Inc., 24; 55 (upd.)
American Ecology Corporation, 77
American Electric Power Company, Inc., V; 45 (upd.)
American Express Company, II; 10 (upd.); 38 (upd.)
American Family Corporation, III
American Financial Group Inc., III; 48 (upd.)
American Foods Group, 43
American Furniture Company, Inc., 21
American General Corporation, III; 10 (upd.); 46 (upd.)
American General Finance Corp., 11
American Girl, Inc., 69 (upd.)
American Golf Corporation, 45
American Gramaphone LLC, 52
American Greetings Corporation, 7; 22 (upd.); 59 (upd.)
American Healthways, Inc., 65
American Home Mortgage Holdings, Inc., 46
American Home Products, I; 10 (upd.)
American Homestar Corporation, 18; 41 (upd.)
American Institute of Certified Public Accountants (AICPA), 44
American International Group, Inc., III; 15 (upd.); 47 (upd.)
American Italian Pasta Company, 27; 76 (upd.)

American Kennel Club, Inc., 74
American Lawyer Media Holdings, Inc., 32
American Library Association, 86
American Licorice Company, 86
American Locker Group Incorporated, 34
American Lung Association, 48
American Maize-Products Co., 14
American Management Association, 76
American Management Systems, Inc., 11
American Media, Inc., 27; 82 (upd.)
American Medical Association, 39
American Medical International, Inc., III
American Medical Response, Inc., 39
American Motors Corporation, I
American National Insurance Company, 8; 27 (upd.)
American Pad & Paper Company, 20
American Pharmaceutical Partners, Inc., 69
American Pop Corn Company, 59
American Power Conversion Corporation, 24; 67 (upd.)
American Premier Underwriters, Inc., 10
American President Companies Ltd., 6
American Printing House for the Blind, 26
American Re Corporation, 10; 35 (upd.)
American Red Cross, 40
American Reprographics Company, 75
American Residential Mortgage Corporation, 8
American Restaurant Partners, L.P., 93
American Retirement Corporation, 42
American Rice, Inc., 33
American Safety Razor Company, 20
American Science & Engineering, Inc., 81
American Seating Company 78
American Skiing Company, 28
American Society for the Prevention of Cruelty to Animals (ASPCA), 68
The American Society of Composers, Authors and Publishers (ASCAP), 29
American Software Inc., 25
American Standard Companies Inc., III; 30 (upd.)
American States Water Company, 46
American Stores Company, II; 22 (upd.)
American Superconductor Corporation, 97
American Technical Ceramics Corp., 67
American Tourister, Inc., 16
American Tower Corporation, 33
American Vanguard Corporation, 47
American Water Works Company, Inc., 6; 38 (upd.)
American Woodmark Corporation, 31
Amerigon Incorporated, 97
AMERIGROUP Corporation, 69
Amerihost Properties, Inc., 30
AmeriSource Health Corporation, 37 (upd.)
AmerisourceBergen Corporation, 64 (upd.)
Ameristar Casinos, Inc., 33; 69 (upd.)
Ameritech Corporation, V; 18 (upd.)
Ameritrade Holding Corporation, 34
Ameriwood Industries International Corp., 17
Amerock Corporation, 53
Ameron International Corporation, 67
Ames Department Stores, Inc., 9; 30 (upd.)
AMETEK, Inc., 9
AMF Bowling, Inc., 40
Amfac/JMB Hawaii L.L.C., I; 24 (upd.)
Amgen, Inc., 10; 30 (upd.); 89 (upd.)
AMICAS, Inc., 69
Amkor Technology, Inc., 69
Amoco Corporation, IV; 14 (upd.)
Amoskeag Company, 8
AMP Incorporated, II; 14 (upd.)
Ampacet Corporation, 67
Ampco-Pittsburgh Corporation 79
Ampex Corporation, 17
Amphenol Corporation, 40
AMR Corporation, 28 (upd.); 52 (upd.)
AMREP Corporation, 21
Amscan Holdings, Inc., 61
AmSouth Bancorporation, 12; 48 (upd.)
Amsted Industries Incorporated, 7
AmSurg Corporation, 48
Amtran, Inc., 34
Amway Corporation, III; 13 (upd.); 30 (upd.)
Amy's Kitchen Inc., 76
Amylin Pharmaceuticals, Inc., 67
Anacomp, Inc., 94
Anadarko Petroleum Corporation, 10; 52 (upd.)
Anaheim Angels Baseball Club, Inc., 53
Analex Corporation, 74
Analog Devices, Inc., 10
Analogic Corporation, 23
Analysts International Corporation, 36
Analytic Sciences Corporation, 10
Analytical Surveys, Inc., 33
Anaren Microwave, Inc., 33
Anchor Bancorp, Inc., 10
Anchor Brewing Company, 47
Anchor Gaming, 24
Anchor Hocking Glassware, 13
Andersen, 10; 29 (upd.); 68 (upd.)
Anderson Trucking Service, Inc., 75
The Anderson-DuBose Company, 60
The Andersons, Inc., 31
Andis Company, Inc., 85
Andrew Corporation, 10; 32 (upd.)
Andrews Kurth, LLP, 71
Andrews McMeel Universal, 40
Andronico's Market, 70
Andrx Corporation, 55
Angelica Corporation, 15; 43 (upd.)
AngioDynamics, Inc., 81
Anheuser-Busch Companies, Inc., I; 10 (upd.); 34 (upd.)
Anixter International Inc., 88
Annie's Homegrown, Inc., 59
AnnTaylor Stores Corporation, 13; 37 (upd.); 67 (upd.)
ANR Pipeline Co., 17
The Anschutz Company, 12; 36 (upd.); 73 (upd.)
Ansoft Corporation, 63
Anteon Corporation, 57
Anthem Electronics, Inc., 13
Anthony & Sylvan Pools Corporation, 56
The Antioch Company, 40
AOL Time Warner Inc., 57 (upd.)
Aon Corporation, III; 45 (upd.)
Apache Corporation, 10; 32 (upd.); 89 (upd.)
Apartment Investment and Management Company, 49
Apex Digital, Inc., 63
APi Group, Inc., 64
APL Limited, 61 (upd.)
Apogee Enterprises, Inc., 8
Apollo Group, Inc., 24
Applause Inc., 24
Apple & Eve L.L.C., 92
Apple Bank for Savings, 59
Apple Computer, Inc., III; 6 (upd.); 36 (upd.); 77 (upd.)
Applebee's International Inc., 14; 35 (upd.)
Appliance Recycling Centers of America, Inc., 42
Applica Incorporated, 43 (upd.)
Applied Bioscience International, Inc., 10
Applied Films Corporation, 48
Applied Materials, Inc., 10; 46 (upd.)
Applied Micro Circuits Corporation, 38
Applied Power, Inc., 9; 32 (upd.)
Applied Signal Technology, Inc., 87
AptarGroup, Inc., 69
Aqua Alliance Inc., 32 (upd.)
aQuantive, Inc., 81
Aquarion Company, 84
Aquent, 96
Aquila, Inc., 50 (upd.)
AR Accessories Group, Inc., 23
ARA Services, II
ARAMARK Corporation, 13; 41 (upd.)
Arandell Corporation, 37
The Arbitron Company, 38
Arbor Drugs Inc., 12
Arby's Inc., 14
Arch Chemicals Inc. 78
Arch Mineral Corporation, 7
Arch Wireless, Inc., 39
Archer Daniels Midland Company, I; 11 (upd.); 32 (upd.); 75 (upd.)
Archie Comics Publications, Inc., 63
Archon Corporation, 74 (upd.)
Archstone-Smith Trust, 49
Archway Cookies, Inc., 29
ARCO Chemical Company, 10
Arctco, Inc., 16
Arctic Cat Inc., 40 (upd.); 96 (upd.)
Arctic Slope Regional Corporation, 38
Arden Group, Inc., 29
Arena Resources, Inc., 97
Argon ST, Inc., 81
Argosy Gaming Company, 21
Ariba, Inc., 57
Ariens Company, 48
Aris Industries, Inc., 16
The Aristotle Corporation, 62
Ark Restaurants Corp., 20
Arkansas Best Corporation, 16; 94 (upd.)
Arkla, Inc., V
Armco Inc., IV

Armor All Products Corp., 16
Armor Holdings, Inc., 27
Armstrong Holdings, Inc., III; 22 (upd.); 81 (upd.)
Army and Air Force Exchange Service, 39
Arnhold and S. Bleichroeder Advisers, LLC, 97
Arnold & Porter, 35
Arotech Corporation, 93
ArQule, Inc., 68
ARRIS Group, Inc., 89
Arrow Air Holdings Corporation, 55
Arrow Electronics, Inc., 10; 50 (upd.)
The Art Institute of Chicago, 29
Art Van Furniture, Inc., 28
Artesyn Technologies Inc., 46 (upd.)
ArthroCare Corporation, 73
The Arthur C. Clarke Foundation, 92
Arthur D. Little, Inc., 35
Arthur J. Gallagher & Co., 73
Arthur Murray International, Inc., 32
Artisan Entertainment Inc., 32 (upd.)
ArvinMeritor, Inc., 8; 54 (upd.)
Asanté Technologies, Inc., 20
ASARCO Incorporated, IV
Asbury Automotive Group Inc., 60
Asbury Carbons, Inc., 68
ASC, Inc., 55
Ascend Communications, Inc., 24
Ascendia Brands, Inc., 97
Ascential Software Corporation, 59
Ash Grove Cement Company, 94
Ashland Inc., 19; 50 (upd.)
Ashland Oil, Inc., IV
Ashley Furniture Industries, Inc., 35
Ashworth, Inc., 26
ASK Group, Inc., 9
Ask Jeeves, Inc., 65
Aspect Telecommunications Corporation, 22
Aspen Skiing Company, 15
Asplundh Tree Expert Co., 20; 59 (upd.)
Assisted Living Concepts, Inc., 43
Associated Estates Realty Corporation, 25
Associated Grocers, Incorporated, 9; 31 (upd.)
Associated Milk Producers, Inc., 11; 48 (upd.)
Associated Natural Gas Corporation, 11
The Associated Press, 13; 31 (upd.); 73 (upd.)
Association of Junior Leagues International Inc., 60
AST Research Inc., 9
Astec Industries, Inc. 79
AstenJohnson Inc., 90
Astoria Financial Corporation, 44
Astronics Corporation, 35
Asurion Corporation, 83
ASV, Inc., 34; 66 (upd.)
At Home Corporation, 43
AT&T Bell Laboratories, Inc., 13
AT&T Corporation, V; 29 (upd.); 68 (upd.)
AT&T Wireless Services, Inc., 54 (upd.)
ATA Holdings Corporation, 82
Atari Corporation, 9; 23 (upd.); 66 (upd.)
ATC Healthcare Inc., 64
Atchison Casting Corporation, 39
The Athlete's Foot Brands LLC, 84
The Athletics Investment Group, 62
Atkins Nutritionals, Inc., 58
Atkinson Candy Company, 87
Atlanta Bread Company International, Inc., 70
Atlanta Gas Light Company, 6; 23 (upd.)
Atlanta National League Baseball Club, Inc., 43
Atlantic American Corporation, 44
Atlantic Coast Airlines Holdings, Inc., 55
Atlantic Energy, Inc., 6
The Atlantic Group, 23
Atlantic Premium Brands, Ltd., 57
Atlantic Richfield Company, IV; 31 (upd.)
Atlantic Southeast Airlines, Inc., 47
Atlantis Plastics, Inc., 85
Atlas Air, Inc., 39
Atlas Van Lines, Inc., 14
Atmel Corporation, 17
ATMI, Inc., 93
Atmos Energy Corporation, 43
Attachmate Corporation, 56
Atwood Mobil Products, 53
Au Bon Pain Co., Inc., 18
The Auchter Company, The 78
Audible Inc. 79
Audio King Corporation, 24
Audiovox Corporation, 34; 90 (upd.)
August Schell Brewing Company Inc., 59
Ault Incorporated, 34
Auntie Anne's, Inc., 35
Aurora Casket Company, Inc., 56
Aurora Foods Inc., 32
The Austin Company, 8; 72 (upd.)
Austin Powder Company, 76
Authentic Fitness Corporation, 20; 51 (upd.)
Auto Value Associates, Inc., 25
Autobytel Inc., 47
Autocam Corporation, 51
Autodesk, Inc., 10; 89 (upd.)
Autologic Information International, Inc., 20
Automatic Data Processing, Inc., III; 9 (upd.); 47 (upd.)
AutoNation, Inc., 50
Autotote Corporation, 20
AutoTrader.com, L.L.C., 91
AutoZone, Inc., 9; 31 (upd.)
Auvil Fruit Company, Inc., 95
Avado Brands, Inc., 31
Avalon Correctional Services, Inc., 75
AvalonBay Communities, Inc., 58
Avco Financial Services Inc., 13
Aveda Corporation, 24
Avedis Zildjian Co., 38
Aventine Renewable Energy Holdings, Inc., 89
Avery Dennison Corporation, IV; 17 (upd.); 49 (upd.)
Aviall, Inc., 73
Aviation Sales Company, 41
Avid Technology Inc., 38
Avis Group Holdings, Inc., 75 (upd.)
Avis Rent A Car, Inc., 6; 22 (upd.)
Avista Corporation, 69 (upd.)
Avnet Inc., 9
Avocent Corporation, 65
Avon Products, Inc., III; 19 (upd.); 46 (upd.)
Avondale Industries, 7; 41 (upd.)
AVX Corporation, 67
Awrey Bakeries, Inc., 56
Axcelis Technologies, Inc., 95
Axsys Technologies, Inc., 93
Aydin Corp., 19
Azcon Corporation, 23
Aztar Corporation, 13; 71 (upd.)
AZZ Incorporated, 93
B&G Foods, Inc., 40
B. Dalton Bookseller Inc., 25
The B. Manischewitz Company, LLC, 31
B/E Aerospace, Inc., 30
B.J. Alan Co., Inc., 67
B.R. Guest Inc., 87
B.W. Rogers Company, 94
Babbage's, Inc., 10
The Babcock & Wilcox Company, 82
Baby Superstore, Inc., 15
Bachman's Inc., 22
Back Bay Restaurant Group, Inc., 20
Back Yard Burgers, Inc., 45
Bad Boy Worldwide Entertainment Group, 58
Badger Meter, Inc., 22
Badger Paper Mills, Inc., 15
Badger State Ethanol, LLC, 83
BAE Systems Ship Repair, 73
Bailey Nurseries, Inc., 57
Bain & Company, 55
Baird & Warner Holding Company, 87
Bairnco Corporation, 28
Baker & Daniels LLP, 88
Baker & Hostetler LLP, 40
Baker & McKenzie, 10; 42 (upd.)
Baker & Taylor Corporation, 16; 43 (upd.)
Baker and Botts, L.L.P., 28
Baker Hughes Incorporated, III; 22 (upd.); 57 (upd.)
Balance Bar Company, 32
Balchem Corporation, 42
Baldor Electric Company, 21; 97 (upd.)
Baldwin & Lyons, Inc., 51
Baldwin Piano & Organ Company, 18
Baldwin Technology Company, Inc., 25
Ball Corporation, I; 10; 78 (upd.)
Ball Horticultural Company 78
Ballantyne of Omaha, Inc., 27
Ballard Medical Products, 21
Ballistic Recovery Systems, Inc., 87
Bally Manufacturing Corporation, III
Bally Total Fitness Corporation, 25; 94 (upd.)
Balmac International, Inc., 94
Baltek Corporation, 34
Baltimore Aircoil Company, Inc., 66
Baltimore Gas and Electric Company, V; 25 (upd.)
Baltimore Orioles L.P., 66
The Bama Companies, Inc., 80
Banana Republic Inc., 25
Bandag, Inc., 19
Banfi Products Corp., 36

Bank of America Corporation, 46 (upd.)
Bank of Boston Corporation, II
Bank of Granite Corporation, 89
Bank of Hawaii Corporation, 73
Bank of Mississippi, Inc., 14
Bank of New England Corporation, II
The Bank of New York Company, Inc., II; 46 (upd.)
Bank of the Ozarks, Inc., 91
Bank One Corporation, 10; 36 (upd.)
BankAmerica Corporation, II; 8 (upd.)
Bankers Trust New York Corporation, II
Banknorth Group, Inc., 55
Bankrate, Inc., 83
Banner Aerospace, Inc., 14; 37 (upd.)
Banta Corporation, 12; 32 (upd.); 79 (upd.)
Banyan Systems Inc., 25
Baptist Health Care Corporation, 82
Bar-S Foods Company, 76
BarclaysAmerican Mortgage Corporation, 11
Barbara's Bakery Inc., 88
Barden Companies, Inc., 76
Bare Escentuals, Inc., 91
Barnes & Noble, Inc., 10; 30 (upd.); 75 (upd.)
Barnes Group Inc., 13; 69 (upd.)
Barnett Banks, Inc., 9
Barnett Inc., 28
Barney's, Inc., 28
Barr Pharmaceuticals, Inc., 26; 68 (upd.)
Barrett Business Services, Inc., 16
Barrett-Jackson Auction Company L.L.C., 88
Barry-Wehmiller Companies, Inc., 90
The Bartell Drug Company, 94
Barton Malow Company, 51
Barton Protective Services Inc., 53
The Baseball Club of Seattle, LP, 50
Bashas' Inc., 33; 80 (upd.)
The Basketball Club of Seattle, LLC, 50
Bass Pro Shops, Inc., 42
Bassett Furniture Industries, Inc., 18; 95 (upd.)
Bates Worldwide, Inc., 14; 33 (upd.)
Bath Iron Works, 12; 36 (upd.)
Battelle Memorial Institute, Inc., 10
Battle Mountain Gold Company, 23
Bauerly Companies, 61
Bausch & Lomb Inc., 7; 25 (upd.); 96 (upd.)
Baxter International Inc., I; 10 (upd.)
Bay State Gas Company, 38
BayBanks, Inc., 12
Bayou Steel Corporation, 31
BB&T Corporation 79
BBN Corp., 19
BDO Seidman LLP, 96
BE&K, Inc., 73
BEA Systems, Inc., 36
Beacon Roofing Supply, Inc., 75
Bear Creek Corporation, 38
Bear Stearns Companies, Inc., II; 10 (upd.); 52 (upd.)
Bearings, Inc., 13
Beasley Broadcast Group, Inc., 51
Beatrice Company, II
BeautiControl Cosmetics, Inc., 21
Beazer Homes USA, Inc., 17
bebe stores, inc., 31
Bechtel Group, Inc., I; 24 (upd.)
Beckett Papers, 23
Beckman Coulter, Inc., 22
Beckman Instruments, Inc., 14
Becton, Dickinson & Company, I; 11 (upd.); 36 (upd.)
Bed Bath & Beyond Inc., 13; 41 (upd.)
Beech Aircraft Corporation, 8
Beech-Nut Nutrition Corporation, 21; 51 (upd.)
Beer Nuts, Inc., 86
BEI Technologies, Inc., 65
Bekins Company, 15
Bel Fuse, Inc., 53
Bel/Kaukauna USA, 76
Belco Oil & Gas Corp., 40
Belden CDT Inc., 76 (upd.)
Belden Inc., 19
Belk Stores Services, Inc., V; 19 (upd.)
Belk, Inc., 72 (upd.)
Bell and Howell Company, 9; 29 (upd.)
Bell Atlantic Corporation, V; 25 (upd.)
Bell Helicopter Textron Inc., 46
Bell Industries, Inc., 47
Bell Microproducts Inc., 69
Bell Sports Corporation, 16; 44 (upd.)
Belleville Shoe Manufacturing Company, 92
Bellisio Foods, Inc., 95
BellSouth Corporation, V; 29 (upd.)
Beloit Corporation, 14
Bemis Company, Inc., 8; 91 (upd.)
Ben & Jerry's Homemade, Inc., 10; 35 (upd.); 80 (upd.)
Ben Bridge Jeweler, Inc., 60
Ben E. Keith Company, 76
Benchmark Capital, 49
Benchmark Electronics, Inc., 40
Bendix Corporation, I
Beneficial Corporation, 8
Benihana, Inc., 18; 76 (upd.)
Benjamin Moore & Co., 13; 38 (upd.)
Benton Oil and Gas Company, 47
Berean Christian Stores, 96
Bergdorf Goodman Inc., 52
Bergen Brunswig Corporation, V; 13 (upd.)
Berger Bros Company, 62
Beringer Blass Wine Estates Ltd., 66 (upd.)
Beringer Wine Estates Holdings, Inc., 22
Berkeley Farms, Inc., 46
Berkshire Hathaway Inc., III; 18 (upd.); 42 (upd.); 89 (upd.)
Berkshire Realty Holdings, L.P., 49
Berlex Laboratories, Inc., 66
Berlitz International, Inc., 13; 39 (upd.)
Bernard C. Harris Publishing Company, Inc., 39
Bernard Chaus, Inc., 27
Bernard Hodes Group Inc., 86
The Bernick Companies, 75
Bernstein-Rein, 92
Berry Petroleum Company, 47
Berry Plastics Corporation, 21
Bertucci's Corporation, 16; 64 (upd.)
Berwick Offray, LLC, 70
Best Buy Co., Inc., 9; 23 (upd.); 63 (upd.)
Best Kosher Foods Corporation, 82
Bestfoods, 22 (upd.)
BET Holdings, Inc., 18
Beth Abraham Family of Health Services, 94
Bethlehem Steel Corporation, IV; 7 (upd.); 27 (upd.)
Better Made Snack Foods, Inc., 90
Betz Laboratories, Inc., I; 10 (upd.)
Beverly Enterprises, Inc., III; 16 (upd.)
The BFGoodrich Company, V; 19 (upd.)
BG Products Inc., 96
BHC Communications, Inc., 26
Bianchi International (d/b/a Gregory Mountain Products), 76
BIC Corporation, 8; 23 (upd.)
Bicoastal Corporation, II
Big A Drug Stores Inc. 79
Big B, Inc., 17
Big Bear Stores Co., 13
Big Brothers Big Sisters of America, 85
Big Dog Holdings, Inc., 45
Big 5 Sporting Goods Corporation, 55
Big Flower Press Holdings, Inc., 21
Big Idea Productions, Inc., 49
Big Lots, Inc., 50
Big O Tires, Inc., 20
Big Rivers Electric Corporation, 11
Big V Supermarkets, Inc., 25
Big Y Foods, Inc., 53
Bill & Melinda Gates Foundation, 41
Bill Barrett Corporation, 71
Bill Blass Ltd., 32
Billing Concepts Corp., 26
Billing Concepts, Inc., 72 (upd.)
Bindley Western Industries, Inc., 9
The Bing Group, 60
Bingham Dana LLP, 43
Binks Sames Corporation, 21
Binney & Smith Inc., 25
Bio-Rad Laboratories, Inc., 93
Biogen Idec Inc., 71 (upd.)
Biogen Inc., 14; 36 (upd.)
Biolase Technology, Inc., 87
Biomet, Inc., 10; 93 (upd.
Biosite Incorporated, 73
Bird Corporation, 19
Birds Eye Foods, Inc., 69 (upd.)
Birkenstock Footprint Sandals, Inc., 12; 42 (upd.)
Birmingham Steel Corporation, 13; 40 (upd.)
BISSELL Inc., 9; 30 (upd.)
The BISYS Group, Inc., 73
BJ Services Company, 25
BJ's Wholesale Club, Inc., 94
BKD LLP, 96
The Black & Decker Corporation, III; 20 (upd.); 67 (upd.)
Black & Veatch LLP, 22
Black Box Corporation, 20; 96 (upd.)
Black Diamond Equipment, Ltd., 62
Black Hills Corporation, 20
Blackbaud, Inc., 85

Blackboard Inc., 89
Blackfoot Telecommunications Group, 60
BlackRock, Inc. 79
Blackwater USA, 76
Blair Corporation, 25; 31
Blessings Corp., 19
Blimpie International, Inc., 15; 49 (upd.)
Blish-Mize Co., 95
Blizzard Entertainment 78
Block Communications, Inc., 81
Block Drug Company, Inc., 8; 27 (upd.)
Blockbuster Inc., 9; 31 (upd.); 76 (upd.)
Blodgett Holdings, Inc., 61 (upd.)
Blonder Tongue Laboratories, Inc., 48
Bloomberg L.P., 21
Bloomingdale's Inc., 12
Blount International, Inc., 12; 48 (upd.)
Blue Bell Creameries L.P., 30
Blue Bird Corporation, 35
Blue Coat Systems, Inc., 83
Blue Cross and Blue Shield Association, 10
Blue Diamond Growers, 28
Blue Heron Paper Company, 90
Blue Martini Software, Inc., 59
Blue Mountain Arts, Inc., 29
Blue Nile Inc., 61
Blue Rhino Corporation, 56
Blue Ridge Beverage Company Inc., 82
Bluefly, Inc., 60
Bluegreen Corporation, 80
BlueLinx Holdings Inc., 97
Blyth, Inc., 18; 74 (upd.)
BMC Industries, Inc., 17; 59 (upd.)
BMC Software, Inc., 55
Boardwalk Pipeline Partners, LP, 87
Boart Longyear Company, 26
Boatmen's Bancshares Inc., 15
Bob Evans Farms, Inc., 9; 63 (upd.)
Bob's Red Mill Natural Foods, Inc., 63
Bobit Publishing Company, 55
Bobs Candies, Inc., 70
Boca Resorts, Inc., 37
Boddie-Noell Enterprises, Inc., 68
Body Glove International LLC, 88
The Boeing Company, I; 10 (upd.); 32 (upd.)
Bogen Communications International, Inc., 62
Bohemia, Inc., 13
Boise Cascade Holdings, L.L.C., IV; 8 (upd.); 32 (upd.); 95 (upd.)
Bojangles Restaurants Inc., 97
Bollinger Shipyards, Inc., 61
The Bombay Company, Inc., 10; 71 (upd.)
The Bon Marché, Inc., 23
Bon Secours Health System, Inc., 24
The Bon-Ton Stores, Inc., 16; 50 (upd.)
Bonneville International Corporation, 29
Bonneville Power Administration, 50
Book-of-the-Month Club, Inc., 13
Books-A-Million, Inc., 14; 41 (upd.); 96 (upd.)
Bookspan, 86
Boole & Babbage, Inc., 25
Booth Creek Ski Holdings, Inc., 31
Boots & Coots International Well Control, Inc. 79
Booz Allen & Hamilton Inc., 10
Borden, Inc., II; 22 (upd.)
Borders Group, Inc., 15; 43 (upd.)
Borg-Warner Corporation, III
BorgWarner Inc., 14; 32 (upd.); 85 (upd.)
Borland International, Inc., 9
Boron, LePore & Associates, Inc., 45
Boscov's Department Store, Inc., 31
Bose Corporation, 13; 36 (upd.)
Boss Holdings, Inc., 97
Boston Acoustics, Inc., 22
The Boston Beer Company, Inc., 18; 50 (upd.)
Boston Celtics Limited Partnership, 14
The Boston Consulting Group, 58
Boston Edison Company, 12
Boston Market Corporation, 12; 48 (upd.)
Boston Professional Hockey Association Inc., 39
Boston Properties, Inc., 22
Boston Scientific Corporation, 37; 77 (upd.)
The Boston Symphony Orchestra Inc., 93
Bou-Matic, 62
Bowne & Co., Inc., 23; 79 (upd.)
The Boy Scouts of America, 34
Boyd Bros. Transportation Inc., 39
Boyd Coffee Company, 53
Boyd Gaming Corporation, 43
The Boyds Collection, Ltd., 29
Boyne USA Resorts, 71
Boys & Girls Clubs of America, 69
Bozell Worldwide Inc., 25
Bozzuto's, Inc., 13
Brach and Brock Confections, Inc., 15
Brach's Confections, Inc., 74 (upd.)
Bradlees Discount Department Store Company, 12
Brady Corporation 78 (upd.)
The Branch Group, Inc., 72
BrandPartners Group, Inc., 58
Brannock Device Company, 48
Brasfield & Gorrie LLC, 87
Brass Eagle Inc., 34
Brazos Sportswear, Inc., 23
Breeze-Eastern Corporation, 95
Bremer Financial Corp., 45
Briazz, Inc., 53
The Brickman Group, Ltd., 87
Bridgeport Machines, Inc., 17
Bridgford Foods Corporation, 27
Briggs & Stratton Corporation, 8; 27 (upd.)
Brigham Exploration Company, 75
Brigham's Inc., 72
Bright Horizons Family Solutions, Inc., 31
Brightpoint, Inc., 18
Brillstein-Grey Entertainment, 80
The Brink's Company, 58 (upd.)
Brinker International, Inc., 10; 38 (upd.); 75 (upd.)
Bristol Hotel Company, 23
Bristol-Myers Squibb Company, III; 9 (upd.); 37 (upd.)
Brite Voice Systems, Inc., 20
Broadcast Music Inc., 23; 90 (upd.)
Broadcom Corporation, 34; 90 (upd.)
The Broadmoor Hotel, 30
Broadwing Corporation, 70
Brobeck, Phleger & Harrison, LLP, 31
Brodart Company, 84
Broder Bros. Co., 38
Broderbund Software, Inc., 13; 29 (upd.)
Bronco Drilling Company, Inc., 89
Bronner Brothers Inc., 92
Bronner Display & Sign Advertising, Inc., 82
Brookdale Senior Living, 91
Brooke Group Ltd., 15
Brooklyn Union Gas, 6
Brooks Brothers Inc., 22
Brooks Sports Inc., 32
Brookshire Grocery Company, 16; 74 (upd.)
Brookstone, Inc., 18
Brother's Brother Foundation, 93
Brothers Gourmet Coffees, Inc., 20
Broughton Foods Co., 17
Brown & Brown, Inc., 41
Brown & Haley, 23
Brown & Root, Inc., 13
Brown & Sharpe Manufacturing Co., 23
Brown & Williamson Tobacco Corporation, 14; 33 (upd.)
Brown Brothers Harriman & Co., 45
Brown Jordan International Inc., 74 (upd.)
Brown Printing Company, 26
Brown Shoe Company, Inc., V; 20 (upd.); 68 (upd.)
Brown-Forman Corporation, I; 10 (upd.); 38 (upd.)
Browning-Ferris Industries, Inc., V; 20 (upd.)
Broyhill Furniture Industries, Inc., 10
Bruce Foods Corporation, 39
Bruegger's Corporation, 63
Bruno's Supermarkets, Inc., 7; 26 (upd.); 68 (upd.)
Brunschwig & Fils Inc., 96
Brunswick Corporation, III; 22 (upd.); 77 (upd.)
Brush Engineered Materials Inc., 67
Brush Wellman Inc., 14
Bruster's Real Ice Cream, Inc., 80
BTG, Inc., 45
Buca, Inc., 38
Buck Consultants, Inc., 55
Buck Knives Inc., 48
Buckeye Partners, L.P., 70
Buckeye Technologies, Inc., 42
The Buckle, Inc., 18
Bucyrus International, Inc., 17
The Budd Company, 8
Budget Group, Inc., 25
Budget Rent a Car Corporation, 9
Buffalo Wild Wings, Inc., 56
Buffets Holdings, Inc., 10; 32 (upd.); 93 (upd.)
Bugle Boy Industries, Inc., 18
Build-A-Bear Workshop Inc., 62
Building Materials Holding Corporation, 52

Bulley & Andrews, LLC, 55
Bulova Corporation, 13; 41 (upd.)
Bumble Bee Seafoods L.L.C., 64
Bundy Corporation, 17
Bunge Ltd., 62
Burdines, Inc., 60
The Bureau of National Affairs, Inc., 23
Burger King Corporation, II; 17 (upd.); 56 (upd.)
Burgett, Inc., 97
Burke, Inc., 88
Burke Mills, Inc., 66
Burlington Coat Factory Warehouse Corporation, 10; 60 (upd.)
Burlington Industries, Inc., V; 17 (upd.)
Burlington Northern Santa Fe Corporation, V; 27 (upd.)
Burlington Resources Inc., 10
Burns International Services Corporation, 13; 41 (upd.)
Burr-Brown Corporation, 19
Burroughs & Chapin Company, Inc., 86
Burt's Bees, Inc., 58
The Burton Corporation, 22; 94 (upd.)
Busch Entertainment Corporation, 73
Bush Boake Allen Inc., 30
Bush Brothers & Company, 45
Bush Industries, Inc., 20
Business Men's Assurance Company of America, 14
Butler Manufacturing Company, 12; 62 (upd.)
Butterick Co., Inc., 23
Buttrey Food & Drug Stores Co., 18
buy.com, Inc., 46
BWAY Corporation, 24
C&K Market, Inc., 81
C & S Wholesale Grocers, Inc., 55
C-COR.net Corp., 38
C-Cube Microsystems, Inc., 37
C.F. Martin & Co., Inc., 42
The C.F. Sauer Company, 90
C.H. Guenther & Son, Inc., 84
C.H. Heist Corporation, 24
C.H. Robinson Worldwide, Inc., 11; 40 (upd.)
C.R. Bard, Inc., 9; 65 (upd.)
C.R. Meyer and Sons Company, 74
C-Tech Industries Inc., 90
Cabela's Inc., 26; 68 (upd.)
Cabletron Systems, Inc., 10
Cablevision Electronic Instruments, Inc., 32
Cablevision Systems Corporation, 7; 30 (upd.)
Cabot Corporation, 8; 29 (upd.); 91 (upd.)
Cache Incorporated, 30
CACI International Inc., 21; 72 (upd.)
Cactus Feeders, Inc., 91
Cadence Design Systems, Inc., 11; 48 (upd.)
Cadmus Communications Corporation, 23
Cadwalader, Wickersham & Taft, 32
CAE USA Inc., 48
Caere Corporation, 20
Caesars World, Inc., 6
Cagle's, Inc., 20
Cahners Business Information, 43
Cal-Maine Foods, Inc., 69
CalAmp Corp., 87
Calavo Growers, Inc., 47
CalComp Inc., 13
Calcot Ltd., 33
Caldor Inc., 12
Calgon Carbon Corporation, 73
California Cedar Products Company, 58
California Pizza Kitchen Inc., 15; 74 (upd.)
California Sports, Inc., 56
California Steel Industries, Inc., 67
California Water Service Group 79
Caliper Life Sciences, Inc., 70
Callanan Industries, Inc., 60
Callard and Bowser-Suchard Inc., 84
Callaway Golf Company, 15; 45 (upd.)
Callon Petroleum Company, 47
Calloway's Nursery, Inc., 51
CalMat Co., 19
Calpine Corporation, 36
Caltex Petroleum Corporation, 19
Calvin Klein, Inc., 22; 55 (upd.)
Cambrex Corporation, 16; 44 (upd.)
Cambridge SoundWorks, Inc., 48
Cambridge Technology Partners, Inc., 36
Camden Property Trust, 77
Camelot Music, Inc., 26
Cameron & Barkley Company, 28
Campbell-Ewald Advertising, 86
Campbell-Mithun-Esty, Inc., 16
Campbell Scientific, Inc., 51
Campbell Soup Company, II; 7 (upd.); 26 (upd.); 71 (upd.)
Campo Electronics, Appliances & Computers, Inc., 16
Canandaigua Brands, Inc., 13; 34 (upd.)
Cancer Treatment Centers of America, Inc., 85
Candela Corporation, 48
Candie's, Inc., 31
Candle Corporation, 64
Candlewood Hotel Company, Inc., 41
Cannon Design, 63
Cannon Express, Inc., 53
Cannondale Corporation, 21
Cano Petroleum Inc., 97
Cantel Medical Corporation, 80
Canterbury Park Holding Corporation, 42
Cantor Fitzgerald, L.P., 92
Cap Rock Energy Corporation, 46
Cape Cod Potato Chip Company, 90
Capel Incorporated, 45
Capezio/Ballet Makers Inc., 62
Capital Cities/ABC Inc., II
Capital Holding Corporation, III
Capital One Financial Corporation, 52
Capitol Records, Inc., 90
Capital Senior Living Corporation, 75
CapStar Hotel Company, 21
Capstone Turbine Corporation, 75
Captain D's, LLC, 59
Captaris, Inc., 89
Car Toys, Inc., 67
Caraustar Industries, Inc., 19; 44 (upd.)
The Carbide/Graphite Group, Inc., 40
Carborundum Company, 15
Cardinal Health, Inc., 18; 50 (upd.)
Cardone Industries Inc., 92
Cardtronics, Inc., 93
Career Education Corporation, 45
CareerBuilder, Inc., 93
Caremark Rx, Inc., 10; 54 (upd.)
Carey International, Inc., 26
Cargill, Incorporated, II; 13 (upd.); 40 (upd.); 89 (upd.)
Carhartt, Inc., 30; 77 (upd.)
Caribiner International, Inc., 24
Caribou Coffee Company, Inc., 28; 97 (upd.)
Carlisle Companies Inc., 8; 82 (upd.)
Carlson Companies, Inc., 6; 22 (upd.); 87 (upd.)
Carlson Restaurants Worldwide, 69
Carlson Wagonlit Travel, 55
Carma Laboratories, Inc., 60
CarMax, Inc., 55
Carmichael Lynch Inc., 28
Carmike Cinemas, Inc., 14; 37 (upd.); 74 (upd.)
Carnation Company, II
Carnegie Corporation of New York, 35
Carnival Corporation, 6; 27 (upd.); 78 (upd.)
Carolina First Corporation, 31
Carolina Freight Corporation, 6
Carolina Power & Light Company, V; 23 (upd.)
Carolina Telephone and Telegraph Company, 10
Carpenter Technology Corporation, 13; 95 (upd.)
CARQUEST Corporation, 29
Carr-Gottstein Foods Co., 17
CarrAmerica Realty Corporation, 56
The Carriage House Companies, Inc., 55
Carriage Services, Inc., 37
Carrier Access Corporation, 44
Carrier Corporation, 7; 69 (upd.)
Carrizo Oil & Gas, Inc., 97
Carroll's Foods, Inc., 46
Carrols Restaurant Group, Inc., 92
The Carsey-Werner Company, L.L.C., 37
Carson Pirie Scott & Company, 15
Carson, Inc., 31
Carter Hawley Hale Stores, Inc., V
Carter Lumber Company, 45
Carter-Wallace, Inc., 8; 38 (upd.)
Carus Publishing Company, 93
Carvel Corporation, 35
Carver Bancorp, Inc., 94
Carver Boat Corporation LLC, 88
Carvin Corp., 89
Cascade Corporation, 65
Cascade General, Inc., 65
Cascade Natural Gas Corporation, 9
Casco Northern Bank, 14
Casey's General Stores, Inc., 19; 83 (upd.)
Cash America International, Inc., 20; 61 (upd.)
Cash Systems, Inc., 93
Castle & Cooke, Inc., II; 20 (upd.)
Casual Corner Group, Inc., 43
Casual Male Retail Group, Inc., 52

Caswell-Massey Co. Ltd., 51
Catalina Lighting, Inc., 43 (upd.)
Catalina Marketing Corporation, 18
Catalytica Energy Systems, Inc., 44
Catellus Development Corporation, 24
Caterpillar Inc., III; 15 (upd.); 63 (upd.)
Catherines Stores Corporation, 15
Catholic Charities USA, 76
Catholic Health Initiatives, 91
Catholic Order of Foresters, 24; 97 (upd.)
Cato Corporation, 14
Cattleman's, Inc., 20
Cavco Industries, Inc., 65
CB Commercial Real Estate Services Group, Inc., 21
CB Richard Ellis Group, Inc., 70 (upd.)
CBI Industries, Inc., 7
CBRL Group, Inc., 35 (upd.); 86 (upd.)
CBS Corporation, II; 6 (upd.); 28 (upd.)
CBS Television Network, 66 (upd.)
CCA Industries, Inc., 53
CCC Information Services Group Inc., 74
CCH Inc., 14
CDI Corporation, 6; 54 (upd.)
CDW Computer Centers, Inc., 16; 52 (upd.)
CEC Entertainment, Inc., 31 (upd.)
Cedar Fair, L.P., 22
Celadon Group Inc., 30
Celanese Corporation, I
Celebrate Express, Inc., 70
Celebrity, Inc., 22
Celera Genomics, 74
Celestial Seasonings, Inc., 16
Celgene Corporation, 67
CellStar Corporation, 83
Cendant Corporation, 44 (upd.)
Centel Corporation, 6
Centennial Communications Corporation, 39
Centerior Energy Corporation, V
Centerplate, Inc. 79
Centex Corporation, 8; 29 (upd.)
Centocor Inc., 14
Central and South West Corporation, V
Central European Distribution Corporation, 75
Central Florida Investments, Inc., 93
Central Garden & Pet Company, 23; 58 (upd.)
Central Hudson Gas and Electricity Corporation, 6
Central Maine Power, 6
Central National-Gottesman Inc., 95
Central Newspapers, Inc., 10
Central Parking Corporation, 18
Central Soya Company, Inc., 7
Central Sprinkler Corporation, 29
Central Vermont Public Service Corporation, 54
Centuri Corporation, 54
Century Aluminum Company, 52
Century Business Services, Inc., 52
Century Casinos, Inc., 53
Century Communications Corp., 10
Century Telephone Enterprises, Inc., 9; 54 (upd.)
Century Theatres, Inc., 31
Cenveo Inc., 71 (upd.)
Cephalon, Inc., 45
Cepheid, 77
Ceradyne, Inc., 65
Cerner Corporation, 16; 94 (upd.)
CertainTeed Corporation, 35
Certegy, Inc., 63
Cessna Aircraft Company, 8; 27 (upd.)
Chadbourne & Parke, 36
Chadwick's of Boston, Ltd., 29
The Chalone Wine Group, Ltd., 36
Champion Enterprises, Inc., 17
Champion Industries, Inc., 28
Champion International Corporation, IV; 20 (upd.)
Championship Auto Racing Teams, Inc., 37
Chancellor Beacon Academies, Inc., 53
Chancellor Media Corporation, 24
Chaparral Steel Co., 13
Charisma Brands LLC, 74
The Charles Machine Works, Inc., 64
Charles River Laboratories International, Inc., 42
The Charles Schwab Corporation, 8; 26 (upd.); 81 (upd.)
The Charles Stark Draper Laboratory, Inc., 35
Charlotte Russe Holding, Inc., 35; 90 (upd.)
The Charmer Sunbelt Group, 95
Charming Shoppes, Inc., 8; 38
Chart House Enterprises, Inc., 17
Chart Industries, Inc., 21; 96 (upd.)
Charter Communications, Inc., 33
ChartHouse International Learning Corporation, 49
Chas. Levy Company LLC, 60
Chase General Corporation, 91
The Chase Manhattan Corporation, II; 13 (upd.)
Chateau Communities, Inc., 37
Chattanooga Bakery, Inc., 86
Chattem, Inc., 17; 88 (upd.)
Chautauqua Airlines, Inc., 38
Checker Motors Corp., 89
Checkers Drive-In Restaurants, Inc., 16; 74 (upd.)
CheckFree Corporation, 81
Checkpoint Systems, Inc., 39
The Cheesecake Factory Inc., 17
Chef Solutions, Inc., 89
Chelsea Milling Company, 29
Chelsea Piers Management Inc., 86
Chemcentral Corporation, 8
Chemed Corporation, 13
Chemfab Corporation, 35
Chemi-Trol Chemical Co., 16
Chemical Banking Corporation, II; 14 (upd.)
Chemical Waste Management, Inc., 9
Chemtura Corporation, 91 (upd.)
CHEP Pty. Ltd., 80
Cherokee Inc., 18
Cherry Lane Music Publishing Company, Inc., 62
Chesapeake Corporation, 8; 30 (upd.); 93 (upd.)
Chesapeake Utilities Corporation, 56
Chesebrough-Pond's USA, Inc., 8
ChevronTexaco Corporation, IV; 19 (upd.); 47 (upd.)
Cheyenne Software, Inc., 12
CHF Industries, Inc., 84
Chi-Chi's Inc., 13; 51 (upd.)
Chiasso Inc., 53
Chiat/Day Inc. Advertising, 11
Chic by H.I.S, Inc., 20
Chicago and North Western Holdings Corporation, 6
Chicago Bears Football Club, Inc., 33
Chicago Board of Trade, 41
Chicago Mercantile Exchange Holdings Inc., 75
Chicago National League Ball Club, Inc., 66
Chicago Review Press Inc., 84
Chick-fil-A Inc., 23; 90 (upd.)
Chicken of the Sea International, 24 (upd.)
Chico's FAS, Inc., 45
Children's Comprehensive Services, Inc., 42
Children's Hospitals and Clinics, Inc., 54
The Children's Place Retail Stores, Inc., 37; 86 (upd.)
ChildrenFirst, Inc., 59
Childtime Learning Centers, Inc., 34
Chiles Offshore Corporation, 9
Chipotle Mexican Grill, Inc., 67
CHIPS and Technologies, Inc., 9
Chiquita Brands International, Inc., 7; 21 (upd.); 83 (upd.)
Chiron Corporation, 10; 36 (upd.)
Chisholm-Mingo Group, Inc., 41
Chittenden & Eastman Company, 58
Chock Full o' Nuts Corp., 17
Choice Hotels International Inc., 14; 83 (upd.)
ChoicePoint Inc., 65
Chorus Line Corporation, 30
Chris-Craft Corporation, 9; 31 (upd.); 80 (upd.)
Christensen Boyles Corporation, 26
The Christian Broadcasting Network, Inc., 52
The Christian Science Publishing Society, 55
Christopher & Banks Corporation, 42
Chromcraft Revington, Inc., 15
The Chronicle Publishing Company, Inc., 23
Chronimed Inc., 26
Chrysler Corporation, I; 11 (upd.)
CHS Inc., 60
CH2M HILL Companies Ltd., 22; 96 (upd.)
The Chubb Corporation, III; 14 (upd.); 37 (upd.)
Chugach Alaska Corporation, 60
Church & Dwight Co., Inc., 29; 68 (upd.)
Church's Chicken, 66
Churchill Downs Incorporated, 29
Cianbro Corporation, 14
Ciber, Inc., 18

CIENA Corporation, 54
CIGNA Corporation, III; 22 (upd.); 45 (upd.)
Cimarex Energy Co., 81
Cincinnati Bell, Inc., 6
Cincinnati Financial Corporation, 16; 44 (upd.)
Cincinnati Gas & Electric Company, 6
Cincinnati Lamb Inc., 72
Cincinnati Milacron Inc., 12
Cincom Systems Inc., 15
Cinemark Holdings, Inc., 95
Cinnabon, Inc., 23; 90 (upd.)
Cintas Corporation, 21; 51 (upd.)
CIPSCO Inc., 6
The Circle K Company, II; 20 (upd.)
Circon Corporation, 21
Circuit City Stores, Inc., 9; 29 (upd.); 65 (upd.)
Circus Circus Enterprises, Inc., 6
Cirrus Design Corporation, 44
Cirrus Logic, Inc., 11; 48 (upd.)
Cisco-Linksys LLC, 86
Cisco Systems, Inc., 11; 34 (upd.); 77 (upd.)
CIT Group Inc., 76
Citadel Communications Corporation, 35
Citfed Bancorp, Inc., 16
CITGO Petroleum Corporation, IV; 31 (upd.)
Citi Trends, Inc., 80
Citicorp Diners Club, Inc., 90
Citigroup Inc., II; 9 (upd.); 30 (upd.); 59 (upd.)
Citizens Communications Company 7; 79 (upd.)
Citizens Financial Group, Inc., 42; 87 (upd.)
Citrix Systems, Inc., 44
City Brewing Company LLC, 73
City Public Service, 6
CKE Restaurants, Inc., 19; 46 (upd.)
Claire's Stores, Inc., 17; 94 (upd.)
CLARCOR Inc., 17; 61 (upd.)
Clare Rose Inc., 68
The Clark Construction Group, Inc., 8
Clark Equipment Company, 8
Classic Vacation Group, Inc., 46
Clayton Homes Incorporated, 13; 54 (upd.)
Clayton Williams Energy, Inc., 87
Clean Harbors, Inc., 73
Clear Channel Communications, Inc., 23
Clearwire, Inc., 69
Cleary, Gottlieb, Steen & Hamilton, 35
Cleco Corporation, 37
The Clemens Family Corporation, 93
Clement Pappas & Company, Inc., 92
Cleveland Indians Baseball Company, Inc., 37
Cleveland-Cliffs Inc., 13; 62 (upd.)
Click Wine Group, 68
Clif Bar Inc., 50
The Clorox Company, III; 22 (upd.); 81 (upd.)
The Clothestime, Inc., 20
Clougherty Packing Company, 72
ClubCorp, Inc., 33
CMG Worldwide, Inc., 89
CMGI, Inc., 76
CML Group, Inc., 10
CMP Media Inc., 26
CMS Energy Corporation, V, 14
CNA Financial Corporation, III; 38 (upd.)
CNET Networks, Inc., 47
CNS, Inc., 20
Coach, Inc., 10; 45 (upd.)
Coach USA, Inc., 24; 55 (upd.)
Coachmen Industries, Inc., 77
The Coastal Corporation, IV, 31 (upd.)
COBE Cardiovascular, Inc., 61
COBE Laboratories, Inc., 13
Coborn's, Inc., 30
Cobra Electronics Corporation, 14
Cobra Golf Inc., 16
Coca Cola Bottling Co. Consolidated, 10
The Coca-Cola Company, I; 10 (upd.); 32 (upd.); 67 (upd.)
Coca-Cola Enterprises, Inc., 13
Coeur d'Alene Mines Corporation, 20
The Coffee Beanery, Ltd., 95
Coffee Holding Co., Inc., 95
Cogent Communications Group, Inc., 55
Cogentrix Energy, Inc., 10
Cognex Corporation, 76
Cognizant Technology Solutions Corporation, 59
Coherent, Inc., 31
Cohu, Inc., 32
Coinmach Laundry Corporation, 20
Coinstar, Inc., 44
Cold Spring Granite Company, 16
Cold Spring Granite Company Inc., 67 (upd.)
Cold Stone Creamery, 69
Coldwater Creek Inc., 21; 74 (upd.)
Cole National Corporation, 13; 76 (upd.)
Cole's Quality Foods, Inc., 68
The Coleman Company, Inc., 9; 30 (upd.)
Coleman Natural Products, Inc., 68
Coles Express Inc., 15
Colfax Corporation, 58
Colgate-Palmolive Company, III; 14 (upd.); 35 (upd.); 71 (upd.)
Collectors Universe, Inc., 48
Colliers International Property Consultants Inc., 92
Collins & Aikman Corporation, 13; 41 (upd.)
Collins Industries, Inc., 33
Colonial Properties Trust, 65
Colonial Williamsburg Foundation, 53
Color Kinetics Incorporated, 85
Colorado Baseball Management, Inc., 72
Colorado MEDtech, Inc., 48
Colt Industries Inc., I
Colt's Manufacturing Company, Inc., 12
Columbia Forest Products Inc., 78
The Columbia Gas System, Inc., V; 16 (upd.)
Columbia House Company, 69
Columbia Sportswear Company, 19; 41 (upd.)
Columbia TriStar Motion Pictures Companies, II; 12 (upd.)
Columbia/HCA Healthcare Corporation, 15
Columbus McKinnon Corporation, 37
Comair Holdings Inc., 13; 34 (upd.)
Combe Inc., 72
Comcast Corporation, 7; 24 (upd.)
Comdial Corporation, 21
Comdisco, Inc., 9
Comerica Incorporated, 40
COMFORCE Corporation, 40
Command Security Corporation, 57
Commerce Clearing House, Inc., 7
Commercial Credit Company, 8
Commercial Federal Corporation, 12; 62 (upd.)
Commercial Financial Services, Inc., 26
Commercial Metals Company, 15; 42 (upd.)
Commercial Vehicle Group, Inc., 81
Commodore International Ltd., 7
Commonwealth Edison Company, V
Commonwealth Energy System, 14
Commonwealth Telephone Enterprises, Inc., 25
CommScope, Inc., 77
Community Coffee Co. L.L.C., 53
Community Health Systems, Inc., 71
Community Newspaper Holdings, Inc., 91
Community Psychiatric Centers, 15
Compaq Computer Corporation, III; 6 (upd.); 26 (upd.)
Compass Bancshares, Inc., 73
Compass Minerals International, Inc. 79
CompDent Corporation, 22
CompHealth Inc., 25
Complete Business Solutions, Inc., 31
Comprehensive Care Corporation, 15
CompuAdd Computer Corporation, 11
CompuCom Systems, Inc., 10
CompuDyne Corporation, 51
CompUSA, Inc., 10; 35 (upd.)
CompuServe Interactive Services, Inc., 10; 27 (upd.)
Computer Associates International, Inc., 6; 49 (upd.)
Computer Data Systems, Inc., 14
Computer Learning Centers, Inc., 26
Computer Sciences Corporation, 6
Computerland Corp., 13
Computervision Corporation, 10
Compuware Corporation, 10; 30 (upd.); 66 (upd.)
Comsat Corporation, 23
Comshare Inc., 23
Comstock Resources, Inc., 47
Comtech Telecommunications Corp., 75
Comverse Technology, Inc., 15; 43 (upd.)
ConAgra Foods, Inc., II; 12 (upd.); 42 (upd.); 85 (upd.)
Conair Corporation, 17; 69 (upd.)
Concentra Inc., 71
Concepts Direct, Inc., 39
Concord Camera Corporation, 41
Concord EFS, Inc., 52
Concord Fabrics, Inc., 16

Concurrent Computer Corporation, 75
Condé Nast Publications, Inc., 13; 59 (upd.)
Cone Mills LLC, 8; 67 (upd.)
Conexant Systems, Inc., 36
Confluence Holdings Corporation, 76
Congoleum Corp., 18
CONMED Corporation, 87
Conn's, Inc., 67
Conn-Selmer, Inc., 55
Connecticut Light and Power Co., 13
Connecticut Mutual Life Insurance Company, III
The Connell Company, 29
Conner Peripherals, Inc., 6
Connetics Corporation, 70
ConocoPhillips, IV; 16 (upd.); 63 (upd.)
Conrad Industries, Inc., 58
Conseco, Inc., 10; 33 (upd.)
Conso International Corporation, 29
CONSOL Energy Inc., 59
Consolidated Delivery & Logistics, Inc., 24
Consolidated Edison, Inc., V; 45 (upd.)
Consolidated Freightways Corporation, V; 21 (upd.); 48 (upd.)
Consolidated Graphics, Inc., 70
Consolidated Natural Gas Company, V; 19 (upd.)
Consolidated Papers, Inc., 8; 36 (upd.)
Consolidated Products Inc., 14
Consolidated Rail Corporation, V
Constar International Inc., 64
Constellation Brands, Inc., 68 (upd.)
Consumers Power Co., 14
Consumers Union, 26
Consumers Water Company, 14
The Container Store, 36
ContiGroup Companies, Inc., 43 (upd.)
Continental Airlines, Inc., I; 21 (upd.); 52 (upd.)
Continental Bank Corporation, II
Continental Cablevision, Inc., 7
Continental Can Co., Inc., 15
The Continental Corporation, III
Continental General Tire Corp., 23
Continental Grain Company, 10; 13 (upd.)
Continental Group Company, I
Continental Medical Systems, Inc., 10
Continental Resources, Inc., 89
Continuum Health Partners, Inc., 60
Control Data Corporation, III
Control Data Systems, Inc., 10
Converse Inc., 9; 31 (upd.)
Cooker Restaurant Corporation, 20; 51 (upd.)
CoolSavings, Inc., 77
Cooper Cameron Corporation, 20 (upd.); 58 (upd.)
The Cooper Companies, Inc., 39
Cooper Industries, Inc., II; 44 (upd.)
Cooper Tire & Rubber Company, 8; 23 (upd.)
Coopers & Lybrand, 9
Copart Inc., 23
The Copley Press, Inc., 23
The Copps Corporation, 32
Corbis Corporation, 31
The Corcoran Group, Inc., 58
Cordis Corporation, 19; 46 (upd.)
CoreStates Financial Corp, 17
Corinthian Colleges, Inc., 39; 92 (upd.)
Corning Inc., III; 44 (upd.); 90 (upd.)
The Corporate Executive Board Company, 89
Corporate Express, Inc., 22; 47 (upd.)
Corporate Software Inc., 9
Corporation for Public Broadcasting, 14; 89 (upd.)
Correctional Services Corporation, 30
Corrections Corporation of America, 23
Corrpro Companies, Inc., 20
CORT Business Services Corporation, 26
Corus Bankshares, Inc., 75
Cosi, Inc., 53
Cosmair, Inc., 8
The Cosmetic Center, Inc., 22
Cosmolab Inc., 96
Cost Plus, Inc., 27
Cost-U-Less, Inc., 51
CoStar Group, Inc., 73
Costco Wholesale Corporation, V; 43 (upd.)
Cotter & Company, V
Cotton Incorporated, 46
Coty, Inc., 36
Coudert Brothers, 30
Council on International Educational Exchange Inc., 81
Country Kitchen International, Inc., 76
Countrywide Credit Industries, Inc., 16
County Seat Stores Inc., 9
Courier Corporation, 41
Cousins Properties Incorporated, 65
Covance Inc., 30
Covanta Energy Corporation, 64 (upd.)
Coventry Health Care, Inc., 59
Covington & Burling, 40
Cowen Group, Inc., 92
Cowles Media Company, 23
Cox Enterprises, Inc., IV; 22 (upd.); 67 (upd.)
Cox Radio, Inc., 89
CPAC, Inc., 86
CPC International Inc., II
CPI Aerostructures, Inc., 75
CPI Corp., 38
CR England, Inc., 63
CRA International, Inc., 93
Cracker Barrel Old Country Store, Inc., 10
Craftmade International, Inc., 44
craigslist, inc., 89
Crain Communications, Inc., 12; 35 (upd.)
Cramer, Berkowitz & Co., 34
Crane & Co., Inc., 26
Crane Co., 8; 30 (upd.)
Cranium, Inc., 69
Crate and Barrel, 9
Cravath, Swaine & Moore, 43
Crawford & Company, 87
Cray Inc., 75 (upd.)
Cray Research, Inc., III; 16 (upd.)
Creative Artists Agency LLC, 38
Credence Systems Corporation, 90
Credit Acceptance Corporation, 18
Cree Inc., 53
Crete Carrier Corporation, 95
Crispin Porter + Bogusky, 83
Crocs, Inc., 80
Crompton Corporation, 9; 36 (upd.)
Croscill, Inc., 42
Crosman Corporation, 62
CROSSMARK 79
Crowley Maritime Corporation, 6; 28 (upd.)
Crowley, Milner & Company, 19
Crown Books Corporation, 21
Crown Central Petroleum Corporation, 7
Crown Crafts, Inc., 16
Crown Equipment Corporation, 15; 93 (upd.)
Crown Holdings, Inc., 83 (upd.)
Crown Media Holdings, Inc., 45
Crown Vantage Inc., 29
Crown, Cork & Seal Company, Inc., I; 13; 32 (upd.)
CRSS Inc., 6
Cruise America Inc., 21
CryoLife, Inc., 46
Crystal Brands, Inc., 9
CS First Boston Inc., II
CSG Systems International, Inc., 75
CSK Auto Corporation, 38
CSS Industries, Inc., 35
CSX Corporation, V; 22 (upd.); 79 (upd.)
CTB International Corporation, 43 (upd.)
CTG, Inc., 11
CTS Corporation, 39
Cubic Corporation, 19
CUC International Inc., 16
Cuisinart Corporation, 24
Cuisine Solutions Inc., 84
Culbro Corporation, 15
CulinArt, Inc., 92
Cullen/Frost Bankers, Inc., 25
Culligan Water Technologies, Inc., 12; 38 (upd.)
Culp, Inc., 29
Culver Franchising System, Inc., 58
Cumberland Farms, Inc., 17; 84 (upd.)
Cumberland Packing Corporation, 26
Cummins Engine Company, Inc., I; 12 (upd.); 40 (upd.)
Cumulus Media Inc., 37
CUNA Mutual Group, 62
Cunard Line Ltd., 23
CUNO Incorporated, 57
Current, Inc., 37
Curtice-Burns Foods, Inc., 7; 21 (upd.)
Curtiss-Wright Corporation, 10; 35 (upd.)
Curves International, Inc., 54
Cushman & Wakefield, Inc., 86
Custom Chrome, Inc., 16; 74 (upd.)
Cutera, Inc., 84
Cutter & Buck Inc., 27
CVS Corporation, 45 (upd.)
Cybermedia, Inc., 25
Cyberonics, Inc. 79
Cybex International, Inc., 49
Cygne Designs, Inc., 25
Cygnus Business Media, Inc., 56

Cymer, Inc., 77
Cypress Semiconductor Corporation, 20; 48 (upd.)
Cyprus Amax Minerals Company, 21
Cyprus Minerals Company, 7
Cyrk Inc., 19
Cystic Fibrosis Foundation, 93
Cytec Industries Inc., 27
Cytyc Corporation, 69
Czarnikow-Rionda Company, Inc., 32
D&H Distributing Co., 95
D&K Wholesale Drug, Inc., 14
D'Agostino Supermarkets Inc., 19
D'Arcy Masius Benton & Bowles, Inc., VI; 32 (upd.)
D.F. Stauffer Biscuit Company, 82
D.G. Yuengling & Son, Inc., 38
D.R. Horton, Inc., 58
Dade Behring Holdings Inc., 71
Daffy's Inc., 26
Dain Rauscher Corporation, 35 (upd.)
Dairy Farmers of America, Inc., 94
Dairy Mart Convenience Stores, Inc., 7; 25 (upd.)
Dairyland Healthcare Solutions, 73
Daisy Outdoor Products Inc., 58
Daisytek International Corporation, 18
Daktronics, Inc., 32
Dal-Tile International Inc., 22
Dale Carnegie & Associates Inc. 28; 78 (upd.)
Dallas Cowboys Football Club, Ltd., 33
Dallas Semiconductor Corporation, 13; 31 (upd.)
Dallis Coffee, Inc., 86
Damark International, Inc., 18
Dames & Moore, Inc., 25
Dan River Inc., 35; 86 (upd.)
Dana Corporation, I; 10 (upd.)
Danaher Corporation, 7; 77 (upd.)
Daniel Industries, Inc., 16
Daniel Measurement and Control, Inc., 74 (upd.)
Dannon Co., Inc., 14
Danskin, Inc., 12; 62 (upd.)
Darden Restaurants, Inc., 16; 44 (upd.)
Darigold, Inc., 9
Darling International Inc., 85
Dart Group Corporation, 16
Data Broadcasting Corporation, 31
Data General Corporation, 8
Datapoint Corporation, 11
Datascope Corporation, 39
Datek Online Holdings Corp., 32
Dauphin Deposit Corporation, 14
Dave & Buster's, Inc., 33
The Davey Tree Expert Company, 11
The David and Lucile Packard Foundation, 41
The David J. Joseph Company, 14; 76 (upd.)
David's Bridal, Inc., 33
Davis Polk & Wardwell, 36
DaVita Inc., 73
DAW Technologies, Inc., 25
Dawn Food Products, Inc., 17
Day & Zimmermann Inc., 9; 31 (upd.)
Day International, Inc., 84
Day Runner, Inc., 14; 41 (upd.)
Dayton Hudson Corporation, V; 18 (upd.)
DC Comics Inc., 25
DC Shoes, Inc., 60
DDB Needham Worldwide, 14
DDi Corp., 97
Dean & DeLuca, Inc., 36
Dean Foods Company, 7; 21 (upd.); 73 (upd.)
Dean Witter, Discover & Co., 12
Dearborn Mid-West Conveyor Company, 56
Death Row Records, 27
Deb Shops, Inc., 16; 76 (upd.)
Debevoise & Plimpton, 39
Dechert, 43
Deckers Outdoor Corporation, 22
Decora Industries, Inc., 31
Decorator Industries Inc., 68
DeCrane Aircraft Holdings Inc., 36
DeepTech International Inc., 21
Deere & Company, III; 21 (upd.); 42 (upd.)
Defiance, Inc., 22
DeKalb Genetics Corporation, 17
Del Laboratories, Inc., 28
Del Monte Foods Company, 7; 23 (upd.)
Del Taco, Inc., 58
Del Webb Corporation, 14
Delaware North Companies Inc., 7; 96 (upd.)
dELiA*s Inc., 29
Delicato Vineyards, Inc., 50
Dell Inc., 9; 31 (upd.); 63 (upd.)
Deloitte Touche Tohmatsu International, 9; 29 (upd.)
DeLorme Publishing Company, Inc., 53
Delphax Technologies Inc., 94
Delphi Automotive Systems Corporation, 45
Delta Air Lines, Inc., I; 6 (upd.); 39 (upd.); 92 (upd.)
Delta and Pine Land Company, 33; 59
Delta Woodside Industries, Inc., 8; 30 (upd.)
Deltec, Inc., 56
Deltic Timber Corporation, 46
Deluxe Corporation, 7; 22 (upd.); 73 (upd.)
DEMCO, Inc., 60
DeMoulas / Market Basket Inc., 23
DenAmerica Corporation, 29
Denbury Resources, Inc., 67
Dendrite International, Inc., 70
Denison International plc, 46
Dentsply International Inc., 10
Denver Nuggets, 51
DEP Corporation, 20
Department 56, Inc., 14; 34 (upd.)
Deposit Guaranty Corporation, 17
DePuy Inc., 30; 37 (upd.)
Deschutes Brewery, Inc., 57
Designer Holdings Ltd., 20
Destec Energy, Inc., 12
Detroit Diesel Corporation, 10; 74 (upd.)
The Detroit Edison Company, V
The Detroit Lions, Inc., 55
The Detroit Pistons Basketball Company,41
Detroit Red Wings, 74
Detroit Tigers Baseball Club, Inc., 46
Deutsch, Inc., 42
Developers Diversified Realty Corporation, 69
DeVito/Verdi, 85
Devon Energy Corporation, 61
DeVry Inc., 29; 82 (upd.)
Dewberry 78
Dewey Ballantine LLP, 48
Dex Media, Inc., 65
The Dexter Corporation, I; 12 (upd.)
DFS Group Ltd., 66
DH Technology, Inc., 18
DHB Industries Inc., 85
DHL Worldwide Express, 6; 24 (upd.)
Di Giorgio Corp., 12
Diagnostic Products Corporation, 73
The Dial Corp., 8; 23 (upd.)
Dial-A-Mattress Operating Corporation, 46
Dialogic Corporation, 18
Diamond of California, 64 (upd.)
Diamond Shamrock, Inc., IV
DiamondCluster International, Inc., 51
Dibrell Brothers, Incorporated, 12
dick clark productions, inc., 16
Dick Corporation, 64
Dick's Sporting Goods, Inc., 59
Dickten Masch Plastics LLC, 90
Dictaphone Healthcare Solutions 78
Diebold, Incorporated, 7; 22 (upd.)
Diedrich Coffee, Inc., 40
Dierbergs Markets Inc., 63
Dietz and Watson, Inc., 92
Digex, Inc., 46
Digi International Inc., 9
Digital Equipment Corporation, III; 6 (upd.)
Digital River, Inc., 50
Digitas Inc., 81
Dillard Paper Company, 11
Dillard's Inc., V; 16 (upd.); 68 (upd.)
Dillingham Construction Corporation, I; 44 (upd.)
Dillon Companies Inc., 12
Dime Savings Bank of New York, F.S.B., 9
DIMON Inc., 27
Diodes Incorporated, 81
Dionex Corporation, 46
Dippin' Dots, Inc., 56
Direct Focus, Inc., 47
Directed Electronics, Inc., 87
DIRECTV, Inc., 38; 75 (upd.)
Discount Auto Parts, Inc., 18
Discount Drug Mart, Inc., 14
Discount Tire Company Inc., 84
Discovery Communications, Inc., 42
Discovery Partners International, Inc., 58
ditech.com, 93
The Dixie Group, Inc., 20; 80 (upd.)
Dixon Industries, Inc., 26
Dixon Ticonderoga Company, 12; 69 (upd.)
DMI Furniture, Inc., 46

Do it Best Corporation, 30
Dobson Communications Corporation, 63
Doctor's Associates Inc., 67 (upd.)
The Doctors' Company, 55
Documentum, Inc., 46
Dolan Media Company, 94
Dolby Laboratories Inc., 20
Dole Food Company, Inc., 9; 31 (upd.); 68 (upd.)
Dollar Thrifty Automotive Group, Inc., 25
Dollar Tree Stores, Inc., 23; 62 (upd.)
Dominick & Dominick LLC, 92
Dominick's Finer Foods, Inc., 56
Dominion Homes, Inc., 19
Dominion Resources, Inc., V; 54 (upd.)
Domino Sugar Corporation, 26
Domino's Pizza, Inc., 7; 21 (upd.)
Domino's, Inc., 63 (upd.)
Don Massey Cadillac, Inc., 37
Donaldson Company, Inc., 16; 49 (upd.)
Donaldson, Lufkin & Jenrette, Inc., 22
Donatos Pizzeria Corporation, 58
Donna Karan International Inc., 15; 56 (upd.)
Donnelly Corporation, 12; 35 (upd.)
Donnkenny, Inc., 17
Donruss Playoff L.P., 66
Dooney & Bourke Inc., 84
Dorian Drake International Inc., 96
Dorsey & Whitney LLP, 47
Doskocil Companies, Inc., 12
Dot Foods, Inc., 69
Dot Hill Systems Corp., 93
Double-Cola Co.-USA, 70
DoubleClick Inc., 46
Doubletree Corporation, 21
Douglas & Lomason Company, 16
Dover Corporation, III; 28 (upd.); 90 (upd.)
Dover Downs Entertainment, Inc., 43
Dover Publications Inc., 34
The Dow Chemical Company, I; 8 (upd.); 50 (upd.)
Dow Jones & Company, Inc., IV; 19 (upd.); 47 (upd.)
Dow Jones Telerate, Inc., 10
DPL Inc., 6; 96 (upd.)
DQE, Inc., 6
Dr Pepper/Seven Up, Inc., 9; 32 (upd.)
Drackett Professional Products, 12
Draftfcb, 94
Drake Beam Morin, Inc., 44
Draper and Kramer Inc., 96
Draper Fisher Jurvetson, 91
Dreams Inc., 97
DreamWorks SKG, 43
The Drees Company, Inc., 41
The Dress Barn, Inc., 24; 55 (upd.)
Dresser Industries, Inc., III
Drew Industries Inc., 28
Drexel Burnham Lambert Incorporated, II
Drexel Heritage Furnishings Inc., 12
Dreyer's Grand Ice Cream, Inc., 17
The Dreyfus Corporation, 70
Dril-Quip, Inc., 81
Drinker, Biddle and Reath L.L.P., 92
DriveTime Automotive Group Inc., 68 (upd.)
DRS Technologies, Inc., 58
Drs. Foster & Smith, Inc., 62
Drug Emporium, Inc., 12
Drypers Corporation, 18
DSC Communications Corporation, 12
DSW Inc., 73
DTE Energy Company, 20 (upd.); 94 (upd.)
DTS, Inc., 80
Dualstar Entertainment Group LLC, 76
Duane Reade Holding Corp., 21
Duck Head Apparel Company, Inc., 42
Ducks Unlimited, Inc., 87
Duckwall-ALCO Stores, Inc., 24
Ducommun Incorporated, 30
Duke Energy Corporation, V; 27 (upd.)
Duke Realty Corporation, 57
The Dun & Bradstreet Corporation, IV; 19 (upd.); 61 (upd.)
Dun & Bradstreet Software Services Inc., 11
Dunavant Enterprises, Inc., 54
Duncan Aviation, Inc., 94
Duncan Toys Company, 55
Dunn-Edwards Corporation, 56
Duplex Products Inc., 17
Duracell International Inc., 9; 71 (upd.)
Durametallic, 21
Duriron Company Inc., 17
Duron Inc., 72
Duty Free International, Inc., 11
DVI, Inc., 51
Dyax Corp., 89
Dycom Industries, Inc., 57
Dyersburg Corporation, 21
Dynamic Materials Corporation, 81
Dynatech Corporation, 13
DynCorp, 45
Dynegy Inc., 49 (upd.)
E! Entertainment Television Inc., 17
E*Trade Financial Corporation, 20; 60 (upd.)
E. & J. Gallo Winery, I; 7 (upd.); 28 (upd.)
E.I. du Pont de Nemours and Company, I; 8 (upd.); 26 (upd.); 73 (upd.)
E.piphany, Inc., 49
E-Systems, Inc., 9
E.W. Howell Co., Inc., 72
The E.W. Scripps Company, IV; 7 (upd.); 28 (upd.); 66 (upd.)
E-Z Serve Corporation, 17
E-Z-EM Inc., 89
Eagle Hardware & Garden, Inc., 16
Eagle-Picher Industries, Inc., 8; 23 (upd.)
Eagle-Tribune Publishing Co., 91
Earl Scheib, Inc., 32
Earle M. Jorgensen Company, 82
The Earthgrains Company, 36
EarthLink, Inc., 36
East Penn Manufacturing Co., Inc. 79
Easter Seals, Inc., 58
Eastern Airlines, I
The Eastern Company, 48
Eastern Enterprises, 6
EastGroup Properties, Inc., 67
Eastland Shoe Corporation, 82
Eastman Chemical Company, 14; 38 (upd.)
Eastman Kodak Company, III; 7 (upd.); 36 (upd.); 91 (upd.)
Easton Sports, Inc., 66
Eateries, Inc., 33
Eaton Corporation, I; 10 (upd.); 67 (upd.)
Eaton Vance Corporation, 18
eBay Inc., 32; 67 (upd.)
EBSCO Industries, Inc., 17; 40 (upd.)
ECC International Corp., 42
Echlin Inc., I; 11 (upd.)
The Echo Design Group, Inc., 68
EchoStar Communications Corporation, 35
Eckerd Corporation, 9; 32 (upd.)
Eclipse Aviation Corporation, 87
Ecolab Inc., I; 13 (upd.); 34 (upd.); 85 (upd.)
eCollege.com, 85
Ecology and Environment, Inc., 39
Eddie Bauer, Inc., 9; 36 (upd.); 87 (upd.)
Edelbrock Corporation, 37
Edelman, 62
EDGAR Online, Inc., 91
Edge Petroleum Corporation, 67
Edison Brothers Stores, Inc., 9
Edison International, 56 (upd.)
Edison Schools Inc., 37
Edmark Corporation, 14; 41 (upd.)
EDO Corporation, 46
Educate Inc. 86 (upd.)
Education Management Corporation, 35
Educational Broadcasting Corporation, 48
Educational Testing Service, 12; 62 (upd.)
Edw. C. Levy Co., 42
Edward D. Jones & Company L.P., 30; 66 (upd.)
Edward Hines Lumber Company, 68
The Edward J. DeBartolo Corporation, 8
Edwards and Kelcey, 70
Edwards Brothers, Inc., 92
Edwards Theatres Circuit, Inc., 31
EFJ, Inc., 81
EG&G Incorporated, 8; 29 (upd.)
Egan Companies, Inc., 94
Egghead.com, Inc., 9; 31 (upd.)
EGL, Inc., 59
eHarmony.com Inc., 71
8x8, Inc., 94
84 Lumber Company, 9; 39 (upd.)
800-JR Cigar, Inc., 27
Eileen Fisher Inc., 61
Einstein/Noah Bagel Corporation, 29
Ekco Group, Inc., 16
El Camino Resources International, Inc., 11
El Chico Restaurants, Inc., 19
El Paso Corporation, 66 (upd.)
El Paso Electric Company, 21
El Paso Natural Gas Company, 12
El Pollo Loco, Inc., 69
Elamex, S.A. de C.V., 51
Elano Corporation, 14
The Elder-Beerman Stores Corp., 10; 63 (upd.)

Electric Boat Corporation, 86
Electric Lightwave, Inc., 37
Electro Rent Corporation, 58
Electromagnetic Sciences Inc., 21
Electronic Arts Inc., 10; 85 (upd.)
Electronic Data Systems Corporation, III; 28 (upd.)
Electronics Boutique Holdings Corporation, 72
Electronics for Imaging, Inc., 15; 43 (upd.)
Elektra Entertainment Group, 64
Element K Corporation, 94
Elephant Pharmacy, Inc., 83
Eli Lilly and Company, I; 11 (upd.); 47 (upd.)
Elizabeth Arden, Inc., 8; 40 (upd.)
Eljer Industries, Inc., 24
Elkay Manufacturing Company, 73
ElkCorp, 52
Ellen Tracy, Inc., 55
Ellerbe Becket, 41
Ellett Brothers, Inc., 17
Elmer Candy Corporation, 88
Elmer's Restaurants, Inc., 42
Elsinore Corporation, 48
Elvis Presley Enterprises, Inc., 61
EMBARQ Corporation, 83
Embers America Restaurants, 30
Embrex, Inc., 72
EMC Corporation, 12; 46 (upd.)
EMCOR Group Inc., 60
EMCORE Corporation, 97
Emerson, II; 46 (upd.)
Emerson Radio Corp., 30
Emery Worldwide Airlines, Inc., 6; 25 (upd.)
Emge Packing Co., Inc., 11
Emigrant Savings Bank, 59
Emmis Communications Corporation, 47
Empi, Inc., 26
Empire Blue Cross and Blue Shield, III
The Empire District Electric Company, 77
Empire Resorts, Inc., 72
Empire Resources, Inc., 81
Employee Solutions, Inc., 18
ENCAD, Incorporated, 25
Encompass Services Corporation, 33
Encore Acquisition Company, 73
Encore Computer Corporation, 13; 74 (upd.)
Encore Wire Corporation, 81
Encyclopaedia Britannica, Inc., 7; 39 (upd.)
Endo Pharmaceuticals Holdings Inc., 71
Energen Corporation, 21; 97 (upd.)
Energizer Holdings, Inc., 32
Energy Brands Inc., 88
Energy Conversion Devices, Inc., 75
Enesco Corporation, 11
Engelhard Corporation, IV; 21 (upd.); 72 (upd.)
Engineered Support Systems, Inc., 59
Engle Homes, Inc., 46
Engraph, Inc., 12
Ennis, Inc., 21; 97 (upd.)
EnPro Industries, Inc., 93
Enquirer/Star Group, Inc., 10
Enrich International, Inc., 33
Enron Corporation, V, 19; 46 (upd.)
ENSCO International Incorporated, 57
Enserch Corporation, V
Entercom Communications Corporation, 58
Entergy Corporation, V; 45 (upd.)
Enterprise Rent-A-Car Company, 6; 69 (upd.)
Entertainment Distribution Company, 89
Entravision Communications Corporation, 41
Envirodyne Industries, Inc., 17
Environmental Industries, Inc., 31
Environmental Power Corporation, 68
Environmental Systems Research Institute Inc. (ESRI), 62
Enzo Biochem, Inc., 41
Eon Labs, Inc., 67
EPAM Systems Inc., 96
Epic Systems Corporation, 62
EPIQ Systems, Inc., 56
Equifax Inc., 6; 28 (upd.); 90 (upd.)
Equistar Chemicals, LP, 71
Equitable Life Assurance Society of the United States, III
Equitable Resources, Inc., 6; 54 (upd.)
Equity Marketing, Inc., 26
Equity Office Properties Trust, 54
Equity Residential, 49
Equus Computer Systems, Inc., 49
Ergon, Inc., 95
Erickson Retirement Communities, 57
Erie Indemnity Company, 35
ERLY Industries Inc., 17
Ernie Ball, Inc., 56
Ernst & Young, 9; 29 (upd.)
Escalade, Incorporated, 19
Eschelon Telecom, Inc., 72
ESCO Technologies Inc., 87
Eskimo Pie Corporation, 21
ESPN, Inc., 56
Esprit de Corp., 8; 29 (upd.)
ESS Technology, Inc., 22
Essef Corporation, 18
Esselte, 64
Esselte Pendaflex Corporation, 11
Essence Communications, Inc., 24
Essex Corporation, 85
The Estée Lauder Companies Inc., 9; 30 (upd.); 93 (upd.)
Esterline Technologies Corp., 15
Estes Express Lines, Inc., 86
Eternal Word Television Network, Inc., 57
Ethan Allen Interiors, Inc., 12; 39 (upd.)
Ethicon, Inc., 23
Ethyl Corporation, I; 10 (upd.)
EToys, Inc., 37
The Eureka Company, 12
Euromarket Designs Inc., 31 (upd.)
Euronet Worldwide, Inc., 83
Europe Through the Back Door Inc., 65
Evans and Sutherland Computer Company 19; 78 (upd.)
Evans, Inc., 30
Everex Systems, Inc., 16
Evergreen International Aviation, Inc., 53
Evergreen Energy, Inc., 97
Everlast Worldwide Inc., 47
Exabyte Corporation, 12; 40 (upd.)
Exar Corp., 14
EXCEL Communications Inc., 18
Excel Technology, Inc., 65
Executive Jet, Inc., 36
Executone Information Systems, Inc., 13
Exelon Corporation, 48 (upd.)
Exide Electronics Group, Inc., 20
Expedia, Inc., 58
Expeditors International of Washington Inc., 17; 78 (upd.)
Experian Information Solutions Inc., 45
Exponent, Inc., 95
Express Scripts Inc., 17; 44 (upd.)
Extended Stay America, Inc., 41
EXX Inc., 65
Exxon Corporation, IV; 7 (upd.); 32 (upd.)
Exxon Mobil Corporation, 67 (upd.)
Eye Care Centers of America, Inc., 69
EZCORP Inc., 43
F&W Publications, Inc., 71
The F. Dohmen Co., 77
F. Korbel & Bros. Inc., 68
F.W. Webb Company, 95
Fab Industries, Inc., 27
Fabri-Centers of America Inc., 16
Facebook, Inc., 90
FactSet Research Systems Inc., 73
Faegre & Benson LLP, 97
Fair Grounds Corporation, 44
Fair, Isaac and Company, 18
Fairchild Aircraft, Inc., 9
Fairfield Communities, Inc., 36
Falcon Products, Inc., 33
Fallon McElligott Inc., 22
Fallon Worldwide, 71 (upd.)
Family Christian Stores, Inc., 51
Family Dollar Stores, Inc., 13; 62 (upd.)
Family Golf Centers, Inc., 29
Famous Dave's of America, Inc., 40
Fannie Mae, 45 (upd.)
Fannie May Confections Brands, Inc., 80
Fansteel Inc., 19
FAO Schwarz, 46
Farah Incorporated, 24
Faribault Foods, Inc., 89
Farley Northwest Industries, Inc., I
Farley's & Sathers Candy Company, Inc., 62
Farm Family Holdings, Inc., 39
Farm Journal Corporation, 42
Farmer Bros. Co., 52
Farmer Jack Supermarkets 78
Farmers Insurance Group of Companies, 25
Farmland Foods, Inc., 7
Farmland Industries, Inc., 48
FARO Technologies, Inc., 87
Farouk Systems Inc. 78
Farrar, Straus and Giroux Inc., 15
Fastenal Company, 14; 42 (upd.)
Fatburger Corporation, 64
Faultless Starch/Bon Ami Company, 55
Fay's Inc., 17
Faygo Beverages Inc., 55

Fazoli's Management, Inc., 76 (upd.)
Fazoli's Systems, Inc., 27
Featherlite Inc., 28
Fedders Corporation, 18; 43 (upd.)
Federal Agricultural Mortgage Corporation, 75
Federal Deposit Insurance Corporation, 93
Federal Express Corporation, V
Federal National Mortgage Association, II
Federal Paper Board Company, Inc., 8
Federal Prison Industries, Inc., 34
Federal Signal Corp., 10
Federal-Mogul Corporation, I; 10 (upd.); 26 (upd.)
Federated Department Stores Inc., 9; 31 (upd.)
FedEx Corporation, 18 (upd.); 42 (upd.)
Feed The Children, Inc., 68
FEI Company 79
Feld Entertainment, Inc., 32 (upd.)
Fellowes Manufacturing Company, 28
Fender Musical Instruments Company, 16; 43 (upd.)
Fenwick & West LLP, 34
Ferolito, Vultaggio & Sons, 27
Ferrara Fire Apparatus, Inc., 84
Ferrara Pan Candy Company, 90
Ferrellgas Partners, L.P., 35
Ferro Corporation, 8; 56 (upd.)
F5 Networks, Inc., 72
FHP International Corporation, 6
FiberMark, Inc., 37
Fibreboard Corporation, 16
Fidelity Investments Inc., II; 14 (upd.)
Fidelity National Financial Inc., 54
Fidelity Southern Corporation, 85
Fieldale Farms Corporation, 23
Fieldcrest Cannon, Inc., 9; 31 (upd.)
Fifth Third Bancorp, 13; 31 (upd.)
Figgie International Inc., 7
Fiji Water LLC, 74
FileNet Corporation, 62
Fili Enterprises, Inc., 70
Film Roman, Inc., 58
FINA, Inc., 7
Fingerhut Companies, Inc., 9; 36 (upd.)
Finisar Corporation, 92
The Finish Line, Inc., 29; 68 (upd.)
FinishMaster, Inc., 24
Finlay Enterprises, Inc., 16; 76 (upd.)
Firearms Training Systems, Inc., 27
Fired Up, Inc., 82
Fireman's Fund Insurance Company, III
First Albany Companies Inc., 37
First Alert, Inc., 28
The First American Corporation, The 52
First Aviation Services Inc., 49
First Bank System Inc., 12
First Brands Corporation, 8
First Cash Financial Services, Inc., 57
First Chicago Corporation, II
First Colony Coffee & Tea Company, 84
First Commerce Bancshares, Inc., 15
First Commerce Corporation, 11
First Data Corporation, 30 (upd.)
First Empire State Corporation, 11
First Executive Corporation, III
First Fidelity Bank, N.A., New Jersey, 9
First Financial Management Corporation, 11
First Hawaiian, Inc., 11
First Industrial Realty Trust, Inc., 65
First Interstate Bancorp, II
The First Marblehead Corporation, 87
First Mississippi Corporation, 8
First Nationwide Bank, 14
First of America Bank Corporation, 8
First Security Corporation, 11
First Solar, Inc., 95
First Team Sports, Inc., 22
First Tennessee National Corporation, 11; 48 (upd.)
First Union Corporation, 10
First USA, Inc., 11
First Virginia Banks, Inc., 11
The First Years Inc., 46
Firstar Corporation, 11; 33 (upd.)
Fiserv Inc., 11; 33 (upd.)
Fish & Neave, 54
Fisher Companies, Inc., 15
Fisher Controls International, LLC, 13; 61 (upd.)
Fisher Scientific International Inc., 24
Fisher-Price Inc., 12; 32 (upd.)
Fisk Corporation, 72
5 & Diner Franchise Corporation, 72
Flagstar Companies, Inc., 10
Flanders Corporation, 65
Flanigan's Enterprises, Inc., 60
Flatiron Construction Corporation, 92
Fleer Corporation, 15
FleetBoston Financial Corporation, 9; 36 (upd.)
Fleetwood Enterprises, Inc., III; 22 (upd.); 81 (upd.)
Fleming Companies, Inc., II; 17 (upd.)
Flexsteel Industries Inc., 15; 41 (upd.)
Flight Options, LLC, 75
FlightSafety International, Inc., 9; 29 (upd.)
Flint Ink Corporation, 13; 41 (upd.)
FLIR Systems, Inc., 69
Florida Crystals Inc., 35
Florida East Coast Industries, Inc., 59
Florida Gaming Corporation, 47
Florida Progress Corporation, V; 23 (upd.)
Florida Public Utilities Company, 69
Florida Rock Industries, Inc., 46
Florida's Natural Growers, 45
Florists' Transworld Delivery, Inc., 28
Florsheim Shoe Group Inc., 9; 31 (upd.)
Flotek Industries Inc., 93
Flour City International, Inc., 44
Flow International Corporation, 56
Flowers Industries, Inc., 12; 35 (upd.)
Flowserve Corporation, 33; 77 (upd.)
Fluke Corporation, 15
Fluor Corporation, I; 8 (upd.); 34 (upd.)
Flying Boat, Inc. (Chalk's Ocean Airways), 56
Flying J Inc., 19
FMC Corporation, I; 11 (upd.); 89 (upd.)
FMR Corp., 8; 32 (upd.)
Foamex International Inc., 17
Focus Features 78
Foley & Lardner, 28
Follett Corporation, 12; 39 (upd.)
Food Circus Super Markets, Inc., 88
The Food Emporium, 64
Food For The Poor, Inc., 77
Food Lion LLC, II; 15 (upd.); 66 (upd.)
Foodarama Supermarkets, Inc., 28
FoodBrands America, Inc., 23
Foodmaker, Inc., 14
Foot Locker, Inc., 68 (upd.)
Foot Petals L.L.C., 95
Foote, Cone & Belding Worldwide, I; 66 (upd.)
Footstar, Incorporated, 24
Forbes Inc., 30; 82 (upd.)
Force Protection Inc., 95
The Ford Foundation, 34
Ford Motor Company, I; 11 (upd.); 36 (upd.); 64 (upd.)
FORE Systems, Inc., 25
Forest City Enterprises, Inc., 16; 52 (upd.)
Forest Laboratories, Inc., 11; 52 (upd.)
Forest Oil Corporation, 19; 91 (upd.)
Forever Living Products International Inc., 17
Forever 21, Inc., 84
FormFactor, Inc., 85
Formica Corporation, 13
Forrester Research, Inc., 54
Forstmann Little & Co., 38
Fort Howard Corporation, 8
Fort James Corporation, 22 (upd.)
Fortune Brands, Inc., 29 (upd.); 68 (upd.)
Fortunoff Fine Jewelry and Silverware Inc., 26
Forward Air Corporation, 75
Forward Industries, Inc., 86
Fossil, Inc., 17
Foster Poultry Farms, 32
Foster Wheeler Corporation, 6; 23 (upd.)
Foster Wheeler Ltd., 76 (upd.)
FosterGrant, Inc., 60
Foundation Health Corporation, 12
Fountain Powerboats Industries, Inc., 28
Four Winns Boats LLC, 96
4Kids Entertainment Inc., 59
Fourth Financial Corporation, 11
Fox Entertainment Group, Inc., 43
Fox Family Worldwide, Inc., 24
Foxboro Company, 13
FoxHollow Technologies, Inc., 85
FoxMeyer Health Corporation, 16
Foxworth-Galbraith Lumber Company, 91
FPL Group, Inc., V; 49 (upd.)
Frank J. Zamboni & Co., Inc., 34
Frank Russell Company, 46
Frank's Nursery & Crafts, Inc., 12
Frankel & Co., 39
Franklin Covey Company, 11; 37 (upd.)
Franklin Electric Company, Inc., 43
Franklin Electronic Publishers, Inc., 23
The Franklin Mint, 69
Franklin Resources, Inc., 9
Franz Inc., 80
Fred Alger Management, Inc., 97
Fred Meyer Stores, Inc., V; 20 (upd.); 64 (upd.)

Fred Usinger Inc., 54
The Fred W. Albrecht Grocery Co., 13
Fred Weber, Inc., 61
Fred's, Inc., 23; 62 (upd.)
Freddie Mac, 54
Frederick Atkins Inc., 16
Frederick's of Hollywood, Inc., 16; 59 (upd.)
Freedom Communications, Inc., 36
Freeport-McMoRan Copper & Gold, Inc., IV; 7 (upd.); 57 (upd.)
Freescale Semiconductor, Inc., 83
Freeze.com LLC, 77
French Fragrances, Inc., 22
Frequency Electronics, Inc., 61
Fresh America Corporation, 20
Fresh Choice, Inc., 20
Fresh Enterprises, Inc., 66
Fresh Express Inc., 88
Fresh Foods, Inc., 29
FreshDirect, LLC, 84
Fretter, Inc., 10
Fried, Frank, Harris, Shriver & Jacobson, 35
Friedman's Inc., 29
Friedman, Billings, Ramsey Group, Inc., 53
Friendly Ice Cream Corporation, 30; 72 (upd.)
Frigidaire Home Products, 22
Frisch's Restaurants, Inc., 35; 92 (upd.)
Frito-Lay North America, 32; 73 (upd.)
Fritz Companies, Inc., 12
Frontier Airlines Holdings Inc., 22; 84 (upd.)
Frontier Corp., 16
Frontier Natural Products Co-Op, 82
Frost & Sullivan, Inc., 53
Frozen Food Express Industries, Inc., 20
Fruehauf Corporation, I
Fruit of the Loom, Inc., 8; 25 (upd.)
Fruth Pharmacy, Inc., 66
Fry's Electronics, Inc., 68
Frymaster Corporation, 27
FSI International, Inc., 17
FTI Consulting, Inc., 77
FTP Software, Inc., 20
Fubu, 29
Fuel Systems Solutions, Inc., 97
Fuel Tech, Inc., 85
FuelCell Energy, Inc., 75
Fujitsu-ICL Systems Inc., 11
Fulbright & Jaworski L.L.P., 47
Funco, Inc., 20
Fuqua Enterprises, Inc., 17
Fuqua Industries, Inc., I
Furmanite Corporation, 92
Furniture Brands International, Inc., 39 (upd.)
Furon Company, 28
Furr's Restaurant Group, Inc., 53
Furr's Supermarkets, Inc., 28
Future Now, Inc., 12
G&K Services, Inc., 16
G-III Apparel Group, Ltd., 22
G. Heileman Brewing Company Inc., I
G. Leblanc Corporation, 55
G.A.F., I
G.D. Searle & Company, I; 12 (upd.); 34 (upd.)
G.I. Joe's, Inc., 30
G.S. Blodgett Corporation, 15
Gabelli Asset Management Inc., 30
Gables Residential Trust, 49
Gadzooks, Inc., 18
GAF Corporation, 22 (upd.)
Gage Marketing Group, 26
Gaiam, Inc., 41
Gainsco, Inc., 22
Galardi Group, Inc., 72
Galaxy Investors, Inc., 97
Galaxy Nutritional Foods, Inc., 58
Gale International Llc, 93
Galey & Lord, Inc., 20; 66 (upd.)
The Gallup Organization, 37
Galyan's Trading Company, Inc., 47
The Gambrinus Company, 40
GameStop Corp., 69 (upd.)
Gaming Partners International Corporation, 93
Gander Mountain Company, 20; 90 (upd.)
Gannett Company, Inc., IV; 7 (upd.); 30 (upd.); 66 (upd.)
Gantos, Inc., 17
The Gap, Inc., V; 18 (upd.); 55 (upd.)
Garan, Inc., 16; 64 (upd.)
Garden Fresh Restaurant Corporation, 31
Garden Ridge Corporation, 27
Gardenburger, Inc., 33; 76 (upd.)
Gardner Denver, Inc., 49
Gart Sports Company, 24
Gartner, Inc., 21; 94 (upd.)
Garst Seed Company, Inc., 86
GateHouse Media, Inc., 91
The Gates Corporation, 9
Gateway, Inc., 10; 27 (upd.); 63 (upd.)
The Gatorade Company, 82
GATX Corporation, 6; 25 (upd.)
Gaylord Container Corporation, 8
Gaylord Entertainment Company, 11; 36 (upd.)
GC Companies, Inc., 25
GE Aircraft Engines, 9
GE Capital Aviation Services, 36
Geerlings & Wade, Inc., 45
Geffen Records Inc., 26
Gehl Company, 19
GEICO Corporation, 10; 40 (upd.)
Geiger Bros., 60
Gemini Sound Products Corporation, 58
Gen-Probe Incorporated 79
GenCorp Inc., 8; 9
Genentech, Inc., I; 8 (upd.); 32 (upd.); 75 (upd.)
General Atomics, 57
General Bearing Corporation, 45
General Binding Corporation, 10; 73 (upd.)
General Cable Corporation, 40
The General Chemical Group Inc., 37
General Cigar Holdings, Inc., 66 (upd.)
General Cinema Corporation, I
General DataComm Industries, Inc., 14
General Dynamics Corporation, I; 10 (upd.); 40 (upd.); 88 (upd.)
General Electric Company, II; 12 (upd.); 34 (upd.); 63 (upd.)
General Employment Enterprises, Inc., 87
General Growth Properties, Inc., 57
General Host Corporation, 12
General Housewares Corporation, 16
General Instrument Corporation, 10
General Maritime Corporation, 59
General Mills, Inc., II; 10 (upd.); 36 (upd.); 85 (upd.)
General Motors Corporation, I; 10 (upd.); 36 (upd.); 64 (upd.)
General Nutrition Companies, Inc., 11; 29 (upd.)
General Public Utilities Corporation, V
General Re Corporation, III; 24 (upd.)
General Signal Corporation, 9
General Tire, Inc., 8
Genesco Inc., 17; 84 (upd.)
Genesee & Wyoming Inc., 27
Genesis Health Ventures, Inc., 18
Genesis Microchip Inc., 82
Genetics Institute, Inc., 8
Geneva Steel, 7
Genmar Holdings, Inc., 45
Genovese Drug Stores, Inc., 18
GenRad, Inc., 24
Gentex Corporation, 26
Gentiva Health Services, Inc. 79
Genuardi's Family Markets, Inc., 35
Genuine Parts Company, 9; 45 (upd.)
Genzyme Corporation, 13; 38 (upd.); 77 (upd.)
The Geon Company, 11
George A. Hormel and Company, II
The George F. Cram Company, Inc., 55
George P. Johnson Company, 60
George S. May International Company, 55
Georgia Gulf Corporation, 9; 61 (upd.)
Georgia-Pacific Corporation, IV; 9 (upd.); 47 (upd.)
Geotek Communications Inc., 21
Gerald Stevens, Inc., 37
Gerber Products Company, 7; 21 (upd.)
Gerber Scientific, Inc., 12; 84 (upd.)
German American Bancorp, 41
Getty Images, Inc., 31
Gevity HR, Inc., 63
GF Health Products, Inc., 82
Ghirardelli Chocolate Company, 30
Giant Cement Holding, Inc., 23
Giant Eagle, Inc., 86
Giant Food LLC, II; 22 (upd.); 83 (upd.)
Giant Industries, Inc., 19; 61 (upd.)
Gibraltar Steel Corporation, 37
Gibson Greetings, Inc., 12
Gibson Guitar Corp., 16
Gibson, Dunn & Crutcher LLP, 36
Giddings & Lewis, Inc., 10
Gilbane, Inc., 34
Gilead Sciences, Inc., 54
Gillett Holdings, Inc., 7
The Gillette Company, III; 20 (upd.); 68 (upd.)
Gilman & Ciocia, Inc., 72
Girl Scouts of the USA, 35
The Gitano Group, Inc., 8

Glacier Bancorp, Inc., 35
Glacier Water Services, Inc., 47
Glamis Gold, Ltd., 54
Glazer's Wholesale Drug Company, Inc., 82
Gleason Corporation, 24
The Glidden Company, 8
Global Berry Farms LLC, 62
Global Crossing Ltd., 32
Global Hyatt Corporation, 75 (upd.)
Global Imaging Systems, Inc., 73
Global Industries, Ltd., 37
Global Marine Inc., 9
Global Outdoors, Inc., 49
Global Payments Inc., 91
Global Power Equipment Group Inc., 52
GlobalSantaFe Corporation, 48 (upd.)
Glu Mobile Inc., 95
Gluek Brewing Company, 75
GM Hughes Electronics Corporation, II
GMH Communities Trust, 87
Godfather's Pizza Incorporated, 25
Godiva Chocolatier, Inc., 64
Goetze's Candy Company, Inc., 87
Gold Kist Inc., 17; 26 (upd.)
Gold'n Plump Poultry, 54
Gold's Gym International, Inc., 71
Golden Belt Manufacturing Co., 16
Golden Books Family Entertainment, Inc., 28
Golden Corral Corporation, 10; 66 (upd.)
Golden Enterprises, Inc., 26
Golden Krust Caribbean Bakery, Inc., 68
Golden State Foods Corporation, 32
Golden State Vintners, Inc., 33
Golden West Financial Corporation, 47
The Goldman Sachs Group Inc., II; 20 (upd.); 51 (upd.)
Golin/Harris International, Inc., 88
Golub Corporation, 26; 96 (upd.)
Gonnella Baking Company, 40
The Good Guys, Inc., 10; 30 (upd.)
Good Humor-Breyers Ice Cream Company, 14
Goodby Silverstein & Partners, Inc., 75
Goodman Holding Company, 42
GoodMark Foods, Inc., 26
Goodrich Corporation, 46 (upd.)
GoodTimes Entertainment Ltd., 48
Goodwill Industries International, Inc., 16; 66 (upd.)
Goody Products, Inc., 12
Goody's Family Clothing, Inc., 20; 64 (upd.)
The Goodyear Tire & Rubber Company, V; 20 (upd.); 75 (upd.)
Google, Inc., 50
Gordmans, Inc., 74
Gordon Biersch Brewery Restaurant Group, Inc., 93
Gordon Food Service Inc., 8; 39 (upd.)
The Gorman-Rupp Company, 18; 57 (upd.)
Gorton's, 13
Goss Holdings, Inc., 43
Gottschalks, Inc., 18; 91 (upd.)
Gould Electronics, Inc., 14
Gould Paper Corporation, 82
Goulds Pumps Inc., 24
Goya Foods Inc., 22; 91 (upd.)
GP Strategies Corporation, 64 (upd.)
GPU, Inc., 27 (upd.)
Graco Inc., 19; 67 (upd.)
Gradall Industries, Inc., 96
Graeter's Manufacturing Company, 86
Graham Corporation, 62
Graham Packaging Holdings Company, 87
GranCare, Inc., 14
Grand Casinos, Inc., 20
Grand Piano & Furniture Company, 72
The Grand Union Company, 7; 28 (upd.)
Granite Broadcasting Corporation, 42
Granite City Food & Brewery Ltd., 94
Granite Construction Incorporated, 61
Granite Industries of Vermont, Inc., 73
Granite Rock Company, 26
Granite State Bankshares, Inc., 37
Grant Prideco, Inc., 57
Grant Thornton International, 57
Graphic Industries Inc., 25
Graphic Packaging Holding Company, 96 (upd.)
Gray Communications Systems, Inc., 24
Graybar Electric Company, Inc., 54
Great American Management and Investment, Inc., 8
The Great Atlantic & Pacific Tea Company, Inc., II; 16 (upd.); 55 (upd.)
Great Harvest Bread Company, 44
Great Lakes Bancorp, 8
Great Lakes Chemical Corporation, I; 14 (upd.)
Great Lakes Dredge & Dock Company, 69
Great Plains Energy Incorporated, 65 (upd.)
Great Western Financial Corporation, 10
Great White Shark Enterprises, Inc., 89
Great Wolf Resorts, Inc., 91
Greatbatch Inc., 72
Grede Foundries, Inc., 38
The Green Bay Packers, Inc., 32
Green Mountain Coffee, Inc., 31
Green Tree Financial Corporation, 11
Greenberg Traurig, LLP, 65
The Greenbrier Companies, 19
Greene, Tweed & Company, 55
GreenPoint Financial Corp., 28
Greenwood Mills, Inc., 14
Greg Manning Auctions, Inc., 60
Greif Inc., 15; 66 (upd.)
Grey Advertising, Inc., 6
Grey Global Group Inc., 66 (upd.)
Grey Wolf, Inc., 43
Greyhound Lines, Inc., I; 32 (upd.)
Griffin Industries, Inc., 70
Griffin Land & Nurseries, Inc., 43
Griffon Corporation, 34
Grill Concepts, Inc., 74
Grinnell Corp., 13
Grist Mill Company, 15
Gristede's Foods Inc., 31; 68 (upd.)
Grolier Incorporated, 16; 43 (upd.)
Grossman's Inc., 13
Ground Round, Inc., 21
Group 1 Automotive, Inc., 52
Group Health Cooperative, 41
Grow Biz International, Inc., 18
Grow Group Inc., 12
GROWMARK, Inc., 88
Grubb & Ellis Company, 21
Grumman Corporation, I; 11 (upd.)
Grunau Company Inc., 90
Gruntal & Co., L.L.C., 20
Gryphon Holdings, Inc., 21
GSC Enterprises, Inc., 86
GSD&M Advertising, 44
GSD&M's Idea City, 90
GSI Commerce, Inc., 67
GT Bicycles, 26
GT Interactive Software, 31
GTE Corporation, V; 15 (upd.)
GTSI Corp., 57
Guangzhou Pearl River Piano Group Ltd., 49
Guardian Industries Corp., 87
Guccio Gucci, S.p.A., 15
Guess, Inc., 15; 68 (upd.)
Guest Supply, Inc., 18
Guida-Seibert Dairy Company, 84
Guidant Corporation, 58
Guilford Mills Inc., 8; 40 (upd.)
Guitar Center, Inc., 29; 68 (upd.)
Guittard Chocolate Company, 55
Gulf & Western Inc., I
Gulf Island Fabrication, Inc., 44
Gulf States Utilities Company, 6
GulfMark Offshore, Inc., 49
Gulfstream Aerospace Corporation, 7; 28 (upd.)
Gund, Inc., 96
Gunite Corporation, 51
The Gunlocke Company, 23
Guardsmark, L.L.C., 77
Guthy-Renker Corporation, 32
Guttenplan's Frozen Dough Inc., 88
Gwathmey Siegel & Associates Architects LLC, 26
Gymboree Corporation, 15; 69 (upd.)
H&R Block, Inc., 9; 29 (upd.); 82 (upd.)
H.B. Fuller Company, 8; 32 (upd.); 75 (upd.)
H. Betti Industries Inc., 88
H.D. Vest, Inc., 46
H.E. Butt Grocery Company, 13; 32 (upd.); 85 (upd.)
H.F. Ahmanson & Company, II; 10 (upd.)
H.J. Heinz Company, II; 11 (upd.); 36 (upd.)
H.J. Russell & Company, 66
H.M. Payson & Co., 69
H.O. Penn Machinery Company, Inc., 96
The H.W. Wilson Company, 66
Ha-Lo Industries, Inc., 27
The Haartz Corporation, 94
Habersham Bancorp, 25
Habitat for Humanity International, 36
Hach Co., 18
Hadco Corporation, 24
Haeger Industries Inc., 88
Haemonetics Corporation, 20
Haggar Corporation, 19; 78 (upd.)

Haggen Inc., 38
Hahn Automotive Warehouse, Inc., 24
Haights Cross Communications, Inc., 84
The Hain Celestial Group, Inc., 27; 43 (upd.)
Hair Club For Men Ltd., 90
HAL Inc., 9
Hal Leonard Corporation, 96
Hale-Halsell Company, 60
Half Price Books, Records, Magazines Inc., 37
Hall, Kinion & Associates, Inc., 52
Halliburton Company, III; 25 (upd.); 55 (upd.)
Hallmark Cards, Inc., IV; 16 (upd.); 40 (upd.); 87 (upd.)
Hamilton Beach/Proctor-Silex Inc., 17
Hammacher Schlemmer & Company Inc., 21; 72 (upd.)
Hamot Health Foundation, 91
Hampshire Group Ltd., 82
Hampton Affiliates, Inc., 77
Hampton Industries, Inc., 20
Hancock Fabrics, Inc., 18
Hancock Holding Company, 15
Handleman Company, 15; 86 (upd.)
Handspring Inc., 49
Handy & Harman, 23
Hanger Orthopedic Group, Inc., 41
Hanmi Financial Corporation, 66
Hanna Andersson Corp., 49
Hanna-Barbera Cartoons Inc., 23
Hannaford Bros. Co., 12
Hanover Compressor Company, 59
Hanover Direct, Inc., 36
Hanover Foods Corporation, 35
Hansen Natural Corporation, 31; 76 (upd.)
Hanson Building Materials America Inc., 60
Happy Kids Inc., 30
Harbert Corporation, 14
Harbison-Walker Refractories Company, 24
Harbour Group Industries, Inc., 90
Harcourt Brace and Co., 12
Harcourt Brace Jovanovich, Inc., IV
Harcourt General, Inc., 20 (upd.)
Hard Rock Cafe International, Inc., 12; 32 (upd.)
Harding Lawson Associates Group, Inc., 16
Hardinge Inc., 25
Harkins Amusement, 94
Harland Clarke Holdings Corporation, 94 (upd.)
Harlem Globetrotters International, Inc., 61
Harley-Davidson Inc., 7; 25 (upd.)
Harleysville Group Inc., 37
Harman International Industries Inc., 15
Harmon Industries, Inc., 25
Harmonic Inc., 43
Harnischfeger Industries, Inc., 8; 38 (upd.)
Harold's Stores, Inc., 22
Harper Group Inc., 17
HarperCollins Publishers, 15
Harpo Inc., 28; 66 (upd.)
Harrah's Entertainment, Inc., 16; 43 (upd.)
Harris Corporation, II; 20 (upd.); 78 (upd.)
Harris Interactive Inc., 41; 92 (upd.)
The Harris Soup Company (Harry's Fresh Foods), 92
Harris Teeter Inc., 23; 72 (upd.)
Harry London Candies, Inc., 70
Harry N. Abrams, Inc., 58
Harry Winston Inc., 45
Harry's Farmers Market Inc., 23
Harsco Corporation, 8
Harte-Hanks, Inc., 17; 63 (upd.)
Hartmann Inc., 96
Hartmarx Corporation, 8; 32 (upd.)
The Hartz Mountain Corporation, 12; 46 (upd.)
Harveys Casino Resorts, 27
Harza Engineering Company, 14
Hasbro, Inc., III; 16 (upd.); 43 (upd.)
Haskel International, Inc., 59
Hastings Entertainment, Inc., 29
Hastings Manufacturing Company, 56
Hauser, Inc., 46
Haverty Furniture Companies, Inc., 31
Hawaiian Electric Industries, Inc., 9
Hawaiian Holdings, Inc., 22 (upd.); 96 (upd.)
Hawk Corporation, 59
Hawkeye Holdings LLC, 89
Hawkins Chemical, Inc., 16
Haworth Inc., 8; 39 (upd.)
Hay House, Inc., 93
Hayes Corporation, 24
Hayes Lemmerz International, Inc., 27
Haynes International, Inc., 88
Hazelden Foundation, 28
HCA - The Healthcare Company, 35 (upd.)
HCI Direct, Inc., 55
HDOS Enterprises, 72
HDR Inc., 48
Headwaters Incorporated, 56
Headway Corporate Resources, Inc., 40
Health Care & Retirement Corporation, 22
Health Communications, Inc., 72
Health Management Associates, Inc., 56
Health O Meter Products Inc., 14
Health Risk Management, Inc., 24
Health Systems International, Inc., 11
HealthExtras, Inc., 75
HealthMarkets, Inc., 88 (upd.)
HealthSouth Corporation, 14; 33 (upd.)
Healthtex, Inc., 17
The Hearst Corporation, IV; 19 (upd.); 46 (upd.)
Heartland Express, Inc., 18
The Heat Group, 53
Hechinger Company, 12
Hecla Mining Company, 20
Heekin Can Inc., 13
Heelys, Inc., 87
Heery International, Inc., 58
HEICO Corporation, 30
Heidrick & Struggles International, Inc., 28
Heilig-Meyers Company, 14; 40 (upd.)
Helen of Troy Corporation, 18
Helene Curtis Industries, Inc., 8; 28 (upd.)
Helix Energy Solutions Group, Inc., 81
Heller, Ehrman, White & McAuliffe, 41
Helmerich & Payne, Inc., 18
Helmsley Enterprises, Inc., 9; 39 (upd.)
Helzberg Diamonds, 40
Hendrick Motorsports, Inc., 89
Henkel Manco Inc., 22
The Henley Group, Inc., III
Henry Crown and Company, 91
Henry Dreyfuss Associates LLC, 88
Henry Ford Health System, 84
Henry Modell & Company Inc., 32
Henry Schein, Inc., 31; 70 (upd.)
Hensel Phelps Construction Company, 72
Hensley & Company, 64
Herald Media, Inc., 91
Herbalife International, Inc., 17; 41 (upd.)
Hercules Inc., I; 22 (upd.); 66 (upd.)
Hercules Technology Growth Capital, Inc., 87
Herley Industries, Inc., 33
Herman Goelitz, Inc., 28
Herman Miller, Inc., 8; 77 (upd.)
Herr Foods Inc., 84
Herschend Family Entertainment Corporation, 73
Hershey Foods Corporation, II; 15 (upd.); 51 (upd.)
The Hertz Corporation, 9; 33 (upd.)
Heska Corporation, 39
Heublein, Inc., I
Hewitt Associates, Inc., 77
Hewlett-Packard Company, III; 6 (upd.); 28 (upd.); 50 (upd.)
Hexcel Corporation, 28
Hibbett Sporting Goods, Inc., 26; 70 (upd.)
Hibernia Corporation, 37
Hickory Farms, Inc., 17
HickoryTech Corporation, 92
High Falls Brewing Company LLC, 74
Highlights for Children, Inc., 95
Highmark Inc., 27
Highsmith Inc., 60
Hilb, Rogal & Hobbs Company, 77
Hildebrandt International, 29
Hill's Pet Nutrition, Inc., 27
Hillenbrand Industries, Inc., 10; 75 (upd.)
Hillerich & Bradsby Company, Inc., 51
The Hillhaven Corporation, 14
Hills Stores Company, 13
Hilton Hotels Corporation, III; 19 (upd.); 62 (upd.)
Hines Horticulture, Inc., 49
Hispanic Broadcasting Corporation, 35
Hitchiner Manufacturing Co., Inc., 23
HMI Industries, Inc., 17
HNI Corporation, 74 (upd.)
Ho-Chunk Inc., 61
HOB Entertainment, Inc., 37
Hobby Lobby Stores Inc., 80

Hobie Cat Company, 94
Hodgson Mill, Inc., 88
Hoechst Celanese Corporation, 13
Hoenig Group Inc., 41
Hoffman Corporation 78
Hogan & Hartson L.L.P., 44
HOK Group, Inc., 59
Holberg Industries, Inc., 36
Holiday Inns, Inc., III
Holiday Retirement Corp., 87
Holiday RV Superstores, Incorporated, 26
Holland & Knight LLP, 60
Holland Burgerville USA, 44
The Holland Group, Inc., 82
Hollander Home Fashions Corp., 67
Holley Performance Products Inc., 52
Hollinger International Inc., 24
Holly Corporation, 12
Hollywood Casino Corporation, 21
Hollywood Entertainment Corporation, 25
Hollywood Media Corporation, 58
Hollywood Park, Inc., 20
Holme Roberts & Owen LLP, 28
Holnam Inc., 8; 39 (upd.)
Holophane Corporation, 19
Holson Burnes Group, Inc., 14
Holt and Bugbee Company, 66
Holt's Cigar Holdings, Inc., 42
Homasote Company, 72
Home Box Office Inc., 7; 23 (upd.); 76 (upd.)
The Home Depot, Inc., V; 18 (upd.); 97 (upd.)
The Home Insurance Company, III
Home Interiors & Gifts, Inc., 55
Home Products International, Inc., 55
Home Properties of New York, Inc., 42
Home Shopping Network, Inc., V; 25 (upd.)
HomeBase, Inc., 33 (upd.)
Homestake Mining Company, 12; 38 (upd.)
Hometown Auto Retailers, Inc., 44
HomeVestors of America, Inc., 77
HON INDUSTRIES Inc., 13
Honda Motor Company Limited, I; 10 (upd.); 29 (upd.)
Honeywell Inc., II; 12 (upd.); 50 (upd.)
Hooker Furniture Corporation, 80
Hooper Holmes, Inc., 22
Hooters of America, Inc., 18; 69 (upd.)
The Hoover Company, 12; 40 (upd.)
HOP, LLC, 80
Hops Restaurant Bar and Brewery, 46
Horace Mann Educators Corporation, 22; 90 (upd.)
Horizon Organic Holding Corporation, 37
Hormel Foods Corporation, 18 (upd.); 54 (upd.)
Horsehead Industries, Inc., 51
Horseshoe Gaming Holding Corporation, 62
Horton Homes, Inc., 25
Horween Leather Company, 83
Hospira, Inc., 71
Hospital Central Services, Inc., 56
Hospital Corporation of America, III
Hospitality Franchise Systems, Inc., 11
Hospitality Worldwide Services, Inc., 26
Hoss's Steak and Sea House Inc., 68
Host America Corporation 79
Hot Stuff Foods, 85
Hot Topic, Inc., 33; 86 (upd.)
Houchens Industries Inc., 51
Houghton Mifflin Company, 10; 36 (upd.)
House of Fabrics, Inc., 21
Household International, Inc., II; 21 (upd.)
Houston Industries Incorporated, V
Houston Wire & Cable Company, 97
Hovnanian Enterprises, Inc., 29; 89 (upd.)
Howard Hughes Medical Institute, 39
Howard Johnson International, Inc., 17; 72 (upd.)
Howmet Corp., 12
HSN, 64 (upd.)
Hub Group, Inc., 38
Hub International Limited, 89
Hubbard Broadcasting Inc., 24; 79 (upd.)
Hubbell Inc., 9; 31 (upd.); 76 (upd.)
Hudson Foods Inc., 13
Hudson River Bancorp, Inc., 41
Huffy Corporation, 7; 30 (upd.)
Hughes Electronics Corporation, 25
Hughes Hubbard & Reed LLP, 44
Hughes Markets, Inc., 22
Hughes Supply, Inc., 14
Hulman & Company, 44
Humana Inc., III; 24 (upd.)
The Humane Society of the United States, 54
Hummer Winblad Venture Partners, 97
Hungarian Telephone and Cable Corp., 75
Hungry Howie's Pizza and Subs, Inc., 25
Hunt Consolidated, Inc., 27 (upd.)
Hunt Manufacturing Company, 12
Hunt Oil Company, 7
Hunt-Wesson, Inc., 17
Hunter Fan Company, 13
Huntington Bancshares Incorporated, 11; 87 (upd.)
Huntington Learning Centers, Inc., 55
Hunton & Williams, 35
Huntsman Chemical Corporation, 8
Huron Consulting Group Inc., 87
Hutchinson Technology Incorporated, 18; 63 (upd.)
Huttig Building Products, Inc., 73
Hvide Marine Incorporated, 22
Hy-Vee, Inc., 36
Hyatt Corporation, III; 16 (upd.)
Hyde Athletic Industries, Inc., 17
Hydril Company, 46
Hypercom Corporation, 27
Hyperion Software Corporation, 22
Hyperion Solutions Corporation, 76
Hyster Company, 17
I.C. Isaacs & Company, 31
Iams Company, 26
IBERIABANK Corporation, 37
IBP, Inc., II; 21 (upd.)
IC Industries, Inc., I
ICF International, Inc., 28; 94 (upd.)
ICN Pharmaceuticals, Inc., 52
Icon Health & Fitness, Inc., 38
Idaho Power Company, 12
IDB Communications Group, Inc., 11
Idearc Inc., 90
Identix Inc., 44
IDEO Inc., 65
IDEXX Laboratories, Inc., 23
IDG Books Worldwide, Inc., 27
IdraPrince, Inc., 76
IDT Corporation, 34
IDX Systems Corporation, 64
IEC Electronics Corp., 42
Igloo Products Corp., 21
IHOP Corporation, 17; 58 (upd.)
IHS Inc. 78
IKON Office Solutions, Inc., 50
Il Fornaio (America) Corporation, 27
Ilitch Holdings Inc., 37; 86 (upd.)
Illinois Bell Telephone Company, 14
Illinois Central Corporation, 11
Illinois Power Company, 6
Illinois Tool Works Inc., III; 22 (upd.); 81 (upd.)
Illumina, Inc., 93
ILX Resorts Incorporated, 65
Image Entertainment, Inc., 94
Imagine Entertainment, 91
Imagine Foods, Inc., 50
Imation Corporation, 20
IMC Fertilizer Group, Inc., 8
ImClone Systems Inc., 58
IMCO Recycling, Incorporated, 32
IMG 78
Immucor, Inc., 81
Immunex Corporation, 14; 50 (upd.)
Imo Industries Inc., 7; 27 (upd.)
IMPATH Inc., 45
Imperial Holly Corporation, 12
Imperial Industries, Inc., 81
Imperial Sugar Company, 32 (upd.)
IMS Health, Inc., 57
In Focus Systems, Inc., 22
In-N-Out Burgers Inc., 19; 74 (upd.)
In-Sink-Erator, 66
InaCom Corporation, 13
Inamed Corporation 79
Incyte Genomics, Inc., 52
Indel Inc. 78
Indiana Bell Telephone Company, Incorporated, 14
Indiana Energy, Inc., 27
Indianapolis Motor Speedway Corporation, 46
Indus International Inc., 70
Industrial Services of America, Inc., 46
Infinity Broadcasting Corporation, 11; 48 (upd.)
InFocus Corporation, 92
Information Access Company, 17
Information Builders, Inc., 22
Information Holdings Inc., 47
Information Resources, Inc., 10
Informix Corporation, 10; 30 (upd.)
InfoSonics Corporation, 81
InfoSpace, Inc., 91
Ingalls Shipbuilding, Inc., 12

Ingersoll-Rand Company Ltd., III; 15 (upd.); 55 (upd.)
Ingles Markets, Inc., 20
Ingram Industries, Inc., 11; 49 (upd.)
Ingram Micro Inc., 52
Initial Security, 64
Inktomi Corporation, 45
Inland Container Corporation, 8
Inland Steel Industries, Inc., IV; 19 (upd.)
Innovative Solutions & Support, Inc., 85
Innovo Group Inc., 83
Input/Output, Inc., 73
Inserra Supermarkets, 25
Insight Enterprises, Inc., 18
Insilco Corporation, 16
Insituform Technologies, Inc., 83
Inso Corporation, 26
Instinet Corporation, 34
Insurance Auto Auctions, Inc., 23
Integra LifeSciences Holdings Corporation, 87
Integrated BioPharma, Inc., 83
Integrated Defense Technologies, Inc., 54
Integrity Inc., 44
Intel Corporation, II; 10 (upd.); 36 (upd.); 75 (upd.)
IntelliCorp, Inc., 45
Intelligent Electronics, Inc., 6
Inter Parfums Inc., 35; 86 (upd.)
Inter-Regional Financial Group, Inc., 15
Interbrand Corporation, 70
Interco Incorporated, III
IntercontinentalExchange, Inc., 95
InterDigital Communications Corporation, 61
Interep National Radio Sales Inc., 35
Interface, Inc., 8; 29 (upd.); 76 (upd.)
Intergraph Corporation, 6; 24 (upd.)
The Interlake Corporation, 8
Intermec Technologies Corporation, 72
INTERMET Corporation, 32, 77 (upd.)
Intermix Media, Inc., 83
Intermountain Health Care, Inc., 27
International Airline Support Group, Inc., 55
International Brotherhood of Teamsters, 37
International Business Machines Corporation, III; 6 (upd.); 30 (upd.); 63 (upd.)
International Controls Corporation, 10
International Creative Management, Inc., 43
International Dairy Queen, Inc., 10; 39 (upd.)
International Data Group, Inc., 7; 25 (upd.)
International Family Entertainment Inc., 13
International Flavors & Fragrances Inc., 9; 38 (upd.)
International Game Technology, 10; 41 (upd.)
International Lease Finance Corporation, 48
International Management Group, 18
International Multifoods Corporation, 7; 25 (upd.)
International Paper Company, IV; 15 (upd.); 47 (upd.); 97 (upd.)
International Profit Associates, Inc., 87
International Rectifier Corporation, 31; 71 (upd.)
International Shipbreaking Ltd. L.L.C., 67
International Shipholding Corporation, Inc., 27
International Speedway Corporation, 19; 74 (upd.)
International Telephone & Telegraph Corporation, I; 11 (upd.)
International Total Services, Inc., 37
Interpool, Inc., 92
The Interpublic Group of Companies, Inc., I; 22 (upd.); 75 (upd.)
Interscope Music Group, 31
Intersil Corporation, 93
Interstate Bakeries Corporation, 12; 38 (upd.)
Interstate Hotels & Resorts Inc., 58
InterVideo, Inc., 85
Intevac, Inc., 92
Intimate Brands, Inc., 24
Intrado Inc., 63
Intuit Inc., 14; 33 (upd.); 73 (upd.)
Intuitive Surgical, Inc. 79
Invacare Corporation, 11; 47 (upd.)
inVentiv Health, Inc., 81
The Inventure Group, Inc., 96 (upd.)
Inverness Medical Innovations, Inc., 63
Invitrogen Corporation, 52
Invivo Corporation, 52
Iomega Corporation, 21
Ionatron, Inc., 85
Ionics, Incorporated, 52
Iowa Telecommunications Services, Inc., 85
IPALCO Enterprises, Inc., 6
Ipsen International Inc., 72
Irex Contracting Group, 90
iRobot Corporation, 83
Iron Mountain, Inc., 33
Irvin Feld & Kenneth Feld Productions, Inc., 15
Irwin Financial Corporation, 77
The Island ECN, Inc., 48
Isle of Capri Casinos, Inc., 41
Ispat Inland Inc., 40 (upd.)
ITC Holdings Corp., 75
Itel Corporation, 9
Items International Airwalk Inc., 17
Itron, Inc., 64
ITT Educational Services, Inc., 33; 76 (upd.)
ITT Sheraton Corporation, III
i2 Technologies, Inc., 87
Ivar's, Inc., 86
IVAX Corporation, 11; 55 (upd.)
IVC Industries, Inc., 45
iVillage Inc., 46
Iwerks Entertainment, Inc., 34
IXC Communications, Inc., 29
J & J Snack Foods Corporation, 24
J&R Electronics Inc., 26
J. & W. Seligman & Co. Inc., 61
J. Alexander's Corporation, 65
J. Baker, Inc., 31
J. Crew Group. Inc., 12; 34 (upd.); 88 (upd.)
J. C. Penney Company, Inc., V; 18 (upd.); 43 (upd.); 91 (upd.)
J. D'Addario & Company, Inc., 48
The J. Jill Group, Inc., 35; 90 (upd.)
J.A. Jones, Inc., 16
J.B. Hunt Transport Services Inc., 12
J.D. Edwards & Company, 14
J.D. Power and Associates, 32
J.F. Shea Co., Inc., 55
J.H. Findorff and Son, Inc., 60
J.I. Case Company, 10
J.J. Keller & Associates, Inc., 81
J.L. Hammett Company, 72
The J. M. Smucker Company, 11; 87 (upd.)
J.P. Morgan Chase & Co., II; 30 (upd.); 38 (upd.)
J.R. Simplot Company, 16; 60 (upd.)
J. W. Pepper and Son Inc., 86
Jabil Circuit, Inc., 36; 88 (upd.)
Jack Henry and Associates, Inc., 17; 94 (upd.)
Jack in the Box Inc., 89 (upd.)
Jack Morton Worldwide, 88
Jack Schwartz Shoes, Inc., 18
Jackpot Enterprises Inc., 21
Jackson Hewitt, Inc., 48
Jackson National Life Insurance Company, 8
Jacmar Companies, 87
Jaco Electronics, Inc., 30
Jacob Leinenkugel Brewing Company, 28
Jacobs Engineering Group Inc., 6; 26 (upd.)
Jacobson Stores Inc., 21
Jacor Communications, Inc., 23
Jacuzzi Brands Inc., 76 (upd.)
Jacuzzi Inc., 23
JAKKS Pacific, Inc., 52
Jalate Inc., 25
Jamba Juice Company, 47
James Avery Craftsman, Inc., 76
James Original Coney Island Inc., 84
James River Corporation of Virginia, IV
Jani-King International, Inc., 85
JanSport, Inc., 70
Janus Capital Group Inc., 57
Jarden Corporation, 93 (upd.)
Jason Incorporated, 23
Jay Jacobs, Inc., 15
Jayco Inc., 13
Jays Foods, Inc., 90
Jazz Basketball Investors, Inc., 55
Jazzercise, Inc., 45
JB Oxford Holdings, Inc., 32
JDS Uniphase Corporation, 34
JE Dunn Construction Group, Inc., 85
Jean-Georges Enterprises L.L.C., 75
Jefferies Group, Inc., 25
Jefferson-Pilot Corporation, 11; 29 (upd.)
Jel Sert Company, 90
Jeld-Wen, Inc., 45
Jelly Belly Candy Company, 76
Jenkens & Gilchrist, P.C., 65
Jennie-O Turkey Store, Inc., 76
Jennifer Convertibles, Inc., 31

Jenny Craig, Inc., 10; 29 (upd.); 92 (upd.)
Jeppesen Sanderson, Inc., 92
Jerry's Famous Deli Inc., 24
Jersey Mike's Franchise Systems, Inc., 83
Jervis B. Webb Company, 24
JetBlue Airways Corporation, 44
Jetro Cash & Carry Enterprises Inc., 38
Jewett-Cameron Trading Company, Ltd., 89
JG Industries, Inc., 15
Jillian's Entertainment Holdings, Inc., 40
Jim Beam Brands Worldwide, Inc., 14; 58 (upd.)
The Jim Henson Company, 23
Jitney-Jungle Stores of America, Inc., 27
JLG Industries, Inc., 52
JLM Couture, Inc., 64
JMB Realty Corporation, IV
Jo-Ann Stores, Inc., 72 (upd.)
Jockey International, Inc., 12; 34 (upd.); 77 (upd.)
The Joffrey Ballet of Chicago, The 52
John B. Sanfilippo & Son, Inc., 14
The John D. and Catherine T. MacArthur Foundation, 34
John D. Brush Company Inc., 94
John Frieda Professional Hair Care Inc., 70
John H. Harland Company, 17
John Hancock Financial Services, Inc., III; 42 (upd.)
The John Nuveen Company, 21
John Paul Mitchell Systems, 24
John Q. Hammons Hotels, Inc., 24
John W. Danforth Company, 48
John Wiley & Sons, Inc., 17; 65 (upd.)
Johnny Rockets Group, Inc., 31; 76 (upd.)
Johns Manville Corporation, 64 (upd.)
Johnson & Higgins, 14
Johnson & Johnson, III; 8 (upd.); 36 (upd.); 75 (upd.)
Johnson Controls, Inc., III; 26 (upd.); 59 (upd.)
Johnson Outdoors Inc., 28; 84 (upd.)
Johnson Publishing Company, Inc., 28; 72 (upd.)
Johnsonville Sausage L.L.C., 63
Johnston Industries, Inc., 15
Johnstown America Industries, Inc., 23
Jones Apparel Group, Inc., 11; 39 (upd.)
Jones, Day, Reavis & Pogue, 33
Jones Intercable, Inc., 21
Jones Knowledge Group, Inc., 97
Jones Lang LaSalle Incorporated, 49
Jones Medical Industries, Inc., 24
Jones Soda Co., 69
Jordache Enterprises, Inc., 23
The Jordan Company LP, 70
Jordan Industries, Inc., 36
Jordan-Kitt Music Inc., 86
Jos. A. Bank Clothiers, Inc., 31
Joseph T. Ryerson & Son, Inc., 15
Jostens, Inc., 7; 25 (upd.); 73 (upd.)
JOULÉ Inc., 58
Journal Communications, Inc., 86
Journal Register Company, 29
JPI, 49
JPMorgan Chase & Co., 91 (upd.)
JPS Textile Group, Inc., 28
j2 Global Communications, Inc., 75
Juicy Couture, Inc., 80
The Judge Group, Inc., 51
Juniper Networks, Inc., 43
Juno Lighting, Inc., 30
Juno Online Services, Inc., 38
Jupitermedia Corporation, 75
Just Bagels Manufacturing, Inc., 94
Just Born, Inc., 32
Just For Feet, Inc., 19
Justin Industries, Inc., 19
JWP Inc., 9
JWT Group Inc., I
K & B Inc., 12
K & G Men's Center, Inc., 21
K'Nex Industries, Inc., 52
K-Swiss, Inc., 33; 89 (upd.)
K-tel International, Inc., 21
Kadant Inc., 96 (upd.)
Kaiser Aluminum Corporation, IV; 84 (upd.)
Kaiser Foundation Health Plan, Inc., 53
Kal Kan Foods, Inc., 22
Kaman Corporation, 12; 42 (upd.)
Kaman Music Corporation, 68
Kampgrounds of America, Inc. 33
Kana Software, Inc., 51
Kansas City Power & Light Company, 6
Kansas City Southern Industries, Inc., 6; 26 (upd.)
The Kansas City Southern Railway Company, 92
Kaplan, Inc., 42; 90 (upd.)
Kar Nut Products Company, 86
Karl Kani Infinity, Inc., 49
Karsten Manufacturing Corporation, 51
Kash n' Karry Food Stores, Inc., 20
Kashi Company, 89
Kasper A.S.L., Ltd., 40
kate spade LLC, 68
Katy Industries, Inc., I; 51 (upd.)
Katz Communications, Inc., 6
Katz Media Group, Inc., 35
Kaufman and Broad Home Corporation, 8
Kaydon Corporation, 18
KB Home, 45 (upd.)
KB Toys, 15; 35 (upd.); 86 (upd.)
Keane, Inc., 56
Keebler Foods Company, 36
The Keith Companies Inc., 54
Keithley Instruments Inc., 16
Kelley Blue Book Company, Inc., 84
Kelley Drye & Warren LLP, 40
Kellogg Brown & Root, Inc., 62 (upd.)
Kellogg Company, II; 13 (upd.); 50 (upd.)
Kellwood Company, 8; 85 (upd.)
Kelly Services Inc., 6; 26 (upd.)
Kelly-Moore Paint Company, Inc., 56
The Kelly-Springfield Tire Company, 8
Kelsey-Hayes Group of Companies, 7; 27 (upd.)
Kemet Corp., 14
Kemper Corporation, III; 15 (upd.)
Ken's Foods, Inc., 88
Kendall International, Inc., 11
Kendall-Jackson Winery, Ltd., 28
Kendle International Inc., 87
Kenetech Corporation, 11
Kenexa Corporation, 87
Kenmore Air Harbor Inc., 65
Kennametal Inc., 68 (upd.)
Kennedy-Wilson, Inc., 60
Kenneth Cole Productions, Inc., 25
Kensey Nash Corporation, 71
Kensington Publishing Corporation, 84
Kent Electronics Corporation, 17
Kentucky Electric Steel, Inc., 31
Kentucky Utilities Company, 6
Kerasotes ShowPlace Theaters LLC, 80
Kerr Group Inc., 24
Kerr-McGee Corporation, IV; 22 (upd.); 68 (upd.)
Ketchum Communications Inc., 6
Kettle Foods Inc., 48
Kewaunee Scientific Corporation, 25
Key Safety Systems, Inc., 63
Key Tronic Corporation, 14
KeyCorp, 8; 93 (upd.)
Keyes Fibre Company, 9
Keys Fitness Products, LP, 83
KeySpan Energy Co., 27
Keystone International, Inc., 11
KFC Corporation, 7; 21 (upd.); 89 (upd.)
Kforce Inc., 71
KI, 57
Kidde, Inc., I
Kiehl's Since 1851, Inc., 52
Kolmar Laboratories Group, 96
Lewis Drug Inc., 94
Lifetouch Inc., 86
LifeWise Health Plan of Oregon, Inc., 90
Kikkoman Corporation, 47 (upd.)
Kimball International, Inc., 12; 48 (upd.)
Kimberly-Clark Corporation, III; 16 (upd.); 43 (upd.)
Kimco Realty Corporation, 11
Kinder Morgan, Inc., 45
KinderCare Learning Centers, Inc., 13
Kinetic Concepts, Inc. (KCI), 20
King & Spalding, 23
The King Arthur Flour Company, 31
King Kullen Grocery Co., Inc., 15
King Nut Company, 74
King Pharmaceuticals, Inc., 54
King Ranch, Inc., 14; 60 (upd.)
King World Productions, Inc., 9; 30 (upd.)
Kingston Technology Corporation, 20
Kinko's, Inc., 16; 43 (upd.)
Kinney Shoe Corp., 14
Kinray Inc., 85
Kintera, Inc., 75
Kirby Corporation, 18; 66 (upd.)
Kirkland & Ellis LLP, 65
Kirshenbaum Bond + Partners, Inc., 57
Kit Manufacturing Co., 18
Kitchell Corporation, 14
KitchenAid, 8
Kitty Hawk, Inc., 22
Kiva, 95
Kiwi International Airlines Inc., 20

KLA-Tencor Corporation, 11; 45 (upd.)
Klasky Csupo Inc. 78
Klein Tools, Inc., 95
Kleiner, Perkins, Caufield & Byers, 53
Klement's Sausage Company, 61
Kmart Corporation, V; 18 (upd.); 47 (upd.)
Knape & Vogt Manufacturing Company, 17
Knight Ridder, Inc., 67 (upd.)
Knight Trading Group, Inc., 70
Knight Transportation, Inc., 64
Knight-Ridder, Inc., IV; 15 (upd.)
Knoll, Inc., 14; 80 (upd.)
The Knot, Inc., 74
Knott's Berry Farm, 18
Knowledge Learning Corporation, 51
Knowledge Universe, Inc., 54
KnowledgeWare Inc., 9; 31 (upd.)
Koala Corporation, 44
Kobrand Corporation, 82
Koch Enterprises, Inc., 29
Koch Industries, Inc., IV; 20 (upd.); 77 (upd.)
Kohl's Corporation, 9; 30 (upd.); 77 (upd.)
Kohlberg Kravis Roberts & Co., 24; 56 (upd.)
Kohler Company, 7; 32 (upd.)
Kohn Pedersen Fox Associates P.C., 57
The Koll Company, 8
Kollmorgen Corporation, 18
Komag, Inc., 11
Koo Koo Roo, Inc., 25
Kopin Corporation, 80
Koppers Industries, Inc., I; 26 (upd.)
Koret of California, Inc., 62
Korn/Ferry International, 34
Kos Pharmaceuticals, Inc., 63
Koss Corporation, 38
Kraft Foods Inc., II; 7 (upd.); 45 (upd.); 91 (upd.)
KraftMaid Cabinetry, Inc., 72
Kraus-Anderson Companies, Inc., 36; 83 (upd.)
Krause Publications, Inc., 35
Krause's Furniture, Inc., 27
Kreisler Manufacturing Corporation, 97
Krispy Kreme Doughnuts, Inc., 21; 61 (upd.)
The Kroger Company, II; 15 (upd.); 65 (upd.)
Kroll Inc., 57
Kronos, Inc., 18
Kruse International, 88
The Krystal Company, 33
K2 Inc., 16; 84 (upd.)
KU Energy Corporation, 11
Kuhlman Corporation, 20
Kulicke and Soffa Industries, Inc., 33; 76 (upd.)
Kurzweil Technologies, Inc., 51
The Kushner-Locke Company, 25
Kyphon Inc., 87
L-3 Communications Holdings, Inc., 48
L. and J.G. Stickley, Inc., 50
L. Luria & Son, Inc., 19
L.A. Darling Company, 92
L.A. Gear, Inc., 8; 32 (upd.)
L.A. T Sportswear, Inc., 26
L.B. Foster Company, 33
L.L. Bean, Inc., 10; 38 (upd.); 91 (upd.)
The L.L. Knickerbocker Co., Inc., 25
L. M. Berry and Company, 80
L.S. Starrett Company, 13; 64 (upd.)
La Choy Food Products Inc., 25
La Madeleine French Bakery & Café, 33
The La Quinta Companies, 11; 42 (upd.)
La Reina Inc., 96
La-Z-Boy Incorporated, 14; 50 (upd.)
LaBarge Inc., 41
LabOne, Inc., 48
Labor Ready, Inc., 29; 88 (upd.)
Laboratory Corporation of America Holdings, 42 (upd.)
LaBranche & Co. Inc., 37
Lacks Enterprises Inc., 61
Laclede Steel Company, 15
LaCrosse Footwear, Inc., 18; 61 (upd.)
LADD Furniture, Inc., 12
Ladish Co., Inc., 30
Lafarge Corporation, 28
Laidlaw International, Inc., 80
Lakeland Industries, Inc., 45
Lakes Entertainment, Inc., 51
Lakeside Foods, Inc., 89
Lam Research Corporation, 11; 31 (upd.)
Lamar Advertising Company, 27; 70 (upd.)
The Lamaur Corporation, 41
Lamb Weston, Inc., 23
Lamonts Apparel, Inc., 15
The Lamson & Sessions Co., 13; 61 (upd.)
Lancair International, Inc., 67
Lancaster Colony Corporation, 8; 61 (upd.)
Lance, Inc., 14; 41 (upd.)
Lancer Corporation, 21
Land O'Lakes, Inc., II; 21 (upd.); 81 (upd.)
LandAmerica Financial Group, Inc., 85
Landauer, Inc., 51
Landec Corporation, 95
Landmark Communications, Inc., 12; 55 (upd.)
Landmark Theatre Corporation, 70
Landor Associates, 81
Landry's Restaurants, Inc., 65 (upd.)
Landry's Seafood Restaurants, Inc., 15
Lands' End, Inc., 9; 29 (upd.); 82 (upd.)
Landstar System, Inc., 63
Lane Bryant, Inc., 64
The Lane Co., Inc., 12
Lanier Worldwide, Inc., 75
Lanoga Corporation, 62
Larry Flynt Publishing Inc., 31
Larry H. Miller Group, 29
Las Vegas Sands, Inc., 50
Laserscope, 67
Lason, Inc., 31
Latham & Watkins, 33
Latrobe Brewing Company, 54
Lattice Semiconductor Corp., 16
Lawson Software, 38
Lawter International Inc., 14
Layne Christensen Company, 19
Lazare Kaplan International Inc., 21
Lazy Days RV Center, Inc., 69
LCA-Vision, Inc., 85
LCC International, Inc., 84
LCI International, Inc., 16
LDB Corporation, 53
LDDS-Metro Communications, Inc., 8
LDI Ltd., LLC, 76
Leap Wireless International, Inc., 69
LeapFrog Enterprises, Inc., 54
Lear Corporation, 71 (upd.)
Lear Seating Corporation, 16
Lear Siegler, Inc., I
Learjet Inc., 8; 27 (upd.)
Learning Care Group, Inc., 76 (upd.)
The Learning Company Inc., 24
Learning Tree International Inc., 24
LeaRonal, Inc., 23
Leaseway Transportation Corp., 12
Leatherman Tool Group, Inc., 51
Lebhar-Friedman, Inc., 55
LeBoeuf, Lamb, Greene & MacRae, L.L.P., 29
LECG Corporation, 93
Lechmere Inc., 10
Lechters, Inc., 11; 39 (upd.)
LeCroy Corporation, 41
Lee Apparel Company, Inc., 8
Lee Enterprises Inc., 11; 64 (upd.)
Leeann Chin, Inc., 30
Lefrak Organization Inc., 26
The Legal Aid Society, 48
Legal Sea Foods Inc., 96
Legent Corporation, 10
Legg Mason, Inc., 33
Leggett & Platt, Inc., 11; 48 (upd.)
Lehigh Portland Cement Company, 23
Leidy's, Inc., 93
Leiner Health Products Inc., 34
LendingTree, LLC, 93
Lennar Corporation, 11
Lennox International Inc., 8; 28 (upd.)
Lenovo Group Ltd., 80
Lenox, Inc., 12
LensCrafters Inc., 23; 76 (upd.)
Leo Burnett Company Inc., I; 20 (upd.)
The Leona Group LLC, 84
Leprino Foods Company, 28
Les Schwab Tire Centers, 50
Lesco Inc., 19
The Leslie Fay Companies, Inc., 8; 39 (upd.)
Leslie's Poolmart, Inc., 18
Leucadia National Corporation, 11; 71 (upd.)
Leupold & Stevens, Inc., 52
Level 3 Communications, Inc., 67
Levenger Company, 63
Lever Brothers Company, 9
Levi, Ray & Shoup, Inc., 96
Levi Strauss & Co., V; 16 (upd.)
Levitz Furniture Inc., 15
Levy Restaurants L.P., 26
Lewis Galoob Toys Inc., 16
LEXIS-NEXIS Group, 33
Lexmark International, Inc., 18; 79 (upd.)
LG&E Energy Corporation, 6; 51 (upd.)

Libbey Inc., 49
The Liberty Corporation, 22
Liberty Livewire Corporation, 42
Liberty Media Corporation, 50
Liberty Mutual Holding Company, 59
Liberty Orchards Co., Inc., 89
Liberty Property Trust, 57
Liberty Travel, Inc., 56
Life Care Centers of America Inc., 76
Life is Good, Inc., 80
Life Technologies, Inc., 17
Life Time Fitness, Inc., 66
LifeCell Corporation, 77
Lifeline Systems, Inc., 53
LifeLock, Inc., 91
LifePoint Hospitals, Inc., 69
Lifetime Brands, Inc., 73 (upd.)
Lifetime Entertainment Services, 51
Lifetime Hoan Corporation, 27
Lifeway Foods, Inc., 65
Ligand Pharmaceuticals Incorporated, 47
Lillian Vernon Corporation, 12; 35 (upd.); 92 (upd.)
Lilly Endowment Inc., 70
The Limited, Inc., V; 20 (upd.)
LIN Broadcasting Corp., 9
Lincare Holdings Inc., 43
Lincoln Center for the Performing Arts, Inc., 69
Lincoln Electric Co., 13
Lincoln National Corporation, III; 25 (upd.)
Lincoln Property Company, 8; 54 (upd.)
Lincoln Snacks Company, 24
Lincoln Telephone & Telegraph Company, 14
Lindal Cedar Homes, Inc., 29
Lindsay Manufacturing Co., 20
Linear Technology, Inc., 16
Linens 'n Things, Inc., 24; 75 (upd.)
Lintas: Worldwide, 14
The Lion Brewery, Inc., 86
Lionel L.L.C., 16
Liqui-Box Corporation, 16
Liquidnet, Inc. 79
Litehouse Inc., 60
Lithia Motors, Inc., 41
Littelfuse, Inc., 26
Little Caesar Enterprises, Inc., 7; 24 (upd.)
Little Tikes Company, 13; 62 (upd.)
Littleton Coin Company Inc., 82
Litton Industries, Inc., I; 11 (upd.)
LIVE Entertainment Inc., 20
Live Nation, Inc., 80 (upd.)
LivePerson, Inc., 91
Liz Claiborne, Inc., 8; 25 (upd.)
LKQ Corporation, 71
Lockheed Martin Corporation, I; 11 (upd.); 15 (upd.); 89 (upd.)
Loctite Corporation, 8; 30 (upd.)
LodgeNet Entertainment Corporation, 28
Loehmann's Inc., 24
Loews Corporation, I; 12 (upd.); 36 (upd.); 93 (upd.)
Logan's Roadhouse, Inc., 29
Logicon Inc., 20
LoJack Corporation, 48
London Fog Industries, Inc., 29
Lone Star Steakhouse & Saloon, Inc., 51
The Long & Foster Companies, Inc., 85
Long Island Bancorp, Inc., 16
Long Island Lighting Company, V
The Long Island Rail Road Company, 68
Long John Silver's, 13; 57 (upd.)
The Longaberger Company, 12; 44 (upd.)
Longs Drug Stores Corporation, V; 25 (upd.); 83 (upd.)
Longview Fibre Company, 8; 37 (upd.)
Loral Space & Communications Ltd., 8; 9; 54 (upd.)
Lost Arrow Inc., 22
LOT$OFF Corporation, 24
Lotus Development Corporation, 6; 25 (upd.)
LOUD Technologies, Inc., 95 (upd.)
The Louisiana Land and Exploration Company, 7
Louisiana-Pacific Corporation, IV; 31 (upd.)
Love's Travel Stops & Country Stores, Inc., 71
Lowe's Companies, Inc., V; 21 (upd.); 81 (upd.)
Lowrance Electronics, Inc., 18
LPA Holding Corporation, 81
LSB Industries, Inc., 77
LSI Logic Corporation, 13; 64
The LTV Corporation, I; 24 (upd.)
The Lubrizol Corporation, I; 30 (upd.); 83 (upd.)
Luby's, Inc., 17; 42 (upd.)
Lucasfilm Ltd., 12; 50 (upd.)
Lucent Technologies Inc., 34
Lucille Farms, Inc., 45
Lucky Stores, Inc., 27
Lufkin Industries Inc. 78
Luigino's, Inc., 64
Lukens Inc., 14
Lunar Corporation, 29
Lund Food Holdings, Inc., 22
Lund International Holdings, Inc., 40
Lutheran Brotherhood, 31
Lydall, Inc., 64
Lyman-Richey Corporation, 96
Lynch Corporation, 43
Lynden Incorporated, 91
Lyondell Chemical Company, IV; 45 (upd.)
M&F Worldwide Corp., 38
M. Shanken Communications, Inc., 50
M.A. Bruder & Sons, Inc., 56
M.A. Gedney Co., 51
M.A. Hanna Company, 8
M.H. Meyerson & Co., Inc., 46
Mac Frugal's Bargains - Closeouts Inc., 17
Mac-Gray Corporation, 44
MacAndrews & Forbes Holdings Inc., 28; 86 (upd.)
MacDermid Incorporated, 32
Mace Security International, Inc., 57
The Macerich Company, 57
MacGregor Golf Company, 68
Mack Trucks, Inc., I; 22 (upd.); 61 (upd.)
Mack-Cali Realty Corporation, 42
Mackay Envelope Corporation, 45
Mackie Designs Inc., 33
Macklowe Properties, Inc., 95
Macmillan, Inc., 7
MacNeil/Lehrer Productions, 87
The MacNeal-Schwendler Corporation, 25
Macromedia, Inc., 50
Macy's, Inc., 94 (upd.)
Madden's on Gull Lake, 52
Madison Dearborn Partners, LLC, 97
Madison Gas and Electric Company, 39
Madison-Kipp Corporation, 58
Mag Instrument, Inc., 67
MaggieMoo's International, 89
Magma Copper Company, 7
Magma Design Automation Inc. 78
Magma Power Company, 11
MagneTek, Inc., 15; 41 (upd.)
MAI Systems Corporation, 11
Maid-Rite Corporation, 62
Maidenform, Inc., 20; 59 (upd.)
Mail Boxes Etc., 18; 41 (upd.)
Mail-Well, Inc., 28
Make-A-Wish Foundation of America, 97
Maine & Maritimes Corporation, 56
Maine Central Railroad Company, 16
Maines Paper & Food Service Inc., 71
Majesco Entertainment Company, 85
The Major Automotive Companies, Inc., 45
Malcolm Pirnie, Inc., 42
Malden Mills Industries, Inc., 16
Mallinckrodt Group Inc., 19
Malt-O-Meal Company, 22; 63 (upd.)
Management and Training Corporation, 28
Manatron, Inc., 86
Mandalay Resort Group, 32 (upd.)
Manhattan Associates, Inc., 67
Manhattan Group, LLC, 80
Manheim, 88
The Manitowoc Company, Inc., 18; 59 (upd.)
Mannatech Inc., 33
Manning Selvage & Lee (MS&L), 76
MannKind Corporation, 87
Manor Care, Inc., 6; 25 (upd.)
Manpower Inc., 9; 30 (upd.); 73 (upd.)
ManTech International Corporation, 97
Manufactured Home Communities, Inc., 22
Manufacturers Hanover Corporation, II
Manville Corporation, III; 7 (upd.)
MAPCO Inc., IV
MAPICS, Inc., 55
Maple Grove Farms of Vermont, 88
Maples Industries, Inc., 83
Marble Slab Creamery, Inc., 87
March of Dimes, 31
Marchex, Inc., 72
marchFIRST, Inc., 34
Marco Business Products, Inc., 75
Marco's Franchising LLC, 86
The Marcus Corporation, 21
Marie Callender's Restaurant & Bakery, Inc., 28
Marine Products Corporation, 75
MarineMax, Inc., 30
Marion Laboratories, Inc., I

Marisa Christina, Inc., 15
Maritz Inc., 38
Mark IV Industries, Inc., 7; 28 (upd.)
Mark T. Wendell Tea Company, 94
The Mark Travel Corporation, 80
Marks Brothers Jewelers, Inc., 24
Marlin Business Services Corp., 89
The Marmon Group, Inc., IV; 16 (upd.); 70 (upd.)
Marquette Electronics, Inc., 13
Marriott International, Inc., III; 21 (upd.); 83 (upd.)
Mars, Incorporated, 7; 40 (upd.)
Mars Petcare US Inc., 96
Marsh & McLennan Companies, Inc., III; 45 (upd.)
Marsh Supermarkets, Inc., 17; 76 (upd.)
Marshall & Ilsley Corporation, 56
Marshall Field's, 63
Marshalls Incorporated, 13
Marshfield Clinic Inc., 82
Martek Biosciences Corporation, 65
Marten Transport, Ltd., 84
Martha Stewart Living Omnimedia, Inc., 24; 73 (upd.)
Martignetti Companies, 84
Martin Franchises, Inc., 80
Martin Industries, Inc., 44
Martin Marietta Corporation, I
MartinLogan, Ltd., 85
Martz Group, 56
Marvel Entertainment Inc., 10; 78 (upd.)
Marvin Lumber & Cedar Company, 22
Mary Kay Inc., 9; 30 (upd.); 84 (upd.)
Maryland & Virginia Milk Producers Cooperative Association, Inc., 80
Maryville Data Systems Inc., 96
The Maschhoffs, Inc., 82
Masco Corporation, III; 20 (upd.); 39 (upd.)
Mashantucket Pequot Gaming Enterprise Inc., 35
Masland Corporation, 17
Massachusetts Mutual Life Insurance Company, III; 53 (upd.)
Massey Energy Company, 57
MasTec, Inc., 19; 55 (upd.)
Master Lock Company, 45
MasterBrand Cabinets, Inc., 71
MasterCard Worldwide, 9; 96 (upd.)
MasterCraft Boat Company, Inc., 90
Match.com, LP, 87
Material Sciences Corporation, 63
The MathWorks, Inc., 80
Matria Healthcare, Inc., 17
Matrix Essentials Inc., 90
Matrix Service Company, 65
Matrixx Initiatives, Inc., 74
Matt Prentice Restaurant Group, 70
Mattel, Inc., 7; 25 (upd.); 61 (upd.)
Matthews International Corporation, 29; 77 (upd.)
Maui Land & Pineapple Company, Inc., 29
Maui Wowi, Inc., 85
Mauna Loa Macadamia Nut Corporation, 64
Maurices Inc., 95
Maverick Ranch Association, Inc., 88
Maverick Tube Corporation, 59
Max & Erma's Restaurants Inc., 19
Maxco Inc., 17
Maxicare Health Plans, Inc., III; 25 (upd.)
The Maxim Group, 25
Maxim Integrated Products, Inc., 16
MAXIMUS, Inc., 43
Maxtor Corporation, 10
Maxus Energy Corporation, 7
Maxwell Shoe Company, Inc., 30
MAXXAM Inc., 8
Maxxim Medical Inc., 12
The May Department Stores Company, V; 19 (upd.); 46 (upd.)
Mayer, Brown, Rowe & Maw, 47
Mayfield Dairy Farms, Inc., 74
Mayflower Group Inc., 6
Mayo Foundation, 9; 34 (upd.)
Mayor's Jewelers, Inc., 41
Maytag Corporation, III; 22 (upd.); 82 (upd.)
Mazel Stores, Inc., 29
Mazzio's Corporation, 76
MBC Holding Company, 40
MBIA Inc., 73
MBNA Corporation, 12; 33 (upd.)
MCA Inc., II
McAfee Inc., 94
McAlister's Corporation, 66
McCarthy Building Companies, Inc., 48
McCaw Cellular Communications, Inc., 6
McClain Industries, Inc., 51
The McClatchy Company, 33; 92 (upd.)
McCormick & Company, Incorporated, 7; 27 (upd.)
McCormick & Schmick's Seafood Restaurants, Inc., 71
McCoy Corporation, 58
McDATA Corporation, 75
McDermott International, Inc., III; 37 (upd.)
McDonald's Corporation, II; 7 (upd.); 26 (upd.); 63 (upd.)
McDonnell Douglas Corporation, I; 11 (upd.)
McGrath RentCorp, 91
The McGraw-Hill Companies, Inc., IV; 18 (upd.); 51 (upd.)
MCI WorldCom, Inc., V; 27 (upd.)
McIlhenny Company, 20
McJunkin Corporation, 63
McKee Foods Corporation, 7; 27 (upd.)
McKesson Corporation, I; 12; 47 (upd.)
McKinsey & Company, Inc., 9
McLane Company, Inc., 13
McLeodUSA Incorporated, 32
McMenamins Pubs and Breweries, 65
McNaughton Apparel Group, Inc., 92 (upd.)
MCN Corporation, 6
MCSi, Inc., 41
McWane Corporation, 55
MDU Resources Group, Inc., 7; 42 (upd.)
The Mead Corporation, IV; 19 (upd.)
Mead Data Central, Inc., 10
Mead Johnson & Company, 84
Meade Instruments Corporation, 41
Meadowcraft, Inc., 29
MeadWestvaco Corporation, 76 (upd.)
Measurement Specialties, Inc., 71
Mecklermedia Corporation, 24
Medarex, Inc., 85
Medco Containment Services Inc., 9
MEDecision, Inc., 95
Media Arts Group, Inc., 42
Media General, Inc., 7; 38 (upd.)
Mediacom Communications Corporation, 69
MediaNews Group, Inc., 70
Medical Information Technology Inc., 64
Medical Management International, Inc., 65
Medical Staffing Network Holdings, Inc., 89
Medicis Pharmaceutical Corporation, 59
Medifast, Inc., 97
MedImmune, Inc., 35
Medis Technologies Ltd., 77
Meditrust, 11
Medline Industries, Inc., 61
Medtronic, Inc., 8; 30 (upd.); 67 (upd.)
Medusa Corporation, 24
Megafoods Stores Inc., 13
Meier & Frank Co., 23
Meijer Incorporated, 7; 27 (upd.)
Mel Farr Automotive Group, 20
Melaleuca Inc., 31
Melamine Chemicals, Inc., 27
Mellon Bank Corporation, II
Mellon Financial Corporation, 44 (upd.)
Mellon-Stuart Company, I
The Melting Pot Restaurants, Inc., 74
Melville Corporation, V
Melvin Simon and Associates, Inc., 8
MEMC Electronic Materials, Inc., 81
Memorial Sloan-Kettering Cancer Center, 57
Memry Corporation, 72
The Men's Wearhouse, Inc., 17; 48 (upd.)
Menard, Inc., 34
Menasha Corporation, 8; 59 (upd.)
Mendocino Brewing Company, Inc., 60
The Mentholatum Company Inc., 32
Mentor Corporation, 26
Mentor Graphics Corporation, 11
Mercantile Bankshares Corp., 11
Mercantile Stores Company, Inc., V; 19 (upd.)
Mercer International Inc., 64
Merck & Co., Inc., I; 11 (upd.); 34 (upd.); 95 (upd.)
Mercury Air Group, Inc., 20
Mercury General Corporation, 25
Mercury Interactive Corporation, 59
Mercury Marine Group, 68
Meredith Corporation, 11; 29 (upd.); 74 (upd.)
Merge Healthcare, 85
Meridian Bancorp, Inc., 11
Meridian Gold, Incorporated, 47
Merillat Industries Inc., 13
Merillat Industries, LLC, 69 (upd.)
Merisant Worldwide, Inc., 70
Merisel, Inc., 12
Merit Medical Systems, Inc., 29

MeritCare Health System, 88
Meritage Corporation, 26
Merix Corporation, 36; 75 (upd.)
Merrell Dow, Inc., I; 9 (upd.)
Merriam-Webster Inc., 70
Merrill Corporation, 18; 47 (upd.)
Merrill Lynch & Co., Inc., II; 13 (upd.); 40 (upd.)
Merry-Go-Round Enterprises, Inc., 8
Mervyn's California, 10; 39 (upd.)
Mesa Air Group, Inc., 11; 32 (upd.); 77 (upd.)
Mesaba Holdings, Inc., 28
Mestek Inc., 10
Metal Management, Inc., 92
Metalico Inc., 97
Metatec International, Inc., 47
Meteor Industries Inc., 33
Methode Electronics, Inc., 13
Metris Companies Inc., 56
Metro Information Services, Inc., 36
Metro-Goldwyn-Mayer Inc., 25 (upd.); 84 (upd.)
Metrocall, Inc., 41
Metromedia Company, 7; 14; 61 (upd.)
Metropolitan Baseball Club Inc., 39
Metropolitan Financial Corporation, 13
Metropolitan Life Insurance Company, III; 52 (upd.)
The Metropolitan Museum of Art, 55
Metropolitan Opera Association, Inc., 40
Metropolitan Transportation Authority, 35
Mexican Restaurants, Inc., 41
MFS Communications Company, Inc., 11
MGA Entertainment, Inc., 95
MGIC Investment Corp., 52
MGM Grand Inc., 17
MGM/UA Communications Company, II
Miami Herald Media Company, 92
Michael Anthony Jewelers, Inc., 24
Michael Baker Corporation, 14; 51 (upd.)
Michael C. Fina Co., Inc., 52
Michael Foods, Inc., 25
Michaels Stores, Inc., 17; 71 (upd.)
Michigan Bell Telephone Co., 14
Michigan National Corporation, 11
Michigan Sporting Goods Distributors, Inc., 72
Micrel, Incorporated, 77
Micro Warehouse, Inc., 16
MicroAge, Inc., 16
Microdot Inc., 8
Micron Technology, Inc., 11; 29 (upd.)
Micros Systems, Inc., 18
Microsemi Corporation, 94
Microsoft Corporation, 6; 27 (upd.); 63 (upd.)
MicroStrategy Incorporated, 87
Mid-America Apartment Communities, Inc., 85
Mid-America Dairymen, Inc., 7
Midas Inc., 10; 56 (upd.)
The Middleby Corporation, 22
Middlesex Water Company, 45
The Middleton Doll Company, 53
The Midland Company, 65
Midway Airlines Corporation, 33
Midway Games, Inc., 25
Midwest Air Group, Inc., 35; 85 (upd.)
Midwest Grain Products, Inc., 49
Midwest Resources Inc., 6
Mikasa, Inc., 28
Mike-Sell's Inc., 15
Mikohn Gaming Corporation, 39
Milacron, Inc., 53 (upd.)
Milbank, Tweed, Hadley & McCloy, 27
Miles Laboratories, I
Millennium Pharmaceuticals, Inc., 47
Miller Brewing Company, I; 12 (upd.)
Miller Industries, Inc., 26
Miller Publishing Group, LLC, 57
Milliken & Co., V; 17 (upd.); 82 (upd.)
Milliman USA, 66
Millipore Corporation, 25; 84 (upd.)
The Mills Corporation, 77
Milnot Company, 46
Milton Bradley Company, 21
Milton CAT, Inc., 86
Milwaukee Brewers Baseball Club, 37
Mine Safety Appliances Company, 31
The Miner Group International, 22
Minerals Technologies Inc., 11; 52 (upd.)
Minnesota Mining & Manufacturing Company (3M), I; 8 (upd.); 26 (upd.)
Minnesota Power, Inc., 11; 34 (upd.)
Minntech Corporation, 22
The Minute Maid Company, 28
Minuteman International Inc., 46
Minyard Food Stores, Inc., 33; 86 (upd.)
Mirage Resorts, Incorporated, 6; 28 (upd.)
Miramax Film Corporation, 64
Misonix, Inc., 80
Mississippi Chemical Corporation, 39
Mitchell Energy and Development Corporation, 7
MITRE Corporation, 26
Mity Enterprises, Inc., 38
MIVA, Inc., 83
MNS, Ltd., 65
Mobil Corporation, IV; 7 (upd.); 21 (upd.)
Mobile Mini, Inc., 58
Mobile Telecommunications Technologies Corp., 18
Mocon, Inc., 76
Modern Woodmen of America, 66
Modine Manufacturing Company, 8; 56 (upd.)
Modtech Holdings, Inc., 77
Moen Incorporated, 12
Mohawk Industries, Inc., 19; 63 (upd.)
Mohegan Tribal Gaming Authority, 37
Moldflow Corporation, 73
Molex Incorporated, 11; 54 (upd.)
Molson Coors Brewing Company, 77 (upd.)
Monaco Coach Corporation, 31
Monadnock Paper Mills, Inc., 21
Monarch Casino & Resort, Inc., 65
The Monarch Cement Company, 72
MoneyGram International, Inc., 94
Monfort, Inc., 13
Monro Muffler Brake, Inc., 24
Monrovia Nursery Company, 70
The Mosaic Company, 91
Monsanto Company, I; 9 (upd.); 29 (upd.); 77 (upd.)
Monster Cable Products, Inc., 69
Monster Worldwide Inc., 74 (upd.)
Montana Coffee Traders, Inc., 60
The Montana Power Company, 11; 44 (upd.)
Monterey Pasta Company, 58
Montgomery Ward & Co., Incorporated, V; 20 (upd.)
Moody's Corporation, 65
Moog Inc., 13
Moog Music, Inc., 75
Mooney Aerospace Group Ltd., 52
Moore Medical Corp., 17
Moore-Handley, Inc., 39
Moran Towing Corporation, Inc., 15
The Morgan Group, Inc., 46
Morgan, Lewis & Bockius LLP, 29
Morgan Stanley Dean Witter & Company, II; 16 (upd.); 33 (upd.)
Morgans Hotel Group Company, 80
Morinda Holdings, Inc., 82
Morningstar Inc., 68
Morris Communications Corporation, 36
Morris Travel Services L.L.C., 26
Morrison & Foerster LLP 78
Morrison Knudsen Corporation, 7; 28 (upd.)
Morrison Restaurants Inc., 11
Morrow Equipment Co. L.L.C., 87
Morse Shoe Inc., 13
Morton International Inc., I; 9 (upd.); 80 (upd.)
Morton Thiokol, Inc., I
Morton's Restaurant Group, Inc., 30; 88 (upd.)
Mosinee Paper Corporation, 15
Mossimo, 27; 96 (upd.)
Motel 6, 13; 56 (upd.)
Mothers Against Drunk Driving (MADD), 51
Mothers Work, Inc., 18
The Motley Fool, Inc., 40
Moto Photo, Inc., 45
Motor Cargo Industries, Inc., 35
Motorcar Parts & Accessories, Inc., 47
Motorola, Inc., II; 11 (upd.); 34 (upd.); 93 (upd.)
Motown Records Company L.P., 26
Mott's Inc., 57
Mountain States Mortgage Centers, Inc., 29
Movado Group, Inc., 28
Movie Gallery, Inc., 31
Movie Star Inc., 17
MPS Group, Inc., 49
MPW Industrial Services Group, Inc., 53
Mr. Coffee, Inc., 15
Mr. Gasket Inc., 15
Mr. Gatti's, LP, 87
Mrs. Baird's Bakeries, 29
Mrs. Fields' Original Cookies, Inc., 27
Mrs. Grossman's Paper Company Inc., 84
MSC Industrial Direct Co., Inc., 71
Mt. Olive Pickle Company, Inc., 44
MTR Gaming Group, Inc., 75
MTS Inc., 37

Mueller Industries, Inc., 7; 52 (upd.)
Mullen Advertising Inc., 51
Multi-Color Corporation, 53
Multimedia Games, Inc., 41
Multimedia, Inc., 11
Murdock Madaus Schwabe, 26
Murphy Family Farms Inc., 22
Murphy Oil Corporation, 7; 32 (upd.); 95 (upd.)
The Musco Family Olive Co., 91
Musco Lighting, 83
Musicland Stores Corporation, 9; 38 (upd.)
The Mutual Benefit Life Insurance Company, III
The Mutual Life Insurance Company of New York, III
Muzak, Inc., 18
MWH Preservation Limited Partnership, 65
MWI Veterinary Supply, Inc., 80
Mycogen Corporation, 21
Myers Industries, Inc., 19; 96 (upd.
Mylan Laboratories Inc., I; 20 (upd.); 59 (upd.)
Myriad Restaurant Group, Inc., 87
Myriad Genetics, Inc., 95
N.F. Smith & Associates LP, 70
Nabisco Foods Group, II; 7 (upd.)
Nabors Industries, Inc., 9
NACCO Industries Inc., 7; 78 (upd.)
Nalco Holding Company, I; 12 (upd.); 89 (upd.)
Nantucket Allserve, Inc., 22
Napster, Inc., 69
NASD, 54 (upd.)
The NASDAQ Stock Market, Inc., 92
Nash Finch Company, 8; 23 (upd.); 65 (upd.)
Nashua Corporation, 8
Nastech Pharmaceutical Company Inc. 79
Nathan's Famous, Inc., 29
National Amusements Inc., 28
National Aquarium in Baltimore, Inc., 74
National Association for Stock Car Auto Racing, 32
National Association of Securities Dealers, Inc., 10
National Audubon Society, 26
National Auto Credit, Inc., 16
The National Bank of South Carolina, 76
National Beverage Corporation, 26; 88 (upd.)
National Broadcasting Company, Inc., II; 6 (upd.); 28 (upd.)
National Can Corporation, I
National Car Rental System, Inc., 10
National City Corporation, 15; 97 (upd.)
National Collegiate Athletic Association, 96
National Convenience Stores Incorporated, 7
National Discount Brokers Group, Inc., 28
National Distillers and Chemical Corporation, I
National Educational Music Co. Ltd., 47
National Envelope Corporation, 32
National Equipment Services, Inc., 57
National Financial Partners Corp., 65
National Football League, 29
National Frozen Foods Corporation, 94
National Fuel Gas Company, 6; 95 (upd.)
National Geographic Society, 9; 30 (upd.); 79 (upd.)
National Grape Cooperative Association, Inc., 20
National Grid USA, 51 (upd.)
National Gypsum Company, 10
National Health Laboratories Incorporated, 11
National Heritage Academies, Inc., 60
National Hockey League, 35
National Home Centers, Inc., 44
National Instruments Corporation, 22
National Intergroup, Inc., V
National Journal Group Inc., 67
National Media Corporation, 27
National Medical Enterprises, Inc., III
National Medical Health Card Systems, Inc. 79
National Oilwell, Inc., 54
National Organization for Women, Inc., 55
National Patent Development Corporation, 13
National Picture & Frame Company, 24
National Presto Industries, Inc., 16; 43 (upd.)
National Public Radio, Inc., 19; 47 (upd.)
National R.V. Holdings, Inc., 32
National Railroad Passenger Corporation (Amtrak), 22; 66 (upd.)
National Record Mart, Inc., 29
National Research Corporation, 87
National Rifle Association of America, 37
National Sanitary Supply Co., 16
National Semiconductor Corporation, II; VI, 26 (upd.); 69 (upd.)
National Service Industries, Inc., 11; 54 (upd.)
National Standard Co., 13
National Starch and Chemical Company, 49
National Steel Corporation, 12
National TechTeam, Inc., 41
National Thoroughbred Racing Association, 58
National Weather Service, 91
National Wine & Spirits, Inc., 49
NationsBank Corporation, 10
Natrol, Inc., 49
Natural Alternatives International, Inc., 49
Natural Ovens Bakery, Inc., 72
Natural Selection Foods, 54
Natural Wonders Inc., 14
Naturally Fresh, Inc., 88
The Nature Conservancy, 28
Nature's Sunshine Products, Inc., 15
Naumes, Inc., 81
Nautica Enterprises, Inc., 18; 44 (upd.)
Navarre Corporation, 24
Navigant Consulting, Inc., 93
Navigant International, Inc., 47
The Navigators Group, Inc., 92
Navistar International Corporation, I; 10 (upd.)
NAVTEQ Corporation, 69
Navy Exchange Service Command, 31
Navy Federal Credit Union, 33
NBD Bancorp, Inc., 11
NBGS International, Inc., 73
NBTY, Inc., 31
NCH Corporation, 8
NCI Building Systems, Inc., 88
NCL Corporation 79
NCNB Corporation, II
NCO Group, Inc., 42
NCR Corporation, III; 6 (upd.); 30 (upd.); 90 (upd.)
Nebraska Book Company, Inc., 65
Nebraska Furniture Mart, Inc., 94
Nebraska Public Power District, 29
Neenah Foundry Company, 68
Neff Corp., 32
NeighborCare, Inc., 67 (upd.)
The Neiman Marcus Group, Inc., 12; 49 (upd.)
Nektar Therapeutics, 91
Neogen Corporation, 94
NERCO, Inc., 7
Netezza Corporation, 69
Netflix, Inc., 58
NETGEAR, Inc., 81
NetIQ Corporation 79
NetJets Inc., 96 (upd.)
Netscape Communications Corporation, 15; 35 (upd.)
Network Appliance, Inc., 58
Network Associates, Inc., 25
Network Equipment Technologies Inc., 92
Neuberger Berman Inc., 57
NeuStar, Inc., 81
Neutrogena Corporation, 17
Nevada Bell Telephone Company, 14
Nevada Power Company, 11
Nevamar Company, 82
New Balance Athletic Shoe, Inc., 25; 68 (upd.)
New Belgium Brewing Company, Inc., 68
New Brunswick Scientific Co., Inc., 45
New Chapter Inc., 96
New Dana Perfumes Company, 37
New England Business Service Inc., 18; 78 (upd.)
New England Confectionery Co., 15
New England Electric System, V
New England Mutual Life Insurance Company, III
New Jersey Devils, 84
New Jersey Manufacturers Insurance Company, 96
New Jersey Resources Corporation, 54
New Line Cinema, Inc., 47
New Orleans Saints LP, 58
The New Piper Aircraft, Inc., 44
New Plan Realty Trust, 11
New Seasons Market, 75
New Street Capital Inc., 8
New Times, Inc., 45
New Valley Corporation, 17
New World Pasta Company, 53
New World Restaurant Group, Inc., 44

New York City Health and Hospitals Corporation, 60
New York City Off-Track Betting Corporation, 51
New York Community Bancorp Inc. 78
New York Daily News, 32
New York Health Care, Inc., 72
New York Life Insurance Company, III; 45 (upd.)
New York Restaurant Group, Inc., 32
New York Shakespeare Festival Management, 93
New York State Electric and Gas, 6
New York Stock Exchange, Inc., 9; 39 (upd.)
The New York Times Company, IV; 19 (upd.); 61 (upd.)
Neways Inc. 78
Newcor, Inc., 40
Newell Rubbermaid Inc., 9; 52 (upd.)
Newfield Exploration Company, 65
Newhall Land and Farming Company, 14
Newly Weds Foods, Inc., 74
Newman's Own, Inc., 37
Newmont Mining Corporation, 7; 94 (upd.)
Newpark Resources, Inc., 63
Newport Corporation, 71
Newport News Shipbuilding Inc., 13; 38 (upd.)
News America Publishing Inc., 12
NewYork-Presbyterian Hospital, 59
Nexstar Broadcasting Group, Inc., 73
Nextel Communications, Inc., 10; 27 (upd.)
NFL Films, 75
NFO Worldwide, Inc., 24
NGC Corporation, 18
Niagara Corporation, 28
Niagara Mohawk Holdings Inc., V; 45 (upd.)
Nichols Research Corporation, 18
Nicklaus Companies, 45
Nicor Inc., 6; 86 (upd.)
NIKE, Inc., V; 8 (upd.); 36 (upd.); 75 (upd.)
Nikken Global Inc., 32
Niman Ranch, Inc., 67
Nimbus CD International, Inc., 20
Nine West Group, Inc., 11; 39 (upd.)
99¢ Only Stores, 25
NIPSCO Industries, Inc., 6
Nitches, Inc., 53
NL Industries, Inc., 10
Nobel Learning Communities, Inc., 37; 76 (upd.)
Noble Affiliates, Inc., 11
Noble Roman's Inc., 14
Noland Company, 35
Nolo.com, Inc., 49
Noodle Kidoodle, 16
Noodles & Company, Inc., 55
Nooter Corporation, 61
Norcal Waste Systems, Inc., 60
NordicTrack, 22
Nordson Corporation, 11; 48 (upd.)
Nordstrom, Inc., V; 18 (upd.); 67 (upd.)
Norelco Consumer Products Co., 26
Norfolk Southern Corporation, V; 29 (upd.); 75 (upd.)
Norm Thompson Outfitters, Inc., 47
Norrell Corporation, 25
Norstan, Inc., 16
Nortek, Inc., 34
North Atlantic Trading Company Inc., 65
The North Face, Inc., 18; 78 (upd.)
North Fork Bancorporation, Inc., 46
North Pacific Group, Inc., 61
North Star Steel Company, 18
Northeast Utilities, V; 48 (upd.)
Northern States Power Company, V; 20 (upd.)
Northern Trust Company, 9
Northland Cranberries, Inc., 38
Northrop Grumman Corporation, I; 11 (upd.); 45 (upd.)
Northwest Airlines Corporation, I; 6 (upd.); 26 (upd.); 74 (upd.)
Northwest Natural Gas Company, 45
NorthWestern Corporation, 37
Northwestern Mutual Life Insurance Company, III; 45 (upd.)
Norton Company, 8
Norton McNaughton, Inc., 27
Norwood Promotional Products, Inc., 26
NovaCare, Inc., 11
NovaStar Financial, Inc., 91
Novell, Inc., 6; 23 (upd.)
Novellus Systems, Inc., 18
Noven Pharmaceuticals, Inc., 55
NPC International, Inc., 40
The NPD Group, Inc., 68
NRG Energy, Inc. 79
NRT Incorporated, 61
NSF International, 72
NSS Enterprises Inc. 78
NTN Buzztime, Inc., 86
Nu Skin Enterprises, Inc., 27; 76 (upd.)
Nu-kote Holding, Inc., 18
Nucor Corporation, 7; 21 (upd.); 79 (upd.)
Nutraceutical International Corporation, 37
NutraSweet Company, 8
Nutrition 21 Inc., 97
NutriSystem, Inc., 71
Nutrition for Life International Inc., 22
NVIDIA Corporation, 54
NVR Inc., 8; 70 (upd.)
NYMAGIC, Inc., 41
NYNEX Corporation, V
O.C. Tanner Co., 69
Oak Harbor Freight Lines, Inc., 53
Oak Industries Inc., 21
Oak Technology, Inc., 22
Oakhurst Dairy, 60
Oakleaf Waste Management, LLC, 97
Oakley, Inc., 18; 49 (upd.)
Oaktree Capital Management, LLC, 71
Oakwood Homes Corporation, 15
Obagi Medical Products, Inc., 95
Oberto Sausage Company, Inc., 92
Obie Media Corporation, 56
Occidental Petroleum Corporation, IV; 25 (upd.); 71 (upd.)
Ocean Beauty Seafoods, Inc., 74
Ocean Spray Cranberries, Inc., 7; 25 (upd.); 83 (upd.)
Oceaneering International, Inc., 63
O'Charley's Inc., 19; 60 (upd.)
OCLC Online Computer Library Center, Inc., 96
Octel Messaging, 14; 41 (upd.)
Ocular Sciences, Inc., 65
Odetics Inc., 14
ODL, Inc., 55
Odwalla, Inc., 31
Odyssey Marine Exploration, Inc., 91
OEC Medical Systems, Inc., 27
Office Depot, Inc., 8; 23 (upd.); 65 (upd.)
OfficeMax, Inc., 15; 43 (upd.)
OfficeTiger, LLC, 75
Offshore Logistics, Inc., 37
Ogden Corporation, I; 6
The Ogilvy Group, Inc., I
Oglebay Norton Company, 17
Oglethorpe Power Corporation, 6
The Ohio Art Company, 14; 59 (upd.)
Ohio Bell Telephone Company, 14
Ohio Casualty Corp., 11
Ohio Edison Company, V
Oil-Dri Corporation of America, 20; 89 (upd.)
Oil States International, Inc., 77
The Oilgear Company, 74
Oklahoma Gas and Electric Company, 6
Olan Mills, Inc., 62
Old America Stores, Inc., 17
Old Dominion Freight Line, Inc., 57
Old Kent Financial Corp., 11
Old National Bancorp, 15
Old Navy, Inc., 70
Old Orchard Brands, LLC, 73
Old Republic International Corporation, 11; 58 (upd.)
Old Spaghetti Factory International Inc., 24
Old Town Canoe Company, 74
Olga's Kitchen, Inc., 80
Olin Corporation, I; 13 (upd.); 78 (upd.)
Olsten Corporation, 6; 29 (upd.)
OM Group Inc. 17; 78 (upd.)
Omaha Steaks International Inc., 62
O'Melveny & Myers, 37
OMI Corporation, 59
Omni Hotels Corp., 12
Omnicare, Inc., 49
Omnicell, Inc., 89
Omnicom Group, Inc., I; 22 (upd.); 77 (upd.)
OmniSource Corporation, 14
OMNOVA Solutions Inc., 59
Omrix Biopharmaceuticals, Inc., 95
On Assignment, Inc., 20
180s, L.L.C., 64
One Price Clothing Stores, Inc., 20
1-800-FLOWERS, Inc., 26
O'Neal Steel, Inc., 95
Oneida Ltd., 7; 31 (upd.); 88 (upd.)
ONEOK Inc., 7
Onion, Inc., 69
Onyx Acceptance Corporation, 59
Onyx Software Corporation, 53

OOC Inc., 97
Openwave Systems Inc., 95
Operation Smile, Inc., 75
Opinion Research Corporation, 46
Oppenheimer Wolff & Donnelly LLP, 71
Opsware Inc., 49
Option Care Inc., 48
Opus Group, 34
Oracle Corporation, 6; 24 (upd.); 67 (upd.)
Orange Glo International, 53
OraSure Technologies, Inc., 75
Orbital Sciences Corporation, 22
Orbitz, Inc., 61
Orchard Supply Hardware Stores Corporation, 17
Ore-Ida Foods Inc., 13; 78 (upd.)
Oregon Chai, Inc., 49
Oregon Dental Service Health Plan, Inc., 51
Oregon Freeze Dry, Inc., 74
Oregon Metallurgical Corporation, 20
Oregon Steel Mills, Inc., 14
O'Reilly Automotive, Inc., 26; 78 (upd.)
Organic Valley (Coulee Region Organic Produce Pool), 53
Orion Pictures Corporation, 6
Orleans Homebuilders, Inc., 62
Ormat Technologies, Inc., 87
Ormet Corporation, 82
Orrick, Herrington and Sutcliffe LLP, 76
Orthodontic Centers of America, Inc., 35
The Orvis Company, Inc., 28
Oryx Energy Company, 7
Oscar Mayer Foods Corp., 12
OshKosh B'Gosh, Inc., 9; 42 (upd.)
Oshkosh Truck Corporation, 7
Oshman's Sporting Goods, Inc., 17
OSI Restaurant Partners, Inc., 88 (upd.)
Osmonics, Inc., 18
O'Sullivan Industries Holdings, Inc., 34
Otis Elevator Company, Inc., 13; 39 (upd.)
Otis Spunkmeyer, Inc., 28
OTR Express, Inc., 25
Ottaway Newspapers, Inc., 15
Otter Tail Power Company, 18
Outback Steakhouse, Inc., 12; 34 (upd.)
Outboard Marine Corporation, III; 20 (upd.)
Outdoor Research, Incorporated, 67
Outdoor Systems, Inc., 25
Outlook Group Corporation, 37
Outrigger Enterprises, Inc., 67
Overhead Door Corporation, 70
Overhill Corporation, 51
Overnite Corporation, 14; 58 (upd.)
Overseas Shipholding Group, Inc., 11
Overstock.com, Inc., 75
Owens & Minor, Inc., 16; 68 (upd.)
Owens Corning Corporation, III; 20 (upd.)
Owens-Illinois, Inc., I; 26 (upd.); 85 (upd.)
Owosso Corporation, 29
Oxford Health Plans, Inc., 16
Oxford Industries, Inc., 8; 84 (upd.)
P&C Foods Inc., 8
P & F Industries, Inc., 45
P.C. Richard & Son Corp., 23
P.F. Chang's China Bistro, Inc., 37; 86 (upd.)
P.H. Glatfelter Company, 8; 30 (upd.); 83 (upd.)
Paccar Inc., I; 26 (upd.)
Pacer International, Inc., 54
Pacer Technology, 40
Pacific Clay Products Inc., 88
Pacific Coast Building Products, Inc., 94
Pacific Coast Feather Company, 67
Pacific Coast Restaurants, Inc., 90
Pacific Ethanol, Inc., 81
Pacific Enterprises, V
Pacific Gas and Electric Company, V
Pacific Sunwear of California, Inc., 28
Pacific Telecom, Inc., 6
Pacific Telesis Group, V
PacifiCare Health Systems, Inc., 11
PacifiCorp, V; 26 (upd.)
Packaging Corporation of America, 12; 51 (upd.)
Packard Bell Electronics, Inc., 13
Packeteer, Inc., 81
Paddock Publications, Inc., 53
Paging Network Inc., 11
PaineWebber Group Inc., II; 22 (upd.)
Palace Sports & Entertainment, Inc., 97
Pall Corporation, 9; 72 (upd.)
Palm Harbor Homes, Inc., 39
Palm Management Corporation, 71
Palm, Inc., 36; 75 (upd.)
Palmer & Cay, Inc., 69
Palmer Candy Company, 80
Palomar Medical Technologies, Inc., 22
Pamida Holdings Corporation, 15
The Pampered Chef, Ltd., 18; 78 (upd.)
Pan American World Airways, Inc., I; 12 (upd.)
Pan-American Life Insurance Company, 48
Panamerican Beverages, Inc., 47
PanAmSat Corporation, 46
Panavision Inc., 24
Pancho's Mexican Buffet, Inc., 46
Panda Restaurant Group, Inc., 35; 97 (upd.)
Panera Bread Company, 44
Panhandle Eastern Corporation, V
Pantone Inc., 53
The Pantry, Inc., 36
Papa Gino's Holdings Corporation, Inc., 86
Papa John's International, Inc., 15; 71 (upd.)
Papa Murphy's International, Inc., 54
Papetti's Hygrade Egg Products, Inc., 39
Pappas Restaurants, Inc., 76
Par Pharmaceutical Companies, Inc., 65
The Paradies Shops, Inc., 88
Paradise Music & Entertainment, Inc., 42
Parametric Technology Corp., 16
Paramount Pictures Corporation, II; 94 (upd.)
PAREXEL International Corporation, 84
Paris Corporation, 22
Parisian, Inc., 14
Park Corp., 22
Park-Ohio Industries Inc., 17; 85 (upd.)
Parker Drilling Company, 28
Parker-Hannifin Corporation, III; 24 (upd.)
Parlex Corporation, 61
Parsons Brinckerhoff, Inc., 34
The Parsons Corporation, 8; 56 (upd.)
Party City Corporation, 54
Pathmark Stores, Inc., 23
Patina Oil & Gas Corporation, 24
Patrick Industries, Inc., 30
Patriot Transportation Holding, Inc., 91
Patterson Dental Co., 19
Patterson-UTI Energy, Inc., 55
Patton Boggs LLP, 71
Paul Harris Stores, Inc., 18
Paul, Hastings, Janofsky & Walker LLP, 27
Paul Mueller Company, 65
Paul Reed Smith Guitar Company, 89
The Paul Revere Corporation, 12
Paul, Weiss, Rifkind, Wharton & Garrison, 47
Paul-Son Gaming Corporation, 66
Paxson Communications Corporation, 33
Pay 'N Pak Stores, Inc., 9
Paychex, Inc., 15; 46 (upd.)
Payless Cashways, Inc., 11; 44 (upd.)
Payless ShoeSource, Inc., 18; 69 (upd.)
PayPal Inc., 58
The PBSJ Corporation, 82
PC Connection, Inc., 37
PCA International, Inc., 62
PCC Natural Markets, 94
PDI, Inc., 52
PDL BioPharma, Inc., 90
PDQ Food Stores, Inc. 79
PDS Gaming Corporation, 44
Peabody Coal Company, 10
Peabody Energy Corporation, 45 (upd.)
Peabody Holding Company, Inc., IV
The Peak Technologies Group, Inc., 14
Peapod, Inc., 30
Pearle Vision, Inc., 13
Peavey Electronics Corporation, 16; 94 (upd.)
PECO Energy Company, 11
Pediatric Services of America, Inc., 31
Pediatrix Medical Group, Inc., 61
Peebles Inc., 16; 43 (upd.)
Peet's Coffee & Tea, Inc., 38
Pegasus Solutions, Inc., 75
Pei Cobb Freed & Partners Architects LLP, 57
Pelican Products, Inc., 86
Pella Corporation, 12; 39 (upd.); 89 (upd.)
Pemco Aviation Group Inc., 54
Pendleton Grain Growers Inc., 64
Pendleton Woolen Mills, Inc., 42
Penford Corporation, 55
Penn Engineering & Manufacturing Corp., 28
Penn National Gaming, Inc., 33
Penn Traffic Company, 13
Penn Virginia Corporation, 85
Pennsylvania Blue Shield, III

Pennsylvania Power & Light Company, V
Pennwalt Corporation, I
PennWell Corporation, 55
Pennzoil-Quaker State Company, IV; 20 (upd.); 50 (upd.)
Penske Corporation, V; 19 (upd.); 84 (upd.)
Pentair, Inc., 7; 26 (upd.); 81 (upd.)
Pentech International, Inc., 29
Penton Media, Inc., 27
Penzeys Spices, Inc. 79
People Express Airlines, Inc., I
Peoples Energy Corporation, 6
PeopleSoft Inc., 14; 33 (upd.)
The Pep Boys—Manny, Moe & Jack, 11; 36 (upd.); 81 (upd.)
Pepper Hamilton LLP, 43
Pepperidge Farm, Incorporated, 81
The Pepsi Bottling Group, Inc., 40
PepsiAmericas, Inc., 67 (upd.)
PepsiCo, Inc., I; 10 (upd.); 38 (upd.); 93 (upd.)
Perdue Farms Inc., 7; 23 (upd.)
Performance Food Group, 31; 96 (upd.)
Perini Corporation, 8; 82 (upd.)
PerkinElmer Inc. 7; 78 (upd.)
Perkins Coie LLP, 56
Perkins Family Restaurants, L.P., 22
Perot Systems Corporation, 29
Perrigo Company, 12; 59 (upd.)
Perry Ellis International, Inc., 41
Perry's Ice Cream Company Inc., 90
The Perseus Books Group, 91
Pet Incorporated, 7
Petco Animal Supplies, Inc., 29; 74 (upd.)
Pete's Brewing Company, 22
Peter Kiewit Sons' Inc., 8
Peter Piper, Inc., 70
Peterbilt Motors Company, 89
Petersen Publishing Company, 21
Peterson American Corporation, 55
PetMed Express, Inc., 81
Petrie Stores Corporation, 8
Petrohawk Energy Corporation 79
Petroleum Helicopters, Inc., 35
Petrolite Corporation, 15
Petrossian Inc., 54
PETsMART, Inc., 14; 41 (upd.)
The Pew Charitable Trusts, 35
Pez Candy, Inc., 38
Pfizer Inc., I; 9 (upd.); 38 (upd.); 79 (upd.)
PFSweb, Inc., 73
PG&E Corporation, 26 (upd.)
Phar-Mor Inc., 12
Pharmacia & Upjohn Inc., I; 25 (upd.)
Pharmion Corporation, 91
Phat Fashions LLC, 49
Phelps Dodge Corporation, IV; 28 (upd.); 75 (upd.)
PHH Arval, V; 53 (upd.)
PHI, Inc., 80 (upd.)
Philadelphia Eagles, 37
Philadelphia Electric Company, V
Philadelphia Gas Works Company, 92
Philadelphia Media Holdings LLC, 92
Philadelphia Suburban Corporation, 39
Philharmonic-Symphony Society of New York, Inc. (New York Philharmonic), 69
Philip Morris Companies Inc., V; 18 (upd.); 44 (upd.)
Philip Services Corp., 73
Philips Electronics North America Corp., 13
Phillips, de Pury & Luxembourg, 49
Phillips Foods, Inc., 63; 90 (upd.)
Phillips International Inc. 78
Phillips Petroleum Company, IV; 40 (upd.)
Phillips-Van Heusen Corporation, 24
Phoenix Footwear Group, Inc., 70
The Phoenix Media/Communications Group, 91
PHP Healthcare Corporation, 22
PhyCor, Inc., 36
Physician Sales & Service, Inc., 14
Physio-Control International Corp., 18
Piccadilly Cafeterias, Inc., 19
PictureTel Corp., 10; 27 (upd.)
Piedmont Natural Gas Company, Inc., 27
Pier 1 Imports, Inc., 12; 34 (upd.); 95 (upd.)
Pierce Leahy Corporation, 24
Piercing Pagoda, Inc., 29
Piggly Wiggly Southern, Inc., 13
Pilgrim's Pride Corporation, 7; 23 (upd.); 90 (upd.
Pillowtex Corporation, 19; 41 (upd.)
The Pillsbury Company, II; 13 (upd.); 62 (upd.)
Pillsbury Madison & Sutro LLP, 29
Pilot Air Freight Corp., 67
Pilot Corporation, 49
Pilot Pen Corporation of America, 82
Pinkerton's Inc., 9
Pinnacle Airlines Corp., 73
Pinnacle West Capital Corporation, 6; 54 (upd.)
Pioneer Hi-Bred International, Inc., 9; 41 (upd.)
Pioneer Natural Resources Company, 59
Pioneer-Standard Electronics Inc., 19
Piper Jaffray Companies Inc., 22
Pitman Company, 58
Pitney Bowes Inc., III; 19; 47 (upd.)
Pittsburgh Brewing Company, 76
Pittsburgh Steelers Sports, Inc., 66
The Pittston Company, IV; 19 (upd.)
Pittway Corporation, 9; 33 (upd.)
Pixar Animation Studios, 34
Pixelworks, Inc., 69
Pizza Hut Inc., 7; 21 (upd.)
Pizza Inn, Inc., 46
Plain Dealer Publishing Company, 92
Plains Cotton Cooperative Association, 57
Planar Systems, Inc., 61
Planet Hollywood International, Inc., 18; 41 (upd.)
Plantation Pipe Line Company, 68
Plante & Moran, LLP, 71
Platinum Entertainment, Inc., 35
PLATINUM Technology, Inc., 14
Plato Learning, Inc., 44
Play by Play Toys & Novelties, Inc., 26
Playboy Enterprises, Inc., 18
PlayCore, Inc., 27
Players International, Inc., 22
Playskool, Inc., 25
Playtex Products, Inc., 15
Pleasant Company, 27
Pleasant Holidays LLC, 62
Plexus Corporation, 35; 80 (upd.)
Plum Creek Timber Company, Inc., 43
Pluma, Inc., 27
Ply Gem Industries Inc., 12
The PMI Group, Inc., 49
PMT Services, Inc., 24
The PNC Financial Services Group Inc., II; 13 (upd.); 46 (upd.)
PNM Resources Inc., 51 (upd.)
Pogo Producing Company, 39
Polar Air Cargo Inc., 60
Polaris Industries Inc., 12; 35 (upd.); 77 (upd.)
Polaroid Corporation, III; 7 (upd.); 28 (upd.); 93 (upd.)
Policy Management Systems Corporation, 11
Policy Studies, Inc., 62
Polk Audio, Inc., 34
Polo/Ralph Lauren Corporation, 12; 62 (upd.)
PolyGram N.V., 23
PolyMedica Corporation, 77
PolyOne Corporation, 87 (upd.)
Pomare Ltd., 88
Pomeroy Computer Resources, Inc., 33
Ponderosa Steakhouse, 15
Poof-Slinky, Inc., 61
Poore Brothers, Inc., 44
Pop Warner Little Scholars, Inc., 86
Pope & Talbot, Inc., 12; 61 (upd.)
Pope Resources LP, 74
Popular, Inc., 41
The Port Authority of New York and New Jersey, 48
Port Imperial Ferry Corporation, 70
Portal Software, Inc., 47
Portillo's Restaurant Group, Inc., 71
Portland General Corporation, 6
Portland Trail Blazers, 50
Post Properties, Inc., 26
Potbelly Sandwich Works, Inc., 83
Potlatch Corporation, 8; 34 (upd.); 87 (upd.)
Potomac Electric Power Company, 6
Potter & Brumfield Inc., 11
Powell's Books, Inc., 40
Power-One, Inc. 79
PowerBar Inc., 44
Powerhouse Technologies, Inc., 27
POZEN Inc., 81
PPG Industries, Inc., III; 22 (upd.); 81 (upd.)
PPL Corporation, 41 (upd.)
PR Newswire, 35
Prairie Farms Dairy, Inc., 47
Pratt & Whitney, 9
Praxair, Inc., 11; 48 (upd.)
Praxis Bookstore Group LLC, 90
Pre-Paid Legal Services, Inc., 20
Precision Castparts Corp., 15

Premark International, Inc., III
Premcor Inc., 37
Premier Industrial Corporation, 9
Premier Parks, Inc., 27
Premium Standard Farms, Inc., 30
PremiumWear, Inc., 30
Preserver Group, Inc., 44
President Casinos, Inc., 22
Pressman Toy Corporation, 56
Presstek, Inc., 33
Preston Corporation, 6
PRG-Schultz International, Inc., 73
Price Communications Corporation, 42
The Price Company, V
Price Pfister, Inc., 70
PriceCostco, Inc., 14
Priceline.com Incorporated, 57
PriceSmart, Inc., 71
PricewaterhouseCoopers, 9; 29 (upd.)
Pride International Inc. 78
Primark Corp., 13
Prime Hospitality Corporation, 52
Primedex Health Systems, Inc., 25
Primedia Inc., 22
Primerica Corporation, I
Prince Sports Group, Inc., 15
Princess Cruise Lines, 22
The Princeton Review, Inc., 42
Principal Mutual Life Insurance Company, III
Printpack, Inc., 68
Printrak, A Motorola Company, 44
Printronix, Inc., 18
Prison Rehabilitative Industries and Diversified Enterprises, Inc. (PRIDE), 53
Pro-Build Holdings Inc., 95 (upd.)
The Procter & Gamble Company, III; 8 (upd.); 26 (upd.); 67 (upd.)
Prodigy Communications Corporation, 34
Professional Bull Riders Inc., 55
The Professional Golfers' Association of America, 41
Proffitt's, Inc., 19
Programmer's Paradise, Inc., 81
Progress Energy, Inc., 74
Progress Software Corporation, 15
The Progressive Corporation, 11; 29 (upd.)
ProLogis, 57
Promus Companies, Inc., 9
Proskauer Rose LLP, 47
Protection One, Inc., 32
Provell Inc., 58 (upd.)
Providence Health System, 90
The Providence Journal Company, 28
The Providence Service Corporation, 64
Provident Bankshares Corporation, 85
Provident Life and Accident Insurance Company of America, III
Providian Financial Corporation, 52 (upd.)
Prudential Financial Inc., III; 30 (upd.); 82 (upd.)
PSI Resources, 6
Psychemedics Corporation, 89
Psychiatric Solutions, Inc., 68
Pubco Corporation, 17
Public Service Company of Colorado, 6
Public Service Company of New Hampshire, 21; 55 (upd.)
Public Service Company of New Mexico, 6
Public Service Enterprise Group Inc., V; 44 (upd.)
Public Storage, Inc., 52
Publishers Clearing House, 23; 64 (upd.)
Publishers Group, Inc., 35
Publix Supermarkets Inc., 7; 31 (upd.)
Pueblo Xtra International, Inc., 47
Puget Sound Energy Inc., 6; 50 (upd.)
Pulaski Furniture Corporation, 33; 80 (upd.)
Pulitzer Inc., 15; 58 (upd.)
Pulte Corporation, 8
Pulte Homes, Inc., 42 (upd.)
Pumpkin Masters, Inc., 48
Pure World, Inc., 72
Purina Mills, Inc., 32
Puritan-Bennett Corporation, 13
Purolator Products Company, 21; 74 (upd.)
Putt-Putt Golf Courses of America, Inc., 23
PVC Container Corporation, 67
PW Eagle, Inc., 48
Pyramid Breweries Inc., 33
Pyramid Companies, 54
Q.E.P. Co., Inc., 65
Qdoba Restaurant Corporation, 93
QRS Music Technologies, Inc., 95
QSC Audio Products, Inc., 56
Quad/Graphics, Inc., 19
Quaker Chemical Corp., 91
Quaker Fabric Corp., 19
Quaker Foods North America, 73 (upd.)
The Quaker Oats Company, II; 12 (upd.); 34 (upd.)
Quaker State Corporation, 7; 21 (upd.)
QUALCOMM Incorporated, 20; 47 (upd.)
Quality Chekd Dairies, Inc., 48
Quality Dining, Inc., 18
Quality Food Centers, Inc., 17
Quality Systems, Inc., 81
Quanex Corporation, 13; 62 (upd.)
Quanta Services, Inc. 79
Quantum Chemical Corporation, 8
Quantum Corporation, 10; 62 (upd.)
Quark, Inc., 36
Quest Diagnostics Inc., 26
Questar Corporation, 6; 26 (upd.)
The Quick & Reilly Group, Inc., 20
Quicken Loans, Inc., 93
Quidel Corporation, 80
The Quigley Corporation, 62
Quiksilver, Inc., 18; 79 (upd.)
QuikTrip Corporation, 36
Quill Corporation, 28
Quintiles Transnational Corporation, 21; 68 (upd.)
Quixote Corporation, 15
The Quizno's Corporation, 42
Quovadx Inc., 70
QVC Inc., 9; 58 (upd.)
Qwest Communications International, Inc., 37
R&B, Inc., 51
R.B. Pamplin Corp., 45
R.C. Bigelow, Inc., 49
R.C. Willey Home Furnishings, 72
R.G. Barry Corporation, 17; 44 (upd.)
R.H. Macy & Co., Inc., V; 8 (upd.); 30 (upd.)
R.J. Reynolds Tobacco Holdings, Inc., 30 (upd.)
R.L. Polk & Co., 10
R. M. Palmer Co., 89
R.P. Scherer, I
R.R. Donnelley & Sons Company, IV; 9 (upd.); 38 (upd.)
Racal-Datacom Inc., 11
Racing Champions Corporation, 37
Rack Room Shoes, Inc., 84
Radian Group Inc., 42
Radiation Therapy Services, Inc., 85
Radio Flyer Inc., 34
Radio One, Inc., 67
RadioShack Corporation, 36 (upd.)
Radius Inc., 16
RAE Systems Inc., 83
Rag Shops, Inc., 30
RailTex, Inc., 20
Rain Bird Corporation, 84
Rainforest Café, Inc., 25; 88 (upd.)
Rainier Brewing Company, 23
Raley's Inc., 14; 58 (upd.)
Rally's, 25; 68 (upd.)
Ralphs Grocery Company, 35
Ralston Purina Company, II; 13 (upd.)
Ramsay Youth Services, Inc., 41
Ramtron International Corporation, 89
Rand McNally & Company, 28
Randall's Food Markets, Inc., 40
Random House, Inc., 13; 31 (upd.)
Range Resources Corporation, 45
Rapala-Normark Group, Ltd., 30
Rare Hospitality International Inc., 19
RathGibson Inc., 90
Ratner Companies, 72
Raven Industries, Inc., 33
Raving Brands, Inc., 64
Rawlings Sporting Goods Co., Inc., 24
Raychem Corporation, 8
Raymond James Financial Inc., 69
Rayonier Inc., 24
Rayovac Corporation, 13; 39 (upd.)
Raytech Corporation, 61
Raytheon Aircraft Holdings Inc., 46
Raytheon Company, II; 11 (upd.); 38 (upd.)
Razorfish, Inc., 37
RCA Corporation, II
RCM Technologies, Inc., 34
RCN Corporation, 70
RDO Equipment Company, 33
RE/MAX International, Inc., 59
Read-Rite Corp., 10
The Reader's Digest Association, Inc., IV; 17 (upd.); 71 (upd.)
Reading International Inc., 70
Real Times, Inc., 66
RealNetworks, Inc., 53

Reckson Associates Realty Corp., 47
Recording for the Blind & Dyslexic, 51
Recoton Corp., 15
Recovery Engineering, Inc., 25
Recreational Equipment, Inc., 18; 71 (upd.)
Recycled Paper Greetings, Inc., 21
Red Apple Group, Inc., 23
Red Hat, Inc., 45
Red McCombs Automotive Group, 91
Red Robin Gourmet Burgers, Inc., 56
Red Roof Inns, Inc., 18
Red Spot Paint & Varnish Company, 55
Red Wing Pottery Sales, Inc., 52
Red Wing Shoe Company, Inc., 9; 30 (upd.); 83 (upd.)
Redback Networks, Inc., 92
Reddy Ice Holdings, Inc., 80
Redhook Ale Brewery, Inc., 31; 88 (upd.)
Redken Laboratories Inc., 84
Redlon & Johnson, Inc., 97
RedPeg Marketing, 73
Reebok International Ltd., V; 9 (upd.); 26 (upd.)
Reed & Barton Corporation, 67
Reeds Jewelers, Inc., 22
Regal Entertainment Group, 59
Regal-Beloit Corporation, 18; 97 (upd.)
The Regence Group, 74
Regency Centers Corporation, 71
Regent Communications, Inc., 87
Regis Corporation, 18; 70 (upd.)
Reichhold Chemicals, Inc., 10
Reiter Dairy, LLC, 94
Rejuvenation, Inc., 91
Reliance Electric Company, 9
Reliance Group Holdings, Inc., III
Reliance Steel & Aluminum Company, 19; 70 (upd.)
Reliant Energy Inc., 44 (upd.)
Relìv International, Inc., 58
Remedy Corporation, 58
RemedyTemp, Inc., 20
Remington Arms Company, Inc., 12; 40 (upd.)
Remington Products Company, L.L.C., 42
Renaissance Learning Systems, Inc., 39
Renal Care Group, Inc., 72
Reno Air Inc., 23
Rent-A-Center, Inc., 45
Rent-Way, Inc., 33; 75 (upd.)
Rental Service Corporation, 28
Rentrak Corporation, 35
Republic Engineered Steels, Inc., 7; 26 (upd.)
Republic Industries, Inc., 26
Republic New York Corporation, 11
Republic Services, Inc., 92
Res-Care, Inc., 29
Research Triangle Institute, 83
Reser's Fine Foods, Inc., 81
Resorts International, Inc., 12
Resource America, Inc., 42
Resources Connection, Inc., 81
Response Oncology, Inc., 27
Restaurant Associates Corporation, 66
Restaurants Unlimited, Inc., 13
Restoration Hardware, Inc., 30; 96 (upd.)
Retail Ventures, Inc., 82 (upd.)
Revco D.S., Inc., V
Revell-Monogram Inc., 16
Revere Electric Supply Company, 96
Revere Ware Corporation, 22
Revlon Inc., III; 17 (upd.); 64 (upd.)
Rewards Network Inc., 70 (upd.)
REX Stores Corp., 10
Rexel, Inc., 15
Rexnord Corporation, 21; 76 (upd.)
The Reynolds and Reynolds Company, 50
Reynolds Metals Company, IV; 19 (upd.)
RF Micro Devices, Inc., 43
RFC Franchising LLC, 68
Rhino Entertainment Company, 18; 70 (upd.)
Rhodes Inc., 23
Rica Foods, Inc., 41
Rich Products Corporation, 7; 38 (upd.); 93 (upd.)
The Richards Group, Inc., 58
Richardson Electronics, Ltd., 17
Richardson Industries, Inc., 62
Richfood Holdings, Inc., 7
Richton International Corporation, 39
Rickenbacker International Corp., 91
Riddell Sports Inc., 22
Ride, Inc., 22
The Riese Organization, 38
Riggs National Corporation, 13
Right Management Consultants, Inc., 42
Riklis Family Corp., 9
Rimage Corp., 89
Ripley Entertainment, Inc., 74
Riser Foods, Inc., 9
Rite Aid Corporation, V; 19 (upd.); 63 (upd.)
Ritz Camera Centers, 34
The Ritz-Carlton Hotel Company, L.L.C., 9; 29 (upd.); 71 (upd.)
Ritz-Craft Corporation of Pennsylvania Inc., 94
The Rival Company, 19
River Oaks Furniture, Inc., 43
River Ranch Fresh Foods LLC, 88
Riverwood International Corporation, 11; 48 (upd.)
Riviana Foods Inc., 27
Riviera Holdings Corporation, 75
Riviera Tool Company, 89
RJR Nabisco Holdings Corp., V
RMH Teleservices, Inc., 42
Roadhouse Grill, Inc., 22
Roadmaster Industries, Inc., 16
Roadway Express, Inc., V; 25 (upd.)
Roanoke Electric Steel Corporation, 45
Robbins & Myers Inc., 15
Robins, Kaplan, Miller & Ciresi L.L.P., 89
Roberds Inc., 19
Robert Half International Inc., 18; 70 (upd.)
Robert Mondavi Corporation, 15; 50 (upd.)
Robert Talbott Inc., 88
Robert W. Baird & Co. Incorporated, 67
Robert Wood Johnson Foundation, 35
Roberts Pharmaceutical Corporation, 16
Robertson-Ceco Corporation, 19
Robinson Helicopter Company, 51
Rocawear Apparel LLC, 77
Roche Bioscience, 11; 14 (upd.)
Rochester Gas and Electric Corporation, 6
Rochester Telephone Corporation, 6
Rock Bottom Restaurants, Inc., 25; 68 (upd.)
Rock-It Cargo USA, Inc., 86
Rock of Ages Corporation, 37
Rock-Tenn Company, 13; 59 (upd.)
The Rockefeller Foundation, 34
Rockefeller Group International Inc., 58
Rockford Corporation, 43
Rockford Products Corporation, 55
RockShox, Inc., 26
Rockwell Automation, 43 (upd.)
Rockwell International Corporation, I; 11 (upd.)
Rockwell Medical Technologies, Inc., 88
Rocky Mountain Chocolate Factory, Inc., 73
Rocky Shoes & Boots, Inc., 26
Rodale, Inc., 23; 47 (upd.)
ROFIN-SINAR Technologies Inc., 81
Rogers Corporation, 61; 80 (upd.)
Rohm and Haas Company, I; 26 (upd.); 77 (upd.)
ROHN Industries, Inc., 22
Rohr Incorporated, 9
Roll International Corporation, 37
Rollerblade, Inc., 15; 34 (upd.)
Rollins, Inc., 11
Rolls-Royce Allison, 29 (upd.)
Roly Poly Franchise Systems LLC, 83
Romacorp, Inc., 58
Roman Meal Company, 84
Ron Tonkin Chevrolet Company, 55
Ronco Corporation, 15; 80 (upd.)
Rooms To Go Inc., 28
Rooney Brothers Co., 25
Roper Industries, Inc., 15; 50 (upd.)
Ropes & Gray, 40
Rorer Group, I
Rosauers Supermarkets, Inc., 90
Rose Acre Farms, Inc., 60
Rose Art Industries, 58
Rose's Stores, Inc., 13
Roseburg Forest Products Company, 58
Rosemount Inc., 15
Rosenbluth International Inc., 14
Rosetta Stone Inc., 93
Ross Stores, Inc., 17; 43 (upd.)
Rotary International, 31
Roto-Rooter, Inc., 15; 61 (upd.)
The Rottlund Company, Inc., 28
Rouge Steel Company, 8
Rounder Records Corporation 79
Roundy's Inc., 14; 58 (upd.)
The Rouse Company, 15; 63 (upd.)
Rowan Companies, Inc., 43
Roy Anderson Corporation, 75
Roy F. Weston, Inc., 33
Royal Appliance Manufacturing Company, 15
Royal Caribbean Cruises Ltd., 22; 74 (upd.)
Royal Crown Company, Inc., 23
RPC, Inc., 91

RPM International Inc., 8; 36 (upd.); 91 (upd.)
RSA Security Inc., 46
RTI Biologics, Inc., 96
RTM Restaurant Group, 58
Rubbermaid Incorporated, III; 20 (upd.)
Rubio's Restaurants, Inc., 35
Ruby Tuesday, Inc., 18; 71 (upd.)
Rudolph Technologies Inc., 94
Ruiz Food Products, Inc., 53
Rural Cellular Corporation, 43
Rural/Metro Corporation, 28
Rush Communications, 33
Rush Enterprises, Inc., 64
Russ Berrie and Company, Inc., 12; 82 (upd.)
Russell Corporation, 8; 30 (upd.); 82 (upd.)
Russell Reynolds Associates Inc., 38
Russell Stover Candies Inc., 12; 91 (upd.)
Rust International Inc., 11
Rusty, Inc., 95
Ruth's Chris Steak House, 28; 88 (upd.)
RWD Technologies, Inc., 76
Ryan Beck & Co., Inc., 66
Ryan's Restaurant Group, Inc., 15; 68 (upd.)
Ryder System, Inc., V; 24 (upd.)
Ryerson Tull, Inc., 40 (upd.)
Ryko Corporation, 83
The Ryland Group, Inc., 8; 37 (upd.)
S&C Electric Company, 15
S&D Coffee, Inc., 84
S&K Famous Brands, Inc., 23
S-K-I Limited, 15
S.C. Johnson & Son, Inc., III; 28 (upd.); 89 (upd.)
Saatchi & Saatchi, 42 (upd.)
Sabratek Corporation, 29
SABRE Group Holdings, Inc., 26
Sabre Holdings Corporation, 74 (upd.)
Safe Flight Instrument Corporation, 71
SAFECO Corporaton, III
Safeguard Scientifics, Inc., 10
Safelite Glass Corp., 19
Safeskin Corporation, 18
Safety Components International, Inc., 63
Safety 1st, Inc., 24
Safety-Kleen Systems Inc., 8; 82 (upd.)
Safeway Inc., II; 24 (upd.); 85 (upd.)
Saga Communications, Inc., 27
The St. Joe Company, 31
St. Joe Paper Company, 8
St. John Knits, Inc., 14
St. Jude Medical, Inc., 11; 43 (upd.); 97 (upd.)
St. Louis Music, Inc., 48
St. Mary Land & Exploration Company, 63
St. Paul Bank for Cooperatives, 8
The St. Paul Travelers Companies, Inc. III; 22 (upd.); 79 (upd.)
Ste. Michelle Wine Estates Ltd., 96
Saks Inc., 24; 41 (upd.)
Salant Corporation, 12; 51 (upd.)
Salem Communications Corporation, 97
salesforce.com, Inc. 79
Salick Health Care, Inc., 53
Salix Pharmaceuticals, Ltd., 93
Sally Beauty Company, Inc., 60
Salomon Inc., II; 13 (upd.)
Salt River Project, 19
Salton, Inc., 30; 88 (upd.)
The Salvation Army USA, 32
Sam Ash Music Corporation, 30
Sam Levin Inc., 80
Sam's Club, 40
Sam's Wine & Spirits, 96
Samsonite Corporation, 13; 43 (upd.)
Samuel Cabot Inc., 53
Samuels Jewelers Incorporated, 30
San Diego Gas & Electric Company, V
San Diego Padres Baseball Club LP 78
Sanborn Map Company Inc., 82
Sandals Resorts International, 65
Sanders Morris Harris Group Inc., 70
Sanderson Farms, Inc., 15
Sandia National Laboratories, 49
Sanford L.P., 82
Santa Barbara Restaurant Group, Inc., 37
The Santa Cruz Operation, Inc., 38
Santa Fe Gaming Corporation, 19
Santa Fe International Corporation, 38
Santa Fe Pacific Corporation, V
Sara Lee Corporation, II; 15 (upd.); 54 (upd.)
Sarnoff Corporation, 57
Sarris Candies Inc., 86
SAS Institute Inc., 10; 78 (upd.)
Saturn Corporation, 7; 21 (upd.); 80 (upd.)
Saucony Inc., 35; 86 (upd.)
Sauder Woodworking Company, 12; 35 (upd.)
Sauer-Danfoss Inc., 61
Saul Ewing LLP, 74
Savannah Foods & Industries, Inc., 7
Sawtek Inc., 43 (upd.)
Sbarro, Inc., 16; 64 (upd.)
SBC Communications Inc., 32 (upd.)
SBS Technologies, Inc., 25
SCANA Corporation, 6; 56 (upd.)
ScanSource, Inc., 29; 74 (upd.)
SCB Computer Technology, Inc., 29
SCEcorp, V
Schawk, Inc., 24
Scheels All Sports Inc., 63
Scheid Vineyards Inc., 66
Scherer Brothers Lumber Company, 94
Schering-Plough Corporation, I; 14 (upd.); 49 (upd.)
Schieffelin & Somerset Co., 61
Schlage Lock Company, 82
Schlotzsky's, Inc., 36
Schlumberger Limited, III; 17 (upd.); 59 (upd.)
Schmitt Music Company, 40
Schenck Business Solutions, 88
Schneider National, Inc., 36; 77 (upd.)
Schneiderman's Furniture Inc., 28
Schnitzer Steel Industries, Inc., 19
Scholastic Corporation, 10; 29 (upd.)
Scholle Corporation, 96
School Specialty, Inc., 68
School-Tech, Inc., 62
Schott Brothers, Inc., 67
Schott Corporation, 53
Schottenstein Stores Corp., 14
Schreiber Foods, Inc., 72
Schuff Steel Company, 26
Schultz Sav-O Stores, Inc., 21; 31 (upd.)
The Schwan Food Company, 83 (upd.)
Schwan's Sales Enterprises, Inc., 7; 26 (upd.)
Schwebel Baking Company, 72
Schweitzer-Mauduit International, Inc., 52
Schwinn Cycle and Fitness L.P., 19
SCI Systems, Inc., 9
Science Applications International Corporation, 15
Scientific-Atlanta, Inc., 6; 45 (upd.)
Scientific Games Corporation, 64 (upd.)
Scientific Learning Corporation, 95
The SCO Group Inc. 78
Scope Products, Inc., 94
The Score Board, Inc., 19
Scotsman Industries, Inc., 20
Scott Fetzer Company, 12; 80 (upd.)
Scott Paper Company, IV; 31 (upd.)
The Scotts Company, 22
Scottrade, Inc., 85
Scotty's, Inc., 22
The Scoular Company, 77
Scovill Fasteners Inc., 24
SCP Pool Corporation, 39
Screen Actors Guild, 72
The Scripps Research Institute, 76
Sea Ray Boats Inc., 96
Seaboard Corporation, 36; 85 (upd.)
SeaChange International, Inc. 79
SEACOR Holdings Inc., 83
Seagate Technology, Inc., 8; 34 (upd.)
Seagull Energy Corporation, 11
Sealaska Corporation, 60
Sealed Air Corporation, 14; 57 (upd.)
Sealed Power Corporation, I
Sealright Co., Inc., 17
Sealy Inc., 12
Seaman Furniture Company, Inc., 32
Sean John Clothing, Inc., 70
Sears, Roebuck and Co., V; 18 (upd.); 56 (upd.)
Seattle City Light, 50
Seattle FilmWorks, Inc., 20
Seattle First National Bank Inc., 8
Seattle Lighting Fixture Company, 92
Seattle Pacific Industries, Inc., 92
Seattle Seahawks, Inc., 92
Seattle Times Company, 15
Seaway Food Town, Inc., 15
Sebastiani Vineyards, Inc., 28
The Second City, Inc., 88
Second Harvest, 29
Security Capital Corporation, 17
Security Pacific Corporation, II
SED International Holdings, Inc., 43
See's Candies, Inc., 30
Sega of America, Inc., 10
Segway LLC, 48
SEI Investments Company, 96
Seigle's Home and Building Centers, Inc., 41
Seitel, Inc., 47
Select Comfort Corporation, 34

Select Medical Corporation, 65
Selee Corporation, 88
The Selmer Company, Inc., 19
SEMCO Energy, Inc., 44
Seminis, Inc., 29
Semitool, Inc., 18; 79 (upd.)
Sempra Energy, 25 (upd.)
Semtech Corporation, 32
Seneca Foods Corporation, 17; 60 (upd.)
Senomyx, Inc., 83
Sensient Technologies Corporation, 52 (upd.)
Sensormatic Electronics Corp., 11
Sensory Science Corporation, 37
Sepracor Inc., 45
Sequa Corporation, 13; 54 (upd.)
Serologicals Corporation, 63
Serta, Inc., 28
Servco Pacific Inc., 96
Service America Corp., 7
Service Corporation International, 6; 51 (upd.)
Service Merchandise Company, Inc., V; 19 (upd.)
The ServiceMaster Company, 6; 23 (upd.); 68 (upd.)
Servpro Industries, Inc., 85
7-11, Inc., 32 (upd.)
Sevenson Environmental Services, Inc., 42
Seventh Generation, Inc., 73
Seyfarth Shaw LLP, 93
SFX Entertainment, Inc., 36
SGI, 29 (upd.)
Shakespeare Company, 22
Shaklee Corporation, 12; 39 (upd.)
Shared Medical Systems Corporation, 14
The Sharper Image Corporation, 10; 62 (upd.)
The Shaw Group, Inc., 50
Shaw Industries, Inc., 9; 40 (upd.)
Shaw's Supermarkets, Inc., 56
Shawmut National Corporation, 13
Sheaffer Pen Corporation, 82
Shearer's Foods, Inc., 72
Shearman & Sterling, 32
Shearson Lehman Brothers Holdings Inc., II; 9 (upd.)
Shedd Aquarium Society, 73
Sheetz, Inc., 85
Shelby Williams Industries, Inc., 14
Sheldahl Inc., 23
Shell Oil Company, IV; 14 (upd.); 41 (upd.)
Sheller-Globe Corporation, I
Shells Seafood Restaurants, Inc., 43
Shenandoah Telecommunications Company, 89
Sheplers, Inc., 96
The Sheridan Group, Inc., 86
The Sherwin-Williams Company, III; 13 (upd.); 89 (upd.)
Sherwood Brands, Inc., 53
Shoe Carnival Inc., 14; 72 (upd.)
Shoe Pavilion, Inc., 84
Shoney's, Inc., 7; 23 (upd.)
ShopKo Stores Inc., 21; 58 (upd.)
Shoppers Food Warehouse Corporation, 66
Shorewood Packaging Corporation, 28
ShowBiz Pizza Time, Inc., 13
Showboat, Inc., 19
Showtime Networks Inc. 78
Shriners Hospitals for Children, 69
Shubert Organization Inc., 24
Shuffle Master Inc., 51
Shure Inc., 60
Shurgard Storage Centers, Inc., 52
Sidley Austin Brown & Wood, 40
Sidney Frank Importing Co., Inc., 69
Siebel Systems, Inc., 38
Siebert Financial Corp., 32
Siegel & Gale, 64
The Sierra Club, 28
Sierra Health Services, Inc., 15
Sierra Nevada Brewing Company, 70
Sierra On-Line, Inc., 15; 41 (upd.)
Sierra Pacific Industries, 22; 90 (upd.)
SIFCO Industries, Inc., 41
Sigma-Aldrich Corporation, I; 36 (upd.); 93 (upd.)
Signet Banking Corporation, 11
Sikorsky Aircraft Corporation, 24
Silhouette Brands, Inc., 55
Silicon Graphics Incorporated, 9
Silver Lake Cookie Company Inc., 95
SilverPlatter Information Inc., 23
Silverstein Properties, Inc., 47
Simmons Company, 47
Simon & Schuster Inc., IV; 19 (upd.)
Simon Property Group Inc., 27; 84 (upd.)
Simon Transportation Services Inc., 27
Simplex Technologies Inc., 21
Simplicity Manufacturing, Inc., 64
Simpson Investment Company, 17
Simpson Thacher & Bartlett, 39
Simula, Inc., 41
Sinclair Broadcast Group, Inc., 25
The Singing Machine Company, Inc., 60
Sir Speedy, Inc., 16
Sirius Satellite Radio, Inc., 69
Siskin Steel & Supply Company, 70
Six Flags, Inc., 17; 54 (upd.)
SJW Corporation, 70
Skadden, Arps, Slate, Meagher & Flom, 18
Skechers U.S.A. Inc., 31; 88 (upd.)
Skeeter Products Inc., 96
Skidmore, Owings & Merrill LLP, 13; 69 (upd.)
skinnyCorp, LLC, 97
Skyline Chili, Inc., 62
Skyline Corporation, 30
SkyMall, Inc., 26
SkyWest, Inc., 25
Skyy Spirits LLC 78
SL Green Realty Corporation, 44
SL Industries, Inc., 77
Sleepy's Inc., 32
SLI, Inc., 48
Slim-Fast Foods Company, 18; 66 (upd.)
SLM Holding Corp., 25 (upd.)
Small Planet Foods, Inc., 89
Smart & Final LLC, 16; 94 (upd.)
SMART Modular Technologies, Inc., 86
SmartForce PLC, 43
Smead Manufacturing Co., 17
Smith & Hawken, Ltd., 68
Smith & Wesson Corp., 30; 73 (upd.)
Smith Barney Inc., 15
Smith Corona Corp., 13
Smith International, Inc., 15; 59 (upd.)
Smith's Food & Drug Centers, Inc., 8; 57 (upd.)
Smith-Midland Corporation, 56
Smithfield Foods, Inc., 7; 43 (upd.)
SmithKline Beckman Corporation, I
Smithsonian Institution, 27
Smithway Motor Xpress Corporation, 39
Smurfit-Stone Container Corporation, 26 (upd.); 83 (upd.)
Snap-On, Incorporated, 7; 27 (upd.)
Snapfish, 83
Snapple Beverage Corporation, 11
Snell & Wilmer L.L.P., 28
Society Corporation, 9
Soft Sheen Products, Inc., 31
Softbank Corporation, 77 (upd.)
Sola International Inc., 71
Sole Technology Inc., 93
Solectron Corporation, 12; 48 (upd.)
Solo Serve Corporation, 28
Solutia Inc., 52
Sonat, Inc., 6
Sonesta International Hotels Corporation, 44
Sonic Automotive, Inc., 77
Sonic Corp., 14; 37 (upd.)
Sonic Innovations Inc., 56
Sonic Solutions, Inc., 81
SonicWALL, Inc., 87
Sonoco Products Company, 8; 89 (upd.)
SonoSite, Inc., 56
Sorbee International Ltd., 74
Soros Fund Management LLC, 28
Sorrento, Inc., 24
SOS Staffing Services, 25
Sotheby's Holdings, Inc., 11; 29 (upd.); 84 (upd.)
Sound Advice, Inc., 41
The Source Enterprises, Inc., 65
Source Interlink Companies, Inc., 75
South Beach Beverage Company, Inc., 73
South Dakota Wheat Growers Association, 94
South Jersey Industries, Inc., 42
Southdown, Inc., 14
The Southern Company, V; 38 (upd.)
Southern Connecticut Gas Company, 84
Southern Financial Bancorp, Inc., 56
Southern Indiana Gas and Electric Company, 13
Southern New England Telecommunications Corporation, 6
Southern Pacific Transportation Company, V
Southern Poverty Law Center, Inc., 74
Southern States Cooperative Incorporated, 36
Southern Union Company, 27
Southern Wine and Spirits of America, Inc., 84
The Southland Corporation, II; 7 (upd.)
Southtrust Corporation, 11

Southwest Airlines Co., 6; 24 (upd.); 71 (upd.)
Southwest Gas Corporation, 19
Southwest Water Company, 47
Southwestern Bell Corporation, V
Southwestern Electric Power Co., 21
Southwestern Public Service Company, 6
Southwire Company, Inc., 8; 23 (upd.)
Sovran Self Storage, Inc., 66
Spacehab, Inc., 37
Spacelabs Medical, Inc., 71
Spaghetti Warehouse, Inc., 25
Spangler Candy Company, 44
Spanish Broadcasting System, Inc., 41
Spansion Inc., 80
Spanx, Inc., 89
Spark Networks, Inc., 91
Spartan Motors Inc., 14
Spartan Stores Inc., 8; 66 (upd.)
Spartech Corporation, 19; 76 (upd.)
Sparton Corporation, 18
Spear & Jackson, Inc., 73
Spear, Leeds & Kellogg, 66
Spec's Music, Inc., 19
Special Olympics, Inc., 93
Specialized Bicycle Components Inc., 50
Specialty Coatings Inc., 8
Specialty Equipment Companies, Inc., 25
Specialty Products & Insulation Co., 59
Spectrum Control, Inc., 67
Spectrum Organic Products, Inc., 68
Spee-Dee Delivery Service, Inc., 93
SpeeDee Oil Change and Tune-Up, 25
Speedway Motorsports, Inc., 32
Speidel Inc., 96
Speizman Industries, Inc., 44
Spelling Entertainment, 14; 35 (upd.)
Spencer Stuart and Associates, Inc., 14
Spherion Corporation, 52
Spiegel, Inc., 10; 27 (upd.)
Spinnaker Exploration Company, 72
Spirit Airlines, Inc., 31
Sport Chalet, Inc., 16; 94 (upd.)
Sport Supply Group, Inc., 23
Sportmart, Inc., 15
Sports & Recreation, Inc., 17
The Sports Authority, Inc., 16; 43 (upd.)
The Sports Club Company, 25
The Sportsman's Guide, Inc., 36
Springs Global US, Inc., V; 19 (upd.); 90 (upd.)
Sprint Corporation, 9; 46 (upd.)
SPS Technologies, Inc., 30
SPSS Inc., 64
SPX Corporation, 10; 47 (upd.)
Spyglass Entertainment Group, LLC, 91
Square D, 90
Squibb Corporation, I
SRA International, Inc., 77
SRAM Corporation, 65
SRC Holdings Corporation, 67
SRI International, Inc., 57
SSOE Inc., 76
STAAR Surgical Company, 57
Stabler Companies Inc. 78
Stage Stores, Inc., 24; 82 (upd.)
Stanadyne Automotive Corporation, 37
StanCorp Financial Group, Inc., 56
Standard Candy Company Inc., 86
Standard Commercial Corporation, 13; 62 (upd.)
Standard Federal Bank, 9
Standard Microsystems Corporation, 11
Standard Motor Products, Inc., 40
Standard Pacific Corporation, 52
The Standard Register Company, 15, 93 (upd.)
Standex International Corporation, 17; 44 (upd.)
Stanhome Inc., 15
Stanley Furniture Company, Inc., 34
The Stanley Works, III; 20 (upd.); 79 (upd.)
Staple Cotton Cooperative Association (Staplcotn), 86
Staples, Inc., 10; 55 (upd.)
Star Banc Corporation, 11
Star of the West Milling Co., 95
Starbucks Corporation, 13; 34 (upd.); 77 (upd.)
Starcraft Corporation, 30; 66 (upd.)
Starkey Laboratories, Inc., 52
Starrett Corporation, 21
StarTek, Inc. 79
Starter Corp., 12
Starwood Hotels & Resorts Worldwide, Inc., 54
Starz LLC, 91
The Stash Tea Company, 50
State Auto Financial Corporation, 77
State Farm Mutual Automobile Insurance Company, III; 51 (upd.)
State Financial Services Corporation, 51
State Street Corporation, 8; 57 (upd.)
Staten Island Bancorp, Inc., 39
Stater Bros. Holdings Inc., 64
Station Casinos, Inc., 25; 90 (upd.)
The Staubach Company, 62
The Steak n Shake Company, 41; 96 (upd.)
Stearns, Inc., 43
Steel Dynamics, Inc., 52
Steel Technologies Inc., 63
Steelcase, Inc., 7; 27 (upd.)
Stein Mart Inc., 19; 72 (upd.)
Steiner Corporation (Alsco), 53
Steinway Musical Properties, Inc., 19
Stemilt Growers Inc., 94
Stepan Company, 30
The Stephan Company, 60
Stephens Media, LLC, 91
Stephens Inc., 92
Stericycle, Inc., 33; 74 (upd.)
Sterilite Corporation, 97
STERIS Corporation, 29
Sterling Chemicals Inc., 16; 78 (upd.)
Sterling Drug, Inc., I
Sterling Electronics Corp., 18
Sterling Software, Inc., 11
Steve & Barry's LLC, 88
Stevedoring Services of America Inc., 28
Steven Madden, Ltd., 37
Stew Leonard's, 56
Stewart & Stevenson Services Inc., 11
Stewart Enterprises, Inc., 20
Stewart Information Services Corporation 78
Stewart's Beverages, 39
Stewart's Shops Corporation, 80
Stiefel Laboratories, Inc., 90
Stillwater Mining Company, 47
Stimson Lumber Company 78
Stock Yards Packing Co., Inc., 37
Stone & Webster, Inc., 13; 64 (upd.)
Stone Container Corporation, IV
Stone Manufacturing Company, 14; 43 (upd.)
Stonyfield Farm, Inc., 55
The Stop & Shop Supermarket Company, II; 24 (upd.); 68 (upd.)
Storage Technology Corporation, 6
Storage USA, Inc., 21
Stouffer Corp., 8
StrataCom, Inc., 16
Stratagene Corporation, 70
Stratasys, Inc., 67
Strattec Security Corporation, 73
Stratus Computer, Inc., 10
Strauss Discount Auto, 56
Strayer Education, Inc., 53
The Stride Rite Corporation, 8; 37 (upd.); 86 (upd.)
Strine Printing Company Inc., 88
The Strober Organization, Inc., 82
The Stroh Brewery Company, I; 18 (upd.)
Strombecker Corporation, 60
Stroock & Stroock & Lavan LLP, 40
Strouds, Inc., 33
Stryker Corporation, 11; 29 (upd.); 79 (upd.)
Stuart C. Irby Company, 58
Stuart Entertainment Inc., 16
Student Loan Marketing Association, II
Stuller Settings, Inc., 35
Sturm, Ruger & Company, Inc., 19
Stussy, Inc., 55
Sub Pop Ltd., 97
Sub-Zero Freezer Co., Inc., 31
Suburban Propane Partners, L.P., 30
Subway, 32
Successories, Inc., 30
Sudbury Inc., 16
Suiza Foods Corporation, 26
Sullivan & Cromwell, 26
The Summit Bancorporation, 14
Summit Family Restaurants, Inc. 19
Sun Communities Inc., 46
Sun Company, Inc., IV
Sun Country Airlines, 30
Sun-Diamond Growers of California, 7
Sun Distributors L.P., 12
Sun Healthcare Group Inc., 25
Sun Hydraulics Corporation, 74
Sun-Maid Growers of California, 82
Sun Microsystems, Inc., 7; 30 (upd.); 91 (upd.)
Sun Sportswear, Inc., 17
Sun Television & Appliances Inc., 10
Sun World International, LLC, 93
SunAmerica Inc., 11
Sunbeam-Oster Co., Inc., 9
Sunburst Hospitality Corporation, 26
Sunburst Shutter Corporation 78

Sundstrand Corporation, 7; 21 (upd.)
Sundt Corp., 24
SunGard Data Systems Inc., 11
Sunglass Hut International, Inc., 21; 74 (upd.)
Sunkist Growers, Inc., 26
Sunoco, Inc., 28 (upd.); 83 (upd.)
SunPower Corporation, 91
The Sunrider Corporation, 26
Sunrise Greetings, 88
Sunrise Medical Inc., 11
Sunrise Senior Living, Inc., 81
Sunterra Corporation, 75
SunTrust Banks Inc., 23
Super 8 Motels, Inc., 83
Super Food Services, Inc., 15
Supercuts Inc., 26
Superior Essex Inc., 80
Superior Energy Services, Inc., 65
Superior Industries International, Inc., 8
Superior Uniform Group, Inc., 30
Supermarkets General Holdings Corporation, II
SUPERVALU Inc., II; 18 (upd.); 50 (upd.)
Suprema Specialties, Inc., 27
Supreme International Corporation, 27
Susan G. Komen Breast Cancer Foundation 78
Susquehanna Pfaltzgraff Company, 8
Sutter Home Winery Inc., 16
Sverdrup Corporation, 14
Swales & Associates, Inc., 69
Swank, Inc., 17; 84 (upd.)
SwedishAmerican Health System, 51
Sweet Candy Company, 60
Sweetheart Cup Company, Inc., 36
The Swett & Crawford Group Inc., 84
SWH Corporation, 70
Swift & Company, 55
Swift Energy Company, 63
Swift Transportation Co., Inc., 42
Swinerton Inc., 43
Swisher International Group Inc., 23
The Swiss Colony, Inc., 97
Swiss Valley Farms Company, 90
Sybase, Inc., 10; 27 (upd.)
Sybron International Corp., 14
Sycamore Networks, Inc., 45
Sykes Enterprises, Inc., 45
Sylvan Learning Systems, Inc., 35
Sylvan, Inc., 22
Symantec Corporation, 10; 82 (upd.)
Symbol Technologies, Inc., 15
Syms Corporation, 29; 74 (upd.)
Symyx Technologies, Inc., 77
Synaptics Incorporated, 95
Synchronoss Technologies, Inc., 95
Syniverse Holdings Inc., 97
SYNNEX Corporation, 73
Synopsys, Inc., 11; 69 (upd.)
SynOptics Communications, Inc., 10
Synovus Financial Corp., 12; 52 (upd.)
Syntel, Inc., 92
Syntex Corporation, I
Sypris Solutions, Inc., 85
SyQuest Technology, Inc., 18
Syratech Corp., 14
SYSCO Corporation, II; 24 (upd.); 75 (upd.)
System Software Associates, Inc., 10
Systemax, Inc., 52
Systems & Computer Technology Corp., 19
T-Netix, Inc., 46
T. Marzetti Company, 57
T. Rowe Price Associates, Inc., 11; 34 (upd.)
TAB Products Co., 17
Taco Bell Corporation, 7; 21 (upd.); 74 (upd.)
Taco Cabana, Inc., 23; 72 (upd.)
Taco John's International, Inc., 15; 63 (upd.)
Tacony Corporation, 70
Tag-It Pacific, Inc., 85
Take-Two Interactive Software, Inc., 46
The Talbots, Inc., 11; 31 (upd.); 88 (upd.)
Talk America Holdings, Inc., 70
Talley Industries, Inc., 16
TALX Corporation, 92
Tambrands Inc., 8
Tandem Computers, Inc., 6
Tandy Corporation, II; 12 (upd.)
Tandycrafts, Inc., 31
Tanger Factory Outlet Centers, Inc., 49
Tanox, Inc., 77
Tapemark Company Inc., 64
Target Corporation, 10; 27 (upd.); 61 (upd.)
Tarragon Realty Investors, Inc., 45
Tarrant Apparel Group, 62
Taser International, Inc., 62
Tasty Baking Company, 14; 35 (upd.)
Tattered Cover Book Store, 43
Taubman Centers, Inc., 75
Taylor Corporation, 36
Taylor Devices, Inc., 97
Taylor Guitars, 48
TaylorMade-adidas Golf, 23; 96 (upd.)
Taylor Publishing Company, 12; 36 (upd.)
TB Wood's Corporation, 56
TBWA/Chiat/Day, 6; 43 (upd.)
TCBY Enterprises Inc., 17
TCF Financial Corporation, 47
Teachers Insurance and Annuity Association-College Retirement Equities Fund, III; 45 (upd.)
TearDrop Golf Company, 32
Tech Data Corporation, 10; 74 (upd.)
Tech-Sym Corporation, 18; 44 (upd.)
TechBooks Inc., 84
TECHNE Corporation, 52
Technical Olympic USA, Inc., 75
Technitrol, Inc., 29
Technology Research Corporation, 94
Technology Solutions Company, 94
TECO Energy, Inc., 6
Tecumseh Products Company, 8; 71 (upd.)
Tee Vee Toons, Inc., 57
Tejon Ranch Company, 35
Tekelec, 83
Teknor Apex Company, 97
Tektronix Inc., 8; 78 (upd.)
Telcordia Technologies, Inc., 59
Tele-Communications, Inc., II
Teledyne Technologies Inc., I; 10 (upd.); 62 (upd.)
Telephone and Data Systems, Inc., 9
Tellabs, Inc., 11; 40 (upd.)
Telsmith Inc., 96
Telxon Corporation, 10
Temple-Inland Inc., IV; 31 (upd.)
Tempur-Pedic Inc., 54
Tenet Healthcare Corporation, 55 (upd.)
TenFold Corporation, 35
Tennant Company, 13; 33 (upd.); 95 (upd.)
Tenneco Inc., I; 10 (upd.)
Tennessee Valley Authority, 50
TEPPCO Partners, L.P., 73
Teradyne, Inc., 11
Terex Corporation, 7; 40 (upd.); 91 (upd.)
The Terlato Wine Group, 48
Terra Industries, Inc., 13; 94 (upd.)
Tesoro Corporation, 7; 45 (upd.); 97 (upd.)
The Testor Corporation, 51
Tetley USA Inc., 88
Teton Energy Corporation, 97
Tetra Tech, Inc., 29
Texaco Inc., IV; 14 (upd.); 41 (upd.)
Texas Air Corporation, I
Texas Industries, Inc., 8
Texas Instruments Inc., II; 11 (upd.); 46 (upd.)
Texas Pacific Group Inc., 36
Texas Rangers Baseball, 51
Texas Roadhouse, Inc., 69
Texas Utilities Company, V; 25 (upd.)
Textron Inc., I; 34 (upd.); 88 (upd.)
Textron Lycoming Turbine Engine, 9
Tha Row Records, 69 (upd.)
Thane International, Inc., 84
Thermadyne Holding Corporation, 19
Thermo BioAnalysis Corp., 25
Thermo Electron Corporation, 7
Thermo Fibertek, Inc., 24
Thermo Instrument Systems Inc., 11
Thermo King Corporation, 13
Thermos Company, 16
Things Remembered, Inc., 84
Thiokol Corporation, 9; 22 (upd.)
Thomas & Betts Corporation, 11; 54 (upd.)
Thomas & Howard Company, Inc., 90
Thomas Cook Travel Inc., 9; 33 (upd.)
Thomas H. Lee Co., 24
Thomas Industries Inc., 29
Thomas J. Lipton Company, 14
Thomas Nelson, Inc., 14; 38 (upd.)
Thomas Publishing Company, 26
Thomaston Mills, Inc., 27
Thomasville Furniture Industries, Inc., 12; 74 (upd.)
Thomsen Greenhouses and Garden Center, Incorporated, 65
Thor Industries Inc., 39; 92 (upd.)
Thorn Apple Valley, Inc., 7; 22 (upd.)
ThoughtWorks Inc., 90
Thousand Trails, Inc., 33

THQ, Inc., 39; 92 (upd.)
3Com Corporation, 11; 34 (upd.)
The 3DO Company, 43
3M Company, 61 (upd.)
Thrifty PayLess, Inc., 12
TIBCO Software Inc. 79
TIC Holdings Inc., 92
Ticketmaster, 76 (upd.)
Ticketmaster Group, Inc., 13; 37 (upd.)
Tidewater Inc., 11; 37 (upd.)
Tiffany & Co., 14; 78 (upd.)
TIG Holdings, Inc., 26
Tilia Inc., 62
Tillotson Corp., 15
Timber Lodge Steakhouse, Inc., 73
The Timberland Company, 13; 54 (upd.)
Timberline Software Corporation, 15
Time Warner Inc., IV; 7 (upd.)
The Times Mirror Company, IV; 17 (upd.)
Timex Corporation, 7; 25 (upd.)
The Timken Company, 8; 42 (upd.)
Tishman Speyer Properties, L.P., 47
The Titan Corporation, 36
Titan International, Inc., 89
Titanium Metals Corporation, 21
TiVo Inc., 75
TJ International, Inc., 19
The TJX Companies, Inc., V; 19 (upd.); 57 (upd.)
TLC Beatrice International Holdings, Inc., 22
TMP Worldwide Inc., 30
TNT Freightways Corporation, 14
Today's Man, Inc., 20
TODCO, 87
Todd Shipyards Corporation, 14
The Todd-AO Corporation, 33
Todhunter International, Inc., 27
Tofutti Brands, Inc., 64
Tokheim Corporation, 21
TOKYOPOP Inc. 79
Toll Brothers Inc., 15; 70 (upd.)
Tollgrade Communications, Inc., 44
Tom Brown, Inc., 37
Tom Doherty Associates Inc., 25
Tom's Foods Inc., 66
Tom's of Maine, Inc., 45
Tombstone Pizza Corporation, 13
Tone Brothers, Inc., 21; 74 (upd.)
Tonka Corporation, 25
Too, Inc., 61
Tootsie Roll Industries, Inc., 12; 82 (upd.)
Topco Associates LLC, 60
The Topps Company, Inc., 13; 34 (upd.); 83 (upd.)
Tops Appliance City, Inc., 17
Tops Markets LLC, 60
Torchmark Corporation, 9; 33 (upd.)
Toresco Enterprises, Inc., 84
The Toro Company, 7; 26 (upd.); 77 (upd.)
The Torrington Company, 13
Tosco Corporation, 7
Total Entertainment Restaurant Corporation, 46
Total System Services, Inc., 18
Totem Resources Corporation, 9
TouchTunes Music Corporation, 97
Tower Air, Inc., 28
Tower Automotive, Inc., 24
Towers Perrin, 32
Town & Country Corporation, 19
Town Sports International, Inc., 46
Townsends, Inc., 64
Toy Biz, Inc., 18
Toymax International, Inc., 29
Toys 'R Us, Inc., V; 18 (upd.); 57 (upd.)
Tracor Inc., 17
Tractor Supply Company, 57
Trader Joe's Company, 13; 50 (upd.)
TradeStation Group, Inc., 83
Traffix, Inc., 61
Trailer Bridge, Inc., 41
Trammell Crow Company, 8; 57 (upd.)
Trane 78
Trans World Airlines, Inc., I; 12 (upd.); 35 (upd.)
Trans World Entertainment Corporation, 24; 68 (upd.)
Trans-Lux Corporation, 51
Transaction Systems Architects, Inc., 29; 82 (upd.)
Transamerica–An AEGON Company, I; 13 (upd.); 41 (upd.)
Transammonia Group, 95
Transatlantic Holdings, Inc., 11
Transco Energy Company, V
Transitions Optical, Inc., 83
Transmedia Network Inc., 20
TransMontaigne Inc., 28
Transocean Sedco Forex Inc., 45
Transport Corporation of America, Inc., 49
TransPro, Inc., 71
The Tranzonic Companies, 37
Travel Ports of America, Inc., 17
The Travelers Corporation, III
Travelocity.com, Inc., 46
Travelzoo Inc. 79
Travis Boats & Motors, Inc., 37
TRC Companies, Inc., 32
Treadco, Inc., 19
Treasure Chest Advertising Company, Inc., 32
Tredegar Corporation, 52
Tree of Life, Inc., 29
Tree Top, Inc., 76
TreeHouse Foods, Inc. 79
Trek Bicycle Corporation, 16; 78 (upd.)
Trend-Lines, Inc., 22
Trendwest Resorts, Inc., 33
Trex Company, Inc., 71
Tri Valley Growers, 32
Triarc Companies, Inc., 8; 34 (upd.)
Tribune Company, IV; 22 (upd.); 63 (upd.)
Trico Products Corporation, 15
Trico Marine Services, Inc., 89
Tilcon-Connecticut Inc., 80
Trident Seafoods Corporation, 56
Trigen Energy Corporation, 42
TriMas Corp., 11
Trimble Navigation Limited, 40
Trinity Industries, Incorporated, 7
TRINOVA Corporation, III
TriPath Imaging, Inc., 77
Triple Five Group Ltd., 49
TriQuint Semiconductor, Inc., 63
Tripwire, Inc., 97
Trisko Jewelry Sculptures, Ltd., 57
Triton Energy Corporation, 11
Triumph Group, Inc., 31
The TriZetto Group, Inc., 83
TRM Copy Centers Corporation, 18
Tropicana Products, Inc., 28; 73 (upd.)
Troutman Sanders L.L.P. 79
True North Communications Inc., 23
True Religion Apparel, Inc. 79
True Temper Sports, Inc., 95
True Value Company, 74 (upd.)
The Trump Organization, 23; 64 (upd.)
TruServ Corporation, 24
TRW Automotive Holdings Corp., 75 (upd.)
TRW Inc., I; 11 (upd.); 14 (upd.)
TTX Company, 6; 66 (upd.)
Tubby's, Inc., 53
Tucson Electric Power Company, 6
Tuesday Morning Corporation, 18; 70 (upd.)
Tully's Coffee Corporation, 51
Tultex Corporation, 13
Tumaro's Gourmet Tortillas, 85
Tumbleweed, Inc., 33; 80 (upd.)
Tupperware Corporation, 28; 78 (upd.)
TurboChef Technologies, Inc., 83
Turner Broadcasting System, Inc., II; 6 (upd.); 66 (upd.)
Turner Construction Company, 66
The Turner Corporation, 8; 23 (upd.)
Turtle Wax, Inc., 15; 93 (upd.)
Tuscarora Inc., 29
Tutogen Medical, Inc., 68
Tuttle Publishing, 86
TV Guide, Inc., 43 (upd.)
TVI, Inc., 15
TW Services, Inc., II
Tweeter Home Entertainment Group, Inc., 30
Twentieth Century Fox Film Corporation, II; 25 (upd.)
24 Hour Fitness Worldwide, Inc., 71
24/7 Real Media, Inc., 49
Twin Disc, Inc., 21
Twinlab Corporation, 34
II-VI Incorporated, 69
Ty Inc., 33; 86 (upd.)
Tyco Toys, Inc., 12
Tyler Corporation, 23
Tyndale House Publishers, Inc., 57
Tyson Foods, Inc., II; 14 (upd.); 50 (upd.)
U S West, Inc., V; 25 (upd.)
U.S. Aggregates, Inc., 42
U.S. Army Corps of Engineers, 91
U.S. Bancorp, 14; 36 (upd.)
U.S. Borax, Inc., 42
U.S. Can Corporation, 30
U.S. Cellular Corporation, 31 (upd.); 88 (upd.)
U.S. Delivery Systems, Inc., 22
U.S. Foodservice, 26
U.S. Healthcare, Inc., 6

U.S. Home Corporation, 8; 78 (upd.)
U.S. News & World Report Inc., 30; 89 (upd.)
U.S. Office Products Company, 25
U.S. Physical Therapy, Inc., 65
U.S. Premium Beef LLC, 91
U.S. Robotics Corporation, 9; 66 (upd.)
U.S. Satellite Broadcasting Company, Inc., 20
U.S. Timberlands Company, L.P., 42
U.S. Trust Corp., 17
U.S. Vision, Inc., 66
UAL Corporation, 34 (upd.)
UAW (International Union, United Automobile, Aerospace and Agricultural Implement Workers of America), 72
UGI Corporation, 12
Ugly Duckling Corporation, 22
UICI, 33
Ukrop's Super Market's, Inc., 39
Ulta Salon, Cosmetics & Fragrance, Inc., 93
Ultimate Electronics, Inc., 18; 69 (upd.)
Ultra Pac, Inc., 24
Ultra Petroleum Corporation, 71
Ultrak Inc., 24
Ultralife Batteries, Inc., 58
Ultramar Diamond Shamrock Corporation, 31 (upd.)
Umpqua Holdings Corporation, 87
Uncle Ben's Inc., 22
Uncle Ray's LLC, 90
Under Armour Performance Apparel, 61
Underwriters Laboratories, Inc., 30
Uni-Marts, Inc., 17
Unica Corporation, 77
Unicom Corporation, 29 (upd.)
Unifi, Inc., 12; 62 (upd.)
Unified Grocers, Inc., 93
UniFirst Corporation, 21
Union Bank of California, 16
Union Camp Corporation, IV
Union Carbide Corporation, I; 9 (upd.); 74 (upd.)
Union Electric Company, V
Union Pacific Corporation, V; 28 (upd.); 79 (upd.)
Union Planters Corporation, 54
Union Texas Petroleum Holdings, Inc., 9
UnionBanCal Corporation, 50 (upd.)
Unique Casual Restaurants, Inc., 27
Unison HealthCare Corporation, 25
Unisys Corporation, III; 6 (upd.); 36 (upd.)
Unit Corporation, 63
United Airlines, I; 6 (upd.)
United Auto Group, Inc., 26; 68 (upd.)
United Brands Company, II
United Dairy Farmers, Inc., 74
United Defense Industries, Inc., 30; 66 (upd.)
United Dominion Industries Limited, 8; 16 (upd.)
United Dominion Realty Trust, Inc., 52
United Farm Workers of America, 88
United Foods, Inc., 21
United HealthCare Corporation, 9
The United Illuminating Company, 21
United Industrial Corporation, 37
United Industries Corporation, 68
United Jewish Communities, 33
United Merchants & Manufacturers, Inc., 13
United National Group, Ltd., 63
United Nations International Children's Emergency Fund (UNICEF), 58
United Natural Foods, Inc., 32; 76 (upd.)
United Negro College Fund, Inc. 79
United Online, Inc., 71 (upd.)
United Parcel Service of America Inc., V; 17 (upd.)
United Parcel Service, Inc., 63; 94 (upd.)
United Press International, Inc., 25; 73 (upd.)
United Rentals, Inc., 34
United Retail Group Inc., 33
United Road Services, Inc., 69
United Service Organizations, 60
United States Cellular Corporation, 9
United States Filter Corporation, 20
United States Pipe and Foundry Company, 62
United States Playing Card Company, 62
United States Postal Service, 14; 34 (upd.)
The United States Shoe Corporation, V
United States Steel Corporation, 50 (upd.)
United States Surgical Corporation, 10; 34 (upd.)
United Stationers Inc., 14
United Talent Agency, Inc., 80
United Technologies Automotive Inc., 15
United Technologies Corporation, I; 10 (upd.); 34 (upd.)
United Telecommunications, Inc., V
United Video Satellite Group, 18
United Water Resources, Inc., 40
United Way of America, 36
Unitil Corporation, 37
Unitog Co., 19
Unitrin Inc., 16; V
Univar Corporation, 9
Universal Compression, Inc., 59
Universal Corporation, V; 48 (upd.)
Universal Electronics Inc., 39
Universal Foods Corporation, 7
Universal Forest Products, Inc., 10; 59 (upd.)
Universal Health Services, Inc., 6
Universal International, Inc., 25
Universal Manufacturing Company, 88
Universal Security Instruments, Inc., 96
Universal Stainless & Alloy Products, Inc., 75
Universal Studios, Inc., 33
Universal Technical Institute, Inc., 81
The University of Chicago Press 79
Univision Communications Inc., 24; 83 (upd.)
Uno Restaurant Corporation, 18
Uno Restaurant Holdings Corporation, 70 (upd.)
Unocal Corporation, IV; 24 (upd.); 71 (upd.)
UnumProvident Corporation, 13; 52 (upd.)
The Upjohn Company, I; 8 (upd.)
Urban Outfitters, Inc., 14; 74 (upd.)
URS Corporation, 45; 80 (upd.)
US Airways Group, Inc., I; 6 (upd.); 28 (upd.); 52 (upd.)
US 1 Industries, Inc., 89
USA Interactive, Inc., 47 (upd.)
USA Mobility Inc., 97 (upd.)
USA Truck, Inc., 42
USAA, 10; 62 (upd.)
USANA, Inc., 29
USF&G Corporation, III
USG Corporation, III; 26 (upd.); 81 (upd.)
UST Inc., 9; 50 (upd.)
USX Corporation, IV; 7 (upd.)
Utah Medical Products, Inc., 36
Utah Power and Light Company, 27
UtiliCorp United Inc., 6
UTStarcom, Inc., 77
Utz Quality Foods, Inc., 72
UUNET, 38
Uwajimaya, Inc., 60
Vail Resorts, Inc., 11; 43 (upd.)
Valassis Communications, Inc., 8; 37 (upd.); 76 (upd.)
Valero Energy Corporation, 7; 71 (upd.)
Valhi, Inc., 19; 94 (upd.)
Vallen Corporation, 45
Valley Media Inc., 35
Valley National Gases, Inc., 85
Valley Proteins, Inc., 91
ValleyCrest Companies, 81 (upd.)
Valmont Industries, Inc., 19
The Valspar Corporation, 8; 32 (upd.); 77 (upd.)
Value City Department Stores, Inc., 38
Value Line, Inc., 16; 73 (upd.)
Value Merchants Inc., 13
ValueClick, Inc., 49
ValueVision International, Inc., 22
Van Camp Seafood Company, Inc., 7
Van's Aircraft, Inc., 65
Vance Publishing Corporation, 64
The Vanguard Group, Inc., 14; 34 (upd.)
Vanguard Health Systems Inc., 70
Vans, Inc., 16; 47 (upd.)
Varco International, Inc., 42
Vari-Lite International, Inc., 35
Varian, Inc., 12; 48 (upd.)
Variety Wholesalers, Inc., 73
Variflex, Inc., 51
Varlen Corporation, 16
Varsity Spirit Corp., 15
VASCO Data Security International, Inc. 79
Vastar Resources, Inc., 24
VCA Antech, Inc., 58
VECO International, Inc., 7
Vector Group Ltd., 35 (upd.)
Veeco Instruments Inc., 32
Veit Companies, 43; 92 (upd.)
Velocity Express Corporation, 49; 94 (upd.)
Venator Group Inc., 35 (upd.)
Vencor, Inc., 16
Venetian Casino Resort, LLC, 47
Ventana Medical Systems, Inc., 75
Ventura Foods LLC, 90

Venture Stores Inc., 12
VeraSun Energy Corporation, 87
Verbatim Corporation, 14; 74 (upd.)
Veridian Corporation, 54
VeriFone Holdings, Inc., 18; 76 (upd.)
Verint Systems Inc., 73
VeriSign, Inc., 47
Veritas Software Corporation, 45
Verity Inc., 68
Verizon Communications, 43 (upd.); 78 (upd.)
Vermeer Manufacturing Company, 17
The Vermont Country Store, 93
Vermont Pure Holdings, Ltd., 51
The Vermont Teddy Bear Co., Inc., 36
Vertex Pharmaceuticals Incorporated, 83
Vertis Communications, 84
Vertrue Inc., 77
VF Corporation, V; 17 (upd.); 54 (upd.)
VHA Inc., 53
Viacom Inc., 7; 23 (upd.); 67 (upd.)
Viad Corp., 73
ViaSat, Inc., 54
Viasoft Inc., 27
VIASYS Healthcare, Inc., 52
Viasystems Group, Inc., 67
Viatech Continental Can Company, Inc., 25 (upd.)
Vicon Industries, Inc., 44
VICORP Restaurants, Inc., 12; 48 (upd.)
Victory Refrigeration, Inc., 82
Videojet Technologies, Inc., 90
Vienna Sausage Manufacturing Co., 14
Viewpoint International, Inc., 66
ViewSonic Corporation, 72
Viking Office Products, Inc., 10
Viking Range Corporation, 66
Viking Yacht Company, 96
Village Super Market, Inc., 7
Village Voice Media, Inc., 38
Vinson & Elkins L.L.P., 30
Vintage Petroleum, Inc., 42
Vinton Studios, 63
Virbac Corporation, 74
Virco Manufacturing Corporation, 17
Virginia Dare Extract Company, Inc., 94
Visa International, 9; 26 (upd.)
Vishay Intertechnology, Inc., 21; 80 (upd.)
Vision Service Plan Inc., 77
Viskase Companies, Inc., 55
Vista Bakery, Inc., 56
Vista Chemical Company, I
Vistana, Inc., 22
VISX, Incorporated, 30
Vita Plus Corporation, 60
Vital Images, Inc., 85
Vitalink Pharmacy Services, Inc., 15
Vitamin Shoppe Industries, Inc., 60
Vitesse Semiconductor Corporation, 32
Vitro Corp., 10
Vivra, Inc., 18
Vlasic Foods International Inc., 25
VLSI Technology, Inc., 16
VMware, Inc., 90
Volcom, Inc., 77
Volt Information Sciences Inc., 26
Volunteers of America, Inc., 66
Von Maur Inc., 64
Vonage Holdings Corp., 81
The Vons Companies, Incorporated, 7; 28 (upd.)
Vornado Realty Trust, 20
Vought Aircraft Industries, Inc., 49
Vulcan Materials Company, 7; 52 (upd.)
W. Atlee Burpee & Co., 27
W.A. Whitney Company, 53
W.B Doner & Co., 56
W.C. Bradley Co., 69
W. H. Braum, Inc., 80
W.H. Brady Co., 17
W.L. Gore & Associates, Inc., 14; 60 (upd.)
W.P. Carey & Co. LLC, 49
W.R. Berkley Corporation, 15; 74 (upd.)
W.R. Grace & Company, I; 50 (upd.)
W.W. Grainger, Inc., V; 26 (upd.); 68 (upd.)
W.W. Norton & Company, Inc., 28
Waban Inc., 13
Wabash National Corp., 13
Wabtec Corporation, 40
Wachovia Bank of Georgia, N.A., 16
Wachovia Bank of South Carolina, N.A., 16
Wachovia Corporation, 12; 46 (upd.)
Wachtell, Lipton, Rosen & Katz, 47
The Wackenhut Corporation, 14; 63 (upd.)
Waddell & Reed, Inc., 22
Waffle House Inc., 14; 60 (upd.)
Wagers Inc. (Idaho Candy Company), 86
Waggener Edstrom, 42
Wah Chang, 82
Wahl Clipper Corporation, 86
Wahoo's Fish Taco, 96
Wakefern Food Corporation, 33
Wal-Mart Stores, Inc., V; 8 (upd.); 26 (upd.); 63 (upd.)
Walbridge Aldinger Co., 38
Walbro Corporation, 13
Waldbaum, Inc., 19
Waldenbooks, 17; 86 (upd.)
Walgreen Co., V; 20 (upd.); 65 (upd.)
Walker Manufacturing Company, 19
Wall Drug Store, Inc., 40
Wall Street Deli, Inc., 33
Wallace Computer Services, Inc., 36
Walsworth Publishing Co. 78
The Walt Disney Company, II; 6 (upd.); 30 (upd.); 63 (upd.)
Walter Industries, Inc., II; 22 (upd.); 72 (upd.)
Walton Monroe Mills, Inc., 8
Wang Laboratories, Inc., III; 6 (upd.)
The Warnaco Group Inc., 12; 46 (upd.)
Warner Communications Inc., II
Warner Music Group Corporation, 90 (upd.)
Warner-Lambert Co., I; 10 (upd.)
Warners' Stellian Inc., 67
Warrantech Corporation, 53
Warrell Corporation, 68
Warwick Valley Telephone Company, 55
The Washington Companies, 33
Washington Federal, Inc., 17
Washington Football, Inc., 35
Washington Gas Light Company, 19
Washington Mutual, Inc., 17; 93 (upd.)
Washington National Corporation, 12
Washington Natural Gas Company, 9
The Washington Post Company, IV; 20 (upd.)
Washington Scientific Industries, Inc., 17
Washington Water Power Company, 6
Waste Connections, Inc., 46
Waste Holdings, Inc., 41
Waste Management, Inc., V
Water Pik Technologies, Inc., 34; 83 (upd.)
Waterhouse Investor Services, Inc., 18
Waters Corporation, 43
Watkins-Johnson Company, 15
Watsco Inc., 52
Watson Pharmaceuticals Inc., 16; 56 (upd.)
Watson Wyatt Worldwide, 42
Watts Industries, Inc., 19
Wausau-Mosinee Paper Corporation, 60 (upd.)
Waverly, Inc., 16
Wawa Inc., 17; 78 (upd.)
Waxman Industries, Inc., 9
WD-40 Company, 18; 87 (upd.)
The Weather Channel Companies, The 52
Weatherford International, Inc., 39
Weaver Popcorn Company, Inc., 89
Webasto Roof Systems Inc., 97
Webber Oil Company, 61
Weber-Stephen Products Co., 40
WebEx Communications, Inc., 81
WebMD Corporation, 65
Weeres Industries Corporation, 52
Wegmans Food Markets, Inc., 9; 41 (upd.)
Weider Nutrition International, Inc., 29
Weight Watchers International Inc., 12; 33 (upd.); 73 (upd.)
Weil, Gotshal & Manges LLP, 55
Weiner's Stores, Inc., 33
Weingarten Realty Investors, 95
Weirton Steel Corporation, IV; 26 (upd.)
Weis Markets, Inc., 15; 84 (upd.)
The Weitz Company, Inc., 42
Welbilt Corp., 19
Welcome Wagon International Inc., 82
The Welk Group Inc. 78
WellChoice, Inc., 67 (upd.)
Wellco Enterprises, Inc., 84
Wellman, Inc., 8; 52 (upd.)
WellPoint Health Networks Inc., 25
Wells Fargo & Company, II; 12 (upd.); 38 (upd.); 97 (upd.)
Wells Rich Greene BDDP, 6
Wells' Dairy, Inc., 36
Wells-Gardner Electronics Corporation, 43
Wendy's International, Inc., 8; 23 (upd.); 47 (upd.)
Wenner Bread Products Inc., 80
Wenner Media, Inc., 32
Werner Enterprises, Inc., 26
West Bend Co., 14

West Coast Entertainment Corporation, 29
West Corporation, 42
West Group, 34 (upd.)
West Linn Paper Company, 91
West Marine, Inc., 17; 90 (upd.)
West One Bancorp, 11
West Pharmaceutical Services, Inc., 42
West Point-Pepperell, Inc., 8
West Publishing Co., 7
Westaff Inc., 33
Westamerica Bancorporation, 17
Westar Energy, Inc., 57 (upd.)
WestCoast Hospitality Corporation, 59
Westcon Group, Inc., 67
Westell Technologies, Inc., 57
Westerbeke Corporation, 60
Western Atlas Inc., 12
Western Beef, Inc., 22
Western Company of North America, 15
Western Digital Corporation, 25; 92 (upd.)
Western Gas Resources, Inc., 45
Western Publishing Group, Inc., 13
Western Resources, Inc., 12
The WesterN SizzliN Corporation, 60
Western Union Financial Services, Inc., 54
Western Wireless Corporation, 36
Westfield Group, 69
Westin Hotels and Resorts Worldwide, 9; 29 (upd.)
Westinghouse Electric Corporation, II; 12 (upd.)
Westmoreland Coal Company, 7
WestPoint Stevens Inc., 16
Westport Resources Corporation, 63
Westvaco Corporation, IV; 19 (upd.)
Westwood One, Inc., 23
The Wet Seal, Inc., 18; 70 (upd.)
Wetterau Incorporated, II
Weyco Group, Incorporated, 32
Weyerhaeuser Company, IV; 9 (upd.); 28 (upd.); 83 (upd.)
WFS Financial Inc., 70
WGBH Educational Foundation, 66
Wham-O, Inc., 61
Wheaton Industries, 8
Wheaton Science Products, 60 (upd.)
Wheelabrator Technologies, Inc., 6; 60 (upd.)
Wheeling-Pittsburgh Corporation, 7; 58 (upd.)
Wheels Inc., 96
Wherehouse Entertainment Incorporated, 11
Whirlpool Corporation, III; 12 (upd.); 59 (upd.)
White & Case LLP, 35
White Castle Management Company, 12; 36 (upd.); 85 (upd.)
White Consolidated Industries Inc., 13
The White House, Inc., 60
White Lily Foods Company, 88
White Rose, Inc., 24
Whitehall Jewellers, Inc., 82 (upd.)
Whiting Petroleum Corporation, 81
Whiting-Turner Contracting Company, 95
Whitman Corporation, 10 (upd.)
Whitman Education Group, Inc., 41
Whitney Holding Corporation, 21
Whittaker Corporation, I; 48 (upd.)
Whole Foods Market, Inc., 20; 50 (upd.)
Wickes Inc., V; 25 (upd.)
Widmer Brothers Brewing Company, 76
Wieden + Kennedy, 75
Wilbert, Inc., 56
Wilbur Chocolate Company, 66
Wilco Farm Stores, 93
Wild Oats Markets, Inc., 19; 41 (upd.)
Wildlife Conservation Society, 31
Wikimedia Foundation, Inc., 91
Willamette Industries, Inc., IV; 31 (upd.)
Willamette Valley Vineyards, Inc., 85
William L. Bonnell Company, Inc., 66
William Lyon Homes, 59
William Morris Agency, Inc., 23
William Zinsser & Company, Inc., 58
Williams & Connolly LLP, 47
Williams Communications Group, Inc., 34
The Williams Companies, Inc., IV; 31 (upd.)
Williams Scotsman, Inc., 65
Williams-Sonoma, Inc., 17; 44 (upd.)
Williamson-Dickie Manufacturing Company, 14; 45 (upd.)
Willkie Farr & Gallagher LLP, 95
Wilmington Trust Corporation, 25
Wilson Sonsini Goodrich & Rosati, 34
Wilson Sporting Goods Company, 24; 84 (upd.)
Wilsons The Leather Experts Inc., 21; 58 (upd.)
Wilton Products, Inc., 97
Winchell's Donut Houses Operating Company, L.P., 60
WinCo Foods Inc., 60
Wind River Systems, Inc., 37
Windmere Corporation, 16
Windstream Corporation, 83
Windswept Environmental Group, Inc., 62
The Wine Group, Inc., 39
Winegard Company, 56
Winmark Corporation, 74
Winn-Dixie Stores, Inc., II; 21 (upd.); 59 (upd.)
Winnebago Industries, Inc., 7; 27 (upd.); 96 (upd.)
WinsLoew Furniture, Inc., 21
Winston & Strawn, 35
The Wiremold Company, 81
Wirtz Corporation, 72
Wisconsin Alumni Research Foundation, 65
Wisconsin Bell, Inc., 14
Wisconsin Central Transportation Corporation, 24
Wisconsin Dairies, 7
Wisconsin Energy Corporation, 6; 54 (upd.)
Wisconsin Public Service Corporation, 9
Wise Foods, Inc. 79
Witco Corporation, I; 16 (upd.)
Witness Systems, Inc., 87
Wizards of the Coast Inc., 24
WLR Foods, Inc., 21
Wm. B. Reily & Company Inc., 58
Wm. Wrigley Jr. Company, 7; 58 (upd.)
WMS Industries, Inc., 15; 53 (upd.)
WMX Technologies Inc., 17
Wolfgang Puck Worldwide, Inc., 26, 70 (upd.)
Wolohan Lumber Co., 19
Wolverine Tube Inc., 23
Wolverine World Wide, Inc., 16; 59 (upd.)
Womble Carlyle Sandridge & Rice, PLLC, 52
Wood-Mode, Inc., 23
Woodcraft Industries Inc., 61
Woodward Governor Company, 13; 49 (upd.)
Woolrich Inc., 62
Woolworth Corporation, V; 20 (upd.)
WordPerfect Corporation, 10
Workflow Management, Inc., 65
Working Assets Funding Service, 43
Workman Publishing Company, Inc., 70
World Acceptance Corporation, 57
World Bank Group, 33
World Book, Inc., 12
World Color Press Inc., 12
World Duty Free Americas, Inc., 29 (upd.)
World Fuel Services Corporation, 47
World Publications, LLC, 65
World Vision International, Inc., 93
World Wide Technology, Inc., 94
World Wrestling Federation Entertainment, Inc., 32
World's Finest Chocolate Inc., 39
WorldCorp, Inc., 10
Worldwide Restaurant Concepts, Inc., 47
Worldwide Pants Inc., 97
Worthington Foods, Inc., 14
Worthington Industries, Inc., 7; 21 (upd.)
WPL Holdings, Inc., 6
WPS Resources Corporation, 53 (upd.)
Writers Guild of America, West, Inc., 92
Wright Express Corporation, 80
Wright Medical Group, Inc., 61
WTD Industries, Inc., 20
Wunderman, 86
Wyant Corporation, 30
Wyeth, 50 (upd.)
Wyle Electronics, 14
Wyman-Gordon Company, 14
Wynn's International, Inc., 33
Wyse Technology, Inc., 15
X-Rite, Inc., 48
Xcel Energy Inc., 73 (upd.)
Xerium Technologies, Inc., 94
Xerox Corporation, III; 6 (upd.); 26 (upd.); 69 (upd.)
Xilinx, Inc., 16; 82 (upd.)
XM Satellite Radio Holdings, Inc., 69
XTO Energy Inc., 52
Yahoo! Inc., 27; 70 (upd.)
Yarnell Ice Cream Company, Inc., 92
The Yankee Candle Company, Inc., 37
YankeeNets LLC, 35
The Yates Companies, Inc., 62
Yellow Corporation, 14; 45 (upd.)

Yellow Freight System, Inc. of Delaware, V
YES! Entertainment Corporation, 26
YMCA of the USA, 31
YOCREAM International, Inc., 47
The York Group, Inc., 50
York International Corp., 13
York Research Corporation, 35
Youbet.com, Inc., 77
YouTube, Inc., 90
Young & Rubicam, Inc., I; 22 (upd.); 66 (upd.)
Young Broadcasting Inc., 40
Young Innovations, Inc., 44
Young's Market Company, LLC, 32
Younkers, 76 (upd.)
Younkers, Inc., 19
Youth Services International, Inc., 21
YRC Worldwide Inc., 90 (upd.)
Yucaipa Cos., 17
Yum! Brands Inc., 58
YWCA of the United States, 45
Zachry Group, Inc., 95
Zacky Farms LLC, 74
Zale Corporation, 16; 40 (upd.); 91 (upd.)
Zanett, Inc., 92
Zany Brainy, Inc., 31
Zapata Corporation, 25
Zappos.com, Inc., 73
Zatarain's, Inc., 64
Zebra Technologies Corporation, 14; 53 (upd.)
Zenith Data Systems, Inc., 10
Zenith Electronics Corporation, II; 13 (upd.); 34 (upd.); 89 (upd.)
ZERO Corporation, 17; 88 (upd.)
Ziebart International Corporation, 30; 66 (upd.)
The Ziegler Companies, Inc., 24; 63 (upd.)
Ziff Davis Media Inc., 12; 36 (upd.); 73 (upd.)
Zila, Inc., 46
ZiLOG, Inc., 15; 72 (upd.)
Zimmer Holdings, Inc., 45
Zingerman's Community of Businesses, 68
Zion's Cooperative Mercantile Institution, 33
Zions Bancorporation, 12; 53 (upd.)
Zipcar, Inc., 92
Zippo Manufacturing Company, 18; 71 (upd.)
Zoltek Companies, Inc., 37
Zondervan Corporation, 24; 71 (upd.)
Zones, Inc., 67
Zoom Technologies, Inc., 18; 53 (upd.)
Zoran Corporation, 77
Zuffa L.L.C., 89
Zumiez, Inc., 77
Zygo Corporation, 42
Zytec Corporation, 19

Uruguay

Administración Nacional de Combustibles, Alcohol y Pórtland, 93
Cooperativa Nacional de Productores de Leche S.A. (Conaprole), 92

Vatican City

Caritas Internationalis, 72

Venezuela

Cerveceria Polar, I
Cisneros Group of Companies, 54
Empresas Polar SA, 55 (upd.)
Petróleos de Venezuela S.A., IV; 74 (upd.)

Vietnam

Lam Son Sugar Joint Stock Corporation (Lasuco), 60

Virgin Islands

Little Switzerland, Inc., 60

Wales

Hyder plc, 34
Iceland Group plc, 33
Kwik Save Group plc, 11

Zambia

Zambia Industrial and Mining Corporation Ltd., IV

Zimbabwe

Air Zimbabwe (Private) Limited, 91

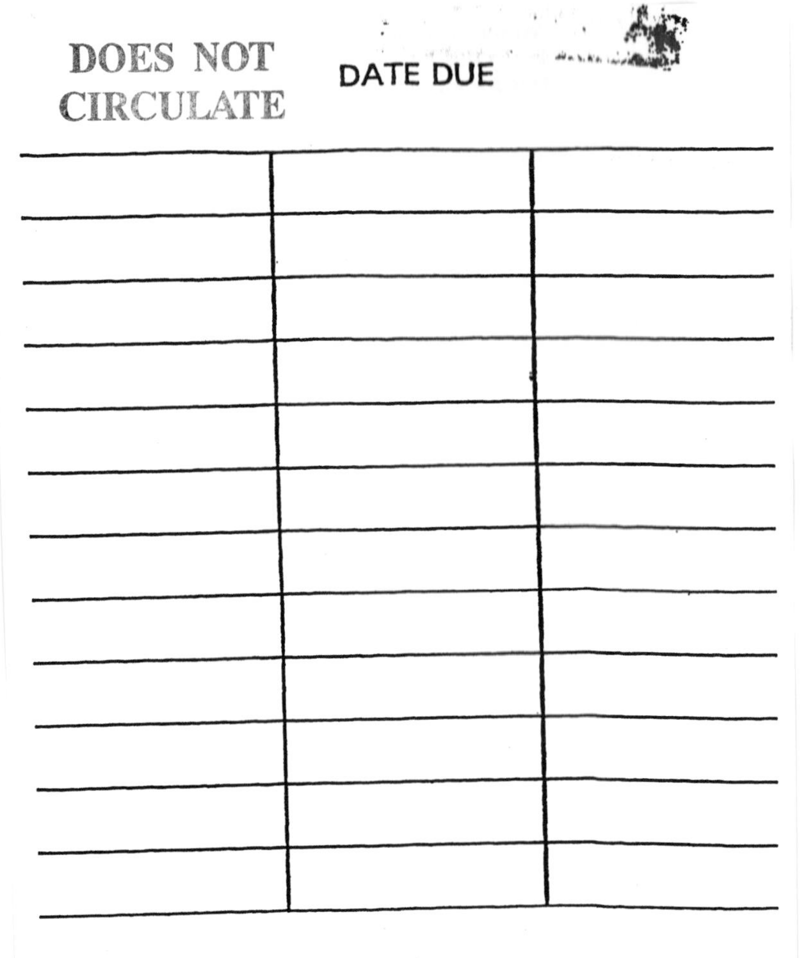

DATE DUE

Form 7 (1/85)